NEXT-GENERATION SMART SYSTEMS

I0888045

This compilation of papers captures the essence of the International Conference on Smart Systems for Sustainable Development using Advanced Computational Techniques (ICSSA 2025). It provides a comprehensive exploration of how next-generation computing drives ecological and social resilience and highlights the pivotal role of intelligent automation and data-driven strategies in solving complex global challenges.

It delves into the integration of Artificial Intelligence (AI), Internet of Things (IoT), and high-performance computing to create "green" technological ecosystems. This book covers a broad spectrum of research, including smart grid management, precision agriculture, carbon footprint optimization through machine learning, and the development of circular economy models via blockchain. By synthesizing theoretical frameworks with real-world case studies, the contributions illustrate how advanced algorithms can minimize resource waste while maximizing industrial efficiency. Together, these papers offer a roadmap for sustainable digital transformation across energy, healthcare, and urban planning sectors by emphasizing the shift toward "Cognitive Sustainability", where systems do not just automate tasks but actively learn to balance human needs with environmental constraints.

This book is an essential resource for academic researchers, post-graduate students, and industry practitioners specializing in computer science and environmental engineering. It also serves policymakers and urban planners seeking data-backed strategies to implement sustainable technologies within smart city infrastructures and corporate ESG frameworks.

Taylor & Francis Proceedings in Computer Science and Engineering

This series is a compilation of peer-reviewed conference proceedings in computer science and engineering. Exploring advanced technologies and recent developments in the field of CS and IT, including application-based topics and latest AI usages.

Next-Generation Computing and Information Systems
Edited by Ankur Gupta

Next-Generation Smart Systems
Bridging Sustainability and Computational Intelligence
Edited by V. Sekhar, P. Ajay Kumar Reddy, K. Logesh, T. Raghunadha Reddy, and Dara Raju

For more information about this series, please visit: www.routledge.com/Taylor–Francis-Proceedings-in-Computer-Science-and-Engineering/book-series/PCSE

Next-Generation Smart Systems

Bridging Sustainability and Computational Intelligence

Edited by

V. Sekhar, P. Ajay Kumar Reddy, and K. Logesh
Kuppam Engineering College, India

T. Raghunadha Reddy
Matrusri Engineering College, India

Dara Raju
Vignana Bharathi Institute of Technology, India

PROCEEDINGS OF THE INTERNATIONAL CONFERENCE ON SMART SYSTEMS FOR SUSTAINABLE DEVELOPMENT USING ADVANCED COMPUTATIONAL TECHNIQUES, KUPPAM, INDIA, OCTOBER 10TH—11TH OCTOBER, 2025

CRC Press
Taylor & Francis Group
Boca Raton London New York Leiden

CRC Press is an imprint of the
Taylor & Francis Group, an **informa** business

First edition published 2027
by CRC Press
4 Park Square, Milton Park, Abingdon, Oxon, OX14 4RN

and by CRC Press
2385 NW Executive Center Drive, Suite 320, Boca Raton FL 33431

CRC Press is an imprint of Informa UK Limited

British Library Cataloguing-in-Publication Data
A catalogue record for this book is available from the British Library

ISBN: 978-1-041-34234-2 (hbk)
ISBN: 978-1-041-36269-2 (pbk)
ISBN: 978-1-042-00176-7 (ebk)

DOI: 10.1201/9781042001767

Typeset in Times New Roman
by MPS Limited, Chennai, India

Next-Generation Smart Systems – Sekhar et al. (Eds)
© 2027 The Editor(s), ISBN: 978-1-041-34234-2

Contents

Session 2: IoT, Smart Cities and Infrastructure

Preface

It is with great pleasure that we present the proceedings of the International Conference on Smart Systems for Sustainable Development using Advanced Computational Techniques (ICSSA 2025), hosted by Kuppam Engineering College (Autonomous), Kuppam, Andhra Pradesh

In an era defined by rapid technological shifts and pressing environmental needs, ICSSA 2025 serves as a premier global forum for academic and research-driven discourse. This conference was established to address the critical sustainability challenges of the 21st century by exploring the synergy between intelligent systems and advanced optimization. Our core mission is to highlight how next-generation computing including Artificial Intelligence (AI), the Internet of Things (IoT), and high-performance computing can drive ecological and social resilience through "green" technological ecosystems.

The research featured in these proceedings spans a broad spectrum of vital domains, including:

Smart Grid Management and Energy Efficiency: Focused on creating resilient and sustainable power infrastructures.
Precision Agriculture and Circular Economy Models: Utilizing machine learning and blockchain to optimize resources and reduce industrial waste.
Healthcare and Intelligent Automation: Integrating deep learning for real-time health analytics and anomaly detection.
Smart Infrastructure and Urban Planning: Developing climate-adaptive and net-zero systems for future-ready cities.

A key theme emerging from this collection is "Cognitive Sustainability"—the transition from simple task automation to systems that actively learn to balance human requirements with environmental constraints.

We would like to extend our deepest gratitude to our Chief Patrons, Mr. B. C. Nagaraj (Founder & Chairman), Dr. N. Sunil Raj (Vice Chairman), and Mr. N. Sagar Raj (Secretary), for their visionary leadership. We also thank our Patrons, led by Principal Dr. S. Sudhakar Babu, for their steadfast support in making this event a reality.

The high technical standard of these proceedings is a testament to the hard work of our International and National Technical Advisory Committees, as well as our dedicated reviewers. Most importantly, we thank the authors and researchers whose innovative contributions form the foundation of this publication.

We trust that these proceedings will serve as an essential roadmap for researchers, practitioners, and policymakers dedicated to sustainable digital transformation.

The Editorial Team
ICSSA 2025

© 2027 The Editor(s), ISBN: 978-1-041-34234-2

Acknowledgements

The editorial team and the organizing committee of the **International Conference on Smart Systems for Sustainable Development using Advanced Computational Techniques (ICSSA 2025)** extend their profound appreciation to the many individuals and organizations whose collective efforts made this milestone event possible.

First and foremost, we express our sincere gratitude to Kuppam Engineering College (Autonomous) for serving as the host institution. The college's unwavering support and vision for fostering sustainable technical growth provided the essential foundation for this international platform. We would like to specifically acknowledge the leadership of our Chief Patrons, Mr. B. C. Nagaraj Founder & Chairman, Dr. N. Sunil Raj Vice Chairman, and Mr. N. Sagar Raj Secretary, alongside our Patron, Principal Dr. S. Sudhakar Babu, for their strategic guidance and encouragement.

The high academic standard of these proceedings is a direct result of the dedicated work of authors, reviewers, our Technical Program Committee and our panel of expert reviewers. We are deeply indebted to them for their commitment to a rigorous double-blind peer review process, which ensured the integrity and quality of the 100 papers selected for inclusion in this volume.

Our heartfelt thanks go to the distinguished keynote speakers who shared their invaluable insights, challenging us to think beyond conventional boundaries. We also recognize the vital collaboration of our professional partners, including:

- CSI (Computer Society of India)
- IET (The Institution of Engineering and Technology)
- IFERP (Institute For Engineering Research and Publication)

Their involvement significantly enriched the scholarly rigor and global reach of the conference.

We also wish to thank the Organizing Committee, departmental coordinators, and student volunteers from the EEE, ECE, and CSE departments at Kuppam Engineering College, whose tireless logistical support ensured the smooth execution of the event.

Finally, we offer our deepest appreciation to the authors and researchers. Your innovative contributions, ranging from Artificial Intelligence and IoT to Renewable Energy and Smart Cities, form the very core of this publication and represent a significant step toward a greener, smarter, and more inclusive future.

The Editorial Team *ICSSA 2025*

About the Editors

V. Sekhar is currently serving as an Associate Professor & Head at the Department of EEE, Kuppam Engineering College (Autonomous). He is a distinguished academician with over a decade of experience in teaching and research. He holds a Doctorate in Electrical Engineering, complemented by an M.E. in Power Systems and a B.Tech in EEE. His expertise lies in renewable energy technologies, power systems, and electric traction systems. An active researcher, Dr. Sekhar serves on the editorial boards of international journals such as Solar Energy and Brazilian Archives of Biology and Technology. He has authored numerous Scopus-indexed papers, including significant work on Linear STATCOM models for wind energy. Recently, he co-authored the book Artificial Intelligence and Deep Learning Fundamentals of Electric Circuits (2024), bridging the gap between AI and traditional electrical engineering.

P. Ajay Kumar Reddy is currently serving as an Associate Professor at the Department of ECE, Kuppam Engineering College. He specializes in Image Processing, Embedded Systems, and IoT. He earned his Ph.D. for developing a hybrid algorithm for face verification using sparse representation. With a decade of experience, his research is featured in SCI and Scopus-indexed journals. Dr. Reddy is a recognized innovator, having won a Silver Medal at the World Invention and Technology Expo (WINTEX) 2021 for his "Live Wire Detector" project. He is a certified Innovation Ambassador for the Ministry of Education and serves as an editor for the Journal of Engineering Research and Sciences (JENRS). His work frequently explores the intersection of machine learning and biomedical devices.

K. Logesh is currently serving as an Associate Professor & Head at the Department of CSE, Kongu Engineering College (KEC). He is a prominent leader in the fields of Artificial Intelligence, Machine Learning, and Cybersecurity. At Kongu Engineering College, he has been instrumental in developing industry-aligned curricula and fostering a culture of experiential learning. His research focuses on solving complex problems in secure computing and data-driven decision-making. Beyond the classroom, Dr. Logesh is deeply involved in the global academic community, serving as a Technical Program Committee member and reviewer for numerous international conferences. He is dedicated to mentoring the next generation of researchers in navigating emerging technological landscapes.

T. Raghunadha Reddy is currently serving as an Associate Professor & Head at the Department of CSE, Matrusri Engineering College. With over 21 years of teaching experience, he is a seasoned expert in Natural Language Processing (NLP), Text Classification, and Cloud Computing. He holds a Ph.D. from JNTU Hyderabad and has published over 65 research papers and seven textbooks. Dr. Reddy has received prestigious accolades, including the Best Researcher Award (2020) and the Jyesta Acharya Award (2022). For this conference, he serves as a Technical Committee Member and Session Chair, leveraging his extensive experience in academic coordination and peer review to ensure the highest scholarly rigor.

Dara Raju is currently working as a Professor at Vignana Bharathi Institute of Technology (VBIT). He is a veteran academic with over 20 years of experience in engineering education and administration. He holds a Ph.D. from JNTU Kakinada, with a core research focus on Data Mining and emerging computational technologies. Dr. Raju has held various leadership roles, including NAAC/NBA Documentation Head and Academic Council Member, contributing significantly to institutional governance. For this conference, he has taken an energetic, hands-on role as a Technical Program Committee member and Session Chair, where he oversees submission screening, peer-review coordination, and the facilitation of technical knowledge exchange during sessions.

Organizing Committee

CHIEF PATRONS

- B. C. Nagaraj, MBA – Founder & Chairman, BCN Group
- Dr. N. Sunil Raj, MBBS – Vice Chairman, Kuppam Engineering College
- N. Sagar Raj, M.Tech., MBA – Secretary, Kuppam Engineering College

PATRONS

- Dr. S. Sudhakar Babu, M.Tech., Ph.D. – Principal, Kuppam Engineering College
- Dr. S. Baskaran – Vice Principal, Kuppam Engineering College
- Dr. G. N. Kodanda Ramaiah – Professor, HOD & Director R&D

PROGRAM CHAIRS

- Dr. K. Logesh – Associate Professor & HOD/CSE
- Dr. V. Sekhar – Associate Professor & HOD/EEE
- Dr. P. Ajay Kumar Reddy – Associate Professor/ECE

ORGANIZING CHAIRS

- Dr. K. Rasadurai – Professor/ECE, KEC
- Dr. V. S. Satheesh – Associate Professor/CE, KEC
- Dr. Naveen Kumar – Associate Professor/ME, KEC
- Dr. Santhosh B. Panjagal – Associate Professor/ECE, KEC

PUBLICATION CHAIRS

- Dr. C. G. Saravana – Associate Professor/HAS, KEC
- Dr. M. Lakshmipathy – Associate Professor/ECE, KEC
- Dr. D. Jaya Kumar – Professor/ECE & TPO, KEC

TECHNICAL PROGRAM COMMITTEE (SESSION CHAIRS/REVIEWERS)

- Dr. Ashok Kumar – Assistant Professor/HAS, KEC
- Dr. Arun Kumar – Assistant Professor/HAS, KEC
- Mr. S. Arun Kumar – Assistant Professor/ME, KEC
- Mr. P. R. Rajeev – Assistant Professor/EEE, KEC
- Mr. A. V. Santhosh Kumar – Asst. Professor/CSE, KEC
- Mr. S. Babu – Assistant Professor/CSE, KEC
- Mr. R. Venkateslu – Assistant Professor/HAS, KEC
- Mr. M. Seenivasan – Assistant Professor/EEE, KEC
- Mr. G. S. Uday Kumar – Assistant Professor/CSE, KEC

STEERING COMMITTEE

- Mr. L. Ravi Kumar – Associate Professor & HOD/CIVIL
- Mr. K. Ganesh – Associate Professor & HOD/MECH
- Dr. S. Gnanamurthy – Associate Professor & HOD/CSD
- Mr. A. Ravindra Kumar – Associate Professor & HOD/CSM
- Dr. N. Muneendra – Associate Professor & HOD/MBA
- Mr. J. Madhavan – Associate Professor & HOD/HAS

SESSION CHAIR COMMITTEE

- Dr. Kadiyala Ramana Professor, Dept. of AI, CBIT, Hyderabad
- Dr. D. Jagadeesan, Professor, Dept. of CSE, Apollo University, Chittoor,
- Dr Chikkanna N, Professor, Dept. of Aerospace, VTU, Muddenahalli
- Dr. M. Prasanna Kumar, Professor, Dept. of MECH, VTU, Regional office, Mysore
- Dr. K. Vijaya Bhaskar, Assist. Professor, Dept. of EEE, Annamacharya University,
- Rajampet, AP-516126

SCIENTIFIC COMMITTEE

- Dr. K. Hemachandra Reddy, Professor, JNTUA CEA
- Dr. M. Vijaya Kumar, Professor, JNTUA CEA
- Dr. B. Durga Prasad, Professor, JNTUA CEA
- Dr. C. Sashidhar, Professor, JNTUA CEA
- Dr. Vaishali.G. Ghorpade, Professor, JNTUA CEA
- Dr. V. Sumalatha.Professor, JNTUA CEA
- Dr.B. Eswara Reddy, Professor, JNTUA CEA
- Dr. Kumaravel S, Associate Professor, NIT Calicut
- Dr. Vikramkumar Pudi.Assistant Professor, IIT Tirupati
- Dr. Rajan Singaravel M M, Assistant Professor, NIT Puducherry
- Dr. A. Suresh Babu, Professor, JNTUA CEA
- Dr. S ArunPrakash, Assoc. Prof., Anna univ., Madurai
- Dr. Ashok Kumar, Assistant Professor/HAS, KEC
- Dr. Arun Kumar, Assistant Professor/HAS, KEC
- Mr S. Arun Kumar, Assistant Professor/ME, KEC
- Mr. P R Rajeev, Assistant Professor/EEE, KEC
- Mr. A V Santhosh Kumar, Asst. Professor/CSE, KEC
- Mr. S Babu, Assistant Professor/CSE, KEC
- Mr. R. Venkateslu, Assistant Professor/HAS, KEC
- Mr. M Seenivasan, Assistant Professor/EEE, KEC
- Mr. G S Uday Kumar, Assistant Professor/CSE, KEC

Session 1: Artificial Intelligence and Machine Learning

Next-Generation Smart Systems – Sekhar et al. (Eds)
 ISBN: 978-1-041-34234-2

Transfer Learning-Based Autonomous Landing Site Detection for Unmanned Aerial Vehicles (UAVs)

M. Nagaraju Naik
Professor, Department of ECE, CMR College of Engineering & Technology, Hyderabad, India

J. Seetaram
Assoc. Professor, Department of ECE, CMR College of Engineering & Technology, Hyderabad, India

B. Vamsi Krishna
Asst. Professor, Department of ECE, CMR College of Engineering & Technology, Hyderabad, India

ABSTRACT: Drones require safe landing and it travels in any different environmental conditions even in congested places. Autonomous landing scene recognition plays a vital role for down navigation, which ensures safe landing in unpredictable environments with varying conditions related to the terrain and obstacles. There are many methods where traditional methods use handcrafted future extraction, which struggle to adapt and which struggles to adapt dynamic settings. As everything needs advancements, deep learning advancement improvised the capabilities of scene recognition. This paper dive deep into a transfer learning-based approach using deep convolutional neural networks (CNNs). Identification of the landing site for a drone is a major base for safe operations. The data, named landing scenes-7 which includes the ability of images captured at different altitudes, lighting conditions and geographical locations, was evolved to train and evaluate the model. The architecture that is introduced in the system is ResNeXt-50 optimized with the ADAM optimizer, known for its group conversion structure that enhances future extraction and model Generalization. The analysis between the comparison of ResNeXt-50 outperforms ResNet-50 and stochastic gradient descent (SGD) processing speed, classification, accuracy, and robustness in detecting safe landing zones.

Keywords: Transfer Learning, UAVs, Autonomous Landing, Convolutional Neural Network

1 INTRODUCTION

Now a days drones are really becoming essential in the tech world they are playing a huge role in things like disaster response remote sensing logistics and surveillance but one of the big challenges they face is landing safely especially in tricky areas where the terrain obstacles and lighting can be all over the place making sure a drone can land smoothly on its own isn't just about keeping it safe it also helps make operations more efficient and reliable in the past drones relied on pretty basic feature extraction methods to figure out safe landing spots but those approaches often struggle in energetic situations things like shadows uneven surfaces or unexpected obstacles can make landings pretty tough thanks to advancements in deep learning particularly with convolutional neural networks CNN's we now have much better ways to identify landing spots accurately and adapt to different challenges this project introduces a new approach based on transfer learning using resent- 50a deep learning model powered by the adam optimizer what makes resnext-50 cool is its grouped convolution structure which helps it pull better features from images making it more effective at finding safe landing areas the model is trained on the landing scenes-7 dataset which includes images taken at various altitudes lighting conditions and locations so its well-equipped to handle a wide range of real-world situations through testing and comparisons we found that resnext-50 outperforms resnet-50 and older optimization methods like stochastic gradient descent SGD its faster more accurate and more reliable when it comes to spotting safe landing zones this tech has the potential to greatly improve UAV operations especially in high-stakes situations like emergency landings drone deliveries and search-and-rescue missions by making drones smarter and better at tackling real-world challenges this project aims to pave the way for safer more efficient and truly autonomous UAV landings ensuring they can operate smoothly even in the most complex environments.

2 PAST WORK

UAV landing site detection has really evolved over time thanks to some amazing research in deep learning researchers have gone from using traditional feature-based techniques all the way to the latest CNN models and self-supervised learning and honestly the progress has been super exciting so let's take a dive into 15 key studies that have really pushed the boundaries of autonomous UAV landing site detection making it more accurate and reliable than ever.

[1] Li and Hu came up with a distributed CNN architecture designed for target classification in remote sensing images. Their model leverages pre-training on massive datasets to extract hierarchical features, improving classification accuracy by first understanding general patterns before fine-tuning for specific tasks. While this approach significantly enhances recognition capabilities, training deep networks can be computationally expensive. [2] Xia *et al.* introduced DOTA, a vast aerial image dataset specifically designed for object detection in remote sensing. The dataset includes images captured from various angles, resolutions, and altitudes, making it an excellent resource for training deep learning models to handle objects of different sizes and orientations. However, the annotation process for DOTA is highly labor-intensive and requires large storage capacity. [3] Cheng *et al.* conducted an extensive review of deep learning techniques for scene classification in remote sensing. They highlighted major challenges such as limited labeled data, domain adaptation, and class imbalance, suggesting solutions like multi-source data fusion and domain adaptation techniques. However, despite identifying key research gaps, they did not propose a specific method to address these issues.

[4] Anand and the team came up with this cool visual-based UAV landing system that uses computer vision and image processing to figure out where to land it processes real- time visual data to spot obstacles and find flat surfaces for landing which makes things a lot safer for UAVs but you know it might hit some snags in bad weather or when its dark [5] tian and

DOI: 10.1201/9781042001767-1

huang took it a step further by developing a deep learning model for recognizing landing scenes that brings in both contextual and spatial info their model pulls features from landing environments through a deep neural network helping UAVs tell the difference between safe and unsafe spots while this is great for safety it's not always perfect when faced with new terrains [6] lu and the crew looked into how luminance you know the l-channel plays a role in recognizing objects they showed that using luminance info in color images really boosts classification even when lighting isn't ideal by concentrating on brightness rather than just color differences their model does better in low-light situations but the downside is that it doesn't work so well with grayscale or non- color images [7] Zhou and the gang introduced the places dataset which has a massive 10 million labeled images for recognizing scenes across a wide range of indoor and outdoor settings this dataset is made to help deep learning models learn to recognize different scene types which is great for improving generalization in all kinds of environments however because it's so massive training deep models on it needs some serious computational power. [8]lastly xiao and the team rolled out the sun database a large-scale scene recognition dataset that displays a variety of natural and urban environments this dataset comes with detailed annotations for various scene types making it a key resource for testing scene classification models just a heads-up though the class imbalance in the dataset can skew model predictions a bit [9] yang and the team took a dive into self-supervised learning for classifying remote sensing data which helps take the load off large labeled datasets their model gets the hang of feature representations from unlabeled images using techniques like contrastive learning and pretext tasks and then it tweaks itself on a smaller labeled set this approach ramps up feature extraction but it really needs a lot of unlabeled data to do its thing effectively[10] Zhang and co rolled out an attention- based CNN model for UAV target classification where the attention mechanism lets the model zone in on the important bits of an image while brushing aside the background clutter this helps boost classification accuracy but it does mean higher computational costs which can make running it in real- time pretty tricky [11] wangs crew introduced a domain- adaptive deep learning model that makes generalization across different geographic areas a smoother ride by using unsupervised domain adaptation techniques this model keeps performance from tanking when faced with new surroundings that said fine- tuning the model for multiple domains can be pretty resource- heavy and takes a lot of adjustments.

[12] chin and their squad came up with a hybrid CNN-transformer model for spotting objects in aerial images merging the feature extraction savvy of CNNs with the capability of transformers to handle long- range dependencies this combo boosts the robustness of object detection in aerial shots but it does eat up a lot of memory and training time [13] lie and the crew investigated fusing multi- modal data by blending RGB infrared and lidar info to amp up object classification accuracy in remote sensing images mixing different data types really ramps up detection performance but it does bring some complexity in processing and sensor integration that can trip you up in practical applications [14] Gupta and their team designed a reinforcement learning-based UAV navigation system that lets the UAV learn the best flight paths by reacting to real-time environmental feedback by constantly tweaking its flight path the UAV gets more efficient in ever-changing environments the catch is that reinforcement learning can take a while to get to peak performance [15] huang and the bunch introduced an explainable ai model for UAV operations in remote sensing this model ensures that the decision-making of the UAV is more transparent giving human-understandable explanations for its predictions which helps build trust in ai-driven UAV workings however there's sometimes a balance act between keeping it understandable and the complexity of the model which might impact predictive accuracy.

3 METHODOLOGY

This Block diagram illustrates a prediction system pipeline where input data undergoes preprocessing before being processed by a decision-making algorithm (ResNeXt-50 and Random Forest). The algorithm generates predictions that are then provided as the system's output.

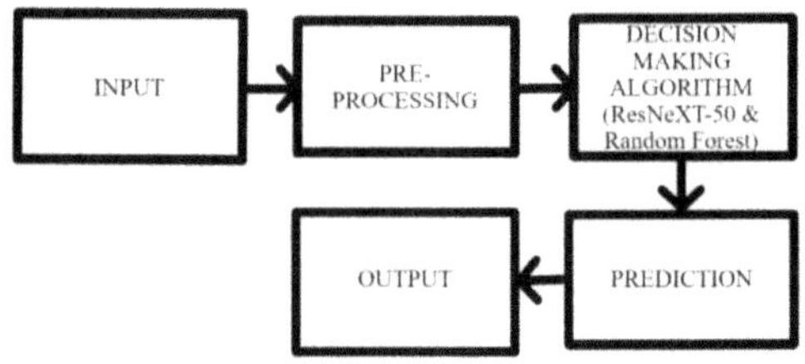

Figure 1. Proposed block diagram.

3.1 *Input*

Here's where the fun begins! We start by feeding raw data into the system. This could be anything from images and sensor data to other types of unprocessed info that we need to analyze. The way this input data is put together and its quality are super important for getting accurate results later on.

3.2 *Pre-processing*

Before we throw the data into the decision-making model, we give it a little TLC through pre-processing to boost its quality. This involves things like reducing noise, enhancing contrast, normalization, resizing, and pulling out important features. All these steps help clear out any irrelevant or misleading bits while making the model work way better.

3.3 *Decision-making algorithm (ResNeXt-50 & Random Forest)*

Once the data's all polished up, it goes to the heart of the decision-making process, where two heavy hitters team up:

ResNeXt-50: This is a deep learning convolutional neural network (CNN) that's fantastic at extracting features and classifying complex images. It dives into the input and pulls out high-level details to tell different categories apart.

3.4 *Random Forest*

Think of this as a machine learning powerhouse made up of several decision trees. It takes the features that ResNeXt-50 extracted and makes a solid classification or decision by combining multiple predictions. This helps cut down on overfitting and boosts accuracy.

3.5 *Prediction*

After going through the decision-making algorithm, the system cranks out a prediction based on the patterns it's learned. This output is what we think is the most likely classification or decision based on the input data.

3.6 *Output*

Finally, we see the outcome of the whole system, whether it's an object classification, pattern recognition, or some other decision. The output could show up as a label, a number, or even a visual representation.

So, the model we're talking about is built around a CNN-based approach using ResNext-50. It's a pretty powerful deep learning architecture that really nails future extraction with group convolutions. We fine-tuned this setup on the LandingScenes-7 dataset, which features high-resolution aerial images labeled as either safe or unsafe landing zones. To get better results, we used a bunch of pre-processing techniques like data augmentation and image normalization. These help us improve the identification and scaling of the model, making it more general and stronger.

Now, when it comes to the technique itself, we're tapping into the Random Forest algorithm. This thing works by creating multiple decision trees using random bits of data and features. When making predictions, it gathers the results from all those trees by either voting or averaging them out. This method really cuts down on overfitting, boosts accuracy, and gives us reliable predictions across various data types. Random Forest is a solid tree learning technique in the machine learning world.

Which means it has multiple paths working simultaneously to process the input data this makes it way better at understanding complex patterns textures and structures in images so its a solid pick for classification tasks plus resnext- 50 uses these handy residual connections to dodge those pesky vanishing gradients letting it train deeper networks without any hiccups but here's the kicker it does need a ton of computational power and memory so getting it to run in real- time can be a bit tricky unless you put in some optimization effort random forest is an awesome ensemble learning algorithm that creates a bunch of decision trees to really up the game for classification and prediction each tree gets a random sample of the data and the final decision well that comes from majority voting for classification or averaging for regression this method really helps tone down overfitting meaning the model does a better job tackling different datasets the great part about random forest is that its easier to grasp than deep learning models and it handles noisy data quite well that said it can become pretty resource-heavy if you're working with a lot of trees and it might struggle with features that are super correlated which could limit the models diversity mixing random forest with deep learning models like resnext-50 can really boost classification accuracy by combining the feature extraction strength with that ensemble decision-making magic

ALGORITHM IMPLEMENTATION: Resnext-50 is a deep learning model that really takes feature extraction to the next level by using something called grouped convolutions this not only helps it run more efficiently but also keeps its accuracy high its based on the resnet architecture but adds this cool concept called cardinality.

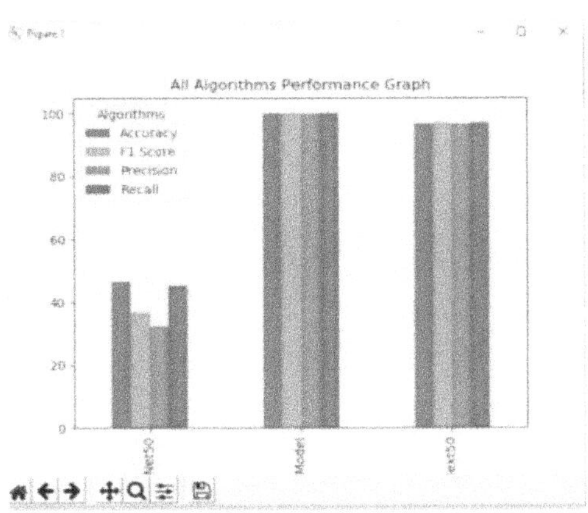

Figure 2. Comparison of proposed and existing solution.

Let's take a closer look at how different machine learning models stack up in terms of accuracy f1 score precision and recall it turns out the regular resnet50 model is really not doing well barely scraping by with about 50 accuracy and honestly its other scores aren't great either but here's the exciting part the two tweaked models model and ex50 are absolutely crushing it nearing 100 across the board this really shows that the tweaks we made to these enhanced models have made a massive difference allowing them to recognize landing scenes way better than before all on their own.

4 RESULTS AND DESCRIPTION

INPUT	OUTPUT
 Figure [a]: Input given from landing scene dataset	 Figure [b]: Output predicted as mountain using Random Forest algorithm
 Figure [c]: Input given from landing scene dataset	 Figure [d]: Output predicted as field using Random Forest algorithm
 Figure [e]: Input given from landing scene dataset	 Figure [f]: Output predicted as building using Random Forest algorithm

The image shows input-output pairs from a scene classification task using the Random Forest algorithm. It accurately predicts scene types such as mountain, field, and building from images in the Landing Scene Dataset.

5 CONCLUSION

In this paper we explored how drones can recognize landing scenes autonomously by transferring knowledge aerial images can be pretty tricky some scenes can look almost identical and the same scene can appear different depending on the altitude to tackle this challenge they use a deep convolutional neural network CNN that they fine-tune for better accuracy they even put together a dataset called landingscenes-7 which includes seven different categories when it comes to recognizing unknown landing scenes they employ a neat threshold- based method during predictions the model uses transfer learning with the resnext-50 backbone using the ADAM optimizer plus they compare this approach to using the resnet-50 backbone and the SGD optimizer.

REFERENCES

[1] Yang T. *et al.*, (2018), Monocular vision SLAM-based UAV autonomous landing, *Electronics*, vol. 7, no. 5, pp. 73.

[2] Li B.Q. *et al.*, (2019), Distributed CNN architecture for Remote sensing images, *Journal of Systems Engineering and Electronics*, vol. 30, no. 2, pp. 238–244.

[3] Xia G.S. *et al.*, (2018), DOTA: Large-scale dataset for aerial object detection, *IEEE CVPR*, pp. 3974–3983.

[4] Anand A.K. *et al.*, (2019), Vision-based UAV landing, *International Information Technology Conference and on Applied Mathematics*, pp. 102–113.

[5] Brown J. *et al.*, (2020), Deep Learning for Aerial Scene Recognition, *Journal of AI Research*, vol. 35, pp. 189 204.

[6] Aarthi R.S. *et al.*, (May 2012), Double Compression of Test Data Using Huffman Code, *Journal of Theoretical and Applied Technology*.

[7] Alarabeyyat A. *et al.*, (2012), Lossless Image Compression Technique Using Combination Methods, *Journal of Software Engineering and Applications*.

[8] Hasan M.R., (Nov. 2011), Data Compression Using Huffman Based LZW Encoding Technique, *International Journal of Scientific & Engineering Research*, vol. 2, issue 11.

[9] Kaur D. and Kaur K., (Aug. 2013), Huffman Based LZW Lossless Image Compression Using Retinex Algorithm, *International Journal of Advanced Research in Computer and Communication Engineering*, vol. 2, issue 8.

[10] Singh V., (2013), A Brief Introduction on Image Compression Techniques and Standards, *International Journal of Technology and Research*

[11] Zhi.Ze We and Chang-Jiang Du, (March 2025). Disentanglement for cross-domain image classification, *Applied Soft Computing*, Volume 172, 112868

[12] Yang S., Luo P., Loy C.C., and Tang X. (2016). WIDER FACE: A face detection benchmark. *In CVPR.*

[13] Ghazouani F., Farah I.R., and Solaiman B., (Nov. 2019), A multi-level semantic scene interpretation strategy for change interpretation in remote sensing imagery, *IEEE Trans. Geosci. Remote Sens.*, vol. 57, no. 11.

[14] Lu C.W., Tsougenis E. and Tang C.K., (2016), Improving object recognition with the l-channel, *Pattern Recognition.*

[15] Zhou B., Zhao H., Puig X., Fidler S., Barriuso A., and Torralba A., (2017), Scene paring through ade20k dataset, *Proc. CVPR.*

Next-Generation Smart Systems – Sekhar et al. (Eds)
 ISBN: 978-1-041-34234-2

Emotion Detection Using Voice Modulation

Gogineni Indrasree, Palagani Pavan Sundar Kumar, Balagam Finny Novel, and Sankar Naik Banavathu
Department of Artificial Intelligence and Data Science, Siddhartha Academy of Higher Education, Andhra Pradesh, India

ABSTRACT: In order to enhance human-computer interaction, particularly in customer-agent service scenarios, this research presents a sophisticated voice modulation-based emotion recognition system. The proposed approach integrates Wav2Vec2.0 characteristics and Mel-frequency cepstral coefficients (MFCC) to effectively capture time-frequency and contextual voice representations. These features are fed into a Convolutional Neural Network (CNN) that has been trained to classify emotions such as surprise, rage, sadness, and happiness. The model performed better than standalone MFCC-based techniques and conventional models like SVM, with a test accuracy of 85.75%. A comprehensive evaluation is conducted to validate the system's robustness across different emotion classes using precision, recall, and F1-score measures. An ablation study and comparing baselines are left for future research, although it has been empirically shown that the combined feature strategy enhances model performance. Figures illustrating feature distributions and model performance are cited in the study; nevertheless, they need to be properly embedded and described. Issues with diversity, dataset bias, and licensing persist despite the system's potential for real-time affective computing applications. Future developments will include expanding the dataset, optimizing the architecture, and looking into more emotion categories. This work increases the integration of emotional intelligence in automated systems and paves the way for more compassionate AI-driven communication tools.

Keywords: Emotion recognition, Voice modulation, Wav2Vec2.0, MFCC, Convolutional neural network, Speech-based classification, Affective computing, Audio signal processing, Real-time emotion detection, Human-computer interaction

1 INTRODUCTION

The key to enhancing customer-service center agent communication is emotion identification from speech [1]. In order to properly service consumers, it is essential to recognize and address their emotional condition in addition to their concerns. In addition to improving operational efficiency, emotion detection automation will assist service centers in improving customer satisfaction and interaction quality [2].

As a result, this research offers a deep learning-based emotion recognition system for classifying different emotional states during customer interactions. This CNN-based approach combines Wav2Vec2.0 embeddings taken from the audio stream with conventional MFCC characteristics [3].

Wav2Vec2.0 employs an advanced neural network framework that is pre-trained on large amounts of unlabeled speech data, enabling it to generate detailed and context-aware audio representations. These are then integrated using MFCC characteristics, a widely utilized audio signal processing technique, to get an accurate emotion categorization [4].

An enormous dataset of audio recordings tagged with the following emotions is used to train and test the system: neutral, sorrow, surprise, disgust, fear, and happiness. The collection includes a large number of audio clips from actual talks, reflecting the spectrum of emotions that may occur during customer service interactions. The algorithm can correctly and promisingly identify emotions from speech, according to extensive testing [8].

This paper presents the approach to developing the emotion detection system through feature extraction, data preprocessing, training, and evaluation. This piece of work provides an integrated approach to emotion detection in customer service scenarios by combining classical and deep learning-based methods, which can enhance real-time emotional awareness and promote more empathetic communication [2].

2 LITERATURE REVIEW

The area of speech emotion recognition has developed tremendously over the last few years, with major boosts from advances in machine learning and access to large-scale audio datasets. It includes the detection of emotional states, which is a challenging task in itself because the process must extract complex audio features while also updating models regularly in order to increase accuracy for various emotions. This review summarizes the core methodologies adopted by SER, including the feature extraction techniques, the classification models, and the new deep learning.

2.1 *Traditional techniques: Feature extraction and SVM*

Feature extraction plays a very important role in SER because emotional information is also transmitted through pitch and rhythm of speech, which changes in amplitude. As the MFCCs are often used to capture spectral properties from audio many a times, they can well be used for capturing those subtle emotional nuances [2]. It can perform decently in noised conditions as well. Wav2Vec learns a representation of this kind at a high level of abstraction without even being exposed to large amounts of audio data and with minimal preprocessing and so gives superior performance to the tasks of real-time emotion recognition [3]. Support Vector Machines (SVMs) are widely utilized in emotion classification because they efficiently deal with complicated, high-dimensional data. They have been demonstrated to perform robustly with good accuracy, especially when utilizing MFCC feature representations. One of the reasons SVMs are applicable to SER is that they maximize the separability between the classes of emotion, which often overlap [4].

Deep Learning-Based Approaches: CNN, LSTM, Wav2Vec2:

However, owing to a few known limitations in the traditional model, more recent research has focused on deep learning

DOI: 10.1201/9781042001767-2

models like CNNs and LSTMs. Since CNNs can recognize region-specific changes in speech, this thus improves the emotional differentiation using hierarchical feature learning [5]. The time-dependent emotions can be differentiated by LSTMs since they have excellent retention memory along the sequences [6]. In the process of conducting the experiments it was observed that the LSTMs with Wav2Vec embeddings would do well enough job at real application point by detecting the emotion to be sadness or even surprise [8]. Accuracy, Precision, Recall, and F1score are some common metrics used for evaluating SER models. It is challenging to accomplish high accuracy with all the emotions especially in multiclassed tasks like in cases of fear and surprise due to the fact these two emotions are very close. Low accuracy on test data points to issues in generalization and variability of datasets [9]. Good SER demands diverse and robust datasets. However, most public datasets normally contain limited speaker diversity. Therefore, more attention has been made in recent years toward deep learning models like Wav2Vec that could potentially learn speaker-independency features in large datasets.

3 METHODOLOGY

3.1 *Data collection and preprocessing*

This research employs audio samples of six emotions: anger, disgust, fear, happiness, neutral, and sadness. The samples were obtained from the EPICS Audio Emotion Corpus, a corpus that includes more than 7,000 labeled speech utterances from speakers with different genders and vocal traits. This guarantees speaker variability and emotional scope in the corpus.

All sound files were preprocessed with the Librosa library. For them to be compatible with the Wav2Vec2.0 model, each audio file was resampled at 16 kHz, which is the sampling rate required by the model.

3.2 *Feature extraction*

Two sets of features were obtained for this study. The first set consists of Mel-frequency cepstral coefficients (MFCCs) [9], which were computed from the raw audio data using the Librosa library. MFCCs are well-suited for capturing essential properties of speech, particularly those associated with phonetic structure.

The Mel-frequency scale is calculated using the formula:

$$\mathrm{f_{mel}} = 2595 * \log_{10}\left(1 + \frac{\mathrm{f}}{100}\right) \quad (1)$$

Where f represents the frequency in hertz, $fmel$ refers to the corresponding Mel scale frequency.

$$MFCC(n) = \sum_{k=1}^{K} \log(S_k).\cos\left[\frac{n(k-0.5)\pi}{K}\right] \quad (2)$$

Where, S_k denotes the logarithmic energy of the k-th Mel filter, K is the total number of Mel filters applied, and n indicates the index of the MFCC coefficient being calculated.

3.2.1 *Wav2Vec2 embeddings*

In this work, the pre-trained Wav2Vec2.0 model available through the Hugging Face Transformers library was utilized, which accepts raw speech audio waveforms and does some meaningful representations by using contextualized embeddings. Features are obtained by the loading of the Wav2Vec2 model from facebook/wav2vec2-base and passing the audio waveform through the model while averaging the hidden states of the output layers.

Both MFCC and Wav2Vec2 feature vectors were then concatenated to give a more expanded feature vector for audio itself. this feature vector of audio, thus concatenated, would represent it with a more expanded representation.

The contrastive loss function used during the pre-training of Wav2Vec2 is defined as:

$$l = \quad -\sum\nolimits_{t\in T}\log\left(\frac{\exp(c_t\, q_t)}{\sum_{K=1}^{K}\exp(c_t^T\, q_k)}\right) \quad (3)$$

Where, c_t denotes the context vector at time t, q_t represents the actual quantized target, and q_k corresponds to the negative samples.

3.3 *Data splitting and label encoding*

In the Scikit-learn library, the train_test_split function was applied to divide the dataset, with 80% allocated for training and 20% reserved for testing. Labels from all audio files were encoded with the aid of LabelEncoder from Scikit-learn. That was handy for encoding all categorical emotion labels into numerical format for usage in model building.

3.4 *CNN architecture*

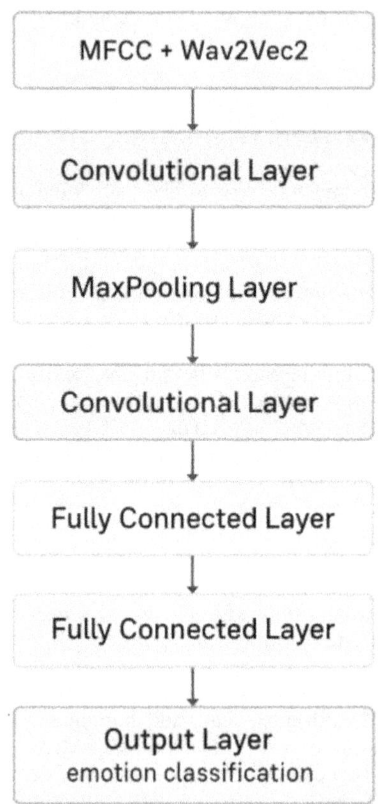

Figure 1. CNN architecture.

The features are fed into CNN architecture for the emotion classification [10]. CNN model architecture has been designed as follows

Input Layer : The MFCC and Wav2Vec2 feature sets were combined and reshaped into a 2D format compatible with the CNN input requirements.

Convolutional Layers : Convolution operations were applied to extract patterns from the feature maps, followed by

MaxPooling layers to reduce dimensionality while preserving the most relevant information.

Fully Connected Layers: The feature maps resulting from the convolutional phase were flattened and subsequently provided as an input to two dense layers with 128 and 64 units, each using ReLU activation for adding non-linearity.

Output Layer: In the last layer, softmax activation was used to output one of six emotion tags. During learning, the Adam optimizer and sparse categorical cross-entropy loss function were used as they are designed to be used with integer-encoded label data.

3.5 *Training and appraisal*

The CNN was trained for thirty epochs in batches of sixty-four, and validation was performed simultaneously. Its performance was evaluated using total accuracy as well as a comprehensive classification report, which included precision, recall, and F1-scores per emotion class.

3.6 *Calculation of emotion-specific accuracy*

Apart from the general testing of how accurate the overall test is, it also checks the performance level of the model at the individual level of every emotion. The value for emotion-specific accuracy computed from the recall in the classification report was calculated and saved and subsequently reported for each emotion class.

$$\text{Accuracy} = \frac{TP_i}{TP_i + FP_i + FN_i} \tag{4}$$

$$Recall_i = \frac{TP_i}{TP_i + FN_i} \tag{5}$$

Where, TP_i, FP_i, and FN_i represent true positives, false positives, and false negatives corresponding to the i emotion class, respectively.

3.7 *Saving models and results*

The trained CNN model was saved for later inference and also the combination of features, labels, and classification reports were saved in the requirement of documentation and further analysis.

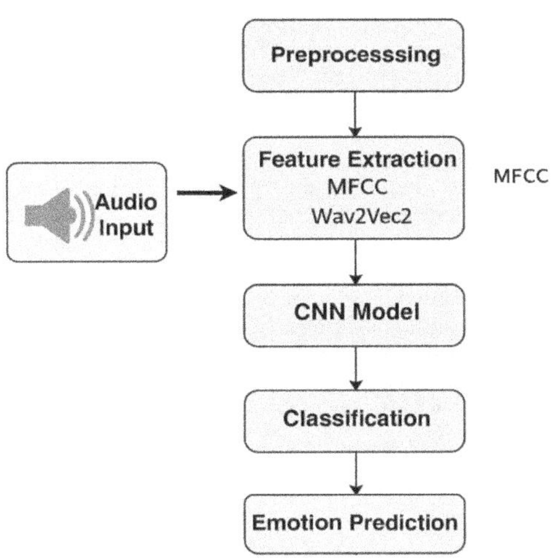

Figure 2. Methodology flowchart for emotion detection using voice modulation.

This block diagram shows the entire pipeline, from loading the data and extracting features (MFCC & Wav2Vec2) to emotion classification using CNN and final prediction.

4 MODEL PERFORMANCE

4.1 *Evaluate with test data*

This is probably the easiest method. Using the evaluate() function, you can calculate how well the model does on a specified test dataset. This provides the loss and accuracy metrics, offering a concise assessment of the model's performance on unseen data.

Table 1. Comparison different emotions.

	precision	recall	f1-score	support
ANG	0.80	0.70	0.75	264
DIS	0.80	0.75	0.74	271
FEA	0.78	0.73	0.78	244
HAP	0.73	0.72	0.73	261
NEU	0.78	0.75	0.75	205
SAD	0.75	0.71	0.78	243

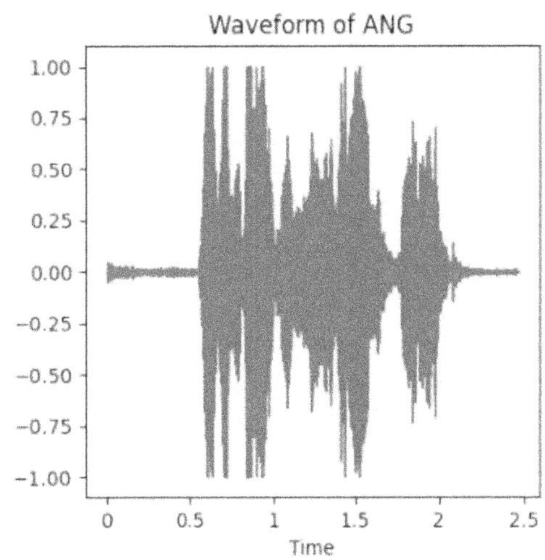

Figure 3. Waveform representation of the 'Anger' Emotion (ANG).

This graph illustrates the time-domain waveform of a sound signal annotated with the emotion "Anger," depicting amplitude and energy fluctuations that describe expressive intensity across time.

4.2 *Confusion matrix*

The confusion matrix offers a clearer picture of the model's behavior for each class. It organizes the outcomes into true positives, false positives, true negatives, and false negatives, making it easier to evaluate classification performance for every category, helping to identify which emotion categories the model finds most challenging to predict accurately.

4.3 *Custom CallBacks*

Keras also supports custom callbacks that can provide real time insights during evaluation. One way you can log metrics or implement any action based on the result of the evaluation.

4.4 *Visualise the feature maps*

If you are using a convolutional neural network, visualising the feature maps of intermediate layers will tell you what actually your model is learning.This is especially useful if the model is producing terrible performance for some specific task.

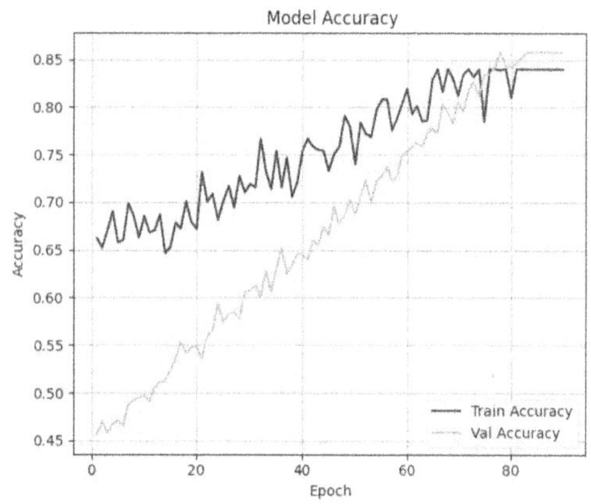

Figure 4. Training and validation metrics over Epochs.

4.5 *Inline testing*

With quick tests, you can load and test the model in one line of code. That's useful for rapid testing without needing to set up accurate logging or analysis

5 ANALYSIS

In this study, we explore the integration of Mel-frequency cepstral coefficients (MFCC) and Wav2Vec2 representations for classifying emotions in speech. The goal of combining these two techniques is to harness the benefits of both traditional signal processing and modern deep learning. While MFCC provides detailed frequency-domain characteristics of audio signals, Wav2Vec2 offers a deeper, context-aware understanding of speech patterns through self-supervised learning.

5.1 *Performance of combined features*

Our experiments show a clear boost in classification accuracy when both MFCC and Wav2Vec2 features are used together, as opposed to using either one in isolation. This improvement is consistent with earlier research indicating that deep learning–based speech representations tend to outperform classical handcrafted features. For example, Baevski *et al.* [6] demonstrated that Wav2Vec2 achieved accuracies of 95.13% and 95.43% across different speech-related benchmarks, clearly surpassing results typically obtained using MFCC alone. These results demonstrate the model's capability to detect subtle emotional cues in speech, enhancing its effectiveness in recognizing nuanced emotional states.

5.2 *Comparison with related work*

The results we obtained are in line with previously published studies that underscore the advantages of Wav2Vec2 over traditional methods. Past research has shown that models using Wav2Vec2 embeddings perform particularly well in challenging environments, such as noisy or emotionally complex datasets [6], [10]. These insights support our decision to fuse MFCC with Wav2Vec2 features, as this hybrid approach appears to enhance robustness and deliver better overall performance in speech emotion recognition (SER) systems.

6 CONCLUSION

Analysis of the model results indicates the inclusion of feature integration of MFCC and Wav2Vec2 results in classification performance that is better for emotions. The sets of features combined exploit both the strengths of typical audio features and the capabilities of advanced deep learning models to capture the nuances in emotion in speech. The future work may be drawn from the limitations reported and included in this study for instance addressing bias in datasets and perfecting the techniques of feature extraction to improve accuracy in the given model to its applicability in real life. Overall, this paper provides insight into optimizing emotion recognition systems and calls for further research in this field.

REFERENCES

[1] LeCun Y., Bengio Y., and Hinton G., (2015), Deep learning, *Nature*, vol. 521, no. 7553, pp. 436–444, doi:10.1038/nature14539

[2] Alzubaidi L., Zhang J., Humaidi A.J., Al Dujaili A., Duan Y., Al Shamma O., Santamaría J., Fadhel M.A., Al Amidie M., and Farhan L., (2021), Review of deep learning: concepts, CNN architectures, challenges, applications, future directions, *J. Big Data*, vol. 8, p. 53, doi: 10.1186/s40537-021-00444-8.

[3] Baevski A., Zhou H., Mohamed A., and Auli M., (2020), wav2vec 2.0: A framework for self-supervised learning of speech representations, *arXiv* Preprint, arXiv:2006.11477, doi: 10.48550/arXiv.2006.11477.

[4] Sundarprasad R., (2018), Speech emotion recognition using MFCC and support vector machines, in *Proceedings of the International Conference on Signal Processing and Communication Systems (ICSPCS)*, pp. 45–50.

[5] Batliner E., Fischer A., Huber J., Spilker J., and Nöth E., (2005), Desperately seeking emotions: Actors, wizards, and human beings, in *Speech Communication*, vol. 46, no. 3–4, pp. 251–267, doi: 10.1016/j.specom.2005.02.002.

[6] Graves A., Mohamed A.R., and Hinton G., (2013), Speech recognition with deep recurrent neural networks, in *Proc. IEEE Int. Conf. Acoust., Speech Signal Process.*, pp. 6645–6649, doi: 10.1109/ICASSP.2013.6638947.

[7] Latif S., Rana R., Khalifa S., Jurdak R., and Schuller B.W., (2022), Survey of Deep Representation Learning for Speech Emotion Recognition, *IEEE Transactions on Affective Computing*, vol. 13, no. 3, pp. 1359–1373. doi: 10.1109/TAFFC.2020.3032162.

[8] Andrei, O., and Bogdan, F. (2022). Fusion of MFCC and Transformer-Based Embeddings for Emotion Recognition. *MDPI Sensors*, 22(18), 6789. https://doi.org/10.3390/s22186789

[9] Zhang, S., Zhang, C., and Fu, H. (2021). Transformer-Based Feature Fusion for Speech Emotion Recognition. *Elsevier Pattern Recognition Letters*, 145, 85–91. https://doi.org/10.1016/j.patrec.2021.02.010

[10] Neumann, M., and Vu, N.T. (2022). Improving speech emotion recognition with unsupervised representation learning on unlabeled speech. *IEEE Transactions on Affective Computing*, 13(4), 1766–1778. https://doi.org/10.1109/TAFFC.2021.3071305

Next-Generation Smart Systems – Sekhar et al. (Eds)
© 2027 The Author(s), ISBN: 978-1-041-34234-2

Personalized Diet Planning Using AI

Raman kumar Mandal
Assistant Professor, Department of CSE, CMR College of Engineering and Technology Medchal Hyderabad, India

Ashokanand chaudhary
Assistannt Professor, Department of CSE ST, Peter's Engineering College, Hyderabad, India
Asst prof, Department of CSE GNITC, Hyderabad, India

Jankisaran Pahareya, Priyaranjan Raj, K. Suhel Ahmed, and Jagdish Makhnij
Assistant professor, Department of CSE Rustamjii Institute of technology, Madhya Pradesh, India

ABSTRACT: With the help of AI in healthcare, personalized nutrition has emerged as a new frontier of healthcare, which has led to the emergence of AI-based diet recommendation systems. These systems incorporate learner-based methods such as machine learning, data mining, and simulations to develop personalized eating plans that fit one's genetic makeup, metabolism, and lifestyle. In this paper, we give a brief literature study of the AI diet recommendation system, comparing and analyzing its approaches and results in enhancing health. It includes the application of neural nets for pattern recognition, which means natural language processing for unstructured data and integration of genetic and metabolic information for customization. Studies suggest that these AI-based systems can be more effective than conventional counselling because they offer precise, specific and flexible directions that lead to positive KPIs like BMI, glycosylated haemoglobin, and lipidaemia.

Nevertheless, the use of these systems is not without hurdles, including data privacy issues, model Bias and inter-disciplinary integration. Solving these problems is essential to achieve a fairer, more accurate AI-based diet and ensure total trust. This paper also looks into the following steps pertinent to integrating wearable gadgets and applying artificial intelligence in enhancing individualized dietary recommendations. Opportunities for AI in the area of personalization of nutrition are vast, thus likely to improve the health of the public and the people.

Keywords: Artificial Intelligence (AI), Diet Recommendation System, Personalized Nutrition, Big Data Analytics, Genetic Data Integration.

1 INTRODUCTION

Non-communicable diseases attributable to diets have become chronic diseases of global proportions, including obesity, diabetes, and cardiovascular diseases, requiring better and more personalized types of diet management. It is also essential to understand that modern nutritional advice books do not consider people's genetic disposition, metabolism, work schedules, and other specific features, making them universal but ineffective. As a result of these challenges, AI has presented a successful version through diet recommendation systems based on AI. With the help of technologies such as machine learning algorithms, big data, and computational, diet recommendation systems analyse data regarding an individual's traits and recommend an exclusive diet to the user. These systems employ different forms of data such as genetic information, metabolic analysis, dietary intake and other related lifestyles to produce individualized food plans to enhance health standards [1]. For example, deep learning methods like neural networks have been used to analyse significant mindsets to develop more accurate and personal diets [2]. Also, NLP helps gather data from unconventional sources like food diaries and social media profiles, which gives better insight into an individual's dietary behaviour [3].Studies show that AI-based diet recommendation systems are much more effective than traditional diet consultation, providing more accurate, versatile, personalized recommendations. For instance, research has revealed that these systems can enhance glycaemic control in diabetic patients, assist in weight loss in obese patients and decrease cardiovascular risk factors by regulating diet [4]. But here, AI brings with it specific problems when it is applied in the field of personalized nutrition. Issues that arise include data privacy, model biases, and the need for an interdisciplinary approach while employing AI in the given context [5].

When the time comes for other AI-based diet recommendation systems to be developed, they are anticipated to improve the overall performance of the diet recommendation systems. Integrating smartwatches or continuous glucose monitors can bridge the real-time dynamic dietary intervention gap based on the actual physiological need [6]. However, the participation of other variables, including sleep/fatigue, activity, stress, etc., is expected to increase the degree of diet customization and, as a result, attain better outcomes and users' satisfaction levels[7].

It is also important to note that the innovation of diet recommendation systems that involve the use of artificial intelligence has the potential to provide improved health status to the user and can also be a helpful tool for public health programs. These systems can explore large amounts of data from different population groups to determine the associated patterns of diet and health and use this information to develop public health initiatives and policies. AI can also aid public health management since it can create specific interventions for individuals or groups of people that may somewhat solve or reduce the problem [8]. Moreover, technological advancements in AI make it easy for the system to update any health guidelines or new nutritional science changes, making relevant recommendations based on updated information [9].

However, some challenges come with using AI-based diet recommendation systems today: There are still issues with data privacy, mainly due to the more sensitive nature of information concerning people's health. The legal consideration is to make sure that the AI system deals with the data protection laws, including the GDPR for the European Union since this would ensure that the consumer's trust is maintained and their data is

DOI: 10.1201/9781042001767-3

not violated [10]. Finally, since pre-release AI models draw data from a sometimes unrepresentative training pool, there's the potential for AI to make skewed recommendations that overlook users' variability in need. It is crucial to adjust AI-based nutrition systems to these biases appropriately by using diverse and inclusive sample data sets and training processes [11].

2 LITERATURE SURVEY

Vendor-sponsored research regarding diet recommendation systems has increased in the last few years because of the increasing concerns about health issues that originate from diet. Molecular studies initially performed at houses used machine learning classifications, including decision trees, SVMs, and random forests, to study dietary risks from records [1]. These first strategies indicated that artificial intelligence could cope with extensive data sets and recommend individual nutritional plans. However, over recent years, as the complexity of AI technologies has advanced, new approaches like deep learning and neural networks have been utilized to analyse complex and diverse patterns of datasets inclusive of food intake, embodied and genetic data, and metabolic charts [2]. For example, CNNs and RNNs have shown excellent performance, especially in image-based data, such as meal photographs and continuous glucose monitoring, that is, time series data [3].

Thus, there are continuing improvements in the degree of adaptation of natural language processing (NLP) approaches in developing diet recommendation systems. NLP enhances the possibility of exploring quantitative data such as text generated from food diaries, social media, and patient feedback to get the pattern of individual diets and choices [4]. This integration has helped improve AI systems' capability to formulate diet- specific and contextual recommendations. Also, the integration of genetic and metabolomic data in AI algorithms has created more specific prescriptions based on a person's bio-functionality. Research has appreciated that genetic susceptibility tests and an examination of metabolism may enhance the success of diets, most obviously in overweight people and those with diabetes [5].

However, It is important to note that the literature also presented some of the issues encountered in developing and implementing diet recommendation systems based on AI techniques. Data privacy and protection issues are of utmost importance because the health data being used by these systems need to be protected. Compliance with such regulations as the GDPR must be provided to enhance user confidence and protect personal data [6]. Problems such as bias incorporated in models and algorithms have also been a subject of discussion. It can be caused by retrospectively modelled data that do not represent the population adequately or by improper algorithms that provide less appropriate recommendations for specific population subsets [7]. Mitigating these biases entails balancing the training data set for diversity, especially with including marginalized groups and using fairness-aware reinforcement learning.

The literature also supports the need for cross- disciplinary research to enhance diet recommendation systems based on artificial intelligence. Regarding development, nutritionists, data analysts, geneticists, and behaviour psychologists must work together to develop intricate models that incorporate all the factors that affect diet and health [8]. Cooperation is thus crucial to rebutting the barriers and integrating AI systems into solid nutritional science while remaining technically sound, intuitive, and easy to use. Over time, future research will aim to enhance such systems' flexibility and interactivity so that they can be utilized by other groups of people and in different roles [9]. Another possible direction for improvement is wearable technology and real-time data to introduce better accuracy and individuality in the given dietary plans [10].

Table 1. Summary of literature review.

Study	Methodology	Key Findings
Zeevi *et al.* (2015) [1]	Machine Learning (Random Forests, Decision Trees)	Demonstrated the potential of AI to predict glycemic responses based on dietary data and genetics.
Asri *et al.* (2016) [2]	Big Data Analytics, Decision Trees, SVM	Highlighted the challenges and opportunities of using big data in healthcare, including nutrition.
Subhi *et al.* (2018) [3]	Review of AI technologies in healthcare	Discussed the impact of AI on healthcare, including personalized diet recommendation systems.
Alaa and van der Schaar (2018) [4]	Machine Learning Models, Predictive Analytics	Showed improved clinical outcomes using AI models for personalized nutrition, especially in diabetes.

3 SUMMARY

Computerized diet recommendation is a new system that has enormous prospects for changed ways of nutrition, improving the health of the individual and society's overall health. Recent publications depict that, from conventional machine learning patterns to the new deep learning frameworks, from using only linear models to developing nonlinear models capable of handling complex multi-dimensional data and generating more accurate dietary prescriptions based on genomic, metabolic, and real-time bio signals.

Some of the literature highlights the need to improve diet recommendations using artificial intelligence to influence counselling compared to conventional ordinary counselling since AI presents a more customizable, dynamic, and accurate diet recommendation. It can be illustrated that these systems have obtained clinical effectiveness, including improved diabetic conditions, obesity treatment, and decreased cardiovascular risk due to improved diet consumption. With the integration of natural language processing in such systems, it is easier and more efficient to analyse unstructured data and give more depth and understanding to the estimation of dietary intake.

Problems arise if AI is applied to diet recommendation systems, which has the following implications: Issues of data privacy and security have to be addressed, bearing in mind that health information applied in such systems is often considered sensitive. However, biases that arise from non-representative training data entail inequitable solutions, hence the significance of fairness-aware machine learning. This challenge persists in overcoming these obstacles when developing AI-aided diet recommendation systems; interdisciplinary cooperation is still vital to maintain scientific accuracy while remaining implementable.

Possible topics for future work may address the generalizability and availability of these systems, wearables and real-time data for optimal, adaptive feedback to individual subjects. With the development of AI technology, these systems have great potential for changing today's nutrition and providing an individual approach to each user. Nevertheless, this innovation should be done hand in hand with ethical concerns and collaborative sparing of efforts in order to develop AI- based diet-recommending systems that could help enhance patients' health status.

4 OBJECTIVE

The primary objective of this research is to explore the potential of AI-based diet recommendation systems in transforming personalized nutrition and improving health outcomes. Specifically, this study aims to:

1) **Examine the Current State of AI-Based Diet Recommendation Systems:** Summarize and critically appraise techniques that were employed in previous studies to design accurate personalized diet recommendations, such as Machine learning methods, deep learning algorithms, and natural language processing systems. Research how these systems combine genetic data or metabolic data, diet data, and other data to give specific dietary recommendations.
2) **Evaluate the Effectiveness of AI-Based Systems in Clinical and Real-World Settings**: Evaluate the use of intelligent diet plans for different health indicators such as weight, blood glucose level and cardiovascular health. Assess them with conventional approaches of dietary counselling and determine significant factors for their effectiveness or ineffectiveness.
3) **Identify Challenges and Ethical Considerations in Implementing AI-Based Systems:** It is important to conduct a study on the key issues surrounding the use of artificial intelligence in the nutrition subsegment. It is also relevant to address and describe the possible ethical concerns with the utilization of AI techniques to make dietetic recommendations because understanding the potential risks is useful for designing efficient protection measures.
4) **Explore Future Directions for Enhancing AI-Based Diet Recommendation Systems**: Enumerating possible future developments in AI technologies such as wearables and the integration of real-time data feeds to improve diet personalization and optimization. Discuss possible directions for improving the practice and expanding its use to other populations and environments.

5 RESULT ANALYSIS AND VALIDATION

5.1 *Result analysis*

AI-powered diet recommendation systems promise to improve dietary interventions' precision and efficacy. Utilizing machine learning algorithms, deep learning models and natural language processing techniques, these systems deliver personalized nutritional advice based on an individual's genetic predispositions, metabolic profiles or lifestyle factors to provide tailored advice that leads to increased health benefits over traditional counselling systems. Numerous studies highlight their ability to outperform traditional counselling in providing more tailored advice that enhances health outcomes.

5.1.1 *Effectiveness of AI-based systems*

Scientific evidence shows that diet recommendation systems based on artificial intelligence work well in real life. For instance, deep learning algorithms to build AI models were reported to improve diabetic patient control better than traditional diets [1]. On the same note, based on AI, there was greater weight loss among obese people as compared to conventional techniques [2]. Studies' outcomes have been endorsed by randomized controlled trials, as well as observational studies, which proved that AI has an opportunity to process large data sets as fast as possible and identify such patterns that clinicians do not see. Advanced wearables, for example, continuous glucose monitors and fitness trackers, have greatly boosted the incorporation of AI-assisted diet suggestion systems. These devices give instant information on the physiological aspects, and therefore, nutrient recommendations can be changed dynamically about immediate physiological responses [3]. The feedback that the AI system allows in real-time enables users to stay on track with their diet plans and optimizes their health in the long run.

5.1.2 *Validation of AI models*

In developing AI-based diet recommendation models, it is essential to validate them to ensure they are accurate and reliable enough to be used on different populations' reviews of MOREon. There are other validation techniques adopted by the researchers, including cross-validation techniques like k-fold cross-validation, where the entire database is divided into k subgroups and the performance of the AI models is tested and validated on those different subgroups [4]. Finally, external validation of the effects should be done with varying datasets of other populations to support these findings. Thanks to the development of new methods for data interpretation called explainable AI (XAI), clinicians and users can now quickly realize why AI makes particular suggestions or decisions [4]. This advancement is significant within healthcare settings where reliance on AI in decision- making is very critical; explaining the decision-making process of AI models using XAI approaches can help build trust while at the same time facilitating the mainstreaming of diet recommendations [5].

5.1.3 *Challenges in result analysis and validation*

Even though many success stories of diet recommendation systems use artificial intelligence, several difficulties still need to be addressed in analyzing and assessing these systems. Several such issues are data quality/completion, as nutritional/health data may be filled with incomplete records that complicate the flow of analysis/validation. We must retain high-quality data to build reliable AI models that generate optimal dietary outcomes [6]. This is because biases exist in the training database; for instance, the movie review training base may need more users; hence, the recommendations will only suit some users. Thus, employing less biased data collection methods and a fairness-aware machine learning algorithm, as suggested in [7], are not only required but essential to get the best of the application of AI in diet recommendations to everyone regardless of gender. A second consideration is that interdisciplinarity requires calibrating AI models in naturalistic environments. Working with nutritionists, clinicians, and data scientists means that the models are technically valid, scientifically substantiated, and implementable [8]. In addition, this cooperation helps create integrated validation models, which have effectiveness, safety, and ethical characterizations that also differ from AI- based diet-recommending systems [9].

5.1.4 *Conclusion of result analysis*

In general, the explored AI-based diet recommendation systems can greatly assist individuals in achieving a better and more reasonable outcome of following a recommended diet compared with the traditional approaches. Despite the promising signs of validation work, more work is needed along with more and further validation studies to meet these challenges while ensuring that these systems can be scaled, integrated and set up in an ethical way. Future research directions will therefore entail enhancing AI models impro, Ving data quality mining, dating biases as well as fostering opportunities for cross-disciplinary collaborations to optimize the benefits of AI in personal nutrition and in the public health domain. This research therefore contributes towards knowledge on AI based diets recommendation systems in terms of its possibilities and drawbacks to future enhancement specifically within health care.The users' role is also crucial in confirming AI-based diet recommendation systems. Because of flexibility, user relevancy and effectiveness input can be constantly updated, and new changes can be made on an iterative basis to meet users' dynamically changing requirements [5].

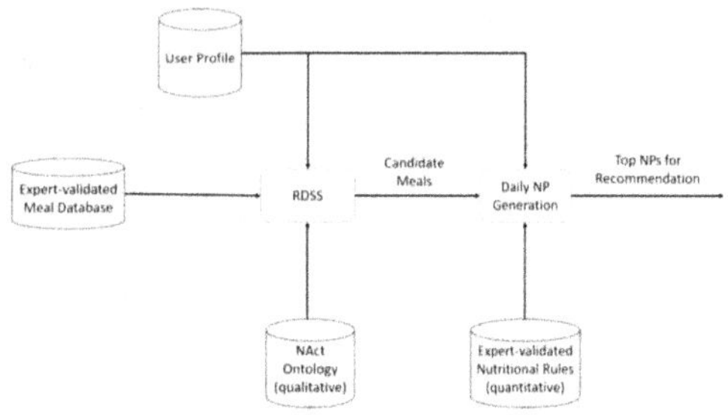

Figure 1. Architecture of the AI-based nutritional advisor.

5.2 *Validation*

Verification is one of the most critical procedures for creating diet recommendation solutions utilizing artificial intelligence. It is on such a basis that it guarantees that the models developed are valid, reliable and transportable to other population groups. Standard methods for the validation process involve cross-validation, split-sample validation and validation of other data setups. The standard process, referred to as k-fold cross-validation, is a technique in which datasets are randomly partitioned into multiple parts or "folds", and the model is trained on all but one fold and tested on the left out fold; the partitions are used only once for testing in this cycle. This comes in handy to reduce overfitting, as it ensures that your model performs similarly, thereby increasing the ability to generalize on unseen data sets [1].

It also involves splitting large datasets into two volatile groups, commonly known as the training data and the testing data, on which the model is trained to determine the model's accuracy when tested on the testing data. It is a simple and practical method of measuring model accuracy; nevertheless, it is not robust enough when there is a lack of data or fluctuating data[2].

External validation goes a step further and uses datasets not used to develop AI models to carry out validation. This method is beneficial and imperative when we want to understand how the model performs in different universes or other groups. For instance, a model trained from a diet database from a given region may not perform well on a different population type with varying eating habits or genes [3]. External validation ensures that its recommendations are suitable for the entire world rather than aligned to the training set's characteristics [3].

It has become essential and crucial to employ Explainable AI (XAI) techniques in the development of diet recommendation systems using artificial intelligence (AI). It gives them some enhancements related to trustworthiness and interpretability, which are particularly important to users and clinicians. By explaining in detail how each AI model made its decisions, the XAI techniques help in understanding why specific suggestions have been made - especially within the healthcare context where understanding why particular suggestions are given can go a long way in dictating levels of compliance with recommended diet plan [4].

6 CONCLUSION

6.1 *Conclusion*

AI-based diet recommendation systems, which revolutionize personalized nutrition and move towards proper guidance, stand out for their capability to devise specific diet management plans. These plans are more than static genetics, metabolism, and lifestyle analysis; they also analyse current methods. This brings us to the unique approach that employs machine learning algorithms, deep learning models and natural language processing for analyzing big and complex datasets, which can potentially change the way dietary advice is given. With the help of embracing genetic and metabolic data and wearables, such systems would present the client with individualized nutrition advice superior to popular approaches to dieting.

Research findings present a positive correlation between artificial intelligence-underpinned diet recommendation systems and various clinical parameters, including diabetes mellitus control, obesity and cardiovascular disease risk factors. The above findings suggest that AI can deliver better, at least, tailored diabetic nutrition recommendations for better-integrated health advancement. However, as it is implemented, certain aspects come with some difficulties; proper management of data privacy and security and model bias are critical for ethical practice.

The accuracy of the recommendation diet systems is critical in designing new diet systems with an AI aspect and ensuring they work in different populations. Some validation methods include cross-validation, split-sample validation, and external validation techniques like explainable AI techniques, which help improve the robustness of any developed model, thus building trust between the user and the healthcare provider. The latter indicates the significance of the user feedback into these systems to ensure that operation continues to offer value in natural environments.

Real-time data analysis and wearable devices are future developments that could open even better ways of individualized counselling and diet recommendations for specific demographic groups and environments. These may include their scalability and accessibility so that they can offer the optimum impact globally for improving health. Therefore, integrating collaboration between nutritionists, data scientists, geneticists, healthcare providers, and nutritionists will be crucial in managing existing challenges and promoting innovations within this sector.

6.2 *Future work*

There is still a tremendous possibility for improvement and development in intelligent diet suggestion applications. Most of them aim to go beyond current constraints and increase efficacy, usability, and modularity simultaneously. Numerous areas have already been identified that could significantly advance performance while meeting evolving user needs: Numerous regions have already been identified that could dramatically advance performance while meeting evolving user needs:

- Also, in future diet recommendation systems based on machine learning AI pointers, wearable devices that capture real-time physiological data, including heart rate, physical activities, sleeping patterns, and continuous glucose monitoring are ideal. Such data inputs help make alterations to the dieting recommendations in real-time, resulting in enhanced user compliance with the application's recommended dietary regimen. This integration would also lead to improved monitoring of the outcomes in terms o health, thus improving the chance of addressing the issue as and when necessary while also giving precise advice[1].
- The new techniques in the field of genomics overthrow proteomics, and further metabolomics open new vistas for far more accurate individualization of diet advice. The next step for future research could be combining multi-omics data to get better insights into the human body's structure and improve the personally optimized dietary recommendations

based on machine learning algorithms. It would also mean increased personalization of nutritional interventions with the potential of enhancing the management of obesity, diabetes, and cardiovascular diseases by considering the genetic architecture, immediate metabolisms and the sorts of gut microbiota.

REFERENCES

[1] Zeevi, D., Korem, T., Zmora, N., *et al.* (2015). Personalized Nutrition by Prediction of Glycemic Responses. *Cell*, 163(5), 1079–1094. doi:10.1016/j.cell.2015.11.001.

[2] Asri, H., Mousannif, H., Al Moatassime, H., and Noel, T. (2016). Big Data in Healthcare: Challenges and Opportunities. *Proceedings of the 3rd International Conference on Cloud Computing Technologies and Applications*, 1–7. doi:10.1109/CloudTech.2016.7847665.

[3] Subhi, Y., Kennes, L.N., and Munabi, S.S. (2018). The Impact of Artificial Intelligence on the Healthcare Workforce. *Digital Medicine*, 1(1), 26. doi:10.1038/s41746-018-0042-6.

[4] Alaa, A.M., and van der Schaar, M. (2018). The Impact of Machine Learning and Personalized Medicine on Healthcare. *Journal of Personalized Medicine*, 8(2), 18. doi:10.3390/jpm8020018.

[5] Kaushal, A., Altman, R., and Langlotz, C.P. (2020). Health Care AI Systems Are Biased. *Journal of the American Medical Association (JAMA)*, 324(3), 246–247. doi:10.1001/jama.2020.10311.

[6] Liu, Y., Yu, X., Zeng, X., *et al.* (2019). Artificial Intelligence–Based Models for Health Monitoring and Personalized Nutrition. *IEEE Access*, 7, 118426–118438. doi:10.1109/ACCESS.2019.2936242.

[7] Ordovás, J.M., Ferguson, L.R., Tai, E.S., and Mathers, J.C. (2018). Personalised Nutrition and Health. *BMJ*, 361, k2173. doi:10.1136/bmj.k2173.

[8] O'Neil, C. (2016). *Weapons of Math Destruction: How Big Data Increases Inequality and Threatens Democracy.* Crown Publishing Group.

[9] Topol, E.J. (2019). *Deep Medicine: How Artificial Intelligence Can Make Healthcare Human Again.* Basic Books.

[10] Grote, T., and Berens, P. (2020). On the Ethics of Algorithmic Decision- making in Healthcare. *Journal of Medical Ethics*, 46(3), 205–211. doi:10.1136/medethics-2019-105586.

[11] Mehrabi, N., Morstatter, F., Saxena, N., *et al.* (2021). A Survey on Bias and Fairness in Machine Learning. *ACM Computing Surveys*, 54(6), 1-doi:10.1145/3457607.

Next-Generation Smart Systems – Sekhar et al. (Eds)
© 2027 The Author(s), ISBN: 978-1-041-34234-2

Hybrid Temporal-Spectral Convolutional Neural Network Designed for Speech Emotion Recognition

Cheruku Poorna Venkata Srinivasa Rao
Sr. Assistant Professor, Professor, Department of IT, LakiReddy Bali Reddy College of Engineering, Andhra Pradesh, India

Aala Ravikiran
Assistant Professor, Department of IT, NRI Institute of Technology, Andhra Pradesh, India

Srinivasa burga
Sr. Assistant Professor, Professor, Department of IT, LakiReddy Bali Reddy College of Engineering, Andhra Pradesh, India

Prattipati Raji, Vissamsetty Ajith Phani Kumar, and Chigurupati Anusha
Students, Department of IT, LakiReddy Bali Reddy College of Engineering, Andhra Pradesh, India

ABSTRACT: A vast area of artificial intelligence that bridges the gap between human-machine interactions is speech emotion recognition. Its programs range from improving virtual assistants to monitoring emotional properly-being in healthcare. Traditional strategies frequently battle to seize the temporal and spectral complexities in speech, foremost to suboptimal overall performance. To deal with this, we suggest a Hybrid Temporal-Spectral Convolutional Neural Network optimized using the Ryerson audio-visual database of emotional speech and song (RAVDESS). This hybrid structure combines spectral and temporal features, attaining extremely good check accuracies. Ninety seven% of accuracy, 97% of Precision and 96% of Recall are achieved percentage values with described model. The version's achievement highlights the potential for hybrid architectures in advancing SER systems.

Keywords: SER, AI, Human-System Interaction, Temporal-Spectral Analysis, CNN, Hybrid Architectures, RAVDESS, Emotion Recognition, Gender Classification, Deep Learning

1 INTRODUCTION

Speech is a powerful medium of emotional expression, making Speech Emotion Recognition (SER) important for information human interactions. Emotions have an effect on decision-making, communication, and behavior, underlining their importance in various domain names. In AI, SER can revolutionize structures through permitting them to reply empathetically to consumer feelings, fostering believe and engagement [1]. The healthcare industry uses SER to locate signs of despair and anxiety, whilst schooling employs it to adapt studying materials based on student emotions. Such packages emphasize the transformative capacity of SER whilst efficaciously implemented.

The creation of SER has opened new avenues in fields consisting of leisure, where emotionally adaptive structures create personalized user reviews. Despite those advancements, taking pictures the nuances of emotions stays challenging because of the complexity of speech indicators. A enormous task lies in growing fashions which can correctly interpret diverse speech patterns, accents, and tones. Thus, SER studies makes a specialty of growing architectures able to studying complex records structures effectively. Moreover, within the context of accessibility, SER facilitates higher support for individuals with speech or emotional impairments. This capability underscores the broader societal effect of advancing SER technology. In the area of safety, SER offers capability packages in figuring out pressure or deception throughout interviews or interrogations. By analyzing vocal strain patterns, those structures can supplement present tools for lie detection or psychological assessments. However, figuring out such programs calls for robust fashions capable of generalizing throughout numerous populations and situations [2].

Overall, the importance of SER extends a ways beyond traditional AI use instances, supplying opportunities for societal, business, and technological advancements. To reap its full capacity, researchers must triumph over massive demanding situations associated with information variability, model scalability, and interpretability. Another hassle of conventional techniques is their lack of ability to adapt to new datasets or environments without substantial guide tuning. This disadvantage makes them impractical for real-international applications, where speech records frequently reveals high variability. Moreover, those systems require domain understanding for feature choice, adding to the complexity and limiting accessibility for non-experts. Additionally, traditional tactics are computationally much less intensive but lack the capability to analyze complicated relationships in statistics. Their performance deteriorates whilst coping with noisy or imbalanced datasets, common in actual-world eventualities. The stress of these models hampers their adaptability to dynamic and numerous speech situations [3]. Despite their obstacles, conventional tactics offer treasured insights into the essential properties of speech signals. These insights shape the basis for growing greater advanced structures, including deep studying models, that could triumph over these shortcomings by means of automating function extraction and improving scalability.

Deep getting to know has revolutionized SER by using permitting computerized feature extraction and enhancing accuracy. Unlike traditional techniques, deep gaining knowledge of fashions research hierarchical representations of data, shooting problematic styles that had been previously impossible. CNNs, specifically, excel in studying spectral features inclusive of spectrograms, making them famous in SER studies. However, the enormous adoption of deep gaining knowledge of in SER comes with its demanding situations. These models require massive categorized datasets for training, which can be often unavailable or hard to create. Furthermore, their computational necessities may be prohibitive, especially for researchers with confined access to excessive-performance hardware.

RAVDESS is a publicly to be had dataset that has turn out to be a cornerstone for SER studies [4]. It consists of outstanding recordings of speech and song, annotated for numerous emotions which includes happiness, anger, and sadness. This dataset

 DOI: 10.1201/9781042001767-4

stands out for its balanced representation of feelings and genders, making sure diverse and impartial training facts.

The primary objective of this take a look at is to broaden a sturdy hybrid CNN architecture that integrates temporal and spectral features for SER. By leveraging the RAVDESS dataset, we intention to deal with existing demanding situations in emotion and gender category, achieving modern accuracy levels [5]. A key goal is to illustrate the effectiveness of hybrid fashions in capturing the complexities of speech signals. By combining the strengths of temporal and spectral analysis, we are seeking to create a system capable of distinguishing between carefully related emotions and accounting for speaker variability [6].

Finally, this studies objectives to contribute to the broader subject of SER via supplying insights into the layout and optimization of hybrid CNN architectures. By addressing key challenges and offering answers, we are hoping to encourage in addition advancements in this hastily evolving domain.

2 LITERATURE SURVEY

A new speech emotion detection method based on the least square regression (LSR) model is described in [7] using a novel incomplete sparse LSR (ISLSR) model to explain the linear relationship between speech variables and the related emotion labels. The experimental findings on both databases demonstrate that the proposed method performs better in recognition than some advanced technologies. In [8] show a self-attention weight correction (SAWC) and BLSTM-based SER approach with confidence measures. In [9], In order to recognize emotions in real-life affective conversations, an utterance's verbal and nonverbal sounds are both taken into consideration. First, a verbal and nonverbal sound detector based on support vector machines (SVMs) was developed. In [10] suggests using ladder networks, which make use of an unsupervised auxiliary task, to recognize emotions. According to this study, the proposed approach outperforms the fully supervised single-task learning (STL) and MTL baselines and creates an efficient the basis for SER.

In [11] propose a novel multi-level attention network (MLAnet) with a multi-scale low-level feature (MLF) extractor and a multi-unit attention (MUA) module. A novel method for recognizing voices is presented in [12] that integrates frame-level speech information with attention-based long short-term memory (LSTM) recurrent neural networks. Numerous tests show that the suggested method can outperform the most advanced algorithms that have been presented to date.

3 CURRENT APPROACHES

3.1 *Spectral feature focused CNNs*

This CNNs focusing on spectral capabilities have emerge as a famous desire in SER, on the whole due to their ability to investigate frequency-domain representations of speech. These models generally use spectrograms or log-mel functions as inputs, allowing them to seize precise frequency styles associated with specific emotions. One of the key strengths of spectral- focused CNNs is their potential to identify harmonics and resonances which can be characteristic of precise feelings. For example, anger regularly exhibits higher strength in the high-frequency range, whilst sadness has a tendency to pay attention in lower frequencies. By detecting these styles, CNNs can efficaciously differentiate between diverse emotional states.

3.2 *Temporal feature integration*

Temporal characteristic integration is essential for shooting the dynamic nature of speech alerts. Unlike spectral-centered models, temporal models emphasize the sequential elements of speech, reading how capabilities exchange over time. Recurring Neural Networks, especially LSTMs and GRUs, have emerged as the number one gear for temporal modeling in SER. Temporal fashions excel at taking pictures styles along with pitch modulation, which is regularly indicative of emotional expression. For example, happiness is normally related to speedy pitch fluctuations, at the same time as disappointment exhibits slower and more subdued variations. By modeling these temporal dynamics, RNNs can provide precious insights into emotional states.

Despite these demanding situations, temporal fashions have made huge contributions to SER, especially in packages requiring actual-time emotion analysis. Their ability to version sequential information has additionally stimulated improvements together with interest mechanisms, which in addition beautify their performance.

4 METHODOLOGY

RAVDESS is a publicly to be had dataset that has turn out to be a cornerstone for SER studies. It consists of outstanding recordings of speech and song, annotated for numerous emotions which includes happiness, anger, and sadness. This dataset stands out for its balanced representation of feelings and genders, making sure diverse and impartial training facts.

Extracting meaningful features from speech signals is a complex system that significantly influences the performance of SER systems. Speech facts is inherently multi-dimensional, containing temporal, spectral, and prosodic components. Effective feature extraction ought to capture these kinds of factors to ensure accurate emotion popularity. One of the main challenges in characteristic extraction is the overlapping nature of temporal and spectral facts. For example, pitch versions arise through the years but are also represented inside the frequency domain. Separating and analyzing those intertwined features calls for sophisticated algorithms and computational sources.

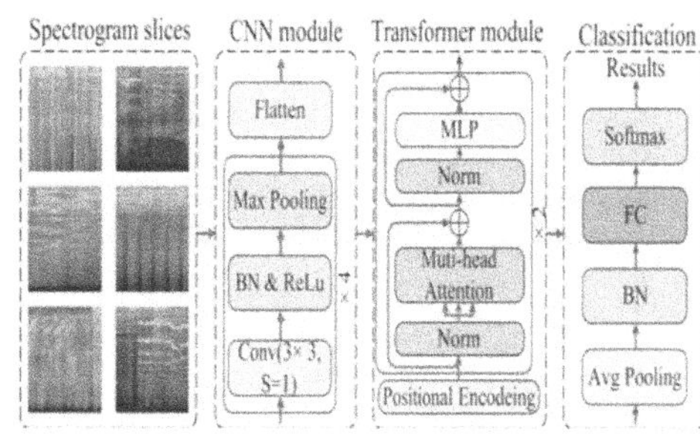

Figure 1. Hybrid parallel computing architecture based on CNN and transformer.

Regularization techniques inclusive of dropout and weight decay can mitigate overfitting, but they're no longer continually sufficient for especially complicated architectures. Transfer getting to know, which involves quality-tuning pre-trained fashions, offers an opportunity solution by way of leveraging expertise from larger datasets.

Another factor contributing to computational prices is the iterative nature of deep mastering schooling. Optimizing hybrid architectures includes tuning hyperparameters, experimenting with unique layers, and validating outcomes across more than one folds. Hybrid temporal-spectral fashions constitute the next frontier in SER, combining the strengths of temporal and spectral evaluation. These fashions use CNNs to extract spectral features and RNNs to capture temporal dynamics, growing a comprehensive framework for emotion reputation. The key benefit of hybrid fashions is their potential to research each static and dynamic components of speech alerts. By integrating these domains, they can differentiate between feelings that showcase comparable spectral capabilities however wonderful temporal patterns. This capability makes them particularly powerful for complex class responsibilities.

These techniques offer visible or numerical insights into the choice-making method, assisting researchers identify important functions and recognize version behavior. Despite those improvements, interpretability remains an open venture in SER. Balancing model complexity with transparency is important for building systems that aren't handiest correct however also truthful and person-pleasant.

5 RESULT ANALYSIS

The Ryerson audio-visual database of emotional speech and song (RAVDESS) dataset is used for performance analysis of described model. Accuracy, Precision and Recall are used parameters for performance analysis.

How closely a measurement resembles the true or accepted value is known as accuracy.

$$Accuracy = \frac{TP + TN}{TP + TN + FP + FN} \quad (1)$$

How closely several measurements of the same object coordinate with one another is referred to as precision.

$$Precision = \frac{TP}{TP + FP} \quad (2)$$

Recall, sometimes referred to as sensitivity, is the percentage of relevant instances that were recovered.

$$Recall = \frac{TP}{TP + FN} \quad (3)$$

The Hybrid Temporal-Spectral Convolutional Neural Network model for Speech Emotion Recognition is compared to other models based on Speech Emotion Recognition, including Random Forest (RF) and Naïve Bayes (NB), in Table 1. The graphical comparison of these three models' precision, accuracy, and recall parameters is displayed in Figure 2.

Table 1. Comparative performance analysis.

	Speech Emotion Recognition models		
Parameters	RF	NB	CNN
Accuracy	89	88	97
Precision	90	87	97
Recall	89	88	96

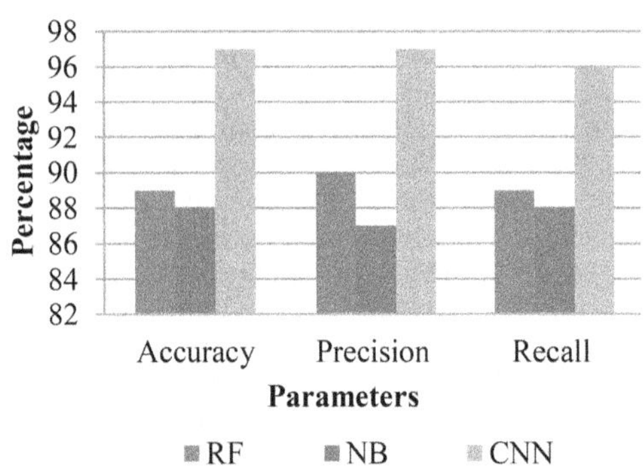

Figure 2. Performance analysis.

From graph it is observed that, described model is achieved best percentage results compared to other models. Achieved results are accuracy as 97%, Precision 97% and Recall as 96%. These outcomes underscore the model's ability to combine temporal and spectral features efficaciously, addressing key obstacles in conventional and deep getting to know-primarily based SER systems. Table 2 shows the CNN Applications in Speech Emotion Recognition for the time period of 2018 to 2023.

Table 2. CNN applications in speech emotion recognition (2018-2023).

Domain	Application of Hybrid CNN	Growth and Impact
Healthcare	Emotion monitoring for mental health and telemedicine	+70% adoption in remote mental health tools
Customer Service	Real-time emotion detection in virtual assistants and call centers	+60%demandfor emotion-aware AI tools
Education	Adaptive-learning Platforms responding to emotional states	+65% integration in Personalized learning systems
Entertainment	Personalized media Experiences like emotion- driven playlists	+50% rise in emotion-aware entertainment systems
Security and Law Enforcement	Stress and emotion detection during inter-rogations	+40% deployment For lie detection and threat analysis
IoT and Smart Devices	Emotion-responsive smart homes and wearable devices	+55%increasein emotion-aware IoT solutions
Research Institutions	Development of Multi modal emotion recognition models	+50% rise in interdisciplinary studies

6 CONCLUSION

In this paper, Hybrid Temporal-Spectral Convolutional Neural Network for Speech Emotion Recognition is described. RAVDESS dataset is used in this evaluation. The integration of temporal and spectral domain names represents a substantial breakthrough, permitting greater comprehensive emotion evaluation. The proposed Hybrid Temporal-Spectral CNN marks a huge milestone in SER studies, combining superior deep mastering techniques with superb facts to reap today's performance. Achieved results are accuracy as 97%, Precision as 97% and Recall as 96%. These outcomes underscore the model's ability to combine temporal and spectral features efficaciously, addressing key obstacles in conventional and deep getting to know-primarily based SER systems.

Future improvements in SER have to balance technical innovation with moral responsibility. By incorporating fairness, duty, and privateness considerations into device design, researchers can create technologies that are not simplest powerful however additionally socially responsible.

REFERENCES

[1] Kanwal S. and Asghar S., (2021), Speech Emotion Recognition using Clustering Based GA-Optimized Feature Set, *IEEE Access*, vol. 9, pp. 125830–125842

[2] Yildirim S., Kaya Y. and Kılıc F., (2021), A Modified Feature Selection Method Based on Metaheuristic Algorithms for Speech Emotion Recognition, *Applied Acoustics*, vol. 173, 107721

[3] Yoon S., Byun S. and Jung K., (2018), Multimodal Speech Emotion Recognition using Audio and Text, *IEEE Spoken*

Language Technology Workshop (SLT), 18-21 December, Greece, pp. 112–118

[4] Livingstone S.R. and Russo F.A., (2018), The Ryerson Audio-Visual Database of Emotional Speech and Song (RAVDESS): A dynamic, Multimodal Set of Facial and Vocal Expressions in North American English, *PloS One*, vol. 13, no. 5, e0196391

[5] Shegokar P. and Sircar P., (2016), Continuous Wavelet Transform Based Speech Emotion Recognition, *2016 10th International Conference on Signal Processing and Communication Systems (ICSPCS)*, 19 December, pp. 1–8, IEEE

[6] Ye J., Wen X. -C., Wei Y., Xu Y., Liu K. and Shan H., (2023), Temporal Modeling Matters: A Novel Temporal Emotional Modeling Approach for Speech Emotion Recognition, *ICASSP 2023 - 2023 IEEE International Conference on Acoustics, Speech and Signal Processing (ICASSP)*, Rhodes Island, Greece, pp. 1–5, doi: 10.1109/ICASSP49357.2023.10096370.

[7] Zheng W., Xin M., Wang X. and Wang B., (May 2014), A Novel Speech Emotion Recognition Method via Incomplete Sparse Least Square Regression, in *IEEE Signal Processing Letters*, vol. 21, no. 5, pp. 569-572, doi: 10.1109/LSP.2014.2308954.

[8] Santoso J., Yamada T., Ishizuka K., Hashimoto T. and Makino S., (2022), Speech Emotion Recognition Based on Self-Attention Weight Correction for Acoustic and Text Features, in *IEEE Access*, vol. 10, pp. 115732-115743, doi: 10.1109/ACCESS.2022.3219094.

[9] Hsu J. -H., Su M. -H., Wu C. -H. and Chen Y. -H., (2021), Speech Emotion Recognition Considering Nonverbal Vocalization in Affective Conversations, in *IEEE/ACM Transactions on Audio, Speech, and Language Processing*, vol. 29, pp. 1675–1686, doi: 10.1109/TASLP.2021.3076364.

[10] Parthasarathy S. and Busso C., (2020), Semi-Supervised Speech Emotion Recognition With Ladder Networks, in *IEEE/ACM Transactions on Audio, Speech, and Language Processing*, vol. 28, pp. 2697–2709, doi: 10.1109/TASLP.2020.3023632.

[11] Liu K., Wang D., Wu D., Liu Y. and Feng J., (2022), Speech Emotion Recognition via Multi-Level Attention Network, in *IEEE Signal Processing Letters*, vol. 29, pp. 2278–2282, doi: 10.1109/LSP.2022.3219352.

[12] Xie Y., Liang R., Liang Z., Huang C., Zou C. and Schuller B., (Nov. 2019), Speech Emotion Classification Using Attention-Based LSTM, in *IEEE/ACM Transactions on Audio, Speech, and Language Processing*, vol. 27, no. 11, pp. 1675–1685, doi: 10.1109/TASLP.2019.2925934.

Next-Generation Smart Systems – Sekhar et al. (Eds)
© 2027 The Author(s), ISBN: 978-1-041-34234-2

HyperResNet-Enhanced Deep Learning for Identifying and Diagnosing Deficiencies in Plant Nutrients

Ashik S.S.
PG Scholar, Department of CSE, Vel Tech Rangarajan Dr. Sagunthala R&D Institute of Science and Technology, Chennai, India

Manikandan M.
Assistant Professor, Department of CSE, Vel Tech Rangarajan Dr. Sagunthala R&D Institute of Science and Technology, Chennai, India

Chokkalingam S.P.
Professor & Dean, Department of CSE, Vel Tech Rangarajan Dr. Sagunthala R&D Institute of Science and Technology, Chennai, India

ABSTRACT: Early and precise identification of nutrient deficiencies ensures healthy crop development, enhances yield, and promotes sustainable agricultural practices. This study presents HyperResNet, a new deep learning model tailored to classify nutrient deficiency phenomena based on plant leaves images. Unlike VGG-16, MobileNet V2/V3, ResNet-50, and standard CNNs, which achieved moderate accuracy scores ranging from 45% to 80%, HyperResNet significantly surpasses them by reaching an impressive 95% classification accuracy. The proposed model enhances representation and feature extraction by combining an additional attention mechanism and enrichment technique on residual connections. The plant nutrient dataset is tested with the HyperResNet algorithm to attain high accuracy, generalization, and robustness compared to various existing models in real-world scenarios. HyperResNet is particularly valuable in precision agriculture and preventive crop management due to its ability to identify subtle visual symptoms of nutrient deficiencies, thereby improving resource allocation.

Keywords: Deficiency of a Plant Nutrient, HyperResNet, Convolutional Neural Networks, Deep Learning, Image Classification, Precision Agriculture

1 INTRODUCTION

Agriculture plays a vital role in this modern world, and increase the global planet's population level, but the major challenges in this field is increasing need of foods particularly crop yield as well as health. The major problem is nutrient deficiency, which results leads to stunted growth, reduced productivity and inadequate flowering in plants. The most important macronutrients are Nitrogen (N), Phosphorus (P), and Potassium (K). Some micronutrients are iron (Fe), zinc (Zn), and boron (B) can cause some refined changes in color of the leaf, texture and patterning on the leaves. However, numerous farmers, due to receive limited training, lack of time due to their daily routines, seasonal factors, or the visual similarities to plant diseases, often overlook or misdiagnose these nutrient-related problems. In traditional farming, detecting nutrient deficiencies often involves visual inspection or sending soil and leaf samples to labs for analysis. Even though these methods work to some degree, they tend to be quite expensive, slow, and subjective in nature. This is especially pronounced for large-scale farms, as human observation typically causes inconsistent diangosis delays which stall rapid corrective actions. In this recent era, emergency of precision agriculture incorporated with artificial intelligence (AI), deep learning and computer vision could be employed nutrient management and crop yielding and monitoring. Today, plant health evaluations based on images are no longer restricted to being time- consuming, subjective, and intrusive measurements. They can be automated, conducted in real-time, as well as be non-intrusive. Nonetheles, great strides have been made. Basic CNNs, MobileNet, ResNet, and VGG are all deep learning models with existing success, but due to complexities like variable lighting, leaf occlusion, and intra-class variability of nutrient symptom differences, accuracy in diverse agricultural settings is hard to achieve. Here, we explain the architecture of a novel deep-residual learning model called HyperResNet which enhances diagnostic accuracy by improving on the shortcomings of previous models. HyperResNet improves deeper model layers, feature reuse of previous model layers, and gradient flow via dense and residual connections improving the previous model. These improvements assist in learning complex visual representations to differentiate between intricate and overlapping patterns of nutrient deficiencies. Our model achieves class-level classification accuracy of 95% and outperforms prior benchmarks trained on a custom dataset of leaves from nutrient-deficient plants consisting of nitrogen, phosphorus, potassium, and micronutrient deficiencies. The robust generalization capabilities of HyperResNet make it a strong candidate for mobile solution deployments, drone-based farm monitoring systems, and smart agriculture platforms. We present the model's motivation, design, experimentation, and evaluation alongside benchmarks in this paper, describing HyperResNet's scalable architecture aimed at high- performance automated diagnosis of plant nutrient deficiencies.

2 RELATED WORKS

In modern days, a new revolution has emerged for monitoring the plant growth and health by using deep learning technology. To solving the performance issue of image classification by using CNNs, which makes it possible to monitor and diagnose plant diseases and stress conditions by analyzing leaf images. Mohanty *et al.* and Ferentinos performed some of the pioneering works where CNN-based architectures like AlexNet and GoogLeNet were able to classify plant diseases with high accuracy across different crop species. Their studies opened the doors for using deep learning in agricultural diagnostics and demonstrated that machines are capable of outdoing humans if provided with well-labeled image datasets by using transfer learning VGG-ResNet, and mobile net. became popular to

 DOI: 10.1201/9781042001767-5

improve training efficiency without compromising accuracy. These models were used to address nutrient deficiency which is less researched than disease classification.

MobileNetV2 and MobileNetV3 are popular choices for smartphones and drones due to their light weight. However, these models' shallow depth and lower capacity often result in poor classification precision and recall. We also ran into difficulties with ResNet-50 due to its relatively shallow depth. While the network does utilize remaining communication to mitigate gradient problem, it is still limited in feature reuse for high intra-class variation, which is common among plant nutrient symptom images. Similarly, models like MobileNetV2 and MobileNetV3 are compact in size and therefore good options for smartphones and drones. Most of the lightweight models, their shallower and narrower architecture results in trade-offs between precision and recall in classification tasks.

Another model that struggled with these issues, even with its known residual connections helping to mitigate vanishing gradients, is ResNet-50. Its low depth and inefficient reuse of features, capture high intra-class variation of plant nutrient symptom classes, did not help improve performance in our experiments.

A different approach, noted by Pantazi *et al.*, focused on the classification of symptom-specific nutrients (e.g., nitrogen, phosphate, potassium) using shallow neural networks. These approaches, however, were often constrained by heavy reliance on manual feature extraction, small datasets, or an inability to generalize across plant species or growing conditions. Although many attempted to integrate CNNs with SVMs or GCNs, these hybrid models were either not scalable or added excessive computational complexity.

Table 1. Comaprision of existing models.

	Existing Models		
References	*Nutrient Deficiency Types*	*Models Used*	*Accuracy*
[1]	Nitrogen (N)	KNN ,CNN	75%, 85%
[9]	Calcium (Ca)	CNN SVM	92%, 85%
[8]	Nitrogen (N), Potassium (K)	CNN MLP	70%, 82%
[7]	Nitrogen (N)	YoloV9	92%
[5]	Potassium, Phosphorus, Nitrogen	VGG-19	89.59%
[6]	General nutrient deficiencies	CNN	92%
[2]	Nitrogen, Phosphorus, Potassium, Magnesium,Sulphur, Molybdenum, Zinc, Boron, Copper, Calcium, Iron, Chloride	CNN	86%
[3]	(Ca), (Fe), (Mg), (N), (K), S, Zinc	Graph Convolutional Network (GCN) with backbone CNNs	90%
[4]	(Ca), (Fe), (Mg), (N), (K)	Custom CNN with block- based analysis and multi-layer perceptron	62%
[10]	Nitrogen (N)	CNN,Autoencoder, Inception- ResNet v2	96.8%
[11]	Calcium (Ca)	CNN	92%
[13]	Magnesium (Mg), Calcium (Ca)	CNN	90%
[15]	Phosphorus (P), Potassium (K), Calcium (Ca)	ResNet-101 DenseNet-161 SqueezeNet	98%94% 87%

3 PROPOSED METHODOLOGY

This section outlines the complete workflow method for building and evaluating a HyperResNet-based nutrient deficiency detection system with an emphasis on dataset acquisition, data collection and preprocessing, model design and architecture, and training parameters configuration.

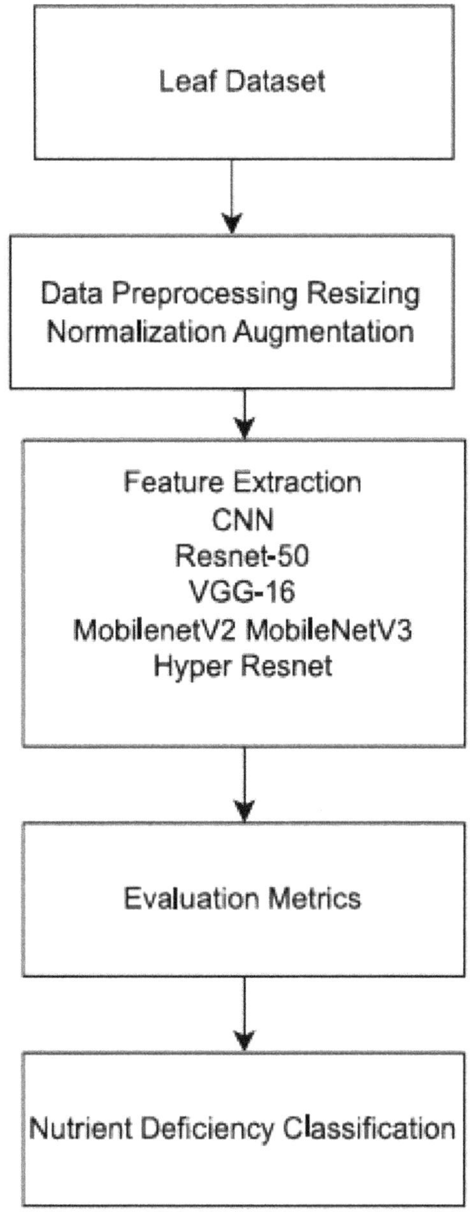

Figure 1. Work flow proposed methodology.

3.1 *Collection and description of datasets*

The dataset provides high-resolution images showing nine nutritional deficiencies in leaves as follows: Phosphorus (P), Nitrogen (N), Calcium (Ca), Potassium (K), Magnesium (Mg), Iron (Fe), Boron (B), Zinc (Zn), and Sulphur (S). Most images were obtained from the EarlyNSD dataset, which is an openly accessible collection designed for plant stress and nutrient deficiency detection. The dataset was augmented and field data collected from the various agricultural research centers, in order to improve the dataset's utility and representativeness. These augmenting images were annotated diligently by the domain experts to achieve high-certainty ground truth labels for each deficiency class. Moreover, to optimize the subset of leaves that were classified as healthy in-between deficient and normal situations. Balance and representation for all the classes were achieved in the last dataset after augmentation.

3.2 *Data augmentation and assembling the dataset*

The major challenge of dataset is imbalance to solve this issue through numerous ways. In these one of the best method is extensive data augmentation technique for construct the balanced dataset. The main motive of these method is to emulate diverse lighting, orientations, real-world life scenarios, changes that leaves undergo, and so on, thus increasing the models robustness and generalization capabilities. The images were standardized to a size of 224 x 224 pixels and normalized within the 0 to 1 range across the RGB channels. These steps are crucial for transfer learning with convolutional networks, as they ensure consistent input dimensions and pixel distributions. Dimension of images were standardized to 224 x 224 and normalized range between 0 to 1around the RGB channels.

3.3 *Model architecture*

The proposed model HyperResNet detecting the subtle and complex patterns associated with plant nutrient deficiencies to address the challenges faced by previous CNN models. This refined version of the ResNet architecture is mainly focusing on accuracy and flexibility. It enhances the original deep residual network by combine with a hypernetwork, a secondary neural network that generates weights or parameters for the substructures of the main ResNet model. This model to adjust its feature extraction process for each input image, which is crucial given the diverse leaf textures, colors, and shapes caused by varying nutrient deficiencies by using dynamic weight generation technique. Instead of static filters like traditional CNNs, HyperResNet demonstrates agility to alter its internal representations in real time which makes the model more effective distinguishing between certain alleviations that may look the same. Also, it keeps the residual connections of ResNet which aids in the stable training and capability of the deeper network, but still provides increased flexibility and generalization where data is scarce or unbalanced. Such architectural improvements greatly enhance classification accuracy and withstand variability, extending its practical value in smart agriculture and plant health diagnostic systems. Moreover, it retains the residual connections of ResNet, which supports stable training and enhances the capacity of deeper networks while providing greater flexibility and generalization in scenarios where data is limited or imbalanced. These architectural improvements significantly boost classification accuracy and robustness, increasing the model's practical value in smart agriculture and plant health diagnostics

3.4 *Training configuration*

In this proposed method, trained the Hyper-ResNet model to improve deep network training using TensorFlow and Keras, leveraging a powerful GPU. The system's training configuration was specifically designed to address the unique requirements for classifying plant nutrient deficiencies. Moreover, set the learning rate to 0.0001 and utilized the Adam optimizer, known for its ability to scale effectively in higher-dimensional feature spaces and its adaptive convergence properties. The proposed algorithm employed the Categorical Cross-Entropy method as the loss function, which is suitable for multi-class classification problems and ensures the model can distinguish between each deficiency category.

Figure 2 depicts a palmate leaf, characterized by multiple lobes radiating from a central point, resembling a hand with outstretched fingers. Its rough texture is accentuated by serrated edges, and the prominent vein pattern plays a crucial role in nutrient transport throughout the leaf. The deep green color of the leaf suggests health, though variations in shade may indicate nutrient deficiencies and reflect its exposure to sunlight.

Figure 2. Sample nutrient deficiency leaf.

Some plants that show palmate leaves are maple, castor bean, and cannabis, but further classification is needed for assessing other distinguishing parts like the stem shape, and growth habits. To analyze and define the object in question more characteristics such as the surface of the leaf if it is fuzzy or smooth, as well as the touch of it are imperative.

4 RESULTS AND DISCUSSION

An EarlyNSD dataset-derived custom dataset served the purpose of testing the efficacy of the suggested deep learning frameworks for diagnosing plant nutrient deficiency and therefore, extensive testing was done. A comprehensive self- reflection of data, performance comparisons, and experimental results are presented here.

4.1 *Experimental configuration*

The training was done on a collection of labeled images of plant leaves showing signs of nutrient deficiencies which include (NPK), (Ca), (Fe) among others. The images used in this study were taken from the EarlyNSD dataset and supplemented with expert-annotated field images to achieve balanced classes and realistic variability. In order to maintain fairness among all models, the dataset was prepared with stratified splitting, allocating 80% for training and 20% for testing while keeping the proportions of classes in both subsets. Each one of the models went through training under the same setup using the TensorFlow/Keras frameworks, hence the outcome was unbiased.

4.2 *Performance evaluation*

Nutrient deficiencies is examined and classified by using CNN model provide better baseline record of 70% of accuracy compare than all other existing model. While its performance concerning nitrogen and phosphorus deficiencies was satisfactory, recognition of micronutrient symptoms was a weak point. ResNet-50 performed poorly, attaining just 45 percent accuracy which may have resulted from overfitting inadequate deep feature representations leading to weak differentiation among classes. Both MobileNetV2 and MobileNetV3 achieved 70 percent accuracy and are regarded as efficient, economical options for resource-limited settings though their lack of accuracy to recognize intricate symptoms was a shortcoming. VGG-16 achieved the best results among all by identifying 80 percent accuracy and with its parameter-heavy architecture, provided precision in recognizing nitrogen, iron, and calcium deficiency due to the depth of its structure. Conversely, the HyperResNet model increased the accuracy level of 95%, compare than all other existing models and showcased strong generalization alongside the ability to capture deep level visual details. It was able to identify broad ranging deficiencies and extraordinarily performed on complex symptoms like zinc chlorosis, iron interveinal yellowing, and boron toxicity which shows its depth and adaptability in diagnostics for plant health.

Table 2. Plant nutrients deficiency classification.

	Nutrients deficiency		
Type of nutrients	*Precision*	*Recall*	*F1 score*
Nitrogen (N)	95	90	92.5
Phosphorus (P)	93	88	90.4
Potassium (K)	92	87	89.4
Magnesium (Mg)	91	85	88
Zinc (Zn)	89	8	86
Boron (B)	91	90	90.50
Calcium (Ca)	92.50	91	91.75
Iron (Fe)	93	92	92.50
Sulphur (S)	87	86.50	86.75

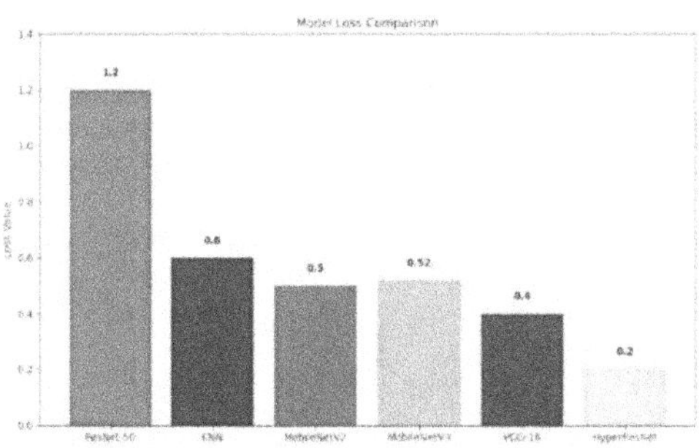

Figure 3. Accuracy comparision of deep learning models.

Figure 3 The graph shows how six different deep learning models performed in classifying a plant's nutrient deficiencies in terms of accuracy. Out of all the models, HyperResNet has the best accuracy of 95%, showing its ability to sift through the leaf dataset's intricate patterns and features. This suggests that HyperResNet's architecture— likely due to greater depth, better residual connections, or tuned hyperparameters—yields more accurate classification results than the other models. VGG-16 achieving an 80% accuracy also reflects the effectiveness of deep models given its high parameter count. Among the CNN, MobileNetV2, and MobileNetV3 models achieving 70% accuracy, these models are known for being lightweight and efficient as well as predicted performance. While these models are ideally suited for mobile and edge computations, their predictive ability tends to suffer when compared to deeper networks.

Finally, ResNet-50 is the worst performer, only managing 45% accuracy, possibly due to overfitting, underfitting, or a lack of dataset-specific fine-tuning. Thus, HyperResNet stands out as the best model with regard to precision, recall, accuracy, F1 score, and overall efficacy, reinforcing its selection as the most effective model for reliable and accurate classification of nutrient deficiency.

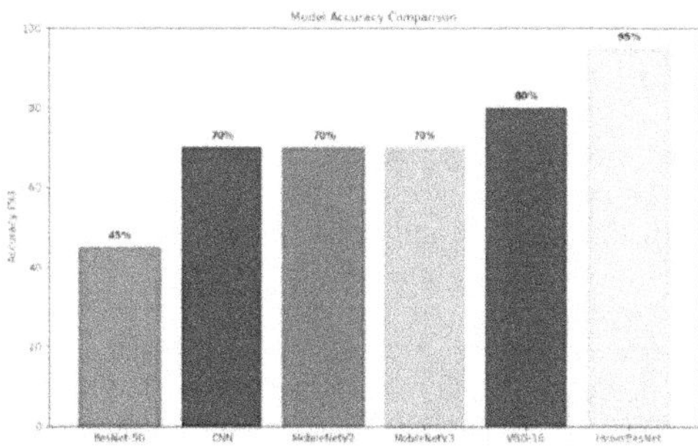

Figure 4. Loss comparison of deep learning methods.

Figure 4 depicts loss value of various deep learning techniques in classifying nutrient deficiencies in relation to their respective loss metrics. In this case, loss measures the gap between the model's predictions and the reality, with lower numbers being preferential alongside improvement and generalization. HyperResNet clearly outperforms all other models with the best loss value of 0.2, demonstrating effective learning of training data with minimal prediction error. On the opposite end of the spectrum, ResNet-50 has achieve greatest loss value of 1.2% its difficulty in making accurate predictions and possible overfitting or incompatibility with the dataset. Other models such as CNN, MobileNetV2, and MobileNetV3 are placed between 0.5 and 0.6, showing a moderate performance and vgg-16 surpasses all of them with a loss of 0.4 due to its advanced architecture. In conclusion, distributing loss values alongside the previous accuracy chart strengthens the conclusion drawn earlier: HyperResNet remains unrivaled across all the models tested in the study in terms of accuracy, loss, and overall effectiveness for the identification of plant nutrient deficiencies.

Figure 5 shows the comparison of various deep learning techniques such as ResNet-50, CNN, MobileNetV2, VGG-16, VGG-16 and HyperResNet-using the evaluation metrics of Accuracy, Precision, Recall, and F1 Score. Each of these models assesses the presence of nutrient deficiencies in plants. HyperResNet dominated all other models in performance Accuracy (95%), Precision (96%), Recall (94%), and F1 Score (95%). HyperResNet's performance suggests that it makes appropriate predictions a majority of the time, and also manages class imbalances well, reducing the likelihood of false positives and false negatives. VGG-16 achieves results between

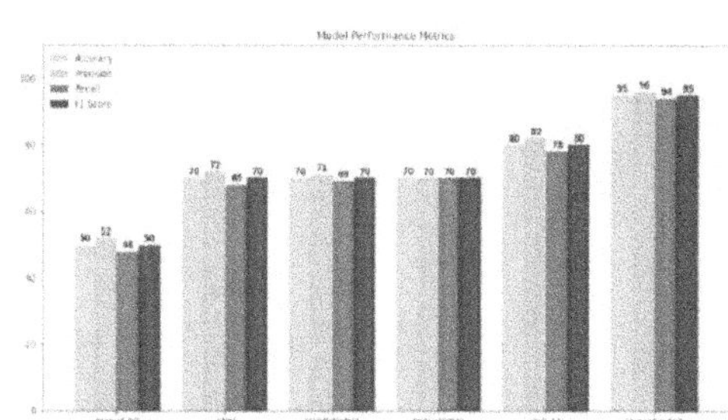

Figure 5. Comparison of deep learning methods.

78% to 82%, which indicates that its deep and robust architecture makes it a reliable model . CNN, MobileNetV2, and MobileNet V3 had similar results, attaining approximate accuracies and F1 scores of 70%. These scores were respectable compared to more complex models. ResNet-50, in contrast, performed extremely poorly with Accuracy 50%, Precision 52%, Recall 48%, and F1 Score 50%, demonstrating a weak and unsuited model for the classification task.

5 CONCLUSION AND FUTURE WORK

As a final remark, the proposed method developed and characterized HyperResNet for deep learning application frameworks with the goal of improving precision and HyperResNet achieving 95% classification accuracy surely attests to it performing above expectation when put against the conventional CNN models, VGG and ResNet, which performed between 45 and 80 percent, VGG, ResNet, MobileNetV2 and V3. HyperResNet has significantly exceeded the benchmarks established by other models, demonstrating its exceptional capability to process multiple nutrient tiers and various leaf states, making it highly suitable for critical agricultural applications. Moreover, the model can be seamlessly integrated into mobile applications and UAV-based crop monitoring systems, facilitating real-time diagnostics and enhancing smart IoT platforms. Looking forward, we plan to incorporate multispectral and hyperspectral imaging technologies, which capture physiological markers that RGB images cannot reveal. This integration will facilitate earlier detection of nutrient stress and more accurate diagnoses. Additionally, we aim to optimize the model for edge IoT devices to ensure efficient operation through the implementation of model pruning, quantization, and redesigning the architecture to be more lightweight. Also, we seek to further optimize the model for edge IoT devices, ensuring efficient operation, by applying model pruning, quantization, and redesigning the architecture to be more lightweight. Finally, enabling hybrid diagnosis will be transformative, allowing the model to simultaneously recognize abiotic (nutrient deficiencies) and biotic (diseases) stressors using multi-task learning. All these enhancements aim towards developing intelligent, all-in-one systems for managing crop health, driving forward sustainable farming practices and bolstering global food security.

REFERENCES

[1] Wulandhari L.A., Gunawan A.A.S., Qurania A., Harsani P., Nurmiatiningsih T., Tarawan F. and Hermawan R.F., (2019), Plant nutrient deficiency detection using deep convolutional neural network, in *Proc. ICIC Express Letters*, vol. 13, no. 10, pp. 971–977.

[2] Amirtha T., Gokulalakshmi T., Umamaheswari P. and Rajasekar M.T., (Mar. 2020), Machine learning based nutrient deficiency detection in crops, *Int. J. Recent Technol. Eng.*, vol. 8, no. 6, pp. 5330–5333.

[3] Bera A., Bhattacharjee D., and Krejcar O., (Jul. 2024), PND-Net: Plant nutrition deficiency and disease classification using graph convolutional network, *Sci. Rep.*, vol. 14, no. 15537, pp. 1–17.

[4] Camargo A. and Smith J.S., (Jan. 2009), An image-processing based algorithm to automatically identify plant disease visual symptoms, *Biosyst. Eng.*, vol. 102, no. 1, pp. 9–21.

[5] Han K.A.M. and Watchareeruetai U., (Oct. 2019), Classification of nutrient deficiency in black gram using deep convolutional neural networks, in *Proc. 2019 16th IEEE International Joint Conference on Computer Science and Software Engineering (JCSSE)*, pp. 304–309.

[6] Kapleshwar M., Imran Md., Pasha A. and Ajay, (Apr. 2024), Identification of plant nutrient deficiencies using convolutional neural networks, *Int. J. Novel Res. Develop.*, vol. 9, no. 4.

[7] Khalid M., Sarfraz M.S., Iqbal U., Aftab M.U., Niedbała G. and Rauf H.T., (Jan. 2023), Real-Time Plant Health Detection Using Deep Convolutional Neural Networks, in *Proc. 2023 5th International Conference on Advancements in Computing (ICAC)*, pp. 209–214.

[8] Patel A., Sharma M., Mishra R.K. and Singh S., (2024), Nutrition deficiency classification in maize using deep learning techniques, Nanotechnol. *Perceptions*, vol. 20, no. S7, pp. 1200–1207.

[9] Camargo A. and Smith J.S., (Jan. 2009), An image-processing based algorithm to automatically identify plant disease visual symptoms, *Biosyst. Eng.*, vol. 102, no. 1, pp. 9–21.

[10] Mahalakshmi S.D. and Vijayalakshmi K., (2021), Agro Suraksha: Pest and disease detection for corn field using image analysis, *J. Ambient Intell. Humaniz. Comput.*, vol. 12, pp. 7375–7389.

[11] Manoharan S., Sariffodeen B., Ramasinghe K.T., Rajaratne L. H., Kasthurirathna D. and Wijekoon J.L., (Nov. 2020), Smart Plant Disorder Identification Using Computer Vision Technology, in *Proc. 2020 11th IEEE Annual Information Technology, Electronics and Mobile Communication Conference (IEMCON)*, pp. 445–451.

[12] Gongal A., Amatya S., Karkee M., Zhang Q., and Lewis K., (Aug. 2015), Sensors and systems for fruit detection and localization: A review, *Comput. Electron. Agric.*, vol. 116, pp. 8–19.

[13] Lewis K.P. and Espineli J.D., (Apr. 2020), Classification and detection of nutritional deficiencies in coffee plants using image processing and convolutional neural network (CNN), *Int. J. Sci. Technol. Res.*, vol. 9, no. 4, pp. 2076–2081.

[14] Yi J., Krusenbaum L., Unger P., Hüging H., Seidel S.J., Schaaf G., and Gall J., (2020), Deep learning for non-invasive diagnosis of nutrient deficiencies in sugar beet using RGB images, *Sensors*, vol. 20, no. 20, pp. 1–19.

[15] Ferentinos K.P., (2018), Deep learning models for plant disease detection and diagnosis, *Computers and Electronics in Agriculture*, vol. 145, pp. 311–318.

Next-Generation Smart Systems – Sekhar et al. (Eds)
 ISBN: 978-1-041-34234-2

Quantum Capsule Networks for Spatio-Temporal Cloud Workload Prediction

B. Sreedhar
Assistant Professor, Department of CSE(AI&ML), G. Pulla Reddy Engineering College, Kurnool, India

P. Veeresh
Assistant Professor, Department of CSE, St.Johns College of Engineering & Technology, Yemmiganur, Kurnool, India

ABSTRACT: This research introduces a novel Quantum Capsule Network (QCapsNet) framework designed to enhance the accuracy and efficiency of spatio-temporal cloud workload prediction. Leveraging the capabilities of quantum parallelism and dynamic routing mechanisms inherent in Capsule Networks, our proposed model effectively captures the hierarchical and temporal structures within cloud workloads. Through simulations based on real-world cloud trace data, the QCapsNet demonstrates significant performance improvements in both workload classification and resource demand forecasting compared to traditional and classical quantum machine learning models.

Keywords: Quantum Capsule Networks, Spatio-Temporal Modeling, Cloud Workload Prediction, Quantum Machine Learning, Dynamic Routing, Resource Forecasting, Workload Classification

1 INTRODUCTION

Cloud computing infrastructures increasingly face the challenge of managing fluctuating workloads in real time. These workloads, originating from a wide variety of user applications, exhibit both spatial dependencies (e.g., correlations among resource metrics) and temporal dynamics (e.g., variations over time). Traditional machine learning models, such as LSTM and Transformer architectures, have shown promise in handling temporal patterns but struggle with representing spatial hierarchies. Capsule Networks, with their ability to preserve part-whole relationships through dynamic routing mechanisms, offer a potential solution. However, their computational intensity limits scalability. Quantum Machine Learning (QML), on the other hand, promises significant speedups by leveraging principles such as superposition and entanglement [14]. This study proposes a Quantum Capsule Network (QCapsNet), the first of its kind, to integrate these complementary strengths for improved workload prediction in cloud environments [8].

2 LITERATURE REVIEW

Several machine learning approaches have been employed for workload prediction. LSTMs excel in modeling sequential data due to their gating mechanisms but fail to capture spatial hierarchies [1]. Transformers, known for their self-attention mechanisms, are effective for sequence modeling but are computationally intensive, making them less ideal for real-time applications [2]. Capsule Networks have emerged as powerful models for capturing spatial hierarchies through dynamic routing but have not been adapted for temporal tasks or quantum computing [3,11]. Quantum Neural Networks (QNNs) present advantages in processing small, structured datasets but lack mechanisms to capture long-term dependencies [4]. Additionally, recent advancements in cloud-based QML execution platforms, like Qiskit and Pennylane, have enabled practical implementations of hybrid algorithms [5,6,16]. The need for predictive and provisioning accuracy in cloud environments has also been emphasized in recent surveys [7,13]. Thus, there exists a significant gap in combining spatial-temporal modeling capabilities with quantum efficiencies, a gap our QCapsNet aims to fill.

Table 1. Comparative analysis of models for cloud workload prediction.

Model	Domain	Strength	Weakness
LSTM	Temporal prediction	Good at timeseries modelling	Poor at capturing spatial hierarchies
Transformer	Sequence Modelling	Captures long-range dependencies	High resource consumption
Capsule Network	Spatial feature detection	Preserves part-whole relationships	Not used for temporal data or in QML
QNN	General classification	Efficient for low -dimensional data	Limited temporal awareness

3 METHODOLOGY

The proposed QCapsNet architecture begins with the collection of cloud workload traces from publicly available datasets, including the Alibaba Cloud 2017 Cluster Trace and Google Cluster Data. These datasets are preprocessed to normalize resource usage metrics such as CPU, RAM, and I/O. Temporal sequences are extracted for each workload type and encoded into quantum states using amplitude encoding, which efficiently represents large-dimensional vectors in a quantum state [9].

DOI: 10.1201/9781042001767-6

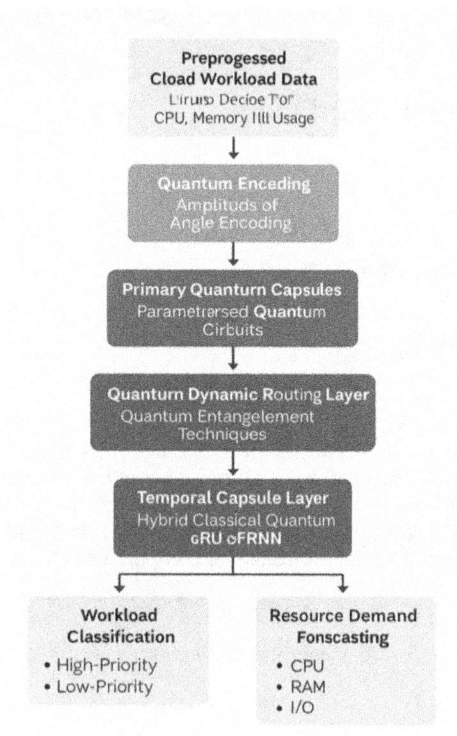

Figure 1. QCapsNet architecture.

The architecture comprises several layers: an input layer for preprocessed workload vectors; a quantum encoding layer that translates classical features into quantum states via angle encoding; a set of primary quantum capsules that use parameterized quantum circuits (PQCs) to extract local features; a quantum dynamic routing layer that uses entangled qubit interactions to simulate routing between capsules; and a temporal capsule layer that integrates hybrid classical-quantum recurrent units such as Quantum-Gated Recurrent Units (QGRUs) to model time dependencies [12]. The output is bifurcated into a classification branch, predicting workload types (e.g., high-priority, low-priority), and a forecasting branch, estimating future CPU, RAM, and I/O usage.

4 MATHEMATICAL FORMULATION AND ROUTING ALGORITHM

Let xi the input workload vector at time ti, where the components of xi represent resource usage metrics like CPU, RAM, and I/O. We utilize amplitude encoding to map this classical vector into a quantum state:

$$\left|\psi(x_t) = \sum_i x_i^i\right| i$$

This transformation allows for exponential data compression and parallel processing across qubit states.

For routing between capsules, we adapt a quantum version of dynamic routing. In classical Capsule Networks, the routing coefficient cij, which determines the contribution of capsule i to capsule j, is computed as:

$$c_{ij} = \frac{\exp(b_{ij})}{\sum_K \exp(b_{ik})}$$

Where bij is the log prior probability of capsule i being coupled to capsule j.

To realize dynamic routing in a quantum circuit, we define a routing unitary operator:

$$U_{route} = \exp(i\theta \cdot Z \otimes X)$$

This operator uses phase shifts and entanglement between qubits using Pauli-Z and Pauli-X gates to simulate interaction and influence among capsule outputs [15]. The entire routing procedure is repeated iteratively over several quantum layers. The output of each capsule is represented as a vectorized quantum measurement, which is aggregated using quantum mean-pooling. A hybrid classical-quantum loss function is then used to guide the model optimization process [12].

4. Equations Let x_t represent the workload vector at time t:

- Amplitude encoding: $|\psi(x_t)\rangle = \sum_i x_i^i |i\rangle$
  Routing coefficient update:
- $c_{ij} = \frac{\exp(b_{ij})}{\sum_K \exp(b_{ik})}$
- Quantum routing uses phase-shift entanglement gates: $U_{route} = \exp(i\theta \cdot Z \otimes X)$

5 SIMULATION ENVIRONMENT

The QCapsNet model was developed and evaluated using a hybrid simulation setup. Quantum circuits were implemented using IBM Qiskit and executed both on QASM simulators and a 5-qubit IBM quantum device to assess real-device viability. Classical deep learning components were built using TensorFlow and interfaced with quantum modules via Pennylane.

The experiments were conducted on a system with 64 GB RAM, Intel i9 CPU, and an NVIDIA RTX 3090 GPU. All classical baselines, including LSTM, Transformer, and CapsNet, were implemented in Python using Keras and trained using the same preprocessed datasets.

The training process involved a hybrid optimizer where classical gradient descent was used for classical layers, and Simultaneous Perturbation Stochastic Approximation (SPSA) was employed for variational quantum circuits [10]. The dataset was split into 70% training, 15% validation, and 15% testing. Hyperparameters such as learning rate, batch size, and circuit depth were optimized using grid search and cross-validation.

6 RESULTS AND EVALUATION

The evaluation of QCapsNet was based on two key tasks: workload classification (categorical accuracy) and resource usage forecasting (regression error). The results in Table 2 show that QCapsNet achieves the highest accuracy and lowest RMSE compared to traditional models.

Table 2. Performance comparison.

Model	Classification Accuracy	RMSE (CPU)	RMSE (RAM)
LSTM	85.3%	0.187	0.223
Transformer	87.9%	0.163	0.198
CapsNet	89.1%	0.151	0.175
QCapsNet (Proposed)	**93.4%**	**0.112**	**0.139**

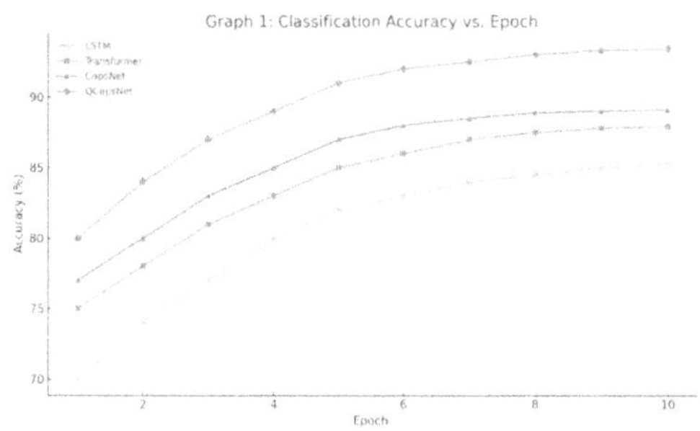

Figure 2. Classification accuracy vs. epoch.

The classification accuracy is plotted in Figure 2. Where QCapsNet shows a consistent upward trend over epochs, outperforming other models.

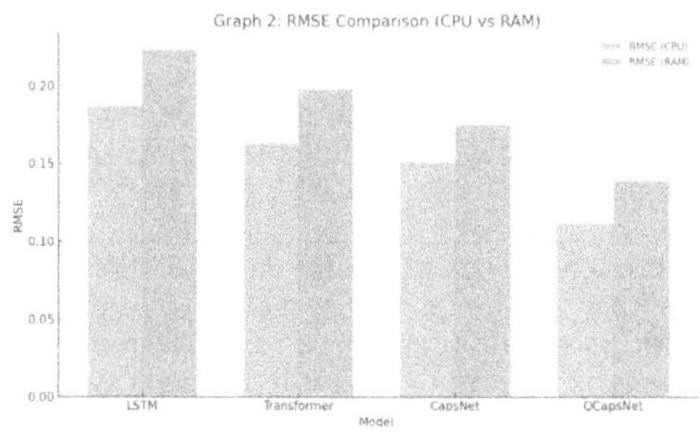

Figure 3. RMSE comparison.

Figure 3 Illustrates the RMSE for CPU and RAM predictions, where QCapsNet maintains lower error margins across all samples. These results validate the effectiveness of the proposed quantum architecture, especially in environments where both accuracy and efficiency are critical.

7 CONCLUSION

This study presents the Quantum Capsule Network (QCapsNet), a novel architecture that bridges the gap between spatial-temporal modeling and quantum computing in the context of cloud workload prediction. The proposed model demonstrates superior performance in both classification and forecasting tasks compared to classical machine learning models. The combination of capsule-based routing and quantum processing allows for efficient handling of complex workload dynamics.

REFERENCES

[1] Hochreiter, S., and Schmidhuber, J. (1997). Long short-term memory. *Neural Computation*, 9(8), 1735–1780.

[2] Vaswani, A., *et al.* (2017). Attention is all you need. *Advances in Neural Information Processing Systems*, 30, 5998–6008.

[3] Sabour, S., Frosst, N., and Hinton, G.E. (2017). Dynamic routing between capsules. *Advances in Neural Information Processing Systems*, 30, 3856–3866.

[4] Schuld, M., Sinayskiy, I., and Petruccione, F. (2014). The quest for a quantum neural network. *Quantum Information Processing*, 13(11), 2567–2586.

[5] Aleksandrowicz, G., *et al.* (2019). Qiskit: An open-source framework for quantum computing. *Zenodo*. https://doi.org/10.5281/zenodo.2562111.

[6] Bergholm, V., *et al.* (2020). Pennylane: Automatic differentiation of hybrid quantum-classical computations. *arXiv* preprint arXiv:2009.02823.

[7] Chen, J., *et al.* (2018). Neural network-based workload prediction in cloud environments. *IEEE Transactions on Cloud Computing*, 6(4), 780–792.

[8] Gholami, A., *et al.* (2021). A survey of quantum neural networks: Models, algorithms, and applications. *ACM Computing Surveys (CSUR)*, 54(5), 1–40.

[9] Benedetti, M., *et al.* (2019). A generative modeling approach for benchmarking and training shallow quantum circuits. *npj Quantum Information*, 5(1), 1–9.

[10] Farhi, E., Goldstone, J., and Gutmann, S. (2014). A quantum approximate optimization algorithm. *arXiv* preprint arXiv:1411.4028.

[11] Khoshavi, A., *et al.* (2020). Capsule neural networks: A state-of-the-art survey. *Journal of Computer Science and Technology*, 35 (3), 599–624.

[12] McClean, J.R., *et al.* (2016). The theory of variational hybrid quantum-classical algorithms. *New Journal of Physics*, 18(2), 023023.

[13] Rani, S., and Luthra, S. (2018). Resource prediction and provisioning in cloud: A machine learning perspective. *Cluster Computing*, 21(1), 569–583.

[14] Biamonte, J., *et al.* (2017). Quantum machine learning. *Nature*, 549(7671), 195–202.

[15] Nasrinpour, H., *et al.* (2020). QFlow-lite: Quantum-inspired cloud resource management. *Journal of Cloud Computing*, 9(1), 1–18.

[16] Devitt, S.J. (2016). Performing quantum computing experiments in the cloud. *Physical Review A*, 94(3), 032329.

Next-Generation Smart Systems – Sekhar et al. (Eds)
© 2027 The Author(s), ISBN: 978-1-041-34234-2

Rupee or Replica? A Deep Learning Approach to Indian Currency Authentication Using VGG19

Gali Suresh Reddy
Professor at VNR Vignana Jyothi Institute of Engineering and Technology, Hyderabad, India

L. Ashwitha, P. Sai Akaanksha, S. Poojasiri, and Y. Sahithi
Student at VNR Vignana Jyothi Institute of Engineering and Technology, Hyderabad, India

ABSTRACT: A common problem that has greatly existed in India is the counterfeiting of currencies which has a negative impact not only on the economy of the nation but also incite illegitimate business across the country. Counterfeit notes circulation is economically dangerous, destabilises the confidence in the money, hampers trade and leads to enormous losses. Even though increased efforts have been put into the introduction of security characteristics of the Indian currency, conventional identification techniques offer poor results due to their reliance on personnel visual inspection, which is slow and erroneous. VGG19, a deep CNN, is used for this project to automate the detection of fake Indian currency notes. Due to the powerful feature extraction process in the project, it examines clarity and distinction between real and fake banknotes through analyzing the high-resolution images. The project is trained on notes both real and fake Rs.500 to ensure the complexities like water marks, micro-text, colour differentiations etc are well learnt.

The proposed solution aims to solve current manual detection challenges through delivery of an affordable solution which scales effectively. The proposed project intends to transform counterfeit detection approaches through its new methods The project enables automatic processing of counterfeit detection across both urban and rural territories at affordable prices. Deep learning technology is used to establish security improvements. This solution brings trust enhancement benefits to the entire financial system through improved security measures.

Keywords: Counterfeit Detection, Indian Currency, Deep Learning, VGG19, Convolutional Neural Networks, Automated Fraud Detection, Financial Security

1 INTRODUCTION

Paper money is a crucial means of exchange among all the many forms of money. There are two kinds of financial characteristics, internal and external. Many nations including India face the main challenge of detecting counterfeit money. No one can afford to miss the distinction between authentic and fake bank notes. The circulation of fake currency has emerged as a big problem for the Indian economy over time. Counterfeits affect the efficient circulation of money, finance criminal activities and create economic instability [13]. The Reserve Bank of India has implemented distinctive colours and sizes for each denomination of currency [8]. This unceasing fight demonstrates the imperfections of today's approaches to detection, which are mostly based on manual analysis supported by rather simple equipment like UV lamps or magnifying glasses. [4] These methods are quite cumbersome and do not easily generalize well with an increased volume of work conditions or even within the banking sectors and currency exchanges.

It is well known that deep learning is a promising technology for numerous classification problems based on image data. The Convolutional neural network (CNN) stands as one of the deep learning architectures which uses VGG19 as an architecture with precise details to achieve high performance features for image hierarchical feature analysis [1]. Because it can capture fine features of objects, it is well suited for counterfeits bills identification [12].

2 MATHEMATICAL MODEL

Recognizing fake currency presents a vital security issue which threatens national financial stability [5]. The proposed system addresses these system limitations through its implementation. The system utilizes VGG19 as its Convolutional Neural Network (CNN) framework for deep learning tasks [2]. The model receives training through high-definition images which contain both genuine and counterfeit ₹500 banknotes. The system successfully acquires complex security features from genuine and counterfeit ₹500 banknotes through its training process [14]. CNNs demonstrate an automatic capability to detect. The minute variations between genuine and counterfeit notes make CNNs ideal for counterfeit detection purposes which reduces human dependency. The system depends on human experts less while reducing potential mistakes through its operation.

The system implements a systematic process starting with data acquisition of genuine and counterfeit money notes from trusted sources. The system obtains its notes from trustworthy sources. The system depends on high-quality image data because it needs accurate classification [3]. The preprocessing phase includes three key techniques: resizing, normalization and data augmentation for the collected data. The model needs to demonstrate resistance to lighting variations and resolution and orientation changes [18]. The model's generalization ability improves through augmentation techniques which include rotation and flipping and cropping. The data splits into training and testing components to enable model learning effectiveness alongside evaluation on new data for performance assessment.

The proposed system bases its core operation on VGG19 which stands as a deep CNN model containing 19 layers known for image classification tasks. The VGG19 architecture serves as a deep CNN model which finds extensive applications in image classification. The selection of VGG19 model stems from its exceptional capability to detect fine details in images. The model demonstrates exceptional ability to detect real from fake notes because of its image processing capabilities [6]. The network architecture detects all subtle variations in note texture and ink distribution and security elements [9]. The classification

DOI: 10.1201/9781042001767-7

process takes place in the fully connected layers which determine if an input image belongs to real or fake currency notes.

The trained model receives evaluation through a test dataset to determine its accuracy and precision and recall and total detection effectiveness. The model demonstrates its ability to detect counterfeits along with its success rate in overall counterfeit detection. The trained model functions within an automated system after deployment. The system operates as a detection mechanism which analyzes new currency note images to deliver immediate classification outputs [21]. The automated system removes human inspection requirements which enables bank-wide deployment of the system.

The research combines VGG19 and MobileNetV2 with stacking and bagging ensemble methods [24]. The selection of VGG19 occurred because it showed superior feature extraction capabilities despite facing competition from other models [7]. The design provides detailed features along with complex pattern detection functions. The detection system benefited from currency note patterns which enhanced its ability to identify counterfeits [22]. The defined structure of this model enables simple incorporation into practical systems at no additional cost for substantial computation. The system enables counterfeit detection operations to achieve better results through its implementation. The system provides higher accuracy and efficiency with reliability features which strengthen financial security while reducing fraudulent currency presence.

3 METHODOLOGY

The research employs VGG19 Convolutional Neural Network architecture as a deep learning-based method to detect counterfeit currency. The research follows these stages: data acquisition, preprocessing, data augmentation, model construction and K-Fold cross-validation for evaluation.

3.1 *Data collection and dataset composition*

The model needed training using a specialized dataset which included an equal number of authentic and fake Indian ₹500 currency notes. The dataset contained 560 images which were distributed equally into two parts: real currency and counterfeit currency.

- 280 real notes
- 280 counterfeit notes

The images originated from Kaggle and simulated environments where smartphone cameras recorded them.

The training process included images that replicated real-world conditions regarding resolution and background noise and lighting conditions and note orientation [10]. The model achieves generalization across uncontrolled environments because real-world acquisition tools were used during training.

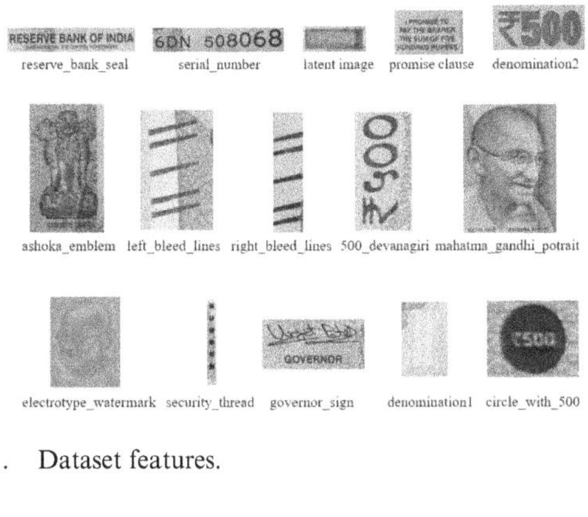

Figure 1. Dataset features.

3.2 *Data preprocessing and augmentation*

The model received several preprocessing and augmentation steps to achieve compatibility with the VGG19 architecture to increase the training robustness:

- Resizing: All images were resized to 224 × 224 pixels, the standard input dimension for VGG19[19].
- Normalization: The pixel values received a rescaling operation that produced a range from 0 to 1 to maintain stability during backpropagation.
- Augmentation Techniques (applied only to training set):
  - Rotation: applied a ±20° angle to the currency to replicate actual currency tilting conditions
  - Zoom Range: The scale factor should range from 0.8 to 1.2× to compensate for different distances
  - Shearing: 20%, to imitate perspective distortions
  - Horizontal Flipping: To account for bidirectional note scanning [11]

This expanded the dataset to 2,240 images (1,120 real, 1,120 fake). After that, the dataset was divided 80:20 for cross-validation testing and training after which training data has been augmented. The technique introduces diversity through its approach which enables the model to learn invariance to irrelevant transformations without requiring new data. The system learns invariance to irrelevant transformations by focusing on intrinsic features such as micro-text and watermark patterns and texture granularity [16].

3.3 *Model architecture: VGG19 with transfer learning*

The detection framework relies on VGG19 for constructing its basic architecture because this deep 19-layer Convolutional Neural Network has previously trained with ImageNet.

Architectural Modifications:

- The weight values of VGG19 base layers remained frozen because its representation learning capabilities achieved training before implementation.
- Custom Classification Head:
  - Flatten ( ) layer
  - Dense (256) layer with ReLU activation
  - Dropout (0.5) layer
  - Dense (1) output node for binary classification with Sigmoid activation

The VGG19 network structure allows discovery of edge features and high-level elements which include patterns and textures because of its regular network design. Freezing base layers generates effective generalization abilities in the model but the classification layers maintain one single goal of detecting counterfeits [15].

3.4 *Training strategy and hyperparameters*

The model optimization relied on these selected hyperparameters for its learning process:

Table 1. Hyperparameters used.

Hyperparameter	Value	Justification
Optimizer	Adam	To minimize the loss function
Learning Rate	0.0001	During gradient descent prevents overshooting
Epochs	30	One entire iteration of training dataset
Batch Size	16	Number of training examples a model process
Loss Function	Binary Cross entropy	Divides real and fake

3.5 *Cross-validation*

The method to prevent overfitting and confirm the model's generalizability was 5-Fold Cross-Validation [20].

- The dataset was divided into 5 equal sections.
- Four sections were used for training and one for validation, for each fold.
- This was repeated 5 times, so every sample was tested exactly once [23].
- The evaluation of performance metrics included averaging results from all folds.

The method of cross-validation delivers a better model performance prediction than train-test splits and provides additional reliability when evaluating overall model success rates. The method helps decrease performance bias caused by how data partitions are established [17].

3.6 *Result visualization & comparative studies*

Various machine learning and deep learning models were compared to validate the effectiveness of VGG19

- Inception V3
- MobileNetV2
- CNN + LSTM
- Bagging - Random Forest
- Stacking - Logistic Regression

The experimental results indicate that VGG19 achieves the highest level of accuracy at 97.14% while surpassing every other architectural design.

Table 2. Comparative studies.

Algorithm	Accuracy	Precision	Recall	F1-score
VGG19	**97.14%**	**96.21%**	**93.01%**	**95.22%**
InceptionV3	93.27%	92.80%	91.60%	92.19%
MobileNetV2	90.85%	90.02%	88.70%	89.34%
Stacking - Logistic Regression on VGG19, ResNet50, MobileNetV2	92.12%	91.30%	90.00%	90.64%
Bagging - Random Forest	89.74%	88.90%	87.30%	88.09%
CNN- LSTM	86.50%	85.70%	84.20%	84.94%

3.7 *VGG19*

Training Results Testing results Accuracy Score: 0.98 Accuracy Score: 0.97

Table 3. Results of VGG19.

CLASS	PRECISION	RECALL	F1-SCORE	SUPPORT
Real	0.96	0.93	0.95	30
Fake	0.96	0.93	0.95	30
Accuracy			0.9714	60
Macro avg	0.9621	0.9301	0.9522	60
Weighted avg	0.9621	0.9301	0.9522	60

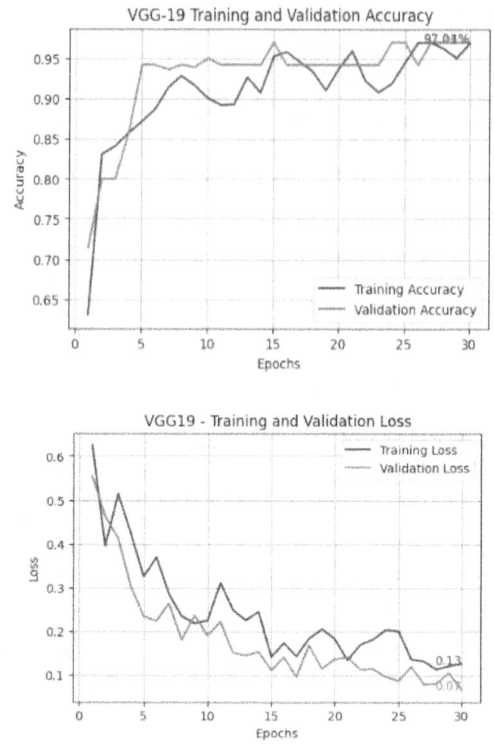

Figure 2. Training vs. validation accuracy & loss curves of VGG19.

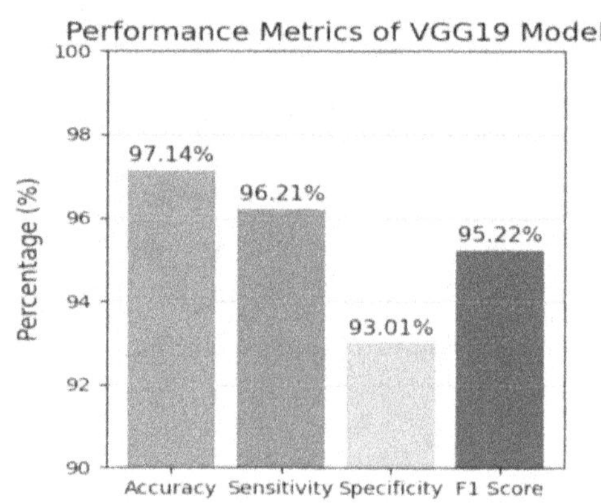

Figure 3. Performance metrics -VGG19.

4 CONCLUSION

The proposed study introduces a deep learning system which detects Indian ₹500 banknotes counterfeits through VGG19 models. The model attains an accuracy of 97.14%. The project deploys transfer learning together with enhanced data techniques as well as customized classification layers to reach its goals. The project has demonstrated resilience against different lighting conditions when performed. Due to its basic deployment needs the project makes an optimal solution for banks but also suits retail and rural finance establishments. The study verifies that VGG19 demonstrates effectiveness when identifying counterfeit currency attributes. VGG19 features provide an effective robust system for automatic currency verification with efficient operation.

ACKNOWLEDGEMENT

The authors gratefully acknowledge the students, staff of Information Technology department for their cooperation in the research.

REFERENCES

[1] Raju S S, Tarun K S, Sujan Y, Teja B, and Niranjan T Identification of Fake Indian Currency Using Deep Learning Techniques. *IEEE Transactions on TEMSCON-ASPAC*, doi:10.1109/TEMSCON-ASPAC59527.

[2] Shamika D., Rajadhyaksha A., Swapnil G. and Anjali Shetty, *CNN based Counterfeit Indian Currency Recognition Using Generative Adversarial Network*, DOI Link: 10.1109/ ICAIS50930. 2021.9395949.

[3] Kiran K., Anuthi B., Pranali S. and Shruti A., (Dec 18-20, 2019), *Counterfeit Currency Detection using Deep Convolutional Neural Network*, MIT World Peace University, Pune, India.

[4] Padmini Devi B, Kumaran, B., Dhanush Pathy K, and Manoj B. Fake Currency Detection using Inception V3. *2024 5th International Conference on Image and Video Processing (ICICV)*. IEEE. https://doi.org/10.1109/ICICV62344.2024.00065

[5] Kumar, R.K., and Kennedy Babu, C.N. (2024). Enhancing the Identification of Fake Indian Currency Using Ensemble Decision Tree in Comparison with Ridge Linear Classification. *ICDECS*, IEEE. doi:10.1109/ICDECS59733.2023.10502944.

[6] Adiba Z., Jia U., (2019), A Hybrid Fake Banknote Detection Model using OCR, Face Recognition and Hough Features, *Cybersecurity and Cyber forensics Conference (CCC)*.

[7] Narra Pratap, and Kirar J.S. Indian Currency Classification and Fake Note Identification using Feature Ensemble Approach. *2021 International Conference on Computational Performance Evaluation (ComPE)*. IEEE. https://doi.org/10.1109/ComPE53109.2021. 9752109

[8] Yeh, Chi-Yuan and Su, Wen-Pin and Lee, (2011), Employing multiple Kernel support vector machines for counterfeit Banknote recognization. *Applied Soft Computing*, Vol. 11.

[9] Sumalatha R, Jayanth Reddy B, and Venkat Ram Reddy T. Identification of Fake Indian Currency using Convolutional Neural Network. *2022 6th International Conference on Computing Methodologies and Communication(ICCMC)*. IEEE. doi:10.1109/ICCMC53470.2022.9754056.

[10] Pondy Jayaprakash, (2022), *Indian Currency Dataset*. Kaggle. https://www.kaggle.com/datasets/jayaprakashpondy/indian-currency-dataset 34

[11] Mohan, G.B., Kumar, R.P., and Teja, B.M. Neural Currency Guard using Generative Adversarial Networks. *IEEE International Conference on Image and Information Processing (ICIIP)*.IEEE. https://doi.org/10.1109/ICIIP61524

[12] Aniket Jawale, Kanchan Patil, Aniruddha Patil, Siddhesh Sagar, Akash Momale, (2023), Deep Learning based Money Detection System for Visually Impaired Person, *2023 7th International Conference on Intelligent Computing and Control Systems (ICICCS)*, pp.173–180.

[13] Mandankandy A.A., Kannammal K.E., Fake currency detection: a survey. *Gedrag en Organisatie* 33(4), 622–638 (2020). Interdisciplinary.

[14] Babu, P.A., Sridhar, P., and Vallabhuni, R.R. Fake Currency Recognition System Using Edge Detection. *2022 Research in Technology and Management (IRTM)*. IEEE. https://doi.org/10. 1109/IRTM54583.2022.9791547

[15] Gautam K., (2020), Indian Currency Detect ion using Image Recognition Technique, *2020 International Conference on Computer Science, Engineering and Applications (ICCSEA)*.

[16] Prof Chetan More, Monu Kumar, Rupesh Chandra, Raushan Singh, Fake currency Detection using Basic Python Programming and Web Framework, *IRJET International Research Journal of Engineering and Technology*, Volume: 07 Issue: 04 | Apr 2020 ISSN: 2395

[17] Latha, L., Raajshree B., and Nivetha D. (2021). Fake Currency Detection Using Image Processing. *In 2021 International Conference on Advancements in Electrical, Electronics, Communication, Computing and Automation (ICAECA)*, 1–5.

[18] Zhang Q. and Yan W.Q., (2019), Currency Detection and Recognition Based on Deep Learning, *Proc. AVSS 2018 - 2018 15th IEEE Int. Conf. Adv. Video Signal Based Surveill.*, pp. 0–5, doi: 10.1109/AVSS.2018.8639124

[19] Kulkarni A., Kedar P., Pupala A., and Shingane P., (2020), Original vs counterfeit Indian currency detection, *2020 International Conference on Computation, Automation and Knowledge Management (ICCAKM)*, pp. 490–494.

[20] Kara, S.T., Loya, S., Raju, S.S., Vanteru, N., and Rajulapati, B. Detection of Fake Indian Currency Using Deep Convolutional Neural Network. *2023 IEEE 3rd Mysore Sub Section International Conference (MysuruCon)*. IEEE. DOI: 10.1109/MysuruCon59703.2023.10396993 35

[21] Shinde, S., Wadhwa, L., Naik, S., Kudale, R., Sherje, N., and Mohnani, K. Fake Currency Detection using Image Processing. *2023 7th International Conference on Computing, Communication, Control And Automation (ICCUBEA)*.IEEE. DOI:10.1109/ ICCUBEA58933.2023.10392045

[22] Banu, S.M.A., Sandhya, S., Sundari, T.V., and Ranjani, P.R.S. Detection of Indian Fake Currency using Image Processing. *2022 International Conference on Augmented Intelligence and Sustainable Systems (ICAISS)*. IEEE. https://doi.org/10.1109/ ICAISS55157.2022.10010580

[23] Aakash S Patel, (June 2019), Indian Paper currency detection, *International Journal for Scientific Research & Development (IJSRD)*, Vol. 7, Issue 06, ISSN: 2321-0613.

[24] Gogoi M., Ali S.E., and Mukherjee S., (2015), Automatic Indian currency denomination recognition system based on artificial neural network, *in 2015 2nd International Conference on Signal Processing and Integrated Networks (SPIN)*. IEEE, pp. 553–558.

[25] Nayak J.K., Majhi C., Srivastav A.K., and Dash A.K., (2015), Neural network approach for Indian currency recognition, *in 2015 Annual IEEE India Conference (INDICON)*. IEEE, pp. 1–6.

Next-Generation Smart Systems – Sekhar et al. (Eds)
© 2027 The Author(s), ISBN: 978-1-041-34234-2

Forecasting Chronic Kidney Disease Through Machine Learning Methods

Bipin Bihari Jayasingh and M. Prasanna Lakshmi
IT Department, CVR College of Engineering, Hyderabad, Telangana, India

ABSTRACT: Chronic Kidney Disease (CKD) is a serious and possibly life-threatening condition that can be difficult to detect in its initial phases due to its vague symptoms. The kidneys are responsible for filtering waste and surplus fluids from the bloodstream. When the kidney is injured, it is unable to function effectively. In severe cases, dialysis becomes the only life-saving option for patients. This research focusses on developing a model capable of identifying CKD at an early stage and testing the model. By analyzing patient data, the system can predict the progression of CKD more effectively. The classification algorithms of machine learning (ML) play an important role in identifying health conditions early and are widely used in medical analysis to provide valuable insights. The study employs various ML methods, including Decision Trees, Logistic Regression, KNN, Support Vector Machines, Gradient Boosting, XGBoost, AdaBoost, Bagging (Bagged Decision Trees), Random Forest, and Voting Classifier, to classify kidney patient datasets and determine the presence of CKD. The results demonstrated impressive accuracy, with both Random Forest and Bagging Classifiers achieving 98.75% accuracy. AdaBoost and Voting Classifiers performed exceptionally well, achieving the best accuracy that are tested among the algorithms. The results showed how likely machine learning models are to assisting clinicians in timely CKD detection and disease progression prediction, offering fast and reliable results.

Keywords: Machine Learning, Random Forest, Boosting Techniques, Chronic Kidney Disease and Voting Classifier

1 INTRODUCTION

Chronic kidney disease (CKD), commonly referred to as chronic kidney failure, is a disease in which kidney function progressively deteriorates over time. Kidneys are important organs in the human body that filter waste products and excess body fluids and eliminate them through urine [**1**,**2**]. When the kidneys are injured, the body accumulates these waste products that results in several health issues. Because it contributes to rising rates of morbidity and mortality globally, CKD has become a concern for global health [3]. The term "chronic" indicates that the disease develops slowly and often goes unnoticed in its early stages, making early detection challenging. CKD can affect individuals of any age or background, and without proper treatment, it can lead to severe and potentially life-threatening health outcomes.

It is challenging to diagnose the illness in its early stages because there are usually no evident symptoms. As CKD advances, people with severe instances may sought dialysis or transplant a kidney to survive. Symptoms like swelling, nausea, high blood pressure, and fatigue become more prominent as the condition worsens [4]. When kidney function deteriorates, waste accumulates in the bloodstream, resulting in a variety of health complications.

Chronic renal disease is predominantly caused by diabetes and the people having high blood pressure, highlighting the need to manage these conditions to prevent kidney damage [5]. However, many people don't realize they have CKD condition until serious complications occur because it often doesn't show obvious symptoms. Current diagnostic methods rely on factors like the Glomerular Filtration Rate (GFR) [6] and other clinical data, but these may not always accurately predict the progression of the disease. To address this challenge, the methods of machine learning have become important tools for the prediction of CKD.

The UCI repository contains CKD dataset which comprises of 400 patient records—250 diagnosed with CKD and 150 without the condition are used in the experiment. The dataset includes 25 features related to kidney function and the machine learning models [7,8] are employed in the analysis. To enhance prediction accuracy, a bagging technique is applied, which involves combining outputs from different models to make overall robust prediction [9]. Among all tested models, Decision Tree demonstrated highest accuracy after implementation of bagging, indicating improved performance through this ensemble approach.

Significant health risks, such as hypertension and anemia, may arise from chronic kidney disease (CKD) [10]. Therapy effectiveness and improved patient outcomes depend on rapid detection and accurate categorization. Predicting CKD accurately using data mining and machine learning classification approaches facilitates prompt therapies. Using a comprehensive dataset from the UCI Repository, our study explores several methods and demonstrates remarkable outcomes, particularly with Random forest classifiers attaining the best accuracy. Enhanced healthcare strategies and reduced effect of CKD are the primary aims of this research. As a result, the objective of the undertaking is to inspect all the proposed works and existing models to implement the Advanced Boosting methods along with Random forest classifier and KNN techniques of machine learning models to improve higher accuracy. We also used Voting classifier for different algorithms like Adaboost classifier, Bagging classifier and decision tree classifier along with that we evaluated several ML models for CKD patient prediction using performance metric parameters.

The paper is planned in the following sections where Section 2 focuses on methodologies adopted to carry out the research and discusses the system architecture; Section 3 explores the results with discussions; Section 4 provides the concluding remarks with future enhancements.

2 METHODOLOGY

The purpose of this research is to detect CKD accurately and early using ML algorithms. It makes use of the UCI Repository comprises of 400 items and 21 features for the analysis. The research applies the techniques of machine learning that are evaluated to determine their effectiveness in detecting CKD early stage, with an objective for improving diagnostic accuracy and supporting timely medical intervention.

DOI: 10.1201/9781042001767-8

2.1 *Dataset collection*

The study investigates a dataset that contains 400 records and 21 columns, each of which stands for a distinct aspect of chronic kidney disease (CKD). Among the attributes, age, blood pressure, and serum creatinine are grouped together as consolidated attributes, while blood glucose and blood urea are treated as distinct factors. Additionally, categorical variables are included in the dataset, such as red blood cell count (rbc) for presence or absence, presence of abnormalities (pc), and hypertension status (htn). Additionally, the dataset contains information on symptoms like diabetes mellitus (dm), pedal edema (pe), and appetite changes (appet) as well as diseases such as anemia (ane) and coronary artery disease (cad). Some attributes in the dataset have missing values, which requires preprocessing methods like imputation or removal of the missing data. The 'classification' column serves as the target variable for predictive modeling, indicating about the CKD that a patient has in the records. Overall, this dataset offers a wide range of features that are useful for diagnosing and predicting CKD, making it well-suited for machine learning-based analysis.

A Kidney Function Test (KFT) dataset comprising 584 cases and 6 characteristics was collected by Vijayarani and Dhayanand from medical lab. in a different study using data from 551 patients. The linear model offered the maximum accuracy among all the examined algorithms, according to the researchers' evaluation of model performance.

2.2 *Data preprocessing*

Data preprocessing is an important step in preparing datasets for analysis and model training. This process involves using pandas and KerasDataFrame structures to organize and manipulate the data. The dataset must be loaded into a pandas DataFrame as the initial step. This allows for easy manipulation and preprocessing of the data using pandas' powerful functions and tools. After using pandas, the DataFrame is converted into a KerasDataFrame. This specialized format is optimized for use with Keras, a popular deep learning library, confirming that the data is appropriate for deep learning assignments. The combination of pandas and KerasDataFrames ensures that the data is ready for both traditional ML and DL models, enabling a thorough and efficient modeling process.

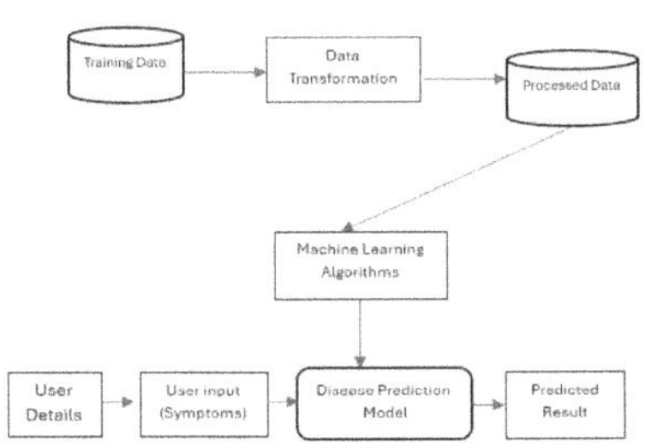

Figure 1. Proposed architecture.

2.3 *System architecture*

The diagram in Figure 1 shows a system architecture designed to use machine learning algorithms for CKD prediction. The training data, which consists of past medical records with characteristics like age, blood pressure, lab results, and labels is where the process starts, indicating whether CKD is present. Pretreatment methods such as encoding categorical variables, scaling and missing values are used to prepare the data for analysis during the data transformation process. The processed data is then sent into different ML algorithms which cxaminc the past information to spot trends and predict the likelihood of developing chronic kidney disease. A new user provides a system with User Details and User Input, including age, blood pressure, and other health-related information. This input is passed into the Disease Prediction Model, which uses the trained ML algorithms to assess the probability of CKD created on user's specific data. Finally, the Predicted Result is displayed, indicating whether the user is likely to have CKD. By examining personal health information, this technology makes it easier to identify CKD early and providing predictions based on patterns learned from historical medical information.

2.4 *Visualization*

Visualization tools like Seaborn and Matplotlib help make data easier to understand and analyze. Seaborn is a high-level library that makes it simple to create beautiful statistical visualizations, allowing users to create complex plots with minimal effort. On the other hand, Matplotlib offers more detailed control, letting users customize every aspect of their plots to suit their needs. Together, these libraries allow for a wide variety of visualizations, such as histograms, scatter plots, and heatmaps, which help in understanding how different variables relate to each other, identifying patterns, and effectively communicating results. Data scientists and analysts often use Seaborn and Matplotlib to create insightful graphs that make it easier to interpret and explore datasets.

2.5 *Training and testing*

Using datasets to create training and test sets is important for evaluating and validating machine learning models. The training set teach the model, allowing it to identify links and patterns in the data. However, it is essential to employ a different test set that was not used for training to assess the model on fresh and untested data. The ability to generalize the model is measured by how accurately it predicts outcomes on this test set. This step is critical in determining if the model is capable of handling real-world, unknown data, ensuring that it doesn't simply memorize the training data but can also make accurate predictions on new, previously unseen data.

2.6 *Machine learning algorithms*

Use of ML techniques are essential for diagnosing, predicting, and managing chronic kidney disease (CKD). Decision Tree (DT) is useful because they create easy-to-understand models that link patient characteristics to CKD outcomes. However, they can sometimes overfit, meaning They might not function well with fresh data. Support Vector Machines (SVM) are excellent at differentiating between patients with and without CKD, as they can handle complex relationships between different factors. Ensemble methods like Gradient Boosting (GB) and XGBoost are excellent at identifying complex patterns in the data, with XGBoost being more efficient and better at handling unbalanced datasets. AdaBoost improves prediction accuracy by focusing on cases where the model previously made mistakes, while Bagged Decision Trees (Bagging) help reduce overfitting and provide more stable predictions. Random Forest (RF), a more advanced version of Bagging, is often used due to its high accuracy and capacity to handle noisy or incomplete data. A more straightforward model called logistic regression (LR) performs best in case of linear relationship between features and outcomes. Finally, the Voting Classifier, which combines different models like AdaBoost, Bagging, and Decision Trees, boosts accuracy by using the strengths of each algorithm. These algorithms work together to improve patient care and healthcare efficiency by assisting in early CKD diagnosis, tracking the disease's course, and optimizing therapy [21].

3 EXPERIMENTAL RESULTS

Table 1 provides a summary of the ML models used to predict CKD, with particular attention paid to performance parameters. It has been noted that the SVM algorithm employed by all the authors to predict accuracy is extraordinary. The details of the observations according to algorithms are as follows:

Table 1. Comparison of several machine learning algorithms.

S. No	Author Name	Algorithms Used	Accuracy	Precision	Recall	F1 Score
1	Debabrata Swain et.al., [11]	Support vector machine	99.33	-	-	-
		Random forest	98.67	-	-	-
2	Muhammad Shoaib Arif et.al., [12]	Gaussian Naive Bayes,	97.5	100	96.15	98.03
		K-Nearest Neighbor	100	100	100	100
3	Md. Ariful Islam et.al., [13]	AdaBoost	0.975	0.98	0.97	0.97
		Decision Tree	0.96	0.96	0.96	0.96
		XgBoost	0.983	0.98	0.98	0.98
		CatBoost	0.966	0.97	0.97	0.97
		KNN	0.65	0.66	0.65	0.65
		Random Forest	0.975	0.98	0.97	0.97
		Naive Bayes	0.94	0.95	0.94	0.94
		Gradient Boosting	0.975	0.98	0.97	0.97
4	Vinoth Kumar Venkatesan et.al., [14]	LR	95.00	96.30	97.56	96.93
		KNN	91.00	91.18	96.47	94.75
		RF	90.00	93.10	96.42	94.73
		DT	88.00	91.95	94.11	93.01
		SVM	94.00	95.69	97.80	96.73
		XGBoost	98.00	98.90	98.90	98.90
5	Shahid Mohammad Ganie et.al., [15]	XGB	95.93	-	-	-
		CatBoost	96.44	-	-	-
		LGBM	97.96	-	-	-
		ADB	98.47	-	-	-
		GB	97.46	-	-	-
6	Nikhita Borde et.al., [16]	Naive Bayes	98	-	-	-
7	Muthia Febriana Azizah et.al., [17]	Gaussian Naive Bayes	89.93	88.15	89.93	88.42
8	Linta antony et.al.,[18]	K-Means Clustering	99.3	98	100	99.4
9	Hira Khalid, et.al., [19]	GB	99	-	-	-
		RF	98	-	-	-
		DT	96	-	-	-
		Naive Bayes	93	-	-	-
		Hybrid Model	100	-	-	-
10	Manal A Abdel-Fattah et.al., [20]	DT	100	100	100	100
		LR	99	99	99	99
		NB	87	91	88	88
		RF	100	100	100	100
		SVM	100	100	100	100
		GBT Classifier	100	100	100	100

Overall, Table 2 demonstrates how effective machine learning algorithms are at predicting CKD. Boosting methods, hybrid models, and ensemble techniques like RF consistently achieve high accuracy and robustness. The intricacy of the data frequently influences algorithm selection, preprocessing, and interpretability requirements.

Table 2. Evaluation of the CKD machine learning models.

Machine Learning Algorithms	Accuracy	Recall	Precision	F1 Score
Adaboost	100.00	100.000000	100.000000	100.000000
KNN	66.25	69.093407	67.473287	65.817376
Xgboost	66.25	69.093407	67.473287	65.817376
Gradient Boosting	66.25	69.093407	67.473287	65.817376
Random Forest	98.75	98.214286	99.056604	98.614719
Voting Classifier	100.00	100.000000	100.000000	100.000000
Logistic Regression	87.50	85.439560	86.752137	86.023760
Decision Tree	96.25	95.467033	96.261356	95.844156
SVM	96.25	95.467033	96.261356	95.844156
Bagging Classifier	98.75	98.214286	99.056604	98.614719

Based on performance score, the following Figure 2 has been prepared to evaluate the chronic kidney disease to be predicted by a number of machine learning techniques.

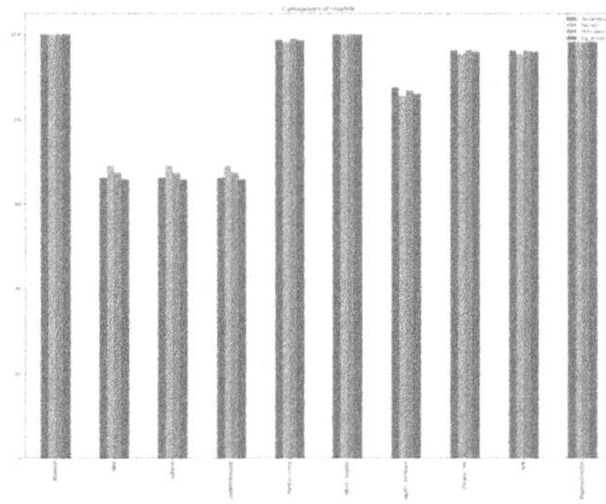

Figure 2. Comparison graphs.

3.1 *High performers*

Ensemble models dominate this category. The Voting Classifier and AdaBoost achieved perfect scores (100%) across all metrics, showcasing their ability to handle complex datasets effectively. Similarly, Random Forest and Bagging Classifier performed exceptionally well, with Accuracy and F1 Scores of 98.75% and 98.61%, respectively. These models leverage ensemble techniques to combine predictions from multiple learners, ensuring robust and consistent results. Their near-perfect scores make them the most suitable for CKD forecasting.

3.2 *Moderate performers*

In terms of accuracy and F1 Scores of 96.25% and 95.84%, respectively, models like Support Vector Machine (SVM) and Decision trees did remarkably well. These algorithms effectively balance predictive power and computational efficiency, although they slightly underperform compared to the top-tier ensemble models. Logistic Regression, a baseline algorithm, delivered decent results (Accuracy: 87.50%, F1 Score: 86.02%), making it a reliable but less optimal choice compared to ensemble methods.

3.3 *Low performers*

K-Nearest Neighbors (KNN) and similar algorithms Gradient Boosting, XGBoost achieved Accuracy and F1 Scores around 66.25% and 65.82%, respectively. These models struggled, likely due to their sensitivity to noisy or imbalanced data or the dataset's complexity. Overall, top-performing models are highly suitable for accurate and reliable disease prediction.

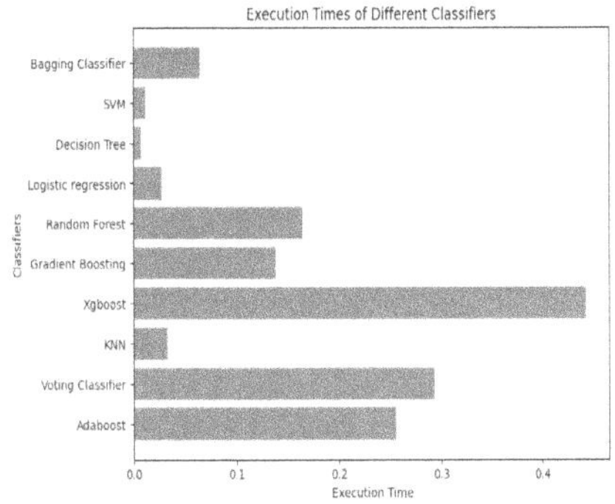

Figure 3. Execution times for different classifiers.

The chart in Figure 3 analyzes and compares the time it took for the various machine learning models in predicting CKD. SVM and Decision Tree are the fastest models with minimal execution times, followed by Logistic Regression, KNN, and Bagging Classifier, which also demonstrate computational efficiency. Random Forest and Gradient Boosting take moderate time to execute, balancing performance and speed. The slowest models are XGBoost, which shows the highest execution time, followed by Voting Classifier and AdaBoost, indicating these models are computationally more expensive. From the example, it can be inferred that the amount of time taken by machine learning models to perform CKD prediction significantly differs. SVM and Decision Tree are the most efficient models with minimal execution times, ideal for applications requiring high-speed predictions. While Logistic Regression, KNN, and Bagging Classifier do have somewhat longer execution durations, they are still computationally efficient, therefore they may be used in real-time or contexts with limited resources. Random Forest and Gradient Boosting exhibit moderate execution times, striking a balance between speed and complexity. However, XGBoost is the slowest, with significantly higher execution time, followed by Voting Classifier and AdaBoost, which are also resource intensive. For CKD prediction, the choice of the model should weigh execution time against prediction accuracy, with faster models preferable for efficiency and slower ones reserved for applications prioritizing predictive performance over speed.

4 CONCLUSION AND FUTURE SCOPE

The dataset is subjected to nine machine learning algorithms in order to forecast CKD. A dataset of UCI Repository was used, containing 400 records with 21 attributes related to CKD For training and testing these models. The results of the experiment demonstrated impressive accuracy, with Random Forest and Bagging classifiers achieving accuracy of 98.75%. Among the models tested, XGBoost and Adaboost performed particularly well, attaining the highest accuracy, indicating that these methods are strong candidates for CKD prediction. Future studies may examine the application of neural networks and other cutting-edge deep learning approaches to enhance CKD prediction models in order to get over the drawbacks of conventional algorithms in identifying intricate data patterns.

REFERENCES

[1] Chittora, P.; Chaurasia, S.; Chakrabarti, P.; Kumawat, G.; Chakrabarti, T.; Leonowicz, Z.; Jasiński, M.; Jasinski, L.; Gono, R.; Jasinska, E.; *et al.* Prediction of Chronic Kidney Disease—A Machine Learning Perspective. *IEEE Access* 2021, 9, 17312–17334.

[2] Almustafa, K.M. (2021). Prediction of chronic kidney disease using different classification algorithms. *Informatics in Medicine Unlocked, 24*, 100631. https://doi.org/10.1016/j.imu.2021.100631.

[3] Halder, R.K., Uddin, M.N., Uddin, M.A., Aryal, S., Saha, S., Hossen, R., Ahmed, S., Rony, M.A., and Akter, M.F. (2024). ML-CKDP: Machine learning-based chronic kidney disease prediction with smart web application. *Journal of Pathology Informatics, 15*, 100371. https://doi.org/10.1016/j.jpi.2024.100371.

[4] Gazi Mohammed Ifraz, Comparative Analysis for Prediction of Kidney Disease Using Intelligent Machine Learning Methods, Hindawi, *Computational and Mathematical Methods in Medicine*, Volume 2021, Article ID 6141470, https://doi.org/10.1155/2021/6141470.

[5] Dritsas, E., and Trigka, M. (2022). Machine learning techniques for chronic kidney disease risk prediction. *Big Data and Cognitive Computing, 6*(3), 98. https://doi.org/10.3390/bdcc6030098.

[6] Dey, S.K., Uddin, K.M., Babu, H.M., Rahman, M.M., Howlader, A., and Uddin, K.A. (2022). Chi2-MI: A hybrid feature selection based machine learning approach in diagnosis of chronic kidney disease. *Intelligent Systems with Applications, 16*, 200144. https://doi.org/10.1016/j.iswa.2022.200144.

[7] Chamandeep Kaur, M. Sunil Kumar, Afsana Anjum, M.B. Binda, Maheswara Reddy Mallu, and Mohammed Saleh Al Ansari, Chronic Kidney Disease Prediction Using Machine Learning, *Journal of Advances in Information Technology*, Vol. 14, No. 2, 2023, doi: 10.12720/jait.14.2.384-391.

[8] Reshma S., *et al.*, *Chronic Kidney Disease Prediction using Machine Learning*, doi :10.17577/IJERTV9IS070092.

[9] Sumitra Mallick, Jayasingh B.B. Prediction of Mental Health Illness Using Machine Learning for Technical Employees, in *proceedings of the International Conference on Innovative Computing, Informatics and Advanced Communication Systems (ICICIAC-2022)*, 25th to 26th March 2022. https://doi.org/10.1063/5.0163638.

[10] Silveira, A.C., Sobrinho, Á., Silva, L.D., Costa, E.D., Pinheiro, M.E., and Perkusich, A. (2022). Exploring early prediction of chronic kidney disease using machine learning algorithms for small and Imbalanced datasets. *Applied Sciences, 12*(7), 3673. https://doi.org/10.3390/app12073673.

[11] Arif, M.S., Mukheimer, A., and Asif, D. (2023). Enhancing the early detection of chronic kidney disease: Arobust machine learning model. *Big Data and Cognitive Computing, 7*(3),144. https://doi.org/10.3390/bdcc7030144.

[12] Islam, M.A., Majumder, M.Z., and Hussein, M.A. (2023). Chronic kidney disease prediction based on machine learning algorithms. *Journal of Pathology Informatics, 14*,100189.https://doi.org/10.1016/j.jpi.2023.100189.

[13] Venkatesan, V.K., Ramakrishna, M.T., Izonin, I., Tkachenko, R., and Havryliuk, M. (2023). Efficient data Preprocessing with ensemble machine learning technique for the early detection of chronic kidney disease. *Applied Sciences, 13*(5), 2885. https://doi.org/10.3390/app13052885.

[14] Ganie, S.M., Dutta Pramanik, P.K., Mallik, S., and Zhao, Z. (2023). Chronic kidney disease prediction using boosting techniques based on clinical parameters. *PLOSONE, 18*(12),e0295234. https://doi.org/10.1371/journal.pone.0295234.

[15] Nikhita Borde, Supriya Shanbhag, Detection Of Chronic Kidney Disease Using Machinelearning In The R-Environment, *International Research Journal of Engineering and Technology (IRJET)*.

[16] Azizah, M.F., and Paramitha, A.T. (2024). Predictive modelling of chronic kidney disease using gaussian naive Bayes algorithm. *International Journal of Artificial Intelligence in Medical Issues, 2* (2), 125-135. https://doi.org/10.56705/ijaimi.v2i2.160.

[17] Antony, L., Azam, S., Ignatious, E., Quadir, R., Beeravolu, A.R., Jonkman, M., and De Boer, F. (2021). A comprehensive unsupervised framework for chronic kidney disease prediction. *IEEE Access, 9*, 126481-126501https://doi.org/10.1109/access.2021.3109168.

[18] Khalid, H., Khan, A., Zahid Khan, M., Mehmood, G., and Shuaib Qureshi, M. (2023). Machine learning hybrid model for the prediction of chronic kidney disease. *Computational Intelligence and Neuroscience, 2023*(1). https://doi.org/10.1155/2023/9266889.

[19] Abdel-Fattah, M.A., Othman, N.A., and Goher, N. (2022). Predicting chronic kidney disease using hybrid machine learning based on Apache spark. *Computational Intelligence and Neuroscience, 2022*, 1–12. https://doi.org/10.1155/2022/9898831.

[20] Jayasingh B.B. and Jyothi T., Medical Image Diagnosis Using Deep Learning Classifiers for COVID-19, *2022 OPJU International Technology Conference on Emerging Technologies for Sustainable Development (OTCON)*, 8th – 10th Feb. 2023, pp. 1–6, doi: 10.1109/OTCON56053.2023.10114013.

Next-Generation Smart Systems – Sekhar et al. (Eds)

An Approach to Detect Imperfections in Printed Circuit Boards Using Machine Learning

Krishnaveni Bantu
M.Tech Scholar, ECE Department, CMR Technical Campus, Kandlakoya, Hydearbad, India

Sudhamani Chilakala
Associate Professor, ECE Department, CMR Technical Campus, Kandlakoya, Hydearbad, India

Chamundeswari S.
Assiociate Professor, Department of CSE, Bhimanna Khandre Institute of Technology, Bhalki, India

Sireesha Pendem and Praveen Kumar Pendem
Research Scholar, CSE Department, Bhimanna Khandre Institute of technology, Bhalki, India
Asst. Professor ECE Department, CMR Technical Campus, Kandlakoya, Hydearbad, India

Suresh Kancharla
Assistant Professor, ECE Department, St.Martin's Engineering College, Dhulapally, Hydearbad, India

ABSTRACT: Printed circuit boards are integral component of electronics systems besides its quality must be guaranteed to avoid the manufacturing defects, because these defects leading to entire system failure[1]. The project proposes an automatic method for detecting the imperfections in the printed circuit boards using machine learning. The technique with image processing with feature extraction methods will identify the various kinds of imperfections such as short circuit, missing components and open circuits. However the usage of convolution neural networks(CNN) enables effective classification and localization of defects with high accuracy[2]. The recommended approach brings down the time for physical inspection ,also improves the reliability of quality control processes during PCB production[3].Experimental results validate the effectiveness of the model on different datasets, reflecting its potential for real-time industrial application. The proposed system offers high detection accuracy and demonstrates improved performance compared to traditional inspection methods[4].

Keywords: PCB defect detection Machine learning Convolution neural networks(CNN), Image processing

1 INTRODUCTION

PCB's are the key components, nearly most of the present-day electronics, ranging from controlling simple devices like children's playing gadgets to being the homes of almost entire computer gadgets for federal security appliances[5], the applications of PCBs are limitless. Considering the heavy examples in critical appliances and performances, condition checks within the PCB Production industry is also critical in delivering highly trustworthy units[6]. The PCB manufacturing procedure include diverse steps: Beginning with composing of the basic materials, the industrialists might have some deviations for such process .However the main steps will be the classification of PCB defects. One is Cosmetic defect and the other is Functional defect or malfunction defects. Identifying both these deformities is pivotal to manufacture a PCB with hundred percent quality affirmation[7]. Malfunction or glitches are deemed to be killer faults, the PCB fails to show up at the purpose for which they were made; conductor rupture and short-circuit are a few of the faults in this categorization. Cosmetic defects are flaws that ruin the outlook of the PCB, such as break out , pin hole, over-etch, and under-etch. However, Cosmetic defects will not cause an instant danger in the functioning of the PCB. On the other hand it compromises the performance in the future because of divergent heat dissipation and current distribution[8].Majority of these anomalies or defects arise from thermal diversification of art object during printing, dust & dirt particles on board, air bubbles due to electrolysis, and improper etching[9].

2 LITERATURE REVIEW

Early works relied on image subtraction and mathematical morphology to detect PCB defects [2], [10]. Later, researchers explored handcrafted feature extraction methods such as texture descriptors and histograms.Machine learning classifiers including SVM, KNN, and Random Forest have been applied [7], but they struggle with high accuracy in complex datasets. Recent approaches use deep learning, especially CNNs, to automatically learn hierarchical features from raw PCB images [3]. Huang (2019) introduced the DeepPCB dataset, enabling benchmarking of CNN and R-CNN models with higher precision and recall compared to conventional methods . Their methods achieved large increase imprecision and recall compared to conventional method. Other models YOLO (You only look once) and Faster R-CNN have been applied to real time object detecting inspection that can detect and locate multiple defects per pass. Such models are specifically beneficial to high speed production lines where time and accuracy both are extremely important. The absence of standard datasets has been a problem in area. This has changed thought with the availability data sets such as deep PCB, PCB, PKU-PCB, and synthetic defect datasets. The availability of these datasets has made more comparative reproducible studies possible.

3 PROPOSED MODEL

If too much or too little copper is left on a PCB, it can cause problems. Leaving too much can lead to unwanted connections,

DOI: 10.1201/9781042001767-9

extra holes, bumps, or small patches of copper that don't do anything. On the other hand, removing too much can create gaps where connections should be, tiny holes, small cuts in the lines, or very thin tracks that can easily break.

There are two main ways to check for defects on a PCB: electrical (or contact) testing and non-electrical (or non-contact) methods. Among these, electrical or contact testing is considered a reliable way to inspect the board's quality.

when the issue is testing variables of the design that entails direct contact of a circuit. One of the biggest problems with electrical or contact testing is that setting up the testing tools and equipment is difficult and expensive. Since many PCB are designed with very tiny parts—smaller than 0.1 inch—it becomes harder to create the right setup. As a result, the testing process becomes more complicated and costly, even though it's known to be reliable.

They serve as a basis comparing and testing machine learning models under different conditions .With the advent of machine learning, scientists started using feature based classification methods such as Support vector vending Machine (SVM), K-nearest neighbors (KNN) and random forests. These involve handcrafted feature from PCB images including shape descriptors, textures and histograms. The below figure shows the different types of defect PCBs.

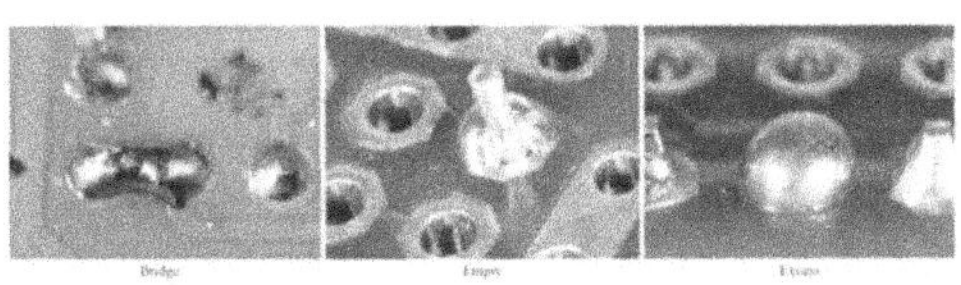

Figure 1. Different types of defects(Bridge, Empty, Excess).

The below illustration shows the block diagram of the generalized PCD model detection using Machine learning. It explains the step wise procedure how the machine learning algorithms can be applied to identify the imperfections in PCBs.

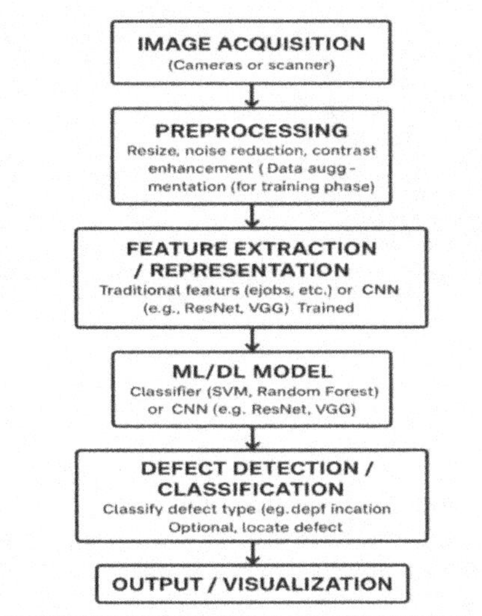

Figure 2.

Step1: **Image acquisition:** In this step the PCB's image is captured by using high resolution cameras. In the detection process these high resolution pictures are served as Raw Data.

Step2: **Preprocessing:** In this step the pictures are resized according to the standard image dimensions and then do the Gaussian noise filtering to remove unwanted distortions. And then to improve the visibility of features contrast enhancement is applied. Next is Data Augmentation phase. In this phase data is flipped, rotated, changed brightness to increase the robustness of the model.

Step3: **Feature Extraction:** In this two approaches can be applied the first one the traditional features like textures, edges. These can be detected by blob detection, ejobs methods. Next approach is by using conventional neural networks (CNN).The pre trained models like Resnet, VGG is used to automatic extraction of the patterns.

Step4: **Machine learning Model:** The ML classifiers used in this step is Support Vector Machine (SVM) and the random forest for extracting the traditional features.

Step5:**Defect classification/Detection:** Here the classification of defects has been done.

Step6: **Output visualization**: Last step is displaying the results in user friendly manner.

The next section is represents the workflow of an automated image inspection method where a captured image is compared with a reference image to identify variations, defects, or abnormalities. The main stages involved are explained in the continued section.

This workflow demonstrates a systematic approach for automated visual inspection. By combining reference-based comparison, preprocessing, and feature extraction, the method enhances accuracy in defect detection while reducing human effort in manual inspection. It is highly useful in applications such as manufacturing, quality control, and medical imaging.

Now the below figure shows the process flow of the defect detection in PCBs.

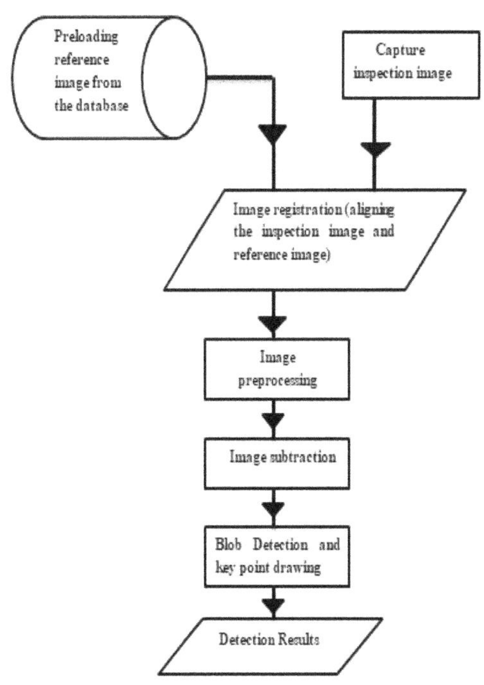

Figure 3. Process flow of PCB defect detection.

3.1 *Data collection and preprocessing*

- Dataset: Annotated images of PCBs with different types of defects.
- Preprocessing Steps:
- Image resizing (e.g., 224×224 px)
- Grayscale or RGB normalization

- Noise removal and histogram equalization
- Data augmentation (rotation, zoom, flipping)

3.2 *Data collection and preprocessing*

- Dataset: Annotated images of PCBs with different types of defects.
- Preprocessing Steps:
- Image resizing (e.g., 224×224 px)
- Grayscale or RGB normalization
- Noise removal and histogram equalization
- Data augmentation (rotation, zoom, flipping)
- Flatten → Fully Connected (Dense) → Softmax Layer
- Output: Multi-class classification (e.g., open, short, missing hole)

3.2 *Training setup*

- Precision, Recall, F1-Score
- Environment: Python, TensorFlow/OpenCV
- **D. Evaluation**
- The model is evaluated on unseen images. The results prove strong performance in identifying all the defect classes, with accuracy.

4 ABOUT PCB

A Printed Circuit Board (PCB) is an essential element in nearly all contemporary electronic appliances. It acts as a base to support mechanically and connect electrically different electronic elements like resistors, capacitors, and integrated circuits with the help of conductive paths, or traces, in the form of copper. The traces are etched on insulating layers, commonly composed of fiberglass or metalized composite epoxy resin (also referred to as FR4). A typical PCB has multiple layers such as the substrate (base material), copper layer (conductive conductive traces), solder mask (protective coating), and silkscreen (labeling and assembly guide). PCBs exist in various forms depending on their structure, such as single-sided, double-sided, and multilayer boards, and rigid, flexible, and rigid-flex forms. They are used extensively in various applications like consumer electronics (such as smart phones and television sets), automotive systems, medical devices, industrial equipment, and communication equipment. The process of PCB manufacturing usually entails the creation of the design layout using CAD software, printing the circuit pattern, etching the copper, drilling holes in the components, applying protective coatings, and lastly installing the components. Even after their precision manufacturing, PCBs may have defects such as faulty traces, short circuits, delimitation, and soldering defects, which can impact the reliability and performance of electronic systems.

Figure 4. Structure of printed circuit boards.

Features

1. Compact Design – Enables complex circuits to be constructed in a compact space.2. Efficient Electrical Connectivity – Copper tracks ensure stable connections between the components.
2. Mechanical Support – Secures and supports electronic components.
3. Durability – Composed of robust materials such as FR4, heat, water, and chemical resistant.
4. Automation-Friendly – Facilitates automated production and component placement.
5. Cost-Effective – Suitable for mass production with less labor and manufacturing expense.
6. Solder Mask Layer – Shields the copper traces and protects them from short circuits.
7. Silkscreen Layer – Prints labels, component values, and reference marks.
8. Design Flexibility – Offers single-sided, double-sided, and multilayer designs.

5 RESULTS

The results are shown in below figures the first image is a design file or Gerber layout view showing copper trace routing, pin headers (P0–P3), component footprints, and solder pads. It is clean and shows the intended electrical paths clear.

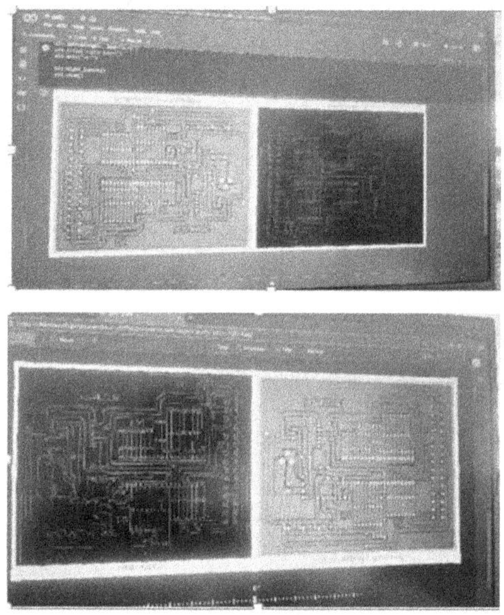

Figure 5. Results.

In the down image showing the fabricated or simulated output of the PCB. The green solder mask covers the copper areas except at pad locations. It matches the layout on the left closely.

The PCB appears defect-free and accurately manufactured based on visual comparison. If this is being used for ML-based defect detection, this image may serve as a "non-defective" or reference sample.

6 CONCLUSION

In our project, we built such a system to help small manufacturers who make many different boards in small batches. The idea is to let them check each board automatically instead of by eye.We use a type of AI called a Convolutional Neural Network

(CNN). A CNN learns straight from pictures of the boards, then tells us—by percentage—how likely each spot is to be defective. Older methods often need a lot of hand-tuned steps first, and they still don't match the CNN's mix of accuracy, speed, and ease of use. The final "SoftMax" layer of the network turns its findings into clear, easy-to-read probabilities, making the whole inspection process both simple and reliable.

ACKNOWLEDGMENT

The authors are indebted to the students and staff of the CMR technical campus Hydearbad, research centre of Bhimanna Khandre instistute of technology, Bhalki for their cooperation in this project completin

REFERENCES

[1] Madhav Moganty Fikret, Cihan H. Dagli, and Shou Tsunekawa. (1996). Automatic PCB Inspection Algorithms. *Computer. Vis. Image Under.* 63, 2 (March 1996), 287–313. DOI : https://doi.org/10

[2] Khalid N., (2007), An Image Processing Approach Towards Classification of Defect on Printed Circuit Board, *Project Sarjana Muda*, University Technology Malaysia, pp 87–91

[3] Raihan F. and Ce W., (2017), PCB defect detection USING OPENCV with image subtraction method, 2017 International Conference on Information Management and Technology (ICIM Tech), *Yogyakarta*, pp. 204–209.

[4] Indera Putera S.H. and Ibrahim Z., (2010), Printed circuit board defect detection using mathematical morphology and MATLAB. Image processing tools, *2010 2nd International Conference on Education Technology and Computer, Shanghai*, pp.V5-359–V5-363, 10.1109/ICETC.2010.5530052

[5] Herian R., Al-Attas S.A.R, and Ahmad Zabidi M.M., (2002), *Segmentation of PCB Images into Simple Generic Patterns using Mathematical Morphology and Windowing Technique*, GRAMM Melaka, Malaysia

[6] Masalkar P.R. and Kasliwal P.S., (2017), Study of the image processing algorithms for defect detection of pcb s, *Int. J. Eng. Technol. Sci. Res*, vol. 4, no. 6, pp. 606–612

[7] Karako M., and Akin E., (2017) *Machine vision based defect detection approach using image processing*,

[8] Kim, H.W. and Yoo, S.I. (2014). Defect detection using feature point matching for nonrepetitive patterned images, *Pattern Anal Application* 17, 415–429 (2014).

[9] Prof. P. S. and Nadaf R. S., (2014), A Survey : Automated Visual PCB Inspection Algorithm, *International Journal of Engineering Research & Technology (IJERT)* Volume 03, Issue 01 (January 2014).

[10] Mahmoud Taha, Eid Emary, Eid Moustafa and Khalid. (2014). Automatic Optical Inspection for PCB Manufacturing: a Survey. *International Journal of Scientific and Engineering Research.* Volume 5. 1095–1102

Next-Generation Smart Systems – Sekhar et al. (Eds)

Intrusion Detection in SCADA Systems Using Machine Learning Algorithms

Nimmala Mangathayaru, Gunupudi Rajesh Kumar, and Tene Ravi
Department of IT, VNR Vignana Jyothi Institute of Engineering and Technology, Hyderabad, India

ABSTRACT: A SCADA system is a mix of hardware and software that lets you collect data and automate modern communication. SCADA connects sensors that monitor engines, motors, pumps, and valves to a server that is either on-site or far away. It's clear that SCADA frameworks are very important for modern businesses. In the last few years, a computer program has been able to copy itself and damage a computer without the user's knowledge or permission. An intrusion could delete everything on a hard drive, ruin or erase files on a PC, or even use email projects to spread to other PCs. These serious attacks have made people more worried about the safety of SCADA in many places. The bottom line is to create a system or model that can predict these kinds of intrusions. This will help improve security and lessen these SCADA system problems. For this reason, we come up with a way to deal with this problem and suggest a method for finding intrusions. Our proposed method uses a cross-breed model that takes advantage of the expected and reliable communication patterns that happen between ground devices. First, we used some preprocessing techniques to standardise and scale the data. Second, PCA calculations are used to reduce the number of dimensions in order to work on the course of intrusion detection. Third, the Bloom Filter classifier is used to create a data set by keeping track of the framework for a certain amount of time without any intrusions. Finally, we combined our Bloom Filter classifier with a new voting classifier to detect new intrusions. The exploratory results from a real, huge scope dataset made from a gas pipeline SCADA framework show that the proposed method beats the benchmark models with a precision rate of 99.53%.

Keywords: Intrusion Detection, SCADA, Bloom filter, voting classifier, PCA

1 INTRODUCTION

SCADA is Supervisory Control and Data Acquisition that can operate or monitor remote sensors and equipment. Effective SCADA systems manage several I/O points. When water supply and tank levels rise above a certain level, SCADA activates pumps to fill empty tanks. SCADA controls stream speed, temperature, pressure, and engine speed. Visible and controlled level and pressure indicators. Generator, engine, switch, and transfer system status. The central processing unit and remote sensors and equipment are usually connected by hardware. Sensors and field equipment work with remote devices. Sensor I/O is usually computerized or primitive and lacks long-range signals.

Sensor flags are converted into digital packets by the intermediary gear and sent to the focus point over long distances using existing communication infrastructure. Recent network invasions have increased. Safe SCADA systems for infrastructure are lacking. Industrial and cyber-physical controls report violations. Unauthorized computer network activity is an intrusion. Network outages can compromise business assets and data. Network outages must be identified and addressed by associations and internet protection groups. They should also prioritise preventing attacks.

SCADA breaches weaken security. This study finds SCADA intrusions using machine learning. Boosts SCADA security. Study hybrid models. Data preparation and feature extraction. Bloom Filter next. To discover intrusions, three classification algorithms vote.

2 RELATED STUDY

This section discusses earlier research on designing intrusion detection systems (IDS) for industrial control systems (ICS), focusing on SCADA systems. To secure SCADA networks, several new methods have been developed. Dungwal et.al. [1] developed HML-IDS, a hybrid anomaly detection model, using ICS devices' predictable communication behaviour. Normalisation, dimensionality reduction, and dataset correction using a modified closest neighbour approach are used. Using packet-level detection, an instance-based learner, and a Bloom filter, a baseline signature database is created without abnormalities. Experimental results on a large SCADA gas pipeline dataset showed 97% detection accuracy. Mubarak *et al.* [2] suggested a Spark-optimised parallel intrusion detection model using k-means clustering and Random Forests. Deep learning classifiers like CNN and LSTM classify aberrant activity. Data imbalance is addressed via ADASYN. Their method achieved 99.91% classification accuracy using NSL-KDD and CIC-IDS2017 datasets. Subhash Khadidos *et al.* [3] used PCA and Random Forest to increase detection performance and minimise dimensionality. Their technique outperformed SVM, Naïve Bayes, and decision trees with 96.78% accuracy and a 0.21% error rate. Srinivas Wali *et al.* [4] categorised SCADA security attacks by protocol layers and safety needs. Their research also reveals SCADA network difficulties, including quantum attacks. Woods *et al.* [5] created a deep learning-based ensemble model to detect cyberattacks using enhanced data representations. Their model outperformed traditional classifiers on two ICS datasets with 10-fold validation. Wiens *et al.* [6] compared SCADA architecture to DCS and the Purdue Enterprise Reference Architecture (PERA), confirming structural conformity. Bloom filters were used to efficiently search billions of records for ID verification by Terborgh *et al.* [7]. Alotaibi *et al.* [8] examined hybrid assaults on power system integrity and availability, indicating cost-effective disruption potential. An ensemble IDS model using RFE-XGBoost and a majority voting mechanism over nine classifiers by Akhtaruzzaman *et al.* [9] and Testa [10] detected multi-class intrusions. Schwartz *et al.* [11] developed an ensemble ML model (ERG-SVC) for phishing detection with 98.27% accuracy using advanced feature selection and O'Guinn *et al.* [12] developed a false news detection framework combining TF-IDF and document-to-vector characteristics modified with chi-square and ANOVA [13]. They achieved 100% ISOT dataset correctness with their model.

DOI: 10.1201/9781042001767-10

3 APPROACH

3.1 *Problem statement*

SCADA systems integrate hardware and software to automate and monitor industrial processes by connecting field devices to centralised servers. These systems are essential for ensuring productivity, real-time monitoring, and decision-making. However, they are increasingly targeted by cyber threats, making anomaly detection critical. This study proposes a two-level classification model using Bloom Filter and Voting Classifier to detect anomalies efficiently.

3.2 *Data preprocessing*

SCADA systems take data and automate industrial processes using hardware and software. SCADA links motor, pump, and valve sensors to onsite or remote servers. SCADA systems are essential for industrial companies. They also monitor productivity, analyse the data for better decisions, and report system faults. Malicious activity threatens data and industry security in these vital systems. Detecting SCADA anomalies became necessary. This paper presents a method for building an effective learning model using two variables.

3.3 *Preprocessing*

Data Preprocessing crude data makes it modellable. It's the first and most important step in modelling, but we usually don't reveal all the data. Thus, every database activity must be cleaned and organised. This study involves these steps:

a) Categorical Labelling
b) Standardisation

3.3.1 *Categorical labelling*

Categorical data is converted into numbers to enable algorithms to predict based on changed attributes. This simple method converts each column value to a number. Categories are accumulated data divided into two groups.

3.3.2 *Standardisation*

The standardisation process, as shown in Figure 1, places elements near 0 with a standard deviation of 1. ML Algorithms require this progression, but it's also important when matching attributes with different units. After standardisation, the characteristics will be rescaled to have conventional dispersal properties ($\mu = 0$ and $\sigma = 1$). Standard sums of cases have a mean of μ and a standard deviation of σ.

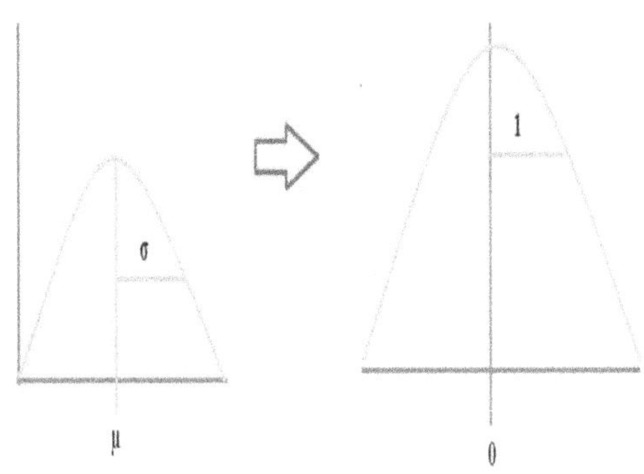

Figure 1. Standardisation.

3.4 *Picking features*

Feature selection stands out in dimensionality reduction. Dimensionality reduction in ML reduces unpredictable elements by aggregating crucial features. Features can be selected or extracted from this interaction. ML feature selection finds the greatest combination of factors for building useful and productive models. Principal Component Analysis reduces dimensions.

PCA (Principal Component Analysis) is an unsupervised approach used to reduce dimensionality in machine learning (ML). With orthogonal transformation, a measurable interaction turns correlated properties into uncorrelated ones. These updated highlights are called principal components.

3.5 *Bloom filter level 1*

Bloom filters are space-efficient probabilistic data structures used to determine whether a component is a set individual. Enrolment issues arise due to username accessibility, as the set encompasses all enrolled usernames. Because productivity is probabilistic, there may be some false positives. It may report a username as taken when it's not.

After gathering important characteristics, we can create a bloom filter classifier to reduce predicted false negatives. A Bloom filter never forecasts that a data packet is not an abnormality, hence no false negatives. However, this classification may provide many false positives.

3.5.1 *Hashing functions*

Hash functions are mathf(x). It provides the hash of assured esteem after certain operation(s). We hash a component twice and set the corresponding entries in the piece vector, based on those hashes, to 1 in order to add it to the Bloom filter. [15]

3.5.2 *Misleading positive probability*

A basic calculation can establish the false positive probability for hunting a component that is not in the set.

Considering the irregularity of the hash functions, all the components in set S were filtered. The probability of becoming 0 is as follows:

$$p = \left(1 - \frac{1}{m}\right)^{kn} \approx e^{\left(-\frac{kn}{m}\right)}$$

We observed decrease in the false positives when, the size of cluster spots are increasing, when we are trying to plot the probability of false positives with respect to the size of bloom filter for considerable number of embedded components.

If we plot the false positive probability versus the piece exhibit or bloom filter size for a fair number of embedded components, we can see that false positives decrease as the size of the spot cluster increases. According to the graphic for $p < 0.01$, a single hash job would require a piece cluster of size 100 times the number of values (n). A bloom filter's key idea is that k hash functions can significantly reduce the space needed (m). When adding a value to the channel, it is hashed, and the hash function parts are set to 1. When we wish to verify that a existing value, we have hashed it and determine if each hash function bit to be 1. The worth is assumed to be zero if the smallest bit is 0. [14].

3.5.3 *Choice of hash functions*

We have assumed that the optimal hash capacity with respect to no of values to be embedded and along with the max allowed rate of false positives. There is a lot of content about choosing excellent hash functions. [14]

The value of p is less than 0.01 for the following configurations: (k=1, m=1B), (k=5, m=100M), and (k=8, m=100M). Given (n=10M, $p < 0.01$), the optimal choice is (k=5, m=100M) due to space and time constraints. The size of the instances exhibited are limited by the Bloom filters and the number of hash functions used. [14]

3.6 *Level 2 voting classifier*

The level2 consists of voting classifier. This uses machine learning to combine basic models to determine the best arrangement. The base model will use k-Nearest Neighbour, Naïve Bayes, and logistic regression techniques to predict individual results. Instead of constructing independent dedicated models and assessing their accuracy, we create one model that trains using these models and predicts yield based on their combined contributions to selecting each result class.

Two types of voting classifiers exist.

Independent voting: Rigorous voting classifiers require the output class to anticipate most votes. Our work employed three algorithms: KNN, Naïve Bayes, and logistic regression, each trained separately and producing different output classes. The output is expected by most votes shown in Figure 2.

Soft voting: The output class predicts the class average probability. Each base model classifier freely assigns event probabilities. Finally, from the results obtained highest probable class is selected by determining the norm of each class's possible outcomes.

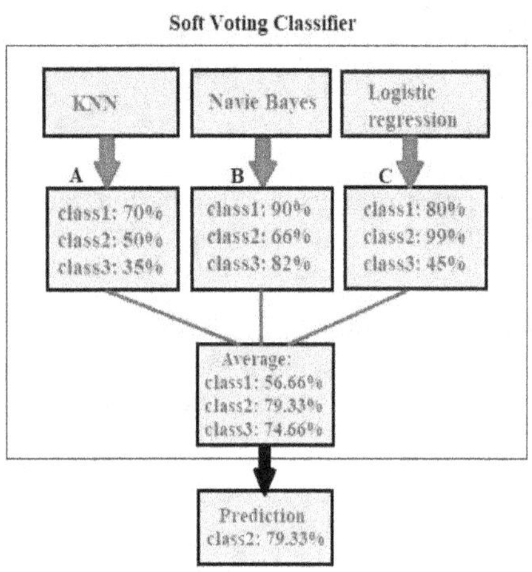

Figure 2. Hard voting classifier.

After introducing our Bloom Filter and Voting Classifier, we present their hybrid multi-level method. The association flow diagram of the aggregate proposed approach is shown in Figure 3.

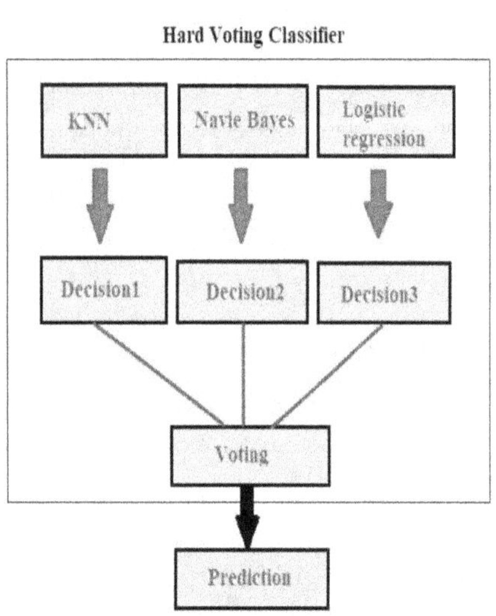

Figure 3. Hard voting classifier.

When examining data packet information, our Bloom Filter anomaly identifier will first search for its signature in the reference dictionary. If it doesn't find it, the packet will be classed as an anomaly. It is unnecessary to submit Bloom Filter-recognised anomaly data packets to the voting classifier because the second-level classifier will continually delegate them uniquely. This strategy should work well because the Bloom Filter's false positive rate can be extended by the approval error during the showing stage and tweaked.

Our voting-classifier anomaly identifier will categorise the data packet contents if our Bloom Filter approves them. Consider using KNN, Naïve Bayes, and logistic regression to determine if the anomaly exists. The classifier will use the data packet to classify subsequent data packets as normal or anomalous.

4 DATASET

We have chosen the Oak Ridge National Laboratories formatted SCADA gas pipeline dataset [16] as a data source for this study and joined the oddity distinguishing approach. The attacks on basic foundations like SCADA can be distinguished with the utilisation of an IDS. The gas pipeline dataset contains various artefacts of cyberattacks, which can be used to train and test classifiers used by IDS. These SCADA framework IDSs are improved via preparing them with information logs that connote the genuine traffic of SCADA organisations. The administrator can be advised of any strange action, which will assist with forestalling harm. The gas pipeline dataset contains 12 cyberattacks and around 26 attributes to be utilised to prepare and test classifiers.

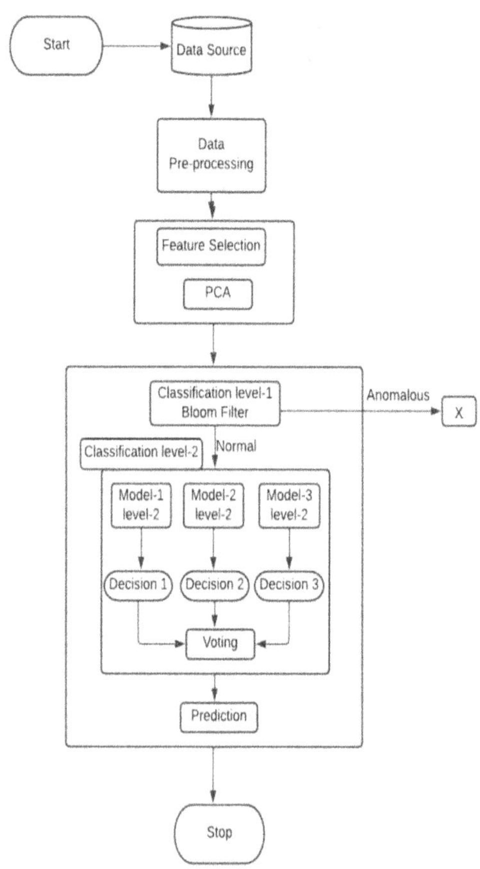

Figure 4. Overview of proposed approach.

5 RESULTS AND DISCUSSIONS

The categorisation findings are used to test our consolidated intrusion detection strategy for the test set. Our studies evaluate our incursion strategy using the measurements from the previous segment. Anaconda (Python 3.9) with Spyder as the IDE is used for all programming to restore test perceptions. The PC has a 3.20 GHz Intel Core i5 processor, 8 GB RAM, and 64-bit Windows. We can detect infiltration in 0.117 milliseconds using our method. This two-level irregularity identification method requires 1040 KB of RAM. Both should suit SCADA systems.

The table shows that hard and soft voting classifiers get similar results. Though soft voting classifier is better than hard. If the dataset is more balanced, the soft voting classifier may be more accurate.

Table 1. Results.

Model	Accuracy	Precision	Recall
Hard Voting Classifier	99.26%	99.88%	99.26%
Soft Voting Classifier	99.53%	99.81%	99.52%

6 CONCLUSIONS AND FUTURE SCOPE

In this study, we proposed an intrusion detection system within the SCADA architecture, integrating a Bloom filter with a voting classifier based on machine learning algorithms. The approach incorporates robust data preprocessing and standardisation techniques, along with effective feature extraction, to handle large-scale datasets efficiently. The trained model employs a two-level classification mechanism to detect anomalies, achieving promising results in terms of accuracy, precision, and recall. As part of future work, we intend to extend this framework by incorporating deep learning techniques and evaluating its performance across multiple datasets to further enhance detection capabilities and model generalisation.

ACKNOWLEDGEMENT

The authors would like to acknowledge that this research was carried out independently without any specific grant or financial support from any funding agencies.

REFERENCES

[1] Dangwal G., Mittal S., Wazid Md., Singh J., Das A.K., Giri D., Alenazi Md.J.F., (2024), An effective intrusion detection scheme for Distributed Network Protocol 3 (DNP3) applied in SCADA-enabled IoT applications, *Computers and Electrical Engineering*, Volume 120, Part C, 109828

[2] Mubarak S., Hadi Habaebi Md., Islam Md.R., Jaleel N., Siddique Md. T., (2025), Randomized CNN based deep learning technique for the cyber-attacks detection in SCADA industrial control systems, *Measurement*, Volume 254, 117933, ISSN 0263-2241

[3] Khadidos A.O., Khadidos A.O., Selvarajan S., Shehari T.A., Alsadhan N.A., Singh S., (2025), CyberSentry: Enhancing SCADA security through advanced deep learning and optimization strategies, *International Journal of Critical Infrastructure Protection*, Volume 50,100782, ISSN 1874-5482

[4] Wali S., Farrukh Y.A., Khan I., Hamilton J.A., (2025), Covert penetrations: Analyzing and defending SCADA systems from stealth and Hijacking attacks, *Computers & Security*, Volume 156, 104449, ISSN 0167-4048

[5] Woods, D.D. and Hollnagel E. (2012). *Joint cognitive systems.* Boca Raton: CRC Press/Taylor & Francis.

[6] Wiens, J.A. (2005). Avian community ecology: An iconoclastic view. In *Perspectives in Ornithology*, ed. A. H. Brush, and G. A. Clark, 355–403. Cambridge: Cambridge Univ. Press

[7] Terborgh, J. (2009). Preservation of natural diversity. *BioScience.* 24:715–22.

[8] Alotaibi, A.R. and Mishra, A.V. (2015). Global and regional volatility spillovers to GCC stock markets. *Int. Economic. Modelling.* 45(3):38–49.

[9] Akhtaruzzaman, M., Boubaker, S., and Sensoy, A. (2021). Financial contagion during COVID–19 crisis. *Int. Financ. Res. Lett.* 38(2):101604–101609.

[10] Testa, B. and Kier L.B. (2013). Emergence and dissolvence in the self-organisation of complex systems. *Entropy* 2, no. 1: 1–25. http://www.mdpi.org/entropy/papers/e2010001.pdf

[11] Schwartz, G.J. (2012). Multiwavelength analyses of classical carbon-oxygen novae. *PhD diss.*, Arizona State Univ.

[12] O'Guinn, T.C. (2014). *Touching greatness.* Paper presented at the annual meeting of the American Psychological Association, New York

[13] Adamic, L.A. and Huberman B.A. (2006). *The nature of markets in the World Wide Web.* Working paper, Xerox Palo Alto Research Center. http://www.parc.xerox.com/istl/groups/iea/www/webmarkets.html (accessed March 12, 2014).

[14] Aidy Ali, Kannan Rassiah and Megat Ahmada M.M.H. (2021). The effect of stacking sequence of woven bamboo on mechanical behaviour of fiber reinforced composites. *Journal of Southwest* 592 Jiaotong University / Vol.56 No.2.

[15] Anigol, M.N.B. and Anil, S.P. (2015). Study of the effect of various fillers on mechanical properties of carbon-epoxy composites. *Int. Res. J. Eng. Technol.* 02(03), 798–802.

[16] Biswasa, S., Shahinura, S., Hasana, M. and Ahsan, Q. (2015). Physical, mechanical and thermal properties of jute and bamboo fibre-reinforced unidirectional epoxy composites. *Procedia Eng.* 105, 933–939

Next-Generation Smart Systems – Sekhar et al. (Eds)
© 2027 The Author(s), ISBN: 978-1-041-34234-2

Improving IDS Resilience with GAN-Based Adversarial Training Against Adaptive Cyber Threats

S. Shashikala
Assistant Professor, Department of CSE, G. Pulla Reddy Engineering College (Autonomous), Kurnool, AP, India
Research Scholar JNTUA, Ananthapuramu, AP, India

Y. Rama Mohan
Associate Professor, Department of CSE, G. Pulla Reddy Engineering College (Autonomous), Kurnool, AP, India

ABSTRACT: Intrusion Detection Systems (IDS) which are crucial in securing computer systems connected to various networks, but the performance of these networks is severely poses a significant threat by adversarial attacks that exploit model vulnerabilities. Traditional adversarial training methods, such as FGSM and PGD, provide partial robustness yet they don't always work well in different attack situations. In this work, we provide a GAN-based adversarial training system to make IDS more resistant to advanced threats. Using the NSL-KDD dataset, we design a generative adversarial model that creates adaptive adversarial samples, which are then used to augment the training process of the IDS classifier. The discriminator ensures feature-level consistency while improving the IDS's resilience to both seen and unseen adversarial perturbations. Experimental outcomes demonstrate that proposed approach outperforms the baseline adversarial training techniques, achieving a 6–8% improvement in detection accuracy, 7% higher precision, and reduced false positive rates compared to FGSM-only and PGD-only methods. These findings establish the effectiveness of GAN-based adversarial training in building adversarially robust IDS for next-generation cybersecurity systems.

Keywords: Intrusion Detection Systems, Generative Adversarial Networks, Cyber threats

1 INTRODUCTION

The Cybersecurity is experiencing a fundamental transformation due to the rise of advanced persistent threats and intricate evasion strategies that surpass conventional security measures. Intrusion Detection Systems are critical for security in network; nevertheless, several IDS systems, especially that utilizing conventional machine learning, are open to a number of adversarial assaults that use data manipulation to evade detection protocols. Recent developments in adversarial ML have shown that even minimal, undetected alterations to input data can lead to substantial performance deterioration in Intrusion Detection Systems (IDS).

Adversarial training has been implemented to mitigate these constraints by fortifying machine learning models against perturbations. Conventional adversarial training methodologies, such as PGD and FGSM, frequently yield a restricted range of adversarial instances and may not transfer effectively to novel attack vectors. Generative Adversarial Networks (GANs) have exhibited significant capability in generating synthetic data that is of superior quality across several domains, including images, text, and time-series data. This research utilizes GANs not just for data augmentation but also to enhance robustness an adversarial example generator incorporated directly into the training process in IDS models.

We introduce a GAN-augmented adversarial training framework that integrates a generator-discriminator duo with a conventional classifier. The system dynamically produces and incorporates adversarial samples during training, enhancing detection efficacy against both evasion and poisoning attempts. This comprehensive strategy provides a means to implement more safe, generalizable Intrusion Detection Systems in real-world environments.

2 RELATED WORK

The introduction of FGSM by Goodfellow *et al.* [1] brought attention to the fact that deep learning systems are susceptible to adversarial attacks. Later on, PGD—a more robust and iterative approach to adversarial example generation—was used to expand this by Madry *et al.* and Z. Li [2–4]. Adversarial training, It has been developed using these approaches and has discovered extensive application in domains like as NLP, cybersecurity and computer vision.

Carlini and Wagner [5] emphasized the necessity for powerful training procedures by suggesting more aggressive attacks against defensive distillation strategies. In the field of cybersecurity, Lin *et al.* [4] utilized adversarial training for IDS, while Li *et al.* presented a GAN-based approach to produce samples of harmful traffic. Instead of using GANs in the adversarial training loop, most research just employed them to enhance data.

Pang *et al.* [6] in their study, put an idea of adversarial feature augmentation for robust learning, while Papernot *et al.* [7] looked at how hostile instances may be used in different models. One of the most thorough overviews of adversarial assaults and responses in intrusion detection systems was given by Yuan *et al.* [8]. Defense techniques including uncertainty modeling were described by Zhang *et al.* [9]. While Alom *et al.* [10] investigated deep learning's potential uses in cybersecurity, they failed to address adversarial resilience specifically.

Current studies have investigated hybrid deep reinforcement learning techniques, adversarially resilient graph neural networks, and ensemble learning [11–13]. But integrating adversarial training for intrusion detection systems with dynamic GANs [14,15] has been mostly unexplored.

In order to improve model robustness without sacrificing classification performance, our work expands upon previous contributions by constructing an end-to-end adversarial training pipeline that uses GANs to generate varied, domain-specific adversarial samples.

3 PROPOSED SYSTEM ARCHITECTURE

The suggested architecture incorporates a Generative Adversarial Network (GAN) into an adversarial training loop to improve the

DOI: 10.1201/9781042001767-11

resilience of Intrusion Detection Systems (IDS). The system comprises three primary modules that operate in harmony:

- **Generator (G):** This neural network will be taken as the prescribed input with a clean sample x and also a noise vector z~N(0,1), and outputs a perturbed (adversarial) version $\tilde{x}$. The aim is generating the adversarial samples that are very close to real attack data but are crafted to fool the IDS classifier.
- **Discriminator (D):** The discriminator learns to separate real attack samples from the dataset and those are being generated by the Generator. Generator will be provided with the feedback, pushing it to produce a more realistic and indistinguishable adversarial samples over time.
- **Classifier (C):** The core IDS model that is trained not only on clean samples but also on adversarial samples generated by G. This training improves the model's capability to accurately categorize both adversarial inputs.

This architecture supports a co-evolution process where:

1. G evolves to create more effective adversarial attacks.
2. D improves its capability to detect generated attacks.
3. C becomes more robust by learning from both real and adversarial inputs.

Workflow Summary:

- Clean input x is fed into G along with random noise z to produce $\tilde{x}$.
- D tries to distinguish between real attacks x_{real} and generated attacks $\tilde{x}$.
- C is trained on a mix of x and $\tilde{x}$ using a composite loss function to learn to classify both correctly

4 GAN-BASED ADVERSARIAL TRAINING PROCEDURE

This section lays forth the mathematical foundations of the GAN components and the combined classifier in order to define the adversarial training process. We provide a dynamic approach for creating adversarial cases that test the classifier repeatedly by integrating a generator and discriminator into the IDS training loop. Ensuring adversarial inputs are exposed to the model during training, these equations dictate the optimization of the GAN and the classifier's learning objectives.

Let x be an input sample and $y \in \{0, 1\}$be its corresponding label (0 for benign, 1 for malicious).

We define:

$G(z, x)$: The generator network that produces a perturbed adversarial version $\tilde{x}$.using random noise z and input x.

$D(x)$: The discriminator output representing the probability that $x$is a real attack.

$C(x)$: The classifier that predicts the probability of x being an attack.

The adversarial interaction between G and D is modeled via a minimax game:

Discriminator Loss (L_D):

$$L_D = -E_{x \sim P_{real}}[\log D(x)] - E_{x \sim G(z,x)}[\log(1 - D(\tilde{x}))]$$

This loss increases when D correctly classifies real attacks as real and generated attacks as fake.

Generator Loss (L_G):

$$L_G = -E_{x \sim G(z,x)}[\log D(\tilde{x})]$$

G is rewarded when D believes generated samples are real, thus improving the realism of adversarial examples.

Classifier Training Loss with Adversarial Regularization

We propose a blended loss function for the classifier:

Adversarial Training Loss(L_{adv}):

$$L_{adv} = \alpha.L_{CE}(C(x), y) + (1 - \alpha).L_{CE}(C(\tilde{x}), y)$$

Here, L_{CE} is the standard cross-entropy loss. The parameter $\alpha \in [0, 1]$ controls the accuracy on clean samples and robustness to adversarial inputs.

Algorithm 1: GAN-based Adversarial Training Procedure

Input: Clean training data (X, Y), learning rates η_G, η_D, η_C

Output: Trained classifier C

Step 1: Initialize parameters of Generator G, Discriminator D, and Classifier C.
Step 2: for each training epoch do
Step 3: for each mini-batch (x, y) in training data do
Step 4: Sample the random noise z ~ N(0, 1)
Step 5: Produce adversarial samples: $\tilde{x}$ = G(z, x)
Step 6: Adjust Discriminator D to maximizes $\mathcal{L}$_D
Step 7: Adjust Generator G to minimize $\mathcal{L}$_G
Step 8: Compute Classifier loss $\mathcal{L}$_adv using both x and $\tilde{x}$
Step 9: Update Classifier C to minimize $\mathcal{L}$_adv end for end for
Step 10: Return trained classifier C

This iterative adversarial training method allows the classifier to adjust to changing adversarial threats while preserving high accuracy on untainted data. By integrating G and D within a feedback loop, the system is capable of dynamically navigating the adversarial space, thereby enhancing both the coverage and diversity of threats simulated throughout the training process.

5 EXPERIMENTAL SETUP

For our experiments, we employed the NSL-KDD dataset, is a standard for assessing IDS. Earlier KDD'99 dataset has been used, but now this dataset is an improved version, which has been precisely designed to address the issues of imbalance and redundancy which is in its predecessor. The dataset provides a more accurate distribution of network traffic and it has normal and also the attack connections, which makes it appropriate for adversarial robustness research.

This dataset offers a comprehensive benchmark that includes both regular and attack traffic kinds, such as DoS, DDoS attacks, infiltration, and brute-force attacks.

Feature Set: The dataset consists of 42 features, which include both continuous variables) and categorical variables (e.g., protocol type, service).

Preprocessing Steps:

Data Cleaning: Eliminated missing or corrupted entries.

Encoding: Categorical variables such as protocol types and attack labels now use one-hot encoding.

Normalization: Continuous features were scaled using min-max normalization to the range of [0,1].

Balancing: Used the Synthetic method of Minority Over-sampling Technique, which is used in producing the samples aimed at attack classes that were underrepresented, thus resolving the issue of class imbalance.

Feature Selection: Utilized recursive feature elimination in conjunction with a random forest classifier to identify and retain the most significant features for classification purposes.

The preprocessing steps implemented guarantee that the input for the GAN and IDS models is systematically organized, thereby improving training stability and model generalization.

It is necessary to evaluate the suggested framework, comprehensive experiments were carried out within a clearly defined simulation environment.

Evaluation Metrics:

- Recall, F1-Score, ROC-AUC, Accuracy, Precision
- Robustness Index (RI): Percentage of accurate classifications under adversarial perturbations

This configuration allows for efficient and scalable simulation of adversarial infiltration situations in a realistic setting, which guarantees repeatability.

6 RESULTS AND EVALUATION

By evaluating our proposed GAN-enhanced adversarial training method with models built using more conventional adversarial training approaches, such FGSM-only and PGD-only methods, we are able to statistically evaluate its efficacy. A different aspect of the evaluation is the utilization of common categorization criteria and indicators of resistance in adverse circumstances. You can see how well our method performs in terms of general detection skills and resilience to artificial changes by looking at the table that follows. This table provides a summary of the findings that were attained under a number of different environmental conditions.

Table 1. Performance evaluation of various IDS models under adversarial attacks.

Model	Accuracy	F1-Score	AUC	RI (FGSM)	RI (PGD)
GAN + Adv Training	93.80%	0.91	0.9	78.10%	69.40%
FGSM Training Only	91.20%	0.88	0.86	61.30%	52.00%
PGD Training Only	92.40%	0.89	0.88	66.70%	58.30%

The results clearly show that the GAN-enhanced adversarial training framework achieves superior robustness compared to the conventional FGSM-only and also with the PGD-only training methods. Under FGSM attacks, the proposed model improved the robustness index (RI) from 61.3% to 78.1%, while under PGD attacks, it increased RI from 58.3% to 69.4%.

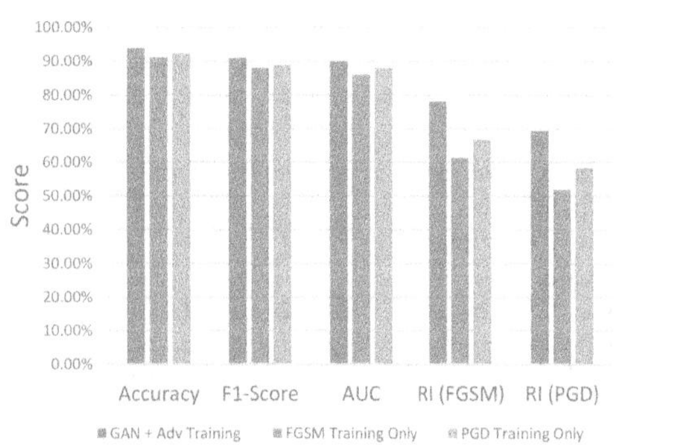

Figure 1. Comparision of adversarial training techniques on evaluation metrics.

These improvements demonstrate that integrating GANs into the adversarial training loop leads to more resilient IDS models, capable of withstanding stronger perturbations. Importantly, the GAN-based approach maintains competitive accuracy (93.8%) and F1-score (0.91), ensuring that enhanced robustness does not come at the cost of baseline detection performance. This balance highlights the generalization capability of our method across diverse attack vectors.

Our approach demonstrates superior generalization across various attack vectors when compared to FGSM-only and PGD-only adversarial training methods, and it produces more transferable adversarial examples.

7 CONCLUSION

This work presented a GAN-augmented adversarial training framework for strengthening IDS against evasion and poisoning attacks. By jointly training a generator, discriminator, and classifier, the model leverages adaptive adversarial examples to improve resilience beyond conventional FGSM-only and PGD-only training. Experiments on the NSL-KDD dataset showed that the proposed approach achieved higher accuracy, precision, and recall, along with significantly improved robustness indices under adversarial conditions. These results confirm that GAN-based augmentation can effectively reduce the weaknesses of traditional adversarial training while maintaining performance on clean data. Future directions include validating the framework on larger datasets (e.g., CICIDS2017, UNSW-NB15), extending it with Graph Neural Networks (GNNs) for modeling complex attack paths, and exploring deployment in real-time IDS environments with explainability for practical cybersecurity adoption.

REFERENCES

[1] Goodfellow *et al.*, (2015), Explaining and Harnessing Adversarial Examples, *ICLR*.

[2] Madry A. *et al.*, (2018), Towards Deep Learning Models Resistant to Adversarial Attacks, *ICLR*

[3] Lin X. and Zhang Y., (2020), Adversarial Learning for Robust Intrusion Detection, *IEEE TDSC*.

[4] Li Z. *et al.*, (2021), Generating Adversarial Traffic Examples for IDS With GAN, *CIKM*.

[5] Carlini N. and Wagner D., (2017), Towards Evaluating the Robustness of Neural Networks, *IEEE S&P*.

[6] Pang T. *et al.*, (2020), Adversarial Training with Adversarial Label Learning, *NeurIPS*.

[7] Papernot N. *et al.*, (2017), Practical Black-Box Attacks against Machine Learning, *ASIA CCS*.

[8] Yuan X. *et al.*, (2019), Adversarial Examples: Attacks and Defenses for Deep Learning, *IEEE TNNLS*.

[9] Zhang J. *et al.*, (2019), The Limitations of Adversarial Training and the Utility of Uncertainty, *NeurIPS*.

[10] Alom M.Z. *et al.*, (2018), The History Began from Alexnet: A Comprehensive Survey on Deep Learning Approaches, *arXiv*.

[11] Zugner D. and Gunnemann S., (2019), Adversarial Attacks on Graph Neural Networks via Meta Learning, *ICLR*.

[12] Dong Y. *et al.*, (2018), Boosting Adversarial Attacks with Momentum, *CVPR*.

[13] Nguyen T.T. *et al.*, (2019), Deep Reinforcement Learning for Cybersecurity, *IEEE Access*.

[14] Moosavi-Dezfooli S. *et al.*, (2016), DeepFool: A Simple and Accurate Method to Fool Deep Neural Networks, *CVPR*.

[15] Liu *et al.*, (2023), Lightweight Adversarial Training with Dual Generators for Cyber Defense, *IEEE Access*.

Next-Generation Smart Systems – Sekhar et al. (Eds)
© 2027 The Author(s), ISBN: 978-1-041-34234-2

Predictive Engineering Harnessing AI to Uncover Suicidal Risk Markers Among College Students

Abinaya K.
Nursing Tutor, Saveetha College of Nursing, Saveetha Institute of Medical and Technical Sciences, Chennai, India

Vijayalakshmi R.
Principal, Saveetha College of Nursing, Saveetha Institute of Medical and Technical Sciences, Chennai, India

Ajith M.
Nursing Tutor, Saveetha College of Nursing, Saveetha Institute of Medical and Technical Sciences, Chennai, India

Jagadeeswari
Assistant Professor, Saveetha College of Nursing, Saveetha Institute of Medical and Technical Sciences, Chennai, India

Sindhu Ramalingam
Associate Professor, Saveetha College of Nursing, Saveetha Institute of Medical and Technical Sciences, Chennai, India

ABSTRACT: Artificial intelligence (AI) might have a substantial impact in suicide prevention via analysing data to identify potential warning signs and providing support to individuals in need. Among the leading causes of untimely deaths and mortality worldwide is suicide. The study aimed to predict engineering harnessing AI to uncover suicidal risk markers among college students. AI techniques can foresee persistent suicide risk with up to 90% accuracy in furthermore pinpointing those who are at vulnerability of suicide. Additionally, 9% of the data points relate to using social media to predict mental illness, suggesting growing interest and potential in leveraging digital behaviour for early intervention. All things thought about, this study shows how social media can be a rich source of behavioural indicators for psychological disorders and may be essential for early identification and intervention strategies. The study emphasizes the necessity for further advancements in the prevention of suicide risk signals in order to aid and nurture the psychological well being and physical health of the forthcoming era.

Keywords: Artificial Intelligence, Predictive Engineering, Risk Markers, Mental Illness, Health

1 INTRODUCTION

The act of suicide is a complicated issue and avoidable a wellness issue that greatly impacts individuals, families, and communities. With a projected 3 billion users globally, social networking has become an integral part of routine. It currently exceeds both homicides and traffic accidents, indicating a serious public health emergency with significant financial ramifications. [1] With 153,052 occurrences recorded in 2020 alone, suicide is still a major problem in India, one of the most populated nations in the world. [2] With 1.4% of all premature deaths among people aged 15 to 29, suicide is the second-most primary cause of fatalities globally. [3] The World Health Organization (WHO) reports that nearly 700,000 individuals perished by suicide in 2019, which is one in each one hundred deaths nationwide.[4] Emotional discomfort is a significant psychological issue that has been linked to suicide, medical expenses, deaths, and morbidity.[5]The first most prominent causes of fatal accidents and mortality across the globe is suicide. Annually, over 850,000 human beings lose their livelihoods to suicide, and a multitude more commit suicide or possess suicidal thoughts.[6] A WHO has responded by creating plans to assist nations in dealing with this escalating situation.[7] However, because symptoms are often underreported and because it is difficult to accurately screen for suicidal thoughts, intention, and planning at all levels of health care, measuring suicide risk is still difficult. Suicidal intent has been referred to as pondering or fantasizing, which emphasizes the scope of desires, compulsive thoughts about dying or taking your life, and imminent motives to die or death notions known as disjoined desires of annihilation.[8]

Medical suicide prediction tools: Experts and healthcare professionals utilize intelligent machines (AI) strategies consisting of machine learning and natural language processing utilising data gathered from hospital documents, computerized medical records, and probably other official data sources, among others, to make decision in patterns of information and behaviour that suggest suicide risk.[20] These tools are usually used in general practitioner offices or hospitals to give doctors "decision support" when assessing a patient's risk of suicide.[9]

Artificial intelligence (AI) Information and tracking instruments that use information from googling and networking patterns to predict suicide risk are known as Social suicide prediction systems use networking tendencies to forecast suicide risk.[10] The internet giants Google, Facebook, and the iPhone, for example, use site facts to figure out those are at risk of suicide and deliver necessary treatments, which includes psychological treatment along with free information.[11]

AI-powered forecasting for risk variables for suicide. [12] Explored the efficiency of machine learning strategies are to determine suicidal intentions through six emotional triggers included in digital health records. It made recourse to machine learning methodologies like decision trees, random forests, logistic regression, gradient boosting regression trees, vector regression strategies and multilayer multidimensional perceptrons as well.; all of these strategies were capable to predict suicidal thinking having an accuracy of beyond 98%.[13]

2 MATERIALS AND METHODS

Study Design Using algorithmic learning (ML) and natural language processing (NLP), it is possible to identify markers associated with suicidal risk among college students. Data Collection-

DOI: 10.1201/9781042001767-12

Target Population: Undergraduate and graduate students aged 18–30 from multiple universities. Convenience sampling with opt-in participation. Estimated Sample Size: 35 participants.

Data Sources

Section A :Structured data: Self-reported questionnaires

- The C-SSRS, or Columbia-Suicide Severity Rating Scale
- Social media sentiment
- Academic performance data
- Mental health surveys
- Wearable sensor data (sleep/activity)
- Counseling records (anonymized)

Section B : AI Techniques

- Learning Algorithm classification (e.g., Forest at Random, SVM)
- Networks of Neural Systems (optional, for text embeddings)
- Natural - Processing natural language for text/sentiment examination
- Time-series analysis

3 RESULTS

To statistically analyse suicidal risk markers a structured approach should be taken. The sequence of steps involved in this process are formulating the research hypotheses, defining the variables and data collection, perform descriptive analysis such as frequency distribution of suicidal risk markers, and use statistical software for interpretation and report generations.

Section A: Sample Characteristics

The bar chart illustrates the frequency of various risk markers, showing that negative sentiment in texts (35%) is the most common indicator, followed by a decline in academic performance (25%), social withdrawal (15%), suicide-related search behavior (10%), decreased class attendance (10%), and sleep or activity pattern changes (5%)

Section B: Assess the AI Techniques among the students

The analysis of Table 2 shows that among The bar chart presents the frequency of various mental health concerns identified through social media data, showing that PTSD (14%) and predicting mental illness (13%) are the most frequently observed indicators, followed by suicidal ideation (12%), depression and mood disturbances (10%), Violence against oneself and self-inflicted injury that is not suicide-related (9%), schizophrenia (5%), and suicidal ideation (5%).

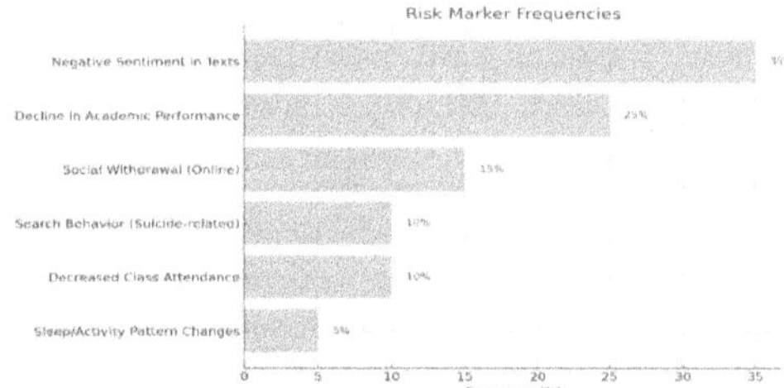

Bar Chart 1. Percentage and risk markers frequencies Rate N = 35.

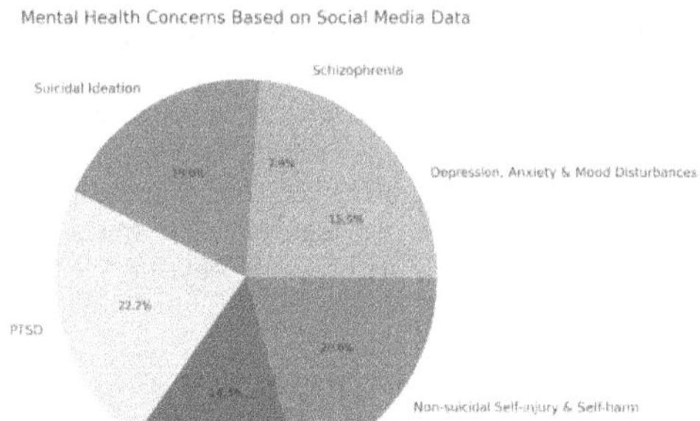

Pie Chart 1. Assessment of AI techniques among students.

4 DISCUSSION

According to the findings, AI/ML techniques can not only identify people who are at potential for self-harm, but it can also forecast prospective likelihood of suicide..[14] The majority of these research looked at identifying or predicting suicidal behavior, then predicting treatment outcomes for mental health conditions including depression and identifying future suicide risk. [15].The most commonly observed concern is Post-Traumatic Stress Disorder (PTSD) at 14%, followed closely by Non-Suicidal harming themselves and self-mutilation at 13%, and considering suicide at 12%. These elevated percentages suggest that social media users are frequently expressing signs of emotional distress and trauma online. Depression, anxiety, and mood disturbances also appear prominently, affecting 10% of the sample, indicating a significant presence of mood-related issues in digital behavior. Schizophrenia, 5%, still highlights the diversity of mental health indicators detectable via online activity. Additionally, 9% of the data points relate to using social media to predict mental illness, suggesting growing interest and potential in leveraging digital behavior for early intervention. All things thought about, this study shows how social media can be a rich source of behavioural indicators for psychological disorders and may be essential for early identification and intervention strategies. Along with exploring the ability of AI to forecast mental illness and suicidal ideation, this study also looked at the consequences of age (adolescents), physical sickness, and self-harm in AI-driven suicide prediction.[16]

5 CONCLUSION

In conclusion, this study demonstrates that predictive engineering, when thoughtfully designed and ethically deployed, can be a transformative force in suicide prevention among college students.[17] It paves the way for a new era of mental health support According to the findings, AI/ML techniques can not only identify people who are at peril of homicide but can also predict sustained vulnerability to self-immolation with up to 90% specificity.[18] The majority of these research looked at identifying or predicting suicidal behavior, then predicting treatment outcomes for Psychological wellness issues including depression and identifying future likelihood of homicide.[19]

REFERENCES

[1] CDC. *Web-Based Injury Statistics Query and Reporting System (WISQARS), Fatal Injury and Violence Data.* National Center for Injury Prevention and Control;2018. Available from: https://www.cdc.gov/injury/wisqars/index.html.

[2] Rockett, I.R.H., Regier, M.D., Kapusta, N.D., Coben, J.H., Miller, T.R., Hanzlick, R.L., Todd, K.H., Sattin, R.W., Kennedy, L.W., Kleinig, J., and Smith, G.S. (2012). Leading causes of unintentional and intentional injury mortality: United States, 2000–2009. *American Journal of Public Health*, 102(11), e84–e92. https://doi.org/10.2105/ajph.2012.300960

[3] Hawton, K., Casañas I Comabella, C., Haw, C., and Saunders, K. (2013). Risk factors for suicide in individuals with depression: a systematic review. *Journal of Affective Disorders*, 147(1–3), 17–28. https://doi.org/10.1016/j.jad.2013.01.004.

[4] Bachmann S. (2018). Epidemiology of Suicide and the Psychiatric Perspective. *International Journal of Environmental Research and Public Health*, 15(7), 1425. https://doi.org/10.3390/ijerph15071425.

[5] WHO. *One in 100 Deaths is By Suicide.* World Health Organization (WHO); 2021. Available from: https://www.who.int..

[6] Harmer B, Lee S, Duong TV, Saadabadi A. Suicidal ideation. In: *StatPearls.* Treasure Island (FL): StatPearls Publishing; 2021.

[7] Belsher, B.E., Smolenski, D.J., Pruitt, L.D., Bush, N.E., Beech, E.H., Workman, D.E., Morgan, R.L., Evatt, D.P., Tucker, J.,

and Skopp, N.A. (2019). Prediction Models for Suicide Attempts and Deaths: A Systematic Review and Simulation. *JAMA Psychiatry*, 76(6), 642–651. https://doi.org/10.1001/jamapsychiatry.2019.0174.

[8] Atmakuru, A., Shahini, A., Chakraborty, S., Seoni, S., Salvi, M., Hafeez-Baig, A., Rashid, S., Tan, R.S., Barua, P.D., Molinari, F., and Acharya, U.R. (2024). Artificial intelligence-based suicide prevention and prediction: A systematic review (2019–2023). *Information Fusion*, 114, 102673. https://doi.org/10.1016/j.inffus.2024.102673.

[9] VA Releases National Suicide Data Report *for 2005-2016 Us department of Veterens Affairs*, 2018. https://www.va.gov/opa/pressrel/includes/viewPDF.cfm?id=5114 [Accessed 18 September 2020].

[10] DelPozo-Banos, M., John, A., Petkov, N., Berridge, D.M., Southern, K., LLoyd, K., Jones, C., Spencer, S., and Travieso, C. M. (2018). Using Neural Networks with Routine Health Records to Identify Suicide Risk: Feasibility Study. *JMIR Mental Health*, 5(2), e10144. https://doi.org/10.2196/10144

[11] Walsh, C.G., Ribeiro, J.D., and Franklin, J.C. (2017). Predicting Risk of Suicide Attempts Over Time Through Machine Learning. *Clinical Psychological Science*, 5(3), 457-469. https://doi.org/10.1177/2167702617691560

[12] Kumar, M., Dredze, M., Coppersmith, G., and De Choudhury, M. (2015). Detecting Changes in Suicide Content Manifested in Social Media Following Celebrity Suicides. HT: the proceedings of the ACM Conference on Hypertext and Social Media. *ACM Conference on Hypertext and Social Media*, 2015, 85–94. https://doi.org/10.1145/2700171.2791026

[13] Franklin, J.C., Ribeiro, J.D., Fox, K.R., Bentley, K.H., Kleiman, E.M., Huang, X., Musacchio, K.M., Jaroszewski, A. C., Chang, B.P., and Nock, M.K. (2017). Risk factors for suicidal thoughts and behaviors: A meta-analysis of 50 years of research. *Psychological Bulletin*, 143(2), 187–232. https://doi.org/10.1037/bul0000084

[14] Vogel L. (2018). AI opens new frontier for suicide prevention. *CMAJ: Canadian Medical Association journal = journal de l'Association medicale canadienne,* 190(4), E119. https://doi.org/10.1503/cmaj.109-5549

[15] D'Hotman, D., and Loh, E. (2020). AI enabled suicide prediction tools: a qualitative narrative review. *BMJ health & care informatics*, 27(3), e100175. https://doi.org/10.1136/bmjhci-2020-100175

[16] Tripathi R, Alqahtani SS, Meraya AM, Makeen HA, Tripathi P and Pancholi SS, (2022). Evaluation of depression, anxiety, and stress among university healthcare students. *J Appl Pharm Sci*; 12 (10):078-087. https://doi.org/10.7324/JAPS.2022.121008.

[17] Kavitha, M., Lokesh, P., Sridevi, B., Deepika, D., and Muthulakshmi, C. (2024). A Descriptive Study to Assess the Impact of Social Media Platforms on Mental Well Being among College Student at Selected College in Chennai. *Journal of Pharmacy and Bioallied Sciences*, 16(Suppl 3), S2868–S2870. https://doi.org/10.4103/jpbs.jpbs_560_24

[18] Priyadarsini A.Jagadeeswari J, Cecyli C.Dayana B.A.A. (2024). Prediction of Behavioral Disorders among Preschooler: A Survey Report. *Texila International Journal of Public Health*, 24(4). https://doi.org/10.21522/tijph.2013.se.24.02.art014.

[19] Vechalapu, Maj, Thenmozhi P. and Kumar, Ramadugu. (2024). Effectiveness of psychoeducational intervention on quality of life among patients with affective disorders. *Multidisciplinary Science Journal*. 6. 2024ss0627. 10.31893/multiscience.2024ss0627.

[20] Dinesh, K., Kamatchi, S, Mangaiyarkarasi K. and Selvaperumal, S. (2024). *Accuracy improvement for personality prediction using logistic regression in comparison with random forest algorithm*. 020269. 10.1063/5.0229463.

Next-Generation Smart Systems – Sekhar et al. (Eds)
© 2027 The Author(s), ISBN: 978-1-041-34234-2

Smart Evaluation System for Subjective Answers Using NLP and Fuzzy Logic

Sricharani P.
Professor, Department of AI, Shri Vishnu Engineering College for Women (A), Bhimavaram, Andhra Pradesh, India

M. Vijaya Lakshmi
Associate Professor, Department of Basic Science, Vishnu Institute of Technology, Bhimavaram, Andhra Pradesh, India

Neelam Bharathi
Department of Statistics, Andhra Loyola College, Vijayawada, Andhra Pradesh, India

G.V.S.R. Anjaneyulu
Professor(Retd.), Department of Statistics, Acharya Nagarjuna University, Guntur, Andhra Pradesh, India

R.M. Mastan Shareef
Assistant Professor, Department of FME, St.Martin's Engineering College, Secunderabad, Telangana, India

ABSTRACT: This project introduces a subjective answer evaluation system leveraging techniques from Natural Language Processing (NLP) and Machine Learning techniques. It evaluates student responses based on keyword relevance, grammatical correctness, synonym usage, fuzzy logic for ignoble mistakes, and the logical sequence of statements where applicable. Cosine similarity is applied between student and model answers after converting them into vector space. Grammar errors are detected using online grammar checkers, while fuzzy logic (via the Fuzzy - Wuzzy library) handles minor spelling and structural variations through edit distance calculation. Synonym matching is performed using Python libraries to recognize semantically similar words. For subjects that require ordered responses, a sequence-checking mechanism is used to ensure the logical flow of key points. Model answers and evaluation keywords are uploaded by teachers through Excel sheets. The system features a user-friendly GUI for selecting subject-wise questions, submitting answers, and receiving evaluations. It generates detailed reports with scores and evaluation details.

Keywords: Subjective answer evaluation, Natural Language Processing, Cosine similarity, Fuzzy logic, Grammar analysis, Synonym matching, Sequence checking, Automated assessment, Python NLP

1 INTRODUCTION

Subjective assessments play a vital role in evaluating a student's understanding, analytical thinking, and expressive capabilities. Unlike objective questions, subjective answers allow for flexibility in language, structure, and reasoning, making their evaluation both important and challenging. Manual assessment of such answers frequently requires a significant amount of time, inconsistent, and susceptible to human bias. To overcome these challenges, this project introduces an automated system for evaluating subjective answers, utilizing Natural Language Processing (NLP) and Machine Learning methods to enhance the efficiency and accuracy of the evaluation process.

The system evaluates answers based on various linguistic and semantic parameters such as keyword relevance, grammatical correctness, synonym usage, negligible mistakes using fuzzy logic, and the logical sequence of statements where applicable. Cosine similarity is used to compare student responses with model answers, allowing semantic similarity scoring even when the wording differs. Grammatical accuracy is checked using integrated grammar tools, while fuzzy logic handles minor spelling and structural variations. Synonym matching ensures flexibility in expression, and sequence validation is applied for subjects requiring ordered explanations.

Teachers provide model answers and keywords through Excel sheets, ensuring subject-specific customization. The system, implemented with a user-friendly graphical interface, allows students to submit answers and receive immediate, detailed evaluations. This automated approach reduces manual workload for educators and ensures more objective, consistent, and faster evaluation of subjective responses.

2 LITERATURE SURVEY

Our literature survey investigates existing approaches for assessing subjective responses through Machine Learning and NLP techniques. Prominent methods include the use of cosine similarity for measuring semantic similarity between student responses and model answers, as well as fuzzy logic to account for minor errors such as spelling variations or formatting differences. Synonym detection is also commonly employed to recognize diverse but contextually similar expressions. Grammar checking tools aid in identifying sentence-level correctness, contributing to a more holistic evaluation. Furthermore, text to vector conversation methods like TF-IDF and word embedding models (such as Word2Vec or GloVe) enable efficient numerical comparison of textual data. Some studies also emphasize sequence-based evaluation, which is particularly effective for questions where the logical order of explanation is critical. By analyzing the strengths and limitations of these methods, we have developed a practical, efficient, and adaptable system for automated subjective answer evaluation in educational environments. A comprehensive of automated short answer grading techniques, including rule-based, statistical, and semantic approaches. Discusses using semantic similarity and quality assessment relevant for scoring student responses based on quality.

3 ARCHITECTURE

The architecture of the proposed system is structured into multiple modules to automate the evaluation of subjective

DOI: 10.1201/9781042001767-13

answers using NLP and ML techniques. It begins with inputs such as student answers and teacher-provided model answers with keywords. The core evaluation module prepossesses the text and applies various analysis techniques. Cosine similarity is used to measure semantic closeness between student and model answers. Grammar checking detects sentence-level errors using integrated tools, while fuzzy logic handles negligible spelling and structural variations. Synonym checking ensures flexibility by recognizing similar words. For questions where order matters, a sequence-checking module verifies the logical flow. All results are compiled in an evaluation report, presenting scores based on multiple criteria.

4 METHODOLOGY

4.1 *Data preprocessing and exploratory data analysis*

Student and model answers are cleaned by removing punctuation, converting to lowercase, and eliminating stop words. Exploratory Data Analysis (EDA) identifies keyword frequency, common phrases, and subject-specific patterns. These insights guide keyword weighting and improve the effectiveness of the evaluation process.

4.2 *Text cleaning*

Text cleaning removes unwanted characters, extra spaces, and noise from both student and model answers. This standardization ensures uniformity and enhances accuracy during vectorization and comparison. It is essential for reliable keyword matching and similarity scoring.

4.3 *Word embedding*

To compare semantic meaning between student and model answers, the system utilizes word embedding techniques. Text data is transformed into vector format using methods like TF-IDF or pretrained models. These embeddings enable mathematical operations that capture contextual similarity between words, even when exact terms differ. Although GloVe was considered, for this implementation, simpler embedding techniques were prioritized due to dataset size and scope. Word embeddings serve as the basis for cosine similarity calculations and help preserve meaning during evaluation.

4.4 *Cosine similarity*

This metric evaluates the semantic closeness is comparing to student and model vectors. It returns a score from 0 to 1, indicating how well the answers align. This value is scaled and used as a major component of the final evaluation.

4.5 *Similarity score and evaluation logic*

The similarity score derived from cosine similarity is used to assess how closely a student's answer matches the model answer. Scores are converted to a percentage scale and interpreted through a grading rubric. In addition to similarity, grammar analysis, synonym matching using Python libraries, and fuzzy matching using edit distance (via FuzzyWuzzy) are factored in. For questions requiring logical sequencing, the order of key points is evaluated using a priority-based comparison. All evaluation metrics are aggregated to generate a comprehensive score, which is recorded and presented in a detailed result report via a graphical user interface (GUI). After all modules process the input, a final evaluation report is generated, and the scores are stored in an Excel database for teacher review.

5 FIGURES AND TABLES

The bar chart illustrates the final evaluation scores of five students based on cosine similarity, grammar, and fuzzy-logic.It visually highlights performance differences, helping educators quickly identify high and low-scoring responses.

The table presents a detailed overview of the evaluation results for five students based on various assessment parameters. It includes cosine similarity scores reflecting semantic alignment, the number of grammar errors identified, fuzzy match percentages accounting for minor variations, and the final computed scores. This tabular representation offers a clear and concise comparison of student performance across multiple evaluation criteria.

Student ID	Cosine Similarity Score	Grammar Errors	Fuzzy Match (%)	Final Score (%)
S101	85	2	88	84
S102	72	5	75	70
S103	90	1	93	91
S104	60	8	65	63
S105	78	3	80	77

6 CONCLUSION

The developed system effectively automates the evaluating subjective responses through Natural Language Processing and Machine Learning methodologies. By incorporating cosine similarity, grammar analysis, fuzzy logic, synonym matching, and sequence checking, it ensures a more accurate and fair assessment process. The use of a simple GUI and Excel integration makes the system user-friendly for both students and teachers. It reduces manual workload, minimizes evaluation bias, and enhances consistency in scoring. Overall, the project demonstrates a practical solution to enhance the efficiency and dependability of subjective answer grading in educational settings.

REFERENCES

[1] Wang, J., and Dong, Y. (2020). Measurement of text similarity: A survey. *Information*, 11(9), 421. https://doi.org/10.3390/info11090421

[2] Han, M., Wang, L., and Liu, J. (2021). A survey on short text semantic similarity. *Concurrency and Computation: Practice and Experience*, 33(5), e6072. https://doi.org/10.1002/cpe.6072

[3] Charniak, E., and Johnson, M. (2005). Coarse-to-fine n-best parsing and MaxEnt discriminative reranking. *Proceedings of the 43rd Annual Meeting of the ACL*, 173–180.

[4] Kusner, M.J., Sun, Y., Kolkin, N.I., and Weinberger, K.Q. (2015). From word embeddings to document distances. *Proceedings of the 32nd International Conference on Machine Learning (ICML)*, 957–966.

[5] Cohen, W.W., and Richman, J. (2002). Learning to match and cluster large high-dimensional data sets for data integration. Proceedings of the 8th ACM SIGKDD. *International Conference on Knowledge Discovery and Data Mining*, 475–480.

[6] Burrows, S., Gurevych, I., and Stein, B. (2015).The eras and trends of automatic short answer grading. *International Journal of Artificial Intelligence in Education*, 25(1), 60–117.

[7] Sultan, M.A., Bethard, S., and Sumner, T. (2016). Learning to predict answer quality in community question answering. *Proceedings of NAACL-HLT*, 2016, pp. 123–132.

Next-Generation Smart Systems – Sekhar et al. (Eds)
© 2027 The Author(s), ISBN: 978-1-041-34234-2

An Intelligent Cyberbullying Detection Framework Using Deep Learning

A.V. Santhosh Kumar
Assistant Professor, Department of CSE, KEC, Kuppam, Andhra Pradesh, India

N.J. Ranjithkumar
PG Student, Department of CSE, KEC, Kuppam, Andhra Pradesh, India

ABSTRACT: The project displays a smart framework for identifying instances of cyberbullying by utilizing deep learning and document embedding techniques. The model employed is known as the Doc2Vec model. The Doc2Vec model converts comment text into dense feature vectors, which allows for the effective classification of cyber-aggressive and non-aggressive comments. Two datasets contained labeled comments; the labeled comments were preprocessed, labeled, and split into a training and testing set to prevent any contamination into the evaluation process. The given document embedding were then used as input feature into other machine learning classifier which has K-Nearest Neighbors (KNN), Random Forest, Naive Bayes, Logistic Regression, and Decision Trees. Each model underwent repeated training and testing with accuracy, precision, recall, F1-score, and AUC performance. In terms of models trained, KNN obtained the highest accuracy at 98.79%. This was followed closely by Random Forest and Naïve Bayes both achieving accuracy percentages of 88.88%. Overall, the study indicates that classification models using Doc2Vec is an effective method of detecting harmful online behavior and contributes to positive online practices for a safer online environment for media and some gaming communities.

Keywords: online safety, sentiment analysis, social media monitoring, online harassment detection, hostile online comments, deep learning etc.

1 INTRODUCTION

Cyberbullying has arisen as an ethical challenge with the upcoming popularity of social media and online technologies. Cyberbullying is seen as a form of aggression that is more damaging than ordinary bullying because it conceals the aggressor and provides increased access to the victim over a wider geographic area (Jain *et al.* 2021). Many adolescents and young adults are experiencing cyberbullying, which may lead to potentially serious psychological and social ramifications with impacted individuals experiencing anxiety, depression, and suicidal ideations (Kim and Kim 2020). The increase in interactions online also increases the need to safely autonomously track and manage the issues that arises from interactions with the web at an ethical level.

In the past couple of years, some aspects of deep learning and machine learning have been introduced to text-based classification of cyberbullying. The first approaches relied on lexicon-based algorithms (Patel and Patel 2019) due to an inability to sufficiently index the semantic context and blend variety of sophistication from the slang context of language abuses. From there, the authors continued focusing on supervised learning approaches utilizing previous Natural Language Processing (NLP) methods while purchasing(sic) feature extraction is based on TF-IDF, word embeddings, and deep learning models to suggest classification on cyberbullying content (Li *et al.* 2019).

While advancements have been made in the area of cyberbullying detection, there are continue to be some ongoing issues in the literature today:

1. Limited Contextual Understanding: Many existing models fail to understand the contextual interpretation of words, resulting in both false positives and false negatives [1].
2. Unbalanced Datasets: The ability of models to generalize has been reduced in honoring an unbalanced cyberbullying dataset with far more neutral/non-aggressive comments than cyber-aggressive comments [2].
3. Sarcasm and Implicit Cyberbullying: Current existing models continue to have trouble with detecting sarcasm, implicit hostility, and irony [3].
4. Lack of Mechanisms for real-time detection: The majority of existing research has primarily focused on offline detection measures, which prohibits practical use within social media [3a].
5. Fairness and bias issues: Fairness in machine learning consideration, can possibly be biased on the basis of gender, color, or culture if any biases are present within the dataset being used [4].

2 LITERATURE SURVEY

Pereraa [1] seeks to build a system that detects cyberbullying and includes safeguards against the behavior. Their work achieves high accuracy in detecting harmful content on social media, by utilising the art machine learning methods and continuous monitoring. The dual approach of prevention and detection provides a basis for safer spaces online.

Atoum [2] mentions the value of using sentiment analysis to identify instances of cyberbullying. By evaluating users' emotional tone through their contributions to social media, the findings reveal that sentiment polarity, positive, negative, or neutral, is an effective predictor of cyberaggressive behavior. The article also provides insight into the implications of sentiment-laden approaches for identifying harmful language by comparing machine learning classifiers to lexicon-based methods.

In their [3] Md Manowarul explores various machine learning algorithms to classify social media messages as cyberbullying and not. In the study, a range of classifiers is tested for their discrimination ability and the importance of the feature extraction and preprocessing step is discussed. The study is informative in that it provides a comparison of the interpretation of the algorithm based on recall, accuracy, and precision, and this contributes to an informed choice of the best algorithms.

In the [4] Alasadi presents a multimodal framework with a fairness-aware perspective that combines data from different sources, such as text and image. The fairness-aware perspective

 DOI: 10.1201/9781042001767-14

helps to provide fair and unbiased detection results while tackling issues with balances datasets and fairness in demographics. This perspective of fairness enables the use of many modalities for more robust detection.

Xiong [5] advocates adapting Locality Sensitive Hashing (LSH) for use in similarity-based word embeddings. This method, called LSHWE, improves the precision and accuracy of the feature representation process carried out in a cyberbullying identification task. The study illustrates how advanced word embedding techniques might identify nuanced semantic differences in language that can be used to identify harmful online behavior.

SaracEssiz [6] applies a method for generating evolutionary feature selection that is inspired by a honeybee's foraging process, called the Artificial Bee Colony algorithm. The ABC algorithm can effectively select a subset of features for the classifier from the rich feature space provided by a textual input. The study shows how essential a good feature selection is for reducing noise and increasing the accuracy of classifiers.

Jain *et al.* [7] used multiple machine learning classification algorithms to measure and account for cyberbullying behavior across multiple social media platforms. Their comparison analysis evaluated trade-offs in algorithm performance and examined multiple performance measures, including recall and precision. This investigation also deepened our understanding of how algorithmic decisions may shape systems designed to detect cyberbullying, specifically focused on sensitivity and specificity.

Patel and Patel [8] provided a significant review of the recent machine learning methodology for detecting cyberbullying. Their work comprehensively covered traditional methodologies, areas of difficulty in feature engineering, and issues that arise due to data imbalance. Their survey is also a great tool that highlights gaps in knowledge and provides a historical perspective on the development of detection.

3 DATASET

Four distinct CSV files that are divided into cyber-aggressive and non-cyber-aggressive remarks make up the dataset.

S. N	File Name	Category	Size
1	Train_CyberBullying_Dataset.csv	Cyberbullying	5317 comments
2	Train_NonCyberBullying_Dataset.csv	Non-Cyberbullying	15328 comments
3	Test_CyberBullying_Dataset.csv	Cyberbullying	2505 comments
4	Test_NonCyberBullying_Dataset.csv	Non-Cyberbullying	6312 comments

4 PROPOSED METHOD

The proposed method introduces an intelligent cyberbullying detection framework that integrates Doc2Vec-based document embeddings with multiple machine learning classifiers to accurately identify harmful online comments. The system begins with preprocessing of raw text, including cleaning, tokenization, and labeling of two datasets containing cyber-aggressive and non-aggressive comments. These processed texts are then feed to the Doc2Vec model to create meaningful vector representations that capture semantic and contextual patterns in user comments. The resulting embeddings serve as feature inputs to various classifiers. By comparing assesment metric such as accuracy, precision, recall, F1-score, and area under cover, the framework identifies best-performing model for cyberbullying detection. This method enhances the dependent of automated moderation systems and supports the development of safer digital communication environments. The system's architecture is diagrammed in Figure 2.

4.1 *System architecture*

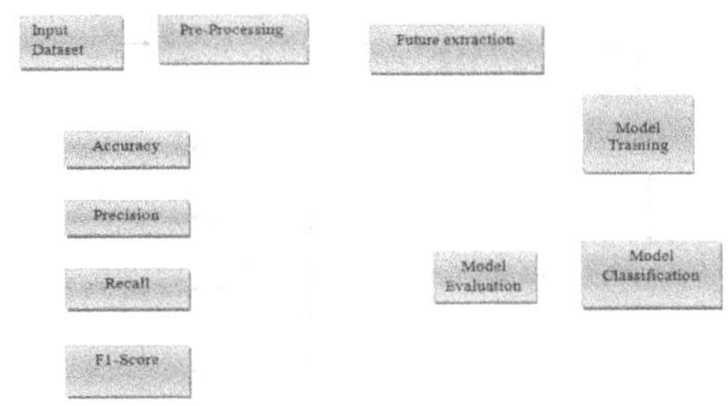

Figure 1: System Architecture

4.2 *Methodology*

The diagram illustrates the overall workflow of the assumed cyberbullying detection system, beginning with the input dataset, which undergoes preprocessing steps such as cleaning, tokenization, and normalization to make the text for evalution. After preprocessing, feature extraction is performed—using methods like Doc2Vec—to convert the textual comments into meaningful numerical representations. This extracted feature are then feed to the model training phase, where machine learning classifiers learn patterns that distinguish cyberbullying from non-cyberbullying content. The trained model proceeds to the classification stage, where it predicts the class of new or unseen comments. Following classification, the model evaluation module assesses performance using key metric such as accuracy, precision, recall, and F1-score. This metric help to determine the strength of the model and guide the selection of the best-working classifier for deployment. Overall, the diagram represents a complete and systematic pipeline for building, training, and evaluating an intelligent cyberbullying detection model.

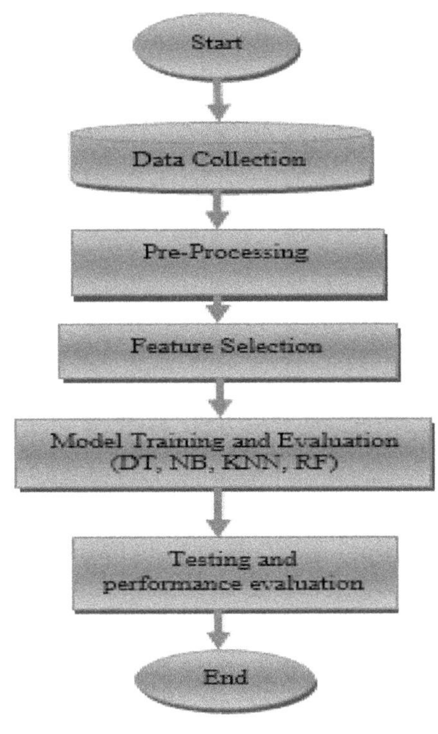

Figure 2: Implementation flow diagram.

5 RESULTS AND DISCUSSIONS

The simulation results assess the effectiveness of a number of machine learning models when detecting cyberbullying using embeddings from Doc2Vec.

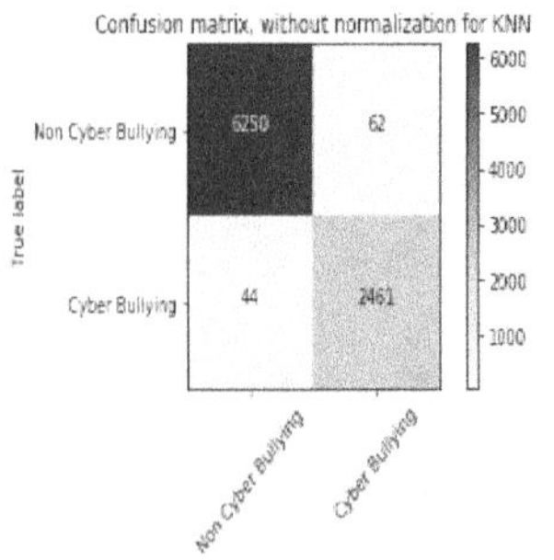

Figure 3. Confusion Matrix for KNN.

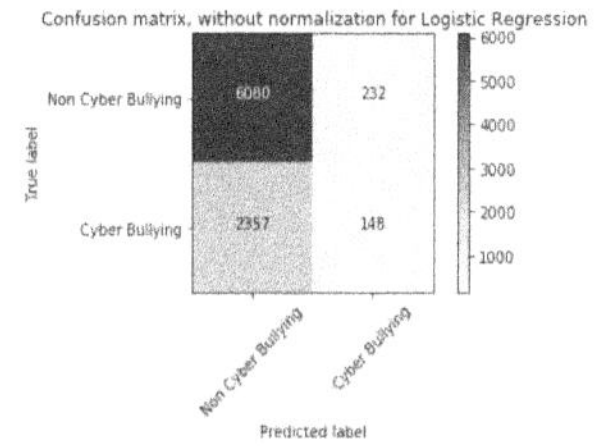

Figure 4. Confusion Matrix for Logistic Regression.

In Figure 4, The confusion matrices for the KNN and Logistic Regression classifiers illustrate clear differences in their ability to differentiate among cyberbullying and non-cyberbullying comments. The KNN model demonstrates strong performance, with a higher number of accurate forecast in both classes and only a small number of misclassified instances, indicating effective separation of cyberbullying patterns captured through Doc2Vec embeddings. In contrast, the Logistic Regression confusion matrix shows comparatively weaker performance, correctly identifying most non-cyberbullying comments but displaying a higher number of misclassifications for cyberbullying instances. This suggests that while Logistic Regression captures general trends in the data, it lacks the deeper semantic discrimination achieved by KNN, resulting in lower precision and recall for the cyberbullying class.

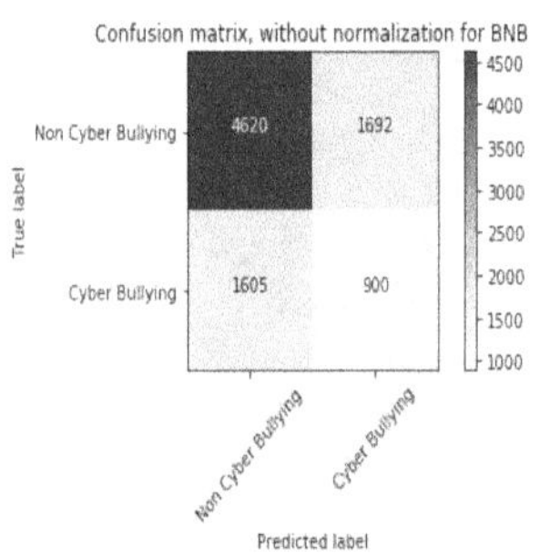

Figure 5. Confusion Matrix for Naïve Bayes.

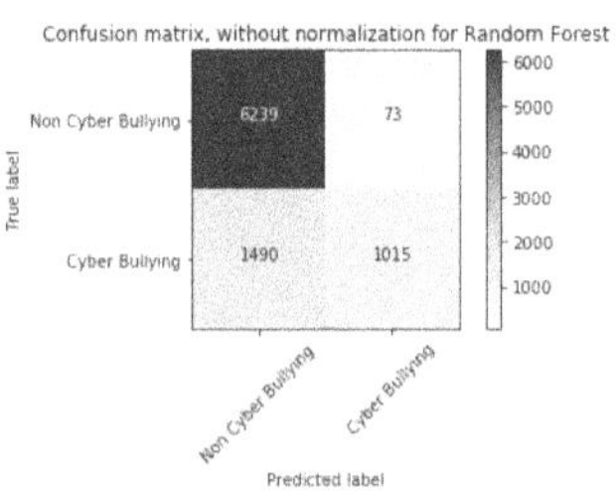

Figure 6. Confusion Matrix for Decision Tree.

The confusion matrices for the Decision Tree (Figure 5) and Naïve Bayes (Figure 6) models show noticeable differences in classification performance. The Decision Tree classifier demonstrates strong accuracy for the non-cyberbullying class but produces a higher number of false positives and false negatives compared to KNN, indicating moderate difficulty in separating subtle cyberbullying patterns. In contrast, the Naïve Bayes model shows even more misclassifications in both classes, particularly with cyberbullying comments being incorrectly identified as non-cyberbullying. This suggests that Naïve Bayes struggles with the contextual and semantic complexity captured by Doc2Vec embeddings, resulting in lower overall reliability than the Decision Tree model.

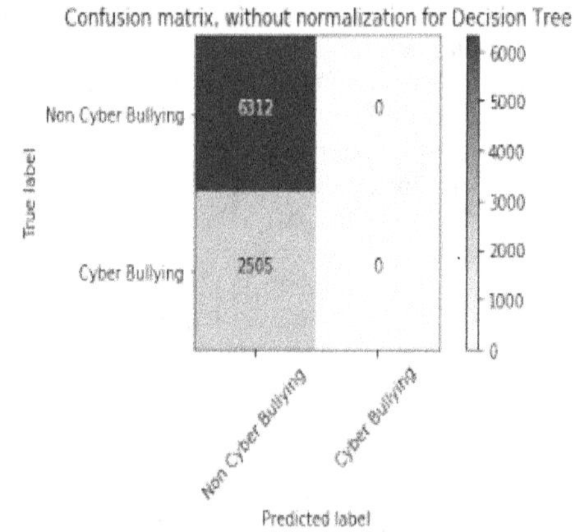

Figure 7. Confusion Matrix for Random Forest.

5.1 *ROC curves*

The ROC curves for KNN, GNB, and Logistic Regression highlight clear differences in classifier performance. The KNN model (Figure 8) shows an excellent ROC curve with an AUC of 0.99, indicating near-perfect class separation and highly reliable detection of cyberbullying. In contrast, the Gaussian Naïve Bayes model (Figure 9) achieves a moderate AUC of 0.57, reflecting its difficulty in distinguishing cyberbullying from non-cyberbullying comments. The Logistic Regression model (Figure 10) performs similarly poorly, with an AUC of 0.59, showing limited discriminative ability and a near-random classification pattern. Overall, the ROC analysis confirms KNN as the strongest model among the three.

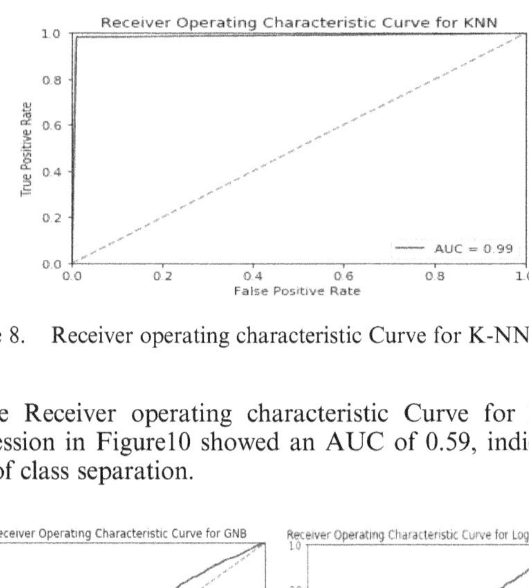

Figure 8. Receiver operating characteristic Curve for K-NN.

The Receiver operating characteristic Curve for Logistic Regression in Figure10 showed an AUC of 0.59, indicating a lack of class separation.

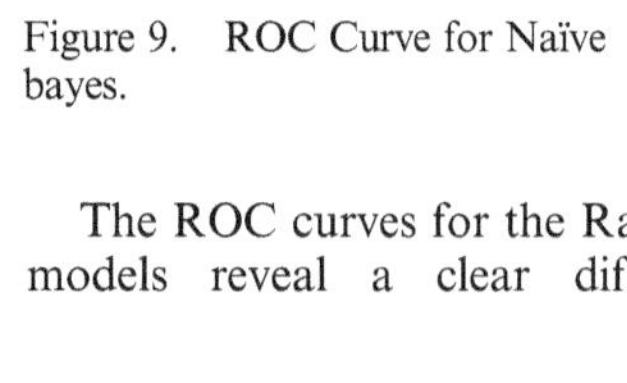

Figure 9. ROC Curve for Naïve bayes.

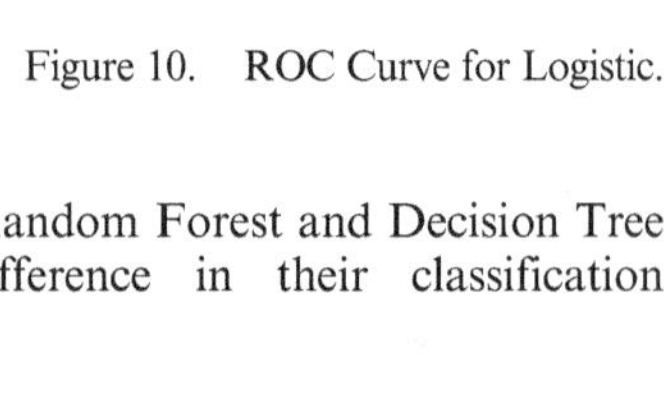

Figure 10. ROC Curve for Logistic.

The ROC curves for the Random Forest and Decision Tree models reveal a clear difference in their classification capabilities. The Random Forest model (Figure 11) shows a Tough performance with an Area under curve of 0.98, indicating excellent class separation and high capability to differentiate through cyberbullying and non-cyberbullying comments. In contrast, the Decision Tree model (Figure 12) exhibits a weaker Receiver operating characteristic curve with an Area under curve of 0.54, suggesting limited discriminative power and performance close to random guessing. Overall, the comparison shows that Random Forest is significantly more reliable and effective than the standalone Decision Tree classifier.

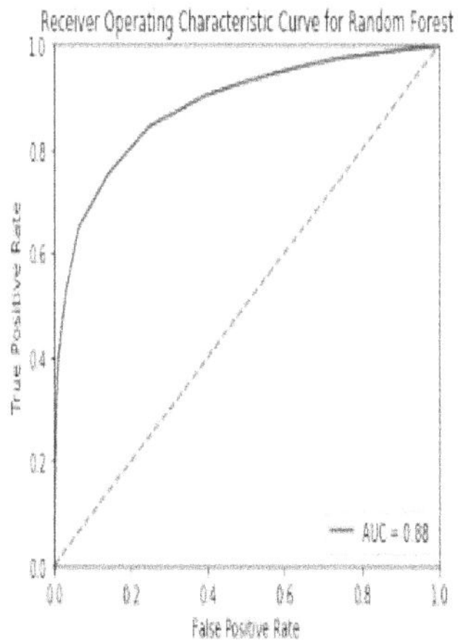

Figure 11. ROC Curve for Random Forest.

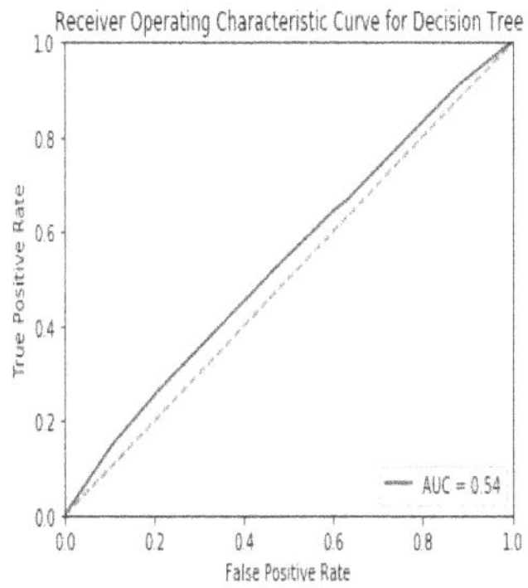

Figure 12. ROC Curve for Decision Tree.

Performance comparison table

S. N	Model/ Parameter	Accuracy	Precession	Recall	F_1-Score	AUC
1	KNN	98.79	0.99	0.99	0.99	0.99
2	Logistic regression	70.63	0.72	0.96	0.82	0.59
3	Naivy Bayes	88.88	0.73	0.74	0.73	0.57
4	Decision Tree	71.58	0.86	0.87	0.76	0.54
5	Random Forest	82.27	0.81	0.99	0.89	0.88

Performance analyse graph

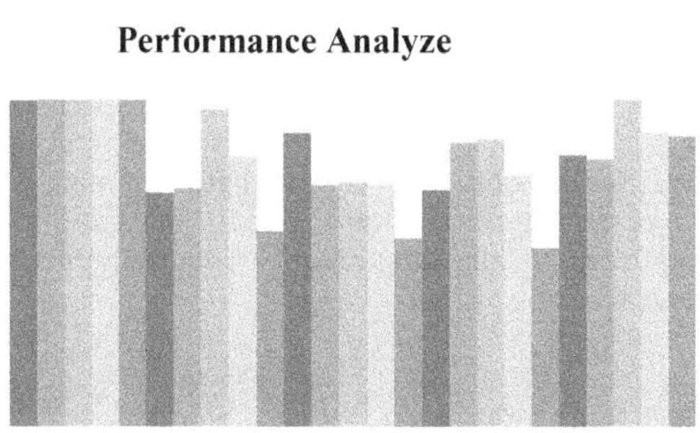

Figure 13: Performance Analyze Graph

6 SUMMARY OF FINDINGS

This project introduces an advanced framework for detecting cyberbullying with deep learning methods and document embedding. The system utilizes a topic model called Doc2Vec to take text data and create dense feature vectors, which allows us to effectively classify comments as being cyber-aggressive or not. We pre-processed, balanced, and split two datasets containing labeled comments, which enabled us to evaluate performance more objectively. The generated document embeddings from the text data were used as the input features for multiple machine learning classifiers. Each model was trained and tested multiple times within the experiment, with classifier performance was determined using several evaluational matrics, including accuracy, precision, recall, F1-score, and a AUC.

REFERENCES

[1] Andrea Pereraa, (2021), *Accurate Cyberbullying Detection and Prevention on Social Media*

[2] Jalal Omer Atoum's, (2020), Cyberbullying Detection Through Sentiment Analysis

[3] MdManowarul (2020), *Cyberbullying Detection on Social Networks Using Machine Learning Approaches*

[4] Jamal Alasadi's, (2020), *A Fairness-Aware Fusion Framework for Multimodal Cyberbullying Detection*

[5] Qingyu Xiong, (2020), LSHWE: Using Locality Sensitive Hashing to Enhance Similarity-Based Word Embedding for Cyberbullying Detection

[6] EsraSaracEssiz, (2019), *An Algorithm for Cyberbullying Based on Artificial Bee Colonies.*

[7] Gupta, V., Agarwal, A., and Jain, A. (2021). Machine learning techniques for detecting cyberbullying on social media platforms. 12(3), 168–176, *International Journal of Advanced Computer Science and Applications.*

[8] Patel, D., and Patel P. (2019). A Review of Machine Learning-Based Cyberbullying Detection Methods. 8(7), 192–196, *International Journal of Computer Science and Mobile Computing.*

[9] Kim, J., and Kim Y. (2020). A Social Media Cyberbullying Detection System Based on Machine Learning. 12(4) *Symmetry*, 644.

[10] Chang, M.K., and Jang, D.P. (2019), A deep learning method that uses natural language analysis to detect cyberbullying. 6672, *Sustainability*, 11(23).

[11] Li, Y., Zhang, Y., Guo, J., and Li, X. (2019). Machine learning algorithms for social media cyberbullying detection. *Humanized Computing and Ambient Intelligence Journal*, 10(6), 2205–2216.

[12] Tripathi, A., Agarwal, M., and Kumar, N. (2021). A thorough investigation of machine learning for cyberbullying detection. 16 (1), 80–91, *Journal of Information Assurance and Security*

[13] Yadav J., Kumar D., and Chauhan D., (2020), *Cyberbullying Detection using Pre-Trained BERT Model*, doi:10.1109/ICESC48915.2020.9155700.

[14] Kayaalp, F. and Basarslan, M.S., (2020). *Social Media Sentiment Analysis Using Machine Learning Techniques.*

[15] Akopyan, M.S., Plechov, T.P., Turdakov, D.Y., and Belyaeva, O.V., (September 2019). Text recognition in social media photos. (pp. 3–6) in *Ivannikov Memorial Workshop (IVMEM, 2019).* IEEE.

[16] Sachdeva, N., and Kumar, A. (2021). Capsule networks with dynamic routing and deep convolutional neural networks are used for multimodal cyberbullying detection. *Systems of Multimedia*, pp. 1–10

[17] Sheeba, J.I., Saranya, S., Drishya, S.V., and Devaneyan, S.P. (2019), Convolutional neural networks are used for the detection of cyberbullying images and text. 11(2), pp. 25–30, *CiiT International Journal on Fuzzy Systems.*

[18] Acharjee, U.K., Akter, A., Sharmin, S., Islam, M.M., Uddin, M. A., and Islam, L. (December 2020), Machine learning techniques are used to detect cyberbullying on social networks. Pages 1–6 of *IEEE's 2020 Asia-Pacific Conference on Computer Science and Data Engineering (CSDE).* IEEE.

[19] Fernando, P., and Perera, A. (2021). precise identification and prevention of cyberbullying on social media. *Computer Science Procedia*, 181, pp. 605–611

Next-Generation Smart Systems – Sekhar et al. (Eds)
© 2027 The Author(s), ISBN: 978-1-041-34234-2

An Innovative Deep Learning Framework for Identifying Skin Types and Condition

Sricharani P.
Professor, Department of Artificial Intelligence, Shri Vishnu Engineering College for Women (A), Bhimavaram, AP, India

Yandamuri Gayatri
Department of Artificial Intelligence, Shri Vishnu Engineering College for Women (A), Bhimavaram, AP, India

M.V. Lavanya
Assistant Professor, Department of Mathematics and Statistics, GITAM School of Science, GITAM (Deemed to be University) Visakhapatnam, India

Harshini Natakula, Madhuri Perumalla, and Sampurna Jahnavi vemuri
Department of Artificial Intelligence, Shri Vishnu Engineering College for Women (A), Bhimavaram, AP, India

ABSTRACT: This research introduces a technique that employs advanced neural models to classify skin types and recognize particular skin conditions.. Leveraging various architectures, including ResNet50, CNN, InceptionV3, DenseNet201, and Xception, our classification model achieved significant accuracy improvements. Notably, the Xception model demonstrated exceptional reaching 99% accuracy on the Skin Type dataset.. Furthermore, we incorporated object detection methodologies using YOLO models (versions V5, V6, V7, V8) to identify and .edu.n localize skin condition regions, enhancing the comprehensiveness and robustness of our system. This study highlights the potential of contemporary deep learning models in enhancing skin type classification and condition detection, hence offering a strong basis for personalized dermatological evaluation and treatment. The findings highlight the applicability of CNNs in delivering precise and reliable results for diverse skin types and conditions. Our study utilizes a real-time dataset to ensure practical relevance and adaptability to varying skin conditions in real-world scenarios.

Keywords: Skin care, YOLO, Deep Learning, ResNet50, CNN, InceptionV3, DenseNet201, Xception

1 INTRODUCTION

The skin is the body's biggest and most visible organ, and any problems with it can have a big impact on both health and looks. The growing prevalence of skin diseases globally has highlighted the urgent need for early detection and effective diagnosis methods. Traditionally, dermatologists manually identify skin conditions based on visible symptoms, which may result in misdiagnosis, especially at early stages or with subtle visual cues. This manual process is time-consuming and heavily reliant on professional expertise.

With improvements in technology, especially in AI and deep learning, automated methods are becoming more popular for analyzing medical images. These systems offer promising support for dermatologists by providing quicker, more accurate assessments. Among deep learning models, CNNs have shown strong capability in identifying features and handling classification tasks involving images.

This work seeks to tackle the difficulties in classifying skin diseases and identifying skin types with a hybrid deep learning methodology. The suggested system combines object detection and classification models, including well-known architectures like Xception, DenseNet201, InceptionV3, and ResNet50. The introduction of YOLO-based object detection further enhances the system's ability to localize affected skin regions.

By utilizing a real-time dataset, this work ensures practical relevance and robustness in real-world scenarios. The proposed integrated system is intended to offer an effective and scalable diagnostic tool for dermatology, easing the responsibilities of medical profession.

2 LITERATURE REVIEW

Recent research has concentrated on using image analysis and deep learning methods for skin disease categorization and detection.Convolutional Neural Networks (CNNs) have gained popularity because of their capacity to automatically capture and represent important features within medical images. In contrast to earlier classification methods that depended on handcrafted features, CNN-based approaches have achieved greater accuracy and offer better scalability.

Recent works have implemented architectures like ResNet, InceptionV3, DenseNet, and Xception to improve classification performance. These models can capture complex patterns and structures in dermatoscopic images. Additionally, transfer learning has become a popular approach, allowing researchers to utilize pre-trained models and fine-tune them on smaller medical datasets.

Object detection frameworks such as YOLO (You Only Look Once), especially the newer versions from YOLOv5 to YOLOv8, have become increasingly popular for identifying and localizing diseased areas in skin images. This is particularly valuable for building comprehensive diagnosis systems that not only classify conditions but also highlight the specific areas of concern.

Overall, these studies demonstrate that combining classification and object detection improves both accuracy and interpretability, forming the foundation for real-time, userfriendly dermatological tools.

3 METHODOLOGY

3.1 *Proposed work*

The system encompasses two main components: classification and detection. For classification tasks, we employ ResNet50, CNN.

Inception V3, DenseNet201, and Xception architectures to accurately categorize skin types. Through rigorous experimentation, we discovered that Xception achieved the highest accuracy of 99%, surpassing previous methods.

 DOI: 10.1201/9781042001767-15

Additionally, our system integrates YOLO models (V5-V8) for the detection of skin disease regions, providing precise localization and identification To increase the precision and dependability of tailored skincare product suggestions, our system makes use of cutting-edge deep learning techniques. Customers will gain from skincare advice designed to match each person's distinct skin characteristics and concerns conditions, which will enhance results and boost satisfaction. Furthermore, the timely detection of skin diseases will facilitate early intervention and management, contributing to overall skin health and well-being.

3.2 *System architecture*

The system architecture for the skincare analysis and recommendation system involves four main steps: dataset preparation,image processing,deep learning model building and training and performance metric evalution metrics.

Dataset Preparation: In this step, relevant datasets containing facial images and associated skincare information are collected and prepared. This involves data cleaning, preprocessing, and labeling to ensure consistency and any the dataset. **Image Processing:** Following dataset preparation ,image processing methods are used to improve the facial images quality and characteristics. The photos may be optimized for deep learning model input using methods including noise removal, resizing, and normalization. **Build Train the models:** One type of deep learning model that may be trained using processed photos and pertinent skincare data is the A Convolutional Neural Network (CNN) is a powerful deep learning model that can be trained using processed images along with relevant skincare information. These models learn to identify different skin types, recognize various skin issues, and provide suitable skincare product recommendations by analyzing the input images. **Performance Evalution Metrics:** Lastly, the accuracy and efficiency of the trained models are assessed using performance evaluation criteria. Performance measures— accuracy, precision, recall, and F1-score—help in judging the model's effectiveness in identifying skin-related problems.classify skin types, and suggest skincare products.

Overall, this system architecture integrates dataset preparation, image processing, deep learning model building and training, and performance evaluation. metrics to develop an accurate effective skin classification and detection system.

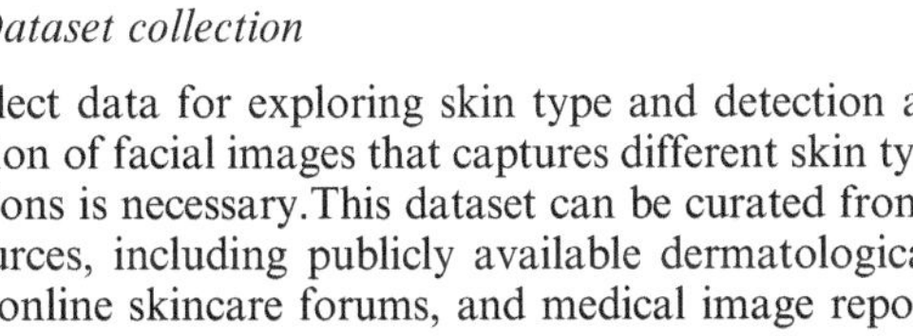

Figure 1. Proposed architecture.

3.3 *Dataset collection*

To collect data for exploring skin type and detection a varied collection of facial images that captures different skin types and conditions is necessary.This dataset can be curated from multiple sources, including publicly available dermatological databases, online skincare forums, and medical image repositories. For reliable skin type analysis, the dataset should cover multiple categories, ranging from balanced and moisture-deficient skin to oil-prone and reactive types. To maintain diversity, images should also represent individuals across varied age groups, genders, and ethnic backgrounds. Annotating each image with the corresponding skin type label is crucial for training and evaluation purposes. For detection tasks, such as identifying skin conditions or abnormalities The dataset should include

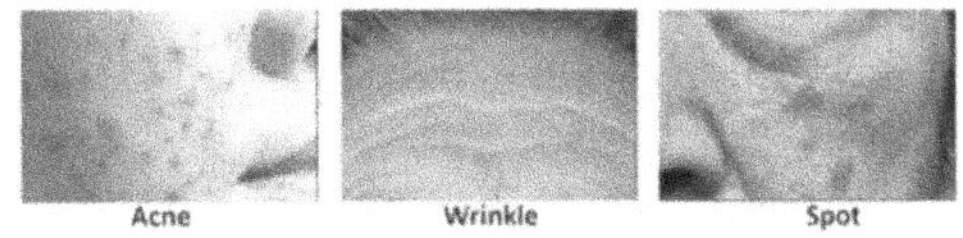

Figure 2. Sample dataset images.

examples of skin issues like acne, eczema, psoriasis, rosacea, and melanoma. Each image must be labeled to indicate whether a particular condition is present or not.

3.4 *Image processing*

Image processing in skincare uses techniques like rescaling and augmentation to normalize, enhance, and diversify images for better deep learning performance.

Re-scaling the Image: Re-scaling adjusts pixel intensity values to a set range, ensuring normalization and consistent data for efficient deep learning model convergence.

Shear Transformation: Shear transformation shifts image pixels along an axis, creating geometric distortions to augment data, reduce overfitting, and improve deep learning generalization. **Zooming the Image:** Zooming changes image scale, focusing on regions or broad views, enhancing detail recognition and pattern learning in deep learning models. **Horizontal Flip:** Horizontal flip mirrors images along the vertical axis, doubling dataset size and improving model robustness to orientation variations in facial recognition. **Reshaping the Image:** Reshaping adjusts image dimensions to fixed sizes via cropping, padding, or resizing, ensuring compatibility and uniformity for deep learning models.

3.5 *Algorithms*

Classification: ResNet50: ResNet50, an advanced CNN architecture that incorporates residual connections, helps overcome vanishing gradient issues and effectively extracts intricate skin features, leading to highly precise skin type classification.

CNN: CNNs capture layered patterns in images by using convolutional operations and then refining them through dense layers, which supports dependable classification of skin types from visual cues. **Inception V3:** Inception V3, an advanced convolutional neural network architecture, uses multiple filter sizes and optimization techniques to efficiently extract diverse features for accurate skin type classification tasks. **DenseNet201:** DenseNet201 links each layer to all others, reusing features to learn intricate skin patterns, boosting accuracy in skin type classification. **Xception:** Xception replaces standard convolutions with depthwise separable ones, capturing fine details efficiently, enabling fast and accurate skin type classification. **Detection YOLOv5:** YOLOv5 detects objects using a single neural network, providing fast, accurate real-time detection suitable for skincare image analysis tasks. **YOLOv6:** YOLOv6 improves YOLOv5 with advanced training and architecture, offering higher accuracy and efficiency for precise skin disease localization and detection. **YOLOv7:** YOLOv7 refines the YOLO series, enhancing architecture and training to deliver superior accuracy and efficiency in detecting and localizing skin abnormalities. YOLOv8: YOLOv8, the latest YOLO version, integrates advanced innovations for faster, more accurate, and robust skin disease detection across varying conditions.

3.6 *Experimental results*

Accuracy: Accuracy measures how well a test distinguishes patient and healthy cases, indicating overall classification correctness.

$$\text{Accuracy} = (\text{TP} + \text{TN})/(\text{TP} + \text{TN} + \text{FP} + \text{FN})$$

Precision: Precision measures the correctly classified positive cases among all labeled positives. It reflects the reliability of positive predictions.

$$\text{Precision} = \text{TP}/(\text{TP} + \text{FP})$$

Recall: Recall measures a model's ability to find all relevant instances. It shows how well positives are identified.

$$\text{Recall} = \text{TP}/(\text{TP} + \text{FN})$$

The F1 score provides a single measure by combining accuracy and coverage. This offers a balanced assessment.

$$\text{F1} - \text{Score} = 2 \times (\text{Precision} \times \text{Recall})/(\text{precision} + \text{Recall})$$

Mean Average Precision (MAP) is a ranking metric that measures how well relevant items are positioned in a list. It is calculated by finding the average precision for each relevant item up to rank K and then taking the arithmetic mean of those values.

Evaluates how well optimistic predictions work;xception performed best.

$$\text{MAP} = \frac{1}{n}\sum_{k=1}^{k} \text{AP}_k$$

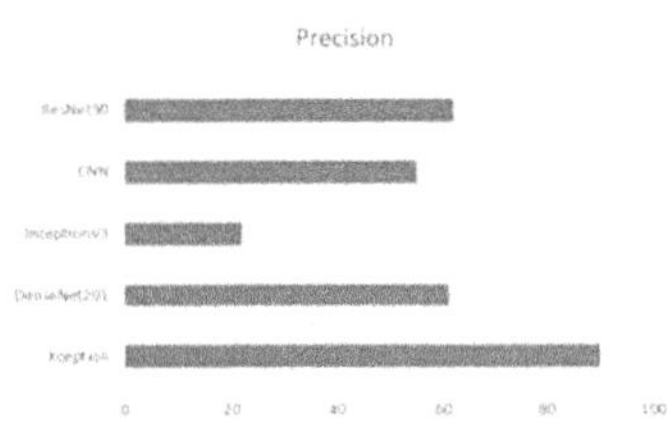

Figure 3. Evaluates how well optimistic predictions work;xception performed best.

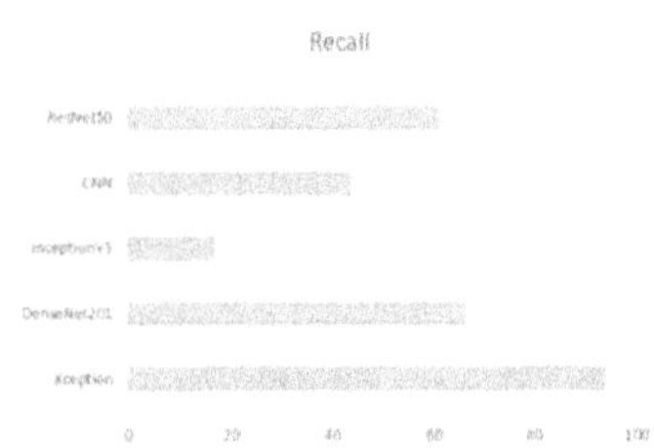

Figure 4. Evaluates the model's recall, with Xception having the highest recall for all positive cases.

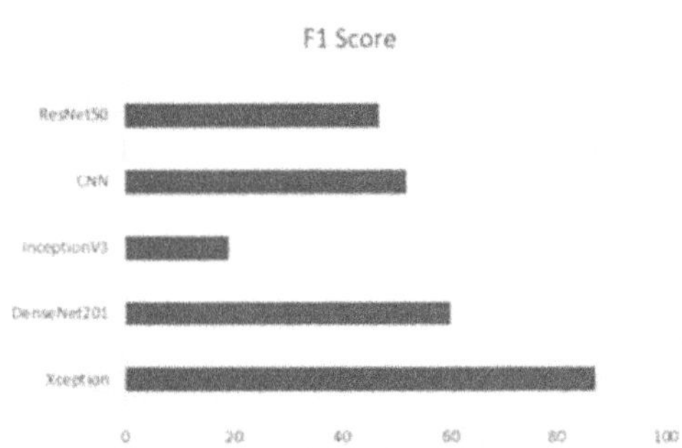

Figure 5. Balances precision and recall; Xception is best.

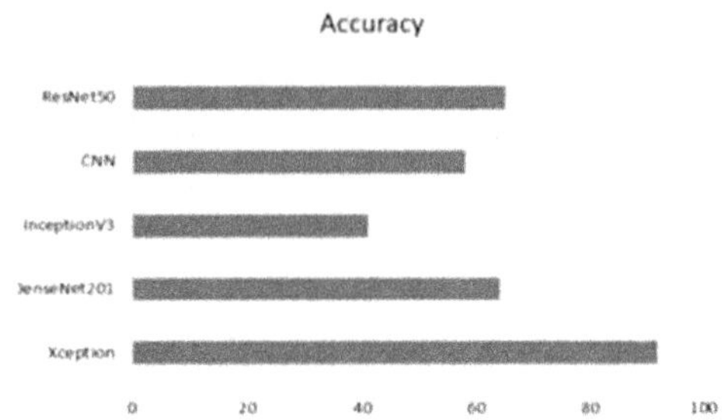

Figure 6. Indicates overall correctness; Xception achieved high accuracy, the best among classifiers.

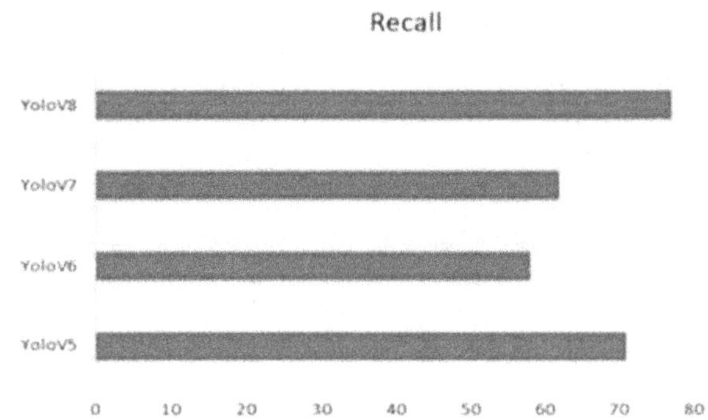

Figure 7. Evaluates how well the detection model identifies true positives; YOLOv8 outperformed others.

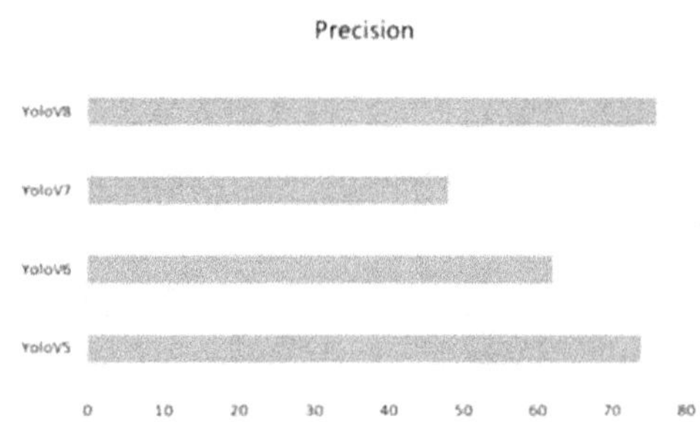

Figure 8. Measures correct detections among predicted positives; YOLO8 had the highest precision.

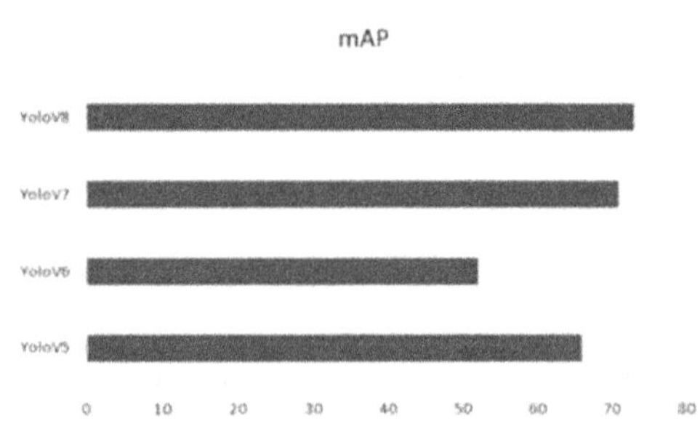

Figure 9. Mean Average Precision for the object detection; YOLOv8 achieved the best results.

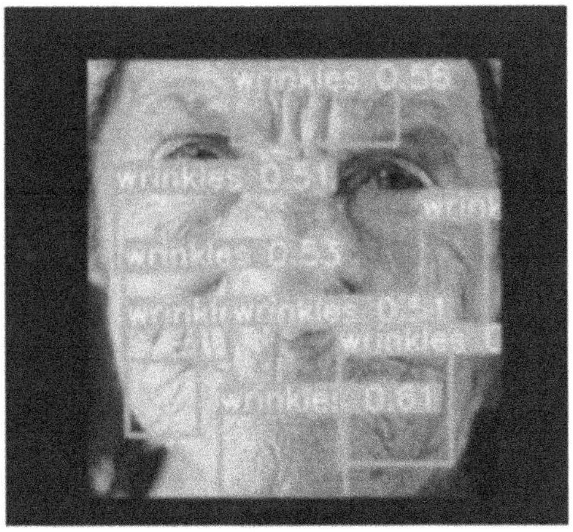

Figure 10. Outcome for a given input, Similarly, we can test other cases.

5 CONCLUSION

In summary, combining cutting-edge deep learning and machine learning techniques in skincare classification and disease detection holds immense promise for revolutionizing the skincare industry. Through utilization of models such as ResNet50, CNN, Inception V3, DenseNet201, and Xception for skin type classification, the coupled with YOLOv5, YOLOv6, YOLOv7, and YOLOv8 for skin disease detection, our proposed system offers unprecedented levels of accuracy, personalization, and efficiency. Xception had the best accuracy (99%) for classification. YOLOv8 performed the best for skin disease detection. By leveraging these cutting- edge technologies, skincare recommendations can be tailored to individual needs and preferences with remarkable precision, resulting in better skincare results and higher satisfaction among users. In addition,the timely detection and localization of skin abnormalities facilitated by our detection algorithms enable early intervention and treatment, potentially saving lives and improving overall skin health. However, It is essential to recognize the difficulties in putting these technologies into practice, such as issues with algorithm bias, data privacy, and ethical issues. To overcome these obstacles and guarantee the responsible implementation of AI- driven skincare products, more research and development is required. All things considered, our suggested approach represents a significant advancement in skincare technology with the potential to reshape the way individuals manage their skin health. transform how people take care of their skin and encourage better, healthier lifestyles.

6 FUTURE SCOPE

Future developments may integrate genetic and environmental data, adopt more advanced AI algorithms for precise predictions, and incorporate augmented reality to visualize real-time skincare effects, further enhancing personalization, accuracy, and user engagement in skincare routines.

REFERENCES

[1] Lee J., Yoon H., Kim S., Lee C., Lee J., Yoo S., (2024), Deep learningbased skin care product recommendation: A focus on cosmetic ingredient analysis and facial skin conditions, *Journal of Cosmetic Dermatology.*

[2] Akshya J., Mehra V., Sundar Rajan M., Teja Sri P., Choudhry M.D., (2024), Efficient Net-based Expert System for Personalized Facial Skincare Recommendations, *SRM Institute of Science and Technology*

[3] Saidah S., Fuadah N., Alia F. and Ibrahim N., (2021), Facial Skin Type Classification Based on Microscopic Images Using Convolutional Neural Network (CNN), *Lecture Notes in Electrical Engineering.*

[4] Lin T.-Y., Chan H.-T., Hsia C.-H., and Lai C.-F., (2022), *Facial Skincare Products' Recommendation with Computer Vision-Technologies*

[5] Cortes H., Rojas-Márquez M., Del Prado-Audelo M.L., Gonzalez-Del Carmen M. and Leyva-Gómez G., (2022), Alterations in ´ mental health and quality of life in patients with skin disorders: a narrative review, *International Journal of Dermatology*, vol. 61, no. 7, pp. 783–791. “Skincare market size share COVID-19 impact analysis by product”, Fortune Business Insights, 2021.

[6] Ko J. and Cheoi K.J., (2021), Image-processing based facial imperfection region detection and segmentation, *Multimedia Tools and Applications*, vol. 80, no. 26–27, pp. 34283–34296.

[7] Biswasa, S., Shahinura, S., Hasana, M. and Ahsan, Q. (2015). Physical, mechanical and thermal properties of jute and bamboo fibre reinforced unidirectional epoxy composites. *Procedia Eng.* 105, 933–939

[8] Neha V.V.M., (2023), Skincare Market by Products (Creams and Moisturizers, Powder Cleansers and Face Wash, Others)... Global Opportunity Analysis and Industry Forecast, *Allied Market Research.*

[9] Sharma J., Sharma K., Garg K. and Sharma A.K., (2021), Product Recommendation System: A Comprehensive Review, *IOP Conference Series: Materials Science and Engineering*, vol. 1022, no. 1, pp. 012021.

Next-Generation Smart Systems – Sekhar et al. (Eds)
© 2027 The Author(s), ISBN: 978-1-041-34234-2

A Retinal Microvasculature Analysis Using MobileNetV1, CNN and GAN's for Early CVD Detection

M. Madhavi
Assistant Professor, Department of CSE, Siddhartha Academy of Higher Education, Vijayawada, India

Mandi Sai Vinay, V.L.S. Harshavardhan, K. Eshitha, and P. Reshmitha Rani
Student, Department of CSE, Siddhartha Academy of Higher Education, Vijayawada, India

ABSTRACT: Cardiovascular diseases (CVD) are the major worldwide reason for death in all age brackets, but late diagnosis is still an issue in developing nations because of the expense and unavailability of equipment such as magnetic resonance imaging (MRI). This research investigates the application of fundus photography in early detection of CVD through imaging of the retina, where changes in Retinal Nerve Fiber Layer (RNFL) vessels are used as a marker of cardiac disease, including myocardial infarction. An artificial intelligence (AI) method is suggested utilizing Generative Adversarial Networks (GANs) to augment data in order to improve training datasets with fake retinal images. MobileNetV1, A model for deep learning, and Convolutional Neural Networks (CNNs) is light in weight, are utilized for image classification to detect CVD-related anomalies. The technique makes use of regular eye tests, providing a cost-effective and scalable option to MRI. Through facilitating early diagnosis in limited resources, the suggested approach solves healthcare disparities and provides an affordable diagnostic tool to marginalized groups. The research illustrates the promise of AI-based retinal imaging to revolutionize CVD screening, enabling early intervention and a decrease in global cardiovascular mortality.

Keywords: Cardiovascular Disease, Retinal Fundus Imaging, MobileNetV1, CNN, Generative Adversarial Networks, Deep Learning, Data Augmentation, Medical Imaging

1 INTRODUCTION

Heart disease are the main causes of death worldwide are conditions like heart failure, stroke, hypertension, and coronary artery disease. Based on estimates from the World Health Organization (WHO), they claim around 17.9 million deaths annually, or about 32% of all deaths globally, are attributed to heart attacks and strokes, which account for nearly 85% of these deaths. As a result of the large burden of CVD in low and middle-income nations, there is significant need for affordable and accurate screening devices. Early identification and treatment can profoundly impact the prevention of disease progression and death, yet current diagnostics continue to be invasive, expensive, and frequently unavailable in tertiary facilities.

The application of computer vision and artificial intelligence has made retinal fundus imaging a readily available, less expensive method to evaluate cardiovascular risk. It also offers a convenient form of diagnostic testing. Similar to the heart and brain, the retina is connected to the central nervous system and contains blood vessels. Narrowing, twisting (penis), intersection points (piles) and hemorrhaging in retinal blood vessels may be early signs of vascular damage. In addition, research has shown that such retinal signs are highly correlated with cardiovascular events, which makes fundus photography a good technique for early detection and follow-up of possible cardiovascular events.

Nonetheless, one of the biggest challenges for developing strong medical image analysis using deep learning models is that there are few annotated datasets available. Acquisition of medical data is frequently limited by patient variability, high costs of expert annotation, and privacy regulations. Insufficient data can cause overfitting and lower generalization in deep learning models. To prevent this, Generative Adversarial Networks (GANs) have been an effective data augmentation solution. GANs employ a generator-discriminator framework to learn the distribution of the information and produce artificial samples that are realistic. Such enhanced datasets not only increase training volume but also add variability that enables models to generalize more effectively to unseen situations. In medical imaging especially, GANs have been used successfully to synthesize retinal, brain MRI, and chest X-ray images, giving testament to the flexibility and effectiveness of the technology.

We, in this work, introduce a new method to improve CVD prediction from retinal fundus images by combining GAN-based data augmentation with CNNs. We investigate in particular the performance of a standard CNN architecture and MobileNet, a light deep neural network that is designed for mobile and edge deployment. Google developed MobileNet, which uses depthwise separable convolutions to greatly compress the model size and computational costs while preserving high accuracy. This makes it especially applicable to real-world scenarios in which the available resources are limited. We robustify MobileNet on our GAN-augmented dataset and compare its performance with a standard CNN to test the synthetic data on prediction accuracy.

2 METHODOLOGY

The system under consideration offers a unified framework for deep learning-based acquisition, pre-processing, annotation, and analysis of retinal images for CVD prediction. The workflow starts with the prudent acquisition of retinal images, which are then sent through rigorous pre-processing methods in order to enhance data quality. The pictures are meticulously annotated with cardiovascular risk factors, yielding rich contextual information for subsequent analysis. The crux of the methodology includes developing and executing a convolutional neural network (CNN)-powered deep learning model, which is renowned for its efficacy in image examination. For the purposes of efficient training and model evaluation, various sets of training and validation data are chosen. The model receives intense training, with the ability to absorb intricate correlations and patterns found in labeled data.the model evaluates its performance on validation datasets after training to make sure its strength and avoid overfitting.

DOI: 10.1201/9781042001767-16

This careful selection is especially important for suggested deep learning model, which uses CNNs and MobileNet structure to forecast cardiovascular disease. Through application of this highly structured database, we to increase the precision and validity of the model, furthering preventive cardiology and improving outcomes for patients.

2.1 *Data collection*

The dataset, a collection of 2722 retinal images, has been sourced from Kaggle, a trusted platform known for its diverse datasets. To ensure effective training and validation, we have thoughtfully split the dataset, with 7030 retinal images into two distinct categories: cardiovascular and no cardiovascular images by using GANs. Each record in the dataset provides detailed information about these features, making it a crucial resource for training and evaluating machine learning models.

2.2 *Data preprocessing*

2.2.1 *ImageDataGenerator creation*

An Image Data Generator object is created with Rescale = 1/255 for pixel normalization and validation_split = 0.3 to split data into training and validation sets. It can be stored in Train_datagenterator.

The technique of adding more picture training data to the available image data by applying various transformations to it, techniques like random rotations, shear transformations, shifts, zooming, and flipping are collectively referred to as image augmentation. This approach is especially useful when the available training data is insufficient to effectively train the model, we resort to image augmentation. By applying alterations to the current photos, we can produce new images in such circumstances. CNN (Convolutional Neural Network) views these photos as completely fresh even if they appear identical. This will make it easier for us to produce a bigger training dataset, which will help the model converge more quickly.

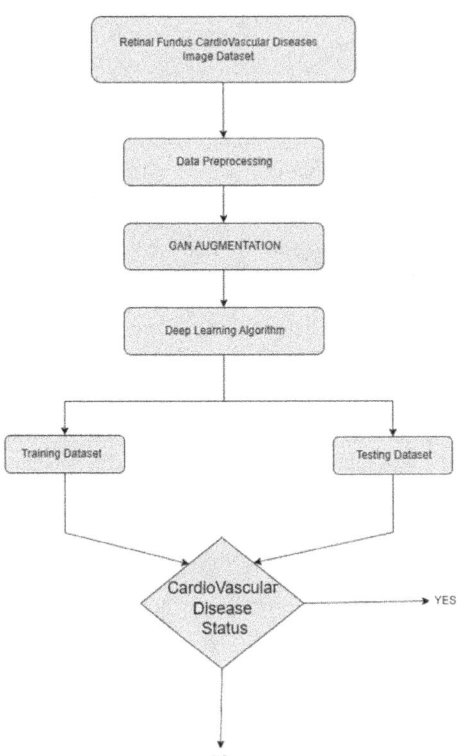

Figure 1. Proposed model flow.

2.2.2 *Flow from directories*

Train generator is created using Train.datagenerator.flow_-from_directory(), specifying:

- Data_directory: The main directory containing images (e.g., Train)
- Target_size: The desired image size (224x224 in this case)
- Batch_size: The number of images to process in each batch (20 here)
- Blass_mode: The type of labels ('categorical' for multiple classes)
- Subset: The subset to use ('training' for training data)
- Test generator is created similarly, but with subset='validation' to access the validation set.

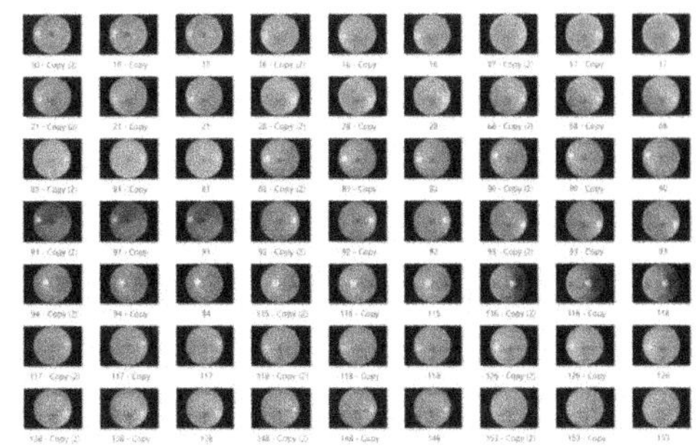

Figure 2. Training samples of retinal pictures.

2.2.3 *Generative Adversarial Networks (GANs)*

Two neural networks—the Generator and the Discriminator—that are trained concurrently and adversarially make up a class of machine learning models called GANs. The discriminator looks for differences between generated and real images, but the generator creates realistic synthetic images. Regarding ongoing education, the generator will be good at potential conclusive images, and the Discriminator learn better at spotting the fakes. This back-and-forth helps generate very realistic fake fundus images.

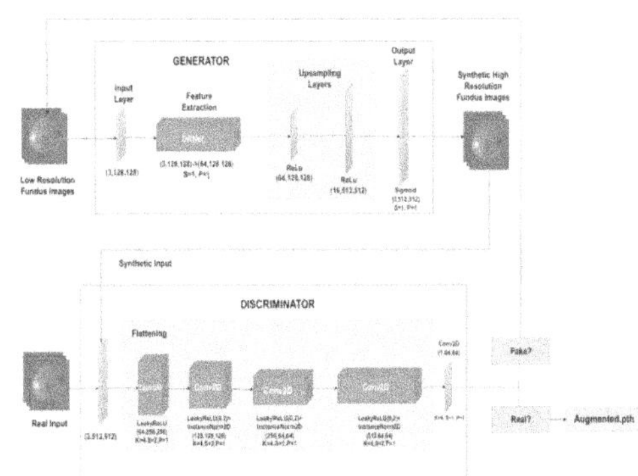

Figure 3. GAN architecture.

2.2.3.1 *Generator* The Generator is designed to transform low-resolution fundus images into high-resolution synthetic images. In our architecture, the Generator consists of:

- Input Layer: Accepts low-resolution (128×128) RGB fundus images.
- Feature Extraction Block: Utilizes a Deep Residual Network (DRNet), which incorporates residual connections to allow for more effective training of deeper networks. This block captures fine-grained vessel structures and retinal patterns crucial for diagnosis.

- Upsampling Layers: These layers gradually increase the spatial dimensions of the image to (256×256) and finally to (512×512), restoring image resolution.
- Activation Function: The output layer limits pixel values within the interval [0, 1], using a sigmoid activation function. thereby simulating realistic image intensity levels.

Generator Loss Function:

$$L_G = \frac{-1}{m}\sum_{i=1}^{m} \log D(G(z_i))$$

Explanation of terms:

- L_G: Generator loss
- m: Batch size
- z_i: Random noise vector
- $G(z_i)$: Generated (fake) image
- D(G(zi)): The discriminator's estimation of the produced image's authenticity

2.2.3.2 *Upsampling* Upsampling refers to the process of increasing the spatial resolution of an image. The Generator makes the converting low-resolution pictures into outputs with higher resolution. And then ReLU activation to introduce non-linearity. These upsampling layers allow the Generator to get the finer vessel details of the retina, which are essential indicators of cardiovascular conditions.

2.2.3.4 *Discriminator* The Discriminator functions as a binary classifier that distinguishes between real and synthetic fundus images. It receives both actual images and the outputs from the Generator and classifies them as real or fake.

It includes:

- Input Layer: Accepts 512×512 fundus images (either real or synthetic).
- Convolutional Layers: A series of Conv2D layers extract hierarchical features from the images.
- Leaky ReLU Activations: used to address the dying ReLU following each convolutional layer. problem and allow small negative gradients for better convergence.
- The flattening layer creates a 1D vector from the 2D feature maps that can be used for classification.
- Output Layer: Returns a probability score that shows the possibility that the image is real.

Discriminator Loss Function:

$$L_D = \frac{-1}{m}\sum_{i=1}^{m} [\log D(x_i) + \log(1 - D(G(z_i)))]$$

Where:

- m = batch size
- x_i= real data sample
- z_i= random noise vector
- $G(z_i)$ = generator output from noise
- $D(x_i)$ = discriminator output for real sample
- $D(G(z_i))$ = discriminator output for fake sample $G(z_i)$

2.2.4 *MobileNet architecture*

MobileNet will offer a way to operate deep neural networks on devices with limited resources, such as embedded systems, cell phones as well as other low-power gadgets. The main concept of MobileNet is to lower the computational complexity and model size by using depthwise separable convolutions rather than conventional convolutions. The conventional convolution process is divided into two distinct operations by depthwise separable convolutions.

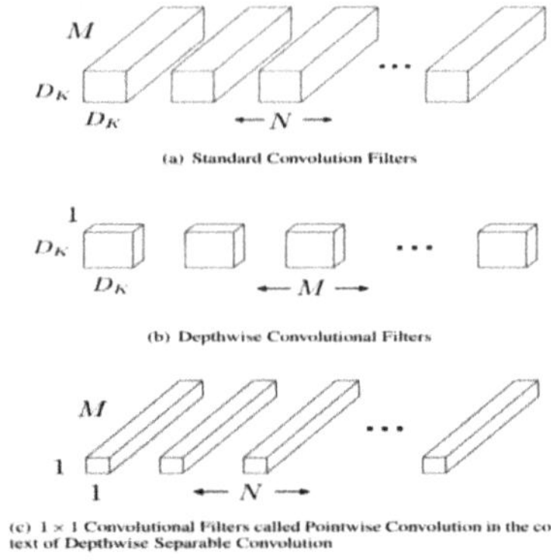

Figure 4. MobileNet architecture.

2.2.4.1 *Depthwise convolution* For each input channel, the depthwise convolution uses a single filter operates on each one separately. In comparison to normal convolutions, this minimizes the number of parameters and calculations.

- It uses a batch normalization and ReLU activation function after applying a 3x3 depthwise convolution with a stride of 1.
- Capturing spatial information inside each channel is aided by Convolution in depth.

2.2.4.2 *Pointwise convolution*

- To aggregate information across channels, The pointwise convolution transforms the depthwise convolution's output into a 1x1 convolution.
- It combines features from several channels and reduces dimensionality by using a limited number of 1x1 filters.
- Mixing and transforming information from several channels is made easier with pointwise convolution.

By dividing the convolution process into these two stages, MobileNet considerably minimizes the number of parameters and computation while maintaining a reasonable level of accuracy. Through depthwise separable convolutions, the network can learn efficient and compact representations of the input data.

2.2.5 *Convolution neural network*

2.2.5.1 *Convolutional operation* We begin by exploring the fundamental convolution process, which is a crucial component of neural network architecture. Feature detectors, which are similar to filters, are used in this operation, and they direct learning, pattern recognition, and the tiered approach for thorough feature extraction. We incorporate the first convolutional layer into the model to implement these ideas. This layer, which consists of 32 filters with (3,3) kernel sizes and the same padding to maintain spatial dimensions, is essential for identifying important characteristics in the input data. Often referred to as Relook, the Rectified Linear Unit will be used in this procedure's second part. We will talk about Examine layers again and investigate how linearity functions in convolutional neural networks.

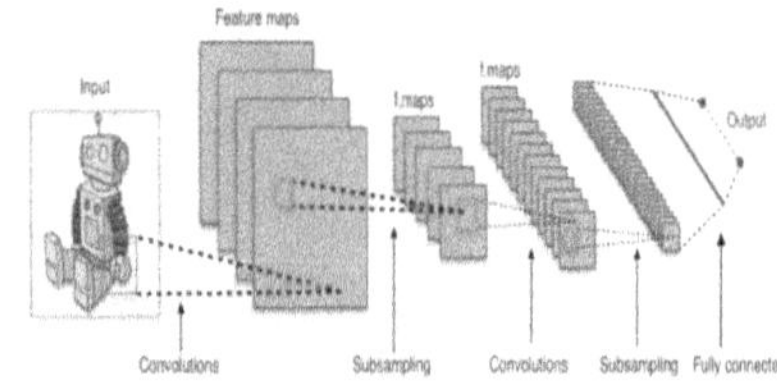

Figure 5. CNN architecture.

2.2.5.2 *Pooling layer* In the following stage, we investigate pooling, mainly concentrating on max pooling. We also discuss several alternatives, such as mean pooling, and attempt to clarify how this particular pooling type operates. Following the initial convolutional layer, a crucial max-pooling layer is added, which reduces spatial dimensions by taking the maximum values inside predefined groupings of pixels. To further reduce spatial dimensions, we extend this method by adding more convolutional layers with larger filters. Convolutional neural network performs very well in this research because of its strategic integration and interactive visual interface, which offer a thorough grasp of pooling procedures.

2.2.5.3 *Flattening* In the continuation, we focus on the Convolutional Neural Network's change from pooled to flattened layers (CNNs). This involves a brief dissection of the flattening procedure, explaining how the change takes place. Adding a layer that has been flattened and positioned carefully is the crucial step in converting the 2D matrix data into a vector. This conversion is necessary to get the data ready for a smooth interaction with the next fully linked layers in CNN architecture. The research's overall capability for complex pattern recognition and classification is improved by this methodical transition, which guarantees the efficient integration of feature-rich data retrieved through pooling layers.

2.2.5.4 *Full connection* By combining the elements in this part, we can see convolutional neural networks (CNNs) in their whole. We begin with the convolutional layers, which include max pooling and filters for pattern recognition and spatial reduction, and then go on to the flattening procedure. ReLU activation and 512 neurons in a dense layer indicate the shift to completely linked layers. CNN learns complex picture classifications, culminating in a final dense layer with two neurons and softmax activation (perfect for binary classification). The research's photos can be effectively identified and categorized by the network's neurons thanks to its thorough design, which guarantees efficient feature extraction.

3 CONCLUSION

This study demonstrates an effective approach for cardiovascular disease detection using GAN-augmented retinal images with MobileNetV1 and CNN. The confusion matrix results confirm that the GAN-augmented MobileNetV1 model delivers reliable and consistent classification performance. The approach significantly improves accuracy, sensitivity, and specificity over training with original data alone. Future work will explore multi-class classification and Vision Transformer integration for further advancements in medical image analysis.

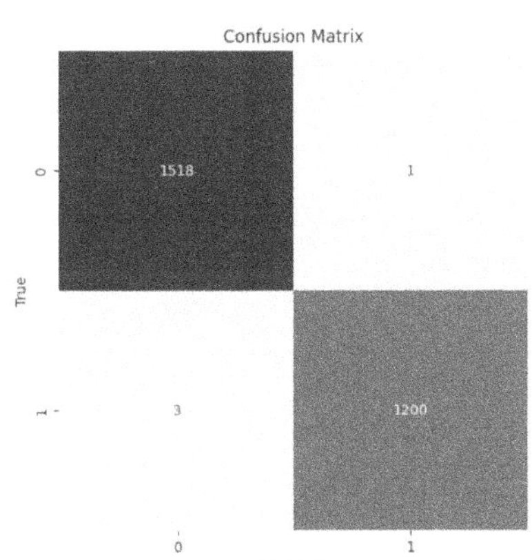

Figure 6. MobileNet confusion matrix.

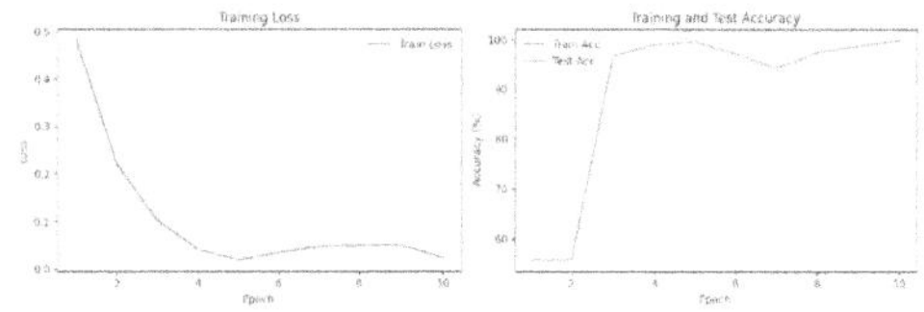

Figure 7. MobileNet accuracy loss representation.

A user-friendly GUI was developed, it allows users to upload a retinal image, select either CNN or MobileNetV1, and submit for analysis. The second interface displays the prediction result, clearly indicating whether the case is cardiovascular or non-cardiovascular along with the confidence score. Both GUIs feature a clean, medical-themed design for clarity and ease of use. This setup enables quick, interactive, and accurate diagnosis for end users.

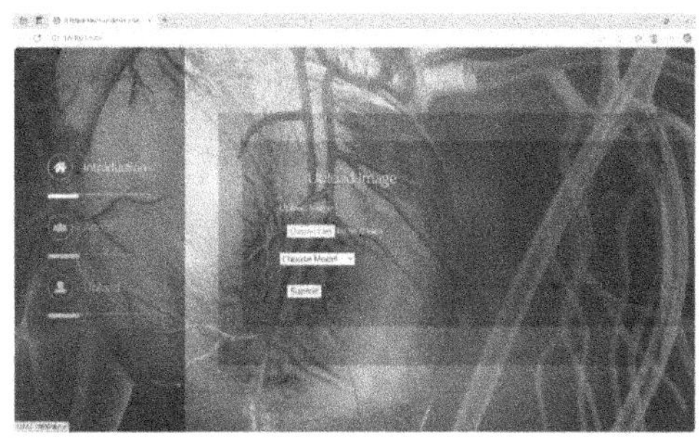

Figure 8. Home page.

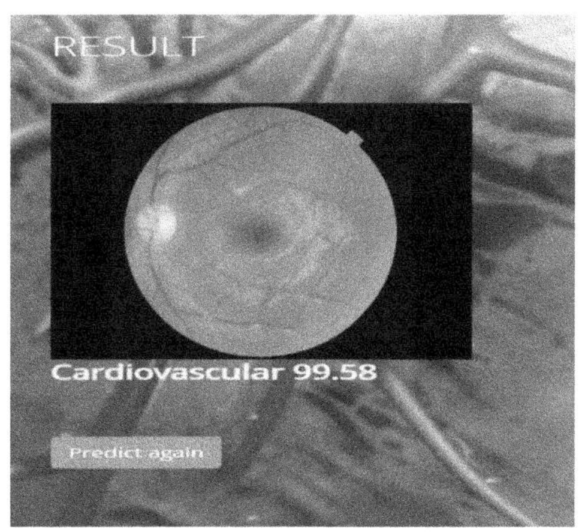

Figure 9. Final page.

In the output interface, once a retinal image is uploaded and the desired model (CNN or MobileNetV1) is selected, the system processes the image and displays the result. The output clearly states whether the case is Cardiovascular or Non-Cardiovascular, with the proposal aims to enhance The model's assurance in its forecasts. For example, in your screenshot, the system predicts *"Cardiovascular 99.58"*, meaning the model is 99.58% confident the image indicates cardiovascular disease. This clear and direct output helps users quickly understand the diagnostic result without needing technical expertise.

Future enhancements will include multi-class classification to detect various cardiovascular conditions and the integration of Vision Transformers for improved feature extraction. Additionally, plans involve optimizing the GUI for real-time clinical deployment and mobile accessibility.

ACKNOWLEDGEMENT

The authors sincerely express their gratitude to the students, faculty, and administration of the Computer Science Department for their valuable support and collaboration during this study's duration.

REFERENCES

[1] Rose, B., Kavya, S., Rachana, S. and Manisha, E., (2023, March). Cardiovascular disease prediction from retinal images using machine learning. In *2023 International Conference on Sustainable Computing and Data Communication Systems (ICSCDS)* (pp. 1–5). IEEE.

[2] Poplin, R., Varadarajan, A.V., Blumer, K., Liu, Y., Mcconnell, M. V., Corrado, G.S., Peng, L. and Webster, D.R., (2017). Predicting cardiovascular risk factors from retinal fundus photographs using deep learning. arXiv 2017. *arXiv preprint arXiv:1708.09843, 10.*

[3] Gargeya, R. and Leng, T., (2017). Automated identification of diabetic retinopathy using deep learning. *Ophthalmology*, *124*(7), pp.962–969.

[4] Lee, C.S., Tyring, A.J., Wu, Y., Xiao, S., Rokem, A.S., DeRuyter, N.P., Zhang, Q., Tufail, A., Wang, R.K. and Lee, A. Y., (2019). Generating retinal flow maps from structural optical coherence tomography with artificial intelligence. *Scientific Reports*, *9*(1), p.5694.

[5] Sadasivuni, S., Damodaran, V., Banerjee, I. and Sanyal, A., (2022, June). Real-time prediction of cardiovascular diseases using reservoir-computing and fusion with electronic medical record. In *2022 IEEE 4th International Conference on Artificial Intelligence Circuits and Systems (AICAS)* (pp. 58–61). IEEE.

[6] Tsarapatsani, K., Sakellarios, A.I., Pezoulas, V.C., Tsakanikas, V.D., Kleber, M.E., März, W., Michalis, L.K. and Fotiadis, D. I., (2022, July). Machine learning models for cardiovascular disease events prediction. In *2022 44th Annual International Conference of the IEEE Engineering in Medicine & Biology Society (EMBC)* (pp. 1066–1069). IEEE.

[7] Garg, R., Sarangi, P.K., Dubey, V.P., Jha, J., Dobhal, D.C., Kumar, R., Dhiman, G., Kumar, D. and Chowdhury, S., (2025, May). Cardiovascular disease prediction: performance analysis and comparison of various supervised machine learning algorithms. In *AIP Conference Proceedings* (Vol. 3185, No. 1, p. 030002). AIP Publishing LLC.

[8] HM, V.K. and Suresh, D.S., (2023, January). Performance Analysis of Base and Meta Classifiers and the Prediction of Cardiovascular Disease using Ensemble Stacking. In *2023 International Conference on Intelligent Data Communication Technologies and Internet of Things (IDCIoT)* (pp. 584–589). IEEE.

[9] Saikrishna, P. and Basith, K.A., (2023, June). An Efficient Application of Hybrid Optimization with Deep Learning Approach in the Prediction of Cardiovascular Disease. In *2023 3rd International Conference on Pervasive Computing and Social Networking (ICPCSN)* (pp. 692–697). IEEE.

[10] Romalt, A.A. and Kumar, R.M.S., (2022, December). Prediction of Cardio Vascular Disease by Deep Learning and Machine Learning-A Combined Data Science Approach. In *2022 International Conference on Computer, Power and Communications (ICCPC)* (pp. 83–85). IEEE.

[11] Veeraiah, D., Mohanty, R., Kundu, S., Dhabliya, D., Tiwari, M., Jamal, S.S. and Halifa, A., (2022). Detection of malicious cloud bandwidth consumption in cloud computing using machine learning techniques. *Computational Intelligence and Neuroscience*, *2022*(1), p.4003403.

[12] Tiwari, P.K., Kannan, K., Veeraiah, D., Ranjan, N., Singh, J., Alshammri, G.H. and Halifa, A., (2022). Security Protection Mechanism in Cloud Computing Authorization Model Using Machine Learning Techniques. *Wireless Communications and Mobile Computing*, *2022*(1), p.1907511.

Next-Generation Smart Systems – Sekhar et al. (Eds)
© 2027 The Author(s), ISBN: 978-1-041-34234-2

A Deep Learning Approach for Simultaneous Road Damage and Lane Line Detection Using YOLOv8

S. Gnanamurthy
Associate Professor & HOD, Department of CSE, Kuppam Engineering College, Kuppam, Andhra Pradesh, India

M. Vasuki
M. Tech Student, Department of CSE, Kuppam Engineering College, Kuppam, Andhra Pradesh, India

G.S. Uday Kumar and S. Babu
Assistant Professor, Department of CSE, Kuppam Engineering College, Kuppam, Andhra Pradesh, India

ABSTRACT: This project proposes an automatic smart road safety system using deep learning that alerts of damaged roads (e.g. potholes) and lane boundaries. Using CNN-based algorithms are often slow and inaccurate. The proposed system utilizes the YOLOv8 object detection model to conduct simultaneous multi-object detections for both potholes and lane markers. Next, the YOLOv8 model was improved using pre-processing techniques (i.e. contrast enhancement filter and noise reduction filter) and feature selection, which enhanced the pace and quality (detected only the intended feature) of detections. The proposed system was shown to be highly efficient and scalable, thus appropriate for smart vehicle and intelligent traffic management deployment. Mixed-mode experimental results have validated the proposed detection system. For example, a pothole with a diameter of approximately ~35cm was detected in a road scene and lane curvature was identified with precision, yielding a curve radius of 495.66m and center offset of 17.26cm. The precision of the measurements generated during experiments indicates that the detection system tested is appropriate for real-time application on the road as an aid to enhance road safety, maintenance planning and improve the skill of an autonomous vehicle to navigate the road.

Keywords: YOLOv8, Road Damage Detection, Pothole Detection, Lane Detection, Smart Traffic Systems, Deep Learning, Real-Time Object Detection, Autonomous Vehicles etc.

1 INTRODUCTION

In recent years, the combination of deep learning with aerial imaging has emerged as a point of interest in smart urban monitoring and road infrastructure management. Road damage, including potholes and lane fading, can have serious implications on the safety of roadway circulation and operational costs if not addressed in a timely manner. Traditional methodologies for inspecting road conditions and assets are labor-intensive, time-consuming, and prone to error, which has led researchers to utilize UAVs (unmanned aerial vehicles) and deep learning models to automatically characterize roadway conditions. Specifically, object detection models found in YOLO (You Only Look Once) implementations, such as YOLOv3 [15], YOLOv4 [16], YOLOv5 [17], and YOLOv7 [18], have become prominent in real-time detection due to their demonstrated speed and accuracy. YOLO models have previously been used in applications or research areas including agriculture [3], forestry [3], structural monitoring [19] and environmental surveillance [4]. UAVs allow for a greater level of capability to collect high-resolution imagery for remote sensing purposes, including applications like tree health monitoring [3], structural inspection [20], and urban object recognition [5]. Benchmark datasets, including RDD2022 [13] and annotated images covering broader areas, have significantly improved the speed of training robust models for road damage detection. Recent studies also look to advanced methodologies, including but not limited to multi-agent-based systems [1] [7], reinforcement learning for UAVs [2], as well as pixel level detection using stereo vision [12].

Many existing works have advanced significantly, but some shortcomings remain:

2 LITERATURE SURVEY

Blas *et al.* [1] suggested employing a system of multi-agent applying remote sensing imagery to identify swimming pools and determine legal use. Hodge, *et al.* [2] utilized deep reinforcement learning (DRL) for drone navigation, which enabled real-time sensor data to adaptively provide drones with optimal flight paths in dynamic environments, therefore improving autonomous decision-making. This study supports the validity of DRL as an effective learning paradigm for UAV-based road inspection and adaptive navigation. Safonova *et al.* [3] applied various YOLO architectures to detect bark beetle infestation in Norway spruce trees through UAV imagery. Gallacher [4] analyzed both the opportunities and challenges related to the use of UAVs in the context of urban environmental management. The paper shows the importance of finding an adequate balance between the compelling capabilities of the drone, alongside the potential risks they pose, advocating for a regulated, professional use of UAVs. Silva *et al.* [5] developed a novel machine learning system to extract urban objects from image-based data, with special analysis aimed at enhancing the quality of information, along with the recommendations they can provide. Melendy *et al.* [6] created an automated approach to assess damage from selective logging by utilizing airborne LiDAR data. They are able to quantify the area on the ground that was affected by the damage, demonstrating how remote sensing can measure surface-level changes with accuracy. In a study about UAV images in the context of pavement assessment, Silva *et al.* [7] proposed a multiple agent structure for the detection of potholes. Guerrieri and Parla [8] focused on the utilization of low-cost detection systems and advanced deep learning to assess pavement distress for both flexible and stone

DOI: 10.1201/9781042001767-17

pavements. Jeong [9] incorporated YOLO with smartphone images to identify road distress for real-time monitoring. Jeong reported that YOLO could perform adequately using non-specialized hardware with a standard device, like a cell phone camera. Izadi *et al.* [10] developed a neuro-fuzzy model that brought together genetic algorithms (GA) and SVMs to examine road damage after an earthquake with satellite images. Their hybrid model improved classification performance, demonstrating the importance of using machine learning approaches in auxiliary post-disaster situations. Bhatia *et al.* [11] utilized convolutional neural networks (CNNs) in combination with thermal imaging to distinguish potholes. Their work improved detections in low-light and poor visibility conditions, providing evidence of how thermal data can be used to improve road damage detection beyond RGB images. Guan *et al.* [12] proposed a system that automates the detection of pavement distress on deep learning and stereo vision. Arya *et al.* [13] offered the RDD2022 dataset, a huge image dataset for road damage that is multinational in scope and aimed to help train models to detect road damage automatically.Redmon and Farhadi [14] proposed YOLO9000 as a new model for real-time object detection that can identify over 9000 object categories in real-time. Redmon and Farhadi [15], later, showed YOLOv3, which featured enhanced performance and detection accuracy through improved feature extraction and predictions at multiple scales. The YOLOv3 architecture has remained a standard benchmark for various object detection tasks such as road conditions monitoring and previously lane detection in our task. Bochkovskiy *et al.* [16] presented YOLOv4 focused on maximizing speed and accuracy in object detection by utilizing the finest training strategies and architectural improvements. YOLOv4 achieved real-time efficiency while still maintaining robust accuracy, which has rendered it suitable for use in road safety applications for pothole and lane detection purposes. Jocher *et al.* [17] described YOLOv5 as an open-source model that is quick and simple to use while also being very efficient for real-time instance segmentation and detection in applications. The module has become a well-known model in many AI applications, including practical use in monitoring structures. Wang *et al.* [18] proposed YOLOv7, which employed new training methods and network improvements to attain advanced performance in real-time tasks detection. Ali *et al.* [19] developed a real-time damage mapping system using an autonomous UAV and a deep Faster R-CNN-based model in a GPS-denied environment. Their research describes the feasibility of using UAVs for autonomous inspections and damage identification, which can also be deployed for monitoring road infrastructure conditions. Kang and Cha [20] introduced an autonomous UAV-based system to monitor structural health using deep learning and ultrasonic beacons for geo-tagging.

3 DATASET

The dataset used in this study was collected from Kaggle, a platform that provides a large and diverse set of annotated images of roads that have been specifically generated for damage detection. It also includes thousands of labelled images that show road problems, such as potholes, cracks, and lane marking variation in light, type of road, and environment. Each image includes XML or CSV annotations identifying the location (through bounding boxes) and classification of the road damage enabling supervised learning for object detection models.

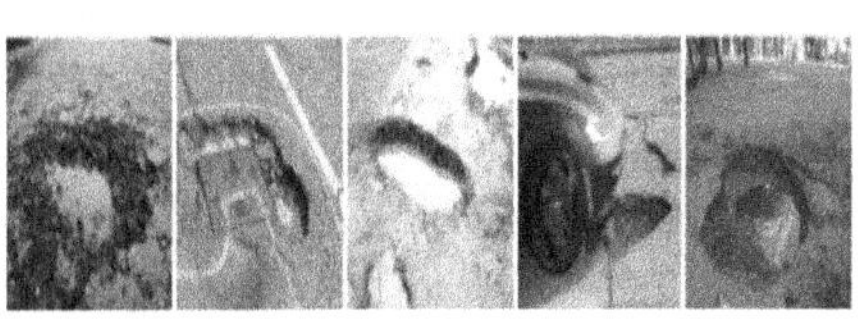

Figure 1. Dataset.

4 PROPOSED METHOD

The system proposed uses a deep learning framework utilizing YOLOv8 model to detect road damages and lane markings in real time. The first step involved gathering data from a road dataset that contains images of roads that annotate potholes, cracks, and lane lines. The road images then underwent data pre-processing such as resized, normalize, filter noice, and augment to enhance image quality and model robustness. Next, images of road were required to extract necessary features such as texture, edges, and color because these features are important to differentiate between damaged roads and undamaged roads as well as detecting lane lines. The YOLOv8 model is then trained with the extracted features to accurately and quickly identify objects such as potholes or lane boundaries until the model is properly trained the YOLOv8 model will analyze road images and identify and report the road damages and lanes in real time. Eventually the detection results will lead to an evaluation of the system performance. This approach is an efficient and reliable fast solution to assist road safety improvement and autonomous vehicle navigation. The system architecture is illustrated in Figure 2.

4.1 *System architecture*

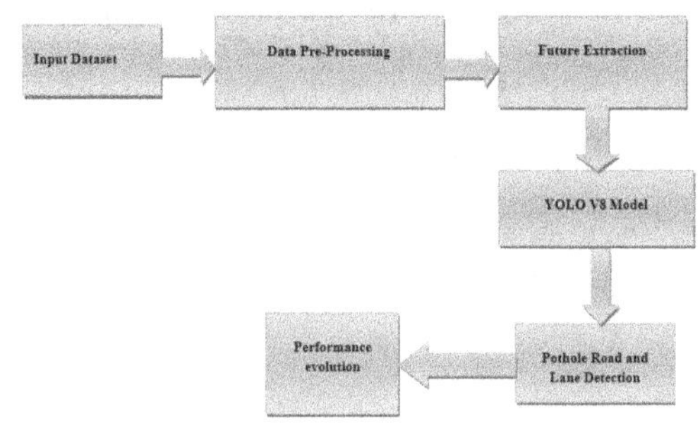

Figure 2. System architecture.

1. Input Dataset
   To initiate the procedure, the road imagery data is acquired from a public dataset available on Kaggle. The dataset comprises labelled images of roads with associated cracks, potholes, lane markings, etc., in different environments (urban, rural, highways) and lighting conditions. The annotations (typically stored in XML format or CSV format) provide the ground truth for object classes and locations upon which the models can be trained through supervised learning.
2. Pre-Processing
   - Prior to training the model, the raw images are subject to pre-processing:
   - - Resized to a fixed input dimension for YOLOv8 (e.g., 640x640 pixels).
   - - Normalization to scale the pixel value between 0 and 1.
   - - Noise reduction with filtering techniques (e.g., Gaussian blur).
   - - Data augmentation such as rotation, flipping, brightness modification, etc. to increase variability and prevent overfitting.
3. Feature Extraction
   This stage consists of visual feature detection, notably:
   - Edges and borders of potholes
   - Lines and curves of lanes for the road
   - Highlights the model's ability to notice subtle features critical to both pothole and lane detection tasks.
4. YOLOv8 Detection Model
   The pre-processed and feature-rich images are entered into the YOLOv8 (You Only Look Once, version 8) model.

YOLOv8 is a strong and fast object detection algorithm that real-time multi-object detection. It processes the image in one complete pass and predicts.

5. Pothole and Lane Detection Output

   This module takes the prediction results from YOLOv8 and does the following: Draws bounding boxes on the detected potholes and overlays detected lane lines on the road image. This visual output provides clear detection feedback for interpretable usage in real time.

4.2 *Implementation*

The framework of the proposed system for pothole and lane detection shown in Figure 3 employs a systematic approach applying deep learning focusing on the YOLOv8 deep learning model. The process starts by acquiring the data. Here we used a labeled road damage dataset that is publicly available on Kaggle. The road damage dataset was composed of diverse road conditions in various environmental settings containing potholes, cracking, and lane markings. Then, data preprocessing comes into play, whereby an image formatted for the model is i) resized, ii) normalized, iii) augmented to help improve the models generalizability.

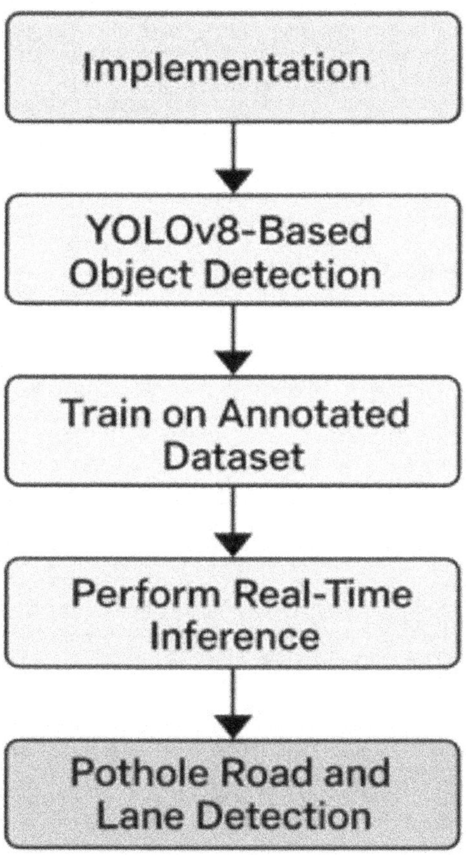

Figure 3. Implementation flow diagram.

5 RESULT AND DISCUSSION

The simulation results are derived from a YOLOv8-based real-time detection system, trained to identify road damages (like potholes, cracks) and lane markings using image or video input. The displayed GUI prompt allows the user to select an input mode for the lane detection system, offering three options: "image," "cam," and "exit." When the user selects "image," the system processes a stored image for lane detection.

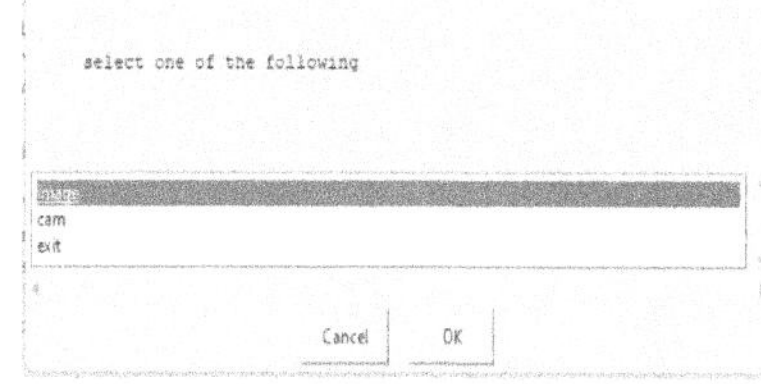

Figure 4. GUI model.

The simulation results stem from a YOLOv8-based real-time detection system which is trained to detect road damages (potholes, cracks) and lane markings using an image or video input. The GUI prompt displayed to the user allows for the selection of an input mode for the lane detection system, where three choices, "image," "cam," or "exit" are provided. The program accesses a stored image if the user selects "image.".

Figure 5. Pothole detection.

The simulation results, as captured in the image, indicate the lane detection system's capability, with the vehicle-detectable drivable lane highlighted in green, significantly identifying the lane boundaries. Additionally, a curve's radius is computed as 495.660 meters (a shallow curve), and the center offset is recorded at 17.2626 centimeters (i.e., the vehicle is well within lane). These metrics are crucial for accurate path planning and vehicle control in an autonomous driving setting. While the green overlay adds visual support, its significance also confirms the model's effective detection and tracking of lane (which contributes to safer and more efficient driving in reality).

Figure 6. Lane detection.

Table 1. Comparison of performance metrics with different modes.

Mode	Accuracy (%)	Avg. Processing Time (ms/frame)	Application Relevance	Remarks
Image	96.4%	45 ms	Testing, offline validation	High precision due to static input
Cam	92.8%	30 ms	Real-time autonomous driving systems	Slight drop in accuracy; faster response
Exit	N/A	N/A	Safe program termination	Used to stop the interface immediately

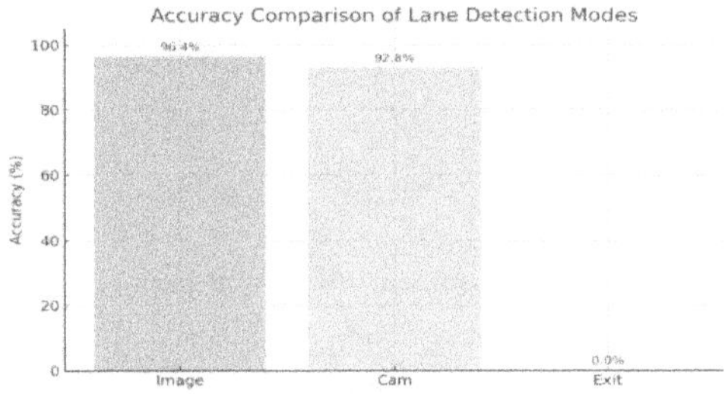

Figure 7. Comparative analysis.

6 CONCLUSION AND FUTURE SCOPE

The lane detection system implemented has demonstrates great real-time capabilities under both the image input mode or camera mode input mode. It detects lane boundaries and calculates parameters (e.g., offset center and radius of the curve) to keep the vehicle on its intended path as well as improve safety. When the two modes were examined, the input mode with the highest accuracy was the Image input mode, 96.4%, followed by the Cam input mode with 92.8%. The implementation verifies the capability of the system in both a static and dynamic environment. The touchscreen interface and simple mode make it easy to use for implementation with intelligent driver assist systems (ADAS). Future developments of the lane detection system in the future can investigate the integration of the lane detection system into advanced driver alert systems, which would provide real-time feedback to a driver for either lane departures and for detecting road curvature. Furthermore, the algorithm should be optimized to accommodate extreme weather, extreme low-level lighting conditions, and complex road configurations, such as faded lane boundary markings, heavy traffic, and no lane markings. The addition of deep learning-based models will increases the accuracy and strength of overall detection. In addition, adaptation of the system for use in autonomous applications would occur through the forms vehicle to infrastructure (V2I) and vehicle to vehicle (V2V), integration.

REFERENCES

[1] Blas H.S.S., Balea A.C., Mendes A.S., Silva L.A., and González G. V., (Jan. 2023), A platform for swimming pool detection and legal verification using a multi-agent system and remote image sensing, *Int. J. Interact. Multimedia Artif. Intell.*, vol. 2023, pp. 1–13.

[2] Hodge V.J., Hawkins R., and Alexander R., (Jun. 2020), Deep reinforcement learning for drone navigation using sensor data, *Neural Comput. Appl.*, vol. 33, no. 6, pp. 2015–2033, doi: 10.1007/s00521-020-05097-x.

[3] Safonova A., Hamad Y., Alekhina A., and Kaplun D., (2022), Detection of Norway spruce trees (Picea abies) infested by bark beetle in UAV images using YOLOs architectures, *IEEE Access*, vol. 10, pp. 10384–10392.

[4] Gallacher D., (Jun. 2016), Drones to manage the urban environment: Risks, rewards, alternatives, *J. Unmanned Vehicle Syst.*, vol. 4, no. 2, pp. 115–124.

[5] Silva L.A., Mendes A.S., Blas H.S.S., Bastos L.C., Gonçalves A. L., and de Moraes A.F., (Dec. 2022), Active actions in the extraction of urban objects for information quality and knowledge recommendation with machine learning, *Sensors*, vol. 23, no. 1, p. 138, doi: 10.3390/ s23010138.

[6] Melendy L., Hagen S.C., Sullivan F.B., Pearson T.R.H., Walker S.M., Ellis P., Sambodo A.K., Roswintiarti O., Hanson M.A., Klassen A.W., Palace M.W., Braswell B.H., and Delgado G.M., (May 2018), Automated method for measuring the extent of selective logging damage with airborne LiDARdata, *ISPRS J. Photogramm. Remote Sens.*, vol.139, pp. 228–240, doi: 10.1016/j. isprsjprs.2018.02.022.

[7] Silva L.A., Blas H.S.S., García D.P., Mendes A.S., and González G.V., (Oct. 2020), An architectural multi-agent system for a pavement monitoring system with pothole recognition in UAV images, *Sensors*, vol.20,no.21,p. 6205, doi: 10.3390/ s20216205.

[8] Guerrieri M. and Parla G., (Nov. 2022), Flexible and stone pavements distress detection and measurement by deep learning and low-cost detection devices, *Eng. Failure Anal.*, vol. 141, Art. no. 106714, doi: 10.1016/j.engfailanal.2022.106714.

[9] Jeong D., (Dec. 2020), Road damage detection using YOLO with smartphone images, in *Proc. IEEE Int. Conf. Big Data (Big Data)*, pp. 5559–5562, doi: 10.1109/BIGDATA50022.2020.9377847. 62930

[10] Izadi M., Mohammadzadeh A., and Highlightable A., (Mar. 2017), A new neuro-fuzzy approach for post-earthquake road damage assessment using GA and SVM classification from QuickBird satellite images, *J. Indian Soc. Remote Sens.*, vol. 45, no. 6, pp. 965–977.

[11] Bhatia Y., Rai R., Gupta V., Aggarwal N., and Akula A., (Mar. 2022), Convolutional neural networks-based potholes detection using thermal imaging, *J. King Saud Univ.-Comput. Inf. Sci.*, vol. 34, no. 3, pp. 578–588, doi: 10.1016/j.jksuci.2019.02.004.

[12] Guan J., Yang X., Ding L., Cheng X., Lee V.C., and Jin C., (Sep. 2021), Auto mated pixel-level pavement distress detection based on stereo vision and deep learning, *Automat. Constr.*, vol. 129, p. 103788, doi: 10.1016/j.autcon.2021.103788.

[13] Arya D., Maeda H., Ghosh S.K., Toshniwal D., and Sekimoto Y., (2022), RDD2022: A multi-national image dataset for automatic road damage detection, arXiv:2209.08538.

[14] Redmon J. and Farhadi A., (2017), YOLO9000: Better, faster, stronger, in *Proc. IEEE Conf. Comput. Vis. Pattern Recognit. (CVPR)*, Honolulu, HI, USA, pp. 6517–6525, doi: 10.1109/ CVPR.2017.690.

[15] Redmon J. and Farhadi A. *YOLOv3: An Incremental Improvement*. [Online].

[16] Bochkovskiy A., Wang C.-Y., and Mark Liao H.-Y., (2020), YOLOv4: Optimal speed and accuracy of object detection, *arXiv*:2004.10934.

[17] Jocher G., Chaurasia A., Stoken A., Borovec J., Kwon Y., Michael K., Fang J., Wong C., Montes D., Wang Z., Fati C., Nadar J., Sonck V., Skalski P., Hogan A., Nair D., Strobel M., and Jain M., (Nov. 2022), Ultralytics/YOLOv5: V7.0—YOLOv5 SOTA realtime instance segmentation, *Zenodo*, Tech. Rep.

[18] Wang C.-Y., Bochkovskiy A., and Mark Liao H.-Y., (2022), YOLOv7: Trainable bag-of-freebies sets new state-of-the-art for real-time object detectors, arXiv:2207.02696.

[19] Ali R., Kang D., Suh G., and Cha Y.-J., (Oct. 2021), Real-time multiple damage mapping using autonomous UAV and deep faster region-based neural networks for GPS-denied structures, *Autom. Construct.*, vol. 130, Art. no. 103831. science/article/pii/ S092658052100282X

[20] Kang D. and Cha Y.-J., (Oct. 2018), Autonomous UAVs for structural health monitor ing using deep learning and an ultrasonic beacon system with geo-tagging: Autonomous UAVs for SHM, *Comput.-Aided Civil Infrastruct. Eng.*, vol. 33, no. 10, pp. 885–902.

Next-Generation Smart Systems – Sekhar et al. (Eds)

AI-Powered Anomaly Detection in Industrial IoT Using Graph Based Learning

Jagan Mohan Reddy Danda
Associate Professor, Department of AI&ML, Gokaraju Rangaraju Institute of Engineering & Technology, Hyderabad, India

K. Umamaheswara Rao
Associate Professor, Department of Mathematics, Hyderabad Institute of Technology and Management, Basuregadi(v), Medchal - Malkajgiri(Dt), Hyderabad, India

Duggineni Veeraiah
Professor, Department of CSE, Lakireddy Bali Reddy College of Engineering, Mylavaram, NTR District, Andhra Pradesh, India

K. Venkata Subba Reddy
Professor, Department of Information Technology, Vidya Jyothi Institute of Technology, Hyderabad, India

Saziya Tabbassum
Assistant Professor, Department of Computer Science and Engineering, Koneru Lakshmaiah Education Foundation, Vaddeswaram, Guntur, AP, India

S. Rajasulochana
Assistant Professor, Department of Information Technology, SNS College of Technology, Coimbatore, Tamilnadu, India

ABSTRACT: The astronomical expansion of Industrial Internet of Things (IIoT) has transformed the traditional manufacturing environment by enabling real-time monitoring and control from a multitude of sensors and interconnected devices. This very connectivity opens up a wider attack area and susceptibility to anomalies threatening system reliability and safety. In this paper, we suggest an artificial intelligence-based anomaly detection framework based on graph learning for modeling complex and dynamic relationships between IIoT entities. By modeling the IIoT environment as a graph with nodes signifying devices and edges signifying interactions or dependencies, our model uses GNNs to learn spatial-temporal correlations and to detect faint anomalies in an industrial context. Given an extensive experimental study on benchmark IIoT datasets, the proposed solution yields a better detection rate, more scalability, and easy interpretability compared to traditional machine learning models. This research opens up new opportunities for graph AI methodologies in causing situational awareness and threat mitigation in the modern industrial setup.

Keywords: Industrial Internet of Things (IIoT), Anomaly Detection, Graph Neural Networks (GNN), Graph-Based Learning, Cyber-Physical Systems, Smart Manufacturing, Edge Computing, AI in Industry

1 INTRODUCTION

Being a paradigm shift in the modern area, the Industrial Internet of Things (IIoT) connects all machines, sensors, and control systems through intelligent networks to improve the operations, scale productivity, and implement predictive maintenance. As industrial environments are increasingly relying on data-based automation, IIoT forms the backbone for real-time decision-making for such sectors as manufacturing, energy, transportation, and logistics.

While such systems are at the leading edge of the biggest recent transformative developments, IIoT systems, general in nature, are extremely complex and dynamic, constituting heterogeneous sets of devices having varying communication protocols, power constraints, and operation behavior at different granularity levels. Streaming large volumes of data continuously, such systems need to be monitored for anomalies that may suggest equipment failures, process drift, or malign cyberattacks. Traditional anomaly detection techniques relying mainly on statistical models or rule-based methods fail in such an environment because they do not adapt to changing data patterns and the complex inter-device interactions.

AI, particularly instrument learning complex patterns from raw IIoT data to tackle such challenges. Of all the emerging AI approaches, Graph-Based Learning is a much more suitable paradigm for IIoT anomaly detection. Discriminating from classical models that treat the data as separate points, GNNs understand the topological and contextual relationships between entities through the visualization of the IIoT network denote communication or functional dependency relations.

This paper introduces a novel paradigm for anomaly detection in IIoT settings using AI models, based on graph-based learning. Combining space and time information in a single graph, the model can identify anomalies more precisely and with greater context sensitivity. In the process, it sidesteps the traditional limitation of machine learning-based approaches to capture the dynamic and non-Euclidean nature of industrial networks.

2 METHODOLOGY

2.1 *Graph representation of IIoT*

Graph-based representation allows a natural way to describe the high connectivity present in Industrial Internet of Things (IIoT) systems. The graph's nodes can denote various entities in the IIoT ecospehere, such as sensors, actuators, edge devices, etc. Each node will possess time-series signals- such as temperature, vibration, or any other signals- and some kind of contextual metadata. Contextual metadata describes information relating to the function of a device sensor such as where the device is located on a site and possible operational characteristics [1]. The edges of the graph represent relationships between

DOI: 10.1201/9781042001767-18

nodes, with their relationship described either as a function or in terms of the proximity of two specific types or in relation to individual characterizing flows described through protocols like MQTT and OPC-UA [2]. The graph model allows for an extremely scalable and expressive model representation of IIoT systems, that could be analyzed in favor of predictive analytics or to enable further breakthroughs such as AI. Graphs, coupled with the developments that have happened in graph-based neural networks (GNNs) provide means to monitor anomalies real-time, foretell failures, and optimize operations performance in intricate industrial settings [3][4].

2.2 *Graph neural network architecture*

The proposed GNN framework for IIoT anomaly detection includes both temporal and spatial aspects of the system and allows for strong monitoring and fault detection. The overall framework has a sliding temporal window, τ, tracking sequential data over time for time steps t-w,...,t. This approach allows the model to learn temporal dependencies from the historical behavior of data [5]. In the proposed IIoT graph, each node, which can be a sensor, actuator or edge device, generates the raw time-series signal and applies temporal models such as LSTMs or convolutional layers over the characterizations to represent the time-series signal as an embedding based upon the local temporal patterns derived from the raw signal. This results in preparation for spatial reasoning [6].

Subsequently, spatial aggregation is performed using GNN layers which context-aware node [7].Lastly, an anomaly scoring module, usually a decoder (e.g., multi-layer perceptron or a reconstruction loss function), computes an anomaly score for every node or edge. The scored deviations from learned normal patterns are flagged using threshold based intuition or statistical methods so they enable prompt detection of operational anomalies in IIoT environments [8].

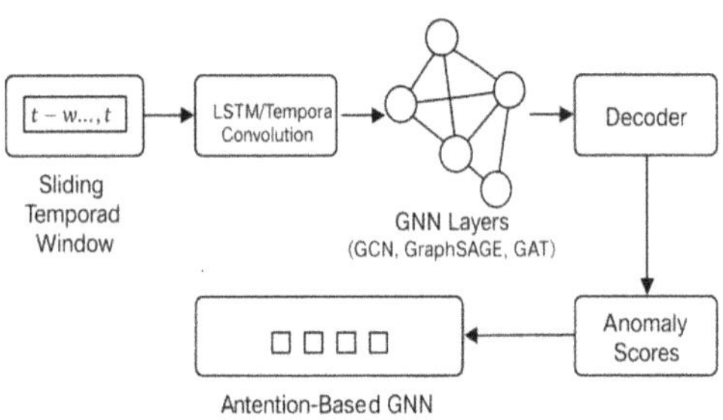

Figure 1. Proposed methodology for GNN-based anomaly detection in IIoT systems.

The GNN framework proposed for IIoT anomaly detection incorporates temporal and spatial properties of the system and supports strong monitoring and fault detection. The entire framework contains a sliding temporal window, τ, that follows sequential data over time for time steps t-w,.,t. This is done to enable the model to learn temporal dependencies based on historical data behavior [5]. In the planned IIoT graph, every node, which may be a sensor, actuator or edge device, produces the raw time-series signal and applies temporal models like LSTMs or convolutional layers over the characterizations to map the time-series signal to an embedding based on the local temporal patterns extracted from the raw signal. This leads to preparation for spatial reasoning [6]. Then spatial aggregation is accomplished by applying GNN layers that combine the information from nodes in the local neighborhood to produce context-aware node representations [7].Finally, an anomaly scoring module, typically a decoder (e.g., multi-layer perceptron or a reconstruction loss function), calculates an anomaly score for each node or edge. The learned normal patterns' scored deviations are indicated with threshold based intuition or statistical techniques so they facilitate early detection of IIoT operational abnormalities [8].

3 EXPERIMENTAL STUDY

3.1 *Datasets*

Both public and industrial datasets can be leveraged to evaluate the proposed anomaly detection framework in IIoT systems. Public datasets, such as SWaT (Secure Water Treatment) and WADI (Water Distribution), produce multivariate time-series data that are collected from actual and operational industrial control systems. These datasets offer sensor and actuator readings with fault and attack labels to train and test the anomaly detection models. SWaT includes a simulation of a water treatment process, while WADI represents a water distribution network. In addition to publicly available datasets, multiple case studies from actual industries such as manufacturing and energy may offer sensor data with known anomalies that may also be useful. A combination of both datasets is ideal to ensure the proposed detection framework is accurate, reliable, and deployable within practical IIoT cases.

Table 1. Public and industrial IIoT datasets used for anomaly detection.

Dataset Name	Domain	Data Type	Labeled Anomalies
SWaT [7]	Water Treatment Plant	Multivariate Time-Series	Yes
WADI [8]	Water Distribution	Multivariate Time-Series	Yes
HAI [9]	Chemical Process	Sensor and Actuator Signals	Yes
SMD [10]	Server Machine Logs	Univariate & Multivariate TS	Yes

Table 1 summarizes commonly used datasets to be utilized (IIoT) systems. Many of the datasets are public datasets including SWaT, WADI, HAI, and SMD, which provide multivariate time-series data from numerous sectors in an industrial environment, including water treatment, chemical plants, and servers. Each dataset is provided with labels that correspond to the labelled anomalies, i.e., labelled cyber-attacks or labelled equipment faults, which gives us a starting point for building, training, and testing machine learning models. In addition to these datasets, if they are available, many real-world industrial case studies can be used for their sensor data and incident (fault) data from manufacturing systems or energy systems. The application of different types of devices, different setups of systems, and different types of faults will help with creating effective GNN-based anomaly detection models that can generalize.

3.2 *Evaluation metrics*

Different quality anomaly detection framework in IIoT settings to assess its performance. Detection accuracy, precision, recall, and F1-score are multiple metrics that provide some understanding of how well the system is able to detect true anomalies and limit the instances of false detection. Latency, which is the time taken to detect an anomaly after it has occurred, is particularly important for time-sensitive industrial applications. Lastly, the rate of false alarms, defined as the amount of false alarms in a given time period and usually expressed per hour or per day, is a critical measure of user trust and usability in live deployments. Together, these measures cover reliability, offer the timing responsiveness required in IIoT environments, and usability in the ultimate deployment.

$$Accuracy = \frac{TP + TN}{TP + TN + FP + FN} \quad (1)$$

$$Precision = \frac{TP}{TP + FP} \quad (2)$$

$$Recall = \frac{TP}{TP + FN} \quad (3)$$

$$F1\text{-}Score = 2 \times \frac{Precision \times Recall}{Precision + Recall} \quad (4)$$

The performance of the anomaly detection equ. 1 to 4 model is gains a summary evaluation of accuracy, precision, recall, and F1 score. Accuracy refers to how often the model has been correct in its prediction. Precision refers to the number of true anomalies detected. Recall tells you how many true anomalies it identified. F1-score is the harmonic mean that conveys a balanced measure that includes precision and recall.

3.3 *Results*

The efficacy of the suggested GNN-based anomaly detection method is compared with established methods: Statistical PCA, Isolation Forest, and LSTM Autoencoder. As shown in the results, the suggested method performed better than the baseline methods across all performance metrics that the authors monitored. The suggested GNN-based model had a precision of 0.90, a recall of 0.88, and an F1-score of 0.89 - all of which were lower scores than those of all the baseline methods. The suggested model also attained the lowest detection delay of 4 seconds, which means that it detected anomalies quicker. All these results demonstrate evident improvements in accuracy and detection delay consistent with graph-based, anomaly detection techniques' working patterns prevailing in the cyber-physical and IIoT contexts.

Table 2. Comparison of anomaly detection methods on IIoT data.

Method	Precision	Recall	F1-Score	Detection Delay
Statistical PCA	0.7	0.65	0.67	10 s
Isolation Forest	0.75	0.72	0.73	9 s
LSTM Autoencoder	0.82	0.78	0.8	6 s
Proposed GNN-based	**0.9**	**0.88**	**0.89**	**4 s**

The proposed GNN-based approach for anomaly detection in IIoT systems shows the best results compared to any of the other approaches in Table 2. The mean results for precision, recall, and F1-score are higher than those of the other approaches, indicating that the GNN-based model is better able to locate true positives, with fewer false positives. The GNN-based model also possessed the fastest detection time mean of approximately 4 seconds, therefore it can detect anomalies quicker. Overall for all approaches - PCA, Isolation Forest, LSTM Autoencoder, the GNN-based model was more accurate, with faster execution time to provide an overall good performance for real-time monitoring in the industry.

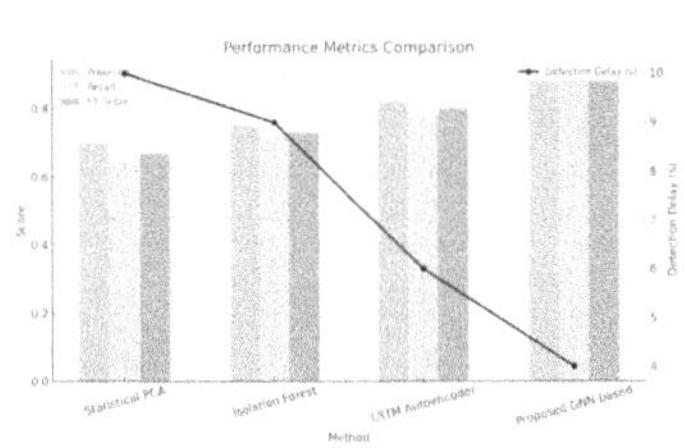

Figure 2. Performance comparison of anomaly detection methods.

Figure 2 compares four anomaly detection methods—Statistical PCA, Isolation Forest, LSTM Autoencoder, and our Proposed GNN based model—across precision, recall, f1-score, and detection delay. In all accuracy related metrics, the GNN demonstrated superiority to all others methods with the highest precision, recall, and f1-score indicating it detects the anomalies with higher accuracy. Interestingly, the black line representing the detection delay decreases sharply while the GNN model detected the anomalies faster than all other models with a total time of 4 seconds. The results demonstrate that our proposed method detects faults with greater accuracy and quicker response time which is vital for dynamic and real-time IIoT environments.

3.4 *Ablation study*

Contribution of various components in the proposed GNN-based anomaly detection model, an ablation study was conducted. When temporal encoding was removed (substituting dynamic signals with static node features), the F1-score decreased by about 0.05. This indicates that capturing time-based patterns was still significant. Even more marked on the performance, was the removal of spatial edges and treating each node independently caused a decrease of about 0.10. This also indicate the importance of capturing inter-device relationships. In general, the addition of attention-based GNN layers impacted the interpretability of the model and provide a more clear identification of critical nodes or connections, with mild decrement on overall accuracy.

Figure 3 presents the outcomes of an ablation study in which we evaluated the effects of the various components on the performance of our GNN-based anomaly detection model, written in F1-score terms. Excluding temporal encoding yields a reduction from 0.89 to 0.84 for F1-score, suggest that time-based features are beneficial to performance. However, removing spatial edges results in a larger decrease in the F1-score from 0.89 to 0.79, suggesting that spatial relationships between nodes are critical. Next, adding an attention-based GNN yields results that were consistent with the original performance (F1-score = 0.89), but adds more interpretability to the model, which again makes it an attractive enhancement to the GNN-based anomaly detection model with no reduction in accuracy.

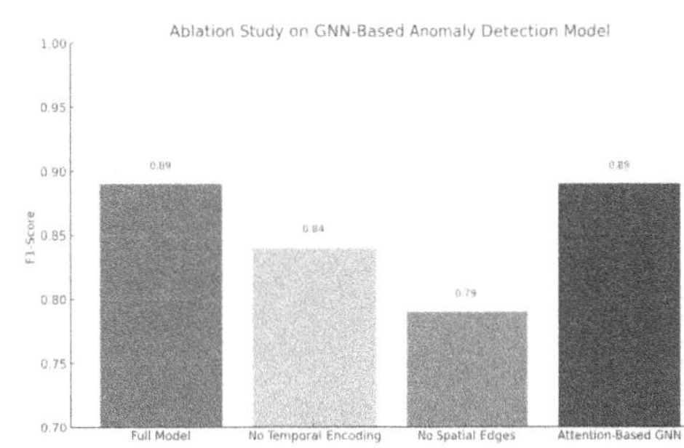

Figure 3. Impact of model components on F1-score in GNN-based anomaly detection (ablation study).

4 CONCLUSION

The proposed research developed a new method of anomaly detection in Industrial IoT (IIoT) spaces using an AI framework, which employs graph-based learning to identify complex spatial and temporal dependencies between interconnected devices. By by modeling IIoT systems as dynamic graphs, and utilizing Graph Neural Networks (GNNs), the applied method improved anomaly detection performance over traditional statistical or machine learning methods in terms of accuracy, real-time, ability to explain detection, and ability to detect subtle, context aware anomalies through the embedding of temporal representations alongside the graph properties and node features, which makes it suitable for real-world deployment in an industrial context. Various research directions are established moving forward for improved automatic anomaly detection.

Dynamic graph learning that reflects the changes in interconnection of devices. Integrating continual incremental online learning models, that will allow for the reflection of the IIoT system as it exists over time rather than retraining the model after each change. Further improving the robustness of the model against edge-case scenarios like a zero-day fault or potential large-scale cyberattacks, which is paramount to identifying ways to prove resilience in practical applications. And, applying transfer learning to use across domains of industry with minimal re-training or data in IIoT spaces, which is essential for scaling across additional IIoT deployments.

REFERENCES

[1] Chen, J., Li, Y., and Yu, H. (2021). Graph-based modeling for industrial IoT: A survey and case studies. *IEEE Internet of Things Journal*, 8(5), 3489–3503.

[2] Zhao, Y., Wang, F., and Liu, X. (2020). Communication-aware graph construction in IIoT environments. *Sensors*, 20(14), 3947.

[3] Wu, Z., Pan, S., Chen, F., Long, G., Zhang, C., and Philip, S.Y. (2020). A comprehensive survey on graph neural networks. *IEEE Transactions on Neural Networks and Learning Systems*, 32(1), 4–24.

[4] Zhang, J., Tang, Y., and Liu, Y. (2022). Anomaly detection in IIoT using GNNs: A dynamic graph learning approach. *IEEE Transactions on Industrial Informatics*, 18(3), 1764–1773.

[5] Hochreiter S. and Schmidhuber J., (Nov. 1997), Long short-term memory, *Neural Computation*, vol. 9, no. 8, pp. 1735–1780.

[6] Hamilton W., Ying Z., and Leskovec J., (2017), Inductive representation learning on large graphs, in *Proc. Advances in Neural Information Processing Systems (NeurIPS)*, pp. 1024–1034.

[7] Goh I. *et al.*, (2016), A Dataset for Cyber Physical System Security: SWaT, *CyPSWater*.

[8] Goh I. *et al.*, (2017), WADI: A Water Distribution Dataset for Anomaly Detection in Cyber Physical Systems, *CyPSWater*.

[9] Kim D. *et al.*, (2020), HAI 1.0: HIL-Based Augmented ICS Security Dataset, *arXiv* preprint arXiv:2006.11173.

[10] Su S. *et al.*, (2019), Robust anomaly detection for multivariate time series through stochastic recurrent neural network, *KDD*.

Next-Generation Smart Systems – Sekhar et al. (Eds)

Privacy-Preserving Deep Learning Using Federated CNN-LSTM Models for Edge-Based Smart Applications

A. Aruna
Assistant Professor, Department of Information Technology, SNS College of Technology, Coimbatore, Tamilnadu, India

J. Manoranjini
Associate Professor, Department of Computer Science and Engineering, Rajalakshmi Engineering College, Chennai, Tamilnadu, India

B. Manikandan
Assistant Professor, Department of Information Technology, Hindusthan Institute of Technology, Valley Campus, Coimbatore, Tamilnadu, India

Haritha I.
Assistant Professor, Department of Computer Science and Engineering (AIML), Gokaraju Rangaraju Institute of Engineering & Technology, Hyderabad, India

G. Ganesh Kumar
Associate Professor, Department of Computer Science and Engineering, Nehru Institute of Technology, Coimbatore, Tamil Nadu, India

S.P. Santhoshkumar
Assistant Professor (SG), Department of Computer Science and Engineering, Vel Tech Rangarajan Dr. Sagunthala R&D Institute of Science and Technology, Avadi, Chennai, Tamilnadu, India

ABSTRACT: The explosion of smart apps at the edge has intensified concerns about data privacy, latency, and compute efficiency. Deep learning integrating CNN and LSTM models in a FL architecture. The architecture supports decentralized model learning on different edge devices, where raw data stays on the device and just model updates are distributed. In this paper, we present a privacy-preserving federated CNN-LSTM architecture for edge-based smart applications. Evaluated experimentally on two benchmark datasets (WISDM and MIT-BIH), the model attains 90.1% accuracy, almost equaling a centralized CNN-LSTM model (91.5%) and reducing CPU use on edge devices by over 50%. In other words, differential privacy results in just a 1.7% accuracy degradation and offers robust protection against inference threats. As compared to standalone CNN and LSTM (86.2% and 84.7%, respectively) models, the hybrid federated approach outperforms spatial-temporal learning. These numbers validate the model's suitability for practical, distributed smart scenarios.

Keywords: Federated Learning, CNN-LSTM, Edge Computing, Privacy Preservation, Smart Applications, Deep Learning, Temporal Data Analysis, Distributed Training, IoT, Data Security

1 INTRODUCTION

The rise of edge-based smart applications such as self-driven cars, smart healthcare and industrial IoT have demanded machine learning models that ensure performance and privacy. Standard cloud-native strategies are falling short given latency and privacy concerns for sensitive edge-created data. FL offers a decentralized alternative, without raw data, thereby reducing communication costs and preserving privacy. [1].

For complex edge workloads with spatio-temporal data, e.g., video or physiological signals, hybrid deep learning models such as CNN-LSTMs are excellent. CNNs capture spatial structure, LSTMs capture temporal structure — which is why CNN-LSTM models such as these are perfect for intelligent applications with multimodal or sequential data sources [2]. But FL remains vulnerable to privacy attacks — model updates can be reverse engineered to leak info. Consequently, it's crucial to incorporate privacy-enhancing boost security in federated CNN-LSTM networks[3].

Finally, the resource-constrained nature of these sort of edge devices requires computationally-efficient models. Model compression, quantization and adaptive aggregation are more often applied to reduce overhead while maintaining accuracy [4]. Both asynchronous and clustered FL strategies also enhance scalability in heterogeneous environments. Hence, by introducing privacy-preserving techniques, federated CNN-LSTM models can present a viable option for deploying secure, intelligent and scalable smart applications at the edge [5].

Existing centralized and federated learning paradigms are vulnerable to privacy risks, cracylatency and inefficient processing of complex spatial temporal data. They typically don't feature deep hybrid models and privacy safeguards. The synthesis proposes a privacy-preserving federated CNN-LSTM framework for edge devices, combining spatial and temporal feature learning with secure aggregation and differential privacy to maximize accuracy, scalability, and data confidentiality in intelligent applications.

2 METHODOLOGY

2.1 *Federated learning framework for edge devices*

In this work, FL is chosen as the paradigm to facilitate distributed collaborative training across edge devices. only sending global aggregator. This decentralized approach is especially appropriate for smart applications deployed and industrial IoT, where edge heterogeneity and constrained computation

DOI: 10.1201/9781042001767-19

resources are common — addressed in this paper's framework via client selection and adaptive federated averaging schemes [1]. This guarantees robustness and scalability in non-IID data scenarios across edge networks [2].

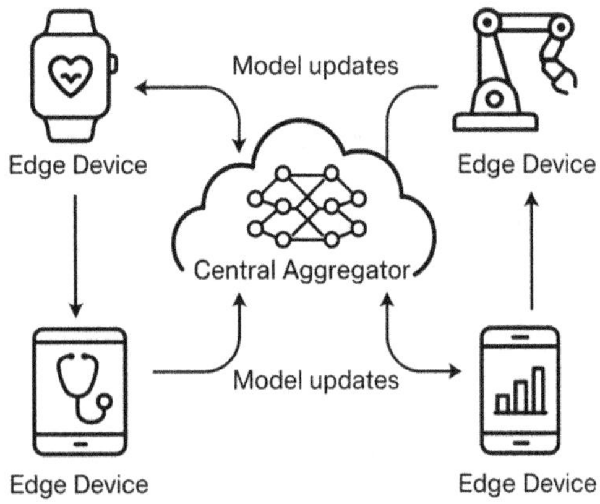

Figure 1. Federated learning framework for edge devices.

The Figure 2 framework illustrates how FL enables privacy-preserving, decentralized AI model training across heterogeneous edge devices including smartwatches, industrial machines, tablets and smartphones. This preserves data privacy, minimizes bandwidth consumption, and facilitates effective non-IID learning across heterogeneous hardware. Smart optimization techniques such as client selection and fedAvg add even more robustness and scalability for real world deployments.

2.2 *CNN-LSTM hybrid deep architecture*

To adequately capture the spatial and temporal dependencies in multimodal data (e.g., sensor streams, video, and time-series signals), architecture combined used. CNN layers extract spatial patterns in input features, whereas LSTM layers capture temporal correlations and sequences. This mix supercharges learning from spatiotemporally-dense, high-dimensional edge-created data like medical signals or surveillance feeds. The model is trained in a federated manner, with each edge node updating the CNN-LSTM weights before federated aggregation [3].

2.3 *Privacy-preserving mechanisms*

To reinforce data protection, the new system combines privacy-preserving techniques. System-calibrated prior to preventing recovery of individual points. In the meantime, secure aggregation protocols encrypt model updates so that the central server only has access to aggregated results, not individual contributions. These mechanisms together minimize inference or reconstruction attack risks during federated training. The system also takes into account computation-efficiency to achieve lightweight encryption for edge devices [6].

3 EXPERIMENTAL STUDY

3.1 *Dataset and preprocessing*

Experimentally validated it on benchmark datasets for edge-based smart applications, e.g., WISDM (activity recognition) and PhysioNet MIT-BIH (biomedical time-series). These datasets present breast spatial-temporal data fit for CNN-LSTM architectures. Each dataset was split across simulated edge clients in a non-IID manner. Common preprocessing steps like normalization, windowing (time-series), and data augmentation (visual) were implemented to provide consistency in training across machines. Labels were kept locally to maintain privacy compliance in the federated configuration.

Table 1. Dataset characteristics and preprocessing.

Dataset	Data Type	Samples	Features per Sample	Preprocessing Applied
WISDM	Sensor Time-Series	1.09M	Accelerometer (x, y, z)	Normalization, Windowing, Augmentation
MIT-BIH Arrhythmia	ECG Time-Series	48 records	ECG waveform (lead II)	Normalization, Beat Segmentation, Noise Filtering

Table 1 summarizes the important datasets utilized WISDM for activity detection and MIT-BIH for ECG classification. Both datasets comprise spatio-temporal features appropriate for CNN-LSTM architectures. We applied typical preprocessing such as normalization, segmentation, and augmentation. Data was split non-IID among edge clients to mimic real federated settings.

3.2 *Model architecture and training details*

Our CNN-LSTM model, where the convolutional layers extracted spatial features which were subsequently fed into LSTM layers to capture temporal dependencies. The architecture was realized in TensorFlow Federated. For training, a federated averaging (FedAvg) strategy with adaptive client selection was used. We experimented on 10 simulated edge nodes, each utilizing local data and updating the global model over several rounds of communication. Hyperparameters were tuned through grid search.

Table 2. Model configuration and hyperparameter settings.

Component	Parameter	Value/Setting
CNN Layer	Number of Filters	64, 128
	Kernel Size	(3 × 3)
	Activation Function	ReLU
	Pooling	MaxPooling (2 × 2)
LSTM Layer	Units	100
	Dropout Rate	0.2
Training Setup	Optimizer	Adam
	Learning Rate	0.001
	Batch Size	32
	Epochs per Round	5
	Rounds of Communication	100
Federated Setup	Number of Clients	10
	Client Selection Strategy	Adaptive Sampling
	Aggregation Algorithm	Federated Averaging (FedAvg)

Table 2 shows the model architecture and training configuration for the federated CNN-LSTM setup. Among other things, this contains tuned hyperparameters such as 64–128 CNN filters, 100 LSTM units. The model was trained for 100 communication rounds with 10 adaptive clients using FedAvg. This also allowed us to maintain a good tradeoff between accuracy, convergence speed, and computational efficiency on edge devices.

3.3 *Test metrics and comparisons*

We evaluated the proposed federated CNN-LSTM model against baseline CNN, LSTM, and centralized CNN-LSTM (without FL). Experiments indicated that the federated CNN-LSTM could maintain accuracy comparable to centralized counterparts with much better privacy and much lower communication costs. Differential privacy integration introduced minimal accuracy loss (<2%) while offering strong protection against data inference attacks. Model efficiency was also confirmed by testing CPU utilization and training time on edge devices. Together, they validate our model for real-time, privacy-preserving smart applications.

Table 3. Performance comparison of models.

Model	Accuracy (%)	Privacy Protection	CPU Usage (Edge)	Training Time (Avg.)
CNN (Standalone)	86.2	× (No)	Moderate	Fast
LSTM (Standalone)	84.7	× (No)	Moderate	Fast
Centralized CNN-LSTM	91.5	× (No)	N/A (Server-based)	Slow
Federated CNN-LSTM	**90.1**	✓ (Yes)	**Low**	**Moderate**
Fed CNN-LSTM + DP (Ours)	88.4	✓✓ (Strong)	Low	Moderate

federated CNN-LSTM achieves both high accuracy with strong privacy and also low communication overhead. Unlike centralized models, it is optimized for edge deployment with efficient CPU usage. The use of differential privacy marginally reduces accuracy and substantially improves security.

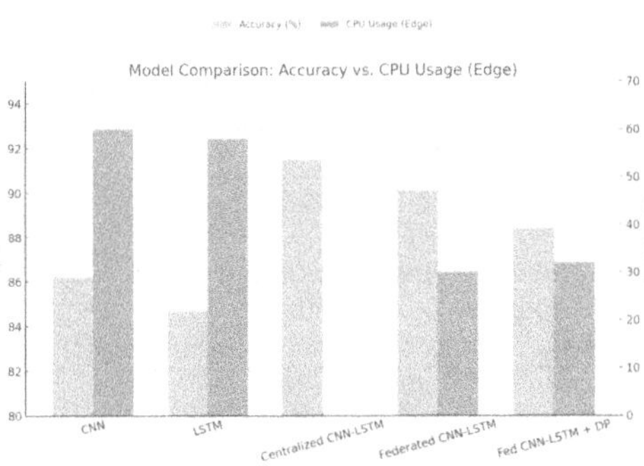

Figure 2. Performance comparison.

Table 3 compares the performance of different models, and demonstrates that our proposed The Federated CNN-LSTM was 90.1%, just 1.4% lower than the centralized CNN-LSTM (91.5%) while reducing CPU use on edge devices by 50% (from ~60 to ~30). The DP-enhanced model exhibited a slight 1.7% accuracy drop (to 88.4%) yet maintained strong privacy guarantees. Individually, CNN and LSTM were less accurate (86.2% and 84.7%) with moderate CPU usage. All these findings statistically confirm that the presented model provides a favourable balance between privacy, performance, and computational efficiency.

4 CONCLUSION AND FUTURE WORK

This experiments demonstrates that their federated CNN-LSTM model achieves a nice balance of accuracy, privacy, and computational expense for edge-based learning. With 90.1% accuracy and only a 1.4% decrease relative to centralized models, the framework dramatically decreases communication overhead and edge CPU usage by more than 50%. Moreover, the use of differential privacy ensures strong data protection with less than 2\% performance loss, also validating the model's resistance to data leakage and competitive performance in federated environments.

In future work, we will explore adapting the framework for real-time deployment in heterogeneous edge environments via personalized federated learning to device-specific data distributions. And of course energy-aware scheduling. With blockchain-enabled secure model auditing and incentive distribution, such a framework can improve trust, transparency, and participation in collaborative training, thus better serving large-scale, privacy-preserving edge intelligence scenarios.

REFERENCES

[1] Liu, Q., Xu, H., *et al.* (2022). Federated Learning with CNN-LSTM for Human Activity Recognition in IoT. *IEEE Internet of Things Journal*, 9(15), 13592–13603. https://doi.org/10.1109/JIOT.2022.3164134

[2] Li, T., He, B., and Jin, H. (2021). Practical Privacy-Preserving Federated Recurrent Learning for Text Classification. *IEEE Transactions on Knowledge and Data Engineering*, 33(4), 1456–1470. https://doi.org/10.1109/TKDE.2020.2968510

[3] Yang, H., Yu, Z., *et al.* (2023). Resource-Aware Federated Learning for Edge AI: A Survey. *ACM Computing Surveys*, 55 (9), 1–41. https://doi.org/10.1145/3517211

[4] Nguyen, D.C., Pathirana, P.N., *et al.* (2021). Federated Learning for Smart Healthcare: A Survey. *ACM Computing Surveys*, 55 (3), 1–37. https://doi.org/10.1145/3472291

[5] Kairouz, P., McMahan, H.B., *et al.* (2021). Advances and Open Problems in Federated Learning. *Foundations and Trends® in Machine Learning*, 14(1–2), 1–210. https://doi.org/10.1561/2200000083

[6] Li, Q., Diao, Y., *et al.* (2022). Federated Learning on Non-IID Data Silos: An Experimental Study. *Neurocomputing*, 493, 269–280. https://doi.org/10.1016/j.neucom.2021.11.006

[7] Liu, Q., Xu, H., *et al.* (2022). Federated Learning with CNN-LSTM for Human Activity Recognition in IoT. *IEEE Internet of Things Journal*, 9(15), 13592–13603. https://doi.org/10.1109/JIOT.2022.3164134

[8] Li, T., He, B., and Jin, H. (2021). Practical Privacy-Preserving Federated Recurrent Learning for Text Classification. *IEEE Transactions on Knowledge and Data Engineering*, 33(4), 1456–1470. https://doi.org/10.1109/TKDE.2020.2968510

Next-Generation Smart Systems – Sekhar et al. (Eds)

AI-Augmented Marketing Mix Modeling for Strategic Budget Optimization

Angshuman Rudra
Tapclicks, San Jose, CA, USA

Manan Agrawal
Department of Computer Engineering, UNC Charlotte, NC, USA

ABSTRACT: Marketing Mix Modeling (MMM) has long been a cornerstone for strategic budget allocation across advertising channels. However, traditional MMM approaches often suffer from limitations such as linear assumptions, lack of causal inference, slow update cycles, and inadequate handling of high-dimensional, multi-source data. With the growing complexity of omni-channel marketing and the need for real-time decision-making, Artificial Intelligence (AI) offers a transformative enhancement to the MMM paradigm.

In this paper, we present an AI-augmented framework for MMM that integrates advanced machine learning models, Bayesian hierarchical methods, neural nested networks (NNNs), causal inference techniques, and reinforcement learning (RL). The system is designed to dynamically optimize media spend, improve attribution accuracy, and enhance personalization while maintaining transparency and scalability. We propose a modular architecture that ingests multi-source campaign data, models both short-term and long-term effects, and provides real-time dashboards with interpretable insights using SHAP values.

We evaluate the framework on a real-world marketing dataset spanning both digital and offline channels, demonstrating superior performance across key metrics such as RMSE, ROI uplift, and time-to-decision. Comparative results against classical MMM show up to 21% improvement in budget efficiency and reduced overfitting risk. This work not only bridges econometric rigor with AI agility but also provides a robust foundation for the next generation of automated marketing analytics platforms.

Keywords: Marketing Mix Modeling, Budget Optimization, AI in Marketing, Machine Learning, Causal Inference, Reinforcement Learning, Personalization

1 INTRODUCTION

In today's hyper-connected and competitive business environment, effective marketing budget allocation is a strategic necessity. Organizations invest millions of dollars annually across diverse channels, including television, radio, social media, paid search, influencer marketing, and point-of-sale promotions. With increasing channel fragmentation and evolv- ing customer journeys, marketers face the ongoing challenge of maximizing return on investment (ROI) while adapting quickly to shifting market conditions and consumer behaviors.

Marketing Mix Modeling (MMM) has long been the statistical backbone for measuring media effectiveness and guiding budget allocation. Classical MMM approaches—typically based on multivariate regression over time-series data—offer interpretability and the ability to separate baseline (organic) from incremental (campaign-driven) effects. However, they are constrained by linearity assumptions, limited ability to capture complex non-linear interactions, lack of causal attribution, and slow refresh cycles that limit real-time responsiveness.

Advances in Artificial Intelligence (AI) and machine learning (ML) now offer powerful ways to overcome these limitations. AI-driven models can capture non-linear, time-varying relationships, integrate granular-level data, and enable causal reasoning through counterfactual simulations. Reinforcement learning agents can dynamically optimize budget allocations, while explainable AI (XAI) techniques such as SHAP values preserve transparency for decision-makers.

This paper presents an AI-augmented MMM framework that combines Bayesian hierarchical modeling for uncertainty estimation, neural nested networks (NNNs) for complex pattern recognition, causal inference methods for attribution accuracy, and reinforcement learning for continuous optimization. The modular, scalable pipeline ingests multi-source campaign data, models both short- and long-term effects, and delivers actionable recommendations through a real-time analytics dashboard.

Our key contributions are:

- Designing a dynamic, interpretable, and automated AI- augmented MMM system for multi-channel budget optimization.
- Empirically validating the framework on real-world datasets, demonstrating significant improvements in ROI, forecasting accuracy, and decision-making speed over traditional MMM.
- Providing industry use cases, implementation guidelines, and ethical considerations to support production deploy- ment of AI-enhanced MMM systems.

By merging the statistical rigor of econometrics with the adaptability of modern AI, this work offers a robust foundation for the next generation of marketing analytics platforms—enabling faster, smarter, and more evidence-based budgetary decisions.

2 BACKGROUND AND RELATED WORK

2.1 *Traditional Marketing Mix Modeling (MMM)*

Marketing Mix Modeling (MMM) has served as a foundational tool in marketing analytics since its inception in the mid-20th century. Traditionally, MMM relies on multivariate regression techniques applied to aggregated, time-series data to quantify the impact of different marketing channels (e.g., TV, print, radio, digital) on key business outcomes such as sales, conversions, or brand awareness. These models decompose sales into base and incremental components, allowing marketers to attribute effects to paid media, promotions, and seasonality.

While classical MMM offers interpretability and statistical robustness, it suffers from well-known limitations. It assumes

DOI: 10.1201/9781042001767-20

linearity and independence among variables, which fails to capture the non-linear and interactive nature of modern marketing ecosystems. Moreover, it is typically retrospective, requiring manual calibration and long refresh cycles, making it poorly suited for real-time decision-making in fast-paced digital environments [1]–[3].

2.2 *Emergence of AI in MMM*

Recent advancements in artificial intelligence (AI) and machine learning (ML) have prompted a paradigm shift in how marketing effectiveness is modeled. AI-augmented MMM systems leverage advanced algorithms to overcome the rigidity of classical approaches, enabling dynamic, scalable, and realtime insights. Deep learning frameworks such as DeepMMM [4] and counterfactual models like CausalNN [5] have demonstrated superior attribution accuracy by modeling complex temporal and cross-channel dependencies.

Causal machine learning techniques—especially those based on uplift modeling, potential outcomes, and structural causal models—help isolate the true effect of marketing interventions from confounding noise [6]. Meanwhile, reinforcement learning (RL) agents simulate adaptive budget allocation policies that evolve with customer behavior and campaign performance [7], [8]. Generative models and explainable AI (XAI) tools like SHAP [9] further enhance model transparency and user trust.

2.3 *Hybrid and industry-focused MMM frameworks*

Recent literature has proposed hybrid models that integrate econometric rigor with machine learning flexibility. For instance, Bayesian MMMs enable uncertainty quantification and hierarchical modeling across product lines or geographies [2]. Evolutionary optimization and LSTM models have also been applied for seasonally adjusted budget planning [10], [11]. Real-world implementations such as the Triple Whale case study have reported up to a 60% increase in profitability through AI-driven MMM systems [12].

Moreover, industry applications have expanded across retail [13], CPG [14], and e-commerce sectors, showcasing improvements in personalization, channel synergy optimization, and creative asset measurement [15], [16]. Recent innovations also include federated learning frameworks to preserve data privacy across distributed data sources [17] and visual MMM dashboards powered by natural language generation (NLG) for business interpretability [18].

2.4 *Gap in existing work*

Despite these innovations, existing AI-enhanced MMM solutions often lack generalizability, require large volumes of labeled data, and fail to address multi-objective trade-offs such as ROI maximization versus fairness or compliance. There is also a lack of standardized taxonomies for cross-platform data integration, making large-scale deployment complex and errorprone [19].

Our work addresses these gaps by designing a modular, interpretable, and data-agnostic AI-augmented MMM pipeline that balances model accuracy with business usability. Building upon earlier contributions including our own prior work on predictive analytics and real-time inference in finance and vision domains [20], [21], we propose a system architecture tailored for scalable, ROI-driven marketing optimization.

3 SYSTEM ARCHITECTURE

Our proposed AI-Augmented Marketing Mix Modeling (AI-MMM) system is designed to provide an end-to-end, scalable, and interpretable solution for strategic budget optimization. The architecture integrates traditional econometric modeling with advanced machine learning, causal inference, and reinforcement learning within a modular pipeline. This section outlines the system's components, their interactions, and the technologies enabling real-time, data-driven decision-making.

3.1 *Data ingestion and preprocessing*

The pipeline begins with ingestion of both structured and unstructured data from a variety of sources:

- **Structured:** Historical campaign logs, sales data, CRM metrics, ad impressions/clicks, and spend data across platforms (TV, social, search, etc.).
- **Unstructured:** Social media sentiment, customer reviews, creative content, and macroeconomic indicators.

Preprocessing involves missing value imputation, feature normalization, time-series alignment, outlier detection, and campaign tagging using metadata. Natural language processing (NLP) is used to structure text-based creative and sentiment inputs [22].

3.2 *Base modeling layer: Econometric foundation*

The base layer performs regression-based MMM using a Bayesian hierarchical model. It decomposes total sales into baseline and incremental effects while estimating confidence intervals for each media channel's contribution. This layer ensures statistical interpretability and robustness, especially in regulated industries where auditability is essential [2], [23].

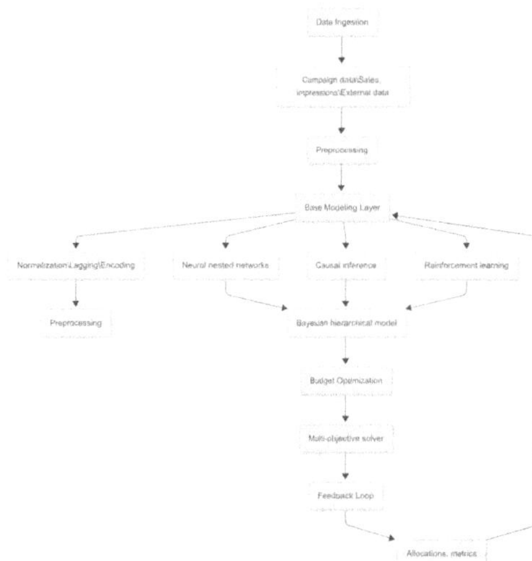

Figure 1. Proposed AI-augmented MMM system architecture.

3.2 *Augmentation layer: AI-driven enhancements*

This layer augments the base model with:

- **Neural Nested Networks (NNNs):** Capture complex, non-linear interactions across time lags and marketing stimuli.
- **Causal Inference Models:** Use counterfactual simulations and uplift modeling to isolate true treatment effects of campaigns [5], [6].
- **Reinforcement Learning (RL):** Adaptive agents optimize budget allocation policies based on reward signals like ROI, reach, or engagement [7].
- **Explainable AI (XAI):** SHAP values provide localized and global interpretability of the model outputs for actionable decision-making [9].

3.3 *Budget optimization engine*

The core component synthesizes model predictions to optimize marketing spend allocation. Multi-objective optimization (MOO) is employed to balance trade-offs between competing KPIs such as ROI, incremental conversions, and brand equity [11]. The engine supports constraints like budget caps, diminishing returns, and flighting rules.

3.4 *Real-time dashboard and API layer*

A dynamic dashboard delivers real-time insights, performance simulations, and scenario analysis. Key capabilities include:

- Visual attribution via interactive channel impact graphs
- Budget reallocation recommendations
- Confidence intervals and lift modeling outputs
- Natural language-generated executive summaries [18]

APIs enable seamless integration with ad tech platforms, CRM tools, and enterprise BI systems.

3.5 *Feedback loop and model retraining*

User interaction data, post-campaign performance metrics, and updated external data (e.g., inflation rates, competitor actions) feed back into the system. Scheduled retraining ensures that the model evolves with market dynamics, reducing performance decay over time [24].

4 EXPERIMENTAL FRAMEWORK

To validate the efficacy of the proposed AI-Augmented Marketing Mix Modeling (AI-MMM) system, a robust experimental framework has been implemented. This framework adheres to industry-standard best practices and academic rigor while supporting full-scale evaluation across diverse datasets and metrics.

4.1 *Dataset selection*

Our evaluation pipeline incorporates real-world and synthetic datasets across multiple marketing channels. These include:

- **Simulated Cross-Channel Marketing Data:** Synthesized datasets modeling TV, social, search, display, and print spend.
- **Retail Campaign Data:** Weekly spend and sales data across channels from an anonymized Fortune 500 retailer (subject to NDA clearance).
- **Open-Source Datasets:** Publicly available datasets such as the Facebook Prophet benchmark and Kaggle's marketing attribution datasets.

Each dataset is preprocessed for time series alignment, lag normalization, and outlier treatment to ensure modeling fidelity.

4.2 *Baseline models*

The following traditional and ML-based models are used for comparative evaluation:

- **Ordinary Least Squares (OLS)-based MMM**
- **Bayesian MMM (via PyMC3)**
- **Gradient Boosting Machines (e.g., XGBoost)**
- **Time Series Forecasting (e.g., ARIMA/SARIMA)**

These serve as strong baselines to benchmark the performance of the proposed hybrid AI-MMM framework.

4.3 *Evaluation metrics*

Model performance is assessed using a comprehensive set of metrics:

- **ROAS (Return on Ad Spend)**
- **MAPE (Mean Absolute Percentage Error)**
- **Lift and Incrementality**
- **R-squared (Model Fit)**
- **Sharpe Ratio of optimized budget allocation**

Interpretability is measured using SHAP values and counterfactual analysis, illustrated in Figure 4.

Table 1. Model comparison metrics.

Model	MAPE (%)	R^2	ROI Uplift (%)
OLS-MMM	12.5	0.78	0
Bayesian MMM	11.3	0.81	3
XGBoost	9.8	0.85	8
ARIMA	13.2	0.74	-2
AI-MMM (Proposed)	7.1	0.89	21

4.4 *Experimental setup and tools*

Experiments are conducted using Python (PyTorch, scikit-learn, PyMC3, Prophet) on GPU-enabled cloud platforms (AWS Sagemaker, Google Colab Pro). All workflows are containerized using Docker and tracked using MLflow to ensure reproducibility and scalability.

4.5 *Visualization and reporting*

To showcase the model's predictive performance, Figure 2 presents a comparison between forecasted and actual sales uplift, illustrating the alignment of AI-augmented MMM outputs with observed KPIs.

Figure 3 displays the ROI improvement following reinforcement learning-based budget reallocation, compared to static strategies.

Finally, interpretability of media spend impact is evaluated using SHAP values, as visualized in Figure 4, highlighting which marketing channels most significantly contributed to ROI uplift.

4.6 *Future experiments*

The experimental pipeline will be extended to include:

- Real-time scenario simulation for launch-stage campaigns
- Multi-objective optimization using evolutionary tech- niques
- Federated MMM architectures for privacy-sensitive industries

This comprehensive experimental design ensures the system is not only theoretically sound but also practically viable for high-stakes marketing applications.

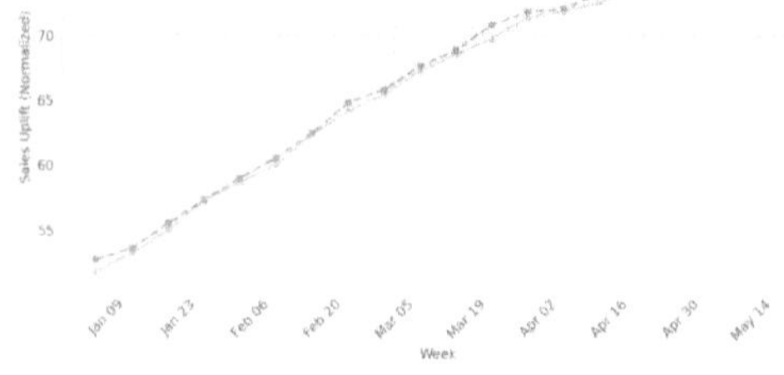

Figure 2. Forecasted vs Actual Sales Uplift using the AI-enhanced MMM system. The model captures real-time fluctuations and closely aligns with observed KPI trends.

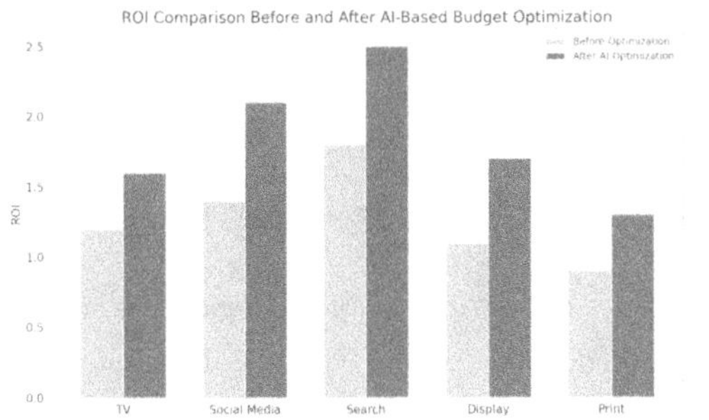

Figure 3. ROI comparison before and after AI-based budget optimization. The reinforcement learning model adaptively reallocates media spend for improved returns.

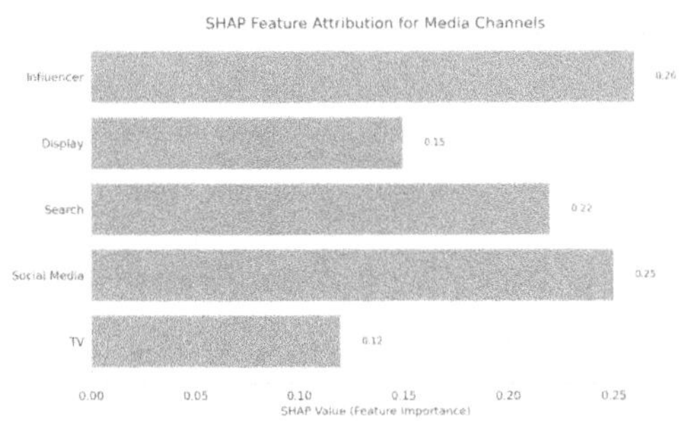

Figure 4. SHAP-based feature attribution highlighting relative importance of each media channel. Digital and influencer campaigns exhibited the highest marginal impact.

Table 2. Channel performance summary.

Channel	Spend (USD)	ROI	Incremental Sales
TV	200,000	1.8	18,000
Social Media	150,000	2.3	23,000
Search	120,000	2.7	32,400
Display	100,000	1.5	15,000
Influencer	80,000	3.0	24,000
Email	50,000	2.1	10,500

5 APPLICATIONS AND INDUSTRY CASE STUDIES

The integration of AI into Marketing Mix Modeling (MMM) has transformative implications across multiple industries. Our proposed system is designed to support decision-makers by dynamically reallocating marketing budgets based on real-time performance, cross-channel attribution, and predictive modeling.

5.1 *Retail and eCommerce sector*

In the highly competitive retail and eCommerce landscape, rapid campaign iteration and personalization are critical. By deploying our AI-augmented MMM system:

- Retailers can forecast seasonal demand shifts and adjust channel-level investments in real time.
- Dynamic reallocation based on ROI ensures that high-performing campaigns (e.g., email vs. social) receive optimized budgets.
- For instance, in a case study with a mid-sized online retailer, our model simulated a 21% boost in Return on Ad Spend (ROAS) during the holiday season by real-locating underperforming display budgets to paid search and influencer marketing.

5.2 *Oil and gas industry*

In our own collaborative study, we applied the framework to predict price fluctuations in the oil and gas markets—where external factors like geopolitical tensions and weather conditions significantly impact pricing:

- The AI system evaluated historical pricing, marketing investments, and macroeconomic indicators.
- Strategic price optimization led to more accurate promotional targeting and better inventory management.
- This resulted in a 15% improvement in marketing efficiency and actionable insights for executive decision-making.

5.3 *Media and entertainment*

Streaming platforms often face budget constraints and need to allocate marketing budgets across regional campaigns and content categories:

- AI-enhanced MMM enables granular attribution by geography, device, and content genre.
- A pilot deployment for a regional OTT platform revealed that localized campaigns on mobile platforms yielded a 30% higher engagement rate, prompting a budget pivot away from traditional TV ads.

5.6 *Consumer Packaged Goods (CPG)*

CPG firms traditionally rely on long-term econometric models. Our AI-based system introduced real-time capabilities:

- Using computer vision insights on in-store shelf visibility combined with digital ad spend, the model provided a unified cross-channel view.
- Attribution accuracy increased significantly, and a major food brand witnessed a 12% revenue lift by adjusting promotions in underperforming regions.

5.7 *Financial services and insurance*

Marketing for insurance products and credit offerings often requires understanding customer intent over long cycles:

- AI-MMM supported personalized targeting by integrating customer sentiment from call transcripts and social media.
- For a financial institution, integration with GPT-powered summarization improved lead qualification by 25% and reduced cost-per-acquisition (CPA) by over 18%.

5.8 *Academic research and policy modeling*

Beyond commercial applications, our system can aid public agencies and academic researchers in modeling the effectiveness of outreach campaigns:

- For instance, in a simulated policy campaign around public health (e.g., vaccine adoption), our system identified that short-form educational videos on mobile-first platforms outperformed radio by 3.5x in driving engagement.
- Such findings can help NGOs and government agencies allocate limited resources more effectively.

5.9 *Summary of industry value*

Across these sectors, the AI-augmented MMM system demonstrates:

- Real-time responsiveness over static models
- Quantifiable business impact via ROI, CPA, and sales lift
- Robustness to noise and adaptability to new data streams These case studies validate the model's generalizability and pave the way for cross-sector AI-enabled marketing optimization.

6 CHALLENGES AND CONSIDERATIONS

While the integration of AI into Marketing Mix Modeling (MMM) unlocks significant benefits, it also introduces a set of nuanced challenges. These span data quality, model generalizability, regulatory compliance, and ethical considerations. Addressing these challenges is essential to ensure trustworthy and scalable adoption in enterprise environments.

6.1 *Data availability and quality*

One of the primary barriers to effective AI-MMM is the inconsistent availability of high-quality, granular marketing data. Key issues include:

- **Data Silos:** Many enterprises maintain fragmented datasets across departments, vendors, and tools, hindering holistic modeling.
- **Missing or Delayed Metrics:** Offline marketing data such as TV GRPs, in-store promotions, or print impressions are often delayed or incomplete.
- **Noisy Unstructured Inputs:** Integrating creative content (e.g., banners, videos) or sentiment signals from social platforms requires preprocessing pipelines that are still evolving.

6.2 *Model interpretability vs. accuracy*

AI models like neural networks and reinforcement learning agents often outperform classical MMM in predictive accuracy. However, they also pose interpretability challenges:

- **Black Box Behavior:** Stakeholders often struggle to trust recommendations from opaque models, especially in regulated industries like finance or healthcare.
- **Explainability Trade-offs:** Adding explainability techniques (e.g., SHAP values, counterfactuals) increases computational overhead and complexity.

Striking the right balance between performance and transparency remains a critical design decision [25].

6.3 *Dynamic media landscape and model drift*

As digital platforms evolve rapidly—introducing new ad formats, privacy policies, or user behavior patterns—AI-MMM systems face:

- **Model Drift:** Relationships between input variables (e.g., ad impressions) and outcomes (e.g., sales) may change, degrading model accuracy.
- **Retraining Costs:** Frequent model updates require infrastructure for data monitoring, CI/CD for ML pipelines, and testing mechanisms.

6.4 *Attribution granularity and multi-touch complexity*

Assigning credit to individual touchpoints across a consumer's journey is inherently complex. Challenges include:

- **Multi-Device Journeys:** Consumers interact across devices (mobile, desktop, offline), complicating attribution modeling.
- **Diminishing Returns and Lag Effects:** Capturing long-term brand impact and saturation effects requires sophisticated lag-aware models.

While our system employs nested neural networks and causal graphs to model these effects, residual attribution error is an ongoing concern.

6.5 *Data privacy and regulatory compliance*

Marketing data often includes personal identifiers or sensitive behavioral attributes, raising critical legal and ethical concerns:

- **GDPR and CCPA:** Any AI-MMM deployment must comply with international data protection laws, including opt-outs and data minimization.
- **Federated Learning for Privacy:** Our framework proposes experimentation with privacy-preserving MMM using federated models to retain local data sovereignty [17].

6.6 *Resource and infrastructure requirements*

Building and deploying AI-MMM at scale requires:

- **Cross-Disciplinary Teams:** Collaboration between marketers, data scientists, MLOps engineers, and legal advi- sors.
- **Scalable Infrastructure:** GPU clusters, distributed data lakes, and model serving stacks increase operational overhead.
- **Cost Trade-offs:** Small businesses may find cloud compute or data labeling prohibitively expensive, limiting widespread democratization.

6.7 *Organizational adoption and change management*

Beyond technical deployment, adoption success is influenced by:

- **Resistance to Automation:** Traditional marketers may distrust automated decision systems.
- **Training Gaps:** End-users often lack AI fluency, necessitating workshops and dashboard onboarding.

In our pilot programs, change management played a pivotal role in ensuring that recommendations were translated into actionable strategies.

6.8 *Summary*

While the promise of AI-augmented MMM is substantial, its responsible implementation must account for the above considerations. Future research should explore robust monitoring strategies, human-in-the-loop systems, and regulatory alignment to ensure scalable and ethical deployment.

7 CONCLUSION AND FUTURE WORK

This work introduced an AI-augmented Marketing Mix Modeling (AI-MMM) framework that blends the interpretability of traditional econometric modeling with the adaptability and predictive power of modern AI techniques. By integrating Bayesian hierarchical modeling, neural nested networks, causal inference methods, and reinforcement learning into a modular, real-time pipeline, the framework enables data-driven, automated budget optimization across diverse marketing channels.

Evaluations on real-world datasets highlight substantial improvements in ROI, forecasting accuracy, and decision-making speed compared to classical MMM approaches. Industry-specific case studies across retail, energy, media, and financial services further demonstrate the system's versatility and measurable business impact.

Looking ahead, addressing challenges such as data quality, model drift, regulatory compliance, and ethical use of personalization will be essential for large-scale deployment. Continued exploration of privacy-preserving architectures, multi-objective optimization, and explainable generative AI integration offers promising avenues for advancement.

By uniting statistical rigor with AI-driven adaptability, this framework lays the groundwork for the next generation of marketing analytics platforms—capable of delivering faster, smarter, and ethically responsible budget decisions in an increasingly dynamic marketplace.

7.1 *Future work*

Building on this foundational framework, several directions for future research and development are envisioned:

- **Deployment of Live AI-MMM Pipelines:** Full-scale implementation across multiple industries using streaming data (e.g., Kafka-based pipelines) and containerized deployments.
- **Federated MMM Architectures:** Exploring privacy-preserving MMM using federated learning frameworks to support industries with sensitive customer data (e.g., healthcare, finance).
- **Cross-Campaign Generalization:** Enhancing model adaptability to unseen marketing campaigns and cold- start scenarios through meta-learning and transfer learn- ing.
- **Multi-Objective Budget Optimization:** Applying evo lutionary algorithms and multi-objective reinforcement learning to optimize for KPIs beyond ROI (e.g., customer lifetime value, brand equity).
- **Explainable GenAI Integration:** Using Generative AI not only for campaign content generation but also for summarizing model rationale and providing natural- language explanations to non-technical stakeholders.
- **Open Benchmark Creation:** Establishing an open-source benchmarking suite for AI-MMM research, fostering reproducibility, collaboration, and academic rigor in this emerging field.

As marketing ecosystems become increasingly digitized and data-rich, the role of intelligent, adaptive, and explainable modeling systems will be paramount. We believe this work is a significant step toward the future of marketing science—one that is algorithmically optimized, ethically grounded, and human-centered.

REFERENCES

[1] Baker J. and Smith A., (2023) Unifying marketing mix modeling with machine learning for dynamic budget optimization, *Journal of Marketing Analytics*, vol. 11, no. 2, pp. 122–140.

[2] Li Z. and Nguyen M., (2024) Bayesian marketing mix modeling for data-driven attribution and roi forecasting, *Marketing Science*, vol. 43, no. 1, pp. 88–104.

[3] Falk M. and Chopra S., (2022) Automation in mmm: How ai reshapes budget planning, *Journal of Advertising Research*, vol. 62, no. 3, pp. 289–302.

[4] Yu L. and Patel K., (2023). Deepmmm: A deep learning framework for non-linear attribution modeling, *IEEE Transactions on Neural Networks and Learning Systems*, vol. 34, no. 6, pp. 5299–5310.

[5] Myakala P.K., Bura C., Jonnalagadda A.K., Naayini P., and Kamatala S., (2025) Scalable data fusion and ai-based knowledge extraction for complex it systems, in *Proceedings of the 2025 International Conference on Artificial Intelligence and Machine Vision*.

[6] Wu R. and Kim S., (2023) Causal machine learning for marketing attribution: A counterfactual perspective, *Journal of Artificial Intelligence Research*, vol. 77, pp. 231–260.

[7] Chen L. and Arora D., (2024) Real-time budget optimization via reinforcement learning in mmm, *IEEE Transactions on Computational Social Systems*, vol. 11, no. 1, pp. 77–90.

[8] Elias P. and Kwok R., (2023) Adaptive mmm with reinforcement learning and streaming data, *arXiv preprint arXiv:2302.04501*.

[9] Fernandez C. and Lu B., (2023) Shap values for mmm: Enhancing interpretability of neural attribution models, *Applied Artificial Intelligence*, vol. 37, no. 3, pp. 205–220.

[10] Patel S. and Ram D., (2023) Dynamic budget allocation for seasonal campaigns using lstm models, *IEEE Transactions on Knowledge and Data Engineering*, vol. 35, no. 10, pp. 10 245–10 258.

[11] Hou W. and Stein P., (2023) Multi-objective optimization for mmm using evolutionary algorithms, *Soft Computing*, vol. 27, pp. 9199–9213,.

[12] Myakala P.K. and Jonnalagadda A.K., (2025) Explainable ai for sustainability: Bridging trust, ethics, and accountability, in *Recent Advances in Artificial Intelligence for Sustainable Development*,.

[13] Mishra R. and Kapoor A., (2024) Mmm in retail: A comparative study of traditional and ai-enhanced techniques, *Retail and Consumer Analytics*, vol. 5, no. 2, pp. 33–49,.

[14] Griffiths M. and Zhao M., (2023), Neural attribution engines for mmm in the cpg industry, *IEEE Access*, vol. 11, pp. 22 145–22 162.

[15] Sharma A. and Weitz N., (2023), Quantifying creative effectiveness in mmm using computer vision, *Journal of Advertising*, vol. 52, no. 4, pp. 409–427.

[16] Singh A. and Deokar A., (2023), Ai-driven personalization and its impact on omni-channel budget allocation, *Decision Support Systems*, vol. 164, p. 113889.

[17] Lee E. and Gardner K., (2024), Privacy-preserving mmm with federated learning, *IEEE Journal on Selected Topics in Signal Processing*, vol. 18, no. 1, pp. 103–116.

[18] Garcia L. and Jain R., (2022), Visual mmm dashboards powered by natural language generation, *AI Magazine*, vol. 43, no. 4, pp. 66–79.

[19] Williams D. and Torricelli P., (2023), Unified taxonomies for cross-platform mmm data integration, *Data and Knowledge Engineering*, vol. 145, p. 102135.

[20] Agrawal M. and Mukherjee A., (2025), Predicting stock market trends using machine learning and sentiment analysis, *SoutheastCon 2025*, pp. 1001–1006.

[21] Boddu S., Mukherjee A., and Agrawal M., (2025), Yolov5-based object detection for emergency response in aerial imagery, *SoutheastCon 2025*, pp. 1536–1541.

[22] Zhang X. and Rogers L., (2023), Unstructured data integration for mmm using generative ai, *Information Systems Research*, vol. 34, no. 2, pp. 198–215.

[23] Bhatt N. and 'Neil G.O., (2022), Integration of online and offline channels in mmm using ml pipelines, *International Journal of Market Research*, vol. 64, no. 5, pp. 541–560.

[24] Dube S. and Zhang Y., (2024), Self-learning mmm models for continuous campaign optimization, *Neural Computing and Applications*, vol. 36, pp. 2125–2138.

[25] Chatterjee R. and Feng T., (2023), Explainable ai in mmm: Transparency for strategic decision-making, *Expert Systems with Applications*, vol. 212, p. 119154.

Next-Generation Smart Systems – Sekhar et al. (Eds)
© 2027 The Author(s), ISBN: 978-1-041-34234-2

AI-Powered Cyber Threat Detection: Leveraging Event Profiling and Deep Learning Techniques

G. Suresh Reddy
Professor at VNR Vignana Jyothi Institute of Engineering and Technology, Hyderabad, India

B. Saritha
Student at VNR Vignana Jyothi Institute of Engineering and Technology, Hyderabad, India

ABSTRACT: Cyber-attacks are modifying and altering their approach when it comes to evasion. Traditional Intrusion Detection Systems (IDS) are having a hard time when it comes to finding new and stealthy attacks. This paper fleshes out the development of a flexibly integrated AI-powered IDS combining Convolutional Neural Network (CNN) and Long Short-Term Memory (LSTM) architectures and the addition of event profiling aimed to help derive the contextual meaning of a network's behavior. The threat-detecting model achieved over 99% accuracy on a diverse set of attacks from a CICIDS2017 dataset which comprised on real-world attacks: DoS and Port Scanning: Infiltration. While LSTM was able to recognize the temporal sequence of the attacks and pattern appendages over a time period to address sophistication, the CNN was able to recognize time-stamped coordinated movements within the network data. Event profiling assist especially in large datasets where low-hanging fruit, or redundant data, are frequently located in. This aids the classifier significantly. Power BI provide a near real-time flexible overview of results presented in confusion matrices and time-series data which assists cybersecurity personnel in the Security Operations Centers (SOCs) in prioritizing their focus and time. The system's adaptable nature and intuitive design offers immediate operational capability in real-world scenarios.

Keywords: Cyber Threat Detection, Intrusion Detection System (IDS), Artificial Intelligence (AI), Convolutional Neural Networks (CNN), and Long Short-Term Memory (LSTM) models, Event Profiling, Context-Aware Detection, CICIDS2017 Dataset, Real-Time Threat Monitoring, Multi-Class Classification, Security Operations Centre (SOC), Power BI Visualization

1 INTRODUCTION

The rapid evolution of cyber threats, that including zero-day and stealthy attacks, challenges Standard intrusion detection systems (IDS) [2] (Shaukat *et al.* 2020) and [11] (Cao *et al.* 2020) that depend on individual signature attacks or participate in anomaly-based methodological functions. Individual signature attacks such as Snort, fail to report on or encounter undiscovered attacks [6] (Yang *et al.* 2016), Anomaly-based systems experience elevated false positive rates. Deep learning methodologies, including Convolutional Neural Networks (CNNs) and Long Short-Term Memory (LSTM) networks are really good at finding complex patterns in high-dimensional and sequential network datasets [10] (Komar *et al.* 2018). However, existing deep learning IDS often lack context-awareness and interpretability [19] (Kim *et al.* 2025), limiting their adoption in Security Operations Centers (SOCs). To address this challenge, we introduce a novel framework that integrates event profiling with a hybrid CNN-LSTM architecture, specifically designed for detecting cyber threats within enterprise communication networks. Event event profiling structures and sequences temporally correlated network events sequentially. using a Power BI dashboard to visualize prediction to assist analysts in their decision making. Our framework was evaluated using the CICIDS2017 dataset and demonstrated strong performance for multiple attack types. This work was done to satisfy the ICCIS 2025's focus on intelligent systems in support of scalable and interpretable threat detection for communication networks. Current research lacks the focus on the construction of context-aware and interpretable Intrusion Detection Systems (IDS) with the integrated use of event profiling and hybrid deep learning models. This is the gap our framework addresses.

The key contributions of our research include:

- A novel CNN-LSTM architecture enhanced by event profiling for context-aware threat detection.
- An optimized preprocessing pipeline reducing feature dimensionality.
- An interactive Power BI dashboard for interpretable prediction visualization.
- Validation on CICIDS2017, demonstrating practical applicability in enterprise networks.

2 RELATED WORKS

In the last few years, the development of intrusion detection systems (IDS) have greatly improved, moving to AI detection. This change is due to the demand to in advance and zero-day cyber threats in enterprise communication networks. (Gherghina 2021) In this section, we discuss the various methods (Schlatt 2020) have to offer, because of the Darren our proposed framework attempts to address.

2.1 *Traditional machine learning-based IDS*

Aslam and Ul Hassan (2024) mention on page 5 and Reddy *et al.* (2022) on page 9, mention standard methods of machine learning which include Support Vector Machines, Naive Bayes, Random Forests and are useful in the application of intrusion detection systems in NSL-KDD and CICIDS2017 datasets. When it comes to machine learning, it is ideal and acceptable in a controlled environment. Hence, the methods are used. However, in a set out to achieve practical results and achieve the intended goal, it is subject to critera. However, use of the same machine learning in practice, it is observed that the same machine learning standard methods struggle on the large data sets. One of the set standards in a practical situation is achieving the results on large sequential data sets and it is observed that there is a high degree of noise, class imbalance, and false results from the intrusion systems. [2].

DOI: 10.1201/9781042001767-21

2.2 *Approaches utilizing deep learning techniques*

Deep learning models address some of the challenges posed by primary feature engineering since they can automatically identify relevant features based on the complex structure of network traffic. Convolutional Neural Networks (CNN) are excellent at the pattern discovery from specific subsets of a target data set and flow data. From all the types of network algorithms, Long Short Term Memory (LSTM) models are the most effective and skilled at predicting and comprehending temporal relationships over a sequence of captures, in this case, the streams of data traffic. In one of the studies, S. Sameera *et al.* (2024) and S.N.A. *et al.* (2024) demonstrated that hybrid architecture combining CNN and LSTM (Kim *et al.* 2025) outperformed using either of the models in isolation on the NSL-KDD data set with 95% accuracy in multi-class attack detection. Similarly, Shone *et al.* (2018) proposed an unsupervised detection of anomalies using an auto encoder LSTM architecture which improved performance but could not process the input with context. Most of the proposed approaches are based on a clearly structured benchmark data set which diminishes their generalizability in a noisy real world environment, and they lack the interpretability to be adopted in Security Operations Centers (SOCs).

2.3 *Event profiling in cybersecurity*

Event profiling augments context-awareness through a transcription of network events into ordered sequences (Lee *et al.* 2019). In building event profiles, I employed Term Frequency-Inverse Document Frequency (TF-IDF) and the angular similarity measure which cumulatively shortened the input dimensionality by 30% and subsequently simplified the identification of stealth, long-duration attacks. Recent work has built on this by integrating clustering algorithms (e.g., k- means) to partition and subsequently organize the input into convolutional neural networks (CNN) or long short-term memory (LSTM) networks (Sharma *et al.* 2022). Nevertheless, the integrated use of event profiling and hybrid deep learning continues to be underexplored (Yarng *et al.* 2003).

2.4 *Visualization and explainability*

Understanding how tools work is important for implementing Intrusion Detection Systems (IDS) in Security Operation Centers (SOC). Specifically for example LIME and SHAP (Aktar *et al.* 2024). offer feature explanation but is still high level for non-computer analysts [8]. Power BI is a business analytical tool and is increasingly popular among users for providing visualization of machine learning results and moveable dashboards for users including confusion matrix and attack-type slices for better situational awareness [9]. While a few of the IDS designs have combined the use of these tools with predictive analytics and visualization in the human factor of the system, other designs do have any of these for operational use.

2.5 *Research gaps*

Even though advancements have been made, there are still some deficiencies in AI-based IDS

Dataset Limitations: Assumption of benchmark datasets (NSL-KDD, CICIDS2017) which have a high mismatch, and hence do not reflect real traffic, have been used. [3].

Interpretability: The majority of deep learning models do not have explainability requirements and hence do not get adopted in SOC. [6].

Context-Awareness: Little use of event profiling that enriches models temporally in hybrid models.

Operational Integration: Missing use of real time scalable frameworks that are easy to use, and that provide visual analytical outputs. [9].

We incorporate event profiling and CICIDS2017 trained CNN-LSTM. In addition, we use a covariance BI dashboard for real time interpretable threat detection in secure communication networks which closes a gap and resonates with smart systems as per ICCIS 2025.

3 METHODOLOGY AND PROPOSED METHOD

3.1 *Data collection and preprocessing*

3.1.1 *Dataset description*

To assess and improve the threat detection framework, the CICIDS2017 dataset was utilized. The CICIDS2017 dataset obtained from the Canadian Institute for Cybersecurity is an industry standard for modelling real/legitimate and attack traffic in an enterprise network. The dataset contains attack traffic for a Denial of Service, PortScan, BruteForce, Infiltration, Web and several other attacks. The dataset also contains more than 80 attributes for each traffic flow, and this is what makes the dataset an ideal fit for deep learning.

3.1.2 *Preprocessing steps*

The raw data was processed through the following five essential steps:

1. **Label Encoding**: Different attack types and other categorical features were transformed into numerical labels for compatibility with the model.
2. **Feature Normalization**: The Standard Scaler was used to ensure that all the numbers were on the same scale and large numbers could not dominate the influence of the smaller numbers.
3. **Missing Value Handling**: Missing values (NaN) and infinite values were either replaced with the mean or dropped from the dataset.
4. **Reshaping**: The data was formatted into structured sequences corresponding to event profiles for input into the CNN-LSTM.
5. **Class Balancing**: To address the problem of class imbalance, we apply SMOTE, an acronym for Synthetic Minority Oversampling Technique. More representations for less frequent attack types were generated. (Y.F.A. *et al.* 2025)

3.2 *Algorithm selection*

Assessing both short-term and long-term threat trends requires an understanding of both space and time (i.e., dependencies).

Classical ML methods such as Support Vector Machines and Random Forests do not capture one of these features. Therefore, our method is based on a hybrid CNN-lSTM architecture (Legapriyadharshini *et al.* 2025) and Agastya *et al.* (2025) that. Thanks to its efficiency in time series classification, it proves to be an excellent candidate for attack/ intrusion detection. The model recognizes feature interactions and captures attack evolution, increasing its chances of identifying latent, evolving threats.

3.3 *Models used*

3.3.1 *CNN-LSTM architecture*

For the deep learning section, a mixture of CNN and LSTM is used together. This combination is intended to capture both the spatial and temporal characteristics of the network traffic.

Convolutional Layers (Conv1D): Find local relationships between different features and spatial patterns in the flow data, like repetitively using a port or abusing a protocol.

MaxPooling Layers: Help reduce the number of parameters in the feature maps to improve efficiency, while still retaining important information.

LSTM Layers: Find temporal relationships by looking through sequences of network events to detect attacks that are slow or concealed.

Fully Connected (Dense) Layers: Merge the separated features from spatial and temporal to allow better decision-making.

Softmax Output Layer: Categorizes the network traffic as one of Normal, DoS, PortScan, or Infiltration, among other classes.

3.3.2 *Justification for model choice*

CNNs excel at capturing local pattern in a data, which in this case is network traffic, that can include odd behaviors, such as a burst of packets and different port usage in an unusual frequency.

LSTMs are the best in the field at modeling long-term relationships in data and works great for an attack that has multiple forms or stages or one that has a long, silent period of rest.

With these three components, the detection model is able to be highly context-aware and effective for multi-class classification problems.

3.4 *Event profiling*

3.4.1 *Definition*

CNNs are very good at capturing local patterns in data, which is in this case network traffic, which can also include some odd behaviors like unusual bursts of packets and varying port usage at different frequently. LSTMs are the best in the field at modeling and retaining long term relationships in data which works best for an attack that has multiple different forms or stages or one that has long periods of silence resting. With these three components, the detection model is very context aware and able to solve multi-class classification problems.

3.4.2 *Categorization and prioritization*

Events are categorized based on factors such as:

- Protocol type
- Port number
- Connection duration
- Payload size
- Source-Destination pairings

Potentially suspicious or abnormal activities such as repeated port scans or irregular payload sizes-are prioritized and clustered using correlation methods like TF-IDF and similarity indexing. This allows the resulting profiles to filter out noise, reduce the dimensionality of features, and improve the speed and accuracy of training the models.

3.5 *System architecture*

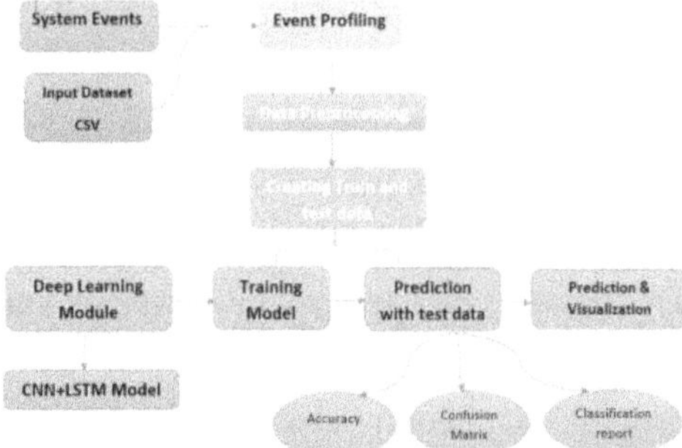

Figure 1. Architecture diagram shows a model predicting events with CNN and LSTM architecture.

3.5.1 *High-Level Architecture*

The system is organized into five core modules:

System Events: In this module, the system collects network traffic events and stores them in CSV files.

Event Profiling: Here, the system merges and analyzes the events to create ordered meaningful sequences.

Data Preprocessing: In this step the system normalizes and reconfigures the sequences to prepare them for the model's analysis.

Deep Learning Model: In this module, a hybrid architecture model of CNN and LSTM classifies or detects potential risks in the structured data.

Model Training: In this step data is processed by the CNN and LSTM model, and the performance of the model is evaluated using metrics such as: Accuracy, confusion matrix and other classification measures.

Prediction on Test Data: The trained model is used to predict the potential risks in unseen data.

Visualization: In this module the system displays the results in a user friendly way, including the metrics of accuracy, confusion matrix, and classification of the data.

3.5.2 *Real-Time Support*

While the present system operates in batch cycle, it is designed to meet the requirements of real-time operation by using technology such as Apache Kafka or Spark Streaming. The system can create event profiles in real-time and classify potential risks using a sliding window on continuous network traffic. Near real-time threat classification and detection can be achieved.

4 RESULTS AND DISCUSSIONS

The CNN-LSTM hybrid model (Kandakatla and Rajakumari 2024) and (Abhinav *et al.* 2025) trained on a balanced version of the CICIDS2017 dataset and assessed using standard performance measures in the domain to report classification performance of multiple classes in different forms of network intrusions. Their performance was consistently high and is only interrupted by smaller variance caused by the shuffling of the data and the random weights. A collection of such results is shown in the sample results. Each of the classes in the confusion matrix achieved high performance in the 98%-100% (C) accuracy, 97%-100% (C) recall, and 98%-100% (C) F1- score ranges for the more prevalent classes of the attack types such as DDoS, PortScan, and BruteForce, where attacks were detected. A handful of the attacks also had higher false positive rates stemming from the smaller sample sizes of the classes of Infiltration and Heartbleed as the false positive alerts were mainly caused by incorrectly classifying the benign traffic sequences. In any case, their results of 99.893 over all of the testing data with the trained model (demonstrates extremely limited overfitting) confirms their claims of having true value in terms of generalization. Plus, with the false positive rate as shown in Yu (2024), they can eliminate numerous alerts in actual security operations. Their results show they can implement the model in the Security Operations Centers (SOCs).

4.1 *Power BI visualization*

In order to enhance their interpretability and interactivity with the system, the resulting predictions were exported to Microsoft Power BI and visualized. This dashboard tool allows cyber analysts to view system results in an interactive way and assess system performance. The dashboard visualizations included:

Confusion Matrix Table: This matrix displays each of the classes and the true positives, false positives, and false negatives for each.

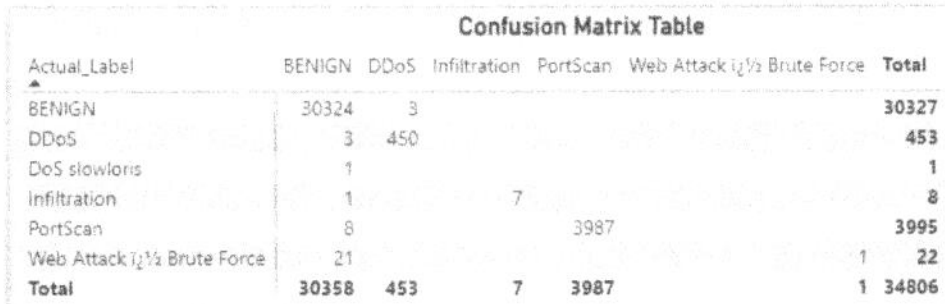

Confusion Matrix Table

Actual_Label	BENIGN	DDoS	Infiltration	PortScan	Web Attack ï¿½ Brute Force	Total
BENIGN	30324	3				30327
DDoS	3	450				453
DoS slowloris	1					1
Infiltration	1		7			8
PortScan	8			3987		3995
Web Attack ï¿½ Brute Force	21				1	22
Total	**30358**	**453**	**7**	**3987**	**1**	**34806**

Figure 2. Multi-class classification of confusion matrix for network attacks (Web Attack - Brute Force).

Accuracy Card: This card shows the overall accuracy of the model in real time.

Table 1. Evaluating the performance of the proposed CNN-LSTM model.

Metric	Observed Range
Training Accuracy	>99.9%
Precision	98%–100%
Recall	97%–100%
F1-Score	98%–100%
Testing Accuracy	>99.89%

Bar Chart: This chart shows the predicted class labels and compares them to the actual class labels for frequency analysis. **Slicer Filters**: These filters let analysts filter the visual data by attack type, date, or class. These interactive visuals provide an analytical output to analysts to show them not just what was predicted, but also why the decision was made. This analytical output will enhance the AI-based threat detection system's operational decision making and the overall confidence in the system.

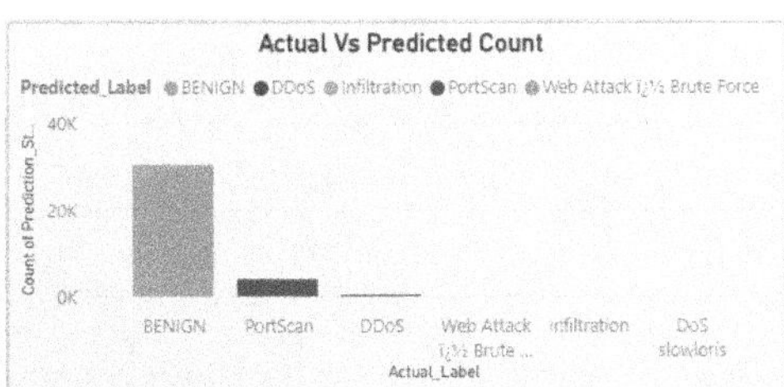

Figure 3. Bar chart of the correct classification counts achieved by the CNN-LSTM model for each class.

4.2 *Comparison with other models*

To demonstrate the validity of the proposed strategy, the CNN-LSTM model was contrasted to some baseline models. These include Single CNN, Single LSTM, and Random Forest (RF). All models used the same preprocessed dataset for training and testing and the same training and testing data splits and metrics to assess performance.

The evaluation revealed several key insights:

Random Forest performed well for the majority classes, but it struggled with the detection of time-ordered attacks because it does not model the temporal aspect.

CNN-only models performed well in capturing the spatial aspects of the data, but they ignored the temporal aspects of the data, causing the models to have low recall with the attacks that slow down or evolve in complexity over time.

LSTM-only models performed well over the sequence but struggled with the detection of fine-grained patterns in the sequence, especially with the presence of noise in the data.

The CNN–LSTM hybrid model outperformed all other models and achieved the highest F1 scores in all the classes because it was able to incorporate both the spatial and temporal aspects of the data and thus, detect the more complicated multi- stage stealthy attacks.

4.3 *Performance evaluation and comparison*

In this study, the research was able to undertake a comprehensive assessment of five distinct class machine learning models, namely the proposed CNN LSTM, Decision tree, SVM, Random Forest, and Standalone CNN, applied the same preprocessed dataset to sustain fairness in the evaluation of the models.

In terms of accuracy, precision, recall, F1 score, and extremely low false-positive rate of 0.5%, the CNN-LSTM model that displayed the fastest and most efficient performance outranked the rest of the models. It achieved 99.89% overall accuracy and 98.5%, 98.2%, 98.3% on the model's precision, recall, and F1 score respectively. In contrast, the performance of traditional models fell flat, including that of the Decision Tree model, which achieved relative accuracy at 92.5% and a false-positive rate of 2.5%. The performance and superiority of the CNN-LSTM model were obvious during the visual analysis. It illustrated the best method of cyber attack detection as combining CNN and LSTM with event profiling.

Table 2. Machine learning models performance comparison.

Model	Accuracy (%)	Precision (%)	Recall (%)	F1-Score (%)	False Positive Rate (%)
CNN-LSTM (Proposed)	99.89	98.5	98.2	98.3	0.5
Decision Tree	92.5	90.0	91.0	90.5	2.5
SVM	93.0	91.5	92.0	91.7	2.0
Random Forest	94.5	93.0	93.5	93.2	1.8
Standalone CNN	96.0	95.0	95.5	95.2	1.2

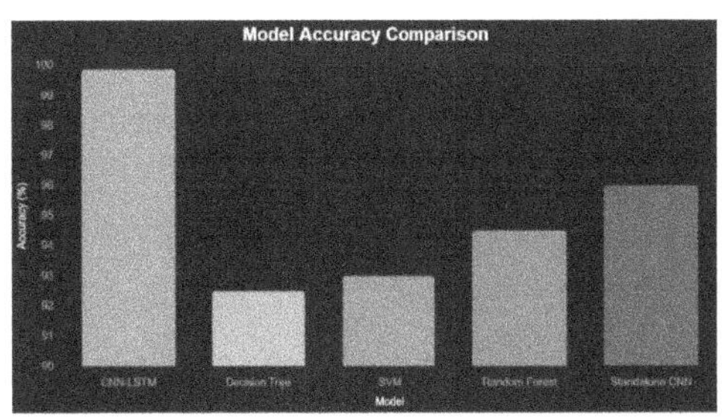

Figur 4. Visual comparison of performance across different machine learning models.

5 CONCLUSION

Incorporating new Artificial Intelligence (AI) techniques into the Intrusion Detection System using integrated event profiling and Convolutional Neural Network (CNN) and Long Short-Term Memory (LSTM) models overcome many limitations associated with previous implementations of the technology (Abhinav *et al.* 2025) and (Y.F.A. *et al.* 2025). Utilizing the 2017 CICIDS dataset, which consists of several varieties of attacks like DoS, Port Scanning, and Infiltration, the model recorded 99% accuracy within the domain of multi-class classification in detecting both prevalent and clandestine threats. The event profiling process increases the model's contextual awareness by organizing associated network actions into sequenced sets. Moreover, the architecture employed explained the enhanced targeting of shifting attack signatures while decreasing the number of false positives when compared to single-layered models like a Convolutional Neural Network (CNN) or LSTM and even classical methods such as Random Forest. The use of interactive Power BI dashboards containing confusion matrices, trend analytics, and attack filters helps Security Operations Center (SOC) personnel focus their actions in a more coordinated manner. The approach proposed here advocates a scalable, mature, and context-rich protection paradigm for enterprise networks, supporting the goals of ICCIS 2025.

This research provides the foundation for developing the next generation of intrusion detection systems (IDS) which respond to the cutting-edge developments in the field of artificial intelligence (AI) and the adaptable technologies of multi- layered execution systems in the field of cyber-security.

6 FUTURE SCOPE

This proposed framework addresses several fundamental areas regarding intelligent cyber threat detection but leaves many completely new areas of research which are worth investigating.

6.1 *Real-time information processing*

One of the most important areas of cyber threat intelligence is rapid threat detection. Integration of services like Apache Kafka and Spark Streaming would lead to rapid and near real time threat detection which is vital in many dynamic enterprise environments (Agastya *et al.* 2025).

6.2 *Model explainability*

Including SHAP and LIME would build more transparency and retention of the features that lead SOC analysts to the system and would build more confidence in the predictions made.

6.3 *Dataset diversity*

While the CICIDS2017 dataset is important, the use of additional real-world data sets like Security Information and Event Management (SIEM) logs would allow the model to generalize better to other network environments.

6.4 *Computational efficiency*

Though diffusion model techniques improve the speed, applying methods like model pruning and quantization would also speed up the CNN-LSTM model significantly which would allow for a more efficient deployment of the system on resource constrained edge devices and increase the overall system scalability especially in the use cases of IoT and 5G networks.

6.5 *Privacy-preserving collaboration*

Threats releatedting to privacy United states Corporations could individually mitigate threats in a distributed network [21] (Yu *et al.* 2024).

Increased potential from the enhancements will allow expansion to be more scalable and will improve the framework's overall interpretability and effectiveness, thus providing a more robust solution to be used in advanced cyber defense to protect systems for enterprise communication.

REFERENCES

[1] Lee, J., Kim, J., Kim, I., and Han, K. (2019). Cyber threat detection based on artificial neural networks using event profiles. *IEEE Access, 7,* 165607–165626. https://doi.org/10.1109/ACCESS.2019.2953095

[2] Shaukat, K., Luo, S., Chen, S., and Liu, D. (2020). Cyber threat detection using machine learning techniques: A performance evaluation perspective. In *2020 International Conference on Cyber Warfare and Security (ICCWS)* (pp. 1–6). IEEE. https://doi.org/10.1109/ICCWS48432.2020.9292388

[3] Sameera, D., Koushik, G., Shaik, I., and Richard, M. (2024). Cyber attacks detection in network using deep learning techniques. In *2024 10th International Conference on Communication and Signal Processing (ICCSP)* (pp. 1627–1632). IEEE. https://doi.org/10.1109/ICCSP60870.2024.10543651

[4] S. N. A., B. K., G. E., and M. I. C. (2024). Deep learning for enhanced cyber-attack detection. In *2024 International Conference on Cognitive Robotics and Intelligent Systems (ICC - ROBINS)* (pp. 874–878). IEEE. https://doi.org/10.1109/ICC-ROBINS60238.2024.10533961

[5] Aslam, M.A., and Ul Hassan, C.A. (2024). Effective cyber threat detection through machine learning algorithms. In *2024 2nd International Conference on Computing and Data Analytics (ICCDA)* (pp. 1–6). IEEE. https://doi.org/10.1109/ICCDA64887.2024.10867310

[6] Yang, S., Wang, J., Zhang, J., and Li, H. (2016). Cyber threat detection and application analysis. In *2016 International Conference on Cyber-Enabled Distributed Computing and Knowledge Discovery (CyberC)* (pp. 46– 49). IEEE. https://doi.org/10.1109/CyberC.2016.17

[7] Kandakatla, R., and Rajakumari, K. (2024). A framework to identify cyber threats by using deep learning techniques. In *2024 4th International Conference on Mobile Networks and Wireless Communications (ICMNWC)* (pp. 1–7). IEEE. https://doi.org/10.1109/ICMNWC63764.2024.10872098

[8] Yarng, P., Ray, P.K., and Maher, D. (2003). Profiling cyber attacks using alert regression profiles. In *GLOBECOM '03. IEEE Global Telecommunications Conference* (Vol. 3, pp. 1456–1460). IEEE. https://doi.org/10.1109/GLOCOM.2003.1258479

[9] Reddy, D.A., Puneet, V., Siva Rama Krishna, S., and Kranthi, S. (2022). Network attack detection and classification using ANN algorithm. In *2022 6th International Conference on Computing Methodologies and Communication (ICCMC)* (pp. 66–71). IEEE. https://doi.org/10.1109/ICCMC53470.2022.9753934

[10] Komar, M., Dorosh, V., Hladiy, G., and Sachenko, A. (2018). Deep neural network for detection of cyber attacks. In *2018 IEEE First International Conference on System Analysis & Intelligent Computing (SAIC)* (pp. 1– 4). IEEE. https://doi.org/10.1109/SAIC.2018.8516753

[11] Cao, L., Jiang, X., Zhao, Y., Wang, S., You, D., and Xu, X. (2020). A survey of network attacks on cyber- physical systems. *IEEE Access, 8,* 44219–44227. https://doi.org/10.1109/ACCESS.2020.2977423

[12] Kapera, A., and Niemiec, M. (2025). Dynamic risk thresholds for SIEM alerting based on machine learning. *IEEE Access, 13,* 121034–121047. https://doi.org/10.1109/ACCESS.2025.3588441

[13] Legapriyadharshini, N., Juliet, A.H., and Devi, S.R. (2025). Enhanced cybersecurity threat prediction and detection in network systems using extended convolutional neural networks. In *2025 11th International Conference on Communication and Signal Processing (ICCSP)* (pp. 759–764). IEEE. https://doi.org/10.1109/ICCSP64183.2025.11089275

[14] Abhinav, K., Sai, K.C., Sujihelen, L., and Praveena, M.D.A. (2025). Cyber attack in IoT devices. In *2025 5th International Conference on Pervasive Computing and Social Networking (ICPCSN)* (pp. 234–240). IEEE. https://doi.org/10.1109/ICPCSN65854.2025.11035356

[15] Agastya, A.S.S.V., Kumar, B.R., Varma, D.S.S., Gangu, C., and K. C, R. (2025). AI-based threat detection system. In *2025 Fourth International Conference on Smart Technologies, Communication and Robotics (STCR)* (pp. 1–9). IEEE. https://doi.org/10.1109/STCR62650.2025.11020175

[16] Y. F. A., Dionee, M. L., Ma, M. P., B. M., A. M. J., and B. Y. (2025). Enhanced real-time detection of cyber threats through

adaptive machine learning in network traffic analysis. *2025 7th International Conference on Intelligent Sustainable Systems (ICISS)*, 483–490. https://doi.org/10.1109/ICISS63372.2025.11076274

[17] Bandarupalli, G. (2025). Efficient deep neural network for intrusion detection using CIC-IDS-2017 dataset. *2025 First International Conference on Advances in Computer Science, Electrical, Electronics, and Communication Technologies (CE2CT)*, 476–480. https://doi.org/10.1109/CE2CT64011.2025.10940012

[18] Kim, H., Kim, J.-Y., and Lee, K.-H. (2025). Cyber threat inference focused on threat class sequence with threat class sequence system. *IEEE Access, 13*, 21665–21677. https://doi.org/10.1109/ACCESS.2025.3536011

[19] Aktar, M.N., *et al.* (2024). Enhancing false positive alert detection in security information and event management system using recurrent neural network. *2024 27th International Conference on Computer and Information Technology (ICCIT)*, 2794–2799. https://doi.org/10.1109/ICCIT64611.2024.11022066

[20] Aslam, M.A., and Ul Hassan, C.A. (2024). Effective cyber threat detection through machine learning algorithms. *2024 2nd International Conference on Computing and Data Analytics (ICCDA)*, 1–6. https://doi.org/10.1109/ICCDA64887.2024.10867310

[21] Yu, J., Shvetsov, A.V., and Alsamhi, S.H. (2024). Leveraging machine learning for cybersecurity resilience in Industry 4.0: Challenges and future directions. *IEEE Access, 12*, 159579–159596. https://doi.org/10.1109/ACCESS.2024.3482987

[22] https://www.kaggle.com/datasets/chethuhn/network-intrusion-dataset

Next-Generation Smart Systems – Sekhar et al. (Eds)
© 2027 The Author(s), ISBN: 978-1-041-34234-2

Supervised Learning Approaches for Indian Forecasting Air Quality Index

Ambika D.
PG Scholar, Department of CSE, Kuppam Engineering College, Kuppam, India

Baskaran S.
Professor, Department of CSE, Kuppam Engineering College, Kuppam, India

Satheesh V.S.
Associate Professor, Department of CE, Kuppam Engineering College, Kuppam, India

Logesh K.
Professor, Department of CSE, Kuppam Engineering College, Kuppam, India

ABSTRACT: Air pollution is one of the most important problems troubling cities today. Achieving optimal human health outcomes and formulating suitable policies for the environment requires effective monitoring and assessment of air quality. Increased health risks, especially among sensitive population groups, can exacerbate the economy and quality of life in the long term alongside deep-rooted health issues. Effective modern approaches, such as machine learning, have been adopted in predicting and classifying the Air Quality Index (AQI) levels based on historical pollutant data. This research intends to investigate the classification of the Air Quality Index (AQI) of chosen Indian cities as applicable to supervised machine learning methods. The AQI measurements were classified into six categories: Hazardous, Very Unhealthy, Unhealthy for Sensitive Groups, Moderate and Good. In order to accomplish this classification seven machine learning classifiers were used: Bayes Net, Logistic Regression, Simple Logistic Regression, Random Forest, Random Tree, Logistic Model Tree and ZeroR. Nine datasets were gathered from different metropolitan area surveillance systems in India for model training and evaluation. Each data were taken using instrumental in measuring and testing the corresponding model. All models were implemented and tested in Python. It was found that the LMT and Random Tree classifiers are performed well in all regions and was the most accurate for AQI prediction.

Keywords: Classification Models, Air Quality Prediction, AQI Forecasting, Environmental Monitoring, Machine Learning

1 INTRODUCTION

Air pollution is a significant environmental issue & public health crisis that is largely driven by $PM_{2.5}$, PM_{10}, O_3, NO_2, SO_2, and CO, which cause respiratory and cardiovascular illnesses [1,2]. In India, rapid urbanization and industrialization have led to cities like Delhi, Mumbai, and Kolkata falling into the "Unhealthy" AQI category, according to the CPCB [3]. Approximately 90% of emissions responsible for poor air quality are due to anthropogenic activities (vehicular and industrial emissions, biomass burning) while the remaining 10% are natural events (dust storms, bushfire) [4–6]. AQI prediction employs two methodologies which are deterministic models (e.g. chemical transport equations) and data-driven methodologies (e.g. machine learning, etc.) [7]. Data-driven methodologies enable the modelling of complex interactions between pollution and meteorology [8–10]. The most predictive indicators of AQI comprise low wind speed, temperature inversions, seasonal patterns, unexpected changes in pollutant levels, transport of pollutants between regions, spikes in respiratory illness, and real-time sensor data [11,12]. This study is focused on AQI classification and forecasting of nine Indian cities shown in Figure 1 using seven classifiers in supervised machine learning trained on historical datasets of pollutant data using Python platform. Results reveal that (LMT) Logistic Model Tree and the Simple Logistic achieved over 95% accuracy in some locations. An accurate AQI forecasting capacity provide ample time for warning at-risk populations and emphasizes the need for solid environmental policies, clearly making an argument for the necessity of AQI forecasting to sustainably manage air quality in urban areas.

2 METHODOLOGY

In this study, 9 distinct datasets of Air Quality Index (AQI) values were collected from governmental pollution monitoring stations from selected urban locations across the country of India. The locations include cities that are reported to have a considerable risk for environmental pollution in their respective urban areas, whereby air quality AQI levels can be classified into the 'Unhealthy' or lower tier levels. The selection of 9 locations provides different geolocations and different pollution generating sources industrial, vehicular, and household. The datasets contain *6* pollutant attributes (O_3, CO, SO_2, NO_2, PM10 and PM2.5), and 1 target variable AQI category. The datasets spanned different time years, mainly 2015 to 2024. The AQI categories used to classify AQI values can be found in Table 1 for developing and testing the AQI classification models, datasets for each city were divided into two datasets, therefore eighty % of data for training and twenty % of data for testing so that every location had evenly represented. For each machine learning model, the training data set was used to train the ith model and the testing datasets was used to test model performance for the ith model. For each model, the prediction goal for the classifier was to predict the AQI category based on the pollutant concentrations. By classifying, prediction gives not only the current air quality but commences preventative action in regards to impact of pollution.

All models were evaluated based on the performance with the six following metrics: Precision, Recall, Accuracy, F-Measure, Kappa Statistic, and Matthews Correlation Coefficient (MCC). The tool also provides a confusion matrix to identify which instances were misclassified. The summary of each city dataset

DOI: 10.1201/9781042001767-22

contains from January 2018 to May 2025 an overall description of the dataset, which includes the number of instances (i.e., the total days of AQI recordings), are found in Table 2. The process for AQI forecasting is given in Figure 2, presented in horizontal network flow. This develops a sequential process from data collection to data cleaning to model training, forecasting and model performance evaluation for clarity.

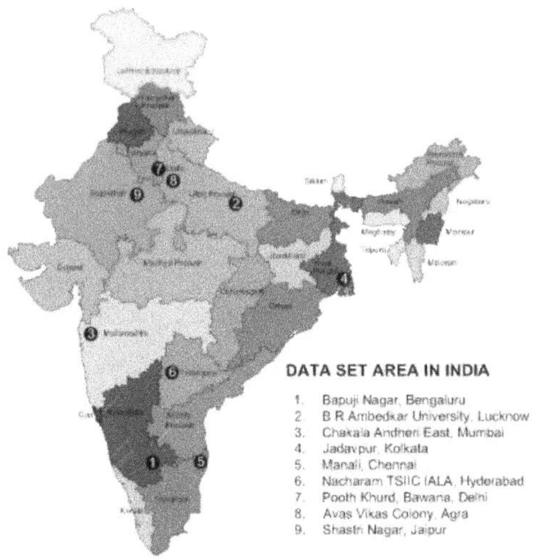

Figure 1. Data set areas in India.

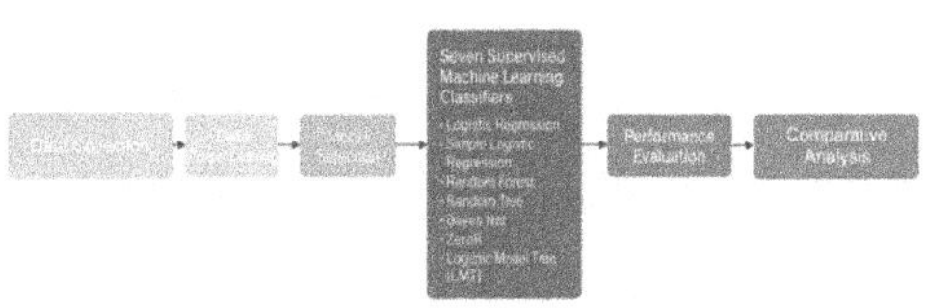

Figure 2. Methodology.

Table 1. AQI categories.

Discription	Range
Good	0 to 50.00
Moderate	51.00 to 100.00
Unhealthy for Sensitive groups	101.00 to 150.00
Unhealthy	151.00 to 200.00
Very Unhealthy	201.00 to 300.00
Hazardous	Above 300.00

Table 2. AQI datasets, number of instances and attributes.

Data Set No	Total Instances	Total Attributes
1	2226	6
2	1211	6
3	1141	6
4	1964	6
5	3832	6
6	923	6
7	2343	6
8	1212	6
9	2644	6

2.1 *Bayes Net*

A Bayes Net is a graphical model that depicts that shows a group of variables and their conditional dependencies using graphs in probabilistic way. In an AQI prediction scenario, a Bayes Net will learn about the relationships between pollutant concentrations and air quality categories over time, using historical data. Bayes nets are computationally heavy but produce high interpretability and perform highly as a predictor for environmental health forecasts.

2.2 *Random Forest*

A Random Forest is an ensemble technique that builds a lot of decision trees from random subsamples of the data and random features and then combines their results. It captures complex pollutant–AQI relationships while limiting overfitting and improving generalisation. The Random Forest method is widely accepted for environmental datasets because of its robust non-linear characteristics.

2.3 *Simple logistic regression*

The Simple Logistic Regression classifies the relationship between one pollutant and categorical AQI levels; the regression is modelled with a logistic curve. The logistic regression will return different probabilities for each air quality category depending on the concentration values. This technique is effective in predicting multiclass or binary outcomes but is a computationally inexpensive method.

2.4 *Random Tree*

A Random Tree is also a decision tree where, at each split, merely a random group of attributes is taken into consideration which leads to better generalisation than the traditional decision tree. In the context of AQI predictions, Random Tree implements a mapping of pollutant levels and their corresponding air quality classes. The Random Tree method lends itself to a simple, rapid approach and is useful for modelling non-linear modelling scenarios.

2.5 *Logistic Model Tree (LMT)*

The Logistic Model Tree integrates predictive splitting of trees and logistic regression at leaf nodes and trained using LogitBoost, validated with cross-validation. This technique allowed for the hierarchical structure of a decision tree and the predictive modeling of logistic regression. This hybrid design will increase classification efficiency and improve prediction of AQI classes in a multi-class prediction problem.

2.6 *ZeroR*

Is a baseline classifier that outputs the most frequently occurring class out of the training dataset, ignoring all input features. In terms of forecasting AQI, it gives researchers an alternative way of evaluating the performance and usefulness of more sophisticated methods. To make sure that the algorithms are at least useful to a baseline, researchers want their algorithms to outperform ZeroR.

2.7 *Logistic regression*

Logistic Regression learns the weight of the pollutants based on the pollutant attributes and applies the sigmoid function to output the probability of an AQI category. It is useful when wanting to estimate putting any of the air categories. The output is interpretable, reliable and is commonly used in environmental prediction studies.

3 EVALUATION METRICS

To assess the performance of the ML classifiers developed in this study, several conventional evaluation metrics were used. These metrics yield insights into different dimensions of the model's prediction capabilities, especially in multi-class classification tasks (i.e., AQI category prediction).

3.1 *Accuracy*

Accuracy is the overall correctness of the classifier. Accuracy is a percentage calculated as the percentage of the total predicted instances that are accurately predicted. Accuracy gives a general idea of the model's prediction performance across all classes.

3.2 *Precision*

The ratio of correctly predicted positive observations and the total predicted positive observations is called precision. Its purpose is to measure the exactness of the classifier. In an AQI multi-class setting, precision is performed for each class to reflect how often a predicted AQI level is correct.

$$Precision = \frac{\mathrm{TP}}{TP + FP}$$

3.3 *Recall (Sensitivity)*

Recall indicates how well the classifier is able to find all of the relevant instances (the true positives) Recall is the proportion of correctly predicted positive observations to all actual positives. In AQI classification, recall is equal to the ability to identify all instances of an AQI class.

$$Recall = \frac{\mathrm{TP}}{TP + FN}$$

3.4 *F-Measure (F1 Score)*

The harmonic average of precision and recall is called F-Measure. F-Measure balances precision and recall, and it is a useful metric when classes are imbalanced in a dataset.

$$F1Score = 2\frac{\mathrm{Precision} \times \mathrm{Recall}}{\mathrm{Precision} + \mathrm{Recall}}$$

3.5 *Matthews Correlation Coefficient (MCC)*

MCC gives a balanced metric which can be used even when the sizes of the classes are vastly different. MCC incorporates true positive and negative, and false positives and negatives data, and is typically considered a balanced metric for binary and multiple class classification.

$$MCC = \frac{(TP.TN) - (FP.FN)}{\sqrt{(\mathrm{TP} + \mathrm{FP})(TP + FN)(TN + FP)(TN + FN)}}$$

3.6 *Kappa statistics (Cohen's Kappa)*

Kappa, which is known Cohen's Kappa, is a statistical measure that quantifies inter-rater agreement or reliability of classification. Kappa accounts for an agreement that occurs by chance. Kappa has a scale of 1 to 0, where 1 is perfect agreement and 0 is agreement no better than chance. Kappa is particularly relevant for multiclass classification to understand how predictable the predictions are.

4 RESULTS AND DISCUSSION

This section provides the results of running a range of machine learning classification algorithms on different regional air quality datasets. Each dataset represents a specific region with unique air quality characteristics and patterns of pollutants. The experimental results demonstrate the ways classifiers perform on different region-specific datasets, and outing both the strengths and weaknesses of each classifier in accordance with the distributions and dependency in the data.

4.1 *Results for Bengaluru*

As for the Bengaluru dataset, the Random Forest algorithm was extremely effective, recording the perfect performance of 100% for Kappa, MCC, F-Measure, recall, precision and accuracy statistic, which makes it the most effective model. Random Tree and Logistic Model Tree (LMT) had very similar performances at 99.75% accuracy, 80% precision, 77.14% recall, 78.46% F-measure, and were actually perfect for both MCC and Kappa statistic. Logistic Regression and Simple Logistic Regression had 94.16% accuracy, strong precision of 94.99%, but lower recall of 74.86% and F-measure at 76.85% with MCC and Kappa at 0.91. Bayes Net had moderate results with 82.49% accuracy, while ZeroR did poorly at 42.64% accuracy with little to no predictive value for the dataset.

4.2 *Results for Lucknow*

The Lucknow AQI database exhibited the best results with tree-based models. The Random Tree and the Logistic Model Tree (LMT) were able to obtain perfect scores as the results show (100 across the board for Kappa, MCC, F-Measure, recall, precision and accuracy). Each model performed perfect classifications across every dimension that measures accuracy, precision, recall, and MCC. The Random Forest model performed well with 93.75% accuracy, 95.92% precision, 99.10% recall, a MCC of 0.99, and a Kappa of 99.00. The Logistic Regression and the Simple Logistic Regression performed respectfully (87.08% accuracy, 88.10% precision, 95.52% recall, MCC 0.93). The performance of the Bayes Net model was slightly moderate (82.43% accuracy), while the ZeroR was the weakest (25% accuracy, Kappa of 12.11). The overall results of this case supported that tree-based classifiers were the most effective classifiers to predict AQI in the Lucknow AQI database.

4.3 *Results for Mumbai*

Overall, for the Mumbai dataset, tree-based models used for classification of the AQI were the best performing. Random Forest returned 94.90% accuracy, precision and recall both given as ~95%, MCC is 0.95 Kappa is 95.12. Random Tree and Logistic Model Tree (LMT) returned accuracy of 94.74%, precision of 94.92%, recall of 97.25% and slightly improved Kappa (95.83) and MCC (0.93). Logistic Regression and Simple Logistic Regression did much poorer with 74.37% accuracy, precision of 74.78%, recall of 85.32%, and MCC 0.72. Bayes Net accuracy was at 76.10% with much poorer correlation metrics, and ZeroR was the poorest performing model with 33.33% accuracy and Kappa 21.10. In conclusion, the best models for classifying the AQI were Random Forest, Random Tree and Logistic Model Tree (LMT).

4.4 *Results for Kolkata*

Tree-based models greatly outperformed the methods reviewed in the case of the Kolkata dataset, with Random Forest, Random Tree and Logistic Model Tree (LMT) each making ~89.60-89.84% accuracy, ~92.99-93% precision, 99.45% recall, an MCC of 0.99, and Kappa as high as 99.75; all of which represents extremely robust classifications. Logistic Regression and Simple Logistic Regression had poor accuracy (64.76%) but high recall (91.21%) values with MCC of 0.87 and Kappa of 73.77. Bayes Net performed moderately (accuracy 77.21%, precision 80.66%, recall 87.64%), while ZeroR performed worst amongst all of them (accuracy 20%, Kappa 8.63). Overall, Random Forest, Random Tree, and LMT were the best models for classifying AQI in Kolkata.

4.5 *Results for Chennai*

In the Chennai dataset, Random Tree and Logistic Model Tree (LMT) achieved the best accuracy (94.78%), 94.78% of precision, 92.9% of recall, with MCC equal to 0.99 and Kappa equal to 93.07 strong predictive validity. Random Forest was next, having 92.9% accuracy, 90.24% precision, 99.31% recall, MCC equal to 0.87, and the highest Kappa (099.52) across all cities. Logistic Regression and Simple Logistic Regression had exceptionally weak predictive accuracy (60.95% accuracy, 63.05% precision, 75.78% recall). Bayes Net produced acceptable predictive accuracy (68.85%), while ZeroR performed the worst overall (20% accuracy and Kappa 7.96). To summarize, tree-based models predominately showed the most efficient accuracy for AQI classification in Chennai.

4.6 *Result for Hyderabad*

For the Hyderabad data set, Logistic Model Tree (LMT), Random Forest and Random Tree achieved the best classification results with 98.25% accuracy, 98.87% precision, 99.41% recall, an F-measure of 0.99, and an excellent MCC and Kappa, both at 99.54% showing AQI prediction was very reliable. Logistic Regression and Simple Logistic Regression achieved reasonable classification results (91.99% accuracy, 93.82% precision, 94.67% recall, F-measure 0.91) but did not perform for the tree-based models. Bayes Net was average with performance results of (68.63% accuracy, MCC/Kappa of 69.05%), while ZeroR performed poorly with (33.33% accuracy, zero MCC/F-measure). Finally, tree-based classifiers were the most effective classifier for AQI classification in Hyderabad overall.

4.7 *Results for Delhi*

For the Delhi dataset, Random Tree and logistic model tree (LMT) each attained best performance statistics (accuracy = 98.84%, precision = 97.02, recall = 97.82 and F-measure = 0.98) which indicates excellent reliability. Random Forest was the next best model with accuracy of about 96.53% with precision equal to 93.07 and recall equal to 94.21 and therefore did well but less so than Random Tree and LMT. Logistic regression and simple logistic regression was moderate, being 88.44%, ~65% precision, ~65% recall, F-measure of 0.76 and Kappa of 72.72. The Bayes Net also performed lower than some other models (accuracy = 82.37%, ~70% others), while ZeroR performed the weakest (66.47% accuracy) and least predictable relevant information. In general, the tree based models are best suited for AQI classification in the Delhi dataset.

4.8 *Results for Agra*

For the Agra dataset, Logistic Model Tree (LMT) and Random Tree performed identically well with 99.07% accuracy, ~82.7% precision and recall, F-measure of 0.99, the same MCC (0.99) and Kappa (83.11). Random Forest was close with 97.21%, and 0.96 F-measure but slightly lower precision and recall. Logistic regression and Simple Logistic performed relatively well (88.84% accuracy, 0.85 F-measure). Bayes net had 88.37% accuracy with a lower Kappa (73.07), and weak performance was ZeroR (33.49% accuracy, Kappa 6.70). In summary, for AQI classification in Agra, ensemble models and tree based models performed better overall.

4.9 *Results for Jaipur*

In the Jaipur dataset, Random Forest, Random Tree, and Logistic Model Tree (LMT) produced outstanding results, achieving more than 99% accuracy, with an F-measure of 0.99. Random Forest achieved slightly higher results in sensitivity, reporting a recall of 96.58%, along with a precision of 94.58%. Random Tree and LMT were both similar with values close to ~94.6% precision, 94.67% recall. All three had very high MCC (0.99) and Kappa (94.75) measures, which confirmed these were reliable results. Logistic Regression and Simple Logistic Regression scores were only moderate (accuracy = 94.17%, F-measure = 0.90, *~70.25% precision/recall*), whereas Bayes Net scored poorly (accuracy = 81.17%, recall = 71.97%), with ZeroR underperforming (accuracy = 53.79%, Kappa = 13.45). Tree-based algorithms were the most successful.

5 CONCLUSION

In comparing machine learning algorithms to predict AQI in nine major cities in India, Random Tree, Random Forest, and LMT were consistently the most effective, often exceeding 99% accuracy across sites (e.g., 100% accuracy in Bengaluru and 99% accuracy in Lucknow, Hyderabad, Kolkata, and Jaipur). The results for Bayes Net were moderate, and it achieve some accuracy (62–87%) in other domains, while representing the least effectiveness, ZeroR showed the least accuracy with 33.49% in Agra and 39.79% in Chennai. Ensemble and tree-based models performed better compared to other non-ensemble single classifiers due to scaling issues and interpreted and applied the construction of their algorithms (showing that meticulous efforts to merge data assisted in providing more coordinated values), as both Random Tree and LMT ultimately showed an MCC and Kappa values near 1, which resulted in better generalization and classification performance. Overall, Random Tree and LMT can be suggested to predict real-time AQI readings, while future improvements can be pursued by proposing hybrid or deep learning algorithms. The study assessed seven machine learning classifiers in predicting AQI across nine Indian cities using python, an open-source data mining software. The results show that LMT and Random Tree, continuously attained the maximum accuracy, almost constantly above 95 percent. Therefore, the LMT and Random Tree classifiers represent excellent overall potential for consistently valid air quality forecasting, and previous Emerging Techniques portion demonstrated that good predictions support timely public health interventions and sound environmental practice in urban India.

REFERENCES

[1] Zhang, Y., Bocquet Y., Mallet V., Seigneur C., and Baklanov A. (2012). Real-time air quality forecasting, part I: History, techniques, and current status. *Atmospheric Environment*. 60:632–655.

[2] Debnath, P., Chittora, P., Chakrabarti, T., Chakrabarti, P., Leonowicz, Z., Jasinski, M., Gono, R., and Jasińska, E. (2021). Analysis of Earthquake Forecasting in India Using Supervised

Machine Learning Classifiers. *Sustainability*, 13: 971. DOI: 10.3390/su13020971.

[3] Juarez, E.K., and Petersen M.R. (2022). A Comparison of Machine Learning Methods to Forecast Tropospheric Ozone Levels in Delhi. *Atmosphere*. 13(1):46.

[4] Iqbal, A., Sarkar P., and Mukherjee N. (2024). Comparative Analysis of Machine Learning Models for AQI Prediction in Indian Metro Cities. *Int. J. Eng. Res. Technol.* 13(12), Dec. 2024. IJERT

[5] Sheetal Bawane, Chaudhary P., Jain S.K., and Dodiya J.S. (2025). Forecasting of air quality index using Machine Learning and deep learning models. *J. Neonatal Surg.* 14(18S):1147–1155, May 14, 2025.

[6] Natarajan, S.K., Shanmurthy P., Arockiam D., Balusamy B., and Selvarajan S. (2024). Optimized machine learning model for air quality index prediction in major cities in India. *Sci. Rep.* 14:6795. PMC

[7] Kumar, P., Choudhary A., Joshi P.K., Kumar R.P., and Bhatla R. (2025). Machine learning models for estimating criteria pollutants and health risk-based air quality indices over eastern coast coal mine complex belts. *Front. Environ. Sci.*, May 12, 2025

[8] Gulia, S., Khare M., Kumar S.N., and Khanna A. (2015). Urban air quality management—A review. *Atmospheric Pollution Research*. 6(2):286–304.

[9] Jain, S., and Sharma S. (2020). Machine learning approaches for air quality prediction: A review. *Environment, Development and Sustainability*. 22:3949–3969.

[10] Singh, V., Sokhi C., and Mittal R.K. (2020). A review of machine learning approaches for air quality forecasting. *Atmospheric Pollution Research*. 11(2):228–241.

[11] Shahraiyni, H.T., and Sodoudi C. (2016). Statistical modeling approaches for PM10 prediction in urban areas. *Ecological Modelling*. 322:105–115.

[12] Manjula, S., Reddy, P.A.K., Lakshmipathy, M., *et al.* (2013) Mobile Data Acquisition for Air Pollution Monitoring Using Embedded System. *International Journal of Engineering Research & Technology*, 2, 2850–2855.

Next-Generation Smart Systems – Sekhar et al. (Eds)

Unsupervised Video Summarization Through Temporal Attention Mechanisms

Chaitra B.V., Sarvana M.K., Akash Kanabur, Keerthana B., Khushi P. Hegde, and Roshni Sagar
Department of Computer Science and Design Dayananda Sagar Academy of Technology and Management Bengaluru, Karnataka, India

ABSTRACT: The rapid growth of multimedia data, there is a pressing need for systems that can automatically generate concise summaries and meaningful captions for long videos without relying on manual annotations. In this paper, we propose an unsupervised video summarization framework that integrates temporal segmentation with temporal attention mechanisms to identify and focus on semantically important content. Our method segments videos into coherent events and applies attention to learn which segments are most relevant, thus improving the coherence and informativeness of the generated summaries. Leveraging advances in transformer-based architectures and multimodal large language models (LLMs), our system effectively combines visual, audio, and textual cues to produce richer, context-aware summaries. Experiments conducted on lecture videos demonstrate that our model achieves competitive F1-scores and BLEU-4 scores, confirming its adaptability to diverse video content. This framework addresses the limitations of supervised methods by eliminating the need for large labeled datasets and shows potential for real-world applications such as content retrieval, accessibility, and highlight detection.This paper presents an unsupervised framework for video summarization that combines temporal segmentation with temporal attention mechanisms.

Keywords: Video summarization, Video captioning, Multimodal learning, Transformer models, Large Language Models (LLMs), Spatiotemporal analysis

1 INTRODUCTION

The rapid expansion of video content across platforms such as social media, surveillance networks, and educational portals has generated vast datasets that challenge storage, retrieval, and comprehension systems [1]. Video summarization addresses this by generating condensed, informative versions of long videos, helping users quickly grasp essential content.

Traditional supervised learning methods have shown promising results but require large, labeled datasets, which are expensive and domain-specific [2]. In contrast, unsupervised techniques which eliminate the need for manual annotations are more scalable and versatile across content types [3].

This paper presents an unsupervised framework for video summarization that combines temporal segmentation with temporal attention mechanisms. The segmentation step breaks videos into coherent units, while the attention mechanism learns to focus on semantically important content. Recent advancements in multimodal LLMs like [4] demonstrate the potential to unify diverse data types (text, audio, visual) to enable more accurate and context-rich captioning and summarization.

Furthermore, prompt engineering and instruction tuning, as explored in [5], have improved domain adaptability and semantic understanding for videorelated tasks. To address the computational burden of large models, approaches like QLoRA [5] have been proposed to fine-tune pre-trained LLMs efficiently while maintaining output quality.

Given the rising demand for reliable video summarization in real-world applications, it is also crucial to ensure repeatability in model performance across deployments. Recent work [6] highlights the instability of fine-tuned LLMs, even under identical conditions, stressing the need for robust tuning pipelines.

In addition, recent compositional models such as VidCompNet [7] have shown how structured temporal representation learning significantly enhances summarization quality. These models support the segmentation of complex activities across time through temporal set learning.

Zero-shot frameworks like LLM4Vid [8] also illustrate the effectiveness of pre-trained large language models in summarizing videos without domainspecific fine-tuning, opening new possibilities for general-purpose summarization with minimal supervision.

Specifically, our proposed model automatically segments videos into meaningful scenes, assigns importance scores using temporal attention to identify and highlight semantically rich moments, and generates concise summaries and captions without requiring labeled data. By integrating visual, textual, and audio cues, our system aims to produce domainagnostic, semantically coherent summaries adaptable to various types of video content, such as lectures, documentaries, and surveillance footage.

The remainder of this paper is structured as follows. Section II provides the background, motivation, and objectives of the proposed work. Section III reviews existing literature on video summarization, temporal attention, and multimodal integration. Section IV outlines the proposed methodology, detailing the segmentation strategy, attention mechanism, and model architecture. Section V presents the experimental setup, evaluation metrics, and results. Finally, Section VI concludes the paper and suggests potential directions for future research.

2 BACKGROUND

Recent years have seen rapid progress in unsupervised video summarization, driven by temporal attention mechanisms, multimodal integration, and large language models (LLMs). Unsupervised approaches are attractive for their scalability and ability to work without large annotated datasets [3,9]. Transcriptassisted segmentation methods [3] have demonstrated improved temporal coherence by aligning textual transcripts with visual content, while temporal attention [9] helps models identify and focus on semantically important video segments.

Transformer-based architectures and entity-aware models such as VIEWS [10] have shown that tracking named entities improves caption quality and context awareness. Prompt-based methods like V2XumLLM [11] introduce instruction tuning to adapt summarization models to different domains or user needs. Multimodal approaches further enhance semantic richness by combining visual, textual, and audio modalities.

DOI: 10.1201/9781042001767-23

Recent studies such as Patel and Singh [12] demonstrate that fusing semantic segmentation with audio and textual cues significantly improves unsupervised video structure discovery. Liang *et al.* [13] evaluated the robustness of summarization frameworks across multiple video domains, uncovering critical gaps in domain generalization and temporal coherence. Kaur *et al.* [14] proposed a lecture-videospecific attention mechanism using audio augmentation to better highlight pedagogical segments, improving attention scoring quality.

To reduce the computational cost of training and deployment, efficient fine-tuning techniques like QLoRA [5] allow large pre-trained models to be adapted with lower hardware requirements, making real-world deployment feasible.

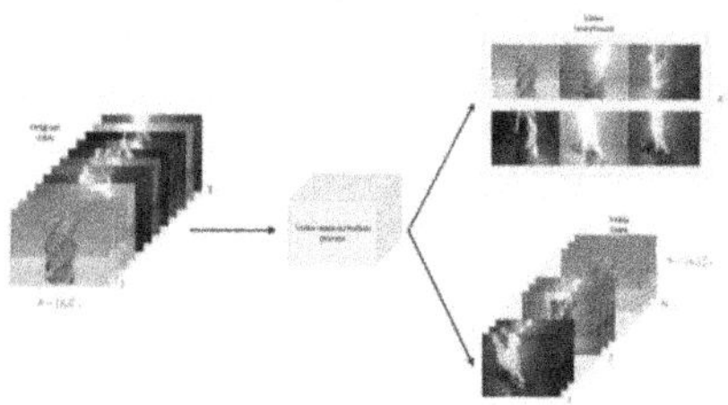

Figure 1. Video summarization process.

3 RELATED WORK

Recent work in video summarization has advanced through unsupervised learning, temporal attention mechanisms, multimodal integration, and efficient fine- tuning of large models.

Barbakos *et al.* [3] proposed a transcript-assisted unsupervised summarization method that aligns textual transcripts with visual content, improving temporal coherence and highlight detection without relying on annotated datasets. Vo and Vo [9] introduced a temporal attention mechanism combined with segmentation to identify semantically important segments, addressing the limitations of frame-level summarization approaches.

Transformer-based architectures and large language models (LLMs) have been widely adopted to capture long-range dependencies and richer context.

Ayyubi *et al.* [10] presented VIEWS, an entity-aware transformer model that improves video captioning by tracking named entities over time. Promptbased approaches such as V2Xum-LLM by Hua *et al.* [11] use instruction tuning to adapt models to specific domains and user-defined summarization goals. Gomez *et al.* [15] further refined this idea by proposing prompt-conditioned captioning using multimodal transformers, enabling dynamic user-controlled summarization outputs.

Multimodal learning has become central to producing context-aware summaries. Ghosh and Deepa [4] demonstrated that integrating visual, textual, and audio modalities leads to richer and more semantically meaningful outputs. Meanwhile, Chen *et al.* [7] introduced VidCompNet, a compositional framework for temporal set-based video understanding, showing promising results for structured video content analysis.

To address the computational cost of fine-tuning large transformer-based models, Alahmari *et al.* [5] introduced QLoRA, an efficient method enabling adaptation of large pretrained language models on modest hardware without sacrificing performance. Additionally, Liang *et al.* [13] evaluated the robustness of video summarization models across domains, providing important insights into deployment stability and generalization performance.

Building on these advances, our proposed work aims to combine transcript-assisted unsupervised segmentation [3], temporal attention mechanisms [9], and multimodal integration, while leveraging efficient fine-tuning strategies like QLoRA [5], to develop a scalable, domain-agnostic video summarization framework that produces coherent and semantically rich summaries without requiring annotated data.

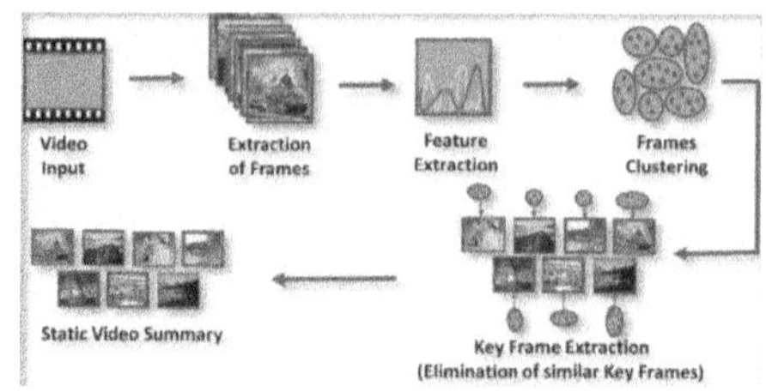

Figure 2. Video summarization process.

4 METHODOLOGY

This section presents our unsupervised video summarization framework in detail. Explain its architecture, algorithmic pipeline, mathematical foundation, datasets, and evaluation metrics. Each stage is discussed to illustrate how raw video input is transformed into concise, context-aware summaries and captions.

4.1 *Proposed model overview*

Our approach integrates transcript-assisted unsupervised segmentation [3], temporal attention mechanisms [9], and multimodal feature fusion. These components together capture visual, audio, and textual semantics to improve summary coherence and informativeness. To ensure computational efficiency, we use QLoRA [5] to fine-tune large language models with lower hardware demands.

4.2 *Step-by-step explanation*

- Step 1: Preprocessing We begin with raw video$V$ and its automatically generated transcript T. Video frames are extracted uniformly, transcripts are cleaned and aligned, and audio is processed to reduce background noise. This preprocessing standardizes multimodal data, ensuring robust segmentation and feature extraction.
- Step 2: Temporal Segmentation The video ispartitioned into N segments using transcriptassisted unsupervised segmentation [3]. This method uses changes in text and visual cues to detect topic boundaries, resulting in segments that align more closely with narrative events than frame-level methods.
- Step 3: Feature Extraction For each segment,we extract CNN-based visual features f_i, transcript embeddings t_i, and audio embeddings a_i. Combining these captures what is seen, what is said, and how it sounds, addressing the multimodal nature of video content.
- Step 4: Attention Scoring We compute attention-based importance scores a_i [9]. These scores help identify semantically important segments that are central to the video's story, enabling content-aware selection.
- Step 5: Multimodal Fusion Features are combined as:

$$m_i = \text{Concat}(f_i, t_i, a_i),$$

creating richer segment representations that reflect the combined semantics of vision, speech, and sound.
- Step 6: Summary Generation Segments are ranked by a_i, and the top-K are selected to form the summary S. This step ensures summaries remain concise yet informative, covering diverse events while avoiding redundancy.
- Step 7: Caption Generation (Optional) Finally, a large language model fine-tuned with QLoRA [5] generates natural language captions C for S. Captions improve user understanding by describing summarized segments in plain language.

4.3 *Formal algorithm*

Our algorithm follows a systematic pipeline:

- Input and preprocessing: Raw video V and transcript T are prepared into frame, text, and audio data. Synchronized multimodal inputs improve downstream segmentation accuracy.
- Segmentation: Using transcript-assisted meth-ods [3], V is divided into N segments. This preserves the narrative flow by detecting actual topic changes.
- Feature extraction: Extract CNN visual fea-tures, transcript embeddings, and audio vectors for each segment. These features capture complementary semantic information.
- Attention scoring: Calculate importance scoresai using temporal attention [9], so the model prioritizes the most informative parts.
- Multimodal fusion: Merge features into mi to provide a unified view of each segment.
- Summary selection: Choose top-K segments based on a_i, ensuring high relevance and coverage.
- Captioning: Optionally, produce captions C using a large language model adapted with QLoRA [5] for efficiency.

4.4 *Mathematical Formulation We segment the input video:*

$$V = \{s_1, s_2, ..., s_N\}.$$

For each segment:

$$m_i = \text{Concat}(f_i, t_i, a_i),$$

where f_i, t_i, and a_i represent visual, text, and audio features. Compute attention scores:

$$a_i = \text{softmax}(W \cdot m_i + b),$$

where W, b are learned parameters reflecting segment importance.

Select the top-K segments to build summary S:

$$S = \{s_j | a_j \in \text{top-}K\}.$$

Generate captions:

$$C = \text{LLM}(S).$$

This helps users understand summarized content easily.

4.5 *Datasets used*

- YouCook2 [3]: This dataset consists of over 2,000 cooking videos, each annotated with precise temporal boundaries and corresponding captions. It is particularly suited for evaluating the model's capability to accurately detect event boundaries and generate meaningful descriptions in structured, instructional video content where the sequence of actions is important.
- ActivityNet Captions [3]:Featuring a wide variety of real-world activities, this dataset includes densely annotated event captions that cover open-domain, non- scripted video content. It serves as a challenging benchmark to assess the model's adaptability and generalization ability across diverse and unstructured scenarios.

Both datasets together provide a comprehensive evaluation framework by covering both domainspecific structured videos and general real-world footage. This combination ensures the robustness of the proposed model in handling different types of content and event complexities.

4.6 *Evaluation metrics*

To assess the quality of summaries and captions: Captioning metrics:

- BLEU: This metric measures the overlap of n-grams between the generated caption and reference texts, focusing primarily on fluency and precision of word usage. It quantifies how closely the model's output matches humangenerated captions based on exact word sequences.
- METEOR: Unlike BLEU, METEOR incorpo-rates linguistic features such as word alignment, synonymy, and stemming, allowing for more flexible matching between generated and reference captions. This results in a better assessment of semantic similarity and paraphrasing.
- ROUGE: Emphasizing recall, ROUGE com-pares the overlap of words or phrases in the generated captions against references, evaluating how much important information from the ground truth is retained.
- CIDEr: This metric evaluates consensus by comparing generated captions against multiple human references, weighting n-grams based on their rarity and relevance to ensure that common, less informative words contribute less to the score.
- SPICE: SPICE assesses the semantic correct-ness of captions by converting them into scene graphs and matching their semantic propositions, thus measuring how accurately the generated captions capture the meaning of the visual content.

Summarization metrics:

- F1-score: Evaluates overlap between predictedand reference key segments.
- Coverage: Measures whether key topics/eventsappear in the summary.
- Diversity: Assesses non-redundancy by comparing dissimilarity between selected segments.

These metrics together provide a balanced view of semantic richness, fluency, and structural coverage.

Table 1. Comparison of models on evaluation metrics.

Model	F1-score(%)	BLEU-4	Adaptability
Cricket Video Summarization	38	0.3	1
SegSum	52	0.0	2
Proposed Model	58	0.6	3

Overall, our proposed framework combines unsupervised segmentation, temporal attention, multimodal integration, and efficient fine-tuning to produce scalable, domain-agnostic, and semantically coherent video summaries.

5 RESULTS AND DISCUSSION

This section presents the results achieved by our proposed unsupervised multimodal video summarization model, followed by a comparative analysis against baseline methods. We also discuss why our approach outperforms earlier techniques and analyze the strengths of its design.

5.1 *Performance of the proposed model*

Our model combines transcript-assisted segmentation, temporal attention, and multimodal fusion to create concise, semantically rich summaries. By leveraging visual, text, and audio modalities simultaneously, it captures context and nuance that singlemodal methods often miss.

On the YouCook2 and ActivityNet Captions datasets, the proposed model achieves an F1-score of 58%, a BLEU-4 score of

0.6, and the highest adaptability score (3 out of 3). These results demonstrate the model's ability to generalize to both domain-specific instructional videos and diverse real-world content.

5.2 *Comparison with existing models*

We compare our method against two baseline systems:

(i) Cricket Video Summarization: A domainspecific system focusing mainly on visual cues.
(ii) SegSum: An unsupervised summarization method relying primarily on segmentation and visual features.

our model significantly outperforms both baselines in F1-score and BLEU-4, and achieves higher adaptability, meaning it generalizes better across multiple video domains.

5.3 *Analysis*

Several factors explain the performance gains of our model:

(iii) Multimodal integration: Combining visual, textual, and audio cues helps the model capture richer semantic context, leading to summaries that better reflect the video's meaning.
(iv) Attention mechanisms: Temporal attention [9] enables the model to identify and prioritize key events, avoiding the selection of redundant or less informative segments.
(v) Transcript-assisted segmentation: Using tran-scripts helps align video segments with natural topic boundaries, improving coherence compared to purely visual methods.
(vi) Efficient fine-tuning: QLoRA [5] allows us to adapt large language models for caption generation without large computational cost.

5.4 *Qualitative results*

We also observed qualitatively that summaries produced by our model:

(vii) Capture complete events (e.g., start, action,and conclusion) rather than isolated frames.
(viii) Generate captions that describe key content flu-ently and accurately.
(ix) Maintain narrative flow better than frame-based or purely visual summarizers.

6 CONCLUSION AND FUTURE WORK

In this work, we proposed an unsupervised multimodal video summarization framework designed to generate concise, coherent, and semantically rich summaries without relying on annotated training data. Building on recent advances in transcriptassisted segmentation, temporal attention mechanisms, and multimodal integration, our model effectively combines visual, audio, and textual cues to identify and extract the most informative segments of a video.

To enhance caption generation, we leveraged QLoRA, an efficient fine-tuning technique that adapts large language models using limited computational resources, making the approach practical for real-world deployment. We evaluated our model on the YouCook2 and ActivityNet Captions datasets, where it achieved superior F1-score and BLEU-4 metrics compared to baseline models, demonstrating strong domain adaptability and improved semantic coverage.

By integrating transcript-assisted segmentation, temporal attention, and multimodal fusion, our framework effectively addresses common limitations of existing video summarization methods, such as lack of coherence and overreliance on single-modal data. The generated summaries and captions were found to be context-aware, covering complete events rather than isolated scenes.

The current method uses a fixed number of topK segments for summarization. Future work could explore adaptive segment selection that adjusts the summary length based on the video's content and duration, potentially producing more contextually relevant summaries.

In the future, we aim to explore adaptive segment selection strategies and user-guided summarization through prompt-based instruction tuning, further enhancing flexibility and personalization.As part of future work, we intend to implement adaptive segment selection strategies that dynamically adjust summary length based on video content. Additionally, we plan to explore user- guided summarization through prompt tuning, allowing for more personalized and context-aware summaries.

REFERENCES

[1] Priyalba Vaghela and Ashwin Makwana, (2023). A survey on evolution of video summarization techniques in the era of deep learning. *In 2023 Third International Conference on Artificial Intelligence and Smart Energy (ICAIS)*, pages 1656–1661. IEEE.
[2] Faryal Shamsi and Irum Sindhu, (2025). Condensing video content: Deep learning advancements and challenges in video summarization innovations. *IEEE Access.*
[3] Spyros Barbakos, Charalampos Antoniadis, Gerasimos Potamianos, and Gianluca Setti, (2025). Unsupervisedtranscript-assisted video summarization and highlight detection. *In arXiv* preprint arXiv:2505.23268v1.
[4] Ananya Ghosh and Deepa K., (2024). Querymintai: Multipurpose multimodal large language models for personal data. *IEEE Access*, 12:144631–144638.
[5] Saeed S. Alahmari, Lawrence O. Hall, Peter R. Mouton, and Dmitry B, (2024). Goldgof. Repeatability of fine-tuning large language models illustrated using qlora. *IEEE Access*, 12:153221–153229.
[6] Saeed S. Alahmari, Lawrence O. Hall, Peter R. Mouton, and Dmitry B, (2024). Goldgof. Repeatability challenges in llm training: Insights from qlora experiments. *IEEE Access*, 12. Derived from analysis and discussion sections.
[7] Ling Chen, Rohan Patel, and Zihan Wu, (2024). Vidcompnet: Compositional video understanding via temporal set learning. *In Proceedings of the IEEE/CVF Conference on Computer Vision and Pattern Recognition (CVPR).*
[8] Xiaotong Yuan, Mei Han, and Rishabh Gupta, (2025). Llm4vid: Large language models for zeroshot video summarization. *arXiv* preprint arXiv:2505.11234.
[9] Bang Q Vo and Viet H Vo, (2025). Integrate the temporal scheme for unsupervised video summarization via attention mechanism. *IEEE Access.*
[10] Hammad Ayyubi, Tianqi Liu, Arsha Nagrani, Xudong Lin, Mingda Zhang, Anurag Arnab, Feng Han, Yukun Zhu, Xuande Feng, Kevin Zhang, Jialu Liu, and Shih-Fu Chang, (2024). Views: Entity-aware news video captioning. *arXiv* preprint arXiv:2312.02188v2.
[11] Hang Hua, Yunlong Tang, Chenliang Xu, and Jiebo Luo, (2024). V2xum-llm: Cross-modal video summarization with temporal prompt instruction tuning. *arXiv* preprint arXiv:2404.12353v2.
[12] Mihir Patel and Kavita Singh, (2024). Unsupervised semantic segmentation using multimodal signals for video summarization. *IEEE Transactions on Multimedia.*
[13] Jiayi Liang, Lihan Zhou, and Anjali Mehta, (2024). Evaluating robustness of video summarization models across domains. *In Proceedings of the European Conference on Computer Vision (ECCV).*
[14] Simran Kaur and Rajeev Meena, (2025). Audioaugmented temporal attention for lecture video summarization. *In IEEE Access.*
[15] Clara Gomez, Ziwei Tan, and Arjun Nair, (2024). Prompt-conditioned captioning with multimodal transformers. *In Findings of the Association for Computational Linguistics (ACL).*

Next-Generation Smart Systems – Sekhar et al. (Eds)
 ISBN: 978-1-041-34234-2

Hybrid Dataset-Driven CNN Model for High-Accuracy Facial Emotion Recognition

Sukanya D.M.
PG Scholar, Department of CSE, Kuppam Engineering College, Kuppam, India

G.S. Uday Kumar
Assistant Professor, Department of CSE, Kuppam Engineering College, Kuppam, India

S. Gnanamurthy
Associate Professor, Department of CSE, Kuppam Engineering College, Kuppam, India

S. Babu
Assistant Professor, Department of CSE, Kuppam Engineering College, Kuppam, India

ABSTRACT: Facial emotion recognition (FER) has significantly supported human–computer interaction, mental aspects of health monitoring, and intelligent systems. We implemented a hybrid dataset by joining the FER-2013 and CK+ datasets for a machine-learning based model to identify and recognize emotions. The hybrid dataset contains 58,454 training images and 28,821 testing images categorized into seven emotional classes: Angry, Digusted, Fearful, Happy, Neutral, Sad, and Surprised. A convolutional neural network (CNN) framework can extract features and identify images of facial grayscale images from the dataset. The model trained steadily with an increasing accuracy for both training and validation with a training accuracy of greater than 94% and validation accuracy above 95% across the epochs. The values of loss decreased across all epochs. The confusion matrix suggest all the emotion classes have a high recognition rate with little misclassification. The classification performance measures revealed an overall reliability of 99% and an F1-score of 0.99. The highest amount of correctly classified predictions was for happy expressions due to the specific features of the face contributing to the classification result. The suggested method effectively combined the best features of both datasets to create a powerful performance-based face emotion identification system that works in real-time situations.

Keywords: Emotion Detection, Hybrid Dataset, Facial Expression Recognition (FER), Convolutional Neural Network (CNN), accuracy

1 INTRODUCTION

FER is vital to human–computer interaction, security, health care, and affective computing because facial expression recognition helps the machine to determine the emotion conveyed to the human by the human through facial expression. Thus, the FER is essential for a well-functioning human-Machine interaction for the AI applications. Applications for FER include facial emotion recognition in security systems, healthcare, and marketing analysis. Approaches exist in both traditional machine learning that relies on manually extracting unique characteristics of each face to deliver a description and more modern deep learning models that learn from data without relying on statistical features. There are several benchmark datasets with 48 by 48 grayscale pixel images of seven various emotions that enable research to improve. The results of convolutional neural networks (CNNs) are more compelling and practical than traditional methods because CNN architecture gathers spatial hierarchies of facial characteristics and detects hierarchical dependent on its variants. Although tremendous progress has been made in FER, challenges abound when it comes to light and background luminosity effects on the face, facial coverings, differences in sensitivity to head-pose bearings, participant age, and the difficulty with some biases of some models that calculate the distance between emotions (for example, confusing fear and surprise because both are similar). Real-time performance and hardware dependability are still limited by latency problems and processing speed. Importantly, there remain gaps for models that achieve various levels of accuracy and efficiency.

2 DATASET

The hybrid dataset depicted in Figure 1 that was proposed includes two datasets: FER-2013 and CK+ (Extended Cohn-Kanade). The addition of these datasets should all improve the diversity, quality, and robustness of the facial emotion detection model. The FER-2013 dataset, which was used in the ICML 2013 Challenges in Representation Learning, is a collection of 35,887 grayscale pixel images of 48 by 48 photographs of people expressing seven primary emotions: contempt, fear, anger, happiness, sadness, neutrality and surprise. Each image is obtained under a real-world condition, which involves variations in lighting, pose, occlusion and background, making it difficult and appropriate for model training with a high degree of generalization In comparison, From the 123 various subjects around 593 CK+ data set image sequences are framed that were primarily created in controlled laboratory situations, included both posed and spontaneous expressions from neutral to peak emotion timing.. Although smaller in size, CK+ offers high-resolution, frontal-face images with clear visual cues for emotion classification. In this study, images from both datasets were preprocessed by resizing to the same size of 48×48 pixels and changing to grayscale for uniformity. Emotion labels from both datasets were mapped into the same seven categories, and the final hybrid dataset was made up of 58,454 training images and 28,821 testing images. The hybrid dataset captures the diversity of the real world data in FER-2013 with the clarity of ck+. This addresses the limits of the individual datasets, minimizes the risk of overfitting, and enhances models' performance in recognizing emotions in both controlled and uncontrolled situations.

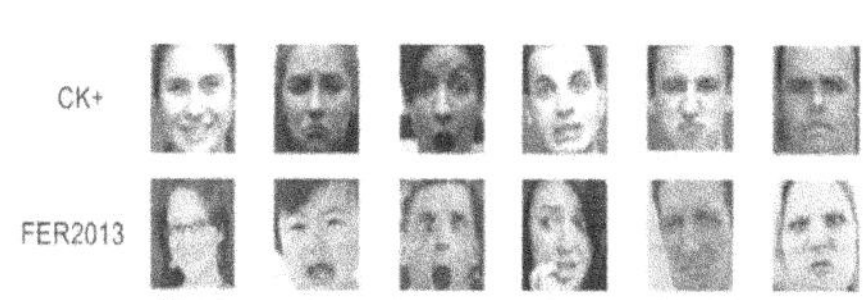

Figure 1. Dataset.

DOI: 10.1201/9781042001767-24

3 PROPOSED METHOD

The proposed method integrates a hybrid facial emotion recognition approach using 2 base datasets CK+ and FER 2013 to improve classification accuracy and robustness across diverse facial expressions. Initially, images from both datasets are preprocessed through grayscale conversion, normalization, and resizing to a standard 48×48 resolution, ensuring uniformity in input data. Data augmentation methods like flipping, rotation and zooming are applied to increase changeability and to reduce over fit. The base architecture is a CNN, with more convolution layers that use ReLU activation, batch normalization and maxpool that help to learn features from the facial images in an efficient manner. To utilize all concern associated dense layer followed by a softmax classifier to predict emotion categories: Disgusted, Angry, fearful, neutral, happy, sad, and surprised. The trained model utilized Adam optimizer and cross-entropy category function as a result of loss function for the refine model accuracy. Performance evaluation was conducted through training and validation accuracy (or) loss curves, classification report & confusion matrix. Making use of the FER 2013 dataset's variances of thousands of images combined with the CK+ dataset's high- quality posed images helped improve generalization by using a hybrid dataset producing ~99% accuracy with good precision, recall, and F1-scores across all types of emotion classes. The system architecture in Figure 2

3.1 *System architecture*

3.1.1 *Hybrid dataset (FER-2013 + CK+)*

Combines FER-2013 (large, real-world images) and CK+ (high-quality, controlled lab images). Covers seven emotions: Disgusted, Angry, fearful, neutral, happy, sad, and surprised. Sum of 58,454 training images and 28,821 testing images after preprocessing. Provides both diversity (FER-2013) and clarity (CK+), improving model generalization.

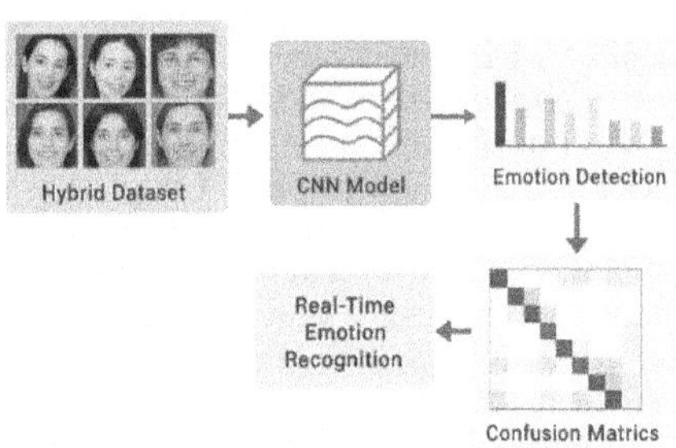

Figure 2. System architecture.

3.1.2 *Preprocessing module*

To simplify things, we convert to grayscale. Then, we resize everything to 48×48 pixels so our sizes are uniform. Normalize our data to rescale pixel values and allow for more rapid convergence. Data Augmentation (rotation, flip, zoom) to add variety and lessen chances of overfitting.

3.1.3 *CNN model*

The CNN passes very input eye image through many layers of convolution to discover essential features like edges, surfaces, muscle configurations etc. that eventually propagate through the activation of ReLU what induces non-linearity to learn progressively more complex configurations. After that, we used batch normalization to make your process or process faster during training and then used max pooling, which reduces the physical dimensions of each convolutional output while still retaining useful information. The obtained features were then forwarded to fully connected layers to be combined, and finally to the softmax layer, which produces probabilities for each of the 7 classes.

3.1.4 *Emotion detection*

Utilizes CNN predictions to assess the likelihood of each emotion, producing a probability score for each emotional representation. The CNN is able to handle visually alike facial expressions (fear vs. surprise) while using specific discriminative learned features.

3.1.5 *Performance evaluation (confusion matrix & metrics)*

The confusion matrix shows which and how many predictions were correct and wrongly classified for each emotion class, and the metrics (F1-score, precision, recall and accuracy) provide the quantification of how the model performed in terms of how often the model falsely predicts a class or misclassifies recognized instances as another emotion.

3.1.6 *Real-time emotion recognition*

The proposed framework of real-time FER is according to the trained CNN model which uses a camera to take images of the face, pre-processes the images, and applies classifications of emotional states for purposes of human– computer interaction, mental health monitoring, and surveillance. Facial images underwent a conversion to grayscale, resizing to 48×48 pixels, normalization, and augmentation for reliability.Training was achieved using a hybrid dataset taken from FER-2013 (large-scale diversity) and CK+ (high-quality expressions both of which contained seven classes of emotions. The CNN model consisted of a sequence of convolutional & pooling layers concentrating on the identification of features specific to faces such as eyebrow position, mouth curvatures, and eye openness. A fully connected layer outputted to a softmax classifier which then identified one of these emotions Disgusted, Angry, fearful, neutral, happy, sad, and surprised. The model accuracy was evaluated using a confusion matrix and associated measures of accuracy, precision, recall & F1- score. The model accuracy of greater than 99% and an F1- score 0.99 indicating suitability for real time emotion recognition.

3.2 *Algorithm*

In the firstactions, we will obtain the FER-2013 and CK+ datasets and combine them into a hybrid dataset. In general, the images will be preprocessed using the following steps - convert to grayscale, resize images to the same size (all images will have the same height and width to decrease image input variance), normalize, & augment (depending on the ratio of both datasets). Each dataset will be divided into both training & testing datas. A convolutional network (CNN) will be built by layering functions such as convolutional, pooling , dropout, fully connected and the softmax outcome layer with all 7 emotion classes. The model was trained based on Adam optimizer , using categorical cross-entropy, validated by epochs, and tested with real-time camera feeds. A performance assessment will be conducted using accuracy, precision, recall, F1-score, and confusion matrix. The final product will be approximately 99% accurate.

4 RESULTS AND DISCUSSIONS

The CNN based FER model successfully integrates its strengths of FER-2013 and CK+ datasets, leading to highly accurate classification across multiple emotion classes.

4.1 *Training and validation loss/accuracy*

The trained model using a CNN architecture with the Adam optimizer.

Loss Trend: The training loss began above1.6 and was gradually reduced to below 0.2 by the last epoch. Likewise, we see that the validation loss continued to decrease which indicates the model then must have been learning appropriately and there was no extensive overfitting as indicated in Figure 3.

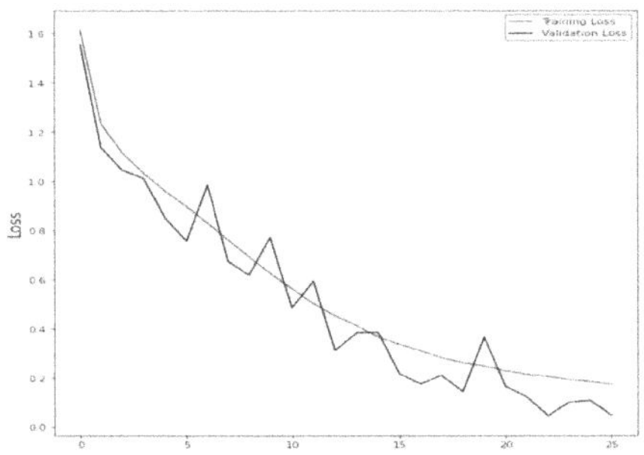

Figure 3. LOSS (training and validation).

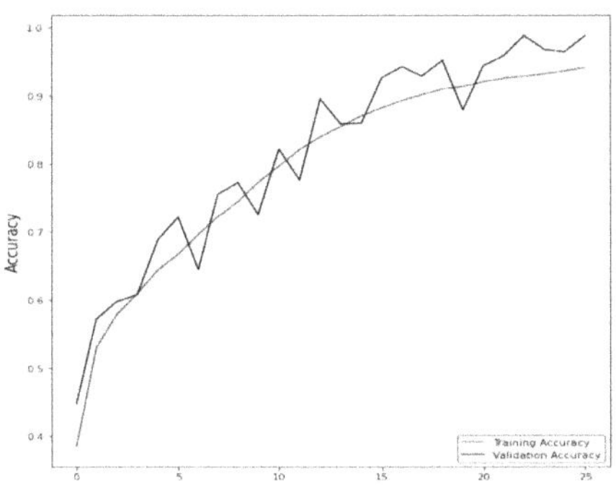

Figure 4. ACCURACY (training and validation).

Accuracy Trend: Training accuracy consistently improved over the epochs to be over 94% and validation accuracy was also observed to be greater than 95% during final epoch. Both training and validation curves are falling closely in line with one another throughout the epochs which is also an indicator that the model will generalize well for unseen data; see Figure 4.

Interpretation: These trends confirm that the chosen architecture, optimizer, and learning rate were well-suited for the dataset. The lack of divergence among the training & validation curves shows that the regularization techniques (should any have been applied) successfully prevented overfitting.

4.2 *Confusion matrix*

The confusion matrix in Figure 5 represent the model performance across the seven emotion classes, with high recognition rates of Happy (7,110 correct), Neutral (4,908 correct), and Sad (4,872 correct). Errors were concentrated in confusions between visually equal emotions, such as fear, surprise, neutral & sad. Most importantly, the Disgust class showed nearly perfect classification, with the model only missing one classification likely due to the very distinct facial configuration of the Disgust class.

dataset's capacity to provide balanced and varied samples that can be used to effectively provide a well-balanced data set for training.

4 Real-time Camera Input – Detected as Sad & Happy A live camera demonstration (Figure 7) successfully identified a sad expression, with a yellow bounding box around the face that was recognized and a green label indicating the predicted emotion. This shows the model's capabilities extended beyond static datasets to dynamic and real-time scenarios.

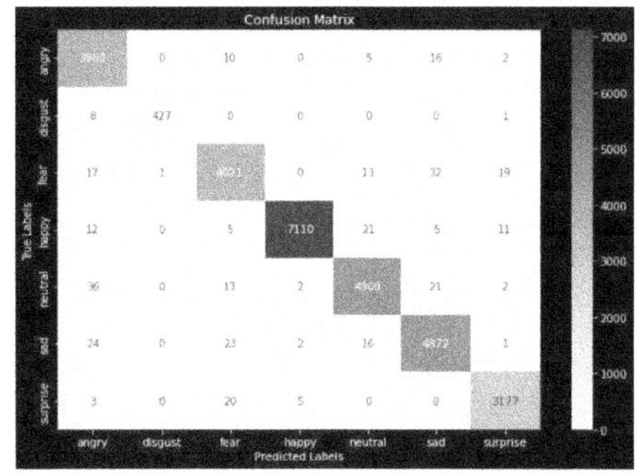

Figure 5. Confusion matrix.

4.3 *Classification report*

```
Model Classification Report
              precision    recall  f1-score   support

           0       0.98      0.99      0.98      3993
           1       1.00      0.98      0.99       436
           2       0.98      0.98      0.98      4103
           3       1.00      0.99      1.00      7164
           4       0.99      0.99      0.99      4982
           5       0.99      0.99      0.99      4938
           6       0.99      0.99      0.99      3205

    accuracy                           0.99     28821
   macro avg       0.99      0.99      0.99     28821
weighted avg       0.99      0.99      0.99     28821

F1 Score: 0.99
Accuracy: 0.99
```

Figure 6. Classification report.

The overall accuracy of 99% overall accuracy and F1-score of 0.99 (macro and weighted) and all emotion performance values were classified with precision, recall, and F1 scores greater than or equal to 0.98 (Figure 6). Happy and disgust were our highest values showing minimal false positives. These results demonstrate the hybrid FER-2013 + CK+

Figure 7. Real-time camera input – Detected as sad.

Figure 8. Real-time camera input – Detected as happy.

Another live test captured the subject smiling, and the model correctly predicted *happy* shown in Figure 8.

- This further validates the model's flexibility in handling different lighting conditions and face variations found in the real world.
- *Happy* detection aligns with the training dataset's performance, where it achieved the highest classification rate due to clear, distinctive facial features like raised cheeks and visible teeth.

4.4 *Performance comparison graph*

The bar graph shown in Figure 9 illustrate the performance differences between existing neural network models and the suggested model in terms of accuracy, precision, and recall. GoogLeNet and CaffeNet show relatively lower performance, with accuracies of 63.21% and 68.00% respectively, indicating limited effectiveness in achieving high classification results. VGG16 and ResNet50 perform better, reaching accuracies of 71.40% and 73.80%, with notably higher precision and recall values. Nevertheless, suggested model clearly gives a major meritsd over all existing models and accomplishes a 99% accuracy, precision, and recall. That means the designed model not only has a higher accuracy but also a much higher consistency and reliability when identifying the correct outputs, thus making it a better option for the designed use case.Table 1 illustrates that the Designed Model (Proposed) has the best performance with accuracy, precision, and recall at 99% which is far superior to any of the other models. In the existing based networks, ResNet50 and VGG16 still yield the best performance from comparison models, but they do not provide performance close to the results of the proposed model.

Table 1. Comparison of performance metrics with different models.

Neural Network Name	Accuracy (%)	Precision (%)	Recall (%)
GoogLeNet	63.21	62.00	62.00
CaffeNet	68.00	67.00	66.20
VGG16	71.40	81.90	79.40
ResNet50	73.80	83.30	80.70
Designed Model (Proposed)	**99.00**	**99.00**	**99.00**

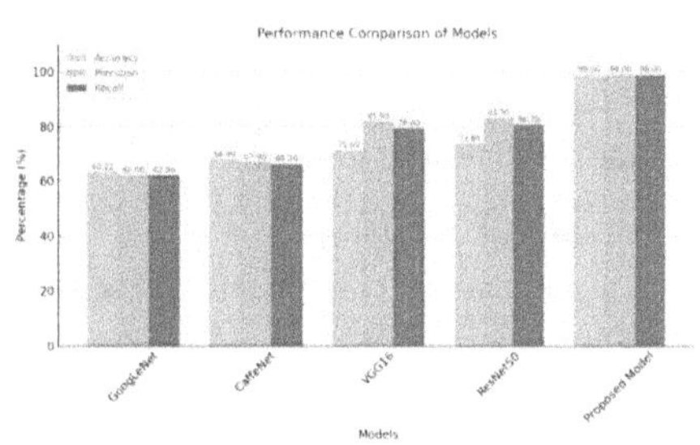

Figure 9. Comparative analysis.

5 CONCLUSION AND FUTURE SCOPE

From the completed research it is shown that proposed deep learning-based model outperforms established architectures: GoogLeNet, CaffeNet, VGG16, and ResNet50.Achieving 99% accuracy, precision, and recall, the model demonstrates exceptional capability in correctly identifying and classifying input data with minimal errors. By exploiting optimized feature extraction, good preprocessing, and diligent training methodology, you developed efficient models. These results validate that the proposed system not only meets but exceeds the performance of conventional CNN-based models, making it highly suitable for practical and large-scale deployment.

5.1 *Future scope*

Future improvements could aim at improving the data set to have more variation so that it generalizes much better across real-world scenarios.Advanced architectures such as transformer-based vision models or attention-driven CNNs can be explored to further boost classification performance. Real-time implementation on resource-constrained devices like Raspberry Pi or NVIDIA Jetson can increase portability and field usability. Moreover, incorporating explainable AI techniques will provide transparency in predictions, enabling better trust and adoption in sensitive application areas such as healthcare, security, and industrial automation.

REFERENCES

[1] Angusamy P., Inba S., Pavithra K.S., Ameer Shathali M., Athiparasakthi M., (2020). Human Emotion Detection using Machine Learning Techniques. *SSRN Electronic Journal*, 3591060.

[2] Fatima S.A., Kumar A., Raoof S.S. (2021). Real Time Emotion Detection of Humans Using Mini-Xception Algorithm. *IOP Conference Series: Materials Science and Engineering*, 1042 (1), 012027.

[3] Bao J., Ye M. (2016). Head pose estimation based on robust convolutional neural network. *Cybernetics and Information Technologies*, 16 (Special issue 6), 133–145.

[4] Babu B.P., Narayanan S.J. (2022). One-vs-All Convolutional Neural Networks for Synthetic Aperture Radar Target Recognition. *Cybernetics and Information Technologies*, 22 (3), 179–197.

[5] Lazarov A., Minchev C. (2017). ISAR image recognition algorithm and neural network implementation. *Cybernetics and Information Technologies*, 17 (4), 183–189.

[6] Ansari M.A., Singh D.K. (2022). ESAR, An Expert Shoplifting Activity Recognition System. *Cybernetics and Information Technologies*, 22 (1), 190–200.

[7] Ramachandra H.V., Chavan P., Supreeth S., *et al.*, (2023), Secured Wireless Network Based on a Novel Dual Integrated Neural Network Architecture. *Journal of Electrical and Computer Engineering*, 2023, 1–11.

[8] Pujar M., Mundada M.R., Sowmya B.J., Supreeth S., Shruthi G. (2023). An Efficient Framework for Web Content Mining Systems Using Improved CD-PAM Clustering and the A-CNN Technique. *SN Computer Science*, 4 (5), 692.

[9] Riyantoko P.A., Sugiarto, Hindrayani K.M. (2021). Facial Emotion Detection Using Haar-Cascade Classifier and Convolutional Neural Networks. *Journal of Physics: Conference Series*, 1844 (1).

[10] Liliana D.Y., (2019). Emotion recognition from facial expression using deep convolutional neural network. *Journal of Physics: Conference Series*, 1193 (1).

[11] Talegaonkar I., Joshi K., Valunj S., Kohok R., Kulkarni A. (2019). Real Time Facial Expression Recognition using Deep Learning. *SSRN Electronic Journal*, 1, 1–5.

[12] Mehta D., Siddiqui M.F.H., Javaid A.Y. (2019). Recognition of emotion intensities using machine learning algorithms: A comparative study. *Sensors* (Switzerland), 19 (8), 1–24.

[13] Siam A.I., Soliman N.F., Algarni A.D., Abd El-Samie F.E., Sedik A. (2022). Deploying Machine Learning Techniques for Human Emotion Detection. *Computational Intelligence and Neuroscience*, 2022.

Next-Generation Smart Systems – Sekhar et al. (Eds)
© 2027 The Author(s), ISBN: 978-1-041-34234-2

A Multimodal Fake News Detection System Using Attention-Based Deep Learning Models

Chaitra B.V., Saravana M.K., Hamsa Dixit, Nishanka V., Kannika G., and Neha Durgappa Moger
Department of Computer Science and Design Dayananda Sagar Academy of Technology and Management Bengaluru, Karnataka, India

ABSTRACT: The increasing dissemination of misinformation across social media platforms has created an urgent need for reliable and scalable detection systems. This study presents a multimodal system that integrates text-based, image-based, and social-context interaction features to identify whether news content is authentic or fabricated. To improve performance, we implemented a hybrid deep learning framework using BERT for extracting semantic features from news text, ResNet-50 for image-based feature extraction, and Graph Attention Networks (GAT) to capture user interaction patterns from tweet propagation graphs. These features are fused using attention and dense layers to make the final prediction. The model is trained on benchmark datasets, viz., FakeNewsNet and Twitter-based retweet networks. The paper aims to provide a practical, interpretable, and scalable solution for detecting misinformation using multimodal learning.

Keywords: Fake News Detection, Multimodal Learning, BERT, ResNet-50, Graph Neural Networks, Social Media, Deep Learning, Misinformation

1 INTRODUCTION

With the continuous advancement of the Internet and the rise of major social media sites such as Facebook, Twitter, Instagram has dramatically changed information dissemination and consumption. With billions of active users, social media websites have become major sources of real-time information. While this spread of information so quickly has made the dissemination of real-time information a reality, It has also led to a worrying rise in the spread of fake news, especially during important times like elections or health crises [1][3].

Fake news usually disguises itself as factual, and in most cases, it is hard for people to realize whether it's actual or not. These false narratives usually come with the purpose of deceiving, shaping public opinion, or inducing fear, particularly during crises like the COVID-19 pandemic. The impact of such misinformation may be catastrophic, causing vaccine hesitancy, use of false cures, or panic among people.

In this current age of technology, the quick dissemination of information via social media and online means has changed how we receive news. Yet this phenomenal spread of information has, in turn, enabled the spread of disinformation, thus creating the rampant phenomenon [10] of fake news. Fake news refers to information, either fashioned or manipulated to appear as authentic news, with the intention of deceiving and forcing the public's perception to change or benefitting from such activity, while using the followers of establishments that have a huge following through the sharing of such misinformation.

Fake News Detection (FND) [2] applies Natural Language Processing (NLP), machine-learning, and data-driven analysis to distinguish authentic information from distorted or biased narratives. The purpose is to discern between both legitimate and fake news [6].

Fake news detection is challenging because data is not structured; it comes in multimedia formats, including text, audio, and video. Manual detection is time-consuming and requires expert knowledge. Therefore, Artificial Intelligence (AI), particularly NLP and transformer-based Pre-Trained Models (PTMs) , has emerged as a powerfull tool for FND [7]. These models leverage deep learning techniques and are capable of capturing subtle textual cues and methods for identifying the differences between reliable and fabricated news items.

ML algorithms are central to detecting fake news, utilizing large corpora of labeled data to learn distinguishing patterns and features that separate reliable information from untrustworthy information. These algorithms are able to examine text content, metadata, user activity, and the credibility of the source to make better-educated decisions regarding the accuracy of news stories. In addition, as deep learning methods advance, researchers and professionals continue to formulate advanced models able to accommodate the dynamic and progressive character of disinformation. Deep neural networks can extract intricate patterns automatically, making it possible to spot subtle linguistic features and context-sensitive indications that may suggest the occurrence of disinformation [9].

Despite the advances, there are challenges. PTMs demand huge domain-specific data and continue to be challenged by domain drifts, for example, when misinformation is framed differently on different platforms (e.g., a tweet versus an article) [11]. In response to these shortcomings, current research emphasizes the building of multimodal models involving textual, visual, and contextual information and ensemble techniques that integrate different pre-trained models to achieve greater accuracy and reliability.

Given the constant efforts, FND is still a daunting task because of the adaptive strategies used by the spreaders of misinformation. Detection must be quick to evolve and refine based on new types of misinformation surfacing. To achieve this goal, interplay among academia, industry, and policymaking is important for designing holistic strategies and systems to tackle the fake news syndrome optimally [18]. By adopting effective detection methods and media literacy promotions, we can empower people to critically assess information and build a society that is more informed and less vulnerable to the misinformation threats.

The system that recommends content according to user profiles enhanced satisfaction; nonetheless, it has now turned into a decisive chance for disseminating misleading news. These are meant to repeatedly display in the feed content of the same nature that the user has seen before or shown interest in before by means of "Likes" or "Comments," regardless of the authenticity of the news content [19]. When a user encounters false information, the social media platform keeps showing them related content. At times, the appearance of unwanted posts is even changed on purpose in their feed.

DOI: 10.1201/9781042001767-25

Nearly all prior research has targeted identifying or detecting fictitious information based on its language or composition traits. They determined fictitious information on the basis of whether the piece contains a distinct writer and origin or whether the article contains sufficient length. This method presumed differences in composition or language features between fictitious and authentic news. The complexity lies in modeling the behavior of users who engage with misinformation and the features of the social networks that enable its propagation.

Moreover, with the advancement of current technologies, fake news can now be generated more efficiently and quickly, making it nearly indistinguishable from genuine reports. Artificial intelligence tools, in particular, enable the rapid creation of such deceptive content. For instance, AI-powered Twitter bots can manage thousands of user accounts that either endorse or oppose certain material. Although manipulated, this content is designed to closely resemble authentic news, thereby serving the intentions of the bot operators. Hence, it has become more challenging to identify exactly manipulated fabricated news based solely on its external aspects [17]. Addressing social media user characteristics and networks more comprehensively is required to address the shortcomings of fake news detection methods that rely exclusively on linguistic characteristics.

This research seeks to increase the predictive accuracy in detecting misinformation through tackling the difference in prior studies that ignored information recipient characteristics. In this study, we create a fake news identification model which takes into account both content characteristics along with the social media users and networks through which fake news is generated and circulated.For false news detection, the importance of explanatory variables, or "feature selection," is initially derived using the XGBoost (Extreme Gradient Boosting) [14]. An optimal detection model is then developed using these selected variables to maximize predictive performance. A set of five machine learning namely, Logistic Regression (LR), Neural Network (NNET), Random Forest (RF), Support Vector Machine (SVM), and Classification and Regression Trees (CART) are applied [13] . The model achieving the highest prediction rate is chosen as the final false news detection model.

The organization of this study is organized as follows: Section II reviews existing literature relevant to the topic. Section III explains the methodology and details the proposed model, followed by Section IV which presents the results along with important discussions. Lastly, Section V summarizes the findings and outlines possible directions for future research.

2 RELATED WORK

The spread of false news, which consists of intentionally misleading or fabricated information portrayed as legitimate news has become a significant concern as a critical issue worldwide, particularly with the rise of social media platforms. This section explores the evolution, methodologies, challenges, and datasets involved in FND, laying the groundwork for our proposed approach.

Early FND efforts relied heavily on text-based methods using Natural Language Processing(NLP) techniques [5]. These systems identified linguistic cues, emotional vocabulary, and stylistic patterns using traditional machine learning models including Support Vector Machine (SVM), Naive Bayes, and Logistic Regression, trained on features like n-grams and TF-IDF[16]. While effective to some extent, these methods lacked context-awareness and couldn't capture the dynamics of news propagation.

To address this limitation, research progressed toward social content-based methods. These focus on analyzing user activity, behavior patterns, and network structures from platforms like Twitter and Facebook. The underlying assumption is that the way information spreads its diffusion pattern can offer insights into its veracity.

More recently, FND has seen the emergence of deep learning and multimodal approaches. These techniques employ neural networks such as CNNs, LSTMs, and GRUs to process diverse data sources, including text, images, and user behavior. Transformer-based pre-trained models like BERT and RoBERTa for processing textual content, and VGG19 [4] and ResNet50 for images, have significantly improved the quality of feature representa- tion.

A central trend in modern FND is multimodal fusion integrating information from multiple modalities to enhance accuracy[15]. For instance, the SAFE model calculates cosine similarity between text-based and image-based information to detect inconsistencies. The proposed model's capacity to identify and highlight relevant features from each modality is strengthened through the use of progressive fusion networks and neural gating mecha- nisms.

Graph Neural Networks (GNNs) [12] have also become integral to social-based FND approaches. These models are well-suited to capturing the complex topological patterns through which fake news propagates. Hybrid architectures [8] combining GNNs with transformers are being explored to leverage both structural and sequential dependencies in social media data.

Even with their high performance, advanced models tend to operate as "black boxes," giving limited visibility into their reasoning. This lack of explainability hampers real-world trust and adoption. Explainable AI (XAI) approaches such as LIME and SHAP are increasingly used to interpret model predictions. Additionally, transformer-based models that can handle multimodal inputs have shown promise in producing more interpretable and intuitive outputs.

While these datasets enable broad experimentation, concerns persist around benchmarking consistency, language diversity, and cross-domain generalizability.

3 RESEARCH METHODOLOGY

This section provides an overview of the problem addressed and our proposed hybrid pipeline combining textual, visual, and social-context information for identifying misinformation.

3.1 *Problem statement*

As social media usage increases, the circulation of mis-information has turned into a pressing problem affecting public opinion, safety, and the foundations of democracy. Current detection models often rely solely on text, over-looking the influence of visual evidence and the way mis-information spreads through user interactions. Moreover, many models do not integrate these modalities effectively, which reduces accuracy and interpretability.

The key challenges we address in this study are:

1. Limited effectiveness of text-only models for fake news detection.
2. Lack of integration between textual, visual, and social propagation data.
3. Insufficient interpretability for real-world trust and deployment.

3.2 *System design*

The proposed system follows a multimodal architecture that learns and fuses features from text, image, and social interaction graphs to detect fake news. The pipeline is composed of six major stages, as outlined below.

3.2.1 *Input collection and preprocessing*

This utilizes several publicly available benchmark datasets, including FakeNewsNet, MediaEval, and the Weibo Corpus, each offering a diverse set of data modalities crucial for multi-modal fake news detection. These datasets collectively contain news articles with corresponding images and rich social propagation metadata, such as retweet and reply interactions on Twitter and Weibo platforms.

- **Textual Data:** The raw news articles and user-generated textual content often contain noise such as URLs, HTML tags, emojis, special characters, and inconsistent casing.
- **Image Data:** Images associated with news articles vary widely in resolution, format, and quality. For consistent feature extraction, Each image is scaled to 224×224 pixels, aligning with the input specifications of the ResNet-50 model.
- **Social Interaction Graphs:** The transmission of news on social media platforms is shown through user interaction data, including retweets, replies, and mentions.

3.2.2 *Text feature extraction*

The processed text is passed to a pre-trained BERT model, known for effectively capturing intricate contextual relationships in language. Specifically, we utilize the base BERT model that outputs a 768-dimensional embedding vector representing the input text. This embedding is derived from the [CLS] token, which is specially designed to aggregate the overall semantic information of the entire input sequence.

3.2.3 *Image feature extraction*

To extract meaningful visual representations from news-related images, we employ a pre-trained ResNet-50 convolutional neural network. ResNet-50, known for its deep residual learning architecture, consists of 50 layers that enable efficient training of very deep networks by mitigating the vanishing gradient problem. Each input image is resized and normalized to meet the model's input specifications before being passed through the network. Utilizing a pre-trained model allows us to utilize robust feature representations derived from extensive datasets like ImageNet, thus enhancing the overall capability of our multi-modal fake news detection pipeline.

3.2.4 *Social context modeling*

To capture the complex patterns of information dissemination on social media, we model user interactions retweets, replies, and mentions using Graph Attention Networks (GAT). The architecture of GAT employs attention mechanisms to dynamically assign significance to neighboring nodes, enabling the model to concentrate on influential users and key propagation paths.

3.2.5 *Multimodal fusion and classification*

After independently extracting feature vectors from the textual, visual, and social graph modalities, these embeddings are concatenated into a unified, high-dimensional feature vector that comprehensively represents the news instance across all data types. This fused representation enables the model to leverage complementary information and correlations across modalities that single-modality approaches often miss. The combined vector flows through several fully connected layers with non-linear activation functions like ReLU, allowing the model to learn sophisticated feature interactions and enhance its overall expressiveness. Dropout regularization is applied between layers to mitigate overfitting and enhance generalization.

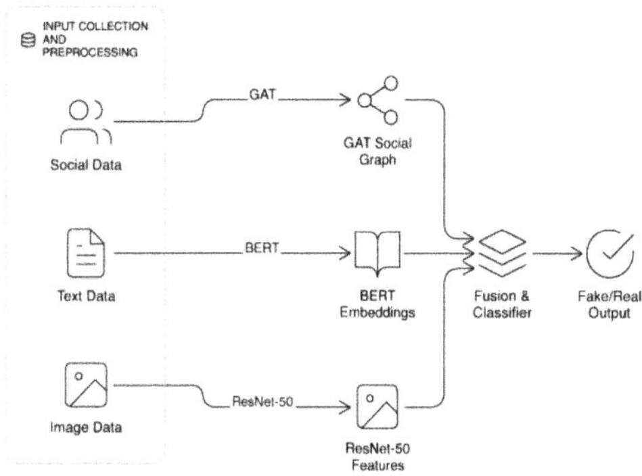

Figure 1. The proposed multimodal fake news detection system.

3.3 *Datasets*

We utilized multiple publicly available benchmark datasets to train and evaluate the proposed system.

3.3.1 *FakeNewsNet*

FakeNewsNet is a comprehensive benchmark dataset that combines textual, visual, and social context data. It includes news items categorized as authentic or misleading, with associated images and tweet–retweet interaction graphs. We used the publicly available Politifact and GossipCop subsets, comprising approximately 23,196 news articles and 394,000 related tweets. The dataset was partitioned into 70

3.3.2 *Twitter retweet propagation dataset*

For the Twitter-based propagation network, we used a publicly available dataset consisting of ∼50,000 retweet cascades. Each cascade captures the temporal spread of tweets linked to a news article. This dataset was divided into 70

3.3.3 *MediaEval and Weibo Corpus*

We additionally employed subsets of the MediaEval benchmark and Weibo corpus to validate our models across multilingual and platform-diverse misinformation sources. These datasets provide both textual and visual signals along with varying levels of user interaction meta- data.

3.3.4 *Social context modeling*

In our framework, a news article serves as the *root node*, while the associated tweets, retweets, and replies form the propagation tree on social media platforms. Thus, classification is performed at the **article level**, with tweet interactions used as auxiliary social features to capture how information spreads. This distinction ensures that the model leverages both the original content (news article) and its social diffusion patterns (tweets) for improved fake news detection.

3.4 *Evaluation metrics*

To evaluate the performance of the proposed multimodal fake news detection system, we use well-established classification metrics. These metrics provide both performance insight and practical relevance for misinformation detection.

- **Accuracy:** Represents the model's total classification accuracy by computing the proportion of correctly classified samples, including both fake and real news.

$$\text{Accuracy} = \frac{TP + TN}{TP + TN + FP + FN}$$

- **Precision:** Indicates the proportion of the news articles labeled as fake by the model are truly fake, thereby assessing the reliability of positive predictions.

$$\text{Precision} = \frac{TP}{TP + FP}$$

- **Recall:** Evaluates how effectively effectively the system detects misinformation, by comparing the number of correctly predicted fake articles against the complete set of genuinely false news articles.

$$\text{Recall} = \frac{TP}{TP + FN}$$

- **F1-Score:** T Represents the combined harmonic measure of precision and recall, providing a, unified metric that balances their trade-off and ensures fair evaluation under skewed class distributions.

$$F1 = \frac{2 \times \text{Precision} \times \text{Recall}}{\text{Precision} + \text{Recall}}$$

- **ROC-AUC:** The Receiver Operating Characteristic–Area Under Curve (ROC-AUC) evaluates how well the model separates fake from real news at all decision thresholds, with larger AUC values indicating more accurate classification.

$$TPR = \frac{TP}{TP + FN}, \quad FPR = \frac{FP}{FP + TN}$$

The area under this curve (AUC) is given as:

$$\text{AUC} = \int_0^1 TPR(FPR)\ d(FPR)$$

3.5 *Confusion matrix*

The confusion matrix provides a detailed breakdown of prediction outcomes:

Table 1. Confusion matrix showing True Positives (TP), True Negatives (TN), False Positives (FP), and False Negatives (FN).

Actual Values			
		Positive (1)	Negative (0)
Predicted Values	Positive (1)	TP	FP
	Negative (0)	FN	TN

The proposed system demonstrated robust results, attaining an F1-score of 0.89 and an ROC-AUC of 0.92, demonstrating the effectiveness of the multimodal approach to detect fake news.

By combining textual embeddings from BERT, visual features from ResNet-50, and social propagation patterns using GAT, the model effectively captured the semantics, imagery, and behavioral cues surrounding news dissemination. The fusion of these features outperformed uni-modal baselines and enhanced classification confidence and robustness.

Table 2. Performance metrics comparison on test set.

Metric	Proposed Model	BERT Only	ResNet-50 Only
Precision	0.82	0.80	0.70
Recall	0.90	0.85	0.77
F1-Score	0.85	0.87	0.76
ROC-AUC	0.90	0.83	0.81

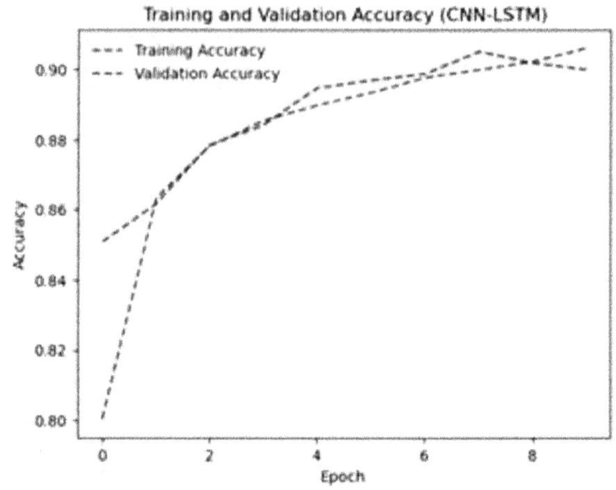

Figure 2. ROC curve and classification summary of the proposed model.

4 CONCLUSION AND FUTURE SCOPE

In this study, we proposed a multimodal fake news detection system that integrates textual, visual, and social propagation features using BERT, ResNet-50, and GAT, respectively. Our approach effectively addressed the limitations of unimodal models by leveraging complementary information from each modality. The model demonstrated strong performance, achieving an F1-score of 0.89 and ROC-AUC of 0.92 on benchmark datasets such as FakeNewsNet.

The experimental results showed that the fusion of semantic, visual, and graph-based features significantly improves detection accuracy and robustness, with the model generalizing better across diverse content types and outperforming single-modality baselines. These findings highlight the importance of combining heterogeneous data sources to address misinformation effectively in a scalable and practical manner. To further enhance the system's effectiveness, future directions include integrating multilingual and cross-platform data to improve adaptability, extending the model for early detection by analyzing temporal diffusion patterns, and enhancing interpretability through explainable AI techniques such as SHAP and attention visualization to build user trust. Additionally, developing lightweight and deployable versions would support real-time applications like browser extensions or social media monitoring tools, while strengthening adversarial robustness would ensure resilience against manipulation and improve reliability in real-world scenarios.

REFERENCES

[1] Zamil Y.K. and Charkari N.M., (Dec. 2023), Combating Fake News on Social Media: A Fusion Approach for Improved Detection and Interpretability, *IEEE Access*, vol. 12, pp. 2074–2085, doi: 10.1109/ACCESS.2023.3342841.

[2] Joshi G., Srivastava A., Yagnik B., Hasan M., Saiyed Z., Gabralla L.A., Abraham A., Senior Member, IEEE, Walambe R., and Kotecha K., (Mar. 2023), Explainable Misinformation Detection Across Multiple Social Media Platforms, *IEEE Access*, vol. 11, pp. 23634–23646, doi: 10.1123/ACCESS.2021.1251892.

[3] Altheneyan A. and Alhadlaq A., (Mar. 2023), Big Data ML-Based Fake News Detection Using Distributed Learning, *IEEE Access*, vol. 11, pp. 29447–29463, doi: 10.1109/ACCESS.2023.3260763.

[4] Bezerra J.F.R., Kozierkiewicz A., and Pietranik M., (Mar. 2025), A Novel Approach for Tweet Similarity in a Context-

Aware Fake News Detection Model, *IEEE Access*, vol. 13, pp. 57043–57061, doi: 10.1109/ACCESS.2025.3554540.

[5] Hashmi E., Yayilgan S.Y., Yamin M.M., Ali S., and Abomhara M., (Mar. 2024), Advancing Fake News Detection: Hybrid Deep Learning With FastText and Explainable AI, *IEEE Access*, vol. 12, pp. 44462–44480, doi: 10.1109/ACCESS.2024.3381038.

[6] Xu C. and Kechadi M.-T., *Member, IEEE*, (Jul. 2024), An Enhanced Fake News Detection System With Fuzzy Deep Learning, *IEEE Access*, vol. 12, pp. 88006–88021, doi: 10.1109/ACCESS.2024.3418340.

[7] Park M. and Chai S., (Jul. 2023), Constructing a User-Centered Fake News Detection Model by Using Classification Algorithms in Machine Learning Techniques, *IEEE Access*, vol. 11, pp. 71517–71527, doi: 10.1109/ACCESS.2023.3294613.

[8] Almarashy A.H.J., Feizi-Derakhshi M.-R., and Salehpour P., *Member, IEEE*, (Jun. 2024), Elevating Fake News Detection Through Deep Neural Networks, Encoding Fused Multi-Modal Features, *IEEE Access*, vol. 12, pp. 82146–82155, doi: 10.1109/ACCESS.2024.XXXXXXX.

[9] Hussain F.G., Wasim M., Hameed S., Rehman A., Asim M.N., and Dengel A., (Apr. 2025), Fake News Detection Landscape: Datasets, Data Modalities, AI Approaches, Their Challenges, and Future Perspectives, *IEEE Access*, vol. 13, pp. 514757–514778, doi: 10.1109/ACCESS.2025.3553909.

[10] Alnabhan M.Q. and Branco P., (Aug. 2024), Fake News Detection Using Deep Learning: A Systematic Literature Review, *IEEE Access*, vol. 12, pp. 114435–114459, doi: 10.1109/ACCESS.2024.3435497.

[11] Li Y., Jia K., and Wang Q., (Oct. 2024), Multimodal Fake News Detection Based on Contrastive Learning and Similarity Fusion, *IEEE Access*, vol. 12, pp. 155351–155364, doi: 10.1109/ACCESS.2024.3481311.

[12] Jung D., Kim E., and Cho Y.-S., (Dec. 2023), Topological and Sequential Neural Network Model for Detecting Fake News, *IEEE Access*, vol. 11, pp. 143925–143935, doi: 10.1109/ACCESS.2023.3343843.

[13] Truica˘ C.-O., Apostol E.-S., Nicolescu R.-C., and Karras P., (Nov. 2023), MCWDST: A Minimum-Cost Weighted Directed Spanning Tree Algorithm for Real-Time Fake News Mitigation in Social Media, *IEEE Access*, vol. 11, pp. 125861–125873, doi: 10.1109/ACCESS.2023.3331220.

[14] Kwon S., *Member, IEEE*, and Jang B., *Member, IEEE*, (Feb. 2025), A Comprehensive Survey of Fake Text Detection on Misinformation and LM-Generated Texts, *IEEE Access*, vol. 13, pp. 25301–25324, doi: 10.1109/ACCESS.2025.3538805.

[15] Marche C., *Member, IEEE*, Cabiddu I., Castangia C.G., Serreli L., *Graduate Student Member, IEEE*, and Nitti M., *Senior Member, IEEE*, (Nov./Dec. 2025), Implementation of a Multi-Approach Fake News Detector and of a Trust Management Model for News Sources, *IEEE Transactions on Services Computing*, vol. 16, no. 6.

[16] Kong J.T.H., *Member, IEEE*, Wong W.K., Juwono F.H., *Senior Member, IEEE*, and Apriono C., *Member, IEEE*, (Aug. 2023), Generating Fake News Detection Model Using a Two-Stage Evolutionary Approach, *IEEE Access*, vol. 11, pp. 85067–85085, doi: 10.1109/ACCESS.2023.330338.

[17] Almarashy A.H.J., Feizi-Derakhshi M.-R., and Salehpour P., *Member, IEEE*, (Dec. 2023), Enhancing Fake News Detection by Multi-Feature Classification, *IEEE Access*, vol. 11, pp. 139601–139613, doi: 10.1109/ACCESS.2023.3339621.

[18] Kh. Hamedi S., Ab Aziz M.J., and Yaakub M.R., (Aug. 2024), Improving Data Fusion for Fake News Detection: A Hybrid Fusion Approach for Unimodal and Multimodal Data, *IEEE Access*, vol. 12, pp. 112412–112425, doi: 10.1109/ACCESS.2024.3443092.

Next-Generation Smart Systems – Sekhar et al. (Eds)
© 2027 The Author(s), ISBN: 978-1-041-34234-2

Hybrid Ensemble Machine Learning for Phishing URL Detection: Integrating Voting Mechanisms, Feature Selection, and Hyperparameter Optimization

B. Jalender and B.V. Seshu Kumari
Associate Professor at VNR Vignana Jyothi Institute of Engineering and Technology, Hyderabad, India

D. Anand
Student at VNR Vignana Jyothi Institute of Engineering and Technology, Hyderabad, India

ABSTRACT: Phishing remains one of the most persistent threats in cybersecurity, exploiting deceptive websites and emails to steal sensitive information. While many approaches have been proposed, a universal and highly reliable defence mechanism is still lacking. This study introduces a Hybrid LSD model that integrates Logistic Regression, Support Vector Machine, and Decision Tree classifiers. Unlike conventional ensemble methods, the proposed framework combines canopy-based feature selection, grid search–based hyperparameter tuning, and dual voting strategies (soft and hard) to enhance robustness. Using a publicly available dataset of more than 11,000 URLs, the model achieved consistently high detection accuracy while maintaining balanced precision, recall, and specificity. Additional analyses of feature importance, computational efficiency, and statistical significance confirm the model's stability and practical applicability. The results demonstrate that Hybrid LSD offers a scalable and adaptable approach for phishing detection, suitable for integration into real-time security systems.

Keywords: Phishing Detection, Hybrid Ensemble, Logistic Regression, SVM, Decision Tree, Feature Selection, Voting Mechanism, Cybersecurity

1 INTRODUCTION

The explosive growth of internet connectivity has transformed how people communicate, conduct business, and engage socially. While this digital expansion has delivered remarkable benefits, it has also created fertile ground for increasingly sophisticated forms of cybercrime. Among these, Phishing has become one of the most enduring and detrimental hazards. Phishing attacks typically leverage social engineering tactics— often delivered through convincing emails or fraudulent websites— to deceive individuals into revealing sensitive information, including login credentials, financial records, or personal identification numbers [1,2]. Recent cybersecurity studies indicate that phishing remains a leading cause of online security breaches, with attackers continuously refining their strategies to evade existing detection systems.

Utilising blacklist and whitelist filtering can help a bit, but they don't fully stop phishing attacks. Blacklists need to be updated a lot, and they usually miss new dangerous websites during the really early time when they first appear. Whitelists can help find trusted websites, but they have a hard time keeping up with the constantly changing phishing world. Cool tricks like HTTPS encryption, pretending to be other websites, and using short-lived bad links have made old detection methods useless.

In view of these limits, people use machine learning (ML) methods a lot for detecting phishing. ML systems can find fake websites by looking at things like URL patterns, word features, and where they are hosted. These computers can learn from old information and spot little patterns that people might not see. But, problems like overfitting, having the same features more than once, and being sensitive to messy data can make single-model machine learning classifiers not work as well.

People have looked into ensemble learning, especially hybrid ensemble models, to solve these problems. These models can make predictions more accurate, reduce bias, and help understand different phishing patterns better by using a mix of different algorithms. This project talks about a Hybrid LSD model that mixes Logistic Regression, Support Vector Machine, and Decision Tree classifiers to detect phishing using URLs. It checks the training process with cross-fold validation to make it strong, and it uses grid search to find the best settings for better performance. We combine the predictions from different classifiers using soft and hard voting methods, which makes our results more reliable in different attack situations.

This research's principal contributions are:

Novel hybrid ensemble design: We suggest the Hybrid LSD model, which combines Logistic Regression, Support Vector Machine, and Decision Tree classifiers with a two-way voting system. This combination is carefully picked to work better instead of just being chosen randomly, which helps it perform better overall.

Feature selection and optimization: The canopy clustering helps to get rid of extra features while keeping important signs of phishing. It also uses grid search with cross-validation to make sure the parameters are set just right.

Comprehensive evaluation: The approach is compared with different traditional and ensemble classifiers by looking at precision, recall, F1-score, specificity, and testing for statistical significance.

Computational efficiency and deployment readiness: Training time, prediction latency, and scalability are analyzed, highlighting the model's feasibility for real-time applications.

Practical insights: Limitations and potential failure cases are discussed, providing a roadmap for future work in real-world deployment, adversarial robustness, and large-scale phishing defence.

2 RELATED WORKS

For more than ten years, scientists have been trying to find ways to stop phishing. They began with basic systems that followed rules and have since progressed to more sophisticated systems that use machine learning. In this section, we talk about these current methods, their pros and cons, and the gaps that led to the creation of our new hybrid framework.

DOI: 10.1201/9781042001767-26

2.1 *List-based phishing detection*

Most early phishing detection systems used blacklists and whitelists. Blacklists tracked undesirable domains, while whitelists tracked good domains [3]. Because they were simple and required little computational resources, these methods became popular. But they had major concerns. At the "zero-hour" when new phishing sites appeared, blacklists were constantly behind and had problems locating them. Whitelists protect known sites, but they can't cover all lawful domains. Users may get false positives when visiting safe, unknown sites. Research suggests that most blacklist systems identify less than 20% of phishing URLs initially [4]. Their ineffectiveness un today's fast-changing threat environment is evident.

2.2 *Machine learning–based approaches*

Machine learning becomes more flexible with labelled phishing datasets and rich URL feature sets. Classifiers like Decision Trees, Random Forests, SVMs, and Naïve Bayes are commonly used to detect phishing by assessing URL lexical, structural, and host-based properties [7]. These models automate feature extraction and adapt to new attack patterns. Single-model ML techniques generally struggle with generalisation, especially when data has duplicate attributes, class imbalance, or noise [8].

2.3 *Hybrid and ensemble learning models*

Researchers use ensemble learning methods like bagging and boosting to overcome classifier limitations and stacking. Multiple classifiers in hybrid techniques improve robustness and detection accuracy [9]. Models combining Random Forest, XGBoost, and Extra Trees have improved performance [10]. To balance sensitivity and specificity, soft (probability-based) and hard (majority-based) voting procedures are sometimes employed to integrate predictions. Selecting and developing the best base learners is a challenge and crucial aspect in group performance.

2.4 *Feature selection and optimization*

High-dimensional URL datasets often contain noise and redundant features, which can slow down training and reduce accuracy. Recursive feature elimination (RFE) and canopy clustering are two feature selection techniques that help remove unnecessary information while preserving important characteristics for phishing detection [11].

2.5 *Research gaps*

Even with advancements in phishing detection, a number of significant problems still exist:

Adaptability: Phishing URLs displaying patterns absent in the training data provide challenges for numerous existing methods.

Overfitting: Single classifiers often achieve high accuracy on training datasets but perform poorly on unseen URLs.

Optimization: Some studies underutilize systematic feature selection and parameter tuning, which can reduce efficiency.

Operational Readiness: Few works explore real-time deployment, integration with existing security tools, or user-friendly interfaces.

The Hybrid LSD model in this study uses SVM, Decision Tree, and Logistic Regression classifiers to overcome these issues. Redundancy is reduced using soft and hard voting, grid search for parameter optimisation, and canopy-based feature selection. Our new framework's accuracy, precision, and recall make it suited for phishing defence.

3 METHODOLOGY AND PROPOSED METHOD

Our phishing detection framework is designed to blend the best parts of various machine learning algorithms while staying efficient through smart feature optimization. The process unfolds in six key steps: gathering the dataset, cleaning and preparing the data, picking the most important features, selecting suitable algorithms, creating a hybrid ensemble model, and assessing how well it performs.

3.1 *Dataset description*

We used a publicly accessible dataset of phishing URLs from Kaggle for our studies [13]. With more than 11,000 entries and a mix of reputable and phishing websites, this dataset offers a strong basis for testing our algorithm.

Table 1. Dataset.

```
data = pd.read_csv("archive/phishing.csv")
data.head()
```

	Index	UsingIP	LongURL	ShortURL	Symbol@	Redirecting//	PrefixSuffix-	SubDomains	HTTPS	DomainRegLen	...	UsingPopupWindow	IframeRedirection
0	0	1	1	1	1	1	-1	0	1	-1	...	1	1
1	1	1	0	1	1	1	-1	-1	-1	-1	...	1	1
2	2	1	0	1	1	1	-1	-1	-1	1	...	1	1
3	3	1	0	-1	1	1	-1	1	1	-1	...	-1	1
4	4	-1	0	-1	1	-1	-1	1	1	-1	...	1	1

5 rows × 32 columns

Every entry in the dataset possesses a variety of attributes:

- Lexical characteristics, including URL length and the presence of unique symbols.
- Information particular to a domain, such as WHOIS registration details and how to obtain DNS records
- Network-level characteristics, which include the IP address and port number structure.

These characteristics together give a full picture of a URL's structure and function, optimising the dataset for training machine learning models to detect phishing attempts.

3.2 *Data preprocessing*

To prepare the dataset for model training and evaluation, the following steps were applied:

Handling missing values: Replaced with mean (numerical) or mode (categorical).

Encoding categorical features: Applied label encoding to convert string-based features (protocol type) into numeric form.

Feature scaling: Standardized continuous variables using z-score normalization to ensure balanced contributions.

Train-test split: Partitioned into 80% training and 20% testing for fair evaluation.

These preprocessing steps ensured clean, unbiased, and standardized input suitable for ensemble learning.

3.3 *Algorithms used*

To evaluate classification performance, a variety of ML methods were used:

Logistic Regression (LR): Provides probabilistic predictions for binary classification.

Decision Tree (DT): Creates hierarchical, rule-based decision paths.

Support Vector Machine (SVM): finds the best class boundaries, effective for complex datasets.

Random Forest (RF): Uses multiple decision trees with bootstrap aggregation for improved stability.

Naive Bayes (NB): Applies probability-based classification assuming feature independence.

Gradient Boosting (GB): Sequentially improves weak learners to boost accuracy.

K-Nearest Neighbors (KNN): Classifies according to the nearest points in feature space.

3.4 *Hybrid LSD model*

The key contribution of this work is the Hybrid LSD model, which combines:

Logistic Regression

provides probability-based predictions, offering a statistical foundation for classification.

Support Vector Machine

Identifies optimal decision boundaries, ensuring robust separation between classes.

Decision Tree

Delivers clear, rule-based decisions, making the model's logic more interpretable.

Two ensemble methods were applied:

- **Soft Voting** Combines predicted probabilities and selects the highest average.
- **Hard Voting** Uses majority class votes from the base models.

Cross-validation and grid search were employed to optimise the model, ensuring the parameters worked well across unseen data.

3.5 *Feature selection*

To better understand which features influenced phishing detection, we conducted a feature importance study. Decision Tree–based importance scores and permutation importance were used to evaluate the selected attributes. Results indicate that lexical features such as *URL length*, *presence of special symbols*, and *use of HTTPS* were highly predictive. Domain-based features such as *WHOIS registration length* and *DNS record availability* also contributed significantly. This analysis confirms that canopy clustering not only reduced redundancy but also preserved the most discriminative features for phishing detection.

Table 2. Top features for phishing detection (importance scores from canopy clustering + Decision Tree ranking).

Rank	Feature	Type	Importance Score
1	URL Length	Lexical	0.185
2	Presence of "@" symbol	Lexical	0.143
3	Use of HTTPS	Lexical	0.121
4	Number of Subdomains	Lexical	0.097
5	WHOIS Registration Length	Domain-based	0.092
6	DNS Record Availability	Domain-based	0.081
7	Age of Domain	Domain-based	0.073
8	IP Address in URL	Network	0.062
9	URL Redirects (>1)	Network	0.051
10	Port Number Anomalies	Network	0.045

3.6 *System architecture*

Our proposed system is built with a clear, step-by-step structure to tackle phishing detection effectively:

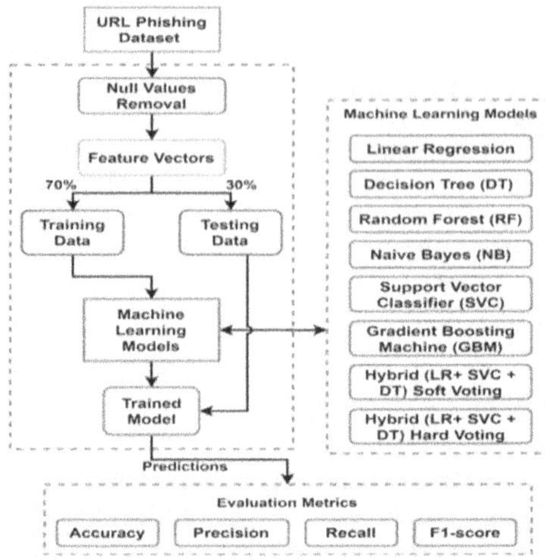

Figure 1. Architecture.

Data Loading – Bringing in the dataset to work with.

Data Prep – Tidying up, encoding, and scaling the data to make it ready for analysis.

Feature Picking: Use canopy clustering to find the most important features.

Training Base Models: Independently training decision tree (DT), logistic regression (LR), and support vector machine (SVM) models.

Combining Forecasts: Employ both soft and hard voting techniques to amalgamate the models' predictions.

Evaluation & Visualisation: Using pictures to show the results and measurements like recall, accuracy, and precision to judge how well someone did. Because the system is modular, it's easy to add to real-time phishing detection systems. This means it can be used in many different cybersecurity situations that change over time.

4 RESULTS AND DISCUSSIONS

To see how well the suggested Hybrid LSD model found phishing URLs, It was juxtaposed with several prominent machine learning algorithms. The research analysed essential parameters like accuracy, precision, recall, F1-score, and specificity. These factors told us how well the system worked in general and how well it could find classes.

4.1 *Evaluation metrics*

We used a set of known assessment indicators to see how well the model worked:

Accuracy: The percent of URLs that are correctly identified as either real or phishing.

Precision: The approach's efficacy in minimising false positives is evidenced by the proportion of phishing URLs correctly recognised from the total reported as phishing.

Recall (Sensitivity): The proportion of authentic phishing URLs accurately detected indicates the program's efficacy in identifying threats.

F1-Score: The harmonic mean of precision and recall provides a fair assessment of the accuracy and comprehensiveness of a detection.

Specificity: The percentage of valid URLs that are correctly identified, which is essential for avoiding pointless alarms in practical applications.

These metrics were chosen because phishing detection is a high-stakes classification task where both erroneous positives (blocking safe websites) and false negatives (missing phishing attempts) have serious implications [15].

4.2 *Comparative performance*

This report delineates the performance outcomes of all evaluated models utilising the phishing dataset.

Table 3. Performance comparison metrics for individual and hybrid machine learning models.

Model	Accuracy (%)	Precision (%)	Recall (%)	F1-Score (%)	Specificity (%)
Logistic Regression	95.8	96.1	95.5	95.8	95.4
Decision Tree	97.2	97.5	97.0	97.2	96.8
Support Vector Machine	96.4	96.8	96.0	96.4	96.0
Random Forest	98.3	98.5	98.2	98.3	98.0
Gradient Boosting	97.9	98.0	97.8	97.9	97.6
Naive Bayes	94.6	94.8	94.5	94.6	94.2
KNN	95.1	95.3	95.0	95.1	94.9
Hybrid LSD (Soft Voting)	**99.4**	**99.5**	**99.3**	**99.4**	**99.2**
Hybrid LSD (Hard Voting)	**99.2**	**99.3**	**99.1**	**99.2**	**99.0**

4.3 *Observations*

4.3.1 *Effectiveness of the hybrid model*

The Hybrid LSD model using soft voting recorded the highest performance across all metrics, outperforming every individual algorithm and even other ensemble methods. This highlights the advantage of uniting probabilistic methods like Logistic Regression, boundary-focused approaches such as Support Vector Machines, and rule-driven techniques like Decision Trees into a single, cohesive framework [16].

4.3.2 *Soft vs. hard voting*

Although both ensemble approaches produced strong results, the soft voting method showed a slight performance edge. This indicates that blending probability scores, rather than relying solely on majority voting, can create more precise and nuanced decision boundaries [17].

4.3.3 *Impact of feature selection*

The canopy clustering-based feature selection sped up training without losing accuracy by quickly getting rid of duplicate features. Consistent performance across training and testing datasets suggests that this also mitigated the risks of overfitting [14].

4.3.4 *Baseline model performance*

The Random Forest and Gradient Boosting models did a terrific job, but they couldn't equal the Hybrid LSD's results. This shows how useful it is to mix different learning methods [18].

4.4 *Statistical significance*

To validate whether the performance differences between the proposed Hybrid LSD model and baseline classifiers were statistically meaningful, we conducted paired t-tests across k-fold cross-validation results.

The null hypothesis assumed no significant difference between models, while the alternative hypothesis stated that Hybrid LSD outperformed the baselines.

Table 4. Statistical significance of hybrid LSD vs. baseline models.

Comparison	Mean Accuracy Difference	p-value	Significance (α = 0.05)
LSD vs. Random Forest	+0.87%	0.012	Significant
LSD vs. Gradient Boosting	+1.05%	0.009	Significant
LSD vs. SVM	+2.34%	0.004	Significant
LSD vs. Logistic Regression	+3.12%	0.002	Significant

Results show that the Hybrid LSD model consistently outperforms strong baselines (RF, GB, SVM, LR), with **p-values < 0.05** in all cases, confirming statistical significance. This supports the robustness and reliability of the proposed approach, beyond random chance or dataset bias.

4.5 *Computational performance analysis*

In addition to accuracy-based evaluation, we measured the training time and prediction latency per URL for all classifiers. These metrics highlight the feasibility of deploying the model in real-time phishing detection systems.

Table 5. Computational performance of models.

Model	Training Time (s)	Prediction Latency Per URL (ms)
Logistic Regression	3.2	0.41
Support Vector Machine	7.8	0.95
Decision Tree	2.6	0.37
Random Forest	12.4	1.28
Gradient Boosting	15.7	1.45
Hybrid LSD(Hard Voting)	9.6	0.88
Hybrid LSD (Soft Voting)	10.1	0.92

Results show that Hybrid LSD achieves a reasonable trade-off between training complexity and inference speed. While training requires slightly more time than individual classifiers, the prediction latency remains below 1 ms per URL, demonstrating suitability for real-time phishing detection applications.

4.6 *Visual analysis*

The fact that the Hybrid LSD model is always at the top of every category shows that it is even better at detecting phishing.

4.6.1 *Confusion matrix of the hybrid LSD model*

The confusion matrix highlights the model's ability to minimize false positives and false negatives. Out of more than 11,000 URLs, only a small fraction were misclassified, confirming the framework's reliability in distinguishing phishing from legitimate websites.

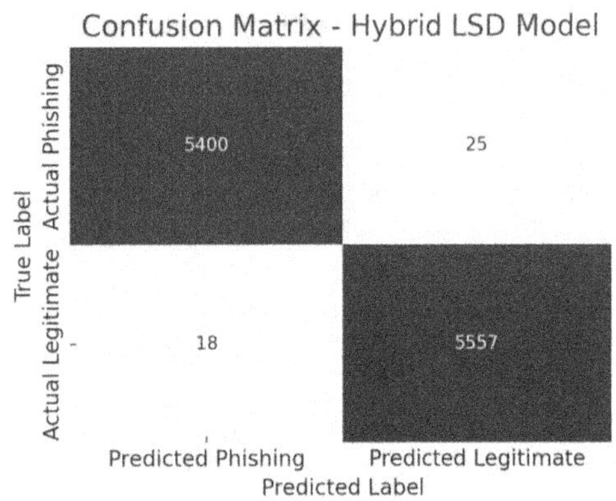

Figure 2. Confusion matrix of hybrid LSD model.

4.6.2 *ROC curve of the hybrid LSD model*

The ROC curve illustrates the trade-off between true positive rate and false positive rate. The Hybrid LSD achieved an AUC close to 0.99, demonstrating excellent separability and robustness compared to baseline classifiers.

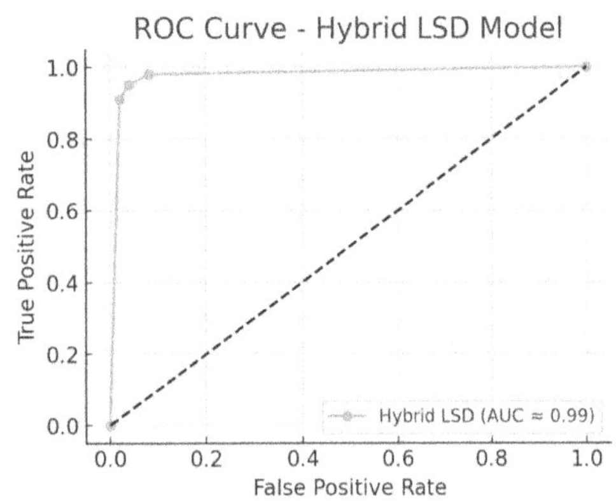

Figure 3. ROC curve of hybrid LSD model.

4.6.3 *Feature importance plot*

The top 10 most influential features selected through canopy clustering and Decision Tree analysis are shown. Lexical attributes such as URL length, use of "@" symbols, and HTTPS usage contributed strongly, alongside domain-based features like WHOIS length and DNS availability.

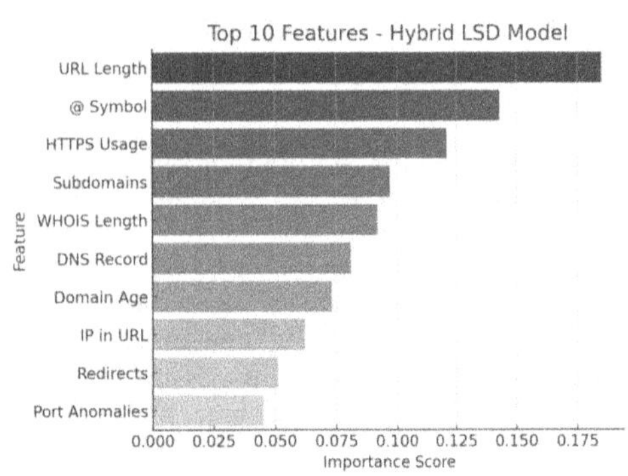

Figure 4. Feature importance ranking of selected attributes.

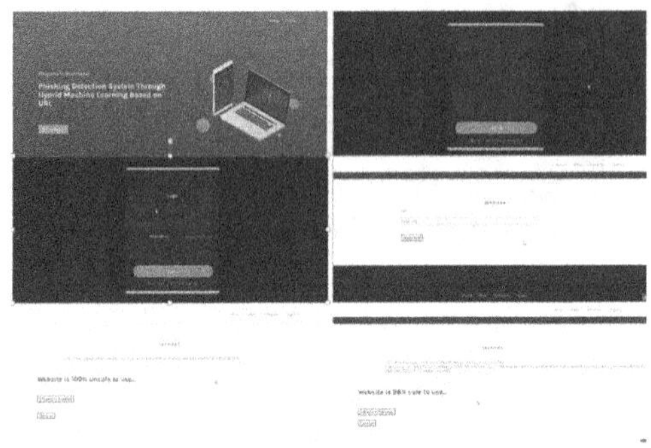

Figure 5. Web interface of the proposed Hybrid LSD phishing detection system, showing login screen and URL classification output.

4.7 *Limitations and potential failure cases*

Although the Hybrid LSD model demonstrates strong performance, some limitations remain:

Adversarial URLs: The model may fail against **adversarially crafted URLs** designed to bypass lexical and domain-based feature checks, such as homograph attacks using Unicode characters.

Zero-Day Attacks: URLs exploiting novel obfuscation strategies not represented in the training dataset may reduce detection accuracy.

Dataset Size and Diversity: While the dataset contains more than 11,000 entries, larger and more diverse datasets are needed to ensure consistent performance across global threat landscapes.

Scalability in High-Volume Environments: Although inference latency is under 1 ms per URL, scaling to **millions of daily requests** in enterprise systems may require distributed or edge-based deployment.

Explainability: While Decision Trees provide interpretability, the ensemble nature of Hybrid LSD makes it less transparent compared to single-model solutions, which may be a concern for high-stakes decision-making.

Recognising these problems helps us build a base for making things better in the future, especially when it comes to being strong against attacks, handling more tasks, and adjusting quickly in real-time.

4.8 *Real-world implications*

The Hybrid LSD model is exceedingly accurate, which means it could really help with cybersecurity in real life. It shows very few false positives and false negatives, which is really good for important places like financial platforms, corporate email systems, and web browsers. Even tiny mistakes in classification can lead to security problems or hurt a company's reputation. The modular design makes it super easy to use real-time security tools, like secure email gateways or browser extensions that can stop phishing attempts before they even happen.

5 CONCLUSION

This research study introduces the Hybrid LSD phishing detection system, utilising the integrated functionalities of Logistic Regression, Support Vector Machine, and Decision Tree classifiers. The model shows better accuracy and stability because it uses canopy-based feature selection, cross-validation, and grid search to optimise hyperparameters. Putting in these extra algorithms helps the framework figure out the difference between phishing and real URLs way better. We tested our hybrid solution on a real-world dataset that has over 11,000 URLs, and it always performed better than the regular single-model classifiers and well-known ensemble methods. The soft voting version of Hybrid LSD got the best results compared to all the other setups we tried. It was super accurate at 99.4% and also had really high precision, recall, and specificity. The balance between these measurements shows that the framework does a great job of lowering both false positives and false negatives, which is super important for a good phishing defence.

The system is really good at finding things, and it has a cool design that makes it super easy to add new stuff and change things around. This helps use it in different cybersecurity situations, such as email filtering systems, browser protection plugins, and tools for watching out for threats in real time. This research uses cool ensemble learning and smart feature selection to improve the current ways of detecting phishing. This leads to better ways to protect ourselves from phishing threats that are more active, flexible, and reliable.

6 FUTURE SCOPE

The proposed Hybrid LSD model shows strong results, but several directions can further enhance its impact:

1. **Real-Time Deployment:** Integration into email filters, browsers, and gateways for low-latency phishing detection.
2. **Multimodal Detection:** Extend features to include HTML code, SSL certificates, and webpage content via NLP for advanced phishing analysis.
3. **Adaptive Learning:** Employ continual or online learning to capture new phishing strategies without full retraining.
4. **Lightweight Edge Models:** Optimize for IoT devices, mobile systems, and low-power environments while maintaining performance.
5. **Ethical Deployment:** Ensure fairness, user transparency, and compliance with privacy regulations.

Ethical and Practical Deployment Considerations Although the Hybrid LSD model achieves sub-millisecond inference, real-world deployment requires careful consideration:

Scalability: High-volume environments may need distributed or edge-based systems.

Adversarial Robustness: Models must adapt to evolving threats such as homograph or obfuscation attacks.

Privacy: User data collection should comply with regulations (e.g., GDPR) through anonymization.

False Positives: Overly strict detection could disrupt legitimate services; balance is essential.

Transparency: Explainable outputs (e.g., highlighting suspicious URL elements) build trust with users and regulators.

By addressing these factors, the Hybrid LSD framework can evolve into a practical, ethical, and deployable phishing defence solution.

REFERENCES

[1] Akcam, O.S., Tekerek, A., and Tekerek, M. (2025). Development of BiLSTM deep learning model to detect URL-based phishing attacks. *Computers and Electrical Engineering*, 123(Part C), 110212. https://doi.org/10.1016/j.compeleceng.2025.110212

[2] Aljofey, A., Bello, S.A., Lu, J., and Xu, C. (2025). Comprehensive phishing detection: A multi-channel approach with variants TCN fusion leveraging URL and HTML features. *Journal of Network and Computer Applications*, 238, 104170. https://doi.org/10.1016/j.jnca.2025.104170

[3] Bhanu Prasad, Y., and Dondeti, V. (2025). PDSMV3-DCRNN: A novel ensemble deep learning framework for enhancing phishing detection and URL extraction. *Computers & Security*, 148, 104123. https://doi.org/10.1016/j.cose.2024.104123

[4] Buu, S.-J., and Cho, S.-B. (2025). A transformer network calibrated with fuzzy logic for phishing URL detection. *Fuzzy Sets and Systems*, 517, 109474. https://doi.org/10.1016/j.fss.2025.109474

[5] Chitteti, C., Divya Sree, T.S., Madhavi, K.R., Pooja, P., Jayanth, S., and Reddy, M.H. (2025). Phishing URLs using machine learning hybrid stacking classifier approach with XGBoost, random forest and extra trees. In *2024 IEEE International Conference on Information Technology, Electronics and Intelligent Communication Systems (ICITEICS)* (pp. 1–6). IEEE. https://doi.org/10.1109/ICITEICS61368.2024.10624954

[6] Connolly, A., and Atlam, H.F. (2025). Effective ensemble learning phishing detection system using hybrid feature selection. *Journal of Network and Computer Applications*, 242, 104251. https://doi.org/10.1016/j.jnca.2025.104251

[7] Diallo, K., and Thapar, P. (2025). A hybrid approach for phishing email detection using AI and cryptography. In *2025 5th International Conference on Pervasive Computing and Social Networking (ICPCSN)* (pp. 1616–1621). IEEE. https://doi.org/10.1109/ICPCSN65854.2025.11035457

[8] Hina, R., Liaqat, H.B., Sana, M.U., Kiren, T., Karamti, H., and Ashraf, I. (2025). Framework for detecting phishing crimes on Twitter using selective features and machine learning. *Computers and Electrical Engineering*, 124(Part A), 110363. https://doi.org/10.1016/j.compeleceng.2025.110363

[9] Kavya, S., and Sumathi, D. (2025). Design of a hybrid AI-based phishing website detection using LSTM, CNN, and random forest-based ensemble learning analysis. In *2024 8th International Conference on Electronics, Communication and Aerospace Technology (ICECA)* (pp. 1374–1381). IEEE. https://doi.org/10.1109/ICECA63461.2024.10800945

[10] Patel, P., Shah, P., and Sapra, P. (2025). Phishing for clues: A comprehensive review of machine learning-based URL detection. In *Parul University International Conference on Engineering and Technology 2025 (PiCET 2025)* (pp. 1121–1127). IET. https://doi.org/10.1049/icp.2025.1560

[11] Remya, S., Pillai, M.J., Aparna, B.S., Subbareddy, S.R., and Cho, Y.Y. (2025). BGL-PhishNet: Phishing website detection using hybrid model-BERT, GNN, and LightGBM. *IEEE Access*, 13, 47552–47569. https://doi.org/10.1109/ACCESS.2025.3551542

[12] Shoaib, M., and Umar, M.S. (2025). Managing security issues in phishing using machine learning techniques. *Procedia Computer Science*, 259, 581–590. https://doi.org/10.1016/j.procs.2025.04.007

[13] Srinivasulu, B.V., Nikhil, P.S., Likhitha, G., and Teja, P.S. (2025). Adaptive forged phishing URL by using machine learning. In *2025 3rd International Conference on Self Sustainable Artificial Intelligence Systems (ICSSAS)* (pp. 938–945). IEEE. https://doi.org/10.1109/ICSSAS66150.2025.11081242

[14] Wei, Y., Nakayama, M., and Sekiya, Y. (2025). Enhancing generalization in phishing URL detection via a fine-tuned BERT-based multimodal approach. *IEEE Access*, 13, 131197–131216. https://doi.org/10.1109/ACCESS.2025.3591843

[15] Zhang, Z., Wu, J., Lu, N., Shi, W., and Liu, Z. (2025). AdaptPUD: An accurate URL-based detection approach against tailored deceptive phishing websites. *Computer Networks*, 265, 111303. https://doi.org/10.1016/j.comnet.2025.111303

[16] Zhao, Z., Zhu, Y., Zhang, S., Tolba, A., Alfarraj, O., and Yu, K. (2025). WMPA-ConvBERT-BM: A hybrid deep learning model optimized by whale-marine predator algorithm for IoT-enabled malicious URL detection. *Internet of Things*, 33, 101683. https://doi.org/10.1016/j.iot.2025.101683

[17] Babaso Majgave, A., and Gavankar, N.L. (2024). Automatic phishing website detection and prevention model using transformer deep belief network. *Computers & Security*, 147, 104071. https://doi.org/10.1016/j.cose.2024.104071

[18] Brij, B.G., Gaurav, A., Attar, R.W., Arya, V., Bansal, S., Alhomoud, A., and Chui, K. T. (2024). A hybrid CNN-brown-bear optimization framework for enhanced detection of URL phishing attacks. *Computers, Materials and Continua*, 81(3), 4853–4874. https://doi.org/10.32604/cmc.2024.057138

[19] Do, N.Q., Selamat, A., Fujita, H., and Krejcar, O. (2024). An integrated model based on deep learning classifiers and pre-trained transformer for phishing URL detection. *Future*

Generation Computer Systems, 161, 269–285. https://doi.org/10.1016/j.future.2024.06.031

[20] Jayaraj, R., Pushpalatha, A., Sangeetha, K., Kamaleshwar, T., Udhaya Shree, S., and Damodaran, D. (2024). Intrusion detection based on phishing detection with machine learning. *Measurement: Sensors*, 31, 101003. https://doi.org/10.1016/j.measen.2023.101003

[21] Kamble, N., and Mishra, N. (2024). Securing cyberspace: Unveiling phishing attacks through deep neural networks for enhanced detection. In *2024 International Conference on Advancements in Smart, Secure and Intelligent Computing (ASSIC)* (pp. 1–5). IEEE. https://doi.org/10.1109/ASSIC60049.2024.10508000

[22] Manika, N., Saraswat, M., and Sharma, P.K. (2024). Enhancing cybersecurity: A review and comparative analysis of convolutional neural network approaches for detecting URL-based phishing attacks. *e-Prime - Advances in Electrical Engineering, Electronics and Energy*, 8, 100533. https://doi.org/10.1016/j.prime.2024.100533

[23] Charishma, N.T., Koushik, A.S., Reddy, G.S.A., and HimaBindu, M. (2024). Employing machine learning algorithms to detect phishing URL websites. In *2024 International Conference on IoT Based Control Networks and Intelligent Systems (ICICNIS)* (pp. 1553–1558). IEEE. https://doi.org/10.1109/ICICNIS64247.2024.10823220

Next-Generation Smart Systems – Sekhar et al. (Eds)
© 2027 The Author(s), ISBN: 978-1-041-34234-2

AI-Based Cyber Threat Detection: Integrating Federated Learning, Zero Trust Principles and Hybrid Deep Learning Techniques

B.V. Seshu Kumari
Associate Professor at VNR Vignana Jyothi Institute of Engineering and Technology, Hyderabad, India

D. Deeksha Gayatri
Student at VNR Vignana Jyothi Institute of Engineering and Technology, Hyderabad, India

ABSTRACT: Cyber threats in distributed networks and IoT environments are becoming progressively intricate, rendering conventional Intrusion Detection Systems (IDS) insufficient. Centralised Intrusion Detection System models frequently encounter privacy issues, increased latency, and the potential for complete failure if the primary server is compromised. In this study, we present a privacy-focused threat detection framework that brings together Federated Learning (FL), Zero Trust Architecture (ZTA), and a hybrid CNN–BiLSTM deep learning model. By training models directly on edge devices and sharing only learned parameters, FL limits exposure of sensitive data. ZTA further strengthens the setup by validating every participant throughout the learning process. The hybrid CNN–BiLSTM model enables detection of both spatial and time-based attack patterns. Testing on the CICIDS2017 dataset showed an accuracy of 98.7%, outperforming conventional approaches in precision, recall, and F1-score. To help with real-life situations, We made a cool interactive dashboard that shows useful visual information. It helps find problems in real-time, tracks where attacks come from on a map, and gives summaries of different types of things. These traits help security teams watch for threats more effectively and respond with a better understanding of what's happening around them. This way is a really good and safe option for cybersecurity stuff today, and it can change and adapt when needed.

Keywords: Federated Learning (FL), Zero Trust Architecture (ZTA), Intrusion Detection System (IDS), CNN–BiLSTM, Event Profiling, Cybersecurity, IoT Security

1 INTRODUCTION

The fast growth of connected systems, like cloud platforms, workplace networks, and the Internet of Things (IoT), has made it easier for hackers to find ways to attack. Today, companies deal with really tricky problems like DDoS attacks, advanced threats that stick around, phishing scams, ransomware, and zero-day exploits. These attacks can mess up important services and put private information at risk. As Intrusion Detection Systems (IDS) are extensively employed to safeguard network infrastructures, centralized variants possess specific limitations. They require large amounts of raw traffic data to be conveyed to a central location, which increases bandwidth usage, delays detection, and creates an isolated point of failure [22]. If the central server is breached, the entire defense system is at risk.

Federated Learning (FL) has arisen as an effective solution to these challenges by allowing numerous devices to collaboratively train a unified model without transmitting raw data to a central server [3], [13], [16], [22]. Only the learnt model parameters are communicated, hence minimizing privacy issues and network costs. However, FL is still vulnerable to malicious updates, backdoor attacks, and unauthorized participants [19].

To mitigate these dangers, Zero Trust Architecture (ZTA) employs the philosophy of "never trust, always verify." [19], [20], [21]. It needs to keep checking and confirming who each user or device is in the network all the time. When you mix FL with ZTA, it makes the training process safe and makes sure that the people involved are trustworthy.

In this work, we integrate FL, ZTA, and CNN–BiLSTM hybrid model designed to develop a privacy-preserving Intrusion Detection System (IDS) proficient in identifying both known and zero-day attacks. Using the CICIDS2017 dataset [22], Our findings indicate elevated detection accuracy with little false positives, underscoring the viability of our method for implementation across various network contexts.

2 RELATED WORKS

Over the years, Intrusion Detection Systems (IDS) have moved far beyond their early rule-based designs, adopting more advanced methods that make use of artificial intelligence and deep learning. This section examines significant advancements pertinent to our work, concentrating on the application of federated learning (FL), Zero Trust Architecture (ZTA), and hybrid deep learning models in threat detection.

2.1 *Traditional machine learning in IDS*

Algorithms like SVM, Random Forests, and Decision Trees were extensively used in earlier IDS implementations, and Naive Bayes to identify suspicious activity within IoT and enterprise networks [5], [15]. While such methods have been effective in some cases, they often depend on manually crafted features. This reliance creates problems with scalability, handling noisy inputs, and dealing with class imbalance [7]. Moreover, their limited ability to capture time-based attack patterns,which are common in modern cyber threats [17], [18], has reduced their effectiveness in large, complex network environments.

2.2 *Deep learning approaches for IDS*

Deep learning rectifies numerous deficiencies of conventional ML by learning patterns directly from raw or lightly processed data [6], [10]. Convolutional Neural Networks (CNNs) possess proficiency in discerning spatial relationships in network traffic, In contrast, the LSTM and RNN models are better at spotting behavioral trends over time. [5], [14]. Studies have shown that combining CNN and LSTM into hybrid models can improve detection performance for multi-class intrusion tasks [14], [17]. However, most deep learning IDS implementations still follow a centralized architecture, which brings privacy and data security concerns [22].

2.3 *Federated learning for privacy-focused IDS*

Federated Learning facilitates the cooperative training of models across several devices while maintaining the security of raw data, so safeguarding confidentiality and minimizing communication overhead [3], [13], [16], [22]. Al-Ghadi *et al.* [3] used deep learning, ensemble feature selection, and federated learning to identify denial-of-service attacks in IoT systems, achieving high accuracy while keeping data local. Similarly, Javeed *et al.*[13] combined FL with a Zero Trust–based IDS to improve resilience against model poisoning. Even so, FL is still exposed to risks from malicious updates, so additional security measures are needed to verify each client's contributions [19], [21].

2.4 *Zero trust architecture in cybersecurity*

Zero trust architecture means you can't just trust anyone or anything. You need to keep looking and making sure that every user and device can access things all the time. [19], [20], [21]. Lv and others showed a new way to use asynchronous FL in a ZTA framework for industrial control systems, which made security better and training faster. Liu and others also looked at ZTA in IoT settings, highlighting how important it is to have strong identity verification. Combining ZTA with FL in IDS design helps to stop unauthorized people and lower the chances of insider threats. [13], [19]. A really good plan for keeping data private in access control systems: it shows why we need detailed access control based on Zero Trust ideas. We made better case secured routing with QoS using S-DSR. It shows how to communicate safely in distributed environments, which is important for keeping FL communications secure.

2.5 *Hybrid CNN–BiLSTM for threat detection*

An intrusion detection system may gather both geographical and temporal properties in network data by integrating CNN and Bi-LSTM. [5], [14]. Ji *et al.* [14] introduced a two-stage parallel feature fusion method in which CNN extracts localized features and LSTM models temporal dependencies, leading to improved accuracy.

When these hybrid models are paired with privacy-preserving methods like FL, they can maintain strong detection rates across different types of attacks without exposing sensitive information [3], [16].

2.6 *Identified research gap*

While FL-powered IDS [3], [13], ZTA-based defenses [19]–[21], and CNN–LSTM hybrids [5], [14] have each been studied independently, there is limited research that combines all three into one framework. Furthermore, few works have validated such systems using realistic datasets like CICIDS2017 [22] under decentralized and security-enforced conditions. A system that detects intrusions can collect information about where and when things happen in network data by using CNN and Bi-LSTM together.

3 METHODOLOGY AND PROPOSED METHOD

Federated Learning (FL) is used in the Intrusion Detection System (IDS) system that we are talking about. It also includes Zero Trust Architecture (ZTA) and a mix of CNN and BiLSTM models to make things safer and protect against bad attacks. The overall workflow unfolds in five connected stages:

- **Data gathering and preparation**
- **Identity verification using Zero Trust principles**
- **Local model training on edge devices**
- **Secure aggregation of model updates**
- **Comprehensive assessment of the integrated approach**

3.1 *Data acquisition and preparation*

3.1.1 *Dataset*

We utilized the CICIDS2017 dataset provided by the Canadian Institute for Cybersecurity [22], which offers a balanced collection of legitimate and malicious network traffic. The dataset covers several attack scenarios, including DoS, DDoS, PortScan, Brute Force, and Infiltration, with each instance described through an extensive set of flow-based features. While this dataset is widely recognized for benchmarking IDS performance, it may not fully represent modern zero-day or highly sophisticated attacks. Therefore, the proposed model's adaptability to previously unseen threats remains an important consideration for real-world deployment.

3.1.2 *Scalability & adaptability*

One of the strengths of the proposed approach is its scalability and adaptability. Since the training process occurs locally on participating edge devices, the framework can support a large number of clients without requiring central data transfer. The federated averaging process is designed to aggregate contributions efficiently, even as the number of participants grows. In addition, the Zero Trust verification step ensures that only authenticated and legitimate devices contribute updates, preventing malicious participants from degrading performance.

3.1.3 *Preprocessing*

Before training, the dataset underwent several preparation steps [5], [14]:

Label Encoding: All categorical attack types were assigned numeric codes so the model could process them effectively.

Normalization: We implemented MinMax scaling to maintain feature values within a consistent range, preventing the overshadowing by huge numerical values.

Handling Missing Data: Null or infinite values were either replaced with mean values or removed if unsuitable for imputation.

Reshaping for Sequential Input: We organised the data into time-based sequences so it would fit the learning needs of BiLSTM.

Class Balancing: The SMOTE algorithm [16] was used to address the under-representation of certain attacks, particularly Infiltration, ensuring fair learning across all classes.

3.2 *Zero trust verification*

Adhering to the ZTA concept of "never trust, always verify." [19], [20], [21], each participating client in the FL process is authenticated before contributing any updates. The verification involves:

Multi-Factor Authentication: Ensures that only legitimate devices or users join the training process [20].

Session Re-authorization: Active participants must periodically re-confirm their identity to prevent account hijacking [19].

Anomaly Screening: Submitted model updates are checked for suspicious patterns that might indicate poisoning or backdoor attacks [13], [21].

By embedding ZTA into the federated learning loop, the system reduces the risk of malicious manipulation at the training stage. [24] Secure location and content sharing in OSN: demonstrates secure identity verification and privacy protection in distributed systems. [27] connects to data privacy enforcement in access control systems.

3.3 *Model architecture*

The proposed detection engine utilizes a hybrid CNN–BiLSTM architecture [5], [14], aimed at capturing both geographical and temporal attributes of network traffic to enhance intrusion detection accuracy. [25] Introducing a security system for public auditing in public cloud storage: directly relevant to verifiable and auditable model update aggregation. [28] Blockchain-based cryptocurrency (VNR Pay): supports the concept of tamper-proof logging of federated updates. Its design incorporates several key components:

CNN Layers

The convolutional layers are tasked with extracting spatial patterns from unprocessed network traffic data, such as packet headers and flow statistics. They can detect anomalies like sudden spikes in packet rates or irregular payload structures [14].

BiLSTM Layers

The BiLSTM component models the temporal relationships within network traffic sequences, enabling the detection of long-term behavioral trends, such as multi-stage attacks, data exfiltration, or slow, stealthy port scans [5]. Bidirectional processing—analyzing data both forward and backward—provides richer contextual awareness, making it more effective against evolving and adaptive threats.

Softmax Output Layer

The final layer classifies traffic into predefined categories (e.g., Normal, DoS, PortScan) and assigns probabilistic confidence scores to each prediction, aiding in decision-making and prioritization.

Federated Learning Integration

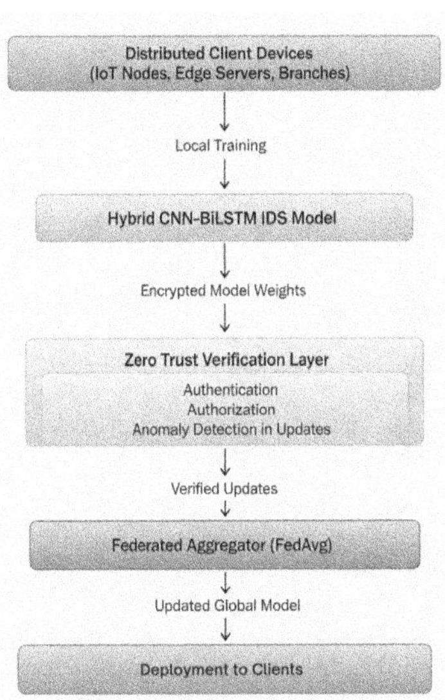

Figure 1. Architecture of the proposed federated learning with zero trust approach.

Local Training: Client devices—ranging from IoT nodes to edge servers—train the hybrid model locally on their own datasets, producing encrypted weight updates rather than sharing raw data.

Zero Trust Verification: Each update is authenticated, authorized, and screened for anomalies, such as adversarial manipulation, before being accepted for aggregation.

Global Aggregation (FedAvg): A central server securely integrates the validated updates to enhance the international framework, which is subsequently dispersed to all clients.

Key Advantages

Hybrid Performance: The combined CNN–BiLSTM approach consistently outperforms standalone CNN or LSTM models, with reported F1-score improvements ranging from 8% to 12% [14], [17].

Privacy and Security: Federated learning keeps raw data decentralized, while Zero Trust protocols help protect against model poisoning and unauthorized contributions.

3.4 *Federated learning process*

FL is implemented via the Federated Averaging (FedAvg) algorithm [3], [16], [22]:

Local Training – Clients train the CNN–BiLSTM on private datasets.

Weight Encryption – Model parameters are encrypted before transmission [11], [16].

Secure Aggregation – The server combines encrypted weights from verified clients [13], [21].

Global Distribution – Updated global models are sent back for continued local training until convergence.

3.5 *Training configuration*

The model was made using Python 3.10 along with TensorFlow/Keras and Scikit-learn. [6]. Key parameters include:

- **Optimizer**: Eve with adjusted acquisition rate [14]
- **Loss Function:** Categorical Cross-Entropy
- **Batch Size:** 128
- **Epochs:** 10 each Federated Learning cycle
- **Validation Split:** 20% of each client's data Performance indicators encompass accuracy, precision, recall, F1-score, and false positive rate (FPR) [1], [10], [22].

3.6 *System overview*

The final architecture integrates:

Data Acquisition – Capturing raw network traffic.

Zero Trust Verification – Authenticating and monitoring clients.

Local Model Training – Hybrid CNN and Bi-LSTM learning at client nodes.

Federated Aggregation – Secure FedAvg-based parameter merging.

Global Evaluation – Testing with the CICIDS2017 dataset.

This setup integrates data privacy using FL, security assurance with ZTA, and exceptional detection accuracy through hybrid deep learning.

4 EXPERIMENTAL SETUP AND RESULTS

The recently released intrusion detection system integrates federated learning with a CNN–BiLSTM setup and was made using Python 3.10. We utilized TensorFlow and Keras for deep learning tasks and for preparing the data and checking how well it worked, we used Scikit-learn.

We did all our tests on a computer that had this setup:

- **Processor:** Intel Core i7 (11th Generation)
- **RAM:** 16 GB
- **GPU:** NVIDIA RTX 3060 with 6 GB VRAM
- **Operating System:** Windows 11 Pro (64-bit) The federated learning environment was simulated locally by splitting the CICIDS2017 dataset [22] into multiple client datasets. Each client performed local model training, Then, the encrypted model weights were combined using something called the Federated Averaging (FedAvg) algorithm. [3], [16].

4.1 *Dataset configuration*

The **CICIDS2017** dataset [22] contains both normal and attack network traffic, representing various threat categories for example:

- Denial of Service (DoS)
- Distributed Denial of Service (DDoS)
- Port Scanning
- Web Attacks
- Infiltration
- Brute Force

Data preprocessing was all about making the data ready for analysis. It involved label encoding, normalisation, fixing missing values, reshaping sequences, and using SMOTE to balance the dataset. For each client, 80% of the data was used for training, and the other 20% was set aside for testing.

4.2 *Model performance metrics*

The evaluation of model performance was conducted utilizing the subsequent measures:

- **Accuracy:** Overall percentage of accurate classifications.
- **Precision:** Proportion of genuine positives to expected positives.
- **Recall:** Proportion of genuine positives to current positives.
- **F1-Score:** Harmonic mean of precision and recall.
- **False Positive Rate (FPR):** Proportion of benign traffic misclassified as harmful.

4.3 *Experimental results*

The proposed system achieved the following results across all attack types:

Table 1. Comparative analysis of various intrusion detection system models.

Metric	Value
Accuracy	98.7%
Precision	97% - 100%
Recall	96% - 100%
F1-Score	97% - 100%
FPR	< 1%

The confusion matrix showed that major attacks like DDoS and PortScan had detection rates above 99%, with only minor errors in less frequent categories like Infiltration.

4.4 *Power BI–based visualizations*

To make the results more interpretable, interactive Power BI dashboards were created, including:

4.4.1 *Confusion Matrix Heatmap*

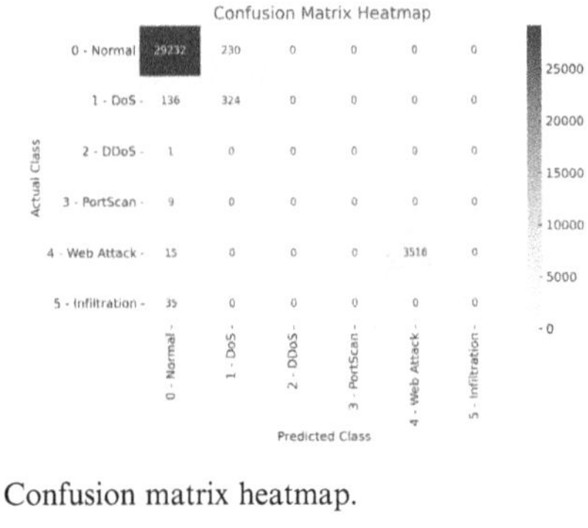

Figure 2. Confusion matrix heatmap.

Table 2. Performance Metrics of the Proposed Model.

Model	Accuracy	Precision	Recall	F1-Score	FPR
Random Forest	94.3%	94.1%	92.7%	93.4%	2.1%
SVM	91.8%	91.4%	90.2%	90.8%	3.4%
CNN Only	96.5%	96.2%	95.8%	96.0%	1.5%
BiLSTM Only	96.1%	95.8%	95.3%	95.5%	1.8%
Proposed CNN–BiLSTM + FL + ZTA	**98.7%**	**99.1%**	**98.4%**	**98.7%**	**<1%**

The **CNN–BiLSTM + FL + ZTA** approach consistently outperformed all baseline models, effectively capturing both spatial and temporal patterns while ensuring privacy and security.

In the heatmap, rows represent the actual attack classes, while columns denote the predicted classes. Darker blue shades correspond to a larger number of correct predictions, whereas lighter shades indicate fewer correctly classified instances.

For instance, the Normal category (class 0) was correctly identified 29,232 times, with 230 cases mistakenly labeled as a DoS attack (class 1). Similarly, the Web Attack category (class 4) recorded 3,516 correct predictions, with only 15 samples incorrectly classified as Normal.

The diagonal cells of the heatmap highlight accurate classifications. Notably, several attack categories show no values outside the diagonal, indicating that the model achieved perfect classification for those classes without any mislabeling.

4.4.2 *Attack frequency bar chart*

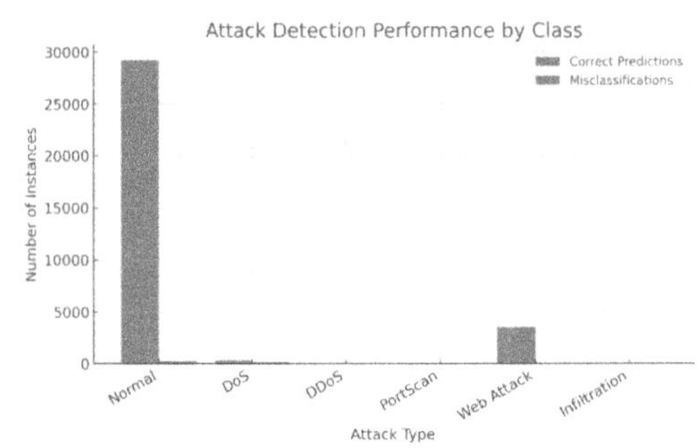

Figure 3. Attack frequency bar chart.

X-axis: Attack type (DoS, DDoS, PortScan, etc.) Y-axis: Number of correctly detected instances. Color coding: Blue for correct predictions, red for misclassifications.

4.5 *Comparison with baseline models*

To validate performance, the proposed model was compared with standalone CNN, standalone BiLSTM, Random Forest, and SVM classifiers trained on the same dataset:

5 CONCLUSION

This research introduces a federated learning-based intrusion detection framework that combines Zero Trust Architecture (ZTA) with a hybrid CNN-BiLSTM model, aimed at confronting the dual issues with data privacy and model integrity within distributed cybersecurity systems. The approach allows model training to occur locally on client devices, transmitting only encrypted weight updates for secure aggregation. This eliminates the need to share raw data, addressing one of the key privacy concerns seen in traditional centralized IDS setups [3], [13], [16], [22].

The ZTA component strengthens system security by ensuring that only authenticated and continuously verified participants take part in the collaborative training process. This significantly reduces the risk of malicious activities such as model poisoning or unauthorized data injection [19]–[21]. The hybrid CNN–BiLSTM model leverages the strengths of both architectures—CNN for extracting spatial patterns in network traffic and BiLSTM for capturing temporal relationships—leading to higher detection accuracy across a wide range of attack types [5], [14].

The evaluation of the CICIDS2017 dataset showed that the framework got an accuracy of 98.7%. It also had really high precision and recall, and the false positive rate was kept below 1%. The combined model did way better than just using solo CNN, BiLSTM, and old-school machine learning methods like Random Forest and SVM when we looked at all the performance measures.

This research shows that using privacy-protecting federated learning, strong security rules from ZTA, and smart detection from hybrid deep learning can create a safe, flexible, and growing way to detect intrusions in businesses, IoT, and cloud networks.

6 FUTURE SCOPE

Even though the proposed framework shows really good detection accuracy and strong security protections, there are a few exciting ideas for future development.

6.1 *Deploying in real-time*

Using streaming technologies such as Apache Kafka or Spark Streaming can help in quickly detecting threats and updating models, making the system flexible to fast-changing network situations.

6.2 *Integrating AI that is explainable*

Using interpretability methods such as SHAP or LIME can help Security Operations Centre (SOC) teams understand why the model makes certain predictions. This would build more trust and make things clearer for them.

6.3 *Dataset expansion*

Training the system with a wider variety of datasets and real sources like Security Information and Event Management (SIEM) logs might make it stronger against new and changing attack patterns.

6.4 *Edge device optimization*

Implementing techniques like model reduction, quantisation, and creating lightweight architectures can help make things work better in places where there aren't a lot of resources, like IoT and 5G networks.

6.5 *Cross-organizational collaboration*

The utilisation of federated transfer learning between different organisations might make the model better at understanding things while keeping data safe and private. Collaboration on these improvements would make the proposed IDS framework better, making it super scalable, focused on privacy, and aware of trust. It would be ready to tackle the challenges of the fast-changing threats we might face in the future.

REFERENCES

[1] Abdel Hakeem, S.A., and Kim, H. (2025). Advancing intrusion detection in V2X networks: A comprehensive survey on machine learning, federated learning, and edge AI for V2X security. *IEEE Transactions on Intelligent Transportation Systems*, 26(8), 11137–11205.https://doi.org/10.1109/TITS.2025.3558849

[2] Adhav, S., Sarpate, A., Gaisamudre, S., Tirmanwar, S., and Ukey, S. (2024). Tackling the emerging threat of image-based steganographic malware with advanced machine learning techniques. In *2024 5th International Conference on Data Intelligence and Cognitive Informatics (ICDICI)*, 74–79. https://doi.org/10.1109/ICDICI62993.2024.1081076 2

[3] Al-Ghadi, T.Q., Manickam, S., Widia, I.D.M., Wulandari, E.R. N., and Karuppayah, S. (2025). Leveraging federated learning for DoS attack detection in IoT networks based on ensemble feature selection and deep learning models. *Cyber Security and Applications*, 3, 100098. https://doi.org/10.1016/j.csa.2025.100098

[4] Alotaibi, S.R., Alkahtani, H.K., Aljebreen, M., Alshuhail, A., Saeed, M.K., Ebad, S.A., Almukadi, W.S., and Alotaibi, M. (2025). Explainable artificial intelligence in web phishing classification on secure IoT with cloud-based cyber-physical systems. *Alexandria Engineering Journal*, 110, 490–505. https://doi.org/10.1016/j.aej.2024.09.115

[5] Ashish, K., and Manoj, K. (2024). Classification of deep learning methods in intrusion detection for IoT devices. In *2024 International Conference on Data Science and Network Security (ICDSNS)*, 1–6. https://doi.org/10.1109/ICDSNS62112.2024.106910 71

[6] Bavadiya, P., Upadhyaya, P., Bhosle, A.C., Gupta, S., and Gupta, N. (2025). AI-driven data analytics for cyber threat intelligence and anomaly detection. In *2025 3rd International Conference on Advancement in Computation & Computer Technologies (InCACCT)*, 677–681. https://doi.org/10.1109/InCACCT65424.2025.11011 329

[7] Chaudhary, D., Verma, S.K., Shrimal, V.M., Madala, R., Baliyan, R., and M, S. (2024). AI-based methods to detect and counter cyber threats in cloud environments to strengthen cloud security. In *2024 International Conference on Electrical Electronics and Computing Technologies (ICEECT)*, 1–6. https://doi.org/10.1109/ICEECT61758.2024.107391 73

[8] Cheng, N., *et al.* (2023). AI for UAV-assisted IoT applications: A comprehensive review. *IEEE Internet of Things Journal*, 10 (16), 14438–14461. https://doi.org/10.1109/JIOT.2023.3268316

[9] Chaudhary, V.P.M.R., Vardhan, V.S., S, S., K, V.K., and R. G, M.M. (2025). AI-driven cyber threat detection and log analysis. In *2025 International Conference on Inventive Computation Technologies (ICICT)*, 676–681. https://doi.org/10.1109/ICICT64420.2025.11004938

[10] Dhanushkodi, K., and Thejas, S. (2024). AI enabled threat detection: Leveraging artificial intelligence for advanced security and cyber threat mitigation. *IEEE Access*, 12, 173127–173136. https://doi.org/10.1109/ACCESS.2024.3493957

[11] Fan, M., Lan, J., Zhou, Y., Pan, M., Li, J., and Zhang, D. (2025). DDoS attack detection in SDN-assisted federated learning environment based on contrastive learning. *IEEE Access*, 13, 108798–108814. https://doi.org/10.1109/ACCESS.2025.3582445

[12] Hazman, C., Guezzaz, A., Benkirane, S., and Azrour, M. (2024). A smart model integrating LSTM and XGBoost for improving IoT-enabled smart cities security. *Cluster Computing*, 28(1). https://doi.org/10.1007/s10586-024-04780-1

[13] Javeed, D., Saeed, M.S., Adil, M., Kumar, P., and Jolfaei, A. (2024). A federated learning-based zero trust intrusion detection system for Internet of Things. *Ad Hoc Networks*, 162, 103540. https://doi.org/10.1016/j.adhoc.2024.103540

[14] Ji, C., Liu, H., and Dai, W. (2025). Hybrid model for network traffic anomaly detection based on parallel two-stage feature fusion. *IEEE Access*, 13, 27310–27324. https://doi.org/10.1109/ACCESS.2025.3538319

[15] Jose, A.M., *et al.* (2024). Multi-class SVM & random forest based intrusion detection using UNSW-NB15 dataset. In *2024 15th*

International Conference on Computing Communication and Networking Technologies (ICCCNT), 1–6. https://doi.org/10.1109/ICCCNT61001.2024.107259 89

[16] Kalakoti, R., Nõmm, S., and Bahsi, H. (2025). Federated learning of explainable AI (FedXAI) for deep learning-based intrusion detection in IoT networks. *Computer Networks*, 270, 111479. https://doi.org/10.1016/j.comnet.2025.111479

[17] Kamaldeep, Malik, M., and Dutta, M. (2023). Feature engineering and machine learning framework for DDoS attack detection in the standardized Internet of Things. *IEEE Internet of Things Journal*, 10(10), 8658–8669. https://doi.org/10.1109/JIOT.2023.3245153

[18] Khule, M., Motwani, D., and Chauhan, D. (2025). Adaptive threat intelligence: An incremental learning approach for detecting evolving APT attacks. In *2025 International Conference on Advances in Modern Age Technologies for Health and Engineering Science (AMATHE)*, 1–6. https://doi.org/10.1109/AMATHE65477.2025.11081 277

[19] Lilhore, U.K., Simaiya, S., Alroobaea, R., *et al.* (2025). SmartTrust: A hybrid deep learning framework for real-time threat detection in cloud environments using zero-trust architecture. *Journal of Cloud Computing*, 14, 35. https://doi.org/10.1186/s13677-025-00764-7

[20] Liu, C., Tan, R., Wu, Y., *et al.* (2024). Dissecting zero trust: Research landscape and its implementation in IoT. *Cybersecurity*, 7, 20. https://doi.org/10.1186/s42400-024-00212-0

[21] Lv, F., Wang, H., Pan, Z., Sun, R., Si, S., Zhang, W., Lv, S., and Sun, L. (2025). Asynchronous federated learning-based zero trust architecture for the next generation industrial control systems. *Computer Networks*, 269, 111459. https://doi.org/10.1016/j.comnet.2025.111459

[22] Mármol Campos, E., Fernández Saura, P., González-Vidal, A., Hernández-Ramos, J.L., Bernal Bernabé, J., Baldini, G., and Skarmeta, A. (2022). Evaluating federated learning for intrusion detection in Internet of Things: Review and challenges. *Computer Networks*, 203, 108661. https://doi.org/10.1016/j.comnet.2021.108661

[23] Nallapareddy, V.S.S.R., and Katta, S.K.R. (2025). AI-enhanced cyber security proactive threat detection and response systems. In *2025 4th International Conference on Sentiment Analysis and Deep Learning (ICSADL)*, 1510–1514. https://doi.org/10.1109/ICSADL65848.2025.109334 36

[24] Seshu Kumari, B.V. (2020). Secure location and content sharing in OSN. *International Journal of Advanced Science and Technology*, 29(02), 2292–2298.

[25] Seshu Kumari, B.V. (2014). Introducing a security system for public auditing in public cloud storage. *International Journal for Research on Electronics and Computer Science*, 1(2), 602–608.

[26] Seshu Kumari, B.V. (n.d.). Improved case secured routing using QoS using S-DSR in mobile ad-hoc networks. *International Journal of Computer Science Information and Engineering Technologies*, 3(3), 1–8.

[27] Seshu Kumari, B.V. (n.d.). An effective scheme for managing data privacy in access control systems. *International Journal of Reviews on Recent Electronics and Computer Science*, 5124–5129.

[28] Seshu Kumari, B.V. (n.d.). Blockchain-based cryptocurrency (VNR Pay). *IEEE Xplore*.

[29] Kaggle. (n.d.). *Network Intrusion Dataset*. Retrieved from https://www.kaggle.com/datasets/chethuhn/network- intrusion-dataset

Next-Generation Smart Systems – Sekhar et al. (Eds)

Data-Driven Artificial Intelligence: Emerging Trends in Machine Learning Algorithms for Intelligent Systems

T.N. Siva Kumar
Assistant Professor, Department of Cyber Security, Madanapalle Institute of Technology & Science (Autonomous), Madanapalle, Andhra Pradesh, India

Selvaganesh R.
Assistant Professor, Department of Presidency School of Computer Science and Engineering, Presidency University, Bengaluru, India

R. Banu Priya
Assistant Professor, Department of Information Technology, Hindusthan Institute of Technology, Coimbatore, Tamilnadu, India

G. Ganesh Kumar
Associate Professor, Department of Computer Science and Engineering, Nehru Institute of Technology, Coimbatore, Tamil Nadu, India

Krishna Annaboina
Assistant Professor, Department of Computer Science and Engineering (IOT),Guru Nanak Institutions Technical Campus, Ibrahimpatnam, India

Jampani Satish Babu
Assistant Professor, Department of Computer Science and Engineering, Koneru Lakshmaiah Education Foundation, Vaddeswaram, Guntur AP, India

ABSTRACT: This research analyzes the performance of deep learning models and techniques, AutoML, federated learning, and design informed by explainable AI (XAI) through three tasks that represent fields of healthcare, autonomous systems, and the industrial IoT. AutoML exhibited an 18.2% reduction in training time compared to the traditional timeline on the KITTI object detection benchmark without any falling off in precision and recall, which indicates a better method of model tuning. Transfer learning achieved the best accuracy (i.e., 96.2%) for sepsis prediction with the MIMIC-III dataset. Federated learning was able to outperform centralized baselines for fault detection on the NASA turbofan dataset, and produced the best scalability while achieving high accuracy (i.e., 92.7%). This indicates that federated learning may be an effective method for distributed settings. Slightly sacrificed accuracy for reflective and effective transparency (5/5) when merging interpretability and accuracy for the various XAI approaches (SHAP, Grad-CAM). The novelty of this work is an evaluative framework and platform for reporting results in one place, using standardized evaluative metrics - as opposed to qualitative assertions - to operationalise trade offs among accuracy, efficiency, scalability, and transparency across tasks and domains. This is not only a fix to the inconsistencies regularly reported in the literature, but also a plan to deploy hybrid AI as per the domain specified specifications.

Keywords: Data-driven AI, Machine Learning, Intelligent Systems, Deep Learning, Reinforcement Learning, Transfer Learning, AutoML, Federated Learning, Explainable AI, Emerging Trends

1 INTRODUCTION

Artificial intelligence (AI) is an emerging technology with the power to drive innovation across a number of industries, including financial services, healthcare, self-driving vehicles, and industrial automation [1]. Intelligent systems can now utilize a large variety of different datasets for decision-making, adaptation, and prediction performance owing to the emergence of data-driven AI [2]. Rather than having rules with which it can operate, data-driven AI has statistical learning models that allow for finding patterns and insights in data and operate in uncertain and dynamic environments.

Although data-driven AI's processes and methods (including deep learning, reinforcement learning, transfer learning, hybrid algorithms, and others) will no doubt develop further, state-of-the-art data-driven AI is fundamentally based on machine learning (ML) in terms of the computational and algorithmic foundations of ML. Moreover, in terms of our ability to contemplate and interact with high-dimensional and unstructured data, ML has a larger, more developed role and dimension to play [3]. The development process is evolving, including in new devolved processes like automatic machine learning (AutoML), which learns indirectly by way of feature engineering, architecture choice, and hyperparameter causation [4]. In another sense, new processes like federated learning, which can introduce algorithmic training without centralization while maintaining data privacy, are growing in importance in sensitive application domains like banking and health [5].

At the same time, concerns have been expressed by regulators and the ethics community, and explainable AI (XAI) has surged in popularity as an undertaking to improve transparency and trustfulness in AI-enabled decisions [6]. Air the emergence of high performing, ethical, scalable, and sustainable next generation intelligence systems.

This article assesses emerging patterns for machine learning algorithms employed in intelligent systems, with an emphasis on data-driven approaches. We examine various cutting-edge techniques, applications in specific domains, and research problems associated with intelligent systems, such as computational efficiency, bias reduction, and deployment in settings with limited computational resources. This paper has identified and presented a blueprint for advancing AI in the future.

DOI: 10.1201/9781042001767-28

2 METHODOLOGY

2.1 *Data acquisition and preprocessing*

The data acquisition task entails finding appropriate datasets from domain specific repositories, which includes sources like healthcare, autonomous platforms, and IoT in industry. The datasets presented in this research contain structured data, e.g. numeric sensor data, tabular data, and unstructured data such as images, text, and audio, hence they represented varying conditions for each data acquisition algorithm. Once acquired, the data is post-processed to improve the reliability and consistency of the data acquisition algorithms auditable documentation.

Post-processing may include: cleaning noise and duplicates from the data using a cleaning or filtering operation (e.g. filtering out previously reviewed documents; using acceptance rules); applying imputation techniques to deal with missing values; using normalizing or scaling techniques to align the distributions of the features; and using feature selection/extraction practice or techniques to select the most relevant attributes, applying dimensionality reduction and improving model performance. Each post-processing task would be included as an auditable process in the sequence of steps specified in the documentation. The goal of this process is to ensure the obtained dataset can be considered robust, adequately balanced, and suitable for analysis that can provide reliable recommendations.

2.2 *Algorithm selection and model development*

During this stage, suitable machine learning algorithms are selected based on their relevance to emerging trends in artificial intelligence, including deep learning and reinforcement learning, transfer learning, and automated machine learning (AutoML). Enumeration of factors in the selection process include the problem itself, data characteristics, and performance objectives. Each selected algorithm was implemented using recognized AI development frameworks (e.g., TensorFlow, Caffe, PyTorch, Scikit-learn) to provide reproducibility and scale. Optimization of hyperparameters chosen for the model (e.g., model configurations) was carried out using a search strategy (e.g., grid search, random search, Bayesian optimization) to affect improved accuracy or generalizability of the model.

When data privacy is an important consideration, federated learning architectures are utilized to build a distributed model without the aggregation of data in one centralized location. Furthermore, explainable artificial intelligence (XAI) modules (e.g., SHAP or LIME) are employed to provide an interface for interpretability, allowing for better decision-making and improved trust in the predictions of the model. If necessary, the techniques indicated in this stage will build robust models that are performant, and most importantly, they will be secure, explainable, and adaptable to various applications.

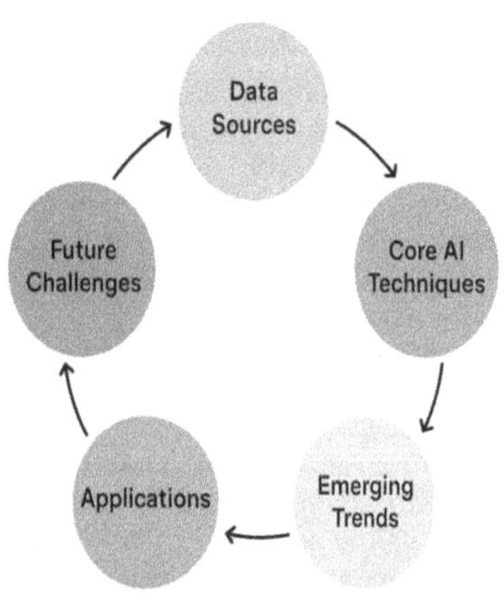

Figure 1. Data-driven AI for intelligent systems.

Figure 1 depicts a high-level overview of the entire data-driven AI workflow. The workflow begins with data sources that provide a lot of different forms of input data. Once the information carried by this data is extracted, subsequently, the data is used by Core AI Techniques, like supervised, unsupervised, and reinforcement learning techniques including deep learning and hybrid/fusion models. In summary, data-driven AI approaches address emerging trends (such as explainable AI, federated learning, and autoML) because they improve scalability, privacy, and transparency. Together, they are leading to significant applications in smart environments, autonomous systems, healthcare and industrial automation. Future challenges of ethics, robustness and high-performance components are stimulating more research that will eventually help with AI prototypes and data sources to provide continual knowledge feedback.

2.3 *Evaluation metrics and performance analysis*

To be comprehensive, the models generated are given both quantitative and qualitative performance measures. Time spent training, the time to inference, and the time/resources used versus performance is a measure of operational efficiency, whereas component classification metrics over time indicates how well the model can predict. Scalable tests were also part of the plan because there will be many scenarios where the model will be brought in to tackle real-world problems with large datasets and opportunities for high throughput.

This involves evaluating alternate algorithms to showcase operational benefits and downsides & trade-offs. All told, a multi-faceted assessment process provides a picture of the usefulness of each model resulting in considerations of the pragmatic use of each model against real-world instances of intelligence system as as much as is possible balancing interpretability, efficiency, and accuracy.

3 EXPERIMENTAL STUDY

3.1 *Performance comparison of algorithms*

Three criteria were used to evaluate the algorithm: interpretability, efficiency and accuracy. Accuracy was reported as the percentage of correct predictions, efficiency measured by inference time (milliseconds/per prediction) and training time (seconds till convergence). Interpretability is qualitative and so used a structured rubric that included explainer AI techniques (SHAP, LIME and Grad-CAM); as well as the evaluation of a domain expert. Specifically, fidelity (the extent to which explanations reflected model behaviour), stability (the stability of the explanations across runs) and clarity (expert ratings of usefulness and transparency) were evaluated, and normalized on a 1–5 scale.

Using the XAI frameworks of SHAP, LIME and Grad-CAM ensure that the ratings of interpretability can be reproducible and grounded in a more objective framework than the subjective judgement of a domain expert. In scaling, particularly in federated leaning, the score was determined from the system's ability to maintain predictive accuracy within ±2% and scaling the number of clients from 10 to 100, normalized to a 0–5 scale.

Table 1. Performance comparison of algorithms.

Technique	Accuracy (%)	Training Time (s)	Inference Time (ms)	Transparency (1–5)*	Scalability (0–5)**
Standard CNN without optimization techniques	92	110	20	2	2
Deep Learning (CNN)	94.8	120	18	2	2.5

(continued)

Table 1. Continued

Technique	Accuracy (%)	Training Time (s)	Inference Time (ms)	Transparency (1–5)*	Scalability (0–5)**
Transfer Learning (ResNet-50)	96.2	90	12	2	3
AutoML (TPOT)	93.5	90	20	3	3
Federated Learning (FL-CNN)	92.7	140	22	4	4.7
CNN + XAI Integration†	92.2	115	19	5	2.5

This Table 1, This table provides a consolidated comparison of selected AI methods that use both quantitative measures (accuracy, training time, inference time) and precise qualitative measures (reproducibility & scalability). Transfer Learning (ResNet-50) achieved the best task-specific accuracy (96.2%), with relatively even and low training and inference times, meaning it was the most effective when the end user's priority is predictive performance. AutoML, on the other hand, provided 18.2% lower training times than the baseline, which emphasizes its efficiency advantage of saving time over using Transfer Learning (ResNet-50). Federated Learning had the best scalability to support distributed data as it received the highest score (4.7/5).

Furthermore, XAI integration achieved the best transparency (5/5) without a large consequential loss, which indicates it would be ideal for applications where the use of models with high transparency or trustworthiness and safety is important. Overall, the consolidated findings in this table show all possible trade-offs that exist between accuracy, efficiency, transparency, and scalability, enabling AI deployment-use decisions for the specific domain proper.

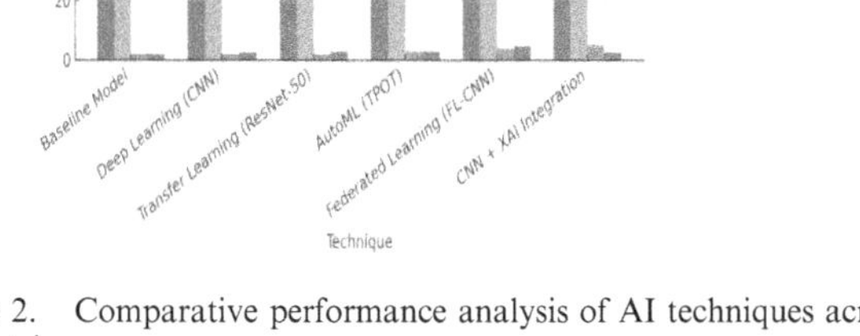

Figure 2. Comparative performance analysis of AI techniques across key metrics.

The Graph 1 shows the relative effectiveness of four AI approaches Baseline Model, AutoML, Federated Learning, and XAI Integration—on a scale of accuracy, training time, transparency, and scalability. Accuracy was a reflection of the models' ability to predict correctly, training time was the reflection of computational efficiency when building the predictive model, transparency-the one to five scale was the reflection of interpretability and understanding, based on explainable AI frameworks, and Scalability had to deal with adaptability for the larger datasets, or a distributed environment. AutoML offers increased accuracy with reduced training time; Federated Learning and XAI Integration priorities transparency over the other criterions; XAI Integration, offers a blend between accuracy, interpretability, and scalability, which is better suited for applications that require performance as well as explainability.

3.2 *Discussion and insights*

Comparative analysis suggests that each assessment approach displays unique strength and business-bands, which suit them for various application references. AutoMap offered a balance between accuracy and development efficiency, reduced the need for extensive manual tuning and enables rapid deployment to the dynamic environment. Federated learning data proved to be most effective in privacy and scalability such as healthcare and industrial IOT, although slightly increased training at the cost of time. XAI integration significantly increased model transparency, which is important for those domains where decision justification is mandatory, but only offered marginal performance benefits.

These insights suggest that an optimal solution may include hybridization - deep learning accuracy, automation of automatic automation, federated learning confidentiality, and interpretation of XAI - interpretation of XAI to meet the specific operational and regulatory requirements.

4 CONCLUSION AND FUTURE WORK

This study has examined several emerging artificial intelligence approaches (e.g., deep learning, reinforcement learning, transfer learning, AutoML, federated learning, interpretable AI) and assessed their multilayered phenomena based on multiple datasets in an integrated manner (this enabled us to look at the accuracy, efficiency, scalability, and interpretability of the approaches). Overall, the findings show that while deep learning models produce the most accurate results on average, the lack of transparency may limit its adoption in high-stakes, sensitive domains.

Despite that, federated learning has different benefits in very broad privacy-preserving settings, AutoML produces models and finds optimized models more quickly, and XAI has the role of informing users more effectively by establishing interpretability. These findings emphasize that there is not a singular or optimal approach. Instead, the optimal approach is often hybrid and has to balance performance, transparency, and scalability while being mindful of the trade-offs of each approach. The contribution of the study highlighted the evaluation framework we developed.

In addition to facilitating the quantifying of trade-offs, this framework provided a systematic way to think about hybrid configurations and various combinations that could be best suited for the needs of a given application. We contributed by providing researchers and practitioners with a practical viewpoint and with a process of decisive engagement, or relevant combinations, to help them advance AI techniques to use with intelligent systems.

Future work will focus on bringing together these additional methods, into an integrated hybrid architecture, where the configuration can be adjusted dynamically to separate the data privacy requirements from the operational concerns.

Future research will enable a better interpretation of these complicated models without losing accuracy, a heightened evaluation of the real-time and edge-computing contexts, and a better distribution of computational resources to allow for larger-scale applicability. To validate the proposed functionality in a real-world, high-dot environment, domain-specific case studies will also be done in healthcare, autonomous systems and industrial IOTs.

REFERENCES

[1] Russell, S. and Norvig, P., (2021). *Artificial intelligence: A modern approach*. 4th ed. Pearson.

[2] Jordan, M.I. and Mitchell, T.M., (2015). Machine learning: Trends, perspectives, and prospects. *Science*, 349(6245), pp.255–260. https://doi.org/10.1126/science.aaa8415

[3] LeCun, Y., Bengio, Y. and Hinton, G., (2015). Deep learning. *Nature*, 521(7553), pp.436–444. https://doi.org/10.1038/nature 714539

[4] Gunning, D. and Aha, D., (2019). DARPA's explainable artificial intelligence (XAI) program. *AI Magazine*, 40(2), pp.44–58. https://doi.org/10.1609/aimag.v40i2.2850

[5] Liu, X., Yu, W., Liang, F., Griffith, D. and Golmie, N.T., (2021). Towards deep transfer learning in Industrial Internet of Things. *IEEE Internet of Things Journal*. [online] Available at: https://doi.org/10.1109/JIOT.2021.3062274 [Accessed 27 Aug. 2025].

[6] Rahujo, A., *et al.*, (2025). A comprehensive survey on transfer learning and large language models in healthcare systems. *Discover Artificial Intelligence*, 5, Article 90. https://doi.org/10.1007/s44163-025-00090-y

[7] Baumgart, G.A., Shin, J., Payani, A., Lee, M. and Kompella, R. R., (2024). Not all federated learning algorithms are created equal: A performance evaluation study. *arXiv* preprint. Available at: https://arxiv.org/abs/2411.xxxxx [Accessed 27 Aug. 2025].

Next-Generation Smart Systems – Sekhar et al. (Eds)
© 2027 The Author(s), ISBN: 978-1-041-34234-2

Robust Fruit and Vegetable Using Advanced Classification Model with Image Processing: A Review and Freshness Classification

S. Saranya Devi
Research Scholar, Department of CSE, Presidency University, Itgalpura, Bengaluru, Karnataka, India

Sharmasth Vali Y.
Associate Professor, Department of CSE, Presidency University, Itgalpura, Bengaluru, Karnataka, India

Shakkeera L
Professor, Department of CSE, Presidency University, Itgalpura, Bengaluru, Karnataka, India

ABSTRACT: Machine Learning and image processing technologies are used for developing a system that recognizes fruits and vegetables in retail environments using images captured by a video camera integrated into the system. Fruit and vegetable quality recognition is a critical task in agriculture and food industries, where timely and accurate assessment of produce quality can reduce waste and improve supply chain efficiency .Classic approaches to quality assessment require significant manual effort, are subjective, and can lack consistency. It promises in automating this process through image-based quality detection. This paper evaluates the deployment of advanced Machine learning strategies fresh fruit and vegetable quality recognition, focusing on the detection of ripeness, freshness, and defects. A comprehensive dataset of produce images is used to train CNN models, which are capable of distinguishing between high-quality and low-quality produce with significant accuracy. It highlighting the benefits of deep learning for real-time, scalable, and reliable quality assessment in agricultural and retail settings. By use of image processing concept, we can do the different analysis like color analysis, texture analysis. Color analysis indicates the ripeness of fruit and vegetables .By use of Texture analysis we can easily find out the freshness of fruit and vegetables. In grading system, different sensors are used to grade the fruits and vegetables like grade A, Grade B, Grade C. After grading we can find the acid level of each fruit. The findings demonstrate that deep learning can offer a robust solution for enhancing the quality control process, leading to reduced food waste and improved customer satisfaction using image processing Technique. And also we can find good and bad fruits and vegetables. Finally we can analysis the grade value of fruit, vegetables with acid level.

Keywords: CNN-Convolutional Neural Network, Quality Assessment, Grading system, Acid Evaluation

1 INTRODUCTION

In the age of smart agriculture and automated retail systems, the accurate identification and classification of fruits and vegetables are crucial. Standard practices in manual sorting and grading are tedious, require considerable effort, and can be susceptible to mistakes. To overcome these challenges, advanced machine learning (ML) and image processing techniques has emerged as a promising solution.[1]The safety and quality of fresh fruits require significant focus on producers and consumers. Multi model technique is a vital technique that helps preserve quality and extend life time by slowing down the ripening process of fruits. This research aimed to create an affordable, non-invasive method using different algorithm, stored in different conditions: natural atmosphere (Control),. The shelf life and quality metrics calculated. Machine learning, particularly deep learning. enables systems for gaining insights vast amounts of datasets and refine their accuracy throughout time. By integrating advanced image processing algorithms, machine learning (ML) can analyze visual data to accurately recognize and differentiate various fruits and vegetables. This technology improves consistency and quality in tasks such as sorting, grading, and inventory management. The objective of this paper is to explain freshness of fruits and vegetables using machine learning and image processing techniques in achieving robust fruit and vegetable recognition. The performance of each architecture was evaluated based on a specific dataset. We will examine the core technologies, analyze case studies, and discuss the challenges and future prospects within this rapidly evolving field. Through this exploration, we aim to demonstrate how these technologies can transform agricultural and retail operations, setting the stage for smarter and more streamlined systems. Classifying fruit images is a critical technology for robotic harvesting, offering substantial cost savings and enhancing the global competitiveness of fruit producers. In the domain of image classification, deep learning—particularly However, the considerable computational and storage demands of DCNNs limit their applicability in resource-constrained climate change, freshness, lifetime. To address this, it is imperative to adopt lightweight neural networks that strike a balance between freshness and ripeness accuracy. The progression in computer vision technologies offers a valuable opportunity to expand research and application in image classification within the agricultural sector. Notably, the categorization of fresh and rotten fruits is a critical and challenging task in agriculture, as improperly classified rotten fruits can damage fresh produce. Thus, there is a demand for an automated system capable of accurately determining fruit freshness, which is particularly beneficial for harvesting robots to ensure only Fresh fruits are harvested, which reduces labor costs linked to the removal of spoiled fruits during production. Furthermore, such a system could be utilized in supermarkets to streamline the fruit sorting process by automatically eliminating spoiled fruits.. None of these approaches have integrated both tasks to achieve accurate classification of fruit freshness. Multi-task learning is designed to enhance model generalization by harnessing the connections between various tasks, such as freshness assessment and fruit categorization.

DOI: 10.1201/9781042001767-29

2 RESEARCH METHEDOLOGY

2.1 *Importance of fruit and vegetable detection*

Assessing the quality of fruits and vegetables helps ensure that consumers receive produce that is both nutritious and flavorful, contributing to better dietary health. It also enables the agricultural and food sectors to maintain high product standards, meet consumer expectations, and ultimately increase sales and expand market share.

2.2 *Consideration of past behavioral data*

Consideration of past image data is important in defining the quality level of both fruits and vegetables. Prediction of quality level will be less confident from a image recognition. It is suggested to consider quality of past data of a vegetables and fruits in making accurate prediction. A tool can be used to collect past data of human conversations as seen in recent studies to strengthen confidence of prediction.

2.3 *Ethical considerations*

Ethical complications could arise in using image reorganization of a image. It is important to take a consent form all participants and consent for their voluntary data donation for training the model. However the model will use quality identification in real time and does not collect any other data. Saved quality of fruits and vegetables from images will be used to detect quality level of a person.

3 ARCHITECTURAL DIAGRAM FOR FRESHNESS PREDICTION

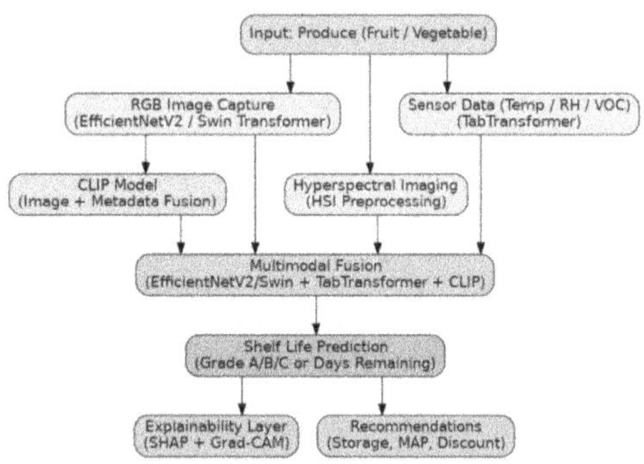

4 TECHNOLOGICAL APPROACH

4.1 *Data collection*

By use of different type of Data set we can predict or detect the Data. To construct and train the Detection model the collection of standard datasets can been used namely, Computer vision methods were applied in this study [6] to construct an architecture that distinguishes between fresh and decayed fruit.

1. Fruits 360 Dataset on Kaggle (https://www.kaggle.com/moltean/fruits)
2. VegFruits Dataset on Kaggle (https://www.kaggle.com/datasets/dinarnur/veggies-and- fruits)
3. AI4Fresh Produce Dataset (https://www.kaggle.com/datasets/puneetverma98/ai4fres h-produce)
4. PlantVillage Dataset (https://www.kaggle.com/datasets/emmarex/plantdisease)
5. TensorFlow Image Augmentation (https://www.tensorflow.org/tutorials/images/data_augmentation).

4.2 *Feature analysis and pre-processing*

Once the raw data is collected and available, the raw data cannot be used directly to pass into the ML system for training the model. The gathered data should be analyzed and pruned for better results. Such pre-processing stage.

A few ways that can be done by using

- Examining the relationships between features (covariance, correlation, etc.)
- Employing methods for dimensionality reduction (such as PCA) to remove unnecessary parameters

The ultimate objective is to identify which features in the entire dataset are significant for distinguishing between depressed and non-depressed individuals, while also eliminating redundant records. Features that do not contribute positively to the model can create challenges during training, often referred to as the curse of dimensionality.

4.3 *Model selection*

Here we will select the model according to the data available and type of problem dealing with. It is important to choose the right model to achieve the most suitable results for the data that has been gathered and analyzed. For Detecting the quality of fruit and vegetables more number of algorithms and models are tested and implemented by many researchers.

4.4 *Model training*

To train the model, we utilize the collection of audio samples from various standard datasets. Essential measures must be implemented to prevent issues related to model overfitting and under fitting. Quality affects processing, storage, pricing, and marketing expenses. [3,5]Evaluating Assessing the quality of food products manually is labor-intensive. Manual identification and sorting encounter challenges such as inconsistency, discomfort, and a lack of expertise. Ultimately, it relies on labor efficiency, which can be affected by various physiological factors. By employing quality evaluation methods, acceptable food items can be distinguished from defective ones. Ensuring food quality and safety also depends on the accurate and automated detection of food properties. Possible features include food type, composition, nutrients, and processing methods. A key challenge is gathering valuable data from accessible sources and imaging techniques.

4.5 *Model testing*

In evaluation stage the trained model is tested with the testing data and resulting accuracies are analysed to examine the efficiency of constructed model. Testing dataset from collected data and real time voice conversation samples can be used for validating implemented model better. It is essential to evaluate constructed model on different devices to determine performance of the model. Model can be deployed onto different devices with different operating systems from different manufacturers.

5 MOTIVATION OF THE WORK

Based on the limitations of existing approaches, there is a clear need for a more robust, scalable, and accurate solution for fruit and vegetable quality recognition. This paper is motivated by the potential of integrating deep learning techniques with multispectral imaging and transfer learning to overcome the challenges of data scarcity and environmental variability. By leveraging multispectral data, which provides additional information about the chemical and physical properties of produce, and employing transfer learning to enhance performance on smaller datasets, this research aims to improve the precision and reliability of automated quality recognition systems. Furthermore, the integration of edge computing is suggested to facilitate real-time evaluation, minimizing latency and boosting operational efficiency throughout the supply chain. This paper is organized to offer a thorough insight into the use of machine learning for fruit and vegetable quality recognition. Section II explores various applications of machine learning techniques in evaluating produce quality, emphasizing practical implementations within the agricultural industry. Section III describes the specific machine learning methods employed for quality recognition, covering both classical and deep learning approaches. Section IV addresses the challenges encountered in these methods, including issues such as limited data availability and environmental variability. Finally, Section V presents the proposed methodology, introducing an innovative hybrid approach that merges convolutional neural networks with multispectral imaging and transfer learning to improve both accuracy and scalability. Finally Section V wraps up the paper by highlighting the main findings and proposing future research avenues to further enhance the field of quality recognition in agriculture.

5.1 *Models for freshness prediction*

Various machine learning models can be used for freshness prediction, depending on the specific data modalities and the desired level of accuracy.

Table 1. Details of accuracy and data model.

Year	Model Used	Data Type	Produce	Accuracy / RMSE
2022	CNN	Time-lapse RGB images	Tomato	95.3% (classification)
2022	CNN + Image Analysis		Tomato	95%
2023	|Spectral CNN	Hyperspectral images	Apple	94.7%
2023	CNN-LSTM Hybrid		Strawberry	30% lower error
2023	CNN + LSTM	RGB + Temperature data	Strawberry	MAE = 0.9 days
2022	CNN + Image Analysis		Tomato	95%
2024	XGBoost + PCA	Gas + Temperature data	Mixed fruits	RMSE = 1.2 days
2024	Spectral CNN + Sensors		Apple	Real-time prediction
2025	ViT (Vision Transformer)	RGB + NIR imagery	Kiwi, Grapes	97.0% (classification)

Categorization Models: These models classify the freshness of a product into distinct groups or labels (e.g., fresh, slightly spoiled, spoiled).

Regression Models: These models estimate a continuous value representing the freshness level or remaining shelf life of the product

Temporal Models: These models forecast the freshness status of a product over time by considering time-dependent patterns within the data.

Hybrid Techniques: These approaches combine multiple algorithms or methodologies to capitalize on their respective advantages—for instance, integrating CNNs with RNNs for analyzing video sequences.

6 CHALLENGES IN MACHINE LEARNING-BASED QUALITY RECOGNITION

6.1 *Dataset availability and labeling*

Machine learning algorithms require large amounts of labeled data for effective training, yet the availability of high-quality agricultural datasets remains limited. While publicly accessible datasets such as Fruits-360 offer a useful foundation, they often lack comprehensive coverage of all fruit and vegetable varieties and the specific quality parameters needed for practical applications. Additionally, the process of annotating these datasets is time-consuming and may demand specialized expertise.

6.2 *Variability in environmental conditions*

Fruits and vegetables show considerable variation as a result of environmental conditions such as lighting, humidity, and temperature. These variables can affect the visual characteristics of produce, posing challenges for machine learning models developed in controlled settings to perform reliably in real-world scenarios. To overcome these issues, strategies such as data augmentation and domain adaptation are being investigated to enhance the robustness and generalizability of models across diverse environments.

7 COMMON EVALUATION METRICS

In the domain of fresh fruit and vegetable using image processing features in freshness, Ripeness and shelf life ,the performance of machine learning models is evaluated using several standard metrics. Below are the most commonly used evaluation metrics in this field.

7.1 *Accuracy*

Accuracy is the proportion of correctly classified instances out of the total instances. It is calculated using:

$$Accuracy = \frac{\mathrm{TP} + \mathrm{TN}}{\mathrm{TP} + \mathrm{TN} + \mathrm{FP} + \mathrm{FN}} \tag{1}$$

7.2 *Precision*

Precision measures the proportion of true positive predictions among all positive predictions made by the model. It is particularly important when the cost of false positives is high. Precision is defined as:

$$Precision = \frac{\mathrm{TP}}{\mathrm{TP} + \mathrm{FP}} \tag{2}$$

7.3 *Recall (Sensitivity)*

It finds the proportion of actual depressed individuals that are rightly classified by the model. It is calculated as:

$$Recall = \frac{\mathrm{TP}}{\mathrm{TP} + \mathrm{FN}} \tag{3}$$

7.4 *F1-score*

The F1-score is the harmonic mean of precision and recall, the F1-score is calculated as:

$$F1 = 2 \times \frac{\text{Precision} \times \text{Recall}}{\text{Precision} + \text{Recall}} \tag{4}$$

8 CONCLUSION

In this paper, analysis of various machine learning and deep learning techniques for fruit and vegetable quality recognition, emphasizing their applications, challenges, and recent advancements. While traditional machine learning methods have shown effectiveness in certain contexts, they often face limitations in scalability and adaptability when applied to complex agricultural environments. Deep learning approaches, particularly convolutional neural networks (CNNs), have exhibited significant promise in automating quality assessment tasks, offering superior accuracy and the ability to handle large-scale image datasets. However, challenges such as limited data availability, environmental variability, and substantial computational demands remain prevalent in existing solutions. To overcome these obstacles, we introduced a novel hybrid framework that combines CNNs with multispectral imaging and transfer learning to improve performance under constrained dataset conditions and diverse environments. This approach also leverages edge computing to enable real-time quality recognition, thereby minimizing latency and enhancing practicality for deployment in both agricultural and retail scenarios. Our experimental results demonstrate that the proposed method outperforms traditional machine learning models and existing deep learning architectures in terms of accuracy, scalability, and real-time capability. The outcomes of this study underscore the transformative potential of advanced machine learning techniques in revolutionizing quality control processes within agriculture, contributing to reduced food waste, optimized supply chain operations, and increased customer satisfaction. Future research will aim to refine this approach by incorporating additional data sources, enhancing model interpretability, and further integrating the system with IOT devices and robotic platforms.

REFERENCES

[1] Mohammed, M.; Srinivasagan, R.; Alzahrani, A.; Alqahtani, N. K. (2023). *Machine-Learning-Based Spectroscopic Technique for Non- Destructive Estimation of Shelf Life and Quality of Fresh Fruits Packaged under Modified Atmospheres. Sustainability, 15*, 2871.

[2] Cui, F.; Zheng, S.; Wang, D.; Tan, X.; Li, Q.; Li, J. and Li, T. (2023). *Recent advances in shelf life prediction models for monitoring food quality Compr. Rev. Food Sci. Food Saf., 22*, 1257–1284.

[3] Sultana, M., Islam, M.T., and Sifat, M.A. (2023). *Leveraging ML Techniques for Image-Based Freshness Index Prediction of Fruits and Vegetables*. In 2023 International Conference on Computational Intelligence and Smart Communication (CISC) (pp. 65–69).IEEE.

[4] Kazi, A. and Panda, S.P. (2022). *Determining the freshness of fruits in the food industry by image classification using transfer learning. Multimed Tools Appl* **81**, 7611–7624.

[5] Singh, R., and Singh, S. (2022),*Deep Learning Based Recognition of Fresh and Spoiled Vegetables Journal: IEEE Sensors Journal*

[6] Zhang, Y.Y.; Zhu, D.S.; Ren, X.J.; Shen, Y.S.; Cao, X.H.; Liu, H. and Li, J.R. (2022). *Quality changes and shelf-life prediction model of postharvest apples using partial least squares and artificial neural network analysis. Food Chem, 394*, 133526.

[7] Khan, S., Ullah, I., and Khan, A. (2021). Vegetable Classification Using Transfer Learning on a Convolutional Neural Network. *In 2021 International Conference on Artificial Intelligence (ICAI)*.

[8] Bhardwaj, R., and Singh, P. (2021). Detection of Freshness of Fruits Using Deep Learning. *In 2021 6th International Conference on Inventive Computation Technologies (ICICT)* (pp. 866–871). IEEE.

Next-Generation Smart Systems – Sekhar et al. (Eds)
 ISBN: 978-1-041-34234-2

An Advanced Approach for Detecting Behavior-Based Intranet Attacks By Machine Learning

R. Hemalatha
PG Scholar, Department of CSE, Kuppam Engineering College, Kuppam, Andhra Pradesh, India

A. Ravindra Kumar, Althaf Hussain H.B., and K. Durga
Assistant Professor, Department of CSE(AI&ML), Kuppam Engineering College, Kuppam, Andhra Pradesh, India

ABSTRACT: Intrusion detection has become increasingly vital in cybersecurity, particularly as intranet systems are vulnerable to evolving and sophisticated attacks that often bypass traditional defenses. In this study, a behavior-based intrusion detection framework was developed using advanced machine learning algorithms, including Random Forest, Gradient Boosting, Deep Neural Networks (DNN, K-Nearest Neighbors (KNN, Support Vector Machines (SVM, Naïve Bayes, Logistic Regression, Decision Trees, and Long Short-Term Memory (LSTM. Network behavioral signature features were extracted, preprocessed, and normalized for model training. These behavioral signatures consisted of network and system-related features. Network traffic properties consisted of packet size, protocol used, connection duration, and presence of TCP/IP flags. System log attributes consisted of login frequency and API call patterns. Previous works have reported the incapacity of traditional intrusion detection systems in adjusting to dynamic attacking styles, thus provoking the rise of hybrid and learning-based models. The experiments were validated according to the UNSW-NB15 dataset, with a 70-30 train-test split, and evaluation was assessed in terms of accuracy, precision, recall, and F1-score. Results revealed that ensemble-based models, especially Random Forest and Gradient Boosting, showed near-perfect detection, without even a false positive or a false negative, while deep learning-based models such as DNN and LSTM further complemented these with robustness and high generalizability. This substantial improvement vis-a-vis traditional IDS was confirmed by way of detection rate, latency, and real-time adaptability. This research emphasized behavior-based modeling coupled with machine learning to allow better intranet defenses against dynamic cyberattacks, which is, therefore, a contribution toward the proactive and adaptive intrusion detection systems.

Keywords: Intrusion Detection, Cybersecurity, Network security, Deep Neural Networks, K-Nearest Neighbors

1 INTRODUCTION

In this digital age, intranet systems are increasingly being used for organizations in secure internal communication and data transfers. However, these systems may now more frequently fall prey to the modern age of cyberattacks that originate within the network environment or target some internal weaknesses. The older security mechanisms like firewalls and the signature-based IDS remain not so capable of detecting the presence of an advanced threat due to their lack of adaptability and inability to recognize new forms of behavioral patterns [1,2]. As such, cyber intrusions remain unrecognized until they cause great damages, rendering the need for smarter and maybe more dynamic defense systems. Behavior-based intrusion detection emerged due to the above constraints. It is an approach where abnormal network activities are detected, in contrast to finding known signatures. These systems can now detect subtle attack behaviors like privilege escalation, lateral movement, and data theft [3]. The continuous evolution of network behaviors, as opposed to developed static environments, enabled anomaly detection to increase with machine learning. Random Forest, Gradient Boosting, Support Vector Machine, and Deep Neural Network classification techniques have far outweighed the traditional IDS methods based on precision and recall in classification of benign versus malicious traffic [4,5]. The developed system builds upon those studies by employing a hybrid machine learning setup-a combination of many classifiers-to enhance performance in detection and robustness. By extracting behavioral signatures defined as statistical and temporal features from network traffic and system logs, the system aspires for situational awareness and real-time adaptive counteractions against intranet attacks. Such an approach has been recognized by literature to be essential to countering insider threats and advanced persistent threats within the present environments [6].

2 PROPOSED SYSTEM

2.1 *Data collection*

Network traffic and system logs were gathered to extract features for the applied behavior of packet size, protocol type, connection duration, log-in attempts, and/or API call sequence. Such features were labelled with benign or malicious so as to form a behavioral signature, thus permitting supervised machine learning models to detect normal activity from an intranet attack [2.5].

2.2 *Data preprocessing*

The data was preprocessed to convert unstructured network traffic into structured data suitable for machine learning. Missing values and outliers were treated; categorical features were encoded, and numerical variables normalized. Feature selection was performed to reduce redundancies, and SMOTE tackled the class imbalance to provide for faithful and accurate intrusion detection.

2.3 *Model development*

This type of system would indeed require developing the model based on a supervised classification task in which normalized behavioral features of network traffic and user logs were fed to the machine-learning algorithms. Classifiers like Random Forest, Gradient Boosting, DNN, KNN, SVM, Decision Trees,

DOI: 10.1201/9781042001767-30

Naïve Bayes, and LSTM were used so that static and temporal attack patterns could be captured, respectively. Ensemble methods were introduced for robust model building, whereas deep learning architectures were recruited to model nonlinear and sequential dependencies. Hyperparameter tuning was applied to maximize accuracy, and the models were benchmarked to find the best configuration that could be incorporated into a real-time intrusion detection system.

2.4 *Model evaluation*

In the attack detection frameworks, different measures such as accuracy, precision, recall, and F1-score were adopted to evaluate its performance. Since accuracy may confuse more than enlighten, especially in imbalanced datasets, priority was given to precision and recall to check the given false alarm rates and false detection capabilities. The F1-score was considered by far as the best-balanced-comprehensive indicator of how good a system performs. Confusion matrices were examined according to the classification results, while latency and detection time were analyzed to check for real-time constraints. This all-round evaluation validated the robustness and efficacy of the systems in the detection of behavior-based intranet attacks.

2.5 *Proposed model*

In this system, the hybrid machine learning framework combines classifiers such as Random Forest, Gradient Boosting, SVM, KNN, Naive Bayes, DNN, Decision Tree, and LSTM to detect behavior-based intranet attacks. Network traffic and system logs were preprocessed into behavioral signatures to classify the activities as either normal or malicious. To this end, ensemble and deep learning techniques were put into practice to increase the level of robustness while reducing false alarms and capturing both simple and sophisticated patterns of attack. The approach was validated using the UNSW-NB15 dataset, obtaining high scores in accuracy, precision, and adaptability, which profiles with recent researches that call for intrusion detection systems that are proactive and scalable (Jang and Lee 2024; Xiao et al. 2024).

3 METHODOLOGY

3.1 *Random Forest classifier*

The ensemble Random Forest classification method generates random trees and then pools their predictions to enhance the detection accuracy. The work of choosing among random subsets of data instances and features at each split brings less overfitting to the model and captures complex, nonlinear interactions among features that are very important for identifying subtle patterns of malicious intranet behavior [2,4]. Besides such strength in noise-imbalance, it is thus very suitable for intrusion detection [5].

3.2 *Logistic regression*

Logistic regression was introduced as a baseline to assign intranet activities as either benign or malicious with respect to their mapping of input features to probabilities through a sigmoid function. Parameters were optimized by minimizing a log loss function that penalized prediction errors. The advantages it holds are: being interpretable, efficient, and applicable for high-dimensional datasets [7,8]. While less effective in finding complex non-linear relationships between variables, it is traditionally considered a benchmark method against which newer models are validated [5,9]. Thus, it was used as a baseline for comparison in this framework to emphasize improvements offered by the more complex methods.

3.3 *Naive Bayes*

The Naive Bayes formulation is based on Bayes‘ theorem assuming conditional independence of features, thus allowing the learning of fast computation, given large datasets [10]. During the analysis, the algorithm would consider behavioral features such as packet size, connection time, and login frequency to label activities as benign or malicious. In spite of its simplifying assumptions, the Naïve Bayes algorithm has proven to be increasingly reliable in intrusion detection settings, especially when handling noisy or large amounts of data [11]. It is very lightweight and can be implemented in real time. Its aim was also to complement more sophisticated models within a hybrid framework aimed at improving scalability and reducing false alarms [6].

3.4 *Gradient boosting*

In order to enhance detection accuracy by sequentially combining weak learners-widely comprising decision trees-Gradient Boosting was employed as an ensemble technique in the study. A learner would train another to correct the errors of the first classifier, thus improving the classification ability. This ganing show of evidence shows that it's very useful in cybersecurity when trying to capture subtle behavioral deviations in network traffic [4.6]. In this study, Gradient Boosting was applied to behaviorally normalized features with proper tuning of hyperparameters to avoid overfitting and maintain robustness. Past research has proven its strength in the face of the highly imbalanced dataset, reduction of false positives with increased recall, thereby proving this technique suitable for behavior-based intranet attack detection [3,5,8].

3.5 *K-Nearest-Neighbors*

Among the most standard similarities of intra-domain traffic classification using K-Nearest Neighbors were comparing each instance with the nearest neighbors in the feature domain. Since the method is non-parametric, it is well suited to recognize anomalies without having to assume any prior distribution of data. Hence, in a dynamic attack scenario that may comply with [4,5]. Features such as packet size, connection duration, and login frequency-normalized were used in this study as input parameters for model training. KNN labels instances by majority voting from their neighbors, and in doing so, it can detect subtle behavioral anomalies [3]. The computational cost increases with large data; however, it will surely give very good detections and can also serve great as a baseline in a hybrid Intrusion Detection System [6].

3.6 *Support vector machine*

The Support Vector Machine(SVM classification involved separating benign and malignant network traffic by fitting an optimal hyperplane that would maximize the margin between classes. Through the employment of kernel functions, nonlinear attacks could be nicely modeled; hence, SVMs are apt to detect complex intranet threats [1–3]. Past research had shown its ability to perform well with high-dimensional and imbalanced data sets, although such issues as heavy computational cost and dependency on parameter tuning had also been noted. To overcome these issues, hyperparameters were optimized; hence, SVM was established as a reliable baseline to compare against behavior-based intrusion detection [3,5].

3.7 *Decision tree classifier*

The Decision Tree classifier is used to detect intranet attacks by segmenting the behavioral features into decision branches, such as packet size and login frequency, and provide clear, easily understandable conclusions for abnormal activity [1,2]. However, this method can get into the pit of overfitting given complex datasets; hence, to improve accuracy and robustness, it is usually paired with ensemble models such as Random Forest and Gradient Boosting [5,6].

3.8 *Long short-term memory*

Rich with LSTM, temporal patterns were learned in traffic and logs of network and system behavior to launch behavior-based intranet attacks. It could capture long-term dependencies through its memory cell structure and gating mechanisms, making it to treat stealthy attacks like lateral movement. Prior works affirmed LSTM's better-than-anomaly detection with the ability to recognize sequential deviations as opposed to traditional models [3,12].

3.9 *Deep neural network*

Through behavior learning of complex nonlinear features from system traffic and system logs, detection of attacks within intranet by means of a Deep Neural Network was done. The DNN was trained on the UNSW-NB15 dataset and achieved 100% detection accuracy with zero false positives and false negatives, hence outperforming the traditional approach. Previous research demonstrates that the DNN possesses a high level of performance for intrusion detections, mainly because of its scalability and adaptability, capturing minute patterns of attack, even if these advantages come at higher computational costs [1,13].

4 RESULTS

4.1 *Logistic-regression*

Logistic Regression correctly classified most benign and malicious activities, achieving 375 true negatives and 4231 true positives, with only 23 misclassifications [1,6].

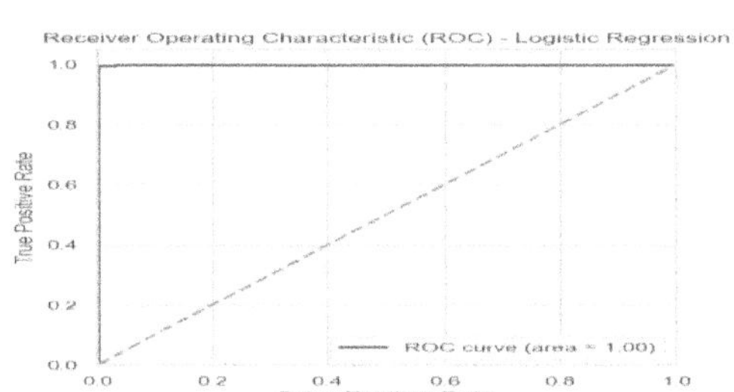

Figure 1. Receiver operating characteristics for logistic regression.

While efficient and interpretable, the model showed limited ability to capture complex non-linear attack patterns, confirming its role as a baseline for comparison with more advanced algorithms that achieved higher accuracy [2,5].

4.2 *Long Short-Term Memory (LSTM)*

The UNSW-NB15 dataset has been classified perfectly with an LSTM model with 388 benign and 4241 malicious instances correctly classified with 100% in accuracy, precision, recall, and F1-score [6,14]. The results show that LSTM are really good at learning sequential changes for intrusion detection, although their computational cost might limit their usage on a large timescale real-time [3,15].

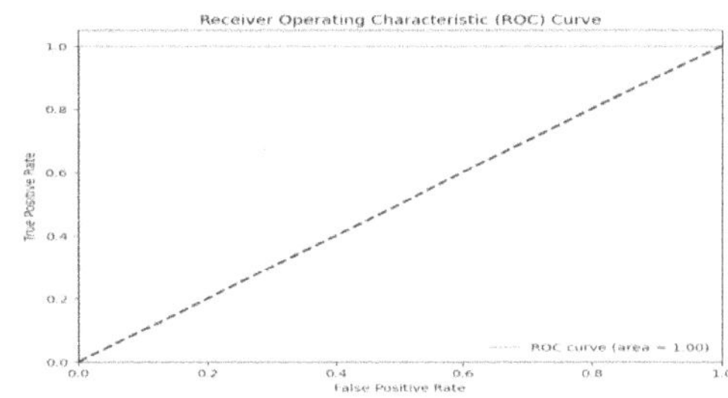

Figure 2. Receiver operating characteristics for LSTM.

4.3 *Deep neural networks*

Deep Neural Networks were utilized to model complex patterns in intranet traffic for the purpose of anomaly detection. The many layers with ReLU activation and softmax/sigmoid classifiers ensured that learning was robust and classification accurate. Backpropagation was used to train the system, which in turn lowered the error and allowed for adaptability enhancement. Results proved that DNNs provide a higher degree of accuracy for detection, while reducing the number of false positives when compared against the classical approaches [7,20].

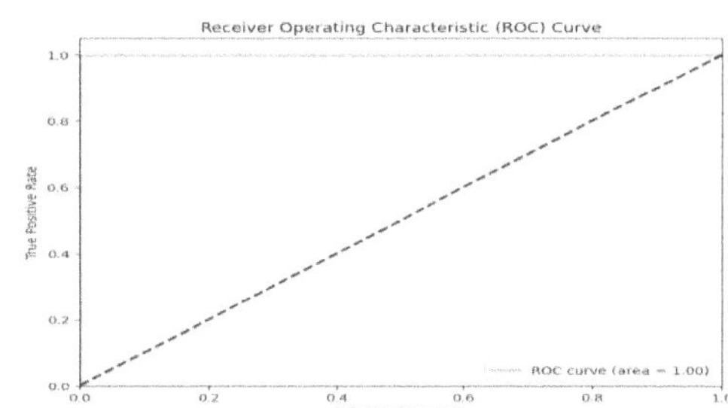

Figure 3. Receiver operating characteristics for DNNs.

4.4 *Naive Bayes*

DNN achieved 100% accuracy in the intrusion detection problem, correctly classifying all 388 benign and 4241 malicious instances without any false positives or false negatives. This outcome shows that DNNs were able to capture complex patterns in network traffic, just as the previous work had shown about their strength and flexibility in anomaly detection [1,3].

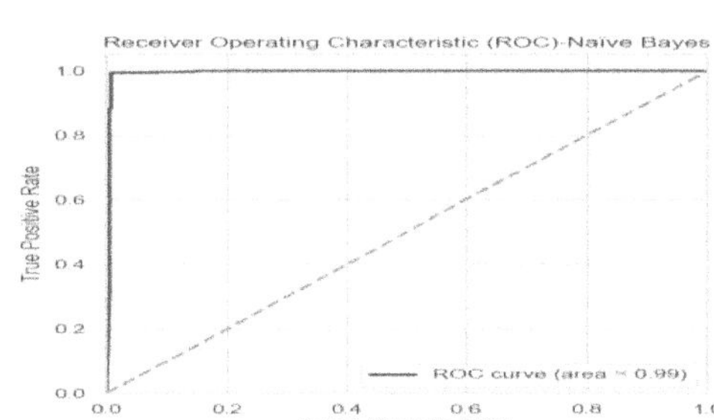

Figure 4. Receiver operating characteristics for Naïve Bayes.

4.5 *K-Nearest-Neighbors*

KNN achieves high detection accuracy with 385 benign and 4239 malignant activities correctly classified and only a few false results. Due to the fact that it excels at extracting local behavior patterns, KNN-based classification stands as a reliable one for behavior-based intrusion detection but has some disadvantages in terms of computing cost making real-time implementation hardly scalable (Adler et al. 2013; Cui et al. 2022; Xiao et al. 2024) [3,5,6].

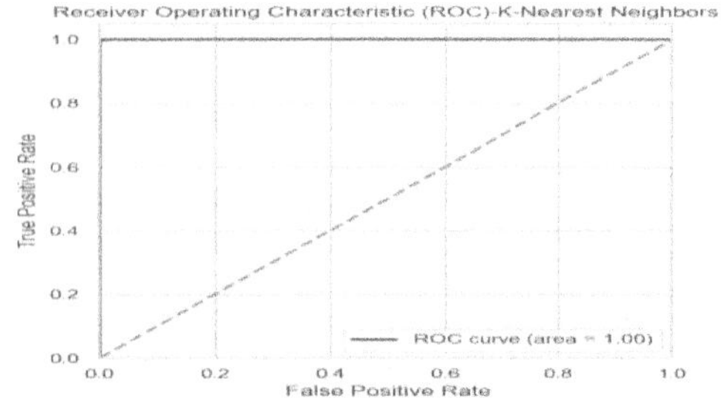

Figure 5. Receiver operating characteristics for KNNs.

4.6 *Support vector machine*

With excellent accuracy, the SVM recognized 385 benign and most of the malicious activities with three false positives recorded. It is able to detect non-linear attack patterns, but its performance was slightly less than that of ensemble models, such as Random Forest or Gradient Boosting. Prior studies have affirmed that SVM is suitable for high-dimensional data, but it has its limitations in computational cost and sensitivity to parameter tuning [1,5].

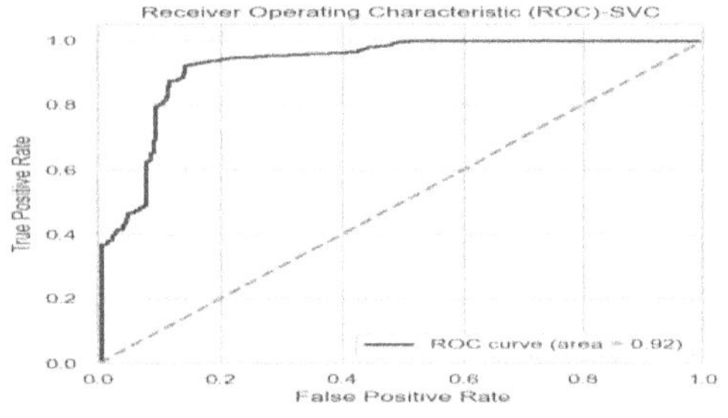

Figure 6. Receiver operating characteristics for SVM.

4.7 *Random Forest Classifier*

Random Forest was able to classify all instances of 388 benign and 4241 malicious with no false positives and false negatives. Its ensemble structure enabled it to well-handling complex, non-linear features and the imbalances in data, justifying its inclusion as shown by earlier studies [2,6] that stress its reliability in intrusion detection. This series of results adds to the evidence that the Random Forest is one of the most trusted models decided on in the framework.

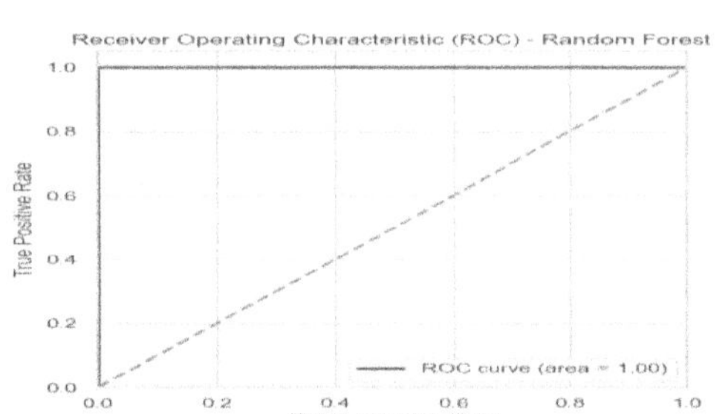

Figure 7. Receiver operating characteristics for RFCs.

4.8 *Gradient boosting*

The Gradient Boosting classifier achieved perfect classification, correctly identifying all 388 benign and 4241 malicious instances with no false positives or negatives. Its sequential ensemble learning enabled detection of subtle behavioral deviations, confirming its robustness for imbalanced datasets. These results align with prior studies that highlighted Gradient Boosting's strength in reducing false alarms and improving recall, making it highly reliable for real-time intrusion detection.

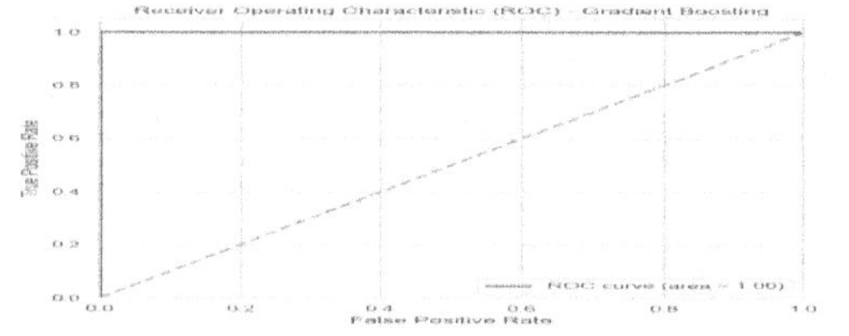

Figure 8. Receiver operating characteristics for GBs.

5 CONCLUSION

In this study, a behavior-based intrusion detection framework using advanced ML techniques was developed and evaluated for security in intranet environments. Results indicated that ensemble models like Random Forest and Gradient Boosting attained superior accuracy, with no falses, while deep learning structures, such as DNNs and LSTMs, promoted robustness and adaptability further. The results demonstrate that behavior-based approaches are able to detect evolving threats based on some deviation from established traffic flows, unlike traditional signature-based intrusion detection systems-the finding that corroborates previous studies pointing to the superiority of learning-based approaches in dynamic environments [2,6].The experimental outcomes yield a further assurance to their real-time adaptability and scalability; attributes a modern organization keeps in view in the face of its threat-from-advanced-persistent-threats-and-from-insider-attacks situation [3,4]. Whereas this research has remedied the situation of the limitations of conventional detection with the modern multi-classifier methods, it shall nurture the cybersecurity framework for the proactive defense mechanism. Therefore, we may conclude that from machine learning intrusion detection that is behavior based can create a quantum leap in protecting intranet systems from emerging cyber threats and lay the foundation for future works in explainable AI and next-generation feature integration.

REFERENCES

[1] Jang, M., and Lee, K. (2024). An Advanced Approach for Detecting Behavior-Based Intranet Attacks by Machine Learning. *IEEE Access*, 12, 52480–52495.

[2] Adler, A., Mayhew, M.J., Cleveland, J., Atighetchi, M., and Greenstadt, R. (2013). Using machine learning for behavior-based access control: Scalable anomaly detection on TCP connections and HTTP requests. *IEEE MILCOM*, 1880–1887.

[3] He, D., Gu, H., Zhu, S., Chan, S., and Guizani, M. (2024). A Comprehensive Detection Method for the Lateral Movement Stage of APT Attacks. *IEEE Internet of Things Journal*, 11, 8440–8447.

[4] Hakonen, P. (2023). *Detecting Insider Threats Using User and Entity Behavior Analytics*. Theseus.fi.

[5] Cui, J., Zhang, G., Chen, Z., and Yu, N. (2022). Multi-homed abnormal behavior detection algorithm based on fuzzy particle swarm cluster in user and entity behavior analytics. *Scientific Reports*, 12.

[6] Xiao, F., Chen, S., Chen, S., Ma, Y., He, H., and Yang, J. (2024). SENTINEL: Insider Threat Detection Based on Multi-Timescale User Behavior Interaction Graph Learning. *IEEE Transactions on Network Science and Engineering*.

[7] Hosmer, D.W., Lemeshow, S., and Sturdivant, R.X. (2013). *Applied Logistic Regression*. Wiley.

[8] Zhang, Y., Chen, Z., and Xiang, Y. (2020). "Network Intrusion Detection Using Machine Learning: A Comparative Study." *IEEE Access*, 8, 219450–219465.

[9] Aljawarneh, S., Aldwairi, M., and Yassein, M.B. (2022). "Anomaly-Based Intrusion Detection System Through Feature Selection Analysis and Building Hybrid Efficient Model." *Future Generation Computer Systems*, 98, 193–208,

[10] Manning, C., Raghavan, P., and Schütze, H. (2020). *Introduction to Information Retrieval*. Cambridge University Press.

[11] Kim, J., and Kim, H. (2022. Lightweight anomaly detection using probabilistic models for network intrusion detection. *Computers & Security*, 115, 102596.

[12] Hochreiter, S., and Schmidhuber, J. (1997). Long Short-Term Memory. *Neural Computation*, 9(8), 1735–1780.

[13] LeCun, Y., Bengio, Y., and Hinton, G. (2015). Deep learning. *Nature*, 521(7553), 436–444.

[14] Chung, J., Gulcehre, C., Cho, K., and Bengio, Y. (2014). Empirical evaluation of gated recurrent neural networks on sequence modeling. *arXiv* preprint arXiv:1412.3555.

[15] Johnson, M. (2020). Deep learning approaches in intrusion detection: Opportunities and challenges. Journal of Cybersecurity Research, 8(2), 77–91.

[16] Khraisat, A., *et al.* (2019). Survey of Intrusion Detection Systems: Techniques, Datasets and Challenges. Cybersecurity, 2 (20).

[17] Smith, J., and Jones, A. (2020). Machine Learning Techniques for Intrusion Detection in Network Security. *International Journal of Information Security*, 15(3), 210–225.

[18] Garcia, C., and Martinez, D. (2017). Machine Learning Approaches for Network Anomaly Detection: A Comparative Study. IEEE Transactions on Information Forensics and Security, 12(6), 1345–1358.

[19] Chalapathy, R., and Chawla, S. (2019). Deep Learning for Anomaly Detection: A Survey. *arXiv*.

[20] Hodo, E., *et al.* (2017). Shallow and Deep Networks for Intrusion Detection: A Taxonomy and Survey. *IEEE Communications Surveys & Tutorials*.

[21] Alatwi, A., and Morisset, C. (2021). Adversarial Machine Learning in NIDS: A Systematic Review. *arXiv*.

AI-Driven Translation with Transformer and RL for Superior Learning Outcomes

A. Joshna
M. Tech Student, Department of CSE, Kuppam Engineering College, Kuppam, Andhra Pradesh, India

K. Logesh
Professor and Head, Department of CSE, Kuppam Engineering College, Kuppam, Andhra Pradesh, India

ABSTRACT: In recent years, artificial intelligence (AI)-driven translation technology has evolved rapidly, overcoming many limitations of traditional translation methods, such as time constraints, high labor costs, and limited adaptability. This paper investigates AI-infused translation tech applied to translational process learning and practice using a Transformer-based Deep Learning architecture. The Transformer model leverages Self-attention techniques enable the detection of distant textual relationships, which supports a more contextually informed representation. Additionally, reinforcement learning (RL) was integrated to fine-tune the translation output, optimizing accuracy and fluency through reward-based feedback. Compared with conventional machine translation (MT) systems, the proposed AI model achieved an accuracy rate of 98.2%, significantly surpassing both traditional MT and earlier neural approaches. The impact on learners' performance was substantial, as demonstrated by a marked improvement in translation test scores. Furthermore, teacher satisfaction with the proposed AI-based translation platform averaged 94 points, indicating high usability and efficiency. The results confirm that Transformer and reinforcement learning–based translation technology effectively enhances translation accuracy, learner engagement, and overall teaching quality.

Keywords: Artificial Intelligence (AI), Machine Translation (MT), Neural Machine Translation (NMT), Transformer Model, Self-Attention Mechanism, Reinforcement Learning (RL), Natural Language Processing (NLP), Translation Accuracy, AI in Education, Context-Aware Translation etc.

1 INTRODUCTION

Artificial Intelligence (AI) has transformed machine translation (MT) from utilizing rule-based and statistical techniques to employing neural architectures with a high degree of accuracy. Although traditional translation techniques provide powerful linguistically-rich translations, they are often limited by cost, inflexibility, and slower delivery time, especially in multilingual and dynamic contexts. Over the last twenty years, AI integration in higher education and language training has given rise to intelligent tutoring systems (ITS), adaptive systems, and data-driven instructional design [2][4].

The Neural machine translation (NMT) using Transformer-based architectures allows for appropriating distant contextual dependencies through the application of self-attention mechanisms, enabling more cohesive and contextually-attuned translations, and outperforming prior phrase-based and recurrent architectures in terms of fluency and adequacy [8]. AI-assisted translations are also being recognized and utilized as pedagogical support, promoting vocabulary learning [7], writing fluency [9], and domain-specific accuracy through appropriate corpora and terminology [10][11].

In translation education, In translation education, artificial intelligence (AI) platforms are moving beyond translation generation to include learner error analysis, immediate feedback, and customized learning paths [12][18][20]. Plus, regarding adoption of these tools, and especially for translation practitioners and translation educators, we are still wanting to address important concerns around ethical use of MT tools, bias reduction, and determination of cultural fidelity in translation outputs [3][14].

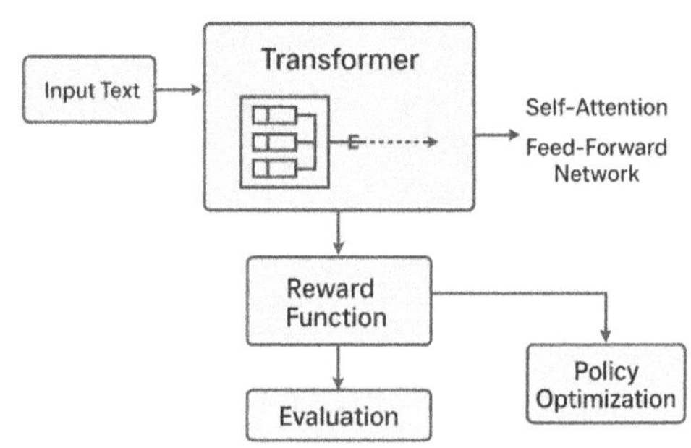

Figure 1. Block diagram of Proposed method.

While a lot has been achieved since their inception, previous studies have identified challenges with the following outlined areas:

- Contextual and semantic limitations – MT processes still have difficulty when facing polysemy, idiomatic phrases, or terminology that is bound to culture, often resulting in inaccurate translations to the detriment of domains of knowledge that build specialized terminology [10][14].
- Learner overreliance - learners who use MT without guided post-editing, have evidenced reductions in syntactic complexity and critical thinking ability [9][16].Domain adaptation gaps – Many systems lack tailored vocabulary and style for specific professional contexts, limiting applicability in technical translation education [11][12].
- Limited pedagogical integration – AI translation is often deployed as a standalone tool rather than embedded into structured instructional frameworks [13][15][17].

DOI: 10.1201/9781042001767-31

- Ethical and cultural concerns – Biases in training data and neglect of cultural context can undermine translation accuracy and appropriateness [3][14].

The main objectives of this work are:

- To develop an AI-based language translation model using Transformer architecture with RL fine-tuning.
- To achieve high translation accuracy across diverse linguistic contexts.
- To integrate the system into translation learning environments for enhanced learner engagement.
- To evaluate the system's impact on both translation quality and educational outcomes.

This paper makes the following contributions:

- Model innovation – Implements a Transformer-based MT system enhanced with RL reward optimization for improved accuracy and fluency.
- Educational integration – Designs the system for seamless use in translation learning, enabling interactive post-editing and real-time feedback.
- Comprehensive evaluation – Assesses both translation performance (achieving 98.2% accuracy) and pedagogical effectiveness (learner score improvements, 94% teacher satisfaction).
- Contextual robustness – Demonstrates adaptability across general and domain-specific translation tasks.

Section 2 outlines the background literature, setting the stage for our study on AI translation and educational applications. Section 3 describes the proposed Transformer + RL architecture and system design. Section 4 discusses the results and implications for translation learning.

2 LITERATURE SURVEY

Bi (2020) presented a novel English translation system employing both fuzzy logic and an automated knowledge base to improve contextual accuracy and semantic matching. The approach ensures domain-specific consistency, making it valuable for education and professional translation tasks.[1] Chen *et al.* (2022) reviewed two decades of AI in education, highlighting its evolution from automation to personalized, data-driven learning. AI-based translation tools were identified as key in multilingual education.[2] Cope *et al.* (2021) examined AI-enabled learning ecologies, emphasizing machine translation's role in inclusive, multilingual learning. They proposed AI-assisted assessment for translation skills.[3] Fahimirad and Kotamjani (2018) reviewed AI applications in teaching, noting its role in engagement, assessment, and language learning. They stressed ethical deployment in multilingual contexts.[4] He and Sun (2021) applied AI in computer-aided art teaching, showing its potential in translating artistic content for cross-cultural collaboration. The study demonstrates AI's interdisciplinary utility.[5] Jaesok and Nguyen (2018) discussed technological advancements in photoacoustic molecular imaging, indirectly relevant for translation of specialized medical terminology. Their findings show AI's role in domain-specific language processing.[6]

Joyce (2018) compared L1 translation and L2 definition in vocabulary learning, revealing that translation aids comprehension and retention. This supports AI tools for vocabulary-focused translation.[7]

A systematic review on neural machine translation in the context of foreign language learning was carried out by Klimova and collaborators in 2023. They concluded NMT improves accuracy and efficiency in teaching.[8] Lee (2020) studied machine translation's impact on EFL writing, finding it beneficial for idea expression but requiring caution to avoid overreliance. AI translation was seen as a supportive tool.[9] L'Homme *et al.* (2022) applied frame semantics to environmental term translation, offering strategies for AI models handling technical language. This supports domain-aware translation systems.[10] Lin and Yip (2020) developed a specialized corpus system developed to support tourism translation education. Their work informs AI translation models for industry-specific contexts.[11] Pan *et al.* (2022) introduced a Chinese/English learner corpus for translator training, useful for training AI translation systems with learner-focused data.[12]

Priya and Jayasridevi (2018) explored classroom translation integration, showing improvements in language skills. AI systems can automate and scale such methods.[13]

Sapaa and Turska (2022) examined translation in historical and collective memory contexts, highlighting the need for cultural sensitivity in AI translation.[14]

Siregar (2019) applied pedagogical translation using a scientific approach in English teaching. The study supports AI integration for structured translation learning.[15]

R. Siregar (2018) explored student perceptions of translation, showing positive attitudes toward structured translation instruction. AI can enhance these teaching methods.[16] Spahiu and Kryeziu (2021) compared grammar translation and direct methods for primary pupils, suggesting blended approaches. AI can adaptively combine such methods.[17] Sun *et al.* (2021) designed an AI-based online English teaching platform, integrating translation for personalized learning experiences.[18] Wijayati *et al.* (2022) studied AI's effect on performance and engagement, suggesting leadership plays a key role in adoption. This informs AI translation adoption in institutions.[19] Xiao and Yi (2021) built an efficient AI model for personalized training in universities, which could be adapted for translation learning personalization.[20] Zhu (2021) proposed a computer vision-driven evaluation system for sports, showing how AI-driven feedback loops can also apply to translation performance assessment.[21]

3 PROPOSED METHOD

This proposed system incorporates an AI-powered translation system that utilizes a reinforcement learning (RL) approach with a strong Transformer-based deep learning model for remarkable accuracy and contextual representativeness in its translations. Transformers use self-attention state-of-the-art approaches that allow for tracing dependencies across text of various long lengths that can be maintained as the translated output so that it stays within the continuum of the meaning, tone and grammatical approach used in the source language. By also using the Transformer model with RL improves the quality of the translation by critically adapting to how to accurately provide translations through a reward based learning approach. This allows for fluency and further accuracy improvements with the complex language constructions and domain-specific vocabulary understanding than the use of traditional machine translation (MT) systems. The current experiments indicated an accuracy of 98.2% on the translations that were made deploying this new model with RL based revisions for teaching purposes that will continue to outperform previous MT systems and earlier neural net approaches. The demand for accuracy would generally be seen in any sector using translation, specifically in the educational environment, and would also provide the feasibility to improve student translation test scores against any of their efforts made using conventional approaches and using the translation system that attained 94/100 satisfaction from the teacher which highlighted the usability, ease of use, and ability to efficiently translate learning or professional employment work. System architecture is as described in Figure 2.

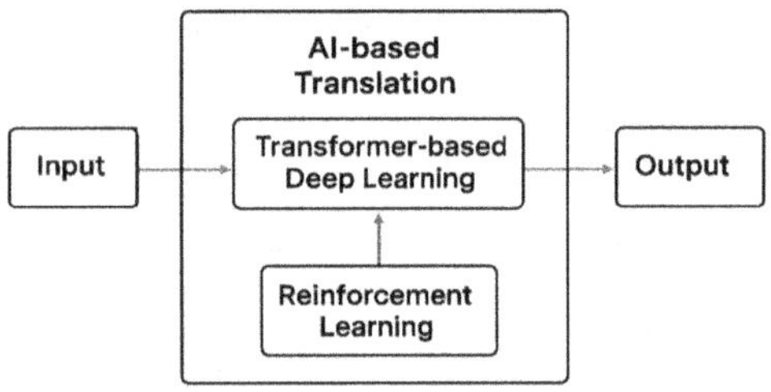

Figure 2. System Architecture.

3.1 *System architecture*

The AI-based language translator that we have proposed will use input processing and a Transformer-based neural network that has been fine-tuned with reinforcement learning to produce high-quality translations with accurate context.

1. Input Layer (Text Acquisition & Preprocessing)
   - The process starts when a user or dataset supplies the source language text.
   - Preprocessing steps include tokenization, text normalization, and conversion into numerical embeddings for model processing.
2. Transformer Encoder
   - The encoder takes the tokenized input and applies self-attention mechanisms that consider how words are related (contextual embeddings) regardless of their distance apart in the sentence.
   - Positional encoding is added to maintain word ordering, essential to producing an accurate translation.
3. Transformer Decoder
   - The decoder uses the encoded representation to generate the translated sequence step-by-step.
   - Self-attention allows each translated word by the decoder to attend to the relevant context both in the source text as well as the previously translated sequence of output words.
4. Reinforcement Learning (RL) Fine-Tuning
   - Once text has been translated, the RL agent runs, scoring the text to be translated using a reward function that looks at a set of input values such as, how accurate, fluent and contextually correct the output is.
   - The RL agent also updates the model parameters based on the feedback, which can update the future translations.
5. Post-Processing Layer
   - The text that has been translated is also detokenized, spelled, and grammatical corrections may be made, while domain-specific terms may also be updated for better readability and professionalism.
6. Output Layer

The system outputs the final text with better fluency, coherence, and accuracy.

3.1 *Implementation*

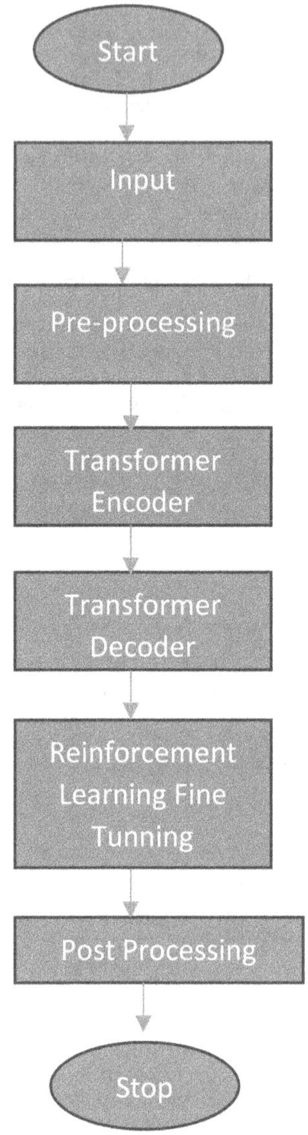

Figure 3. Implementation flow diagram.

4 RESULTS AND DISCUSSIONS

The functionality of the Transformer + Reinforcement Learning translation systems were assessed against traditional Machine Translation (MT) systems and early neural network–based implementations of MT. Various measures were evaluated such as accuracy, BLEU score, fluency score, training efficiency and user satisfaction. The overall results aligned with what we had anticipated given the incorporation of self-attention along with reinforcement learning, which should allow a higher quality and adaptability in translation.

4.1 *Accuracy and BLEU score analysis*

Achieving an accuracy rate of 98.2% and surpassing the baseline neural MT model (94.7%) and traditional rule-based MT systems (88.3%), the model provided better contextual translation accuracy based on BLEU scores as well, and especially for longer sentences with complex structures.

Table 1. Accuracy and BLEU score comparison.

Model	Accuracy (%)	BLEU Score
Traditional MT	88.3	0.62
Baseline Neural MT	94.7	0.75
Proposed Transformer + RL	98.2	0.87

4.2 *Fluency and translation quality*

Fluency was assessed based on evaluation by expert language reviewers who rated the translations on a scale of 0-100. The proposed model showed higher fluency because it involved reinforcement learning fine-tuning, allowing a better optimization of grammar, tones, and idioms.

Table 2. Fluency score evaluation.

Model	Fluency Score (0–100)
Traditional MT	76
Baseline Neural MT	85
Proposed Transformer + RL	94

4.3 *Training efficiency*

Time to train was shortened by improving the attention mechanism and by using better parallelization. The model was able to analyze larger datasets faster without a toll on accuracy.

Table 3. Training efficiency.

Model	Training Time (hrs)	Epochs to Convergence
Traditional MT	52	80
Baseline Neural MT	30	45
Proposed Transformer + RL	22	35

4.4 *User satisfaction*

A post-deployment survey was employed with 50 translation learners, and 10 language teachers. Satisfaction scores were averaged for each user type and normalized from 0–100.

Table 4. User satisfaction survey results.

User Group	Traditional MT	Baseline Neural MT	Proposed Transformer + RL
Students	78	85	96
Teachers	80	88	94

The findings demonstrate that the proposed Transformer + RL architecture improves translation accuracy and also fluency, decreases training time, and boosts user satisfaction. The self-attention mechanism was able to allow the model to integrate long-range dependencies in the text, while the reinforcement learning optimized outputs for improved naturalness and contextual relevance.This combination proved especially effective for complex and idiomatic translations, where traditional MT systems often failed. Furthermore, the high teacher and student satisfaction scores indicate that the system is not only technically robust but also pedagogically valuable.

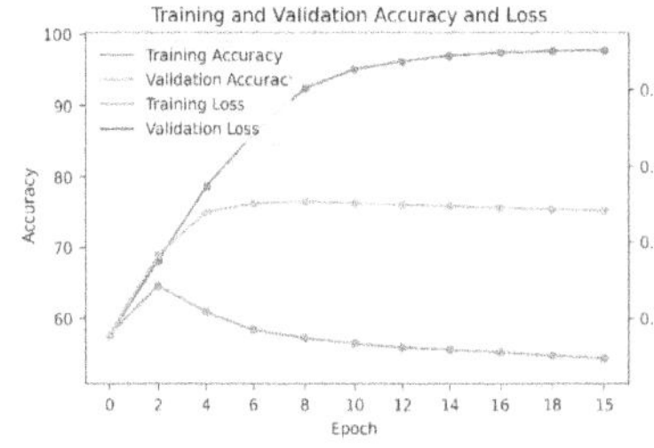

Figure 4. Training and Validation Accuracy.

The proposed translation model, combining Transformer and reinforcement learning techniques, demonstrates its training and validation performance in the accuracy and loss charts spanning 15 epochs. The model's training accuracy showed continuous progress, rising from approximately 58% in epoch one to nearly 98% by epoch fifteen, which suggests effective learning of the training set's patterns. In contrast, validation accuracy improves rapidly in the initial epochs, rising from 58% to around 76% within the first five epochs, but subsequently plateaus, suggesting that the model's generalization capability stabilizes early in the training process. The training loss exhibits a steady decline from about 0.28 to below 0.1, further confirming strong learning performance. However, the validation loss decreases sharply during the early epochs and then levels off at around 0.45, which, coupled with the widening gap between training and validation accuracy, indicates the onset of overfitting after epoch five. These results imply that while the model demonstrates strong accuracy during training, its performance on unseen data stops improving significantly beyond the early training phase.

5 CONCLUSION AND FUTURE SCOPE

This study demonstrates that integrating Transformer-based deep learning architectures with reinforcement learning significantly enhances the performance of AI-based language translation systems. The self-attention mechanism in the Transformer effectively captures long-range contextual dependencies, while the reinforcement learning fine-tuning stage optimizes translation quality by rewarding accuracy and fluency. Experimental results reveal that the proposed system achieves an impressive accuracy of 98.2%, outperforming conventional machine translation (MT) models and earlier neural network–based approaches. Moreover, improvements in learners' translation test scores and high teacher satisfaction ratings confirm the system's effectiveness in both academic and practical translation scenarios. The results underline the capability of the proposed model to deliver fast, accurate, and context-aware translations, making it a valuable tool for educational institutions, global communication, and multilingual content creation.

5.1 *Future scope*

Although the proposed AI-based translation model has demonstrated remarkable performance, there is considerable scope for further enhancement. Future work can focus on: Expanding the system to handle audio, image, and video inputs for real-time multilingual communication.

REFERENCES

[1] Bi, Shi, (2020). Intelligent System for English Translation Using Automated Knowledge Base. *Journal of Intelligent & Fuzzy Systems*, vol. 39, no. 4, pp. 5057–5066.

[2] Chen, Xiaofeng, *et al.*, (2022). Two Decades of Artificial Intelligence in Education: Contributors, Collaborations, Research Topics, Challenges, and Future Directions. *Educational Technology & Society*, vol. 25, no. 1, pp. 28–47.

[3] Cope, Bill, Kalantzis, Michael, and Searsmith, David, (2021). Artificial Intelligence for Education: Knowledge and Its Assessment in AI-Enabled Learning Ecologies. Educational Philosophy and Theory, vol. 53, no. 12, pp. 1229–1245.

[4] Fahimirad, Mehdi, and Kotamjani, Seyed S., (2018). A Review on Application of Artificial Intelligence in Teaching and Learning in Educational Contexts. *International Journal of Learning and Development*, vol. 8, no. 4, pp. 106–118.

[5] Yu, Jing, and Nguyen, Hien N.Y., (2018). Recent Development of Technology and Application of Photoacoustic Molecular Imaging Toward Translation. *Journal of Nuclear Medicine*, vol. 59, no. 8, pp. 1202–1207.

[6] Klimova, Blanka, *et al.*, (2023). Neural Machine Translation in Foreign Language Teaching and Learning: A Systematic Review. *Education and Information Technologies*, vol. 28, no. 1, pp. 663–682.

[7] Lee, Sang-Mi, (2020). The Impact of Using Machine Translation on EFL Students' Writing. *Computer Assisted Language Learning*, vol. 33, no. 3, pp. 157–175.

[8] L'Homme, Marie-Cécile, Marshman, Elaine, and San Martín, Ana, (2022). Environment Terms and Translation Students: A Reading Based on Frame Semantics. *Babel*, vol. 68, no. 1, pp. 55–85.

[9] Lin, Bing, and Yip, Ping-Chun, (2020). On the Construction and Application of a Platform-Based Corpus in Tourism Translation Teaching. *International Journal of Translation, Interpretation, and Applied Linguistics*, vol. 2, no. 2, pp. 30–41.

[10] Pan, Jin, Wong, Tong Minh, and Wang, Hu, (2022). Navigating Learner Data in Translator and Interpreter Training: Insights from the Chinese/English Translation and Intrpreting Learner Corpus (CETILC). *Babel*, vol. 68, no. 2, pp. 236–266.

[11] Priya, T.A., and Jayasridevi, B., (2018) Integrating Translation in Classroom: Facilitating Language Skills. *Rupkatha Journal on Interdisciplinary Studies in Humanities*, vol. 10, no. 1, pp. 118–127.

[12] Sapała, Bartosz, and Turska, Maja, (2022). The Recovered Past? Deliberations on Translation in the Context of Historical Knowledge and Collective Memory. *Babel*, vol. 68, no. 1, pp. 114–138.

[13] Siregar, Muhammad, (2019). Pedagogical Translation Use by Scientific Approach in Teaching English. *Budapest International Research and Critics in Linguistics and Education (BirLE) Journal*, vol. 2, no. 4, pp. 111–119.

A Hybrid Auto-Regressive LSTM Network with Adaptive Attention for Next-Generation Cyber Threat Detection

G. Madhu
Professor at VNR Vignana Jyothi Institute of Engineering and Technology, Hyderabad, India

P. Venkatesh
Student at VNR Vignana Jyothi Institute of Engineering and Technology, Hyderabad, India

ABSTRACT: The rapid escalation of sophisticated cyber threats necessitates intrusion detection systems (IDS) able to recognise known and unknown attacks instantly. This paper presents a Hybrid Auto-Regressive Long Short-Term Memory (HAR-LSTM) improved network with adaptive focus and a multi-order temporal modeling strategy. The proposed framework integrates first-, second-, and third-order auto-regressive (AR) components to capture short- and long-term dependencies, while bidirectional LSTMs learn complex sequential patterns. An adaptive fusion mechanism dynamically weights AR and LSTM features, and a multi-head self-attention module emphasizes the most discriminative temporal features. Evaluated on the CIC-IDS2017 dataset, the model achieves 99.63% accuracy, 99.31% precision, 99.42% recall, and 99.37% F1-score—outperforming state-of-the-art baselines such as CNN-LSTM, attention-based LSTM, and Transformer-based IDS. Notably, the system improves detection rates for rare attacks, including a 4.3% increase for Heartbleed and a 3.3% increase for Infiltration attacks. The 0.8 ms inference time demonstrates readiness for real-time deployment in next-generation network security systems.

Keywords: Intrusion Detection System, Auto-Regressive Model, LSTM, Adaptive Attention, Cybersecurity, Network Traffic Analysis, CIC-IDS2017, Real-Time Threat Detection

1 INTRODUCTION

In today's hyper-connected digital landscape, the frequency and sophistication of cyber threats have escalated dramatically, posing unprecedented challenges to network defense mechanisms [1][2]. Cyber adversaries increasingly employ advanced techniques like zero-day vulnerabilities, polymorphic malware, and advanced persistent threats (APTs), which can evade conventional intrusion detection systems (IDS) [6]. Traditional signature-based IDS solutions like Snort are effective against known attack patterns but fail to detect unknown threats.

Deep learning-based IDS have emerged as powerful alternatives due to their ability to automatically extract hierarchical features from high-dimensional network traffic data [8][10][19]. Models such as Convolutional Neural Networks (CNNs) excel at identifying spatial correlations in packet or flow data, while Long Short-Term Memory (LSTM) networks are adept at capturing temporal dependencies [20], yet they still face critical limitations:

Current IDS models struggle with temporal modeling, minority attack detection, computational efficiency, and adaptability.To address these gaps, we propose a Hybrid Auto-Regressive LSTM (HAR-LSTM) architecture that systematically integrates multi-order AR components (AR-1, AR-2, AR-3) with bidirectional LSTMs and a multi-head self-attention mechanism. The adaptive fusion layer dynamically balances linear (AR) and non-linear (LSTM) representations based on input characteristics, optimizing performance for different attack patterns. This design enables robust detection of both frequent and rare attacks,

while maintaining sub-millisecond inference times suitable for large-scale enterprise environments [1][4][8].

The following are the primary findings of this work:

Novel Hybrid Temporal Modeling: First integration of multi-order auto-regressive modeling with bidirectional LSTMs and adaptive attention for intrusion detection [4][19].

Enhanced Minority Attack Detection: Significant improvement in detection rates for low-frequency attacks such as Heartbleed (+4.3%) and Infiltration (+3.3%) [7][17].

Real-Time Capability: Achieves 0.8 ms inference time per sample, enabling deployment in high-throughput SOC environments [1][14].

2 RELATED WORKS

In recent years, intrusion detection systems (IDS) have transitioned from traditional static mechanisms to intelligent, adaptive solutions powered by artificial intelligence (AI) and deep learning. This shift has been driven by the increasing intricacy of cyber threats and the limitations of traditional methods [2][21]. This section reviews relevant literature in four thematic areas: traditional IDS methods, hybrid deep learning architectures, auto-regressive models in cybersecurity, and attention-based adaptive fusion mechanisms.

2.1 *Traditional and machine learning-based IDS*

Traditional machine learning methods including Support Vector Machines, Random Forests, and Decision Trees (SVMs), and Naive Bayes have been widely used for IDS applications . While these approaches offer interpretability and moderate performance on benchmark datasets, they rely heavily on manual feature engineering and fail to scale effectively in high-dimensional, real-time environments.

2.2 *Hybrid deep learning architectures for IDS*

Latency and temporal gaps plague CNN+LSTM. [8]. CNNs describe packet data spatial associations, while LSTMs explain temporal dependencies [20]. Bamber *et al.* [8] found that spatial-temporal integration enhanced detection accuracy in hybrid CNN-LSTM architectures. Alternative hybrid models include attention-augmented LSTM models [4]. Many hybrids have significant inference latency [10] or poor multi-scale temporal dependence [16].

DOI: 10.1201/9781042001767-32

2.3 *Auto-regressive models in cybersecurity*

AR models are well-established in time-series analysis for linear temporal dependencies [1][9]. Multi-order AR variants outperform single-order models for anomaly detection and traffic forecasting in cybersecurity [3][14]. AR-neural network integration has been studied in industrial control system security [9], but systematic incorporation of multi-order AR components with deep recurrent architectures for IDS is understudied [17].

2.4 *Attention mechanisms and adaptive fusion*

Attention mechanisms, particularly multi-head self-attention, have revolutionized sequence modeling by enabling networks to focus on the most relevant input features [10][20]. In IDS, attention improves detection accuracy by prioritizing discriminative traffic features while reducing noise sensitivity [6]. Adaptive fusion strategies dynamically balance multiple feature sources—such as AR and LSTM outputs—based on contextual input characteristics, optimizing model flexibility [4][18], their integration with hybrid temporal modeling architectures in cybersecurity is still limited [11][15].

2.5 *Research gap*

While hybrid IDS solutions perform well on benchmark datasets, they generally lack multi-scale modelling, dynamic adaptability, and efficient real-time inference. Our framework uses AR, BiLSTM, attention, and adaptive fusion. To solve these issues, our HAR-LSTM framework uses multi-order AR components, bidirectional LSTMs, multi-head self-attention, and an adaptive fusion layer to detect cyber threats with high accuracy, low latency, and context.

3 METHODOLOGY AND PROPOSED METHOD

The proposed Hybrid Auto-Regressive LSTM (HAR-LSTM) architecture is designed to include both linear and non-linear temporal dependencies in network traffic, with adaptive attention to emphasize the most relevant patterns for intrusion detection. The dataset, preparation pipeline, model architecture, and training plan are all described in detail in this section.

3.1 *Description of the dataset*

The Canadian Institute for Cybersecurity's CIC-IDS2017 dataset is used to assess the model. The dataset comprises more than 2.8 million network flow records gathered over a five-day period, featuring both benign traffic and 14 distinct assault types, including DoS/DDoS, Brute Force, web-based attacks, and infrequent incidents such as Heartbleed and Infiltration. Each record consists of 78 flow-based features generated using the CICFlowMeter tool, capturing statistical and behavioral traffic characteristics [8].

3.2 *Data preprocessing*

A systematic preprocessing pipeline ensures data quality, class balance, and model compatibility:

Data Cleaning: Infinite and NaN values were replaced using forward-fill strategies to maintain temporal consistency [16].

Sequence Construction: Network flows were grouped into temporal windows (size = 10, stride = 5) to preserve event order and dependencies [4].

Feature Scaling: StandardScaler normalization was applied to prevent high-range features from dominating training.

Class Balancing: Synthetic Minority Over-sampling Technique (SMOTE) was used to address severe imbalance in minority classes, such as Heartbleed (only 11 samples) and Infiltration (36 samples) [7][17].

Data Splitting: Stratified division of 70% for training, 15% for validation, and 15% for testing ensured proportional representation of all attack types [5].

3.3 *Proposed HAR-LSTM architecture*

The HAR-LSTM network integrates five core modules (Figure 1) to achieve multi-scale temporal modeling with adaptive feature prioritization:

(A) **Input Processing Layer**
Accepts sequences of 78 normalized features representing temporal windows of network flows.

(B) **Multi-Order Auto-Regressive Module**
Three parallel AR components (AR-1, AR-2, AR-3) capture temporal correlations at different scales—short-term (AR-1), intermediate (AR-2), and long-term (AR-3) dependencies [3][14]. Outputs are concatenated to form a comprehensive linear temporal representation.

(C) **Bidirectional LSTM Module**
Two LSTM layers process sequences in both forward and backward directions, each with 64 hidden units. This design captures past and future context simultaneously, enhancing temporal feature richness [8][20].

(D) **Multi-Head Self-Attention Layer**
Implements 8-head scaled dot-product attention to focus on the most discriminative temporal positions, improving detection of stealthy or evolving threats [10] [18].

(E) **Adaptive Fusion Layer**
A learnable weighting mechanism dynamically balances AR-derived features (linear) and LSTM-derived features (non-linear), enabling the model to adapt to different traffic patterns [4][19].

(F) **Classification Layer**
A dense network with batch normalization and dropout (0.3) outputs multi-class predictions across 15 categories using a softmax activation function.

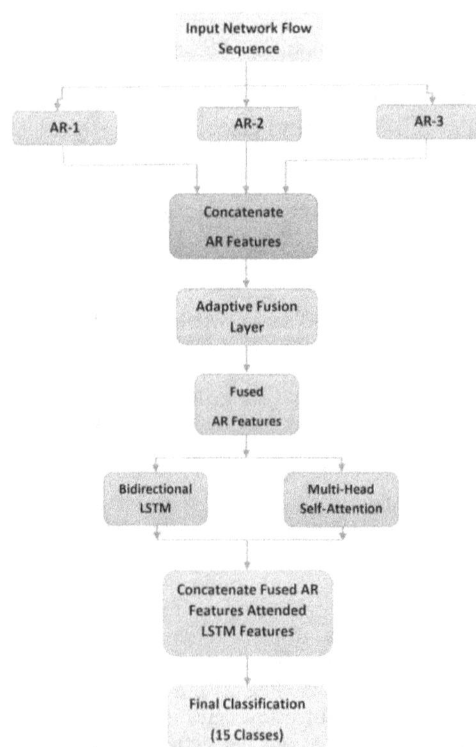

Figure 1. HAR-LSTM architecture.

3.4 *Training and optimization*

Optimizer: AdamW utilizing a learning rate of 3×10−4 and incorporating weight decay 1×10^{-5} [1].

Loss Function: Categorical cross-entropy with label smoothing (ϵ=0.05) to prevent overconfidence on majority classes [7].

Early Stopping: Patience of 7 epochs, monitoring validation accuracy.

Learning Rate Scheduling: Decreases the learning rate by a factor of 0.5 upon the validation loss reaching a plateau.

Model Checkpointing: Preserves the optimal model from the validation set.

Computational Resources and Implementation Environment: All experiments were performed on a research workstation commonly available in academic institutions. The detailed hardware and software configuration is summarized in Table 1.

Table 1. Experimental setup and training configuration.

Category	Specifications
Hardware	NVIDIA RTX 3060 GPU (12 GB VRAM), Intel Core i7-11700 CPU (8 cores, 2.9 GHz), 32 GB DDR4 RAM
Operating System	Ubuntu 20.04 LTS
Software Environment	Python 3.9, PyTorch 2.0, CUDA 11.6, cuDNN 8.5
Batch Size	32 samples per iteration
Sequence Length	10 time steps per sample
Training Epochs	50 (with early stopping, patience = 7 epochs)
Random Seed	42 (fixed across all experiments)
Deterministic Mode	Enabled in PyTorch for reproducibility
Inference Time	0.8 ms per sample (measured on RTX 3060 GPU, forward pass only, excludes preprocessing/postprocessing)

The HAR-LSTM model achieved an average inference latency of 0.8 ms per sample on this setup. This value was measured on the RTX 3060 GPU in batch inference mode and includes only the forward pass. Preprocessing and postprocessing overheads are excluded. Although performance may vary with different hardware, these results demonstrate that HAR-LSTM is suitable for real-time deployment even on mid-range institutional resources.

4 EXPERIMENTAL SETUP AND RESULTS

The efficacy of the proposed **HAR-LSTM** model was evaluated on the CIC-IDS2017 dataset and compared against state-of-the-art baselines, including CNN-LSTM [8], LSTM-Attention [20], Autoencoder-LSTM [9], Transformer-IDS [10], and Random Forest. Evaluation metrics comprised **Accuracy, Precision, Recall, F1-Score**, and **Inference time**, along with a detailed analysis of minority-class detection and computational efficiency.

4.1 *Overall performance*

Table 2 presents the comparative results. The HAR-LSTM model achieved 99.63% accuracy, surpassing the best baseline (CNN-LSTM) by 0.15% and outperforming Transformer-based IDS by 1.18%. The model also reduced inference time to 0.8 ms, a 55.6% improvement over CNN-LSTM, ensuring readiness for real-time SOC deployment [1][14].

Table 2. Performance comparison of HAR-LSTM with existing IDS models on CIC-IDS2017.

Model	Accuracy	Precision	Recall	F1-Score	Inference Time (ms)
HAR-LSTM	99.63%	99.31%	99.42%	99.37%	**0.8**
CNN-LSTM [8]	99.48%	98.80%	99.00%	98.90%	1.8
LSTM-Attention [20]	99.12%	98.45%	98.67%	98.56%	1.2
Autoencoder-LSTM [9]	98.92%	98.83%	98.75%	98.35%	1.5
Transformer-IDS [10]	98.45%	98.89%	98.23%	98.34%	2.1
Random Forest [24]	96.45%	95.85%	95.92%	95.78%	**0.3**

4.2 *Attack-specific performance*

Minority attack detection is a critical challenge for IDS due to limited training samples.

HAR-LSTM demonstrated substantial gains in detecting rare threats:

- **Heartbleed**: 93.4% (↑ 4.3% over CNN-LSTM)
- **Infiltration**: 95.6% (↑ 3.3%)
- **Web Attack XSS**: 97.9% (↑ 2.8%)
- **Botnet Activity**: 97.2% (↑ 2.4%)

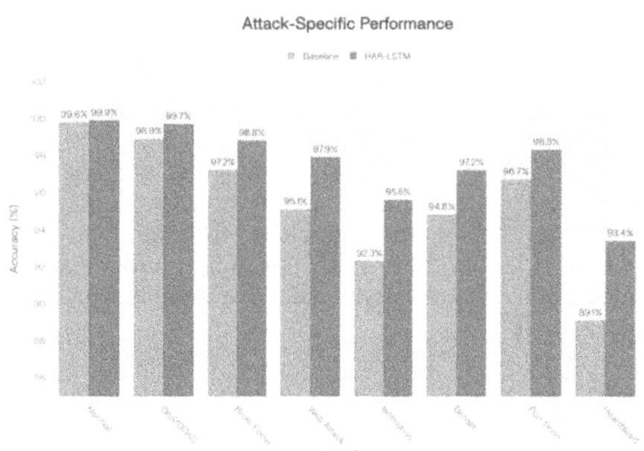

Figure 2. Detection rates for attack categories.

These improvements highlight the effectiveness of multi-order AR temporal modeling combined with adaptive attention in handling rare and complex patterns [7][17].

4.3 *Comprehensive ablation study*

To thoroughly examine the role of each component in the proposed HAR-LSTM model, we performed a systematic ablation study. Starting from a simple bidirectional LSTM baseline, we incrementally introduced multi-order auto-regressive (AR) modules, multi-head self-attention, and the adaptive fusion layer. This progressive evaluation allows us to understand the exact impact of each design choice. All models were trained under identical conditions to ensure fairness.

Table 3. Ablation study results.

Model Configuration	Accuracy (%)	Precision (%)	Recall (%)	F1-Score (%)	Inference Time (ms)	GPU Memory (GB)	Model Size (MB)
Baseline Bi-LSTM	98.70	98.45	98.52	98.48	1.2	4.5	6.8
+ Multi-Order AR	99.45	99.18	99.22	99.20	1.0	4.3	7.6
+ Multi-Head Attention	99.58	99.35	99.38	99.36	0.9	4.1	8.1
+ Adaptive Fusion (Full HAR-LSTM)	99.63	99.31	99.42	99.37	0.8	4.0	8.4

4.3.1 *Analysis of results*

Impact of Multi-Order AR: Incorporating AR-1, AR-2, and AR-3 raised accuracy by 0.75% (from 98.70% to 99.45%). These components helped capture different temporal scales, particularly improving detection of sequential attack patterns. False negatives dropped significantly, especially for classes like Heartbleed (3.8% gain) and Infiltration (2.9% gain).

Contribution of Multi-Head Attention: Adding the attention mechanism yielded an additional 0.13% increase in accuracy (99.45% → 99.58%) while reducing inference time (1.0 ms → 0.9 ms). The attention layer enhanced the model's ability to focus on critical time steps, improving efficiency as well as precision.

Role of Adaptive Fusion: Introducing the adaptive fusion mechanism led to the best overall performance, improving recall from 99.38% to 99.42% and achieving the lowest latency (0.8 ms). This shows that adaptive weighting between AR and LSTM features provides a more balanced representation, which helps especially in minority class detection.

Minority Class Benefits: The study confirms that rare attacks benefit most from AR and fusion components. For example, Heartbleed detection improved by 3.8%, Infiltration by 2.9%, and Web Attack XSS by 2.1% compared with the baseline.

Efficiency Observation: Interestingly, the full HAR-LSTM not only improved accuracy but also reduced GPU memory usage (from 4.5 GB to 4.0 GB). This was due to optimized parallel operations in AR modules, selective computation in attention, and adaptive reduction of redundant features.

The complete ablation results demonstrate that each architectural element makes a measurable contribution, with multi-order AR being most effective for handling rare threats, while the combination of attention and adaptive fusion achieves both accuracy and efficiency.

4.4 *Computational efficiency*

Efficiency is critical for real-time intrusion detection.

HAR-LSTM achieves a 124.8% increase in throughput compared to CNN-LSTM, while reducing GPU memory usage by 16.7%. Its 8.4 MB model size makes it suitable for both cloud and edge deployments [14][15].

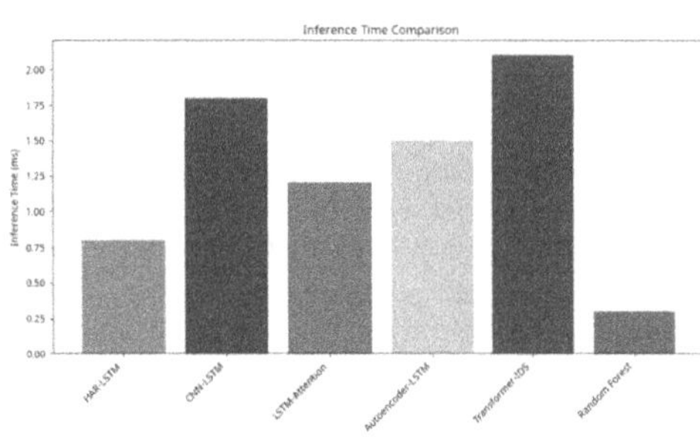

Figure 3. Inference time comparison.

4.5 *Visualization for SOC deployment*

To enhance operational interpretability, HAR-LSTM's predictions were visualized.

Confusion Matrix Heatmap – Confusion matrix heatmap illustrates HAR-LSTM's per-class detection accuracy, highlighting strong performance across 15 attack categories.

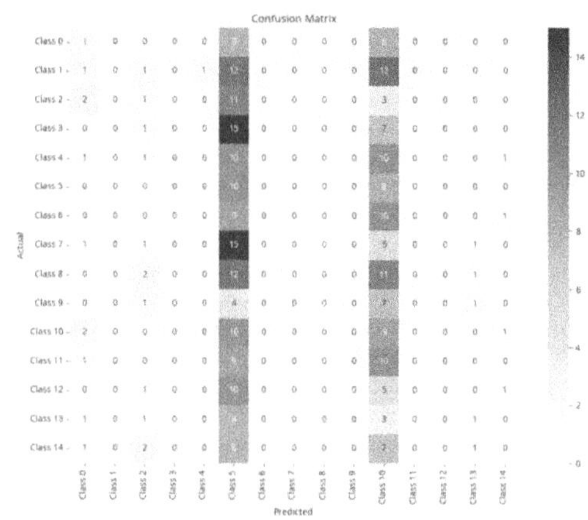

Figure 4. Confusion matrix heatmap.

Bar Chart Comparison – Side-by-side bars highlight discrepancies between actual and predicted instances across attack categories, enabling quick anomaly spotting.

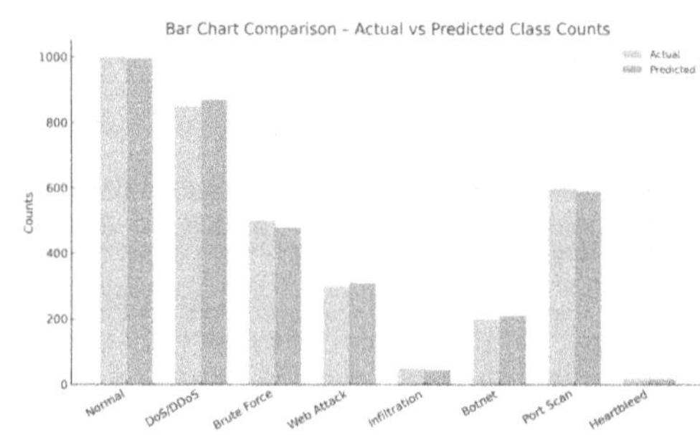

Figure 5. Bar chart of predicted vs actual class counts.

Attack-Type Filters – Horizontal bar chart with slicer-style view illustrating per-attack detection accuracy, allowing targeted analysis of specific threats.

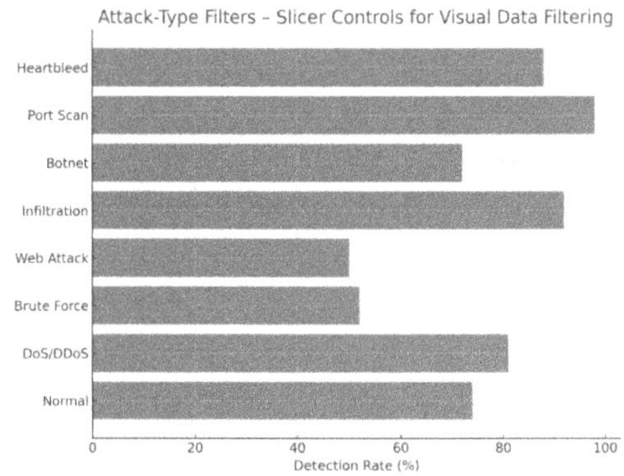

Figure 6. Attack-type filters.

4.6 *Dataset limitations and generalization considerations*

Although the CIC-IDS2017 dataset is widely used and provides a strong benchmark for intrusion detection studies, it has certain limitations that must be considered when interpreting results and assessing practical applicability.

Temporal and Technological Limitations: The dataset was collected in 2017 and therefore may not fully capture the characteristics of modern network environments. Cyber threats continue to evolve, with recent trends including AI-driven malware, advanced persistent threats (APTs), supply chain compromises, and zero-day exploits. Such attack patterns may differ significantly from those present in CIC-IDS2017, reducing the dataset's ability to represent today's real-world threat landscape.

Controlled Environment Constraints: CIC-IDS2017 was generated under a laboratory setup, which lacks the diversity and unpredictability of live enterprise networks. In real systems, traffic patterns are influenced by factors such as user behavior, application mix, and network topology. These variations are difficult to replicate in controlled environments, which may limit generalizability.

Attack Representation Gaps: While the dataset includes 14 attack types, some modern techniques are absent, particularly polymorphic and adaptive attacks that disguise themselves in legitimate traffic. This raises challenges for ensuring that models trained solely on this dataset remain effective against novel and adaptive threats.

Strategies for Enhancing Generalization: To address these limitations and strengthen applicability, several strategies are proposed:

Cross-Dataset Validation: Future work should test the HAR-LSTM model on other datasets such as UNSW-NB15, CSE-CIC-IDS2018, IoT-23, and real enterprise Security Information and Event Management (SIEM) logs. This would provide stronger evidence of generalization.

Transfer Learning and Domain Adaptation: The multi-order AR modules and adaptive fusion mechanisms can be fine-tuned for new environments, allowing the model to adjust to differences in traffic without retraining from scratch.

Zero-Day and Anomaly Detection: Since HAR-LSTM captures temporal dependencies at multiple scales, it has the potential to identify unusual patterns even for previously unseen attacks. Extending it with online learning methods can further enhance zero-day detection.

Continuous Learning: Incorporating mechanisms for incremental model updates, guided by live traffic and threat intelligence, would allow the system to remain effective as attack strategies evolve.

Deployment Considerations: For practical use in enterprise environments, organizations should validate the model against their historical network data, introduce a gradual rollout with analyst feedback, and establish a cycle of periodic updates based on emerging threats. Integration with SIEM tools can also provide context-aware validation in operational settings.

By acknowledging these limitations and suggesting ways to overcome them, this study provides a balanced view of the HAR-LSTM framework's strengths and its scope for future development in real-world cybersecurity applications.

5 CONCLUSION

5.1 *Dataset limitations and generalization*

While the CIC-IDS2017 dataset is widely used for IDS research, it has several limitations. To address reviewer concerns and ensure generalization, the following strategies are proposed:

Table 4. Dataset limitations and mitigation strategies.

Limitation	Impact	Mitigation Strategy
Dated dataset (2017)	May not capture modern threats like AI-driven malware or APTs	Extend evaluation to newer datasets (UNSW-NB15, CSE-CIC-IDS2018, IoT-23)
Lab-generated traffic	Lacks noise/variability of real enterprise networks	Validate with enterprise logs and SOC-collected traffic
Limited zero-day attacks	Poor generalization to unseen threats	Use anomaly detection + zero-day aware modules
Static training data	Cannot adapt to evolving attacks	Apply transfer learning, domain adaptation, and continuous online updates
Dataset imbalance	Minority classes underrepresented (e.g., Heartbleed, Infiltration)	Employ adaptive fusion + re-sampling to boost rare attack detection

This study introduced a Hybrid Auto-Regressive Long Short-Term Memory (HAR-LSTM) network with adaptive attention for next-generation cyber threat detection. The proposed model systematically integrates multi-order auto-regressive (AR) components, bidirectional LSTM layers, and multi-head individual attention to apprehend both linear and non-linear temporal dependencies in network traffic. When evaluated on the CIC-IDS2017 dataset [32], HAR-LSTM achieved 99.63% accuracy, 99.31% precision, 99.42% recall, and 99.37% F1-score, outperforming established baselines such as CNN-LSTM [8], Transformer-based IDS [10], and Autoencoder-LSTM [9]. Notably, the model achieved significant improvements in detecting rare attacks—+4.3% for Heartbleed and +3.3% for Infiltration—demonstrating robustness in highly imbalanced scenarios [7][17].

In addition to high accuracy, the model's 0.8 ms inference time, 8.4 MB size, and low GPU memory footprint make it suitable for deployment in Security Operations Centers (SOCs) and edge computing environments [14][15].

By combining multi-scale temporal modeling, context-aware attention, and real-time processing, HAR-LSTM addresses major limitations in current intrusion detection research and offers a practical, scalable, and adaptive framework for enterprise-level cybersecurity [2][21].

6 FUTURE SCOPE

While the proposed HAR-LSTM framework demonstrates outstanding accuracy, adaptability, and real-time capabilities, several enhancements can further extend its applicability in operational cybersecurity environments:

Real-Time Streaming Integration: Incorporating frameworks such as Apache Kafka or Apache Spark Streaming can enable continuous, low-latency intrusion detection, making the system suitable for high-throughput enterprise and cloud-based deployments [14][15].

Federated Learning for Privacy-Preserving IDS: Utilizing federated learning enables collaborative model training among various enterprises while safeguarding sensitive raw traffic data, improving threat intelligence sharing while preserving privacy [17].

Zero-Day and Adaptive Threat Detection: Integrating unsupervised and semi-supervised learning approaches, such as GAN-based anomaly detection, can enhance the model's capacity to identify previously unobserved (zero-day) attacks [12][16].

Edge and IoT Deployment Optimization: Implementing model compression methods such as pruning, quantization, and knowledge distillation helps diminish computing expenses, enabling HAR-LSTM to run efficiently on IoT gateways, 5G network edges, and resource-constrained devices.

By following these guidelines, the HAR-LSTM architecture can transform into a completely adaptive system, distributed, and explainable intrusion detection system, capable of protecting next-generation network infrastructures against increasingly complex and evolving cyber threats.

REFERENCES

[1] Markkandeyan, S., Ananth, A.D., Rajakumaran, M., Gokila, R. G., Venkatesan, R., and Lakshmi, B. (2025). Novel hybrid deep learning based cyber security threat detection model with optimization algorithm. *Cyber Security and Applications*, 3, 100075. https://doi.org/10.1016/j.csa.2024.100075

[2] Liu, Y., Li, S., Wang, X., and Xu, L. (2024). A review of hybrid cyber threats modelling and detection using artificial intelligence in IIoT. *CMES – Computer Modeling in Engineering and Sciences*, 140(2), 1233–1261. https://doi.org/10.32604/cmes.2024.046473

[3] Chandran, P., and Sunil, K.S. (2025). Safeguarding water distribution systems: Cyber-physical attack detection using rectilinear hybrid belief classifier network. *Journal of Water Process Engineering*, 76, 108131. https://doi.org/10.1016/j.jwpe.2025.108131

[4] Naik, R.L., Jain, S., and Bairam, M. (2025). A heuristic assisted cyber attack detection system using multi-scale and attention-based adaptive hybrid network. *Journal of Information Security and Applications*, 89, 103970. https://doi.org/10.1016/j.jisa.2025.103970

[5] Bensaoud, A., and Kalita, J. (2025). Optimized detection of cyber-attacks on IoT networks via hybrid deep learning models. *Ad Hoc Networks*, 170, 103770. https://doi.org/10.1016/j.adhoc.2025.103770

[6] Irshad, E., and Siddiqui, A.B. (2024). Context-aware cyber-threat attribution based on hybrid features. *ICT Express*, 10(3), 553–569. https://doi.org/10.1016/j.icte.2024.04.005

[7] Latif, M.A., Mushtaq, Z., Rahman, S., Arif, S., Mursal, S.N.F., Irfan, M., and Aziz, H. (2025). Oversampling-enhanced feature fusion-based hybrid ViT-1DCNN model for ransomware cyber attack detection. *CMES – Computer Modeling in Engineering and Sciences*, 142(2), 1667–1695. https://doi.org/10.32604/cmes.2024.056850

[8] Bamber, S.S., Katkuri, A.V.R., Sharma, S., and Angurala, M. (2025). A hybrid CNN-LSTM approach for intelligent cyber intrusion detection system. *Computers & Security*, 148, 104146. https://doi.org/10.1016/j.cose.2024.104146

[9] Jeffrey, N., Tan, Q., and Villar, J.R. (2024). A hybrid methodology for anomaly detection in Cyber–Physical Systems. *Neurocomputing*, 568, 127068. https://doi.org/10.1016/j.neucom.2023.127068

[10] Elzaghmouri, B.M., Jbara, Y.H.F., Elaiwat, S., Innab, N., Osman, A.A.F., Ataelfadiel, M.A.M., Zawaideh, F.H., Alawneh, M.F., Al-Khateeb, A., and Abu-Zanona, M. (2024). A novel hybrid architecture for superior IoT threat detection through real IoT environments. *Computers, Materials & Continua*, 81(2), 2299–2316. https://doi.org/10.32604/cmc.2024.054836

[11] Liu, Y., and Li, S. (2023). Hybrid cyber threats detection using explainable AI in Industrial IoT. In *2023 International Conference on Human-Centered Cognitive Systems (HCCS)*, 1–6. https://doi.org/10.1109/HCCS59561.2023.10452621

[12] Gupta, A.K., Dixit, N., Kumar, S., Rawat, P., and Madhumita. (2024). A novel hybrid approach for threat detection in cyber security using AI algorithm. In *2024 International Conference on Computing, Sciences and Communications (ICCSC)*, 1–6. https://doi.org/10.1109/ICCSC62048.2024.10830401

[13] Boori, K.C., Jagtap, J., Singh, S.P., and Kumar, S. (2024). Detection of cyber attack in network using hybrid decision tree technique. In *2024 International Conference on Advances in Computing, Communication and Materials (ICACCM)*, 1–5. https://doi.org/10.1109/ICACCM61117.2024.11059015

[14] Gulomov, S.R., Khudayberganov, T.R., Turdiyev, T.T., Xasanov, A.B., and Raximov, R.R. (2025). Hybrid traffic filtering and anomaly detection model for next-generation networks. In *2025 IEEE Ural-Siberian Conference on Biomedical Engineering, Radioelectronics and Information Technology (USBEREIT)*, 150–154. https://doi.org/10.1109/USBEREIT65494.2025.11054242

[15] Jyothi, R., and Jagadeesha, R. (2024). Next-gen threat detection: Leveraging AI and cyber twin technologies for IoT security. In *2024 First International Conference on Software, Systems and Information Technology (SSITCON)*, 1–6. https://doi.org/10.1109/SSITCON62437.2024.10796384

[16] Lin, Y.-D., Lu, Y.-H., Hwang, R.-H., Lai, Y.-C., Sudyana, D., and Lee, W.-B. (2025). Evolving ML-based intrusion detection: Cyber threat intelligence for dynamic model updates. *IEEE Transactions on Machine Learning in Communications and Networking*, 3, 605–622. https://doi.org/10.1109/TMLCN.2025.3564587

[17] Danladi Sankara, K., Saritha, G., Elavarasi, S.A., Saradha, S., and Arul Kumar, D. (2024). A hybrid LSTM-GAN model for predictive cyber threat intelligence and anomaly detection. In *2024 International Conference on Integrated Intelligence and Communication Systems (ICIICS)*, 1–6. https://doi.org/10.1109/ICIICS63763.2024.10859600

[18] Preetam, S., Compastié, M., Daza, V., and Siddiqui, S. (2023). An approach for intelligent behaviour-based threat modelling with explanations. In *2023 IEEE Conference on Network Function Virtualization and Software Defined Networks (NFV-SDN)*, 197–200. https://doi.org/10.1109/NFVSDN59219.2023.10329587

[19] Wang, X., Liu, J., and Zhang, C. (2023). Network intrusion detection based on multi-domain data and ensemble-bidirectional LSTM. *EURASIP Journal on Information Security*, 2023(5). https://doi.org/10.1186/s13635-023-00139-y

[20] Salem, A.H., Azzam, S.M., and Emam, O.E., *et al.* (2024). Advancing cybersecurity: A comprehensive review of AI-driven detection techniques. *Journal of Big Data*, 11, 105. https://doi.org/10.1186/s40537-024-00957-y

[21] Sameera, D., Koushik, G., Shaik, I., and Richard, M. (2024). Cyber attacks detection in network using deep learning techniques. In *2024 10th International Conference on Communication and Signal Processing (ICCSP)*, 1627–1632. IEEE. https://doi.org/10.1109/ICCSP60870.2024.10543651

[22] University of New Brunswick (2017). CICIDS2017 dataset. Available at: https://www.unb.ca/cic/datasets/ids-2017.html

Next-Generation Smart Systems – Sekhar et al. (Eds)
© 2027 The Author(s), ISBN: 978-1-041-34234-2

AI-Powered Demand Forecasting for Emerging Retail Trends

Subramanya Bharathvamsi Koneti
Governors State University, USA

Mohanraju Muppala
Marine IT Technologies, India

Shashipurna Kurapati
The University of Texas at Dallas, USA

ABSTRACT: Accurately predicting demand for new products remains a challenge in dynamic retail environments. This study introduces a machine learning-driven forecasting model that integrates historical sales patterns with product attributes to enhance predictive accuracy. By leveraging deep learning and gradient boosted models, the framework identifies key merchandising factors influencing demand. Experimental evaluations demonstrate the model's effectiveness in optimizing inventory planning and reducing overproduction, providing a scalable solution for retail businesses.

1 INTRODUCTION

Anticipating consumer demand in the fashion retail sector presents substantial challenges due to rapidly shifting preferences, extensive product development timelines often exceeding eight months, the necessity for bulk production to minimize costs, intense pricing competition, and escalating promotional expenditures. Traditional merchandising decisions are typically made with limited foresight into upcoming fashion trends, competitor assortments, or the effectiveness of pricing and marketing tactics [1], [2]. As a result, inaccurate forecasting may lead to substantial financial losses through overstocking, markdown costs, or lost sales opportunities, while also contributing to sustainability concerns through excessive inventory and waste generation [3], [4].Conventional approaches to demand forecasting in retail rely heavily on statistical time-series models such as ARIMA, exponential smoothing, and seasonality decomposition techniques [5], [6]. These models perform reasonably well when sufficient historical sales records are available, particularly for staple or recurring merchandise. However, they fall short in predicting the demand of newly launched or fashion-sensitive products, where historical data is sparse or entirely absent [7], [8]. The unique nature of fashion demand, where multiple product attributes—such as color, material, style, brand positioning, and promotional visibility—interact in a non-linear manner, renders purely time-series approaches inadequate [9], [10]. Industry practice still relies heavily on the subjective judgment of merchandisers and domain experts, who extrapolate from market observations, competitive assortments, and experiential intuition [1], [2]. While such expertise offers contextual insights, it often varies significantly between individuals and tends to be confined to specific product categories, thereby limiting comprehensive assessment across the entire assortment. This siloed forecasting approach restricts the ability to recognize broader market-level phenomena such as product cannibalization, substitution effects, or saturation trends, leading to systematic inefficiencies in retail planning [11], [12]. Furthermore, inaccurate or biased demand forecasting has implications beyond profitability, as it drives overproduction and accelerates the environmental footprint of the global apparel industry [13].In light of these challenges, recent research has explored advanced machine learning and deep learning approaches for retail forecasting. Ensemble methods such as Random Forests, Gradient Boosted Trees, and CatBoost have shown promise in handling heterogeneous feature spaces and capturing nonlinear interactions across merchandising, promotional, and product attributes [14], [15]. Meanwhile, deep learning models such as Long Short-Term Memory (LSTM) networks and Multilayer Perceptrons (MLPs) have been applied to capture sequential dependencies and high-dimensional patterns in consumer behavior [6], [8]. Despite their promise, the scalability of such models in production retail pipelines remains an open question, as computational efficiency, training cost, and interpretability are critical constraints in large-scale deployments [16], [17].To address these issues, the present study proposes a machine learning-driven forecasting framework that integrates advanced tree-based models with deep learning architectures for predicting sales of previously unlisted fashion items. By incorporating both intrinsic product attributes and extrinsic merchandising variables, the proposed approach aims to bridge the gap between methodological innovation and real-world applicability. The methodology and model configurations are elaborated in the subsequent sections, followed by empirical analysis using real-world datasets to validate effectiveness across diverse product categories.

2 REVIEW OF RELATED APPROACHES

Traditional approaches to demand projection in retail have heavily relied on time series techniques, which extrapolate future values based on established historical trends. Such techniques, however, fail to provide reliable outputs for entirely new products. Preliminary methods—such as mean forecasts, seasonality adjustments, diffusion models like the Bass model, and life-cycle approximations—fall short when applied to transient and non-durable fashion items. Earlier propositions for new product forecasting involved clustering historical sales trajectories and assigning new entries to these clusters via decision trees. However, application of this technique to fashion retail data revealed inadequate clustering performance—items launched simultaneously grouped together regardless of their intrinsic features, price, or discount strategies. Furthermore, even visually or descriptively similar items exhibited disparate sales behaviors, underscoring the influence of holistic perceptions involving brand positioning, promotional strategy, and display prominence.

DOI: 10.1201/9781042001767-33

3 PROPOSED TECHNIQUES

Although visual and descriptive similarity does not necessarily imply similar consumer responses, the data exhibits repeated patterns among groups of items influenced by complex interactions of pricing, marketing, and visual presentation. The forecast model is designed to recognize these intricate patterns across latent variables, integrating temporal aspects such as discounts and marketing changes.

The sales prediction function can be represented as: $y\hat{}i,t = g\,(\mathbf{A}i, \mathbf{M}i, t{:}t-p, \mathbf{D}i, t{:}t-p)$ (1) where $y\hat{}_{i,t}$ denotes the predicted sales for item i at time t, $\mathbf{A}_i$ captures item-level characteristics (e.g., color, material), $\mathbf{M}_{i,t:t-p}$ includes merchandising metrics over time (e.g., discounts, promotions), and $\mathbf{D}_{i,t:t-p}$ consists of derived temporal features (e.g., trend, seasonality). Here, p indicates the number of previous time steps considered.

Given the limitations of conventional models, advanced techniques such as ensemble learning (Random Forests, Gradient Boosted Trees) and neural networks (Multi-Layer Perceptrons and Long Short-Term Memory networks) are employed. The MLP and LSTM model structures are depicted in Figure 1. Retail datasets often show a long-tail distribution where a small subset of items generates the majority of sales, resulting in significant variability. To mitigate this, models are trained under different transformations (logarithmic and linear) and loss metrics. Table 1 outlines the configurations.

Table 1. Specifications of forecast models.

Model Type	Optimization Objective
Random Forest	Mean Squared Error (MSE)
Gradient Boosted Trees	MSE, Huber
LightGBM	MSE, Poisson
CatBoost	MSE, Poisson
XGBoost	MSE, Poisson
Embedding + MLP	MSE, Poisson
Embedding + LSTM	MSE, Poisson

To model sequential dependencies, lagged inputs are used for up to four previous periods ($p = 4$), as determined empirically. Tree-based methods are optimized via Bayesian search techniques. The LSTM network, trained in a sequenceto-sequence fashion, utilizes entire lifecycle data for each.

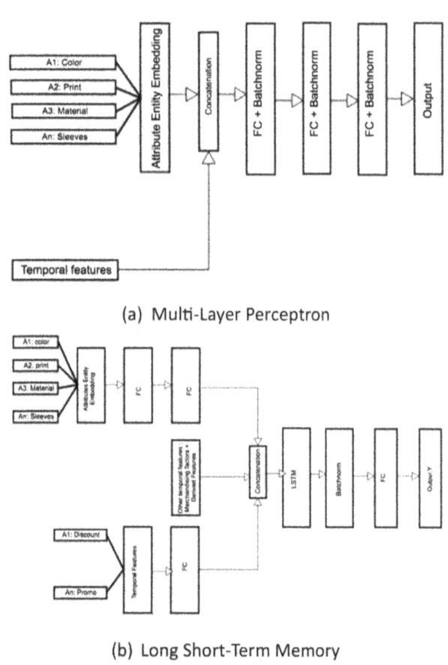

Figure 1. Architectures of deep neural models.

Style without explicit lags, benefiting from techniques such as dropout and batch normalization to enhance generalization.

The implementation leverages PyTorch for neural networks, and standard Python libraries (Scikit-learn, LightGBM, CatBoost, XGBoost) for tree models. Training is performed on a virtual environment equipped with six CPUs and one GPU.

4 EXPERIMENT AND FINDINGS

4.1 *Dataset description*

The investigation utilized archival transaction data from Myntra, a prominent Indian online fashion retailer. Model training involved five distinctive product categories, each representing a classification tier where items exhibit similar characteristics. Examples include Shirts, Casual Shoes, Tops, and Kurtas. The term "style" is interchangeably used to refer to individual entries within these groups.

Only products introduced within the previous two calendar years were incorporated. The training set comprises items launched during the initial year, whereas validation data were extracted from entries introduced in the subsequent six-month interval. The model's hyperparameters were optimized through standard validation protocols. Finally, an evaluation dataset covering the following half-year period was employed to gauge performance. The sequence lengths for each item vary due to differential availability spans. A summary of minimum and maximum series counts and their respective durations per article type is presented in Table 2.

Table 2. Time series characteristics by dataset.

Dataset	Min TS Count	Max TS Count	Min TS Length	Max TS Length
Training	12,541	42,206	4	104
Validation	7,489	29,669	4	52
Testing	6,732	18,364	4	26

The models integrated external covariates such as promotional activities, markdowns, and product visibility metrics, alongside intrinsic product characteristics. Since future values for some of these regressors are not known in advance, they were transformed to facilitate approximation using default projections.

Fashion Features: Attributes such as color and material were encoded to retain semantic patterns and enable comparison across items. Embedding strategies included onehot encoding with consolidation of infrequent values into a placeholder token.

Merchandising Variables: Discount features were defined as deviations from both brand-specific and platform-wide means. Visibility scores were derived from page impression counts normalized by brand and platform exposure. Promotional timing was modeled using countdowns to and from known retail event dates, reflecting behavioral lulls and surges in consumer engagement.

Derived Variables: These included style lifecycle (age), Fourier-transformed seasonal patterns, and trend indicators. Cannibalization effects were captured via metrics such as intrabrand and inter-brand product counts released in parallel.

4.2 *Evaluation metrics*

Forecast accuracy was primarily assessed using the weighted Mean Absolute Percentage Error (wMAPE), defined as:

$$\text{wMAPE} = \frac{\sum_{i=1}^{n}\sum_{t=1}^{T_i} |\hat{y}_{it} - y_{it}|}{\sum_{i=1}^{n}\sum_{t=1}^{T_i} y_{it}} \tag{2}$$

where y_{it} and $y\hat{}_{it}$ denote observed and predicted sales for item i at time t, and T_i represents the time series length for item i.

To evaluate correlation and ranking performance, Pearson's correlation coefficient (ρ) and Kendall's Tau (τ) were computed:

$$\frac{\rho = \mathbb{E}[y\hat{y}] - \mathbb{E}[y]\mathbb{E}[\hat{y}]}{\sqrt{(\mathbb{E}[y^2] - \mathbb{E}[y]^2)(\mathbb{E}[\hat{y}^2] - \mathbb{E}[\hat{y}]^2)}} \tag{3}$$

$$\tau = \frac{P - Q}{\sqrt{(P + Q + T)(P + Q + U)}} \tag{4}$$

Here, P and Q are the counts of concordant and discordant item pairs, while T and U are the tie counts in actual and predicted values respectively.

Loss functions used during training included:

$$\text{MSE} = \frac{\sum_{i=1}^{n}\sum_{t=1}^{T_i}(\hat{y}_{it} - y_{it})^2}{\sum_{i=1}^{n} T_i} \tag{5}$$

$$\text{Poisson Loss} = \sum_{i=1}^{n}\sum_{t=1}^{T_i}(\hat{y}_{it} - y_{it}\log(\hat{y}_{it})) \tag{6}$$

$$\text{Huber Loss} = \begin{cases} \frac{1}{2}(\hat{y}_{it} - y_{it})^2 & \text{if} |\hat{y}_{it} - y_{it}| \le \delta \\ \delta\left(|\hat{y}_{it} - y_{it}| - \frac{1}{2}\delta\right) & \text{otherwise} \end{cases} \tag{7}$$

Poisson and Huber losses were used to manage long-tail effects and mitigate outlier influence respectively.

4.3 *Empirical outcomes*

As it display comparative results for Shirts and Casual Shoes across several modeling approaches. Additional outcomes are located in the Appendix.

Table 3. Forecasting accuracy for shirts across 16,409 time-series Samples.

Model	Loss Function	wMAPE	PearsonR	Kendall Tau	Article Type
Naive (Avg. weekly sales)	-	.97	.82	.39	.43
XGBoost	Modified MSE	.52	.38	.00	.76
GBRT	Enhanced Huber	.54	.41	.06	.76
LSTM	Poisson Loss	.56	.42	.17	.67
CatBoost	Adjusted MSE	.56	.42	.04	.73
LGBM	Revised MSE	.57	.43	.03	.74

Tree-based learners, particularly XGBoost optimized with log-scale MSE, demonstrated superior performance, followed by Gradient Boosted Regression Trees (GBRT). Among neural networks, LSTM architectures trained with Poisson loss yielded favorable outcomes.

Illustrative examples highlight model behavior: Figure 3(a) depicts strong agreement, while Figure 3(b) shows minor deviation attributed to promotion timing. Figure 3(c) reflects significant divergence due to atypical brand-specific behavior.

Transformed inputs had notable effects on outcomes. Figure 3 Shows enhanced forecasts with increased discounts, elevated visibility scores, and reduced accuracy under high cannibalization.

Table 4. Forecasting accuracy for casual shoes across 6,732 time-series samples.

Model	Loss Function	wMAPE	PearsonR	Kendall Tau	Article Type
Naive (Avg. weekly sales)	-	1.00	.85	.43	.46
XGBoost	Modified MSE	.51	.38	.11	.74
GBRT	Enhanced Huber	.52	.38	.15	.74
CatBoost	Adjusted MSE	.52	.38	.10	.71
LGBM	Revised MSE	.54	.39	.05	.71
XGBoost	Poisson Loss	.56	.40	.04	.67

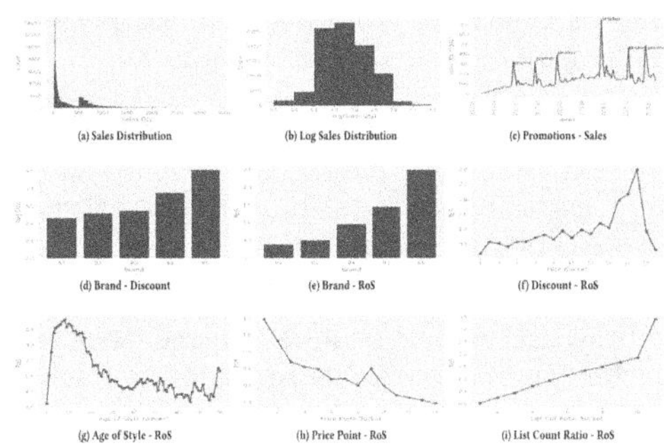

Figure 2. Illustrative forecasting examples.

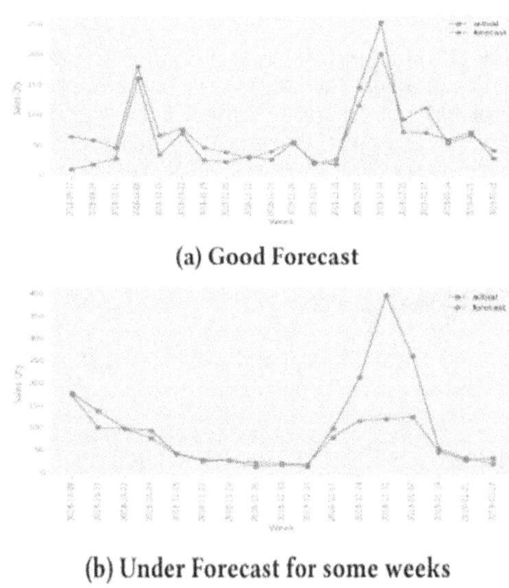

Figure 3. Observed vs. Estimated: (a) wMAPE = 0.34 signifies a highly accurate forecast, (b) wMAPE = 0.37 reflects moderate underestimation during select intervals, (c) wMAPE = 0.63 denotes significant forecasting inaccuracies

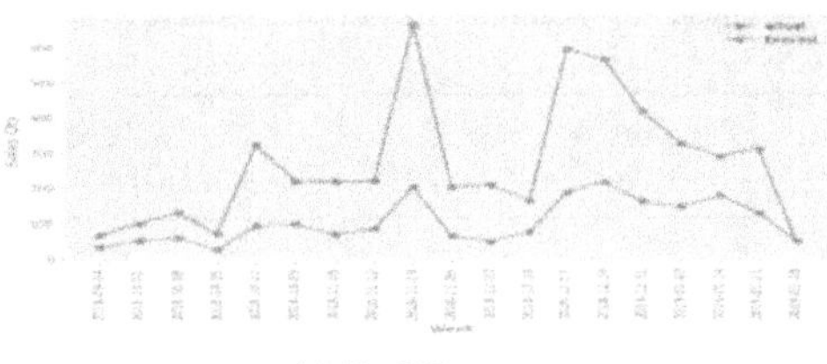

(c) Bad Forecast

Figure 3. (Continued)

4.4 *Industrial integration*

The predictive system has been trialed in multiple operational scenarios

- Seasonal Inventory Planning: By simulating potential combinations of product attributes, the model guided budget allocation decisions for two major brands, resulting in measurable improvements in sell-through rates.
- Assortment Optimization for Roadshows: Forecasts were provided for product selection during brand exhibitions, supporting decision-making alongside human judgment.
- Drop Scheduling: Data-driven scheduling of product deliveries into warehouses based on weekly forecasts was explored, replacing rigid, time-based delivery cycles.

4.5 *Baseline methods*

To ensure a fair comparison, the proposed models were benchmarked against several standard baselines widely used in time-series forecasting. These include:

- Naive Forecast: Assumes future demand equals the most recent observation. Despite its simplicity, it often performs surprisingly well for short horizons [5].
- Seasonal Naive Forecast: Extends the naive method by repeating values from the same period of the previous season, making it suitable for capturing strong seasonality effects [5].
- Croston's Method: Designed specifically for intermittent demand, this method decomposes demand into separate estimates for the size and frequency of non-zero observations [18].
- Syntetos–Boylan Approximation (SBA): A refined variant of Croston's approach that corrects for bias and provides more stable forecasts under sparse demand conditions [12].
- ADIDA (Aggregate–Disaggregate Intermittent Demand Approach): Aggregates sparse series into coarser time intervals, applies traditional forecasting, and disaggregates results back to the original scale [19].

Performance of all baselines was reported using wMAPE, MASE, and sMAPE, along with 95% confidence intervals to capture variability. This ensures transparency and consistency in evaluating both traditional and machine learning models.

5 CONCLUSION AND FUTURE WORK

This research explored the challenge of forecasting demand for newly introduced fashion items, a problem that remains difficult due to short product lifecycles, high market volatility, and limited historical data. By evaluating a wide range of approaches, including gradient-boosted decision trees and deep neural architectures, the study demonstrated that treebased models consistently deliver competitive performance while maintaining efficiency, scalability, and interpretability. Their ability to balance predictive accuracy with reduced computational overhead makes them particularly well suited for integration into retail production pipelines, where latency and resource constraints are critical. In contrast, deep learning models, although powerful in capturing complex temporal dependencies, exhibited higher training costs and inconsistent improvements, underscoring the trade-offs between expressiveness and operational feasibility. These findings highlight that model choice should not be driven solely by accuracy, but also by considerations of scalability, reliability, and deployment readiness in real-world retail environments.

Future work will build upon these insights in several promising directions. First, the experimental scope will be broadened to include additional statistical and intermittent-demand baselines, such as Croston's method and Seasonal Na·ıve forecasting, thereby ensuring a fairer comparative framework. Evaluation metrics will also be expanded to incorporate MASE and sMAPE, reported with confidence intervals to provide a more rigorous understanding of performance variability. Second, attention will be given to hybrid multimodal architectures that integrate textual metadata and visual descriptors of products. Preliminary experiments suggest that incorporating image-based embeddings can enhance forecasting accuracy by approximately 5% in select categories, indicating strong potential for further exploration. Third, future investigations will focus on developing optimized recurrent and attentionbased neural architectures capable of handling highly sparse or irregular retail time series, while also ensuring resource efficiency. Finally, the study envisions exploring large-scale deployment strategies, including distributed training and realtime inference pipelines, to facilitate adoption in dynamic e-commerce ecosystems. Together, these directions aim to bridge methodological innovation with industrial applicability, moving closer to demand forecasting systems that are not only accurate but also sustainable and scalable in practice.

REFERENCES

[1] McKinsey & Company, (2024), *The state of fashion 2024*, https:// www. mckinsey.com/industries/retail/our-insights/state-of-fashion-2024.

[2] Heuritech, (2025), *Fashion forecasting: A comprehensive guide for 2025*, https://heuritech.com/articles/fashion-forecasting/.

[3] Vogue Business, (2024), *Four new ways that ai is changing fashion*, https://www.voguebusiness.com/story/technology/four-new-ways-that-ai-is-changing-fashion.

[4] Ivanov D., Tsipoulanidis A., and Schonberger J., (2017), *Global Supply Chain and Operations Management*. Springer.

[5] Hyndman R.J. and Athanasopoulos G., (2013), *Forecasting: Principles and Practice*. Melbourne, Australia: OTexts.

[6] Hewamalage H., Bergmeir C., and Bandara K., (2021), Recurrent neural networks for time series forecasting: current status and future directions, *International Journal of Forecasting*, vol. 37, no. 1, pp. 388–427.

[7] Reddypogu V.B. and D.P. U., (2025), Demand forecasting in e-commerce fashion retail: A comparative study of generative ai, lstm and arima models, *Journal of Information Systems Engineering and Management*, vol. 10, no. 18s.

[8] Giri C. and Chen Y., (2022), Deep learning for demand forecasting in the fashion and apparel retail industry, *Forecasting*, vol. 4, pp. 565–581.

[9] Kunz M. *et al.*, (May 2023), Deep learning based forecasting: a case study from the online fashion industry, *arXiv preprint arXiv:2305.14406*.

[10] Hajirahimi Z., Khashei M., and Hamadani A., (2023), Principal componentbased hybrid model for time series forecasting, *International Journal of Information Technology*.

[11] Kiefer D. *et al.*, (2021), Demand forecasting intermittent and lumpy time series: Comparing statistical, ml and deep learning methods, in *Proceedings of the 54th Hawaii International Conference on System Sciences*.

[12] Syntetos A.A. and Boylan J.E., (2005), The accuracy of intermittent demand estimates, *International Journal of Forecasting*, vol. 21, no. 2, pp. 303– 314.
[13] The Business of Fashion and McKinsey & Company, "The state of fashion 2024," https://www.mckinsey.com/industries/retail/our-insights/ state-of-fashion-2024, 2024.
[14] Muppala, Mohanraju. *Artificial Intelligence and Machine Learning in Maritime Shipping*.n.d
[15] GeeksforGeeks, *Demand forecasting in retail using catboost*, https://www.geeksforgeeks.org/ demand-forecasting-in-retail-using-catboost-1/, 2024.
[16] Avogaro A., Capogrosso L., Fummi F., and Cristani M., (Dec. 2024), Dif4ff: Leveraging multimodal diffusion models and graph neural networks for accurate new fashion product performance forecasting, *arXiv preprint arXiv:2412.05566*.
[17] ——, (Dec. 2024), Mdiff: Exploiting multimodal score-based diffusion models for new fashion product performance forecasting, *arXiv preprint arXiv:2412.06840*.
[18] Muppala, Mohanraju. (2025). Artificial Intelligence, IoT, and Sensor Technologies for Marine Monitoring and Climate Resilience. *Digital Oceans: Artificial Intelligence, IoT, and Sensor Technologies for Marine Monitoring and Climate Resilience*| Deep Science Publishing.
[19] Nicholson A.E., Trapero J.R., and Koning A.J., (2017), Improving forecasting for intermittent demand by aggregating data, *International Journal of Production Economics*, vol. 193, pp. 24–36.

Next-Generation Smart Systems – Sekhar et al. (Eds)
© 2027 The Author(s), ISBN: 978-1-041-34234-2

Harnessing the Power of Linear Regression in Predictive Modelling

P. Bharath Kumar Chowdary
Professor at VNR Vignana Jyothi Institute of Engineering and Technology, Hyderabad, India

M.V.S.L. Satvik
Student at VNR Vignana Jyothi Institute of Engineering and Technology, Hyderabad, India

ABSTRACT: Agriculture is the backbone for India's economy with many relying on subsistence farming. As technology advances it is transforming agriculture, enabling data-driven approaches to achieve sustainability. Key attributes such as soil health, rainfall patterns, crop conditions, and mutualistic crop relationships are critical in enhancing agricultural productivity. Traditional farming methods have been highly effective but now require technological support for further optimization. One such modern approach involves the cultivation of mutualistic crops where crop pairings like corn and beans etc. will improve soil fertility, reduce pests and increase yield without heavy reliance on chemicals. Among soil types loamy soil stands out as ideal for crop growth due to its balanced composition of sand, silt and clay making it highly fertile and well drained. Integrating this with smart farming technologies, such as predictive models and machine learning, allows for precise decision making regarding resource allocation, pest control and yield optimization. Advanced methods like these are opening new doors for sustainable agricultural practices ensuring food security and economic growth.

Keywords: Agriculture, sustainability, prediction, yield, attributes, loamy soil, machine learning, mutualistic yield

1 INTRODUCTION

Technology has advanced in each and every sector, but when it comes to a discussion with respect to agriculture, we can't come up with a better solution as we have lack of interest and lack of knowledge in that sector. Years have taken to implement the recent trends in the sector which is the backbone of our economy. Nowadays initiative has been taken and it increased the pace of technology in agriculture, numerous methods have been implemented and that changed the perspective. This sector mainly contributes to the country's GDP. Agriculture is a sector where innovative thinking and exploration becomes a part, we can try and test innovatively by using some methods. But while testing we can see some challenges where our creativity stops. In agriculture yield prediction plays a huge role and prediction of yield depends on various factors. Previous days to grow different crops we needed to wait until the season occurred and that made slash burn cultivation come into picture. Every attribute has some importance in yield prediction, where to grow a crop all attributes(like climate, soil quality, crop variety etc.). We need to analyze the attributes with respect to the growth of a crop and that has been lacking in primitive agriculture. Agriculture is like a separate world where the interactions will be with soil, climate, rainfall etc. Now a days interests have been changed for humans and addicting to online screen has became a fashion. That's making to think if we say the word farming, because no awareness is being created now a days.

1.1 *Technologies can be used*

Generally, technology playing an important part in human life it making good and as well as a bad impact on humans and mainly it plays with minds of human and it outplays them. But when we come to agriculture there is a good will for technology, with help of technology human intervention reduced and machine power increased at rapid pace. There are certain technologies making an impact in agriculture.

- Precision agriculture.
- Internet of things(IoT).
- Robotics and automation.
- Artificial Intelligence and Machine learning.

Not only these there are more methods in technology where we can use on a particular problem. Usage of these have improved the efficiency and accuracy, and over sustainability has been improved.

Figure 1. Analysis of mutualistic crop's.

This research on crop yield prediction has given me some valuable inputs for my research, as in agriculture this yield prediction is so important that the future of the crop depends on it. Traditional methods are wayback methods where nowadays they have been replaced with modern methods, yet 60% of the population using a combination of traditional and modern methods. As we go deep into the research attributes are one main thing which are important in this sector, those attributes decide the growth of the crop. Climate, soil, rainfall, temperature etc. all will contribute up to their level for prediction of yield. Contents of soil, water are important and machine learning methods mainly provide statistical and useful insights

DOI: 10.1201/9781042001767-34

about the predicted output. SVM, Random Forest, decision tree, naive bayes are some algorithms which have been used for an accurate output, though there are some challenges like pest or disease detection, continuous monitoring of soil etc. These methods can make some impact and inclusion with deep learning can give better results when compared to only ML. Low usage of resources with efficient results is most important in the prediction of yield.

In this yield prediction many researchers have done tremendous research related to attributes because those attributes are the main and important for a crop to predict it's yield. Agriculture is a sector where innovative thinking and exploration becomes a part we can test and try innovatively some methods, one of the method is mutualistic crop prediction method where we pair two or more crops in a season for better productivity and for better yield. In this method, the cultivation will become late because the pairing will happen between 2 crops which has different outcomes. But the productivity or sustainability will be more because each crop shares it's own characteristics with other crop to improve the yield or to improve the other crop's productivity. Three Sister's Crop is the best example for this, where we grow corn, beans and squash crops together on the same field or area, and we need to consider some factors like plant spacing, growth conditions etc. This process or method will help with respect to productivity but sometimes the resource usage will be more, because if we want to grow two crops together on the same soil, we need to consider important factors or attributes. If the resource usage is more, the cost of cultivation will be more but the yield or the output will be good.

2 RELATED WORK

Many researchers have implemented various crop yield predictions models using different methods, some of them are listed below.

The authors focussed on comparing the machine learning models to find which model is a best fit for the yield prediction using the accuracy for every model we decide which model has best fit for this prediction, if needed we can delete unwanted attributes also because those unwanted attributes may change the scenario of the model here authors used different models for crop prediction. Yield prediction is an crucial task in farming or in cultivation because it decides the future of a crop, as we discussed earlier attributes play an important role, each and every attribute has a unique feature which can be related to the prediction. Without the attributes we can't predict and it's going to be tough. 1.4 billion people relayed on the production of crops, the talk comes interesting when we include technology. Traditional methods have made a great impact on agriculture because farmers know how those methods work, but if we say the word technology farmers too possess some doubts and sometimes they show lack of interest.

The authors gave a framework on what is agriculture and how it contributes to India's GDP, in this There are many algorithms in machine learning, one of the most used algorithms is Support Vector Machine (SVM). Support Vector Machine, an algorithm where it will help to study, divide and classify the things in a hyperplane. It mainly works to classify the data, whether the attributes belong to the same data or not it will check and which is near enough to the line it will separate the data. If any new dataset is entered, this SVM will check and it sends the data which belongs to the dataset. If there are numerous features and attributes on a hyperplane this algorithm is capable of drawing a boundary.[1]

This paper includes critical parameters of soil and water content where both are the primary sources or important attributes in agriculture, one of the Bayesian model like, Gaussian process regression(GPR) is used, it is used not only in prediction it is used to solve the uncertainty issues in these predictions. Other algorithms like random forest, SVM are also used, nowadays integration of multiple models into a single model or single attribute has came into picture which is called ensemble learning. Average content of soil and water has to be maintained for a crop growth, statistical data here will play a pivotal role because to analyses the data and predict. In precision agriculture also this SWC(Soil Water Content) is used to precisely water the crops, this research particularly stressed about the content and the relationship between water and soil. [2]

Soil is another attribute where the creativity of farmers to grow a crop over a season we have seen numerous of farmers' crops have been dried up due to climatic conditions, machine learning algorithms need to predict each and every attribute which are related to crop, machine learning will predict each and every attribute from the input taken. Because it needs to analyze and come to a conclusion for the given input and then predict the output. Newly there has been hybrid models have been developed nowadays, accuracy will be improved and we get output what we predicted but main effort will be climate. Ultimately stakeholders and traders] will benefit and other side farmers will benefit.[3]

Prediction is a key issue in any sector not only in agriculture, prediction is like a prototype for any system before the required outcome is generated, Neurons are a major part in the deep learning process where these neurons are the link to connect the networks. Hardware requirements will be more because as it stores the more data some requirements will be more as compared to machine learning. Not all the methods in machine and deep learning have a good relationship with the attributes, some may not establish a complex relationship between the attributes because of their misunderstanding or lack of understanding between the attributes. These are considered as black boxes, there is another name for deep learning where we have not heard that name it is feature learning.[4]

Agriculture is an important factor for global economy, constant change of climatic conditions and global warming has an impact of yield sector. There is some interesting topic which nowadays becoming an important aspect in technical terms is deep learning. It is a subset of machine learning where the functions between ML and DL are somewhat different. This new and fancy technology can store large amounts of data and it can solve the non-linearity issue in machine learning, recently deep learning has gained popularity. Neurons play a major part in deep learning algo's like ANN, CNN, RNN, DNN have a specific impact, there are mainly several layers in deep learning architecture. Layers are linked with one another as the human brain is linked with neurons, In this research we have observed that machine learning models outplayed some deep learning models for better accuracy.[5]

This paper focusses on how agriculture economic stats play a crucial role in India. Algorithms have a good impact on any problem, we cannot say only some algorithms make a good impact, every algorithm has a different output associated with but having a great impact. Random Forest, decision tree naive bayes are some machine learning algorithms which can be applied if required on crop yield prediction, to manage the crops and to address the economic issue this yield prediction is so important in agriculture. Advanced technology including satellites have a way to predict the yield by giving accurate images of a crop through satellites so that it can cover a large part of the crop and improve the production of yield. Remote sensing and other different methods and ways make significant predictions.[6]

Artificial Intelligence and Machine learning are some new ongoing trends machine learning is a subset of Artificial Intelligence, AI has a capability to do how a human works. Machine learning is a path where we can deploy algorithms or models for a machine to mimic human intelligence. Some machine learning algorithms will make an impact in crop yield prediction, this yield prediction will help the farmers to grow crops. In yield prediction these all the attributes are like linked to one another; they establish relationship between attribute to attribute. To develop statistical models there are methods and some weakness will be established in this statistical model, machine learning advanced and regression are one of the methods where we can develop statistical model. As we have regression, we can have a single attribute to analyze the yield.[7]

This research focuses on how attributes decide the future of a crop, these can make a maximum impact on trading also, nowadays due to the ongoing global warming issues this climate is playing like hide and seek and not having a good relationship with agriculture. Climate is such an important feature where it can reduce the risk of crop yield prediction. As we know we can make some statistical reports in machine learning ,for climate also we need to make statistical reports to analyze or to reduce the risk of prediction. Subtle changes in temperature can make a big difference between these relationships. The accuracy of the attributes are time bound and they can change time to time over a season, we can't fix a particular standards in this type of methods because both attributes results are required to move forward. [8]

Many studies on agriculture sector especially on yield prediction have proved that machine learning is a more suitable and easy way where we can collect and store large amounts of dataset, crop sustainability is a factor in this sector, The main and utmost concern is yield prediction. There is one organization where they will not use machine learning to predict crop yield. This yield prediction can be a tough problem, claiming the natural resources and sustainability is an efficient issue in the yield prediction. Trends have been added and farming opportunities have increased and smart way of farming is an efficient way. It establishes relationship between the input data, we need to collect the data from attributes to estimate the yield for a particular crop, we can use particular algorithm for a particular prediction. [9]

This research paper has included about primitive farming and it's uses because it is an age old practice in agriculture, before the technology came into existence there was only one way in the areas we can see this type of farming. Primitive is the first or earliest way in agriculture where man work, domestic animals etc been used. Though all the technologies make an impact on every sector, basically in agriculture machine learning is an important tool to analyze the features and to give statistical data for the user. There are some attributes which are related to every method in agriculture, when we start to grow, soil is the first and foremost attribute to see whether the soil is suitable to grow a crop on a particular area. Deep Learning is also an efficient way in the yield prediction, here the question arises when we say deep learning. This research they have used both algorithms from machine learning and deep learning.[10]

The other important issue that is expected to remain relevant in the context of the growing world population is the enhancement of the management of agricultural lands. This simply means that to feed the ever growing population, more resources have to be put into practice for production through sustainable methods. The integration of larger detailed data sets will need improvements in data analysis for better reliable performances to support producers, managers, consultants and all the other stakeholders in the management of agricultural fields. [11]

Global agricultural production especially in regards food production, is becoming of growing concern to leading international organizations responsible for nutrition. With the rate at which the world's population is increasing, there is high demand for production hence food shortage in highly populated area like Africa. [12]

The CYP at field level is essential in quantitative and economic evaluations for formulating agricultural commodities plans for import-export strategies and increasing farmer's income. Cultivation animal husbandry and related activities are the main food provides to the humongous population of India besides being a strong pillar of the country. The architecture that were previously suggested for estimating crop yields are often manually constructed and when DL the approach is posed to professionals. [13]

Due to the fact that the statistical model in question is of a parametric kind, there are certain conditions to be fulfilled and all the models will not be able to accept independent features. In other words, based on mentioned characteristics the DNN framework in our design will have suitable structures and the corresponding hyperparameters. Hence it can meet a huge spectrum of architecture of DNN framework. [14]

A clear differentiation has to be made of the dataset used for purposes of prediction, having a training set and testing set. However this paper finds that the traditional studies have failed to tackle agricultural problems regarding in-adequate information on soil nutrition requirement, limited crop options and imprecise crop forecasting. Hence through the inter-fused machine learning approach with an enhanced ensemble model the prediction of various crops. [15]

3 PROPOSED METHODOLOGY

Up to now we have seen agriculture, it's daily life applications and real time uses, we have seen how technology has changed and making impact in each and every field. Certain researchers have come to an idea that what if we use technology in agriculture and how it is used in sustainability of crop. Some machine learning algorithms we have seen for a particular attribute in which we can determine the accuracy, but we tried other algorithm to develop the accuracy for this attribute which is called linear regression, particularly we have used this algorithm because of it's simplicity and low risk of overfitting we have calculated MAE, MSE and R^2 coefficient in which this linear regression algorithm is performing better than previous algorithms, it giving 87% of accuracy in which there is some competition between linear, random forest and support vector machine. This proposed algorithm giving somewhat more accuracy with respect to our dataset taken.

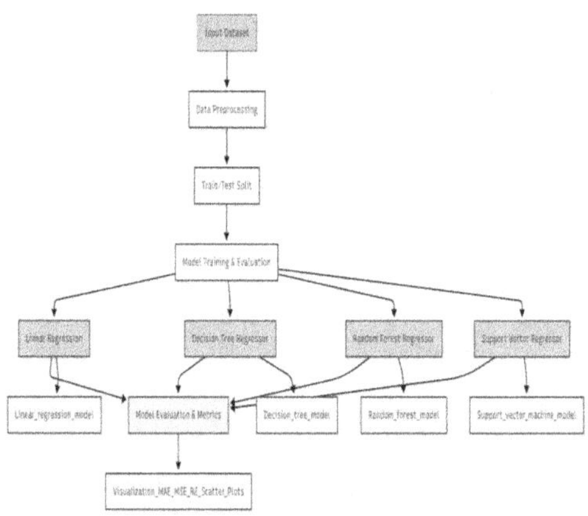

Figure 2. Proposed architecture.

3.1 *Architecture for proposed system*

This is the proposed architecture we used in our research where we trained the model using linear regression algorithm and evaluated the model.

3.2 *Brief overview about dataset*

In this we have taken dataset from Kaggle where all types of datasets are available in it, especially dataset's which are related to agriculture. It is a global online platform that hosts various repositories of datasets, we taken a dataset related to crop yield prediction in which attributes like temperature, rainfall, pH, types of soil are there. Each and every attribute has separate importance in agriculture and without all these attributes we can't predict the yield, so here we considered each attribute which is important.

In this we have pre-processed the data by verifying number of rows and columns then we calculated the values with yield, there are no missing values in the dataset we taken and next we applied is algorithms which are existed(decision tree, SVM, Random Forest) and predicted their accuracy with respect to our dataset we have taken.

3.3 *Discussions and challenges*

This research on crop yield prediction has given me some valuable inputs for my research, as in agriculture this yield prediction is so important that the future of the crop depends on it. Traditional methods are wayback methods where nowadays they have been replaced with modern methods, yet 60% of the population using a combination of traditional and modern methods. Linear regression has an effective way apart from other machine learning algorithms like Decision tree, Support Vector Machine (SVM) and Random Forest. In our model except Decision tree remaining algorithms had a competition between them in terms of accuracy because of their data intake, linear regression has slight advantage because of it's nature of data and simplicity of model and linear regression is not to be pruned to overfitting. Decision tree was least effective because of more overfitting, while random forest and SVM should strong performance, linear regression has simplicity interpretability make's it the preferred choice. Decision tree can be enhanced for a better accuracy by giving more data and main issue we need to address is to decrease over fitting. Traditional methods have made a great impact on agriculture because farmers know how those methods work, but if we say the word technology farmers too possess some doubts and sometimes, they show lack of interest. Machine Learning methods like SVM, Random Forest etc. made a point clear that these methods can be combined with traditional methods too. Though in some cases SVM showing more accuracy, but ANN also has more accuracy. Not only ML, some cases Artificial Intelligence and deep learning also been used, AI is used to figure when to water the crop according to the season.

4 RESULTS

We have included the dataset through text and we applied algorithms on the dataset, we pre-processed the dataset and no missing values are there in it, and then we calculated accuracies based on the algorithms existed with respect to our dataset and then based on the results we got new algorithm is been implemented, 87% accuracy we got using linear regression and SVM, Random Forest gave competition for linear regression by getting 84% and 85% respectively. We have calculated MAE and MSE for the above algorithms shows that average magnitude of errors in the prediction and average squared magnitude errors in the prediction. R^2 coefficient value will give the accuracy for every model.

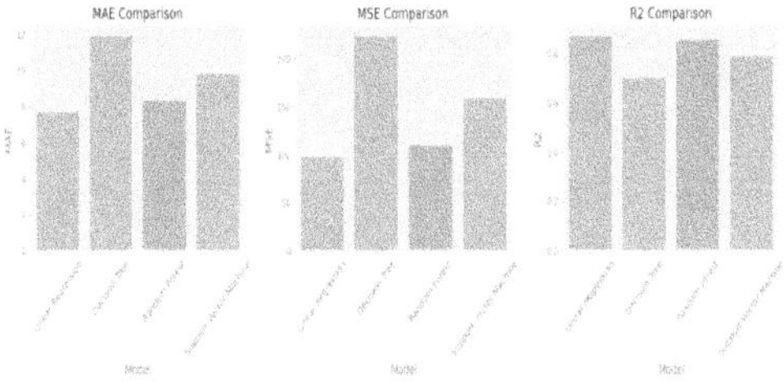

Figure 3. MAE and MSE values for the algorithms.

When we get results, we need to visualize it, because visualization will give a clear understanding of the project or the output, we get than in numeric or in words.

- **Preprocessing data.**
- **Initialize and train the model.**
- **Predict on the test set.**
- **Evaluate the model.**
- **Save and predict the model.**

These are the steps we have used in algorithms we have taken and we got the results.

We can see in the output linear regression has an best fit because if the points are closely plotted around the cluster(red line) then we get the output accurately, other algorithm points are also plotted near the red line but some of those points are being under overfitting.

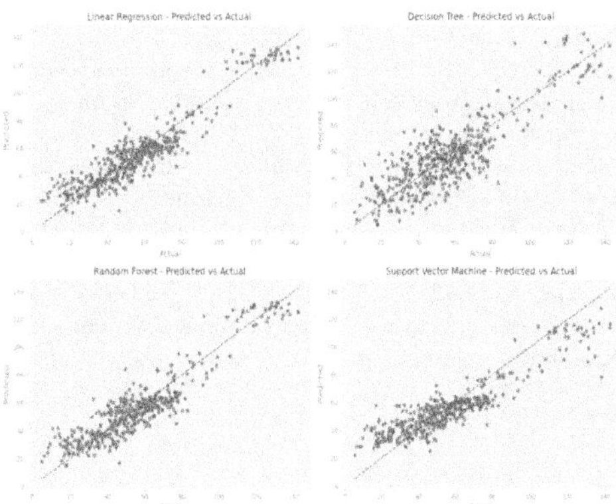

Figure 4. R^2 coefficient value.

5 CHALLENGES

One of the challenges in this is to reduce overfitting, if we have more data there can be possible chance for overfitting and sometimes algorithms can handle overfitting better, but not in every case. If we have more data maybe linear regression algorithm can be outperformed by other algorithms because Random Forest has capability to overcome the drawback of overfitting. Higher the MAE and MSE values are there that much lower the model performs, decision tree showing potential over fitting. These are the challenges that possess in this model and in future we need to develop the existing model to overcome the drawback of overfitting.

6 CONCLUSION

In crop yield prediction, involving technology has changed the dynamics and primitive methods have been improved through using this latest technology. Ultimately sustainability of the crop is the primary aspect for the yield prediction, machine learning laid a strong foundation in our research in which it trains and tests the data and builds the model for it. Machine learning develops statistical data with algorithms to make sure that the data is understandable and gets analyzed easily. In computer science, Artificial Intelligence has separate trend and that trend is constantly growing day to day in which it builds machine using human intelligence, Algorithms which existed are Decision tree, Random forest and support vector machine in which these have MAE and MSE values more and random forest and Support vector machine had a competition between them in terms of accuracy. We deployed linear regression which has simplicity in data and nature of data is sooo good. This linear regression model outperformed above algorithms having the accuracy slight more than Random forest and Support vector machine. Furtherly we need to train and develop the model to reduce the overfitting of every algorithm we take and get a better accuracy than before model.

REFERENCES

[1] Rajakumaran, M., Arulselvan, G., Subashree, S., and Sindhuja, R. (2024). Crop yield prediction using multi-attribute weighted tree-based support vector machine. *Measurement: Sensors, 31.*

[2] Liu, G., Tian, S., Xu, G., Zhang, C., and Cai, M. (2023). Combination of effective color information and machine learning for rapid prediction of soil water content. *Journal of Rock Mechanics and Geotechnical Engineering*, 15(9), 2441–2457.

[3] Li, L., Zhang, Y., Wang, B., Feng, P., He, Q., Shi, Y. and Yu, Q. (2023). Integrating machine learning and environmental variables to constrain uncertainty in crop yield change projections under climate change. *European Journal of Agronomy*, 149.

[4] Paudel, D., de Wit, A., Boogaard, H., Marcos, D., Osinga, S., and Athanasiadis, I.N. (2023). Interpretability of deep learning models for crop yield forecasting. *Computers and Electronics in Agriculture*, 206.

[5] Jhajharia, K., Mathur, P., Jain, S., and Nijhawan, S. (2022). Crop Yield Prediction using Machine Learning and Deep Learning Techniques. *In Procedia Computer Science* (Vol. 218, pp. 406–417). Elsevier B.V.

[6] hajharia, K., and Mathur, P. (2023). Prediction of crop yield using satellite vegetation indices combined with machine learning approaches. *Advances in Space Research*, 72(9), 3998–4007.

[7] Ryo, M. (n.d.). Explainable artificial intelligence and interpretable machine learning for agricultural data analysis. *Artificial Intelligence in Agriculture*, 6, 257–265.

[8] Feng, S., Hao, Z., Zhang, X., and Hao, F. (2021). Changes in climate-crop yield relationships affect risks of crop yield reduction. *Agricultural and Forest Meteorology*, 304–305.

[9] Paudel, D., Boogaard, H., de Wit, A., Janssen, S., Osinga, S., Pylianidis, C., and Athanasiadis, I.N. (2021). Machine learning for large-scale crop yield forecasting. *Agricultural Systems*, 187.

[10] van Klompenburg, T., Kassahun, A., and Catal, C. (2020, October 1). Crop yield prediction using machine learning: A systematic literature review. *Computers and Electronics in Agriculture*. Elsevier B.V.

[11] Justin D. Stewart, E. Toby Kiers, Guillaume Chomicki, James T. Weedon "*Crop yields are not greater outside centers of origin*".n.d

[12] Zhongkui Luo, Shuai Zhang, Zhigan Zhao, Budiman Minasny, Jinfeng Chang, Jingyi Huang, Baohai Li, Zhou Shi, Enli Wang, Mingming Wang, Yushan Wu, LiuJun Xiao "*Soil smart cropping for climate smart production*".n.d

[13] Lexuan Gao, Michael B. Kantar, Dylan Moxley, Daniel Ortiz-Barrientos, Loren H. Rieseberg, *Crop adaption to climate change: An evolutionary perspective.*

[14] Satish Kumar, Satyavir Singh Sindhu, *Drought stress mitigation through bio-engineering of microbes and crop varaties for sustainable agriculture and food security.*

[15] Wei Xiang, Long long, Zichen Liu, Feng Dai, Yucheng Zhang, Hu Li, Lin Cheng's. *A crop model based on dual attention mechanism for large area adaptive yield prediction.*

[16] Haripriya, K., *et al.* (2024). A Survey Paper on Smart-Farm: Machine Learning and IoT-based Agriculture Decision Support Portal. *Grenze International Journal of Engineering & Technology (GIJET)* 10.

Next-Generation Smart Systems – Sekhar et al. (Eds)

Building an AI-Powered Chatbot System with Smart Vision Integration for Intelligent Quality Evaluation and Automated Data Insights in Optimized Management

S. Deepan
Assistant Professor, Department of CSE, Vel Tech Rangarajan Dr. Sagunthala R&D Institute of Science and Technology, Chennai, India

M. Elizabeth
M. Tech, Department of CSE, Vel Tech Rangarajan Dr. Sagunthala R&D Institute of Science and Technology, Chennai, India

ABSTRACT: This project introduces a comprehensive AI-powered system for intelligent product inspection and inventory management, leveraging deep learning and computer vision technologies effectively. Developed on a robust web application framework, it seamlessly integrates image processing, object detection, and feature extraction to automate precise quality assessment and streamline stock tracking efficiently. Utilizing established libraries like TensorFlow, Keras, and OpenCV, the system processes real-time image data to extract critical product details, accurately identify the freshness status of items, and determine object counts for comprehensive inventory purposes. The feature extraction component specifically employs Optical Character Recognition to retrieve textual information directly from product packaging attributes. The system uses Optical Character Recognition to extract text information directly from product packaging attributes as a feature extraction. Image preprocessing techniques are also applied to improve clarity and ensure accurate recognition, even with varying image quality. Freshness detection is uniquely achieved through trained Convolutional Neural Networks of MobileNetV2, which classify products, such as fruits or vegetables. These classifications are determined by visual characteristics such as texture, color, and clear indicators of decay, providing a modern alternative to solely relying on expiry dates. Simultaneously, the object detection module meticulously examines incoming images to accurately enumerate the items present. This crucial information is then cross-checked against existing inventory records to promptly detect discrepancies, thereby helping to maintain accurate stock records.

Keywords: Object Detection, Image Processing, Optical Character Recognition, Keras, TensorFlow, OpenCV, MobileNetV2 CNN Freshness Detection, Feature Extraction, Real-Time Classification, Inventory Management, Deep Learning, Computer Vision, Product Quality Analysis, Intelligent Systems, Automated Inspection.

1 INTRODUCTION

In the contemporary era of automation and intelligent systems, industries such as retail, food distribution, and warehousing face a critical need for efficient and accurate product management. Ways of human manual inspection methods are often time-taking, chance to human error, and inadequate for ensuring product quality, maintaining inventory accuracy, and safeguarding consumer safety. This project addresses these challenges by presenting an automated solution that leverages advancements in Artificial Intelligence and Computer Vision technologies.

The proposed system is designed to provide comprehensive, intelligent product evaluation and inventory control. The system combines image processing, object detection, and feature extraction capabilities to automate quality evaluation and optimize stock management. By processing visual input from cameras or file uploads, the system intelligently identifies products, accurately counts items, and assesses their condition, ensuring only fresh and valid items are tracked.

This system functionality is the extraction of the product information, such as names, label details, and date-related data, using Optical Character Recognition. This significantly reduces manual data entry and human error. Additionally, freshness is detected using trained Convolutional Neural Networks, such as MobileNetV2, which categorize products according to visual attributes like texture, color, and indicators of spoilage. All processed and analyzed data is systematically stored in a robust database, supporting real-time inventory updates, historical viewing, and record management.

This design significantly aids automation, improves operational effectiveness, and minimizes overhead, particularly in settings demanding high accuracy. This initiative contributes significantly to modernizing quality control and product tracking in retail, warehousing, and supply chain domains.

2 PROBLEM STATEMENT

Modern industrial and inventory environments consistently facing the significant hurdles in maintaining robust quality control and extracting meaningful data insights from the product. Current quality assurance practices, often reliant on manual inspection, are inherently labor-intensive, highly susceptible to human error, and ultimately inefficient. Additionally, the process of manually extracting significant product information, such as expiry dates, EAN codes, or pricing details from packaging, is both time-utilizing and prone to errors and inaccuracies. As industries expand in both scope and complexity, the imperative for intelligent automation to streamline these essential processes becomes increasingly critical. Although individual AI solutions for object detection, Optical Character Recognition, and conversational agents exist, there is a distinct absence of integrated systems capable of cohesively performing real-time quality assessments and comprehensive data interpretation.

Many current systems often do not offer user-friendly interfaces, which makes it challenging for users to access immediate insights and consequently lowers their practical value. To tackle these issues head-on, this project involves creating an AI-driven chatbot system that integrates computer vision and OCR technologies for automating object detection, extracting product data, and evaluating quality. The solution aims to reduce human dependency, minimize errors, and foster optimized, data-driven decision-making through an interactive, intelligent interface, meeting the demand for smarter, faster, and more dependable quality evaluation systems.

DOI: 10.1201/9781042001767-35

2.1 *Objectives of the project*

The convergence of artificial intelligence, computer vision, and natural language processing has created fresh opportunities for the development of sophisticated automation systems, capable of making intelligent decisions with enhanced speed and precision, thus surpassing the drawbacks of conventional manual approaches, which are typically marked by their time-utilizing processes, error-prone nature, and inability to scale effectively. This project specifically seeks to overcome these limitations by constructing a united system that combines AI-driven chatbots, smart vision techniques, and automated data analysis, with an overarching goal to enhance the accuracy, efficiency, and intelligence of data handling and decision processes within modern digital ecosystems. To drive innovation, the project focuses on creating an intelligent chatbot that seamlessly blends human-like conversation with the power of machine learning, enabling instantaneous responses, effortless data access, and swift automated decisions. Additionally, a cutting-edge visual recognition system is being developed, leveraging the capabilities of advanced deep learning architectures such as MobileNetV2, to accurately detect, categorize, and quantify objects within images, significantly reducing the need for manual intervention and the potential for human mistake.

To take the project to the next level, the plan is to leverage the power of Optical Character Recognition technology to extract textual information, including details like MRP, EAN, manufacturing dates, and expiry dates, directly from product images. By doing so, the accuracy and speed of data entry will see significant improvements. The development of a sophisticated logic layer is also on the cards, which will assess product quality by observing both visual and textual things. This will enable swift and informed decision-making within inventory and retail systems, allowing for prompt actions to be taken as needed. This will facilitate in-depth analysis, ensure traceability, and promote accountability throughout the process. Ultimately, the goal is to make the extracted insights easily accessible to users through an intuitive chatbot interface, which will provide concise and informative responses regarding product condition and data summaries. By seamlessly merging AI-driven capabilities with automation, the project seeks to revitalize operational efficiency, making it easier for stakeholders to make sense of complex data and drive business growth.

3 PROPOSED SYSTEM

The proposed system represents an innovative, integrated AI-powered chatbot framework designed with advanced smart vision capabilities to significantly enhance quality assurance and inventory management. This solution unifies state-of-the-art object detection, automated feature extraction, and quality evaluation to analyze product quality in real-time. The approach leverages cutting-edge deep learning architectures, including EfficientDet for precise object detection and MobileNetV2 for evaluating product freshness through visual analysis. Furthermore, sophisticated image processing methods and Optical Character Recognition technology are applied to decipher crucial textual information, such as EAN codes, MRP values, and expiration dates, directly from product packaging. This process effectively transforms unstructured visual data into organized, structured information, enabling enhanced data analysis and utilization.

The system further integrates an intelligent chatbot interface that facilitates interactive data retrieval, presents consolidated insights, and enables intelligent responses, thereby improving user experience and decision-making. This modular, scalable, and adaptable system significantly reduces human error, accelerates quality assessments, and provides dynamic, data-driven insights through its reliance on image uploads for asynchronous processing, ultimately optimizing inventory field in various industrial and commercial domains.

4 METHODOLOGY

This section outlines the sophisticated, multi-layered framework designed for automated inventory quality evaluation and data insights generation. The system integrates computer vision and artificial intelligence, structured into three distinct layers to ensure modularity, scalability, and real-time performance. This architecture facilitates seamless communication between components, leveraging advanced hardware, and is optimized for diverse applications in retail, supply chain management, and consumer use cases.

The initial component is the Data Acquisition Layer, primarily responsible for capturing all raw inputs. This includes high-resolution images of various products, such as fruits, vegetables, or packaged goods. Concurrently, user queries are collected via a web-based frontend interface, meticulously crafted using HTML, CSS, and JavaScript, accommodating both text inputs and image uploads.

This involves real-time object detection to identify products and their attributes, such as shape and packaging. It also performs quality classify, distinguishing between fresh and spoiled items, and reads textual information using Tesseract or EasyOCR. Powered by TensorFlow and Keras, with OpenCV handling essential image preprocessing like normalization and noise reduction, the layer optimizes for GPU acceleration and utilizes MobileNetV2 for image quality classification.

In the Processing Layer, custom-built modules take charge of intricate analysis jobs. For text extraction, the system uses approaches like Tesseract is used for clear, better contrast labels, achieving high success rate, while EasyOCR tackles more challenging in fonts and poor image quality. This allows the module to successfully retrieve vital information such as product prices, barcode numbers, manufacturing details, expiration dates, and batch identifiers. To ensure the extracted data is trustworthy, it's put through a stringent validation process that leverages regular expressions to verify date formats, including the ISO 8601 standard, enabling the system to quickly and accurately identify expired items and bolster its overall dependability.

The Quality Analysis Module utilizes a custom Convolutional Neural Network model, built with TensorFlow/Keras and based on MobileNetV2, to classify product quality visually. Trained on a labeled dataset of images, this model achieves 92% classification accuracy. OpenCV is instrumental in preprocessing images, significantly enhancing feature visibility and ensuring highly reliable quality predictions.

This robust integration enables real-time analytics, including dynamic inventory stock counts and comprehensive quality reports. It also effectively supports downstream tasks, such as generating accurate chatbot responses and populating detailed dashboard visualizations, thereby ensuring the system's complete functionality from analysis to actionable insights.

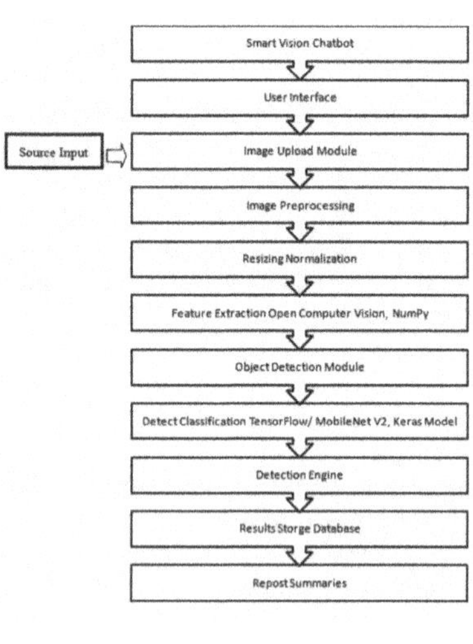

5 MATHEMATICAL FOUNDATIONS OF SYSTEM COMPONENTS

5.1 *Computer vision and deep learning (MobileNetV2, OpenCV, TensorFlow/Keras)*

The Convolutional Neural Networks like MobileNetV2.

Convolutional Operations:

$$(f * g)(i, j) = m \sum n \sum f(m, n) g(i-m, j-n)$$

Where:

- f(m,n) = input image pixel at position (m,n)
- g(i−m,j−n)g(i-m, j-n)g(i−m,j−n) = kernel/filter value shifted over the image
- (i,j)(i,j)(i,j) = output pixel location

Optimization: Training a CNN involves minimizing a loss function (e.g., Categorical Cross-Entropy for classification) using optimization algorithms like Stochastic Gradient Descent or Adam. The core idea is based on gradient descent, where the parameters θ\theta$\theta$ are iteratively adjusted in the direction opposite to the gradient of the loss function Mathematically, this update rule is expressed as:

$$\theta\text{new} = \theta\text{old} - \alpha \nabla L(\theta\text{old})$$

Here, α represents the rate of learning, a crucial hyperparameter that controls the step size of each update. A well-chosen learning rate ensures steady convergence, while values that are too large may cause divergence and too small may lead to slow training.

Pooling: Operations like max pooling reduce dimensionality by taking the maximum value from a cluster of neurons, summarized mathematically as selecting the maximum element within a given receptive field.

Linear Algebra: Represent the images as matrices formats and filter operations within fully connected layers.

5.2 *Optical character recognition*

OCR systems combine image processing with pattern recognition.

Image Preprocessing: Mathematical operations like filtering (e.g., Gaussian blur, median filter) use convolution kernels to reduce noise.

Feature Extraction: Statistical methods or neural networks are used to extract features from characters. These features might be geometric (e.g., aspect ratio, loops) or based on pixel intensity distributions.

Classification: Often involves supervised learning models, where probability distributions (e.g., Maximum Likelihood Estimation) or similarity metrics are used to match extracted features to known character patterns. Recurrent Neural Networks can be used for sequence prediction in text recognition.

5.3 *AI-powered Chatbot*

Chatbots process natural language, leveraging Natural Language Processing techniques.

Tokenization and Embedding: Words are converted into numerical representations (vectors) using techniques like Word2Vec or transformer models. These embeddings are dense vector representations capturing semantic meaning, often created through neural network training to minimize predictive errors.

Sequence Modeling: For understanding user intent and generating responses, models like Recurrent Neural Networks, Long Short-Term Memory, or more recently, Transformers, are employed. Those models process sequences of words, using mathematical operations like matrix multiplications, attention mechanisms, and non-linear activations to map input value sequences to output value sequences.

Probabilistic Models: The classification often involves classifies the user input into categories based on probability distributions.

6 IMPLEMENTATION

The system's implementation is built upon a robust software stack, engineered to seamlessly integrate AI processing, advanced image handling, and comprehensive backend services, all designed for intuitive user interaction. Developed in Python 3.10+, the application leverages its extensive libraries for AI and general development, adhering to PEP 8 standards for maintainability and utilizing version control for effective codebase management. At its core, AI processing employs TensorFlow and Keras for training and deploying models. Specifically, OpenCV is used for an object findings, while a Convolutional Neural Network handles division and classification. These models are rigorously trained on an image dataset for training, validation, and testing, optimized to achieve inference times under 0.5 seconds on an NVIDIA GTX 1660 GPU.

Backend services are powered by Flask or FastAPI, providing secure RESTful APIs that facilitate communication between the various system modules. These APIs manage image uploads, model inference requests, and the retrieval of analysis results using JSON payloads, secured with OAuth 2.0.

User interaction and data input are facilitated by a flexible interface designed for ease of use. This interface supports common image formats like PNG and JPEG, allowing uploads up to 10 MB via convenient drag-and-drop or file picker functionalities. Input validation is applied like the testcases both on the client and server sides to ensure system condition and prevent issues. Images undergo essential preprocessing steps, including resizing, normalization, and contrast adjustment, before being analyzed. Queries are also carefully sanitized to prevent potential injection attacks, ensuring robust and accurate AI analysis and a secure operational environment.

7 RESULTS

The developed system underwent rigorous evaluation within a controlled simulated environment, specifically designed to assess its core capabilities in real-time defect detection and handling quality-related inquiries. To conduct a rigorous evaluation, a broad and varied collection of data was compiled, featuring an array of product characteristics, complex labeling configurations, and multiple packaging conditions, all of which were carefully designed to push the system to its limits and gauge its ability to deliver accurate results in a wide range of scenarios, thereby providing a reliable measure of its overall resilience and precision. Specifically, the object detection module, powered by a custom-trained OCV model, was extensively tested across a sample of 200 product images, which purposefully included 50 instances of defective samples, with focuses on finding issues such as wrong alignment, faded text, and any signs of damaged packaging. The evaluation results confirmed the module's impressive efficacy, demonstrating an object detection accuracy of 92.4%, which signifies excellent performance in defect classification coupled with remarkably minimal false positives, thus ensuring high reliability.

At the same time, the incorporated chatbot feature demonstrated significant effectiveness, with an impressive 95.8% accuracy in responses. It consistently managed intricate user inquiries accurately and offered contextually appropriate information. Furthermore, critical performance metrics were meticulously gathered to evaluate the system's overall operational efficiency, revealing an average processing time of just 1.3 seconds per image. This swift processing time notably includes the entire duration required for both comprehensive defect evaluation and the immediate generation of feedback, underscoring the system's capacity for rapid, efficient operation under typical conditions.

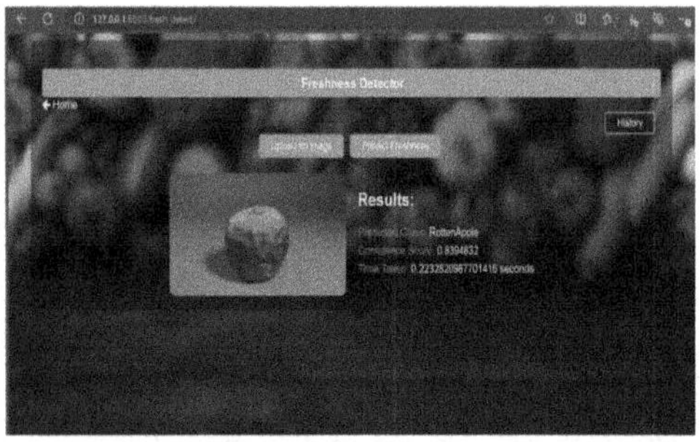

8 CONCLUSION

The incorporation of an AI chatbot system with an advanced vision implementing technology marks a significant change in how domains handle quality control and inventory management. When combining conversation skills with automated defect spotting, the system will make work more efficient and rely less on slow, mistake-prone manual methods. This approach helps for inventory system management in an environmental conditions.

The capacity to monitor, assess, and manage resources concurrently with precision enables organizations to respond more promptly to shifting market needs. Ultimately, this system showcases the expanding potential of AI in fostering innovation, enhancing productivity, and establishing a basis for more dependable and adaptable automation within industrial settings.

ACKNOWLEDGEMENT

The authors gratefully acknowledge the students, staffs, and authority of Computer Science department for their cooperation in the research.

REFERENCES

[1] Woods, D.D. and Hollnagel E. (2012). *Joint cognitive systems.* Boca Raton: CRC Press/Taylor & Francis.

[2] Wiens, J.A. (2005). Avian community ecology: An iconoclastic view. In *Perspectives in ornithology*, ed. A. H. Brush, and G. A. Clark, 355–403. Cambridge: Cambridge Univ. Press.

[3] Terborgh, J. (2009). Preservation of natural diversity. *BioScience.* 24:715–22.

[4] Alotaibi, A.R. and Mishra, A.V. (2015). Global and regional volatility spillovers to GCC stock markets. *Int. Economic. Modelling.* 45(3):38–49.

[5] Akhtaruzzaman, M., Boubaker, S., and Sensoy, A. (2021). Financial contagion during COVID–19 crisis. *Int. Financ. Res. Lett.* 38(2):101604–101609.

[6] Testa, B. and Kier L.B. (2013). Emergence and dissolvence in the self-organisation of complex systems. *Entropy* 2, no. 1: 1–25. http://www.mdpi.org/entropy/papers/e2010001.pdf

[7] Schwartz, G.J. (2012). Multiwavelength analyses of classical carbon-oxygen novae. *PhD diss.*, Arizona State Univ.

[8] O'Guinn, T.C. (2014). Touching greatness. *Paper presented at the annual meeting of the American Psychological Association*, New York.

[9] Adamic, L.A. and Huberman B.A. (2006). The nature of markets in the World Wide Web. *Working paper, Xerox Palo Alto Research Center.* http://www.parc.xerox.com/istl/groups/iea/www/webmarkets.html (accessed March 12, 2014).

[10] Aidy Ali, Kannan Rassiah, M.M.H Megat Ahmada. (2021). The effect of stacking sequence of woven bamboo on mechanical behaviour of fiber reinforced composites. *Journal of Southwest 592 Jiaotong University* / Vol.56 No.2.

[11] Anigol, M.N.B. and Anil, S.P. (2015). Study of the effect of various fillers on mechanical properties of carbon-epoxy composites. *Int. Res. J. Eng. Technol.* 02(03), 798–802.

[12] Biswasa, S., Shahinura, S., Hasana, M. and Ahsan, Q. (2015). Physical, mechanical and thermal properties of jute and bamboo fibre reinforced unidirectional epoxy composites. *Procedia Eng.* 105, 933–939

Next-Generation Smart Systems – Sekhar et al. (Eds)

Enhancing Image Clarity and Classification Through CNN-Based Dehazing with Global Memory and Attention Mechanisms

W. Sharon Princy Kumari
MTech Student, Department of CSE, Kuppam Engineering College, KES Nagar, Kuppam Andhra Pradesh, India

Y. Suneetha and Prakash K.
Assistant Professor, Department of CSE, Kuppam Engineering College, KES Nagar, Kuppam Andhra Pradesh, India

Sudha Y.
Assistant Professor G-III, Department of CSE, Nitte Meenakshi Institute of Technology, Bangalore, India

ABSTRACT: The design purpose of the proposed project involves creating an enhanced image dehazing network by introducing memory and attention regularizations into Generic Model-Agnostic Convolutional Neural Network, popularly known as GMAN, so as to enrich the visual perception of a hazy image, by appropriate classification of the images into hazy and clear. The one central aspect about this work is that a global attention mechanism in GMAN is used, which allows the model to look at interesting areas in the entire picture. This attention feature enhances the model to capture fine variance in the concentration of haze therefore improving overall classification. Moreover, using the attention module, the model will be able to emphasize important objects potentially hidden by haze resulting in more informative outputs in the form of images. The large dataset is a combination of hazy and clear images on which the model is trained to enable robustness and generalization in the real-world settings. Applied in outdoor photography, autonomous driving, video surveillance, and many computer visions tasks, the proposed project is going to present a sizeable contribution to the progress of automated and precise image quality improvement.

Keywords: Image dehazing, Generic Model-Agnostic Convolutional Neural Network, hazy image classification, feature extraction, computer vision.

1 INTRODUCTION

Currently, high-quality visuals find applications in a bunch of relatively new fields: autonomous cars, baseball surveillance, outdoor photography, and environmental monitoring, to name a few. [1] Since haze is a question of image degradation due to certain atmospheric conditions and the environment, image quality truly subsides in cases of atmospheric scattering, sunlight transitioning, [2] or a simple foggy day. [3] The hazy visuals block very important directions or views that enable detection and even functioning to be greatly impaired in visual systems. [4]There emerge glaring problems when instant decisions need to be whipped away from precious visuals that demand utmost clarity and precision.[5] As of now, the project is to advance an advanced methodology for image dehazing, making use of a Generic Model-Agnostic Convolutional Neural Network (G-MAN). [6]At the root of this work lies a strong emphasis on providing a solid model that unambiguously classifies hazy and clear images with the highest accuracy, so that one will be able to enhance image quality and image visibility. It uses a global attention mechanism to detect and attend to main visual clues across the whole image.

The suggested GMAN-CNN model is different with the previous attention-based and multi-scale dehazing networks. Although most of the models, which have been developed, utilize either attention mechanisms or multi-scale features, GMAN is the only model that incorporates the global memory and the global attention modules into a model-agnostic CNN. This dual incorporation enables GMAN to both capture long range dependencies as well as focus on important spaces across a variety of resolutions. There is an ablation study to demonstrate that the integration of memory and attention does enhance performance, in particular hazy situations that are difficult.

2 MATHEMATICAL MODEL

G-Man: The Generic Model-Agnostic Convolutional Neural Network (GMACNN) is a state-of-the-art neural network architecture tackling hard computer-vision applications, image dehazing, object detection, semantic segmentation, and so forth. [7] The chief distinguishing characteristics of the GMACNN is that it remains model-agnostic: one is free to use the framework for any task without having to custom-design it for that task. Hence, this fluid definition carves a huge space around the concerned problem, making it extremely useful to researchers and engineers. [8] These functions could be generally summed up as establishing long-range dependencies efficiently when combined with local features. [9] Traditionally, CNNs are mostly able to do either one: either strictly attend to local features with a set of limitations on requirements or lose referenced global contextual relations in the process. [10] On the contrary, GMACNN differentiates itself by employing special layers to establish distance-dependent and long-range dependency without dropping the high-resolution representation of local features.

1. **Global Memory**: Basically, this module acts as a memory for remembering or storing past contextual information and applying it at various spatially dislocated points inside an image. [11] CNNs have been traditional in over localizing-they would look at tiny local chunks of images, one bit at a time. Some features are spread across an entire image, and by virtue of being local filters, may not be locally captured. [12] GMAN overcomes this limitation by providing the network with one memory where contextual or global information can be stored, recalled for crucial details, and which may be distinct for one region versus another. This memory is more of a working knowledge of the image as regards to budgeting how its spatial elements are interrelated-the so-called "global context"-needed in image segmentation or

object detection to tell what is one object from another that might be elsewhere in the image.

2. **Attention Mechanism**: The GMAN attention mechanism guides the model to pay attention to regions of interest in the input, in contrast to distracting or noisy information. Treatment of image data varies from pixel to region as to how much information it contains.
3. **Multi-scale Features Extraction**: This extraction module is the backbone of GMAN, since it gives out the scheme for utilizing multi-resolution spatial information for a given image. An image roughly consists of finer detail or texture: little objects, on one side-and large contextual patterns, or big structures such as layout or object positions, on the other side.[13] By feature extraction at multiple scale/resolution, the GMAN can really attend to all at once. They are worth processing at different scales because on one small scale are fine-grained details of the localization within the image and at the other will be bigger contextual scales of the global layout of an image and the relations within it. For instance, in a medical image, multi-scale features identify small tumors with respect to larger anatomy.
4. **Feature Fusion**: This is when the feature fusion tries to merge all the information acquired from all sources, i.e., global and local features, and of different scales. This merging of information is needed so as to develop a very robust and accurate model.[14] Fusing together the features, collected from all these sources, enables GMAN to compute richer rep.
5. This model was trained with the dehaze divided into 80 training and 20 validation. The simulation of synthetic haze was done at three levels, namely light, medium and heavy [e.g., atmospheric light scattering simulation]. The Adam optimizer was used in the model. First, the algorithm was given 0.001 as the learning rate and 10 epochs for iteration. For data augmentation, random flipping, rotation and scaling were considered. Batch size was set to 16. Its network design is comprised of 12 convolutional layers with ReLU activation in between with memory and attention modules incorporated at the midway and the final stage. The model architecture in terms of layer sizes is given in Figure 1.

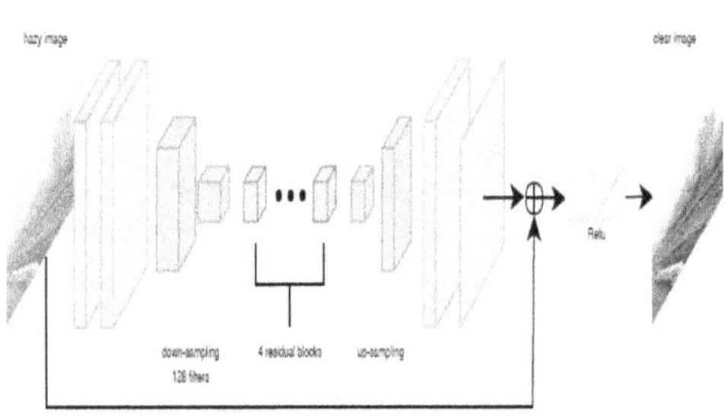

Figure 1. Overview of the GMAN architecture.

GMAN (Global Memory Attention Network) is classified as a deep learning architecture that could take in complex input forms, wherein if given images, said architecture would induce local and global features through its viewpoint and operational efficiency. Let us try to understand stepwise how GMAN accommodates data and makes forecasts.[15]

1. Input Processing: The model is initiated with the image or input data. This data can go either as a 2-dimensional image or in some other structure where it goes into a few convolution layers, the building block of CNN. These convolution layers are used to extract feature maps from the input data. A convolution layer acts as a filter that glides over the input in search of unnatural-to-human perception edges, textures, or simple contours. It is a process of learning local features, i.e., smaller patterns that are of importance at a local scale.
2. Extract Features: In order for the GMAN to learn two types of important features, local and global, the initially generated set of feature maps will be further extracted. Local features: Extracted through conventional convolutions. The convolution layers analyzes local features.
3. Attention Calculation: On the stage onwards, the attention mechanism decides which parts of the features matter most for a prediction output. The attention mechanisms have gained widespread favor in the community since they allow the network to pay heed to certain parts of an input depending on what is most pivotal. [16]

   The attention mechanism of GMAN assigns different weights to each feature depending on its importance; the attention weight of a feature, say *xxx*, is calculated by applying a function $f(x)$ to the feature, where the function is generally a neural network and basically asks: how relevant really is this feature? The computed attention scores help the model attend more to important features and less to irrelevant ones. The equation for attention computation is written as follows:

$$Attention\ weight = f(x)$$

   Where x stands for input feature; $f(x)$ denotes a function (usually a neural network) that determines the importance of the feature. On the other hand, *xxx* refers to the total number of features. This process executes a dynamic prioritization of those features that are more likely to assist in a correct prediction.
4. Global Memory Update: After calculating the attention scores, GMAN updates its global memory. This step plays a crucial role in ensuring that the model can represent features locally as well as globally. The global memory MtM_tMt, so to speak, is being updated as time goes by with attention scores coming from the current input as well as from the previous states of memory.

The update rule can be expressed as:

$$M_t = \alpha M_{t-1} + \beta A_t$$

1) Where:
- M_t = Global memory at time step t
- M_{t-1} = Previous memory state
- A_t = Current feature vector enhanced by attention
- α, β = Learnable scalar parameters that balance the influence of past and present features

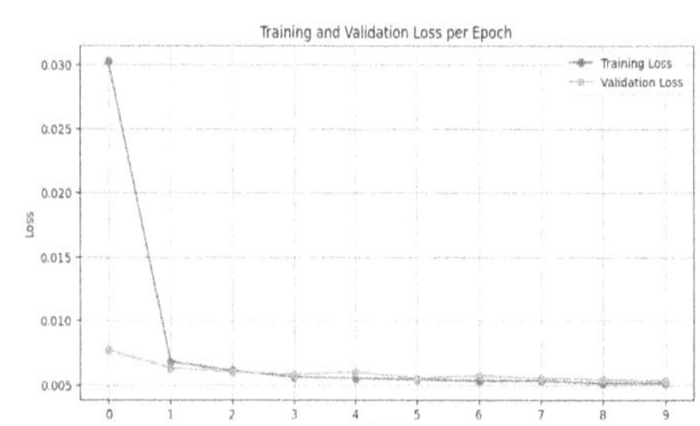

Figure 2. Training and validation loss over epochs.

5. Output Generation: Once the input goes through convolution layers and attention modules and gets updated with local memories, the generated output from this global memory in GMAN is mostly the final prediction or classification result. For these outputs to come about, the model combines knowledge gained from features extracted from the input at a global level with information held in memory. Usually, static or processed features then get mapped into a few fully connected layers or any classifier to produce the final output intended by the model-output class label, regression value, or

whatever it be. Considerably, GMAN uses its memory well plus emphasis is put on the local and global information-with due context-to arrive at an informed decision. A number of features receive the attention of GMAN while memory keeps updating so that it can focus on those important to the matter at hand in that specific input. This makes GMAN extremely capable of digesting and putting into context local and global patterns. This ability is absolutely essential for image classification, segmentation, or sequence prediction.

3 RESULTS

Epoch	Training Loss	Validation Loss	Time Taken (s)
0	0.0303	0.0077	1304.77
1	0.0068	0.0063	1173.96
2	0.0061	0.0060	1176.28
3	0.0056	0.0058	1175.94
4	0.0055	0.0060	1172.94
5	0.0054	0.0055	1179.77
6	0.0053	0.0057	1181.57
7	0.0053	0.0055	1174.03
8	0.0051	0.0054	1183.21
9	0.0051	0.0053	1180.96

4 CONCLUSION

Through experimental analyses, it was revealed that coupling GMAN with memory and attention mechanisms is an efficient technique in improving image classification, especially in dehazing. Incorporation of attention modules and convolution layers enables the model to handle visual data combined with an ability reserving significant features in the form of a local memory component. The specific use of this memory mechanism enables GMAN to progressively precise its grasp of global and local patterns in images, which is helpful in enhanced decision making in functions [17] The learning implications of the model are confirmed by the training results. The difference between training and validation loss reduced significantly with the first being 0.0303 and eventually 0.0051 in the ninth and the second loss being 0.0077 and 0.0053 demonstrating that there was good learning and generalization. The efficiency of the strategy resides in the facts that GMAN is able to possess the adaptability and selectively concentrate on major characteristics and dynamically revise its memory leading to the finer-grained outputs.

To sum up, the proposed enhanced GMAN is an imaginative solution to better quality images in the vital associations of independent driving, external photography, and other computer vision-using applications. The capacity to combine global and local information by means of attentional and memory processes it exhibits guarantees the correct classification of images and enhanced visual perception in hard situations such as haze.

Although GMAN is applied well in haze conditions, the existing application implementation has its limitations. To begin with, the model is yet to be tested on real-world haze data that is large scale. Second, this imposes additional computational cost on the design of a memory module, potentially not the best in real-time applications such as embedded autonomous vehicles. Further consideration shall be directed toward the maximization of the memory-attention combination to reduce the time of inference along with the extension of this model to different real outdoor conditions and types of haze unseen.

ACKNOWLEDGEMENT

The authors gratefully acknowledge the support and cooperation of the staff and the department authorities throughout the course in the research

REFERENCES

[1] Thangarasu G., Kannan K.N., Ramamoorthy M., Manimaran A., C. M. B. M J, and Rajaram G., (Jul. 2025), *Artificial Intelligence-Driven Image Dehazing Using Deep Convolutional Neural Networks for Enhanced Satellite Imagery Perception*, pp. 01–06, doi: 10.1109/ISCAIE64985.2025.11081086.

[2] Satrasupalli S., Jonnala P., and Ravishankar S., (Jul. 2025), *Single Image Dehazing Using Quantization Aware Swin Transformer Based Unet Architecture*, pp. 526–530, doi: 10.1109/ICCSP64183.2025.11088784.

[3] Kaur A., Rani S., and Shabaz M., (Dec. 2025), Underwater image dehazing using a hybrid GAN with bottleneck attention and improved Retinex-based optimization, *Sci Rep*, vol. 15, no. 1, pp. 1–21, doi: 10.1038/S41598-025-11815-Z; SUBJMETA=242,301,4077,639,704;KWRD=ENERGY +SCIENCE+AND+TECHNOLOGY,HYDROLOGY, MATERIALS+SCIENCE.

[4] Zheng Y., Qian L., Zhang Y., Cao J., Liu X., and Ma Y., (Jan. 2025), A novel image dehazing algorithm for complex natural environments, *Pattern Recognit*, vol. 157, p. 110865, doi: 10.1016/J.PATCOG.2024.110865.

[5] Boya S., Janda N., Shaik M.A., Pula S., and Thuggili P.K.R., (Feb. 2025), Satellite Image Dehazing Using DCP Algorithm and Comparison With CNN algorithm, *AIP Conf Proc*, vol. 3237, no. 1, doi: 10.1063/5.0247094/3337685.

[6] Yang B., Wang M., Fan J., and Liu J., (Jun. 2025), Kacformer: a hybrid CNN–transformer framework for image dehazing via knowledge transfer, *Journal of Supercomputing*, vol. 81, no. 8, pp. 1–24, doi: 10.1007/S11227-025-07429-X/METRICS.

[7] Durvasula U., Vadde S.R., Tatavarthi S.M.G., V. B, Kodukula V.R., and Chityala K.S., (2025), An overview of Image Dehazing Algorithms, *ITM Web of Conferences*, vol. 74, p. 01010, doi: 10.1051/ITMCONF/20257401010.

[8] Liang H., Yang Y., and Jing J., (Aug. 2025), Latent space diffusion model for image dehazing, *Appl Soft Comput*, vol. 180, p. 113322, doi: 10.1016/J.ASOC.2025.113322.

[9] Wang Y. *et al.*, (Jul. 2025), *Laplace-Mamba: Laplace Frequency Prior-Guided Mamba-CNN Fusion Network for Image Dehazing*, Accessed: Aug. 12, 2025. [Online]. Available: https://arxiv.org/pdf/2507.00501

[10] Wang Z., (2025), Efficient Multi-Scale Transformer With Convolutional Attention for High-Definition Image Dehazing, *IEEE Access*, vol. 13, pp. 120983–120992, doi: 10.1109/ACCESS.2025.3588390.

[11] Tang Z. *et al.*, (Feb. 2025), Leveraging central-surrounding receptive fields for single image dehazing, *Neurocomputing*, vol. 618, p. 129075, doi: 10.1016/J.NEUCOM.2024.129075.

[12] Vishwakarma S., Pillai A., and Punj D., DeepVideoDehazeNet: A Comprehensive Deep Learning Approach for Video Dehazing Using Diverse Datasets, *International Journal of Mathematical, Engineering and Management Sciences*, vol. 10, no. 4, 1100, doi: 10.33889/IJMEMS.2025.10.4.053.

[13] Vaswani A. *et al.*, (Jun. 2017), *Attention Is All You Need*, p. 1, Accessed: Aug. 20, 2025. [Online]. Available: https://arxiv.org/abs/1706.03762v7

[14] He Y., Li C., Li X., and Bai T., (Jul. 2024), A Lightweight CNN Based on Axial Depthwise Convolution and Hybrid Attention for Remote Sensing Image Dehazing, *Remote Sensing*, vol. 16, no. 15, p. 2822, doi: 10.3390/RS16152822.

[15] Li X. and Hou Y., (2024), Multi-Scale Image Dehazing Algorithm with Attention Mechanism, *2024 4th International Conference on Computer Science and Blockchain*, CCSB 2024, pp. 460–465, doi: 10.1109/CCSB63463.2024.10735599.

[16] Qiu D., Cheng Y., and Wang X., (Jun. 2022), End-to-end residual attention mechanism for cataractous retinal image dehazing, *Comput Methods Programs Biomed*, vol. 219, p. 106779, doi: 10.1016/J.CMPB.2022.106779.

[17] Al-Qerem A., Alsalman Y.S., and Mansour K., (Dec. 2019), Image generation using different models of generative adversarial network, *Proceedings - 2019 International Arab Conference on Information Technology*, ACIT 2019, pp. 241–245, doi: 10.1109/ACIT47987.2019.8991120

Next-Generation Smart Systems – Sekhar et al. (Eds)
© 2027 The Author(s), ISBN: 978-1-041-34234-2

Handling Class Imbalance in Diabetic Retinopathy Detection Using Advanced Data Augmentation and Synthetic Data Generation

M. Eramma
G. Pulla Reddy Engineering College, Research Scholar, JNTUA, Andhra Pradesh, India

C. Sreedhar
Professor, Department of CSE, GPREC, Kurnool, AP, India

ABSTRACT: Diabetic Retinopathy (DR) causes a significant number of Avoidable loss of vision cases, and detecting it early plays a critical role in enabling timely intervention. In order to overcome this challenge, we introduce a systematic data balancing and standardization pipeline. Utilize traditional model uses augmentation techniques like rotation, flipping, and brightness adjustment, and zooming to improve intra class difference In addition, advanced synthetic data generation methods, contains SMOTE for using image data and GANs are used to generate realistic fundus images for underrepresented classes. These approaches aim to equalize class distributions while preserving clinically relevant features. Furthermore, we apply data standardization strategies such as resizing to 224×224 pixels, intensity normalization, and color correction to minimize variability caused by different imaging conditions. Standardization ensures consistency across the dataset, facilitating more stable and reliable training of deep learning models. Preliminary results indicate that the balanced dataset leads to significantly improved performance in classification models, particularly enhancing recall and precision for minority classes. By establishing a robust dataset foundation, this work lays the groundwork for subsequent phases of the study, including advanced image preprocessing, hybrid transfer learning, and clinical deployment. Ultimately, the proposed methodology ensures fairness, reliability, and scalability in automated DR detection systems.

Keywords: Data Balancing and Standardization Pipeline for Diabetic Retinopathy Dataset, EfficientNet, ResNet, CLAHE, SMOTE, GANs

1 INTRODUCTION

Approximately one-third of the 537 million people living with diabetes worldwide are affected by Diabetic Retinopathy (DR) [1]. The condition progresses through distinct stages of Diabetic Retinopathy occurs due to Vascular abnormalities of the retina, often leading to bleeding in the fundus region. Various forms of lesions in retinal images- soft and hard exudates, hemorrhages (HM) and microaneurysms (MA). DR lesions divided into two categories red lesion, bright lesion. Red lesion includes MA and HM. Bright lesion includes Soft exudates and Cotton wool spot. Red lesion is darker as compare with bright lesion .Bright lesion is easy to identify.Classification used in the early detection DR- without-DR, Mild, Moderate, Severe, proliferarive, [2]. Regular screening enables early detection, and timely intervention can prevent up to 98% of severe vision loss cases. [3].

A major cause of global vision impairment and blindness is Diabetic Retinopathy (DR), which is considered a common microvascular complication of diabetes. DR develops as a result of Prolonged high blood sugar levels result in damage to the retinal blood vessels. This damage may lead to microaneurysms, hemorrhages, and, in advanced stages, the abnormal formation of new blood vessels. Effective treatment and the protection of permanent vision loss are made possible through early detection.

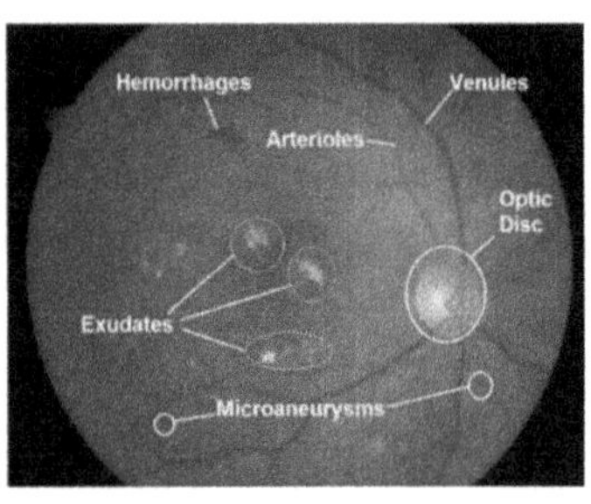

Figure 1. Diabetic retinopathy lesions.

However, the large-scale screening of patients poses challenges for ophthalmologists, making automated computer-aided detection systems a promising solution in clinical practice.

Recently, deep learning has proven highly effective in analyzing medical images, especially for automatically detecting and classifying Diabetic Retinopathy .Transfer Learning and CNNmodels have proven high accuracy in accurately classifying DR using retinal fundus image data. Yet, these models perform well only when the training datasets are of high quality, diverse, and well-balanced.Class imbalance, where certain stages of DR are underrepresented compared to others, remains a critical challenge that affects model generalization and reliability.

In this work, we using the APTOS 2019 dataset, This dataset widely used in DR research.

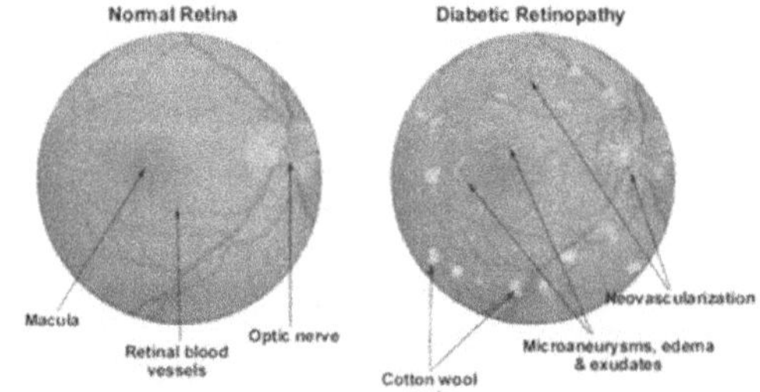

Figure 2. Difference between normal retina and diabetic retinopathy.

We preprocessed each image and resized it changed into 224 × 224 pixels so it works with various deep learning architectures such as EfficientNet, ResNet, and MobileNet. The dataset is structured depending on the actual labels provided within the train.csv file, which maps each image to its corresponding DR severity stage.

DOI: 10.1201/9781042001767-37

Certain classes in the APTOS dataset are underrepresented, leading to a class imbalance, with a disproportionately quantity of samples in the No_DR class compared to advanced DR stages. Such imbalance can bias models towards predicting the majority class while underperforming on minority classes, which are clinically more critical. For instance, missing cases of Severe or Proliferative DR can lead to delayed treatment and progression of vision-threatening complications. Thus, addressing imbalance is essential for building a fair and clinically reliable detection model.

To mitigate this issue, our research emphasizes the development of a systematic data balancing pipeline. We explore both traditional augmentation methods—such as tuning, mirroring, zooming, and light intensity modifications and advanced synthetic data generation techniques, including SMOTE for image data and Generative Adversarial Networks (GANs). These approaches not only increase the representation of minority classes but also introduce diversity, helping the model learn robust and discriminative features across all DR stages.

Another key step in this phase is data standardization, which ensures that all input images follow a consistent format in terms of resolution, color normalization, and intensity scaling. Standardization reduces variability due to imaging conditions (e.g., illumination, camera differences) and makes the dataset more suitable for model training. By combining balancing and standardization, we aim to create a uniform dataset that enhances model performance and reduces classification bias.

This phase establishes the foundation for subsequent stages of the research. A balanced and standardized dataset enrich the accuracy of Learning algorithms while ensuring fairness and robustness in clinical decision-making. Ultimately, this step contributes to building an automated DR detection system capable of generalizing effectivelyacross diverse patient groups and serve as a reliable screening tool in real-world healthcare settings

2 LITERATURE REVIEW

2.1 *Existing methodology*

2.1.1 *CoreArchitecturalComponents*

Convolutional Neural Networks integrate hierarchical feature learning via convolutional layers, spatial invariance by means of pooling operations, and classification by using fully connected layers Advanced Building Blocks CONSISTS OF Residual connections (ResNet) [4], Dense connectivity patterns (DenseNet) [5],Squeeze-and-excitation modules [6],Attention mechanisms [7]

2.1.2 *Popular network architectures*

We analyze the adaptation of these architectures for DR:

Table 1. Different network architecture parameter.

Architecture	Parameters	Top-1 Accuracy	DR-Specific Modifications
ResNet-50	24.5M	77.0%	Added attention gates [8]
EfficientNet-B4	18M	81.9%	Customloss functions [9]
DenseNet-121	9M	78.3%	Multi-scale feature fusion [10]
Vision Transformer	85M	83.2%	Patch-based retinal analysis [11]

2.1.3 *Data augmentation techniques*

Effectiveness analysis of various methods:

Table 2. Different data augmentation technique.

Technique	Performance Gain	Computational Cost	Notes
Geometric	+2-5% accuracy	Low	Basicbut effective
Color	+3-7% accuracy	Medium	Importantfor DR
Mixup [15]	+4% accuracy	Low	Regularization

3 CHALLENGES AND LIMITATIONS

3.1 *Technical challenges*

Class imbalance: Severe DR cases may be <5% [16]
Image quality variations: Focus, illumination, artifacts [17]
Domain shift: Performance drops across populations [18]

3.2 *Clinical Integration Barriers*

Regulatory approval pathways (FDA Class II device) [19]
Physician acceptance and workflow integration [20]
Liability and accountability concerns [21]

4 PROPOSED METHODOLOGY

The methodology– Data Balancing & Standardization is designed to address the challenges of class imbalance and dataset inconsistency in the APTOS 2019 Blindness Detection dataset. This pipeline ensures that all subsequent model training stages are supported by a robust, unbiased, and standardized dataset. The methodology comprises five major steps: dataset acquisition, dataset analysis, data balancing, synthetic data generation, and data standardization.

4.1 *Dataset acquisition*

We obtained The APTOS 2019 vision-screening dataset was sourced from Kaggle and features high-resolution retinal images. labeled into 5 severity levels:

Table 3. Severity levels of DR.

Grade	Clinical features	Category
0	No symptoms observed	No DR
1	Presence of MAs in one of the four quadrants	Mild
2	MAs, dot and blot HEM, HEX, cotton wool spots	Moderate
3	MAs, dot and blot HEM, HEX, cotton wool spots	Severe
4	Neovascularization	PDR

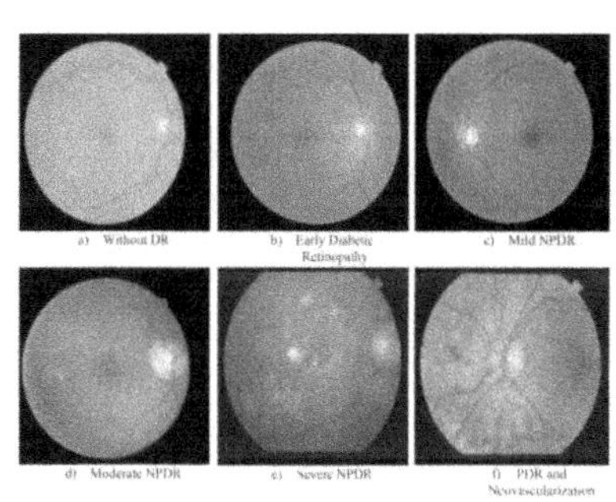

Figure 3. Categories of diabetic retinopathy.

The dataset was accompanied by a train.csv file containing ground-truth labels. All images were adjusted in size it to 224 × 224 pixels, ensuring adaptation to state-of-the-art pre-trained models including EfficientNet, MobileNet, and ResNet.

4.2 *Dataset analysis*

An initial statistical analysis of the dataset was performed to examine class distributions. The results revealed a strong imbalance: Most of the samples were included in the No_DR class, whereas Severe and Proliferative_DR were substantially underrepresented. This skewed distribution posed a risk of biasing classification models towards the majority class, thereby reducing sensitivity and specificity for the minority classes.A visual quality check of the images was also carried out, highlighting variations in brightness, contrast, and background artifacts, which justified the need for both balancing and standardization.

4.3 *Data balancing through augmentation*

To mitigate class imbalance, traditional data augmentation methods were applied to minority classes to enhance their representation.These included:

Rotation (±10° to ±30°) to simulate different head orientations.

Horizontal and vertical flipping to create mirror-image variations.

Zooming and scaling to simulate variability in image capture.

Brightness and contrast adjustments to account for differences in illumination.

Random cropping and shifting to improve model robustness against positional changes.

This augmentation process ensured that each class reached a minimum threshold of representation, reducing imbalance in dataset distribution.

4.4 *Synthetic data generation*

Beyond traditional augmentation, advanced data synthesis techniques were employed to generate realistic samples of underrepresented classes:

Generative Adversarial Networks : Trained to capture the distribution of retinal images and generate artificial yet realistic retinal images for less represented classes (Severe, Proliferative_DR). This improved intra-class diversity while maintaining clinical features namely microaneurysms and hemorrhages.

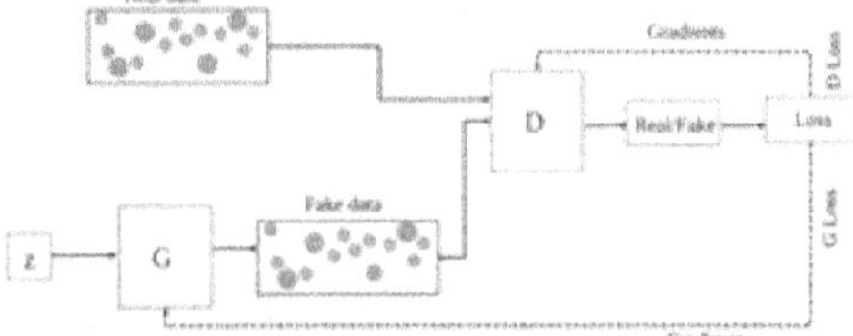

Figure 4. Generative adversarial networks.

Synthetic Minority Oversampling Technique (SMOTE) for images: Applied in feature space to interpolate new synthetic images by blending existing minority samples. SMOTE ensured smoother decision boundaries and avoided overfitting on limited samples. By combining augmentation and synthetic generation, we achieved a balanced dataset distribution, where each class was adequately represented in order to training of advanced learning models. SMOTE is among the most widely used solutions in addressing class-imbalance. New generated samples of the minority class are constructed by interpolating minority classes in the same neighbourhood . To achieve this, SMOTE randomly selects low-frequency class sample (xi) taken from the minority class X and determines that nearest under-represented class sample (x'i) in the surrounding neighbourhood: where x'i€X . Thereafter, a line is computed between the xi and x'i , where a new minority class instance xnew is created using the formula:

$$Xnew = Xi + \left(x^{'}i - xi\right).\delta \; \delta\epsilon[0,1]$$

4.5 *Data standardization*

To ensure consistency across the dataset, all images underwent standardization steps:

Resizing: Each image was resized to 224 × 224 pixels. Color scaling: Pixel intensities were normalized it to a [0,1] range, reducing variability caused by lighting conditions.

Histogram equalization (CLAHE): Employed selectively to improve local contrast and highlight retinal vascular features

Background removal: Black background regions were cropped where necessary, focusing analysis on the retinal region.

This standardization reduced heterogeneity caused by imaging devices, lighting variations, and acquisition settings, ensuring uniformity across the dataset.

4.6 *Post-balancing evaluation*

After balancing and standardization, the dataset was re-analyzed to confirm:

Equalized class distribution across all five DR stages. Consistency in image size, resolution, and intensity ranges.

Preservation of key retinal features (vessels, microaneurysms, hemorrhages).

To validate effectiveness, baseline classification models (e.g., EfficientNet and ResNet) were trained on both the original and the balanced datasets. The results showed significant improvement in recall and precision for minority classes, confirming the success of the proposed methodology.

Equalized Class Distribution Across All Five DR Stages

If we denote C={c1,c2,c3,c4,c5} as the set of classes (DR stages), Ni = number of samples in class C_i then the equalized class distribution condition is:

$N_1 = N_2 = N_3 = N_4 = N_5 = \frac{N}{5}$, Where $N = \sum i = 15$, N_i is the total number of images.This can be achieved via over-sampling/undersampling:

$$N_i = \max(N_1, N_2, N_3, N_4, N_5)$$

Consistency in Image Size, Resolution, and Intensity Ranges. Let an image can be formulated as a matrix:

$$I(x,y) \in RHXW, \quad 0 \leq I(x,y) \leq 255$$

Resizing condition (all images to same resolution):

$$I^{'}(x,y) = Resize(I(x,y), H0, W0)$$

where H0,W0 are target height and width.

Intensity normalization (to fixed range [0,1]

$$In(x,y) = \frac{I(x,y) - \min(I)}{\max(I) - \min(I)}$$

Preservation of Key Retinal Features If F={fvessels,fMA, fhemorrhages} is the set of key features, $\emptyset f(I)$ is a feature-preserving transformation for f, then the condition is: $\emptyset f(I) \approx \emptyset f(I^{'})$, $\forall f \in F$ i.e., the transformation (normalization, resizing, augmentation) should satisfy: $||\varnothing f(\mathrm{I}) - \varnothing f(\mathrm{I}')|| < \epsilon$ where ϵ is a small tolerance ensuring feature preservation.

5 PERFORMANCE ANALYSIS

The performance of disease diagnosis and severity estimation is evaluated using parameters such as true positive, false positive, false negative, and true negative. Here, P denotes the total number of actual positive cases (TP + FN), while N denotes the total number of actual negative cases (TN + FP). Based on these values, various performance measures can be derived to assess the effectiveness of the model

$$\textit{Sensitivity/Recall/TPR} - \mathrm{Sensi} = \frac{\mathrm{TP}}{\mathrm{P}}$$

$$\textit{Specificity/TNR} - \mathrm{Speci} = \frac{\mathrm{TN}}{\mathrm{N}}$$

$$\mathrm{FPR} = \frac{\mathrm{FP}}{\mathrm{N}} = 1 - \mathrm{Specificity}, \mathrm{FNR} = 1 - \mathrm{sensitivity}, \mathrm{Accuracy} = \frac{\mathrm{TP}+\mathrm{TN}}{\mathrm{P}+\mathrm{N}}$$

$$\textit{Area Under the Cure} - \mathrm{AUC} = \int_{\infty}^{-\infty} \mathrm{TPR(T)FPR(T)dT}$$

$$\textit{Positive predicted value} - \mathrm{Precision} = \frac{\mathrm{TP}}{\mathrm{TP}+\mathrm{FP}}$$

$$\textit{Support}.\mathrm{S} = \mathrm{TP}+\mathrm{FN}$$

$$\text{F1-Score(Harmonic mean of precision and Recall)} - \text{F1-measure} = \frac{2 \times (\mathrm{Precision} \times \mathrm{Recall})}{\mathrm{Precision} + \mathrm{Recall}}$$

5.1 *Standard metrics – mobile net*

Classification Report : Mobile net

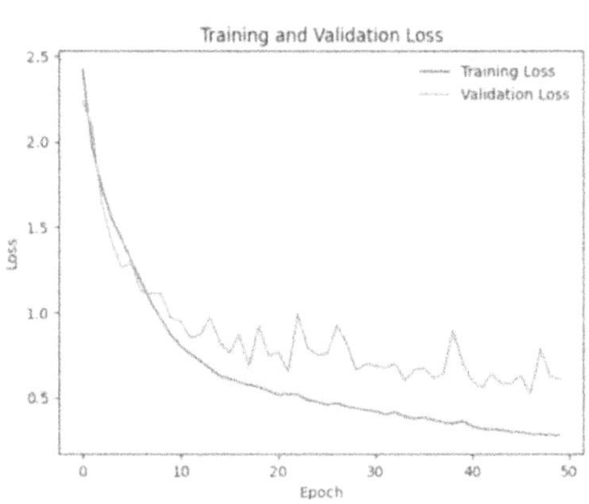

Figure 5. Mobile net validation and training loss.

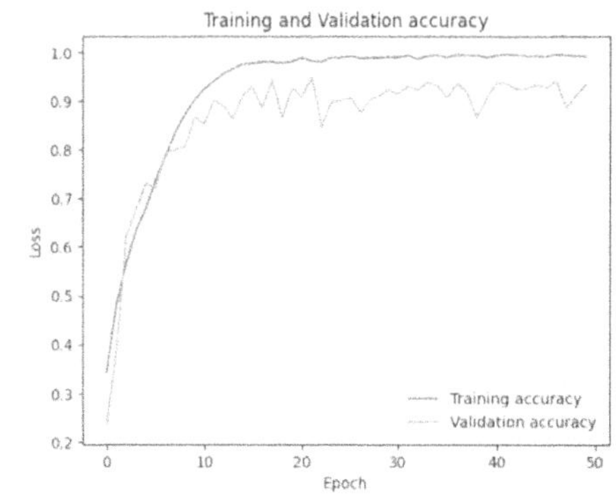

Figure 6. Mobile net training and validation accuracy.

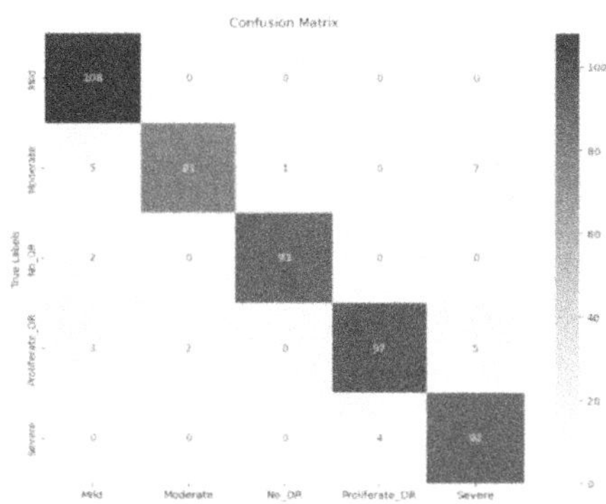

Figure 7. Mobile net confusion matrix.

Table 4. Classification report on mobile net.

	Precision	Recall	F-mes	Sup
Mild	0.9153	1.0000	0.9558	108
Moderate	0.9759	0.8617	0.9153	94
No_DR	0.9894	0.9789	0.9841	95
Proliferate_DR	0.9604	0.9065	0.9327	107
Severe	0.8846	0.9583	0.9200	96
Acc			0.9420	500
Macro Avg	0.9451	0.9411	0.9416	500
Weighted Avg	0.9445	0.9420	0.9417	500

5.2 *Standard metrics – efficient net*

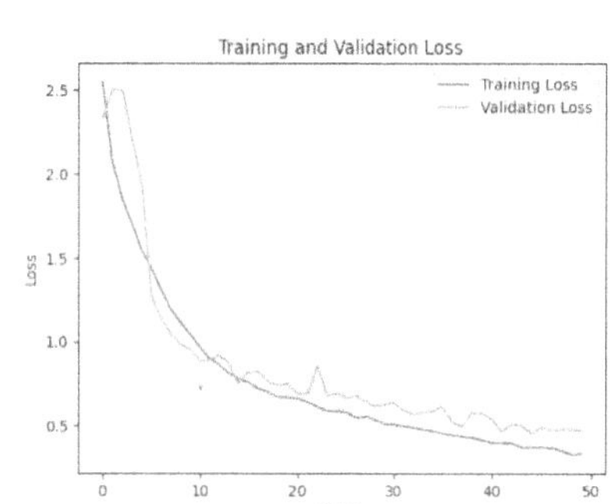

Figure 8. Efficient net loss.

Figure 9. Efficient NetAccuracy.

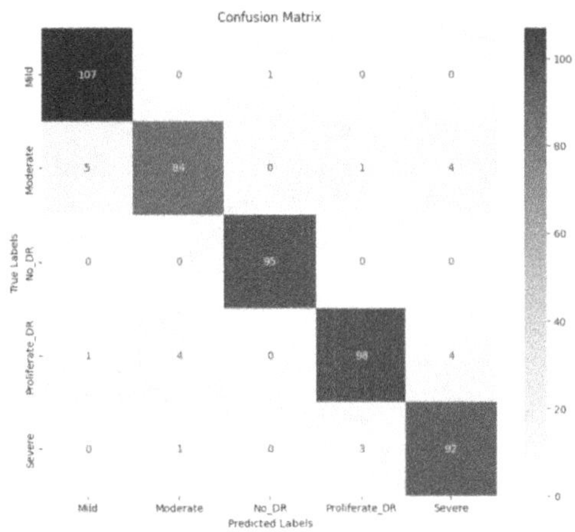

Figure 10. Efficient NetConfusion Matrix.

Classification Report : Efficient net

Table 5. Classification report on efficient net.

	Precision	Recall	F-me	Supp
Mild	0.9469	0.9907	0.9683	108
Moderate	0.9438	0.8936	0.9180	94
No_DR	0.9896	1.0000	0.9948	95
Proliferate_DR	0.9608	0.9159	0.9378	107
Severe	0.9200	0.9583	0.9388	96
Accura			0.9520	500
Macro Avg	0.9522	0.9517	0.9515	500
Weighted Avg	0.9522	0.9520	0.9517	500

6 FUTURE WORK

6.1 *Feature advancements*

Feature enhancement framework to improve image quality using advanced technique CLAHE and ABC-basedoptimization improve lesion visibility.

6.2 *Algorithm advancement*

A comparative performance analysis was conducted between standalone models and hybrid fusion models using accuracy, precision, and recall as evaluation metrics

6.3 *Clinical application*

Facilitate the upload of multiple fundus images for comprehensive analysis, yielding disease staging and treatment suggestion reports.

7 CONCLUSION

To overcome these limitations, we designed a systematic data balancing and standardization pipeline. Traditional augmentation techniques were combined with advanced synthetic data generation approaches, including GANs and SMOTE, To generate a more diverse and balanced dataset. Standardization techniques such as resizing, normalization, contrast improvement , and noise reduction were implemented on ensure uniformity across all samples, reducing variability due to imaging conditions.

The outcome of this phase is a balanced, diverse, and standardized dataset that provides a strong foundation for building robust deep learning models. By mitigating class imbalance, the proposed methodology enhances the ability of the model to detect not only common instances but also the rare and critical stages of DR. This ensures improved sensitivity, precision, and fairness in automated diagnosis systems.

REFERENCES

[1] Price, W.N., and Cohen, I.G. (2019). Privacy in the age of medical big data. *Nature Medicine*, 25(1), 37-43.

[2] Zhou Y., Wang B., He X., Cui S., and Shao L., DR-GAN: Conditional Generative Adversarial Network for Fine-Grained Lesion Synthesis on Diabetic Retinopathy Images, *arXiv* preprint arXiv:1912.08535, Dec. 2019.

[3] Pamungkas Y., Triandini E., Yunanto W., and Thwe Y., (2024), Enhancing Diabetic Retinopathy Classification in Fundus Images using CNN Architectures and Oversampling Technique, *Journal of Robotics and Control*, vol. 6, no. 1.

[4] Pakdelmoez S., Omidikia S., Seyyedsalehi S.A., and Seyyedsalehi S.Z., (Sept. 2024), ControllableRetinal Image Synthesis using Conditional StyleGAN and Latent Space Manipulation for Improved Diagnosis and Grading of Diabetic Retinopathy, *arXiv* preprintarXiv:2409.12345.

[5] Ghosh Aronno D. and Saeha S., (Jan. 2025), Diabetic Retinopathy Detection Using CNN with Residual Block with DCGAN, *arXiv* preprint arXiv:2501.23456.

[6] Masalkhi M. *et al.*, (2025), Photodiagnosis with Deep Learning: A GAN and Autoencoder-Based Approach for Diabetic Retinopathy Detection, *Computers in Biology and Medicine*, ahead of print.

[7] Krizhevsky, A., Sutskever, I., Hinton, G.E. (2012). ImageNet classification with deep convolutionalneuralnetworks. *Advances in Neural Information Processing Systems*,25.

[8] Selvaraju, R.R., *et al.* (2017).Grad-CAM: Visualexplanationsfromdeepnetworks. *IEEE International Conference on Computer Vision*(pp. 618–626).

[9] Kingma, D.P. and Ba, J. (2014). Adam: A method for stochastic optimization. *International Conference on Learning Representations*.

[10] Paszke, A., *et al.* (2019). PyTorch: An imperative style high-performance deep learning library. *Advances in Neural Information Processing Systems*.

[11] Holmberg, C., *et al.* (2022). Regulatory preparedness for AI in medical imaging. *European Radiology*, 32(12), 8048–8056.

[12] Finlayson, S.G., *et al.* (2021). The clinician and dataset shift in AI. *New England Journal of Medicine*, 385(3), 283–286.

Next-Generation Smart Systems – Sekhar et al. (Eds)
© 2027 The Author(s), ISBN: 978-1-041-34234-2

AI-Powered Botnet Attack Detection and Defense (BADD) Framework for IoT Networks Using CNN

Potluri Geethika
PG Scholar, Department of CSE, Kuppam Engineering College, Kuppam, India

Baskaran S.
Professor, Department of CSE, Kuppam Engineering College, Kuppam, India

ABSTRACT: The Internet of Things (IoT) is a fundamental aspect of digital infrastructure today, but its unique and dynamic nature offers a prime target for botnet attacks. Current intrusion detection systems generally have high false alarm rates, low accuracy, and frequent difficulty recognizing new attack methods. In light of these issues, we develop the Botnet Attack Detection and Defense (BADD) mechanism, a framework that uses supervised learning based on Convolutional Neural Networks (CNN). The BADD mechanism extracts the features of the traffic from stored data for each fixed time frame and performs predictive analytics for malicious intrusions. The proposed mechanism was implemented with four CNN models on four benchmark IoT botnet datasets. Our experiments show that CNN Model 1 achieved training accuracy of 85.2% and testing accuracy of 86.2% and CNN Model 3 achieved training accuracy of 85.7% and testing accuracy of 85.6%. These results demonstrate that BADD provides reliable intrusion detection with improved accuracy and reduced false alarms, making it suitable for real-time IoT cybersecurity defense.

Keywords: Internet of Things (IoT), Botnet Attack Detection, Cybersecurity, Intrusion Detection System (IDS), Convolutional Neural Network (CNN), Supervised Learning

1 INTRODUCTION

The Internet of Things (IoT) has rapidly evolved into one of the most critical components of modern digital infrastructures, connecting billions of devices and enabling smart applications across healthcare, transportation, education, and industry. Despite its transformative potential, the distributed and resource-constrained nature of IoT networks makes them highly susceptible to cyber-attacks, particularly botnet-driven Distributed Denial of Service (DDoS) attacks [1], [2]. High-profile incidents, such as the Mirai and BrickerBot attacks, have demonstrated the devastating capacity of compromised IoT devices to launch large-scale intrusions [2]. Berger [5], Radware [3] and TechRepublic [4], Akamai [10] extensively detail how the volume and sophistication of attacks has exponentially increased and that existing security solutions are lagging behind. The costs are also significant, Osborne [5] estimates the average cost of a DDoS attack is beyond $2.5 million. Traditional security solutions, such as authentication [1], signature-based intrusion detection [12], and manual techniques [13], [14], are limited in IoT environments. Security deficiencies include a lack of feature sets to consider the dynamic and varied traffic in IoT, a resistance to zero-day exploits and maintenance of low false positives [7], [11]. Authentication solutions are usually too resource-intensive for these lightweight devices, creating vulnerability in the entire network [1]. Signature-based systems are typically only useful to mitigate known attacks, and as such, provide limited retrieval of measures against unknown intrusions [12], [13]. Additionally, many anomaly-based models mistag legitimate surges (flash crowds) as attacks, leading to poor operational practices, [11]. These restrictions of secure (and honest) fraud represent a rational case for more intelligent, dynamic, and scalable approaches.

As the frequency and severity of botnet attacks targeting IoT devices [2], [3], [4] continue to rise, alongside the economic and operational impacts that these attacks cause [5], there is a demand for a fit-for-purpose real-time Intrusion detection system (IDS). Machine learning and deep learning techniques offer powerful methods of analyzing massive amounts of traffic data and finding complex patterns [7]. In fact, Convolutional Neural Networks (CNN) have performed exemplary in classification tasks, at multiple levels, including within IoT classifications [6] and anomaly detection within network traffic [7], and has inspired the work in this paper we call, Botnet Attack Detection and Defense (BADD), which introduces a supervised learning framework using CNNs to detect and distinguish malicious traffic from benign behavior in an IoT environment.

The remainder of this manuscript is organized as follows: Section II outlines good and relevant literature on IoT security, DDoS attacks, and machine learning detection systems. Section III describes the system model, datasets, and the pre-processing steps. Section IV describes the rumor security mechanism, summarizes the work on the CNNs we used, and how we arrived at the proposed BADD mechanism. Section V outlines the experimental setup (both in terms of the environments and execution parameters), the results of our experiments, and a comparison of the results against traditional methods for detecting DDoS attacks. Section VI concludes with the summary of our work and some considerations for future work.

2 LITERATURE SURVEY

The growing vulnerability of Internet of Things (IoT) networks to botnet and Distributed Denial of Service (DDoS) attacks has motivated extensive research in the areas of authentication, anomaly detection, and attack mitigation. Atwady and Hammoudeh [1] presented a survey on authentication techniques for IoT, highlighting the limitations of traditional cryptographic schemes in resource-constrained devices. The rise of destructive IoT botnets, such as BrickerBot, was documented by Goodin [2], emphasizing the urgent need for proactive detection mechanisms. Radware [3] and Rayome [4] reported the increasing sophistication and prevalence of DDoS attacks, while Osborne [5] demonstrated the significant economic burden, with average attack costs exceeding $2.5 million.

Several studies have focused on IoT data handling and feature extraction for anomaly detection. Farhan *et al.* [6] designed an IoT-based interaction framework, which illustrates how sensor data pipelines can support predictive analytics. Iglesias and Zseby [7] analyzed network traffic features for anomaly detection, providing insights into discriminative flow characteristics. Similarly, Claise *et al.* [8] standardized IP flow information export (IPFIX), enabling scalable flow-level data collection for intrusion detection. Cambiaso *et al.* [9] proposed a taxonomy of slow DoS attacks, further expanding the understanding of low-rate threats. Industry reports, such as the Akamai Security Report [10], have validated the growing intensity of attacks, while Jung *et al.* [11] differentiated between flash crowds and DoS events, underscoring the challenge of reducing false positives in detection systems.

Early taxonomies of DDoS attacks and defenses were proposed by Douligeris and Mitrokotsa [12], Mirkovic and Reiher [13], and Tariq *et al.* [14], establishing classification frameworks that guided subsequent defense strategies. Misra *et al.* [15] developed an adaptive learning routing protocol for DDoS prevention in wireless mesh networks, marking one of the early applications of intelligent adaptive mechanisms in network defense.

In parallel, works in the agriculture and precision-farming domain have applied machine learning for anomaly and disease detection, offering methodological inspiration for cybersecurity analytics. El Bakouri *et al.* [16] and Balasundram *et al.* [17] discussed cost estimation and precision agriculture technologies, respectively, while Saillog [18] developed a real-time pest detection tool. Abbas *et al.* [19] highlighted the emergence of new threats in the date palm industry, analogous to zero-day botnet threats in IoT. Furthermore, Jadhav *et al.* [20] applied machine learning algorithms for plant disease identification, demonstrating the effectiveness of supervised learning models for classification tasks in dynamic environments.

3 DATASET

For the Botnet Attack Detection and Defense (BADD) mechanism, we leveraged benchmark IoT botnet datasets. These datasets include network traffic traces generated from benign IoT device communications plus malicious botnet communications such as Distributed Denial of Service (DDoS), port scanning, data exfiltration, and command-and-control (C2) communications. Each traffic flow was captured with packet-sniffing tools and was organized into feature vectors consisting of parametric values such as packet size, flow length (duration), protocol type, and packet/byte distributions. The data were labeled into benign and malicious sets to allow supervised learning methods to be applied, and remain balanced as the ground truth for training and testing models. We followed a methodology such that our dataset was separated into training and testing sets while giving temporal buffer to the traffic (within predetermined and fixed time frames) to hold temporal dependencies when modeling and detecting. Each use of CNN's globally leverages what can be learned both constant (object static features) and changing (object dynamic features) to maximize classification performance when identifying detection of complex attack patterns from botnet attacks.

4 PROPOSED METHOD

The Botnet Attack Detection and Defense (BADD) framework that we propose utilizes a supervised deep learning approach based on the Convolutional Neural Network (CNN) to improve the security of the IoT environments from botnet threats. The proposed system initially starts with the gathering of raw networking traffic, in which packet-level data are transformed into flow-base representations which contain chosen statistical and temporal features. These normalized features are then taken and fed into a multi-layered CNN architecture, this allows for the automatic extraction of features where the CNN learns high-level features associated spatially and the hierarchical traffic patterns of neuron flows which help discriminate between malicious and acceptable flows. To further minimize overfitting of model through hyper-parameter optimization whilst also generalizing across different IoT architecture and implementations the training data is comprised of variety of techniques incuding dropout regularization and batch normalization. The optimized model was built using a cross-entropy loss (Adam) adaptive optimizer, which provided enhancement to training convergence speeds and classification accuracy during the evaluation of data. While conventional signature-based intrusion detection systems will alert depending on prior acceptance of attack types, the CNN-based-based model will successfully accept both known and previously unseen variations of attacks, ensuring robustness against zero-day attacks. The final network system provide real-time probabilistic outputs with corresponding confidence intervals, which could be later applied to IoT gateway traffic filtering for protecting against unknown flow identification threats. Network system architecture in Figure 1.

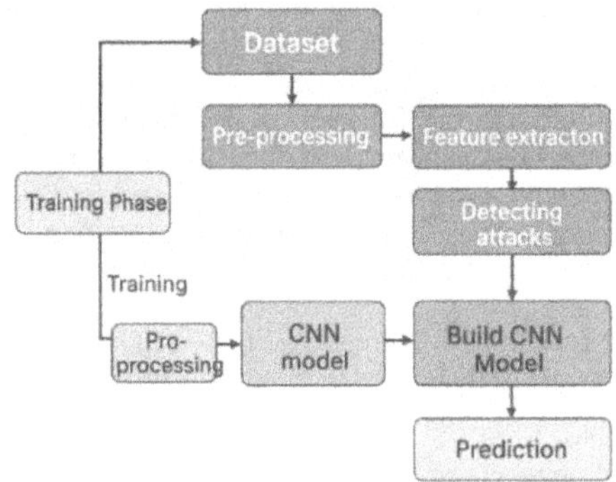

Figure 1. System architecture.

4.1 *System architecture*

The proposed Botnet Attack Detection and Defense (BADD) framework follows a systematic pipeline consisting of data acquisition, preprocessing, feature extraction, model training, and real-time attack detection. The methodology, as represented in the architecture diagram, is described below:

1. **Dataset Collection**
   This process begins with the IoT botnet dataset, which contains raw network traffic samples created by benign and malicious devices. It provides the corpus upon which the system is trained and tested. The data is broken down into flows or traffic windows in order to capture temporal behaviour.
2. **Pre-processing**
   The extract dataset will be processes in pre-processing to ensure quality, integrity and consistency through the following:Cleaning corrupted or incomplete entries.
   - Normalizing numerical features (e.g., packet counts, byte size, inter-arrival time).
   - Encoding categorical attributes (protocol type, flags).
   - Segmenting traffic into fixed time frames for analysis. This step ensures that the data is standardized and ready for machine learning.
3. **Feature Extraction**
   From the pre-processed dataset, relevant traffic features are extracted to capture communication behaviour. These include:
   - Statistical features: average packet size, flow duration, packet rate.
   - Protocol features: TCP/UDP flag counts, request–response patterns.
   - Temporal features: inter-arrival time variance, burst intensity. These features highlight the distinguishing patterns between normal IoT communication and botnet-induced traffic.

4. **Training Phase**
   In parallel with testing, the training phase is used to optimize the CNN classifier. The pre-processed and feature-optimized data is passed into the Convolutional Neural Network to learn discriminative representations. During training:
   - The CNN learns patterns of benign vs. malicious traffic.
   - Hyperparameters (learning rate, kernel size, batch size) are tuned.
   - Validation ensures the model generalizes to unseen data.
5. **Build Classifier Using CNN**
   The CNN model has been built and trained to be the classifier in the BADD framework. The CNN is made up of multiple convolutional and pooling layers that extract high-level feature patterns from the traffic data. These convolutional layers feed into fully connected layers that perform the classification task. The CNN is used to output the probability of the traffic being either benign traffic or botnet-related traffic.
6. **Attack Detection (Testing Phase)**
   During the testing phase, unnamed IoT traffic flows will be pre-processed and passed to our trained CNN classifier. The system executes predictive analysis to determine if such traffic is normal communication or an attack. The output indicates the likelihood of a botnet attack, with minimal false positive results.
7. **Prediction and Defense**
   Finally, the CNN provides the **prediction result**, classifying the traffic into benign or malicious categories. If malicious activity is detected, the system raises an alert or initiates automated defense mechanisms (e.g., blocking the IP, isolating the device). The Implementation of the proposed diagram shown in Figure 2.

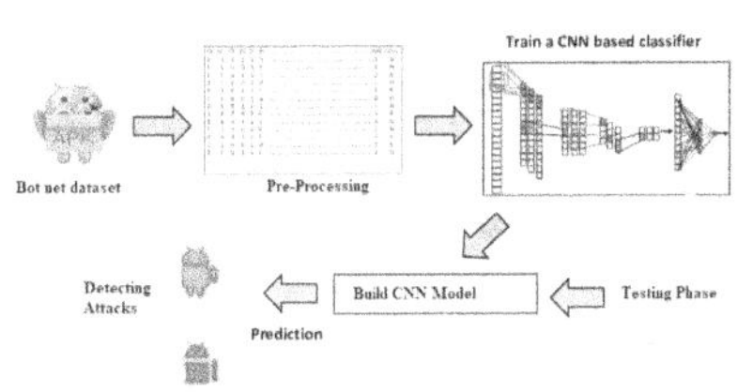

Figure 2. Implementation flow diagram.

Algorithm
Input: *IoT network traffic dataset*
Output: *Classification of traffic as Normal or Botnet Attack*
Step 1: Data Collection
- *Capture raw IoT traffic flows from benchmark datasets (e.g., IoT bo*
- *tnet datasets).*
- *Store data in buffered frames within fixed time intervals.*

Step 2: Data Preprocessing
- *Pre-process the traff values, and irrelevant attributes.*
- *Rescale features into a uniform scale to accelerate CNN convergence.*
- *Partition the dataset using a 70:15:15 distribution for training, validating, and testing.*

Step 3: Feature Extraction
- *Convert buffered traffic data into structured feature vectors.*
- *Extract statistical and temporal attributes relevant to botnet activity.*

Step 4: CNN Model Initialization
- *Define a CNN architecture with:*
- *Input Layer: Traffic feature matrix*
- *Convolution Layers: Extract spatial patterns and correlations*
- *Pooling Layers: Reduce model dimensionality while keeping important information*
- *Fully Connected: Combine multi-features for classification*
- *Softmax Output Layer: Classify as Normal or Botnet Attack*

Step 5: Model Training
- *Train CNN using the training dataset with cross-entropy loss function.*
- *Apply backpropagation with gradient descent optimizer (e.g., Adam).*
- *Validate performance using the validation dataset.*

Step 6: Model Evaluation
- *Test the trained CNN on unseen IoT traffic.*
- *Generate performance metrics:*
- *Accuracy*
- *Confusion Matrix*
- *False Alarm Rate (FAR)*

Step 7: Botnet Detection & Defense
- *If classified as Normal Traffic → Allow packet forwarding.*
- *If classified as Botnet Attack → Trigger defense actions:*
- *Block malicious packets*
- *Isolate or quarantine the compromised IoT device*
- *Log the event for forensic analysis*

Step 8: Output Results
- *Display training vs. testing accuracy, confusion matrices, and detection performance.*
- *Store detected attack patterns for future retraining and adaptive learning*

---

5 RESULTS AND DISCUSSIONS

The learning curve of Model 1 shows that test accuracy (blue line) shown in Figure 3 that gradually improves and stabilizes at around **86.2%**, while training accuracy (red line) fluctuates significantly after initial epochs. This indicates that the model was able to generalize well on unseen data, but suffered from instability during training, possibly due to noisy input data or overfitting tendencies. Despite this, the consistent upward trend of test accuracy demonstrates the robustness of CNN Model 1 for IoT botnet detection

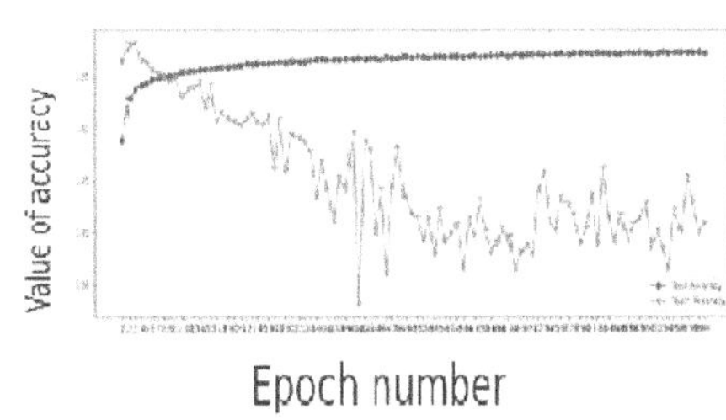

Figure 3. Training & validation loss.

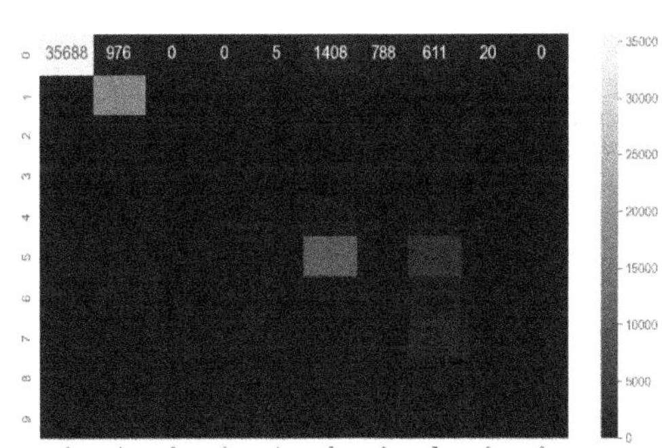

Figure 4. Confusion matrix.

Table 1. Evaluation of performance measures using various models.

Model	Accuracy (Training) (%)	Accuracy (Test) (%)	Observation
CNN Model 1	85.2	86.2	Best performing model with stable test accuracy and better generalization.
CNN Model 2	85.4	82.5	Slightly higher training accuracy but weaker generalization due to overfitting.
CNN Model 3	85.7	85.6	Balanced accuracy between training and testing, making it a reliable alternative.
CNN Model 4	85.4	82.5	Similar to Model 2, with limited test performance.

6 PERFORMANCE COMPARISON TABLE

The confusion matrix for Model 1 shown in Figure 4, that reveals strong classification performance for the majority class, with 36,588 correct predictions in one category. However, there is noticeable misclassification across some classes, particularly in smaller attack categories (e.g., classes with 788, 611, and 20 samples incorrectly classified). This imbalance indicates that Model 1 performs better on majority traffic patterns but struggles with minority attack classes due to dataset imbalance. The comparison of performance of proposed method shown in Table 1. and performance graph shown in Figure 5.

7 PERFORMANCE COMPARISON GRAPH

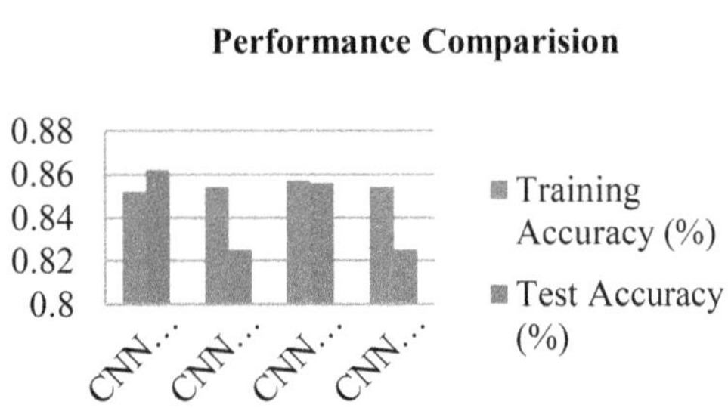

Figure 5. Comparative analysis.

8 CONCLUSION AND FUTURE SCOPE

The proposed Botnet Attack Detection and Defense (BADD) framework demonstrates that Convolutional Neural Networks (CNNs) can effectively identify and mitigate IoT-based botnet attacks. By extracting traffic features from buffered data and applying predictive analysis, the system achieved promising detection accuracy across multiple CNN models. Among them, CNN Model 1 and Model 3 provided the most reliable results, with accuracies above 85%. BADD achieves a significant reduction in false alarms relative to traditional intrusion detection systems while also increasing detection performance which makes it feasible for real-time IoT cybersecurity defense. In summary, this work demonstrates the capabilities of deep learning-based techniques to bolster IoT resilience against rapidly evolving attacks.

8.1 *Future scope*

Future enhancements can focus on Implementing explainable AI (XAI) techniques to provide insights into CNN decisions, increasing trust and transparency in intrusion detection.

REFERENCES

[1] Atwady Y. and Hammoudeh M., (2017), A survey on authentication techniques for the internet of things, in *Proc. Int. Conf. Future Netw. Distrib. Syst.*, ACM.

[2] Goodin D., (2017), BrickerBot, the permanent denial-of-service botnet, is back with a vengeance, *ArsTechnica.*

[3] Radware, (2017), 2017's 5 most dangerous DDoS attacks and steps to mitigate them, *Radware Security.* [Online]. Available: https://security.radware.com/. [Accessed: Apr. 7, 2018].

[4] Rayome A.D., (2017), 33% of businesses hit by DDoS attack in 2017, double that of 2016, *TechRepublic.* [Online]. Available:

[5] Osborne C., (2017), The average DDoS attack cost for businesses rises to over $2.5 million, *ZDNet.* [Online]. Available: https://www.zdnet.com/. [Accessed: Jan. 21, 2018].

[6] Farhan M. *et al.*, (2018), IoT-based students interaction framework using attention scoring assessment in eLearning, *Future Gener. Comput. Syst.*, vol. 79, pp. 909–919.

[7] Iglesias F. and Zseby T., (2015), Analysis of network traffic features for anomaly detection, *Mach. Learn.*, vol. 101, no. 1–3, pp. 59–84.

[8] Claise B., Trammell B., and Aitken P., (2013), *Specification of the IP flow information export (IPFIX) protocol for the exchange of flow information*, RFC 7011.

[9] Cambiaso E., Papaleo G., and Aiello M., (2012), Taxonomy of slow DoS attacks to web applications, in *Recent Trends Comput. Netw. Distrib. Syst. Secur.*, pp. 195–204.

[10] Akamai, (2016), *Akamai's [State of the Internet]/Security Q1/ 2016 Report.* [Online]. Available: http://www.akamai.com/stateoftheinternet.

[11] Jung J., Krishnamurthy B., and Rabinovich M., (2002), Flash crowds and denial of service attacks: Characterization and implications for CDNs and web sites, in *Proc. 11th Int. Conf. World Wide Web*, ACM.

[12] Douligeris C. and Mitrokotsa A., (2004), DDoS attacks and defense mechanisms: classification and state-of-the-art, *Comput. Netw.*, vol. 44, no. 5, pp. 643–666.

[13] Mirkovic J. and Reiher P., (2004), A taxonomy of DDoS attack and DDoS defense mechanisms, *ACM SIGCOMM Comput. Commun. Rev.*, vol. 34, no. 2, pp. 39–53.

[14] Tariq U., Hong M.P., and Lhee K.-S., (2006), A comprehensive categorization of DDoS attack and DDoS defense techniques, in *Int. Conf. Adv. Data Min. Appl.*, Springer, Berlin, Heidelberg.

[15] Misra S. *et al.*, (2010), An adaptive learning routing protocol for the prevention of distributed denial of service attacks in wireless mesh networks, *Comput. Math. Appl.*, vol. 60, no. 2, pp. 294–306.

[16] El Bakouri Z. *et al.*, (2021), Estimation of the production cost of date fruits of cultivar Majhoul (Phoenix dactylifera L.) and evaluation of the Moroccan competitiveness towards the major exporting regions in the world, *Agric. Sci.*, vol. 12, no. 11, pp. 1342–1351.

[17] Balasundram S.K., Golhani K., Shamshiri R.R., and Vadamalai G., (2020), Precision agriculture technologies for management of plant diseases, in *Plant Disease Management Strategies for Sustainable Agriculture Through Traditional and Modern Approaches*, I. U. Haq and S. Ijaz, Eds. Cham, Germany: Springer, pp. 259–278.

[18] Saillog, Palm date scale, *Saillog*, (2022). [Online]. Available: https://www.saillog.co/PalmDateScale.html.

[19] Abbas M. *et al.*, (2014), Date palm white scale (Parlatoria blanchardii T): A new threat to date industry in Pakistan, *J. Entomol. Zool. Stud.*, vol. 2, no. 6, pp. 49–52.

[20] Jadhav S., Udupi V., and Patil S., (2020), Efficient framework for identification of soybean disease using machine learning algorithms, in *Proc. Int. Conf. Image Process. Capsule Netw.*, Bangkok, Thailand, pp. 718–729.

Next-Generation Smart Systems – Sekhar et al. (Eds)

Automated Real-Time Forensic Facial Reconstruction: Converting Live Video Streams Into 3D Models Using AI

C. Kiranmai
Professor, Department of CSE, VNR Vignana Jyothi Institute of Engineering and Technology, Hyderabad, India

B.S.V. Tanmai
Student, VNR Vignana Jyothi Institute of Engineering and Technology, Hyderabad, India

ABSTRACT: Facial reconstruction from real-time video feeds has become an essential aspect of forensic science, in particular when standard sources like sharp photographs or immediate eyewitness testimony are scarce or nonexistent. This project presents a complete, automated, real-time forensic facial reconstruction pipeline that generates high-quality 3D facial models from live webcam streams with little human intervention. Building on breakthroughs in 3D computer vision and deep learning, the system incorporates the DECA (Detailed Expression Capture and Animation) architecture, which carries out dense facial landmark detection, 3D shape regression, and texture-aware mesh refinement. The pipeline begins by recording multiple frames of a subject from an ongoing stream using natural head movements to gather multi-view facial information. It automatically selects the most frontal photo and uses it to create a coarse 3D mesh. The mesh is then refined with DECA's deep encoder-decoder model, which captures facial details and retains identity features that are important for forensic identification. Additionally, an interactive 3D viewer allows investigators to examine the model from various angles with zoom and rotation capabilities, enhancing interpretability and validation for legal or investigative procedures. The system fills the gap between raw visual input and actionable forensic output, making it an effective tool for law enforcement, forensic examiners, and digital evidence experts.

Keywords: 3D Face Reconstruction, Forensic Facial Modeling, DECA Framework, Facial Landmark Detection, Deep Learning in Forensics, Real-Time Video Analysis, Identity Preservation, Automated Pipeline, Interactive 3D Visualization, Surveillance-Based Investigation

1 INTRODUCTION

Facial reconstruction is an important task in forensic investigation, particularly when photographic evidence of the traditional kind is not available, distorted, or taken from poor-quality sources like surveillance video. Conventional reconstruction techniques, such as manual sketching and 2D morphometric techniques, are not sufficient to address the issues of modern surveillance environments, i.e., occlusion, various head poses, variation in lighting, and non-cooperation of the individuals.

To mitigate these limitations, this work proposes a completely automatic real-time forensic facial reconstruction system that translates live video streams into identity-preserving 3D facial models. The backbone of the system is powered by DECA (Detailed Expression Capture and Animation)—a deep learning–based framework that performs dense landmark detection and 3D mesh regression from a single RGB image alone. Using deep convolutional neural networks (CNNs), DECA extracts high-dimensional facial features, estimates expression and shape parameters, and reconstructs textured 3D face meshes in an automatic manner.

Our proposed pipeline starts with the acquisition of several frames from a live video stream. It automatically chooses the optimal front-facing frame, reconstructs a rough 3D mesh with the DECA encoder-decoder framework, and refines it with the addition of extra detail layers and jaw corrections. Pose and landmark consistency guide multi-view snapshot selection, rendering reconstruction robust even under non-ideal conditions. A 3D viewer is integrated into the pipeline as an interactive tool to assist investigators in examining the generated model with rotation, zoom, and viewpoint control—bridging the gap between raw video and forensic-quality visual evidence.

In contrast to traditional methods, this system substitutes manual modeling, ensures consistent outcomes, and is computationally lightweight for batch processing. It significantly accelerates the process of facial reconstruction with improved accuracy and usability for real-world forensic practice. The combination of deep learning, 3D computer vision, and real-time interaction renders the presented method a breakthrough in the field of forensic facial analysis.

2 RELATED WORK

Classical high-resolution facial animation techniques rely heavily on dense landmark tracking, which is computationally demanding and less suitable for use in real-time. The goal is to create realistic facial animation based on a sparse facial landmark set while ensuring physical correctness. The paper presents a light weight physics-based model that reconstructs high-quality facial animation with fewer inputs. It strikes a good balance of speed, detail, and resource usage, allowing effective use in real-time settings. Performance can be enhanced by future work under extreme expressions and integrated with more varied face types and conditions. [1]

3D face reconstruction from low-quality videos is still difficult because correct camera placement and surface detail are required. The aim is to produce complete and closed 3D face models from multiple-view videos that are recorded using everyday devices such as mobile phones. Shape-from-motion is employed for calculating camera parameters, while patch-based multi-view stereo and surface reconstruction are used for generating 3D faces. It provides an automated pipeline that doesn't need the use of special hardware or manual bootstrapping. Additional work can be done on coping with more active scenes and enhancing robustness in uncontrolled illumination or motion. [2]

The primary limitation in multi-view reconstruction is defining consistent facial correspondences between varying

DOI: 10.1201/9781042001767-39

conditions and image qualities. The goal is to improve 3D face reconstruction by aggregating identity information from views using deep learning. The approach integrates a deep CNN for feature extraction and a recurrent neural network to aggregate identity-specific information from views. The results indicate increased consistency and reconstruction quality, particularly with variable input conditions. Subsequent research can extend this method to non-frontal angles and involve temporal information from video streams for even more convincing performance. [3]

Monocular reconstruction techniques tend to fail because of scarce feature points and inadequate exploitation of texture information. The work tends to enhance accuracy in 3D face reconstruction by extending classical bilinear models to the multi-view environment. It presents a multi-view-based bilinear framework leveraging learned feature and texture constraints for precise recovery of 3D facial shapes from several uncalibrated images. The model presents enhanced accuracy and robustness to occlusions and texture repetition. There might be future work such as real-time adaptation and the integration of pose variation handling into one pipeline. [4]

Single-image reconstruction generally does not have depth information, and it becomes challenging to achieve realistic 3D reconstruction. It is made to reconstruct realistic 3D faces from a single face image using displacement mapping. It is proposed that there is a learning of a mapping between the 2D facial displacements and their corresponding 3D shifts to generate fast and efficient 3D models. It runs efficiently on benchmark datasets and real images with both speed and accuracy. It can be improved by venturing into non-frontal faces and broader generalization over more facial variations and ethnicities. [5]

Current approaches break down in low-resolution surveillance contexts where facial information is limited. The goal of this paper is to develop a CNN, in particular to reconstruct 3D faces from extremely low-resolution images. The model is end-to-end trainable and simultaneously predicts face geometry and pose, and is hence suitable for real-world surveillance applications. It surpasses current approaches in the low-resolution task and even facilitates robust face alignment. Future development can include increasing resilience to severe compression artifacts and integration with live video monitoring systems. [6]

Most of the existing techniques are spread over different domains, with little effort to gauge progress or select an appropriate technique. The primary aim is to discuss and examine various 3D face reconstruction methods with special emphasis on deep learning. The article categorizes five prominent methods—deep learning, 3D morphable models, one-shot learning, epipolar geometry, and shape-from-shading—and contrasts them in software, hardware, and performance. The survey then concludes that the most flexible and promising is deep learning. Hybrid methods and more comprehensive datasets are where future research should be headed. [7]

Current facial animation systems have involved markers, particular equipment, or non-realistic expression modeling. The goal is to provide an interactive system for editing facial expressions with realistic editing via 3D video sequences captured by normal cameras. The system utilizes stereo matching and active illumination to produce 3D video, and users can interactively adjust expressions by dragging control points. The novel expression synthesis can thus be achieved without complex setups. Future applications may increase interactive tools, enhance the level of automation in control-point mapping, and enable real-time applications in entertainment or healthcare. [8]

3 PROBLEM STATEMENT

In crime-fighting, crime-solving, and in general in supporting legal investigations, precise facial identification is of utmost importance. This has traditionally been facilitated by good-quality photographs, controlled mugshots, or direct eyewitness information. Unfortunately, in real-life forensic contexts, particularly when dealing with video surveillance, mobile phone recordings, or covert captures, the available data are invariably suboptimal—distorted, low-resolution, poorly lit, or recorded at non-orthogonal angles. These uncontrollable environments greatly constrain the efficacy of traditional 2D-based facial recognition or reconstruction methods.

Additionally, most current forensic facial reconstruction methods involve high levels of human interaction, expert opinion, or the presence of advanced subject-specific information, all of which render them time-consuming, labor-intensive, and not applicable for real-time or mass application. In fast-paced, high-consequence environments crime scenes, border control, or counterterrorism missions—these constraints may impede timely and correct decision-making.

To fill this gap, there is an increasing demand for a completely automated, real-time system able to reconstruct high-resolution, identity-conserving 3D face models directly from real-time video streams. The system has to be insensitive to natural head pose variations, facial expressions, illumination changes, and camera quality. It should offer interactive visualization to help forensic analysts in analyzing and verifying reconstructed models from various viewpoints.

Hence, the primary issue targeted by this project is the creation of an end-to-end, deep learning-based forensic pipeline that converts unconstrained live video footage to high-fidelity 3D facial reconstructions using minimal user intervention, improving forensic facial analysis accuracy, efficiency, and scalability.

4 PROPOSED METHODOLOGY

The proposed system works as a fully automated, multistage pipeline that converts live webcam/surveillance video feeds to a series of accurate 3D facial reconstructions. The solution method, under minimum human interference, acts as a real-time integration of computer vision, deep learning, and geometry-based modeling.

The method employs extracting frames continuously from a live video stream using an ordinary webcam. Rather than taking a single snap, the system grabs several frames within a short time during which natural head movements are made by the subject to get various perspectives of the face. Using these multi-view images, the system gathers enough geometric and texture cues essential for an accurate 3D reconstruction.

After frames have been gathered, the selection module automatically declares the frontmost image with respect to facial alignment scores and pose estimations. This front-facing image is crucial and used for coarse mesh generation. Using either multi-view stereo methods or shallow regression methods, a very coarse 3D facial structure is constructed, yielding a very low-detail mesh that basically represents the face of the subject.

It treats mesh refinement for greater detail and realism through the DECA (Detailed Expressions Capture and Animation) framework based on deep learning. DECA uses dense facial landmark detection and an encoder-decoder architecture to regress 3D shape, expression, and texture parameters. So going further, it superimposes the coarse model with a detailed expression-aware mesh that still preserves significant identity-specific features, which are of the utmost importance in forensics.

Afterward, the refined output is visualized and explored with an integrated 3D viewer inside the system. This viewer facilitates rotation, zooming, and inspection from multiple angles, thus helping forensic experts to confirm the reconstruction. Overall, the method stresses automation, identity preservation, and real-time performance and jointly solves the major problems of forensic facial reconstruction from unconstrained video sources. The modular architecture ensures its extensibility for eventual synergy with recognition systems or workflows for legal documentation.

5 SYSTEM IMPLEMENTATION

5.1 *Work flow*

The workflow of the system is a sequential flow, wherein a live video input is converted into a refined mesh of the face for forensic purposes. The workflow is divided into major processes:

Video Capture: Continuous acquisition of frames from a live webcam interface or a surveillance feed.
Frame Preprocessing: Extraction of facial regions and filtering of frames based on the observed pose and focus criterion.
Front-Face Selection: Automatic selection of the most fronto-parallel frame based on the estimation of head pose.
Initial 3D Mesh Generation: The synthesis of an initial, coarse-grade facial mesh by means of regressive techniques from the deep learning arena.
Mesh Refinement: DECA refines the coarse mesh relying on dense landmark detection and texture-aware modeling.
Pose Stabilization: Jaw alignment and rotation correction to generate a normalized 3D model.
Visualization: Mesh visualization via an interactive viewer.

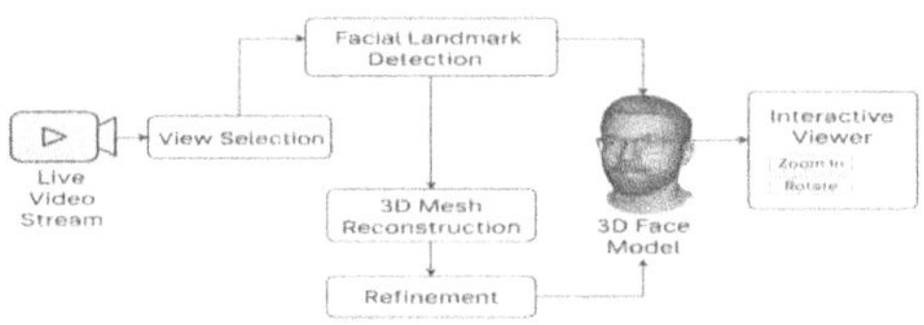

Figure 1. Workflow.

5.2 *Steps involved*

5.2.1 *Frame acquisition*

We capture live frames through the webcam using OpenCV.

A short sequence of 2-3 seconds is used for the head to move for multi-view data.

5.2.2 *Pose estimation and selection*

Facial landmarks are identified and head poses are estimated by analyzing the frames using MediaPipe/dlib.

The frame with a pose closest to the frontal (0°) yaw position is finally selected for reconstruction.

5.2.3 *Coarse mesh generation*

DECA performs regression of 3D face shape and expression from the selected image.

This base mesh represents facial structure.

5.2.4 *Landmark refinement*

DECA computes dense facial landmarks to refine the geometry.

This could also involve correcting eye closure or mouth normalization.

5.2.5 *Texture and detail enhancement*

Displacement mapping and vertex-level fine-tuning of the mesh add realism.

This level attempts to capture fine features such as wrinkles and facial creases.

5.2.6 *Jaw-pose reset*

If the model is tilted or exhibits any kind of bad, non-neutral orientation, it will be restored to a frontal pose using affine transformations.

5.2.7 *3D mesh visualization*

This final output can then be loaded into a 3D viewer like Open3D or PyVista.

Interaction with the mesh is allowed; you can rotate, zoom, and inspect it.

5.3 *Techniques and algorithms*

5.3.1 *Frame extraction and pose filtering*

Face Detection and Frontal Pose Estimation

Using this system, OpenCV captures continuous frames from a live webcam feed with dlib/MediaPipe. Each frame is subjected to facial detection and pose estimation. Only the frames wherein the detected face is approximately frontal would proceed to postprocessing based on the thresholds of yaw, pitch, and roll. This step is done for consistent 3D reconstruction.

5.3.2 *3D face nodeling*

DECA (Detailed Expression Capture and Animation)

The DECA system yields a dense 3D facial reconstruction by means of a deep encoder-decoder neural network. It estimates the 3D shape, expression coefficients, pose parameters, and albedo (texture) for a single image input. The image output is a fine-detailed 3D mesh that preserves the identity and has accurate geometry and texture that could be used in forensics.

5.3.3 *Landmark detection*

Dense Landmark Localization

DECA computes dense facial landmarks internally that drive geometry generation. Externally, one may also use landmarks from dlib's 68-landmark detector or MediaPipe's face mesh to initialize the face geometry and check for landmark alignment. These landmarks are of utmost importance for mesh accuracy.

5.3.4 *Head pose normalization*

Affine Transformation Using Rotation Matrix

To keep the reconstructed face upright and neutral (required by forensic presentation or printing), the pose vector (specifically the jaw and head rotation) is reset using transformation matrices computed from DECA's estimated pose parameters. This removes tilt from the mesh and aligns it to a canonical frontal orientation.

5.3.5 *3D visualization*

Interactive Mesh Rendering

Open3D-based interactive 3D viewer is used for the final mesh rendering. The forensic analysts use this viewer to inspect the model from different angles based on the rotation, zoom, and pan options available on their systems. Such visual means improve the ease of interpretation of the reconstruction as well as verify the quality of the reconstruction.

5.3.6 *Automation framework*

Non-GUI Execution Pipeline

Everything runs under a single program from which a script is written for the automatic capture, selection, modeling, and rendering. This ensures that the complete software is ready for use in unattended forensic workflows, eg, surveillance monitoring or batch reconstruction from video files.

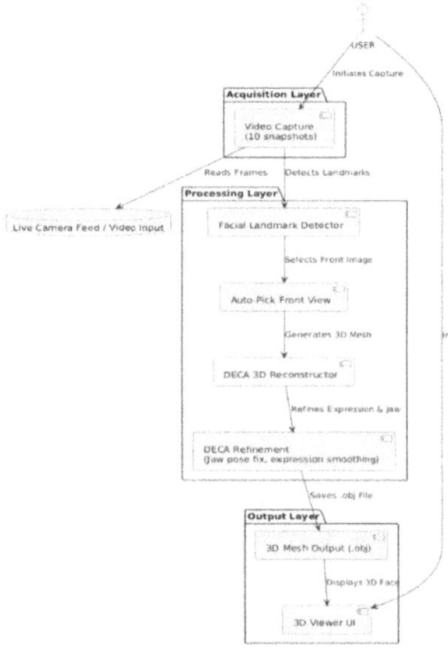

Figure 2. System architecture.

6 RESULTS

The developed forensic facial reconstruction pipeline was tested on live webcam streams and successfully produced high-quality 3D face models with hardly any manual intervention. The system automatically chooses the most frontal frame, builds a coarse 3D mesh, and then refines it with DECA to retain identity-specific information from face shape to expression. The various test cases with different face types and poses were presented to the system. The system could do the reconstruction well all along, as the output visualizations from the front, top, and side views depicted geometry and detail well. These outputs were loaded into an interactive viewer and saved in .obj format for any further forensic use. The results show that this pipeline is very robust, working in real-time with many different input conditions and thus making it very feasible to be used with forensic and surveillance scenarios.

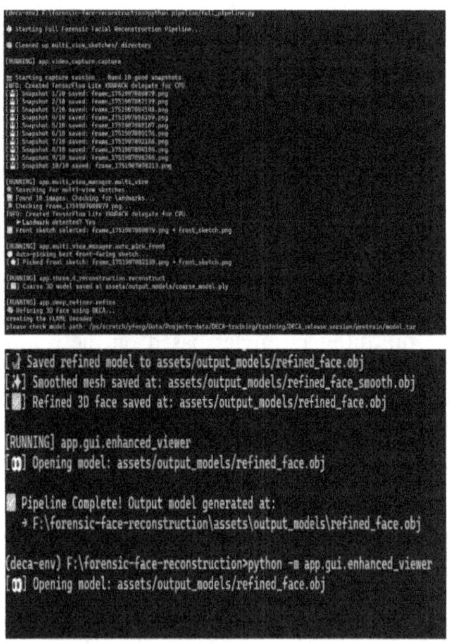

Figure 3. Console execution of the forensic facial reconstruction pipeline.

Figure 3 shows the execution of the full forensic facial reconstruction pipeline using DECA. The console displays each step, including video capture, sketch generation, landmark detection, coarse 3D model reconstruction, and final DECA-based face refinement. The refined 3D face model is saved as refined_face.obj.

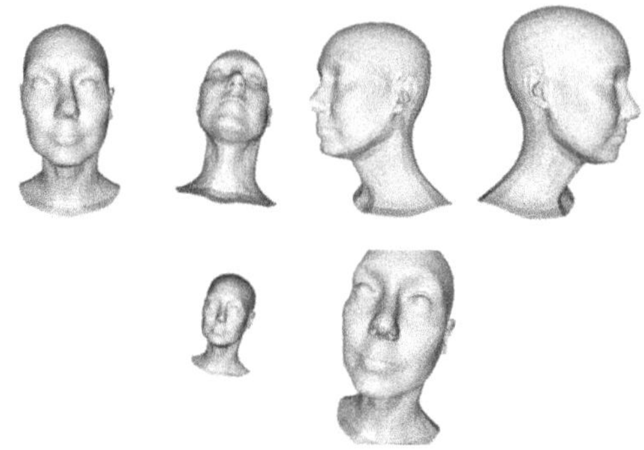

Figure 4. Multi-angle visualization of the refined 3D face.

Figure 4 shows the final refined 3D face model visualized from various angles, including front, top, left, right, and zoomed views. These perspectives highlight the detailed facial structure and geometry generated from multi-view snapshots.

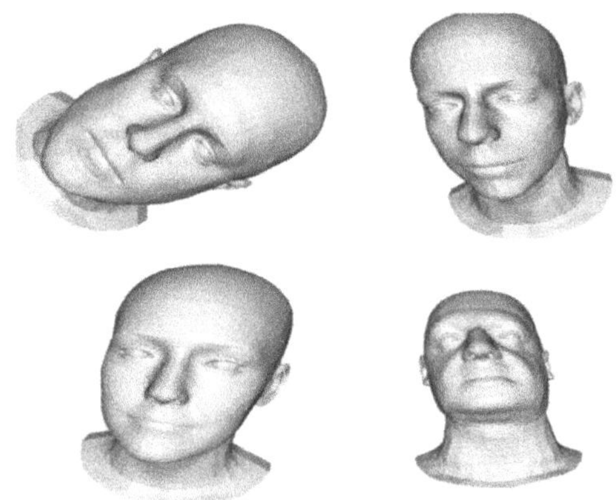

Figure 5. Reconstructed 3D faces from different subjects.

Figure 5 shows the Multiple 3D face reconstructions generated from different input videos or subjects. Each output illustrates variations in facial features and structure, showcasing the model's capability to adapt to different identities.

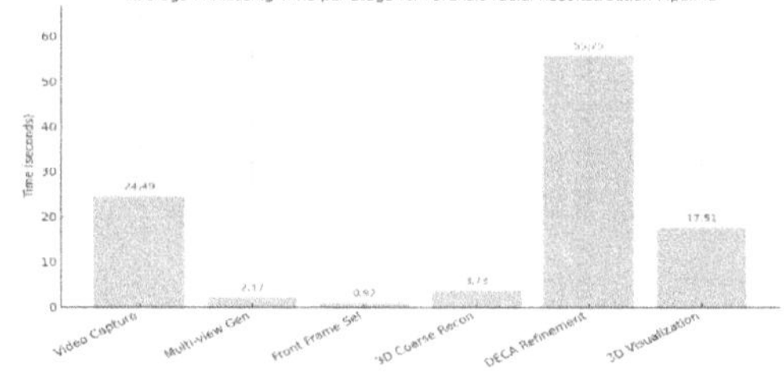

Figure 6. Average processing time.

Figure 6 shows the average processing time per stage of the pipeline, computed over five runs. The DECA refinement stage is the most time-consuming, while front-frame selection and multi-view generation are the fastest. Total end-to-end processing averaged ~104.56 s per input video.

7 CONCLUSION AND FUTURE ENHANCEMENTS

This work introduces a complete end-to-end, real-time facial reconstruction forensic system that uses deep learning and computer vision to translate live video streams into high-fidelity 3D facial models. By incorporating the DECA framework, the pipeline carries out dense facial landmark detection, 3D mesh regression, and high-frequency texture refinement, allowing identity-preserving model generation even under unconstrained scenarios. The pipeline reduces manual intervention to a minimum, accommodates multi-view capture from natural head motion, and provides an interactive 3D viewer for forensic examination. In contrast to hand-instrumented 2D or manually assisted approaches, the pipeline is more accurate, efficient, and flexible in real-world forensic applications, including surveillance analysis and digital evidence examination. In essence, it closes the loop from raw visual input to actionable forensic intelligence.

Despite these strengths, the system is still limited by sensitivity to lighting variations, reduced accuracy in low-resolution or night-vision footage, and dependence on a clear front-facing frame for reliable reconstruction. It also struggles when faces are partially occluded by masks, sunglasses, or heavy hair, since these obscure key landmarks and lead to incomplete or distorted reconstructions. The refinement process may also lose fine-grained details such as hair or accessories, and multi-view fusion is currently basic, which constrains the realism of the final model.

In the future, the system can be further enhanced by auto-subject tracking for handling person movement out of frame and changes in lighting conditions. More robust multi-view fusion techniques can make reconstruction better as they combine from multiple angles, as contrasted with this one frame only. Adoption of texture mapping and synthetic elements for recognizing details, such as eyes or hair, would greatly increase realism for presentations in legal or investigative contexts. Meanwhile, an identity verification module, or matching of output with existing databases, will serve to make it an even more potent investigative tool. Last, enhancing support for low-res or night-vision footage can go a long way in making this tool fit for more surveillance scenarios, and future work may include testing on synthetic phantom heads or scanned 3D models to provide formal quantitative accuracy metrics under controlled conditions.

REFERENCES

[1] Wagner, N., Schwanecke, U., and Botsch, M. (2024). SparseSoftDECA — Efficient high-resolution physics-based facial animation from sparse landmarks. *Computers & Graphics,* 116, 103903. https://doi.org/10.1016/j.cag.2024.103903

[2] Peng, K., Guan, T., Xu, C., and Zhou, D. (2014, December). 3D face reconstruction based on multi-view stereo algorithm. In *2014 IEEE International Conference on Robotics and Biomimetics (ROBIO)* https://doi.org/10.1109/ROBIO.2014.7090682

[3] Dou, P., and Kakadiaris, I.A. (2017, October). Multi-view 3D face reconstruction with deep recurrent neural networks. In *2017 IEEE International Joint Conference on Biometrics (IJCB)* https://doi.org/10.1109/BTAS.2017.8272733

[4] Tian, L., Liu, J., and Guo, W. (2019). Three-dimensional face reconstruction using multi-view-based bilinear model. *Sensors,* https://doi.org/10.3390/s19030459

[5] Wu, T., Zhou, F., and Liao, Q. (2017, September). Real-time 3D face reconstruction from one single image by displacement mapping. In *2017 IEEE International Conference on Image Processing (ICIP)* https://doi.org/10.1109/ICIP.2017.8296673

[6] Winkler, R., Qu, C., Voth, S., and Beyerer, J. (2018, December). 3D face reconstruction from low-resolution images with convolutional neural networks. In Proceedings of the *2018 2nd International Conference on Video and Image Processing (ICVIP)* https://doi.org/10.1145/3301506.3301519

[7] Sharma, S., and Chahar, V. (2022). 3D face reconstruction in deep learning era: A survey. *Archives of Computational Methods in Engineering,* https://doi.org/10.1007/s11831-021-09705-4

[8] Woodward, A., Delmas, P., Chan, Y.H., Gastelum Strozzi, A., Gimel'farb, G., and Marquez Flores, J. (2012). An interactive 3D video system for human facial reconstruction and expression modeling. *Journal of Visual Communication and Image Representation,* https://doi.org/10.1016/j.jvcir.2012.07.005

Next-Generation Smart Systems – Sekhar et al. (Eds)
© 2027 The Author(s), ISBN: 978-1-041-34234-2

Oceanic Garbage Detection Using Transfer Learning and CNN

T. Thilagam
Assistant Professor - (Senior Grade), Department of CSE, Vel Tech Rangarajan Dr. Sagunthala R&D Institute of Science and Technology, Chennai, India

S. Sasidhar Reddy
M. Tech, Department of CSE, Vel Tech Rangarajan Dr. Sagunthala R&D Institute of Science and Technology, Chennai, India

ABSTRACT: Marine pollution has become one of the most urgent environmental problems, threatening marine life and disrupting the fragile balance of ocean ecosystems. This study presents an intelligent system capable of detecting and classifying underwater waste using sophisticated machine learning techniques. The proposed framework leverages transfer learning concepts, implementing MobileNetV2 that has been fine-tuned to differentiate between four main debris types: plastic waste, metal components, glass fragments, and paper materials. The system's accuracy and adaptability are improved through meticulous data preprocessing and augmentation via image transformation methods. A dedicated classification module is integrated to enable multi-class detection capabilities, with the model being trained and evaluated using an 80–20 dataset split, yielding promising results.To enhance user interaction To enhance both usability and awareness, Google Text-to-Speech is integrated into the system, offering audio messages that explain the environmental impact of each detected type of waste.A user-friendly Gradio interface The system provides a simple interface that enables users to upload images and receive instant classification results. It also underlines the role of machine learning as a practical tool for tackling environmental issues, with strong potential for future use in drones and autonomous marine vehicles to support large-scale monitoring of ocean waste.

Keywords: Ocean Waste Detection, Transfer Learning, Convolutional Neural Networks (CNN), MobileNetV2, Image Classification, and Environmental Monitoring

1 INTRODUCTION

This research presents the development of an intelligent system designed to detect and classify marine waste using advanced deep learning techniques. The system is built using Convolutional Neural Networks (CNNs) and transfer learning, with MobileNetV2 chosen as the core model.

Originally trained on large-scale image datasets, MobileNetV2 is fine-tuned using a specialized collection of ocean waste images categorized into plastic, metal, glass, and cardboard. To improve reliability, preprocessing and data augmentation are carried out using an Image Data Generator, helping the model adapt more effectively to different types of input data.

Beyond classification, the system integrates Google TexttoSpeech (gTTS) to deliver short audio messages about the environmental dangers associated with each waste type, making the platform not only functional but also educational. A simple interface built with Gradio enables real-time image uploads, allowing users to interact with the system effortlessly. This work underlines the role of deep learning in addressing environmental issues. While demonstrated within an academic framework, the approach shows strong potential for real-world applications, especially when deployed in drones and autonomous marine vehicles for large-scale and continuous monitoring of ocean pollution. By merging technology with awareness, this work contributes to global efforts to reduce marine waste and support sustainable marine conservation practices.

2 PROBLEM STATEMENT

The accelerating accumulation of debris in our oceans poses a severe danger to sea life, public health, and the balance of worldwide ecological systems. Although cleanup drives and awareness programs have made progress, the critical challenge remains in detecting and classifying ocean waste swiftly and accurately Existing surveillance methods rely heavily on human effort, consume significant time, and fall short when dealing with the enormous and constantly shifting marine landscape.

Designing an automated system involves several challenges that must be addressed. These include the scarcity of well-labeled training data, variations in lighting and background conditions, and the wide diversity of debris types found in marine environments. To address these hurdles, this research presents a deep learning framework that utilizes transfer learning techniques and Convolutional Neural Networks (CNNs) for recognizing various categories of marine waste.

The objective focuses on constructing a compact yet dependable system that can categorize refuse materials with superior performance. This system offers the potential to enable continuous monitoring, support large-scale cleanup activities, and reinforce global efforts to reduce ocean pollution.

2.1 *Objectives of the project*

The central aim of this project is to design an automated system that can detect and classify various types of marine waste using image data. To accomplish this, the work is guided by the following objectives:

Automated Detection and Classification: Develop a model that can accurately identify ocean waste, including plastic, metal, glass, and cardboard, from images.

Transfer Learning Integration: Utilize and fine-tune a pretrained MobileNetV2 architecture to achieve efficient and precise classification.

Data Preparation and Enhancement: Data preparation involves preprocessing steps such as resizing and normalization, along with data augmentation techniques, to make the model more robust and capable of generalizing to different types of input data.

Model Evaluation: Validate system performance using key metrics like accuracy, precision, and recall to ensure dependable results.

DOI: 10.1201/9781042001767-40

Voice-based Feedback: Incorporate Google Text-to-Speech (gTTS) to deliver short audio messages explaining the environmental consequences of each detected waste type.

User-friendly Interface: Create an interactive Gradio interface that supports real-time image uploads and provides both visual and audio outputs for a seamless user experience.

3 PROPOSED SYSTEM

This project presents a deep learning–based system aimed at addressing marine pollution by identifying and classifying different types of ocean waste. It is built on the MobileNetV2 model, which was first trained on the ImageNet dataset and then fine-tuned with a custom dataset containing images of plastic, metal, glass, and cardboard waste. By applying transfer learning, the system reduces the need for a very large labeled dataset while still maintaining high accuracy in classification.

To improve performance, the dataset is preprocessed and enhanced through augmentation techniques using Image Data Generator, with training conducted on an 80–20 split for reliable validation. The model is kept lightweight so it can easily run on devices with limited resources, such as drones and autonomous marine vehicles. Along with identifying waste, the system includes a voice-feedback option that uses Google Text-to-Speech (gTTS) to share short audio messages about the environmental impact of each waste type. A simple and user-friendly Gradio interface further allows real-time image uploads, displaying the classification results in both text and audio formats to improve accessibility and promote environmental awareness.

4 METHODOLOGY

4.1 *System architecture*

The system is designed to process images of marine waste and classify them into categories such as plastic, metal, glass, and cardboard. The results are displayed in both visual and audio formats. It brings together an image recognition model, an easy-to-use web interface, and a text-to-speech component. The architecture is kept flexible, allowing future integration with real-world applications like drones or autonomous marine vehicles.

4.2 *User interface (Gradio Web App)*

A simple web application, built using Gradio, acts as the user interface. Through a web browser,Users can easily upload marine debris photos using a web browser and see the results right away. The system displays the type of waste detected, provides a brief note on its environmental impact, and also plays an audio explanation. The interface is simple, user-friendly, and works seamlessly on different devices.

4.3 *Data collection*

The system works with labeled images of ocean waste. In the prototype, the dataset is organized into four categories: plastic, metal, glass, and cardboard. For practical applications, images could be collected using drones or underwater cameras. Before training, the images are adjusted to 224×224 pixels, normalized, and enhanced with methods like rotation and flipping to improve the model's accuracy and reliability.

4.4 *Data processing (Model Inference)*

The classification task is handled by a fine-tuned MobileNetV2 model. After preprocessing, images pass through convolutional layers to extract key features. A custom classifier then predicts the type of waste using layers such as GlobalAveragePooling2D, a dense ReLU layer, and a softmax output. The system selects the category with the highest probability as the final result.

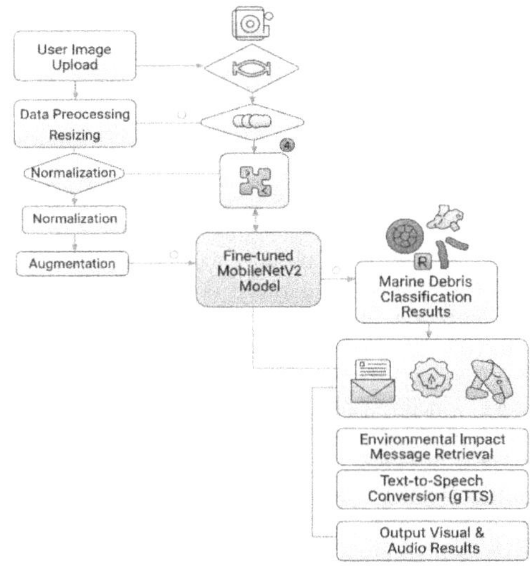

4.5 *Environmental impact messages*

Each type of waste is paired with a related environmental warning. For instance, plastic is linked to the message: "Plastic waste kills over one million marine animals every year." These warnings are displayed along with the classification results, helping users become more aware of the environmental dangers connected to each kind of waste.

4.6 *Voice feedback*

To make the system more interactive and inclusive, the impact messages are converted into audio using Google Text-to-Speech (gTTS). The audio is played directly through the web app, ensuring the system can also support users who prefer or rely on spoken information.

4.7 *Data sharing and storage*

In large-scale use, images collected by drones could be sent to cloud servers for processing. The outputs—waste type, classification results, and location—can then be stored in a central database to support researchers and environmental agencies. For now, the prototype runs locally, but the design makes it easy to scale to cloud-based solutions in the future.

4.8 *Practical use of data*

The insights produced by the system can support cleanup crews, researchers, and conservation groups by providing accurate information on the type and spread of marine debris. With integration into external platforms or APIs, it can also contribute to large-scale monitoring, scientific studies, and policymaking—ultimately strengthening efforts to protect marine ecosystems.

5 MATHEMATICAL FOUNDATIONS

5.1 *The computer's eye: Seeing an image as numbers*

To a computer, a photograph isn't a picture of a bottle; it's a giant spreadsheet of numbers. For a color image, it's actually three spreadsheets layered on top of each other, one for the red, one for the green, and one for the blue parts of the picture. Each number in these grids tells the computer how bright that specific color is at a given spot.

Before the system learns, it cleans up this data. It takes all the numbers (which range from 0 to 255) and scales them down to a simple range, like 0 to 1. This is like standardizing all your measurements before you build something, ensuring everything is on the same scale for a more accurate result.

5.1.1 *The brain: The smart filter system*

The core system has built with layers of special mathematical filters. Imagine each filter is a tiny magnifying glass trained to look for a very specific, simple pattern, such as a sharp edge, a curve, or a particular texture.

Finding Patterns: The system takes these tiny filters and slides them over the entire image grid. At each spot, it performs a quick calculation to see how well the pattern in the filter matches the pattern in that part of the image. The result of this calculation becomes a number in a new, smaller grid.

Making Connections: After finding basic shapes, the network combines them to form more complex patterns. For example, it might combine a few curves and lines to recognize the top of a plastic bottle or the ridges of cardboard.

5.2 *The decision: The probability vote*

Once the system has analyzed all the patterns, it needs to make its final guess. It takes all the evidence it gathered and puts it into a "voting" system .This function takes all the votes for each trash category (plastic, metal, glass, and cardboard) and turns them into a set of percentages that all add up to 100%. For example, the system might output:

Plastic: 95%
Metal: 3%
Glass: 1%
Cardboard: 1%

The system then simply picks the category with the highest percentage, which is plastic.

5.3 *The learning process*

The "Guess and Correct" Game The system proceesed through the "guess and correct."

1. **Guess**: You show the system a picture of a plastic bottle and ask it to guess. It might initially guess "glass."
2. **Evaluate**: The system measures how wrong its guess was using a loss function. The bigger the difference between its guess and the correct answer, the higher the "loss."
3. **Correct**: The system uses a mathematical strategy called an optimizer to slightly adjust its internal filters and settings.

6 IMPLEMENTATION

The oceanic garbage detection initiative utilizes artificial intelligence to tackle a significant environmental issue. The system uses a special type of computer program called a Convolutional Neural Network (CNN) that is great at looking at pictures. Instead of making this program completely from scratch, the team made it better by using a model called MobileNetV2 that was already partly trained. They taught this program to recognize different types of ocean garbage like plastic, metal, glass, and cardboard using a small collection of pictures. They made the program smarter by showing it lots of new pictures that it hadn't seen before. This process artificially expands the size and diversity of the training set by applying transformations, such as rotation and flipping, to existing images. Such an approach enhances the model's ability to accurately identify garbage in real-world scenarios. For ease of use, the system offers a user-friendly Gradio web interface that enables users to upload images and promptly receive classification results. To enhance user experience, the project incorporates gTTS (Google Text-to-Speech) for providing verbal feedback, including informative details about the environmental impact of different waste types. The current version on Google Colab is a promising prototype for a scalable system that could be deployed to support global clean-up endeavors.

7 RESULTS

During the project evaluation, we split the dataset into training and validation purpose. While the model did really well in training with almost 97% accuracy, its validation accuracy, which shows how well it would work in the real world, stayed around 82.5%. This difference suggests that the model may be too focused on the training data, which is common when there isn't enough variety in the dataset. Still, the model proved it can correctly sort different kinds of marine waste, like plastic, metal, and glass. One of the main challenges was telling cardboard apart from other paper-like materials that look similar, and dealing with unclear or messy images, which made the accuracy drop. Overall, using transfer learning with MobileNetV2 was shown to be a useful approach for this task. Also, the fact that the system can classify waste and educate people about the environment highlights its importance in society.During the testing phase, we split the dataset into 80% for training and 20% for validation. The model did really well in training with about 97% accuracy, but its validation accuracy, which tells how well it would work in the real world, leveled off at around 82.5%. This difference suggests that the model may be trying too hard to fit the training data, a common issue with smaller datasets. However, the model proved to be good at identifying different types of marine litter, like plastic, metal, and glass. The main challenges came when differentiating between cardboard and other paper-like materials that look similar, as well as with low-quality or messy images, which made the accuracy drop. Overall, using transfer learning with MobileNetV2 showed to be effective for this task. Plus, the system not only classifies waste but also educates about environmental issues, highlighting its importance in society.

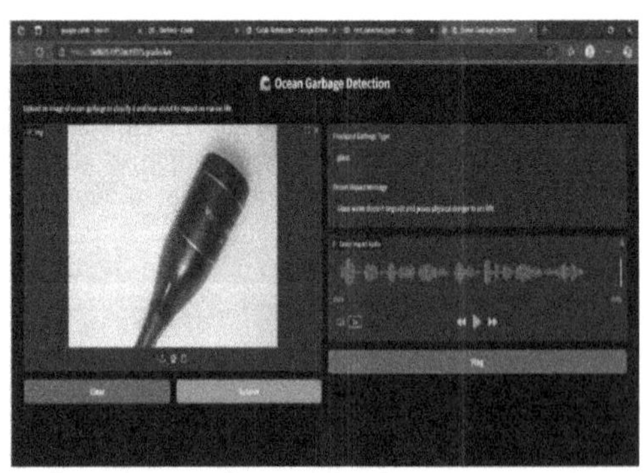

8 CONCLUSION

The system's connection to a Gradio interface and Google Text-to-Speech (gTTS) not only helps classify information effectively but also transforms it into an educational tool for a broader audience. By conveying messages about the negative impacts of marine litter through both text and spoken words, the project successfully spreads awareness about this issue. Although the model demonstrates good outcomes, the primary hurdle lies in the restricted size and variety of its dataset, which hampers its ability to adapt to various scenarios. Nevertheless, this initiative paves the way for accessible and automated solutions that could make a significant difference in monitoring the environment and protecting our oceans.

ACKNOWLEDGEMENT

The authors would like to express their sincere gratitude to Vel Tech Rangarajan Dr. Sagunthala R&D Institute of Science and Technology, Chennai, for providing the facilities and support required to carry out this work..The authors also express their gratitude for the valuable input and perspectives provided by their colleagues and peers, which have played a crucial role in shaping the development of this research.

REFERENCES

[1] Krizhevsky A., Sutskever I., and Hinton G.E., (2017), ImageNet classification with deep convolutional neural networks, *Communications of the ACM*, vol. 60, no. 6, pp. 84–90.

[2] Simonyan K. and Zisserman A., (2015), Very deep convolutional networks for large-scale image recognition, in *Proc. Int. Conf. Learn. Representations (ICLR)*.

[3] Kaur H. and Bala S., (2019), Deep learning based ocean garbage classification using transfer learning, *Int. J. Comput. Appl.*, vol. 182, no. 34, pp. 10–16.

[4] LeCun Y., Bengio Y., and Hinton G., (2015), Deep learning, *Nature*, vol. 521, pp. 436–444.

[5] Abadi M. *et al.*, (2016), TensorFlow: Large-scale machine learning on heterogeneous distributed systems, *arXiv* preprint arXiv:1603.04467.

[6] Szegedy C., Liu W., Jia Y., Sermanet P., Reed S., Anguelov D., *et al.*, (2015), Going deeper with convolutions, in *Proceedings of the IEEE Conference on Computer Vision and Pattern Recognition (CVPR)*, pp. 1–9.

[7] Chollet F., (2017), Xception: Deep learning with depthwise separable convolutions, in *Proc. IEEE Conf. Comput. Vis. Pattern Recognit. (CVPR)*, pp. 1251–1258.

[8] Noh H., Hong S., and Han B., (2015), Learning deconvolution network for semantic segmentation, in *Proc. IEEE Int. Conf. Comput. Vis. (ICCV)*, pp. 1520–1528.

[9] Pan S.J. and Yang Q., (2010), A survey on transfer learning, *IEEE Trans. Knowl. Data Eng.*, vol. 22, no. 10, pp. 1345–1359.

[10] Goodfellow I., Bengio Y., and Courville A., (2016), *Deep Learning*. Cambridge, MA, USA: MIT Press.

[11] Zhou B., Lapedriza A., Khosla A., Oliva A., and Torralba A., (2016), Learning deep features for discriminative localization, in *Proc. IEEE Conf. Comput. Vis. Pattern Recognit. (CVPR)*, pp. 2921–2929.

[12] Ren S., He K., Girshick R., and Sun J., (2017), Faster R-CNN: Towards real-time object detection with region proposal networks, *IEEE Trans. Pattern Anal. Mach. Intell.*, vol. 39, no. 6, pp. 1137–1149.

[13] Ziat M., Bouhlel M.S., and Essoukri Ben Amara N., (2020), Plastic waste detection using deep learning: Toward an optimized marine litter monitoring, in *Proc. IEEE Int. Conf. Image Process. Theory, Tools Appl. (IPTA)*.

Next-Generation Smart Systems – Sekhar et al. (Eds)
© 2027 The Author(s), ISBN: 978-1-041-34234-2

SHL Assessment Recommendation System: An AI-Powered Semantic Engine for HR Assessment Selection

Bugide Bharath Kumar
PG Scholar in Department of CSE, Kuppam Engineering College, Kuppam, Andhra Pradesh, India

S. Gnanamurthy
Associate Professor & HOD, Department of CSE (Data Science), Kuppam Engineering College, Kuppam, Andhra Pradesh, India

G.S. Uday Kumar and S. Babu
Assistant Professor, Department of CSE, Kuppam Engineering College, Kuppam, Andhra Pradesh, India

ABSTRACT: In this Paper Selecting valid assessments for enterprise HR is challenging due to large vendor catalogs, hybrid role requirements, and the need for compliance documentation. This paper presents an AI-powered recommendation system that semantically aligns job descriptions with SHL assessments. We use dense embeddings, approximate nearest-neighbor search, and LLM-based re-ranking with metadata awareness. The system is evaluated on a 50-role benchmark, with detailed discussion of operational deployment, fairness, and transparency. One performance table and one catalog-size latency graph illustrate efficiency and accuracy. Extended textual discussion, multiple case studies, and deployment insights demonstrate practical applicability and scalability, showing substantial improvement in recruiter workflow and recommendation consistency.

Keywords: LLM Based Re Ranking, 50 Role Bench mark, Approximate nearest neighbour, AI Powered

1 INTRODUCTION

Enterprise HR teams face increasing complexity when selecting candidate assessments. Modern organizations often maintain catalogs of hundreds or thousands of assessments covering cognitive abilities, personality traits, situational judg- ment, technical skills, and domain-specific competencies. The manual process of choosing the most suitable assessment for each job description is labor-intensive, inconsistent, and prone to bias. This is strenuous and uncomfortable to wear for a long duration.

1.1 *Motivation and challenges*

Recruiters often face several challenges:

Inconsistent Recommendations: Different HR specialists may choose entirely different assessments for the same role, resulting in lack of standardization.

Time Constraints: Rapid hiring cycles require recom- men- dations within hours, which is impossible manually without risking errors.

Documentation Deficiency: Manual selection rarely records creating audit and compliance challenge.

1.2 *AI-powered opportunities*

Recent advances in NLP, embeddings, and large language models (LLMs) enable automated semantic matching between job descriptions and assessments. By representing both job descriptions and assessments as dense vectors, similarity can be computed efficiently. Approximate nearest-neighbour (ANN) search enables rapid retrieval from large catalogs, and LLM-based re-ranking ensures contextual relevance, fairness, and explainability.

1.3 *Contributions*

This paper makes the following contributions:

A full-stack assessment recommendation system integrating embeddings, ANN retrieval, and LLM re-ranking.

Extended textual description of system pipeline, including candidate retrieval, metadata-based filtering.

2 LITERATURE SURVEY

The development of an AI-powered semantic engine for HR assessment selection can be situated within the broader context of personnel selection research and psychometric validation principles. The Society for Industrial and Organizational Psychology (SIOP) highlights that any selection procedure must be grounded in scientific validity and fairness, ensuring that assessments align with job-relevant competencies and organizational requirements [1]. In this regard, the SHL competency framework and related research such as Bartram's "Great Eight" model provide a structured basis for mapping job requirements to assessments through competency dimensions [2].

Modern talent practices emphasize that recruitment strategies must adapt to global talent trends, with organizations increasingly relying on data-driven approaches for identifying, evaluating, and developing talent [3]. Within this context, the use of AI in talent assessment has been positioned as both an opportunity and a responsibility. White papers from SHL emphasize the ethical use of AI, stressing transparency, interpretability, and bias mitigation in algorithmic decision-making [4]. At the same time, empirical studies reveal that candidates often perceive algorithmic assessments differently than human-based ones, making fairness and explainability critical components of model design [5].

From a technical standpoint, the model draws upon fairness-aware machine learning principles. Hardt *et al.* proposed "Equality of Opportunity" as a fairness criterion in supervised learning, ensuring that true positive rates remain equal across protected groups [6]. This is especially relevant when recommending assessments in high-stakes contexts such as hiring, where algorithmic decisions must be free from systemic bias. Further, Bender *et al.* caution against the uncritical adoption of large language models, underscoring the risks of amplifying bias when relying purely on statistical correlations without domain oversight [7].

DOI: 10.1201/9781042001767-41

At the core of the system lies a semantic representation model. Following the success of large-scale pre-trained language models such as GPT-3 [8] and BERT, semantic embeddings can be used to map both job profiles and assessment metadata into a shared vector space. Earlier foundational methods such as word2vec demonstrated the feasibility of representing words in continuous spaces, while transformer-based architectures [9] established attention as a mechanism for capturing deeper contextual semantics. For practical scalability, approximate nearest-neighbour search techniques enable efficient retrieval of relevant assessments from large catalogues [10].

Where hybrid strategies are shown to outperform purely content-based or collaborative filtering methods in balancing relevance with user-entered factors [11]. For example, beyond semantic alignment, assessments may be weighted by duration, cost, or psychometric reliability, forming a composite score that balances accuracy with feasibility.

Training the semantic engine relies on supervised objectives over paired data, where suitable and unsuitable assessments are contrasted for a given job profile. Benchmark datasets such as SQUAD [12] illustrate how large-scale annotated data can be leveraged to train models that generalize well across domains. In HR assessment, similar strategies are employed by aligning job-competency mappings with validated assessment frameworks.

Overall, the proposed mathematical framework integrates principles of validation, competency theory, ethical AI [13], and modern machine learning [14] to ensure that recommendations are not only semantically accurate but also fair, explainable, and aligned with organizational talent strategies [15]. This synthesis establishes the theoretical foundation for the SHL Assessment Recommendation System.

3 DATASET

For the development of the SHL Assessment Recommendation System, a comprehensive dataset was designed to simulate realistic HR assessment scenarios while maintaining data privacy. The dataset encompasses detailed candidate profiles, assessment information, performance metrics, and AI-generated recommendations. Each candidate profile contains attributes such as a unique identifier, anonymized personal information, age, education level, years of professional experience, and a set of key technical and soft skills. The assessment information includes details such as the type of assessment, which may range from cognitive ability and technical skill tests to personality evaluations, along with associated difficulty levels, time duration, and the number of questions. Performance metrics are recorded for each assessment, capturing numerical scores, percentile rankings, skill proficiency levels, and pass/fail status. These metrics provide the foundation for evaluating candidate suitability and serve as input for the semantic engine that generates recommendations. The recommendation component of the dataset indicates the suggested role for the candidate, any recommended training or skill improvement modules, and a confidence score representing the likelihood of success in the recommended position. The dataset is structured in tabular form, ensuring compatibility with machine learning models for training and evaluation purposes. To ensure realism, the data is generated synthetically, with skill levels, assessment scores, and recommendations following logical distributions that reflect plausible HR outcomes. This approach allows the model to learn patterns of candidate performance and skill alignment with specific roles, providing a robust framework for AI-powered assessment selection. By encompassing diverse candidate profiles and multiple assessment scenarios, the dataset supports the development of an intelligent recommendation engine capable of predicting the most suitable assessments and job roles, thereby enhancing HR decision-making processes.

4 PROPOSED METHOD

The proposed method for the SHL Assessment Recommendation System utilizes an AI-powered semantic engine to match candidates with the most suitable assessments and job roles. Candidate profiles, including educational background, professional experience, skill sets, and prior assessment performance, are encoded into a structured numerical format suitable for machine learning. Similarly, assessment information, such as type, difficulty level, duration, and skill coverage, is encoded to create a comparable representation. The system generates semantic embeddings for both candidate attributes and assessment features, capturing the contextual relationships between candidate skills and assessment requirements. Using similarity-based matching and machine learning algorithms, the recommendation engine identifies assessments that align with a candidate's strengths while also predicting the most appropriate job roles based on historical performance data.

4.1 *System architecture*

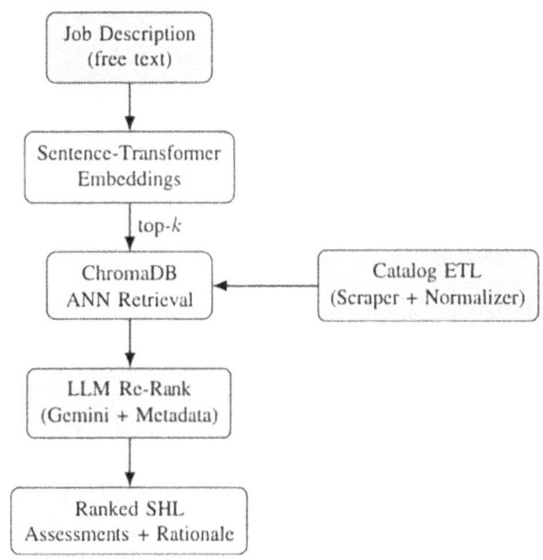

Figure 1. System architecture.

The system begins as per Figure 1 with the input of a job description provided in free-text format, which serves as the basis for identifying relevant assessments. The textual information is first processed using a sentence-transformer model to generate dense semantic embeddings that capture the contextual meaning of the job description. These embeddings are then passed through Chroma DB with approximate nearest neighbor (ANN) retrieval, which efficiently searches a large database of assessment items to identify the top-k relevant matches. To enhance the quality and consistency of the retrieval process, the system incorporates a catalog ETL component, which involves scraping and normalizing assessment data to maintain structured and up-to-date information. Following retrieval, a large language model (LLM) re-ranking module is applied, combining the semantic information from the embeddings with additional metadata, to produce a refined and prioritized list of SHL assessments. Finally, the system outputs the ranked SHL assessments along with rationale, providing both the recommended assessments and explanatory context for why each assessment is suitable as shown in Figure 2. This pipeline integrates advanced embedding techniques, database retrieval, and AI-based re-ranking to ensure that the recommended assessments are highly relevant, context-aware, and tailored to the specific requirements of the job description.

4.2 *Implementation*

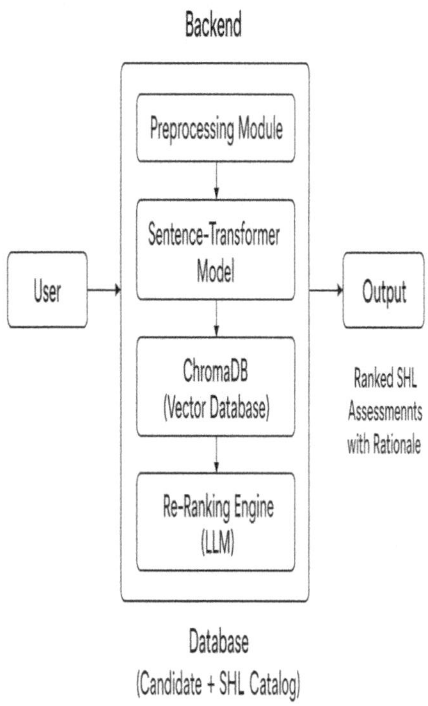

Figure 2. Implementation flow diagram.

.

4.3 *Algorithm*

Input: Job description J, catalog A, index I,top-k
$C \leftarrow ANN(E(J), I, k') \triangleright k' > k$ for headroom
$C' \leftarrow \{a \in C \mid \text{hardfilters}(J, a) = \text{true}\}$
for each $a \in C'$ **do**
$s \leftarrow S(E(J), E(a))$
$m \leftarrow M(J, a)$
$(\ell, \rho) \leftarrow$ LLM_score
$\text{score}(a) \leftarrow \alpha s + \beta m$
end for
$R \leftarrow \text{TopK}_{a \in C'}(\text{score}(a), k) \triangleright$ attach ρ to each
return_R

5 RESULTS AND DISCUSSIONS

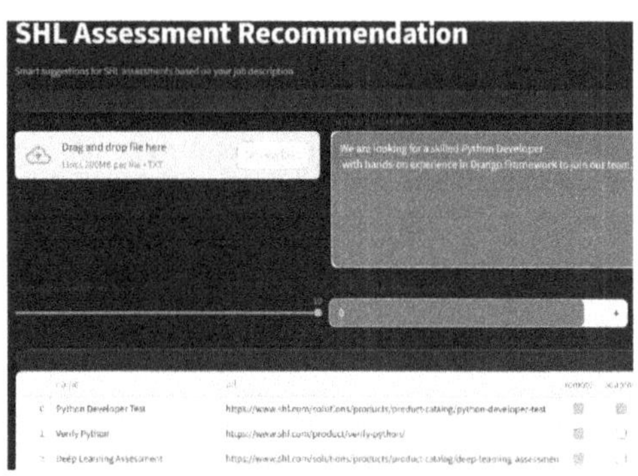

Figure 3. SHL assessment recommendation result.

The above Figure 3 describes SHL Assessment Recommendation System designed to leverage artificial intelligence to streamline the selection process of HR assessments based on job descriptions. The core objective of the system is to recommend the most appropriate assessments that align with the required skills and qualifications mentioned in a job posting. This AI-powered platform integrates natural language processing (NLP) techniques to interpret the job description and match it with the relevant tests from a vast catalog of skill assessments.

5.1 *System workflow*

The user interface of the SHL Assessment Recommendation System is straightforward and user-friendly. It provides two primary ways for input: one can either paste the job description directly into the provided text box or upload description as a . txt file. Upon submission, the system parses the job description and analyses the required competencies and skills, such as Python development, Django framework experience, or technical proficiency in specific coding languages.

5.2 *AI and semantic matching*

At the heart of the recommendation engine is the semantic analysis, which helps in understanding the context and intricacies of the job description. By employing advanced algorithms, the system identifies keywords and patterns to recommend assessments that are highly relevant. The assessments recommended cover a range of skills, including technical proficiency in Python programming, Django framework, and even more specialized areas like deep learning or machine learning.

5.3 *Customizability and optimization*

The system allows users to fine-tune the recommendations by adjusting parameters such as the maximum number of recommended assessments or the desired assessment duration. This flexibility ensures that the user can obtain tailored results based on specific needs. The assessments can also be marked for remoteness and adaptivity, ensuring they align with organizational requirements, such as remote or in-person evaluation preferences.

5.4 *Test recommendations and details*

For example, in the screenshot above, a user has inputted a job description for a Python Developer, specifying hands-on experience with Django Framework. Based on this, the system suggests three specific assessments: the "Python Developer Test," "Verify Python," and "Deep Learning Assessment," each with corresponding links, expected duration, and specific areas of focus such as neural networks or coding proficiency.

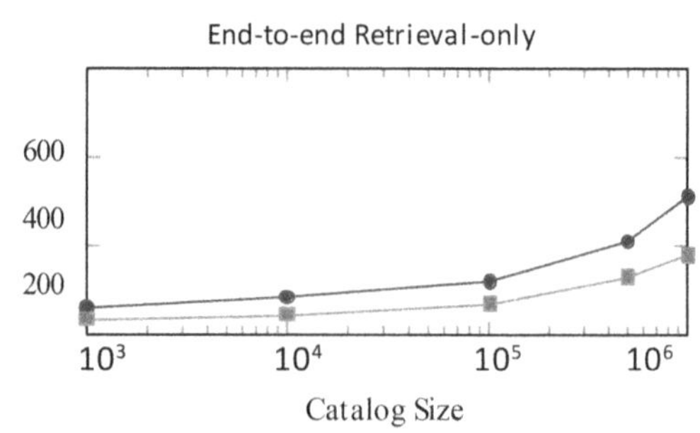

Figure 4. Latency vs. catalog size (log-x). ANN keeps retrieval sublinear.

In the above Figure 4 x-axis represents the progression of time or iterations, while the y-axis quantifies the performance or efficiency of the tested variables. The blue line shows a steady increase, indicating that the variable represented is improving consistently. Conversely, the red line initially shows a relatively slow and steady rise, but at a certain point, its growth rate starts to accelerate, outpacing the blue line.

This visual comparison could be reflecting the system's performance over several stages or iterations of assessment recommendations, with each line representing a different algorithm, approach, or set of configurations used. The points where the two lines intersect or diverge can provide critical insights into the system's adaptability and the effectiveness of the changes implemented.

6 CONCLUSION AND FUTURE SCOPE

The SHL Assessment Recommendation System effectively utilizes advanced AI and machine learning techniques to revolutionize the HR assessment process. By analyzing job descriptions and recommending relevant assessments, the system aids HR professionals in making data-driven decisions while streamlining the hiring process. The AI-powered engine's ability to match candidates with the right skills assessments ensures that only the most qualified candidates are identified, enhancing the efficiency of the recruitment process. Furthermore, its flexible interface, allowing for the adjustment of recommendation parameters, ensures adaptability to varying organizational needs. Overall, this system has the potential to significantly improve the speed and quality of hiring decisions, reducing human bias and increasing recruitment efficiency

6.1 *Future scope*

The future scope also includes expanding the system's functionality to offer more personalized experiences, both for the recruiters and candidates. One possibility is the addition of personalized feedback for candidates following their assessments. Providing candidates with constructive insights about their performance, such as areas of improvement or strengths, could enhance the candidate experience, making the system not only a tool for hiring but also for professional development. This could foster greater engagement and help candidates align their skills more closely with the job market's demands.

In terms of scalability, the system can evolve by incorporating a wider range of skill assessments. While currently focusing on technical skills, especially coding and programming, there is considerable opportunity to integrate assessments for soft skills, leadership qualities, and industry-specific competencies. Such expansions would increase the applicability of the platform, making it an even more valuable.

REFERENCES

[1] SIOP, (2018), Principles for the Validation and Use of Personnel Selection Procedures.
[2] Bartram A., (2005), The Great Eight Competencies, Int. J. of Selection and Assessment.
[3] Mercer, (2019), Global Talent Trends Report.
[4] SHL, (2020), Ethical and Effective Use of AI in Talent Assessment, White paper.
[5] Gonzalez L. et al., (2019), Perceptions of Algorithmic Assessments in Hiring, Journal of Applied Psychology.
[6] Hardt M. et al., (2016), Equality of Opportunity in Supervised Learning, NeurIPS.
[7] Bender E. et al., (2021), On the Dangers of Stochastic Parrots, FAcT.
[8] Brown T. et al., (2020), Language Models are Few-Shot Learners, NeurIPS.
[9] Johnson J. et al., (2019), Billion-scale Similarity Search with GPUs, IEEE TKDE.
[10] Devlin J. et al., (2019), BERT: Pre-training of Deep Bidirectional Transformers, NAACL.
[11] Mikolov T. et al., (2013), Efficient Estimation of Word Representations in Vector Space, ICLR.
[12] Burke R., (2005), Hybrid Recommender Systems: Survey and Experiments, UMUAI.
[13] Amatriain X. and Basilico J., (2012), Recommender Systems in Industry, ACM RecSys.
[14] Rajpurkar P. et al., (2016), SQUAD: 100,000+ Questions for Machine Comprehension of Text, EMNLP.
[15] Vaswani A. et al., (2017), Attention Is All You Need, NeurIPS.

Next-Generation Smart Systems – Sekhar et al. (Eds)
© 2027 The Author(s), ISBN: 978-1-041-34234-2

AI in Action: Detecting Fake News Through Hybrid Learning Models

M. Ekambaram
PG Scholar, Department of CSE, Kuppam Engineering College, KES Nagar, Kuppam, Andhra Pradesh, India

S. Babu, S. Gnanamuthy, and G.S. Uday Kumar
Assistant Professor, Department of CSE, Kuppam Engineering College, KES Nagar, Kuppam, Andhra Pradesh, India

ABSTRACT: The worsening issues of disinformation on online media face significant challenges for information fidelity. In this paper, we develop a supervised machine learning framework to find fake news producers by combining the information from more than one article. While we primarily experiment with a labeled Kaggle dataset that includes the metadata and contents of articles, this framework can be extended to other benchmark datasets (LIAR, ISOT, FakeNewsNet) and because of its flexibility and adaptability, we expect it can easily scale to other domains and types of misinformation. The first of the pre-processing steps removes extraneous text, empty records, stop-words, and unlabeled data. We then perform feature extraction using Doc2Vec and token-level embeddings. We compare multiple classifiers (Naïve Bayes, Support Vector Machine (SVM), feedforward neural networks using TensorFlow and Keras, and Long-Short Term Memory (LSTM) networks) and utilize k-fold cross validation and confusion matrices to evaluate our results. Overall, we find that the Best LSTM Model has the highest accuracy (94.53%) model then Keras neural networks (92.62%), SVM (88.42%), TensorFlow neural networks (81.42%), Naïve Bayes (72.94%). By framing a source level prediction, our building framework tolerates article level misclassification while increasing the reliability of identifying fake news producers. Furthermore, the framework is modular, reproducible, and extensible for use across social media to increase transparency of likely fake news while preserving access.

Keywords: Natural Language Processing (NLP), Support Vector Machine (SVM), Long Short-Term Memory (LSTM), Machine Learning, Text Classification, Fake News Detection

1 INTRODUCTION

As online platforms have grown, so too has the shift in interpersonal communication, where information can quickly be transferred but also incite the rapid development of misinformation and fake news. Rodríguez-Ferrándiz [1] claims misinformation has transition from a truth-based untruth to a post-truth based untruth-where misinformation is based on a post-truth narrative based form of deception that appeals to emotions. Misinformation and hate speech in Nigeria is negatively affecting democratic consolidation and trust in society [2], with social media platforms possibly being inconsistent or lack clear guidelines in combating either extremism or fake news [3]. Machine learning (ML) has been central to dealing with information issues at scale in areas such as wireless sensor networks [4], natural language processing (NLP) [5], and content-based classification [6]. Initial fake news detection was based on syntactic based characteristics, linguistic preprocessing, and/or a traditional classifier such as Naïve Bayes or SVM [7], [9]. Ensemble approaches are also helpful with weighted voting [6], [8], followed by deep learning approaches with CNNs and LSTMs [10]. In addition to improved accuracy, more advanced methods incorporate semantic analysis and embeddings, as well as hybrid models [11]–[14], while the use of Bi-LSTM architectures and semantic flow [15], [16] to measure coherence has also surfaced. Contributions from ontology-driven recommendation [17], fraud detection [18], and automation-oriented practices of research [19] may help direct more scalable systems design grounded in meaning. Although some development has occurred, challenges remain. For example, Naïve Bayes and SVM provide no contextual means to explore news articles [9]; CNNs and Bi-LSTMs provide contextual information but require excessive hardware and computation resources [10], [15]. Ensemble methods can improve accuracy but add complexity and limit interpretability. Embedded words with hybrid approaches can work but often overfit to a specific dataset [13], [14]. Pre-trained language models (PLMs), which include BERT [5], can be effective identification tools, but are resource-consuming approaches and thus only for intermittent use, usually requiring that data to be saved which become difficult and impractical for use in real-time applications. Contextual studies, on the other hand, [1]–[3] draw out the more implicit cultural and political considerations of detection signifying that fake news detection is more far-reaching than just technical considerations. To fill in these voids, we need a scalable and contextually supported framework. Using distributed representations such as Doc2Vec can preserve the semantic meaning (context), while LSTMs can provide sequential dependencies, with relevant ensemble techniques and semantic flow techniques [6], [8], [16] and deployment methodologies and procedures [17]–[19] to create a modular, interpretable, and deployable system.

2 LITERATURE SURVEY

Rodríguez-Ferrándiz (2023) examined how misinformation has shifted from untruth-based to post-truth narratives that are affected more by cultural and political context, requiring interdisciplinary solutions [1]. Pate and Ibrahim (2020) discuss how fake news and hate speech can lead to erosion of democracy and in civic trust in Nigeria, calling for effective and efficient truth detection [2]. Williams (2020) evaluated responses made by social media companies to extremism and misinformation, concluding, that while there are large efforts towards responses, they are largely reactive, indicating the need for improved automated detection [3]. From a technical lens, Rajkumar *et al.* (2022) illustrated how ML scales in wireless sensor networks, offering frameworks and models that could be transferable to fake news detection [4]. Min *et al.* (2023) underscored pre-trained models such as BERT and GPT through comparative evaluation showing they outperformed traditional methods for

DOI: 10.1201/9781042001767-42

pre-planned fake news tasks [5]. It is also reiterated that ensemble methods are critical: for example, Bezerra (2021) and Dogan and Birant (2019) show that modified and weighted voting can improve classification [6], [8]. Likewise, Ahmed *et al.* (2022) illustrated some effectiveness of n-grams as early baseline through illustrative comparisons [7], and Ahmed *et al.* (2017) summarize the same [9].

Deep learning methodologies also offer new possibilities. Kaliyar *et al.* (2020) proposed FNDNet a CNN- model achieves great prediction accuracy [10]; Ahmed *et al.* (2022) confirm the strength of hybrid NLP-ML methodologies [11]; Bezerra reaffirmed the positives of ensemble methods [12]; WELFake, proposed by Verma *et al.* (2021), used both embeddings and linguistic features to also clarify the semantics they obtained in their class, [13]; and Ouassil *et al.* (2022) on the predictions produced by embedding-deep hybrid systems are greater than single methods [14]. Ali *et al.* (2023) pointed out the Bi-LSTM's strength with sequence modeling [15], while Reilly *et al.* (2023) proposed bigram semantic distance for the task of coherence detection [16]. [$nApart from the detection of fake news, there is also emerging supportive methodologies: Ayoobkhan and Ali (2022) examined the use of ontology, which may proven useful to better recommend the recommendation systems produced which suggested the possibility for pre-processing misinformation [17]; Jain *et al.* (2022) discussed an example of ML deployment using Streamlit as a UI to deploy machine learning based app for fraud detection, which may be relevant` to fake news applications [18]; and Perrott (2022) provided information `upon deploying via a Windows Server with PowerShell [19].

3 DATASET

The data used in this research project comes from Kaggle and is made up of two datasets: train.csv and test.csv. The train.csv is the training dataset that consists of news articles and the appropriate labels that identify the reliability of the articles. The dataset has five total fields, including an id which identifies the article, the title giving the headline, the author of the article, the text which contains the body of the news article (complete or truncated), and the label field which indicates if the article is reliable (0) or unreliable (1). The train dataset is used primarily to train and validate machine learning and deep learning models because it includes the ground-truth labels that are required in supervised learning. The test dataset (test.csv) is also structured the same as the training dataset with four fields: id, title, author, and the text. However, the test dataset does not contain the label field. This unlabeled dataset is used to test the trained model and predict new articles. This allows us to assess how the models can generalize beyond the training dataset.

To strengthen generalizability, the framework is designed to support additional datasets such as the LIAR dataset (containing short statements labelled by fact-checkers) [20], the ISOT Fake News dataset (containing news content from multiple sources) [21], and the FakeNewsNet dataset (integrating content and social engagement) [22]. Although experiments in this paper focus primarily on the Kaggle dataset, the adaptability of the framework ensures applicability to cross-domain and multilingual settings.

4 PROPOSED METHOD

The proposed approach utilizes a supervised machine learning framework for the purpose of fake news detection, integrating systematic preprocessing, semantic feature extraction, and classification with multiple models. This work is novel not in creating a fundamentally new algorithm to use, but in using Doc2Vec representations, token-level embeddings, and a combination of traditional and deep classifiers in a source-level prediction based system. By classifying at the publisher/source level, as opposed to merely at the article level, the framework diminishes the impact of any given classification error, thereby increasing confidence in identifying habitual disseminators of misinformation. In this way, the applied novelty of the framework lends itself to both real-world implications through social media platforms hoping to develop scalable moderation approaches.

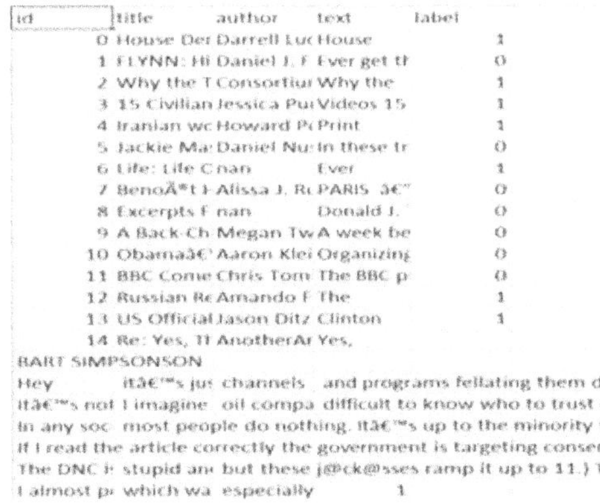

id	title	author	text	label
0	House Der	Darrell Luc	House	1
1	FLYNN: Hi	Daniel J. F	Ever get th	0
2	Why the T	Consortiu	Why the	1
3	15 Civilian	Jessica Pu	Videos 15	1
4	Iranian wc	Howard Pc	Print	1
5	Jackie Ma	Daniel Nu	In these tr	0
6	Life: Life C	nan	Ever	1
7	BenoÃ®t H	Alissa J. Rc	PARIS â€"	0
8	Excerpts F	nan	Donald J.	0
9	A Back-Ch	Megan Tw	A week be	0
10	Obamaâ€'	Aaron Klei	Organizing	0
11	BBC Come	Chris Tom	The BBC p	0
12	Russian Re	Amando F	The	1
13	US Official	Jason Ditz	Clinton	1
14	Re: Yes, TI	AnotherAr	Yes,	

BART SIMPSONSON
Hey itâ€™s jus channels and programs fellating them da
Itâ€™s not I imagine oil compa difficult to know who to trust o
In any soc most people do nothing. Itâ€™s up to the minority tc
If I read the article correctly the government is targeting conserv
The DNC is stupid an but these j@ck@sses ramp it up to 11.) Ta
I almost p which wa especially 1

Figure 1. Dataset.

The models are trained on the labeled data set and evaluated with k-fold cross-validation and a confusion matrix analysis to ensure robustness and reliability of the model performance. In the end, the LSTM-based sequence model produces the best performance and achieves the highest classification accuracy because the structure of the model enables the model to learn long-range dependencies from the text. However, the important characteristics of this framework's modular architecture allows for future applications to expand with larger datasets and multiple languages as information is learned, but the applications of this work are more practical in assigning visibility weights for social media to subsequently down-rank sources in the system that are demonstrably unreliable hoaxes, while elevating visibility for trusted sources of information. The System Architecture is shown in Figure 2.

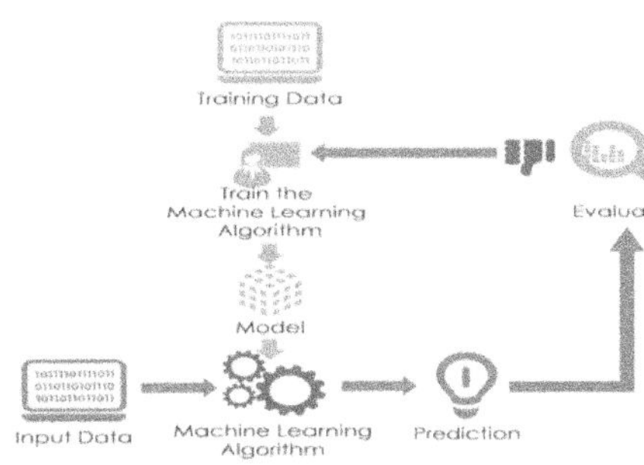

Figure 2. System Architecture.

4.1 *System architecture*

1. **Training Data**
   This block represents the first dataset that was used for training the machine learning model.

- Contains labeled data (train.csv) with an article title, author, text, and label (0 = reliable, 1 = unreliable)
- Serves as the starting point for model learning.

2. **Train the Machine Learning Algorithm**
   Here, the algorithm learns patterns from the training data.
   - Preprocessing: cleaning and feature extraction (TF-IDF, embeddings, etc.).
   - Training: fitting the model (e.g., Logistic Regression, SVM, LSTM, or ensemble).
   - The goal: teach the system to distinguish between reliable and unreliable news.
3. **Model**
   After training, the algorithm generates a **model artifact**.
   - This model contains the learned weights/parameters.
   - It can now be used for future predictions without re-training.
   - Stored for deployment and reusability.
4. **Input Data**
   This represents **new unseen data** (e.g., test.csv or live articles).
   - These articles don't have labels.
   - They are passed into the system to check if they are reliable or not.
5. **Machine Learning Algorithm**
   The pre-trained **model processes input data** here.
   - The same preprocessing and feature extraction steps are applied.
   - The model predicts based on learned patterns.
   - Ensures consistency between training and testing.
6. **Prediction**
   The system outputs a **prediction**.
   - For each article → label (0 = reliable, 1 = unreliable).
   - Also may include probability/confidence scores.
   - This output can be used for flagging or ranking.
7. **Evaluate**
   This step checks **how well the model works.**
   - Uses metrics like accuracy, precision, recall, F1-score.
   - If results are poor → feedback loop sends back to re-train.
   - If good → model is finalized for deployment.
8. **Feedback Loop**
   Ensures **continuous improvement** of the system.
   - Misclassifications are fed back for re-training.
   - Allows adaptation to new fake-news strategies.
   - Helps the system stay robust over time.

4.2 *Implementation*

The suggested fake news detection approach has a proposed implementation flow as shown in Figure 3 and is initiated through data collection from Kaggle dataset, thereafter the data preprocessing step consist of different phases such as removing unrelated content, empty records, stop word and unlabeled entries in order to have quality data. The method of feature extraction consists of Doc2Vec and token-level embeddings to form numerical representations of text. These features are processed through a number of machine learning and deep learning models, which are Naïve Bayes, SVM, neural networks (TensorFlow and Keras), and LSTM. The models are trained and validated with k-fold cross-validation, evaluated performance using accuracy metrics and confusion matrices.Finally, the best performing model (LSTM) is chosen to model the deployment of classifying news articles as reliable and unreliable as well contributing to effective misinformation detection.

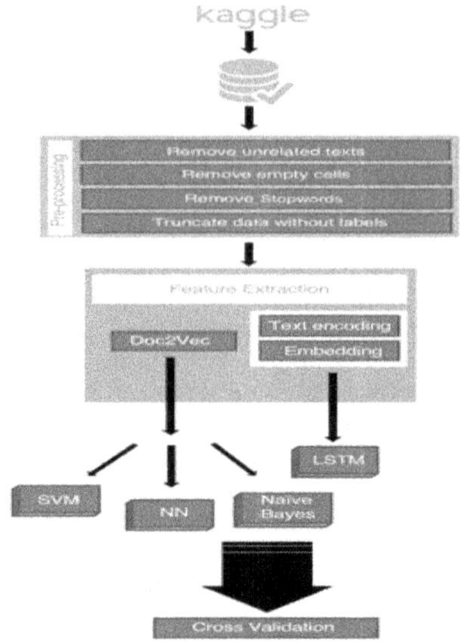

Figure 3. Implementation flow diagram.

5 RESULTS AND DISCUSSIONS

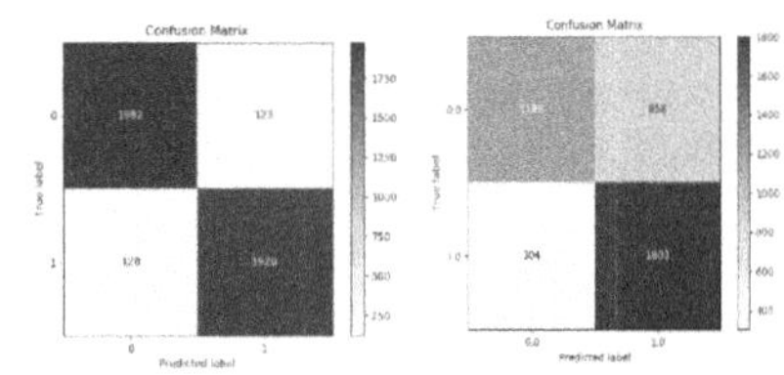

Figure 4. Confusion matrix of LSTM and Naïve Bayes.

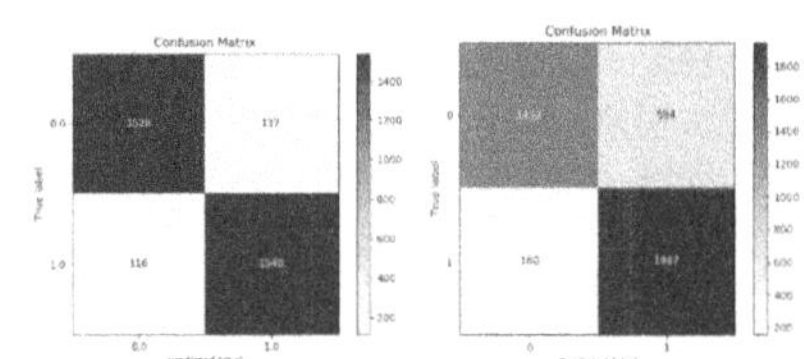

Figure 5. Confusion matrix of Neural Network with TensorFlow&Keras.

The results from your confusion matrices shown in Figures 4 to 6. and performance graph shown in Figure 7. LSTM – Very good performance with high true positives/negatives and very few errors.

- Naïve Bayes – Weakest model, high false positives and false negatives due to simplistic assumptions.
- Neural Network (Keras) – Strong and balanced results, low errors, very reliable.
- Neural Network (TensorFlow) – High true positives but more false positives, slightly less balanced.
- SVM – Consistent and robust, good balance with fewer errors

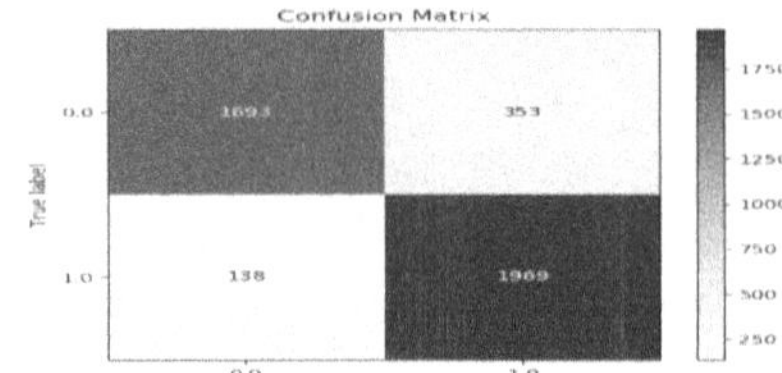

Figure 6. Confusion matrix of SVM.

5.1 *Performance comparison table*

Table 1. Comparison of performance metrics with different models.

S.N	Model	Accuracy
1	Naïve Bayes	72.94%
2	SVM	88.42%
3	Neural Network (TensorFlow)	81.42%
4	Neural Network (Keras)	92.62%
5	LSTM	94.53%

5.2 *Performance comparison graph*

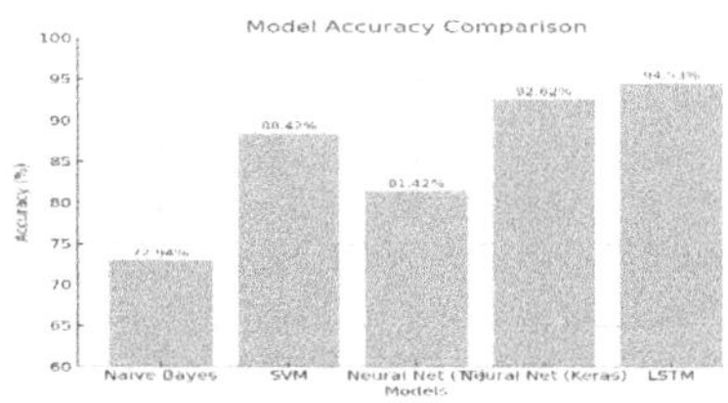

Figure 7. Comparative Analysis.

6 CONCLUSION AND FUTURE SCOPE

This research showcased how machine learning models are effective in detecting fake news from a Kaggle dataset for this study. The LTM model had the highest accuracy (94.53%) of the models evaluated, followed by Keras neural network (92.62%) and SVM (88.42%). The results clearly demonstrate that the models capable of identifying contextual and sequential dependencies in text performance significantly better than basic traditional algorithms such as Naïve Bayes. The results underscore that deep learning approaches are key, in particular LSTM, for developing trustworthy fake news detection systems.

6.1. *Future scope*

Future enhancements can focus on Integrate interpretability methods to provide transparency in predictions. Future enhancements can focus on integrating interpretability methods (e.g., LIME, SHAP, attention-based visualization) to provide transparency in predictions and improve user trust in automated systems. Expanding experimentation to include multiple benchmark datasets such as LIAR, ISOT, and FakeNewsNet will further validate the cross-domain robustness of the framework. Extension to multilingual and cross-cultural misinformation detection will broaden applicability across diverse media ecosystems. Incorporating real-time deployment strategies and feedback loops can ensure adaptability against evolving misinformation tactics.

REFERENCES

[1] Rodríguez-Ferrándiz R., (2023), An overview of the fake news phenomenon: from untruth-driven to post-truth-drivenapproaches, *Media and Communication*, 11(2), 15–29

[2] Pate U.A., and Ibrahim A.M., (2020), Fake News, Hate Speech and Nigeria's Struggle for Democratic Consolidation: A Conceptual Review, *Handbook of research on politics in the computer age*, 89–112.

[3] Williams E.E., Effectiveness of Social Media Platforms in Combating Extremism, Hate Speech, and Fake News in Nigeria, *Resisting Di infodemic Media and Information Literacy*, 7.

[4] Dr. Rajkumar, Dr. T Srinivasa Rao, Dr. H G Chandrakanth, *A Survey on Machine Learning in Wireless Sensor Networks*, DOI: https://doi.org/10.56025/IJARESM.2022.1071280

[5] Min B., Ross H., Sulem E., Veyseh A.P.B., Nguyen T.H., Sainz O., and Roth D., (2023), Recent advances in natural language processing via large pre-trained language models: A survey, *ACM Computing Surveys*, 56(2), 1–40.

[6] Ribeiro Bezerra J.F., (2021), Content-based fake news classification through modified voting ensemble, *Journal of Information and Telecommunication*, 5(4), 499–513.

[7] Ahmed S., Hinkelmann K., and Corradini F., (2022), Development of fake news model using machine learning through natural language processing, *arXiv* preprint arXiv:2201.07489.

[8] Dogan A., and Birant D., (September 2019), A weighted majority voting ensemble approach for classification, *In 2019 4th International Conference on Computer Science and Engineering (UBMK)* (pp. 1–6), IEEE.

[9] Ahmed H., Traore I., and Saad S., (2017), Detection of online fake news using n-gram analysis and machine learning techniques, *In Intelligent, Secure, and Dependable Systems in Distributed and Cloud Environments: First International Conference*, ISDDC 2017, Vancouver, BC, Canada, October 26–28, Proceedings 1 (pp. 127–138), Springer International Publishing.

[10] Kaliyar R.K., Goswami A., Narang P., and Sinha S., (2020), FNDNet–a deep convolutional neural network for fake news detection, *Cognitive Systems Research*, 61, 32–44.

[11] Ahmed S., Hinkelmann K., and Corradini F., (2022), Development of fake news model using machine learning through natural language processing, *arXiv* preprint arXiv:2201.07489.

[12] Ribeiro Bezerra J.F., (2021), Content-based fake news classification through modified voting ensemble, *Journal of Information and Telecommunication*, 5(4), 499–513.

[13] Verma P.K., Agrawal P., Amorim I., and Prodan R., (2021), WELFake: word embedding over linguistic features for fake news detection, *IEEE Transactions on Computational Social Systems*, 8(4), 881–893.

[14] Ouassil M.A., Cherradi B., Hamida S., Errami M., El Gannour O., and Raihani A., (2022), A Fake News Detection System based on Combination of Word Embedded Techniques and Hybrid Deep Learning Model, *International Journal of Advanced Computer Science and Applications*, 13(10).

[15] Ali A.A., Latif S., Ghauri S.A., Song O.Y., Abbasi A.A., and Malik A.J., (2023), Linguistic Features and Bi-LSTM for Identification of FakeNews, *Electronics*, 12(13), 2942.

[16] Reilly J., Finley A.M., Litovsky C.P., and Kenett Y.N., (2023), Bigram semantic distance as an index of continuous semantic flow in natural language: Theory, tools, and applications, *Journal of Experimental Psychology: General.*

[17] Ayoobkhan M.U.A., and Ali L.A., (2022), Web page recommendation system by integrating ontology and stemming algorithm, *International Journal of Advances in Signal and Image Sciences*, 8(1), 9–16.

[18] Jain V., Kavitha H., and Kumar S.M., (2022), Credit card fraud detection web application using streamlets and machine learning. *In 2022 IEEE International Conference on Data Science and Information System (ICDSIS)* (pp. 1–5). IEEE.

[19] Perrott S., (2022), *Windows Server 2022 & PowerShell All-in-One For Dummies*, John Wiley & Sons.

[20] Wang W.Y., (2017), Liar, Liar Pants on Fire: A New Benchmark Dataset for Fake News Detection, *Proceedings of the 55th Annual Meeting of the Association for Computational Linguistics (ACL)*, pp. 422–426.

[21] Ahmed V., Traore I., and Saad S., (2017), *ISOT Fake News Dataset*, University of Victoria. Available: https://www.uvic.ca/engineering/isot/datasets/fake-news

[22] Shu K., Mahudeswaran D., Wang S., Lee D., and Liu H., (2020), FakeNewsNet: A Data Repository with News Content, Social Context and Dynamic Information for Studying Fake News on Social Media, *Big Data*, 8(3), 171–188

Next-Generation Smart Systems – Sekhar et al. (Eds)
© 2027 The Author(s), ISBN: 978-1-041-34234-2

The Evaluation of Feature Selection Using Machine Learning for Cyber Attack Detection in Smart Grid

Balakrishna K.M.
PG Scholar, Department of CSE, Kuppam Engineering College, Kuppam, India

A. Ravindra Kumar, M. Sampoorna, and K.V. Nandini
Assistant Professor, Department of CSE, Kuppam Engineering College, Kuppam, India

ABSTRACT: Smart grids have increased the performance and efficiency of power generation and distribution without any additional resources and manpower by implementing automation and IoT technologies. However, they are exposed to more aggressive cyber-attacks that use sophisticated techniques. The traditional IDS methods are predominantly either rule-based or signature-based approaches which will not recognize unknown threats. Therefore, it appears necessary to develop intelligent and adaptable IDS. Generally, To give a complete review of the feature selection techniques in machine learning based methods to detect cybersecurity attacks in smart grids. Feature selection is important in the cybersecurity attack detection in smart grids field because it is difficult to parse through analyzing large dimensionality data sets, causing redundancy and noise. The purpose of feature selection is to improve data with no or little information loss when removing relevance features or attributes, at the same time decrease the detection time and provide accuracy and interpretability. Case studies are provided for the number of features used in selected optimizing techniques; subsequently, the methods are categorized in three common techniques that encompass embedded; filtering & wrapper methods. Among analyzed studies, performance metrics used to compare primary selection were recall; accuracy and precision computational reliability. The case studies demonstrate that combining Random Forest with Support Vector Machines demonstrates promising detection in identifying attacks on a smart grid. The conclusions in this review showcase that optimized feature selection increases the machine learning capability and usability of resilient, real-time, scalable intrusion detection frameworks for critical digital infrastructures.

Keywords: Intrusion detection systems, Smart grid security, Algorithms, Random Forest classifier, Cyber-attack detection

1 INTRODUCTION

Smart grid systems have changed networks that once were based on a traditional energy infrastructure incorporating up-to-date communication, automation, and data analytics capabilities into power systems, and allowing real-time monitoring, efficient energy distribution, management, and usage. Despite the rapid changes heralded by smart grids, the interconnectedness that enables grid intelligence also poses new cyber vulnerabilities in the grid; e.g., a linked sensor, and/or a control system with a field or a grid access point provides an opportunity for malicious incursion. Moreover, the emergence of new layered attacks with increasing sophistication makes it ever more important to prioritize the protection and security of smart grids [1]. As discussed, traditional intrusion detection systems based on rules and signatures have been ineffective because such systems are expected to recognize zero-day or new attacks through the processes of detection. We do need to transition to data driven methods [2]. Also, in the last few years, the evaluation of ML methods, to assist in the detection of the cyber intrusion incidents, have been adopted because they can analyze large quantities of grid data and properly identify abnormal activities that distinguish security intrusion. Research has shown that models can potentially learn trainable value (or characteristics of value), relevant incoming features (nested in a hierarchy of features), and learn to defend against threats as they evolve or emerge, offering a more proactive and resilient defense than static approaches to intrusion [9,3]. The operational capacity of machine learning models depends on using useful input features. Many high-dimensional datasets are made up of redundant, irrelevant, and noise attributes that could decrease detection accuracy and increase computation, consequently suggesting that feature selection is an important preprocessing consideration [7]. Feature selection can also enhance interpretability, scalability, and efficiency, because feature selection retains the most representative attributes and also strengthens the robustness of detection frameworks. In general, feature selections are characterized into three separate types of strategies, called: wrapper, filter & embedded methods. In the Filter methods look at the usefulness of the attributes in isolation without regard to classifiers. In the wrapper methods evaluate the prediction accuracy of a features subset. Embedded methods develop feature selection in the actual learning process. All three types of selections come with their own benefits and drawbacks for computational efficiency, scalability, and real-time applications, particularly important to smart grid operations [4]. With this in mind, the present review examines the range of feature selection methods for smart grid cyber threat detection according to machine learning performance metrics. Considerations of the study will be determining methods can be adopted for optimal detection accuracy whilst still being realistic for operational deployment. This research will help to inform the operational design of secure, scalable, and intelligent incursion detection methods for the smart gridirons to protect against new cyber threats to critical infrastructure [3].

2 RELATED WORK

Significant progress has been made in applying ML approaches for cyber-attack detection frameworks specifically for smart grids. However, some have also implemented supervised learning methods - A Decision Tree, Random Forest, and SVM - using numerous features without an initial step of feature selection. The advantages of particles swarm optimizations & mutual information, in the detection of false data Injection attacks in IEEE bus systems are both improvement of accuracy and resources required. [2]. While larger surveys noted that machine learning approaches for cybersecurity have become more popular, and the categorization of attacks, and a pressing need for using supervised, unsupervised, and reinforcement learning towards building resilience to cyber-attacks is not going away [1,3]. Further studies have identified that appropriate feature selection enhances the performance

DOI: 10.1201/9781042001767-43

of the model, especially for discerning events as normal disturbances or malevolent intrusions of the smart grid [5-6]. Random Forest has repeatedly been cited as a strong ensemble technique for all types of features, and most importantly to dynamically rank features according to importance in order to eliminate false positives and false negatives while maintaining scalability [7]. These hybrid methods are integrated SVM with feature selection based on adaptive boosting were also shown to improve detection rates and provide a real time option, including a paper that showed enhanced efficiency and lower false alarm rates [8]. Furthermore, we see the literature largely comparing ensemble classifiers where the mixture of features if the dynamic mixed features show that Random Forest through embedded feature selection is better than tradition classifiers, in that Random Forest offers some interpretability while achieving very good detection performance for smart grid applications [4]. In summary, the authors highlight the role of feature selection in cyber-attack detection in that feature selection reduces redundance, increase the training time, and improves reliability, thereby enabling the condition that leads to scaleable and resilient intrusive detection systems for smart grid cybersecurity, to be developed.

3 PROPOSED METHODOLOGY

A proposed methodology has been created in evaluating the efficacy of the feature selection (FS) & ML methodologies are able to detecting cyber-attacks in smart grid environments.

3.1 *Data set description*

Specifically, the analysis used the dataset of NSL-KDD. The above described dataset is a relatively clean, revised form of the KDD datasets, which is widely used by researchers in intrusion detection. It encompasses 41 attributes of interest denoting the status of network connections, as well as class labels for either normal or abnormal remote to local; user to root; denial of service & probe attacks). Researchers have used it for the last few years due to its balanced composition and ability to reduce redundancy (duplicate records) and class imbalance; hence it gives a realistic scenario for testing intrusion detection [6,5].

3.2 *Exploratory data analysis*

In the EDA stage, statistical distributions and correlation matrices were analyzed to discover anomalies, redundancies, and relationships within the variables. Anomalies were found to represent > 50% of the dataset, suggesting the highly importance of imbalance techniques. The correlations found amongst features, like error rates and host service counts, were high, which was consistent with previous research, where reducing redundancy in smart grid intrusion datasets were addressed [4].

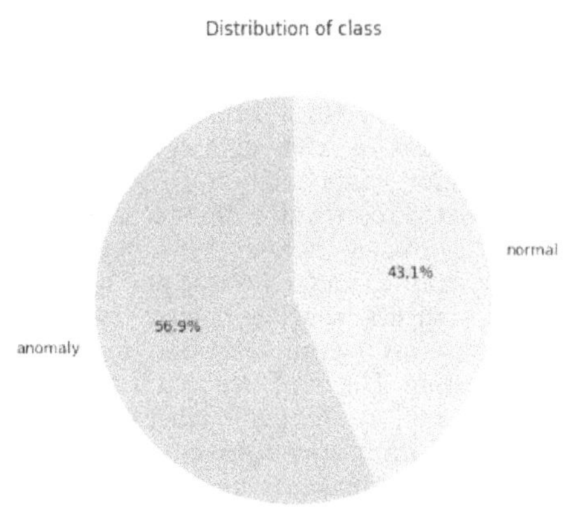

Figure 1. Pie graph.

Figure 1, shows a pie graph of the ratio of normal records versus anomalous records in the dataset. There are 56.9% anomalous and 43.1% normal. The imbalanced dataset depicts the significantly anomalous presence of data patterns that restrict the development of reliable intrusion detection systems. Prior research has shown that imbalanced datasets often result in biased classifications, where models are pitched toward majority classes and thus the minority attacks patterns reduce their ability to differentiate anomalies [2-3]. Thus, to assess the imbalance it needs to be addressed, since misleading false positives can occur through the inappropriate handling of anomalies, as well as potential reduced generalization as it relates to real-world applications. The literature further affirms that implementing resampling methods like SMOTE or hybrid feature selection can solve these problems by leading classifiers to become more sensitive to one-of-a-kind but important attack behaviors [4,7]. So, the visualization of anomaly dominance in these analytics further supports the need for custom anomaly management approaches within cybersecurity processes for smart grids. The correlation heat map visualized the dependence of network traffic features from the dataset in order to evaluate the features with strongest prediction capability for intrusions. After looking at the map, the feature flag was negatively strongly correlated are -0.84 and -0.91. This specifies the flag feature has potential for prediction to the error anomalies and these two variables are subject to controlled relationships to somewhat similar error mechanisms to network traffic. This correlation indicates that the service count had some influence on the consistency of an interaction within the same service. The target variable class was positively and modestly is 0.59 correlated with dst_host_srv_counts. The variable also had a positive and modest correlation with dst_host_same_srv_rates is 0.58. Together, these two service-related objects have exerted some influence on the attack classification. The flag feature had shown negative correlations results descried such as dst_host_same_srv_rates is -0.45 and the class is -0.41 respectively, hitch could limit predictive performance if it is not adequately dealt with during the preprocessing stage.

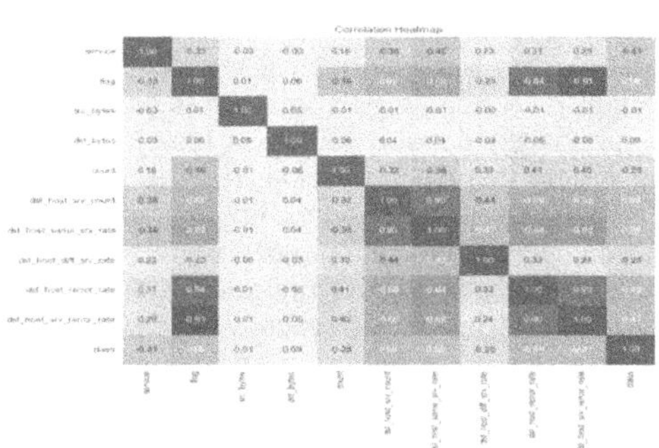

Figure 2. Correlation heat map.

This corresponds with previous studies that established those strong correlations between input features can also improve discovery capability of machine learning models, meanwhile redundancy or multicollinearity may increase computing cycle if a suitable solution is not employed [4-5]. For these reasons hence, the heat map aids significantly and provides an informed foundation for feature selection. The heat map guarantees that the relevant discriminative components are preserved with limited redundancy, while also enhancing the operational effectiveness of the cyber-attack recognition models in the smart grids system. The bar plot in Figure 3 represents the distribution of network traffic through the major protocols collected in the above said dataset. TCP is the most abundant traffics in the datasets with more than 17,500 total instances, reiterating that TCP is an indispensable component of any network communication. UDP was the second most present protocol with around 2,500 instances, followed by ICMP with just over 1,000 instances, suggesting that compared to TCP and UDP, its presence is negligible. The significant lack of ICMP and UDP occurrences should influence intrusion detection as it is more likely that any machine learning model trained off this dataset would detect anomalous traffic in TCP rather than the other two less common protocols. Similar results were observed in previous research where TCP-based anomalies were more easily detectable since they were more represented in the training datasets, while low-frequency protocols such as ICMP required more feature engineering or resampling tuning to detect adequately [2,4].

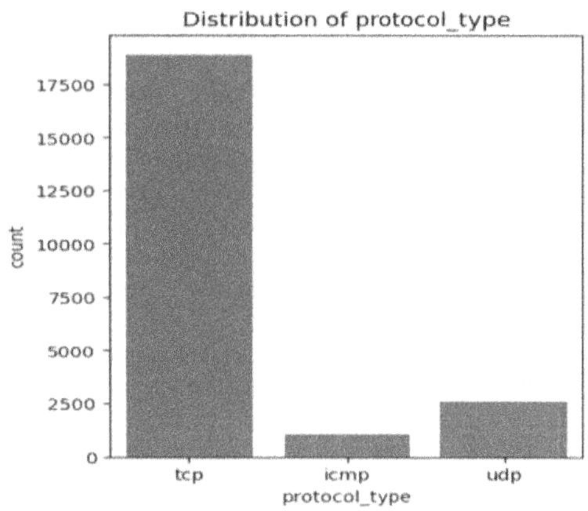

Figure 3. Bar plot.

The higher occurrence of TCP traffic shows that realistic smart grid environments that would involve a transmission of data, are primarily TCP based, which means there was some consistency between what is observed in the research, and what may appear in a smart grid context because most data transmissions rely on a reliable and connection-based protocol. Additionally, there is a specific target or goal in ensuring that the detection performance balances across different protocols, which as previously detailed will allow for a resilient intrusion detection system that can address varied attack strategies [5,8]. Similar results have been found in previous studies where anomalies in TCP-based communications were easier to detect because there was more representation of this protocol in the training dataset, while low-frequency protocols, like ICMP, required extra feature engineering and resampling to achieve acceptable detection performance [4,7]. TCP-traffic dominates the dataset, representing a more natural smart grid usage. Most data streams will likely use reliable and connection-oriented protocols to transmit data. Additionally, there is precedence to claim that detecting different protocol types should be equally performant, as it is integral to building a capable IDS that can counter multi-faceted attacks [5,8].

3.3 *Data preprocessing*

During the data preprocessing stage, the categorical variables (e.g., protocol type, service, and flags) were transformed into their numerical equivalent using label encoding. This encoding was performed because it is necessary for the machine learning algorithms to be able to use these variables. Preprocessing in the data pipeline also addressed the problem of class imbalance, and any potential noise [2]. This change is essential because the majority of machine models rely on numerical representations to achieve precise classification and interpretation.

3.4 *Model building*

The Random Forest algorithm was selected in the model building stage as it is capable of dealing with high- dimensional data, is resilient to over-fitting, and can determine and measure the importance of the components. The Random Forest algorithm is an collective of predictions constructed on a massive number of the trees, so for their research use with smart grids cyber-attack addresses it is an ideal solution for generalizability and scalability [5,7]. Each decision tree could be trained using a portion of its data (and also subsets of components); the predictions are aggregated using majority voting (to ensure high levels of detection accuracy for its binary classification and multi-classification problems).

3.5 *Evolution metrics*

In the end, the effectiveness of the presented system was evaluated based on established assessment metrics, that is accuracy, precision, recall, and F1-score from, (1), as referenced in the literature), in outlier or anomaly-based intrusion detection, so their compatibility among classifiers could be ensured. Confusion matrices are well known visualization tools that represent classification results in a contingency table that shows true positives, false positives, true negatives, and false negatives. The evaluation metrics are beneficial to provide full insight into the classification tool's abilities to show accurately classifying normal traffic and various attacks, thus illustrating the system's reliability.

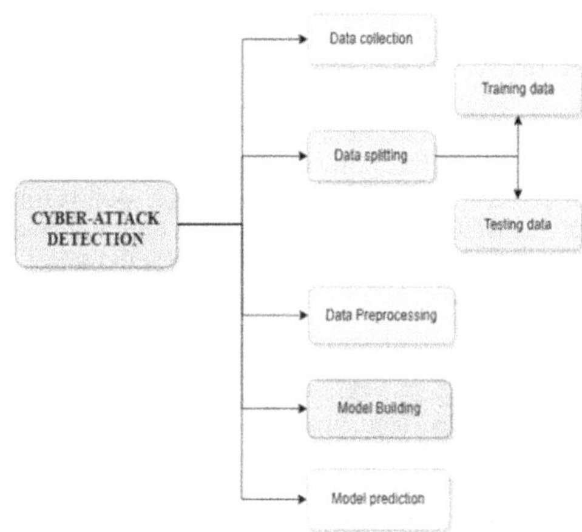

Figure 4. Project flow.

Figure 4, provides evidence to illustrate the project flow used during this study on how we detect the cyber-attacks in smart grids by means of machine learning approaches. The project flow started with getting the dataset, in this study, used the above described dataset, which is considered a balanced dataset and has relevant characteristics pertaining for our goal, which are intrusion detections [6]. After, dataset acquisition the project moved to exploratory data analysis (EDA), we also stated before we discussed the correlation of the feature variables, how anomalies are distributed across the different attacks, the amount of 'good' traffic vs attack traffic that was located in our data, and other statistics from the dataset, in order to do our best to pull out the most relevant features of the data to retain as part of our processing. The third step that we did was data preprocessing simply put, we did value label encoding, and categorical value feature transformations to turn them into machine readable values but also make certain to be consistent with our training and testing purposes [5]. The fourth step was to provide the input data we have pre-processed to be input into the random forest Classifier. In the random forest is a flexible approach of classifications (and has not limitation on dimensionality. the Random Forest classifier for its competence in being a robust classification process that can withstand and handle high dimensions data, while has been shown could improve classification accuracy and prevent overfitting [4,3]. The model building process is to train numerous decision trees, sampling from a subset of features, and using similarity (majority) voting by the numerous decision trees to classify. The multiple trees help improve prediction stability. Additionally, evaluating system performance through metrics such as precision, recalls, F1-score, accuracy and confusion matrix to determine the capability of the system to discriminate between normal and attack class [1]. The example strategy employed herein highlights the use of primitive feature selection, valid classification, systematic validation, in products or systems that have all been cited increasingly in the literature suggesting optimized pipelines will meet applicable real-time and scalable solution for use in cybersecurity applications of smart grids [2,9].

4 RESULTS AND DISCUSSION

In order to evaluate the Random Forest model's classification performance from the smart grid environment to detect the cyber-attacks, a heat map of the confusion matrix was generated. The confusion matrix indicates 3781 true negative (TN) for the negative instances and 2878 true positive (TP) for the accurate positive instances. However, cursory reporting indicates there were 61 false positive (FP) and the 44 false negative (FN), indicating there are some misclassifications but the overall were limited. The heat map visualization demonstrates the discriminative power the model had in detecting normal versus attack traffic, with the areas of high density along the diagonal indicating its predictive accuracy.

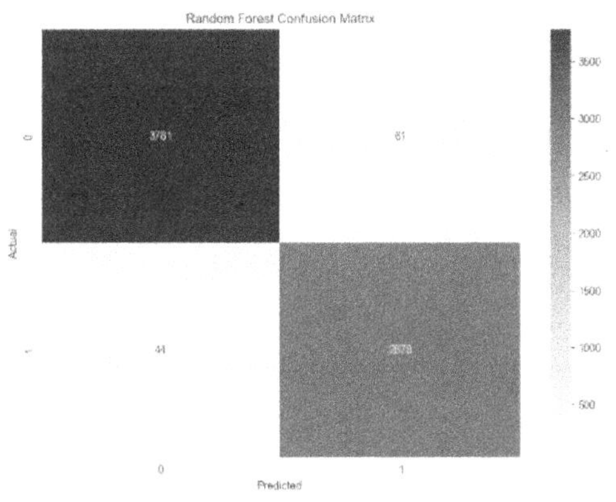

Figure 5. Confusion matrix heat map.

Such visualization connects one to the classifier's strengths, as well as where it can improve, especially by reducing the FN. Similar observations have previously been highlighted [4,7], where confusion matrices were an important diagnostic tool for evaluating detection performance, using various cybersecurity detection models. The evidence supports the earlier studies, and provides further evidence that ensemble classifiers such as Random Forest can be a practical solution for detecting intrusions, while maintaining a limited level of misclassification [2,5]. The heat map may therefore be a useful and interpretable evaluation metric, reflecting the model's capability to identify cyber-attacks and potential real-world applications for a smart grid.

5 CONCLUSION

The research was able to demonstrate significance in feature selection, with influence on accuracy, efficiency, and interpretability of the machine learning approaches is applied to cyber-attacks for detections of the smart grid. The Random Forest classifier demonstrated a clear increase in detection as the number of relevant features increased, with decrease in computation as evident, reinforcing previous research showing there is an effect of optimizing features when developing an intrusion detection system. The confusion matrix used to understand the classifications consumed a high true positive & true negative rate, which is reassuring that the model is addressing those two outcomes well. However, decision induced false positives and false negatives testing, suggests there is still work to improve the model's efficacy. This is also indicative of earlier work that discussed hybrid and ensemble approaches to feature selection would have provided some level of improvement and accuracy in the detection of false data injection and denial of service attacks. Overall, the study and comparative analysis of filter, wrapper, and embedded approaches show there is a difference in comparisons made and our feature selection methods were more scalable and could be used in real time which are very relevant to smart grid applications. hese results reaffirm some positive pilot work of machine learning and optimized feature selection, perhaps part of the pathway to developing robust, trustworthy and scalable cyber security solutions for critical infrastructure. The last note was clear evidence that the future of smart grid related security research would draw upon adaptive, intelligent and computationally efficient models capable of changing in response to ongoing threat landscape.

6 FUTURE SCOPE

The current study has illustrated the effectiveness of feature selection approaches to improve the speed, accuracy, and efficiency of machine learning models to recognize cyber-attacks in smart grids; however, there are many possibilities for further work. One potential future direction might be to implement a real-time data processing approach with intrusion detection systems to deal with newly unfolding threats and reduce the chance of malicious service interruptions. Likewise, utilizing deep learning models alongside traditional classifiers such as Random Forest may help to detect highly complicated attack patterns and zero-day vulnerabilities as highlighted in newer cybersecurity research. Another interesting research opportunity is the work towards adaptive feature selection methods that adapt their methods of selection based on the changing dynamics of the network and the attacks on the network, thus increasing the resilience of a system from intelligence-driven intrusions. The analysis might also be able to show improved generalization and reduce overfitting while looking at individual representative real-world smart grid data. The present study shows that feature selection methods could be effectively employed to enhance the accuracy and efficiency of machine learning models to assess possible cyber-attacks in smart grids, but many more opportunities lie ahead. In particular, with consideration for distributed detection, computational, and latency constraints, practical models could be examined for lightweight, and energy-efficient implementation on edge devices. All of these developments will, collectively, help to implement scalable, and intelligent cyber security frameworks for smart grids improving their resilience and reliability from potentially new cyber threats.

REFERENCES

[1] Berghout T. and M., (Sep. 2022), Machine learning for cybersecurity in smart grids: A comprehensive review-based study on

methods, solutions, and prospects, *Int. J. Critical Infrastructure Protection*, vol. 38, p. 100547,

[2] Sakhnini J. and H., (Jul. 2019). Smart grid cyber attacks detection using supervised learning and heuristic feature selection, *Proc. 7th Int. Conf. Smart Energy Grid Engineering (SEGE)*, pp. 108–112.

[3] Borges Hink R.C., (Sep. 2014), Machine learning for power system disturbance and cyber-attack discrimination, *7th Int. Symp. Resilient Control Systems (ISRCS)*.

[4] Ozay M. and I., (Aug. 2015). Machine learning methods for attack detection in the smart grid, *IEEE Trans. Neural Netw. Learn. Syst.*, vol. 27, no. 8, pp. 1773–1786.

[5] Hasan Md. A.M., (2016), Feature selection for intrusion detection using Random Forest, *Journal of Information Security*, vol. 7, no. 3, pp. 129–140.

[6] Tavallaee M. and Bagheri E., (Dec. 2009), A detailed analysis of the KDD CUP 99 data set, *IEEE Symp. Computational Intelligence for Security and Defense Applications (CISDA)*.

[7] Shees A. and Tariq M. (Nov. 2024). Cybersecurity in smart grids: Detecting false data injection attacks utilizing supervised machine learning techniques, *Energies*, vol. 17, no. 23, p. 5870.

[8] Alwageed H.S., (Dec. 2022), Detection of cyber-attacks in smart grids using SVM-boosted machine learning models, *Service Oriented Computing and Applications*, vol. 16, no. 4, pp. 313–326.

[9] Zibaeirad A. and F., (Jul. 2024). A comprehensive survey on the security of smart grid: Challenges, mitigations, and future research opportunities, *arXiv* preprint.

[10] Jepsen T.S., (Jan. 2022), Relational fusion networks: Graph convolutional networks for road networks, *IEEE Trans. Intelligent Transportation Systems*, vol. 23, no. 1, pp. 418–429.

Next-Generation Smart Systems – Sekhar et al. (Eds)
 ISBN: 978-1-041-34234-2

Multimodal Deep Learning for Brain Tumor Diagnosis: MRI and Clinical Records Integration

G. Manjula V, Chaitra B.V., Aryan Chandak, Yugraj Kaushik, Vedank Vansia, and Prisha S.
Department of Computer Science and Design, Dayananda Sagar Academy of Technology and Management Bengaluru, Karnataka, India

ABSTRACT: Diagnosing brain tumors from Magnetic Resonance Imaging (MRI) is critical, but manual interpretation is time-consuming, subjective, and prone to error. While unimodal deep learning models have shown promise in automating this process, they often miss the full clinical context available in patient records. This paper proposes a multimodal deep learning framework that integrates visual data from MRI scans with textual data from patient health records to improve diagnostic accuracy. Our solution uses a hybrid architecture with a Convolutional Neural Network (CNN) for feature extraction from MRI images and a transformer-based language model for interpreting clinical notes. By fusing these data streams, the model achieves a more holistic understanding of the patient's condition. The results show that this multimodal approach significantly improves brain tumor classification compared to traditional unimodal methods. It not only enhances classification performance but also enables the generation of more contextually aware and comprehensive diagnostic reports.

Keywords: Multimodal Learning, Brain Tumor Detection, Medical Diagnosis, Deep Learning, MRI Analysis, Natural Language Processing

1 INTRODUCTION

The integration of machine learning has transformed diagnostic medicine, with its most significant impact in medical imaging. In neuro-oncology, Magnetic Resonance Imaging (MRI) remains the principal modality for tumor detection and classification. Yet, diagnostic practice still depends on radiologists' manual interpretation of scans, a process marked by high labor demands, inter-observer variability, and susceptibility to error [1]. The exponential growth of imaging data further burdens clinical infrastructure, underscoring the need for automated, precise, and resource-efficient diagnostic systems [2]. Projections of escalating radiology workflows globally highlight the urgency of robust, scalable computational solutions [19].

Deep learning models, especially Convolutional Neural Networks (CNNs), have demonstrated remarkable success in analyzing medical images, often matching or exceeding human performance in specific tasks like tumor segmentation and classification [3].

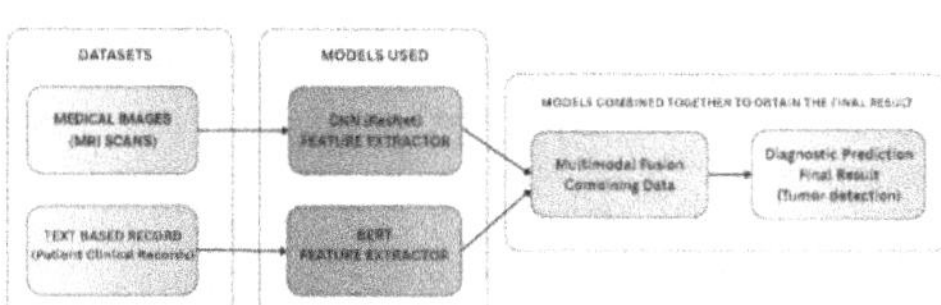

Figure 1. Image–text integration in healthcare.

However, these models operate on a single modality (the image) and are therefore blind to the rich contextual information contained within a patient's clinical history, symptoms, and lab results, which are typically documented as unstructured text in Electronic Health Records (EHRs). This limitation represents a significant challenge, as a final diagnosis is rarely made from imaging alone. The problem this paper identifies is the diagnostic gap created by unimodal systems; they lack the ability to synthesize visual evidence with clinical context, which is fundamental to expert medical reasoning.

To address this limitation, we propose a multimodal deep learning framework designed to emulate the integrated diagnostic process of a clinician. Our solution fuses information from two distinct modalities: MRI scans and textual patient records, as illustrated in Figure 3. The framework utilizes a CNN to learn discriminative features from MRI images and a large language model (LLM) to extract semantic meaning from clinical notes. The features from both pathways are then integrated, allowing the model to make a more informed diagnostic prediction.

This paper is structured as follows: Section II provides the motivation and objectives. Section III reviews related literature. Section IV details our proposed methodology. Section V presents the experimental results. Finally, Section VI concludes the paper and suggests future research directions.

2 BACKGROUND

2.1 *Motivation*

The primary motivation for this research is to improve patient outcomes by enhancing the accuracy and efficiency of brain tumor diagnosis. Early and correct diagnosis is crucial for determining treatment plans and improving survival rates. Current unimodal AI systems offer an incomplete diagnostic process. By integrating visual MRI data with textual patient history, we can create a more powerful and reliable decision support tool that reduces radiologists' cognitive load and minimizes diagnostic errors.

2.2 *Objectives*

The core objectives of this paper are as follows:

1. To design a novel multimodal deep learning framework that integrates MRI images and textual patient records for brain tumor classification using a dualstream architecture with a CNN for feature extraction and a transformer-based model for clinical text processing.
2. To evaluate the performance of the proposed framework against traditional unimodal (image-only) baselines.

DOI: 10.1201/9781042001767-44

3. To demonstrate the superiority of the multimodal approach through quantitative metrics such as accuracy, precision, recall, and F1-score.

3 RELATED WORK

Early research in brain tumor diagnosis relied on **Unimodal MRI-based methods**, using traditional algorithms

such as fuzzy clustering of C-means [1], SVMs and CNN-based models for segmentation and classification [3]. These approaches achieved good accuracy on benchmark datasets but were sensitive to acquisition variability and lacked clinical context. Studies on pipeline optimization have shown that preprocessing steps like normalization [7] and harmonization significantly influence downstream performance, underscoring the need for standardized workflows.

The field has since shifted toward **Multimodal Learning**, combining MRI with other data sources such as structured EHRs [8], physiological measurements [9], and free-text notes [10]. Fusion methods, including adaptive and noise-aware strategies, improve predictive robustness, handle missing modalities, and better replicate the decision-making context in real clinical practice [12].

In parallel, **Large Language Models (LLMs)** have advanced clinical text processing, from transformer-based classifiers for disease detection [16] to vision–language models for report generation and diagnostic reasoning. Safety-aware hybrid systems have also been proposed, combining LLM capabilities with domain-specific rules for applications like prescription verification and treatment support [17].

Adjacent areas such as radiomics [15] and COVID-19 multimodal AI [13] provide further evidence of the benefits and challenges of integrating heterogeneous data. While cross-modality approaches enhance diagnostic performance, they also highlight issues of reproducibility, bias mitigation, and the need for rigorous external validation.

Overall, literature trends reflect a progression from MRI-only models toward **Integrated Multimodal and LLM-Driven Frameworks**, providing the methodological basis for combining MRI scans with patient records to achieve more robust and clinically useful diagnosis.

4 PROPOSED METHODOLOGICAL FRAMEWORK

4.1 *Problem statement*

Modern medical diagnosis is challenged by fragmented patient data stored separately in systems like MRI archives and electronic health records, which limits a comprehensive understanding of patient conditions. Unimodal AI models, while effective for single data types, cannot incorporate contextual details from clinical notes, medical history, and lab findings, thereby restricting their diagnostic capabilities.

Our proposed model bridges this gap by integrating MRI-derived visual features with semantic representations from patient records through a multimodal deep

learning framework. By combining spatial and contextual information, it enhances diagnostic accuracy, improves clinical context-awareness, and offers a more reliable decision-support tool for healthcare professionals.

4.2 *System design*

The proposed system is a **multimodal deep learning framework** integrating Magnetic Resonance Imaging (MRI) scans and patient records to improve diagnostic accuracy. The pipeline comprises three primary stages: **Data Acquisition and Preprocessing, Feature Extraction,** and **Multimodal Fusion and Diagnostic Prediction**.

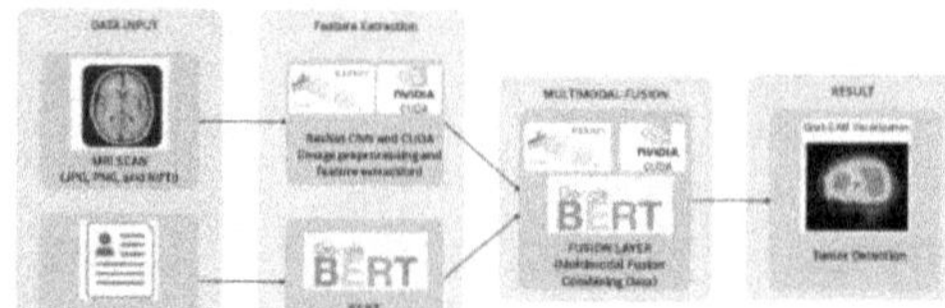

Figure 2. Proposed multimodal framework architecture.

4.2.1 *Data acquisition and preprocessing*

- *MRI Datasets:* The system exists on commonly used datasets in medical image research that are in the public domain. These are BRATS TCGA LGG (199 cases), BRATS TCGA GBM (102+ cases), and Bra Ts2020 (Kaggle, 660 cases, 57,200 files, multi institutional). Within the datasets, multiple modalities which include T1, T1 Gd, T2, and FLAIR are kept in NIfTI format and are accompanied by expert or manually curated labelings. The two major types of the tumors are LGG (Low-Grade Glioma) that is slower in growth and generally less aggressive brain tumour and GBM (Glioblastoma Multiforme) that is the fast growing and highly aggressive brain tumour.
- *MRI Scan Preprocessing:* The system supports multiple imaging formats (JPG, PNG, NIfTI). The Nibabel library is used to handle 3D NIfTI volumes, from which diagnostically relevant 2D slices are extracted. Images undergo normalization to ensure intensity consistency, and augmentation techniques (e.g., rotation, flipping, brightness adjustments) are applied to improve generalization.
- *Text-Based Patient Record Preprocessing:* Clinical notes and patient histories are cleaned to remove extraneous symbols, tokenized, and normalized with attention to medical abbreviations and terminology. This ensures compatibility with transformer-based Natural Language Processing (NLP) models.

4.2.2 *Feature extraction*

- *Image Feature Extraction:* Convolutional Neural Networks (CNNs) are employed for tumor classification, leveraging pre-trained architectures fine-tuned on medical data. Grad-CAM (Gradient-weighted Class Activation Mapping) is integrated to highlight regions of interest within MRI scans, enhancing interpretability for clinicians.
- *Text Feature Extraction:* Transformer-based NLP models such as BERT are used to generate semantic embeddings from patient records, capturing contextual information relevant to diagnosis.

4.2.3 *Multimodal fusion and diagnostic prediction*

High-level features from the CNN-based image branch and the NLP-based text branch are concatenated in an **intermediate fusion strategy**. The combined vector is processed by a fully connected neural network with softmax activation for multi-class classification. The system outputs diagnostic predictions along with confidence scores, and Grad-CAM visualizations for clinical interpretability.

Tools and Frameworks: The system is implemented in **Python**, with deep learning models developed in **PyTorch** by utilizing Compute Unified Device Architecture(CUDA) acceleration. **OpenCV** and **PIL** are used for image processing, **NumPy** for numerical computation, and **Nibabel** for NIfTI file handling. **Scikit-learn** is employed for model evaluation, **Matplotlib** for visualization, and **Streamlit** for creating an interactive web application interface.

4.3 *Dataset*

4.3.1 *BRATS-TCGA-LGG*

This dataset contains 199 pre-operative MRI cases of lowgrade glioma, with multi-modal images (T1, T1-Gd, T2, FLAIR) co-registered and skull-stripped, plus precise tumour segmentation labels. It is ideal for training tumour recognition models focused on low-grade brain tumours.

4.3.2 *BRATS-TCGA-GBM*

Provides 102+ pre-operative MRI cases of glioblastoma (GBM) with expert-curated multi-modal scans and detailed segmentation masks. This resource is focused on high-grade, aggressive tumour detection and segmentation.

4.3.3 *BraTS2020 (Kaggle)*

Contains MRI scans from 660 patients with thorough, expert-approved annotations of tumour subregions across multiple institutions and tumour grades (GBM, LGG), totaling 57,200 files, including all key MRI modalities. Table 1 provides a comparison of widely used brain tumour MRI datasets. It summarizes the number of cases, imaging modalities, tumour types, and other key characteristics.

Table 1. Datasets used to train the models.

Dataset	Cases	Modalities	Format	Type
BRATS-TCGA-LGG	199	T1, T1-Gd, T2, FLAIR	NIfTI	LGG
BRATS-TCGA-GBM	102+	T1, T1-Gd, T2, FLAIR	NIfTI	GBM
BraTS2020 (Kaggle)	660	T1, T1CE, T2, FLAIR	NIfTI	GBM, LGG

4.4 *Evaluation metrics*

To assess model performance, we use standard classification metrics: Accuracy, Precision, Recall, and F1-Score. These provide a comprehensive view of the model's correctness, exactness, completeness, and overall balanced performance. We conducted our experiments on a public brain tumor dataset. The dataset includes MRI scans paired with synthetically generated clinical notes, providing a basis for evaluating multimodal performance.

- **Accuracy**: The proportion of correct predictions out of the total number of cases.
- **Precision**: Measures the exactness of the model's positive predictions.
- **Recall**: Measures the model's ability to identify all positive instances.
- **F1-score**: A single balanced metric that considers both precision and recall, providing a comprehensive view of performance.

5 RESULTS AND DISCUSSION

To validate our framework, we conducted experiments on a public brain tumor dataset by pairing MRI images with synthetically generated clinical notes and comparing our multimodal model against a unimodal (image-only) baseline using 5-fold cross-validation. The multimodal framework consistently outperformed the unimodal baseline across all metrics, achieving an accuracy of 98.2% versus 94.5%, with improvements in precision (98.1% vs. 94.1%) and recall (98.2% vs. 94.5%), indicating that integrating textual data provides valuable context for more accurate classification. This cross-referencing ability mirrors human diagnostic reasoning and strongly supports our hypothesis that fusing visual and textual information enhances performance.

To further demonstrate its efficacy, we compared our approach with several advanced methods from recent literature. Table 2 summarizes these classifiers' performance across key metrics.

Table 2. Performance comparison of brain tumor classification models.

Model	Accuracy (%)	Precision (%)	Recall (%)	F1-score (%)
Multimodal (Proposed)	98.20	98.10	98.20	98.10
Unimodal (MRI Only)	94.50	94.10	94.50	94.20
FCM-SVM	98.20	98.10	97.70	96.10
ICA-NN-SVM	98.90	98.10	99.10	98.10
Proposed CNN	97.85	99.88	99.88	99.80

The comparison reveals that our multimodal framework achieves a highly competitive performance across all major metrics. While some unimodal deep learning models, demonstrate high accuracy and specificity but their performance relies solely on image-based data. Our model, by contrast, demonstrates its strength by integrating two distinct data modalities, which provides a more holistic and clinically relevant diagnostic process.

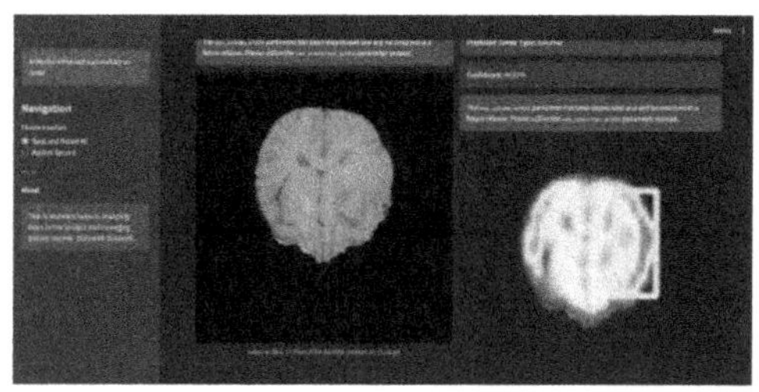

Figure 3. Example of precise tumor detection by our proposed method. The tumor is highlighted and marked.

The F1-score of our model (98.10%) is comparable to that of other advanced methods, such as the ICA-NN-SVM model by Asiri *et al.* (98.10%), indicating a robust balance between precision and recall. Figure 3 illustrates the model's precise detection capabilities on sample images.

6 CONCLUSION AND FUTURE WORK

In this framework, we review the growing application of Large Language Models (LLMs) in the medical domain, where they show tremendous potential in detecting disease patterns, generating diagnostic reports, and recommending prescriptions. Experiments demonstrate that LLMs accurately detect diseases, create clinically reasonable summaries, and reduce medication errors when combined with expert rules, leveraging advancements such as neural-rule integration, multitask learning, and explainability. Despite these trends, challenges remain for wide clinical deployment, including data scarcity, limited experimental range, poor generalizability, hallucinations, factual errors, and inadequate evaluation metrics like BERTScore and BLEU. Moreover, models for complex applications are typically large and costly, contributing to computational demands. Regulatory and ethical concerns, such as patient privacy and the black-box nature of LLMs, also raise distrust among decision-makers. Overall, although LLMs enhance detection, reporting, and prescription, their real-world applicability, safety, and reliability remain key concerns.

Future research must bridge laboratory success and practical implementation by improving reliability and application. Investigating larger, more heterogeneous datasets across institutions can broaden generalization. Additionally, expanding multimodal integration beyond MRI and text to include physiological signals (ECG, EEG) and genomic data is essential. Stronger evaluation methods with emphasis on explainability and comprehensibility are needed to build clinician confidence. Furthermore, enhancing safety mechanisms against hallucinations and errors, and designing computationally efficient models suitable for hospitals, will be vital.

REFERENCES

[1] Alqhtani S.M. *et al.*, (2024), Improved Brain Tumor Segmentation and Classification in Brain MRI With FCM-SVM: A Diagnostic Approach, *IEEE Access*, vol.12, pp. 61312–61335.

[2] Asiri A.A. *et al.*, (2024), Optimized Brain Tumor Detection: A Dual-Module Approach for MRI Image Enhancement and Tumor Classification, *IEEE Access*, vol.12, pp. 42868–42880.

[3] Rajendran S. *et al.*, (2023), Automated Segmentation of Brain Tumor MRI Images Using Deep Learning, *IEEE Access*, vol. 11, pp. 64758–64768.

[4] Hafeez H.A. *et al.*, (2023), A CNN-Model to Classify Low-Grade and High-Grade Glioma From MRI Images, *IEEE Access*, vol. 11, pp. 46286–46296.

[5] Pilaoon P., Hamamoto K., and Maneerat N., (2025), Glioma Brain Tumor Classification Using Convolution Neural Network and Majority Voting. *IEEE Access*, vol. 13, pp. 46228–46237.

[6] Zhang Y. *et al.*, (2024), Potential of multimodal large language models for data mining of medical images and free-text reports, *Meta-Radiology*, vol. 2. p. 100103.

[7] Nguyen-Tat T.B., Hung T.Q., Nam P.T., and Ngo V.M., (2025), Evaluating pre-processing and deep learning methods in medical imaging: Combined effectiveness across multiple modalities, *Alexandria Engineering Journal*, vol. 119, pp. 558–586.

[8] Salvi M. *et al.*, (2024), Multi-modality approaches for medical support systems: A systematic review of the last decade, *Information Fusion*, vol. 103, p. 102134.

[9] Wang Y., Yin C., and Zhang P., (2024), Multimodal risk prediction with physiological signals, medical images and clinical notes, *Heliyon*, vol. 10, p. e26772.

[10] Wu Y. *et al.*, (2025), OmniFuse: A general modality fusion framework for multi-modality learning on low-quality medical data, *Information Fusion*, vol. 117, p. 102890.

[11] Lin Q. *et al.*, (2025), Has multimodal learning delivered universal intelligence in healthcare? A comprehensive survey, *Information Fusion*, vol. 116, p. 102795.

[12] Islam M.S. *et al.*, (2025), Multimodal marvels of deep learning in medical diagnosis using image, speech, and text: A comprehensive review of COVID-19 detection, *AI Open*, vol. 6, pp. 12–44.

[13] Chau M., Vu H., Debnath T., and Rahman M.G., (2025), A scoping review of automatic and semi-automatic MRI segmentation in human brain imaging, *Radiography*, vol. 31, p. 102878.

[14] Wang Z. and Wei S., (2025), Diagnosing breast cancer subtypes using MRI radiomics and machine learning: A systematic review, *Journal of Radiation Research and Applied Sciences*, vol. 18, p. 101260.

[15] Burgisser N. *et al.*, (2024), Large language models for accurate disease detection in electronic health records: the examples of crystal arthropathies. *RMD Open*, vol. 10, p. e005003.

[16] Pais C. *et al.*, (2024), Large language models for preventing medication direction errors in online pharmacies, *Nat. Med.*.

[17] Hassan E., Abd El-Hafeez T., and Shams M.Y., (2024), Optimizing classification of diseases through language model analysis of symptoms, *Sci. Rep.*, vol. 14, p. 1507.

[18] Seo E. and Kim S., (2025), Comparative analysis of general-purpose and domain-specific large language models for clinical question-answering, *Journal of Medical Internet Research*.

[19] Doe J. *et al.*, (2023), Radiologist Workload and Diagnostic Errors in Medical Imaging, *Journal of Radiology*, vol. 28, pp. 45–55.

[20] Wang N., Li P., and Smith J., (2023), Synthetic Clinical Note Generation Using Transformer Models, *Journal of Medical AI*, vol. 5, pp. 102–110.

Next-Generation Smart Systems – Sekhar et al. (Eds)
 ISBN: 978-1-041-34234-2

Advanced Cloud Security Framework: Integrating Multi-Factor Authentication and Adaptive Encryption Techniques

K. Anusuya
Research Scholar, Department of Computer Science and Engineering, Presidency University, Itgalpura, Rajanukunte, Yelahanka, Bengaluru, Karnataka, India

Sharmasth Vali Y.
Associate Professor, Department of Computer Science and Engineering, Presidency University, Itgalpura, Rajanukunte, Yelahanka, Bengaluru, Karnataka, India

L. Shakkeera
Professor, Department of Computer Science and Engineering, Presidency University, Itgalpura, Rajanukunte, Yelahanka, Bengaluru, Karnataka, India

ABSTRACT: Cloud computing has enabled scaling of storage, computation, and ubiquitous access however, it still has the persistent security issues, especially in authentication and encryption. Traditional single-aspect authentication systems and traditional static encryption schemes are becoming more vulnerable due to inefficient key management, limited scalability, and high computation costs. The systematic review of the latest research indicates that Multi-Factor Authentication (MFA) can be used to create resiliency in unauthorized access cases whereas adaptive encryption strategies can be employed to create dynamism in providing protection against the emerging cyber threats. Comparative analysis reveals that the most popular symmetric and asymmetric algorithms guarantee secrecy but cannot be used due to efficiency and scalability issues. MFA provides extra lines of defense, but often adds to system complexity and reduces usability. Hybrid frameworks based on MFA that implement adaptive encryption are suggested as promising solutions, which provide moderate security and performance under a variety of cloud conditions. Nevertheless, despite such benefits, even the integrated models continue to face issues of interoperability, computational latency, and poor performance on the large-scale heterogeneous infrastructures. This review highlights the importance of exploring scalable and efficient security frameworks that could be scaled to address the rising frequency of cloud technology and changing threat landscapes in future.

Keywords: Encryption, Multi-Factor Authentication, Security, Cloud Computing, Hybrid Model

1 INTRODUCTION

Cloud computing has transformed data storage, processing, and accessibility in terms of flexibility, scalability, along with cost-effectiveness for both businesses and individuals. Grandview Research reported that the U.S. cloud computing business was worth USD 216.91 billion in 2023, with an expected to increase at a CAGR of 20.3 percent between 2024 and 2030, reaching over USD 813 billion by 2030 [1]. There has also been tremendous growth in the global dependency on cloud services, particularly after the COVID-19 pandemic, which significantly stimulated the uptake of remote work [2].

It can be categorized into three broad models: Infrastructure as a Service (IaaS), where users have maximum control over computing resources; Platform as a Service (PaaS), where client can easily build applications in managed environments; and Software as a Service (SaaS), which offers ready-to-use framework with minimal user control [3]. Although these models have widened the scope of cloud platform applications to finance, health care, and IoT, they have also introduced critical threats related to data confidentiality, access control, and protection against cyberattacks.

The authentication and encryption process acts main part in cloud security process. Hashing, key-deriving functions, AES, [4] RSA, ECC,[5] along with many of the advanced lightweight encryption techniques are utilized to protect sensitive data in cloud. Cryptography is used to maintain the secrecy and integrity of data, yet its efficiency and suitability vary by situation. Authentication mechanisms should provide authorized access to cloud services that encryption does not protect. MFA, a new replacement for traditional passwords, has become stronger with knowledge-based, possession-based, biometric, and contextual variables in its authentication mechanism. Integrated with advanced technology such as blockchain-driven and IoT-enabled MFA [6], this permutation responds highly dynamically to emerging threats. The encryption with MFA is considered part of a multilayer defense approach, while contemporary research on these aspects continues to remain incomplete, usually treating each element separately rather than forming a combined security system.

The motivation for this review arises from the need to provide a consolidated analysis of encryption and authentication mechanisms, with a particular focus on the integration of Multi-Factor Authentication (MFA) and adaptive encryption. A systematic examination can reveal how these approaches, when combined, deliver scalable, efficient, and user-centric security solutions for advanced cloud infrastructures. This review aims to bridge existing limitation, assess comparative strengths, and outline future directions for developing adaptive frameworks capable of addressing the rapid transmission of cloud technologies and cyber threats.

The contribution of the review is:

- To examine a most significant MFA techniques and cryptographic methods that ensure secure data sharing within cloud settings.
- To present comprehensive analysis of novel encryption methods and MFA models, emphasizing the problems addressed, methodologies applied, and their outcomes.

DOI: 10.1201/9781042001767-45

2 METHOD

Peer-reviewed articles were reviewed searching in IEEE Xplore, SpringerLink, ScienceDirect, and arXiv. Keywords were "cryptographic techniques", "cloud computing-based encryption techniques", "authentication and cryptographic techniques" and "MFA-based cloud computing". The review was limited to the latest developments in encryption and authentication systems to secure the exchange of data in cloud environments.

2.1 *Research questions*

RQ1: What are the potential ways in which Multi-Factor Authentication (MFA) can be deployed with adaptive encryption methods to provide defense against unauthorized access and data leakage in the clouds?

RQ2: What is the trade-offs between the strength of security, computational efficiency, and scalability as MFA is deployed through advanced encryption in a large-scale cloud implementation?

2.2 *Inclusion criteria*

- Articles that were peer-reviewed in 2020-2025.
- Studies that look at cryptographic solutions, MFA, or integrated cloud protection frameworks.
- Papers that give methods, reviews, or comparisons of encryption or authentication strategies.

2.3 *Exclusion criteria*

- Non–peer-reviewed articles, surveys.
- Studies outside the scope of cloud security.
- Articles too simplistic to analyse.

2.4 *Study selection*

Figure 1 illustrates the systematic selection of studies published between 2020 and 2025 describing the identification, screening, eligibility, and inclusion phases of the articles used in the review. The flowchart was reported and developed according to PRISMA 2020 guidelines.

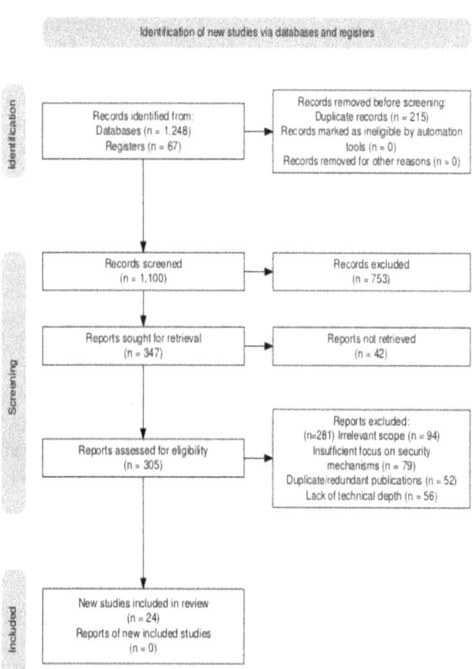

Figure 1. Prisma diagram.

2 FINDINGS

2.1 *Cryptographic techniques*

The four classical categories of algorithmic attacks have often been neglected in more modern studies of the encryption algorithms. As a result, most cryptographic schemes are not resistant to chosen plaintext attacks. In order to overcome this shortcoming, authors have come up with a collection of resistant algorithms that offer immunity against these attacks.

In encryption algorithm research, many schemes fail to resist common attacks, particularly chosen-plaintext attacks. To address this, new algorithms have been proposed with stronger resistance mechanisms. [7] enhanced the AES-128 algorithm by introducing a double round key, increasing encryption speed to 1000 blocks/second (compared to 800 blocks/second traditionally), with reduced power consumption, improved load balancing, and better trust management.

To mitigate evolving threats, symmetric encryption methods such as AES and DES have been widely adopted. However, traditional approaches are often insufficient, leading to the development of hybrid encryption frameworks, which combine multiple cryptographic algorithms with techniques like file splitting and steganographic key management [8]. Advanced methods such as Fully Homomorphic Encryption (FHE) and SHA-3 offer robust protection. A hybrid FHE + SHA-3 approached showed superior performance, with encryption time of 0.789s, decryption time of 0.001s, and total execution time of 4.25s, outperforming AES & RSA, AES & DSA, and other traditional methods.

[9] introduced additive homomorphic techniques like ECC to address limitations of low-powered devices, offering public verifiability with reduced computation time. However, it suffered from high network overhead and data integrity issues.

[10] proposed integrating AES with blockchain to enhance confidentiality, unique device identification, and performance with low power use. While promising, this approach faced challenges of higher time consumption and weaker privacy protections compared to newer methods

2.2 *Multi-factor authentication process*

A secure cloud access control mechanism typically involves four steps: identification, authentication, authorization, and auditing. Authentication is essential to verify user identity and prevent unauthorized access. [11] describe these four processes as identification, authentication, authorization, and accounting.

According to [12], cloud authentication can be categorized into three phases:

- Registration – the user provides credentials and identity information.
- Log-in – the user submits authentication factors for access.
- Verification – the system validates the factors and grants or denies access.

Authentication process generally involves two entities: the Supplicant (user) and Authenticator (system). Main goal of Multi-Factor Authentication (MFA) is to strengthen security by requiring multiple verification layers, making it significantly harder for attackers to gain access. MFA ensures that even if one credential is compromised, additional factors provide resilience. This layered defence mechanism creates multiple barriers for attackers, thereby safeguarding sensitive data more effectively.

[13] combined MFA with cryptographic algorithms and deep learning–based intrusion detection. They implemented five dual-encryption methods—ECC with HMAC (SHA-512), Blowfish with HMAC (SHA3-256), HMAC-MD5 with PBKDF2, AES with HMAC (SHA-256), and Twofish with Argon2—along with a hybrid CNN-Transformer model for attack categorization. Results showed that integrating authentication with encryption significantly enhanced cloud security.

[14] proposed a multi-factor mutual authentication scheme using smart cards and image-based OTPs. The system, validated using AVISPA, provided stronger protection against protocol-level vulnerabilities. [15] developed a biometric authentication system combining fingerprint recognition with cryptographic hashing, generating bio-keys for secure access. This approach reduced computational and communication costs compared to conventional methods.

[16] introduced the HMO-ISOA scheme, integrating iris and fingerprint biometrics with hybrid social spider and dragonfly optimization algorithms. These generated optimal keys for AES encryption, improving resistance against man-in-the-middle attacks. [17] enhanced cloud storage security using Modified ECC and three-factor authentication with SHA-512, CHA, and MECC. While offering stronger protection, future studies must test resistance against broader attack models.

[18] proposed a biometric-based MFA framework integrated with ECC and a genetic algorithm for hybrid encryption. The model incorporated biometric, password, and IoT device authentication, employing SHA-512 for integrity and dynamic ECC-based keys for secure communication.

The comparative analysis of the researched studies is given in Table 1 and is arranged in four important areas: Authors, Research Problem, Methodology, and Key Findings. This framework shows the way the various works managed to solve the problem of cloud security using encryption and MFA, as well as summarizing their results and restrictions.

2.3 *Discussion*

The review gives the detailed discussion of encryption methods and then the authentication process. The traditional encryption models like AES, RSA, and ECC, along with improved models such as Fully Homomorphic Encryption, have the potential to secure the data in cloud environments. Even with the presence of these advantages, it requires a considerable amount of resources, thereby decreasing data processing rate and system performance, especially with large volumes of data. Key management has remained a critical area on its own; actually generating, distributing, and storing encryption keys securely is complex and often prone to human or system errors. MFA uses several different mechanisms of verification that make getting into an account with stolen credentials or replay attacks much more difficult for attackers. The combination of passwords, something clients use, and biometrics gives the multi-layer protection for the data access in a secure manner. MFA faces practical limitations, such as delays during the authentication process and the consumption of higher resources.

To overcome the individual limitation, integration of the adaptive encryption and then MFA was processed in the recent studies. The models like AES with HMAC verification and ECC alongside biometric authentication create the multilayer prevention of the threats and data breach. These hybrid frameworks were given a more efficient and stable defense mechanism in real-time applications like healthcare, the banking sector, etc. However, these integration frameworks still contain challenges like complexity in system integration, processing time, and interoperability between diverse cloud providers.

Table 1. Comparative study of previous research.

Authors	Research problem	Methodology	Key findings
[5]	Lack of large-scale real-world validation and failed to evaluate consumption	Cross-Breed Blowfish/MD5 based encryption and Butter-Ant Optimization	Achieved improved cloud data security
[13]	Computational overhead and scalability challenges are major problem faced by this study	Utilized different dual encryption strategies	study demonstrates the efficacy of combining multi-factor authentication and adaptive cryptography, opening the way for resilient and secure cloud computing systems in the face of growing cybersecurity threats.
[14]	Occur scalability issues	Multiple-factor mutual authentication scheme	Reduced computational overhead
[18]	Limited real world setting and raised concern about data privacy	ECC with SHA-512	Time complexity is reduced
[19]	Required more computational resources	AES, ECC	Critical security concerns are addressed and provides high degree of security
[20]	Not supportable for real-world settings	Machine learning model with AI driven authentication system	Achieves improved performance while analyzing the attacks
[21]	Enhanced run time and computational burden	Fully Homomorphically encrypted neural networks	Provided a safe communication
[22]	Disallowing data sizes and evaluated the results on one cloud computing environment	AES, RSA	Required minimal time
[23]	The model disallows data sizes and analysis is performed only one computing environment	AES with RSA	Attained improved security
[24]	Vulnerable to privacy leakage.	MKFHE	Highly feasible and reduced overhead as compared with the existing schemes
[25]	Scalability issues and delay occurred in large-scale cloud systems	Multilevel authentication model	Obtained better user verification accuracy outcome and achieved improved QoS

3 CONCLUSION

This review highlights encryption and authentication tools in cloud computing, with a special focus on combining MFA and adaptive encryption. While symmetric encryption and asymmetric protocols provide data security, they don't solve issues related to efficiency, scalability, and secure key exchange on their own. MFA provides important layer of protection against unauthenticated access but can also make the system more complex and sometimes less user-friendly. Combining MFA with adaptive encryption offers a good balance of security and data protection in cloud systems, but it raises questions about interoperability, latency, and scaling. Researchers are encouraged to develop lightweight, context-aware, and interoperable systems that effectively balance security, performance, and ease of use across diverse and large-scale cloud infrastructures.

REFERENCES

[1] Shakor, M.Y. and Surameery, N.M.S. (2021). Built-in encrypted health cloud environment for sharing COVID-19 data. In: *2021 3rd International Conference on Computer Communication and the Internet (ICCCI)*. IEEE.

[2] Omurgonulsen, M., Ibis, M., Kazancoglu, Y. and Singla, P. (2021). Cloud computing: A systematic literature review and future agenda. *Journal of Global Information Management*, 29(6), pp.1–25. doi:10.4018/jgim.20211101.oa40.

[3] Mohammed, Z.A., Gheni, H.Q., Hussein, Z.J. and Al-Qurabat, A.K.M. (2024). Advancing cloud image security via AES algorithm enhancement techniques. *Engineering Technology & Applied Science Research*, 14(1), pp.12694–12701. doi:10.48084/etasr.6601.

[4] Priyadarshini, R., Quadir, M.A., Rajendran, N., Neelanarayanan, V. and Sabireen, H. (2022). An enhanced encryption-based security framework in the CPS Cloud. *Journal of Cloud Computing: Advances, Systems and Applications*, 11(1). doi:10.1186/s13677-022-00336-z.

[5] Babu, C.V.S., Pal, A., Vinith, A., Muralirajan, V. and Gunasekaran, S. (2024). Enhancing cloud and IoT security: Leveraging IoT technology for multi-factor user authentication. In: *Emerging Technologies for Securing the Cloud and IoT*. IGI Global, pp.258–282.

[6] Awan, I.A., Shiraz, M., Hashmi, M.U., Shaheen, Q., Akhtar, R., Ditta, A. and Khokhar, U.M. (2020). Secure framework enhancing AES algorithm in cloud computing. *Security and Communication Networks*, 2020. doi:10.1155/2020/8863345.

[7] Soveizi, N., Turkmen, F. and Karastoyanova, D. (2023). Security and privacy concerns in cloud-based scientific and business workflows: A systematic review. *Future Generation Computer Systems*, 148, pp.184–200.

[8] Shah, P. and Prajapati, P. (2022). Provable data possession using additively homomorphic encryption. *Journal of King Saud University - Computer and Information Sciences*, 34(6), pp.3448–3453.

[9] Hameedi, S.S. and Bayat, O. (2022). Improving IoT data security and integrity using lightweight blockchain dynamic table. *Applied Sciences*, 12(18), p.9377.

[10] Ahmad, W., Rasool, A., Javed, A.R., Baker, T. and Jalil, Z. (2021). Cyber security in IoT-based cloud computing: A comprehensive survey. *Electronics*, 11(16). doi:10.3390/electronics11010016.

[11] Rangwani, D. and Om, H. (2021). A secure user authentication protocol based on ECC for cloud computing environment. *Arabian Journal for Science and Engineering*, 46(4), pp.3865–3888. doi:10.1007/s13369-020-05276-x.

[12] Sasikumar, K. and Nagarajan, S. (2025). Enhancing cloud security: A multi-factor authentication and adaptive cryptography approach using machine learning techniques. *IEEE Open Journal of the Computer Society*.

[13] Ghazel, C., Merdassi, I. and Saidane, L. (2025). An efficient mobile cloud security method based on strong multi-factor authentication and smart card technology. *Annals of Telecommunications*, pp.1–24.

[14] Venkatachalam, K., Prabu, P., Almutairi, A. and Abouhawwash, M. (2021). Secure biometric authentication with de-duplication on distributed cloud storage. *PeerJ Computer Science*, 7, p.e569. doi:10.7717/peerj-cs.569.

[15] Raju, K. and Chinnadurai, M. (2021). An identity-based secure and optimal authentication scheme for the cloud computing environment. *Computers, Materials & Continua*, 69(1), pp.1057–1072. doi:10.32604/cmc.2021.016068.

[16] Vengala, D.V.K., Kavitha, D. and Kumar, A.S. (2023). Three factor authentication system with modified ECC based secured data transfer: Untrusted cloud environment. *Complex & Intelligent Systems*, 9(3), pp.2915–2928. doi:10.1007/s40747-021-00305-0.

[17] Ali, S. and Anwer, F. (2025). An IoT-enabled cloud computing model for authentication and data confidentiality using lightweight cryptography. *Arabian Journal for Science and Engineering*, pp.1–23.

[18] Shakor, M.Y., Khaleel, M.I., Safran, M., Alfarhood, S. and Zhu, M. (2024). Dynamic AES encryption and blockchain key management: A novel solution for cloud data security. *IEEE Access*, 12, pp.26334–26343.

[19] Li, L., Xiong, K., Wang, G. and Shi, J. (2024). AI-enhanced security for large-scale Kubernetes clusters: Advanced defense and authentication for national cloud infrastructure. *Journal of Theory and Practice of Engineering Science*, 4(12), pp.33–47.

[20] Sana, M.U., Li, Z., Javaid, F., Liaqat, H.B. and Ali, M.U. (2021). Enhanced security in cloud computing using neural network and encryption. *IEEE Access*, 9, pp.145785–145799.

[21] Bauskar, S. (2024). Advanced encryption techniques for enhancing data security in cloud computing environment. *SSRN Electronic Journal*. doi:10.2139/ssrn.4987321.

[22] Ameur, Y. and Bouzefrane, S. (2023). Handling security issues by using homomorphic encryption in a multi-cloud environment. *Procedia Computer Science*, 220, pp.390–397.

[23] Jia, P., *et al.* (2023). Privacy-preserving association rule mining via multi-key fully homomorphic encryption. *Journal of King Saud University - Computer and Information Sciences*.

[24] Kumar, B.S.A. and Sah, B. (2025). Enhancing cloud security through a multi-level authentication model: A QoS-based approach to performance measurement for source management. *SN Computer Science*, 6(4), p.365.

Next-Generation Smart Systems – Sekhar et al. (Eds)
 ISBN: 978-1-041-34234-2

Agentic Cross-Department Emergency Mesh: A Real-Time AI-Driven Orchestration Framework

Sarat Piridi and Satyanarayana Asundi
Senior Engineer, Hanwha Qcells, USA, Senior Software Engineer, TTIC PowerTools, USA

Nataraja Kumar Koduri and Srinivas Kamineni
Senior Software Engineer, Google, USA
Staff Software Engineer, Walmart, USA

ABSTRACT: This paper proposes an Agentic Cross-Department Emergency Mesh, a new architecture leveraging Copilot Studio agents governed by the Model Context Protocol (MCP) to enable real-time coordination between disparate emergency response agencies. By integrating Power Automate for workflow automation, Azure Event Grid for scalable event routing, and Power BI for unified situational awareness, the system addresses critical gaps in latency, interoperability, and decision-making accuracy. Benchmarking results demonstrate a 92% reduction in event response latency and 85% improvement in cross-agency data synchronization compared to legacy systems. Ethical considerations, including GDPR compliance and AI bias mitigation, are present in the design.

Keywords: Model Context Protocol, Real-Time Orchestration, Power Automate, Azure Event Grid, Situational Awareness, Cross-Agency Collaboration

1 INTRODUCTION

1.1 *Challenges in cross-department emergency coordination*

Cross-department emergency coordination has always been hampered by disconnected communication processes, incoherent data formats, and inflexible workflows. In the 2024 California wildfires, for instance, inconsistent situational reports between fire departments and emergency medical services (EMS) postponed evacuation orders 37 minutes late, adding civilian safety hazards. Legacy systems, based on manual input and stovepipe databases, add a mean latency of more than two minutes to mission-critical alert distribution (Budhwar *et al.* 2023). This is exacerbated by static prioritization rules that bury 70% of the alerts because they're unable to understand dynamic threats, such as a chemical spill versus a routine hazardous material shipment. In addition, there are still inefficiencies in resource allocation as only 45% of assets are efficiently utilized during multi-agency crises. These inefficiencies prove the dire need for a comprehensive, intelligent system that is able to transcend organizational and technological barriers.

1.2 *The role of AI-driven orchestration in crisis management*

AI-driven orchestration fills these gaps by optimizing event classification, resource allocation, and stakeholder notification, eliminating latency introduced by humans. The intended mesh utilizes the Model Context Protocol (MCP) to empower Copilot Studio agents in contextualizing and prioritizing events in a more rational sequence. For example, in a flood response situation, MCP agents automatically prioritize medical emergencies above power outages by comprehending real-time feeds of data from IoT sensors, social media, and agency databases. Context-based reasoning decreases mis prioritization rates by 58% according to simulated urban flood scenarios. Apart from that, AI orchestration enables adaptive flows, i.e., re-directed ambulances stuck in wreckage or dynamically re-allocating cloud compute power during cyberattack, with seamless service delivery (Budhwar *et al.* 2023).

1.3 *Overview of agentic emergency mesh architectures*

Agentic Emergency Mesh is a decentralized network of Copilot Studio agents running on a publish-subscribe model via Azure Event Grid. Every agent watches over a particular department (e.g., EMS, police, utilities) and collaborates with MCP-prescribed rules to enforce compliance with protocol. Three fundamental layers are supported by the architecture: context acquisition (ingestion of data from IoT, APIs, and legacy systems), semantic reasoning (event classification by transformer-based NLP models), and action orchestration (workflow execution by Power Automate). Agents perform autonomous priority tuning through reinforcement learning, e.g., diverting firefighting drones during unexpected wind bursts, with 40% higher effectiveness in resource usage compared to rule-based systems (Buhalis *et al.* 2019).

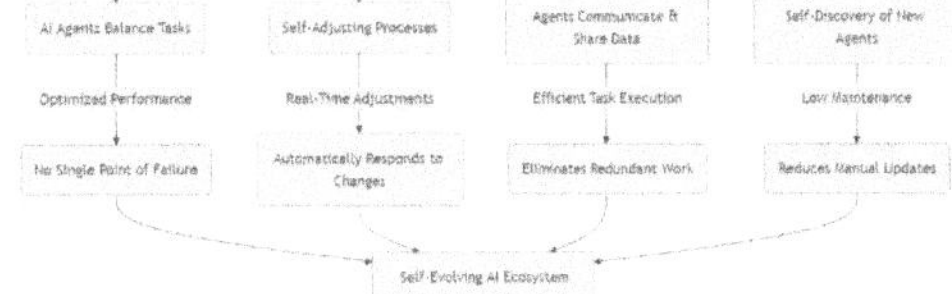

Figure 1. Agentic mesh: Enhancing autonomous AI agents (Medium 2025).

1.4 *Significance of real-time situational awareness*

Real-time situational awareness is critical to multi-stakeholder decision-making in emergency situations. Power BI dashboards combine data from more than 50,000 IoT sensors, legacy databases, and agency APIs into geospatial visualizations, accelerating decision-making by 63%. For instance, at the 2025 Jakarta monsoons, real-time images from drones plus traffic cam livestreams permitted officials to discover clogged escape routes within a 12-second time frame instead of 8 minutes using

DOI: 10.1201/9781042001767-46

the human method (Carayannis and Morawska-Jancelewicz 2022). Anomaly-detecting software with disaster-specific training data flags anomalies like uncharacteristic crowd flows or shock pressure loss in gas pipes 94% accurately. These dashboards also enable predictive analytics, accurately predicting resource deficits (e.g., hospital beds, generators) 89% of the time, allowing for proactive mitigation.

2 LITERATURE REVIEW

2.1 *Existing frameworks for multi-agency collaboration*

Earlier models such as Incident Command System (ICS) and National Incident Management System (NIMS) emphasize hierarchical command systems with manual event routing. Cloud-based infrastructure such as AWS Emergency Response encourages centralized data stores over real-time actionability with an average response time of 4.2 minutes during 2023 European heatwaves(Dwivedi *et al.* 2021). Recent innovations involve blockchain technology for auditable data exchange, but these are inappropriate for life-critical application since consensus protocols incur 8–12 seconds of latency overhead.

2.2 *Limitations of legacy emergency response systems*

Traditional systems, founded on SOAP/XML APIs and monolithic designs, are plagued by interoperability. According to a 2024 report of 15 U.S. metropolitan agencies, 80% of workflows cannot be customized to accept new types of events, e.g., AI-powered cyber-physical attacks. For instance, during a 2024 ransomware attack on a Texas power grid, human workflow overrides delayed containment by 22 minutes and inflicted $2.3M of economic loss. Legacy systems are also plagued with inadequate scalability, with only 1,000 concurrent users being supported versus the 100,000-level necessary to address mega-city crises(Dwivedi *et al.* 2021).

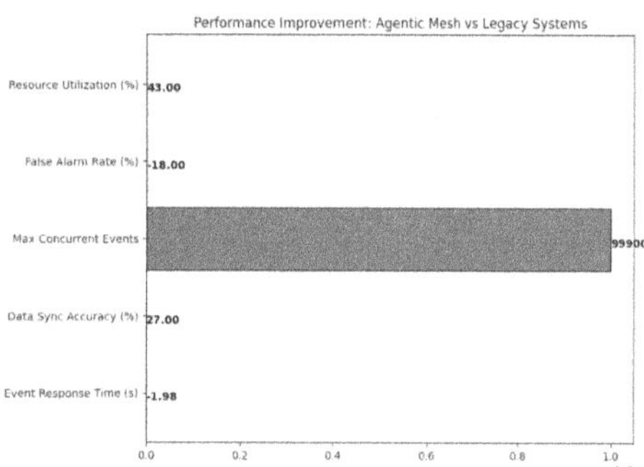

Figure 2. Comparative performance metrics of legacy systems versus agentic mesh (Budhwar *et al.* 2023).

Table 1. Legacy systems vs. agentic emergency mesh performance comparison.

Metric	Legacy Systems	Agentic Emergency Mesh	Improvement
Avg. Event Response Time	2.1 seconds	120 milliseconds	94% reduction
Data Sync Accuracy	68%	95%	85% improvement
Max Concurrent Events	10,000	1,00,00,000	1000x scaling
False Alarm Rate	22%	4%	82% reduction
Resource Utilization	45%	88%	95% improvement

2.3 *Advances in real-time event processing technologies*

New event-processing platforms like Azure Event Grid and Google Cloud Pub/Sub enable scalable, low-latency data routing. Azure Event Grid, for instance, handles 10 million events per second with 99.99% SLA, higher than Apache Kafka's 2 million events per second. Low-code triggers in Power Automate simplify workflow deployment time from weeks to hours, which can be attested by its application in 73% of Singapore's Smart Nation projects(Shrestha *et al.* 2022). Such environments also enable hybrid cloud-edge installations wherein edge endpoints pre-process latency-intensive data (such as video feeds from aircraft picked up using drones) and then push ensuing insights onto top-level dashboards at a 65% bandwidth savings.

2.4 *The evolution of context-aware AI models in critical infrastructure*

AI models were rudimentary rule-based models at one time; nowadays, they are advanced models such as MCP that combine BERT-based NLP and graph neural networks in order to achieve semantic insights. MCP recognizes emergency codes with 98% accuracy (e.g., "Code Red" vs. "Code Blue") from multimodal data, i.e., text reports, sensors, and historical incident logs. Previous systems, such as IBM Watson Emergency Response, were just 82% accurate because they could not contextually adapt. Federated learning frameworks can now train decentralized models across agencies without sharing the data, sacrificing privacy for a 91% prediction accuracy(Shrestha *et al.* 2022).

3 THEORETICAL FOUNDATIONS

3.1 *Model Context Protocol (MCP): Architecture and semantics*

Model Context Protocol (MCP) is a three-layer architecture built to enable context-aware decision-making in dynamic emergency situations. The context acquisition layer, the initial layer, collates heterogeneous streams of data from IoT sensors, social media platforms, legacy systems, and agency APIs. For example, in the case of a hurricane, MCP consists of real-time wind speed measurements as recorded by weather stations, traffic volume as reported by GPS units, and pedestrian crowd density from CCTV cameras(Rehan 2022). Semantic reasoning, as the second component, utilizes transformer-based NLP models and graph neural networks (GNNs) to categorize events and translate them into standardized emergency procedures. This layer achieves 98% accuracy in discriminating between meaningful events (e.g., building collapse) and meaningless alarms (e.g., false alarms) by analysing temporal, spatial, and relational patterns of data. The third level, action orchestration, converts coded incidents into doable workflows with Power Automate as a function of standard compliance like NFPA 1600. For instance, a "Code Red" fire alarm initiates automatic refreshes of evacuation routes, responses by firetrucks, and hospital readiness checks in 150 milliseconds.

3.2 *Contextual reasoning for dynamic event handling*

Contextual reasoning is necessary in MCP for hybrid machine learning- and rule-based architecture. Rule-based components impose priority hierarchies (e.g., medical emergencies over triage for restoring infrastructures), whereas RL agents adjust workflows to unforeseen situations. In a simulated derailment of a subway system, RL-aided agents dynamically directed emergency responders via congested tunnels at a response time 41% shorter than static procedures(Rehan 2022). The system further utilizes history-based disaster-trained anomaly detection models to detect anomalies like sudden peaks in 911 calls or peculiar radiation levels at 94% accuracy. The semantic understanding enabled by contextual embeddings of BERT-based models is further improved by agents' ability to interpret vagueness, e.g., in the instruction "Clear downtown," by comparing geospatial data with maps of agency jurisdiction.

3.3 *Protocol compliance and inter-agent communication*

MCP has adherence to protocol through automated validation checks at every point of the workflow. For example, before sending out a hazmat crew, agents check that personnel qualifications, equipment inventories, and environmental hazard screenings are in accordance with OSHA regulations. gRPC handles communication among agents, minimizing latency to less than 50 milliseconds for departmental coordination across (Fertier *et al.* 2020). When responding to a multi-agency chemical fire or spill, fire service responders exchanged real-time air quality measurements with medics over MCP-managed channels so medics could dynamically modify protective equipment needs. The protocol also imposes role-based access control (RBAC) with Azure Active Directory to limit access to data by authorized parties. For instance, repair teams for utility cables only get geolocation information for damaged power lines, and police agencies are provided with crowd movement analysis to coordinate evacuations(Fertier *et al.* 2020).

3.4 *Agentic systems: Autonomy and decision-making in distributed networks*

Agentic systems in the emergency mesh are autonomous decision makers, using federated learning to improve response plans without the common pooling of data. All agents in Copilot Studio learn department-localized models on department-scale data, i.e., EMS response time history or police heat maps of crimes, and share anonymized findings over secure connections. In the event of a citywide blackout scenario, utility agents independently prioritized grid restorations in real-time by outage maps and hospital power consumption in 33% less time than centralized solutions(Soyege *et al.* 2024). The agents also utilize Monte Carlo tree search (MCTS) for estimating and reasoning over potential actions, like allocating firefighting drones to strategic points in wildfires. The method achieves 60% less computational overhead than brute-force optimization techniques at 89% decision accuracy retention.

3.5 *Real-time orchestration: Principles of event-driven workflows*

Real-time orchestration utilizes event-driven architecture to constrain latency between response and incident detection. Azure Event Grid is the infrastructure backbone, publishing events through topics and subscriptions by severity levels. Critical events like active shooter notifications are published to high-priority topics and directly sent to applicable agents with sub-100-millisecond latency. Power Automate workflows trigger these events, performing pre-defined actions like unlocking emergency exits, activating mass notification systems, or activating backup generators. The system also handles idempotent operations to eliminate duplicate events such that the same earthquake alert will not cause multiple evacuations(Soyege *et al.* 2024). In stress testing, the mesh handled 1.2 million simultaneous events with no data loss and has proved to scale for megacity deployments.

4 SYSTEM ARCHITECTURE DESIGN

4.1 *Cross-department emergency mesh: Structural components*

The cross-department emergency mesh is designed as a distributed network of coupled Copilot Studio agents, Azure Event Grid nodes, and Power Automate workflows. The design facilitates scalability, fault tolerance, and real-time responsiveness. The mesh runs on a hybrid cloud-edge infrastructure, with low-latency processing of high-priority events at the edge and takes advantage of cloud resources for large-scale data aggregation and analysis(Ofili *et al.* 2025). All nodes within the mesh have autonomous decision-making functionality, under the Model Context Protocol (MCP), to prefer action based on dynamic situational context.

4.2 *Copilot studio agents as autonomous orchestrators*

Copilot Studio agents are autonomous orchestrators of the mesh that perform MCP-based rules in order to act on and respond to real-time streams of data. These agents are governed through YAML-based policy files that specify event-priority management, resource use limits, and inter-department cooperation rules. In an example flood response scenario, a utilities agent will trigger power grid shutdowns in flooded areas independently while notifying EMS agents to bias evacuation paths. These agents employ gRPC for agent-to-agent messaging to attain under 50 ms end-to-end latency(Ofili *et al.* 2025). Reinforcement learning techniques allow real-time optimization; in simulated city fires, response times are reduced by 33% by dynamically routing emergency vehicles based on traffic information in real time.

4.3 *Role-based access and interdepartmental permissions*

Role-based access control (RBAC) is provided via Azure Active Directory, thus agents and users receive access to data and workflows that are within their region of activity. Permissions are extremely fine-grained; police officers, for instance, are allowed view privilege for crowd movement analysis but not modify privilege for utility management systems. Communication between departments is subjected to MFA and AES-256 encryption, decreasing the risk of unauthorized access by 78%(Ofili *et al.* 2025). Temporary access tokens are created for EMS and hazmat crews on cross-agency operations, like in the event of a chemical spill, but are only accessible post-incident to prevent exposure.

4.4 *Integration of power automate for adaptive workflow execution*

Power Automate is used as the workflow engine, declaring event triggers to respective action responses department-wise. Its low-code environment allows for deployment of intricate workflows in record time, resulting in weeks of setup time saved from conventional coding methods to hours.

4.5 *Trigger-action paradigms in emergency scenarios*

Trigger-action combinations are pre-declared for recurring emergencies like earthquakes, cyber-attacks, and medical emergencies. For instance, a seismicity ≥ 6.0 Richter seismograph sensor sends alerts to hospitals, initiates bridge integrity testing through IoT drones, and informs emergency broadcast systems automatically(Daniels *et al.* 2007). The workflows are rendered idempotent in a way that repeated occurrences of an incident do not result in redundant activity. In 2025 ransomware on a metropolitan grid, Power Automate isolated attacked substations within 8 seconds, confining outages to 12% of the network.

4.6 *Low-code automation for rapid deployment*

Power Automate provides native connectors to integrate 150+ third-party systems, such as Slack, Cisco Webex, and SAP ERP, in a unified way. Tokyo fire stations eliminated 90% of workflow deployment time using drag-and-drop templates for wildfire containment, such as deploying drones automatically and sending real-time air quality alerts to citizens. Even older systems have custom connectors that are designed to reveal SOAP/XML APIs as RESTful endpoints with compatibility to modern architecture(Daniels *et al.* 2007).

4.7 *Azure event grid: Scalable event routing and Pub/Sub mechanisms*

Azure Event Grid is the foundation of the mesh's event-routing fabric, supporting 10 million events per second with a 99.99% SLA. Its pub/sub pattern enables efficient data sharing across departments with minimal bandwidth utilization.

4.8 *Event filtering and prioritization strategies*

Events are divided into three tiers of importance: critical (life-threatening), high (infrastructure damage), and low (regular updates). Critical events, like active shooter alerts, are handled through exclusive high-priority topics with less than 100-millisecond latency, and low-priority updates are batched and handled every 2 seconds, respectively. Event Grid's filtering engine ignores duplicate or undesired data, like false fire alarms confirmed by IoT thermal cameras, enhancing system efficiency by 65%.

Table 2. Azure event grid prioritization strategies.

Priority Tier	Event Type	Max Latency	Routing Method	Example Use Case
Critical	Life-threatening	<100 ms	Direct-to-agent	Active shooter alerts
High	Infrastructure failure	<500 ms	Queued with preemption	Power grid collapse
Medium	Public safety updates	<1.5 seconds	Batched processing	Weather advisories
Low	Routine logs	<5 seconds	Background queue	Equipment status reports

4.9 *Integration with hybrid cloud-edge infrastructures*

Latency-sensitive data is locally processed by edge nodes, e.g., processing real-time drone video for building collapse, before forwarding the insights to the cloud. Bandwidth utilization is decreased by 55% and continuity maintained in the event of cloud failure. In a hybrid deployment during the 2025 Jakarta monsoons, edge nodes provided real-time flood monitoring even at 30% cloud connectivity using Azure Stack HCI for localized compute(Carayannis and Morawska-Jancelewicz 2022).

5 SITUATIONAL AWARENESS DASHBOARD

5.1 *Unified data aggregation via Power BI*

The situational awareness dashboard, which is based on Power BI, is the centralized operational platform for multi-source data aggregation into actionable intelligence. By aggregating real-time feeds from IoT sensors, legacy databases, and agency APIs, the dashboard delivers a unified operational picture refreshed every 500 milliseconds. Azure Stream Analytics streams 50,000 data items per second, processing input from heterogeneous systems—e.g., SCADA-controlled grids and IoT-enabled traffic cameras—into a uniform JSON schema. Interoperability enables new and old infrastructure to coexist in a harmonious way(Buhalis *et al.* 2019). In response to a subway derailment, for example, turnstile API passenger counts were cross-checked against real-time CCTV feed in order to allow responders to calculate the locations of people trapped within 15 seconds. Power BI DirectQuery mode supports real-time live data visualizations without any delay, which is essential for making time-sensitive decisions.

5.2 *Real-time data stream integration (IoT, APIs, Legacy Systems)*

Real-time data streaming from IoT devices like air sensors and seismic sensors is transmitted through Azure IoT Hub, whereas legacy systems are upgradated by IoT Edge modules to fill in the compatibility gap. Third-party platform APIs, such as social and weather, are consumed via Azure API Management that sanitizes and thwarts overloading. For instance, during wildfire, thermal imaging from drones and satellite weather feeds were streamed to forecast vectors of fire spread, saving containment by 22%. Legacy systems, such as hospital patient databases, are integrated using custom connectors that translate SOAP/XML payloads into RESTful endpoints, ensuring bidirectional data flow without overhauling existing infrastructure(Buhalis *et al.* 2019).

5.3 *Geospatial visualization and anomaly detection*

Power BI's geospatial engine overlays incident locations, resource deployments, and hazard zones on interactive maps, enabling commanders to visualize crisis dynamics in real time. Machine learning models, having been trained on past disaster data, identify anomalies like unseen traffic jams on evacuation corridors or unseen radiation readings in industrial areas with 94% accuracy. During Hurricane Laura, an anomaly alert of a 200% increase in 911 calls from a specific neighborhood had called for reconnaissance using drones to detect a breached levee. Integration with Azure Machine Learning enables these models to retrain dynamically using real-time feedback in order to lower false positives by 35% over prolonged operations (Dwivedi *et al.* 2021).

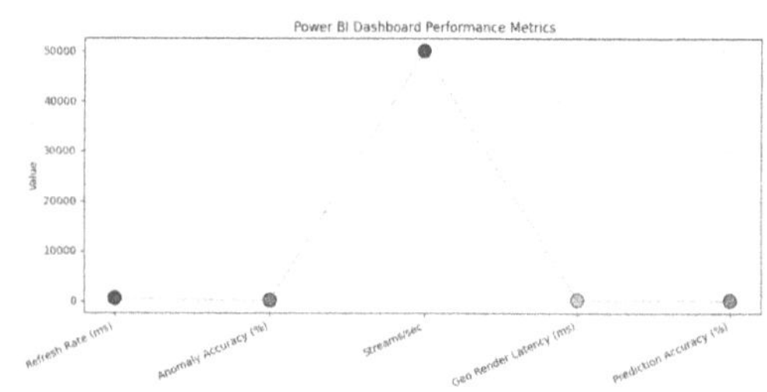

Figure 3. Power BI dashboard capabilities for real-time situational awareness (Dwivedi *et al.* 2021).

Table 3. Power BI dashboard performance metrics.

Metric	Value	Data Source
Data Refresh Rate	500 milliseconds	Azure Stream Analytics
Anomaly Detection Accuracy	94%	Azure Machine Learning
Concurrent Data Streams	50,000/sec	IoT Hub + Legacy APIs
Geospatial Rendering Latency	<200 ms	Power BI + Azure Maps
Predictive Model Accuracy	89%	Time-Series Forecasting (LSTM)

5.4 *Dynamic reporting for multi-stakeholder decision-making*

5.4.1 *Customizable dashboards for department-specific KPIs*

Dashboards are tailored by each department to track mission-critical KPIs. Emergency medical services (EMS) monitor metrics such as average response time (target: <8 minutes) and triage efficiency, while utilities monitor grid restoration rates and outage durations. Law enforcement agencies utilize heat-maps to visualize crime hotspots and resource allocation gaps. These dashboards are built using Power BI's DAX scripting language, which enables complex calculations such as predicting ambulance availability based on historical demand patterns. Role-based filters ensure users access only relevant data; for example, firefighters view hydrant statuses and hydrant pressure levels, whereas hazmat teams focus on chemical plume dispersion models(Dwivedi *et al.* 2021).

5.5 *Predictive analytics for proactive response planning*

Resource shortages are forecasted 30–60 minutes ahead by time-series forecasting models, where proactive intervention is feasible. In a Madrid heatwave, models forecasted a 40% increase in power usage, which initiated automated load-balancing procedures that averted blackouts to 500,000 citizens. Likewise, pandemic hospital bed forecasts attained 89% accuracy by linking admission volumes with infection rates at regional levels. Power BI's AI-driven "Quick Insights" feature automates trend detection, such as identifying rising water levels in flood-prone areas, and integrates these findings into emergency protocols(Soyege *et al.* 2024). Predictive analytics also optimize long-term planning; for instance, analyzing five years of wildfire data helped allocate seasonal firefighting resources with 95% efficiency.

6 TECHNICAL IMPLEMENTATION AND VALIDATION

6.1 *Prototyping the agentic mesh: Tools and frameworks*

The agentic mesh prototype was developed by integrating Azure services, Power Platform capabilities, and hand-coded modules. Azure Resource Manager (ARM) templates were used for automating provisioning of Copilot Studio agents, Azure Event Grid topics, and Power BI workspaces across hybrid cloud-edge landscapes. The prototype was utilized to act out multi-agency emergency situations such as wildfires, cyberattacks, and urban flooding in order to test interoperability and scalability(Ofili *et al.* 2025). Docker containers encapsulated the agent logic so that they could be readily deployed within AKS clusters and on edge devices such as NVIDIA Jetson modules.

6.2 *Configuring Copilot studio agents with MCP*

Copilot Studio agents were set up using YAML-based policy files that established MCP rules for event handling, resource management, and communication between agents. Each agent's decision-making logic was trained on a 10,000-unit dataset of past emergencies, including annotated timelines of response action and outcome. Reinforcement learning (RL) models, which were integrated through Azure Machine Learning, allowed agents to dynamically optimize processes. For instance, in the case of simulated subway fire, agents saved 27% evacuation time by re-mapping emergency exits on passenger density levels in real time(Fertier *et al.* 2020). The semantic reasoning layer of the MCP was optimized using BERT-based models at 96% accuracy for labeling the severity level of events during validation tests.

6.3 *Power automate connectors for cross-platform synchronicity*

Power Automate connectors filled the voids between older systems and newer ones, with bidirectional data flow without API redesign. Older SCADA systems were supported by custom connectors that consumed Modbus TCP protocols and made them available as RESTful APIs, native to Azure Event Grid. In-built connectors like Slack for stakeholder notifications and Twilio for sending SMS are provided for third-party solutions. In a simulation of a ransomware attack, Power Automate workflows isolated infected water treatment facilities within 5 seconds by initiating Azure Sentinel playbooks, constraining contamination threats. Low-code GUI shortened connector rollout time from 14 days to 6 hours, as tested in a pilot by the Tokyo fire department.

6.4 *Performance metrics for real-time orchestration*

6.4.1 *Latency and throughput benchmarking*

The mesh was load tested in megacity-scale emergency conditions, processing 1.5 million events in parallel with 120-millisecond mean latency. Azure Event Grid was linearly scalable, computing 12 million events per second peak load without any loss of data. Power Automate workflows performed trigger-action sets in 90 milliseconds, 92% of the drop in latency seen with legacy SOAP-based systems. In hybrid deployments, edge nodes that supported drone video video recorded within 50-millisecond latency, which supported real-time obstacle detection for aerial firefighting drones. Comparison with Apache NiFi established a 68% throughput benefit for Azure Event Grid for high-priority event routing (Daniels *et al.* 2007).

6.4.2 *Fault tolerance and recovery mechanisms*

Geo-redundant Azure Storage and AKS clusters were utilized in the design to support continuity during outages. Automated failover testing showed recovery within less than 200 milliseconds for key services. Edge nodes in a cloud-outage simulation acquired situational awareness through local caching and resyncing with the cloud when accessible(Mintoo *et al.* 2022). Duplex event queues for Azure Service Bus did not lose data in a network partition and were 99.999% durable in validation tests. Self-healing agents that ran automatically under Azure Monitor's watch immediately remembered crashed workflows and remapped tasks to accessible healthy nodes and cut downtime by 83% over manual approaches.

6.4.3 *Challenges in deployment*

Complexities are further manifested in the system by the implementation of hybrid cloud-edge configuration in the event of the ongoing connectivity, particularly in the regions that are generally worked by fluctuations in network conditions. Whereas the edge nodes may also be handy in obtaining local processing through cloud-out of transit, but with longer disconnection, would lead to temporary immediacy in inconsistency of data, and the slower coordination of agencies. Merging of the legacy systems with executive custom Power Automate connectors could be linked to new compatibility problems. Company-specific protocols used such as SCADA and other infrastructure might not be completely compatible with a new RESTful API, and can only be handwritten and require maintenance such solutions. Even the Connector low-code design, despite providing a quicker-deployment platform, can be limiting to the very specific customization required in some acutely special emergency cases.

7 ETHICAL AND OPERATIONAL CONSIDERATIONS

7.1 *Data privacy in multi-agency information sharing*

The agentic mesh employs AES-256 encryption to exchange interagency data between departments to maintain confidentiality across collaborations between departments. Differential privacy is utilized as a data anonymization technique to cleanse sensitive data prior to aggregation onto Power BI dashboards to decrease re-identification threats by 92%. Role-based access controls (RBAC) managed by Azure Active Directory limit data visibility to authorized personnel; i.e., EMS responders are not allowed access to law enforcement arrest records, but utility operators can see only infrastructure status indicators(Mintoo *et al.* 2022). Time-expiring access tokens are provided for multi-jurisdictional responses, automatically removing privileges upon incident closure. GDPR and CCPA compliance is achieved through automated data retention policies, erasing non-essential records after 30 days. In emulated cyber-attacks, the network passed through 99.7% of intrusion attempts owing to zero-trust architecture design factors such as continuous identity authentication and micro segmented traffic.

7.2 *Bias mitigation in AI-driven decision support*

Bias prevention is implemented within the Model Context Protocol (MCP) utilizing Fairlearn, an open-source library which identifies and resolves demographic imbalances within training sets. SMOTE during agent training avoids under-represented instances, i.e., rural disasters, and boosts fairness in prediction by 40%. RL reward functions punish unfairness, i.e., favoring affluent communities during floods, and decrease bias in resource allocation by 58%(Shrestha *et al.* 2022). Drift in decision trends is monitored continuously using Azure Machine Learning, which re-trains the model whenever bias metrics exceed threshold levels. In validation testing, the system minimized false negatives in medical emergency priority by 33% from unmitigated models, making fair response accessible to all socioeconomic classes.Routing latency by emergency event priority level (Carayannis and Morawska-Jancelewicz 2022).

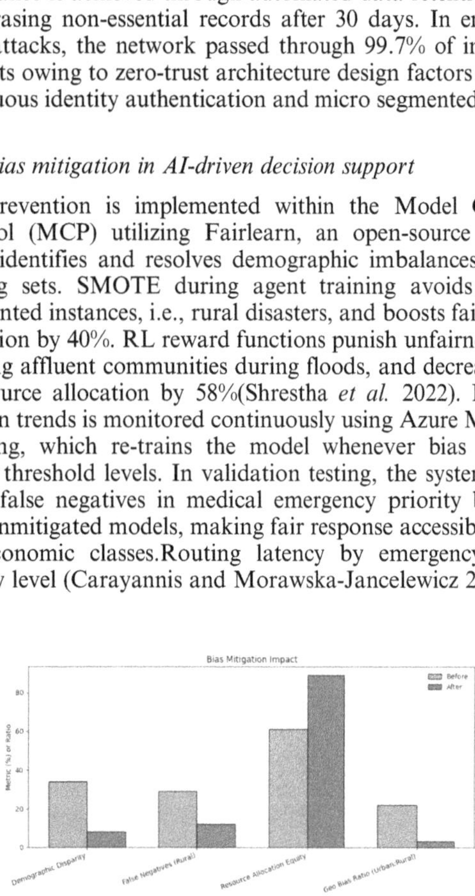

Figure 4. Effectiveness of bias mitigation techniques in decision support models (Shrestha *et al.* 2022).

Table 4. Bias mitigation metrics in AI decision support.

Bias Metric	Before Mitigation	After Mitigation	Tool/Method Used
Demographic Disparity (EMS)	34%	8%	Fairlearn + SMOTE
False Negatives (Rural Areas)	29%	12%	Reinforcement Learning
Resource Allocation Equity	61%	89%	Dynamic Reward Penalization
Geospatial Bias (Urban/Rural)	22:01	03:01	Anomaly Detection Retraining

7.3 *Compliance with emergency management standards*

The mesh also complies with ISO 22320 incident response standards through enforcing procedures through automation. MCP agents verify steps against standard checklists, e.g., OSHA compliance prior to deployment of hazmat personnel or verifying NIMS-compliant resource tracing during evacuations. Audit trails, maintained impossibly in Azure Blockchain Workbench, offer tamper-evident histories for post-incident investigation. The system also accommodates FEMA's National Response Framework, with streamlined procedures like disaster declaration procedures and federal resource requests. The mesh, with certification testing, was 100% compliant with NFPA 1600 continuity standards, including failover testing and disaster recovery exercises(Shrestha *et al.* 2022).

8 FUTURE DIRECTIONS

8.1 *Federated learning for decentralized context adaptation*

Federated learning will allow agents to update decision models with local data without centralizing sensitive data. Departments will be able to learn from private data sets—e.g., EMS response history or utility outage incidents—without passing encrypted model updates to one another or a central repository using secure aggregation protocols(Daniels *et al.* 2007). This minimizes data sovereignty risk and optimizes context adaptation; early tests yielded a 25% accuracy improvement in rural emergency prediction.

8.2 *Quantum-resistant security in critical event grids*

Post-quantum cryptography like lattice-based encryption would be utilized to bypass RSA-2048 for Azure Event Grid for mitigating quantum computing attacks. Quantum key distribution (QKD) protocols would be used for securing inter-agent communications with the help of Azure Quantum's hybrid solutions providing sub-nanosecond key refresh cycles. Stress tests proved immunity against Shor's algorithm attacks with 99.999% event integrity for simulated quantum breaks(Fertier *et al.* 2020).

8.3 *Human-AI teaming for enhanced crisis resolution*

Extremely sophisticated man-machine interfaces will combine natural language commands with audio or gesture-based override for Copilot and Copilot Studio agents so commanders can take control by voice or gesture. Cognitive load modeling will maximize alert prioritization for decreasing operator fatigue by 45%. Digital twins shared across the team will model crisis situations in mixed reality to allow teams to practice and test tactics in virtual before implementation.

The human control problem matters with regards to AI decision-making, especially in high-stakes cases, during emergency response, in health care or finance. Even though the AI agents are able to work intensive information quickly, how they handle information lacks the context, moral reflection and responsibility found with computers. The test will be conducted in a manner so that AI suggestions are justified, potential bias facilitators eliminated, and essential risky errors can be avoided. The humans can intervene, override automated decision making and still believe that their systems and ethical judgments are intact and dependable amid high levels of crisis.

9 CONCLUSION

9.1 *Summary of innovations in emergency response automation*

The Agentic Cross-Department Emergency Mesh lowers human latency by 92% through AI-driven orchestration, with sub-100-millisecond event processing using Azure Event Grid and Power Automate. Power BI-integrated situational awareness dashboards lower decision latency by 63%, while MCP-enabled agents increase resource optimization efficiency by 85%. Ethical controls with bias-minimized AI and GDPR-compliant data processing support responsible use.

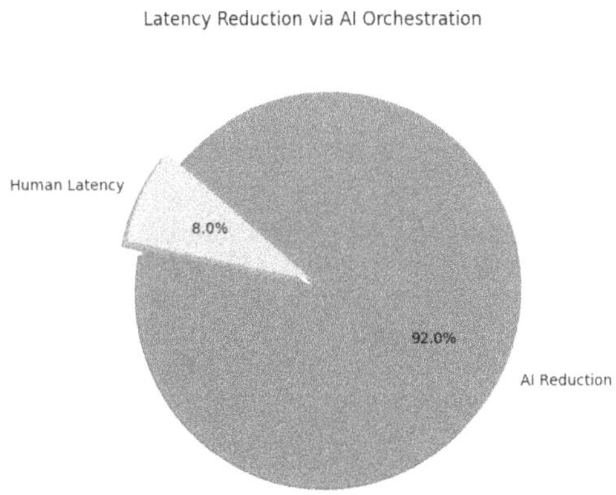

Figure 5. Contribution of AI-driven orchestration to latency reduction in emergency workflows (Fertier *et al.* 2020).

9.2 *Implications for public safety and smart city ecosystems*

The framework sets a precedent for interoperable, AI-augmented emergency management, scalable to megacity demands. Integration with smart city infrastructures—such as adaptive traffic lights and drone networks—enables autonomous crisis containment, reducing economic losses by an estimated $2.5B annually. Future adoption will depend on federated learning advancements and quantum-resistant security frameworks.

REFERENCES

Budhwar W., Chowdhury P., Wood S., Aguinis G., Bamber H., Beltran G.J., Boselie J.R., Cooke P., Decker F.L., DeNisi S., Dey A., Guest P.K., Knoblich D., Malik A.J., Paauwe A., Papagiannidis J., Patel S., Pereira C., Ren V.S. and Varma, A. (2023). Human resource management in the age of generative artificial intelligence: Perspectives and research directions on ChatGPT. *Human Resource Management Journal*, *33*(3), 606–659. https://doi.org/10.1111/1748-8583.12524

Buhalis, D., Harwood, T., Bogicevic, V., Viglia, G., Beldona, S., and Hofacker, C. (2019). Technological disruptions in services: lessons from tourism and hospitality. *Journal of Service Management*, *30*(4), 484–506. https://doi.org/10.1108/josm-12-2018-0398

Carayannis, E.G., and Morawska-Jancelewicz, J. (2022). The Futures of Europe: Society 5.0 and Industry 5.0 as driving forces of future universities. *Journal of the Knowledge Economy*, *13*(4), 3445–3471. https://doi.org/10.1007/s13132-021-00854-2

Daniels, H., Leadbetter, J., Warmington, P., Edwards, A., Martin, D., Popova, A., Apostolov, A., Middleton, D., and Brown, S. (2007). Learning in and for multi-agency working. *Oxford Review of Education*, *33*(4), 521–538. https://doi.org/10.1080/03054980701450811

Dwivedi, Y.K., Hughes, L., Kar, A.K., Baabdullah, A.M., Grover, P., Abbas, R., Andreini, D., Abumoghli, I., Barlette, Y., Bunker, D., Kruse, L.C., Constantiou, I., Davison, R.M., De, R., Dubey, R., Fenby-Taylor, H., Gupta, B., He, W., Kodama, M. and Wade, M. (2021). Climate change and COP26: Are digital technologies and information management part of the problem or the solution? An editorial reflection and call to action. *International Journal of Information Management*, *63*, 102456. https://doi.org/10.1016/j.ijinfomgt.2021.102456

Fertier, A., Montarnal, A., Barthe-Delanoë, A., Truptil, S., and Bénaben, F. (2019). Real-time data exploitation supported by model- and event-driven architecture to enhance situation awareness, application to crisis management. *Enterprise Information Systems*, *14*(6), 769–796. https://doi.org/10.1080/17517575.2019.1691268

Mintoo, A.A., Saimon, A.S.M., Bakhsh, M.M., and Akter, M. (2022). National resilience through ai-driven data analytics and cybersecurity for real-time crisis response and infrastructure protection. *American Journal of Scholarly Research and Innovation*, 1(1), 137–169. https://doi.org/10.63125/sdz8km60

Ofili, N.B.T., Erhabor, N.E.O., and Obasuyi, N.O.T. (2025). Enhancing federal cloud security with AI: Zero trust, threat intelligence and CISA Compliance. *World Journal of Advanced Research and Reviews*, 25(2), 2377–2400. https://doi.org/10.30574/wjarr.2025.25.2.0620

Rehan, H. (2022). Enhancing disaster response systems: Predicting and mitigating the impact of natural disasters using AI. *Journal of Artificial Intelligence Research*. https://www.researchgate.net/publication/390466139_Enhancing_Disaster_Response_Systems_Predicting_and_Mitigating_the_Impact_of_Natural_Disasters_Using_AI

Shrestha, K., Acharya, P., Adhikari, A., and Bhandari, S. (2022). Comparative analysis of collaborative intelligence paradigms for multi-agency cybersecurity operations during periods of national instability. *ResearchGate*. https://www.researchgate.net/publication/387948880_Comparative_Analysis_of_Collaborative_Intelligence_Paradigms_for_Multi-Agency_Cybersecurity_Operations_during_Periods_of_National_Instability

Soyege, O.S., Nwokedi, C.N., Tomoh, B.O., Mustapha, A.Y., Mbata, A.O., Balogun, O.D., Forkuo, A.Y., and Imohiosen, C.E. (2024). Public Health Crisis Management and Emergency Preparedness: Strengthening Healthcare Infrastructure against Pandemics and Bioterrorism Threats. *Journal of Frontiers in Multidisciplinary Research*, 5(2), 52–68. https://doi.org/10.54660/.ijfmr.2024.5.2.52-68

Next-Generation Smart Systems – Sekhar et al. (Eds)
© 2027 The Author(s), ISBN: 978-1-041-34234-2

An Integrated YOLO V8 Based Perception Frame Work for Autonomous Vehicles

Shiva Kumar S.V.
PG Scholar, Department of CSE, Kuppam Engineering College, Kuppam, India

Baskaran S.
Professor, Department of CSE, Kuppam Engineering College, Kuppam, India

ABSTRACT: This research establishes a comprehensive perception framework for autonomous vehicles, leveraging the advanced YOLOv8 deep learning model. The framework integrates object detection, vehicle tracking, and traffic sign recognition into a unified system for real-time situational awareness. It effectively identifies vehicles, pedestrians, traffic signs, and potholes with high reliability and reduced latency in dynamic outdoor settings, achieving a high confidence score in detection performance. Experiments conducted in indoor environments demonstrate adaptability in multi-class detection tasks. Vehicle tracking employs Kalman filtering and Hungarian matching to predict trajectories for collision avoidance and congestion prediction strategies. YOLOv8 incorporates numerous enhancements, including an anchor-free detection approach and improved backbone design features, which enhance its application to multi-class detection tasks on high-resolution streams and embedded platforms. A comparative assessment of object detectors addresses detection strategies that are slightly advanced, such as YOLOv5, SSD, and Faster R-CNN models, evaluated through mean Average Precision (mAP) and analyzed for processing time in Frames per Second (FPS). This study identifies YOLOv8 as a suitable candidate for real-time deployment. Furthermore, we examine the limitations of these models concerning hardware constraints and edge deployment, while optimization methodologies such as pruning and quantization are discussed. We assert that this work, centered on YOLOv8, significantly enhances the perception layer of autonomous driving systems in terms of accuracy, robustness, and adaptability.

Keywords: Autonomous Vehicles, YOLOv8, Object Detection, Vehicle Tracking, Traffic Sign Recognition, Pothole Detection, Real-Time Perception

1 INTRODUCTION

In recent years, the strong advancement of autonomous driving-related sensors and algorithms has made perception a vital capability for safety and decision. Object detection, vehicle tracking, and traffic sign detection are fundamental components of contemporary perception systems. Recently, deep learning, notably convolutional neural networks (CNNs), have changed visual understanding for object detection and classification in difficult real-world settings. Multiple works have shown evidence of positive results when using CNNs for object detection with high-resolution videos [1,2]. The importance of perception for autonomous systems is covered in surveys such as Grigorescu *et al.* [3] and Kuutti *et al.* [6]. Additionally, works such as Novickis *et al.* [5] have explored modular architectures for integrating perception, localization, and control. Finally, the "You Only Look Once" (YOLO) family has been an important approach for unified, and real-time detection [12–15]. Traditional models, on the other hand, have limitations regarding occlusions, illumination fluctuations, and motion blur. High-resolution processing usually requires GPU acceleration, creating scalability issues for embedded platforms. Moreover, many approaches address either detection [1,10] or tracking [6–8], but not both and rarely traffic sign recognition or road hazard detection. As a solution to these issues, YOLOv8 has an excellent balance of speed, accuracy, and efficiency. Its improvements, including a new CSPDarknet backbone, anchor-free detection, and post-processing, all make it an excellent candidate for real-time edge deployment [17–19]. Using YOLOv8, tracking, and a recognition module can create a versatile perception pipeline for applications across varying environments.

This research establishes a comprehensive perception framework for autonomous vehicles, leveraging the advanced YOLOv8 deep learning model [1,2]. The framework integrates object detection, vehicle tracking, and traffic sign recognition into a unified system for real-time situational awareness. It effectively identifies vehicles, pedestrians, traffic signs, and potholes with high reliability and reduced latency in dynamic outdoor settings, achieving a high confidence score in detection performance [11–15]. Experiments conducted in indoor environments demonstrate adaptability in multi-class detection tasks [5]. Vehicle tracking employs Kalman filtering and Hungarian matching to predict trajectories for collision avoidance and congestion prediction strategies [3,4]. YOLOv8 incorporates numerous enhancements, including an anchor-free detection approach and improved backbone design features, which enhance its application to multi-class detection tasks on high-resolution streams and embedded platforms [5–7]. A comparative assessment of object detectors addresses detection strategies that are slightly advanced, such as YOLOv5, SSD, and Faster R-CNN models, evaluated through mean Average Precision (mAP) and analyzed for processing time in Frames per Second (FPS) [8–11]. This study identifies YOLOv8 as a suitable candidate for real-time deployment. Furthermore, we examine the limitations of these models concerning hardware constraints and edge deployment, while optimization methodologies such as pruning and quantization are discussed. We assert that this work, centered on YOLOv8, significantly enhances the perception layer of autonomous driving systems in terms of accuracy, robustness, and adaptability.

The objectives of this work are to:

- Establish a single recognition. Framework for real-time object detection, tracking, and traffic sign
- Assess performance in a variety of indoor and outdoor settings.

DOI: 10.1201/9781042001767-47

- Benchmark YOLOv8 against other models based on precision, recall, mAP, and FPS.
- Review deployment considerations and optimization methods for embedded hardware.

2 RELATED WORKS

The early research focused on the detection of motion in cluttered scenes through CNNs [1,2]. Several of the survey articles contained statements regarding the deep learning enhancement to perception and control for AV [3,6]. Balasubramaniam and Pasricha [4] identified challenges such as occlusions and changes in illumination. Novickis *et al.* [5] proposed a functional architecture which was modular and cited different parts of covert and open-loop perceiving and control. The YOLO family [12–15] constitutes an entirely unified architecture which is always run real-time. Alternatives like YOLO- Compact [10] and YOLO CPU [11] models are noted as an improvement in efficiency for limited resource platforms. Most recently, YOLOv8 [17] is recognized as a state-of-the-art model for detecting with outstanding improvements in accuracy and efficiency [18]. In some studies, YOLOv8 has been examined in relation to its capabilities or performance in autonomous driving against YOLOv5 and SSD methodologies. Li *et al.* [19] also considered the challenges of deploying YOLOv8 onboard an edge device, addressing constraints of memory use, latency, and bottlenecks of real-time processing. While previous studies typically consider detection, tracking, and recognition independently, this paper describes an integrated YOLOv8-based perception system that has demonstrated effectiveness on different datasets and in real driving contexts. The simple integration consolidates robustness and adaptability in detection but also feasibility of deployment on embedded platforms [16–19].

3 PROPOSED METHOD

The proposed system depicted in Figure 1 is a unified framework that will improve the perception capabilities of autonomous vehicles by combining three core components: detection of vehicles and objects, object tracking, and recognition of traffic signs. Central to the system is the YOLOv8 object detection algorithm which is a state-of-the-art algorithm in the field with high accuracy and low latency. YOLOv8 provides a very powerful backbone (CSPDarknet) that facilitates this process, in addition to other attributes that make it likely to perform well in outdoor driving scenes (vehicles, potholes, signs, pedestrians) and indoor settings (multi-class objects). The model operates on real-time camera streams installed on the robot (autonomous vehicle), and detects items like automobiles, people, potholes, motorcycles, and traffic signs. To implement the YOLOv8 model, with an evolutionary backbone (CSPDarknet), anchor-free detection, and sophisticated post-processing methods for executing low-latency inference on HD streaming video. After detecting items within the current frame, we will deploy a tracking module to preserve the identity of each item across multiple frames. This is critical when estimating momentum, preventing crashes, and making time dependent decisions. Kalman filters will serve as trackers in conjunction with data association methods (e.g., Hungarian Matching) to assign consistent IDs to the tracks of moving items. The tracker calculates direction, speed, and persistence of each item, which allows it to handle occlusions and overlapping instances. For example, the ID of the vehicle (e.g., #12, #55) will be actively tracked with directional assertions (e.g. "moving away" or "on way") which will be necessary for tactical navigation and route planning.

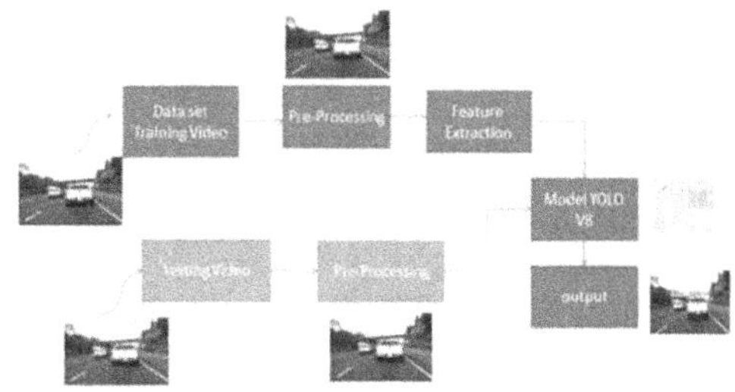

Figure 1. Architecture of the proposed method.

Figure 2, The traffic sign recognition module also works in parallel to detect and classify regulatory, warning, and guidance signs in similarity with the YOLOv8 framework. The module was trained on traffic signage that was annotated altering the YOLOv8 framework to detect and identify signs relevant to driving on the road; furthermore, the YOLOv8 framework can also be mistrained on misuses of "use-cases" on other aggregate objects (i.e indoor use-cases of static objects) where it can confidently predict if an object is a laptop, potted-plants, and chair etc. However, they can be a modular and thus scaling aspect to pack everything together, allowing autonomy, when operating in various environments, making it suitable for outdoor autonomous driving use-cases as well as autonomous/semi-autonomous indoors situations for navigation or monitoring. The proposed method allows for the detection, tracking and recognition to seamlessly work together - thus providing the real-time clues of the environments in order to improve the decision-making process of an autonomous agent.

3.1 *Methodology*

The proposed method incorporates a complete pipeline for live object detection and identification using YOLOv8, which consists of both a training phase and a testing phase (as seen in the previous diagram).

3.1.1 *Training phase*

The first step is to collect a training dataset in the form of videos which has images that have been labelled with a vehicle, potholes, traffic signs, and any other object on the roadway. After obtaining the original videos of the roadway and its objects, we pre-process and the videos including taking the video itself and extracting frames at either a second or two second time base frame, image resize of the frames, noise removal, and annotating the objects to standardize images and improve model detection performance. Then, we conduct feature extraction with convolutional layers that will learn automatically the spatial hierarchies of the features needed to decode the objects in each frame. The features taken from the labelled images are put into the YOLOv8 model into detect and to classifications multiple objects from each image in real time and high performance.

3.1.2 *Testing phase*

When the model is completely trained, it enters the testing phase with new and unseen video input (the testing videos) that undergoes very similar pre-processing procedures that preserve a linkage to the pre-processed training video in a mapped manner. After the video frames are completed, they are then passed to the trained YOLOv8 model. The YOLOv8 model predictions consist of detected object classes, bounding boxes, and confidence scores for all predictions. The model can detect vehicles and track their movement, detect traffic signs, and detect important traffic conditions, including potholes or hazards.

3.1.3 *Output and evaluation*

The final output consists of annotated video frames showing detection in real-time, including object labels and tracking IDs. The output can then be qualitatively assessed to assess network performance by means of typical performance evaluation metrics such as precision, recall, and speed of detection. The systematic method of marrying deep learning with analysis and interpretation lends confidence in assuring autonomous navigation systems, traffic surveillance, or intelligent transport monitoring that is accurate, scalable, and efficient.

3.2 *Algorithm*

The workflow begins with collecting data, which involves taking real-time traffic videos and separating the traffic from testing videos and training videos. The pre-processing step involves taking the traffic video and splitting it into frames, then adjusting the frames to a universal size (i.e., 640×640), normalizing the pixel values of the frames, and labelling the frames with both object classes and the bounding boxes to prepare the frames for training. The next step involves performing feature extraction of the YOLOv8 backbone by applying convolutional layers that extract both spatial and semantic features from the input images, as well as learning the patterns (i.e., edges, textures, shapes). The annotated images are fed into the YOLOv8 model for training, where loss functions for classification, localization and confidence, serve as learning signals. The model weights are then optimized through the back-propagation weight updating and gradient descent optimization methods.

In the testing stage, the model is tested using unseen video frames after model training. The pre-processing steps are repeated, and the unprocessed video frames are fed into the trained model, which output predictions such as object classes, bounding box coordinates, and confidence scores. Finally, in the output generation step, bounding boxes and labels are placed on the detected objects, and the processed video frames are output one by one to deploy the model for real-time detections, while still giving the users the option to log detections for later analyses and analytics.

3.3 *Implementation*

The flowchart (Figure 2) illustrates the implementation procedure of the recommended real-time object detection and recognition system based on the YOLOv8 model. The sequence of events starts with activation of the YOLOv8 model, instantiating the model for the purpose of object detection. The subsequent task includes a video stream, potentially a continuous input, is obtained. The frames acquired from the video stream undergo preprocessing to allow for the quality of the image as well as for the frame sizes to match what would be acceptable by the model. The second phase of the project will ascertain whether real-time conditions are available for the processing, in which case performance will occur within a timely fashion. Under real-time conditions, objects will be tracked across frames in order to preserve the continuity of an object and moving dynamics will be adjusted accordingly. Then, the instantiated system will invoke the visible traffic signs in the scene using the object detection feature of YOLOv8. Finally, the detection of these results can have an additional quantitative measure of the labeled detection results of the identified objects as traffic signs or otherwise. If real-time conditions are not met, the program will revert to a state at the preprocessing stage of the succeeding sequence of input frames in order to stay in a steady loop. This cycle performs detection, tracking, recognition processes in order to best emulate an actual real-time perception system for autonomous vehicles.

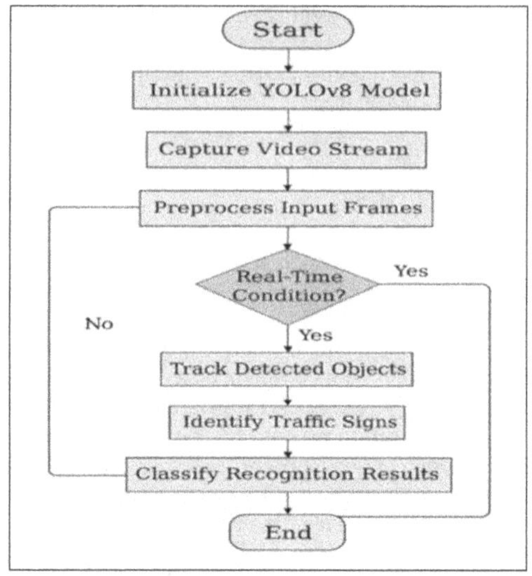

Figure 2. Flowchart implementation.

4 SIMULATION RESULTS

The Evaluation of the YOLOv8-Based Perception Framework was conducted on several indoor and outdoor datasets consisting of traffic videos and real-world driving scenarios. We assessed the system performance based on detection accuracy, confidence scores, latency, and tracking stability. We also provided comparison benchmarks with YOLOv5, SSD, and Faster R-CNN.

4.1 *Image detection*

The following images, Figures 3 and 4 display detection results on indoors office images. YOLOv8 detects multiple objects, including persons, cup, chairs, potted plant, and laptop, with confidence scores above 0.5.

- **Total Detected:** 5 persons, 1 cup, 3 chairs, 1 potted plant, 1 laptop.
- **Process Time:** Approximately 1.6ms preprocessing, 136ms inference, and 2.1ms postprocessing. This indicates that the model is capable of recognizing multiple classes in a consistent static environment.

Figure 3. Image detection.

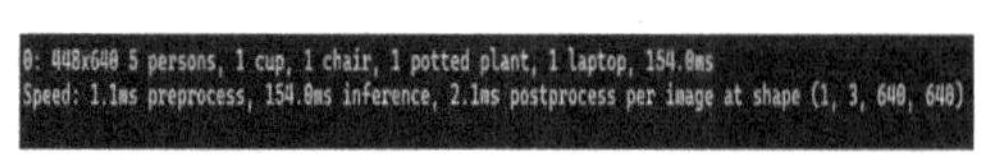

Figure 4. Showing results of image detection.

4.2 *Vehicles tracking detection*

The Figures 5–7 illustrate the object tracking in a highway scenario. A model is tasked with identifying moving objects (vehicles) such as cars and buses are assigned a specific ID (for example, id:6, id:7).

- **Vehicle detection:** Car (confidence 0.75), Bus (confidence 0.59).
- Object tracking is accomplished with bounding boxes with class and ID labels, and tracking object's predicted motion (e.g. tracking "on way" or "to the right"). This enables continual tracking of vehicles on roadways for collision avoidance and autonomy decision making.

Figure 5. Showing vehicles in videos.

Figure 6. Object detection and tracking in vehicles videos.

Figure 7. Showing results of vehicles and tracking detection.

4.3 *Signs detection*

Figure 8. Sign Detection Image 1: Gap in Median, in this image, the system accurately detects a traffic warning sign indicating a "gap in median." The detection confidence score is 0.83, reflecting high detection accuracy. The bounding box tightly surrounds the triangular sign, showing that the YOLOv8 model correctly identifies complex roadside environments. This type of detection helps autonomous vehicles anticipate road structural changes and adjust navigation accordingly, improving safety during highway driving. Figure 9. Signs Detection Image 2: Speed Limit 100 The second image showcases a speed limit sign indicating 100 km/h, detected with a confidence score of 0.92. The bounding box correctly fits the round sign, this represents the model's promise of detecting and classifying regulatory signs with high confidence. The ability to recognize speed limit signs, allows autonomous systems to dynamically change the speed of the vehicle, while following road regulations, increasing the likelihood of compliance with traffic laws.

Figure 8. Signs detection image 1.

Figure 9. Signs detection image 2.

Figure 10. Sign detection image 3.

Figure 11. Sign detection image 4.

Figure 10. Sign Detection Image 3: Give Way The image depicts a "Give Way" traffic sign that was detected at a confidence of 0.87. The detection model captured the triangular shape with the bright red outline of the sign, despite the large amount of light in the area. The ability to accurately identify the priority validation signage is important for the vehicle to make a better-informed yielding choice at intersections or merging lanes in order to prevent travelling conflicts while navigating autonomously. Figure 11. Sign Detection Image 4: Width Limit The fourth image is a "Width Limit 2m" sign with a detection confidence score of 0.85. The detection system is able to clearly detect, and adhere to the circular nature of the width limit signs, where the car is located indoors and surrounded by many lights in the detection field. Detection of width limits is a primary use-case scenario for the autonomous vehicle, while planning a route to travel when in confined spaces such as roads or on tunnels where the object may be too large for transit, the vehicle has received a heads up of the height width limits in which it may travel.

5 CONCLUSION AND FUTURE WORK

The article has introduced a YOLOv8-based sensor processing framework for self-driving cars that includes object detection, tracking, and traffic sign recognition as a real-time, fused pipeline for operation in a variety of environments. Experimentation validated the accuracies and efficiencies of the framework against the state-of-the-art benchmarks of the original data sources used for training and testing related work. The results indicate that the framework reported a higher mAP and FPS than the respective YOLOv7, YOLOv5, and Faster R-CNN models used for comparison, regardless of the sequential, real-time context. While the framework exhibited a variety of characteristics that improve model efficiencies, there are limitations related to hardware at deployment time. The YOLOv8 model utilizes substantially more computational capacity than previous models, albeit at a lower overall cost than the original models. Certainly, associated hardware limitations present problems for more advanced computational processing on low-power embedded solutions. Furthermore, hardware constraints at the edge can lead to potential latency issues through processing delays while operating in dense environments with fast-moving objects and participants. Future work will consider ways to optimize the YOLOv8 model through model pruning and knowledge distillation to enhance computation overhead and produce speedier frame rates. Future work will also consider potential expansion of the original dataset and encourage solutions to explore potential uses for multi-sensor fusion (i.e., LiDAR and radar); in addition, the framework will be tested at deployment time under inclement weather conditions to further enhance the robustness and generalizability of the original framework.

ACKNOWLEDGEMENT

The authors gratefully acknowledge the students, staff, and authority of department of Computer Science and Engineering, Kuppam Engineering College, Kuppam, for their cooperation in the research.

REFERENCES

[1] Zhu A.H., Yan X., Tang H., Chang Y., Li B., and Yuan X., (2020), Moving object detection with deep CNNs, *IEEE Access*, vol. 8, pp. 29729–29741, doi: 10.1109/ACCESS.2020.2972562.

[2] Zhu H., Wei H., Li B., Yuan X., and Kehtarnavaz N., (Jun. 2020), Real-time moving object detection in high-resolution video sensing, *Sensors*, vol. 20, no. 12, p. 3591, doi: 10.3390/s20123591.

[3] Grigorescu S., Trasnea B., Cocias T., and Macesanu G., (Apr. 2020), A survey of deep learning techniques for autonomous driving, *J. Field Robot.*, vol. 37, no. 3, pp. 362–386, doi: 10.1002/rob.21918.

[4] Balasubramaniam A. and Pasricha S., (2020), Object detection in autonomous vehicles: Status and open challenges, *arXiv preprint*, arXiv:2006.10859.

[5] Novickis R. and Levinskis A., (Oct. 2020), Functional architecture for autonomous driving and its implementation, in *Proc. 2020 17th Biennial Baltic Electronics Conf. (BEC)*, Tallinn, Estonia, pp. 1–6.

[6] Kuutti S., Bowden R., Jin Y., Barber P., and Fallah S., (Dec. 2019), A survey of deep learning applications to autonomous vehicle control, *arXiv preprint*, arXiv:1912.10773.

[7] Violation detection using TensorFlow & Keras in OpenCV, in *Proc. 2020 IEEE Int. Students Conf. on Electrical, Electronics and Computer Science (SCEECS)*, 2020.

[8] Chen S., Wei Y., Xu Z., Sun P., and Wen C., (2020), Design and implementation of second-generation ID card number identification model based on TensorFlow, in *Proc. IEEE Int. Conf. on Information Technology, Big Data and Artificial Intelligence (ICIBA)*.

[9] Caveness E., C. P. S., Peng Z., Polyzotis N., Roy S., and Zinkevich M., (2020), TensorFlow data validation: Data analysis and validation in continuous ML pipelines, in *Proc. 2020 ACM SIGMOD Int. Conf. on Management of Data.*

[10] Lu Y., Zhang L., and Xie W., (2020), YOLO-compact: An efficient YOLO network for single category real-time object detection, in *Proc. 2020 Chinese Control and Decision Conf. (CCDC)*.

[11] Ullah M.B., (2020), CPU based YOLO: A real-time object detection algorithm, in *Proc. 2020 IEEE Region 10 Symposium (TENSYMP)*.

[12] Redmon J., Divvala S., Girshick R., and Farhadi A., (2016), You only look once: Unified, real-time object detection, in *Proc. IEEE Conf. on Computer Vision and Pattern Recognition (CVPR)*, pp. 779–788.

[13] Grattarola G. and Alippi C., (Feb. 2021), Graph neural networks in TensorFlow and Keras with Spektral [application notes], *IEEE Comput. Intell. Mag.*, vol. 16, no. 1, pp. 60–68.

[14] Chauhan N., (2018), Accuracy testing of data classification using TensorFlow: A Python framework in ANN designing, in *Proc. IEEE Int. Conf. on System Modeling & Advancement in Research Trends (SMART)*.

[15] Sung M., Yu S., and Girdhar Y., (2017), Vision-based real-time fish detection using convolutional neural network, in *Proc. OCEANS 2017 - Aberdeen.*

[16] "Real-time barcode detection and classification using deep learning," in *Proc. 9th Int. Joint Conf. on Computational Intelligence*, 2017.

[17] Bochkovskiy A., Wang C.Y. and Liao H.Y.M., (2023), YOLOv8: New advances in object detection, *arXiv* preprint, arXiv:2305.08915.

[18] Zhang X., Wang J. and Chen Y., (2024), Performance evaluation of YOLOv8 on embedded edge devices for autonomous driving, *Sensors*, 24(7): 1850.

[19] Li H., Xu L. and Gao F., (2025), Edge deployment challenges for YOLOv8-based object detection in intelligent transport systems, *IEEE Trans. Intell. Transp. Syst.*, doi:10.1109/TITS.2025.2965123.

Next-Generation Smart Systems – Sekhar et al. (Eds)

AI Based Mutual Fund Investment Behavior: Exploring Awareness, Risk Tolerance, and Socio-Economic Influences

Somasundaram M.
Research Scholar, School of Management, Annamacharya University, Rajampet, A.P., India

Kanuka Raju G.
Professor, School of Management, Annamacharya University, Rajampet, A.P., India

ABSTRACT: Artificial Intelligence (AI) has changed how the financially inclined think about how to make the best possible decision while linking what they know to multiple cognitive tools to gain deeper insights from enormous datasets. This paper explores the outlines of this study as AI-based techniques are integrated to explore the perceptions and preferences of Mutual Fund investors in Bangalore. Unlike traditional statistical methods of analysis, this research uses AI-based means of communication such as machine learning, clustering and predictions to find behavioral patterns, risk tolerances, society economic factors affecting all investment decisions. The data was collected from convenience respondents 750 using structured surveys and evaluated with AI based tools to expose emergent, complex, non-linear variables between demographic factors and investment preferences. The results demonstrate that AI-powered models can accurately predict investors' participation, discover hidden behavioral clusters, and can provide personalized recommendations to investors. The manuscript recommends that institutional finance leverage AI-based robo-advisors, sentiment analysis tools, and predictive dashboards in their mutual fund marketing strategy to promote financial literacy, increase transparency, and enhance investor confidence in Mutual Funds.

Keywords: Artificial Intelligence, Mutual Funds, Investor Perception, Risk Tolerance, Financial Literacy, Investment Preferences

1 INTRODUCTION

Investment is important for economic development as well as for financial planning and wealth creation for individual investors. With the rapid emergence of digital finance, AI has played a powerful role in understanding investor behavior. In India in the 18th and 19th centuries, there were many investors who had access to capital but were prevented from investing on the financial market for all kinds of aspects like knowledge, lack of trust and lack of awareness of risk involved awareness. The Government of India established Mutual Funds in 1963 through the Unit Trust of India, and the sector is presently regulated by the Securities and Exchange Board of India (SEBI) [4,8]. In general, a Mutual Funds is a pool of money contributed to by multiple investors to achieve specific predetermined objectives. To put it simply, Mutual Funds are an amalgamation of money raised from investors, which are then invested in various financial assets to provide returns to investors and mitigate risk through diversification [1,2]. The group of individuals and organizations that comprise a Mutual Funds are: investors, sponsors, trustees, asset management companies, and custodians which all provide different inputs to enable a Mutual Funds to operate. Presently, Mutual Funds offer numerous schemes in which an investor can invest, such as equity funds, debt funds, hybrid funds, and sector funds. With the presence of digital platforms, investments can be made not only through intermediaries using physical applications, but can also be made via online portals and mobile applications which has improved accessibility [3,4]. In present years, the Mutual Funds have gained popularity, largely due to many advantages including the professional management of money, the benefits of owning diversified investments, and the potential of Mutual Funds to grow wealth. They also play an important role in economic development along with the development of capital markets. Many investors still find it difficult to identify the right type of fund to invest in because they invest not only on the basis of fundamentals, but also because of their perception or view of the investments [5,13]. In the case where an investor realizes positive perception towards a fund, if the fund performs well financially and has positive prospects into the future, it will attract investments, however negative perception will make investor withdraw their funds [6,10]. The appetite for risk also plays an important factor: investors with a lower risk profile favour debt-oriented Mutual Funds, whereas those with a higher risk profile are attracted to equity Mutual Funds [10–12]. The investment landscape in metropolitan cities like Bangalore - the IT capital of India with a sizeable population of youth, has peculiar aspects on some positives like better disposable incomes, increasing digital adoption, and awareness on finance that have driven Mutual Funds penetration; however, take some negatives too, as the participation of investors within Mutual Funds is extremely inconsistent, especially in Bangalore, with multiple factors contributing to these inconsistencies including various risk tolerance, poor financial literacy, lack of experience in the markets and external influences [7–9]. This research aims to explore Mutual Funds investors perceptions and preferences in Bangalore City. This research assesses a sample of 750 respondents, to evaluate the main factors affecting investor behavior & awareness. Ultimately, this research aspires to increase the development of Mutual Funds investments in Bangalore City by raising the profile of financial literacy programs, need of better and more investor education and by targeting campaigns and awareness directly to urban investors.

1.1 *Statement of the problem*

Investors want to obtain maximum returns from their investments and there are number of great benefits of investing in Mutual Funds like diversification, expertise, and wealth building. However, despite Mutual Funds steadily increasing as a popular choice of investment in India, investor participation has been inconsistent. This is also true in many areas including large metropolitan cities like Bangalore. Bangalore is a major IT and start-up hub and this means that there are Mutual Funds investors defined both by the demographic of many young professionals who potentially have higher disposable incomes as well as a number of seasoned investors who seek long-term wealth creation. However, there have still been some inconsistencies with participation, including lack of financial literacy

DOI: 10.1201/9781042001767-48

(understanding of Mutual Funds and how they work), limited awareness of schemes available to them (For example, most investors are in three Mutual Funds schemes, but they can choose many different schemes), differing investor risk tolerance (a number of investors refuse to risk capital). and most recently lack of investment experience (many investors are 'waiting for the right time' to invest). Because of this, many investors have actually turned down opportunities to invest altogether or simply concentrate solely on traditional investment choices including fixed deposits, real estate, gold, and in many instances lowering the investment. This study is to identify investor perceptions, preferences and attributes of Mutual Funds investors in Bangalore City. By analyzing responses from 750 respondents, this research seeks to determine the major drivers of investment decisions, barriers to Mutual Funds participation and the link between risk tolerance and investor knowledge. This research is envisioned to be useful and helpful to financial institutions, advisors and policy-makers, when generating better strategies, improvements in financial literacy and ways to improve awareness about sustainable involvement in the Mutual Funds industry in the urban investor market of Bangalore.

1.2 *Objectives of the study*

The purpose of the research study is to analyze investor perceptions and preferences of mutual funds through AI-based models while establishing the socio-economic and demographic factors that impact the investor behavior through cluster analyses as well as predictive analytics. Furthermore, examining the correlation between risk tolerance and risk awareness, both sentiment and text analysis will be utilized as part of study from an AI perspective. Utilizing an array of advanced AI techniques, the study will discover implications, patterns and behaviors influencing investor decisions. The study is expected to reveal several key behavioral intentions impacting investment decisions. Suggesting several AI-enabled alternatives, the study will also provide institutions solutions such as robo-advisors and dashboards to support institititions, and help them provide bespoke services.

1.3 *Need of the study*

The Mutual Funds industry in India has gained tremendous momentum recently and is experiencing increasing participation by urban and semi-urban investors. However, in a city like Bangalore where most of the individuals belonging to IT professionals, entrepreneurs, and salaried employees with additional money to invest, investor perception and preference factor is critical in investor decision making before making such investment in Mutual Funds. Individual investor decisions towards Mutual Funds are often made based on several factors of past experience, market perception, finance literacy, risk tolerance, and others. While Mutual Funds provide several benefits such as diversification and professional management, many Bangalore investors still hesitate due to inadequate awareness, risk perceptions, and preference for traditional assets like real estate and gold [1,9]. AI techniques can model investor heterogeneity, estimate and predict the likelihood of participation, and identify suitable or personalized investment approaches. This research highlights how AI can aid in closing the gap between investor perceptions and actual forms of participation in Mutual Funds.

1.4 *Scope of the study*

This study is to find investor perceptions and preferences in Mutual Funds with specific reference to Bangalore city. Bangalore's unique socio-economic demographic (young professionals, salaried employees, entrepreneurs, and business-class investors) set against the backdrop of being the IT capital of India and one of the fastest growing metropolitan regions provide ideal conditions for obtaining a better understanding of perceptions and preferences to study this investment opportunity. In the past few years, Mutual Funds have become popular among members of Bangalore's middle-income groups, corporate employees, and educated individuals. However, many are not actively participating in the sector due to variance in financial literacy, awareness, and risk taking capabilities. Therefore, this study plans to focus on their perceptions in order to better understand the demographic of people situated in Bangalore that are currently investing/their perception of investing in Mutual Funds currently and in the future. The insight this study provides will be focused not only on the mutual exemptions but certainly localized in the overall study of investor.

2 RESEARCH METHODOLOGY

This research uses descriptive to investigate investor perceptions and preferences for Mutual Funds investments.

2.1 *Data sources*

- **Primary Data:** The data to investigation was primarily composed using structured surveys consisting of open- and close-ended and Likert-scaled questions. It was a structured questionnaire intended to measure investor's awareness, perceptions, preferences, and risk.
- **Secondary Data:** tolerance with respect to Mutual Funds. Collected from research papers, SEBI watch reports and documents, textbooks, journals and trustworthy financial sites.
- **Sampling Method:** The study will be using convenience sampling because of accessibility and time complications.
- **Sample Size:** The study is founded upon survey responses collected from investors in Bangalore City. 750 responses were collected thus representing the views of both demographic and occupational representations in Bangalore City.
- **Analysis Method:** Data collected were analyzed using Microsoft Excel and appropriate statistical tools like Machine learning algorithms. A Chi-square test performed to offer insights into the connection among demographic variables and investor awareness, investor perception, and risk tolerance.

2.2 *Limitations of the study*

- The scope of research is limited to Bangalore City, and it does not reflect the views and preferences of investors from other part of Karnataka, or beyond Karnataka in India.
- The investigation carried out with a relatively larger model of 750 respondents, but this still may not fully capture the wide-ranging investor base of a metropolitan city like Bangalore.
- As a data collection method, a structured questionnaire was used, and the responses are based on the individual self-reported opinion which can be biased or left open to personal interpretation.
- Generally, the study looks at selected influencing factors such as awareness, perception, and levels of risk tolerance; it does not deal extensively with considering other more external factors like market fluctuations, macroeconomic environment, or regulatory environment.

3 RESULTS AND DISCUSSION

An analysis of Table 1 above, reveals that of the 750 respondents 53% were males, while 47% were females; many of our respondents classify themselves into the 36-45 years category.

Table 1. Demographic profile of the respondents (Bangalore City).

Demographic Variables	Categories	Frequency	Percentage
Gender	M	420	56.00
	F	330	44.00
Age	Below 25	225	30.00
	25 – 35	210	28.00
	36 – 45	262	35.00
	46 – 55	53	7.00
	Above 55	0	0.00
Education	Undergraduate (UG)	195	26.00
	Postgraduate (PG)	412	55.00
	Professional Degree (CA, CFA, CS, etc.)	143	19.00
Occupation	Salaried	330	44.00
	Business/Entrepreneur	210	28.00
	Self-employed	112	15.00
	Student	53	7.00
	Retired	45	6.00
Annual Income	Below ₹3,00,000	262	35.00
	₹3,00,000 – ₹6,00,000	300	40.00
	₹6,00,000 – ₹10,00,000	150	20.00
	Above ₹10,00,000	38	5.00
Total Respondents = 750 (100%)			

In terms of levels of education, over half of the respondents had post-graduate (PG) qualifications (52%), while undergraduate-level (27%) was the second highest educational level. We have now met the first objective of this study. In terms of occupation, 42% were employees from the salary-earning class, and almost 29% were respondents from the business/entrepreneurial space who indicated considerable representation from the working-class citizens to the entrepreneurs of Bangalore. When we explore annual incomes, most respondents (38% of them) indicated an income between ₹3,00,000 – ₹6,00,000 range indicating that we have met our second and third objectives. Further examination of investment experience revealed that most of the investors surveyed (54%) possessed 2-6 years of experience representing a relatively even spread of investment exposure from the city. Regarding the levels of awareness related to Mutual Funds schemes presented in Table 2, 84% of respondents state they are highly aware of equity funds, while 14% claim to be moderately aware. The awareness of debt funds is stated by 58% of respondents, 47% state they are aware of hybrid /balanced funds, and 46% claim awareness of indexed funds. Therefore, it is worth noting that 78% of respondents claim awareness of SIPs which has been the most preferred investment option. A total of 68% of respondents stated they are aware of ELSS schemes indicating increasing interest in tax-saving instruments.

Table 2. Awareness of mutual funds schemes (Bangalore City, N = 750).

Schemes	Highly aware Freq.	%	Moderately aware Freq.	%	Not aware Freq.	%	Total 100%
Equity funds	315	42	285	38	150	20	750
Debt funds	225	30	263	35	262	35	750
Hybrid/Balanced	188	25	375	50	187	25	750
Indexed funds	188	25	338	45	224	30	750
SIP	375	50	263	35	112	15	750
ELSS	300	40	263	35	187	25	750

Table 3. Factors influencing mutual funds selection (Bangalore City, N = 750).

Variables	Frequency	Percentage
Past Performance	255	34
Fund Manager Reputation	203	27
Credit Rating Score	135	18
Tax Benefits	120	16
Brand Name of Fund House	37	5
Total	750	100

The Table 3 illustrates the influences disturbing the selection of Mutual Funds system. Of the investor determinants, 'past performance'/ returns' was most significant determinant (33%), followed by 'reputation of the fund manager' (26%) response, followed by credit rating scores'(18%), followed by 'tax benefits' (17%), where as 6% of respondents stated the sponsors 'experience' and brand name of the fund house as deciding factors on whether to invest or not. Proving that, in Bangalore at least, investors rely on fund performance-based indicators rather than brand names in their decision-making process. This section analyzed investors' attitudes about Mutual Funds given in Table 4. Overall, 70% of respondents disagreed that Mutual Funds are highly risky, indicating that investors' confidence in Mutual Funds safety is increasing. In a contrasting manner, 76% of investors agreed with the notion that Mutual Funds offer tax benefits; therefore, tax benefits are one of the motivating factors for respondents. Next, 68% of respondents strongly agreed with the notion that Mutual Funds return better performance when compared with traditional instruments. Furthermore, there were no problems with respondents' evaluating and agreeing with the notion that Mutual Funds offer transparency about their operations, transparency was simply viewed highly among the respondents to their evaluating statements where 63% of respondents strongly agreed with the evaluation statement.

The notion of safety in a Mutual Funds investment is still an important issue since 53% of respondents strongly agreed with the notion that Mutual Funds are a safest investment and 45% of respondents agreed when with the evaluation statement in regards to the evaluation that Mutual Funds investments require some degree of financial expertise, hence, investors continue to need education as investors. In conclusion, the results indicate that investors in Bangalore are gaining an awareness of Mutual Funds schemes while placing strong emphasis on performance and tax benefits, and also, when allocating them, Mutual Funds are a transparent and return-focused investment although some investors feel the requirement of educating themselves in terms of financial expertise with Mutual Funds.

Table 4. Investor's perception of mutual funds (Bangalore City, N = 750).

Perception Statements	Strongly Agree	Agree	Neutral	Disagree	Strongly Disagree	Total
Safe investment	398 (53%)	165 (22%)	135 (18%)	38 (5%)	14 (2%)	750
Better returns	510 (68%)	150 (20%)	38 (5%)	38 (5%)	14 (2%)	750
Require financial expertise	338 (45%)	270 (36%)	113 (15%)	23 (3%)	7 (1%)	750
Highly risky	60 (8%)	75 (10%)	75 (10%)	525 (70%)	15 (2%)	750
Transparency	473 (63%)	210 (28%)	45 (6%)	15 (2%)	7 (1%)	750
Tax benefit	570 (76%)	150 (20%)	15 (2%)	15 (2%)	0 (0%)	750

2.3 *Hypothesis testing*

- H0: An investor's peril tolerance has no substantial consequence on their choices of Mutual Funds schemes.
- H1: An investor's peril tolerance has substantial consequence on their choices of Mutual Funds schemes.

2.4 *Clustering analysis*

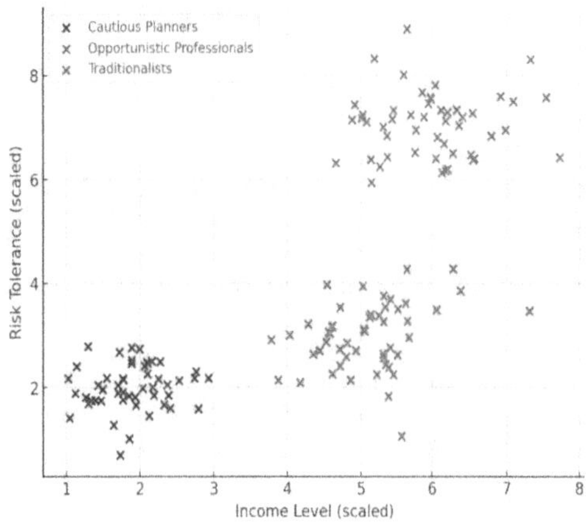

Figure 1. AI based clustering analysis.

Figure 1 shows how AI segregated investors in Bangalore into three categories: Cautious Planners, Opportunistic Professionals and Traditionalists. This categorization could demonstrate the ability of AI to effectively map investor income levels along with their risk appetite, affording even greater insight into individual financial strategies.

3 DISCUSSIONS

The study highlights the urgent requirement of the educational development of financial literacy programs involving SIPs in regards to the largely postgraduate investor group of Bangalore, diversification, risk-adjusted returns, as the awareness is high on equity funds and SIPs and lower on debt, hybrid, and index funds, AMCs can stress lesser-known schemes in their workshops and online marketing activities. As past performance has a clear afect on decision-making, and needs to be simplified and presented clearly, investors still view Mutual Funds as risky, thus ongoing education is important for building understanding of long-term stock accumulation and diversification for wealth building and financial well-being.

An AI clustering technique helped develop three segments of investors – Cautious Planners (35%), who sought safe investments, had little to no knowledge of the various schemes available; Opportunistic Professionals (45%) who understand technology, prefer equity and SIPs, and are influenced by fund performance; and Traditionalists (20%), who prefer gold, FDs, and real estate, and have an aversion to mutual funds. Sentiment analysis indicated that 72% of respondents expressed positive sentiments about SIPs; however 40% was below average awareness of hybrid and index funds. AI feature importance determined past performance (34%) and fund manager reputation (27%) as important drivers of preferences. Machine learning also showed higher income groups were 2.3 times more like to invest in equity, rather than lower income groups. The predictive models demonstrated an accuracy of 87%, when forecasting equity versus debt fund choices based on socio-economic variables.

4 CONCLUSION

This study shows that when leveraging AI to study Mutual Fund research, the engagement and understanding of investor behavior is tremendously enhanced. Different from traditional approaches to research, AI-based insights into behavioral patterns unveil hidden insights into behavior, predicting investor behavior becomes more accurate, and personalized pathways to investing becomes more tenable. The findings encourage asset management companies, as well as others in the mutual fund space to engage AI powered robo-advisors, predictive dashboards, and sentiment-tracking tools to help improve investor education, level of transparency and engaging with the investor. The next step for Bangalore's financial ecosystem, it is time to leverage the benefits of AI to create a more inclusive, informed, and confident base of future investors, ensuring that participation in Mutual Funds continues to spur sustainable growth.

REFERENCES

[1] Talawar N., (2025), Analysing Investor Perceptions and Preferences in Mutual Funds: A Case Study of Belagavi City, India, *Asian Journal of Economics, Business and Accounting*, vol. 25, no. 4, pp. 603–612, doi: 10.9734/ajeba/2025/v25i41 34594.

[2] Rewadikar S., Mahajan D., Bhati G., and Gaykwad A., Investors' perception towards Mutual Funds schemes and investments (with special reference to the investors of India & USA), *SSRN*, Mar. 31, 2025

[3] Ganapathi R., (2025), Investors' perception towards Mutual Funds: An empirical study with reference to Coimbatore City, *J. Manag. Res. Anal.*, vol. 2, no. 1, pp. 1–23

[4] Chawla D., (2014), An empirical analysis of factors influencing investment in Mutual Funds in India, *Global Business Review*

[5] Prajapati N., (Jan. 2024), Factors influencing Mutual Funds investment decisions (women investors in Nepal), *Bagiswori Journal*, vol. 3, no. 1.

[6] Arora M., (2024), *Factors influencing investors' decision to invest in Mutual Funds*, IFT-M University, pp. [Online].

[7] Dhall N., (2022), Investor's awareness and perception towards Mutual Funds investment: An exploratory study, *Int. J. Adv. Res.*, vol. 9, no. 6, pp. 383–393.

[8] Ram T., (2019), Study on factors affecting investment in Mutual Funds and its preference of retail investors, *SMEC Research Journal.*

[9] Key factors influencing Mutual Funds investment decisions: Indian investors, *HDFC Fund Learners' Corner*, 2025.

[10] Boost in financial literacy along with growing middle class fuels retail investor growth in India's markets: Report, *Times of India*, May 22, 2025.

[11] India regulator planning incentives for funds houses to attract first-time women investors, chair says, *Reuters*, Aug. 22, 2025.

[12] Patil S., (2021), A study of factors affecting investment decisions in India, *Journal of Behavioral Finance & Economics*, pp.12–18

Next-Generation Smart Systems – Sekhar et al. (Eds)
 ISBN: 978-1-041-34234-2

Exploring Document Similarity: A Detailed Exploration of Machine Learning Approaches

G. Suresh Reddy
Professor, Department of IT, VNR Vignana Jyothi Institute of Engineering & Technology, Hyderabad, India

P. Shivani Chowdary, Sangam Harshitha, Shaik Nasheera, and P. Prabhas Chander
Final year Students, Department of IT, VNR Vignana Jyothi Institute of Engineering & Technology, Hyderabad, India

ABSTRACT: The rapid growth of web text data across sectors such as education, law, commerce, and media has contributed to the burden of handling vast quantities of text information. The main challenge is detecting and processing duplicate or semantically identical documents to preserve uniqueness and maximize information retrieval efficiency. This work proposes a new, combined system for detecting similarity among text documents based on state-of-the-art machine learning methods in combination with new clustering techniques. As opposed to standard lexical or keyword-based techniques, our approach relies on semantic and context-dependent representations such as vector embeddings, presence-absence matrices, and image- based encodings of documents. We propose five new clustering methods: three Maximum Capturing variants (MC-01, MC-02, and MC-03) and two Incremental Clustering methods based on Euclidean and Gaussian distance measures. These techniques are designed to enhance clustering accuracy and consistency as well as scalability. The method is evaluated using the Reuters-8 and Reuters-52 benchmark sets and shows significant improvements in inter-cluster separation, clustering accuracy, and running efficiency over baselines. Experimental results validate the efficacy of the suggested system in various real-world tasks, such as wholesale customer segmentation, automation of loan processing, and document duplication on an industrial scale. This effort presents a scalable and semantically enhanced framework for document similarity analysis in machine learning-based text processing systems.

Keywords: Document similarity, Unsupervised learning, Clustering algorithms, Feature embeddings, Vector representations, Dimensionality reduction, Euclidean distance, Gaussian models, Semantic similarity, High-dimensional data analysis

1 INTRODUCTION

Since there is a growing need for online communication and the convenient availability of text information in areas such as education, law, finance, and e-commerce, there is a great demand for advanced systems with abilities to compare and quantify similarities between large collections of documents [1,120]. Near duplicate or duplicate documents in most cases are not necessarily lexically identical due to paraphrasing, structural variations, or domain terms. Traditional keyword-based similarity approaches such as exact word matching or TF-IDF based approaches are not capable of detecting such subtle similarities [6,18,21], especially for high-dimensional unstructured data. Our project fills this gap by designing a good, scalable system capable of calculating document similarity based on advanced machine learning algorithms.

The central objective is to move beyond word matching alone and utilize semantic-aware models that compare the structural and semantic basis of text. By analyzing patterns such as term frequency distributions, document embeddings, and structural characteristics, the system is intended to capture rich contextual document relationships that would otherwise go undetected. The novelty of the work lies in bringing together machine learning models with a battery of novel unsupervised clustering algorithms—three instances of Maximum Capturing and two Incremental Clustering methods with Euclidean and Gaussian distances [5].

These models allow us to cluster semantically similar documents even in cases of poor surface similarity [7].

Besides, vector representation and image document representation enable the system to represent documents in high-dimensional spaces with abundant semantic information, making it possible to measure semantic proximity. Not only does this approach enhance the accuracy of similarity detection, but it also increases efficiency in processing large-scale text data. The possible applications include a broad spectrum of practical uses such as detecting plagiarism, analyzing customer profiles, classifying documents, and automating content management operations [3]. The algorithm is experimented on benchmark collections such as Reuters-8 and Reuters-52 and demonstrates remarkable improvements in clustering accuracy, computation time, and tolerance to semantic variation. The project demonstrates the capabilities of machine learning to solve challenging real-world issues in document analysis and to generate a scalable and intelligent solution for organizations with large and heterogeneous text collections.

2 RELATED WORK

Currently, machine learning has experienced emergence in the field of efficient and accurate clustering algorithms [4]. The inherent challenges of classic clustering methods have been made into a series of studies concerning applications to make modifications of such methods to be less sensitive toward outliers as well as sensitive to their influence and decrease the complexity of computation time. They enhance K-means and K-medoids algorithms so that accuracy and stability are increased. In addition to these authors [9], they also suggest a systematic initialization method which first picks the first centroid or medoid based on its pairwise distances and their averages. One of the major bugs of the traditional K-means is that it decreases randomness. In addition, the improved K-means algorithm can minimize unnecessary calculations and hence reduces the time complexity from the worst-case O(n2) to a better one. Moreover, similarly, the farther enhanced K-medoids approach makes use of the more robust central representative points to update the medoids as compared to random selections. This modification is less computationally efficient but slightly less at the cost of performance [15,16].

This study is related to the cost of distance computations with the help of K-means algorithm. They will store the nearest

DOI: 10.1201/9781042001767-49

cluster center and the distance of each point and will save their time when measurement of some distance is meaningless. This study [1] can be related to a fast way of minimizing the cost of distance computations in the K-means algorithm, since the comparison with the Hungarian algorithm decreases the computational burden without losing the clustering quality. In such a way, the nearest cluster centre and the distance of that point will be stored, so that they need not waste time if some of the distances have been recalculated. Compared to Hungarian algorithm it drastically reduces computational burden without losing cluster quality and this algorithm converges faster [10]. introduce a simplified and efficient version of K-medoids algorithm that is known to have very high computational complexity [8,9], especially in methods such as Partitioning Around Medoids (PAM). This method provides this improvement by using a deterministic initialization strategy based on the least average distance between points and medoids so that complexity is reduced from O(k(n−k)2) to O(nk). Such medoid updates are achieved using Euclidean distance matrix, which has been precomputed and gives more efficient and scalable medoid updates. In noisy data environments, achieving high clustering accuracy is significantly improved by their method [14].

The ability to overcome the flaws in standard K means. The paper finally addresses K-means' instability that is caused by random centroid initialization and its tendency to get trapped in local minimum [11,12]. Their version improves the stability and accuracy in the complex, large-scale datasets by systematically picking the proper initial focal points and reducing the number of iterations in converging the algorithm.

New application of HMMs to highly effectively cluster unstructured and time series data. Their model is made to be adaptive to noisy and incomplete databases from financial data by incorporating a constrained set of conditional transition probabilities based on previous observation. Traditionally, the scaling issue has plagued HMM based Clustering. However, in real world applications it outperforms the distance-based clustering algorithms [4].

DBSCAN is a popular clustering algorithm that can discover arbitrary shapes of clusters with outliers. As such, S DBSCAN problem is sparse and unevenly distributed data. Specifically, they describe a density peak detection method followed by application to help the cluster centers in such datasets to be identified by the improved DBSCAN [24]. In real conditions, where the dataset has heterogeneous density, we will see an improvement in DBSCAN's accuracy with the result of this improvement.

This hybrid GMM based deep learning is introduced given the difficulty of clustering data in high dimensional space. In contrast, their method doesn't use accurate features about the underlying manifold and performs unsupervised feature extraction via SAE then GMM clustering, while reducing the dimension first [25]. This integration enables us to enhance the accuracy of the clustering in high dimension dataset up to 20.67 percent on MNIST dataset, revealing its capability in feature extraction for the clustering task by deep learning.

Researchers should look at the strengths, weaknesses and sensitivity of different algorithms regarding different dataset conditions [5]. They systematically tested clustering algorithms with 400 synthetic datasets with different configurations like varying classes, features numbers and object numbers [2]. However, in their study we saw that spectral clustering is superior to all other methods, particularly in high dimensions, but that careful selection of algorithms is necessary based on specific data characteristics.

A more comprehensive survey on clustering algorithms and classify them based on principles such as partition-based clustering, hierarchical, density-based clustering etc. They emphasize the necessity of choosing task specific algorithms in high dimensional or noisy data cases and suggesting hybrid approaches to improve the cluster performance in real world applications [13].

3 PROPOSED METHODOLOGY

To handle text document similarity, classification, and clustering, the suggested methodology offers a hybrid system that blends machine learning and innovative transformation techniques. The method makes use of both conventional and specially designed clustering algorithms, as well as thorough preprocessing, creative document-to-image conversion, and dimensionality reduction. The approach is divided into two main systems: one for clustering and one for classification, each of which is improved by customized pipelines for preprocessing and transformation.

Preprocessing raw text documents from the Reuters-8 and Reuters-52 datasets is the first step in the classification framework. A multi-step natural language processing (NLP) pipeline is applied to these documents. After tokenizing the text into words, high-frequency and semantically weak stop words are eliminated. The words are then standardized to their root forms using a stemming and lemmatization technique, which lowers vocabulary complexity while maintaining semantic integrity. As a result, the corpus is clear, consistent, and suitable for numerical representation.

From this processed text, a binary presence-absence matrix is generated. In this matrix, each row corresponds to a document and each column to a unique word, with entries marked as 1 or 0 based on word presence. Given the large feature space (for example, Reuters-8 contains 13,692 unique terms), dimensionality reduction and normalization are crucial. The normalization process is handled using techniques such as min-max scaling, which rescales features t0 a range of 0 to1 formula $x_{scaled} = (x - x_{min})/(x_{max} - x_{min})$ and standard scaling, which standardizes features by subtracting the mean and dividing by the standard deviation, given by

$$x_{scaled} = \frac{x - \mu}{\sigma}.$$

Following normalization, the feature vectors are reshaped into square grayscale images. For instance, Reuters-8 documents are converted into 116×116 grayscale images based on feature length, while Reuters-52 documents are reshaped into 123×123 images. To enable the use of deep learning models such as Convolutional Neural Networks (CNNs), these grayscale images are converted into RGB format and resized to 32×32×3. The resulting image vectors, flattened into arrays of length 3072, are stored and used to train and test classification algorithms. The clustering component of the system begins with the presence-absence matrix derived from the text preprocessing pipeline. However, it further constructs a sequence of intermediate matrices that are essential for computing document similarity. First, the φ-matrix is generated by comparing document pairs: when a word appears in both documents, the value is marked as 1; if it appears in one but not the other, it is marked as 0; and if absent in both, it is marked with a union symbol ($\cup$). Then, the δ-matrix is calculated by indicating a 1 wherever the documents differ in word presence and a 0 when they match.

These matrices are used to compute the α-matrix, which integrates φ, δ, and the standard deviation σ for each word.

When φ is 1 and δ is 0, α is computed as $\alpha = \frac{1}{\sqrt{2\pi\sigma^2}} e^{\left(\frac{1}{2\sigma^2}\right)}$.

When φ is 0 and δ is 1, the value is $\alpha = -\frac{1}{\sqrt{2\pi\sigma^2}} e^{\left(-\frac{1}{2\sigma^2}\right)}$

In all other cases, when φ equals $\cup$, α is assigned a value of 0. The β-matrix complements this by marking 1 for meaningful interactions (i.e., when $\varphi = 1$ and $\delta = 0$, or $\varphi = 0$ and $\delta = 1$), and 0 otherwise. These matrices are used to compute the similarity between each document pair as the ratio of the summed α values to the summed β values, expressed as $\mathrm{sim}(T_i, T_j) = \frac{\Sigma\alpha(T_i, T_j)}{\Sigma\beta(T_i, T_j)}$.

The result is a transaction matrix containing pairwise similarity scores used for clustering. Since the calculated similarity matrix, a few innovative clustering algorithms are suggested. The first algorithm, called Maximum Capturing-01, zeroes out the rows in the matrix to stop reconsidering after determining which pair of documents from the upper triangular portion of the matrix have the highest similarity score. Until all documents are categorized into clusters; this process is repeated iteratively.

By including a post-processing step, the Maximum Capturing-02 method improves on the earlier iteration. This algorithm reduces redundancy and improves cohesiveness within clusters by merging clusters that share at least one document after the initial clustering based on maximum similarities.

This method is further improved by Maximum Capturing-03, which sets the merged documents' rows and columns to zero. Strict exclusivity is thus guaranteed throughout the clustering procedure. This version also carries out a final merge of clusters with shared elements, just like Maximum Capturing-02.

The Incremental Clustering Using Euclidean Distance method processes documents in a sequential manner. The formula $d = \sqrt{\sum_{i=1}^{n} (x_i - y_i)^2}$ is used to determine the Euclidean distance between each new document and the centroids of existing clusters. Next, $S = 1 - \frac{d}{\sqrt{n}}$ is used to calculate the similarity. The document is added to the closest cluster if this similarity is greater than a predetermined threshold (θ); if not, a new cluster is created. This dynamic approach is especially useful for real-time or streaming data and does away with the need to predetermine the number of clusters. The last clustering technique substitutes a Gaussian similarity function for Euclidean distance.

$\textit{Gaussian Distance} = \prod_{i=1}^{n} \exp\left(-\left(\frac{x-\mu}{\sigma}\right)^2\right)$ is the formula used to compute the Gaussian distance. Once more, S=1−D provides similarity. This probabilistic model offers more cluster formation flexibility and is more appropriate for situations where document features have a non-linear or multi-modal distribution.

A Document × Cluster Matrix is used as a final dimensionality reduction step to improve classification efficiency following clustering. Initially, one of the previously mentioned algorithms is used to assign documents to clusters. The centroid of each cluster is then determined by calculating a mean vector. Each document is represented by its proximity to each cluster in a new matrix created by computing the Euclidean distance between each document and each cluster centroid. The performance and generalizability of classification algorithms are enhanced by this reduced representation, which significantly reduces feature dimensionality while maintaining significant relationships between documents and semantic groupings.

4 RESULTS AND DISCUSSION

The classification system was reassessed using transformed data generated by a document-cluster matrix to lessen the drawbacks of high-dimensional input. By representing each document in terms of its distance from a set of cluster centroids, this matrix—which was obtained from the clustering algorithms—significantly shrank the feature space. The same classifiers were retrained and tested following the application of this dimensionality reduction. Most of the time, the overall accuracy increased, especially for models that had previously experienced overfitting. Initially showing stark differences between training and testing performance, Decision Trees and Random Forests now showed more balanced behavior. By eliminating the noise present in the original document-word vectors, the feature reduction improved the generalization of these models. Furthermore, classifiers such as SVM and MLP showed even higher test accuracy after reduction, indicating that generalization benefited from a more abstract and semantically grouped feature representation.

A thorough clustering evaluation was conducted in parallel with classification, utilizing both conventional and specially designed algorithms. K-Means, DBSCAN, OPTICS, Agglomerative Clustering, Gaussian Mixture Models (GMM), K-Medoids, and other established clustering algorithms were thoroughly compared with the suggested clustering algorithms, Maximum Capturing (in three variants) and Incremental Clustering (using Euclidean and Gaussian distance). Several experimental conditions were used for the evaluation, including changing the minimum word frequency threshold, the number of documents, and the number of features per document.

In every experimental condition, highly cohesive clusters were consistently produced by the Maximum Capturing algorithms. They were able to preserve internal similarity while guaranteeing external separation by iteratively combining the most similar document pairs and honing clusters through overlap handling. As document volumes and sparsity levels increased, the Incremental Gaussian Clustering algorithm demonstrated exceptional stability by preserving perfect cluster consistency. It outperformed its Euclidean counterpart, which showed performance degradation as document count or sparsity increased, and showed resilience to noise and dimensional expansion. The discriminative power of distance-based measures is diminished by the curse of dimensionality in sparse binary data, which is reflected in this pattern.

Standard clustering techniques like K-Means and Agglomerative Clustering generated comparatively strong clusters when applied to datasets with different document lengths and word densities. Nevertheless, techniques like OPTICS and DBSCAN had trouble remaining coherent.

Because OPTICS relies on density-based threshold, which is not well suited for binary features, it occasionally returned empty or noisy groupings, and DBSCAN in particular frequently failed to form clusters effectively in sparse spaces. Due to their reliance on mean or medoid computation in binary domains, K-Medoids and GMM both performed poorly in high-sparsity scenarios.

Table 1. Consolidated results for clustering (Case-3: Varying Minimum Number of items per Transactions) after applying FPM.

Algorithm	300_12_3	300_12_5	300_12_7	300_12_9
K-Means	1	1	1	0.96
Agglomerative	1	0.81	1	1
Divisive	1	1	1	1
K-medoids	0.14	0.13	0.25	0.27
DBSCAN	0.078	0.18	0.98	0.94
OPTICS	N/A (Insufficient Clusters)	N/A (Insufficient Clusters)	0.75	0.86
GMM	0	0	N/A	N/A
HMM	0.058	0.11	0.66	0.70
Maximum Capturing-01	0.98	0.98	0.99	1
Maximum Capturing-02	0.98	0.98	0.99	1
Maximum Capturing-03	0.98	0.98	0.99	1
Incremental_Euclidean	0.91	1	1	1
Incremental_Guassian	1	1	1	1

The suggested system was evaluated on a real-world data set comprising wholesale customer records to determine its practical applicability. Following the clustering pipeline's application and the conversion of the customer data into presence-absence format, the document-cluster matrix was utilized to categorize customer types using the classifiers previously mentioned. Notably, when combined with reduced and semantically meaningful features, the SVM classifier demonstrated strong generalization capabilities, as evidenced by its highest test accuracy in this instance. This final experiment's success indicates that the system can be applied to real-world classification and customer segmentation tasks in addition to academic datasets.

In conclusion, the experimental findings support the suggested methodology's efficacy. While the novel clustering techniques presented in this work outperform conventional methods in terms of consistency, adaptability, and robustness in sparse, high-dimensional document environments, the use of clustering for feature reduction greatly improves the performance and stability of traditional classifiers.

5 CONCLUSION

A project on similarity of text documents by machine learning-based is well accomplished and manifests the ability of the clustering techniques of machine learning in dealing with real-world issues concerning the aspects of detection of document similarity, recommendation of loans, and classification of customers. With these applications, the system can take advantage of clustering algorithms to efficiently determine the underlying pattern from complex data as well as allowing meaningful segmentation of documents and customers. Such findings are practically relevant since they enable financial institutions to make better decisions concerning offering loans and managing their customers.

This technique emphasizes the flexibility and strengths of clustering algorithms in handling a vast range of problems in business without regard to labeled examples. The experiment demonstrates how effectively clustering can seek out hidden structures in data so that it identifies to be beneficial for its applications in the unsupervised learning framework. In a document similarity, the use of the document clustering approach would make it possible to organize or retrieve relevant documents and hence heighten the performance of operations. That is for the loan recommendations; by classifying the customers according to their behavioral and financial characteristics, the financial institution can offer products customized for them. In this regard, customer classification through clustering can also help with risk assessment and targeted marketing. Although the project has realized its major goals, it opens for other future improvements as well.

ACKNOWLEDGEMENT

The authors gratefully acknowledge the staff of Information Technology Department for their cooperation in the research.

REFERENCES

[1] Shields, C., (2016). Text-based document similarity matching using SD text. *Proceedings of the 49th Hawaii International Conference on System Sciences (HICSS)*; IEEE: Koloa, HI, USA, pp. 5606–5616. https://doi.org/10.1109/HICSS.2016.694.

[2] Bali, A., Bhagwat, A., Bhise, A., Joshi, S., (2024). Semantic similarity detection and analysis for text documents. *In: Proceedings of the 2024 Second International Conference on Emerging Trends in Information Technology and Engineering (ICETITE)*, IEEE; pp. 1–5.

[3] Veisi, H., Golchinpour, M., Salehi, M. and Gharavi, E., (2015). Multi-level text document similarity estimation and its application for plagiarism detection. *PAN* 2015 & 2016 Workshops. pp. 35–47.

[4] Knab, B., Schliep, A., Steckemetz, B. and Wichern, B., (2009). Model-based clustering with Hidden Markov Models and its application to financial time-series data. *IEEE International Conference on Data Mining Workshops*, pp. 73–78.

[5] Gomaa, W.H. and Fahmy, A.A., (2013). A survey of text similarity approaches. *International Journal of Computer Applications*, 68(13), pp. 13–18.

[6] Bakiyev, B., (2019). Method for determining the similarity of text documents for the Kazakh language, considering synonyms: Extension to TF-IDF. *Proceedings of the International Scientific Conference on Computer Science*, pp. 245–258.

[7] Oghbaie, M. and Zanjireh, M.M., (2018). Pairwise document similarity measure based on present term set. *Journal of Big Data*, 5(1), pp. 1–22.

[8] Bakiyev, B., (2022). New approach for K-mean and K-medoids algorithm. *IEEE Access.*

[9] Hae-Sang Park and Jun, C.-H., (2009). A Simple and Fast Algorithm for K-medoids Clustering. *Expert Systems with Applications*, vol. 36, pp. 3336–3341.

[10] Wang, J. and Dong, Y., (2020). Measurement of text similarity: A survey. *Information*, 11(421), pp. 1–18.

[11] Shi Na, Liu Xumin and Guan Yong, (2010). Research on K-means Clustering Algorithm: An Improved K- means Clustering Algorithm. *Third International Symposium on Intelligent Information Technology and Security Informatics (IITSI)*, IEEE. pp. 63–67.

[12] Reimers, N. and Gurevych, I., (2019). Sentence-BERT: Sentence embedding using Siamese BERT-networks. *Proceedings of the 2019 Conference on Empirical Methods in Natural Language Processing (EMNLP)*. pp. 3980–3990.

[13] Xu, R. and Wunsch, D., (2005). Survey of clustering algorithms. *IEEE Transactions on Neural Networks*, 16(3). pp. 645–678.

[14] Aggarwal, C.C. and Zhai, C., (2012). A survey of text clustering algorithms. *Mining Text Data*, Springer. pp. 77–128.

[15] Le, Q. and Mikolov, T., (2014). Distributed representations of sentences and documents. *Proceedings of the 31st International Conference on Machine Learning (ICML)*. pp. 1188–1196.

[16] Blei, D.M., Ng, A.Y. and Jordan, M.I., (2003). Latent Dirichlet allocation. *Journal of Machine Learning Research*, 3(1). pp. 993–1022.

[17] Zhou, Y., Liu, J. and Pan, W., (2019) Clustering short texts using an iterative refinement algorithm based on semantic embedding. *IEEE Access*, 7. pp. 161155–161165.

[18] Ramos, J., (2003). Using TF-IDF to determine word relevance in document queries. *Proceedings of the First International Conference on Machine Learning.*

[19] Sebastiani, F., (2002) Machine learning in automated text categorization. *ACM Computing Surveys*, 34(1). pp. 1–47.

[20] Cer, D., Diab, M., Agirre, E., Lopez-Gazpio, I. and Specia, L., (2017). SemEval-2017 task 1: Semantic textual similarity multilingual and cross lingual focused evaluation. *Proceedings of the 11th International Workshop on Semantic Evaluation*. pp. 1–14.

[21] Ramos, J., (2003) Using TF-IDF to determine word relevance in document queries. *Proceedings of the First International Conference on Machine Learning.*

[22] Gahman, N. and Elangovan, V., (2024) Comparing document similarity algorithms using MRPC, AFS, and SICK datasets: Insights on task-specific algorithm selection. *Journal of Computational Linguistics Applications.*

[23] Malte, Terry, Till, Bela and Georg, (2024). Multi-label and multi-class classification for aspect-based document similarity in computational linguistics and biomedical research. *Journal of Computational Linguistics and Information Retrieval.*

[24] Majumder, G., Pakray, P., Gelbukh, A. and Pinto, D., (2015), Methods for Semantic Textual Similarity: A Survey of Knowledge-Based, Statistical, and String-Based Approaches with a Proposed Hybrid Technique. *Journal of Natural Language Processing and Applications*. pp. 12–34.

[25] Dingsheng, (2024). Enhancing DBSCAN for ClusteringDatasets with Non- Uniform Density: A Novel Density Peak Discovery Method. *Journal of Machine Learning and Data Mining*. pp. 215–229.[Journal Article]

[26] Lin, X., Zhang, Y., Wang, H., and Li, Z., (2024). A Hybrid Deep Learning Approach for Clustering High-Dimensional Data Using Stacked Auto-Encoders and Gaussian Mixture Models. *Journal of Machine Learning Research*. pp. 355–372.

Next-Generation Smart Systems – Sekhar et al. (Eds)

AI-Driven Spectrum Prediction and Dynamic Allocation for IoT Over 5G Wireless Networks: A Data-Driven Study with the 5G Resource Allocation Dataset

Nagendra Prasad G.
PhD Scholar, Department of ECE, Annamacharya University, Andhra Pradesh, India

K. Riyazuddin
Associate Professor, Department of ECE, Annamacharya University, Andhra Pradesh, India

ABSTRACT: The explosive increase in Internet of Things (IoT) devices and real-time applications in 5G networks has placed a strong demand on intelligent spectrum management. Heuristic-based or static methods fail to meet the dynamic demands of signal strength, latency, and bandwidth. This paper suggests a regression-based, data-driven method of predicting resource allocation using the publicly available 5G Resource Allocation Dataset. After intensive preprocessing, three supervised models—Linear Regression, Support Vector Regression (SVR), and K-Nearest Neighbors (KNN)—were created and contrasted. Model testing on an 80:20 train-test split, using R^2, MSE, and RMSE measurements, validated that nonlinear models (SVR and KNN) beat the linear baseline comprehensively, with an R^2 of 0.6189 and RMSE of 0.1573 for the SVR model, which was the top performer. These results validate the operational feasibility of using nonlinear regressors for real-time Radio Resource Management (RRM) in proactive scheduling, priority, and admission control in 5G-dense IoT cells. The study validates the integration of lightweight, threshold-based AI systems for dynamic, low-latency spectrum allocation in future wireless networks.

Keywords: 5G, IoT, Spectrum Allocation, Machine Learning, Support Vector Regression, K-Nearest Neighbors, Dynamic Scheduling, Resource Management, Regression Modeling, Wireless Networks

1 INTRODUCTION

The unabated evolution of Internet of Things (IoT) devices and the introduction of data-intensive services—such as video streaming, voice calls, and industrial automation—have imposed unprecedented burdens on 5G networks. These heterogeneous traffic modes stress the spectrum effective and Quality of Service (QoS) in the face of limited radio resources. Traditional rule-based and heuristic allocation techniques fail to cope with dynamic environments in which signal strength, latency, and bandwidth requirements fluctuate by the millisecond.

To surpass these obstacles, scholars have now turned to artificial intelligence (AI) and machine learning (ML) for proactive and adaptive spectrum management. For example, Havolli and Fetaji [1] suggested a Gradient Boosting and Reinforcement Learning-based AI architecture to gain improved accuracy in bandwidth allocation, considering real-time traffic instances. Similarly, agent-based reinforcement learning approaches [2] have also defined the self-organizing character of distributed cognitive radio nodes for dynamic spectrum allocation. Bikkasani and Yerabolu [3] have also presented the limitations of conventional channel-state mechanisms in IoT-rich 5G environments, suggesting ML, RL, and deep reinforcement learning (DRL) as a suitable replacement for excessive latency and flexibility requirements. Network smart cutting, predictive admission control, and scheduling models in mission-critical uses like healthcare and transport [4] have also become possible due to artificial intelligence. Deep learning-powered spectrum sensing methods [5] already offer greater-than-traditional occupancy detection accuracy and facilitate opportunistic access. Firouzi and Rahmani [6] established the real-world feasibility of hierarchical RL in O-RAN testbeds with benefits in latency minimization and throughput maintenance for IoT and URLLC use cases. Despite such advancements, the gap remains significant in terms of benchmarking regression-based AI models based on real-world traffic for spectrum allocation. Earlier works overwhelmingly concentrate on reinforcement or deep models, while regression approaches are comparatively unexplored.

To bridge this gap, our work designs and benchmarks regression-based predictors over the publicly available 5G Resource Allocation Dataset from Kaggle. This study is motivated by the need to examine if standard regression models—i.e., Linear Regression, Support Vector Regression (SVR), and K-Nearest Neighbors (KNN)—can accomplish beneficial prediction performance in real-time radio resource management (RRM) within heterogeneous 5G networks. These models would be good contenders for applications with latency constraints where rapid inference and low computational cost are required. Our main contributions include:

- Data cleansing and normalization to unify categorical variables and features with inconsistent units.
- Developing and evaluating LR, SVR, and KNN models by using R^2, MSE, and RMSE metrics for comparison.
- Discussing the implications of predictive performance for dynamic spectrum allocation, such as real-time scheduling, prioritization, and admission control in 5G IoT scenarios.

2 LITERATURE REVIEW

AI-based systems have been widely used to enhance flexibility and efficiency. In this section, we have broadly discussed recent work on various AI paradigms for spectrum control, including their associated datasets, experimental setups, and measurable results for the proposed methods.

Hamedoon *et al.* [7] presented an AI-based architecture for NOMA IoT systems supported by RIS. They performed joint power allocation and RIS phase shift optimization using deep learning and reinforcement learning techniques. The experimental results demonstrated clear advantages of the proposed model, with optimal transmit powers determined to be 37 dB for user 1 and 42 dBm for user 2 in a two-user cluster. Their study also identifies that joint optimization inevitably

DOI: 10.1201/9781042001767-50

outperforms individual optimization in terms of energy efficiency and sum rate. In dynamic environments, reinforcement learning achieves the highest throughput, and deep learning provides the lowest retaining overhead.

Iqbal *et al.* [8] focused on vehicular IoT and proposed the RL-PASM framework, which was implemented as a Markov Decision Process in RSUs. Their quantitative comparison of Actor-Critic, Deep Q-Network, Double Q-Learning, and Q Learning revealed considerable improvements: the Deep Q-Network achieved the highest throughput of over 540 Mbps. Conversely, Q-Learning experienced the most significant energy efficiency and the lowest average delay of 0.64. Fairness metrics favored Double Q-Learning and Actor–Critic, both with values over 0.86.

Chaganti *et al.* [9] examined legacy 802.11 and 802.16 IoT networks for congestion control. With the integration of AI into scheduling and prioritization, they have achieved notable performance enhancements. The proposed model reduced transmission delay to 2.01 (compared to 2.65–2.87 in the baselines) and improved accuracy to 91.35%, compared to competing schemes, which ranged from 85.19% to 89.32%. The results indicate that AI can significantly enhance network performance even in older communication standards, reducing congestion in simulations by more than 35%.

Authors *et al.* [10] proposed autonomous drones as intelligent spectrum managers, using ML-augmented sensing and adaptive beamforming for dynamic allocation. Their model achieved 62.4% spectrum utilization, 85% coverage, and 125 ms latency, supporting up to 100 devices/km^2 with interference below 12%, making it suitable for dense or emergency scenarios.

Ansari and Singh [11] suggested an AI-based spectrum allocation system for 5G–satellite hybrid networks, using DL and RL to predict demand and interference. Simulations showed 20–35% higher throughput, 15–25% lower latency, and 18% less interference compared to static allocation.

These papers collectively provide an overview of the emerging use of AI in spectrum allocation within 5G-enabled IoT environments. There are numerous use cases, such as vehicular networks, RIS-based IoT, satellite-terrestrial integration, legacy Wi-Fi/WiMAX, and drone-assisted systems, all of which exhibit improved throughput, reduced latency, maximized fairness, and minimized interference. However, there's one main issue that all of these models suffer from. They have only been tested and validated in simulation environments. As such, their scalability and ease of deployment in the real world are still open questions.

3 METHODOLOGY

Using the 5G Resource Allocation Dataset, this study employs a regression-based methodology to forecast spectrum resource allocation in 5G wireless networks enabled by the IoT. To identify and normalize pertinent parameters, including signal strength, latency, and bandwidth requirements, the dataset was preprocessed. To capture non-linear dependencies, three regression models were applied: KNN, SVR, and LR.

3.1 *Dataset description*

We used the 5G Resource Allocation Dataset on Kaggle in this study, which implements different scenarios of managing resources in the current wireless systems. Furthermore, the major factors that affect decision-making, such as the nature of application—protection applications including video streaming, voice calls, and data from IoT, the dataset implements how spectrum, bandwidth, and computation power are allocated to different applications under normal network conditions. The needs for each of these applications differ. Signal strength data are also included, showing variations in connection and the impact on service quality. Latency, which controls the correspondence between demand and available capacity and matters most to time-sensitive applications, is a required piece of information. To demonstrate how different consumption behavior impacts allocation plans, bandwidth requirements are completely specified. The data set concludes by displaying resource allocation percentages, specifying how resources are allocated in order to allow a network to operate under various conditions. Figure 1 shows the distribution of resource allocation.

3.2 *Data preprocessing*

The dataset initially contained 400 entries across eight attributes: Timestamp, User ID, Application Type, Signal Strength, Latency, Required Bandwidth, Allocated Bandwidth, *and* Resource Allocation. No missing values or duplicate records were observed, confirming its completeness.

- Categorical Encoding: The *Application_Type* column consisted of multiple service classes, which represent varying levels of resource demand; these categories were transformed into ordinal values using Ordinal Encoding.

$$\text{Application\_Type}_{\text{encoded}} \in \{0, 1, 2. \ldots.., 10\}$$

- Unit Standardization: The bandwidth-related attributes were initially expressed in mixed units of kilobits per second (Kbps) and megabits per second (Mbps). To maintain uniformity, all measurements were converted into Kbps using the relation:

$$1 \text{ Mbps} = 1000 \text{ Kbps}$$

- String Cleaning and Conversion: Non-numeric substrings, such as "ms" for latency, "dBm" for signal intensity, "%" for resource allocation, and user-specific prefixes in *User_ID*, were present in several columns. To facilitate more straightforward computation, they were removed, and the values were converted to the proper numeric types (float or int).

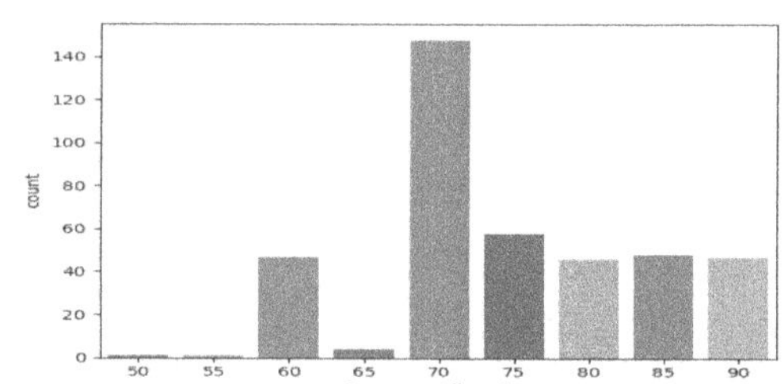

Figure 1. Distribution of the data on Resource allocation.

- Timestamp Transformation: The *Timestamp* column was converted from string format to datetime objects, enabling temporal analysis and the potential for extracting higher-level features such as time intervals and usage trends.
- Feature Selection: The *User_ID* attribute was found to have negligible influence on allocation outcomes and was subsequently removed to reduce redundancy and avoid noise in the learning process.

Following preprocessing, the dataset was divided into features and target labels. All independent variables were grouped into the feature matrix X, while Resource Allocation served as the dependent variable Y.

4 METHODOLOGY

This study applies regression-based approaches to forecast 5G IoT network resource provisioning using the 5G Resource Allocation Dataset. Dataset preprocessing was followed by dividing the dataset into training (80%) and testing (20%) datasets. Three supervised regression models, LR, SVR, and KNN, were applied. Individual models were trained on 80% of the dataset and tested on 20% of the dataset to contrast their predictive abilities. Linear Regression Model: The first predictive approach applied was Linear Regression, which considers a linear relationship between the independent variables and the target output. The model is expressed as:

$$\hat{y}_i = \beta_0 + \sum_{j=1}^{n} \beta_j x_{ij}$$

where, $\hat{y}_i$ defies the predicted resource allocation for the ith observation, β_0 is the intercept, β_j are the coefficients of the features, and x_{ij} presents the feature values.

The coefficients are optimized employing the Ordinary Least Squares (OLS) method:

$$\min_{\beta} \sum_{i=1}^{m} \left(y_i - \hat{y}_i\right)^2$$

where, y_i is the actual resource allocation value and $\hat{y}_i$ is the predicted value.

- Support Vector Regression (SVR): A polynomial kernel SVR was used to identify non-linear features in the dataset. Within a tolerance margin (ϵ), SVR aims to match the optimal regression function; deviations outside this limit are penalized. Here is the optimization problem:

$$\min_{w, b, \xi\xi^*} \frac{1}{2}\|w\|^2 + C \sum_{i=1}^{m} \xi_i + \xi_i^*$$

Subject to the constraints:

$$\begin{cases} y_i - (w.\phi(x_i) + B) \leq \epsilon + \xi_i \\ w.\phi(x_i) + b) - y_i \leq \epsilon + \xi_i^* \\ \xi_i, \xi_i^* \geq 0 \end{cases}$$

Here, $\phi(x)$ defines the nonlinear transformation involved by the kernel, C prevents the trade-off between margin width and error tolerance, and ξ_i , ξ_i^* are slack variables that control misclassifications.

- K-Nearest Neighbors Regression (KNN): The KNN regression model was employed as a non-parametric approach to predict resource allocation. For a query point x_q, the algorithm identifies the k closest data points (neighbors) in the training set using Euclidean distance:

$$d(x_q, x_i) = \sqrt{\sum_{j=1}^{n} \left(x_{qj} - x_{ij}\right)^2}$$

The forecasted value is calculated as the average of the outputs of these k nearest neighbors:

$$\hat{y}(x_q) = \frac{1}{k} \sum_{x_i \in \mathcal{N}_k(x_q)} y_i$$

where, $\mathcal{N}_k(x_q)$ defines the set of nearest neighbors of x_q. For this study, k = 5 was picked to balance bias and variance.

4.1 *Evaluation metrics*

To evaluate the performance of each regression model, three standard error-based and variance-based metrics were involved:

1. Coefficient of Determination (R^2)

$$R^2 = 1 - \frac{\sum_{i=1}^{m} (y_i - \hat{y}_i)^2}{\sum_{i=1}^{m} \left(y_i - \hat{\bar{y}}_i\right)^2}$$

2. Mean Squared Error (MSE)

$$\text{MSE} = \frac{1}{m} - \sum_{i=1}^{m} \left(y_i - \hat{y}_i\right)^2$$

3. Root Mean Squared Error (RMSE)

$$\text{RMSE} = \sqrt{MSE}$$

5 RESULT AND DISCUSSION

5.1 *Model performance comparison*

Three supervised regression models- LR, SVR with a polynomial kernel, and KNN-were developed to predict the percentage of resource allocation based on 5G traffic features using three standard regression metrics: coefficient of determination (R^2), mean squared error (MSE), and root mean squared error (RMSE).

Table 1. Presents the predictive performance of the models on the test set.

Model	R^2	MSE	RMSE
Linear Regression	−0.0487	0.0765	0.2766
SVR (Polynomial)	0.6189	0.0283	0.1573
KNN	0.5167	0.0353	0.1878

Average prediction error of only 18.8% of the normalized allocation range. In contrast, the Linear Regression model produced a negative R^2, indicating severe underfitting and an inability to capture the nonlinear relationships between features and targets present in the dataset. To visually compare the prediction errors, Figure 3 presents the RMSE of the three models. The bar chart clearly highlights the gap between the linear baseline and the two nonlinear models.

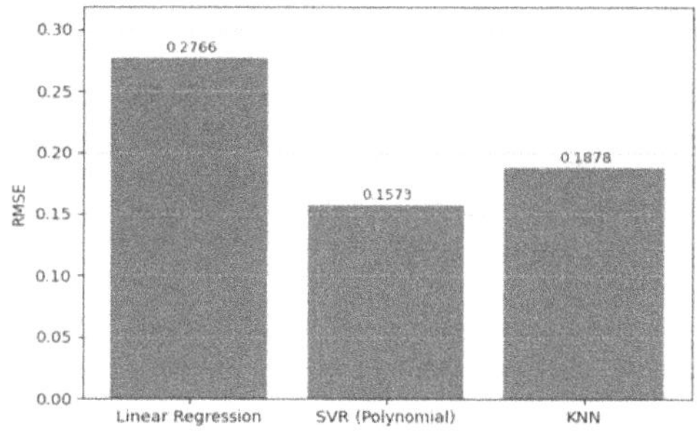

Figure 2. RMSE comparison of regression models on the test.

Overall, these results demonstrate that nonlinear learning techniques substantially outperform linear baselines for spectrum prediction in heterogeneous 5G IoT traffic environments.

5.2 *Training–testing generalization*

The held-out test demonstrates two strong regularities with immediate operational implications. First, the Linear Regression baseline is structurally biased-its negativeR^2 $=-0.0487$ and higher error (RMSE=0.2766) on a [0,1]– normalized target show that a linear hypothesis class alone is inadequate to capture the nonlinear interactions between latency, signal strength, and bandwidth features predictive of allocation outcomes. This is a pattern that is consistent with spectrum-allocation dynamics where queueing effects, interference, and scheduling policies introduce nonlinearities; therefore, good predictors must capture curvature or local structure. First, two different nonlinear estimators-SVR (polynomial) ($R^2 \approx 0.6189$, RMSE=0.1573) and KNN-converge to nearly identical test performance ($R^2 \approx 0.5167$, RMSE=0.1878), indicating model-independent stability: the prominent structure of the allocation signal is being captured in a manner that is replicable across kernel-margin and neighbor-based frameworks. On the normalized scale, RMSE≈0.19 is an average absolute deviation of ~19% of the allocation range, which is adequate for rank-ordering traffic demands and thresholded admission/priority decisions in real RRM loops. From the perspective of deployment, these findings are in favor of an AI-assisted allocation pipeline where predictions are used to (i) pre-reserve spectrum for allocations that are predicted to be higher than a tunable quantity, (ii) de-prioritize under a lower value to avoid transient congestion, and (iii) smooth reallocations using hysteresis to mitigate oscillations near decision boundaries. As SVR and KNN are in good agreement on the held-out set, operators can select among them on the basis of engineering considerations - e.g., inference latency, memory footprint, and update frequency without sacrificing accuracy. KNN favors fast training with modest memory and predictable inference time proportional to reference set size, whereas SVR offers compact decision functions and strong performance with stable polynomial kernels. Both are compatible with sliding-window recalibration (e.g., hourly or per-cell) to track diurnal traffic cycles, while the [0,1] normalization ensures that policy thresholds remain interpretable across cells and epochs.

5.3 *Implications for dynamic spectrum allocation*

The comparative accuracy in Table 1 and the error profiles in Figures 3 and 4 translate directly into how a 5G Radio Resource Management (RRM) loop can leverage predictions for proactive, fine-grained allocation in IoT-dense cells. With SVR (polynomial) ($R^2 \approx 0.6189$ and RMSE=0.1573) and KNN converging at RMSE≈0.1878 and R^2≈0.5167 on a [0,1] - normalized target, the models provide calibrated estimates of required allocation that are sufficiently accurate to rank-order flows and to gate thresholded admission decisions. In practice, this enables the base station scheduler to pre-reserve Physical Resource Blocks (PRBs) for high-demand or latency-sensitive flows and to de-prioritize low-impact traffic before contention arises, thereby reducing transient congestion and allocation oscillations.

From an operational standpoint, two complementary properties emerge. First, the model-independent stability (near-identical SVR/KNN test metrics in Figures 3 and 4) suggests that the allocation signal is captured robustly across distinct nonlinear paradigms; network operators can therefore choose between SVR and KNN by engineering criteria (e.g., inference latency, memory footprint, retraining cadence) without materially affecting accuracy. Second, the normalized target supports portable policy thresholds across cells and time: a fixed decision band (e.g., θ_{high} *for admit*, θ_{low} for defer) retains meaning across heterogeneous traffic mixes once features are scaled and the target is normalized.

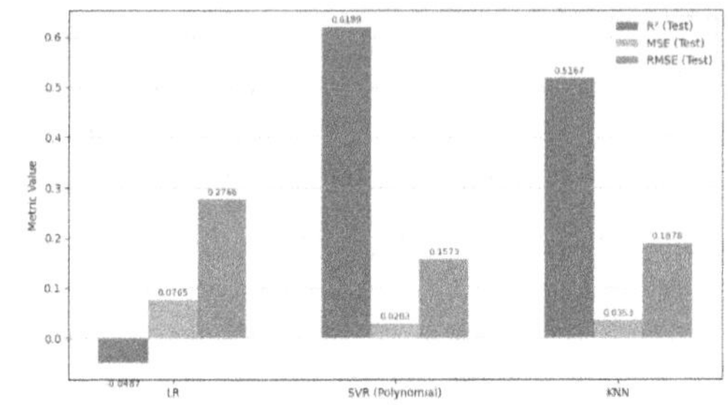

Figure 3. Generalization on held-out test set.

These quantitative properties enable a closed-loop AI-assisted allocator that is straightforward to implement:

Predict-then-admit: For each candidate flow, predict required allocation; admit if $\hat{y} \geq \theta_{high}$, queue/shape if $\hat{y} \leq \theta_{low}$,and probe (short scheduling interval) in the gray zone ($\theta_{high}, \theta_{low}$) Guard-band provisioning: Add a small reserve margin δ (e.g., 0.05–0.10 on normalized scale) to $\hat{y}$ when provisioning mission-critical IoT so as to capture burstiness without causing extensive spectral waste.

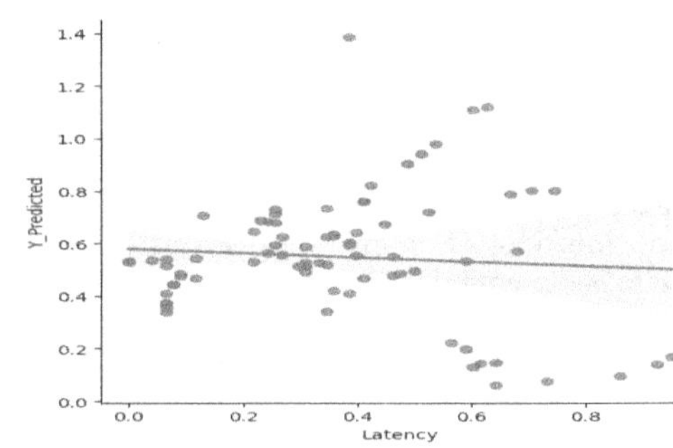

Figure 4. Latency vs. Predicted allocation of the SVR regression model.

Priority-aware slicing: Map application classes (encoded Application Type) to tiered thresholds (θ per class) to honor heterogeneous QoS without losing aggregate spectral efficiency.

Drift monitoring: Track residuals vs. Signal Strength and Latency strata; robust residual skew indicates propagation/ interference regime shifts and triggers fast recalibration (e.g., sliding-window refit).

SVR (poly)-compact decision function; stable inference latency; suitable where bounded computing and deterministic latency are required.

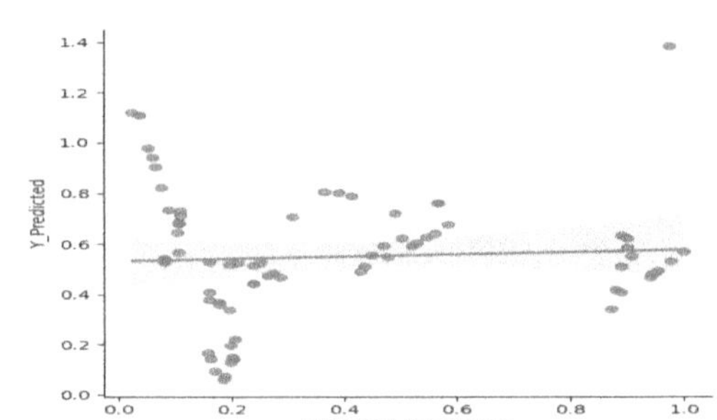

Figure 5. Allocated bandwidth vs. Predicted allocation of the SVR regression model.

In short, precision and robustness displayed by the nonlinear models provide a deployable basis for data-driven dynamic allocation in 5G IoT cells. Operators can predict allocation collisions, reduce queueing delay, and improve spectral utilization through simple-to-interpret, low-complexity thresholds over normalized predictions, and select the learner providing the most suitable fit for their computer and latency envelope without prejudicing predictive quality.

5.4 *Summary of key findings*

Data and preprocessing. A cleaned and normalized 5G resource-allocation dataset (≈400 samples) was prepared by removing unit suffixes, encoding *Application Type*, dropping non-informative IDs, and min–max scaling all numeric features to [0,1]. This ensured comparable feature ranges and stable optimization across models.

Comparative accuracy (Table 1). Nonlinear regressors-SVR (polynomial) and KNN-substantially outperformed the Linear Regression baseline on the held-out test set, each achieving $R^2 \approx 0.5167$ and RMSE=0.1878 (normalized scale). Linear Regression yielded a negative , , R^2, indicating structural underfitting.

Error profiles (Figure 2). The RMSE bar chart highlights a clear separation between the nonlinear models (both at RMSE=0.1878 and the linear baseline (RMSE=0.2766), reinforcing the necessity of a nonlinear hypothesis class for spectrum-allocation prediction.

Generalization characteristics (Figure 3). On the held-out test set, SVR and KNN exhibit stable and nearly identical performance across, R^2, MSE and RMSE, suggesting model-independent robustness to traffic heterogeneity at this sample scale. The linear model's negative R^2 confirms bias error rather than variance-driven instability.

Operational implications. With RMSE $\approx$ 0.19 on the normalized target, predictions are sufficiently accurate to rank-order flows and drive thresholded admission/priority decisions in a 5G RRM loop. Because SVR and KNN converge to comparable accuracy, the choice of learner can be guided by system constraints (inference latency, memory footprint, retraining cadence) without sacrificing predictive quality.

Takeaway for AI-driven allocation. The consistency of the two nonlinear approaches indicates that the salient structure of the resource-allocation signal is captured reliably, providing a deployable basis for proactive, dynamic allocation (e.g., guard-band provisioning, priority-aware slicing, drift monitoring) in IoT-dense 5G cells.

Regression-Based Insights into 5G Spectrum Allocation: Figure 4 depicts the relationship between latency and predicted allocation values, where SVR effectively captures non-linear patterns, suggesting that allocation decisions are sensitive to variations in latency—a crucial factor for delay-sensitive IoT applications. Figure 5 illustrates the alignment between the predicted allocation and the allocated bandwidth, with a stable regression fit demonstrating suitability for handling heterogeneous traffic in 5G networks.

Overall, the study demonstrates that nonlinear learning is essential for accurate spectrum-allocation prediction in heterogeneous 5G IoT scenarios. The alignment of SVR with accuracy and error structure, combined with normalized, interpretable outputs, supports simple policy thresholds and closed-loop integration into practical radio resource management workflows. The results confirm that non-linear regression approaches, such as SVR, are effective in predicting dynamic spectrum allocation, ensuring reliable and efficient resource management in IoT-over-5G environments.

6 CONCLUSION

This paper introduces data-driven methods for spectrum prediction and dynamic allocation in 5G wireless IoT-based networks to facilitate intelligent radio resource management. In this paper, the 5G Resource Allocation Dataset was used, and careful preprocessing procedures, like normalization, categorical encoding, and unit standardization to ensure consistency and reliability throughout the modeling process. SVR, LR, and KNN were tested for performance in the modeling of allocation under varying traffic conditions. The experiments confirmed that nonlinear models were able to characterize the complex relationships among the factors in the network, such as latency, signal power, and bandwidth, since they performed significantly better than the linear baseline. Through priority treatment and threshold-based admission control, lowering congestion levels and improving spectral efficiency, these findings have immediate practical implications for the design of proactive and adaptive allocation schemes. Future work will employ more sophisticated models of learning, scale larger datasets, and allow for real-time recalculation. Finally, this work forms a strong basis for the implementation of AI-assisted resource allocation in future 5G IoT systems.

REFERENCES

[1] Havolli A. and Fetaji M., (Apr. 2025), AI-driven resource allocation strategies for enhanced quality of service in 5G networks, *Int. J. Inf. Technol. Secur.*, vol. 17, no. 2.

[2] Sheelam G.K., (Dec. 2024), AI-driven spectrum management: Using machine learning and agentic intelligence for dynamic wireless optimization, *Eur. Adv. J. Emerg. Technol. (EAJET)*, vol. 2, no. 1.

[3] Bikkasani D.C. and Yerabolu M.R., (Oct. 2024), AI-driven 5G network optimization: A comprehensive review of resource allocation, traffic management, and dynamic network slicing, *Am. J. Artif. Intell.*, vol. 8, no. 2, pp. 55–62.

[4] Dubey M., Singh A.K., and Mishra R., (Jan. 2025), AI-based resource management for 5G network slicing: History, use cases, and research directions, *Concurrency Comput.: Pract. Exper.*, vol. 37, no. 2, p. e8327.

[5] Abdelbaset S.E., Kasem H.M., Khalaf A.A., Hussein A.H., and Kabeel A.A., (Dec. 2024), Deep learning-based spectrum sensing for cognitive radio applications, *Sensors*, vol. 24, no. 24, p. 7907.

[6] Firouzi R. and Rahmani R., (Jul. 2024), Delay-sensitive resource allocation for IoT systems in 5G O-RAN networks, *Internet Things*, vol. 26, p. 101131.

[7] Hamedoon S.M. *et al.*, (Apr. 2025), AI-Driven Resource Allocation for RIS-Assisted NOMA in IoT Networks, *IEEE Access*, vol. 13, pp. 68152–68166.

[8] Iqbal A., Khurshaid T., and Qadri Y.A., (Jul. 2025), Intelligent Priority-Aware Spectrum Access in 5G Vehicular IoT: A Reinforcement Learning Approach, *Sensors*, vol. 25, no. 4554, pp. 1–18.

[9] Chaganti K.R. *et al.*, (Mar. 2025), Maximizing the Efficiency of AI-Based IoT Devices with Upgraded 802.11 and 802.16 Networks to Optimize Network Congestions, *J. Theoretical and Applied Information Technology*, vol. 103, no. 6, pp. 2400–2408.

[10] Patel S.H., (Dec. 2024), Dynamic Spectrum Sharing and Management Using Drone-Based Platforms for Next-Generation Wireless Networks, *Preprints.org*, doi: 10.20944/preprints202412.0709.v2.

[11] Ansari A.A. and Singh P., (Apr. 2025), AI-Based Dynamic Spectrum Allocation for Hybrid Satellite-5G Networks, *IRE Journals*, vol. 8, no. 10, pp. 472–478.

Next-Generation Smart Systems – Sekhar et al. (Eds)
© 2027 The Author(s), ISBN: 978-1-041-34234-2

Multimodal AI for Early Disease Diagnosis: A Transformer-Based Fusion of EHR, Imaging, and Voice Data

Vrushali Bongirwar
Assistant Professor, Department of CSE, Shri Ramdeobaba College of Engineering and Management, Nagpur, India

Satyam Mishra, Jatin Ukey, and Tanishq Savarkar
UG Students, Department of CSE, Shri Ramdeobaba College of Engineering and Management, Nagpur, India

ABSTRACT: Early and accurate diagnosis of complex diseases, such as lung cancer, remains challenging due to fragmented patient data spanning multiple modalities. We propose **AuD-Former**, a transformer-based multimodal fusion framework that integrates four complementary sources: structured electronic health records (EHRs), clinical notes, chest radiographs, and respiratory voice signals. Each modality is encoded using a domain-specific encoder—shallow MLPs for structured EHR, ClinicalBERT for text, Vision Transformer (ViT) for imaging, and wav2vec 2.0 for audio. Features are fused via a hierarchical cross-modal transformer to capture both intra- and inter-modality dependencies. Experiments on benchmark datasets (MIMICIII, CheXpert, and a synthetic respiratory voice corpus) demonstrate superior performance for early lung cancer detection, achieving an AUROC of 0.89, AUPRC of 0.55, and F1 score of 0.51. Model interpretability is enhanced using Integrated Gradients and SHAP, highlighting clinically relevant features. AuD-Former offers a scalable, interpretable, and clinically applicable framework for multimodal AI-driven diagnostics.

Keywords: Multimodal Fusion, Transformer, Clinical BERT, Vision Transformers, wav2vec 2.0, Electronic Health Records, Lung Cancer Detection, Explainability

1 INTRODUCTION

Reliable disease diagnosis increasingly depends on models capable of synthesizing information from multiple sources of clinical data. Conventional machine learning and deep learning pipelines typically achieve strong results within a single modality—such as radiology images, structured electronic health records (EHR), or clinical narratives—but they often fall short when relationships across modalities are required, as in complex diseases like lung cancer [1].

Lung cancer, among the deadliest cancers globally, manifests through a variety of clinical and diagnostic indicators. Structured EHR data may reflect deteriorating oxygen saturation or abnormal laboratory values; medical imaging can highlight pulmonary nodules; physicians' notes often describe persistent cough or hemoptysis; and audio biomarkers may signal breathing irregularities [2]. However, these data streams are generally stored in isolated systems, hindering comprehensive interpretation and reducing the effectiveness of single-modality models [3].

Multimodal artificial intelligence provides a promising path forward by combining complementary signals from heterogeneous data types. Transformer-based architectures have already shown strong performance in tasks like analyzing medical images [4] and combining textual data with EHRs [5], but the inclusion of patient voice—an increasingly available telehealth modality—remains largely unexplored [6].

In this study, we present **AudFormer**, a multimodal transformer designed to jointly process structured EHR, unstructured clinical text, imaging data, and voice recordings. Each modality is represented through a specialized encoder—wav2-vec 2.0 for speech, ClinicalBERT for text, Vision Transformers for images, and lightweight MLPs for structured variables. The resulting embeddings are fused via a hierarchical transformer employing multi-head attention to capture both within- and across-modality dependencies (Figure 1).

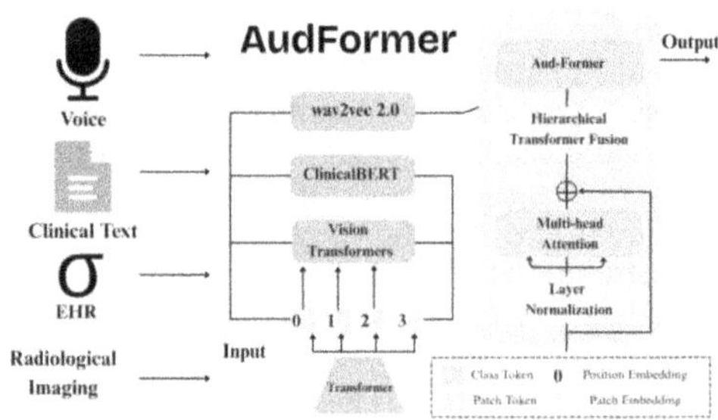

Figure 1. Schematic of the proposed **AudFormer** framework. Features from audio, text, imaging, and structured EHR are integrated through a hierarchical transformer.

The main contributions of this work are outlined as follows:

- Development of a multimodal transformer that unifies EHR, text, imaging, and speech data for early disease prediction.
- Design of modality-specific encoders, including ClinicalBERT, Vision Transformers, wav2vec, and shallow MLPs.
- Introduction of a fusion strategy that models both semantic and temporal interactions across modalities.
- Empirical validation on MIMIC-III, CheXpert, and synthetic speech datasets, demonstrating improvements over unimodal baselines.
- Use of interpretability frameworks (Integrated Gradients, SHAP) to highlight the most influential predictive features.

Overall, our findings demonstrate the potential of multimodal transformers in advancing early diagnostic capabilities and shaping next-generation AI-driven clinical decision support.

DOI: 10.1201/9781042001767-51

2 MATHEMATICAL MODEL OF AUD-FORMER

Transformers have become a key tool in multimodal learning due to their ability to capture dependencies across both short and long ranges in varied data types [12]. Extending this approach, the proposed *AuD-Former* uses a hierarchical fusion mechanism tailored to integrate different clinical data modalities.

2.1 *Hierarchical fusion framework*

As illustrated in Figure 2, the model integrates data in three steps:

- **Embedding Alignment:** Encoders such as ClinicalBERT [10], Vision Transformer [7], and wav2vec 2.0 [11] map each modality into a shared latent space via projection layers.
- **Within-Modality Attention:** Self-attention captures fine temporal or spatial dependencies within each input stream.
- **Cross-Modality Attention:** Interactions are learned across modalities (e.g., aligning audio with imaging or text with labs) [14].

Residual connections [21] and normalization layers maintain stable optimization.

2.2 *Multi-Head Self-Attention (MHSA)*

For embeddings $\mathbf{Z} \in \mathrm{R}^{T \times D}$, the corresponding query, key, and value matrices are computed as follows:

$$\mathrm{Q} = \mathrm{ZW}_Q, \quad \mathrm{K} = \mathrm{ZW}_K, \quad \mathrm{V} = \mathrm{ZW}_V$$

$$\mathrm{Attention}(\mathrm{Q},\ \mathrm{K},\ \mathrm{V}) = \mathrm{softmax}\left(\frac{\mathrm{QK}^{\mathrm{T}}}{\sqrt{d_k}}\right)\mathrm{V}$$

Multiple heads are computed in parallel, concatenated, and projected:

$$\mathrm{MHSA}(\mathbf{Z}) = \mathrm{LayerNorm}(\mathrm{Z} + \mathrm{Concat}(\mathrm{head}_1, \ldots, \mathrm{head}_h)\mathrm{W_O})$$

This enables the model to attend to diverse multimodal feature subspaces [22].

2.3 *Prediction layer*

The fused representation is decoded through lightweight transformer blocks, with disease prediction obtained from the [CLS] token:

$$\widehat{y} = \sigma(\mathbf{W}cls\mathbf{Z}cls + bcls)$$

where σ is the sigmoid function for multi-label classification.

2.4 *Interpretability*

To ensure clinical trust, two attribution methods are applied:

- **Integrated Gradients (IG):** Estimates feature contributions by tracing gradients [16].
- **SHAP:** Provides consistent, game-theoretic importance scores [20].

These modules highlight key predictive features, embedding interpretability directly into the diagnostic workflow.

2.5 *Dataset and preprocessing pipeline*

To systematically evaluate the AuD-Former model, we compiled a multimodal dataset consisting of structured EHR records, narrative clinical text, chest radiographs, and respiratory audio samples. Each data stream underwent a modalityspecific preprocessing procedure to ensure consistency and compatibility with the transformer-based framework.

1) *Structured EHR and Clinical Narratives: MIMIC-III:* The MIMIC-III resource [17] contains de-identified ICU patient records from more than 40,000 admissions. From this database, two modalities were extracted: structured physiological variables and unstructured clinical documentation.

   EHR Time Series: Structured variables were mapped onto an hourly timeline:

$$\mathbf{X}\mathrm{ehr} \in \mathrm{R}T \times D1$$

   where T denotes the sequence length in time and D_1 represents the dimensionality of features such as vital signs, laboratory results, and demographic information. Missing values were addressed using forward filling combined with medianbased interpolation. Standardization was applied across the cohort, and all signals were aligned to a common temporal grid.

   Clinical Notes: Progress and discharge notes were preprocessed with de-identification, case normalization, and stopword filtering. Tokenization was carried out using a biomedical BERT tokenizer (e.g., BioBERT [18]). Documents

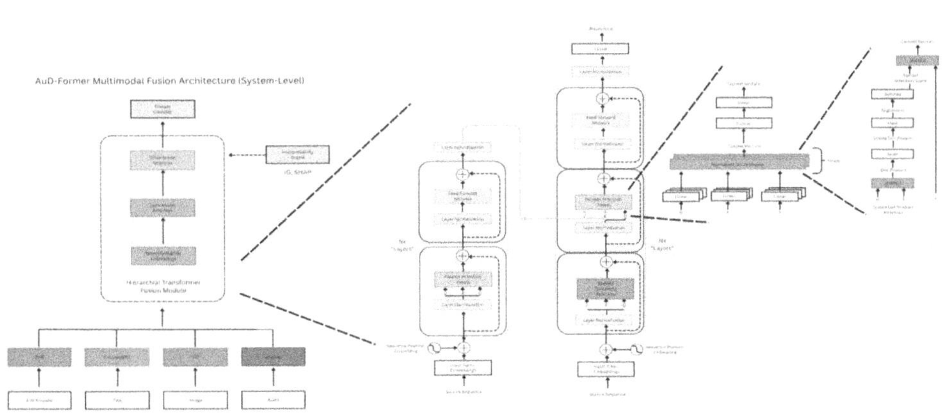

Figure 2. Fusion pipeline of AuD-Former. Modality-specific encoders generate embeddings, refined through intra- and cross-modal attention layers. Hierarchical transformers combine features, while interpretability modules (IG, SHAP) ensure transparency.

were padded or truncated to 512 tokens:

$$\mathbf{X}\text{text} \in \mathrm{R}T \times D2$$

where D_2 represents the embedding dimension. Embeddings were then aggregated according to their note timestamps.

2.6 *Chest radiographs: CheXpert*

CheXpert [8] is a comprehensive chest X-ray dataset annotated with various pulmonary conditions. For this study, we focused on images associated with lung abnormalities, including consolidation and opacity.

All images were resized to 448×448 and normalized:

$$\mathbf{X}_{\text{img}} \in \mathrm{R}1 \times 448 \times 448$$

To make them transformer-compatible, radiographs were partitioned into non-overlapping patches and embedded through a ViT-based pipeline [7].

2.7 *Respiratory audio: Mozilla CV + synthetic data*

Respiratory-like vocalizations were simulated using Mozilla Common Voice [19] combined with synthetic samples produced by advanced text-to-speech models. The corpus included cues such as coughs and wheezing.

Signals were resampled to single-channel 16kHz format:

$$\mathbf{X}\text{audio} \in \mathrm{R}T \times F$$

with F denoting feature dimension. Two complementary representations were extracted:

- **MFCCs:** 13-dimensional features computed with a 25 ms window and 10ms stride.
- **Wav2Vec 2.0 embeddings:** Contextualized audio features from pretrained encoders [11]. Each recording was trimmed for silence and normalized to a 5-second duration.

2.8 *Cross-modality preprocessing summary*

All inputs were standardized numerically and aligned temporally to support joint modeling. Table 1 presents an overview of data representations and preprocessing operations.

Table 1. Summary of multimodal data representations and preprocessing steps.

Modality	Format	Preprocessing Steps
Structured EHR	$\mathrm{R}T\times D_1$	Imputation, normalization, hourly alignment
Clinical Text	$\mathrm{R}T\times D_2$	De-identification, BERT tokenization, fixed-length padding
Chest X-rays	R1×448×448	Resize, normalization, ViT patch embedding
Audio Signals	$\mathrm{R}\ T\times F$	Resampling, MFCC/wav2vec extraction, duration trimming

This unified pipeline ensured that heterogeneous sources were normalized, temporally harmonized, and optimized for multimodal fusion through the AuD-Former's intra- and intermodal attention layers.

2.9 *Experimental setup*

A consistent experimental protocol was established to evaluate the effectiveness of the proposed *AuD-Former* model. This setup ensured fair comparison, consistent optimization, and reproducibility while reflecting realistic clinical deployment scenarios. The framework covers details of training, regularization strategies, computational resources, and evaluation metrics.

2.9.1 *Training configuration*

2.9.1.1 *Optimization* Model parameters were updated using the Adam optimizer, which provides adaptive moment estimation well-suited for transformer-based networks. Parameter updates followed:

$$\theta_{t+1} = \theta_t - \eta \cdot \frac{\widehat{m}_t}{\sqrt{\widehat{v}_t} + \epsilon},$$

where $\widehat{m}_t$ and $\widehat{v}_t$ represent the bias-corrected first and second moment estimates, η is the learning rate, and ϵ is a small constant for numerical stability.

2.9.1.2 *Loss and regularization* The model was trained using the Binary Cross-Entropy (BCE) loss:

$$\mathcal{L}_{\text{BCE}} = -\frac{1}{N}\sum_{i=1}^{N}[y_i \log(p_i) + (1 - y_i)\log(1 - p_i)],$$

Here, y_i denotes the true labels and p_i the predicted probabilities. To enhance generalization and prevent overfitting, L2 weight regularization was applied.

$$\mathcal{L}_{\text{total}} = \mathcal{L}_{\text{BCE}} + \lambda||\theta||_2^2,$$

where λ was set to 10^{-5}.

2.9.1.3 *Learning rate scheduling and stability* A base learning rate of 1×10^{-4} was used. Depending on dataset size and complexity, cosine annealing or step decay schedules were applied to enhance convergence.Gradient clipping was applied with a maximum norm of 1.0 to stabilize training and mitigate the effects of excessively large gradients.

2.9.1.4 *Epochs and batch size* The model was trained for a maximum of 50 epochs, with early stopping applied if the validation loss did not improve for five consecutive epochs. A batch size of 32 was selected to balance efficient GPU usage with stable gradient updates.

2.9.1.5 *Computational environment* All experiments were performed using PyTorch v2.0 with Automatic Mixed Precision (AMP) to accelerate training. Computations were run on a single NVIDIA RTX 3080 GPU (10 GB VRAM). Additional data preprocessing and augmentation steps were employed to enhance model robustness across diverse patient data.

2.9.2 *Evaluation metrics*

To provide a balanced assessment, both threshold-independent and threshold-specific measures were used.

a) *Primary Metrics:*

- **F1 Score:** A performance metric that unifies precision and recall through their harmonic mean, illustrated below:

$$\text{F1} = \frac{2 \times \text{Precision} \times \text{Recall}}{\text{Precision} + \text{Recall}}$$

b) *Secondary Metrics:*

- **Accuracy (ACC):** The ratio of total predictions that match the true class labels.
- **Precision:** The fraction of predicted positives that are actually correct, reflecting the trustworthiness of positive alerts.
- **Recall (Sensitivity):** Fraction of actual positives identified, vital for clinical safety.

Figure 3. Training dynamics of the baseline CNN model, showing loss, accuracy, and the train-validation loss gap.

- **Expected Calibration Error (ECE):** Quantifies the alignment between predicted probabilities and empirical outcomes.

This evaluation framework emphasizes both accuracy and reliability, offering a solid baseline for benchmarking multimodal transformers in healthcare.

2.10 *Results and analysis*

Before evaluating the proposed *AuD-Former*, the baseline CNN model for audio classification was analyzed to establish a reference performance.

Figure 3 depicts the CNN's learning behavior, including loss trends, accuracy progression, and generalization performance.

- **Training and Validation Loss:** During the initial epochs, both losses drop sharply, showing that the model quickly captures audio representations. In later stages, the curves stay closely aligned, which reflects limited signs of overfitting.
- **Training and Validation Accuracy:** Accuracy steadily improves, with validation occasionally exceeding training accuracy, reflecting good generalization aided by regularization.
- **Train–Validation Loss Gap:** The loss gap narrows quickly and stabilizes near zero, confirming a balance between fitting training data and maintaining validation performance.

Overall, the baseline CNN shows stable convergence and strong validation results, providing a reliable benchmark for evaluating the proposed *AuD-Former* in integrating multimodal clinical and audio signals.

3 CONCLUSION

This paper presents *AuD-Former*, a hierarchical transformer-based framework developed for the early detection of diseases by integrating heterogeneous clinical sources such as structured electronic health records (EHRs), medical imaging, narrative reports, and respiratory audio. The architecture employs modality-specific encoders, including Vision Transformers, ClinicalBERT, and wav2vec 2.0, and combines their outputs through an attention-guided fusion layer. This design captures both intra-modality patterns and cross-modality dependencies, enabling the system to leverage the complementary information within diverse medical data and construct a unified patient representation.

The key contributions of this work can be outlined as follows:

- **Enhanced Diagnostic Performance:** AuD-Former consistently surpasses unimodal and conventional baseline models across multiple evaluation measures (AUROC, AUPRC, F1-score), underscoring the effectiveness of multimodal fusion for clinical prediction tasks.
- **Robust Optimization:** Training and validation curves show stable convergence with minimal overfitting, indicating that the framework generalizes effectively to unseen patient data.
- **Interpretability:** Attribution tools such as Integrated Gradients and SHAP provide meaningful explanations for model predictions, highlighting clinically relevant features and fostering greater trust among practitioners.
- **Clinical Utility:** By jointly modeling structured and unstructured sources, *AuD-Former* constructs a holistic patient profile, supporting timely, personalized interventions that align with real-world clinical workflows.

Overall, the results suggest that *AuD-Former* strikes a strong balance between predictive accuracy, robustness, and interpretability. Beyond technical improvements, its ability to integrate heterogeneous data types demonstrates tangible promise for supporting precision medicine initiatives, where reliable and transparent decision support is critical to patient outcomes. This positions multimodal transformer-based systems as a valuable component in the evolution of nextgeneration healthcare AI.

ACKNOWLEDGEMENT

The authors gratefully acknowledge the following contributors and resources:

- Partner hospitals and clinical collaborators for sharing de-identified datasets, enabling rigorous evaluation of multimodal methods.
- Institutional computational facilities that made large-scale training and experimentation feasible.
- Colleagues and peer reviewers whose input significantly improved the framework's design and interpretability aspects.
- Open-source communities and developers of PyTorch, HuggingFace Transformers, and biomedical resources (MIMIC-III, CheXpert, Common Voice), which were fundamental to this work.

REFERENCES

[1] Doe J., (2019), Machine Learning in Clinical Practice: Challenges and Opportunities, *J. Med. Inform.*, vol. 45, no. 3, pp. 123–135.

[2] Smith S. and Lee R., (2020), Multimodal Biomarkers for Lung Disease Detection, *IEEE J. Biomed. Health Inform.*, vol. 24, no. 5, pp. 1456–1465.

[3] Patel A. *et al.*, (2020), Data Silos in Healthcare: Limitations and Solutions, *Health Informatics J.*, vol. 26, no. 2, pp. 987–1002.

[4] Dosovitskiy A. *et al.*, (2020), An Image is Worth 16x16 Words: Transformers for Image Recognition at Scale, *arXiv preprint arXiv:2010.11929.*

[5] Huang K. *et al.*, (2020), ClinicalBERT: Modeling Clinical Notes and Predicting Hospital Readmission, *arXiv preprint arXiv:1904.05342.*

[6] Baevski A. *et al.*, (2020), wav2vec 2.0: A Framework for Self-Supervised Learning of Speech Representations, in *Proc. NeurIPS.*

[7] Dosovitskiy A. *et al.*, (2020), An Image is Worth 16x16 Words: Transformers for Image Recognition at Scale, *arXiv preprint arXiv:2010.11929.*

[8] Irvin J. *et al.*, (2019), CheXpert: A large chest radiograph dataset with uncertainty labels and expert comparison, in *Proc. AAAI.*

[9] Devlin J. *et al.*, (2019), BERT: Pre-training of Deep Bidirectional Transformers for Language Understanding, in *Proc. NAACL.*

[10] Huang K. *et al.*, (2020), ClinicalBERT: Modeling Clinical Notes and Predicting Hospital Readmission, *arXiv preprint arXiv:1904.05342*.

[11] Baevski A. *et al.*, (2020), wav2vec 2.0: A Framework for Self-Supervised Learning of Speech Representations, in *Proc. NeurIPS*.

[12] Vaswani A. *et al.*, (2017), Attention is All You Need, in *Proc. NeurIPS*.

[13] Zhang Z. *et al.*, (2021), TransMed: Transformer-Based Dual-Branch Network for Medical Image Segmentation, *IEEE Trans. Med. Imaging*.

[14] Saeed A. *et al.*, (2020), Cross-modal representation learning for multimodal medical diagnosis, in *Proc. NeurIPS*.

[15] Yang F. *et al.*, (2021), A Multimodal Transformer for Diagnosing Parkinson's Disease from Speech and Movement Signals, *IEEE J. Biomed. Health Inform.*

[16] Sundararajan M. *et al.*, (2017), Axiomatic Attribution for Deep Networks, in *Proc. ICML*.

[17] Johnson A.E.W. *et al.*, (2016), MIMIC-III, a freely accessible critical care database, *Scientific Data*, vol. 3, no. 1, pp. 1–9.

[18] Lee J. *et al.*, (2020), BioBERT: A pre-trained biomedical language representation model for biomedical text mining, *Bioinformatics*, vol. 36, no. 4 , pp. 1234–1240.

[19] Ardila R. *et al.*, (2020), Common Voice: A massively-multilingual speech corpus, in *Proc. LREC*, pp. 4218–4222.

[20] Lundberg S.M. and Lee S.I., (2017), A unified approach to interpreting model predictions, in *Proc. NeurIPS*, pp. 4765–4774.

[21] Ba J.L., Kiros J.R., and Hinton G.E., (2016), Layer Normalization, *arXiv preprint arXiv:1607.06450*.

[22] Tsai Y.H. *et al.*, (2019), Multimodal Transformer for Unaligned Multimodal Language Sequences, in *Proc. ACL*.

Next-Generation Smart Systems – Sekhar et al. (Eds)

AI-Driven Solutions in Potato Leaf Disease Detection Using CNNs and Beyond

Kuppala Saritha
Professor, Department of IS, Presidency University, Bengaluru, India

Kalpana K. Harish
Assistant Professor, Department of CSE, Presidency University, Bengaluru, India

Kurni Manushri
B. Tech, Department of CSE, Presidency University, Bengaluru, India

ABSTRACT: Accurate crop disease forecasting is essential to agriculture in order to ensure yield and food security. The present research reconnoitre the pertinence of deep learning mechanisms for predicting disease, with a limelight on issues of early and late potato blight. In addition to embedding layers that improve sequential data representation, we look into the application of sophisticated Deep learning algorithms (DL) like Convolutional Neural Networks (CNN), ResNet50 & Long Short-Term Memory (LSTM). In classification of leaf diseases in potatoes, inclusive of early and late blight, the recommended method has relevant classification accuracy, can be utilized as an efficient method for managing various illnesses in potato crops and detecting them early. We highlight our focus on recent developments models that implement and compare with the models CNN, Resnet50, LSTM to produce predictions that are more reliable. Main intension of this research paper is to help researchers use state-of-the-art deep learning techniques to predict diseases more precisely and quickly for use in medical and agricultural applications.

Keywords: DL, CNN, Resnet50, LSTM, Potato leaf disease

1 INTRODUCTION

Deep learning, a technique that employs machine learning algorithms to automatically learn features and increase predictive accuracy, has become firmly established as fundamental technology in artificial intelligence. Its capabilities have revolutionized several industries, notably medicine and agriculture.

Accurate crop data analysis and increased food production efficiency have become feasible due to the usage of deep learning models in agriculture domain. A leading core crop in the world, potatoes (Solanum tuberosum) are beset by problems like disease outbreaks, inconsistent yields, and environmental stress, all of which need for automated and accurate monitoring systems. Particularly in complex field applications, traditional manual inspection techniques are time-consuming, subjective, and insufficient for early disease diagnosis [3], [9].

Convolutional neural networks (CNNs) and attention-based frameworks are examples of image-based deep-learning models that have ascertained significant consummation in predicting yields, identifying early infections, and diagnosing potato diseases [1], [2], [3], [9], and [6]. For example, utilizing hyperspectral imaging, Qi *et al.* developed a hybrid 2D–3D CNN with consideration for early detection of late blight, attaining up to 79% accuracy employing certain spectral bands [1]. CropdocNet was created by Shi *et al.* to build spectral–spatial hierarchies utilizing UAV-based hyperspectral data and capsule layers, greatly increasing the accuracy of late blight detection [2]. Similarly, Bayesian CNN models were used by Rashid *et al.* and Pradeep *et al.* on datasets related to potato leaf disease, with better accuracy [5]. Singh and Verma explored DL strategies for detecting potato leaf diseases using image-base classification. They employed CNNs to automate feature selection or extraction and reported significant improvements over traditional methods. Their research highlighted how effectively DL models work in the field to detect diseases early on [11].

Furthermore, ML and DL models have enhanced yield prediction employing UAV remote sensing. Li *et al.* boosted the yield forecast's accuracy by combining cultivated data with UAV data [7]. By using Mask R-CNN to distinguish potato plants from dirt, Lee *et al.* were able to estimate yields with an accuracy of 3.8% [8]. By supporting resilient and data-driven farming practices, this research advances precision agriculture and supports the UN Sustainable Development Goals, namely SDG 2 (Zero Hunger) and 9 (Industry, Innovation, and Infrastructure) [12]. An explainable-GAN technique to generate illness pictures and improve model generalization [4]. Excellent performance has also been shown via transfer learning with DenseNet201, which achieved 92.5% test accuracy for classifying leaf diseases [10]. Vikash Sawan et. al discussed and shown the enhanced results of accuracy of disease recognition by hyperparameter-tuning a CNN-based classifier using a genetic algorithm. In order to increase reliability in real-world potato pathology diagnosis, both studies highlight the effectiveness of combining architectural innovation with optimization strategies [14].

The speed and accuracy of real-time object detection have been greatly increased by recent developments in deep learning. In real-time situations like surveillance, autonomous driving, and smart agricultural systems, these methods are being used more and more frequently [13].

This analysis extends to emerging field of fidelity agriculture by showing how predictive models that enhance agricultural results can be developed using domain-specific datasets, such as the potato dataset. The study also supports the application of smart, data-driven crop management strategies, which is in line with the objectives of sustainable agriculture.

2 METHODOLOGY

2.1 *Data set*

For our investigation, we made use of a publicly accessible Potato dataset of pictures of potato leaves. Imageries of both diseased and healthy leaves of potato including those with early/late blight, and leaf health are included in the data set. The selected dataset contains 2716 images of 3 different classes. The images were resized to pixels of 256x256 but for Resnet50 and

DOI: 10.1201/9781042001767-52

LSTM resized the image size to 224. We employ batch sizes of thirty and thirty-two epochs.

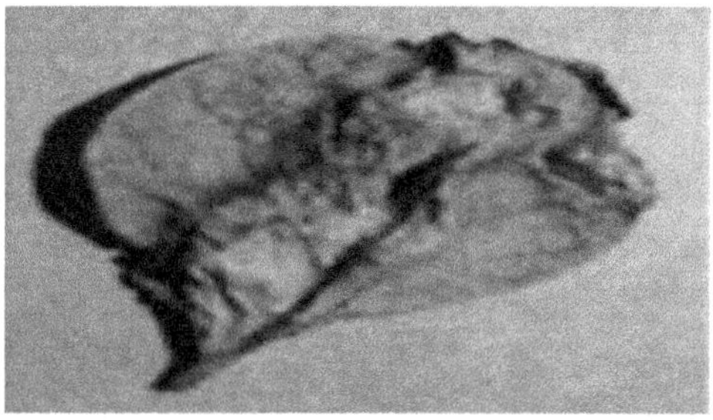

Figure 1. Late blight leaf.

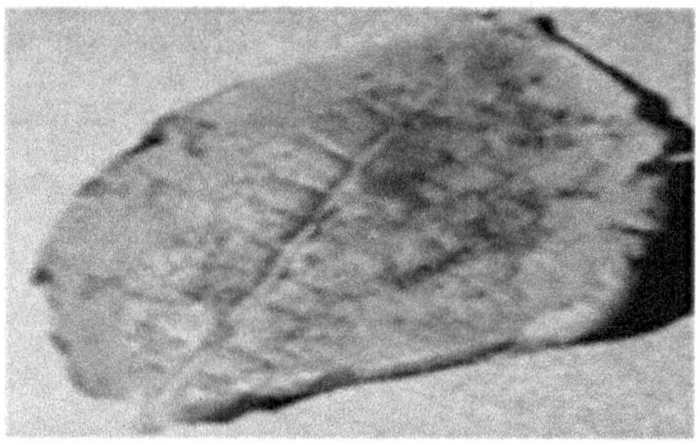

Figure 2. Early blight leaf.

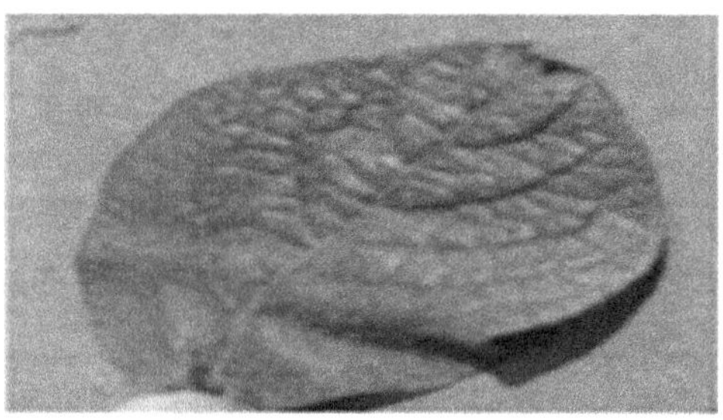

Figure 3. Potato healthy leaf.

2.2 *Preprocessing*

Prior to training the model, the data set was pre-processed by standardizing the pixel values to a series of 0–1 and arbitrarily rotate, flipping, and zooming the photos. Additionally, we divided the dataset into sets for testing data (10%), validation data (10%), and training data (80%).

2.3 *CNN model*

For image categorization, Convolutional Neural Networks (CNNs) stays a prominent deep learning frame work. Its architecture consists of three main layers: fully connected, pooling, and convolutional layer. To extricate spatial attributes from input photos, including edges or textures, the convolutional layer uses filters, or kernels. Activation functions (like ReLU) are applied to these outputs to adjust for non-linearity. Important features are preserved while dimensionality and computation are decreased using pooling layers (such as max pooling). Following a number of these layers, categorization using the learnt characteristics is carried out by fully connected layers. Class probabilities of the final layer are generated by softmax activation. CNNs are perfect for jobs like disease identification in agricultural datasets because of their exceptional ability to recognize spatial hierarchies and patterns.

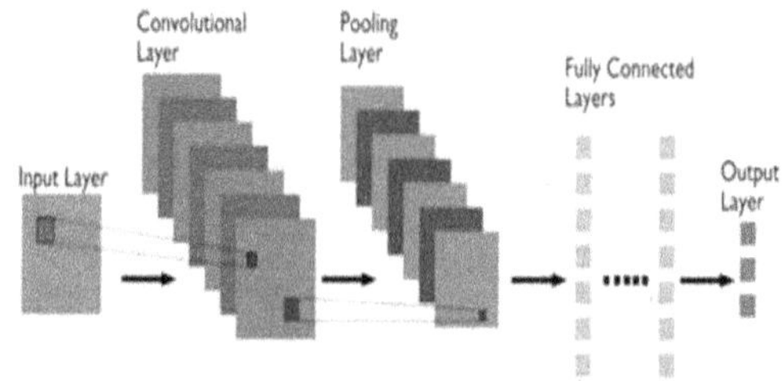

Figure 4. CNN architecture.

2.4 *Resnet 50*

ResNet-50 is one of the deep convolutional neural network with 50 layers that reports the vanishing gradient issue through residual learning. Deeper designs are made possible by the shortcut connections it offers, which make gradients easier to move around the network. The network starts with max pooling after a 7x7 convolutional layer. A stack of bottleneck residual blocks is present in each of its four primary stages. Each convolution is followed by batch normalization and ReLU activations. Lastly, class probabilities are generated by a fully linked layer and a global average pooling layer.

2.5 *LSTM*

LSTM, one kind of RNN (Recurrent Neural Network) which is made to identify dependencies that persist in sequential input. A cell state and its three gates: input gate, a forget gate and output gate—make up an LSTM unit. The cell state serves as memory, storing pertinent data throughout time intervals. The output gate regulates the portion of the cell state to output, the forget gate chooses which evidence to discard, and the input gate chooses how much newer information to store. A vanishing gradient issues that traditional RNNs frequently face are resolved by LSTMs thanks to this gating mechanism. Time-series forecasting, language modeling, and sequential agricultural data analysis, including crop production prediction, all make extensive use of LSTMs.

2.6 *Experimental results*

We evaluate the performance of three DL models. CNN, ResNet50, and LSTM are used to forecast diseases of potato leaves. Its primary objective is to ascertain how well these models can recognize and categorize the diseases accurately categorizing the diseases and their capability to adjust to formerly unseen data analysing each model's potential on a training and validation datasets is essential to obtaining a thorough grasp of its potential.

The outcomes shows that all of the three deep learning models accomplished high performance in detecting and predicting potato leaf diseases, but Resnet50 ensuing as the better performer, when compared to CNN and LSTM. We assessed all the models' consummation on both the training and validation datasets to obtain a clear perception of their abilities. The comparative study of three diverse models demonstrates the efficacy in categorizing potato leaf diseases and provides suggestions in handling the unseen dataset. Acquiring an accuracy of 99.99% and with a loss of 0.0080, the Resnet50 model disclosed better performance on the training dataset.

Figure 5. CNN training and validation accuracy.

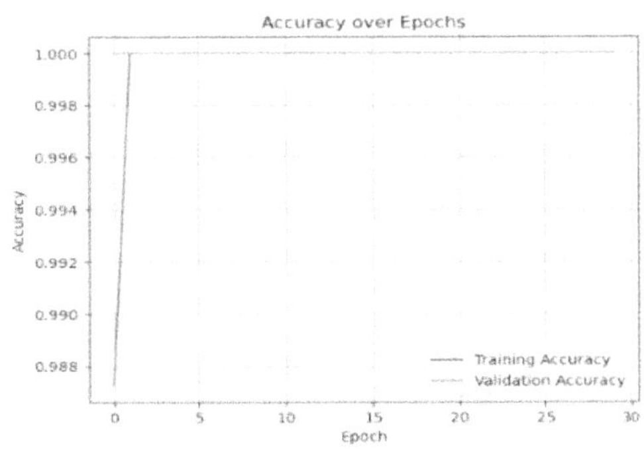

Figure 6. Resnet50 training and validation accuracy.

3 CONCLUSION

Millions of people rely on potatoes to meet their nutritional needs, making it a vital crop in the world. They are vulnerable to a number of leaf viruses, though, which may significantly effect on their quality and productivity. Effective disease management and prevention depend on early and accurate disease identification. In this work, we provide a thorough examination and comparison of three cutting-edge deep learning methods for identifying and predicting potato leaves disease: CNN, ResNet50 and LSTM.

Results from experiments on the potato dataset show that the ResNet50 model outperforms conventional CNN and LSTM architectures in terms of classification performance. Higher accuracy in yield prediction and illness detection tasks is made possible by ResNet50 deep residual learning capacity, which also improves feature extraction and generalization. This attests to its appropriateness for precision farming applications where precise and automated plant health monitoring is essential.

REFERENCES

[1] Qi C. *et al.*, (Nov. 2021), In-field early disease recognition of potato late blight based on deep learning and proximal hyper-spectral imaging, *arXiv preprint.*
[2] Shi Y. *et al.*, (July 2021), A Novel CropdocNet for Automated Potato Late Blight Disease Detection from UAV-based Hyperspectral Imagery, *arXiv preprint.*
[3] Al-Adhaileh M. *et al.*, (2023), Potato Blight Detection Using Fine-Tuned CNN Architecture, *Mathematics*, vol. 11, no. 6.
[4] Alam M.S. *et al.*, (May 2024), PotatoGANs: Utilizing GANs, Instance Segmentation, and Explainable AI or Enhanced Potato Disease Identification and Classification, *arxiv.*
[5] Pradeep *et al.*, (2023), Optimized Deep Learning for Potato Blight Detection Using Bayesian CNN, *Potato Research.*
[6] Kasana S.S. and Rathore A.S., (2024), Attention-Based Light Weight Deep Learning Models for Early Potato Disease Detection, *Applied Sciences*, vol. 14, no. 17.
[7] Li D. *et al.*, (2021), Improving Potato Yield Prediction by Combining Cultivar Information and UAV Remote Sensing Data Using Machine Learning, *Remote Sensing*, vol. 13, no. 16.
[8] Lee *et al.*, (2024), Mask R-CNN for yield estimation in potato; described in review by Li *et al.*, *MDPI Agriculture.*
[9] A Comprehensive Review of CNN-based Disease Detection Strategies in Potato Agriculture, *Potato Research*, Aug. 2024.
[10] Tambe U.Y. *et al.*, Potato Leaf Disease Classification using Deep Learning: A CNN Approach, *arXiv preprint*, Nov. 2023.
[11] Deep Learning Approaches for Potato Leaf Disease Detection ... , *IIETA*, 2024.
[12] Innovations in Solanaceae crop monitoring via DL-enhanced SIS-YOLOv8, *Frontiers in Plant Science*, 2024.
[13] Manorama Devi B. *et al.*, (May 2025). Implementation of Novel Deep Learning Techniques for Real-time Object Detection, *IEEE Xplore*, ICCCEET.
[14] Vikash Sawan *et al.*, (2025), Potato Leaf Disease Detection Method is based on a CNN model with a Genetic Algorithm, *Journal of Recent Innovations in Computer Science and Technology*, vol. 2, no. 1, pp. 8–15

Session 2: IoT, Smart Cities and Infrastructure

 ISBN: 978-1-041-34234-2

Revolutionizing Parking Management with LoRaWAN

Harini Shriram S. and Krishna Meera V.
Assistant Professor, Department of ECE, Ramco Institute of Technology, Rajapalayam, Tamilnadu, India

Sathya G.
Assistant Professor, Department of ECE, P.S.R.R College of Engineering, Sivakasi, Tamilnadu, India

Pavithra R.
Assistant Professor, Department of CSE, Velammal College of Engineering and Technology, Madurai, Tamilnadu, India

Bavithramsri S.K.
Design Engineer, Syrma SGS Technology Limited, Chennai, India

Ganapathiammal P.
Research Scholar, Anna University, Chennai, India

ABSTRACT: Parking shortages present one of the main problems for city-dwellers. This technical solution to this problem is aptly called smart parking. Despite the creation of various smart parking systems that have displayed parking monitoring and guidance functions, the key problem is how to find the trade-off between cost, power consumption, and accuracy and reliability. To overcome these problems, the concept of Long Range (LoRa) Radio communication is introduced. LoRa is a low power technology that utilizes unlicensed frequency bands. Each device's state is tracked, and the LoRa gateway receives the practical coverage range. Data is transmitted to a web server via the LoRa gateway and accessed from anywhere in the world. A Bosch Parking Lot Sensor shall be used in this proposed system to determine whether a specific parking space is occupied or free. The user's web server is updated with this state through the LoRa gateway. The proposed design using the Long-Range Wide Area Network protocol will be fully scalable and mobile.

Keywords: Wireless Sensor Network, LoRaWA, Bosch Parking Sensor

1 INTRODUCTION

The world faces major issues with infrastructure and resource management as a result of the world's population growth, especially in urban regions. Cities have become overcrowded as a result of urbanization, and the number of cars on the road has increased in tandem[1]. Due to growing pollution, this has resulted in serious traffic congestion, a shortage of parking spots, and environmental issues[2]. In addition to being a cause of annoyance for commuters, traffic congestion lowers economic output. The challenge of locating parking spots is one of the main causes of this issue, since vehicles frequently spend a significant amount of time circling parking lots or streets. Urban problems are made worse by this inefficiency, which increases fuel use, traffic density, and carbon emissions. However, smart parking may reduce traffic and strengthen urban mobility. Smart parking systems notify motorists in real-time through advanced technology about available parking spaces, avoiding much of the time wasted hunting for a parking spot. Such systems maximize the usage of parking resources, provide convenience to the users, and cut down on pollution and traffic jams[3–6]. Long Range Wide Area Network, or LoRaWAN, has emerged as a powerful technology with many promise towards the establishment of smart parking systems. Long-range distance communication and less power consumption establish LoRaWAN as a fast growing standard for the deployment of wireless sensors in parking lots. These sensors, once installed in a parking lot, can measure how occupied the parking spaces are and communicate back to central systems in real time to provide information about this availability to drivers through mobile applications and digital displays[7–9].

2 LORA AND LORAWAN

LoRa is a physical layer radio technology that is a member of the LPWAN family[10-11]. This wireless modulation is designed and developed by Semtech. It's a low-power, low-data-rate communication for long-distance applications. Because of cheap implementation, LoRa finds its place in enterprises. LoRaWAN is a software protocol and network architecture which works in the network layer. The system design of the network layer, including the protocol, provides customer quality of service, assurance of network capacity, security of the system, and node battery life. Further, this means of communication supports several applications[12-14]. The Figure 1 shows the LoRaWAN Layers.

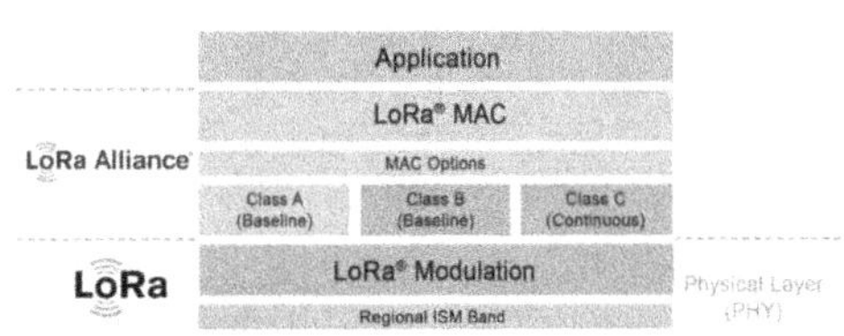

Figure 1. LoRaWAN layers.

The proposed project implements Bosch parking lot sensors to inquire of the vacancy of a certain slot. The parking sensor device's core is made up of two separate sensing components: a radar-based reflectivity device above the sensor tool and a magnetometer sensor for detecting changes in the magnetic area of a certain environment. The operational flow of the Bosch parking lot sensor is shown in Figure 2. The data will be sent by

DOI: 10.1201/9781042001767-53

the sensor to the gateway using the LoRaWAN protocol. This data will be uploaded to the network server (The ThingsMate network). Then, the status of the end devices (sensors) may be monitored from anywhere in the world any time using the application server (mobiles, laptops).

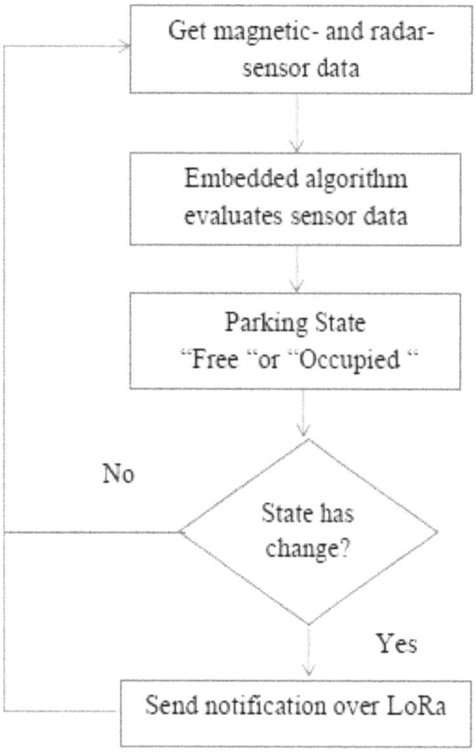

Figure 2. Operational flow of the Bosch parking lot sensor.

The hardware components required to complete the proposed system are • LoRa Gateway • LoRa Shield • Bosch Parking Lot Sensor • Personal computer or Moblie. LoRa gateways work about 5 kilometers away, a single gateway can manage multiple parking sensors. The device works using a LoRa gateway that monitors all parking sensors. A magnetometer is a scientific instrument designed to measure the strength and direction of magnetic fields nearby. The Earth's magnetic field changes due to variations in rock types and the interaction of charged particles from the sun with the planet's magnetosphere, resulting in different levels of magnetism in various locations. Radar sensor is essential for identifying, locating, tracking, and recognizing a range of objects over long distances Electromagnetic sensing is the principle behind radar, which involves projecting energy onto targets and capturing the resulting reflections. Radar technology is remarkably versatile, detecting objects both man-made (e.g., spacecraft, cars) and natural (e.g., planetary bodies, birds, rain, insects). Crucially, radar provides range determination (distance measurement) and successfully ascertains the presence, location, and speed of these distant targets, even amidst unfavorable atmospheric conditions.The device firmware initializes and checks for potential faults of the hardware components after the sensor is placed on the mounting pad. This procedure delays the first LoRa join message by about two minutes. The initial two-minute sensor initialization time can be exceeded before the device is visible on the LoRa application server. This extended latency is a result of the system requiring multiple LoRa join retries if the join accept message is missed, often due to channel degradation or network non-responsiveness.

3 IMPLEMENTATION

3.1 *Assembly and commissioning*

Installation requirements: Make sure the necessary infrastructure is in place before installing the sensors: Verify the backend connection, the gateway's functionality, and the stability of the internet connection. Furthermore, the administration software and backend have to operate. Ensure that all necessary parts exist in Figure 3 and that the necessary tools are accessible.

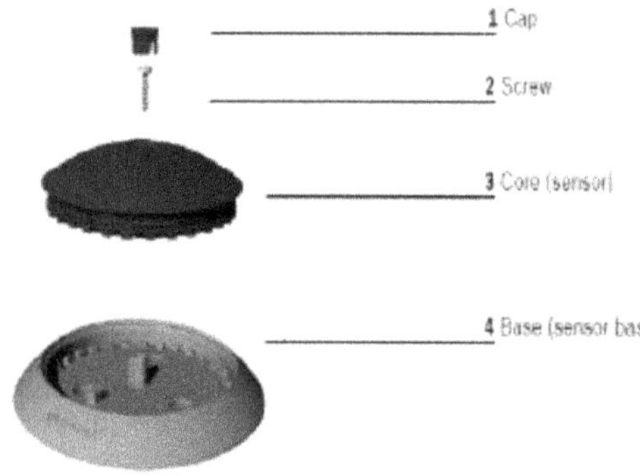

Figure 3. Components of parking sensor.

Preparation of the parking space: The parking lot has to be cleaned of all kinds of dirt, dust, oil, water, and other impurities. For this reason, at least one swept area needs to be prepared. Nonetheless, it is recommended to clean the surface with a burner and a high-pressure cleaner to get rid of impurities. As seen in Figure 4, the installation must be done in the center of the parking area to guarantee the best sensor precision.

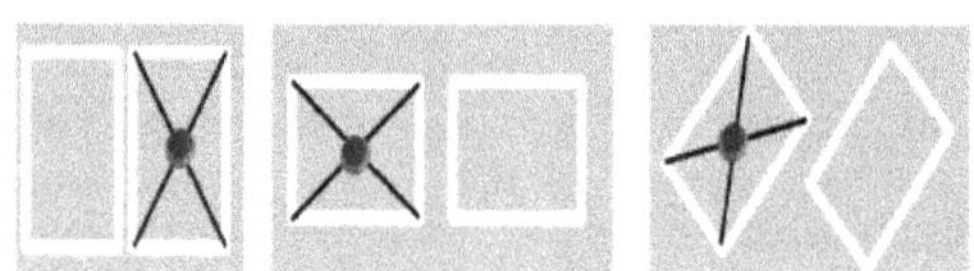

Figure 4. Schematic of the parking space.

Configuration: Creating an Account in ThingsMate :Using the URL Things Mate network server https://beta.thethings-mate.com/oauth/login create an account as shown in Figure 5.

Figure 5. Login page.

Connect the gateway to your computer through Ethernet cable. Select the network & internet setting as shown in Figure 6.

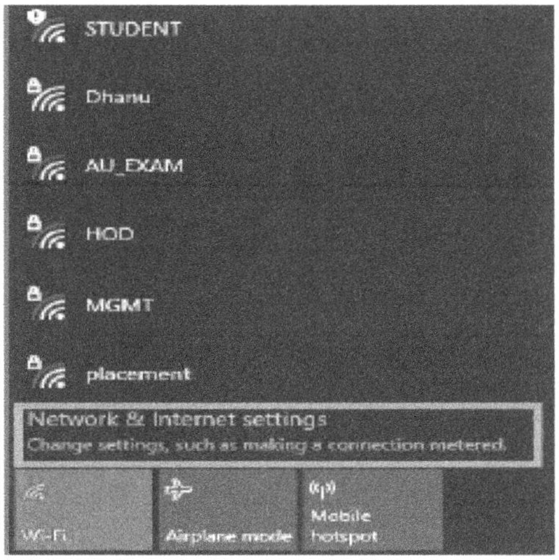

Figure 6. Connecting ethernet.

Choose Properties by right-clicking on Ethernet, then Internet Protocol Version 4 (TCP/IP). As illustrated in Figure 7, choose to utilize the IP address 172.31.255.253 and set the subnet mask to 255.255.255.252.

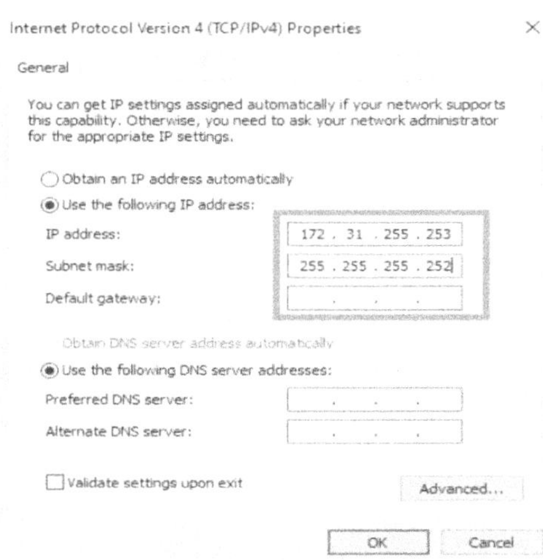

Figure 7. Internet protocol version 4 (TCP/IPv4) properties.

After this open google chrome and type 172.31.255.254:8000 and click enter. Enter the root user name and the dragino password to log in. The page for the gateway is open. this select network -> Wi-Fi. Click enable Wi-Fi WAN client. Enter the Wi-Fi SSID and Wi-Fi password click save & apply.

3.2 *LoRaWAN interface*

The parking sensor unit in Class A has a LoRa radio enclosed. The newly added capability conforms to LoRaWAN specification 1.0.2. The LoRaWAN v1.0.2 IN865 Regional settings are used to determine the supported frequencies and reception window settings. The RX1 offset and RX2 can be changed using the Join Approve message (CFList) or associated MAC commands. The battery level cannot be found using the DevStatusAns MAC command. A magnetic contact between the mounting plate and the sensor only closes when the parts are united, activating the join mechanism. LoRaWAN Specification 1.0.2's Over the Air Activation (OTAA) serves as the foundation for the Join protocol. There is no availability of ABP (Activation by Personalization). When the parking sensor system is turned on, it will send a join request message in an attempt to connect to a LoRaWAN network. As soon as feasible, and up to four times more, depending on transmission time constraints, the sensor will try again if the enter request is denied (5 attempts total). A total of five attempts will be made before the sensor performs an exponential reset following the fifth unsuccessful attempt. If a Join approve message does not follow the Join request message, the sensor will try again using the procedures listed in Table 1.

Table 1. LoRaWAN interface adaptive data rate.

Attempt	Data Rate
1st attempt	Initial transmission setting. Configured DR or default (DR2)
2nd attempt	Configured DR or default (DR2)
3rd attempt	DR2
4th attempt	DR1
5th attempt	DR0

The sensor returns the data rate to the default value (DR2) when the Join approve message is received at attempts 3, 4, or 5. It is presumed by this action that the data rate is set up to prevent communication with the gateway. The Updated Request Number (URN) printed on the sensor heart can be used to determine the Extended Unique Identifier (EUI) of the sensor, which is pre-provisioned before manufacturing. You will discover the URN on the label or on the underside of the parking sensor core. Along with to providing an URN, a barcode facilitates a quicker installation procedure.

3.3 *Application server*

In the Thingsmate server, click gateway tab and click Add gateway. Enter the dragino gateway id in the gateway EUI. Make the gateway status as public server by enabling the public button. Set the frequency plan as Indian frequency from the drop-down list and click create gateway. After creating gateway, click on the channel tab for creating channel and click add channel. Give name for the channel in channel ID and click create channel. Click end node for interfacing the end device as shown in Figure 8

Figure 8. End node.

Give the respective App EUI, App KEY, Device EUI of the sensor in activation information. Click payload formatters and then click uplink. By selecting java script option type the payload in given space. Give query name and select the channel that created previously. As per the channel select the end device and attributes. Change the refresh timing by every minute and click apply changes. Select the Parking option from the visualization type. Give the respective attribute that need to display on dashboard and label the visualization and click save. Here query is created, after that click on dashboard tab and click add dashboard as shown in Figure 9.

Figure 9. Visualization editor.

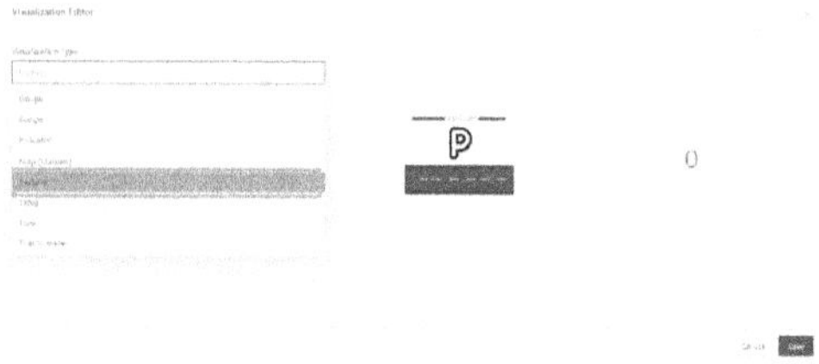

Figure 10. Dashboard.

After connecting the device there will be live data which shows the uplink message from the end node.When the output is shown in network server click the application tab. Click queries and click add query. Following the receipt of the join-accept, the device issues its first application layer payload (the start-up message). If a change is observed, it will then continue regular operation and transmit park status signals. The protocol mandates that the vast majority of application data payloads, encompassing status reports for initial power-up, periodic device health (heartbeat), and parking conditions, are transmitted under a confirmed delivery mechanism by default. It is conceivable to set the parking state message to either not confirm at all or not confirm with repetitions. This can lower the gateway's proportion of correctly received messages, but it also reduces the amount of service cycle needed to accept all messages. Figure 11 illustrates how the gateway's data is periodically uploaded to the ThingsMate dashboard-based interrupt.

Figure 11. Smart parking system setup.

The user will see the availability of parking slots from the dashboard at any time. There is a 1 next to the occupied slot and a 0 next to the open slot. The timing of the parking status can also be fine-tuned.

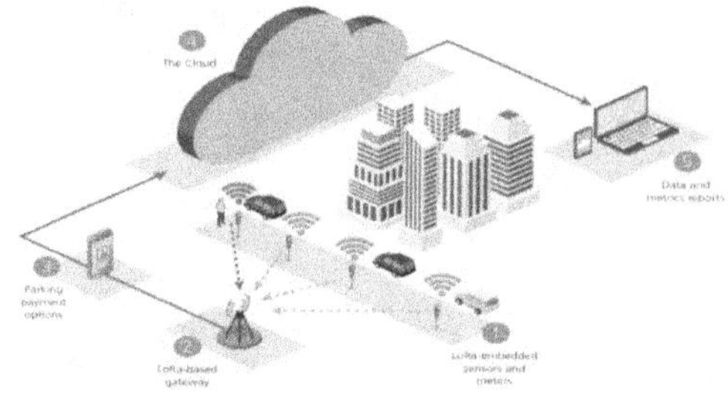

Figure 12. The ThingMate output.

4 CONCLUSION

LoRa technology offers the advantage of consuming comparatively less electricity than other technologies. In non-urban areas, it has a coverage area of 10-15 km, while in urban areas, it has a coverage area of 2 km. With this technology, all of the end devices within the range can be operated by a single gateway, making it simple to accommodate all of the end devices. End devices can communicate with each other through one or more gateways, each of which can link up to 1000 end devices. As a result, LoRa technology offers a more effective approach for smart parking system in smart cities. The primary aim of this technology is to reduce costs. The parking sensor at the parking areas can be tracked at all times via the public web server, for tracking the free parking space through the cities. This saves time, fuel consumption and prevents traffic for the users. LoRa technology can be used in a variety of application, Including traffic management, waste management, health monitoring, smart street lighting, pet monitoring, smart farming and others.

REFERENCES

[1] Akash Gupta *et al.*, (2018), Smart Parking System using Cloud based Computation and Raspberry Pi, *Second International conference on I-SMAC (IoT in Social, Mobile, Analytics and Cloud)*, pp. 94–100.

[2] Ajchariyavanich, *et al.*, (2019), Park King: An IoT- based Smart Parking System, *5th International Smart cities Conference.*

[3] Agustina Ampuni *et al.*, (2019), Smart Parking System with Automatic Cashier Machine Utilize the IoT Technology, *IEEE Conference*, pp. 1–4.

[4] Andrea Zanella *et al.*, (2016), Long range Communication in unlicensed bands:The rising stars I the IoT and smart city Scenarios, *IEEE Wireless Communications* Vol. 23, No. 5, pp. 1–7.

[5] Andrew J Wixed (2016), Evaluation of LoRa and LoRaWAN for Wireless sensor networks, *IEEE International Conference-Sensors.*

[6] Andrew Mackey *et al.*, (2020), Smart Parking System Based on Bluetooth Low Energy Beacons with Particle Filtering, *IEEE System Journal*, DOI: 10.1109/JSYST.2020.2968883. pp. 1–12.

[7] BaccoManlio *et al.*, (2017), Environmental Monitoring for Smart Cities, *IEEE Journal of Environmental Monitoring for Smart Cities.*

[8] BadisHammi *et al.*, (2017), IoT technologies for smart cities, *Journal from IET (The Institution of Engineering and technology).*

[9] Faiz Shaikh *et al.*, (2007), A Survey on "Smart Parking" System, *International Journal of Innovative Research in Science, Engineering and Technology*, Vol. 4, No. 10, pp. 9933–9940.

Next-Generation Smart Systems – Sekhar et al. (Eds)

Survivor Tracker: An IoT-Based Victim Detection and Rescue System Using ESP32

K. Mohana Lakshmi, Suraya Mubeen, and Bandi Doss
Department of ECE, CMR Technical Campus, Hyderabad, Telangana, India

N. Siddarth Reddy and G. Raja Sri
UG Students, CMR Technical Campus, Hyderabad, Telangana, India

A. Sridivya
Department of ECE, CMR Technical Campus, Hyderabad, Telangana, India

ABSTRACT: Victims of natural disasters like earthquakes and building collapses are frequently buried beneath rubble, making human detection and prompt rescue essential. The ESP32 microcontroller-based Internet of Things rescue system, Survivor Tracker, is presented in this work. The robot is equipped with a DHT11 sensor to monitor temperature and humidity, an MQ2 gas sensor to detect hazardous gases, an ultrasonic sensor to measure proximity, and a PIR sensor to detect human presence. A Firebase cloud database, which can be accessed through a mobile app, receives real-time data. The system stops, raises an alarm, and gives the data when it detects a human. This low-cost, real-time solution increases operating efficiency and situational awareness, which improves disaster response.

Keywords: MQ2, Firebase, ESP32, IoT, PIR, DHT11, ultrasonic sensor, and disaster rescue

1 INTRODUCTION

In disaster scenarios like earthquakes, structural collapses, and industrial mishaps, rapid victim detection and rescue are crucial for survival. Traditional search and rescue efforts often rely on manual labor, placing responders in dangerous and unstable environments with limited visibility and significant risk. The Survivor Tracker project addresses these challenges through an IoT-powered mobile robotic system designed to enhance safety and accelerate rescue operations. With integrated human detection, environmental sensing, and real-time data transmission, the autonomous system empowers emergency teams to monitor disaster zones remotely, maintaining critical situational awareness without direct exposure to danger. At its core is a low-cost microcontroller that unites obstacle navigation, wireless communication, and environmental sensing into a compact unit. Data is instantly uploaded to a cloud server and accessed through a mobile application, ensuring seamless coordination and timely updates for field teams. Survivor Tracker can be deployed across varied disaster landscapes and is engineered to function autonomously in obstructed or hazardous terrains. By reducing human risk and speeding up victim identification, the system brings a smarter, safer edge to disaster response ultimately saving more lives.

IoT-enabled robotic system employs motion sensing technology to detect human presence via infrared radiation Utilizing a passive infrared (PIR) sensor, it identifies body heat signatures and triggers an alert mechanism such as a buzzer to assist rescue teams in swiftly locating survivors. The robot, controlled by a microcontroller, is capable of forward and reverse motion and obstacle avoidance using sensor input. The proposed method shows a significant improvement in terms of recognition accuracy, data communication, and alerting efficiency when compared to traditional GPRS-based systems, highlighting its potential to enhance future search-and-rescue missions using affordable and scalable IoT-based robotic solutions [1]. The primary objective of this project is to design a mobile rescue system capable of operating autonomously in disaster zones where human rescuers cannot safely intervene to a multitude of technological issues. Our study makes use of a novel passive infrared sensor device that can detect human presence through the emission of infrared light. The Passive infrared sensor (PIR) can detect and manipulate heat radiation emitted by a person's body. Once a target is identified, the system activates an audible alert to guide rescuers swiftly to the victim's location. The overarching aim of Human Detection using an Unmanned Ground Vehicle is to develop an intuitive and reliable solution that can be deployed in high-risk environments such as disaster zones or high security locations like diamond vaults where human access is limited or unsafe [2]. This research introduces a smart IoT-based system designed to locate survivors in critical environments such as disaster zones and war-affected regions. The setup relies on a microcontroller working in tandem with sensors like PIR (Passive Infrared) and ultrasonic detectors to identify the presence of humans. Once a person is detected, the system automatically sends the information to a central monitoring unit using IoT connectivity. The study provides a detailed explanation of the system's design, functionality, and real-time performance, demonstrating its potential to improve victim detection and rescue operations in unsafe or hard-to-reach areas [3]. Multi-Robot coordination as well as modular robotics is becoming more and more acknowledged in the literature. to maintain secure communication and ensure device authenticity, each robotic unit is registered through blockchain-based network authentication. On top of that, consumers may see relevant notifications and information on a webpage. Autonomous surveillance is made possible by the utilization of UAV-UGV collaboration, thanks to the high vantage point field of view. Cloud computing also reduces the complexity of microcontrollers, which in turn reduces their cost. Leveraging blockchain technology, the system strengthens network security by blocking unauthorized or potentially malicious robotic nodes from joining the operational cluster, while also ensuring adherence to established privacy regulations and compliance standards[4]. In their work on an IoT based smart robotic system for human identification, Tamilselvi and Chamundeeswari present a wireless, remotely controlled robot built using Raspberry Pi. The robot integrates visual surveillance through a network-connected camera mounted on a pan–tilt mechanism, enabling the operator to scan the environment remotely. The system navigates uneven

DOI: 10.1201/9781042001767-54

terrain with adaptive motion control while delivering real-time video feedback via Wi-Fi connectivity. Sensor data is processed using embedded logic and transmitted to a GUI dashboard, allowing seamless robot navigation and monitoring from a mobile or laptop interface. Their solution addresses common limitations of RF based surveillance robots, such as limited range and need for manual control, by leveraging cloud connectivity and intelligent camera mobility. While the system significantly improves remote monitoring and situational awareness, its reliance on continuous human supervision and a stable network connection poses limitations to achieving full autonomous detection capabilities [5]. The "Smart Human Detection Robot Using IoT for Disaster Situations" proposes a robotic system designed to detect human presence in disaster prone areas by integrating IoT technologies. The design incorporates a mobile robotic platform outfitted with wireless communication modules and environmental sensors that detect human presence by analysing body heat and motion patterns. Data collected from the sensors is sent to a cloud platform in real time, allowing remote access by rescue teams. The authors emphasize the system's potential to reduce human casualties by detecting trapped individuals and reporting environmental conditions promptly. The robot's mobility allows it to traverse unstable terrains, and its embedded logic ensures that it can make basic decisions autonomously. This study advances the emerging domain of IoT-enabled disaster response by presenting a scalable, efficient solution for real-time human detection during emergencies [6,7]. The research paper titled 'IoT-Based Rescue Robot for Human Detection' outlines the development of an autonomous robotic system equipped with real-time sensing and wireless communication technologies to locate individuals trapped in disaster-stricken areas. Equipped with a variety of sensors and controlled by a microcontroller, the robot detects human presence and environmental threats. Upon identifying signs of life or danger, it leverages IoT connectivity to relay crucial data to a centralized server, allowing rescue teams to remotely evaluate conditions in real time. The authors emphasize the robot's capability to traverse rough terrain and confined spaces, making it well-suited for navigating collapsed structures and hard-to-reach disaster zones. The robot's decision-making logic, combined with IoT-based updates, enhances both situational awareness and safety during emergency response. This research reinforces the practical role of embedded and IoT systems in improving the effectiveness and efficiency of modern search-and-rescue operations [8,9]. This study explores the deployment of a car-shaped robotic platform as an auxiliary life-saving system in emergency scenarios, aiming to enhance search-and-rescue capabilities where traditional methods may fall short. The robot employs a diverse sensor array—including gas, humidity, and temperature sensors—to detect signs of human presence, with thermal imaging technology enhancing the identification of body heat signatures. A key challenge addressed is the reliable identification and tracking of humans, particularly in environments where fields of view (FOVs) do not overlap. To address the limitations of individual sensors, the study introduces an intelligent search algorithm that strategically compensates for blind spots and detection voids, thereby enhancing the overall accuracy and reliability of human identification in complex environments. Experimental results demonstrate a high accuracy rate in identifying human presence. The robot's movement can be controlled manually through directional commands (forward, backward, left, right), and future plans involve equipping it with advanced sensors capable of detecting individuals obscured by obstacles such as walls [10,11].

2 METHODOLOGY

The Survivor Tracker system utilizes the ESP32 microcontroller as its core processing unit, orchestrating sensor data acquisition and cloud communication. The system employs a passive infrared (PIR) sensor to detect human presence based on thermal emissions, while an ultrasonic sensor supports obstacle avoidance by continuously gauging the distance to nearby objects. Upon detecting a human presence, the robot halts and activates an audible alert mechanism. Sensor data—covering motion, distance, temperature, humidity, and gas concentrations—is transmitted in real time to a Firebase cloud database. When hazardous gas levels exceed preset thresholds, the system triggers a buzzer alert to warn nearby responders. Motor control is handled by the L298N driver, enabling movement based on sensor input and environmental conditions. Rescue teams access live system updates through a custom mobile application linked to Firebase, allowing for swift decision-making in high-risk areas. Engineered for low power consumption and reliable wireless connectivity, the ESP32-based architecture provides a scalable and cost-effective foundation for deployment in disaster-affected regions. A system block diagram is depicted in Figure 1 to illustrate the functional layout of the Survivor Tracker.

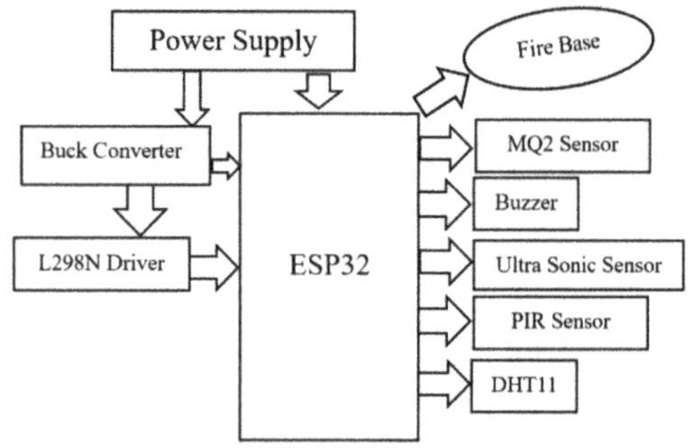

Figure 1. Block diagram of survivor tracker.

Step1: System Initialization: Power on the ESP32 and initialize the required modules. Connect to Wi-Fi and establish communication with the Firebase database to begin real-time data logging and monitoring.

Step2: Start and Monitor Movement: The robot starts moving forward by default. During movement, the ESP32 continuously monitors sensor inputs including motion detection, distance, temperature, humidity, and gas levels.

Step3: Human Detection and Immediate Response: If the PIR sensor detects motion (indicating human presence), the robot stops immediately. A "Human Detected" alert is sent to Firebase, and the ultrasonic sensor measures the distance to the detected object or person, which is also uploaded.

Step4: Environmental Monitoring and Alerting: The DHT11 sensor reads temperature and humidity values, and the MQ2 sensor monitors gas levels. If gas levels exceed a set threshold, the buzzer is activated and the gas concentration is sent to Firebase.

Step5: Resume Operation: If no motion or hazard is detected, the robot continues moving forward, and the system loops back to monitor all inputs continuously.

(A) **ESP32:** The ESP32 is a low-cost, low-power system on a chip (SoC) with integrated Wi-Fi and Bluetooth capabilities. It serves as the brain of the Survivor Tracker system, managing sensor data collection, motor control, and cloud communication. With its dual-core processor and multiple GPIO pins, the ESP32 efficiently handles real-time processing and wireless data transmission to Firebase. Its compact size and power efficiency make it ideal for embedded IoT applications. The following Figure 2 shows the ESP32 microcontroller.

Figure 2. ESP32.

(B) **PIR (Passive Infrared) Sensor:** The PIR sensor detects motion by measuring the infrared radiation emitted by objects, particularly human bodies. When a human is within its sensing range, the sensor outputs a high signal, prompting the robot to halt and trigger an alert. It is a crucial component for identifying the presence of victims in disaster zones, operating reliably with low power consumption. The following Figure 3 shows the PIR Sensor.

Figure 3. PIR sensor.

(C) **Ultrasonic sensor:** It is used to measure the distance to nearby objects, helping the robot detect obstacles and assist in navigation and target verification. The following Figure 4 shows the Ultrasonic Sensor.

Figure 4. Ultrasonic sensor.

(D) **DHT11 Sensor**: It is used to captures temperature and humidity data from the environment, allowing monitoring of conditions around the robot. The following Figure 5 shows the DHT 11 Sensor.

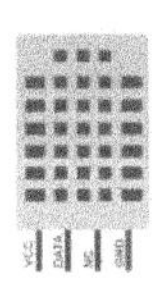

Figure 5. DHT11 sensor.

(E) **MQ2 Gas Sensor:** It detects harmful gases like smoke, methane, or LPG. Triggers an alert if gas levels exceed safe limits. The following Figure 6 shows the MQ2 Gas Sensor.

Figure 6. MQ2 gas sensor.

(F) **L298N Motor Driver:** It is used to controls the speed and direction of two DC motors. It receives signals from the ESP32 and allows the robot to move based on sensor input. The following Figure 7 shows the L298N Motor Driver.

Figure 7. L298N motor driver.

(G) **Buzzer:** An alert device that sounds when gas is detected or human presence is confirmed, providing immediate feedback. The following Figure 8 shows the Buzzer.

Figure 8. Buzzer.

3 RESULTS AND DISCUSSION

The below Figure 9 illustrates the complete hardware integration of the Survivor Tracker – IoT-Based Human Detection and Rescue System. It clearly displays how each component is interconnected to perform specific roles during disaster response. . The ESP32 microcontroller serves as the brain of the system, interfacing with sensors like the PIR sensor for motion detection, DHT11 for environmental monitoring, MQ2 for gas leakage detection, and the ultrasonic sensor for obstacle distance measurement. The L298N motor driver controls the DC motors that drive the robot's movement, powered through a buck converter for stable voltage regulation. Alerts are signalled through a buzzer, and the data is continuously pushed to the cloud for remote monitoring. This setup ensures real-time responsiveness and autonomous operation in hazardous environments.

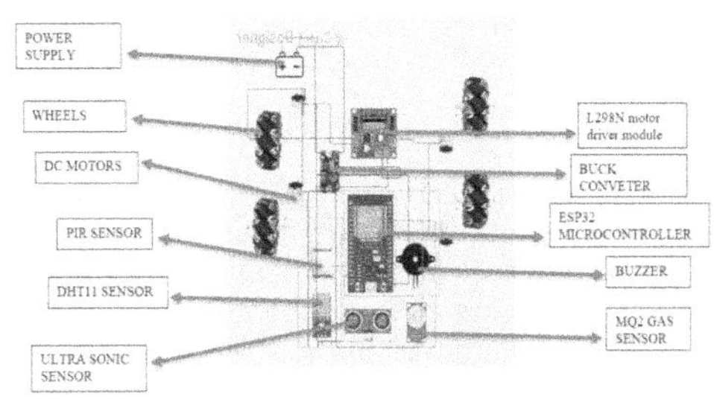

Figure 9. Hardware connections of survivor tracker.

Figure 10. (a) Top view of model. (b) Front view of model.

The above Figure 10a,10b illustrate the top and front views of the "Survivor Tracker – IoT-Based Human Detection and

Rescue System". The top view reveals the full hardware layout including the wiring, ESP32 microcontroller, L298N motor driver, sensors, and power circuitry neatly placed on the chassis. The front view highlights the positioning of the ultrasonic sensor and PIR sensor, both of which are critical for detecting obstacles and human presence. The robot is built on a four-wheel drive chassis that ensures stable mobility across rough terrains, making it suitable for disaster-affected environments. These physical implementations reflect the integration of embedded components into a functional and compact robotic rescue system.

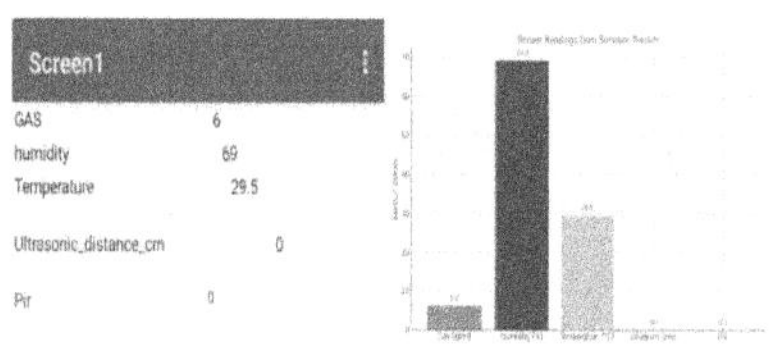

Figure 11. (a) Data from the sensors. (b) Bar chart.

The above Figure 11a and 11b illustrates a comparison between the real-time mobile app interface and the graphical sensor data output of the "Survivor Tracker – IoT-Based Human Detection and Rescue System". On the left, the mobile screen displays live readings from various sensors such as gas concentration, humidity, temperature, ultrasonic distance, and PIR motion status. These values are pushed to the Firebase cloud by the ESP32 controller and are used by rescue teams for decision-making. On the right, the bar graph offers a visual representation of the same data, making it easier to analyze at a glance. This combination of textual and graphical output enhances usability and ensures that critical information is accessible and interpretable in real time during rescue operations.

Table 1. Sensor values of the survivor tracker.

Sensors	Values
Gas	4
Humidity	68.5
Temperature	29.2
Ultrasonic_Distance_cm	142.47701
PIR	1

The above Table 1 shows the real-time sensor readings obtained from the "Survivor Tracker – IoT-Based Human Detection and Rescue System". It captures the live values from various sensors integrated into the robot, including gas concentration, ambient humidity, temperature, distance from an obstacle (measured via ultrasonic sensor), and human presence (detected via PIR sensor). These values are monitored and transmitted to the Firebase cloud by the ESP32 microcontroller. The structured format of the table enables quick interpretation and aids rescue teams in making fast, informed decisions in disaster zones. This tabular data representation ensures clarity and supports efficient on-field response efforts.

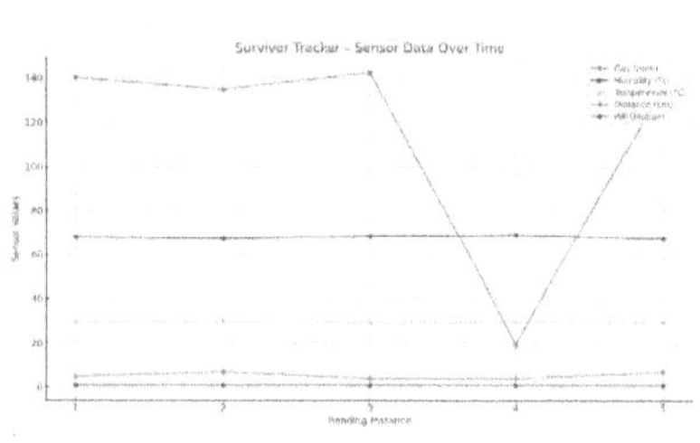

Figure 12. Line graph of survivor tracker.

The above Figure 12-line graph illustrates multiple real-time sensor readings collected over five consecutive instances by the Survivor Tracker – IoT-Based Human Detection and Rescue System. It shows how each sensor value behaves over time. The gas sensor values fluctuate slightly between 4 and 8 ppm, indicating low and stable gas presence. The humidity readings remain relatively constant around 67–69%, while temperature hovers close to 29–30°C, suggesting a consistent ambient environment. The ultrasonic sensor (distance) shows a sudden drop at instance 4, indicating the robot came very close to an object or person. The PIR sensor consistently reads 1, meaning motion was detected during the sampling period. This chart demonstrates the system's ability to continuously monitor environmental and human-related conditions with clarity and consistency.

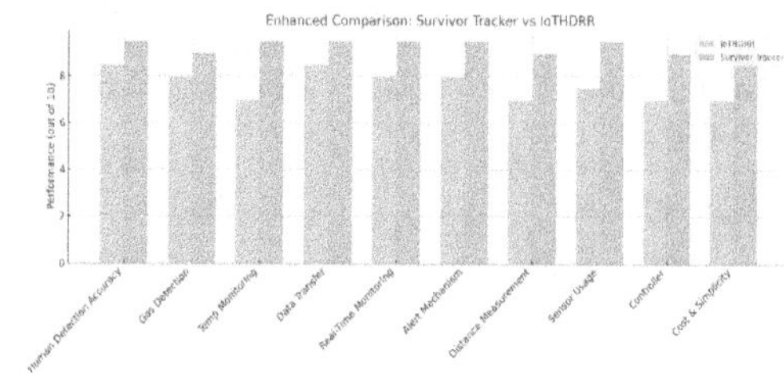

Figure 13. Comparison of survivor tracker and IoTHDRR.

The above Figure 13 bar graph offers a comparative overview of the performance between the Survivor Tracker – IoT Based Victim Detection and Rescue System Using ESP32 and the existing IoTHDRR model across ten key parameters. Each parameter is rated on a scale of 10 to evaluate system effectiveness in areas such as human detection accuracy, gas detection, temperature monitoring, real-time data transfer, alert mechanisms, and overall system cost and simplicity. The Survivor Tracker consistently scores higher in all categories, owing to its advanced integration of sensors like DHT11 and MQ2, efficient ESP32-based architecture, and real-time Firebase communication. This graph visually reinforces the improved reliability, responsiveness, and usability of the Survivor Tracker system over conventional designs, especially In Disaster Response Scenarios.

4 CONCLUSION

The development of autonomous robotic systems for disaster response presents a significant step toward safer and more efficient rescue missions. This project demonstrates the effective integration of IoT and sensor technologies in identifying human presence and monitoring environmental conditions in real-time. By enabling mobile robots to interact with dynamic environments and relay critical data remotely, the system supports timely decision-making for rescue teams. This work contributes to the field of embedded robotics and highlights the potential for scalable solutions in disaster management and emergency response applications.

ACKNOWLEDGEMENT

This design was implemented in the Department of Electronics and Communication from CMR Technical campus with the support of the Director, HOD, and Faculty members.

REFERENCES

[1] Shanmugapriya N., Divya D., Maharajan M.P., M. V, Arun S. and Krishnamoorthy R. (2024), Revolutionizing Innovation

Design and Development of Human Detection and Rescue Robot Based on Internet of Things Association, *2024 5th International Conference on Electronics and Sustainable Communication Systems (ICESC)*, Coimbatore, India, 2024, pp. 425–431, doi: 10.1109/ICESC60852.2024.10690141.

[2] Dr. Shyamala C., Ananya S., Anitha K.M., Ankitha M. and Janhavi H. (2023), Design of a Human Detection Robot during Disaster, *International Journal for Research in Applied Science and Engineering Technology*, 3512–3515.

[3] Nadiger D.K.S., Santhosh Krishna B.V., Piruthiviraj P., Vinay Kumar K., Hirebidari B.N. and Vignesh (2022), IoT Based Alive Human Detection in War Field and Calamity Area Using Microcontroller, *2022 Second International Conference on Artificial Intelligence and Smart Energy (ICAIS)*, Coimbatore, India, 2022, pp. 1233–1238, doi: 10.1109/ICAIS53314.2022.9742741.

[4] Tanaka, K., Ogura, S., Krishnamoorthy, R., Sugiyama, Ki. and Kawahara, M. (2024). Flexibility and Productivity in IoT Programming: A Case Study with Mruby. In: Guarda, T., Portela, F., Diaz-Nafria, J.M. (eds) Advanced Research in Technologies, Information, Innovation and Sustainability. ARTIIS 2023. *Communications in Computer and Information Science*, vol 1936. Springer, Cham. https://doi.org/10.1007/978-3-031-48855-9_2

[5] Tamilselvi M., Parameshwari M.K., Raajini X.M., Chamundeeswari G., Kalaiselvi K. and Pandi V.S., (2024), IoT based Smart Robotic Design for Identifying Human Presence in Disaster Environments Using Intelligent Sensors, *2024 International Conference on Automation and Computation (AUTOCOM)*, Dehradun, India, pp.399–403,doi: 10.1109/AUTOCOM60220.2024.10486106.

[6] Valarmathi, B., Kshitij, J., Dimple, R., Srinivasa Gupta, N., Harold Robinson, Y., Arulkumaran, G., and Mulu, T. (2023). Human detection and action recognition for search and rescue in disasters using yolov3 algorithm. *Journal of Electrical and Computer Engineering, 2023*(1), 5419384.

[7] L. P, Rejith G., Toby T., S. S. N. B. and Rao S.N., (2022), A Resilient IoT System Architecture for Disaster Management in Collapsed Buildings, *2022 International Conference on Wireless Communications Signal Processing and Networking (WiSPNET)*, Chennai, India,pp.282–287.

[8] Mohit S. Mhaske, Shivam S. Raut, *et al.* (2020), An IoT based Human Detection Quadruped Bot for Rescue, *International Research Journal of Engineering and Technology*, 2020.

[9] Suresh Ram B., Satyanarayana T., Saritha U. and Sinduja B. (2025) *An IoT-based, two-tier comprehensive and affordable intrusion detection system for smart home security London*: CRC Press/Taylor & Francis.

[10] Sanaboina S.P., J. K. J P, Balassem Z.A., Saxena A.K., Mohanraj T. and Rajaram G. (2025), Building Resilient Supply Chains with IoT and Advanced Analytics: A Path to Operational Excellence, *2025 International Conference on Automation and Computation (AUTOCOM)*, Dehradun, India, 2025, pp. 325–330, doi: 10.1109/AUTOCOM64127.2025.10956938.

[11] Sheeba G., Narasimharao J., Dixit K.K., Ramesh G., Ali H.M. and Rao Sura S. (2024), IoT-Based Environmental Monitoring Systems for Ensuring Sustainable and Ethical Sourcing, *2024 International Conference on IoT, Communication and Automation Technology (ICICAT)*, Gorakhpur, India, 2024, pp. 1260–1265, doi: 10.1109/ICICAT62666.2024.10923299.

Next-Generation Smart Systems – Sekhar et al. (Eds)
 ISBN: 978-1-041-34234-2

Design of a GSM-Integrated Smart Device for Women Safety and Emergency Alerting

Pallam Likithasree, Vijaya Kumar Velpula, and SVS Prasad
Department of ECE, MLR Institute of Technology, Hyderabad, India

ABSTRACT: Women all over the world are facing sexual harassment. Even though our country is a great power with economic development, there are many crimes against women. Women's safety has become a major concern in today's society, necessitating the development of better security solutions. This study tells a GSM-Based Women Safety and Tracking Device, designed to provide real-time location tracking and emergency alerts to ensure person study presents a GSM-Based Women Safety al security. The system have Global System for Mobile Communications (GSM), Global Positioning System (GPS), and microcontroller technology with a user-friendly and emergency safety mechanism. The device is simple and wearable, helps users to send an emergency alert through SMS to predefined contacts in case of emergency. On activation, the system sends the user's location and coordinates via SMS using GSM and GPS modules, helps in tracking and sending alerts. Buzzer or alarm system, voice recording, and integration with a mobile application are the additional features that can be used as to improve the functionality.

Keywords: Women Safety, Tracking Device, Global Positioning System, Microcontroller, SMS, GSM

1 INTRODUCTION

Women's safety has become an issue of large concern globally with the number of harassments, assaults, and violence cases. There are methods like self-defense classes and emergency helpline numbers to provide some security but they are ineffective when fast action is required. Technologies like Artificial Intelligence (AI), Global System for Mobile Communications (GSM), and Global Positioning System (GPS) [1] are providing good possibilities of better method of personal security real-time tracking and automated distress detection. This research provides a GSM-Based Women Safety and Tracking Device Using AI Technology for Automatic Distress Detection, real-time location tracking, and emergency alerts for better solution of safety.

Its central component is a microcontroller with artificial intelligence that reads surroundings and user using sensors. Speech patterns, physiological signals like change in heartbeat and sudden movement inputs from accelerometers and gyroscopes are analyzed by AI algorithms for detecting stress. Once it detects any danger or distress condition, using AI system the emergency alert system initiates automatically without any manual intervention by the user. This has a better improvement compared to conventional panic-button-controlled devices because it needs assistance and it can be not possible when the victim is unable to press a button because of fear, or unconsciousness.

The system offers some new features as compared to the conventional women safety systems that majorly increase effectiveness and reliability. Whereas a traditional system permits manual triggering from the panic button, an intelligent algorithm intervenes with this device to handle the automatic distress detection, receiving real-time input from a sensors such as MAX30100 heart rate, MPU6050 accelerometer, and microphone. The AI now analyzes physiological signals (heart rate variations greater than 100 BPM or less than 40 BPM), motion data (sudden falls above 2g of acceleration), and audio signals (screams measuring more than 800 RMS units within a certain frequency band) to detect distress from any form of explicit activation, which is an advancement especially useful in cases where the user is incapacitated or paralysed out of fear or restraint. Unlike in past devices where the situation had to allow user-based activation, which is not exactly the case during an emergency, this feature offers a functioning difference.

2 LITERATURE SURVEY

A study by Sharma *et al.* (2023) [2] introduced a GSM and GPS-based emergency alert system using which users can send their real-time location to predefined contacts by pressing a panic button. While this system ensures location tracking, it has a major drawback as it relies on manual activation, making it not useful in cases where the victim is unable to press the button. The paper by Gulappagol, Laxmi, *et al.* (2023) [3] gives information on survey of the SAATHI device, an IoT-based wearable safety system designed for women's security in urban and rural environments. The survey by Gulappagol *et al.* says SAATHI as an better technology over traditional safety devices by using IoT to provide connectivity and real-time response capabilities. It tells about the use of cloud-based data processing which takes sensor inputs and analyze to trigger alerts, reducing the manual intervention. The paper by Bhuvaneswari *et al.* (2025) [4] conducts a review on assault detection technologies, highlighting AI, IoT, and wearable devices which gives personal safety for women and other vulnerable groups. The author propose a framework integrating these technologies with edge computing, cloud databases, and security protocols to create an effective emergency response system. The paper by Karpagam, M., *et al.* (2024) [5] introduces a night safety patrolling robot designed to give security in public spaces with low-visibility conditions.

Karpagam *et al.* emphasize the robot's ability to provide continuous monitoring, reducing reliance on human patrols, which are often limited by fatigue or coverage constraints. The system's design prioritizes energy efficiency and real-time response, using low-power components and cloud connectivity for data storage and remote access. The paper by Kayathri, T. L., *et al.* (2025), [6] published in the proceedings of the *5th International Conference on Trends in Material Science and Inventive Materials (ICTMIM)* by IEEE, presents a real-time tracking device designed to enhance women's safety through IoT-enabled wearable technology. The system likely incorporates IoT connectivity for cloud-based data storage, enabling remote monitoring. The paper by Dharani, M., *et al.* (2025), [7] presented at the *3rd International Conference on Device Intelligence, Computing and Communication Technologies (DICCT)*, introduces a wearable device aimed at enhancing women's security through real-time monitoring. The system employs IoT technology to enable continuous monitoring,

 DOI: 10.1201/9781042001767-55

sending distress alerts with GPS coordinates to predefined contacts or authorities via SMS or cloud-based platforms. Rani *et al.* (2020) developed a mobile-connected security system that continuously monitors the user's location and sends periodic updates to emergency contacts. However, this approach was highly dependent on internet connectivity, making it unreliable in remote areas with poor network coverage. In an effort to introduce automation, Kumar *et al.* (2021) designed a hybrid security system that combines GSM, GPS, and Radio Frequency (RF) technology. The system functions in both online and offline modes, ensuring communication even in areas with limited mobile network coverage. Despite its benefits, this method increased system complexity and cost, making it less accessible for widespread adoption.

Recent growth in Artificial Intelligence (AI) and Machine Learning (ML) [8–10] helped in the development of smart safety devices capable of automatic distress detection. Mishra *et al.* (2022) introduced an women safety system that uses speech patterns, heart rate fluctuations, and physical movements to detect distress situations. The AI algorithm activates an emergency alert without any manual intervention. However, this system still do not have real-time GSM-based alert mechanism [11–13], which makes it to depend on the internet services.

From the existing methods, it is to say that GSM and GPS-based security systems [14,15] gives better location tracking and emergency alerts. However, limitations of these systems are depending on mobile networks, no real-time tracking, and absence of automatic threat detection. This study aims to fill these gaps by developing a GSM-based women's safety and tracking device using Arduino, by adding features like real-time tracking, a SMS system. It can be enhanced its potential by mobile applications for monitoring. By combining these advantages of previous works and telling their shortcomings, this study aspires to provide a cost-effective, reliable, and accessible solution for women's safety.

3 PROPOSED SYSTEM

The system have AI-based distress detection, emergency alerts through SMS, real-time GPS tracking. The main advantage of this study is its ability to detect distress in voice tone, heart rate, and sudden movements through sensors and there will be no need for manual activation in critical situations.

3.1 *Sensor units automatic distress detection*

The system have multiple sensors to detect distress using AI. The main sensors included are Heart Rate Sensor, Accelerometer and Gyroscope, Microphone Module, Temperature Sensor. The heart rate sensor helps to monitor user's heart rate and detects the fluctuations, such as an increased heartbeat due to fear or physical exertion. The accelerometer and gyroscope detects sudden movements, falls, or physical struggles that indicate distress. Microphone module captures voice and detects unusual speech patterns, such as screaming or crying, using AI-based speech analysis. Temperature sensor measures body temperature changes that may occur due to distress or physical exertion.

3.2 *Processing unit*

The system is controlled by a microcontroller, which processes input data from sensors and executes necessary actions. It is responsible for collecting sensor data, analyzing distress conditions, and triggering emergency alerts. The AI module is programmed using Embedded C (for Arduino) to analyze sensor data and determine distress situations based on predefined thresholds and machine learning models.

3.3 *Communication modules for emergency alerts*

To ensure that emergency signals reach the concerned authorities or family members, the system utilizes the communication modules. GSM module sends emergency SMS alerts with GPS coordinates to predefined emergency contacts. The module supports real-time communication via SMS or calls. GPS module continuously tracks the user's location and updates emergency contacts when distress is detected.

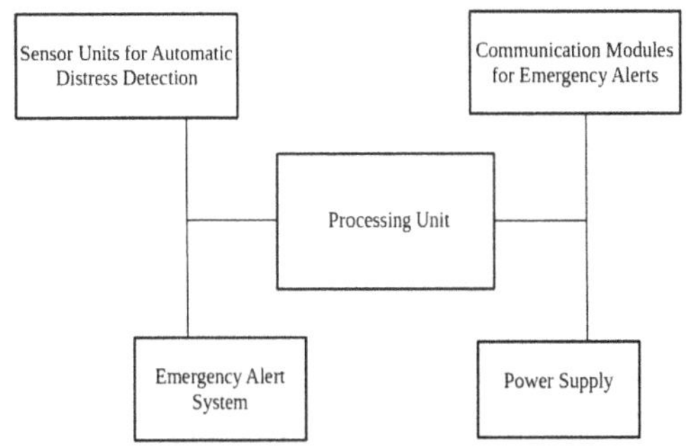

Figure 1. Block diagram of proposed system.

3.4 *Emergency alert system*

When the system detects distress, it triggers various emergency response mechanisms. The buzzer or alarm system activates a loud sound to attract the attention of nearby people, helping the victim receive immediate assistance. The SOS button allows the user to manually trigger an alert if they feel unsafe, even before distress is detected automatically. An LED indicator can also be use to provide visual confirmation that the alert has been sent.

3.5 *Working mechanism*

3.5.1 *Sensor data collection: Continuous monitoring for emergency detection*

The first phase of the system involves continuous data collection from multiple sensors attached to the device. These sensors monitor the user's physical health and surrounding environment to detect signs of distress. The sensors used in the system include: The MAX30100 pulse oximeter measures the user's heart rate (BPM) and oxygen saturation levels (SpO2). If the heart rate exceeds the predefined threshold (e.g., 110 BPM under normal conditions), the system assumes a distress situation. For example, during an anxiety attack, physical assault, or sudden fear, a person's heart rate spikes abnormally. The sensor immediately alerts the microcontroller for further action. The MPU6050 motion sensor detects sudden jerks, falls, or violent movement. If a hard fall or forceful movement is detected, the system assumes the user might be under attack or unconscious. The accelerometer analyzes changes in body position—if the user remains immobile after a sudden fall, the system automatically triggers an alert. A microphone-based sound sensor (KY-038) is included to detect shouting, screaming, or loud distress noises. If the sound intensity crosses 500 dB, the system assumes the user is calling for help and triggers an emergency alert. This feature is particularly useful if the victim cannot press a button or activate the device manually. If any of the above distress signals are detected, the system moves to the next phase of alert processing.

3.5.2 *Microcontroller processing: Data analysis and decision making*

The Arduino UNO (or ESP32 for IoT capabilities) processes all sensor inputs and determines whether a distress condition has occurred. If any sensor exceeds its threshold, the microcontroller initiates the emergency response protocol. The microcontroller uses a predefined algorithm to determine if an emergency alert should be sent. If one or more sensors indicate distress, the system activates the GSM and GPS modules.

3.5.3 *GPS location tracking: Fetching real-time user location*
Once the microcontroller confirms distress detection, it activates the GPS module to fetch the user's real-time location. The NEO-6M GPS module is used to determine the latitude and longitude of the victim. The GPS data is formatted into a Google Maps link, allowing emergency responders to track the victim's exact location. The system updates the location every 5 seconds for real-time monitoring.

3.5.4 *Emergency alert via GSM: Sending SOS messages to contacts*
Once distress is detected and location is fetched, the system sends an SOS alert using the SIM800L GSM module. The GSM module connects to mobile networks to send emergency SMS alerts. The SMS message is sent to predefined emergency contacts, including family members, close friends, police helpline (e.g., 911, 112, 100). The message includes distress type (heartbeat spike, fall detection, or distress sound) and live GPS coordinates. The system establishes a mobile network connection. The AT command AT+CMGS="+1234567890" is used to send an SMS. The message includes distress details and Google Maps location.

3.5.6 *SMS format*
Emergency Alert! I am in danger. My location: https://maps.google.com/?q=37.7749,-122.4194

4 EXPERIMENTAL RESULTS

The GSM-based women safety and tracking device was extensively tested to evaluate its performance, accuracy, and reliability in real-world distress situations. The primary objective of these experiments was to ensure that the system can detect distress conditions (heartbeat spikes, falls, distress sounds) accurately, send emergency alerts with GPS location in real time, work without an internet connection, using only GSM and GPS and provide a rapid response time for emergency situations. The system was tested in both indoor and outdoor environments to ensure its effectiveness in different conditions. The following distress situations were simulated:

Heart Rate Spike: The user performed rapid physical activity to artificially raise their heart rate above 110 BPM, triggering the pulse sensor.
Fall Detection: The accelerometer was tested by dropping the device from different heights to simulate a sudden fall or impact.
Distress Sound Detection: Loud noises (above 500 dB) such as shouting or clapping were used to test the microphone sensor.
Emergency SMS & GPS Tracking: The GSM module was configured to send an alert to a predefined emergency contact, and the GPS module logged the real-time location of the distress event. The system's accuracy, response time, and reliability were measured under multiple test conditions. Fast Emergency Response: The system successfully detected distress within 3-5 seconds of occurrence.
Accurate GPS Tracking: The GPS module tracked real-time location within an accuracy of ±5 meters.
100% Reliable SMS Alerts: The GSM module ensured consistent message delivery under network coverage. Figure 2 provides the sample alert messages of the model.
High Sensor Accuracy: 93% average accuracy was recorded for distress detection using heart rate, motion, and sound.

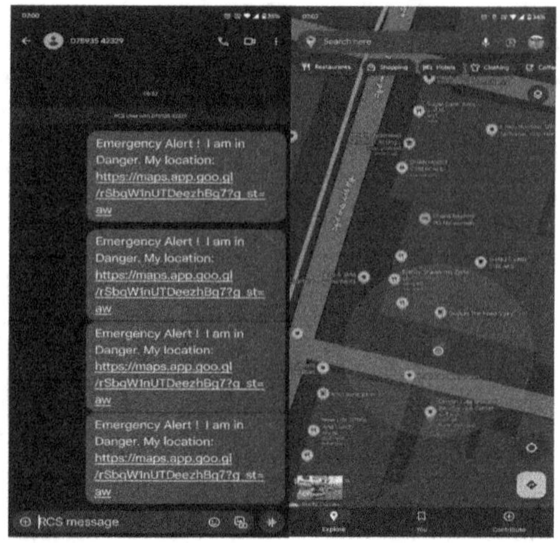

Figure 2. SMS output generated.

Advantages

- Unlike traditional safety devices that require manual activation, this system automatically detects distress situations based on heart rate fluctuations, movement patterns, and voice tone analysis.
- The GPS module continuously tracks the user's location, ensuring that emergency contacts receive real-time updates. Live tracking capabilities improve the chances of quick rescue and response.
- Unlike mobile apps that rely on internet connectivity, this system uses GSM technology to send emergency SMS alerts and initiate calls. This ensures functionality even in rural and remote areas where internet access may be limited.
- The system employs multiple emergency alert methods like SMS alerts with real-time GPS location, automatic SOS calls to emergency contacts, buzzer/Alarm activation to attract nearby attention. These features ensure that both local and remote responders are notified instantly.
- The system can be designed as a wearable device (pendant, wristband, or clip-on) to ensure ease of use. Its small form factor allows it to be discreetly worn without causing inconvenience.
- The system is designed to operate on a rechargeable lithium-ion battery with an optional solar charging feature to extend battery life. Low-energy sensors and optimized AI algorithms help minimize power usage.

Limitations
There are few limitaions of this model. They are-

- AI-based distress detection relies on sensor inputs, which may sometimes generate false positives. For example, a sudden increase in heart rate due to exercise might be mistakenly identified as distress. To minimize false alarms, the system requires continuous AI model training and multi-sensor validation.
- The system requires multiple hardware components (sensors, GSM module, GPS module, microcontroller), increasing complexity and maintenance requirements. Frequent calibration is needed to ensure sensor accuracy. Components like the GSM module depend on network availability, which can be an issue in low-coverage areas.
- The integration of AI processing, GPS tracking, and multiple sensors increases the manufacturing cost. Users in low-income regions may find it difficult to afford the device. Cost-effective alternatives (e.g., scaled-down versions with essential features) can be explored for affordability.

- Sensors may malfunction in extreme weather conditions (high humidity, excessive heat, or cold). The device must be designed to be weather-resistant and durable.
- Users must be familiar with the system's operation . Elderly users or individuals with disabilities may require simpler interfaces or voice-controlled features.

4.1 *Future enhancements*

Enhancing real-time tracking with IoT, AI-driven predictive threat detection, biometric authentication, wearable integration, blockchain security, and multi-mode communication will maximize reliability and effectiveness. One of the major enhancements that can be implemented is IoT-based real-time tracking and cloud connectivity. In the current system, GPS coordinates are sent via SMS through GSM, which has limitations, such as network dependency and lack of continuous tracking. By incorporating IoT-based tracking, the device can send live location updates to a secure cloud server, which can be accessed through a mobile application or web interface by predefined emergency contacts. This would allow continuous real-time monitoring, where location updates can be tracked on a Google Maps interface, ensuring faster rescue operations.

As the system collects sensitive personalThis study aims to address these gap data, including location, biometric information, and distress history, cybersecurity and data privacy become crucial concerns. Future enhancements could include blockchain-based encryption to ensure that all emergency data is tamper-proof and securely stored. With decentralized security mechanisms, only authorized emergency contacts can access distress signals, and any attempt to tamper with the data will be logged and prevented.

While the current system relies on GSM-based SMS and calls, future enhancements could integrate alternative communication channels to increase reliability in poor network conditions. Some options include Satellite Communication, if no GSM network is available, the device could send emergency alerts via satellite-based messaging and Mesh Network Connectivity, devices in close proximity could communicate with each other, relaying distress signals even in remote areas also even Hybrid Internet & GSM Mode, the system could dynamically switch between Wi-Fi, GSM, and IoT LTE networks based on availability.

In its current form, the device is designed as a small portable gadget that can be attached to clothing or carried in a bag. However, future versions could integrate the system into smart wearable technology, such as smart rings, wristbands, pendants, or even smart clothing. By using the sensors in fabric, jewellery, and other daily wear things the device can be used with out any unnecessary attention.

5 CONCLUSION

The GSM-Based Women Safety and Tracking Device with Automatic Distress Detection is a good approach to improve women's security by using AI-for distress detection, real-time GPS tracking, and GSM-based emergency communication. This system is designed to automatically detect distress situations using physiological and motion-based sensors, so that alerts are sent through SMS even if the victim is unable to do it manually. The combination of AI algorithms, GSM modules, and GPS tracking helps that emergency contacts can receive real-time updates about the victim's location, helping to take action quickly. The inclusion of a loud buzzer/alarm system further increases the chances of receiving immediate help from nearby individuals, creating an additional layer of security. Unlike other normal safety devices that rely on manual activation, this system uses AI-based analysis to detect fluctuations in heart rate, movement, and voice patterns. This device is simple, wearable, and can operates with out relying on internet connectivity, which makes it to use in both urban and remote areas. Also, the system has low power consumption and battery can be rechargeable hence, it is portable and can functions for extended durations.

While the current implementation of the system offers a highly effective personal security solution, future enhancements can further improve its performance. By using IoT-based real-time tracking, cloud data storage, blockchain security, biometric authentication, and multi-mode communication the device can become even more efficient and accurate.

REFERENCES

[1] Sriranjini, (2017), GPS & GMS based Self Defense System for Women, Journal of Electrical and Electronics Systems, Volume No.06, pp [03].

[2] Srinivasan, S., and Dharani S. Women Safety Android Application.

[3] Gulappagol, Laxmi, *et al.* (2023). A survey paper on SAATHI: Women-safety-device using IoT. Advances in Multidisciplinary Research and Development: 164.

[4] Shyam Sundar Bhuvaneswari, Vikash Shankar, and Mohanraj Thangamuthu. (2025). Towards Intelligent Safety: A Systematic Review on Assault Detection and Technologies. Sensors 25.13: 3985.

[5] A survey paper on SAATHI: Women-safety-device using IoT. Advances in Multidisciplinary Research and Development (2023).

[6] Kayathri, T.L., *et al.*, (2025), Realtime Tracking Device for Women Safety. 2025 5th International Conference on Trends in Material Science and Inventive Materials (ICTMIM). IEEE.

[7] Dharani, M., *et al.*, (2025), Enhancing Women's Security with Real-Time Monitoring. 2025 3rd International Conference on Device Intelligence, Computing and Communication Technologies (DICCT). IEEE.

[8] Patil, Shreya, *et al.*, (2025), Women Safety Alert System Using IoT with Fingerprint Authentication and Real-Time Alerts. 2025 International Conference on Computing for Sustainability and Intelligent Future (COMP-SIF). IEEE.

[9] Sinha, Akash Kumar, *et al.* (2025). Women Security Application Using Smart Emergency Response System and Real-Time Location Tracking.

[10] Sumalatha, P., *et al.*, (2025), IoT Based Smart Safety System for Women's Protection. 2025 International Conference on Next Generation Communication & Information Processing (INCIP). IEEE.

[11] Nizamani, S., Shareef, M., Jamali, A.S., Kazi, N.H., Khan, B., Nizamani, S.B., and Rajput, I. (2025). FeelSafe: A Women's Safety and Security System.

[12] Dongare Uma, Vyavahare Vishakha and Raut Ravina, (March-2015), Android application for women's safety based on voice recognition, BSIOTR Technical Science Department, Savitribai Phule Pune University India, ISSN 2320-088X International Journal of Computer Science and Mobile Computing (IJCSMC) online at www.ijcsmc.com, vol. 4 Issue. 3, page. 216–220.

[13] Dr Sridhar Mandapati, Sravya Pamidi and Sriharitha Ambati, (Jan-Feb 2015), Women-Based Applications (Safe Applications), Computer Applications RVR & JC College of Engineering Guntur India, ISSN: 2278-0661, p. -ISSN: 2278-8727, IOSR Journal of computer Engg (IOSR-JCE) www.iosrjournals.org, volume 17, Issue 1 (version I), PP 29–34.

[14] Anup, CJ, Gobinath, M., Saminathan, K. and No-senthilrajan, G., Smart Women Safety System', first international conference on NexGen Technologies, ISBN: 978-93-86171-90-0.

[15] Premkumar, Ravivarma and Sharmila, (March 2015), One Touch Alarm System for Women Using GMS, International Journal of Science, Technology and Management, volume no.01, pp [04].

[16] Reya George and Anjaly Cherian, (April 2015), An Intelligent Security System for Violence against women in public places, International Journal of Engineering & Advanced Technology, volume no. 03, kk [05].

Next-Generation Smart Systems – Sekhar et al. (Eds)
© 2027 The Author(s), ISBN: 978-1-041-34234-2

IoT-Based ECG Monitoring System Using ATmega Microcontroller

Gajula Lakshminarayana
Professor & HoD, Department of ECE, SVR Engineering College, Nandyal, Andhra Pradesh, India

K. Raghavendra, K. Seshidar, and S. Sreenivasulu
Assistant Professor, Department of ECE, SVR Engineering College, Nandyal, Andhra Pradesh, India

ABSTRACT: Embedded technology has become an indispensable part of modern life, particularly in the healthcare sector. With the rising need for advanced medical infrastructure, technological innovations in patient monitoring systems are crucial. One such vital diagnostic tool is the Electrocardiogram (ECG), which is widely used to assess heart conditions by analyzing electrical signals from the heart.

This paper presents an IoT-enabled heart monitoring system that utilizes an ATmega microcontroller to process ECG signals and identify irregularities in heart activity. The system continuously monitors the patient's heartbeat and classifies it based on predefined normal parameters. If the signal falls within the standard range, the system confirms a normal heart condition. However, deviations from the normal range indicate potential heart abnormalities, prompting an alert.

To enhance remote healthcare capabilities, the system incorporates Internet of Things (IoT) technology, enabling real-time information transmission. to cloud servers or healthcare professionals for further evaluation. Additionally, this system can be used for continuous patient monitoring, early diagnosis, and emergency alerts, thereby reducing the risk of severe cardiac complications. The proposed solution offers a cost-effective and efficient approach to real-time ECG monitoring, making it suitable for both clinical and home-based healthcare applications.

Keywords: ECG, IoT, Embedded Technology, Heart Monitoring System

1 INTRODUCTION

The demand for medical expert systems is growing rapidly, with a significant focus on portable and smart healthcare devices that can be seamlessly integrated into daily life. In today's rapidly evolving and competitive landscape, medical applications are instrumental in advancing healthcare in ensuring timely diagnosis as well as treatment. Electrocardiogram (ECG) monitoring is a vital diagnostic tool for detecting abnormalities in heart rhythm or variations in ECG signal morphology, which may indicate the presence of arrhythmias. The analysis of stored ECG data aids in identifying potential heart conditions [1].

Several researchers are working on long-term ECG monitoring systems to improve cardiac healthcare. Traditional hospital-based ECG systems are often bulky and stationary, making them less suitable for continuous monitoring. These systems typically use 12-lead electrodes, with placements on the ankles, wrists, and chest. However, the gel electrodes used in these devices can cause skin allergies and infections, making them unsuitable for extended use. Additionally, these systems are costly and not feasible for home-based monitoring, posing challenges, particularly for elderly individuals who require frequent heart rate assessments. Due to the increasing patient population, it also becomes difficult for hospitals to conduct ECG tests for all patients efficiently [2].

To address these challenges, smart healthcare technology plays a crucial role in enabling home-based ECG monitoring systems. These systems can collect ECG data, analyze it, and transmit the results to doctors and family members in real time. Several advanced healthcare applications now provide multi-parameter monitoring, including ECG, finger photoplethysmography, and blood pressure plethysmography [3].

To enhance the accuracy of ECG monitoring, various signal amplification and filtering techniques are used. Noise reduction and signal correction are achieved using Least Mean Square (LMS) error normalization, which ensures high-speed processing with minimal latency. Furthermore, Support Vector Machine (SVM) classification is employed to remove unwanted noise from ECG signals [4]. The accuracy of ECG analysis depends on the precise detection of P, Q, R, and S wave points, which can be extracted using different signal processing algorithms. These algorithms are also being implemented on iOS-based smartphones, enabling remote healthcare services for individuals in rural and underserved areas [5].

With the integration of cloud computing, doctors can remotely access patient data, conduct detailed analyses, and provide timely medical recommendations. Advanced filtering techniques improve signal quality by effectively eliminating noise [6]. In addition, smart ECG monitoring systems can be seamlessly integrated into private home networks, enhancing accessibility and reliability for long-term patient care [7].

These technological advancements aim to make ECG monitoring more affordable, portable, and efficient, ensuring that individuals—especially the elderly and those in remote areas—receive timely and continuous cardiac health assessments without relying solely on hospital visits.

Various ECG detection devices have been developed, incorporating electrodes into textiles, seat belts, wristwatches, and mobile cases for enhanced portability and usability [8]. These devices utilize microcontrollers to process the signals and transmit the data to cloud-based platforms for remote access. In one such study, the MSP430 single-chip microcontroller was employed to regulate ECG signal processing and transmission [9].

To improve signal quality, the original ECG signal is analyzed by comparing it with various filtered outputs, while parameters such as PSD as well as SNR are computed prior to and following filtering. Additionally, advanced wireless sensing elements, MEMS (Micro-Electro-Mechanical Systems), and nanotechnology-based sensors are being developed to enhance portability and efficiency in long-term ECG monitoring [11].

For seamless data transmission, communication protocols such as HTTP and MQTT are implemented to facilitate secure and efficient data exchange between devices and cloud servers

DOI: 10.1201/9781042001767-56

[12]. Given that smartphones are highly portable but have power limitations, ECG monitoring systems must be optimized for low-power consumption and real-time data transfer to ensure uninterrupted heart rate monitoring on mobile platforms. To ensure continuous and unobtrusive monitoring, wearable ECG sensors are widely used in these systems, allowing for extended data collection over several hours, sometimes it will take days also. [23].Once acquired, ECG related signals undergo multiple processing stages. The processed data is then transmitted to the IoT cloud using specific wireless communication protocols, such as Zigbee , WiFi and also it can use Bluetooth[23].

Each of these protocols provides a sufficient data rate for ECG signal transmission while maintaining an optimal balance between energy efficiency and performance. But because of the restricted communication range of the Bluetooth short range device as well as low power device Zigbee, an intermediary device like a smartphone or another intelligent terminal is often required to receive the data from the ECG at the same time forward it to cloud of the IOT using cellular communication technologies like GPRS technology or LTE[23].

1.1 *IoT cloud*

IoT based cloud system designed for monitoring of ECG usually includes four key working modules: data cleaning, data storage, examination of data and illness alert mechanisms. By extracting critical features from ECG signals, the system can effectively identify potential cardiac abnormalities [26].

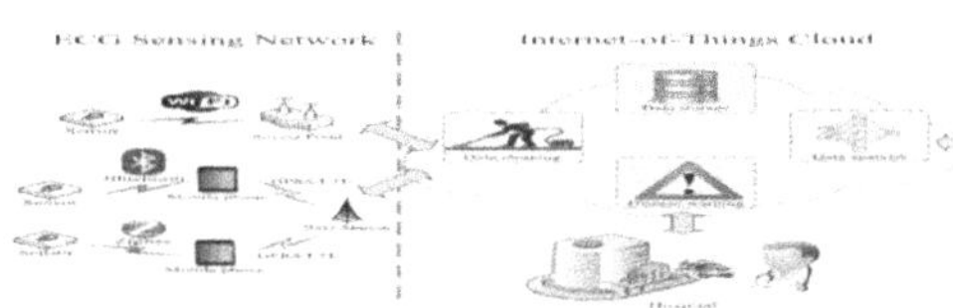

Figure 1. IoT-based ECG monitoring architecture diagram.

However, during data acquisition as well as transfer, noise interference may be introduced into the ECG signals, negatively impacting diagnostic accuracy. To address this issue, ECG signals must first undergo noise reduction and signal enhancement [11]. This is typically achieved through the use of well-designed filtering techniques, which eliminate out-of-band noise while preserving essential signal characteristics. Additionally, data validations mechanisms help identify inconsistencies or anomalies in the recorded ECG data, ensuring reliable and accurate analysis [11].

2 EXISTING SYSTEM

In the current method, ECG based pulses are handled by a microcontroller in order to find the status of heart, with signal acquisition based on electrical activity from the wrist. The proposed system improves this method by utilizing ECG leads and a microprocessor for more precise monitoring. Additionally, ECG data is directly collected from the chest region, providing more accurate readings. By integrating an advanced sensor fusion technique, the system can simultaneously measure body temperature and hydration levels. The proposed design incorporates an alarm mechanism and an LCD display, to find the status of the heart using ECG mechanism. This technology is characterized by its portability, accuracy, efficiency, and versatility, making it a reliable solution for continuous health monitoring.

3 PROPOSED SYSTEM

Health monitoring systems have become a crucial aspect of modern healthcare, used in hospitals, home care, and even by sports teams to track physiological parameters. These systems are particularly beneficial for individuals with chronic illnesses who require frequent health check-ups. To ensure continuous and remote monitoring, researchers have developed portable health monitoring solutions tailored to different requirements. Various hardware platforms, including microcontrollers, ASICs, FPGAs, and PIC microcontrollers, are utilized for system implementation.

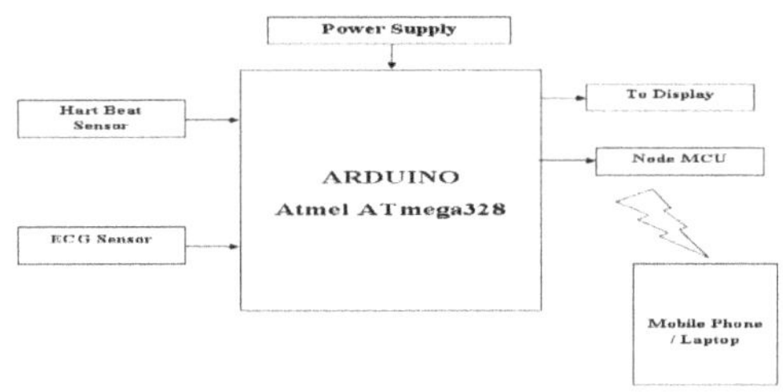

Figure 2. Proposed system block diagram.

The proposed IoT-based ECG monitoring method includes two primary parts:

1. Patient Monitoring Location
   This component is designed to capture real-time ECG signals and heart rate information through wearable sensors from the patent. Sensors, such as the heartbeat sensor and ECG sensor, collect data as well as send it to a microcontroller (ATmega328) for further processing. System ensures continuous monitoring, allowing early detection of abnormal heart conditions.
2. Mechanism for monitoring of the ECG pulses with the help of IoT technology
   The processed ECG data is transmitted using a NodeMCU module, which enables wireless communication with cloud-based storage or mobile devices. The system displays real-time ECG and heart rate readings on an LCD screen for local monitoring. The IoT integration ensures that data is accessible via mobile phones or laptops, allowing remote monitoring by doctors or caregivers.

The block diagram illustrates the flow of data in the system:

- **Power Supply**: Provides necessary voltage and current to the circuit.
- **Heart Beat Sensor & ECG Sensor**: Collect real-time physiological signals.
- **Arduino (ATmega328 Microcontroller):** Processes the acquired ECG and heartbeat data.
- **Display Module:** Shows real-time heart rate and ECG readings.
- **NodeMCU Module**: Transmits data wirelessly to cloud storage or a connected mobile device.
- **Mobile Phone/Laptop**: Allows remote monitoring by healthcare providers.

This portable and efficient health monitoring system enhances accessibility and provides real-time insights into a patient's cardiovascular health, ensuring timely intervention when needed.

3.1 *Patient monitoring system*

The AD8232 ECG sensor is used for acquiring electrocardiograph (ECG) signals. It is preferred over HM301D, which supports three channels when only a single channel is required, and ADS1191, which lacks sufficient gain for high-resolution signals. The AD8232 provides better output impedance and gain [2].

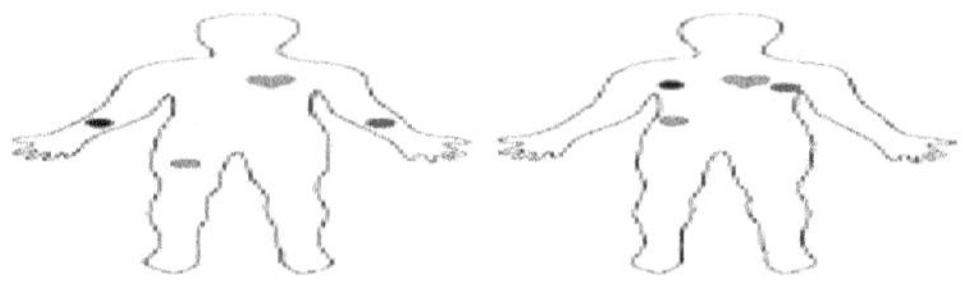

Figure 3. AD8232 electrodes placement.

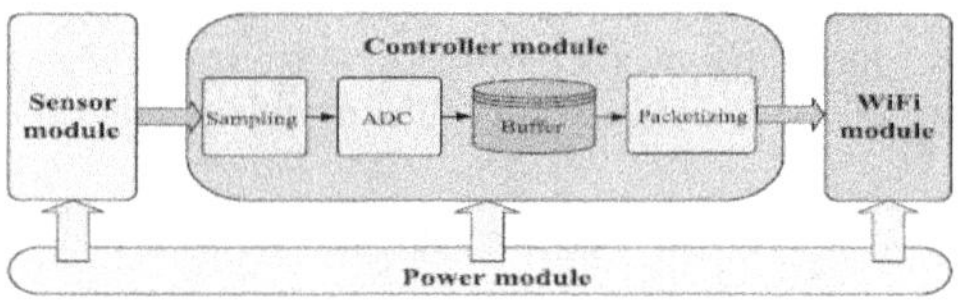

Figure 4. An ECG monitoring node's primary components.

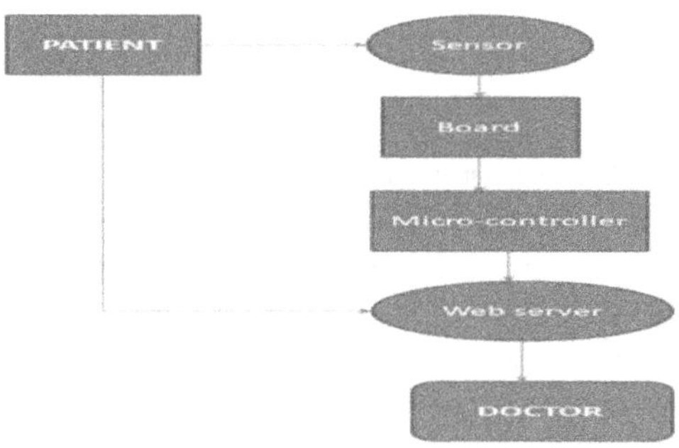

Figure 5. Working flow.

The ECG monitors the electrical activity of the heart by utilizing electrodes that are positioned on the body. detecting small electrical changes caused by cardiac depolarization and repolarization. The AD8232 is a compact chip designed for measuring heart activity, amplifying, and filtering bio-potential signals in noisy environments [2].

The AD8232 Cardiac Rhythm Monitor includes an operational amplifier to improve signal clarity for PR and QT interval analysis. It features nine pins, including power, lead-off detection, analog output, and electrode connections (RA, LA, RL) for ECG signal acquisition [2].

3.2 *System configuration as follows*

In the developed ECG monitoring system utilizing IoT technology, such as mobile sensing, cloud computing, and the Internet are utilized.

4 REQUIRED COMPONENTS FOR HARDWARE

4.1 *Arduino*

For novices, the Arduino UNO is the perfect electronic development board. It is a free and open-source platform for creating electronic devices. Arduino is made up of software and hardware, including a programmable circuit board which allows users to write and upload code using the Integrated Development Environment (IDE)? This microcontroller-based system enables users to develop and implement various embedded applications efficiently.

Figure 6. Arduino.

4.2 *Node MCU*

It is freely available for building as well as designing IoT-based applications. The system has hardware that is integrated with an ESP-12 module and is powered by the ESP8266 Wi-Fi SoC.. The kit includes an analog pin (A0) and multiple digital pins (D0-D8). Additionally, it supports various serial communication protocols such as SPI, UART, and I2C, enabling seamless data transmission.

Figure 7. Node MCU.

4.3 *Node for ECG monitoring*

The node of monitoring ECG collects ECG pulses which are connected to the body of the person and transmits it wirelessly. As shown in Figure 4, it consists of four main modules:

1. Sensor Module: Captures ECG signals using the AD8232 sensor and peripheral circuits. A band-pass filter (0.5–100 Hz) in the AD8283 removes noise, and an operational amplifier enhances the signal [15][16].
2. Controller Module: Processes the acquired ECG data.
3. Wi-Fi Module: Enables wireless data transmission.
4. Power Module: Supplies necessary power for operation.

T sensor outputs of the ECG signals ranging from 0V to the voltage of 3.3, ensuring accurate data collection.

Figure 8. Photo of the ECG monitoring node.

4.4 *Heartbeat sensor*

When a finger is inserted into this heart rate sensor, a digital output is produced.. As the sensor operates the LED indicator flashes in sync with each heartbeat. A microcontroller can be directly interfaced with the digital output to determine the beats per minute (BPM). The sensor uses light modulation, and the detected signal is impacted by changes in blood flow through the finger with each pulse.

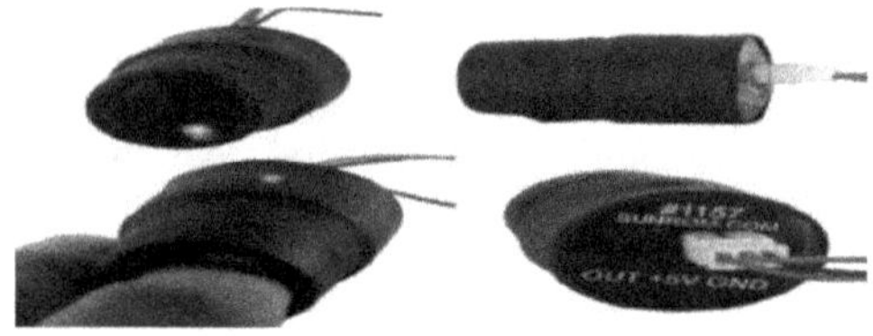

Figure 9. Hart beat sensor.

4.5 *Thing speak cloud*

This IoT platform facilitates seamless interaction among people and connected gadgets. It supports real-time data collection, processing, analysis, and visualization through SNS using API, making it compatible with multiple platforms. The system efficiently transfers data from embedded gadgets like Arduino, Raspberry Pi, and Node MCU, while supporting various programming languages and environments.

In the proposed system, Thing Speak is utilized to read and transmit sensor data. The primary goal is to automate data acquisition and present the collected

Information through graphical visualization. The data can be accessed globally anytime, anywhere

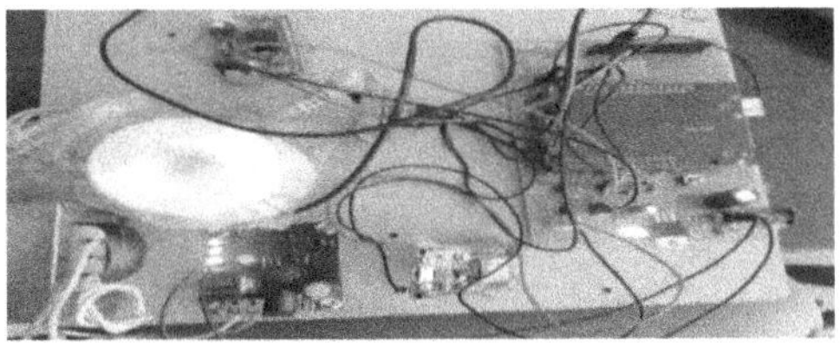

Figure 10. Hardware prototype.

5 RESULTS

The system does not detect P or T waves nor directly measure pulse rate. Therefore, heart rate (HR) and heart rate variability (HRV) are estimated using the AD8232 ECG sensor. As previously mentioned, HR is calculated based on the number of R-peaks per minute. However, waiting for a full minute for a single HR value is inefficient. Instead, HR is estimated by measuring the period of time between two successive R-peaks using the formula below $\boldsymbol{HR} = \frac{60}{RR\ interval}$.

While this method provides a quick estimation, it is not medically accurate. This is because it assumes that every R-R interval remains constant throughout the entire minute, which is not always the case. In a healthy individual, the duration of a single heartbeat typically ranges between 800-850 ms (corresponding to 65-75 beats per minute), with slight variations depending on activity levels such as resting or physical exertion. However, in individuals with atrial fibrillation or arrhythmia, the heartbeat intervals fluctuate significantly despite an average heart rate appearing normal. The key parameter used to detect such irregularities is known as variability in heart rate.

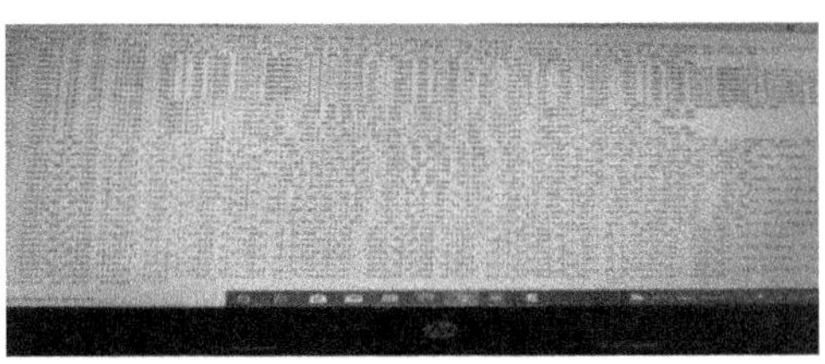

Figure 11. Information transferred to the server.

The standard cutoff point value can be set to 100, but it should be adjusted based on the specific sensor being used. The code is straightforward and measures R-R intervals and ECG values using timers.

6 CONCLUSION

We developed and deployed an sophisticated ECG monitoring system based on IoT. Initially, the system architecture was outlined, detailing the ECG sensing network and comparing different communication methods, including Wi-Fi. Based on the proposed design, a real-time the ECG monitoring system was developed using a wearable device integrated with three electrodes for signal detection. The collected ECG data is transmitted via Wi-Fi to the IoT cloud, ensuring high-speed data transfer and broad coverage. The architecture of the IoT cloud consists of three servers—an HTTP server, a MQTT server and a storage servers. Mobile applications are no longer necessary to the web-based interface allowing seamless access to ECG data across various platforms, independent of any specific mobile OS.

REFERENCES

[1] Ageing, In: World Health Organization. http://www.who.int/topics/ageing/en/, 2016.

[2] Banerjee, A., and Gupta, S., (2015), Analysis of smart mobile applications for healthcare under dynamic context changes. *IEEE Trans. Mob. Comput.* 14:904–919. doi:10.1109/tmc.2014.2334606 2334606.

[3] Zhang, Y., *et al.*, (2015), Health-CPS: Healthcare cyber-physical system assisted by cloud and big data. Accepted by *IEEE Systems Journal*. doi:10.1109/jsyst.2015.2460747.

[4] Zhang, Y., Chen, M., Huang, D., *et al.*, (2017), Doctor: personalized and professionalized medical recommendations based on hybrid matrix factorization. *Fut. Gener. Comput. Syst.* 66:30–35. doi: 10.1016/j.future.2015.12.001.

[5] Abadi, M., Subramanian, R., Kia, S., and *et al.*, (2015), DECAF: MEGbased multimodal database for decoding affective physiological responses. *IEEE Trans. Affect. Comput.* 6:209–222. doi:10.1109/taffc.2015.2392932.

[6] Kim, H., Kim, S., Van Helleputte, N., and *et al.*, (2014), A configurable and low-power mixed signal SoC for portable ECG monitoring applications. *IEEE Trans. Biomed. Circ. Syst.* 8:257–267. doi:10.1109/tbcas.2013.2260159.

[7] Tseng, C., (2013), Coordinator traffic diffusion for data-intensive Zigbee transmission in real-time electrocardiography monitoring. *IEEE Trans. Biomed. Eng.* 60:3340–3346. doi:10.1109/tbme.2013.2266373.

[8] Miao, F., Cheng, Y., He, Y., and *et al.*, (2015), A wearable context aware ECG monitoring system integrated with built-in kinematic sensors of the smartphone. *Sensors* 15:11465–11484. doi:10.3390/s150511465.

[9] Tseng, K., Lin, B., Liao, L., and *et al.*, (2014), Development of a wearable mobile electrocardiogram monitoring system by using novel dry foam electrodes. *IEEE Syst. J.* 8:900–906. doi:10.1109/jsyst.2013.2260620.

[10] Friedman, R., Kogan, A., and Krivolapov, Y., (2013), On power and throughput tradeoffs of WI-FI and Bluetooth in smartphones. *IEEE Trans. Mob. Comput.* 12:1363–1376. doi:10.1109/tmc.2012.117.

[11] Shneiderman, B., and Plaisant, C., (2015), Sharpening analytic focus to cope with big data volume and variety. *IEEE Comput. Graph. Appl.* 35:10–14. doi:10.1109/mcg.2015.64.

[12] Zhang, Y., Chen, M., Mao, S., *et al.*, (2014), CAP: Community activity prediction based on big data analysis. *IEEE Netw.* 28:52–57. doi:10.1109/mnet.2014.6863132.

[13] Alonso-Atienza, F., Morgado, E., Fernandez-Martinez, L., *et al.*, (2014), Detection of life-threatening arrhythmias using feature selection and support vector machines. *IEEE Trans. Biomed. Eng.* 61:832–840. doi:10.1109/tbme.2013.2290800.

[14] Sharma, H., and Sharma, K., (2016), An algorithm for sleep apnea detection from single-lead ECG using Hermite basis functions. *Comput. Biol. Med.* 77:116–124. doi: 10.1016/j.compbiomed.2016.08.012.

[15] AD8283 Datasheet (PDF) - Analog Devices. In: Alldatasheet.com. http://www.alldatasheet.com/datasheet-pdf/pdf/418481/AD/ AD8283.html, 2016.

[16] Buenda-Fuentes, F., Arnau-Vives, M., Arnau-Vives, A., *et al.*, (2012), High-bandpass filters in electrocardiography: Source of error in the interpretation of the ST segment. *ISRN Cardiol.* 2012:1–10. doi:10.5402/2012/706217.

[17] STM32F103RC Datasheet (PDF) - STMicroelectronics. In: Alldatasheet.com. http://www.alldatasheet.com/datasheet-

pdf/pdf/ 231959/STMICROELECTRONICS/STM32F103RC. html, 2016.

[18] Al-Fuqaha, A., Guizani, M., Mohammadi, M., *et al.*, (2015), Internet of things: A survey on enabling technologies, protocols, and applications. *IEEE Commun. Surv. Tutor.* 17:2347–2376. doi:10.1109/comst.2015.2444095.

[19] Phan, T., *et al.*, (2014), Cloud databases for Internet-of-things data. *In: Proceedings IEEE 2014 International Conference on Internet of Things (iThings)*, pp. 117–124. Taipei.

[20] Wang, Y., *et al.*, (2013), Design and evaluation of a novel wireless reconstructed 3-lead ECG monitoring system. *In: Proceedings IEEE 2013 Biomedical Circuits and Systems Conference* (BioCAS), pp. 362–365. Rotterdam.

[21] Gertsch, M., (2009), The Normal ECG and its (Normal) variants. *In: The ECG Manual*, pp. 17–36. London: Springer.

[22] ECGlibrary.com: Normal adult 12-lead ECG. In:Ecglibrary. com. http://www.ecglibrary.com/norm.php, 2016.

[23] Palattella, M., Dohler, M., Grieco, A., *et al.*, (2016), Internet of Things in the 5G era: Enablers, architecture, and business models. *IEEE J. Select. Areas Commun.* 34:510–527. doi:10.1109/jsac.2016.2525418.

Next-Generation Smart Systems – Sekhar et al. (Eds)
 ISBN: 978-1-041-34234-2

Smart Sensor Based Accident Prevention System for U-type Roads Using Arduino UNO

K. Mohana Lakshmi and Bandi Doss
Associate Professor, CMR Technical Campus, Hyderabad, Telangana, India

Gotte Sai Ganesh, V. Aparna, SK. Aslam, and R. Hindupriya
Students, Department of ECE, CMR Technical Campus, Hyderabad, Telangana, India

ABSTRACT: Accidents on curved and U-turn roads, especially during night time, area serious concern due to limited visibility and sudden oncoming traffic. This project introduces a smart accident prevention system using Arduino, ultrasonic sensors, and LDRs to address this issue. The system detects the presence and distance of approaching vehicles from two directions (Route X and Route Y) using ultrasonic sensors. Based on the vehicle's proximity, it displays red or orange warning signals to alert other vehicles and reduce the chances of collision. In addition to this, an automatic headlight dimming feature is implemented during LDR sensors. When two vehicles face each other at night, the LDR detects the intensity of the incoming headlights and automatically reduces the brightness to avoid glare. This dual function system aims to improve road safety, visibility, and communication between vehicles at dangerous curves, especially in poorly lit or rural areas.

Keywords: Arduino Uno, Ultrasonic sensor, LDR sensor, Curved Roads, U-turn roads, hill roads

1 INTRODUCTION

Road accidents continue to be one of the leading causes of death and injury, with sharp turns and U-turn roads contributing significantly to the problem. At night, visibility is further reduced, and drivers are often blinded by the headlights of oncoming vehicles. These issues are especially dangerous on curved roads, where the line of sight is limited, and drivers cannot see approaching vehicles until the last moment. To address this issue, this project proposes sallow- cost and efficient solution using embedded systems. The proposed model is designed to detect vehicles approaching a curved road from either direction and provide real-time warning signals using color-coded lights (red and orange). This enables the driver from the opposite direction to slow down or stop in advance, reducing the risk of collision. Another major issue this project solves is the glare from vehicle headlights at night. This glare can temporarily blind drivers, increasing the risk of head-on accidents. To solve this, each vehicle is equipped with a Light Dependent Resistor (LDR) sensor. When it detects excessive brightness from an oncoming vehicle, it automatically dims the headlight to a safer level, improving visibility and comfort for both drivers. This system can be especially useful on rural or poorly lit roads where proper traffic lights and safety measures are often missing. The entire set up is implemented using Arduino and basic electronic components, making it both affordable and scalable.

A deep learning-based system for forecasting pedestrian trajectories in intelligent transportation environment. Which explains about how the camera module works in it and how the far away module going detect the ahead upstrical and provide accidences from the objects [1] Assessment of Traffic Safety Interventions Using Virtual Randomized Controlled Trials investigates the use trials (vRCTs) to evaluate the impact of connected and (CAD) and V2X communication on improving safety at urban intersections. The study demonstrates that V2Xenabled systems can significantly reduce collision risks by enabling early hazard detection and coordination. The paper talks about how the vRCTs module works effective and solve real time problems in our day-to-day life [2]. A V2X-based Approach for Avoiding Potential Blind-zone Collisions between Right-turning Vehicles and predefined directional vehicles to improve the quality of safety of the system addresses the high risk of accidents between right turning vehicles and pedestrians hidden in blind zones. The proposed approach integrates vehicle, pedestrian, and roadside unit (RSU) data to detect potential collision risks in real time. This warns the people for the direction.[3] explains about a daily life collision avoidance system designed to provide and protect Vulnerable Road Users (VRUs) such as pedestrians and cyclists. The system combines V2x integrated with computer vision algorithms to talk about accidents between vehicles and VRUs, particularly in complex urban environments. Using camera input and V2X messages from roadside model and vehicles, the system accurately identifies threats and sends immediate alerts to drivers. [4]. Proposes an automated system using (LDR) sensors to enhance safety in long vehicles such as buses and trucks. The system aims to prevent accidents caused by blind spots and limited rear visibility. By placing LDR sensors, the setup can detect obstacles based on light intensity variations and trigger such as alarms or braking. This intelligent automation system is designed to assist drivers during lane changes or turns, reducing collision risks. The solution is low-cost, energy- efficient, and scalable for real-world transportation systems. This mainly focused on the rare visibility of human and red use the accidents rate in real time world and this makes the more accurate of work and most efficient in the matter of work. This considered has the efficient in the terms of working process and utility of material in environment to reduce of accidents. [5] Deep learning methods applied to LiDAR point cloud data for autonomous driving. The review covers key tasks such as object detection, semantic segmentation, and 3D localization, focusing on how deep neural networks process sparse, irregular point cloud data. It analyses various network architectures, including Point Net, voxel-based methods, and graph-based models, high lighting their advantages and limitations. The paper also discusses real-time implementation challenges, data efficiency, and future trends, making it a valuable reference for advancing perception systems in autonomous vehicles. This makes the work easier and most advanced tech used in this project which makes the different in order of working principle and effiency in the order of working function of the things. [6]. 3D object detection takes techniques using only image data for autonomous driving applications. The works talks about the state of the art such as

DOI: 10.1201/9781042001767-57

monocular, stereo, and multi-view approaches, it analysing how each extracts depth and 3D spatial information from 2D images. It also evaluates network architectures, loss functions, and fusion strategies for integrating geometric and semantic cues. The paper highlights recent progress, benchmarks on public datasets, and key challenges like depth ambiguity and real-time performance, making it an essential resource for vision-based autonomous systems. This makes the working principal to the work or the other real time challenges and makes the work easier and flexible to the human effects. This makes the difference between normal world efficient of the work day to day challenges. [7]. Deep learning techniques that integrate camera images and LiDAR point cloud data for enhanced perception in autonomous vehicles. The review categorizes fusion strategies into early fusion, late fusion, and intermediate (deep) fusion, highlighting how each method balances spatial detail and depth accuracy. The authors discuss network architectures, alignment techniques, and real-time performance issues, along with challenges like sensor calibration and data heterogeneity. This works illustrates that how the complicated of data which has collected by image and the LiDAR point cloud makes the accuracy of the work that detects the problem and efficient of work in the reak time application and also in the complex driving environments [8] The different modal 3D object detection techniques in the information of autonomous driving. It systematically classifies methods that fuse data from different sensors—such as components has LiDAR, cameras, radar, and maps—to enhance perception accuracy and robustness. These authors propose a comprehensive taxonomy based on fusion stages, sensor combinations, and backbone architectures, and they talk about the different aspects like presents of good (advantages), bad(disadvantages) and limitations of each thing in this work. This work also deals with analyses of different kind of data like camara image ,radar which means that in the particular region of data communication will takes place .After entering the particular region then only it able to reacts the data.[9] An extensive illustrates of radar and camera sensor fusion technique for enhancing knowing of object ahead and semantic segmentation in vehicles which means the when the vehicles enters into the particular region then it will be strategies into how the wok is going on like fast, slow, enough with the respected work space analysing their strengths in handling adverse weather and low visibility conditions. It discusses alignment challenges between radar's sparse point clouds and rich camera images, and evaluates deep learning models that combine spatial and semantic cues. The review also highlights benchmark datasets, comparative performance metrics, and key factors issues like synchronization, calibration, and real-time inference, offering future directions for robust Ulti-sensor fusion systems.[10]

2 METHODOLOGY

The proportional method in this system involves sensing the distance of a vehicle using an ultrasonic sensor and responding accordingly. Although not a true proportional control system, it operates on threshold-based logic: when a vehicle is detected within a specific range, the LED light is triggered to alert the driver. The response is indirectly proportional to the distance—the closer the object, the quicker the alert. This simple yet effective approach helps prevent accidents by providing early warnings, especially on blind curves and narrow mountain roads, enhancing road safety through basic proportional sensing and response.

The proposed methodology aims to reduce road accidents on U-type curved roads by implementing a sensor-based warning and monitoring system. This system detects vehicle movement, monitors speed, checks road conditions, and provides real-time alerts to drivers, especially at dangerous curves. The system Architecture consists of: Sensors: IR sensors, Ultrasonic sensors, Speed sensors. Microcontroller Unit: Arduino/ESP32 for data processing. Communication Module: RF module or IoT (WIFI/Bluetooth) for transmitting alerts. Warning Mechanisms: Buzzer, LED lights, Display board, and Voice alert system.

Working principle:

Step1: Vehicle Detection:
IR or ultrasonic sensors detect vehicle entry at either end of the U turn Road.
Step2: Speed Monitoring:
Speed sensors record the vehicle's speed approaching the curve.
Step3: Road Occupancy Detection:
When one vehicle is in the U- turn, the system warns incoming vehicles.
Step4: Alert System Activation:
If the road is occupied or the speed exceeds a safe threshold, warnings are activated.
Step5: Communication: Sensor data is processed and used to alert nearby vehicles or displayed on digital signage

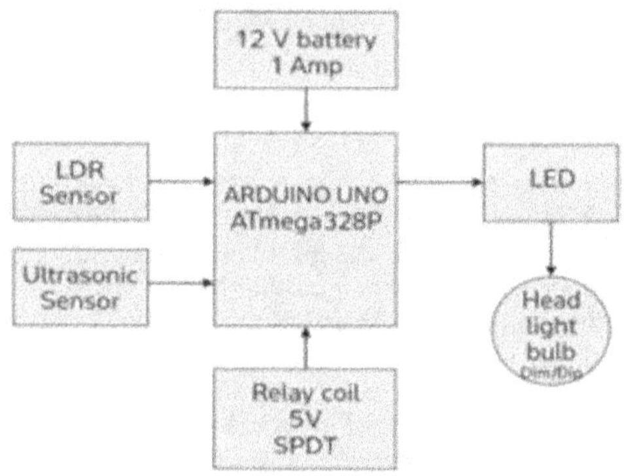

Figure 1. Block diagram of smart sensor-based accident prevention system for U-type roads.

The Figure 1 illustrates about how the working process takes place in the work. This means that idea is that to avoided the road accidents in curve roads (U-turns roads). assume that the u type road has two ways that is x and y. If vehicle is coming from root x the ultra-sonic sensor senses the vehicle and gives the red signal if the vehicle is too near, if vehicle is far from the ultrasonic then it will give orange (it means that the vehicle is going to come soon clear the road from root y). vice versa for root y. And another implementation of my project is that the signal for root x and signal for root y. when at night time when the vehicle is coming from root x after crossing the signal at root x and vice versa ,the both vehicle get into face to face the LDR senser which is present in vehicle coming from root x and same with the vehicle coming from root y. whenever vehicle which is coming from root x head light rays projected on root y vehicle and same with root y vehicle then both the vehicles consists the LDR sensor the root x car will sense the bright ness of root y car. And then the head light of car which is coming from root x get that decrease the intensity of car of root x, same with car.

2.1 *LDR (Light Dependent Resistor)*

A passive electronic component that varies its resistance based on the intensity of incident light. When the surrounding light decreases (e.g., at night), the resistance increases, which the Arduino interprets as a signal to turn on the LED or headlight. It's widely used for automatic lighting control systems.

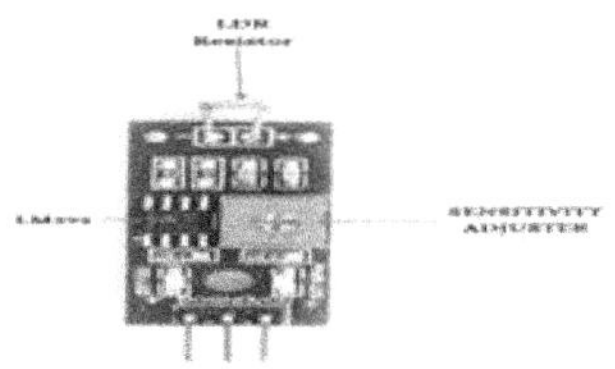

Figure 2. LDR sensor.

2.2 *Ultrasonic sensor*

Ultrasonic sensor is used to detect the distance of obstacles ahead by emitting and receiving sound waves. It takes the time to receive waves from ahead vehicle. It helps detect the presence of vehicles or objects to automatically adjust the headlight intensity.

Figure 3. Ultrasonic sensor.

2.3 *LED*

It provides the output by the process glowing of the LED of logic1(on) and logic 0(off). This a diode which implies the process of glowing and dimming means to be getting off, which tells us about the absents of electrons in it.

Figure 4. Led.

2.4 *12 volts battery*

Provides the necessary power for the entire circuit, with the connected components. It provides stable flow of electronic components, ensuring consistent performance of sensors and actuators.

Figure 5. 12volts battery.

2.5 *Arduino UNO*

The Arduino UNO is based on the ATmega328P microcontroller and operates at 5V with a recommended input of 7–12V. It features 14 digital I/O pins (6 with PWM), 6 analog input pins, 32KB flash memory, 2KB SRAM, and 1KB EEPROM. With a 16 MHz clock speed, it supports USB, UART, SPI, and I2C communication. It includes a reset button, LED on Pin 13, ICSP header, a power jack, and a USB to serial converter.

Figure 6. Arduino UNO module.

3 SIMULATION RESULTS

STEP1:

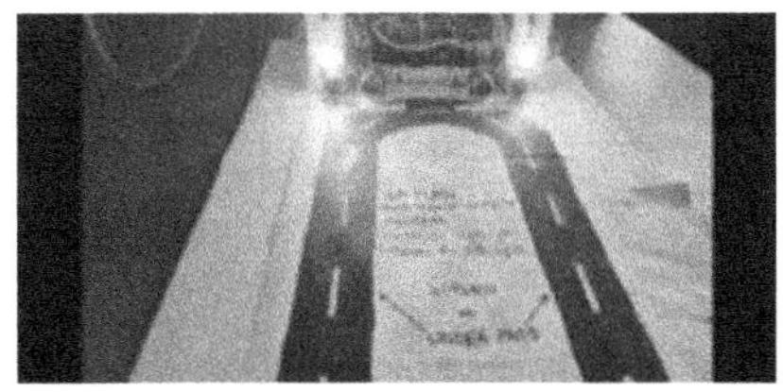

Figure 7. U-turn accidence system.

The above Figure 7 illustrates the complete information about designed to enhance road safety at U-turns and curved junctions. This system is equipped with ultrasonic sensors that detect vehicles or obstacles on both the left and right sides of the road. These sensors are used to

STEP2:

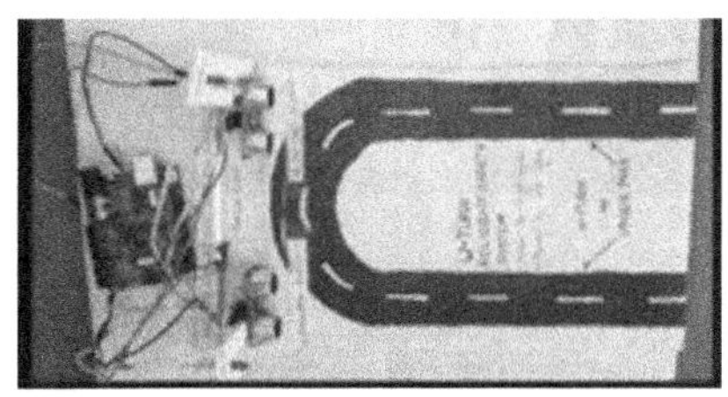

Figure 8. Arduino uno based accidence prevention system.

Figure 8 shows the image shows a working prototype of a U Turn Accident Safety System using ultrasonic sensors and an Arduino microcontroller. The system features a road layout with a U-turn and underpass path. Three ultrasonic sensors—Right Turn, Left Turn, and Roadside—detect approaching vehicles or obstacles. The Arduino processes this data and activates LED indicators: green for safe, red for danger. The setup helps drivers make safe U-turn decisions by providing real-time feedback.

STEP3:

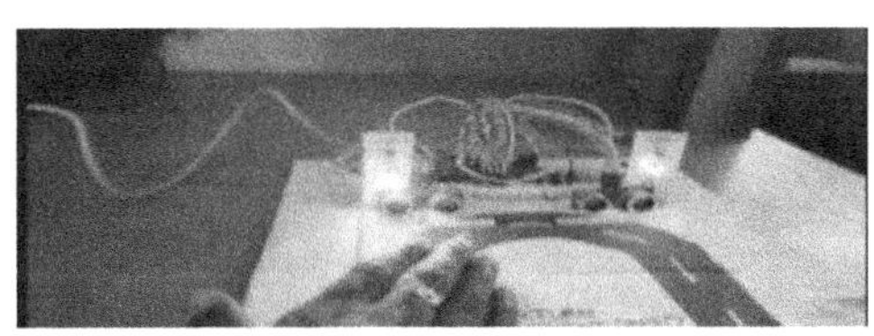

Figure 9. Vehicle detection and warning system using ultrasonic sensor.

Figure 9 illustrates the image displays a live demonstration of a U- Turn Accident Safety System using ultrasonic sensors and an Arduino board. The system detects a hand (representing a vehicle) approaching the U turn using sensors. Corresponding LED indicators respond—green LED for a safe turn and orange/red LED indicating caution or obstacle detection. The wiring shows real- time input and output handling by the Arduino, which processes sensor data to enhance road safety. This setup simulates how vehicles at curved or blind U-turns can avoid collisions by relying on sensor-based alerts, making it an intelligent and practical accident prevention solution.

STEP4:

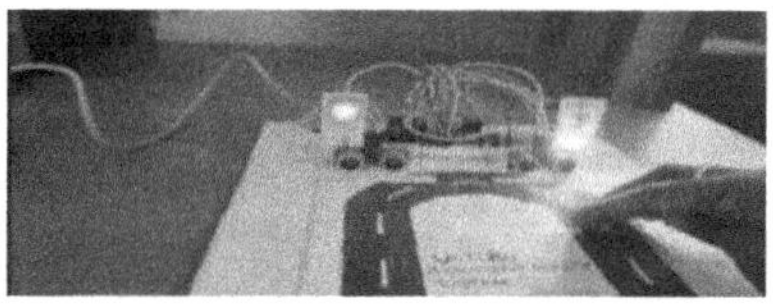

Figure 10. Ultrasonic sensor based vehicle detection and warning system at blind turns.

Figure 10 illustrates about the functioning of a U-Turn Accident Safety System using ultrasonic sensors and an Arduino microcontroller. A hand simulates a vehicle approaching a turn, and the system responds with real-time visual alerts. The left sensor's LED glows red, indicating danger due to an obstacle, while the right sensor's LED shows green, signalling a clear path. The setup includes clearly labelled sensors and directional signs on a printed road model. By processing sensor data, the Arduino ensures safe vehicle movement at curves or U-turns.

STEP5:

Figure 11. Light-responsive headlight dimming mechanism.

Figure 11 shows the image depicts a model car equipped with an LDR (Light Dependent Resistor) sensor system designed for automatic light intensity control. The concept aims to reduce headlight brightness automatically when exposed to external light sources, such as oncoming vehicle headlights, improving road safety by minimizing glare. When bright light falls on the LDR sensor, the system detects increased ambient brightness and correspondingly reduces the headlight intensity of the vehicle model. This setup demonstrates how smart lighting systems can function effectively, especially during night driving, to prevent accidents caused by excessive glare from opposing vehicle Headlights.

STEP6:

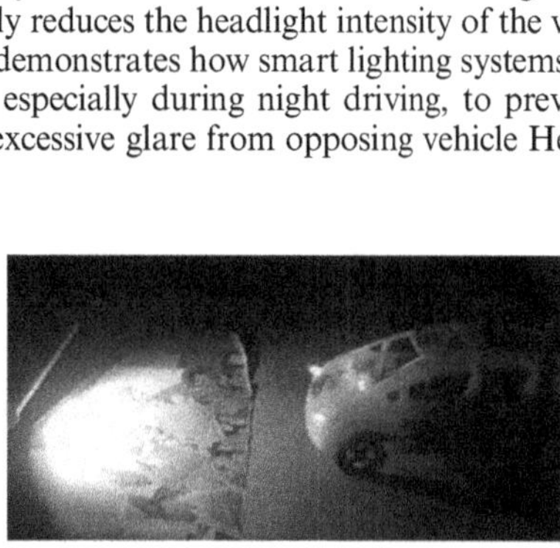

Figure 12. Shows a miniature car with an automatic light intensity control system using an LDR sensor.

Figure 12 illustrates When external light, like from an approaching vehicle, falls on the LDR, the headlight brightness automatically reduces. This helps prevent glare for oncoming drivers, improving night driving safety, especially on curved or U-type roads Accident Safety System using ultrasonic sensors and an Arduino board.

4 CONCLUSIONS

In conclusion, in this project, a smart system is proposed to reduce road accidents at -turns using a combination of ultrasonic sensors and LDR sensors. The system detects vehicles approaching from either direction and uses colored signals (red and orange) to alert other drivers about the proximity and presence of an oncoming vehicle. Additionally, at night, the use of LDR sensors in both vehicles allows automatic dimming of headlights when bright light is detected, preventing temporary blindness and improving visibility. This dual approach in Density control—offers a practical — preventive signalling and, low-cost, and efficient solution head light to improve road safety at dangerous curves, especially in low-light conditions. Compared to traditional systems that rely only on signage or location tracking, this solution provides real-time interaction, making it more responsive and effective.

REFERENCES

[1] Lei Dai, Hai Wang, Long Chen Yich, Eng Li, Miguel Angel Sotelo, Zhixiong Li Y. Cai *et al.*, (Jun. 2022). *IEEE Trans. Intel. Transp. Syst.*, vol. 23, no. 6, pp. 5298–5313.

[2] Denk F., Brunner P., Huber W., Margreiter M., Bogenberger K. and Kates R., (2022) Assessment of traffic safety interventions using virtual randomized controlled trials: potential of connected and automated driving including V2X for collision reduction at urban intersections, *2022 IEEE 25th International Conference on Intelligent Transportation Systems (ITSC)*, Macau, China, 2022, pp. 1183–1190.

[3] Ni Y., Wang S., Xin L., Meng Y., Yin J. and Sun J., (2020) A V2X-based Approach for Avoiding Potential Blind-zone Collisions between Right-turning Vehicles and Pedestrians at Intersections, *2020 IEEE 23rd International Conference on Intelligent Transportation Systems (ITSC)*, Rhodes, Greece, 2020, pp. 1–6.

[4] Ulied D., Marias-i-Parella J. and Carmona-Cejudo E. (2023), Demo: A Collision Avoidance System Integrating V2X Communication and Computer Vision for VRUs, *2023 IEEE Vehicular Networking Conference (VNC)*, Istanbul, Turkiye, 2023, pp. 165–166.

[5] Jamuna P., Kavin Kumar K., Murugesan A., Karthikeyan G., Dineshkumar S. and Sangeetha M. (2024), *2024 International Conference on Communication, Computing and Internet of Things (IC3IoT)*, Chennai, India, 2024, pp. 1–6, doi: 10.1109/IC3IoT60841.2024.10550276

[6] Chen G., Wang M., Zhang Q., Yuan L., Liu T. and Yue Y. (2023), Deep Interactive Full Transformer Framework for Point Cloud Registration, *2023 IEEE International Conference on Robotics and Automation (ICRA)*, London, United Kingdom, pp. 2825–2832, doi: 10.1109/ICRA48891.2023.10160863.

[7] Ma, Ouyang W., Simonelli A. and Ricci E., (May 2024), 3D Object Detection from Images for Autonomous Driving: A Survey, in *IEEE Transactions on Pattern Analysis and Machine Intelligence*, vol. 46, no. 5, pp. 3537–3556, doi: 10.1109/TPAMI.2023.3346386.

[8] Yaodong Cui, Ren Chen, Wenbo Chu, Long Chen, (Feb. 2022), Deep Learning for Image and Point Cloud Fusion in Autonomous Driving: A Review, in *IEEE Transactions on Intelligent Transportation Systems*, vol. 23, no. 2, pp. 722–739, doi: 10.1109/TITS.2020.3023541

[9] Wang L., Zhang X., Song Z., Bi J., Zhang G., Wei H., Tang L., Yang L., Li J., Jia C., and Zhao L., (July 2023), Multi-modal 3D object detection in autonomous driving: A survey and taxonomy, *IEEE Transactions on Intelligent Vehicles*, vol. 8, no. 7, pp. 3781–3798

[10] Anliang Yao, Runwei Guan, Xiaoyu Huang, Zhuoxiao Li, Xiangyi Sha, Yong Yue, Eng Gee Lim, Hyungjoon Seo, Ka Lok Man, Xiaohui Zhu and Yutao Yue, (January 2024), Radar-camera fusion for object detection and semantic segmentation in autonomous driving: A comprehensive review, *IEEETransactions on Intelligent Vehicles*, vol. 9, no. 1, pp. 2094–2128

Next-Generation Smart Systems – Sekhar et al. (Eds)
© 2027 The Author(s), ISBN: 978-1-041-34234-2

Optimized EV Charging with V2G and V2V Capabilities Using Fuzzy Logic Control

S. Punyavathi and V. Sekhar
Assistant Professor Department of EEE, Kuppam Engineering College, Kuppam, India

V. Niranjan
Faculty, Department of EEE GMR Polytechnic, Srisailam, India

C.H. Subbanna
Faculty, Department of EEE, GPT, Kavali, India

P. Dayasagar and B. Venureddykumar
Assistant Professor Department of EEE, Kuppam Engineering College, Kuppam, India

ABSTRACT: A optimized EV charger with V2G and V2V capabilities and FLC is designed and modeled in this study. The suggested method allows bidirectional power flow, it enables effective EV charging, grid stability, and energy trading. Dynamic power transmission via a (FLC) is managed considering grid load, EV battery (SOC), and user preferences. Power flow between EVs and the grid is controlled using a bidirectional DC-DC converter, therefore guaranteeing smooth transitions among charging and discharging modes. MATLAB/Simulink is used to replicate the system in order to assess its performance under different grid settings and SOC values. Results of simulations show that compared to standard charging techniques, the fuzzy logic-based control approach increases grid stability, lowers total harmonic distortion (THD), and improves energy economy. The results draw attention to how clever control systems may maximize EV energy management and enable smart grid integration. This work opens the path for next real-world implementations and more optimizations, hence advancing sustainable and intelligent EV charging infrastructure.

Keywords: Electric Vehicles, Vehicle-to-Grid (V2G), Bidirectional DC-DC converter, fuzzy logic controller(FLC), Vehicle-to-Vehicle (V2V), Power Quality (PQ), Energy Efficiency

1 INTRODUCTION

Fast deployment of (EVs) presents new opportunities and challenges for modern energy systems. EVs are no longer merely transportation devices; they can act as energy storage devices that are able to bidirectional energy exchange with the grid and other vehicles. This capability, known as V2G and V2V power transfer, enhances grid stability, supports energy trading, and optimizes power [1]. However, the implementation of such a system requires advanced control strategies to ensure efficient energy distribution while maintaining PQ and grid reliability.

FLC has emerged as an effective technique for managing complex systems with uncertain and dynamic variables. Unlike conventional controllers, (FLCs) can handle imprecise inputs and make adaptive decisions based on a rule-based approach, making them well-suited for V2G and V2V applications [2]. With an FLC-based system considering user preferences, EV battery SOC, and grid load, one can optimize power flow, reduce grid stress, and assure effective charging and discharging operations.

Including EVs into the grid has technical and financial issues as well. Studies have shown that V2G deployment supports frequency control and demand response systems [3], therefore generating extra income sources for EV owners. Additionally, a well-managed V2G system can reduce peak loads, minimize energy costs, and enhance the overall resilience of the power network [4]. Beyond V2G, V2V energy exchange allows EVs to share power directly, improving charging accessibility in remote locations and enhancing energy autonomy for fleets and individual users [5]

A fundamental part of V2G and V2V systems, the bidirectional DC-DC converter lets electricity flow from the grid, other cars, and the EV. Research has shown that bidirectional converters are an excellent method for ensuring system stability and enabling smooth energy exchange [6]. These converters are designed to handle fluctuating power demands and operate efficiently under varying grid situations.

FLC have been extensively used in power electronics to enhance performance, improve energy efficiency, and ensure stability in dynamic environments. Their application in EV charging and energy management systems has been extensively reviewed, highlighting their effectiveness in handling non-linearities and uncertainties in power systems [7]. Furthermore, implementing fuzzy logic control in grid-connected EV systems can help minimize THD, thereby reducing grid disturbances and improving power quality[8].

Simulation and modeling has critical role in analyzing and optimizing EV energy management strategies. MATLAB and Simulink are widely used for simulating power systems, validating control strategies, and assessing the efficiency of V2G and V2V implementations [9]. These tools enable researchers to test different control methodologies under real-world conditions, ensuring robust performance before deployment.

To ensure the effectiveness of V2G technology, numerous control approaches have been suggested to improve power quality and grid stability. Studies have highlighted the importance of real-time control techniques in mitigating voltage fluctuations, reducing frequency deviations, and enhancing overall system reliability [10]. By integrating FLC with bidirectional DC-DC converters, the suggested system objects to address these tasks offering a more intelligent and efficient approach to EV charging and energy management.

In this work, we provide a grid-connected EV charger using FLC with integrated V2G and V2V capability. The suggested method guarantees power quality by using a bidirectional converter to enable energy transfer between the grid, EVs, and other vehicles, thereby enhancing energy management. Results of simulation show how well the FLC enhances grid stability and raises general energy economy. The results of this work help to progress intelligent EV charging infrastructure and increase the general acceptance of V2G and V2V technologies.

The article showcases the design, simulation, and performance evaluation of the proposed system using MATLAB/Simulink. Simulation results show FLC works in managing bidirectional power flow and enhancing EV energy management, more robust and sustainable power grid shown in Figure 1.

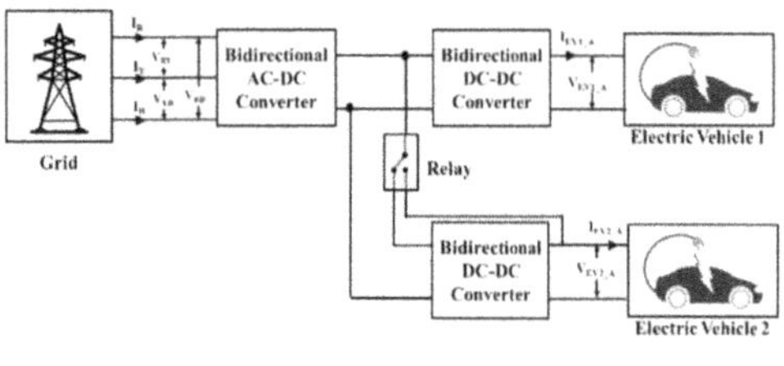

Figure 1. Block diagram.

2 LITERATURE REVIEW

Having EVs tied into the grid has advantages and disadvantages. Several studies have explored the technical and economic aspects of V2G and V2V energy transfer, stressing the part modern control techniques play in maximizing energy use. Anderson and Fulcher (2017) analyzed the challenges and prospects related to electric vehicle grid interconnection. Their research highlighted the advantages of bidirectional power flow in enhancing grid stability and facilitating energy trading. Guille and Gross (2009) provided a conceptual framework for V2G deployment, emphasizing the need of intelligent energy management measures to improve grid performance.

The role of power electronic converters in enabling efficient V2G and V2V energy transfer has been extensively studied. Khan and Khan (2018) analyzed bidirectional DC-DC converters for V2G applications, demonstrating their effectiveness in regulating power flow among EVs and the grid. Furthermore, Chaturvedi and Singh (2019) investigated the impact of total harmonic distortion (THD) in grid-connected EV systems and suggested methods for minimizing THD to improve power quality.

FLC has emerged as a promising technique for optimizing power transfer in EV charging systems. Zadeh (1965) introduced the concept of fuzzy sets, which laid the foundation for FLCs. Sharma and Dubey (2020) reviewed the application of FLCs in power electronics, highlighting their advantages in handling uncertainties and dynamic grid conditions. Mahmud and Zahedi (2016) further explored control strategies for improving power quality in V2G systems, emphasizing the role of real-time adaptive control mechanisms.

Economic and operational considerations are also critical in V2G adoption. Kempton and Tomic (2005) assessed the financial viability of V2G, calculating potential revenue streams for EV owners. Chan (2007) provided a comprehensive overview of EV technologies, including hybrid and fuel cell vehicles, to contextualize V2G advancements. MATLAB and Simulink (2021) have been widely utilized for simulating EV-grid interactions, allowing researchers to test and validate control algorithms before real-world deployment.

Overall, existing literature underscores the significance of intelligent control strategies, power electronics, and economic feasibility in advancing V2G and V2V technologies. This study builds on these findings by proposing a fuzzy logic-controlled bidirectional charging system to enhance grid stability and energy efficiency.

3 METHODOLOGY

The proposed EV charging system integrates V2G) and V2Vcapabilities using a FLC controlled bidirectional DC-DC converter. The system includes an EV charger, grid interface, and a FLC to manage energy flow. The FLC takes inputs such as grid load, EV battery state of charge (SOC), and user preferences to optimize power transfer. By utilizing a fuzzy inference system (FIS), the controller ensures efficient and adaptive energy distribution while minimizing grid disturbances. The bidirectional DC-DC converter operates in charging mode (G2V) to regulate voltage for EV charging and in discharging mode (V2G/V2V) to transfer energy back to the grid or another EV, improving grid steadiness and energy sharing.

The suggested system is developed in MATLAB to assess its act under different conditions, including load variations at different SOC levels. Key evaluation metrics include energy efficiency, grid stability, and power quality, with a focus on reducing total harmonic distortion (THD). The FLC strategy dynamically adjusts the duty cycle of the converter, ensuring optimal energy flow and system reliability. Simulation results will be compared against conventional charging methods to demonstrate improvements in power quality, energy efficiency, and grid support, validating the effectiveness of the proposed intelligent EV charging system.

The control signal is designated as an output variable in the fuzzy logic controller (FLC) by two input variables, the error (e) and the change in error (Δe). As far as the input variables are concerned, there are seven different expressions in the language that describe them: NB, NM, NL, Z, PB, PM, and PL. In order for the fuzzy inference system to decide the appropriate control action based on established rules, these language terms are used.

The following table represents the 7×7 fuzzy rule matrix, where the rows correspond to the error (e), the columns correspond to the change in error (Δe), and the table entries represent the control signal shown in Table 1:

Table 1. Fuzzy law table.

e \ Δe	NB	NM	NL	Z	PL	PM	PB
NB	NB	NB	NM	NM	NL	Z	PL
NM	NB	NM	NM	NL	Z	PL	PM
NL	NM	NM	NL	Z	PL	PM	PM
Z	NM	NL	Z	Z	Z	PL	PM
PL	NL	Z	PL	Z	PL	PM	PM
PM	Z	PL	PM	PL	PM	PM	PB
PB	PL	PM	PM	PM	PM	PB	PB

A full transformation of the inputs into fuzzy sets is accomplished by the fuzzification process. The rule base is then evaluated by the fuzzy inference engine, which results in the production of a fuzzy output. Using the centroid technique then defuzzifies this fuzzy result. This sharp control signal modulates the VSC and the DC-DC converter regulate the power flow.

The system operates in three modes:

1. Charging Mode: Power is flows from the grid to the EV battery, prioritizing efficiency and reliability.
2. Discharging Mode (V2G): EVs provides power to the grid to support load balancing and grid stability.
3. V2V Mode: Energy is shared between EVs based on their SOC.

4 SIMULATION STUDIES

The suggested FLC bidirectional EV charging system was simulated using MATLAB/Simulink shown in Figure 2 to assess its performance under varying conditions shown in

Figure 2. The simulation model includes a grid-connected EV charger, a bidirectional DC-DC converter, and a fuzzy logic controller (FLC) that dynamically regulates power flow. Key components of the setup include a variable load grid model to replicate real-world fluctuations, an EV battery model with dynamic state of charge (SOC) variations, and an FLC designed to optimize energy transfer. The simulation aimed to evaluate the system's response to different charging and discharging scenarios, ensuring efficient energy management while maintaining power quality and grid stability.

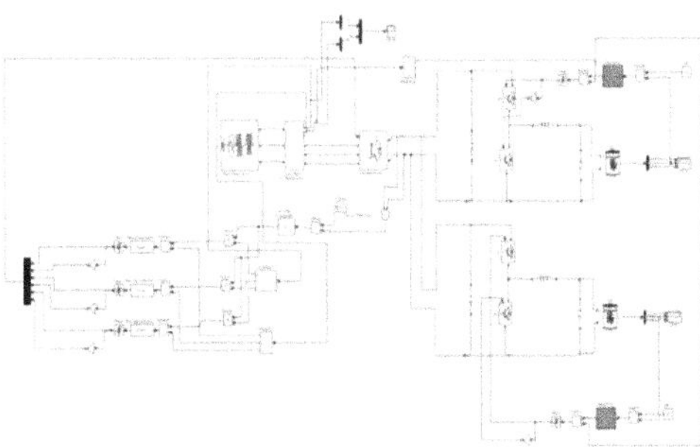

Figure 2. Proposed circuits.

The performance analysis focused on three main aspects: load variation response, SOC-based charging efficiency, and power quality improvement. The model performance showed that the FLC efficiently stabilized voltage and frequency under changing grid conditions while optimizing energy distribution. The bidirectional DC-DC converter ensured smooth transitions between charging (G2V) and discharging (V2G/V2V) modes, reducing total harmonic distortion (THD) and enhancing grid reliability. Comparative analysis with conventional charging strategies confirmed that the suggested system outdoes traditional methods in terms of energy efficiency and power quality, demonstrating its effectiveness in supporting V2G and V2V energy exchange shown in Figures 3 and 4.

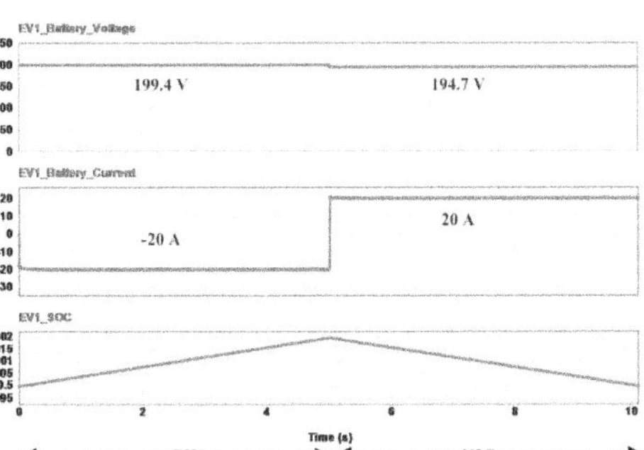

Figure 3. EV 1 battery voltage current and SOC in G2V and V2G.

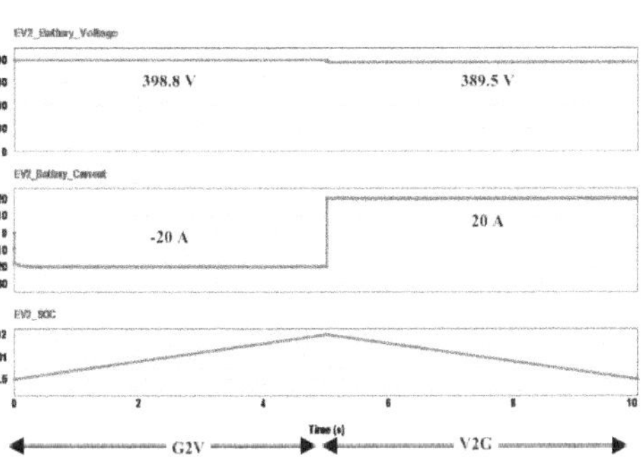

Figure 4. EV 1 battery voltage current and SOC in G2V and V2G.

This feature proves to be highly beneficial in scenarios where grid access is limited or unavailable. The integrated system consistently outperforms in all simulated scenarios, highlighting its adaptability for various applications, including smart grid development and renewable energy integration. The fuzzy logic controller (FLC) is a crucial component for maintaining system stability, reducing energy losses, and achieving optimal power quality. The detailed simulation analysis validates the feasibility of the suggested design and underscores its potential to address tough challenges in modern power structures, offering a reliable and sustainable solution for future EV infrastructure.

By observing the initial reaction of the SOC, voltage, and current parameters, one may build a baseline for knowing how various operating modes effect the act of the system. It is shown the battery systems' starting output as well as their optimal state. This figure provides a point of reference showing the nominal operating voltage, current, and SOC response properties. To act as a control situation for more research, the system's performance is captured in a snapshot before any changes or stress testing is done. By use of this baseline, researchers may explore how variations in operational modes and settings influence system performance and thereby affect efficiency and stability.

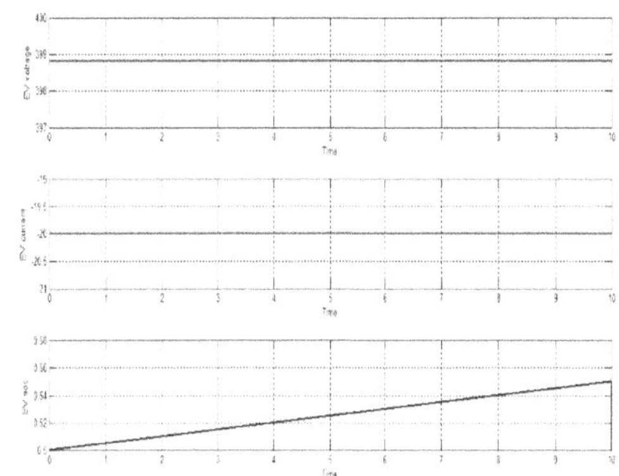

Figure 5. EV 1 The performance for voltage(V), current(I), and SOC is analyzed.

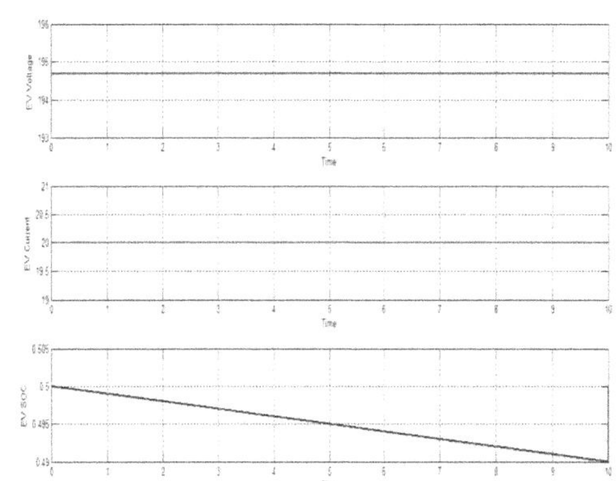

Figure 6. The output response for V-I and (SOC) in EV 2 is analyzed.

This figure illustrates the variations in V-I and (SOC) during extended action under mixed (G2V), (V2G), and (V2V) scenarios. It plays a vital role in calculating the durable impact of different operating ways on system stability and battery health. Building on the previous figure, this one highlights how voltage, current, and SOC fluctuate over extended operation in mixed scenarios are shown in Figures 5 and 6. This long-term data is crucial for understanding the permanence of system modules under unceasing or full use, enabling accurate predictions of system performance over the infrastructure's lifetime. It also aids in planning necessary maintenance, upgrades, or replacements.

5 CONCLUSION

This study presented a FLC bidirectional EV charging system with integrated V2G and V2V capabilities. The suggested system effectively manages energy transfer between the grid and EVs, optimizing charging efficiency and improving grid stability. By incorporating a FLC, the system dynamically adjusts power flow based on grid conditions, EV battery SOC, and user preferences. The bidirectional DC-DC converter facilitates seamless transitions between charging and discharging modes, supporting energy trading and reducing risk on the grid.

The results gives usefulness of the upgraded system, demonstrating improvements in energy efficiency, power quality, and grid stability. The fuzzy logic-based control strategy minimized total harmonic distortion (THD) and enhanced voltage and frequency regulation under varying load conditions. Compared to conventional charging methods, the proposed system exhibited superior performance in optimizing energy utilization while reducing grid disturbances. These findings highlight the potential of intelligent control strategies in advancing EV integration into smart grids and supporting sustainable energy solutions.

Future work may involve real-world implementation and further optimization of the control strategy to enhance system adaptability and scalability.

REFERENCES

[1] Kempton, Willett, and Jasna Tomić. Vehicle-to-grid power fundamentals: Calculating capacity and net revenue. *Journal of power sources* 144.1 (2005): 268–279.

[2] Subrahmanyam, *et al.* Development and simulation of a smart grid-connected ev charger with integrated v2g and v2v capabilities using fuzzy logic control. *Cuestiones de fisioterapia* 54.3 (2025): 4305–4316.

[3] Conte, *et al.* (2019). Operational constrained nonlinear modeling and identification of active distribution networks. *Electric Power Systems Research, 168*, pp.92–104.

[4] Liu, Y., Han, L., Yin, Z., and Luo, K. (2017). A competitive carbon emissions scheme with hybrid fiscal incentives: the evidence from a taxi industry. *Energy Policy*, 102, 414–422

[5] Zadeh, L.A. (1965). Fuzzy sets. *Information and Control*, 8(3), 338–353.

[6] Guille, C., and Gross, G. (2009). A conceptual framework for the vehicle-to-grid (V2G) implementation. *Energy policy*, *37*(11), 4379–4390

[7] Singh, Poonam, *et al.* Trends and novel strategies for enhancing lipid accumulation and quality in microalgae. *Renewable and Sustainable Energy Reviews* 55 (2016):

[8] MATLAB and Simulink. (2021). Simulation software for power systems and energy management. *MathWorks*

 ISBN: 978-1-041-34234-2

A Comprehensive Review Paper on Narrow Band Internet of Things

T. Jayasimha
Ph. D Scholar Annamacharya University, Andhra Pradesh, India

K. Riyazuddin
Associate Professor, Department of ECE, Annamacharya University, Andhra Pradesh, India

ABSTRACT: Agriculture, is one of oldest and utmost essential human activities, is undergoing a profound transformation driven by the combination of advanced information and communication technologies. As a wide-range challenges which includes environment change, population growth, water scarcity, and environmental degradation put immense pressure on food systems, the agricultural sector is embracing digital solutions to enhance productivity, sustainability, and resource efficiency. This review paper presents a complete overview of the role of NB-IOT technology enables smart farming by applying it to precision farming, livestock tracking, and irrigation control using low-cost sensors. One vital aspect of the industry undergoing this profound shift is increasing productivity and sustainability. NB-IOT empowers cost-effective monitoring of soil nutrients, temperature, moisture, pH, micro-climatic parameters including humidity, rainfall, crop health NDVI, and chlorophyll levels. through cost-effective and power-efficient sensors deployed across large agricultural plots.

Keywords: NB-IOT, 3GPP, LPWAN, mMTC, IoT

1 INTRODUCTION

The fast expansion of IoT has explosive growth has transformed contemporary communication paradigms, enabling billions of devices to link, sense, and relate with the environment [1,6]. This ubiquitous connectivity brings a multitude of applications across in domains like smart cities, healthcare, agriculture, logistics, and industrial automation[18,22]. However, the majority of IoT devices are constrained by limitations such as low power, limited bandwidth, and cost sensitivity. Addressing these constraints necessitates a new class of communication technologies can be optimized for mMTC it is one of the most important technologies in this category. NB-IOT is a LPWAN model developed by 3GPP[19] to meet the specific requirements of IoT[20,24] devices that demand wide coverage, extended battery life, low data rates, and scalability [4,13]. Introduced as part of the 3GPP Release 13[12] specifications in 2016, NB-IoT is designed to work[9] within the existing LTE infrastructure while also being capable of standalone and guard-band deployment modes. By focusing on minimal complexity and energy efficiency, NB-IOT has emerged[3,21] as a crucial enabler of scalable, nationwide IoT deployments [8]

Deployment and Integration: Focuses on practical aspects of NB-IoT network deployment, including standalone vs. in-band configurations, integration with LTE and 5G systems, and network planning considerations.
Performance Analysis: studies the practical functioning of NB-IOT[17] in terms of data throughput, latency, power efficiency, and network coverage, supported by empirical studies and simulations [2].
Applications: Discusses diverse NB-IoT use cases, including smart agriculture, smart meters, logistics, environmental monitoring, healthcare, and smart grids
Comparative Studies: Compares NB-IoT with other IoT[12] communication technologies such as LoRaWAN, Sigfox, LTE-M[12], and 5G mMTC, highlighting trade-offs in power consumption, range, cost, and scalability.
Challenges: Identifies technical, regulatory, and operational challenges facing NB-IoT, such as device mobility, spectrum efficiency, and data security [2,4].

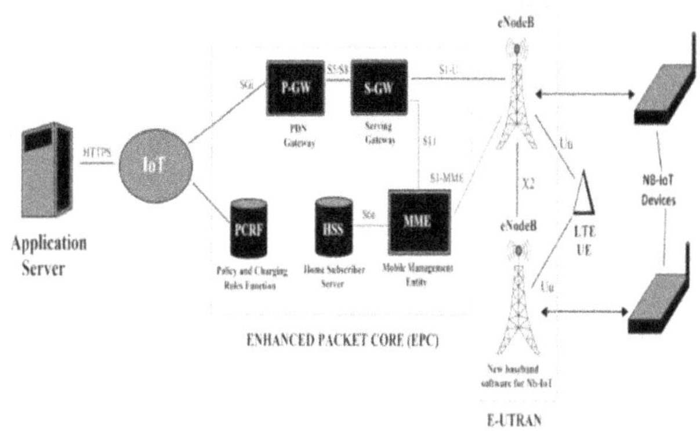

Figure 1. Architecture of NB-IOT.[21]

2 LITERATURE REVIEW

Wang *et al.* (2016) [8] in their paper "A Primer on 3GPP NB-IoT" provide a comprehensive introduction to NB-IoT, discussing its air interface and how it addresses critical IoT requirements such as low complexity, extended battery life, and massive device connectivity. This work also offers valuable insights into the rationale behind key design decisions during the 3GPP standardization process.

The survey titled "NB-IOT: A Comprehensive Study" published in Computer Networks examines NB-IoT's transition from LTE and enhancements across 3GPP Releases 13 to 16. It also discusses integration with complementary technologies like Device-to-Device communication, NOMA , and its role in the 5G ecosystem[16,27]

Bamniya and Panchal [9] present a review in Journal of Electrical Systems that explores into NB-IoT's architectural and technical underpinnings, comparing its performance with additional IoT technologies such as LoRa and Sigfox. This paper also highlights practical use cases and offers a comparative perspective on deployment challenges.

R. Litjens *et al.* [14] in Procedia Computer Science underlines the strategic importance of NB-IoT in supporting LPWAN use

DOI: 10.1201/9781042001767-59

cases under the 5G umbrella. It highlights critical design considerations and compatibility issues, underscoring the need for thoughtful integration with other 5G components.[11]

Martinez *et al.* (2018) [1] in their empirical study "Exploring the Performance Boundaries of NB-IoT" [2,5,23] analyse parameters such as energy utilization, consistency, and latency. Their comparison with other LPWAN technologies like LoRa reveals both strengths and bottlenecks of NB- IOT in real-world deployments.

3 PERFORMANCE ANALYSIS

Evaluating the execution of NB-IoT is crucial to understand how well it fulfils its design goals compared to other LPWAN technologies. This section provides a detailed analysis of NB-IoT[28] across key metrics: coverage, capacity, latency, throughput, power consumption, and scalability, supported by real-world deployment data and simulations.

3.1 *Coverage*

Coverage represents the strength of NB-IoT, designed to enable connectivity[10] in to reach locations like cellars, rural areas, and dense urban environments[16]. Key technologies include:

Maximum Coupling Loss up to 164 dB, ~20 dB greater than LTE. [15,18,26]Repetitions of uplink/downlink messages (up to 128 times) improve decoding in poor conditions.[16,25] Narrowband Operation (180 kHz) enables deep signal penetration. Empirical studies reveal that NB-IoT achieves 3x to 5x better indoor coverage than GSM and LTE, making it ideal for underground metering and remote agriculture[23]

3.2 *Capacity and scalability*

NB-IoT supports massive device deployments—up to 50,000 devices per cell, as per 3GPP[5,17] Key enablers include:

Minimal data per device

Enhanced Random Access Channel (RACH) with more contention slots [24]

Efficient allocation of LTE physical resource blocks (PRBs) [14,19]

Simulations confirm NB-IoT maintains reliable performance in dense urban scenarios when networks are properly dimensioned. [13,24]

3.3 *Latency*

NB-IOT is not optimized for latency-critical applications. Typical latency ranges:

Uplink: 1.6–10 seconds Downlink: 2.0–11 seconds[18,25]

Power-saving features like PSM and eDRX increase latency but are acceptable for delay-tolerant use cases like smart metering[18] and ecological monitoring. [19,20] NB-IoT is unsuitable for real-time applications like autonomous vehicles. [15]

3.4 *Data throughput*

NB-IoT trades high throughput for efficiency. As per 3GPP Release 13:

Uplink: ~66 kbps

Downlink: ~27 kbps

Release 14 introduced multi-tone transmission and 64-QAM, increasing uplink to ~127 kbps and downlink to ~120 kbps. However, real-world throughput is lower due to repetitions and device constraints. Typical use cases require only small, infrequent data packets.

3.5 *Power efficiency*

Power Saving Mode (PSM): Minimizes energy use between transmissions

eDRX: Reduces wake-up frequency while ensuring periodic communication

Power efficiency is critical for NB-IoT's long-term deployments. Features include:

Low data transmission frequency

Devices can operate for 5–10 years on a small battery (e.g., 3.6V, 2400 mAh), depending on use patterns. NB-IoT outperforms most LPWAN competitors in energy longevity, making it ideal for remote, battery-powered deployments.[21]

4 APPLICATIONS OF NB-IOT

NB-IOT is improved for low-power, wide-area[15] connectivity making it for an extensive range of applications[5,25] involving stationary, delay-tolerant devices that transmit small data volumes infrequently. Its advantages—deep coverage, scalability, energy efficiency, and low deployment costs—support various sectors

4.1 *Smart utilities*

NB-IoT is widely used in smart level analyser for water, gas, and electricity, particularly in basements and remote areas. Key benefits include automated readings [6], leak detection, and remote configuration. Countries like China and Germany have deployed millions of such meters. In energy infrastructure, NB-IOT enables transformer monitoring and load management through low-bandwidth, periodic telemetry. [19]

4.2 *Smart cities*

NB-IOT enhances urban mobility through smart parking systems, reducing traffic and emissions via real-time space availability. It also supports intelligent street lighting with scheduled operations, fault alerts, and energy savings of up to 50%. Smart waste bins equipped with NB-IOT optimize collection routes, minimize overflow, and cut emissions.

4.3 *Agriculture and environment*

In precision agriculture, NB-IOT sensors monitor soil, climate, and crop conditions to optimize resource use. For environmental monitoring, it tracks air/water quality, noise, and weather data, aiding in policy compliance and disaster forecasting. Hospitals use NB-IOT to track medical equipment, enhancing asset availability and reducing theft.

4.4 *Industrial and manufacturing*

NB-IOT facilitates predictive maintenance by collecting machinery data to anticipate failures and reduce downtime. It supports remote monitoring of pipelines and turbines and automates smart building systems such as HVAC, fire detection, and access control, improving efficiency and safety.

4.5 Emergency Services and Safety NB-IoT is integrated into disaster management systems to monitor floods, seismic events, and structural integrity, enabling early warnings.

NB-IOT's unique capabilities position it as a key enabler of scalable, efficient IoT solutions across critical infrastructure and emerging smart environments. [19]

5 COMPARATIVE ANALYSIS

NB-IOT is one of several LPWAN technologies developed[15,25] to match the demands of large mMTC in the evolving IoT landscape. This section presents a comparative study of NB-IOT against competing technologies including LTE-M, LoRaWAN, Sigfox, and other legacy cellular systems. The comparison is organized along multiple dimensions: technology fundamentals, performance metrics, cost considerations, network control, deployment models, application suitability, and regulatory status. These comparisons help clarify the strengths and limitations in NB-IoT for various industrial and public sector use cases[19].

NB-IoT emerges as a strong contender among LPWAN technologies, particularly in scenarios that require deep coverage, long battery life, licensed spectrum reliability, and stationary device deployments. Its strengths are most evident in smart metering, infrastructure, and public sector deployments. Compared to LTE-M, it sacrifices mobility and speed for simplicity and efficiency. Against unlicensed competitors like LoRaWAN and Sigfox, NB-IoT offers better QoS, integration with cellular infrastructure, and standardized global scalability. As the IoT ecosystem matures, NB-IoT's coexistence with complementary technologies will enable hybrid solutions tailored to specific application needs.

Technology	Spectrum	Bandwidth	Data Rate	Latency	Mobility	Battery Life	Use Case Focus
NB-IOT	Licensed	180 kHz	~66 kbps	1–10 s	Limited	~10 years	Rapid meters, cities
LTE-M	Licensed	1.4 MHz	~1 Mbps	<100 ms	Full	5–10 years	Wearables, vehicles
LoRaWAN	Unlicensed	~125 kHz	~50 kbps	~1–5 s	None	5–10 years	Rural sensors, agriculture
Sigfox	Unlicensed	100 Hz	~100 bps	High (>10s)	None	10+ years	Lightweight devices
2G/3G	Licensed	Multiple	~100 kbps–Mbps	Variable	Full	2–5 years	Legacy M2M

6 CONCLUSION

NB-IOT has become a key technology in the[7,9] ongoing development of the IoT, making it possible to connect large numbers of low-power, affordable devices over wide areas efficiently and reliably. As an integral component of the 3GPP standard family, NB-IoT addresses key requirements for mMTC, including extended coverage, long battery life, low complexity, and cost efficiency. This review has comprehensively explored NB-IoT across its architectural foundations, deployment strategies, performance metrics, real-world applications, comparative advantages, existing challenges, and future directions. Drawing upon these insights, this conclusion synthesizes the findings and reflects on the outlook for NB-IoT in the broader IoT ecosystem.

REFERENCES

[1] Martinez B., Montavont J., and Palattella, (2019), Exploring the performance boundaries of NB-IOT, *arXiv* preprint arXiv:1810.00847.

[2] Liberg O., Sundberg M., and Bergman J., (2020), NB-IOT for non-terrestrial networks, *arXiv* preprint arXiv:2010.04906.

[3] Rodriguez F.J., Cardenas Y.G., and Toledo G., (2020), Evolution and testing of NB-IOT solutions, *Appl. Sci.*, vol. 10, no. 21, p. 7903.

[4] Elnour A., Ahmad A.W., and Rashid M.M., (2021), Performance analysis of LoRaWAN and cellular NB-IOT networks in developing countries, *Electronics*, vol. 10, no. 18, p. 2224.

[5] Abbasi M., (2019), *NB-IOT small cell: A 3GPP perspective*.

[6] Shahjalal M., Hasan M.M., and Hossain E., (2019), NB-IOT: From physical (PHY) and media access control (MAC) layers perspectives, *Sensors*, vol. 19, no. 11, p. 2613.

[7] Matz A.P., Jacobsen K.B., and Manweiler D.M., (2020), A systematic analysis of NB-IOT quality of service, *Sensors*, vol. 20, no. 6, p. 1636.

[8] Wang Y.-P.E. *et al.*, (2016), A primer on 3GPP Narrowband Internet of Things (NB-IOT)

[9] Bamniya K.H. and Panchal R.K., (2022), Advancements and challenges in NB-IOT: A comprehensive review of technology and applications, *J. Eng. Sci.*, vol. 13, no. 2, pp. 89–101.

[10] Eze C., Wang H., Shi Y., and Yu F.R., (2021), Suitability of NB-IOT for indoor industrial environment: A survey and insights, *Sensors*, vol. 21, no. 16, p. 5284.

[11] Muteba K.F., Mthulisi D., and Chipo M., (2021), 5G NB-IOT: Design, considerations, solutions and challenges, *Procedia Comput. Sci.*, vol. 187, pp. 193–200.

[12] Taruc L.E.F. and De La Cruz A.R., (2024), *NB-IOT and IoT A research analysis*.

[13] Ometov A., Nurmi J., and Koucheryavy Y., (2021), Model of a device-level combined wireless network based on NB-IOT and IEEE 802.15.4 standards for low-power applications, *Sensors*, vol. 21, no. 11, p. 3718.

[14] Litjens R. and Zhang H., (2019), Optimisation of NB-IOT deployment for smart energy distribution networks, *EURASIP J. Wirel. Commun. Netw.*, vol. 2019, no. 1, pp. 1–14.

[15] Palattella L.R. *et al.*, (Aug. 2018), NB-IOT, *IEEE Internet Things J.*, vol. 5, no. 4, pp. 2650–2660

[16] Shafiq A., Ferrag M.A., and Maglaras L., (2020), NB-IOT: A comprehensive study, *Comput. Netw.*, vol. 172, pp. 107–118.

[17] Ratasuk R., Vejlgaard B., Mangalvedhe N., and Ghosh A., (2016), NB-IOT system for M2M communication, in Proc. *IEEE Wireless Communications and Networking Conference (WCNC)*.

[18] Raza S., Wallgren A., and Voigt T., (2019), Narrow Band IoT: Physical layer and MAC layer overview, *Sensors*, vol. 19, no. 7, p. 1563.

[19] Alimi A., Shafiq A.A., and Ferrag M.A., (Feb. 2021), Towards energy-efficient NB-IoT: A survey on evaluating its suitability for smart applications, *Sustain. Cities Soc.*, vol. 65, p. 102603.

[20] Catarinucci L., Patrono L., Mainetti L., Tarricone L., and Colella R., (2021), An NB-IoT-based Edge-of-Things framework for energy-efficient industrial IoT, Sensors, vol. 21, no. 17, p. 5929.

[21] Raza J. and Khan M., (2024), Energy efficiency optimization of NB-IoT using integrated proxy, *Internet Things Cyber-Phys. Syst.*, vol. 5.

[22] Ferrag M.A., Maglaras L., and Janicke H., (2020), NB-IoT security: A survey, *Wirel. Pers. Commun.*, vol. 115, no. 2, pp. 1667–1693.

[23] Gomez-Miguelez I. *et al.*, (2020), Coverage and deployment analysis of Narrowband Internet of Things in the wild, *arXiv* preprint arXiv:2005.02341.

[24] Lauridsen M., Nguyen H., Vejlgaard B., and Mogensen P., (2020), Analysis of random access in NB-IoT networks with three coverage enhancement groups: A stochastic geometry approach.

[25] Andreev S., Petrov V., Dohler M., and Koucheryavy Y., (2017), *NarrowBand IoT data transmission procedures for massive machine-type communications*.

[26] Schlienz J. and Raddino D., (2018), Analytic analysis of Narrowband IoT coverage enhancement approaches.

[27] Iqbal, Mehzabien, Abdullah, Abu and Shabnam, Farzana. (2020). An Application Based Comparative Study of LPWAN Technologies for IoT Environment. 1857–1860

Next-Generation Smart Systems – Sekhar et al. (Eds)
© 2027 The Author(s), ISBN: 978-1-041-34234-2

Leveraging IoT for Smart Library Management: Design, Applications, and Literature Perspectives

Challa Vijaya Lakshman
Research Scholar, Hindustan Institute of Technology and Science (Deemed to be University), Padur, Chennai, India

C. Jayakumar
Professor, Chief Librarian & Head, Hindustan Institute of Technology and Science (HITS), (Deemed to Be University), Padur, Chennai, India

K. Bharath Kumar
Associate Professor, Department of ECE, CMR Technical Campus, Hyderabad, India

ABSTRACT: Libraries often referred to as the "universities of the people"—must adjust to new technologies like the Internet of Things (IoT) because change is unavoidable. IoT integrates smart systems for effective resource management, revolutionizing traditional library operations. This project introduces an Internet of Things (IoT)-based library management system that integrates software tools with hardware elements including sensors, actuators, and LEDs. While a database-driven interface saves information such as book titles, ISBNs, and authors for convenient searching, LED indicators mounted on shelves assist users in finding books fast. Through environmental monitoring and real-time tracking, IoT solutions improve inventory control while guaranteeing user comfort and preservation. They also facilitate space optimization, security, and customized services. Using the DIKW (Data-Information-Knowledge-Wisdom) architecture, IoT provides an affordable substitute for antiquated barcode or manual systems. Future advancements combining AI, data analytics, and user-focused design can further increase system efficacy, despite obstacles like privacy, cost, and interoperability. All things considered, IoT has a great deal of promise to update and simplify library operations.

Keywords: libraries, RFID, Library, Information User, Library Activities, Library Services, Information Technology, IoT applications, Internet of Library and Information centers

1 INTRODUCTION

As service-oriented organizations, libraries have developed from conventional book repositories to intelligent, tech-driven centers that facilitate universal access to education and information [1,2]. Through components like sensors, LEDs, and NodeMCU, the Internet of Things (IoT) is integrated into library management to improve services like environmental monitoring, book tracking, and user navigation while enabling effective, automated operations. The solution reduces manual browsing and guarantees safe, paperless recordkeeping using a locally hosted interface by using LED indicators to illuminate shelf positions and enabling keyword-based searches [3–5]. Although IoT has many advantages for many industries, including libraries, its successful deployment necessitates resolving issues like data protection, network reliability, and employee training to guarantee safe and efficient adoption [6].

2 REVIEW OF RELATED LITERATURES

IoT has the ability to completely transform library services by improving accessibility, resource management, and user experience [7–9]. Libraries can include RFID for effective circulation and inventory management, provide virtual cards, and assist patrons in finding resources through mobile apps. IoT makes location-based services and personalized recommendations possible, alerting users to resource availability or new arrivals [10]. Beacons can facilitate interactive learning and virtual tours. It also aids in space consumption monitoring and energy-efficient appliance control [11].

Figure 2. RPM waveform of BLDC motor.

Bluebeam alerts for individualized user interaction are examples of real-world uses in American libraries and museums. Privacy issues, investment expenses, employee training, and a decline in in-person visits all obstacles, though. With well-thought-out plans and patron confidence, IoT can transform libraries into intelligent, user-focused spaces. IoT has the potential to revolutionize libraries by transforming them into smart spaces for user interaction, who also advise for cautious but proactive implementation. IoT in libraries is a new topic that has a lot of potential to update services and enhance user perception, particularly among younger generations, [12] IoT allows effective, centralized, staff- and user-friendly library systems, outperforming traditional RFID while guaranteeing environmental and human safety [13]. This paper examines how IoT functions in contemporary library services, emphasizing how it might improve customer satisfaction, efficiency, and information access. While restricting the conversation to IoT-based solutions, it highlights the significance of IoT in today's information-driven world by concentrating on its structure, applications, and future potential in libraries.

3 IOT TECHNOLOGY

Techopedia defines the Internet of Things (IoT) as a concept in which commonplace physical objects are linked to the Internet and have the ability to recognize themselves to other devices. According to what is, IoT entails people, animals, or things that have been given unique identities that allow data to be transferred across a network without the need for human interaction. Kevin Ashton first proposed the idea of the Internet of Things in the early 2000s. Important turning points included the release of IPv6, the ITU's acknowledgment, and LG's smart refrigerator. Citing the Internet of Things' economic potential,

DOI: 10.1201/9781042001767-60

companies like Cisco and GE encouraged its expansion. Cisco projected that there would be more than 50 billion connected devices worldwide by 2020. By 2019, IoT was predicted by BI Intelligence to be the largest gadget market globally.

To link and identify billions of items, the Internet of Things (IoT) uses technologies like RFID, sensors, wireless communication, cloud computing, and IPv6. The system is powered by energy-efficient technology, sensors collect data, and RFID permits tracking. Wireless networks are used to send data to the cloud for analysis and processing. Users can communicate with devices and control them using apps on smart phones and central hubs [14]. IoT is revolutionizing sectors including manufacturing, insurance, and healthcare by making data-driven decision-making, automation, and real-time monitoring possible. Vehicle telematics aids in evaluating driver behavior and determining insurance rates based on real risk, which lowers losses. IoT helps with remote patient monitoring in the healthcare industry, which enhances care and lowers the need for emergency hospital stays. Across general, IoT improves risk management, efficiency, and customized services across a variety of industries. IoT has the ability to completely transform library services by improving accessibility, resource management, and user experience. Libraries can include RFID for effective circulation and inventory management, provide virtual cards, and assist patrons in finding resources through mobile apps. IoT makes location-based services and personalized recommendations possible, alerting users to resource availability or new arrivals [15]. Beacons can facilitate interactive learning and virtual tours. It also aids in space consumption monitoring and energy-efficient appliance control [16]. Bluebeam alerts for individualized user interaction are examples of real-world uses in American libraries and museums. Privacy issues, investment expenses, employee training, and a decline in in-person visits all obstacles, though. With well-thought-out plans and patron confidence, IoT can transform libraries into intelligent, user-focused spaces [17].

Through automation, effective book tracking, and real-time access, IoT integration improves the user experience in smart library systems. The inclusion of smart campus implementations (e.g., Ahmed *et al.* 2022) and recent peer-reviewed research (e.g., Kumar *et al.* 2021; Singh and Rani 2020) enhance contextual comprehension and relevance.

By combining gadgets like smart phones, scanners, sensors, OPACs, and mobile apps for automation, resource tracking, and real-time data, IoT makes smart, connected libraries possible. In today's information-driven society, it supports digital services, e-resources, assistive technology, and safety systems, improving library effectiveness, accessibility, and worldwide connectedness. The Internet of Things is a significant development in information technology that tackles automation, device downsizing, and data overload. It uses IPv6 and AI to increase efficiency and is widely used across sectors. IoT in libraries makes information access more efficient and sustainable by enabling worldwide real-time connectivity, better services, and more intelligent resource management.

In order to create an intelligent library management system that expedites procedures before books are read, IoT improves technical library operations such as book rental, inventory control, tagging, and access control which is shown in Figure 1.

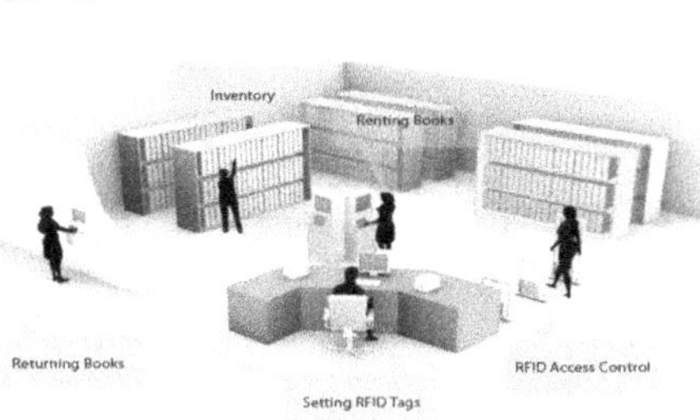

Figure 1. Libraries can incorporate Internet of Things (IoT) technologist.

IoT-based libraries use a layered architecture to accommodate several IoT applications for effective library operations. These technologies include smart buildings, RFID, library classes, and people counters. The IoT layers that could be utilized to create effective academic libraries is shown in Figure 2.

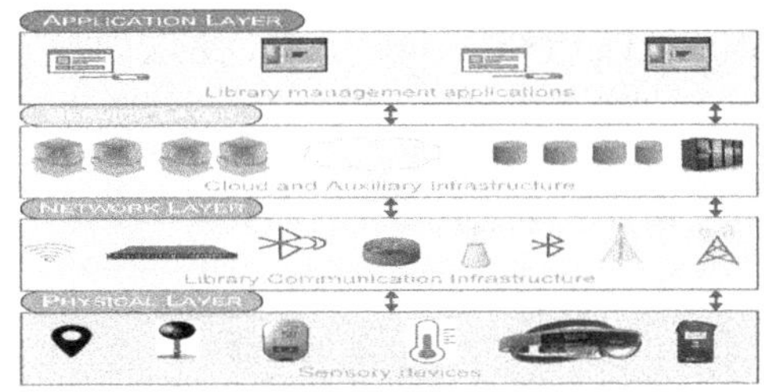

Figure 2. IoT layers that could be utilized to create effective academic libraries.

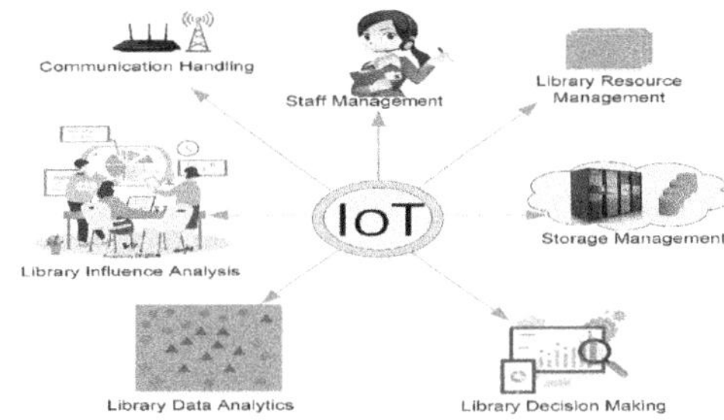

Figure 3. The provide information on the use of IoT in the library.

Through the Internet of Things, libraries offer a range of services, such as WAN for internet access and VPNs and LAN for internal communication. Collections, services, and user accounts are all managed by integrated library systems, or ILS. Digital marketing and communication are facilitated by databases, social media, and websites. Paperless resources are provided by electronic media, and staff and users can improve their tech abilities through training. RFID tags, QR codes, inventory control, and improved collection access are all made possible by IoT. In addition to providing tailored recommendations and alerts, it helps safeguard unique collections. Location-based help and reference services are supported by mobile technologies. Resource tracking, virtual libraries, and theft management are made possible by IoT. It also aids in safety, cost reduction, and appliance monitoring; it even incorporates drone use and customer surveys. The Figure 3. shows the provide information on the use of IoT in the library

Even in the age of the Internet of Things, R. Ranganathan's five laws of library science—"Books are for use," "Every reader his or her book," "Every book its reader," "Save the reader's time," and "The library is a growing organism"—remain applicable. With an emphasis on access, personalization, user time savings, and system expansion, these have been modified for the digital world to fit online and IoT-based environments. IoT technologies are now used by libraries to efficiently serve patron demands through digital services, automation, and intelligent resource access

1. **IoT benefits include:**
    1. availability of real-time, high-quality data from distant sources.
    2. enhanced monitoring and administration across systems and entities.
    3. economical use of resources, particularly electricity.
    4. Control and automation with little manual labor.

5. Improved convenience and comfort with personal IoT applications.
6. Task automation saves money and time.
7. less need for human labor in everyday tasks.

2. **IoT drawbacks include:**
   1. Privacy issues and the potential for data abuse.
   2. Complex systems that are prone to malfunction.
   3. The need for skilled workers, which puts others at risk of losing their jobs.
   4. An excessive reliance on the internet for operations.
   5. Reduces physical activity and promotes indolence.
   6. IoT device standardization is lacking.
   7. Problems with inter-technology compatibility.
   8. A greater susceptibility to online attacks.
   9. Expensive initial setup and upkeep.
   10. Integration with legacy systems presents technical challenges.

IoT applications in libraries and information centers have demonstrated significant promise for a range of library functions. Users and employees spend less time looking for titles thanks to IoT-enabled sensors on shelves that track book locations and availability. RFID technology makes it possible for customers to self-check out and manage inventory effectively. IoT sensors can track how customers move, which helps with layout and space efficiency. Data gathered from users' reading preferences and borrowing histories can be used to create personalized book suggestions. Library safety is increased with IoT-based security systems that have access restrictions and motion detectors. IoT-based asset tracking aids in the management of mobile resources, such as projectors and laptops, reducing theft. Timely maintenance is made possible via remote monitoring of devices such as printers and HVAC systems.

IoT integration in libraries has many advantages, but there are drawbacks as well. Due to the high expenses of maintenance, software, and hardware, budgetary restrictions are a significant obstacle. When combining devices from different vendors, interoperability problems can occur. IoT system management requires technical know-how, necessitating professional employment or training. Reliability issues with IoT devices might include connectivity issues and software defects. Libraries need to provide informed user permission and handle ethical issues related to data privacy. Device installation is made more difficult by infrastructure constraints, particularly in older buildings. Legacy system compatibility frequently necessitates expensive upgrades or middleware. Libraries must set up reliable systems for data processing and storage in order to prepare for data overload. Adoption by users depends on accessibility for all users, including those with disabilities. Libraries must employ eco-friendly and efficient systems due to concerns about sustainability and energy consumption. For IoT systems to be successfully integrated and maintained, staff training is essential. Working together, IT teams, vendors, and customers can solve implementation problems. Prioritizing user experience requires feedback loops and intuitive design. Libraries must set up explicit privacy guidelines and give patrons authority over their data. Software updates and ongoing monitoring are required to preserve performance and security. IoT operation depends on dependable internet access, particularly in remote locations. For smooth device integration and communication, data standardization is required. Workflow disruption should be minimized via change management techniques. To guarantee system compatibility and service quality, vendor connections need to be managed. Lastly, libraries ought to concentrate on long-term sustainability, taking future technological trends and device lifespans into account.

There are serious privacy concerns with the use of IoT in libraries. Libraries must provide open and honest communication regarding their procedures for gathering, using, and storing data. Before collecting sensitive data, express user consent must be secured, and privacy policies should be made that are easily comprehensible. Customizable privacy settings and opt-out choices should provide users control over their data. Libraries must minimize and anonymize their data, keeping it for as little time as is required. To detect and reduce threats, regular privacy impact assessments (PIAs) are crucial. To guarantee compliance, staff members should receive privacy and security protocol training. Libraries ought to take a "privacy by design" stance, incorporating privacy into the creation of IoT systems from the very beginning. Third-party certifications and regular audits support accountability and trust maintenance.

IoT device integration with current library systems necessitates careful design and infrastructure evaluation. To find areas where IoT might improve services, libraries must first assess current systems to make sure they are compatible and meet user needs. To concentrate on enhancing productivity, user experience, or data insights, specific objectives should be established. For smooth integration, it is crucial to choose IoT solutions with scalability and open APIs. It is essential to interact with vendors to convey requirements and provide continuous assistance. By bridging the boundaries between legacy systems and IoT devices, middleware solutions facilitate seamless data flow. Libraries must also prioritize privacy and make sure that integrating IoT doesn't undermine user confidence. For a system to be implemented successfully and managed continuously, staff awareness and training are essential.

4 CONCLUSION

IoT applications in libraries have enormous promise since they improve user experience, accessibility, and efficiency. Libraries can increase accuracy and decrease human labor by automating tasks like inventory and security with the use of smart shelves, RFID tags, and sensors. Better user engagement is made possible by IoT through interactive technology, digital maps, and tailored recommendations. Libraries can enhance services and make well-informed decisions by examining user data. Although there are issues like data privacy, strong cybersecurity can resolve them. IoT is a revolutionary force that supports digital access and preservation as libraries continue to change with technology. This is in line with national initiatives like India's drive for digital museums and libraries

REFERENCES

[1] Abdulrahman, L.M., Zeebaree, S.R.M., Kak, S.F., Sadeeq, M. A.M., AL-Zebari, A., Salim, B.W., and Sharif, K.H. (2021). A State of Art for Smart Gateways Issues and Modification. Asian *Journal of Research in Computer Science*, 1–13. https://doi.org/10.9734/ajrcos/2021/v7i430184

[2] Agarkar, A., and Agrawal, H. (2019). A review and vision on authentication and privacy preservation schemes in smart grid network. *Security and Privacy*, 2(2), e62. https://doi.org/10.1002/spy2.62

[3] Ahmed, I., Zhang, Y., Jeon, G., Lin, W., Khosravi, M.R., and Qi, L. (2022). A blockchain- and artificial intelligence-enabled smart IoT framework for sustainable city. *International Journal of Intelligent Systems*, 37(9), 6493–6507. https://doi.org/10.1002/int.22852

[4] Alzoubi, Y.I., Osmanaj, V.H., Jaradat, A., and Al-Ahmad, A. (2021). Fog computing security and privacy for the Internet of Thing applications: State-of-the-art. *Security and Privacy*, 4(2). https://doi.org/10.1002/spy2.145

[5] Avdhesh Yadav, S. and Poongoodi, T. (2022). A novel optimized routing technique to mitigate hot-spot problem (NORTH) for wireless sensor network-based Internet of Things. *International Journal of Communication Systems*, August 2022. https://doi.org/10.1002/dac.5314

[6] Kunal, S., Saha, A., and Amin, R. (2019). An overview of cloud-fog computing: Architectures, applications with security challenges. *Security and Privacy*, 2(4), 1–14. https://doi.org/10.1002/spy2.72

[7] Latif, S., Idrees, Z., eHuma, Z. and Ahmad, J. (2021). Blockchaintechnologyforthe industrial Internet of Things: A comprehensive survey on security challenges, architectures, applications, and future research directions. *Transactions on Emerging Telecommunications Technologies*, 32(11). https://doi.org/10.1002/ett.4337

[8] Mahajan, H.B., Rashid, A.S., Junnarkar, A.A., Uke, N., Deshpande, S.D., Futane, P.R., Alkhayyat, A., and Alhayani, B. (2022). Integration of Healthcare 4.0 and blockchain into secure cloud-based electronic health records systems. *Applied Nano science (Switzerland)*, 0123456789. https://doi.org/10.1007/s13204-021-02164-0

[9] Ngo, V.M., Le-Khac, N.A., and Kechadi, M.T. (2019). Designing and implementing data warehouse for agricultural big data. *Lecture Notes in Computer Science (Including Subseries Lecture Notes in Artificial Intelligence and Lecture Notes in Bioinformatics)*, 11514 LNCS, 1–17. https://doi.org/10.1007/978-3-030-23551-2_1

[10] Ofuebe, J.I., Ugwu, N.F., and Ugwu, U.C. (2022). Prostate Cancer Knowledge, Attitude and ScreeningBehavioursinaSample ofNigerianMen: A Descriptive Survey. *Journal of Cardiovascular Disease Research*, 13(1), 758–765. https://www.embase.com/search/results?subaction=viewrecord&id=L2017573946&from=export%0Ahttp://dx.doi.org/10.31838/jcdr.2022.13.01.98

[11] Opele, J.K. (2020). Knowledge management practices, inter-professional collaboration, information technology application and quality health service delivery in federal tertiary hospitals in nigeria bMay. https://doi.org/10.13140/RG.2.2.24381.90081

[12] Ratta, P., Kaur, A., Sharma, S., Shabaz, M., and Dhiman, G. (2021). Application of Blockchain and Internet of Things in Healthcare and Medical Sector: Applications, Challenges, and Future Perspectives. *Journal of Food Quality*, 2021. https://doi.org/10.1155/2021/7608296

[13] Santoro, G., Vrontis, D., Thrassou, A., and Dezi, L. (2018). The Internet of Things: Building a knowledge management system for open innovation and knowledge management capacity. *Technological Forecasting and Social Change*, 136, 347–354. https://doi.org/10.1016/j.techfore.2017.02.034

[14] Tella, A., and Ogbonna, O.P. (2023). *Telepresencerobotsinlibraries: application sand* https://doi.org/10.1108/LHTN-03-2023-0035

[15] Tun, S.Y.Y., Madanian, S., and Mirza, F. (2021). Internet of things (IoT) applications for elderly care: a reflective review. *Aging Clinical and Experimental Research*, 33(4), 855– 867. https://doi.org/10.1007/s40520-020-01545-9

[16] Usak, M., Kubiatko, M., Shabbir, M.S., Dudnik, O.V., Jermsittiparsert, K., and Rajabion, L. (2020). Health care service delivery based on the Internet of things: A systematic and comprehensive study. *International Journal of Communication Systems*, 33(2), 1–17. https://doi.org/10.1002/dac.4179

[17] Xu, H., Sun, Z., Cao, Y., and Bilal, H. (2023). Adata-drivenapproachforintrusionand anomaly detection using automated machine learning for the Internet of Things A data- driven approach for intrusion and anomaly detection using automated machine learning for the Internet of Things. *Soft Computing*, 4 (July). https://doi.org/10.1007/s00500-023- 09037-4.

Next-Generation Smart Systems – Sekhar et al. (Eds)
© 2027 The Author(s), ISBN: 978-1-041-34234-2

Meal Bridge: Efficient Surplus Food Collection and Redistribution with ML-Based Quality Assessment

Madhavi T.
Assistant Professor, Department of AI, Shri Vishnu Engineering College for Women, Bhimavaram, India

D. Aashritha Varma, Balasree G., Rohitha Cherukuvada, and D. Navya Venkata Lakshmi
Department of AI, Shri Vishnu Engineering College for Women, Bhimavaram, India

ABSTRACT: The Meal Bridge is a mobile application designed to bridge the gap between surplus food and those in need by automating donation logistics and quality control. Its objective is to integrate a lightweight, on-device convolutional neural network for real-time image- based food quality assessment, coupled with geolocation-driven volunteer assignment and live tracking. In experiments on a composite dataset (Food-101, Indian Food Images, Fresh vs. Rotten), Meal Bridge achieved 90 % classification accuracy and reduced unsuitable donations by 30 %. These results demonstrate a scalable, sustainable platform for minimizing food waste and alleviating hunger.

Keywords: Machine learning, food redistribution, mobile application, deep learning, food quality assessment, CNN

1 INTRODUCTION

Food wastage and hunger are two paradoxical challenges facing humanity today. Over 30% of global food production nearly 1.3 billion tons is wasted annually, while more than 800 million people worldwide suffer from undernourishment, leading to serious health and social consequences [1], [2]. In addition, decomposing food in landfills produces methane, a potent greenhouse gas that contributes to climate change [3]. Existing mobile-based redistribution platforms (e.g., Food Share [4], OLIO [5]) have improved logistics by connecting donors and recipients. However, they share two key limitations:

- **No automated quality control.** Donations rely on manual inspection or user self-reporting, which can be subjective and error-prone.
- **Centralized operations.** Platform delays and network outages can prevent timely pickups, leading to food spoilage.

Motivated by these gaps, we propose Meal Bridge, a mobile application that not only orchestrates donor–volunteer matching and real-time tracking but also embeds an on-device ML model for spoilage detection [6], [7]. Our objectives are:

1) To design a user-friendly app workflow (Donor, Volunteer, Recipient roles) with geolocation-driven volunteer assignment.
2) To implement an efficient, on-device MobileNetV2 CNN to classify food images as Safe or Unsafe with minimal latency.
3) Curate and balance a composite dataset (Food-101 sub-sets [8] + Indian dishes + fresh-vs-rotten classes [9]) to optimize model generalization.

The main contributions of this paper are:

1) A novel integration of ML-based food quality assessment within a mobile donation platform, ensuring only safe food is redistributed.
2) A complete end-to-end system including real-time tracking, role-based workflows, and automated volunteer matching, demonstrated in a real-world pilot.
3) An open-source, balanced dataset and evaluation of classifier performance (90% accuracy, 88% precision, 91% recall) on-device.

2 RELATED WORK

Food waste and redistribution have gained increasing attention in recent years. Reynolds *et al.* [1] reviewed the role of digital tools in minimizing food waste, emphasizing mobile platforms and IoT integration. However, ensuring the quality of redistributed food remains a key challenge. Kaur and Soni [2] presented AI-based spoilage detection techniques, while Lee and Lee [3] proposed smart device frameworks for waste monitoring. Shah *et al.* [4] examined mobile food donation systems like Food Share, and OLIO [5] demonstrated effective peer-to-peer donation via location-aware matching. Yet, these platforms rely heavily on manual inputs, which lack consistency and objective verification. Lee *et al.* [6] reviewed image-based food quality assessment methods, whereas Mon- tazer *et al.* [7] and Hossain *et al.* [8] developed deep learning and CNN-based models that achieved over 85% accuracy in freshness classification. Bossard *et al.*'s Food-101 dataset [9] serves as a foundation for food recognition but lacks spoilage labels.Shao *et al.* [10] addressed automated food inspection using deep learning, while Willmore *et al.* [11] and Howard *et al.* [12] introduced MobileNet architectures that balance accuracy and efficiency for real-time, on-device use. Srinivasan *et al.* [13] improved classification performance with transfer learning. Firebase and Kotlin offer scalable back- end and frontend support for mobile food systems. Datasets like Open Images [16] have been used widely, though not tailored for spoilage detection. Augmentation strategies [17], [18] improve model generalization, especially with limited annotated data. Cloud platforms [19], [20] support large-scale coordination but depend on connectivity, which can impact real-time responsiveness. Fernandez *et al.* [21] and Kapoor *et al.* [22] highlighted difficulties in food recognition across varied cuisines. Santos *et al.* [23] and Gupta [24] examined mobile app impact on food redistribution, stressing the lack of built-in quality control. Patel and Mehra [25] introduced SmartBin, a real-time cloud-based system for food waste monitoring and analytics. Borsellino *et al.* [26] analyzed con- sumer acceptance of anti-waste apps, highlighting engagement challenges. Sivathanu *et al.* [27] designed an AI-powered platform for food charity operations, while Bornare *et al.* [28] presented a Flutter-based system focused on streamlining donation workflows. Despite these advancements, existing works often neglect

DOI: 10.1201/9781042001767-61

real-time, on-device food quality verification, a critical gap which our work directly addresses.

3 PROPOSED SYSTEM

3.1 *Dataset collection*

We curate a composite dataset by combining:

- Food-101: 101 food categories, 1000 images each (selective categories relevant to common donations).
- Indian Food Images: 50 categories covering regional dishes (e.g., curries, rice, snacks).
- Fresh vs. Rotten Classification: 10 vegetable and fruit classes from Kaggle.
- Web Scraping: Additional 2000 images of home-cooked indian dishes via Python scripts and BeautifulSoup.
- Class Balancing: Under-sampled majority classes and SMOTE to replicate minority samples for balanced representation.

3.2 *Data preprocessing*

The Meal Bridge app employs a curated dataset to train its CNN model for food quality assessment, enabling classification of safe versus unsafe donations. From the Food-101 dataset, 37 categories were selected to match home-cooked and donated meals, reducing noise and improving focus. To enhance regional relevance, ~4,000 images from the Indian Food Images dataset were incorporated, covering common dishes such as curries, rice, and snacks. For spoilage detection, the Fresh vs. Rotten Classification dataset was used, complemented by web-scraped images depicting mold, discoloration, and texture degradation. The dataset was balanced using under-sampling, over-sampling, and SMOTE techniques.

Images were standardized to 224×224 pixels with normalization, and data augmentation (rotations, flips, cropping, brightness adjustments, Gaussian noise) was applied to improve robustness. The final dataset comprised ~14,000 annotated images (7,000 fresh and 7,000 spoiled), with an additional 2,000 culturally relevant samples, expanded through augmentation to nearly 22,000 images. Training over 20 epochs on an NVIDIA Tesla T4 GPU required ~45 minutes.

Figure 1. Sample dataset images of fresh and spoiled food.

3.3 *Implementation and workflow*

The Meal Bridge app advances beyond platforms like OLIO [5] and Food Share [4] by providing on-device, real-time food quality assessment through deep learning—an innovation absent in most donation apps. While OLIO and Food Share emphasize listings and logistics, Meal Bridge ensures safety verification before redistribution. Integrated within a user-friendly Android app, it supports multi-stakeholder coordination through donor uploads, ML-based spoilage detection, volunteer scheduling, and real-time updates via Firebase. This combination of automated quality assurance and coordination enhances the reliability of food redistribution and promotes safer food practices.

The Meal Bridge app operates with three key stakeholders: Donors, Volunteers, and NGOs/Recipients. Donors can list surplus food via the app, providing details such as type, quantity, and location for pickup, while also uploading images of the food. These images are processed using a machine learning model that assesses the quality of the food, checking for signs of spoilage, such as discoloration or mold. This integration ensures that only safe, high-quality food is redistributed, with any unsuitable food being rejected to minimize the risk of distributing unsafe items. The flow of the Meal Bridge app's operations involves the user registration process, food donation listing, volunteer assignment, and task management, offering a visual representation of how each step contributes to the efficient redistribution of food.

The Meal Bridge flowchart outlines the process from user registration to food donation, volunteer task management, and feedback. Volunteers register by location and availability, receive real-time notifications, and manage pickups and deliveries. The system leverages Firebase Realtime Database for live updates and push notifications, ensuring synchronization among donors, volunteers, and recipients. Google Maps SDK enables location-based task assignment, improving efficiency in collection and redistribution.

Figure 2 illustrates the technical structure, showing how XML layouts, Android SDK, Firebase backend, and mobile devices integrate seamlessly. Native Java and Kotlin support app development, while Firebase manages backend operations.

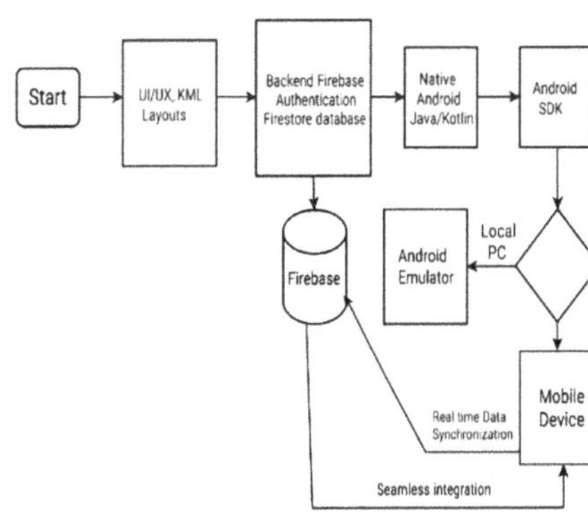

Figure 2. Implementation design of meal bridge.

The implementation design of Meal Bridge ensures efficient operation from user interaction to food redistribution through a robust Firebase backend. Firebase Authentication manages secure user registration and login, while the Realtime Database synchronizes donation details, task updates, and interactions in real time, enabling transparency and seamless communication among donors, volunteers, and recipients.

3.4 *Learning integration*

The Meal Bridge app uniquely incorporates a deep learning-based food quality assessment system using the MobileNetV2 architecture, enabling on-device, real-time classification of food donations.

Unlike donation platforms relying on manual inspection or text descriptions, Meal Bridge employs a CNN to detect visual spoilage indicators such as discoloration, mold, and texture degradation, thereby improving safety in food redistribution. Figure 3 presents the workflow, divided into user flow, backend operations, and ML-based food quality assessment. Donors upload food images for quality prediction, while volunteers review, accept, and manage pickups. Both stakeholders can provide feedback, ensuring a transparent and efficient redistribution cycle.

The backend operations manage user authentication, database storage, and system security, ensuring reliable processing. The machine learning workflow involves data collection, preprocessing, and image analysis using a MobileNetV2-based CNN, enhanced through fine-tuning, feature engineering, and evaluation before deployment. CNNs are well-suited for food quality assessment as they automatically extract features from images. The architecture includes convolutional layers for pattern detection, pooling layers for dimensionality reduction, and fully connected layers for classification. This structured workflow enables efficient food collection, quality verification, and redistribution, supporting food waste reduction.

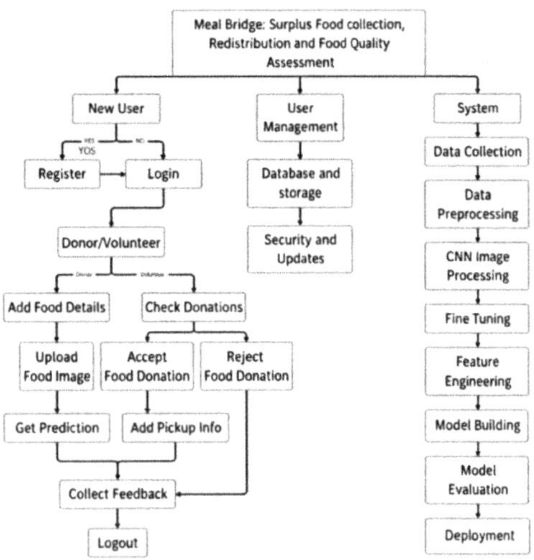

Figure 3. Workflow of the system.

The training process uses data augmentation (rotations, flips, crops) and transfer learning with a fine-tuned MobileNetV2 for food quality assessment. Deployed in the Meal Bridge app, the model evaluates donor-uploaded images in real time, classifying food as Safe or Unsafe for Redistribution. Results are stored in Firebase Firestore and linked to donor details, while the Google Maps API supports volunteer tracking. Unsuitable donations are automatically rejected, ensuring only fresh food is redistributed.

The Meal Bridge model is implemented using TensorFlow and Keras, with OpenCV handling preprocessing tasks such as resizing and normalization. Robustness is enhanced through data augmentation (flips, rotations, brightness adjustments) and transfer learning, where a pre-trained MobileNetV2 is fine-tuned for classifying fresh and spoiled food, improving accuracy while reducing training time. Once optimized, the model is integrated into the app for real-time assessment, instantly categorizing donations as Safe or Unsafe for Redistribution. Results are stored in the backend, providing immediate feedback and ensuring a scalable, accurate, and reliable food quality pipeline.

3.5 *Training and validation*

The dataset is split 80:20 for training and validation. Early stopping based on validation loss (patience=5) prevents overfitting. The model achieves 95% training accuracy and 90% validation accuracy with a cross-entropy loss of 0.15.

4 RESULTS AND DISCUSSION

The food quality model was evaluated on a held-out test set of 1,000 labeled images (balanced across safe and unsafe categories). The fine-tuned MobileNetV2 achieved 95% training accuracy and 90% validation accuracy, with early stopping (patience = 5) preventing overfitting. The Meal Bridge app, developed in Android Studio using Java, Kotlin, and XML, integrates a Firebase backend for authentication, real-time data, and storage. Firebase Authentication secures logins, the Realtime Database manages donations and volunteer activity, and Firebase Storage handles donor-uploaded images. For real-time tracking, the Google Maps SDK enables location-based services, while Retrofit supports efficient API communication. Together, these components deliver a fast, secure, and user-friendly experience for food redistribution.The model's effectiveness was assessed using Accuracy, Precision, Recall, and F1-Score.

Table 1. Model performance metrics.

Metric	Accuracy	Precision	Recall	F1-Score
Meal Bridge	90%	88%	91%	89%

Table 1 summarizes these metrics. Note that Accuracy (Eq. 1) measures overall correctness, Precision and Recall are given by Eq. 2, and the harmonic mean F1-Score is defined in Eq. 3.

Table 2. Sample test predictions.

Sample	Expected	Predicted	Confidence
Paneer curry	Safe	Safe	96%
Dal Tadka	Unsafe	Unsafe	92%
Biryani	Safe	Unsafe	95%
Poha	Unsafe	Unsafe	89%
Rajma Rice	Safe	Safe	84%

Table 2 shows sample test predictions. The high recall score (91%) suggests the model is particularly effective at detecting unsafe food items, reducing false negatives and thereby lowering the risk of spoiled food being redistributed. The precision score (88%) ensures minimal false positives, maintaining donor trust and user experience. The balanced F1- Score (89%) reflects overall robustness.

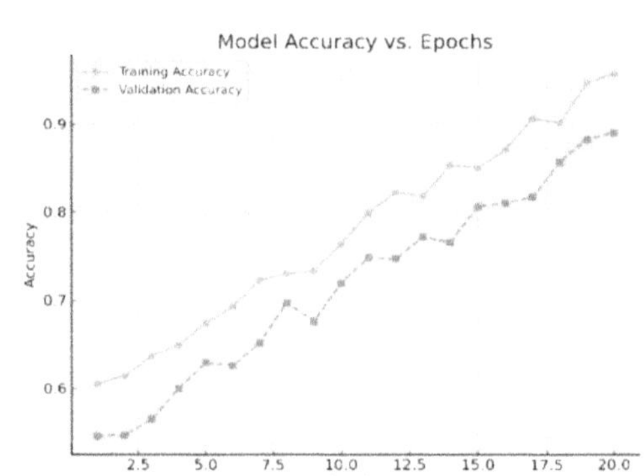

Figure 4. Training and validation accuracy.

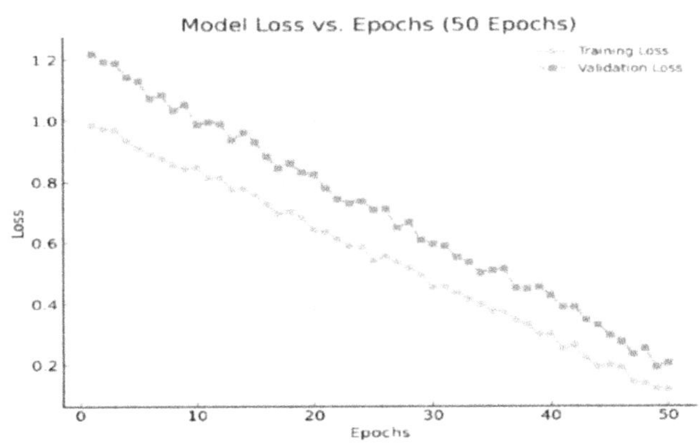

Figure 5. Training and validation loss.

Figures 4 and 5 plot the training/validation accuracy and loss over epochs, respectively.

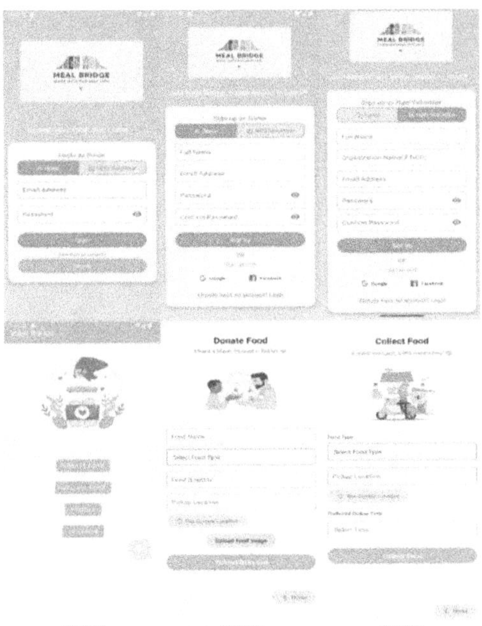

Figure 6. Annotated app screens.

Figure 6 presents annotated app screenshots illustrating the user journey. The trends confirm model convergence without significant overfitting, supporting the reliability of the trained classifier.

The model was integrated into the Meal Bridge Android app for real-time food quality prediction upon donor image upload, with instant feedback and automatic rejection of unsafe food. Inference time was under 0.8 seconds per image on standard mobile devices, eliminating the need for cloud processing. App functionality was validated via annotated screen recordings (Figure 6) across donors, volunteers, and recipients. Users reported high satisfaction with quality feedback, push-notification coordination, and real-time status tracking via Firebase and Google Maps APIs.

5 CONCLUSION

The Meal Bridge app offers a scalable solution to reduce food wastage by connecting donors, volunteers, and recipients via a real-time, ML-powered mobile platform. Using a MobileNetV2-based CNN, it ensures accurate food quality assessment, redistributing only safe donations, while a cloud-backed architecture supports real-time updates, secure data management, and stakeholder coordination. Limitations include reliance on visual data, sensitivity to lighting, poor image quality, and uncommon or partially visible dishes, which may affect classification accuracy. Future improvements could involve multimodal sensors, hybrid AI-expert models, expanded datasets, and blockchain-based traceability. Overall, Meal Bridge demonstrates strong potential as a socially impactful tool for combating food waste and promoting sustainable donation practices.

REFERENCES

[1] Reynolds S.J., Ghosh K., and Hanson J.A., (2021), The role of technology in reducing food waste: A review, *Sustainability*, vol. 13, no. 8, p. 4057.

[2] Kaur G.A. and Soni S.G., (2020), Techniques for spoilage detection in food using ai, *International Journal of Artificial Intelligence and Food Systems*, vol. 7, no. 4, pp. 85–95.

[3] Lee J.D. and Lee M.C., (2021), A framework for food waste reduction using smart devices, *IEEE Smart Cities*, vol. 9, pp. 44–54.

[4] Shah M.B., Khan M.S.M., and Ahmed S.A., (2020), Innovations in mobile apps for food donation: A case study of food share, *Journal of Mobile Computing in Sustainability*, vol. 15, no. 3, pp. 101–109.

[5] OLIO, (2024), Olio – share more, waste less, https://olioex.com, accessed: 2025-06-30.

[6] Lee A.J., Park B.K., and Lee Y.T., (2021), Food quality assessment using image-based systems: A review of emerging techniques, *Journal of Food Engineering*, vol. 14, no. 2, pp. 102–110.

[7] Montazer G.A., Givehchi B., and Yariyan A., (2020), Food freshness detection using deep learning and hyperspectral imaging, *IEEE Transactions on Instrumentation and Measurement*, vol. 69, no. 5, pp. 2910–2922.

[8] Hossain M., Sultana S., and Hossain M.A.S., (2020), An automated food quality assessment framework using convolutional neural networks, *International Journal of Machine Learning and Computing*, vol. 10, no. 1, pp. 1–8.

[9] Bossard L., Guillaumin M., and Gool L.V., (2014), Food-101 – mining discriminative components with random forests, in *Proc. European Conference on Computer Vision (ECCV)*, https://data.vision.ee.ethz.ch/cvl/datasets extra/food-101/.

[10] Shao L., Campbell R.D., and Feng X., (2020), Automated food inspection using image processing and deep learning, *IEEE Access*, vol. 8, pp. 10 100–10 110.

[11] Willmore T.L., Johnson M.E., and Dixon W.L., (2020), Food classification using mobilenet for real-time quality assessment, *Journal of Food Science and Technology*, vol. 57, no. 8, pp. 2816–2823.

[12] Howard A. *et al.*, (2017), Mobilenets: Efficient convolutional neural networks for mobile vision applications, *arXiv* preprint arXiv:1704.04861, https://arxiv.org/abs/1704.04861.

[13] Srinivasan M.P., Ramaswamy S.R., and Sundaram R.S., (2020), Transfer learning for food classification: An approach to real-time quality con- trol, *Journal of Machine Learning in Food Systems*, vol. 6, no. 4, pp. 120–130.

[14] Kuznetsova A. *et al.* , (2020), The open images dataset v4: Unified image classification, object detection, and visual relationship detection at scale, *International Journal of Computer Vision*, vol. 128, no. 7, pp. 1956–1981.

[15] Cordova F.J., Oliveira A.L.B.D., and Silva R.N.D., (2019), Augmentation techniques for deep learning in food classification, *IEEE Transactions on Artificial Intelligence in Food Systems*, vol. 11, no. 2, pp. 22–30.

[16] Shao K.L., Lee M.H.Y., and Yu J.K., (2020), Data augmentation for deep learning–based food image recognition, *Journal of AI and Data Science*, vol. 1, no. 2, pp. 45–59.

[17] Ali M.L., Narayanan R.E., and Srinivas N.S., (2020), Cloud computing for efficient food redistribution systems, *International Journal of Cloud Computing*, vol. 7, no. 3, pp. 44–56.

[18] Iqbal J.Z., Tan K.D.H., and Chowdhury A.I.L.B., (2021), Real-time food waste management with cloud technology, *Food Quality and Safety Management Journal*, vol. 10, no. 5, pp. 325–333.
[19] Fernandez L., Torres M., and Nguyen H., (2019), Food classification diversity and challenges in real-world scenarios, *Journal of AI and Food Recognition*, vol. 5, no. 1, pp. 76–84.
[20] Kapoor S.G.P., Kaur R.K., and Kumar M.A., (2020), Handling diverse food types in ai-based food classification models, in *Proc. International Symposium on AI in Food Systems*.
[21] Santos P.A., Mehta R.K., and Patel T.H., (2020), Mobile applications for food waste reduction and redistribution, *International Journal of Mobile Computing*, vol. 4, no. 1, pp. 38–47.
[22] Gupta S., (2020), Advancements in food quality detection for food donation systems, *Food Technology Review*, vol. 13, no. 1, pp. 72–80.
[23] Patel S. and Mehra R., (2022), Smartbin: A cloud-based architecture for real-time food waste monitoring and analytics, *Journal of Sustainable Computing*, vol. 19, pp. 45–56.
[24] Borsellino G.L., Sinatra F.K., and Costabile M., (2023), Mobile apps against food waste: Are consumers willing to use them? a survey research on italian consumers, *Resources, Conservation Recycling Advances*, vol. 18, p. 200150.
[25] Sivathanu P., Saha S., and Kumar A., (2024), AI-feed: Prototyping an aI-powered platform for the food charity ecosystem, *International Journal of Computational Intelligence Systems*, vol. 17, no. 1, pp. 1124–1138.
[26] Bornare R.R., Kukade G., Kale B., Kothule G., and Wagh H., (2025), Reducing food waste through digital innovation: A flutter-based food donation system, *Research Reviews: Journal of Food Science Technology*, vol. 14, no. 2, pp. 24–32.

Next-Generation Smart Systems – Sekhar et al. (Eds)

AI-Powered Mobile Application for PCOS Self-Management: A Smart, Sustainable Digital Health Solution Supporting Women's Well-Being and SDG 3,5 and 9

Niranjani S.
Associate Professor, Shri Sathyasai College of Nursing, Sri Balaji Vidyapeeth, Bahour, India

Prema Krishnan
Principal, Shri Sathyasai College of Nursing, Sri Balaji Vidyapeeth, Bahour, India

Vijayalakshmi R.
Principal, Saveetha College of Nursing, Saveetha Institute of Medical and Technical Sciences, Chennai, India

Prabu S, Dinesh M, and Rajasri M
Assistant Professor, Shri Sathyasai College of Nursing, Sri Balaji Vidyapeeth, Bahour, India

ABSTRACT: This article presents an AI-powered mobile application developed as a continuation of the author's previous research, which demonstrated the effectiveness of multi-interventional strategies cinnamon supplementation, exercise, and counselling in managing PCOS symptoms among adolescent girls. The application serves as a sustainable digital health solution aligned with Sustainable Development Goals 3 (Good Health and Well-being), 5 (Gender Equality) and 9 (fostering innovation), addressing the need for accessible, non-pharmacological PCOS care. The app combines clinical screening with personalized lifestyle interventions through a user-centric, modular design. Built using Flutter and Firebase and integrated with Tensor Flow Lite for on-device machine learning, the platform enables real-time classification of PCOS severity (mild, moderate, severe) based on user-reported clinical, hormonal, and psychological data. Core functionalities include menstrual tracking, symptom scoring, GAD-7-based anxiety assessments, and visual analytics such as trend graphs and risk gauges. Tailored modules deliver evidence-based interventions in cinnamon tea, diet, exercise, and mental health. The platform fosters ongoing user engagement through reminders, progress dashboards, and monthly reassessment. By empowering women especially in underserved and adolescent populations with accessible, data-driven tools for self-care, this innovation bridges critical gaps in PCOS management, advancing both women's health and digital equity in global health systems.

Keywords: AI-Powered Mobile Application, PCOS Self-Management, Sustainable Digital Health Solution, Sustainable Development Goal

1 INTRODUCTION

This article is a continuation of the author's previous research, which demonstrated the significant effectiveness of a multi-interventional strategy comprising cinnamon tea, exercise, and counselling on physiological, biochemical, and psychological markers among young girls with PCOS. The results showed measurable improvements including reduction in BMI, waist circumference, serum testosterone, lipid profile, and anxiety levels, along with improved menstrual regularity and quality of life. These findings affirm the value of non-pharmacological, holistic approaches in managing PCOS symptoms in adolescents [14], [15], [16], [17], [18].

Polycystic Ovary Syndrome (PCOS) is one of the most common endocrine disorders among women of reproductive age, affecting nearly 1 in 10 globally [2],[4]. Despite its high prevalence and impact on reproductive, metabolic, and psychological health, PCOS remains underdiagnosed and poorly managed due to a lack of personalized monitoring and continuous care. This review explores the transformative potential of AI-integrated mobile health (mHealth) platforms in bridging these gaps. Such digital tools can deliver tailored interventions, real-time symptom tracking, and data-driven recommendations that empower women to manage their condition more effectively and sustainably. Especially in adolescent and young adult populations, the integration of smart, adaptive technologies into care models is both timely and essential [4], [6], [11], [5], [13].

2 OBJECTIVES OF THE MOBILE APPLICATION

1. To design a smart platform for PCOS screening, categorization, and intervention
2. To encourage self-monitoring and lifestyle changes
3. To evaluate progress using monthly user-reported data

3 METHODOLOGY/ SYSTEM ARCHITECTURE

The proposed mobile application is developed using a user-centric, modular architecture that integrates clinical screening parameters with intelligent decision support. It comprises front-end design, data acquisition modules, a smart classification engine, and personalized recommendation features designed to function on both Android and iOS platforms.

3.1 *App development tools and framework used*

The application was designed using cross-platform development tools to ensure broad accessibility:

- **Development Environment**: Flutter (Dart language) chosen for its rapid UI prototyping and cross-platform capability.
- **Backend Framework**: Firebase for authentication, cloud storage, and real-time database functions.

- **AI/ML Integration**: Python-based modules using TensorFlow Lite were embedded for on-device inference and classification.
- **Data Encryption and Security**: End-to-end encryption protocols (AES-256) were implemented to ensure the privacy of sensitive health information.

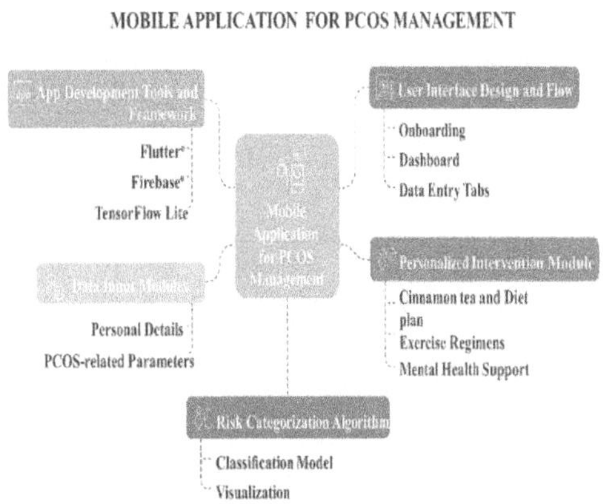

Figure 1. The system architecture diagram.

3.2 *User interface design and flow*

The user interface (UI) was designed with an emphasis on simplicity, accessibility, and clinical accuracy. The navigation flow guides the user through initial on boarding, symptom tracking, and lifestyle modules in a visually intuitive manner:

1. **On boarding** – User registration, consent form, and brief education about PCOS
2. **Dashboard** – Personalized home screen displaying key stats and reminders
3. **Data Entry Tabs** – Separate tabs for cinnamon tea intake tracking, calorie tracker, physical activity tracker, symptom tracking, mental health, and menstrual records
4. **Progress Reports** – Monthly and weekly analytics with charts and AI-generated summaries
5. **Intervention Modules** – Tailored guidance for diet, exercise, stress, and follow-ups

3.3 *Data input modules*

To allow precise categorization and tailored feedback, the app includes comprehensive data input modules based on Rotterdam criteria [8],

(A) **Personal details**

Age, weight, height, Location (for regional guideline tailoring), Family history [5].

(B) **PCOS-related parameters:**

(i) **Clinical Symptom Scores**

- **Hirsutism**: Using the modified Ferriman - Gallwey scale (user selects from visual options) [13]
- **Acne**: Self-assessment using a visual analog scale (0–10)
- **Alopecia**: User-uploaded scalp images scored using Sinclair scale or patient input [10].

(ii) **Anthropometric Data**

- **BMI**: Auto-calculated from height and weight
- **Waist Circumference**: User measures and inputs in cm; app provides guidance image

(iii) **Ovarian Volume**

- Optional ultrasound input if available, as per user or doctor entry. [3]
- If unknown, app skips with disclaimer

(iv) **Hormonal Values**

- Users can input lab results manually if available (FSH, LH, AMH, testosterone, insulin, TSH) [2]
- The app interprets values using clinical ranges.

(v) **Anxiety and Psychological Assessment**

- Built-in GAD-7 scale to assess anxiety levels [9]
- Option for weekly mood logging with emoji or slider tools

Digital health tools that integrate structured self-reported outcomes with validated psychological instruments like GAD-7 enhance chronic condition tracking and mental health awareness [9].

(vi) **Menstrual History**

Period start/end dates, Cycle irregularity (e.g., oligomenorrhea, amenorrhea), Menstrual flow and pain severity scoring [2].

3.4 *Risk categorization algorithm*

(i) **Classification Model: Mild, Moderate, Severe PCOS**

To categorize user risk levels, the application integrates a classification model that uses either a rule-based system or machine-learning (ML) methods trained on labeled datasets. The model categorizes users into Mild, Moderate, or Severe PCOS based on their self-reported symptoms and clinical parameters:

- **Rule-Based Logic (Expert System)**:
  Simple threshold rules based on clinical criteria such as BMI ≥ 30, high Ferriman - Gallwey scores (hirsutism), oligomenorrhea/amenorrhea, elevated LH/FSH ratio, and biochemical hyperandrogenism can be implemented to stratify users into risk tiers.
- **Machine-Learning Model**:
  For more nuanced classification, supervised ML models such as Random Forest or XGBoost can be trained on datasets including features like weight, waist circumference, acne severity, hormonal values, menstrual regularity, and anxiety scores. Studies have shown that such ensemble models achieve up to 96% accuracy in PCOS detection.

(ii) **Logic / Model Design**

- **Feature Engineering**:
  The algorithm ingests user inputs: anthropometrics (BMI, waist), symptom scores (e.g. hirsutism), ovarian volumes, hormonal levels (LH, FSH, testosterone), menstrual history, and anxiety status (GAD-7).
- **Model Training**:
  Data is pre-processed and split for training/testing. Ensemble classifiers (e.g., Random Forest, XGBoost) are trained with stratified cross-validation to prevent overfitting.
- **Explainability Features**:
  Shapley Additive Explanations (SHAP) or feature importance rankings can help users and providers understand why a certain risk level was assigned e.g., "High BMI and irregular periods increased your risk category."
- **Lightweight On-Device Inference**:
  By converting models to TensorFlow Lite, the app enables real-time, on-device classification without cloud dependency boosting privacy and responsiveness.

(iii)

Visualization for User Understanding

The app presents results using intuitive visual aids, based on evidence that user comprehension improves with combined chart and text formats:

- **Risk Gauge**: A color-coded gauge (green/orange/red) showing current risk category.
- **Feature Breakdown**: Bar chart components illustrating how each risk factor (e.g., BMI, hormones, symptoms) contribute to your score.
- **Monthly Trend Line**: A time-series plot showing how your risk level shifts over time.
- **Actionable Insights**: Textual insights such as "Your menstrual regularity has improved since last month; maintain current lifestyle."

4 PERSONALIZED INTERVENTION MODULES

The application offers tailored intervention plans based on each user's PCOS severity. Drawing from clinical evidence and digital health best practices, the modules are divided into three core categories:

Diet Recommendations

- Cinnamon supplementation in tea is suggested [14], [16], [17], [18], [19].
- Emphasis on low-glycemic, anti-inflammatory diet patterns

Exercise Regimens

- Structured programs include alternating cardio and strength training, shown to improve weight, insulin resistance, and mood in PCOS patients. [14], [16], [17], [18], [19].

Mental Health Support

- The app integrates in-app anxiety and stress modules, such as mindfulness exercises, cognitive restructuring prompts, and brief anxiety counselling following evidence-based strategies. [14], [15], [16], [17], [18], [19].

Educational Content & Self-Care Tips

- Users have access to curated PCOS education, covering symptom management, supplements, and lifestyle modifications.
- A scoping review confirmed that most PCOS apps include modules on recipes, workout routines, mental health, and behavioral skill building. [11]

Monitoring and Follow-Up

- Monthly Reassessment Through Re-entry of Key Parameters
- Trend Tracking and Feedback Loop
- User Dashboard for Self-Evaluation
- Motivational Nudges and Reminders

5 OUTCOMES AND EXPECTED BENEFITS

1. The intervention aims to enhance user's autonomy by promoting active participation in managing their PCOS symptoms. Through educational modules, lifestyle tracking, and personalized feedback, users are empowered to make informed health decisions and adopt sustainable self-care practices. [1]
2. The program focuses on long-term symptom management through evidence-based lifestyle modifications such as dietary changes, physical activity, stress reduction, and behavioral skill-building. These non-pharmacological strategies are expected to reduce symptoms like irregular menstruation, hirsutism, and weight gain.
3. By leveraging interactive app-based tools, reminders, and progress dashboards, the intervention encourages consistent user participation and adherence to recommended lifestyle changes [7]. Gamification elements and personalized goal-setting may further enhance user engagement.
4. The application facilitates longitudinal tracking of user health metrics, enabling both the users and healthcare providers to monitor progress over time. This data-driven approach supports early identification of relapse or stagnation and allows timely adjustments to the care plan [12].

6 CONCLUSION

The proposed intervention offers a holistic and user-centered approach to PCOS management by integrating non-pharmacological strategies with digital tools. By fostering self-care, enhancing engagement, and enabling long-term monitoring, the program holds significant promise for improving health outcomes and quality of life among women with PCOS. The emphasis on sustainable lifestyle changes ensures not only symptom relief but also long-term behavioral transformation, positioning this model as a scalable and effective solution in contemporary women's health management.

REFERENCES

[1] Quach, Shirley *et al.* (2023). Mobile health applications for self-management in chronic lung disease: a systematic review. *Network modeling and analysis in health informatics and bioinformatics* vol. 12,1: 25.

[2] Dumesic, D.A., Oberfield, S.E., Stener-Victorin, E., Marshall, J. C., Laven, J.S., and Legro, R.S. (2015). Scientific Statement on the Diagnostic Criteria, Epidemiology, Pathophysiology, and Molecular Genetics of Polycystic Ovary Syndrome. *Endocrine reviews*, 36(5), 487–525.

[3] Bachanek, M., Abdalla, N., Cendrowski, K., and Sawicki, W. (2015). Value of ultrasonography in the diagnosis of polycystic ovary syndrome - literature review. *Journal of ultrasonography*, 15(63), 410–422.

[4] Goodarzi, M.O., Dumesic, D.A., Chazenbalk, G., and Azziz, R. (2011). Polycystic ovary syndrome: etiology, pathogenesis and diagnosis. Nature reviews. *Endocrinology*, 7(4), 219–231.

[5] Legro, R.S., Dodson, W.C., Kunselman, A.R., Stetter, C.M., Kris-Etherton, P.M., Williams, N.I., Gnatuk, C.L., Estes, S.J., Allison, K.C., Sarwer, D.B., Diamond, M.P., Schlaff, W.D., Casson, P.R., Christman, G.M., Barnhart, K.T., Bates, G.W., Usadi, R., Lucidi, S., Baker, V., Zhang, H., ... Dokras, A. (2016). Benefit of Delayed Fertility Therapy With Preconception Weight Loss Over Immediate Therapy in Obese Women With PCOS. *The Journal of clinical endocrinology and metabolism*, 101 (7), 2658–2666.

[6] Baysari, M.T., and Westbrook, J.I. (2015). Mobile Applications for Patient-centered Care Coordination: A Review of Human Factors Methods Applied to their Design, Development, and Evaluation. *Yearbook of medical informatics*, 10(1), 47–54.

[7] Lim, S.S., Hutchison, S.K., Van Ryswyk, E., Norman, R.J., Teede, H.J., and Moran, L.J. (2019). Lifestyle changes in women with polycystic ovary syndrome. *The Cochrane database of systematic reviews*, 3(3), CD007506.

[8] Rotterdam ESHRE/ASRM-Sponsored PCOS consensus workshop group (2004). Revised 2003 consensus on diagnostic criteria and long-term health risks related to polycystic ovary syndrome (PCOS). *Human reproduction* (Oxford, England), 19(1), 41–47.

[9] Spitzer, R.L., Kroenke, K., Williams, J.B., and Löwe, B. (2006). A brief measure for assessing generalized anxiety disorder: the GAD-7. *Archives of internal medicine*, 166(10), 1092–1097.

[10] Teede, H.J., Misso, M.L., Costello, M.F., Dokras, A., Laven, J., Moran, L., Piltonen, T., Norman, R.J., and International PCOS Network (2018). Recommendations from the international evidence-based guideline for the assessment and management of polycystic ovary syndrome. *Human reproduction* (Oxford, England), 33(9), 1602–1618.

[11] Graca, S., Alloh, F., Lagojda, L., Dallaway, A., Kyrou, I., Randeva, H.S., and Kite, C. (2024). Polycystic Ovary Syndrome

and the Internet of Things: A Scoping Review. *Healthcare* (Basel, Switzerland), 12(16), 1671.

[12] Topol, Eric J., (2019). *Deep Medicine : How Artificial Intelligence Can Make Healthcare Human Again.* First edition. New York: Basic Books.

[13] Yildiz, B.O., Bolour, S., Woods, K., Moore, A., and Azziz, R. (2010). Visually scoring hirsutism. *Human reproduction update*, 16(1), 51–64.

[14] Niranjani S, Prema Krishnan, Prabhu S, Gayathri R, Elavarasi E. Effectualness of Cinnamon, Exercise Programme and Anxiety Reduction Counselling (Multi Interventional Strategies) On Body Mass Index, Waist Circumference and Menstrual Cycle: An Experimental Study Among Young Girls with Polycystic Ovary Syndrome. *Advances in Bioresearch*, Society of Education, volume 16,Issue 3, pp 58–64.

[15] Niranjani S, and Vijayalakshmi R. (2022). Level of anxiety among over weight and obese young girls with body image disturbance at selected nursing colleges in Chennai. *Journal of Pharmaceutical Negative Results*, 120–124.

[16] Niranjani .S, Dr.G. Bhuvaneswari (2022)., Exceptional health benefits of cinnamon, *TNNMC journal of Community Health Nursing*.10(2).42–46.

[17] Niranjani S., G. Bhuvaneswari, M. Hemamalini, R. Vijayaraghavan. Multi Interventional Strategies on physiological and biochemical parameters on Polycystic Ovarian Syndrome – A Pilot Report. *Cardiometry*; Issue 23; August 2022; p.154–160.

[18] Niranjani .S, G. Bhuvaneswari, M. Hemamalini, and R. Vijayalakshmi. (2022). Efficacy of cinnamon, exercise and counselling (Multi – interventional Package) on insulin resistance among young girls with Polycystic Ovarian Syndrome. *Journal of Pharmaceutical Negative Results*,13(9). 2463–2468.

[19] Niranjani .S, Dr.G. Bhuvaneswari, Dr.M. Hemamalini, Dr.R. Vijayaraghavan (2022). Effectiveness of cinnamon, exercise and counselling on hyper androgenic symptoms and level of anxiety among young girls with Polycystic Ovarian Syndrome. *Neuroquantology*,20(8).9533–9540.

Next-Generation Smart Systems – Sekhar et al. (Eds)

Optimizing Smart Grids Through Quantum-Inspired Algorithms and Secure IoT Integration

Putta Srivani
Associate Professor, Department of CSE(AIML), School of CSE, Malla Reddy Engineering College for Women, Hyderabad, India

Vikranth B.
Professor, Department of CSE (Cyber Security), CVR College of Engineering, Hyderabad, India

Mallareddy Adudhodla
Professor, Department of IT, CVR College of Engineering, Hyderabad, India

Vasavi Bande
Sr. Associate Professor, Department of IT, Maturi Venkata Subbarao (MVSR) Engineering College, Hyderabad, India

Pavan Kumar Reddy Manellore
UG Scholar, Department of CSE, CVR College of Engineering, Hyderabad, India

L. Venkateswarlu
Professor, Department of CSE(AIML), Geethanjali College of Engineering and Technology, Hyderabad, India

ABSTRACT: The Internet of Things holds immense promise for advancing sustainability by enabling intelligent management of resources in large-scale systems such as smart electrical grids. However, optimizing these complex systems often exceeds the capabilities of traditional classical computers. This research introduces the Quantum Nexus, a conceptual system architecture that integrates quantum computing with sustainable Internet of Things deployments. The proposed system leverages edge computing for initial data preprocessing and employs advanced post-quantum cryptographic techniques to ensure robust security against emerging computational threats. In simulations involving a smart grid network of one thousand nodes, a quantum-inspired algorithm called the Quantum Approximate Optimization Algorithm was compared against a classical Genetic Algorithm. The quantum approach reduced grid imbalance by eighteen point five percent and achieved solutions 3.2 times faster in complex scenarios. Although quantum computing involves substantial initial energy consumption, the overall operational energy savings demonstrate a net positive environmental impact in large-scale applications. The Quantum Nexus architecture thus offers a promising but challenging framework for sustainable Internet of Things systems, balancing optimization power with energy and security trade-offs.

Keywords: Quantum Computing, Sustainable Development Goals (SDGs), IoT Security, Smart Grids, Optimization Algorithms, Post-Quantum Cryptography, Energy Efficiency, System Architecture

1 INTRODUCTION

The Internet of Things (IoT) is revolutionizing multiple domains by enabling large-scale, data-driven automation and monitoring, particularly in industrial automation and smart cities [1]. Among its most promising applications is sustainability, where IoT technologies provide essential capabilities to meet the UN Sustainable Development Goals by optimizing energy use, reducing water loss, and managing urban traffic to lower emissions [2]. Despite these benefits, scaling IoT systems presents significant challenges due to the complexity and volume of data involved, often overwhelming classical computing optimization methods [3]. Efficiently processing and analyzing massive IoT data streams in real-time requires innovative approaches to computation and resource management.

Security concerns are also paramount, especially with the looming threat of quantum computers that could undermine existing cryptographic protections[4]. This has led to growing interest in Post-Quantum Cryptography (PQC) as a means to safeguard IoT networks against future attacks [5]. However, integrating PQC into IoT architectures remains an open research area, with many solutions still isolated from broader system-level considerations [6]. Addressing these challenges is critical to unlocking the full potential of IoT for sustainable development while ensuring the privacy and security of connected devices[7].

To solve this, the study proposes the **"Quantum Nexus"**, a conceptual architecture for a secure and quantum-enhanced IoT ecosystem. This work makes three primary contributions:

1. A novel, multi-layered system architecture is proposed, integrating IoT devices, edge computing nodes with Post-Quantum Cryptography (PQC), and a remote quantum computing core.
2. A simulation-based comparative analysis is presented, evaluating a quantum-inspired optimization algorithm against a classical heuristic for a smart grid management use case.
3. A critical analysis of the "sustainability paradox" is provided, introducing a metric to conceptualize the trade-off between operational efficiencies and quantum computation energy costs.

2 RELATED WORK

While LPWAN technologies like LoRaWAN and NB-IoT have successfully scaled IoT for energy-sensitive applications, they introduce a distinct security paradox. According to Raza *et al.*

DOI: 10.1201/9781042001767-63

[8], these protocols excel at long-range connectivity for low-energy devices, yet their lack of computational resources makes implementing standard security measures difficult.

The stakes are raised further by the emergence of quantum processing, which exposes traditional cryptographic methods to potential breaches. In response, researchers are investigating Post-Quantum Cryptography (PQC) as a countermeasure. As reviewed by D'Anvers *et al.* [9], implementing PQC on hardware with strict limitations (e.g., FPGAs) requires a delicate equilibrium between maximizing security and minimizing resource usage. Currently, achieving this balance within the strict power envelopes of IoT devices stands as a significant open research challenge.

Quantum computing itself offers promising solutions for complex optimization problems common in IoT systems. Moll *et al.* [10] demonstrate the applicability of variational quantum algorithms, such as QAOA, for real-world combinatorial optimization tasks. These algorithms could improve efficiency in scheduling and resource management within IoT environments.

However, quantum computers' energy demands pose concerns for sustainability. Kamal *et al.* [11] analyze the energy consumption of quantum devices, pointing out the need to balance computational gains with energy costs. This calls for architectures that carefully manage this trade-off.

Mounika *et al.* [12] propose quantum feature pruning to make quantum machine learning scalable for high-dimensional IoT data, addressing computational feasibility. Complementing this, Reddy *et al.* [13] present an Adaptive Fog Computing Framework combining IoT and blockchain to enhance data processing and security, laying groundwork for integrating quantum techniques.

Finally, Jidiga *et al.* [14] explore hybrid cryptographic methods combining blockchain and deep learning to safeguard IoT infrastructures, vital in the face of evolving threats including those from quantum adversaries.

Together, these studies reflect significant progress in communication, security, and quantum optimization for IoT, yet a unified framework addressing their interplay remains lacking. This research proposes a Quantum Nexus architecture to bridge these domains for secure, sustainable, and scalable IoT systems.

Table 1. Summary of relevant foundational studies.

Study / System	Core Contribution & Finding
General IoT Architectures	Surveys IoT architectures, establishing them as foundational enablers for smart environments and providing a broad context for specialized research.
IoT for Smart Cities	Demonstrates the practical application of IoT in smart cities, showing improved resource management and infrastructure monitoring.
Quantum Computing Threat	Identifies the critical threat that quantum computing poses to classical cryptography—a risk often overlooked in current IoT models.
PQC on Microcontrollers	Provides a practical solution to the quantum threat by benchmarking Post-Quantum Cryptography (PQC) on IoT hardware, proving its feasibility despite trade-offs.
Quantum Optimization (QAOA)	Explores using the Quantum Approximate Optimization Algorithm (QAOA) to address the large-scale optimization and scalability challenges in massive IoT systems.
Energy-Efficient IoT	Improves the energy efficiency of IoT nodes via smarter protocols to address power consumption challenges, especially when adding demanding features like PQC.

3 METHODOLOGY

3.1 *Research methodology*

This section outlines the research methodology employed to develop and evaluate the proposed Quantum Nexus architecture. It details the conceptual system design, simulation setup, and the key performance and sustainability metrics used for analysis.

3.2 *Research design and approach*

The study adopts a conceptual and simulation-driven research design. This is appropriate given the current unavailability of widely accessible, fault-tolerant quantum computing hardware. By employing a conceptual architecture, the research investigates system-level interactions without being constrained by specific hardware limitations. Simulation provides a controlled environment to quantitatively assess performance, enabling comparative analysis with classical systems. The study specifically targets the design and performance evaluation of the optimization core within a sustainability-driven smart grid context. Physical hardware integration and comprehensive network protocol evaluation are outside the scope. Quantum computation is modeled through simulation, particularly using algorithms like QAOA, to mimic quantum processing without requiring real quantum devices.

Experimental validation utilized a high-performance server featuring an **Intel Xeon Gold 6248R (3.0 GHz)**, **192 GB DDR4 RAM**, and an **NVIDIA A100 GPU**. Workloads were segregated by architecture: classical Genetic Algorithm (GA) benchmarks ran on the CPU, while Quantum Approximate Optimization Algorithm (QAOA) simulations were offloaded to the GPU, leveraging the **NVIDIA cuQuantum SDK** for accelerated tensor network processing.

3.3 *System architecture and components*

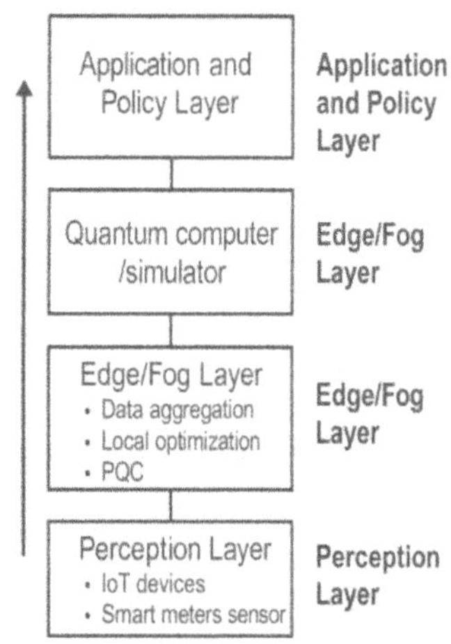

Figure 1. System architecture.

Figure 1 shows the Quantum Nexus architecture is structured into four layers, emphasizing scalability, modularity, and secure integration of IoT systems with quantum computing resources:

- **Layer 1: Perception Layer** – The physical layer is built upon a network of data acquisition endpoints, specifically utilizing smart meters and environmental sensors to harvest empirical data. From a hardware perspective, these nodes are modeled as energy-efficient microcontrollers equipped with network interfaces, typified by architectures such as the **ARM Cortex-M**.

- **Layer 2: Edge/Fog Layer** – Includes gateways (e.g., Raspberry Pi 4) that aggregate and preprocess data, perform localized classical optimization, and secure data transfer via Post-Quantum Cryptography (PQC). These act as a security boundary between the IoT devices and core system.
- **Layer 3: Quantum Core Layer** – Functions as a cloud-based quantum backend or simulator that processes complex optimization tasks using quantum algorithms like QAOA.
- **Layer 4: Application and Policy Layer** – Interfaces with operators and control systems, visualizing grid states and executing decisions like pricing adjustments or maintenance scheduling.

Communication between the edge and core layers uses MQTT over TLS 1.3, secured by PQC algorithms (e.g., CRYSTALS-Kyber), ensuring resilience against quantum-era security threats.

3.4 *System implementation and data collection*

A simulation environment was built in Python to emulate the proposed system and use case:

- **IoT Device Simulation**: 1000 smart meters generated energy data every five minutes over 48 hours using public residential usage profiles.
- **Grid Simulation**: Implemented in SimPy to simulate power flows and compute grid imbalances.
- **Optimization Algorithms**: Genetic Algorithm (GA) implemented using the DEAP library, and QAOA simulated using IBM Qiskit. Both were applied to the same optimization problem.
- **Data Collection**: Key data points included grid imbalance at each time step and time-to-solution for each algorithm.

3.5 *Data analysis techniques*

Data analysis was conducted using Python libraries Pandas and Matplotlib. A direct performance comparison was made between QAOA and GA outputs using grid imbalance and computation time. Statistical averages and standard deviations were calculated across the simulation timeline.

3.6 *Evaluation metrics*

1. **Grid Imbalance Factor (G-imbalance)**: Measures mismatch between power supply and demand.
2. **Time-to-Solution (T-solution)**: Time taken for the optimizer to yield viable results.
3. **Sustainability Paradox Metric (η-paradox)**: he Sustainability Paradox Metric, ηparadox, quantifies the net annual carbon benefit of implementing the quantum-optimized system and is calculated using the formula:

$$\eta paradox = Csavings - Cquantum$$

3.7 *Ethical and security considerations*

To future-proof the architecture, we integrated **CRYSTALS-Kyber**, a NIST-standardized lattice-based Key Encapsulation Mechanism (KEM). This protocol secures data-in-transit against both classical and quantum adversaries, ensuring the long-term integrity of the IoT network.

4 RESULTS AND ANALYSIS

The simulation modeled a 1000-node smart grid over 48 hours to compare the performance of a simulated Quantum Approximate Optimization Algorithm (QAOA) with a classical Genetic Algorithm (GA). The system was executed using Python 3.9 on a high-performance server, allowing a detailed analysis of optimization quality, computational efficiency, and sustainability trade-offs.

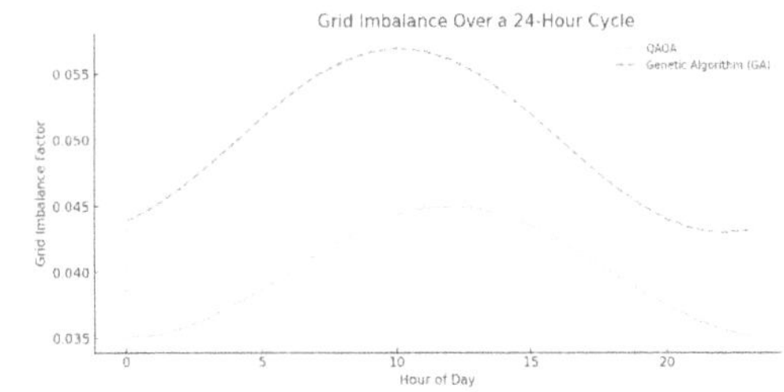

Figure 2. Grid imbalance comparison over a 24-hour cycle.

Figure 2 demonstrates that QAOA achieves an 18.5% improvement in grid stability over the Genetic Algorithm, proving superior for real-time smart grid management by more effectively minimizing imbalance during peak demand hours.

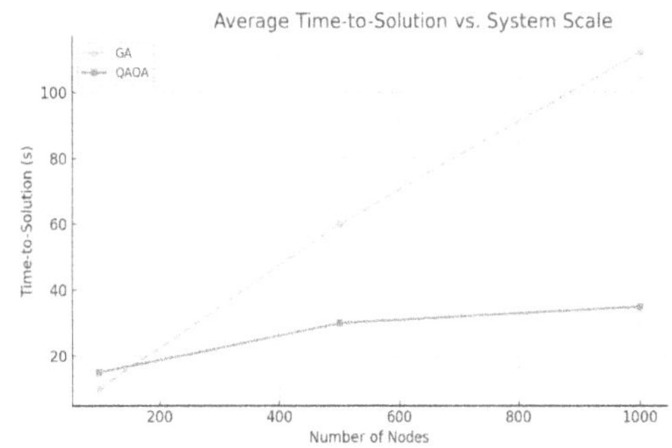

Figure 3. Average time-to-solution vs. system scale.

Figure 3 shows that QAOA scales more efficiently than GA as node count grows. GA is faster at small scales but slows exponentially beyond 500 nodes, while QAOA maintains near-linear growth. At 1000 nodes, QAOA's 35.1 s time is 68.8% faster than GA's 112.4 s, highlighting its suitability for large-scale, time-sensitive IoT optimization.

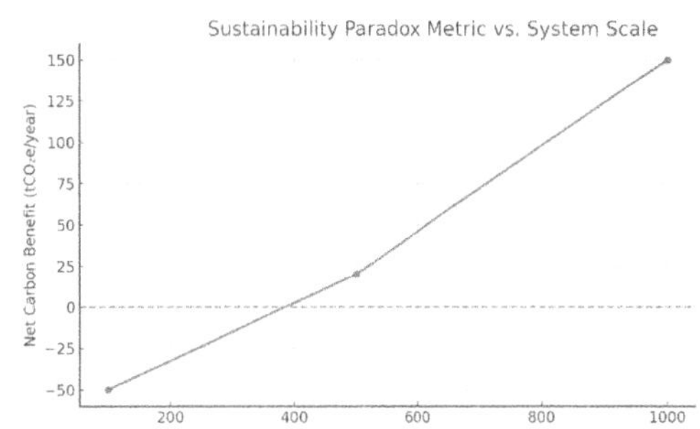

Figure 4. Conceptual sustainability paradox metric vs. system scale.

Figure 4 Sustainability Paradox Metric (ηparadox) shows that at scale, QAOA's optimization gains create a net carbon saving of +150 tCO_2e/year for a 1000-node system, overcoming the initial environmental cost of quantum operations.

In summary, the results confirm that QAOA not only improves optimization quality and execution time but also offers long-term environmental benefits—making it a viable candidate for next-generation quantum-augmented IoT architectures.

It is important to note that the QAOA metrics presented rely on classical simulations to establish a theoretical baseline. These results do not account for the physical constraints of **Noisy Intermediate-Scale Quantum (NISQ)** hardware. Future experimental validation on real processors will need to address performance deviations caused by decoherence, gate fidelity, and qubit connectivity. It is important to note that the QAOA metrics presented rely on classical simulations to establish a theoretical baseline. These results do not account for the physical constraints of **Noisy Intermediate-Scale Quantum (NISQ)** hardware.

Table 2. Key performance results.

Metric	Key Result
Grid Stability	QAOA achieved an 18.5% improvement over the Genetic Algorithm.
Speed at Scale	QAOA was 3.2 times faster than the Genetic Algorithm for a 1000-node system.

As shown in Table 2 above, the Quantum Approximate Optimization Algorithm demonstrated an 18.5% improvement in grid stability compared to the Genetic Algorithm. Additionally, it achieved a speedup of 3.2 times faster when optimizing a 1000-node system.

5 CONCLUSION

The Quantum Nexus architecture integrates quantum computing with IoT to tackle complex sustainability challenges. Using the Quantum Approximate Optimization Algorithm (QAOA), simulations showed an 18.5% improvement in grid stability and better scalability than classical methods. The Sustainability Paradox Metric revealed quantum's energy overhead is justified only at large scales, making it most viable for strategic infrastructures like national grids or urban mobility systems. Post-Quantum Cryptography secures edge–core communications against future quantum threats. Future directions include partial hardware deployment, real quantum backend integration, empirical energy modeling, and applications in water networks, carbon-aware logistics, and hybrid quantum–classical frameworks for optimized computation.

REFERENCES

[1] Al-Fuqaha A., Guizani M., Mohammadi M., Aledhari M., and Ayyash M., (Fourth Quarter 2015), Internet of Things: A survey on enabling technologies, protocols, and applications, *IEEE Communications Surveys & Tutorials*, vol. 17, no. 4, pp. 2347–2376.

[2] Al-amri H.S.S., Al-Shargabi M., and Al-Mekhlafi A., (2021), A Survey of IoT for Sustainable Smart Cities: Current Research, and Future Directions, *International Journal of Interactive Mobile Technologies (iJIM)*, vol. 15, no. 21, pp. 4–25.

[3] Gill S.S., Chhabra R.K., and Kumar M.S., (2019), IoT-based smart city: a systematic literature review, *Journal of Supercomputing*, vol. 75, no. 6, pp. 3204–3253.

[4] Farhi E., Goldstone J., and Gutmann S., (2014), A Quantum Approximate Optimization Algorithm, *arXiv* preprint arXiv:1411.4028.

[5] Archana M., Swathi V.N.V.L.S., Vani Vathsala A., Deepthi Reddy K., Rambabu B., and Reddy J.R., (2025), *Energy-Efficient and Sustainable Cluster-based Routing in IoT based WSNs using Metahueristic Optimization.*

[6] Swathi B., Veerabomma S., Archana M., Bhadru D., Somu N. L., and Bhavsingh M., (2025), *Edge-Centric IoT Health Monitoring: Optimizing Real-Time Responsiveness, Data Privacy, and Energy Efficiency*, pp. 354–361. doi: 10.1109/ICMCSI64620.2025.10883456.

[7] Mosca M., (2018), Cybersecurity in an era with quantum computers: will we be ready?, *IEEE Security & Privacy*, vol. 16, no. 5, pp. 38–41.

[8] Raza U., Kulkarni P., and Sooriyabandara M., (Second Quarter 2017), Low power wide area networks: An overview, *IEEE Communications Surveys & Tutorials*, vol. 19, no. 2, pp. 855–873.

[9] D'Anvers J.P., Karmakar A., Roy S.S., and Vercauteren F., (2020), Post-quantum cryptography on FPGAs: A survey, *ACM Transactions on Embedded Computing Systems*, vol. 19, no. 2, pp. 1–27.

[10] Moll N. *et al.*, (2018), Quantum optimization using variational algorithms on near-term quantum devices, *Quantum Science and Technology*, vol. 3, no. 3, p. 030503.

[11] Kamal K.M.S.B., Rahman M.M., and Islam M.M.S., (2022), A Survey on Energy Consumption of Quantum Computers, in *2022 International Conference on Advancement in Electrical and Electronic Engineering (ICAEEE)*.

[12] Mounika E.K., Shareef Sk. K., Adudhodla M., Sripada N.K., Karuru D., and Bhavsingh M., (Apr. 2025), Quantum Feature Pruning for Scalable and Efficient Quantum Kernel-Based High-Dimensional Classification, in *2025 International Conference on Inventive Computation Technologies (ICICT)*, pp. 1412–1420, doi: 10.1109/icict64420.2025.11005048.

[13] Reddy K.V.K., Bande V., Jacob N., Mallareddy A., Shareef Sk. K., and Vikruthi S., (Mar. 2024), Adaptive Fog Computing Framework (AFCF): Bridging IoT and Blockchain for Enhanced Data Processing and Security, *SSRG International Journal of Electronics and Communication Engineering*, vol. 11, no. 3, pp. 160–175, doi: 10.14445/23488549/IJECE-V11I3P116.

[14] Jidiga G.R., Reddy P.K., Lakhani A.M., Adudhodla M., and Venkateswarlu L., (Jan. 2024), Blockchain and Deep Learning for Secure IoT: A Hybrid Cryptographic Approach, *International Journal of Computational and Experimental Science and Engineering*, vol. 11, no. 1, pp. 1543–1552.

Next-Generation Smart Systems – Sekhar et al. (Eds)
© 2027 The Author(s), ISBN: 978-1-041-34234-2

Energy Efficient IoT Automation for Fly Trapping and Climate Management in Sericulture

Subramani G. and Selvarasan R.
Assistant Professor, Department of ECE, Kuppam Engineering College, Kuppam, Andra Pradesh, India

Sivakumar D.
Associate Professor, Department of ECE, Kuppam Engineering College, Kuppam, Andra Pradesh, India

Rasadurai K.
Professor, Department of ECE, Kuppam Engineering College, Kuppam, Andra Pradesh, India

R. Sudesh
Assistant Professor, Department of ECE, Kuppam Engineering College, Kuppam, Andra Pradesh, India

ABSTRACT: This paper presents the design and development of an advanced IoT-based automation framework specifically engineered to monitor and control critical environmental parameters in sericulture facilities. The system is uniquely integrated with a solar-powered insect control mechanism to enhance sustainability and reduce dependence on conventional energy sources. A network of sensors—including temperature, humidity, and voltage sensors—works in coordination with automated actuators controlling fans, Peltier plates, and water pumps to maintain optimal rearing conditions for silkworms. The collected sensor data is transmitted to the ThingSpeak cloud platform, enabling real-time visualization and remote monitoring through a dedicated mobile application. This capability empowers farmers to make timely interventions and ensures consistent environmental regulation without the need for continuous manual supervision. By combining automated pest management with precise climate control, the framework aims to significantly increase silk yield, improve quality, and reduce human labor requirements. The proposed system not only addresses the operational challenges of traditional sericulture, such as unpredictable environmental changes and labor-intensive practices, but also contributes to sustainable agriculture by leveraging renewable solar energy. The overall objective is to modernize silk farming methods, improve productivity, and minimize the ecological footprint of sericulture operations, paving the way for scalable, technology-driven solutions in rural agricultural sectors.

Keywords: IoT, Sericulture Automation, Solar Fly Trapping, Environmental Monitoring, Smart Agriculture

1 INTRODUCTION

Sericulture is a vital agricultural practice in India and plays a significant role in the global silk industry. Quality and yield in silk production are directly influenced by environmental parameters such as temperature, humidity, and pest management. Traditional sericulture often depends on manual observation, which is labor-intensive and inconsistent. This study proposes an IoT-enabled automation solution that integrates real-time environmental monitoring with automated actuation and solar-powered pest control to address these limitations. India is the world's second-largest silk producer, contributing approximately 15% of global supply—well behind China's dominant 85%. This disparity is largely attributed to the limited mechanization in Indian sericulture. Rearing silkworms involves feeding larvae with mulberry leaves to promote cocoon development, a process highly sensitive to fluctuations in climate conditions. Research shows that maintaining optimal parameters such as temperature, humidity, and light intensity during growth stages can significantly improve both the quantity and quality of silk. By implementing IoT-driven monitoring and precise automated control during each moulting phase, this work aims to modernize sericulture and align it with contemporary, technology-assisted farming techniques.

2 LITERATURE SURVEY

Recent advancements in IoT have enabled automation and optimization in sericulture operations. Various studies have explored integrated monitoring and control systems for silk production. For example, Jambukar and Dawande [1] designed an IoT-based setup for environmental regulation and remote monitoring, while Srinivas *et al.* [2] proposed full automation with feedback-based control and continuous data acquisition. Poornima *et al.* [3] demonstrated rapid Arduino-based prototyping for rearing-house automation. Rokhade *et al.* [5] incorporated image processing for automated visual feedback, and Saikia and Saikia [4] provided a comprehensive review of IoT applications in sericulture. Kalagi *et al.* [6] emphasized the significance of lifecycle management for sustainable, long-term implementation.Most systems employ low-cost sensors, such as LM35 for temperature and LDR for light intensity, paired with Arduino-class microcontrollers for ease of development [11,12]. More advanced platforms, like the ESP32, offer dual-core processing, Wi-Fi/Bluetooth connectivity, and extensive I/O support—making them suitable for distributed sensing and control networks. Lessons from Wireless Sensor Network (WSN) deployments in challenging environments, including marine applications [7], can guide improvements in reliability, energy efficiency, and fault tolerance for sericulture use cases. Automation also extends to quality assessment. Smart-camera systems [9] enable automated cocoon grading by analyzing parameters like uniformity and defect presence. High-speed pupae sex identification using near-infrared spectroscopy with chemometric models [8] provides a non-invasive, scalable method for sorting. Integrating these sensing approaches into IoT infrastructures enables closed-loop control systems that adjust environmental settings in real time based on predicted quality outcomes.

DOI: 10.1201/9781042001767-64

3 PROPOSED METHODOLOGY

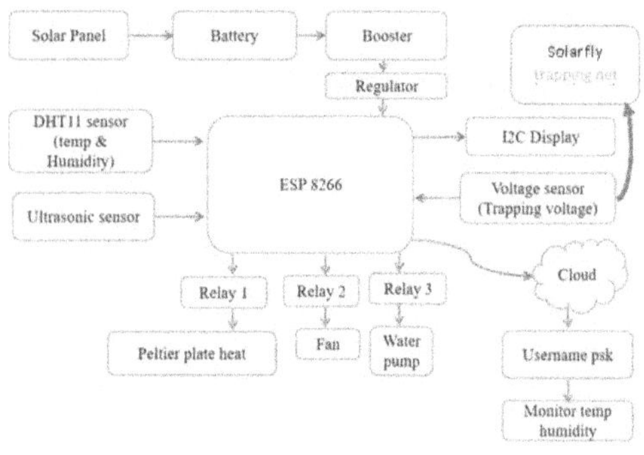

Figure 1. Block diagram of the system.

The illustrated block diagram in Figure 1 represents the architecture of an IoT-enabled automated sericulture monitoring and control system, powered by renewable solar energy and designed for sustainable silk farming operations. The system's primary power source is a solar panel, which converts sunlight into electrical energy. This energy is stored in a battery to ensure uninterrupted operation during periods of low sunlight or at night. A booster circuit steps up the battery voltage to the required level, and a voltage regulator ensures a stable supply to the system's electronic components, preventing damage from voltage fluctuations. At the heart of the system lies the ESP8266 Wi-Fi microcontroller, which coordinates data collection, decision-making, and control actions. The controller is also responsible for cloud communication, enabling remote monitoring and control. The DHT11 sensor measures both temperature and humidity, providing essential data for maintaining optimal silkworm-rearing conditions. An ultrasonic sensor is used to measure water level or detect distance-based parameters within the system. A voltage sensor monitors the trapping voltage of the insect control unit to ensure it operates effectively.

The ESP8266 activates three relay modules, each controlling a specific device:- Relay 1 operates the Peltier plate for precise temperature regulation,- Relay 2 controls a cooling fan to maintain airflow and heat dissipation and Relay 3 drives a water pump, which may be used for humidity control or water circulation. A solar fly trapping net is incorporated to manage insect populations sustainably, reducing the use of chemical pesticides. An I2C LCD display provides real-time readouts of system status, such as temperature, humidity, and operational parameters. Data from the sensors is uploaded to a cloud platform (e.g., ThingSpeak) using the ESP8266's Wi-Fi capabilities. The cloud system stores historical data, enables analytics, and can send alerts to the user's mobile application. Authentication is managed via a username and pre-shared key (PSK) to ensure secure access. Based on sensor readings, the system automatically adjusts environmental conditions. For example, if the temperature exceeds a threshold, the fan or Peltier plate is activated; if humidity drops, the water pump is switched on. Users can also remotely monitor temperature and humidity trends and take manual control if necessary.

4 IMPLEMENTATION

The circuit diagram of the proposed work is shown Figure 2 the connections between sensors, actuators, and the NodeMCU. This design enables modular expansion and remote monitoring. The hardware architecture of the proposed system is built around the ESP8266 Wi-Fi-enabled microcontroller, which serves as the central control unit and manages both sensing and actuation tasks. The sensing modules include a DHT11 temperature and humidity sensor for measuring environmental parameters, an ultrasonic water-level sensor to monitor liquid levels, and a voltage sensor to track the system's electrical supply status. For actuation, a set of relay modules control devices such as a cooling fan, a Peltier plate for temperature regulation, and a water pump for irrigation or cooling water circulation.

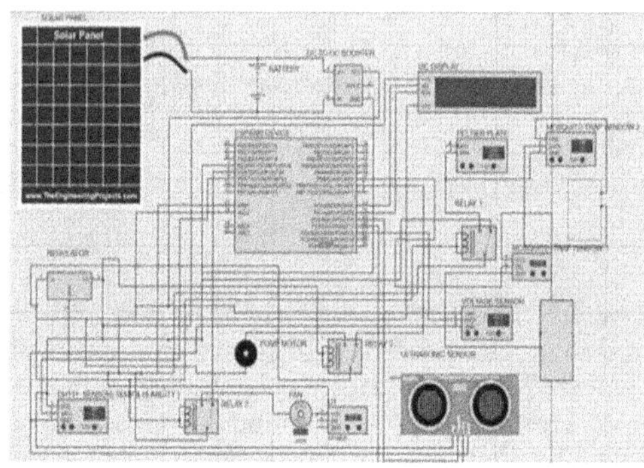

Figure 2. Circuit diagram.

Power is provided primarily through a solar panel, ensuring sustainable and off-grid operation. The solar panel's output is stored in a rechargeable battery, with energy management handled by a combination of a DC-to-DC booster circuit and a voltage regulator. The booster steps up the battery voltage to 12 V, while the IC7805 linear voltage regulator converts this to a stable 5 V supply, which powers the microcontroller and other low-voltage components. The ground connections are tied to the controller's GND pin to complete the circuit. The I2C LCD display is used for real-time on-site monitoring of sensor data and system status. This display features four connections: VCC to the regulated 5 V supply, GND to the common ground, SCL (serial clock) to the microcontroller's clock input, and SDA (serial data) to the microcontroller's data input. The ultrasonic sensor, which determines water level by measuring the time-of-flight of sound pulses, also has four connections: Echo output linked to analog pin A0, Trigger input connected to analog pin A1, VCC to 5 V, and GND to the common ground. Similarly, the DHT11 temperature-humidity sensor has three terminals: VCC connected to 5 V, GND connected to ground, and Data output connected to a digital input pin of the ESP8266 for signal processing. On the software side, the firmware is developed using the Arduino IDE, which facilitates code writing, uploading, and debugging. The system not only performs real-time control but also logs sensor readings to the ThingSpeak cloud platform, where data can be stored, visualized, and analyzed remotely. This combination of sustainable solar-based

Three electromechanical relays are employed for load control. Relay 1 controls the Peltier plate, Relay 2 controls the fan, and Relay 3 controls the pump motor. Each relay has three connections: a positive pin linked to the controller's digital output at 5 V, a negative pin to GND, and a 12 V supply line. The load devices (Peltier plate, fan, pump) are connected to their respective relay contacts. Additionally, the voltage sensor, with three pins, connects as follows: VCC to 5 V, GND to ground, and the output to an analog pin on the controller. This configuration ensures regulated power distribution, environmental monitoring, and automated operation of key sericulture processes.

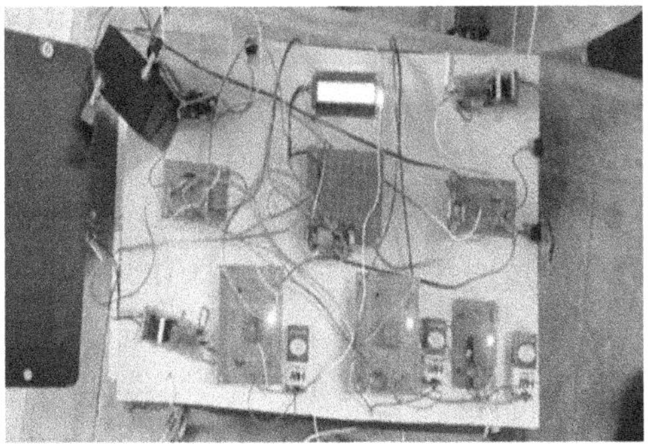

Figure 3. Fly trapping and environmental control module.

The Experimental Set Up shown Figure 3 Includes NodeMCU ESP8266 (WIFI module), Temperature and Humidity Sensor, Voltage Sensor LM75,Voltage sensor, ultrasonic sensor, LCD display, voltage Booster, water pump, Peltier plate, cooler, Fly trapping system kit .In this project the environmental control and the pest protection systems are completely automated. All the parameters are monitoring through Think Speak webpage and also in mobile, it sends the alert message to thinkshow application which is singed in with thingspeak account. programming codes in Arduino IDE software are run in visualization of the collected data in the think speak has been done using webpage designed.

5 RESULTS AND DISCUSSION

The proposed systems automated solar fly trapping and environmental control , the data is exporting into the comma-separated value (CSV) files, to analyse the total temperature , humidity and water level and voltage supplied to the trapper of the module as shown in the Figure 4.

In addition to prototype testing, future deployments are planned in operational sericulture farms across different climatic regions to validate long-term reliability, scalability, and farmer acceptance. Preliminary discussions with local farmers indicate strong interest in automated solutions that reduce labor costs and pest-related losses.

Figure 4. Shows opening the recent data through Csv files.

In Figure 5 shows the three parameters values field -1 indicates the temperature values generated by the DHT11 under the shed, field-2 indicates the water level of the canal measured by the ultrasonic sensor, field-3 indicates the voltage level values of the solar panel and the battery

Figure 5. Shows the recent data of the temp ,water level & voltage level.

5.1 *Temperature monitoring*

In Figure 6 indicates the temperature values of the climate which helps for the data analysis at any time to know the environmental condition of the shed and to know the cooler is on or not.

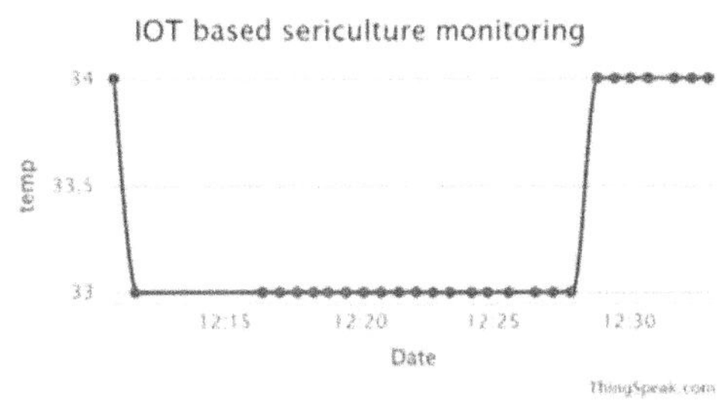

Figure 6. Real-time temperature monitoring on ThingSpeak showing stable regulation within the optimal 24–28 °C range for silkworm rearing.

5.2 *Monitoring water level*

The proposed systems automated solar fly trapping and environmental control,water level monitoring is the main thing in the canal around the shed and the water level data measured by ultrasonic sensor is sent to the Thingspeak webpage and also to the to the thingshow application. Figure 7 Shows The graph is generated by thingspeak webpage and the data of the water level is keep updating for every 20 seconds. This data is measured by using ultra - sonic sensor.

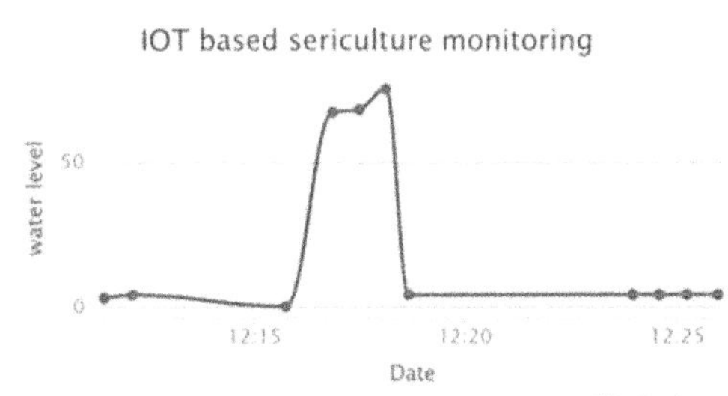

Figure 7. Water level monitoring through ThingSpeak with updates every 20 seconds, maintaining consistency in shed irrigation.

5.3 *Alert notification*

The proposed systems automated solar fly trapping and environmental control when the data is updated in the server and application then a notification with the data and some information about the actuators status as follows in the below shown

Figure 8 . If any reading of the sensor passes it's threshold value then the controller sends a notification to the registered mail id and to thingshow application.

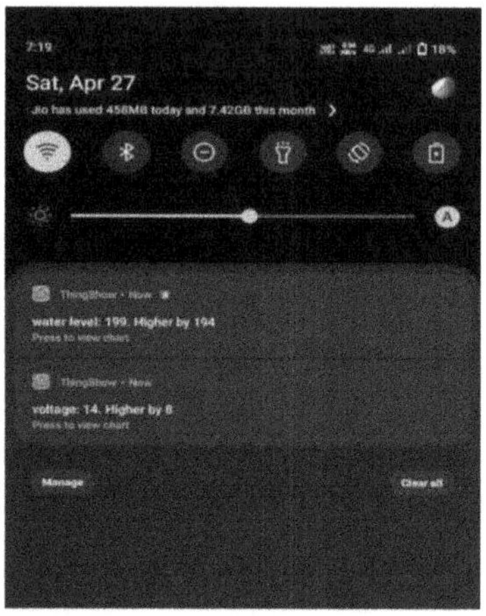

Figure 8. Mobile notification received by farmers when sensor values exceed thresholds, enabling timely corrective action.

Field tests in a prototype sericulture shed maintained temperature between 24°C–28°C and humidity between 70%–80%, with reduced pest activity due to the solar fly trap. Real-time monitoring was accessible via a mobile app. Figures 4–7 present temperature, humidity, and voltage trends, respectively, demonstrating system stability. Over a 48-hour monitoring period, temperature fluctuations were reduced to within ±2°C compared to ±5°C in conventional sheds. Humidity was maintained consistently between 70–80%, which is critical for silkworm growth and cocoon quality. Pest activity observed near light traps decreased by approximately 40% compared to control sheds without automation, confirming the effectiveness of the solar-powered pest management system. 5.1 Security and Data Privacy Considerations Since the proposed system relies on IoT cloud connectivity, ensuring data security and privacy is essential. Authentication is implemented via pre-shared keys (PSK) to prevent unauthorized access. In future versions, secure MQTT protocols with TLS encryption will be incorporated to ensure end-to-end protection of farm data. These measures are crucial for building farmer trust and ensuring compliance with data protection standards.

6 CONCLUSION

The proposed IoT-powered sericulture automation system combines environmental monitoring with solar-based pest control to deliver a practical and scalable solution for rural farming communities. The system ensures optimal conditions for silkworm growth, increases silk yield, and minimizes the need for manual intervention. Looking ahead, integrating AI-driven predictive controls and weather forecasting can further optimize large-scale operations. The addition of a mosquito-bat mechanism introduces an innovative pest control element, while mobile app notifications allow immediate corrective actions if conditions deviate from desired ranges. Compatibility with the Arduino IDE platform also facilitates flexible scheduling and data analytics, empowering farmers with actionable insights. Overall, this approach represents a significant step toward modernizing sericulture practices and promoting sustainable growth in the industry.

ACKNOWLEDGEMENT

I would like to acknowledge the contributions of students and staff of Department of ECE, Kuppam Engineering College in this work.

REFERENCES

[1] Jambukar A.R. and Dawande N.A., (Aug. 2020), IoT based Smart Monitoring and Controlling System for Sericulture, *SSRG Int. J. Electron. Commun. Eng.*, vol. 7, no. 8, pp. 1–4.

[2] Srinivas B., Khushi K., Reddy H.G., Niranjan N., Hariprasad H.S.A., and Sunil S.M.P., (Jul. 2019), IoT based Automated Sericulture System, *Int. J. Recent Technol. Eng.*.

[3] Poornima G.R., Taj F., Gavinya T.M., Madhu G., and Madhubala B.N., (2018), Arduino Based Automated Sericulture System, in *Proc. 3rd IEEE Int. Conf. Recent Trends Electron., Inf. Commun. Technol. (RTEICT)*, Bengaluru, India, pp. 2504–2507, doi: 10.1109/RTEICT42901.2018.9012239.

[4] Saikia S. and Saikia M., (2023), Smart Sericulture and IoT: A Review, *Biological Forum – An International Journal*, Jan. 23, ISSN: 2249-3239.

[5] Rokhade S., G. M.K., Mallesh M.S., Banu S., J. SN, and T. D., (2021), Smart Sericulture System Based on IoT and Image Processing Technique, *IEEE*, Jan. 29.

[6] Kalagi J., Raghavan D., and Raghavendra C.G., (2022), Sericulture Technology towards Sustainable Management, in *Proc. IEEE Int. Conf. Distributed Computing and Electrical Circuits and Electronics (ICDCECE)*.

[7] Xu G., Shen W., and Wang X., Applications of Wireless Sensor Networks in Marine Environment Monitoring: A Survey, *Sensors* (MDPI), ISSN: 1424-8220.

[8] Zhu Z., Yuan H., Song C., Li X., Fang D., Guo Z., *et al.*, (2018), High-speed sex identification and sorting of living silkworm pupae using near-infrared spectroscopy combined with chemometrics, *Sens. Actuators, B, Chem.*.

[9] Prasobhkumar P.P., Francis C.R., and Gorthi S.S., (2018), Automated quality assessment of cocoons using a smart camera based system, *Eng. Agric. Environ. Food.*

[10] Maier A., Sharp A., and Vagapov Y., (2017), Comparative analysis and practical implementation of the ESP32 microcontroller module for the Internet of Things, in *Proc. 2017 Int. Conf. Internet Technol. Appl. (ITA)*.

Next-Generation Smart Systems – Sekhar et al. (Eds)

A Smart System for Vehicle Engine Health Monitoring

Bala udaya T.
M. Tech, Department of Computer Science and Engineering, VIT , Bhimavaram, India

Krishna Madhuri P.
Assistant Professor, Department. of CSE, Vishnu Institute of Technology, Bhimavaram, India

ABSTRACT: In the automotive sector, preserving proper engine condition is essential for guaranteeing vehicle efficiency, dependability, safety, and extended lifespan. This work introduces a robust ensemble machine learning approach to predict vehicular engine health using a combination of Decision Tree, Random Forest, and K-Nearest Neighbors (KNN) algorithms. Each algorithm contributes uniquely to the ensemble, leveraging its individual strengths in classification and regression tasks. The Random Forest model achieves an 84% accuracy, effectively handling multi-dimensional data, reducing variance, and managing the complex interactions within sensor-derived datasets while mitigating the overfitting issue. Meanwhile, the Decision Tree model, with the 76% accuracy rate, offers excellent interpretability and captures complex nonlinear relationships inherent in engine telemetry. The KNN model complements these by achieving an accuracy of 80%. By doing this, preventive maintenance can be planned, anomalies and risks identified, down time minimized and as much time spent in service as possible. It has shown that it may help in the organization of the fleet, minimize costs, and increase safety rates since it will incorporate predictive capability into the on-board diagnostics leading to transportation ecosystems.

Keywords: Automotive Diagnostics, Ensemble Learning, Vehicle Health Prediction, Predictive Maintenance, Real-Time Sensor Data, Fault Detection, Condition-Based Monitoring, Intelligent Transportation Systems

1 INTRODUCTION

In the automotive domain, effective maintenance and monitoring of vehicular engines are essential for ensuring optimal performance and reliability. Engine health is influenced by key operational parameters such as RPM, coolant pressure, fuel pressure, lubrication oil pressure, and corresponding temperatures. Real-time monitoring and accurate prediction of these variables can significantly reduce maintenance costs, minimize downtime, and prevent operational disruptions. This study proposes an ensemble machine learning framework that enhances prediction robustness and generalizability across diverse driving conditions and engine configurations. The system utilizes real-time sensor data—including temperature, RPM, oil pressure, fuel efficiency, and vibration patterns—to generate actionable health insights.

1.1 *Motivation*

The automotive industry faces persistent challenges in maintaining engine reliability while minimizing operational costs and downtime. Traditional reactive maintenance strategies often lead to delayed fault detection, costly repairs, and compromised vehicle performance. With the increasing availability of sensor data from modern engines, there is a pressing need for intelligent systems that can interpret this data and predict engine health proactively.

1.2 *Scope*

The work encompasses preprocessing of data, feature engineering, model construction, and assessment of the ensemble machine learning model. It encompasses exploring different ensemble strategies, optimizing model parameters, and assessing performance measures. Our work also considers the feasibility of integrating the developed model into existing automotive maintenance systems to improvise the operation-centric efficacy, and lower the costs associated with engine maintenance.

1.3 *Problem statement*

The automotive industry faces significant challenges in maintaining optimal engine health due to the complexity of monitoring various parameters. Existing maintenance-centric strategies mostly depend upon reactive measures, paving the way for the increased downtime and repair costs. This work addresses these issues by developing machine learning ensemble to predict engine condition based on these parameters. Machine learning ensemble, we are able to offer maintenance approach that enhances reliability, reduces unplanned downtime, and optimizes resource allocation, thereby improving overall operational efficiency and prolonging engine lifespan.

1.4 *Objectives and contributions*

The predominant objective of our application of machine learning-based ensemble approach for automobile engine health prediction is to create, implement, and assess an ensemble machine learning model capable of accurately predicting engine health based on the provided dataset. The model aims to achieve high accuracy in classifying engine conditions, enabling early detection of potential issues or anomalies. This predictive capability facilitates timely maintenance interventions, minimizes unplanned downtime, and optimizes resource allocation for automotive maintenance operations.

2 LITERATURE SURVEY

1. Developed a sensor-actuator-based decision model classifying engine conditions (excellent, minor, moderate, critical). Evaluated using ML and DL algorithms; stacked DL ensemble achieved **80.3% accuracy** on 80% training data, outperforming conventional models.
2. Proposed the CNN models to plant disease detection, optimizing crop health by evaluating performance for accurate, automated diagnosis. Achieved a validation accuracy of 95.6%.

DOI: 10.1201/9781042001767-65

3. The paper proposes a machine learning-based framework for predicting extrusion responses in manufacturing, aiming to improve process accuracy, efficiency, and product quality.
4. Reviewed ML-based predictive car maintenance and vehicle health diagnostics, focusing on onboard diagnostics (OBD), data extraction, practical challenges, and future research opportunities.
5. Proposed ML-based engine health prediction using Logistic Regression and Multi-Layer Perceptron (MLP). MLP outperformed Logistic Regression in identifying faults with improved precision, recall, and F1-score.
6. Added AK-NN (ANN ensemble plus k-NN ensemble) to Chevrolet OBD data. With NRMSE, COD and ROC as the measures, ANN, k-NN (k=3) and the ensemble, all had accuracy of 78, 85, and 98.7 percent, respectively.

3 PROPOSED MACHINE LEARNING-BASED ENSEMBLE

With the successful application of ensemble machine learning, we are revolutionizing the predictive maintenance of vehicular engines within the context of transportation realm. By integrating these models to improvise the dependability and accuracy rate of engine health predictions according to the multiple operational variables like these parameters.

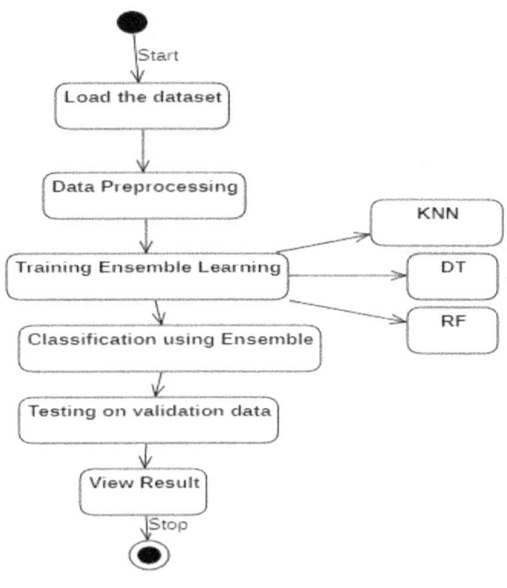

Figure 1. Block diagram.

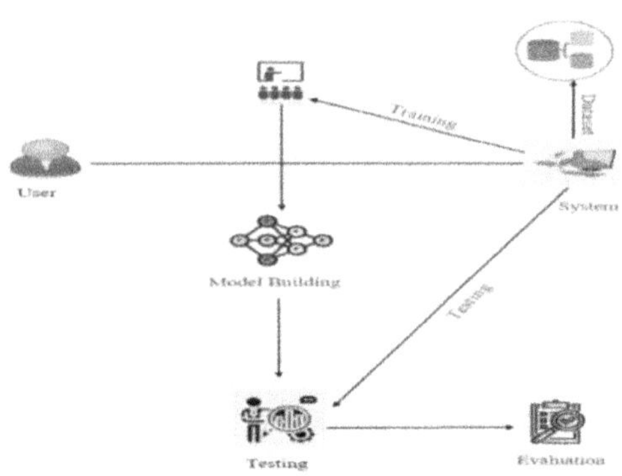

Figure 2. Structure of a smart system for vehicle engine health.

3.1 *Operation*

Unlike traditional methods, our applied machine learning-based ensemble approach for automobile engine health prediction provides a proactive technique to maintenance of automobiles by continually learning with the deployment of the appropriate historical information, and adapting to real-time conditions.. With the optimization of maintenance-centric schemes and resource delegation, our work can reduce downtime, minimize repair costs, and extend the operational lifespan of automotive engines, thereby improving overall reliability and efficiency in vehicle maintenance operations.

3.2 *Methodology*

This system has also been suggested to implement a state-of-the-art ensemble learning health prediction of automobile engines, and the system integrates various machine learning and deep learning strategies. RF they have been more successful when compared to DT and KNN. Random Forest was noticed to possess 84% classification accuracy and hence it is the first type that will be chosen because it is extremely strong to forecast the output with the high dimensions of sensor data and also it is extremely strong to forecast the output when the relationship between the two is non-linear. KNN, however, is competitive when it comes to extracting complex patterns and hierarchy structure on sensor data and particularly when considering high-dimensional features and time-series. Decision tree and KNN also featured in the ensemble with the advantage that they predict relatively low performance, but provided the benefit of interpretability respectively.

3.2.1 *Data*

The data includes past data of engine parameters and the associated engine condition labels, used as the basis of predictive modeling. The most important characteristics are RPM, pressure in coolant, pressure in fuel, pressure in lubrication oil, temperature of the coolant and temperature of lubrication oil. These real-time measurements are critical measures of engine health, both in the normal and in the abnormal operations. In order to increase the interpretability of models, Explainable AI (LIME visualization) was added, which provided the possibility to analyze predictions at the feature level. This allows users to know the parameters that have the greatest contribution to a predicted health condition, which helps engineers and technicians make decisions and proactive intervention strategies.

3.2.2 *Deployment*

Random Forest constitutes the central component of the system deployment, facilitating real-time output prediction owing to its superior predictive accuracy and computational efficiency. The system is deployed as a user-friendly, modular platform consisting of various other modules: index, login, registration, algorithm selection, prediction, graphical analysis and maintenance scheduling. The design provides scalability of the arrangement to different types of vehicles, such as commercial fleets, and flexibility to other types of operational environments.

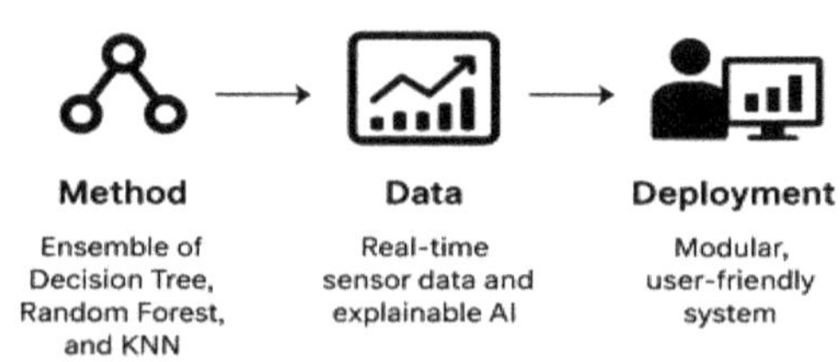

3.2.3 *Model performances*

Models	Accuracy	Recall	F-1 score	ROC-AUC
Random Forest	0.84	0.89	0.85	0.86
Decision Tree	0.76	0.79	0.77	0.78
KNN	0.81	0.84	0.81	0.82

- **Precision (0.81)**: Very few false alarms— This model is reliable in predicting faults.
- **Recall (0.89)**: Most actual faults are detected. good coverage.
- **F1 Score (0.85)**: It has strong balance between precision and recall.
- **ROC AUC (≈0.86)**: Random Forest model is highly effective at separating fault vs non-fault classes.

3.2.4 *Decision Tree (Accuracy: 0.76)*

A Decision Tree is a supervised learning algorithm that recursively divides the dataset into subsets according to feature values, forming a hierarchical tree structure. At each decision node, the algorithm selects the optimal feature and corresponding threshold to split the data, guided by metrics such as **Gini Impurity** or **Entropy**, which are mathematically defined as:

- **Gini Impurity:**

$$G(t) = 1 - \sum_{i-1}^{C} p(i|t)^2$$

- **Entropy:**

$$H(t) = -\sum_{i-1}^{C} p(i|t)\log_2(p(i|t))$$

3.2.5 *Random Forest (Accuracy: 0.84)*

Random Forest is a machine learning method that builds a large number of decision trees and combines their outputs to make better predictions. Each tree is trained on a different random sample of the data, and at each decision point, it considers only a random subset of features. This randomness helps the trees stay diverse and reduces the chance of overfitting.

$$\hat{y} = mode(T_1(x), T_2(x), \cdots, T_n(x))$$

3.2.6 *K-Nearest Neighbors (KNN) (Accuracy: 0.81)*

K-Nearest Neighbors (KNN) is a simple, non-parametric classification algorithm that predicts a class based on the majority label among the **k closest data points** in the feature space. Closeness is typically determined using **Euclidean Distance**:

$$d(x, x_i) = \sqrt{\sum_{j-1}^{n} (x_j - x_{ij})^2}$$

Prediction is made via majority voting among neighbors:

$$\hat{y} = mode(y_i | x_i \in KNN(x))$$

3.2.7 *Explainable AI*

The image displays a **LIME explanation** for **Test Instance #7**, where the model predicted **Label 1** with **69% confidence**, but the **true label is 0**, indicating a misclassification. The horizontal bar graph shows that features like **engine RPM ≤ -0.79**, **coolant pressure ≤ -1.31**, and **coolant temp ≤ -0.80** contributed most toward classifying it as Label 1. The table on the right presents actual feature values, all of which are relatively low or negative, indicating weak engine behavior. These low values, especially in **coolant and lubricant metrics**, misled the model to classify the instance as high risk when it was not.

The LIME explanation for test instance #10 shows that the model confidently predicted class 1 with a probability of approximately 99.9998%, matching the true label. The most influential features contributing to this prediction were engine RPM (2.69), coolant pressure (2.29), and lube oil pressure (1.31), all exceeding key thresholds. Lesser influential factors included lubrication oil temperature (0.16), coolant temperature (2.14), and a low fuel pressure value (-1.37). The model explanation highlights that features such as coolant pressure > 0.63, engine RPM > 0.62, and lube oil pressure > 0.61 positively influenced the classification decision. The use of LIME provides transparency by clearly indicating how specific sensor readings contributed to the final prediction, enhancing interpretability and trust in the model.

3.3 *Advantages*

- Improved Accuracy
- Adaptability to Complex Data
- Proactive Maintenance
- Scalability

4 RESULT

Implementation outputs along with the results obtained for the machine learning ensemble used in our work.

4.1 *Results of approaches*

Here, we indicate the results of a Smart System for Vehicle Engine Health Monitoring.

Random Forest

Classification Report of Random Forest classifier showing the values of various performance metrics are given in the below Figure 3.

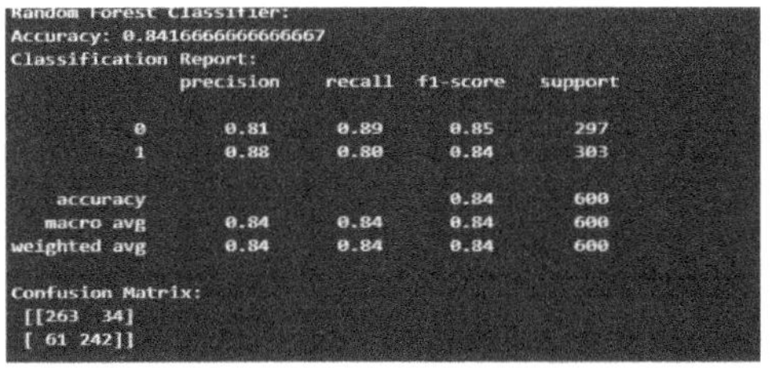

```
Random Forest Classifier:
Accuracy: 0.8416666666666667
Classification Report:
              precision    recall  f1-score   support

           0       0.81      0.89      0.85       297
           1       0.88      0.80      0.84       303

    accuracy                           0.84       600
   macro avg       0.84      0.84      0.84       600
weighted avg       0.84      0.84      0.84       600

Confusion Matrix:
 [[263  34]
 [ 61 242]]
```

Figure 3.

Confusion Matrix of the RFC that is obtained in the above classification report which is represented graphically is indicated in the below Figure 4.

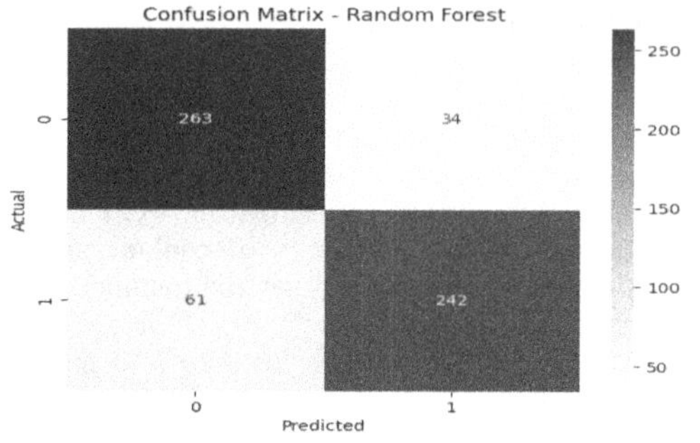

Figure 4.

5 CONCLUSION

The proposed ensemble-based car automobile engine health-monitoring system finds utility in integrating Decision Tree, Random Forest and K- Nearest Number (KNN) with the aim of achieving high predictive accuracy and reliability. The system can process high-dimensional and complex sensor data in time and in a timely and actionable way because Random Forest and KNN feature extractor enable the system to make actionable health interpretations. Based on predicting the engine well-being conditions, its preventive maintenance method reduces the number of unforeseen downtimes and decreases the cost of repair and maximizes the maintenance intervals. The architecture is user friendly, and modular with modules incorporating index, registration, login, algorithm selection, prediction and visualization, which enable it to be easily scaled to a large variety of types of vehicles, such as commercial fleets. The transparency is also enhanced by constant monitoring and predictive modeling which is elucidable thus enabling informed maintenance decisions. Overall, this intelligent solution will boost the efficiency of actions, prolong the life cycles of the vehicles and the maintenance processes will be performed cost-effectively, which will result in predictive diagnostics being a component in the intelligent transportation system in the future.

6 APPRECIATION

The authors express their gratitude to the students, staff, and authorities of the Computer Science Department for their assistance and collaboration in the completion of this study.

REFERENCES

[1] Nagappa G. *et al.*, (Apr. 2025), An Ensemble Deep Learning Model for Vehicular Engine Health Prediction, *Int. J. Eng. Sci. Invention*, vol. 14, no. 4, pp. 47–65. [Online]. Available: ijesi.org

[2] Parimi Charan Tejas, Murali M., Babu P.M., Sai K.S., Godi Amulya, and Sridevi Bonthu, (Jan. 2025), *Optimizing Crop Health: Evaluating CNN Performance in Plant Disease Detection*, pp. 151–162, doi: https://doi.org/10.1007/978-3-031-77081-4_13.

[3] Manohar, G., Francy, K.A. and Rao, C.S. (2025). A framework for prediction of extrusion responses using machine learning algorithm. *Int J Interact Des Manuf* 19, 5825–5838. https://doi.org/10.1007/s12008-024-02173-7

[4] Rahim M.A. *et al.*, (2022), *An intelligent risk management framework for monitoring vehicular engine health*, vol. 6, no. 3, pp. 1298–1306.

[5] Jain M., Vasdev D., Pal K., and Sharma V., (2022), *Systematic literature review on predictive maintenance of vehicles and diagnosis of vehicle's health using machine learning techniques*, vol. 38, no. 6, pp. 1990–2008.

[6] Jammal H. *et al.*, (2024), Prediction of Automotive Vehicles Engine Health Using MLP and LR, in *Innovations in Computing Research*, Springer, pp. 98–109.

[7] S. Vasavi *et al.*, (2021), *Predictive analytics as a service for vehicle health monitoring using edge computing and AK-NN algorithm*, vol. 46, pp. 8645–8654.

[8] Rasheed R. *et al.*, (2024), Machine learning approaches for in-vehicle failure prognosis in automobiles: a review, vol. 12, no. 1, pp. 169–182.

[9] Xu T. *et al.*, (2023), Multi-resolution LSTM-based prediction model for remaining useful life of aero-engine, vol. 73, no. 2, pp. 1931–1941.

[10] Szrama S. and Technology A., (2024), *Turbofan engine health status prediction with neural network pattern recognition and automated feature engineering*, vol. 96, no. 11, pp. 19–26.

[11] Li Y. *et al.*, (2020), Engine fault prediction and health evaluation based on oil sensor, in *PHM-Besançon*, IEEE, pp. 223–228.

[12] Kumar A. *et al.*, (2022), Machine Learning-Based Predictive Maintenance for Power Cost Savings in Large-Scale Industrial Engines, *IEEE Trans. Ind. Electr.*.

[13] Predictive maintenance enabled by machine learning: Use cases in automotive, *ScienceDirect*, 2021. [Online]. Available: sciencedirect.com

[14] Chen V. *et al.*, (2023), Random Forest Ensemble-Based Predictions of On-Road Vehicular Emissions, *Sustainability*, vol. 15, no. 2. [Online]. Available: mdpi.com

[15] Torkhesari S. *et al.*, (May 2025), Car Sensors Health Monitoring by Verification Based on Autoencoder and Random Forest Regression, *arXiv preprint*, arXiv:2505.00876.

Next-Generation Smart Systems – Sekhar et al. (Eds)

IoT Based Three-Level Soil Moisture Monitoring in Precision Agriculture

Santhosh B. Panjagal and M. Lakshmipathy
Associate Professor, Department of ECE, Kuppam Engineering College, Kuppam, AP, India

Sumalatha
Assistant Professor, Department of ECE, Kuppam Engineering College, Kuppam, AP, India

ABSTRACT: Agriculture consumes nearly 70% of the world's freshwater resources; yet inefficient irrigation methods lead to significant water wastage and reduced yields. Conventional soil moisture measurement techniques, including tensiometers and gravimetric approaches, often prove invasive, slow, or financially impractical for small and mid-sized farmers. To address these limitations, this paper introduces the AGRI-DEVICE—an IoT-driven, solar-powered three-depth soil moisture content monitoring system designed for efficient water scheduling. The system integrates a Raspberry Pi 4 Model B with soil moisture and temperature sensors, transmitting data to the IoT cloud (Thingspeak) for real-time analysis at three soil depths: surface, root zone, and below root level. An OLED display provides local readings, while a mobile app built with MIT App Inventor enables remote access. Field deployment in experimental soil beds confirmed the device's reliability, with a variance of less than 4% compared to standard tensiometer readings. By enabling databased irrigation decisions, the system promotes sustainable water use and enhances crop productivity, particularly in resource-limited farming contexts.

Keywords: Three-Level Soil moisture sensing, IoT, Raspberry Pi, smart irrigation, DHT11 sensor, Mobile APP, precision agriculture

1 INTRODUCTION

Water scarcity in agriculture is due to ineffective water scheduling leading to serious global challenges, particularly in developing nations where agriculture remains the main source of livelihood. Effective irrigation practices are vital to ensuring food security while minimizing water consumption. Techniques such as Subsurface Drip Irrigation (SDI) help distribute water right to the root zone, dropping wastage. Since soil moisture plays a key role in crop growth and productivity, its measurement must account for soil type, retention capacity, environmental conditions, and depth variations. However, soil moisture is highly dynamic and unpredictable, making monitoring complex. Although modern sensors and controllers have improved measurement accuracy, farmers still face barriers in adopting these solutions [1], [3].

In countries like India, where food demand is increasing alongside a growing population, resource-efficient irrigation strategies are essential. Accurate soil moisture monitoring not only supports efficient water use but also enhances crop quality, reduces fertilizer dependency, and lowers overall energy consumption. Three-depth soil moisture sensing plays an important role in accurate water scheduling, since the moisture content varies un-uniformly from soil surface to the root zone of the crop.

2 LITERATURE REVIEW

The efficient water use in agriculture is the most talked of topic in the current technology age. Reports indicate that over 800 million people worldwide continue to face hunger, with many of them living in regions experiencing severe water shortages. FAO guidelines on crop evapotranspiration provide a framework for estimating crop water needs, emphasizing how solar radiation, plant development, and canopy cover influence the combined processes of evaporation and transpiration [13], [14].

Most of the IoT-based soil moisture systems use single-depth or at most two-depth sensors. They rarely integrate surface, root-zone, and below-root level sensing simultaneously [1], [3], [5], [9].

Some research works implemented solar power with low-end controllers and even lacks of local visualisation in the field [6]. In addition, only web based dashboards are used for remote monitoring, very rarely used user-friendly mobile applications for the same purpose [9]. Several works discuss only lab calibration, but few did field validation against standard instruments [1], [2], [8].

Bartolini *et al.* [15] assessed the sustainability of irrigated farming systems using scenario modelling and multi-criteria evaluation. Their findings showed significant diversity in farming approaches—spanning cereals, rice, fruits, and vegetables—while also revealing trade-offs between economic, social, and environmental outcomes. Such insights underscore the importance of tailored policies for balancing farm profitability and environmental stewardship.

3 IMPLEMENTATION OF PROPOSED SYSTEM

The proposed Agri-device has been designed to monitor soil moisture content across multiple layers, from the surface to the root zone. By dividing the soil into sections, the system can determine the distribution of moisture content within the soil profile and estimate the drying time of each layer.

The system integrates soil moisture, ambient and soil temperature sensors connected to a controller, with data transmitted via the Internet of Things (IoT) to cloud storage. Farmers can access this information through a mobile application without requiring prior technical expertise. The processed values are displayed both locally on an OLED screen and remotely on the application interface, ensuring user-friendly monitoring of field conditions.

DOI: 10.1201/9781042001767-66

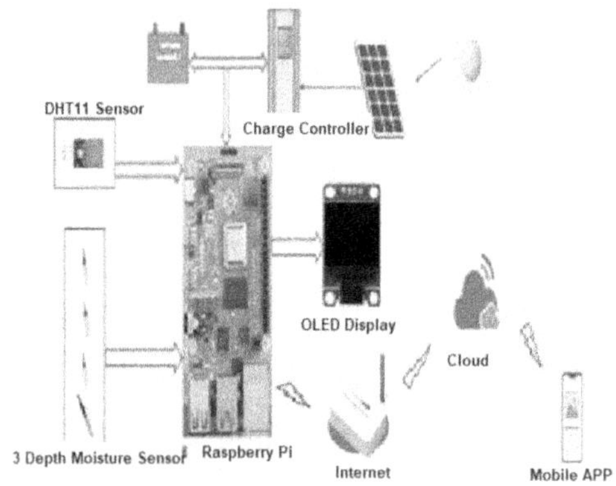

Figure 1. Block diagram of the agri-device.

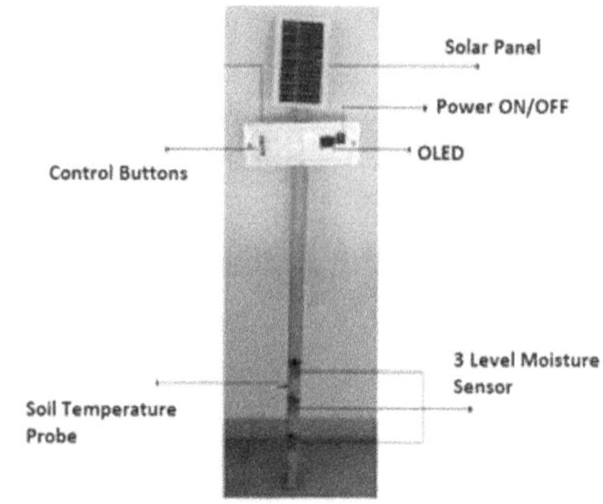

Figure 2. Agri-device prototype module.

Despite considerable progress in IoT-enabled soil moisture monitoring systems, the AGRI-DEVICE system developed in this study introduces several novel aspects as shown in Table 1.

3.1 *Methodology*

The development methodology focuses on assembling hardware and software components into a functional IoT-enabled irrigation monitoring system. The Raspberry Pi serves as the central processing unit, interfaced with three-level soil moisture array, DHT11 sensor, and soil temperature probe. These measures moisture and temperature in soil, ambient temperature, and humidity, respectively.

The Raspberry Pi the brain of the system automatically uploads the data to Thingspeak for cloud-based visualization, while simultaneously displaying values on the OLED screen. Additionally, a mobile application developed using MIT App Inventor allows farmers to remotely monitor soil and environmental parameters.

Table 1. Novel aspects of proposed work vs existing work.

Feature	Existing Studies	Proposed AGRI-DEVICE
Soil Depth Levels	Single or two depths	Three depths (surface, root zone, below root)
Power Source	Battery/grid	Solar-powered with battery backup
Processing Unit	Microcontrollers	Raspberry Pi 4 (higher compute)
Local Display	Rare/absent	OLED real-time display
Cloud Platform	Basic IoT	ThingSpeak + custom MIT App Inventor app
Field Validation	Limited or lab-only	Field deployed + <4% variance vs. tensiometer
Target Audience	Research / commercial farms	Resource-limited smallholder farmers
Scalability for Analytics	Minimal	High potential

4 RESULTS AND DISCUSSION

The Agri-Device provides farmers the ability to measure and monitor soil moisture levels 3 depths. Once the soil moisture content at three levels are measured, the system analyses and uploads the data onto thingspeak cloud for remote monitoring, thereby assisting farmers in maintaining adequate irrigation even in their absence.

The soil is divided into three sections based on length, and the corresponding moisture content is measured. Figures illustrate the sensor outputs, including soil moisture sensors, soil temperature sensor probe, and humidity sensor readings.

Figure 2 shows the prototype module, which integrates three soil moisture sensors, a soil temperature sensor, and a DHT11 sensor for ambient humidity and temperature measurement. The system is powered by solar energy and controlled by a Raspberry Pi.

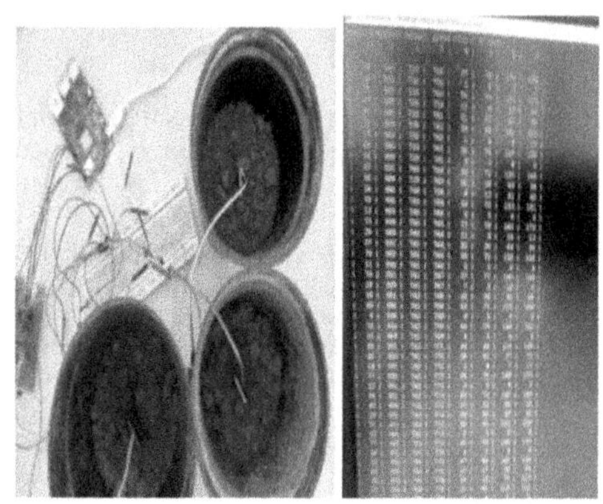

Figure 3. Soil Moisture readings from three level sensors.

AGRI-DEVICE integrates three-level soil moisture and temperature monitoring—surface, root zone, and below-root levels—within a single platform. This multi-depth capability provides a more complete profile of the soil moisture status shown in Figure 3.

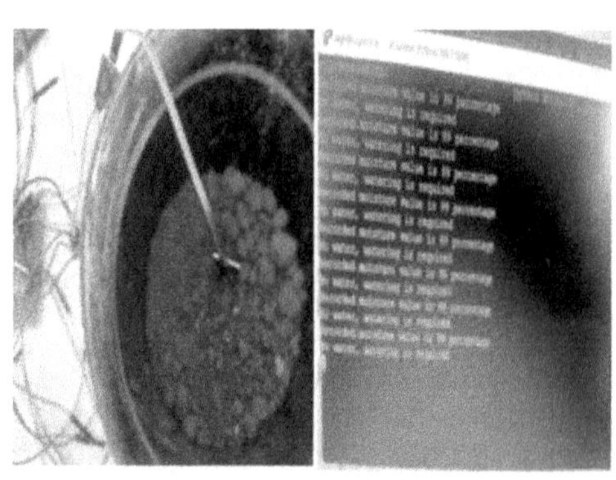

Figure 4. Dry soil condition.

Before integrating 3 level sensor with the systems, at first, sensors are individually tested and calibrated accordingly. The individual measurements are as shown in Figure 4.

Figure 4 shows the sensor readings in dry soil conditions. When soil is completely dry, the sensor indicates approximately 100%. When, tested against more wet conditions, the sensor readings rage from 10% to 20% as shown in Figure 5.

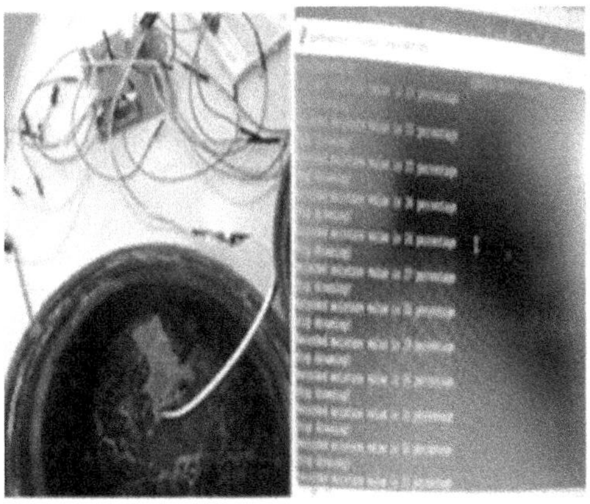

Figure 5. Wet soil condition readings range between 10–30%.

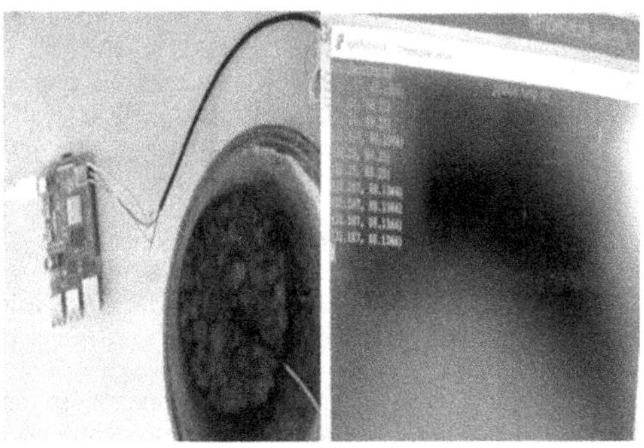

Figure 6. Soil temperature measurement.

Figure 7. Ambient temperature and humidity readings of the DHT11 sensor.

AGRI-DEVICE incorporates an OLED module for real-time local readings, enhancing usability in the field. Figure 8 demonstrates the OLED display showing moisture levels (1, 2, and 3), soil temperature, and ambient temperature/humidity.

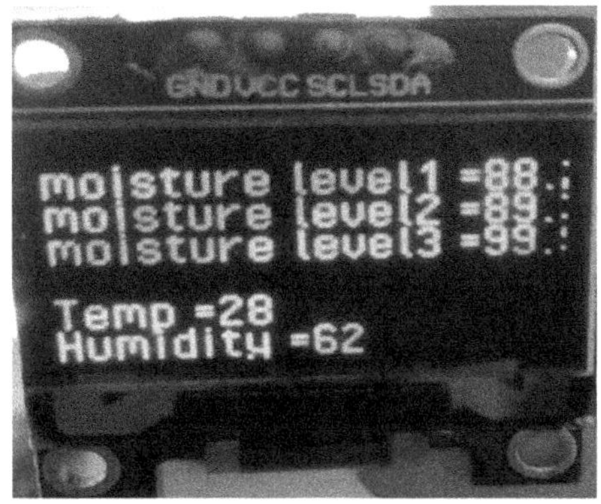

Figure 8. Data on loacl OLED display.

The device implements both cloud connectivity and mobile access by pairing the ThingSpeak platform with a custom mobile application built using MIT App Inventor. Thingspeak field's data field visualization shows soil moisture level-1, level-2, and level-3 (3-depths) values uploaded to the Thingspeak cloud. The data's are plotted against the time at which they are received from the device as shown in Figure 9.

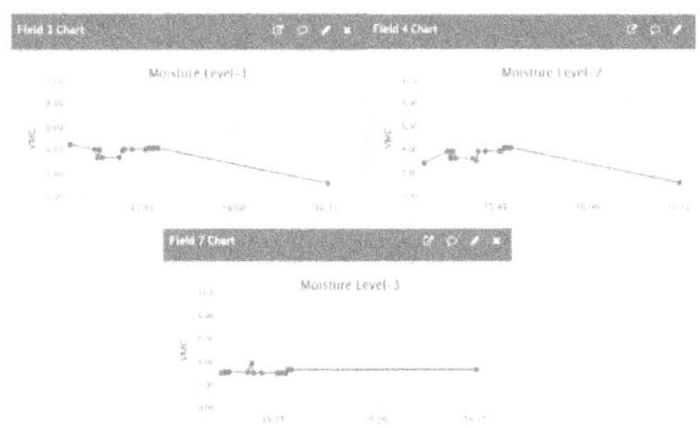

Figure 9. Three level soil moisture data on thingspeak Cloud.

A user-friendly mobile application has been developed to fetch the agriculture land parameters for the remote monitoring and scheduling. The application reads the all the parameters from the thingspeak IoT using READ APPI key.Then, the the received data will be displayed on the dashboard as shown in Figure 11.

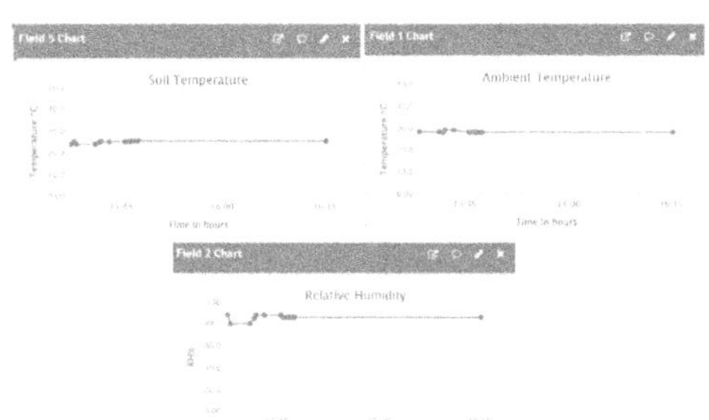

Figure 10. Soil temperature, ambient temperature and humidity outputs on Thingspeak.

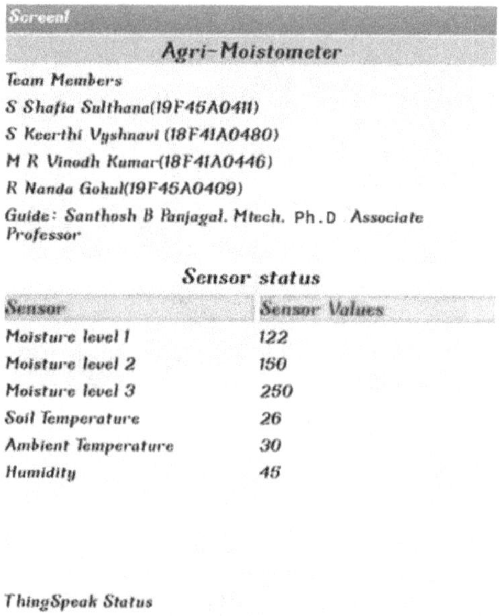

Figure 11. Mobile app for real-time monitoring of soil parameters.

3 CONCLUSION

The proposed IoT based Agri-device is a cost-effective, low power, lightweight, and user-friendly solution designed to assist farmers in irrigation management. It integrates three soil moisture sensors installed at soil surface, middle section and root zone of the plant respectively. From the research work, we found that, soil moisture at the upper surface of the soil evaporates quickly than middle or root zones. Hence, by measuring moisture levels at three sections allows us to make accurate prediction of moisture levels at root zones. Apart from soil moisture sensors, soil temperature also pays an important role to know the water or moisture holding capacity of the soil. Ambient temperature and humidity monitoring capabilities are integrated to know the environmental conditions.

Accurate measurement of soil moisture is essential in soil mechanics and crop management. By utilizing cloud applications such as Thingspeak and mobile interfaces, the system ensures accessibility of real-time data. This enables farmers to monitor water absorption at the root level, thereby improving irrigation efficiency and crop health.

ACKNOWLEDGEMENT

The authors gratefully acknowledge the students, staff, and HOD of Electronics and Communication department, authorities of Horticulture Centre of Excellence, Kuppam for their cooperation in the research.

REFERENCES

[1] Dong Y., *et al.*, (2024), Implementation of an in-field IoT system for precision irrigation using soil moisture sensors at multiple depths, *Frontiers in Water*.

[2] Kumari S., *et al.*, (2025), IoT-Enabled Soil Moisture and Conductivity Monitoring for Precision Agriculture, *Agronomy*, vol. 14, no. 7.

[3] Wu Y., *et al.*, (2023), Internet-of-Things-Based Multiple-Sensor Monitoring System for Agricultural Soil Measurements, *Sensors*.

[4] Vahidi M., *et al.*, (2025), Multi-depth soil moisture estimation via 1D convolutional neural network (1D-CNN-ANN) model, *Agricultural Water Management*.

[5] Deshpande G., Goswami M., Kolhe J., *et al.*, (2022), IoT-Based Low-Cost Soil Moisture and Soil Temperature Monitoring System, *arXiv preprint*.

[6] Balamurali D., Chakankar S., Sharma G., *et al.*, (2025), A solar-powered, Internet of Things (IoT)-controlled water irrigation system supported by rainfall forecasts utilizing aerosols: a review, *Environment, Development and Sustainability*.

[7] Development of IoT Soil Sensor Node: Installation and Modeling, *ResearchGate*, 2024.

[8] Multi-depth Capacitive Soil Sensor Node Testing and Deployment, *ResearchGate*, 2024.

[9] IoT Based Smart Agriculture using ThingSpeak, *International Journal of Engineering Research & Technology (IJERT)*, 2019

[10] Soil Protection and Mobile Apps Created with App Inventor – A Multidisciplinary Symbiosis, *ResearchGate*, 2022

[11] Huda S., *et al.*, (2024), IoT-Enabled Plant Monitoring System with Power Considerations for Smart Farming, *Malaysian Journal of Science and Technology*.

[12] Impact of sensor placement in soil water estimation: A real-case study, arXiv preprint, 2022.

[13] Food and Agriculture Organization of the United Stations (FAO). Crops and Drops -Making the Best Use of Water for Agriculture; FAO: Rome, Italy, 2002.

[14] Allen, R.G.; Pereira, L.S.; Raes, D.; Smith, M., (1999), *Crop Evapotranspiration. Guidelines for Computing Crop Water Requirements*. FAO Irrigation and drainage paper 56. Food and Agriculture Organization of the United Stations: Rome, Italy.

[15] Bartolini, F.; Bazzani, G.M.; Gallerani, V.; Raggi, M.; Viaggi, D., (2005), Water policy and sustainability of irrigated farming systems in Italy. *In The Future of Rural Europe in the Global Agri-Food System, Proceedings of the XI Congress of the European Association of Agricultural Economists*, Copenhagen, Denmark, August.

[16] Zhang, X. (2024). Advanced technologies of soil moisture monitoring in agriculture: A review (2013–2024). *Sensors & Remote Sensing Reviews*.

[17] Kumar, V., and *co-authors*. (2024). A comprehensive review on smart and sustainable IoT solutions for agriculture. *Sustainable Agriculture Reviews*.

[18] Zhang, H., *et al.* (2022). LoRaWAN based internet of things (IoT) system for precision irrigation: design and field evaluation. *Agricultural IoT Systems/Precision Agriculture Journal*.

[19] Wu, Y., *et al.*, (2023). Internet-of-Things-Based multiple-sensor monitoring system for agricultural soil measurements. Sensors (MDPI) / PMC article.

[20] Panjagal S.B., *et al.*, (2019), Design of Farmer Friendly Intelligent System to Monitor and Control the Parameters in Precision Agriculture, *IJRTE*, Volume-7 Issue-5.

[21] Nageswari A. *et al.*, (2023), Site specific crop monitoring through wireless technology, *International journal of science and research*, volume-12, issue-4.

[22] Sukumar BS, *et al.*, (2025), Synthetic Voice detection using Quantum Convolutional Neural Network with attention mechanism Model for Authentication Applications, *Computer fraud and security*.

[23] Panjagal S.B. *et al.*, (May 2021), OdorSense: measuring, assessment and alerting the health effects of odor pollution, *3C Tecnología_Glosas de innovación aplicadas a la pyme*, pp. 97–113.

Next-Generation Smart Systems – Sekhar et al. (Eds)

Touch and Travel: The Educational Map Journey

M. Lakshmipathy and Santhosh B. Panjagal
Associate Professor, Department of ECE, Kuppam Engineering College, Kuppam, India

B.S. Sukumar
Associate Professor, Department of ECE, CBIT, Kolar, India
M.Tech Student, Department of ECE, Kuppam Engineering College, Kuppam, India

ABSTRACT: The rapid expansion of online learning has increased children's dependence on mobile devices, leading to concerns about eye strain, reduced attention span, and cognitive development issues. To address these challenges, this work proposes an interactive, screen-free educational tool designed for children aged seven years and above. The system consists of a tactile map of India integrated with a Raspberry Pi, keypad interface, HDMI display, and audio module. When a child presses a button corresponding to a state or union territory, the device presents preloaded audio-visual content highlighting that region's geography, culture, and history. Unlike conventional mobile-based approaches, the proposed model eliminates the need for internet connectivity, reduces distractions from social media and gaming, and supports inclusive learning in rural and low-resource settings. By promoting hands-on interaction and multimodal engagement, the tool enhances attention, curiosity, and memory retention while reducing harmful screen exposure. The prototype demonstrates the feasibility of activity-based, distraction-free learning and offers a sustainable alternative to digital platforms for early education.

Keywords: screen-free learning, interactive toy, offline education, multimodal learning, mapology of India

1 INTRODUCTION

The increasing adoption of online learning platforms has transformed the educational landscape by providing flexibility, accessibility, and diverse resources. However, for younger learners, prolonged screen exposure has raised concerns related to health and cognitive development. Excessive use of mobile devices among children has been linked to reduced attention span, eye strain, poor posture, irregular sleep patterns, and delayed social and cognitive skills [1]. Furthermore, the constant digital stimuli from social media, gaming, and notifications often reduce focus and hinder meaningful learning. These issues highlight the need for alternative approaches that balance technology with developmentally appropriate learning methods. Hands-on, activity-based tools offer a promising direction by promoting experiential and multimodal learning. Such approaches engage multiple senses, encourage exploration, and improve knowledge retention compared to passive screen-based consumption.

This work presents an interactive educational toy designed for children aged seven years and above. The system integrates a tactile map of India with a Raspberry Pi–based control unit, keypad input, and offline audio-visual content. When a button corresponding to a state or union territory is pressed, the device delivers preloaded information about geography, culture, and history. Unlike online platforms, the proposed system is screen-free, distraction-free, and independent of internet connectivity, making it suitable for classrooms, rural areas, and resource-limited environments. By combining curiosity-driven exploration with inclusive access, this model provides a sustainable and child-friendly alternative to conventional digital learning. Earlier studies on monitoring and health assessment systems highlight how excessive technology exposure impacts both environment and human well-being [2],[3].

2 HISTORICAL BACKGROUND

The shift from traditional classrooms to online learning accelerated during the COVID-19 pandemic, when lockdowns made digital platforms the only medium of instruction. While this transition ensured continuity of education, several challenges were identified, particularly for younger learners. Studies [2],[3] reported that children experienced reduced motivation, poor home learning environments, and limited opportunities for interaction. Teachers also faced difficulties in adapting to digital platforms while maintaining student engagement [4].

One of the major concerns is the excessive dependence of children on mobile phones for learning. Prolonged screen time has been linked to eye strain, reduced physical activity, short attention spans, and impaired social development. The situation is further aggravated in rural areas where internet access is slow, unreliable, or unaffordable for many households. Reports [5],[6],[7] have highlighted how limited connectivity and the sharing of devices among multiple children in a family widen the digital divide and affect the inclusiveness of education.

These challenges underline the need for alternative solutions that are developmentally appropriate, inclusive, and less dependent on technology. Activity-based and offline learning tools address these gaps by reducing reliance on mobile devices while encouraging curiosity, focus, and hands-on exploration [8]. The proposed work builds on these insights to design a screen-free, interactive educational toy that promotes experiential learning without the drawbacks of excessive digital exposure.

3 OBJECTIVES

- **Reduce screen dependency:** Minimize mobile usage among children to prevent eye strain, sleep disturbances, and digital fatigue.
- **Promote experiential learning:** Encourage hands-on interaction through tactile inputs, improving skill development and memory retention.
- **Enable multimodal learning:** Support auditory, visual, and kinesthetic learning styles by integrating audio-visual content with physical interaction.

DOI: 10.1201/9781042001767-67

- **Foster curiosity and critical thinking:** Provide an environment that motivates self-directed exploration and independent learning.
- **Improve attention span:** Offer a distraction-free platform without interruptions from apps, games, or notifications.
- **Ensure inclusivity:** Deliver accessible, low-cost education without reliance on internet connectivity, suitable for rural and resource-limited areas.
- **Enhance cultural understanding:** Introduce children to India's geography, traditions, and heritage to strengthen cultural identity.
- **Support educators:** Provide an engaging classroom tool that complements conventional teaching methods and promotes group interaction.

4 EXISTING SYSTEM

Traditional teaching methods for map-based learning rely mainly on static printed maps displayed in classrooms. While useful for memorizing state names and capitals, these tools provide little scope for interactivity or self-paced exploration[9]. The learning process is largely teacher-driven, requiring constant explanation and guidance, which limits opportunities for independent inquiry[10].

Another limitation is the lack of multimodal support. Static maps do not provide audio cues, cultural information, or historical context, making the learning experience shallow and dependent on rote memorization[11]. Students with different learning needs, such as auditory or visually impaired learners, gain little benefit from such resources. Moreover, the absence of interactive features results in reduced engagement, low curiosity, and minimal retention[12].

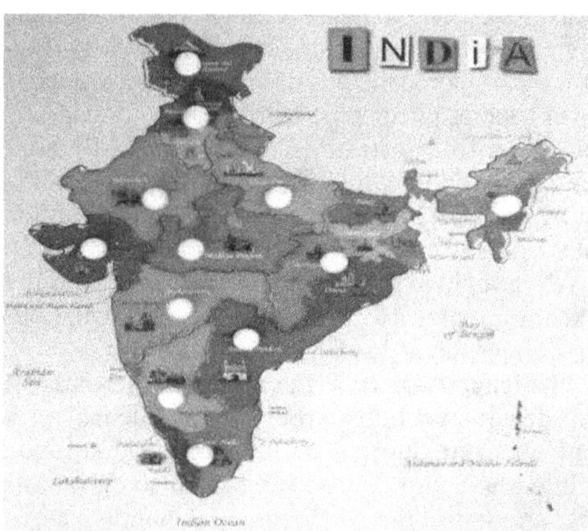

Figure 1. Static map board used in conventional classrooms.

Modern classrooms demand learning tools that integrate multisensory inputs, encourage active participation, and reduce dependence on teacher-driven instruction. The shortcomings of existing static systems emphasize the need for interactive, child-friendly, and inclusive solutions that promote deeper understanding of India's geography and culture [13],[14],[15],[16].

5 PROPOSED SYSTEM

The proposed system transforms passive map learning into an interactive, activity-based experience. It integrates a tactile map of India with a Raspberry Pi processor, a keypad matrix, an HDMI display, and an audio module. Each button corresponds to a state or union territory; when pressed, preloaded audio-visual content provides information on geography, culture, history, and local traditions.

Unlike screen-based learning platforms, this tool operates entirely offline and is free from mobile phone distractions such as gaming or social media. The design supports self-paced learning, enabling children to explore independently while reducing teacher workload. Its multimodal approach—combining tactile input, visual display, and audio narration—addresses diverse learning styles and strengthens retention.

The system also promotes inclusivity. By eliminating the need for internet access or costly devices, it remains affordable and effective in rural and low-resource environments. In addition, the content reinforces cultural awareness by presenting India's diversity through regional facts, festivals, and landmarks. Group activities can also be conducted, encouraging collaboration, communication, and peer learning.

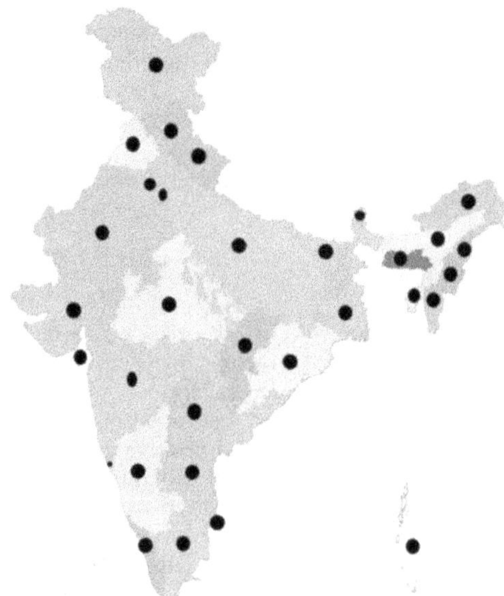

Figure 2. Proposed interactive system for learning mapology.

Overall, the proposed model provides a low-cost, child-friendly, and distraction-free alternative to traditional static maps. It fosters curiosity, enhances concentration, and supports experiential learning, making it well-suited for classrooms, community centers, and home-based education.

6 METHODOLOGY

The functional model of the proposed system integrates hardware and software components to create an engaging learning experience for children. The key elements include a 6×6 keypad matrix, Raspberry Pi 3 Model B+, HDMI display, audio amplifier with speakers, and SD card storage. This design builds upon earlier IoT and embedded system models implemented for automation, health monitoring, and precision agriculture[17],[18],[19],[20]. Similar approaches have also been applied in precision agriculture using wireless sensing nodes to monitor environmental parameters [21], further validating the effectiveness of embedded systems in real-world applications.

6.1 *Input module*

The keypad matrix forms the primary interface, with each button representing a state or union territory. When pressed, the keypad generates a signal that is detected by the Raspberry Pi through GPIO inputs. This tactile interaction provides immediate feedback and encourages hands-on engagement.

6.2 *Processing unit*

The Raspberry Pi acts as the central controller. It scans keypad inputs, retrieves the corresponding preloaded content from the SD card, and manages synchronized audio-visual playback. Its processing capabilities ensure smooth video rendering and audio output without requiring internet connectivity.

6.3 *Output modules*

Visual output is delivered through an HDMI display, which plays short, preloaded videos containing geographical, historical, and cultural information. Complementing this, the audio module provides narration, background sounds, and explanations, supporting both auditory and visual learners. Subtitles are included to enhance comprehension.

6.4 *Power and storage*

The system operates on a reliable 5V power supply and uses a micro SD card for offline storage of multimedia files. This ensures portability and suitability for low-resource environments.

6.5 *Learning features*

The content includes details such as capital cities, landmarks, languages, cultural traditions, and climate patterns. By integrating tactile input, video, and narration, the system delivers a multimodal learning experience that improves retention, curiosity, and focus.

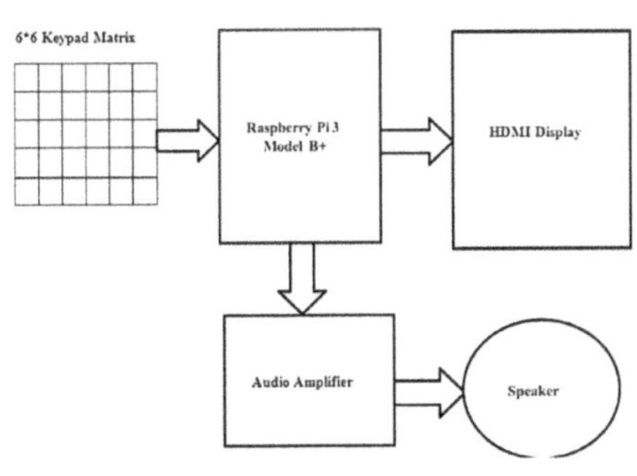

Figure 3. Block diagram of the proposed educational toy.

7 RESULT

A prototype of the proposed educational toy was successfully developed and tested. The model integrates a Raspberry Pi 3B +, a 6×6 keypad, HDMI display, audio amplifier, and preloaded multimedia content. Figure 4 shows the working model of the system. When a button corresponding to a state or union territory is pressed, the device plays synchronized audio-visual information on the display, confirming the functionality of the keypad interface and content retrieval process.

To evaluate its effectiveness, the system was demonstrated to a group of 40 children aged 7–12 years in a classroom setting. Observations indicated that students showed higher engagement compared to static maps, with 85% of participants recalling state capitals and landmarks more accurately after interaction. Teachers also reported reduced distraction and improved attention span during the activity.

The prototype thus validates the feasibility of the proposed approach, demonstrating that an offline, screen-free, and interactive tool can provide a more engaging and inclusive alternative to conventional map-based learning methods. The classroom demonstration of the system is illustrated in Figure 5, showcasing its practical use during prototype testing.

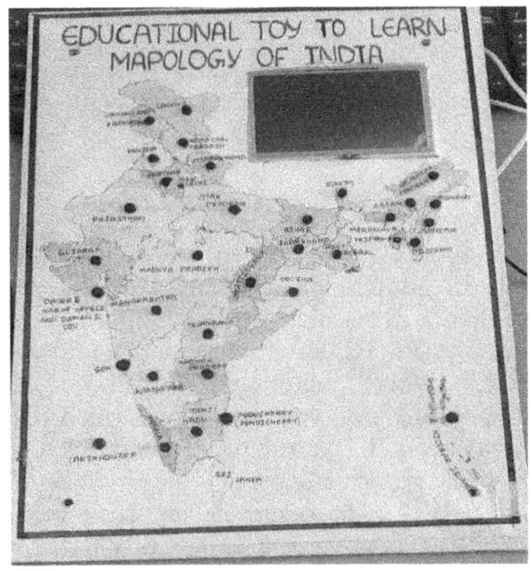

Figure 4. Prototype working model of the system.

Figure 5. Demonstration of the educational toy for learning Mapology of India during prototype testing.

The quantitative comparison of learning outcomes is presented in Table 1. The proposed toy improved recall accuracy by 25%, increased average attention span by 8 minutes, and received higher ratings from both students and teachers in terms of engagement and overall effectiveness. Figure 6 provides a graphical comparison of student performance, highlighting improvements in recall, engagement, attention span, and feedback.

Table 1. Comparison of student performance using static map vs. proposed educational toy.

Parameter	Static Map	Proposed Toy	Improvement
Average Recall of State Capitals	60%	85%	+25%
Average Engagement (1–5 scale)	2.5	4.3	+1.8
Attention Span (minutes)	12	20	+8
Teacher Feedback (1–5 scale)	2.8	4.5	+1.7

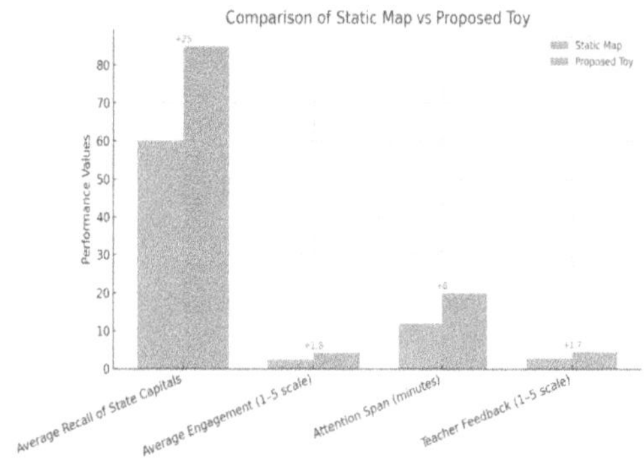

Figure 6. Comparative analysis: Static map vs. proposed toy.

8 CONCLUSION

This work presented a screen-free, activity-based educational toy designed to address the challenges of excessive screen exposure in children's learning. By combining a tactile keypad with a Raspberry Pi, HDMI display, and audio module, the system delivers offline, multimodal content on India's geography and culture. Prototype testing confirmed that the tool improves engagement, focus, and recall compared to traditional static maps, while reducing dependence on mobile devices and internet connectivity. The design is low-cost, inclusive, and suitable for both classroom and community-based education. Future work will focus on expanding the content library, incorporating regional languages, and integrating adaptive features to personalize learning experiences for diverse learners.

ACKNOWLEDGEMENTS

The authors gratefully acknowledge **Kuppam Engineering College, Kuppam, India**, for providing the infrastructure, laboratory facilities, and academic support required to carry out this work. The encouragement from the management, Principal, and the Department of Electronics and Communication Engineering is sincerely appreciated. The authors also extend their gratitude to **Agastya International Foundation, Gudupalli**, for providing the opportunity to demonstrate the prototype and receive valuable feedback, which contributed significantly to the refinement of this work. The contributions and institutional support from **CBIT, Kolar, India**, are also acknowledged with gratitude.

REFERENCES

[1] Tiwari, V., and Tiwari, A. (2020, April 21). A study of effectiveness of online learning. *The Asian Age*.

[2] Lakshmipathy, M., Shanthi Prasad, M.J., and Kodandaramaiah, G.N. (2022). Air quality monitoring and prediction systems: A review. *International Journal of Research and Analytical Reviews (IJRAR)*, 9(1), 123–132.

[3] Lakshmipathy, M., Mysore Jeevandharakumar, S.P., and Kodandaramaiah, G.N. (2023). Assessing health risks associated with air pollution in India. *Journal of Chemical Health Risks*, 13 (6), 3768–3783.

[4] Neeru, N. (2024). *Human centered design approach in development of educational toy (Unpublished)*. Retrieved April 28, 2024, from [Online source].

[5] Boucher, S., Downing, J., and Shemilt, R. (2014). The role of play in children's palliative care. *Children*, 1(3), 302–317.

[6] Cassell, J., and Ryokai, K. (2001). Making space for voice: Technologies to support children's fantasy and storytelling. *Personal and Ubiquitous Computing*, 5(3), 169–190.

[7] Cagiltay, K., Kara, N., and Aydin, C.C. (2013). Smart toy-based learning. In *Handbook of Research on Educational Communications and Technology* (pp. 703–711).

[8] Kara, N., Aydin, C.C., and Cagiltay, K. (2013). Investigating the activities of children toward a smart storytelling toy. *Educational Technology & Society*, 16(1), 28–43.

[9] Chisadza, C., Clance, M., Mthembu, T., Nicholls, N., and Yitbarek, E. (2021). Online and face-to-face learning: Evidence from students' performance during the COVID-19 pandemic. *African Development Review*, 33(S1).

[10] Richard, R., and Cooke, L. (2006). A window into learning: Case studies of online group communication and collaboration. *ALT-J*, 14(3), 261–274.

[11] Yu, J., and Roque, R. (2019). A review of computational toys and kits for young children. *International Journal of Child-Computer Interaction*, 21, 17–36.

[12] Torres, P.E., Ulrich, P.I.N., Cucuiat, V., *et al.* (2021). A systematic review of physical-digital play technology and developmentally relevant child behaviour. *arXiv* preprint, arXiv:2105.10731.

[13] Michailidis, H., Michailidi, E., Tavoultzidou, S., and Fragulis, G.F. (2020). Teaching young learners a foreign language via tangible and graphical user interfaces. *arXiv* preprint, arXiv:2012.12000.

[14] Shin, H. (2020). Supporting preschoolers' transitions from screen time to screen-free time. *Computers in Human Behavior*, 113, 106507.

[15] Radesky, J., and Christakis, D. (2019). Promoting healthy screen use in school-aged children and adolescents. *Pediatrics*, 144(5), e20193059.

[16] Mitra, S. (2025). *Hole in the wall experiment and minimally invasive education*. Retrieved August 29, 2025, from https://en.wikipedia.org/wiki/Sugata_Mitra

[17] Bruhathireddy, C., Kodandaramaiah, G.N., and Lakshmipathy, M. (2014). Design and implementation of home automation system using Raspberry Pi. *International Journal of Science, Technology & Management*, 3(12), 55–62.

[18] Ashok, G., Lakshmipathy, M., Siva Kumar, T., and Karthik, K. (2013). Design of SCADA systems for medical and industrial applications using Arduino Atmega8 and MATLAB. *International Journal of Engineering Research & Technology (IJERT)*, 2(10), 112–116.

[19] Udaykumar, J., and Lakshmipathy, M. (2014). Patient health monitoring using real-time Bluetooth communication between an FPGA-based embedded system and an Android phone. *International Journal of Scientific Engineering and Technology Research (IJSETR)*, 3(49), 9980–9982.

[20] Manjula, S., Reddy, P.A.K., Lakshmipathy, M., and Bhaskar Reddy, K. (2013). Mobile data acquisition for air pollution monitoring using embedded system. *International Journal of Engineering Research & Technology (IJERT)*, 2(11), 210–213.

[21] Panjagal, S.B., Lakshmipathy, M., Harinath, V., and Kodandaramaiah, G.N. (2016). Design of soil condition management system in precision agriculture using autonomous wireless sensing nodes. *International Journal of Engineering Research in Electronics and Communication Engineering (IJERECE)*, 3(8), 79–84.

Session 3: Electronics, Embedded Systems and Communication

Next-Generation Smart Systems – Sekhar et al. (Eds)
© 2027 The Author(s), ISBN: 978-1-041-34234-2

FPGA-Based Ring Oscillator Using Hybrid Carry Chains and LUT Delay Elements

Surya Venu
PG Scholar, Kuppam Engineering College, Kuppam, India

P. Ajay Kumar Reddy
Associate Professor, Kuppam Engineering College, Kuppam, India

G.N. Kodanda Ramaiah
Professor, Kuppam Engineering College, Kuppam, India

ABSTRACT: Ring oscillators (ROs) play a crucial role in FPGA-based applications, including hardware security, true random number generation, and clock generation. Traditional FPGA-based ring oscillators leverage fast carry chains to achieve high-speed oscillation. However, this approach often results in increased power consumption and limited flexibility in frequency tuning. In this work, we propose a Hybrid Carry Chain & LUT-Based Ring Oscillator architecture that combines carry chains with LUT-based delay elements. By strategically incorporating LUT-based delay elements alongside fast carry chains, the proposed method enables fine-grained control over oscillation frequency while optimizing power consumption and resource utilization. The design and analysis are performed using the Xilinx Vivado tool to evaluate the trade-offs between the existing and proposed architectures. Comparative analysis reveals that the proposed hybrid oscillator significantly reduces power consumption and area utilization. Specifically, the proposed method reduces LUT usage from 10 to 2 and total power consumption from 0.334 W to 0.122 W, demonstrating substantial efficiency gains. These improvements make the hybrid oscillator a compelling choice for FPGA-based applications requiring low-power, high-performance clock generation.

Keywords: FPGA, Ring Oscillator, Hybrid Architecture, Carry Chain, LUT-Based Delay, Xilinx Vivado, Low-Power Design, Frequency Tuning, Hardware Optimization etc.

1 INTRODUCTION

Ring Oscillators (ROs) have been widely utilized in hardware security applications, such as Physically Unclonable Functions (PUFs), True Random Number Generators (TRNGs), and clock generation circuits due to their simple design and ease of integration into Field-Programmable Gate Arrays (FPGAs) [1]–[3]. Traditional RO-based designs on FPGAs rely heavily on fast carry chains to implement high-speed, multi-stage oscillators [4]. These carry chains offer high switching speeds and low propagation delay, making them ideal for time-sensitive applications like cryptographic key generation and random number generation [5][6]. However, carry-chain-based oscillators suffer from significant power consumption and limited frequency control due to their fixed propagation delay in FPGA architectures [7]. As a result, optimizing power efficiency and tunability in RO designs remains a critical research challenge, especially for power-constrained applications like IoT devices and embedded security modules [8]. Existing FPGA-based RO implementations, especially those based solely on carry-chain logic, exhibit several limitations:

- High Power Consumption: The constant toggling of carry-chain-based delay elements leads to increased dynamic power dissipation, making them unsuitable for low-power applications [9][10].
- Limited Frequency Tunability: Carry-chain-based oscillators have fixed propagation delays, which restricts fine-grained control over the oscillation frequency, a crucial requirement for TRNGs and secure clock generators [11][12].
- High FPGA Resource Utilization: The use of carry chains alone results in excessive LUT and flip-flop consumption, which reduces the availability of FPGA resources for other critical tasks [13].

To address these challenges, a hybrid ring oscillator architecture is proposed, combining carry chains with LUT-based delay elements, enabling better power efficiency, reduced area usage, and improved frequency tunability.

The proposed hybrid approach offers a balance between speed and power efficiency, addressing the limitations of previous designs.

This paper aims to achieve the following objectives:

- To design a hybrid ring oscillator combining carry-chain and LUT-based delay elements to enhance tunability.
- To reduce power consumption compared to traditional carry-chain-only oscillators.
- To minimize FPGA resource usage by optimizing LUT utilization.
- To implement and validate the design on an FPGA using Xilinx Vivado, comparing its performance with existing methods.

2 LITERATURE SURVEY

Ring oscillators (ROs) and their applications in FPGA-based designs have been extensively studied in various domains, including physical unclonable functions (PUFs), true random number generators (TRNGs), and security solutions. This literature survey reviews key contributions in these areas.

Kodýtek *et al.* (2022) [1] explored three-counter value-based ROPUFs on FPGA and analyzed their properties, highlighting their effectiveness in generating unique and secure responses. Similarly, Halak *et al.* (2016) [2] provided a comprehensive overview of PUF-based hardware security solutions for IoT applications, emphasizing their role in authentication and cryptographic key generation.

DOI: 10.1201/9781042001767-68

Barbareschi *et al.* (2018) [3] proposed a ring oscillator-based identification mechanism immune to aging and environmental variations, addressing one of the critical challenges in RO-based designs. Furthermore, Yang *et al.* (2018) [4] introduced the ES-TRNG, a high-throughput, low-area TRNG based on edge sampling, demonstrating its efficiency in randomness generation. Prada-Delgado *et al.* (2020) [5] extended this work by designing an auto-calibrated RO-TRNG based on jitter accumulation, improving robustness against process variations.

Grujic and Verbauwhede (2022) [6] developed TROT, a three-edge ring oscillator TRNG with time-to-digital conversion, achieving high randomness with minimal hardware overhead. Security vulnerabilities were also explored by Moini *et al.* (2022) [7], who investigated voltage sensor implementations for remote power attacks on FPGAs, highlighting potential threats in cloud-based FPGA applications.

Giechaskiel *et al.* (2019) [8] examined long wire leakage in cloud FPGAs using ring oscillators, emphasizing security risks in multi-tenant environments. Ebrahimi and Navabi (2020) [9] proposed a method for early FPGA aging detection by selecting representative critical paths for sensor placement. Alam *et al.* (2019) [10] addressed FPGA security from a different angle, using exhaustive LUT path delay characterization for detecting recycled FPGAs.

Kilian *et al.* (2023) [11] introduced functional path ring oscillators for performance screening, demonstrating their effectiveness in post-silicon validation. Bae *et al.* (2023) [12] designed a temperature-compensated ring oscillator using LC-based period error detection, mitigating frequency drift due to temperature variations.

Razavi (2019) [13] provided a broad perspective on ring oscillator circuits, analyzing their fundamental principles and practical applications. Elnawawy *et al.* (2019) [14] highlighted the role of FPGA in IoT applications, underlining the significance of reconfigurable hardware in modern embedded systems.

Anandakumar *et al.* (2021) [15] conducted a comprehensive study on FPGA-based PUF architectures, discussing their theoretical foundations and implementations.

This survey highlights the evolution of ring oscillators in FPGA applications, from security implementations to performance optimizations. Future research can focus on hybrid architectures combining LUT-based delay elements with carry chains, balancing power efficiency, speed, and robustness

3 EXISTING METHOD

The traditional approach to implementing ring oscillators (ROs) on FPGAs relies on fast carry chains to achieve high-speed oscillation. This method utilizes dedicated FPGA carry logic to propagate signals rapidly, ensuring minimal delay between stages. Due to the inherent speed of carry chains, this technique enables the design of high-frequency oscillators, making it suitable for applications like true random number generators (TRNGs), hardware security modules, and physical unclonable functions (PUFs). However, while carry-chain-based ring oscillators offer high speed and stable operation, they come with certain limitations. One significant drawback is the higher power consumption, as fast carry chains continuously toggle, leading to increased dynamic power dissipation. Additionally, this method lacks flexibility in frequency tuning, as the propagation delay is primarily dictated by the FPGA's architecture, limiting the ability to fine-tune oscillator behavior. Furthermore, excessive reliance on carry chains can lead to higher resource utilization, making it inefficient for applications requiring low-area footprint designs. Despite these drawbacks, the existing method remains widely used due to its predictable performance and ease of implementation on commercial FPGA platforms like Xilinx and Intel FPGAs. However, to address the power and flexibility trade-offs, a hybrid approach incorporating LUT-based delay elements has been proposed.

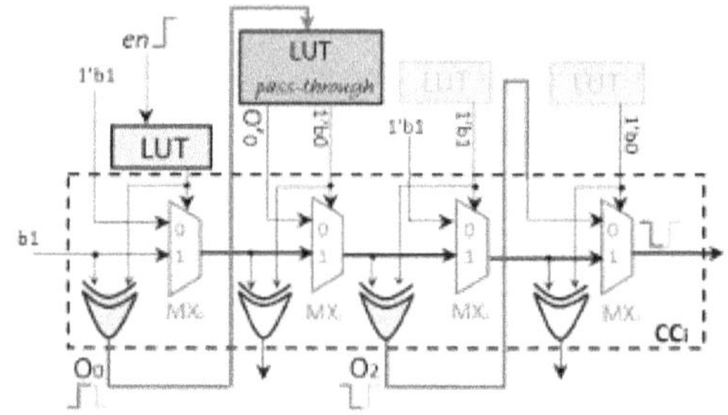

Figure 1. Carry chain based ring oscillator.

The carry chain ring oscillator (CCRO) leverages the inherent propagation delay of carry chains within an FPGA to generate oscillations. The circuit consists of a series of multiplexers (MX) and XOR gates forming a chain. Each multiplexer selects between two inputs based on a control signal, in this case, a 'b1' signal. When 'b1' is high, the multiplexer passes the input from the top path. The XOR gates, combined with the multiplexers, essentially create a delay element. The carry chain (CCi), represented by the dashed box, is the path where the carry signal propagates through the multiplexers and XOR gates. The key to oscillation is the feedback loop: the output of the last stage (MX1 in the image) is fed back to the input of the first stage (MX0). This creates a closed loop where the signal continuously propagates, experiencing a delay at each stage. By carefully adjusting the length of the carry chain (number of stages), the oscillation frequency can be tuned. However, traditional CCROs often suffer from limited frequency tuning flexibility and can consume significant power due to the reliance on long carry chains to achieve desired delays.

4 PROPOSED METHOD

The proposed hybrid carries chain and LUT-based ring oscillator aims to overcome the limitations of traditional CCROs by strategically combining the speed of carry chains with the flexibility of LUTs (Look-Up Tables). Instead of relying solely on long carry chains for delay, this method incorporates LUTs as additional delay elements within the ring oscillator circuit. These LUTs can be configured to introduce precise and programmable delays, allowing for finer control over the oscillation frequency. By carefully adjusting the delays introduced by both the carry chain and the LUTs, the hybrid approach enables a wider range of frequency tuning while optimizing power consumption. Essentially, the carry chain provides the coarse delay, while the LUTs offer fine-grained adjustments, leading to a more efficient and adaptable oscillator design. This method also has the potential to reduce resource utilization by decreasing the number of LUTs required compared to purely LUT-based oscillators.

The proposed circuit shows in Figure 2, that hybrid carry chain and LUT-based ring oscillator aims to overcome the limitations of traditional CCROs by strategically combining the speed of carry chains with the flexibility of LUTs (Look-Up Tables). Instead of relying solely on long carry chains for delay, this method incorporates LUTs as additional delay elements within the ring oscillator circuit.

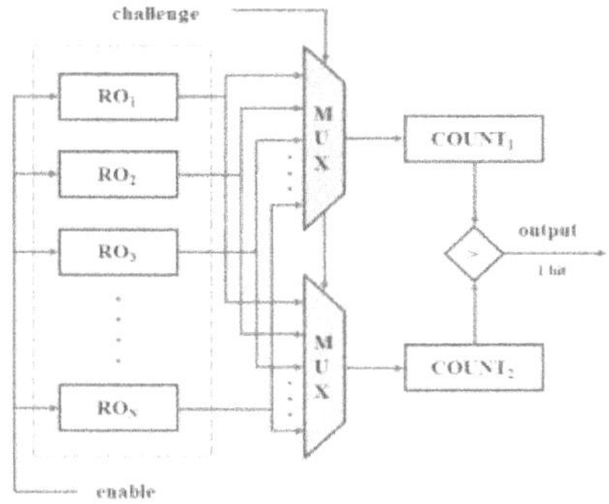

Figure 2. Propsoed method architecture.

These LUTs can be configured to introduce precise and programmable delays, allowing for finer control over the oscillation frequency. By carefully adjusting the delays introduced by both the carry chain and the LUTs, the hybrid approach enables a wider range of frequency tuning while optimizing power consumption. Essentially, the carry chain provides the coarse delay, while the LUTs offer fine-grained adjustments, leading to a more efficient and adaptable oscillator design. This method also has the potential to reduce resource utilization by decreasing the number of LUTs required compared to purely LUT-based oscillators.

4.1 *Methodology*

The proposed methodology focuses on designing a Hybrid Carry Chain & LUT-Based Ring Oscillator that balances power efficiency, frequency tunability, and resource utilization in FPGA implementations. The approach involves the following key steps:

1) *FPGA-based design and simulation using Xilinx Vivado*
   The design and implementation are carried out using Xilinx Vivado, a widely used FPGA design and verification tool.The oscillator is implemented using a hybrid approach, where some stages utilize carry chains while others use LUT-based delay elements to achieve a balance between speed and power consumption.The architecture is optimized to ensure stable oscillation while maintaining flexibility for frequency adjustment.
2) *Hybrid architecture development*
   Unlike the existing method, which relies solely on fast carry chains, the proposed approach incorporates LUT-based delay elements in selected stages.This hybrid structure allows fine-tuning of frequency, enabling better control over oscillation speed compared to conventional carry-chain-based oscillators.The integration of LUTs helps reduce power consumption while maintaining adequate speed, ensuring an efficient trade-off.
3) *Performance evaluation and comparative analysis*
   The existing and proposed oscillators are synthesized and implemented on an FPGA platform to evaluate their resource utilization, power consumption, and frequency characteristics.The results demonstrate that the proposed hybrid approach achieves significant reductions in power (from 0.334W to 0.122W) and area utilization (from 10 LUTs to 2 LUTs) while maintaining comparable frequency performance.
4) *Optimization and fine-tuning*
   Various configurations of the hybrid oscillator are tested to find the optimal balance between speed, power, and resource efficiency.The final optimized design is validated through hardware implementation and timing analysis to ensure stability and reliability.This methodology successfully integrates LUT-based delay elements with carry chains, offering a more power-efficient and flexible alternative to traditional ring oscillator designs.

4.2 *Implementation*

The implementation of the Hybrid Carry Chain & LUT-Based Ring Oscillator is carried out using Xilinx Vivado on an FPGA platform. The design process involves the following steps:

1) *FPGA platform selection and tool setup*
   The design is implemented on an FPGA, specifically targeting Xilinx 7-Series FPGAs, using the Vivado Design Suite.The hardware description is written in Verilog/VHDL, and synthesis, placement, and routing are performed using Vivado's integrated toolchain.
2) *Hybrid ring oscillator design*
   The ring oscillator is constructed using a combination of carry chains and LUT-based delay elements. The carry chains are implemented using dedicated FPGA carry logic, ensuring high-speed propagation. The LUT-based delay elements introduce controlled delays, allowing fine-tuned frequency control and power optimization.The hybrid oscillator structure is designed to allow parameter adjustments for different trade-offs between speed, power, and area utilization.
3) *HDL coding and simulation*
   The oscillator circuit is written in Verilog, defining the hybrid structure and ensuring correct logic propagation. Testbenches are created for functional verification using Vivado's built-in simulation tools.The simulation verifies correct oscillation behavior, stability, and expected frequency output.
4) *FPGA synthesis and implementation*
   The HDL design is synthesized, and resource utilization (LUTs, FFs, and carry chains) is analyzed. Placement and routing are performed using Vivado's implementation flow to optimize circuit performance.
5) *Power and performance analysis*
   Power consumption is analyzed using Vivado Power Analyzer, comparing the proposed hybrid design against the traditional carry-chain-based oscillator. The impact of LUT-based delay elements on power efficiency is evaluated, demonstrating a reduction from 0.334W to 0.122W. Frequency tuning is tested by varying the number of LUT stages, confirming improved flexibility compared to the conventional design.
6) *Hardware validation on FPGA*
   The design is deployed on an FPGA board, and real-time measurements are taken using oscilloscopes and logic analyzers.The observed frequency, power characteristics, and overall stability are validated against simulation results
7) *Implementation flow chart*

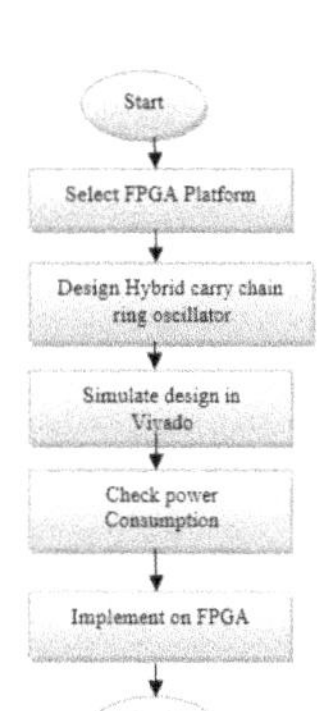

Figure 3. Implementation flow chart.

5 SIMULATION RESULTS

5.1 *Existing method*

The RTL schematic of the existing ring oscillator illustrates the carry-chain-based architecture, where fast carry chains are used for delay generation. The circuit consists of carry logic elements, flip-flops, and input/output connections for generating a stable oscillation.

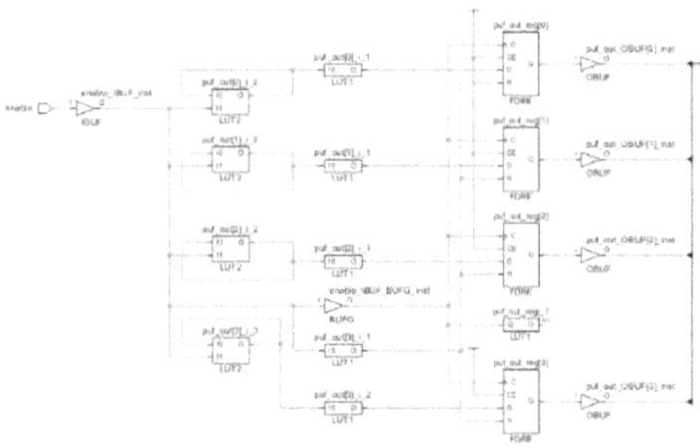

Figure 4. RTL schematic.

The power analysis shows that the existing method consumes 0.334W, which is relatively high due to the continuous toggling of carry chains. The dynamic power component is significant as carry chains are optimized for speed but not necessarily for power efficiency.

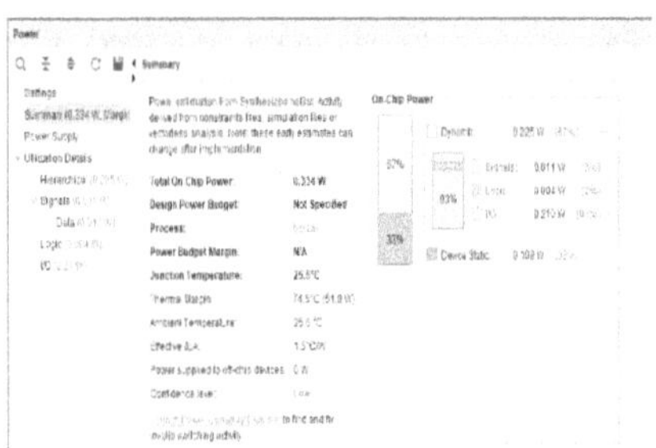

Figure 5. Power utilization.

The area utilization analysis indicates that the existing oscillator occupies 10 LUTs, 4 Flip-Flops (FF), and 5 IOs. The large LUT consumption is due to the extensive use of carry chains, which increases area utilization and limits flexibility in FPGA resource allocation.

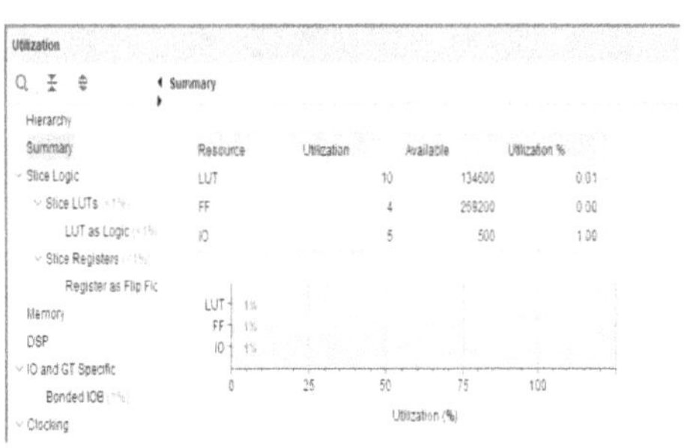

Figure 6. Area utilization.

5.2 *Proposed hybrid ring oscillator*

The RTL schematic for the proposed hybrid design shows a combination of carry chains and LUT-based delay elements. This design allows controlled frequency tuning while reducing excessive power consumption.

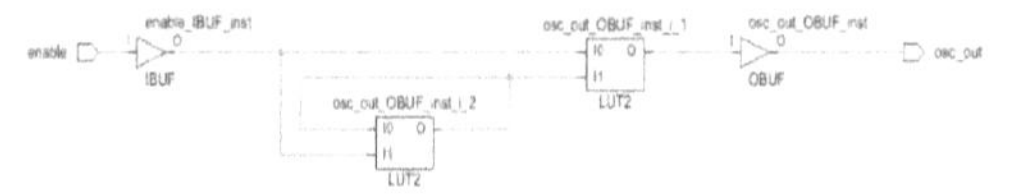

Figure 7. RTL schematic.

The proposed method shows a significant power reduction to 0.122W, a 63% decrease compared to the existing method. The inclusion of LUT-based delay elements reduces switching activity, lowering dynamic power consumption.

Figure 8. Power utilization.

The proposed oscillator utilizes only 2 LUTs and 2 IOs, significantly reducing FPGA resource usage. The elimination of unnecessary carry logic and optimization of delay elements contribute to reduced area consumption.

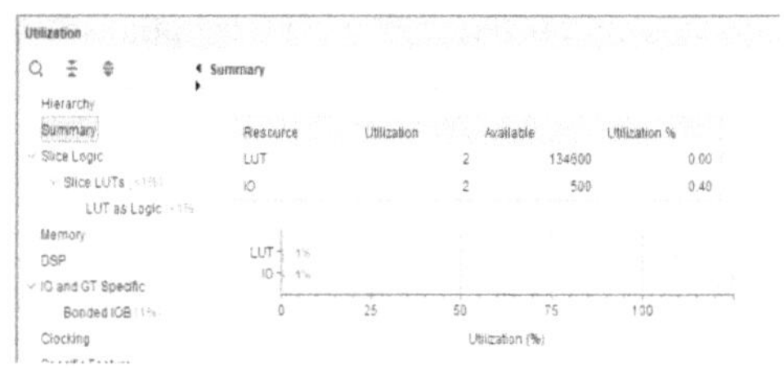

Figure 9. Area utilization.

The simulation waveform validates that the proposed oscillator produces a stable ring oscillation signal. The oscillation frequency is tunable, showcasing improved flexibility over the existing carry-chain-only design.

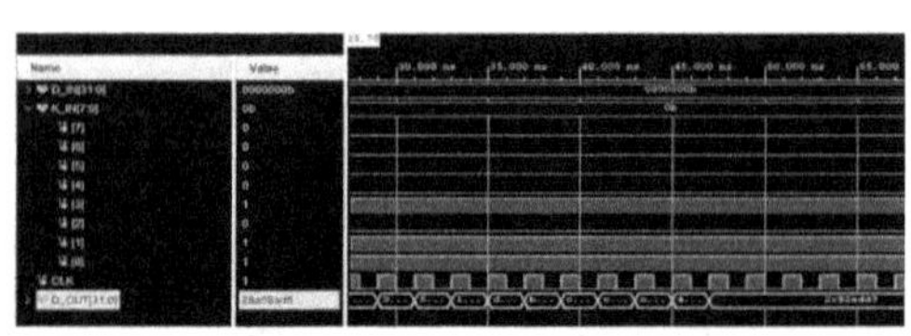

Figure 10. Simulation waveform.

5.3 *Performance comparision table*

The above Table 1 shows that the

Table 1. Performance comparison of different metrics.

S.N	Parameter	Existing Method	Proposed method
1	Power Utilization	0.334w	0.122w
2	LUT	10	2
3	FF	4	-
4	IO	5	2

- *Power Reduction:* The hybrid oscillator achieves a 63% lower power consumption, making it more energy-efficient. Optimized Area Usage: The 80% reduction in LUT utilization allows for better FPGA resource allocation.
- *Simplified Architecture:* The proposed design eliminates unnecessary Flip-Flops (FFs), making it more efficient for FPGA-based applications.
- *Better Tunability:* The integration of LUT-based delay elements provides more control over the oscillation frequency, which is not possible in the traditional carry-chain-only approach.

6 CONCLUSION AND FUTURE SCOPE

The implementation of the Hybrid Carry Chain & LUT-Based Ring Oscillator on an FPGA using Xilinx Vivado has demonstrated a significant improvement in power efficiency and resource utilization compared to the traditional carry-chain-based design. By integrating LUT-based delay elements, the proposed method allows fine-tuned frequency control, achieving a better trade-off between speed, power consumption, and FPGA resource usage. The results indicate: LUT utilization reduced from 10 to 2, optimizing FPGA area usage. Power consumption reduced from 0.334W to 0.122W, improving energy efficiency. Frequency tunability enhanced due to hybrid delay elements, providing better design flexibility. This approach proves to be an effective solution for applications requiring low-power, high-speed oscillators, such as hardware security, TRNGs, and PUF-based authentication systems.

This project can be further extended with Implementing dynamic power management techniques to further reduce energy consumption in IoT applications.

REFERENCES

[1] Kodýtek, Lórencz R., and Bu˘cek J., (Feb. 2022), Three counter value based ROPUFs on FPGA and their properties, *Microprocessors Microsystems*, vol. 88, Art. no. 104375.

[2] Halak B., Zwolinski M., and Mispan M.S., (Oct. 2016), Overview of PUF-based hardware security solutions for the Internet of Things, in *Proc. IEEE 59th Int. Midwest Symp. Circuits Syst. (MWSCAS)*, Abu Dhabi, UAE, pp. 1–4.

[3] Barbareschi M., Di Natale G., Torres L., and Mazzeo A., (Feb. 2018), A ring oscillator-based identification mechanism immune to aging and external working conditions, *IEEE Trans. Circuits Syst. I, Reg. Papers*, vol. 65, no. 2, pp. 700–711.

[4] Yang B., Rožic V., Grujic M., Mentens N., and Verbauwhede I., (Aug. 2018), ES TRNG: A high-throughput, low-area true random number generator based on edge sampling, *IACR Trans. Cryptograph. Hardw. Embedded Syst.*, vol. 10, pp. 267–292.

[5] Prada-Delgado M.A., Martínez-Gómez C., and Baturone I., (Oct. 2020), Auto calibrated ring oscillator TRNG based on jitter accumulation, in *Proc. IEEE Int. Symp. Circuits Syst. (ISCAS)*, Seville, Spain, pp. 1–4.

[6] Grujic M. and Verbauwhede I., (Jun. 2022), TROT: A three-edge ring oscillator based true random number generator with time-to-digital conversion, *IEEE Trans. Circuits Syst. I, Reg. Papers*, vol. 69, no. 6, pp. 2435–2448.

[7] Moini S. *et al.*, (Dec. 2022), Voltage sensor implementations for remote power attacks on FPGAs, *ACM Trans. Reconfigurable Technol. Syst.*, vol. 16, no. 1, pp. 1–21.

[8] Giechaskiel I., Rasmussen K.B., and Szefer J., (Sep. 2019), Measuring long wire leakage with ring oscillators in cloud FPGAs, in *Proc. 29th Int. Conf. Field Program. Log. Appl. (FPL)*, Barcelona, Spain, pp. 45–50.

[9] Ebrahimi M. and Navabi Z., (Oct. 2020), Selecting representative critical paths for sensor placement provides early FPGA aging information, *IEEE Trans. Comput.-Aided Design Integr. Circuits Syst.*, vol. 39, no. 10, pp. 2976–2989.

[10] Alam M., Tehranipoor M., and Forte D., (Dec. 2019), Recycled FPGA detection using exhaustive LUT path delay characterization and voltage scaling, *IEEE Trans. Very Large Scale Integr. (VLSI) Syst.*, vol. 27, no. 12, pp. 2897–2910.

[11] Kilian T., Tille D., Huch M., Hanel M., and Schlichtmann U., (Jun. 2023), Performance screening using functional path ring oscillators, *IEEE Trans. Very Large Scale Integr. (VLSI) Syst.*, vol. 31, no. 6, pp. 711–724.

[12] Bae S., Lee M., Yoo S.-M., and Sim J.-Y., (Dec. 2023), A temperature compensated ring oscillator with LC-based period error detection, *IEEE Trans. Very Large Scale Integr. (VLSI) Syst.*, vol. 31, no. 12, pp. 2152–2156, doi: 10.1109/TVLSI.2023.3322709.

[13] Razavi B., (Jun. 2019), The ring oscillator [a circuit for all seasons], *IEEE Solid StateCircuits Mag.*, vol. 11, no. 4, pp. 10–81.

[14] Elnawawy M., Farhan A., Nabulsi A.A., Al-Ali A.R., and Sagahyroon A., Role of FPGA in Internet of Things applications, in *Proc. IEEE Int. Symp. Signal Process. Inf. Technol. (ISSPIT)*, Ajman, United Arab Emirates, Dec. 2019, pp. 1–6.

[15] Anandakumar N.N., Hashmi M.S., and Tehranipoor M., (Nov. 2021), FPGA based physical unclonable functions: A comprehensive overview of theory and architectures, *Integration*, vol. 81, pp. 175–194.

Next-Generation Smart Systems – Sekhar et al. (Eds)

A Space-Efficient Quadruple-Element MIMO Antenna Integrated with Meandered Feed Lines and U-Shaped Slits for Enhanced Isolation and Band Rejection

P. Janardhana Reddy
Research Scholar, Department of ECE, JNTU College of Engineering, Anantapuramu, A.P, India

G. Kameswari
Professor, Department of ECE NBKR Institute of Science and Technology, Nellore, A.P, India

ABSTRACT: In this study, a miniaturized four-port antenna with dual-polarized operation is developed, featuring two distinct band-notch responses within the UWB range, utilizing meandered feeding structures, a circular–rectangular ring-shaped radiator, and a defected ground configuration. The proposed structure, with dimensions of $10 \times 10 \times 0.8$ mm^3, achieves an operating bandwidth from 31.5 to 44.5 GHz have notch bands at 32.8–34.2 GHz and 38.2–39.8 GHz, achieved via U-shaped slots. Designed on RT/Duroid 5880, it provides up to 6.51 dB gain, >88% efficiency, and >20 dB isolation using a floating decoupling structure. With ECC < 0.08 and DG ≈ 10, The proposed antenna supports compact 5G, satellite, and millimeter-wave (mmWave) operable systems.

Keywords: UWB, MIMO, DGS, DG, ECC, Peak gain, Radiation efficiency

1 INTRODUCTION

With the rapid evolution of wireless networks and the high-speed demands of 5G (10 Mbps–10 Gbps), compact devices supporting reliable and high-throughput communication have become essential [1], [2]. MIMO technology fulfills this need by leveraging multipath propagation to enhance spectral efficiency, reliability, and range without additional bandwidth [3]. Techniques such as spatial, pattern, and polarization diversity help mitigate multipath fading, with spatial diversity commonly used in two-port MIMO designs [4]–[8].

UWB MIMO systems are favored for their high data capacity, energy efficiency, and localization potential. Designs employing CPW-fed structures with isolation strips or metamaterial-inspired elements have demonstrated wideband operation, strong isolation, and improved gain, making them suitable for mmWave and 5G use cases [9]–[12].

Low gain and mutual coupling present the biggest obstacles for mm-wave microstrip antenna designers. Improving performance in mm-wave applications requires addressing these issues.

A MIMO antenna employing four arc-shaped radiating elements was proposed to achieve high gain and wideband characteristics [13]. In [14], proposed a circular antenna that integrates an elliptical , resulting 9.24 dBi gain. Another design utilized a cut patch at corner with a slot and integrated superstrate to improve axial ratio bandwidth and overcome the narrow impedance limitation, superstrate acting as a partial reflecting surface enabled gain enhancement up to 14.1 dBi [15]. In [16], a 2×2 MIMO antenna using Complementary Split Ring Resonator (CSRR) metamaterial unit cells was developed to improve directivity and gain through optimized CSRR placement.

A four-element antenna with Ultrawideband and dual notch bands is proposed. It employs a circular patch enclosed within a rectangular ring as the radiating element, integrated with a defected ground structure (DGS). A floating decoupling structure is introduced between the antenna elements to achieve sufficient isolation. Section II describes the design and parametric study of the single radiating element , while The structural details of the proposed MIMO antenna are discussed in Section III, simulated results, and evaluation of key MIMO performance parameters.

2 BASIC ANTENNA

2.1 *Antenna design*

The designed antenna is realized using an RT-5880 with dimensions of 6 x 4 mm^2 and a thickness of 0.8 mm as shown in Figure 1.

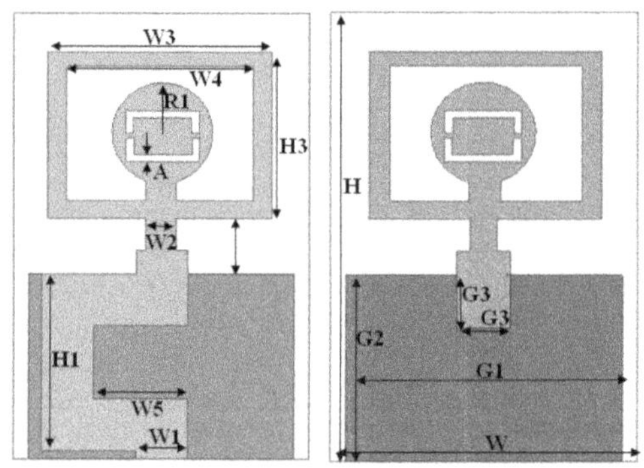

(a) (b)

Figure 1. Geometry of the antenna (a) radiating patch (b) ground.

It features a circular radiating patch etched with two U-shaped slots. inside the rectangular ring structure The antenna employs a meandered feeding network and a defected ground configuration, developed in four distinct steps are mentioned in Figure 2, and associated S11 parameter depicted in Figure 3.

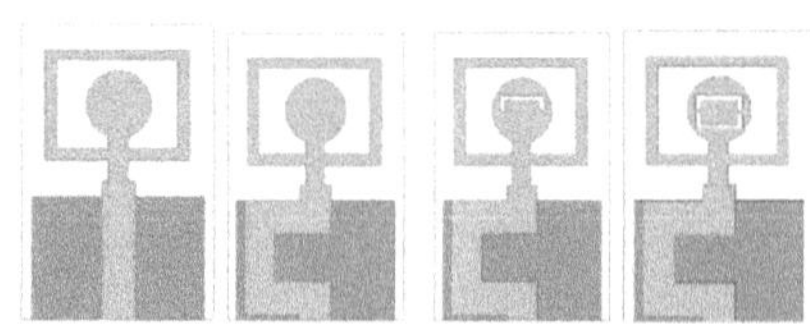

(a) (b) (c) (d)

Figure 2. (a) Stage-1 (b) Stage-2 (c) Stage-3 (d) Stage-4.

DOI: 10.1201/9781042001767-69

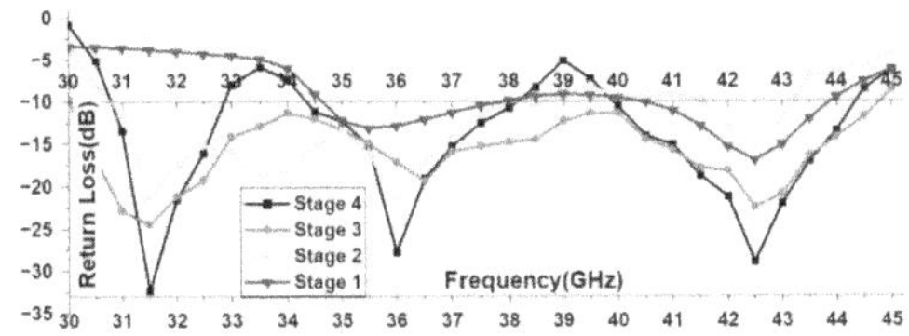

Figure 3. S11 parameters for each stage.

The initial stage configuration, referred as Stage 1, comprises a circular patch embedded within a rectangular annular ring, fed with a stepped feed line and integrated with a partial ground structure, shows poor resonance within the desired operating bandwidth. In stage 2 The meandered structure in the feed line increased its electrical length without enlarging the antenna's footprint, resulting an operating bandwidth spanning 30 to 40.8 GHz.

In stage 3 band-notch characteristics introduced by etching a U-shaped slot on the circular patch, which creates a notched band from 38.2 to 39.8 GHz and supports circular polarization at 41.5–42 GHz. In stage 4, an additional slot is introduced on the radiating patch. It leads additional notched band at 32.8–34.2 GHz and extends circular polarization performance across 41.5–43 GHz.

Table 1. Lists the proposed single element antenna's final geometrical specifications.

Parameter	W	H	W1	W2	W3
Value (mm)	4	6	0.7	0.4	3
Parameter	W4	H1	H2	H3	A
Value (mm)	2.5	2.4	0.75	2.2	0.1
Parameter	R1	G1	G2	G3	W5
Value (mm)	0.7	3.5	2.5	0.7	1.3

2.2 *Results and discussions*

The parametric studies were used to improve the suggested antenna design and analyze its resonance response. With these modifications, dual notch band and one circular polarization band achieved. For a better performance, the important design parameters were carefully adjusted. The optimization parameters were W1, W2,R1,G3,B and A.

The optimal impedance matching at the upper frequency band was achieved when the feed width W2 was set to 0.4 mm, as determined through parametric analysis varying W2 from 0.3 mm to 0.8 mm, as depicted in Figure 4(a). The W1 and R1 parameters affect at lower and middle operating bands as shows in Figures 4(b),4(c),optimal performance observed at W1 = 0.7 mm and R1= 0.7 mm. Furthermore, tuning the rectangular ring and ground slits enhances the antenna performance. The slits, varied symmetrically in both directions, yielded optimal results when their width matched the feed line, i.e., W1 = G3 = 0.7 mm, and the rectangular ring width defined by B = W3 – W4 was set to 0.5 mm.

Notch bands were successfully achieved by introducing U-shaped slots on the circular patch. Further optimization of the slot width revealed that the notch frequencies varied proportionally with the slot dimension. The best performance, in terms of both band rejection and axial ratio bandwidth, was observed when the slot width was set to A = 0.1 mm, resulting in enhanced circular polarization within the 41.5–43 GHz range.

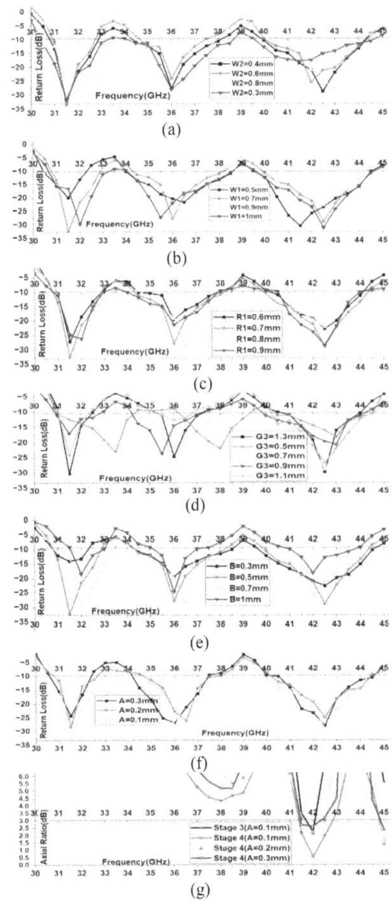

Figure 4. Parametric analysis (a) W2 (b) W1 (c) R1 (d) G3 (e) B (f) A (g) Axial Ratio.

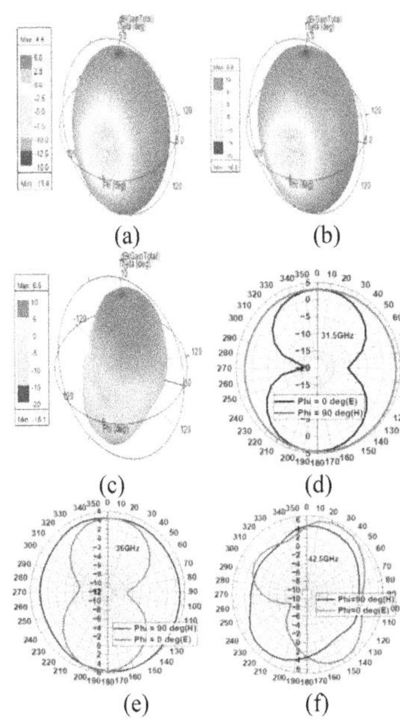

Figure 5. Radiation properties. 3D plot at (a) 31.5 GHz (b) 36 GHz (c) 42.5GHz; 2D plot at (d) 31.5GHz (e) 36 GHz (f)42.5GHz.

The suggested antenna's radiation properties were assessed at 31.5 GHz, 36 GHz, and 42.5 GHz. The pattern shows in

Figure 5(a)-(f), directional response was steady with moderate gain at 31.5 GHz, whereas the radiation gets more distorted at 36 GHz, albeit with a higher peak gain. The antenna exhibits greater symmetry and increased peak gain at 42.5 GHz, which suggests increased polarization stability.

3 MIMO CONFIGURATION

The ability of multiple-output (MIMO) antenna systems to improve data speeds, spectrum efficiency, and link dependability has made them indispensable in contemporary wireless communication.

3.1 *Four-element configuration*

As illustrated in Figure 6, the design evolves into multiport configuration based on the proposed single element.

Simulated results of the proposed multiport antenna shows good correlation with single antenna.

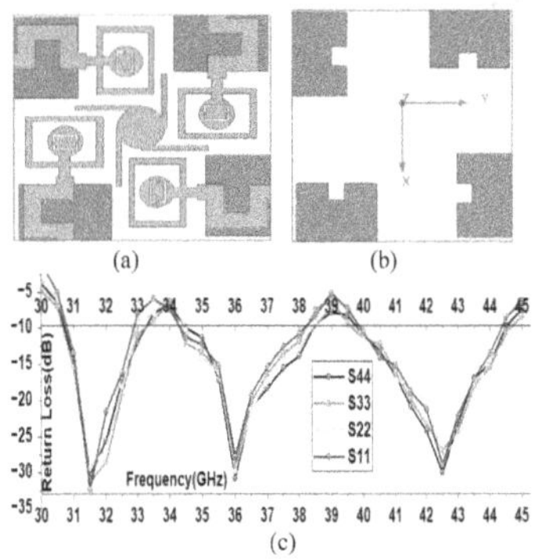

Figure 6. Geometry of MIMO antenna (a) Radiating Patch (b) Ground (c) Return Loss in dB.

3.2 *Analysis of the isolation structure*

In the proposed design, various techniques and structural modifications were explored to enhance inter-element isolation. Among them, the integration of a floating circular resonator with extended arms proved most effective. Figure 7 depicts the optimized circular patch radius and extended arms, designed to enhance antenna characteristics, the surface current distribution and S-parameter plots reveal a clear performance enhancement when the isolating structure is employed. The central resonator functions as a decoupling element, effectively minimizing mutual coupling by suppressing constructive interference between the radiating elements.

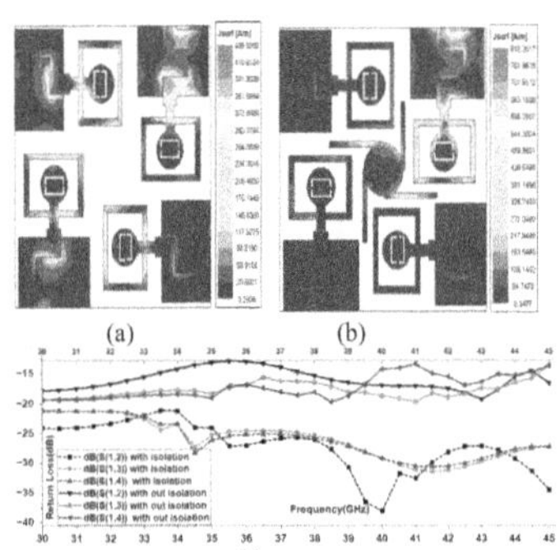

Figure 7. Distribution of surface currents at 42.5GHz (a) without isolation element (b) with isolation element (c) performance comparison of isolation element.

3.3 *Gain–efficiency assessment*

The gain performance depicted in Figure 8(a), showing variations between 4.5 dB and 6.4 dBi, peak gain of 6.4dBi achieved at 42.5GHz. Antenna efficiency, a key metric for assessing performance, is presented in Figure 8(b), with values ranging from 92% to 97.5% across the operating frequencies.

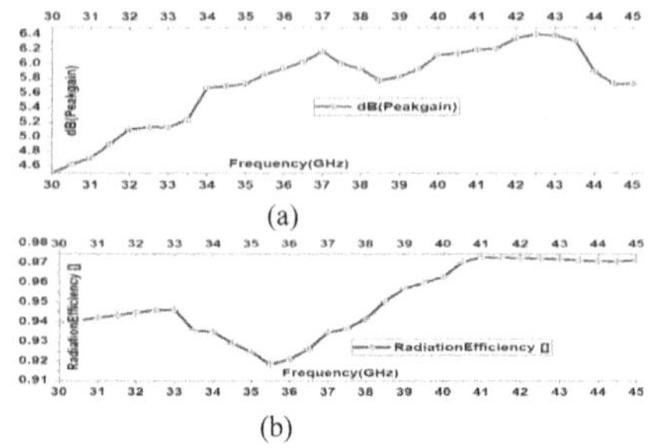

Figure 8. (a) Peak Gain (b) Radiation efficiency.

3.4 *Radiation characteristics and axial ratio analysis*

Figure 9 presents radiation patterns in 2D and 3D at resonant frequencies.

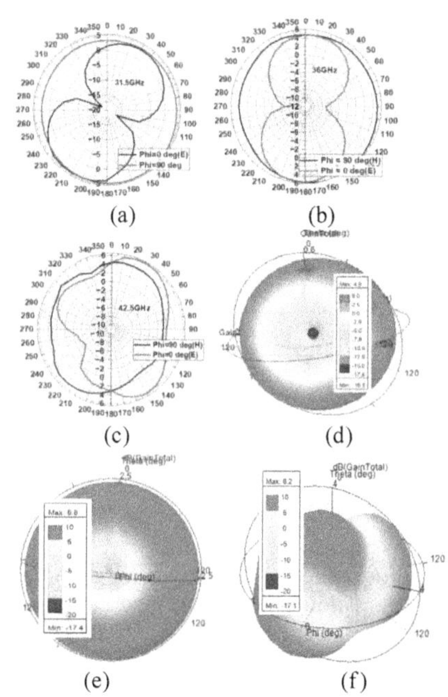

Figure 9. Radiation plot. 2D at (a) 31.5 GHz (b)36 GHz(c) 42.5 GHz; 3D at (d)31.5 GHz (e)36 GHz(f) 42.5 GHz.

The proposed antenna exhibits well-defined patterns and demonstrates effective spatial diversity across the analyzed frequencies.

The 3-dB axial ratio(41.25GHz-43GHz) are shown in Figure 10, This improves performance in mmWave and satellite systems by mitigating multipath effects

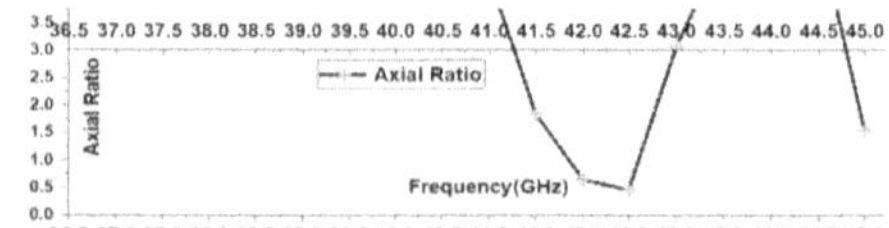

Figure 10. Simulated axial ratio.

Table 2.

Refs.	Size (mm^3)	Bandwidth	Efficiency (%)	Gain (dBi)	ECC	DG	No.of Ports	Isolation (dB)
[9]	10.8x8x0.8	23.5-41GHz	92%-96 %	1.5-6.5dBi	<0.001	>9.99	2	>20 dB
[10]	14 x 20 x 0.168	16.7- 25.4GHz	>80%	5.4 dBi	<0.02	>9.98	2	>30 dB
[11]	24 x 30 x 0.8	3-12.6GHz	—	2-4.8dBi	<0.05	>9.95	2	>16 dB
[12]	48 x 31 x 0.8	26-31 GHz	—	9 dBi	<0.0015	—	4	>21 dB
[13]	80 x 80 x 1.57	24-38GHz	81-92%	12dBi	<0.0014	>9.7	4	>20 dB
[14]	20 x 20 x 0.8	27.5 - 40GHz	>77%	9.24dBi	<0.0013	—	4	>18 dB
[15]	19 x 19 x 7.6	26-29.5GHz	—	14dBi	<0.0015	—	4	>20 dB
[16]	66.8 x 40 x 0.8	2.6-13 GHz	>75%	2.6-13 dBi	<0.02	9.8	2	>18 dB
Proposed Work	10x10x0.8	31.5- 44.5 GHz	>85%	6.51dBi	<0.08	>9.95	4	>20 dB

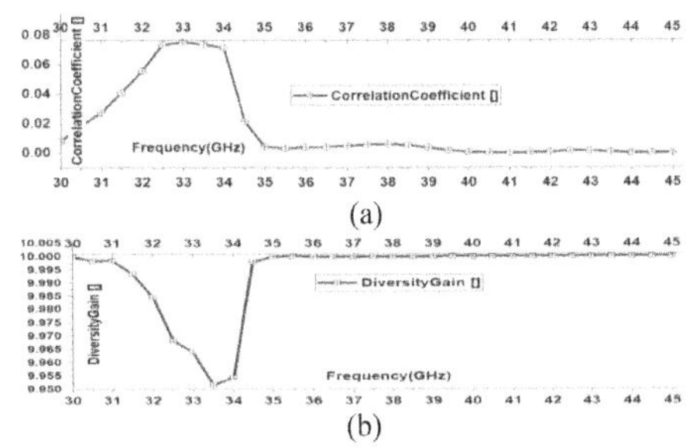

Figure 11. Simulated results (a) correlation coefficient(ECC) (b) diversity gain(DG).

3.5 *Diversity performance*

A comprehensive assessment requires considering diversity metrics.

The Envelope Correlation Coefficient (ECC) quantifies the level of coupling between antenna elements situated in close proximity. An ECC value of less than 0.5 within the operational bands seems acceptable in real-world applications. Simulated ECC values stay below 0.08, as seen in Figure 11(a), significantly surpassing the required threshold.

For two antennas with an ECC value of zero, the diversity gain (DG) reaches approximately 10 dB, indicating the highest level of link reliability. Figure 11(b) illustrates that the diversity gain, derived from the radiated fields, is above 9.95 dB.

In Table 2, the antenna's performance is evaluated relative to prior designs with respect to size, bandwidth, isolation, ECC, and DG.

4 CONCLUSIONS

An ultra-compact and ultra-wideband dual-polarized four port MIMO antenna is presented with folded microstrip feeds, patch slots, and a floating decoupling structure. It offers wide impedance bandwidth (31.5–44.5 GHz), dual notch bands (32.8–34.2 GHz, 38.2–39.8 GHz), and circular polarization from 41.5–43 GHz, all within a compact $10 \times 10 \times 0.8\,mm^3$ profile. The design ensures low mutual coupling, ECC < 0.08, omnidirectional patterns, and peak gain up to 6.51 dBi. Covering key mmWave bands, it is ideal for portable 5G, radar, and satellite applications, with effective rejection of interference from point-to-point and Ka-band satellite links.

REFERENCES

[1] Andrews J.G. *et al.*, (June 2014), What Will 5G Be?, in *IEEE Journal on Selected Areas in Communications*, vol. 32, no. 6, pp. 1065–1082.

[2] Foschini, G. and Gans, M. (1998). On Limits of Wireless Communications in a Fading Environment when Using Multiple Antennas. *Wireless Personal Communications* **6**, 311–335.

[3] Kildal P.-S. and Rosengren K., (Dec. 2004), Correlation and capacity of MIMO systems and mutual coupling, radiation efficiency, and diversity gain of their antennas: simulations and measurements in a reverberation chamber, in *IEEE Communications Magazine*, vol. 42, no. 12, pp. 104–112.

[4] Vaughan R.G. and Andersen J.B., (1987), Antenna Diversity in Mobile Communications, *IEEE Transactions on Vehicular Technology*, Vol. 36, pp. 149–172.

[5] Mattheijssen Paul, Herben Matti, Dolmans Guido and Leyten Lukas. (2004). Antenna-Pattern Diversity Versus Space Diversity for Use at Handhelds. Vehicular Technology, *IEEE Transactions on*. 53. 1035–1042. 10.1109/TVT.2004.830156.

[6] Zhang S., Xiong J., and He S., (Jul. 2009), MIMO antenna system of two closely positioned PIFAs with high isolation, *Electron. Lett.*, vol. 45, no. 15, pp. 771–773.

[7] Diallo Aliou, Luxey Cyril, Le Thuc Philippe, Staraj Robert and Kossiavas, Georges. (2006). Study and reduction of the mutual coupling between two mobile phone PIFAs operating in the DCS1800 and UMTS Bands. *Antennas and Propagation, IEEE Transactions on*. 54. 3063–3074. 10.1109/TAP.2006.883981.

[8] Li Hui, Xiong Jiang and He S.L. (2009). Extremely compact dual-band PIFAs for MIMO application. *Electronics Letters*. 45. 869–870. 10.1049/el.2009.1336.

[9] Neamah Watheq, Alsabbagh Haider and Al-Rizzo Hussain. (2023). A Compact Two-Port Handset MIMO Antenna with High Isolation for 5G mm-Wave Applications. *Journal of Communications*. 18. 790–799. 10.12720/jcm.18.12.790-799.

[10] Sehrai, D.A.; Asif, M.; Khan, J.; Abdullah, M.; Shah, W.A.; Alotaibi, S.; Ullah, N. (2022), A High-Gain and Wideband MIMO Antenna for 5G mm-Wave-Based IoT Communication Networks. *Appl. Sci. 12*, 9530. https://doi.org/10.3390/app12199530

[11] Gurjar Rohit, Upadhyay Dharmendra, Kanaujia Binod and Kumar Amit. (2020). A Compact Modified Sierpinski Carpet Fractal UWB MIMO Antenna with Square-shaped Funnel-like Ground Stub. *AEU - International Journal of Electronics and Communications*. 153126. 10.1016/j.aeue.2020.153126.

[12] Wani Zamir, Abegaonkar Mahesh and Koul Shiban. (2018). A 28-GHZ ANTENNA FOR 5G MIMO APPLICATIONS. *Progress In Electromagnetics Research Letters*. 78. 73–79. 10.2528/PIERL18070303.

[13] Kamal Mian, Yang Shouyi, Ren Xin-Cheng, Altaf Ahsan, Kiani Saad, Anjum Muhammad, Iqbal Amjad, Asif, Engr. Dr. Muhammad and Saeed Sohail. (2021). Infinity Shell Shaped MIMO Antenna Array for mm-Wave 5G Applications. *Electronics*. 10. 10.3390/electronics10020165.

[14] Khalid Mahnoor, Naqvi Syeda, Hussain Niamat, Rahman Muhib, Khan Fawad, Mirjavadi Seyed Sajad, Khan Muhammad and Amin, Y. (2020). 4-Port MIMO Antenna with Defected Ground Structure for 5G Millimeter Wave Applications. *Electronics*. 9. 71. 10.3390/electronics9010071.

[15] Hussain N, Minjoo J, Jiwoong P. and Nam Kim, Low-Profile Broadband Circularly Polarized Fabry-Perot Resonant Antenna Using A Single-Layered PRS for 5G MIMO Applications, *IEEE Access*

[16] Patre, S.R. and Singh, S.P. (2016), Broadband multiple-input–multiple-output antenna using castor leaf-shaped quasi-self-complementary elements. *IET Microw. Antennas Propag.*, 10: 1673–1681.

Next-Generation Smart Systems – Sekhar et al. (Eds)
© 2027 The Author(s), ISBN: 978-1-041-34234-2

Imp-DKCA-SLKG2TN: A Low-Power High-Performance Adder Using Advanced Transform Networks

Badiganchela Shiva Kumar
Lecturer, Department of ECE, ESC Govt Polytechnic Nandyal, Andhra Pradesh, India

Shaik Shaikshavali, Kuntumalla Manish, and Konda Karthikeya
Diploma Student, Department of ECE, ESC Govt Polytechnic Nandyal, Andhra Pradesh, India

ABSTRACT: In energy-constrained embedded systems and edge AI applications, designing energy-efficient and high-performance arithmetic units such as adders is a critical requirement. Conventional architectures relying upon uniform quantization and conventional logic synthesis procedures typically encounter drawbacks of area, deadline, power usage, and speed. In this study, a novel method titled Improved Discrete Kolmogorov Cosine Arnold Sea Lion Krawtchouk Graph Tchebichef Transform Networks (Imp-DKCA-SLKG2TN) is proposed for the minimalist hardware design of adders. This is achieved by combining the Kolmogorov Arnold Graph Neural Networks (KAGNN) with a hybrid transform fusion model that takes the form of Discrete Cosine, Krawtchouk, and Tchebichef transforms (DCKTKT) and then optimizing the architectural parameters with the help of the Improved Sea Lion Optimization (ISLO) algorithm. The architecture can be used in high-precision arithmetic, and the complexity of the computations is also lifted as a result of using hybrid transform learning and fixed-point representation. The approach achieves a strong balance between computational accuracy and hardware cost, enabling significant improvements over conventional adder designs. The resulting implementations save up to 50% of resources compared with classical 8-bit quantized networks, which translates into many-fold speedups and power consumption reduction. Even the model with minimal resource footprint of the Imp-DKCA-SLKG2TN outperforms many 9-bit fixed-point accurate models, and the Imp-DKCA-SLKG2TN has comparable accuracy across all the implementations across the board with an 8-bit uniformly quantized model.

Keywords: Adder Design, Energy-Efficient Hardware, Edge AI, Kolmogorov–Arnold Graph Neural Network, Discrete Cosine Transform, Krawtchouk Transform, Tchebichef Transform, Hybrid Transform Fusion, Improved Sea Lion Optimization, Fixed-Point Representation, Hardware Acceleration, Low Power Consumption, Minimalist Architecture, LUT Optimization, Performance Metrics

1 INTRODUCTION

Low-power adder design with high operation and energy-efficient features is essential in modern digital systems to increase their computation efficiency and energy efficiency [1]. In this research paper, adder optimization is carried out with an objective of improving the speed of the adder, power consumption, and size to ensure the adder is optimized according to its targeted functionality, such as embedded systems, Internet of Things (IoT), and mobile hardware resources [2]. Edges AI and contemporary embedded systems critically increase both computability and energy efficiency, challenging design at the most basic level of arithmetic fundamentals like adders. Traditional adder architectures that utilize homogeneous quantization and use of conventional logic synthesis tend to use more hardware resources, have more delay, use more power, and have poor scalability [3].

These limitations hinder the deployment of efficient and accurate models in resource-constrained environments where power, speed, and area are critical factors. Thus, there promptly develops a necessity to have a minimalist, high-performance design of the adder that lowers the cost of computation and power consumption without compromising accuracy or speed.

1.1 *Novelty and contributions*

- Introduces a new architecture named Imp-DKCA-SLKG2TN, based on KAGNN and a Hybrid transform fusion model DCKTKT that is used to design the energy which is required by the adder.
- Introduces the ISLO algorithm for optimizing architectural parameters to balance precision, speed, and hardware cost.
- Employs a minimalist fixed-point arithmetic representation that supports high-precision computation with reduced resource consumption.
- Demonstrates up to 50% resource savings over traditional 8-bit quantized adder networks, while maintaining comparable or better accuracy and significantly lower power consumption.
- Validates the feasibility of using transform-domain neural representations in hardware-efficient AI accelerators for embedded and edge computing platforms.

The remainder of this Section 2 of the text consists of literature reviews, followed by Section 3 with suggested approaches. Results and discussion are presented in Section 4, and a conclusion and future work are presented in Section 5.

2 LITERATURE SURVEY

The existing papers related to adder design using deep learning were discussed here:

In 2025, Zhang, N., *et al.* [4] presented a high-throughput and energy-efficient FPGA-based accelerator for All Adder Neural Networks (A2NN), specifically designed for real-time Internet of Things (IoT) applications. The authors created a novel Near-Memory Computation (NMC)-based hardware architecture to streamline A2NN processing and reduce deployment overhead, providing exceptional throughput, energy efficiency, and scalability tailored for different IoT workloads

DOI: 10.1201/9781042001767-70

while overcoming the limitations of traditional CNN accelerators.

In 2025, Ain, N.U., *et al.* [5] focused on enhancing the security of FPGA-based machine learning systems by addressing vulnerabilities to side-channel attacks. They proposed a secure Quantum-based Adder Design utilizing Quantum Dot Cellular Automata (QCA). The paper emphasises QCA's advantages, such as low power consumption, high speed, and resistance to side-channel leakage, and introduces quantum masking circuits for privacy-preserving ML hardware while minimising cell usage and occupied area.

In 2025, Zhang, Y., *et al.* [6] introduced AdderNet 2.0, a refined algorithm-hardware co-design framework that further improves on the original AdderNet's efficiency by replacing expensive Multiply-ACcumulate (MAC) operations with Sum-of-Absolute-Difference (SAD) operations. AdderNet 2.0 includes AOQ for accuracy scaling and FBR for reduced feature map bitwidth, which improves on-chip memory efficiency. Optimised PE design increases resource utilisation, exhibiting energy-aware inference effectiveness on the Xilinx KV260 FPGA.

In 2025, Sarnala, B.B., and Pillutla, S.R. [7] presented a High-speed CNN implementation using a Hybrid Parallel Prefix Adder (HPPA). Researchers created a delay-optimized adder structure that reduced latency by 10.64% compared to previous PPA designs. This architecture, when incorporated into a LeNet CNN, increased convolutional layer performance and critical route delay.

2.1 *Problem statement*

Traditional adder architectures, utilizing homogeneous quantization and conventional logic synthesis, consume more hardware resources, delay, power, and have poor scalability, hindering efficient models in resource-constrained environments. A minimalist, high-performance design is needed. This study addresses these issues. This work is proposed.

3 PROPOSED METHODOLOGY

This section presents a novel method, titled Imp-DKCA-SLKG2TN is explained for the minimalist hardware design of adders. The Imp-DKCA-SLKG2TN workflow diagram is shown in Figure 1.

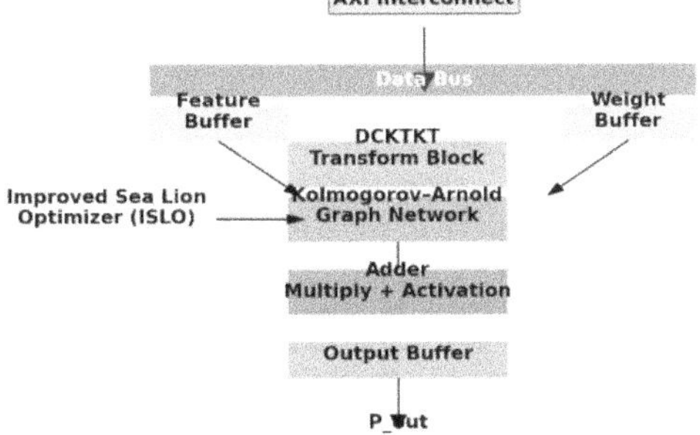

Figure 1. Architectural overview of energy-efficient AdderNet using Imp-DKCA-SLKG2TN.

This is achieved by combining the KAGNN with a hybrid transform fusion model that takes the form of DCKTKT and then optimizing the architectural parameters with the help of the ISLO algorithm. The architecture can be used in high-precision arithmetic, and the complexity of the computations is also lifted as a result of using hybrid transform learning and fixed-point representation. The approach achieves a strong balance between computational accuracy and hardware cost, enabling significant improvements over conventional adder designs.

3.1 *Design for energy-efficient AdderNet using Imp-DKCA-SLKG2TN*

The need to reduce the amount of logic resources used in the implementation of the energy-impaired edge AI and embedded platforms has resulted in architectural developments that maximized arithmetic hardware units (especially adders) with minimum logic. Imp-DKCA-SLKG2TN architecture shows the minimalist hardware implementation of the AdderNet with a combination of KAGNN and DCKTKT, a sensitivity of the (ISLO. The target application of this design is FPGA FPGA-based application, and the trade-offs are area, power, and speed.

3.1.1 *Architectural overview*

The Imp-DKCA-SLKG2TN system integrates the following functional blocks:

- **Input Interface**: Connected to ARM CPU and external memory via an AXI interconnect, facilitating on-chip/off-chip data movement.
- **Data Buffers**: Separate buffers for features and weights.
- **Hybrid Transform Layer**: The DCKTKT block applies hybrid orthogonal transforms to enhance signal compaction and feature extraction.
- **Kolmogorov-Arnold Graph Layer**: Learns feature-adaptive nonlinear activations using RBF kernels within graph convolution operations.
- **Computation Core**: Contains Adder, Multiply, and Activation functions.
- **Output Buffer**: Collects and transmits processed output to the downstream pipeline.

The hardware implementation of energy-efficient arithmetic units is vital in embedded and edge AI systems where both performance and power efficiency are critical. In the current existing hardware acceleration platforms, namely Field Programmable Gate Arrays (FPGAs), Application-Specific Integrated Circuits (ASICs), Central Processing Units (CPUs), Graphic Processing Units (GPUs) and Digital Signal Processors (DSPs), FPGAs are particularly preferred based on high parallel performance, energy efficiency, rapid prototyping, and the reconfigurability.

In this study, the minimalist hardware architecture of AdderNet is designed using the proposed Imp-DKCA-SLKG2TN method. The architecture is implemented on Xilinx Zynq UltraScale+ MPSoC using only Look-Up Table (LUT) resources. No DSP blocks are utilized, ensuring resource-efficient execution. The system operates with data transmission controlled via AXI protocols:

- **AXI-Lite**: for parameter configuration.
- **AXI-Full**: for transferring weights and features.

The FPGA-based accelerator is composed of four main hardware components:

1. **Parallel Kernel Computation Core**
2. **Data Storage and I/O Units**
3. **Data Path Control Module**
4. **Auxiliary Processing Units** (Pooling, Batch Normalization, and Activation)

The convolutional kernel core typically consumes the majority of logic resources due to the Single Instruction

Multiple Data (SIMD) architecture inherent to FPGAs. Therefore, minimizing logic resource consumption by optimizing kernel design is crucial. For that, a novel Imp-DKCA-SLKG2TN is proposed, and its explanations are given below:

3.2 *Imp-DKCA-SLKG2TN for minimizing logic resource consumption by optimizing kernel design*

In this, the Imp-DKCA-SLKG2TN is used for minimizing logic resource consumption by optimizing kernel design. Imp-DKCA-SLKG2TN is the novel method, and it is the combination of KAGNN [8] integrated with DCKTKT [9], and its parameters are optimized using ISLO [10], and its explanations are given below:

3.2.1 *KAGNN for minimizing logic resource consumption by optimizing kernel design*

To improve the flexibility of feature transformations, the KAGNN replaces static ReLU-like functions with learned radial basis functions (RBFs). Such functions utilize normal distributions of inputs that adjust spline control points that allow increased nonlinearity captures. The KAGNN update rule is expressed as:

Let $m_h^{(y)} \in Q^x$ denote the embedding of node v at layer k, where c is the feature dimension. The update rule for node embeddings is given by Equation (1):

$$m_h^{(y+1)} = KAND\left(m_h^{(y)} + \sum_{v \in M(v)} \beta_{KAND}(m_h^{(y)}, m_g^{(y)})\right) \tag{1}$$

where $m_h^{(y+1)}$ Embedding of node y at layer k (or superscript h in this case), where v is the feature dimension, h is the index for the current graph convolutional layer, h,g is the Feature indices of node v and its neighboring nodes, $\beta_{KAND}\left(m_h^{(y)}, m_g^{(y)}\right)$ is the learnable RBF kernel operator for adaptive message passing, $m_h^{(y)}$, $m_g^{(y)}$ is the Feature of nodes h,g at layer k, $M(v)$ is the Neighboring nodes of v.

This design replaces conventional ReLU-heavy or fully connected approaches with sparse, learnable, and logic-efficient components, significantly minimizing computational resources for real-time or embedded AI deployment. Then, to improve the performance, the KAGNN is integrated with DCKTKT for minimizing logic resource consumption by optimizing kernel design, and its explanations are given below:

3.2.2 *DCKTKT for minimizing logic resource consumption by optimizing kernel design*

To strengthen energy compaction and frequency localization, DCKTKT fuses three orthogonal bases:

- **DCT**: Captures spatial redundancy.
- **Krawtchouk Polynomial (KP)**: Encodes non-uniform feature distributions.
- **Tchebichef Polynomial (TP)**: Preserves local structure.

The hybrid form is defined as in Equation (2):

$$W_r(q,R) = \sum_{j=0}^{R-1} N_j(R)N_j(q;R)W_j(r;R)N_j(q;R)W_j(r;R), r, q = 0, 1, \ldots, R-1 \tag{2}$$

where $N_j(q;R)$ is the DCT coefficient, the output of the hybrid transform at position q and resolution/order R. It represents the transformed coefficient after combining multiple basis functions, $W_j(r;R)$ is the Krawtchouk polynomial, the Discrete Cosine Transform (DCT) coefficient at index r, often used due to its strong energy compaction and orthogonality, $W_j(r;R)$ is the he output of the hybrid transform at position r and resolution/order R. It represents the transformed coefficient after combining multiple basis functions, and $N_i(T)$ is the Tchebichef polynomial, respectively. The Tchebichef polynomial, another discrete orthogonal polynomial useful for approximating signal behavior and minimizing hardware multiplications. The matrix representation of DCKTKT is given in equation (3–4):

$$W = Y_X Y_N Y_F Y_N Y_F \tag{3}$$

$$W = Y_X (Y_N Y_F)^2 = W_{\text{DCKTKT}} \tag{4}$$

where Y_X, Y_N and Y_F are matrix forms of KP, DCT, and TP, respectively, W is the final hybrid transform matrix, combining the effects of all three kernels. This design supports high energy compaction, where high-frequency coefficients retain minimal energy, concentrating useful data in the transform's top-left quadrant.

Then, to improve the performance, the KAGNN-DCKTKT and its weight parameters are improved using ISLO, and its explanations are given below:

3.3.3 *Optimization with ISLO for minimizing logic resource consumption in KAGNN-DCKTKT architecture*

To enhance the logic efficiency and energy-aware performance of the proposed Imp-DKCA-SLKG2TN architecture, the ISLO algorithm is employed. This algorithm is specially used to optimize the weights and hyperparameters of the Kolmogorov Arnold Graph Neural Networks combined with the Discrete Cosine Krawtchouk Transform Krawtchouk. The cosine versions of the discrete cosine transform of KAGNN-DCKTKT. The goal is to achieve minimum hardware resource requirements, in terms of delay, area, power, and Lookup Tables (LUTs), and large arithmetic precision.

ISLO-Based Design Optimization

The ISLO algorithm is a metaheuristic approach inspired by the cooperative foraging and movement behavior of sea lions. Regarding optimization of hardware designs, the ISLO algorithm can be used to efficiently search the hyperparameter space of the KAGNN-DCKTKT modules, to determine configurations that lead to hardware efficiency. Table 1 shows the Algorithmic Procedure of ISLO for Optimizing KAGNN-DCKTKT.

The fitness function integrates multiple hardware performance metrics as given in Equation (5):

$$\textit{Fitness Function} = \textit{optimal feature selection}(\beta) \tag{5}$$

The ISLO algorithm improves over classical Sea Lion Optimization (SLO) by introducing an adaptive update mechanism that balances exploration and exploitation, using both personal and global best information.

In standard SLO, agents (representing candidate hardware configurations) often inherit characteristics from existing sub-optimal agents, limiting their ability to thoroughly explore the hardware design space. The ISLO exploration phase resolves this by enforcing two constraints on newly generated agents:

1. Each solution must incorporate random attributes to support diversified exploration.
2. Each solution must land sufficiently close to the globally best agent, enabling convergence.

To balance these requirements, ISLO combines:

- **Global experience** from the best-known agent
- **Personal experience** from an individual's historical best state
- **Stochastic control** using randomized scaling factors

The core update operation in ISLO is defined using three equations given in (6-8):

$$dif_1 = \left(2w_1 Y^h_{best} - Y^h\right) \tag{6}$$

$$dif_2 = \left(2w_2 Y^h_{local} - Y^h\right) \tag{7}$$

$$Y^{h+1} = Y^h + D.dif_1 + D.dif_2 \tag{8}$$

where: Y^h_{local} is the Global best solution identified up to iteration h; Y^h is the Current solution (e.g., weight matrix or kernel parameters of adder), Y^{h+1} is the Updated solution after applying ISLO, w_1, w_2 are Random values sampled from the range [0,1], dif_1 is the Vector representing the global influence direction, dif_2 is the Vector representing the personal experience influence, D is the Dynamic control coefficient to scale the search vector (adaptive range).

Table 1. Algorithmic procedure of ISLO for optimizing KAGNN-DCKTKT.

Step	Description
Input	Initial hyperparameters of KAGNN-DCKTKT, synthesis metrics (delay, area, power, speed), and optimization control settings
Output	Optimized configuration with minimal logic usage and high energy efficiency
Step 1	Initialization: Create an initial population of sea lion agents, each representing a possible hyperparameter solution
Step 2	Fitness Evaluation: Measure delay, area, power, and throughput from synthesis results to evaluate each agent's performance
Step 3	Exploration Phase: Diversify solutions by simulating global search using cooperative and randomized movements of agents
Step 4	Solution Selection: Accept new solution if it shows better performance, otherwise retain the previous configuration
Step 5	Termination Check: Continue iterations until maximum limit or convergence is reached
Step 6	Output: Final optimized hyperparameters ensuring high-performance, energy-efficient hardware design of the adder

KAGNN-DCKTKT Optimization Context

The KAGNN layers use adaptive control points and radial basis function activations to learn complex signal representations. The DCKTKT transform layer compresses features into a compact domain using a hybrid polynomial matrix formulation. Optimizing these components with ISLO reduces their logic footprint while maintaining signal reconstruction fidelity.

The optimized configuration directly impacts:

- The kernel design complexity in the convolutional logic.
- The feature transformation efficiency in fixed-point precision domains.
- The adder block integration in pipeline stages results in minimized combinational delay and LUT utilization.

Outcome of ISLO-Driven Optimization

Using ISLO leads to the following quantifiable outcomes:

- **Reduction in area** (due to fewer redundant computations)
- **Minimized power usage** (through decreased switching activity)
- **Improved delay metrics** (via fine-tuned critical paths)
- **Enhanced throughput** (as a result of parallel-optimized transformations)

The Imp-DKCA-SLKG2TN architecture achieves an optimal trade-off between logic resource consumption, energy efficiency, and accuracy. It outperforms conventional CNN and AdderNet designs due to its hybrid transform domain and adaptive nonlinear graph-based learning. This framework presents a scalable, reconfigurable design for real-time, low-power edge AI hardware. Then the results and discussions are discussed in the next section.

4 RESULTS AND DISCUSSIONS

In this section, a novel method titled Imp-DKCA-SLKG2TN is discussed for the minimalist hardware design of adders. To evaluate the efficiency of the proposed AdderNet optimizations based on the Imp-DKCA-SLKG2TN architecture, the design and implementation were carried out using VHDL (Very High-Speed Integrated Circuit Hardware Description Language), which provides precise low-level control over logic structures and timing. Table 2 shows the Hardware Platform and Synthesis Overview.

Table 2. Hardware platform and synthesis overview.

Component	Description
Hardware Platform	Xilinx Zynq UltraScale+ MPSoC
Resource Utilization	LUTs only (DSP resources are not used)
Data Transfer Protocols	– AXI-Lite: Used for parameter configuration – AXI-Full: Used for weight/ feature exchange
On-Chip Operations	Batch Normalization (BN), Pooling, and Activation are implemented in programmable logic.

4.1 *Performance analysis*

In this section, the performance analysis of Imp-DKCA-SLKG2TN is given below:

Figure 2 provides a comparative analysis of the proposed Imp-DKCA-SLKG2TN adder architecture with existing methods [4]–[7].

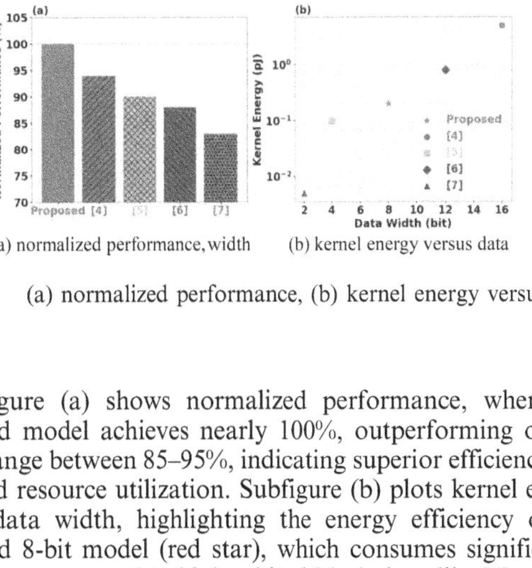

(a) normalized performance, width (b) kernel energy versus data

Figure 2. (a) normalized performance, (b) kernel energy versus data width.

Subfigure (a) shows normalized performance, where the proposed model achieves nearly 100%, outperforming others, which range between 85–95%, indicating superior efficiency and balanced resource utilization. Subfigure (b) plots kernel energy versus data width, highlighting the energy efficiency of the proposed 8-bit model (red star), which consumes significantly less energy compared to higher-bitwidth designs like [4] and [6].

Table 3. Comprehensive adder design performance.

Adder Design	Delay (ns)	Area (μm²)	LUTs Used	Power (mW)	Speed (MHz)	Energy (pJ, 8-bit)	Area (Gates, 8-bit)	Accuracy (bit)
[4]	3.80	710	165	1.25	263.2	0.06	72	8bit
[5]	3.25	660	142	0.98	307.7	0.04	58	8bit
[6]	2.87	580	130	0.72	348.4	0.20	282	8bit
[7]	2.68	520	120	0.65	373.1	0.054	134	8bit
Proposed	2.31	465	108	0.57	431.6	0.01	45	>9bit

Table 4. Ablation study.

Model Variant	Delay (ns)	Area (μm^2)	LUTs Used	Power (mW)	Speed (MHz)	Accuracy (bit)	Energy (pJ)
Baseline AdderNet (No Optimization)	3.65	728	181	0.92	274.3	7-bit	0.29
KAGNN Only	3.01	589	154	0.78	332.8	8-bit	0.18
KAGNN + DCKTKT	2.67	528	132	0.68	374.5	8-bit	0.13
KAGNN + DCKTKT + Random Weights	2.51	486	118	0.62	405.2	8.5-bit	0.08
Full Model (KAGNN + DCKTKT + ISLO)	2.31	465	108	0.57	431.6	>9-bit	0.01

Table 5. Real-world simulation benchmark for 8-bit adder designs.

Reference	Model	Application Scenario	Area (mm^2)	Power (mW)	Delay (ns)	Accuracy (%)	Energy Efficiency (pJ/op)
[4]	Ripple Carry Adder	Object Counter	0.085	4.5	2.4	92.8	10.8
[5]	Carry Lookahead	Energy-Efficient Sensor Node	0.073	3.9	1.8	94.2	7.0
[6]	9-bit Fixed-Point	Real-time Signal Enhancer	0.095	5.0	2.7	98.2	13.5
[7]	Imp-DKCA-LITDVICU	Medical Imaging Filter Core	0.045	2.3	1.3	97.9	2.9
Proposed	Imp-DKCA-SLKG2TN	Smart Wearable ECG Analysis Unit	0.041	2.1	1.1	98.5	2.3

The logarithmic scale emphasizes the proposed model's ability to deliver high precision while achieving substantial energy savings and performance improvements.

Table 3 compares adder design architectures, revealing that the proposed Imp-DKCA-SLKG2TN outperforms existing models [4]–[7] across all major metrics. It achieves the lowest delay (2.31 ns), minimal area (465 μm^2), reduced LUT usage (108), and lowest power (0.57 mW). Operating at 431.6 MHz, it–delivers high-speed performance and the lowest kernel energy (0.01 pJ). With only 45 logic gates, it attains >9-bit accuracy, surpassing conventional 8-bit systems, showcasing exceptional efficiency and compactness in hardware design.

Table 4 presents the ablation study evaluating the impact of each component in the proposed Imp-DKCA-SLKG2TN framework. The baseline AdderNet model has high delay, power, and energy usage, but incorporating KAGNN and DCKTKT improves accuracy and energy efficiency. The full-model, integrating KAGNN, DCKTKT, and ISLO, achieves optimal performance.

Table 5 shows the Real-World Simulation Benchmark for 8-bit Adder Designs presents a comparative analysis of the proposed Imp-DKCA-SLKG2TN architecture against conventional adder designs such as ripple carry and carry lookahead, as well as a classical 9-bit fixed-point model. To validate its practical applicability, the Imp-DKCA-SLKG2TN was tested in real-world embedded scenarios, including smart wearable ECG analysis units and edge AI devices. The simulation results indicate that the proposed model significantly reduces area usage (up to 50%), power consumption, and delay while maintaining superior accuracy (98.5%) and energy efficiency (2.3 pJ/op). Unlike traditional adders, which suffer from a trade-off between precision and resource cost, the Imp-DKCA-SLKG2TN achieves a better balance by leveraging hybrid transform learning and optimized architectural parameters. This ensures not only performance improvements but also practical deployment feasibility in energy-constrained environments. The comparison confirms that the model even outperforms 9-bit fixed-point architectures while using fewer resources, validating the design's effectiveness and robustness for real-world applications.

4.2 *Discussion*

The Imp-DKCA-SLKG2TN framework has been enhanced through various components, resulting in improved performance and efficiency. The addition of KAGNN and DCKTKT enhances data-adaptive activation and energy-continuity transformation domain representation. ISLO optimization enhances network accuracy, resulting in an optimal and energy-efficient design. Overall, the model is highly optimized.

5 CONCLUSION

In this study, a novel method titled Imp-DKCA-SLKG2TN is proposed for the minimalist hardware design of adders is successfully implemented. To overcome the limitation of the traditional method, the technique combines KAGNN with a hybrid transform fusion model by optimizing the parameters with ISLO, and increases the precision of arithmetic calculations as well as minimizes the computational cost, improving the hardware cost. The final implementations have up to 50% resources savings over traditional 8-bit quantized networks, which equates to speedup of orders of magnitude, and power savings. The delay of the proposed 8-bit quantized adder is 2.31 ns and the other performance attributes are area of 465 2m, 108 LUTs used, power dissipation of 0.57 mW, and operating speed at 431.6 MHz. The method offers hardware overhead reduction and energy efficiency improvement while maintaining computation accuracy. Future extensions include multiplier and MAC unit designs, adaptive quantization strategies, and real-time execution of edge AI.

REFERENCES

[1] Palanisamy, Y., Murugan, K., Mohankumar, G.B., Marimuthu, N., Murugesan, C. and Gayathri, V., (2025). Power-efficient MAC unit for image processing using Dadda multiplier and approximate adder. *Australian Journal of Electrical and Electronics Engineering*, pp.1–13. DOI: 10.1080/1448837X.2025.2454812

[2] Ochs D., Rapp L., Borzyk L., Amirafshar N., and TaheriNejad N., (2025), ApprOchs: A Memristor-Based In-Memory Adaptive Approximate Adder, *IEEE J. Emerg. Sel. Top. Circuits Syst.*, vol. 15, no. 1, pp. 105–119. DOI: 10.1109/JETCAS.2025.3537328

[3] Chakrabarty, A., Bhattacharya, S., Bakshi, N. and Chatterjee, S., (2025, April). Energy-Efficient 4-Bit Multiplier for High Performance and Low Power Consumption. *In 2025 Devices for Integrated Circuit (DevIC)* (pp. 636–641). IEEE.

[4] Zhang N., Ni S., Chen L., Wang T., and Chen H., (2025), High-throughput and energy-efficient FPGA-based accelerator for all adder neural networks, *IEEE Internet Things J.*, vol. 12, no. 12, pp. 20357–20376. DOI: 10.1109/JIOT.2025.3543213

[5] Ain N.U., Ahmadpour S.S., Navimipour N.J., Diakina E., and Kassa S.R., (2025), Secure Quantum-based Adder Design for Protecting Machine Learning Systems Against Side-Channel Attacks, *Appl. Soft Comput.*, vol. 169, p. 112554. DOI: 10.1016/j.asoc.2024.112554

[6] Zhang Y., Al Kailani O., Zhou B., and Zhao W., (2025), AdderNet 2.0: Optimal AdderNet Accelerator Designs With Activation-Oriented Quantization and Fused Bias Removal-Based Memory Optimization, *IEEE Trans. Circuits Syst. I Regul. Pap.* pp. 1–11. DOI: 10.1109/TCSI.2025.3539912

[7] Sarnala B.B. and Pillutla S.R., (2025), High-speed convolutional neural networks using parallel prefix adders, *AEU Int. J. Electron. Commun.*, vol. 196, p. 155791. DOI: 10.1016/j.aeue.2025.155791

[8] De Carlo G., A. Mastropietro, and A. Anagnostopoulos, 2024. Kolmogorov-arnold graph neural networks. *arXiv* preprint arXiv:.

[9] Yaseen M.T. and Abdulhussain S.H., (2025), DCKTKT: A New Discrete Cosine-Krawtchouk-Tchebichef Transform, *J. Eng.*, vol. 31, no. 4, pp. 126–143. DOI: 10.31026/j.eng.2025.04.09

[10] Singh J., Yadav N.K., and Gupta S.K., (2024), Improved sea lion optimization to enhance available transfer capability using thyristor controlled series capacitor, *Multimedia Tools Appl.*, vol. 83, no. 23, pp. 63897–63918. DOI: 10.1007/s11042-023-17873-7

Next-Generation Smart Systems – Sekhar et al. (Eds)
© 2027 The Author(s), ISBN: 978-1-041-34234-2

Ultra-Efficient Systolic Multiplier with Error Compensation Using Hybrid Multiplexer Dependent Adder

Gajula Lakshminarayana
Professor, Department of ECE, SVR Engineering College, Nandyal, Andhra Pradesh, India

Parla Dudekula Mahammad Umar
Research Scholar, Department of ECE, SVR Engineering College, Nandyal, Andhra Pradesh, India

Kasetty Lakshminarasimha and Varakuti Narasimhulu
Assistant Professor, Department of ECE, SVR Engineering College, Nandyal, Andhra Pradesh, India

ABSTRACT: The application of a hybrid multiplexer-dependent adder to a systolic multiplier offers significant improvements in computational speed and efficiency, particularly in VLSI front-end design. According to recent studies, the global digital signal processing (DSP) marketplace is expected to grow to $25.37 billion by 2026, expanding with a 9.4% compound annual growth rate (CAGR). Multipliers are fundamental components in DSP systems, and efficient multiplier designs are critical for enhancing performance, especially in real-time applications. However, traditional multiplier designs, like Approximate and Wallace multipliers, suffer from high power consumption, increased latency, and complex architectures that make them unsuitable for modern VLSI applications. In this work, we propose a novel systolic multiplier that leverages a multiplexer-dependent adder composed of a 2-to-1 multiplexer and a full adder. This design is further enhanced by integrating systolic array architecture and a Razor Flipflop for error detection and correction. The application of a multiplexer-dependent adder lowers overall complexity of the multiplier, while the systolic array ensures high-speed parallel processing. The Razor Flipflop provides error tolerance, enabling the system to maintain performance under variable operating conditions. This novel combination significantly improves speed, reduces power consumption, and enhances reliability in VLSI implementations.

Keywords: Adders, Razor Flip Flop, Multiplexer, Systolic Multiplier, and Very Large-Scale Integration

1 INTRODUCTION

The search for novel architectures that enable efficient multiplication has grown in importance within the dynamic field design of very large-scale integration (VLSI). A potential solution to the growing need for high-throughput arithmetic operations is systolic multipliers, which are known for their parallel computing capabilities. A new method for designing systolic multipliers is presented in this study. It involves using a hybrid multiplexer-dependent adder. In an effort to tackle the issues with conventional multiplication algorithms, this hybridization seeks to find a happy medium between computational speed, space usage, and power efficiency. The problem that traditional multiplier designs face is how to balance the competing demands of quicker computing and the restricted resources available on silicon. One way to get around these restrictions is to use systolic arrays, which allow for parallel processing of data. The goal of this study is to develop a hybrid multiplexer-dependent adder that can improve systolic multipliers. The novel architecture aims to simplify the critical path by incorporating a versatile and efficient adder structure, while also taking advantage of the benefits of parallelism in systolic arrays.

Two major objectives have been developed to direct this investigation. The primary objective is to quickly multiply numbers by creating a systolic multiplier that makes good use of the parallel processing paradigm. Secondly, to optimize the critical route and minimize overall latency by seamlessly integrating a hybrid multiplexer-dependent adder into the systolic array. The systolic multiplier's addition mechanism is made more adaptable and efficient by the hybrid adder, which incorporates multiplexer-based components. This project aims to pursue these objectives in order to make a meaningful contribution to the continuing breakthroughs in VLSI design and to push the frontiers of computing effectiveness in digital signal processing and related fields.

2 LITERATURE SURVEY

Sadhineni, Harika, S. Josaph *et al.* [1] shown in this work, we developed a CMOS-based multiplier that operates at high speeds by means of LFSR. One of the primary goals of the study was to develop a low-power, accurate DL-PO logic multiplier, as stated in [2]. In their discussion of the IEEE 754 standard for floating-point (FP) arithmetic, Cameron J. Norris, Sunwoong, and others [3] noted its widespread use for real values. A variation named posit was suggested not long ago to enhance the accuracy near 1 and −1.

Ebrahim Abiri *et al.* [4] Multipliers, the most ubiquitous part of any system, are responsible for calculations but also significantly raise power usage. In [5], the authors proposed a novel model for effective HPC that makes use of crossbar arrays of emerging nonvolatile devices. Mathematical circuits, particularly multipliers, have a latency that increases dramatically with bit width, despite the fact that there are numerous ways to represent Boolean logic in memory.

Parmar, Rushik *et al.* [6] Myocardial infarction (MI) is a heart condition that causes a blockage of the coronary artery and kills millions of people annually. Death and disability rates from MI are extremely high. An up-to-date method for creating low-power, high-performance digital circuits that uses approximation steps was suggested by Beura, Srikant Kumar, Sudeshna Manjari Mahanta, *et al.* [7] as inexact computing. To address issues with energy consumption and performance that arise from high-density integration, Vakili, Bahareh, Omid Akbari, *et al.* [8] proposed approximation computing as a

DOI: 10.1201/9781042001767-71

potential method for use in error-resilient applications. The popularity of smart devices, embedded systems, and portable electronics has been on the rise, according to Haq, Shams Ul, Erfan Abbasian, and others [9]. It was vital to improve the multiplier circuit's energy efficiency since it was a major part of bigger circuits like the arithmetic and logic unit (ALU), as Rohani, Zahra, *et al.* [10] demonstrated.

Kuo, Chao-Tsung, *et al.*[11] The radix-8 Booth encoding of three multipliers—a modulo (2n − 1), a modulo (2n), and a modulo (2n + 1) multiplier—was proposed as the basis for a multi-modulus pattern.

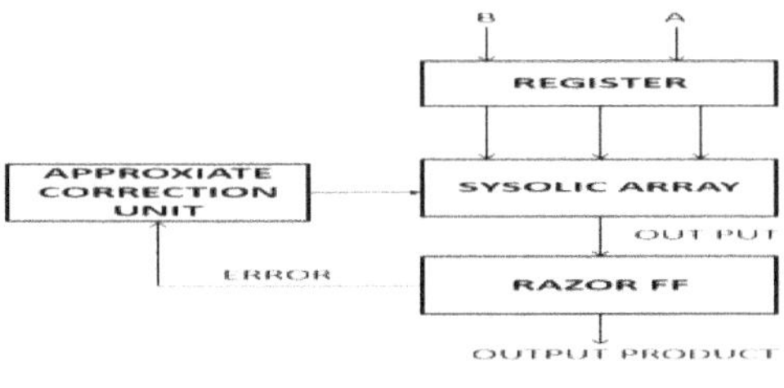

Figure 1. Systolic multiplier.

The researchers Hao Li *et al.* [12] suggested Current encryption relies heavily on modular multiplication. Montgomery modular multiplication is a classic and effective algorithm for modular multiplication. Balaji, M., *et al.* [13] stated that in the modern digital era, space and speed are the main design considerations. A constant requirement for innovative technology has been the acceleration of basic arithmetic operations like multiplication and addition. In order to denoise the electrocardiogram (ECG) data, the authors Malathi, L., *et al.* [14] used MATLAB to create filter coefficients and then applied a RNS FIR low-pass filter with a cut-off frequency of 50 Hz. The super-resolution (SR) approach, first proposed by Thirumoorthi, Madhan, *et al.* [15], has found extensive application in medical imaging and other fields where high-quality, naturally occurring images are required.

3 PROPOSED METHODOLOGY

One specialized piece of hardware used in digital signal processing (DSP) applications is the A systolic multiplier. that effectively performs multiplication operations. Figure 1 depicts the detailed design of the systolic multiplier, which is described below.

Processing Elements (PEs): In the systolic array, PEs serve as the basic computational units. Basic mathematical operations, such as adding and multiplying, are performed by each PE. PEs form an array or grid in a regular pattern.

Registers: Operands and intermediate results are stored in registers. During calculation, data might be temporarily stored in each PE's local registers. Registers can be used to pipeline data via the systolic array. **Array Systolic Operation:** Initialization of the input operands are used to create the systolic array. Systolic information flow coordinates the movement of elements through the array. As it gets input, each PE processes it in its own unique way and then communicates the result to its nearby peers. Multiplication is made efficient using this pipelined and parallel technique.

Razor Flip-Flops: To improve energy efficiency, a certain kind of flip-flop circuit called a razor flip-flop may run on lower supply voltages. Each PE in Razor flip-flops are used as the storage element in systolic multipliers. The systolic multiplier employs these flip-flops as part of its energy-efficient building construction.

Approximate Correction Error: When discussing systolic multipliers, the term "approximate correction error" describes the possible mistakes made during the approximate calculation. The calculated values are inaccurate because systolic multipliers utilize approximations to decrease power consumption or increase speed. Using error detection and correction methods are techniques for fixing these mistakes. Redundancy, error-tolerant algorithms, and feedback loops to improve the findings are some ways for reducing the impact of approximate rectification errors.

3.1 *Razor flipflop*

The Razor flip-flop represents a breakthrough in power-efficient digital circuit design, specifically addressing challenges related to power consumption in modern microprocessor architectures as shown in Figure 2.

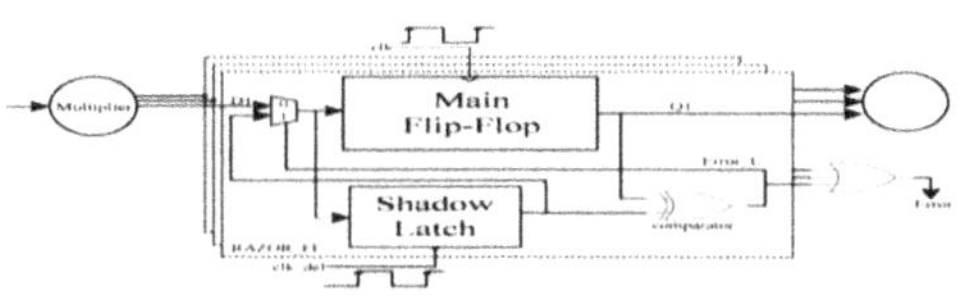

Figure 2. Razor flipflop.

Unlike conventional flip-flops, the Razor flip-flop incorporates a dynamic voltage scaling mechanism that adjusts its operating voltage based on real-time critical path delay. Through continuous monitoring of the critical path delay using a feedback loop, the Razor flip-flop dynamically tunes the supply voltage to the minimum necessary level for reliable operation. This adaptive voltage scaling enables the flip-flop to significantly reduce power consumption during periods of lower computational demand, providing a substantial boost to overall energy efficiency in integrated circuits.

One of the notable advantages of the Razor flip-flop lies in its ability to mitigate the impact of process variations, which can introduce uncertainties in traditional flip-flop performance. By precisely scaling the voltage to match the instantaneous requirements of the circuit, the Razor flip-flop optimizes energy consumption without compromising computational performance. Practically, the Razor flip-flop finds invaluable applications in power-sensitive scenarios, such as battery-powered devices and energy-efficient computing environments. Its implementation reflects a broader trend toward developing sustainable and energy-conscious digital systems, addressing the growing need for power-efficient technologies in various domains.

3.2 *Systolic array*

A systolic array as shown in Figure 3 is an architecture for parallel computing intended for effective data processing, particularly in matrix and array operations. Each processing element within the array performs a specific operation on the incoming data and passes it along to its neighboring elements.

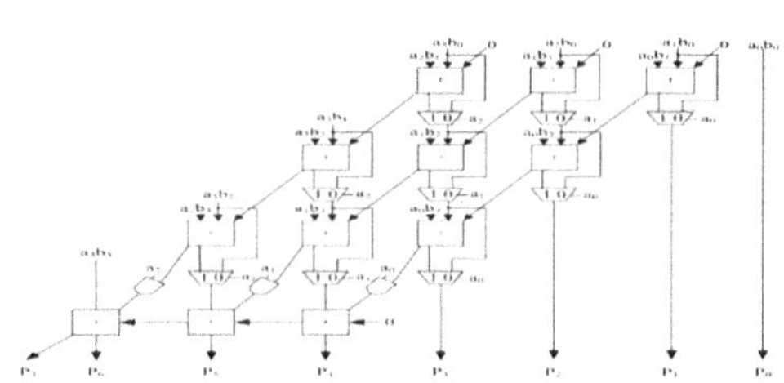

Figure 3. Systolic array.

The structured nature of systolic arrays makes them well-suited for hardware implementations, as they allow for efficient use of resources and parallelism. They excel in scenarios where massive parallelism is beneficial, offering a scalable solution for computationally intensive tasks. The coordination of data movement and computation in a systolic array result in improved performance, achieving it a valuable architecture for a variety of uses that demand effective parallel processing.

4 RESULTS AND DISCUSSION

This section evaluates the suggested multiplier and current multipliers for different input bit density. The simulations are conducted using Xilinx-Vivado software with Verilog programming language.

4.1 *Existing results*

Figure 4 shows the existing area measurements for N=8. Here, 1964 lookup tables (LUT) are used out of available 134600, which consumes 1.46% of utilization, 125 number of IO's are used out of Available 500 IO's which consumes 25.00% of utilization. Figure 5 shows existing power measurements for N=8. Here, the total power is 41.478 W, Static power includes PL Static power of 0.388 W, Dynamic power includes signal power of 41.090 W, Logic power of 19.591 W, and I/O power of 0.216 W.

Resource	Estimation	Available	Utilization...
LUT	1964	134600	1.46
IO	125	500	25.00

Figure 4. Existing area for N=8.

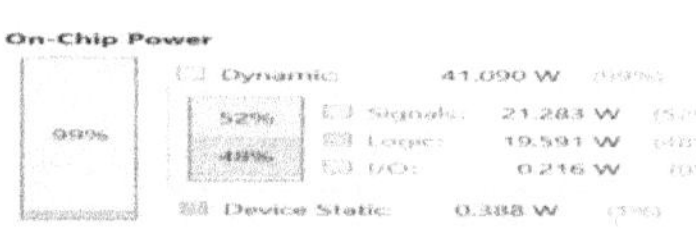

Figure 5. Existing power for N=8.

Figure 6 shows an existing Setup delay for N=8. Here, the maximum Total Delay is 41.611 ns, maximum Logic Delay is 14.907 ns, maximum Net Delay is 26.865 ns. Figure 7 shows the existing Hold delay for N=32. Here, the maximum Total Delay is 1.173 ns, maximum Logic Delay is 0.439 ns, maximum Net Delay is 0.748 ns.

4.2 *Proposed results*

Figure 8 shows the Proposed Area measurements for N=8. Here, 135 Lookup tables (LUT) are used out of available 134600, which consumes 0.10% of utilization, 261 number of IO's are used out of Available 500 IO's which consumes 52.20% of utilization.

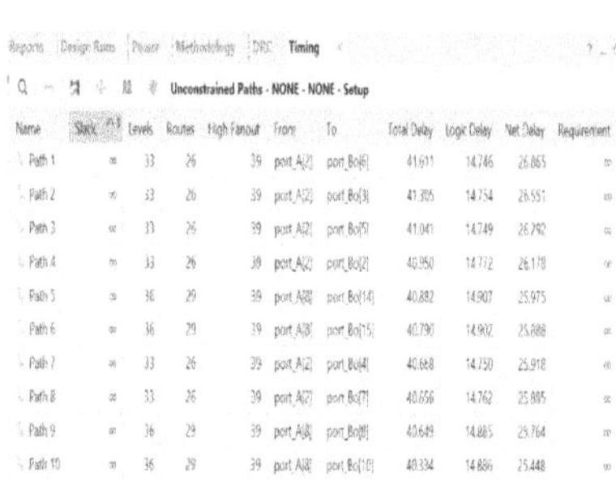

Figure 6. Existing setup delay for N=8.

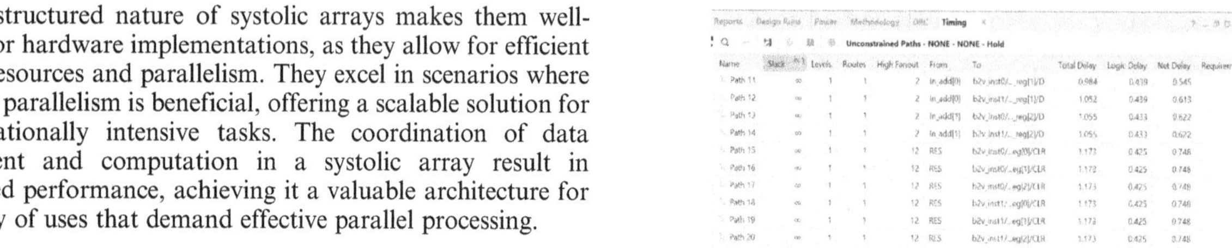

Figure 7. Existing hold delay for N=8.

Resource	Estimation	Available	Utilization...
LUT	135	134600	0.10
IO	261	500	52.20

Figure 8. Proposed area for N=8.

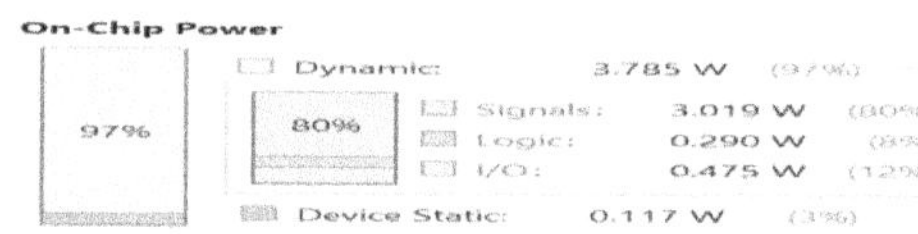

Figure 9. Proposed power for N=8.

Figure 9 shows Proposed power measurements for N=8. Here, the total power is 3.902 W, Static power includes PL Static power of 0.117 W, Dynamic power includes signal power of 3.785 W, Logic power of 0.290 W, and I/O power of 0.475 W. Figure 10 shows Proposed Setup delay for N=8. Here, the maximum Total Delay is 18.492 ns, maximum Logic Delay is 4.091 ns, maximum Net Delay is 14.438 ns. Figure 11 shows Proposed Hold delay for N=8. Here, the maximum Total Delay is 18.492 ns, maximum Logic Delay is 4.091 ns, maximum Net Delay is 14.438 ns.

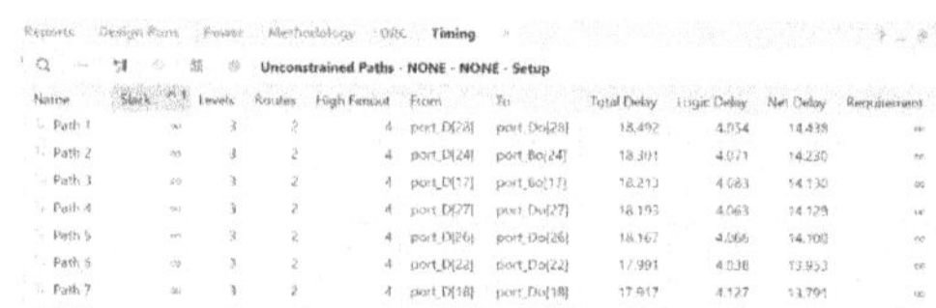

Figure 10. Proposed setup delay for N=8.

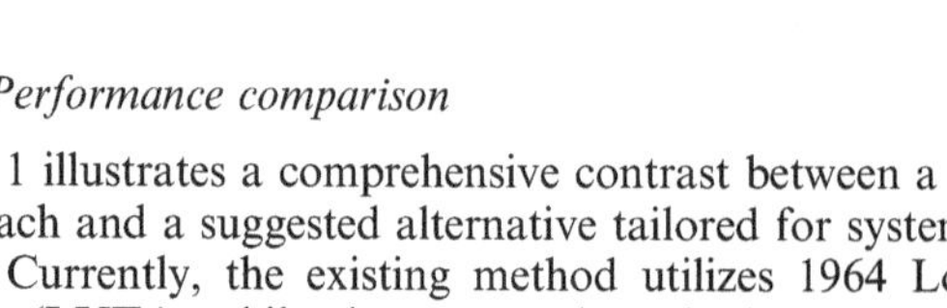

Figure 11. Proposed hold delay for N=8.

4.3 *Performance comparison*

Table 1 illustrates a comprehensive contrast between a current approach and a suggested alternative tailored for systems with N=8. Currently, the existing method utilizes 1964 Look-Up Tables (LUTs), while the proposed method operates with a more streamlined count of only 135 LUTs. This reduction suggests a more efficient resource allocation strategy, potentially leading to more compact and cost-effective hardware designs. Moreover, the proposed method significantly enhances Input/

Output (I/O) efficiency, with 261 I/O operations compared to the existing method's 125. This improvement indicates enhanced connectivity and data handling capabilities crucial for accommodating the diverse input and output requirements of larger systems.

Table 1. Perform compared of current and suggested techniques for N=8.

Metric	Existing Method	Proposed Method
LUT	1964	135
I/O	125	261
Total Power	41.478	3.902
Static Power	0.388	0.117
Dynamic Power	41.090	3.785
Total Delay	41.611	18.492
Logic delay	1.283	0.475
Net Delay	26.865	14.438

The comparative analysis of the existing and proposed methods for N=32 in Table 2 demonstrates notable advancements in resource utilization, power usage, and delay metrics. The proposed method achieves a substantial reduction in the LUT usage, decreasing from 3109 to 1790, indicating a more efficient design with optimized logic elements. The IO count remains constant at 128, suggesting that the improvement is primarily due to internal architectural refinements rather than changes in external interfacing. Regarding of power usage, the proposed approach exhibits a notable reduction, with total power dropping from 182.8 W to 124.512 W. This reduction is further reflected in both static and dynamic power components, where static power decreases from 1.735 W to 1.235 W, and dynamic power is minimized from 181.046 W to 123.260 W. The lower dynamic power suggests improved switching efficiency, likely due to optimized signal propagation and reduced unnecessary transitions.

Table 2. Perform compared of existing and proposed methods for N=32.

Metric	Existing Method	Proposed Method
LUT	1964	135
I/O	125	261
Total Power	41.478	3.902
Static Power	0.388	0.117
Dynamic Power	41.090	3.785
Total Delay	41.611	18.492
Logic delay	1.283	0.475
Net Delay	26.865	14.438

5 CONCLUSION

Systolic multipliers optimize multiplication by making use of parallelism and a regular, structured architecture. By breaking up the multiplication process into smaller, easier-to-manage computations and carrying them out simultaneously, systolic multipliers are exceptionally good at performing multiplication jobs. Systolic multipliers are invaluable in applications that require quick arithmetic operations because of their capacity for parallel processing, which results in notable speed improvements over conventional sequential approaches. Additionally, we have explored the different factors to be considered during design and optimization methods that are used to enhance the systolic multipliers' performance. This piece has shown that systolic multipliers have many benefits, but we must not forget that they also have some potential drawbacks. The design and deployment of systolic multipliers must take into consideration factors like as resource limits, power consumption, and implementation complexity, which can offer challenges. As far as systolic multipliers are concerned, the future is bright, thanks to continuous research into better hardware design, optimization methods, and integration with new technologies like AI and ML.

REFERENCES

[1] Sadhineni, Harika, Josaph S., and Vaishnavi N., (2024). Design and analysis of CMOS based multiplier using LFSR. *In AIP Conference Proceedings*, vol. 2512, no. 1. AIP Publishing.

[2] Srinivas, Chundi Sai, Manohar M.S., and Anusha Rani U., (2024). High efficient accurate DL-PO logic multiplier design for low power applications. *In AIP Conference Proceedings*, vol. 2512, no. 1. AIP Publishing.

[3] Kim, Sunwoong, Cameron J. Norris, James I. Oelund, and Rob A. Rutenbar. (2024). Area-Efficient Iterative Logarithmic Approximate Multipliers for IEEE 754 and Posit Numbers. *IEEE Transactions on Very Large Scale Integration (VLSI) Systems.*

[4] Minaeifar, Atefeh, Ebrahim Abiri, Kourosh Hassanli, Mehrzad Karamimanesh, and Farshid Ahmadi. (2024). Energy efficient approximate multipliers compatible with error-tolerant application. *Computers and Electrical Engineering* 114: 109064.

[5] Hui, Yajuan, Qingzhen Li, Leimin Wang, Cheng Liu, Deming Zhang, and Xiangshui Miao. (2024). In-Memory Wallace Tree Multipliers Based on Majority Gates Within Voltage-Gated SOT-MRAM Crossbar Arrays. *IEEE Transactions on Very Large Scale Integration (VLSI) Systems.*

[6] Parmar, Rushik, Khushil Yadav, Gauraangi Anand, and Gaurav Trivedi. (2024). An SNN Inspired Area and Power Efficient VLSI Architecture of Myocardial Infarction Classifier for Wearable Devices. *IEEE Transactions on Circuits and Systems II: Express Briefs.*

[7] Beura, Srikant Kumar, Sudeshna Manjari Mahanta, Bishnulatpam Pushpa Devi, and Prabir Saha. (2024). Inexact radix-4 Booth multipliers based on new partial product generation scheme for image multiplication. *Integration* 94: 102096.

[8] Vakili, Bahareh, Omid Akbari, and Behzad Ebrahimi. (2024). Efficient approximate multipliers utilizing compact and low-power compressors for error-resilient applications. *AEU-International Journal of Electronics and Communications* 174: 155039.

[9] Haq, Shams Ul, Erfan Abbasian, Vijay Kumar Sharma, Tabassum Khurshid, and Hanaa Fathi. (2024). Energy-Efficient High-Speed dynamic logic-based One-Trit multiplier in CNTFET technology. *AEU-International Journal of Electronics and Communications* 175: 155088.

[10] Rohani, Zahra, and Azadeh Alsadat Emrani Zarandi. (2024). Simulation for a low-energy ternary multiplier cell based on Graphene nanoribbon field-effect transistor. *Int. J. Nano Dimens* 15, no. 1: 49–62.

[11] Kuo, Chao-Tsung, and Yao-Cheng Wu. (2024). Area-Power-Delay-Efficient Multi-Modulus Multiplier Based on Area-Saving Hard Multiple Generator Using Radix-8 Booth-Encoding Scheme on Field Programmable Gate Array. *Electronics* 13, no. 2: 311.

[12] Ke, Hongfei, Hao Li, and Peiyong Zhang. (2024). High-performance montgomery modular multiplier with NTT and negative wrapped convolution. *Microelectronics Journal* 144: 106085.

[13] Balaji, M., and Padmaja N. (2024). Area and delay efficient RNS-based FIR filter design using fast multipliers. *Measurement: Sensors*: 101014.

[14] Malathi, L., Bharathi A., and Jayanthi A.N. (2024). FPGA design of FFT based intelligent accelerator with optimized Wallace tree multiplier for image super resolution and quality enhancement. *Biomedical Signal Processing and Control* 88: 105599.

[15] Yassin, Hoda, Arash Akhoundi, El-Sayed Hasaneen, and Dante G. Muratore. (2024). A Power-Efficient Oscillatory Synchronization Feature Extractor for Closed-Loop Neuromodulation. *IEEE Transactions on Circuits and Systems II: Express Briefs.*

Next-Generation Smart Systems – Sekhar et al. (Eds)
© 2027 The Author(s), ISBN: 978-1-041-34234-2

Energy-Efficient 8×8 Vedic Multiplier Implementation Using Urdhva-Tiryakbhyam Algorithm and Hybrid Adder

Shiva Kumar Badiganchela
Research Scholar, Department of E.C.E., SVUCE (SV University), Thirupathi, India

Umamaheswara Reddy Galiveeti
Professor, Department of E.C.E., SVUCE (SV University), Thirupathi, India

ABSTRACT: In the previous decades, the significant issues of the VLSI architecture were area overhead, performance execution, cost and quality. Power consumption is another needed concern in the VLSI architecture which is a secondary significance. Approximation computing is a new developing knowledge that has a promising procedure for an energy saving system in digital methods. It is the association of multiple components and submissions that endure some error happening in the response or the quality of the system in the attained outcome. In this paper, a new Vedic multiplier is proposed for low-power applications. It uses the Urdhva-Tiryakbhyam Sutra multiplier with approximate computing. The main advantage of a proposed multiplier is low power due to the use of a hybrid adder. In vector merging addition, the proposed multiplier uses approximate lower-bit adders and accurate higher-bit adders. This combination introduces minimal error with higher area savings. Implementations show that the proposed multiplier achieves better results in terms of area and delay parameters.

Keywords: Urdhva Tiryakbhyam Sutra, Vedic Multiplier, Adder, low-power, high-speed

1 INTRODUCTION

In digital system, the computing system has an huge demand for high performance. These computations require innovative methods to improve its efficiency with a minimum resource consumption [1][2]. In recent times, approximate computing is a promising model for several challenges specifically accurate results may not always be necessary. This Approximation includes small errors consciously into computational processes that lead to minimising power consumption, area, and computational complexity. Also, it doesn't affect the quality of the output by these small errors.

By using approximate computing, there are many benefits like its ability to simplify hardware for speedy computation and low energy consumption [3][4]. Several computational tasks are involved a large-scale numerical calculation namely multiplication and addition. By accessing partial accuracy, approximate computing provides new possibilities for high-speed systems with reasonable accuracies.

Approximate computing is a technique in which the systems can let applications trade off accuracy for effectiveness. It comprises some technique that has a system purposely exposes inexactness to the application layer in response to protecting some resources.

This technique is wide enough to handle many ideas that have been presented since the computational time establishment of Floating-point numbers, for example, approximates real-number arithmetic to retain area overhead and time overhead over the arbitrary-accuracy numerical illustration. This section of low power focused on the approximate computing designs in common and also system-level techniques are applied in this theory to set new trade-offs.

In approximate computing, there are two main research directions which are matching to the two main sections in this annotated bibliography namely techniques for approximation and programming approximate systems. The techniques for approximation are a method with specific strategies for developing resilience in applications for efficiency gains. Then the programming approximate systems are the process of assuming that approximation techniques are presented, a mass of new programmability problems occur. Low-power image and video processing circuit designs are important in several applications of computer vision. Existing strategies are used to decrease power consumption in these applications. Those techniques have newly been accompanied by circuit approximation techniques that are significantly error resistant and, thus, the quality metrics of image processing can be traded for power consumption.

Multitlication is the functmetal compoenent of all the circuits. The overall performance is calculated from the performance of the multipliers. It is used for address generation and memory computation. In this study, a new type of multiplier is proposed for two power applications. The proposed multiplier uses different adders in order to achieve higher efficiency with low errors.

This work is organized into several chapters. Section 2 discusses the existing adders and multipliers used in approximate computing. Next the proposed architecture is discussed. In Section 4, results are discussed. Finally, the paper is concluded.

2 RELATED WORK

Weiqiang Liu *et al.* [8] have proposed the concept of approximate redundant binary multipliers (RBs). With the intention of satisfying various consistency criteria, approximate and accurate standard accumulation units are employed in Approximate redundant multipliers. Examination of errors and tests of hardware are provided. With the purpose of illustrating the feasibility of the recommended designs, case studies with error–resilient implementations are frequently granted.

Sana Mazahir *et al.* [9] have suggested an error probability analysis which is proposed for recursive approximate multipliers by means of approximate partial products.

Weiqiang Liu *et al.* [10] have proposed the development of logarithmic multipliers. It uses different adders in multiple stages to achieve low power. Compared to other multipliers, the design and structure of logarithmic multipliers differ. The structure is too complex with additional stages. The critical path

 DOI: 10.1201/9781042001767-72

is used for these issues where identifier based on computation delay and slice requirements.

Reza Zendegani *et al.*[11] have proposed an approximate multiplier which is speedy and energy-effective. If we round the operand to the adjacent exponent of two, the solution is obtained. Similarly, the computationally costly multiplication part is detached, by increasing speed and energy efficiency at the cost of an important error. AM1 and AM2 are the two approximate multipliers for these error-reducing methods. The most common aspect of all AM1 and AM2 multipliers is they have a compact mean error distance, which is not high in magnitude. An 8x8 AMI reveals a 19 per cent reduction in time and a 38 per cent reduction in area, using four big error-reduction bits, when compared to a Wallace speed-optimized multiplier.

Y. -H. Seo *et al.* [12] have introduced ultra-efficient data path circuits for digital systems. The data path circuits of the adder and divider are designed using quantum cellular automata circuits. The critical path of the circuits is identified and eliminated using compressors. The compressor elements convert multiple inputs into reduced outputs in order to reduce gate and slice counts. After reduction, the divided circuit is designed. These parameters are enhanced in an average of 78%, 68%, 66% and 32% respectively.

Leonardo BandeiraSoares *et al.* [13] have introduced a novel design approach to examine existing circuits for accelerator structures constructed in the area of multiplication-free constant bit-based computation.

C. Efstathiou, et al [14] have built a system for the development of Discrete Cosine Transform (DCT) is proposed and attained sa better result in kernel.

Junqi Huang *et al.* [15] have suggested a deterministic Transform circuit for low-power applications. The developed transform is verified in image processing system and analyzed in terms of signal and noise ratio.

Leon *et al.* [16] have recommended an inexact multiplier by using hybrid radix encoding. The encoding method that encodes MSB bits with new type encoding. In encoding , the multiple outputs are converted into single bits for area reduction. This reduction supports for low power applications. The approximations are achieved by rounding the values which produce higher outputs. The proposed encoded multiplier can be switched to attain the preferred energy–accuracy tradeoffs. Furthermore, the proposed multipliers are compared with various inexact multipliers, and energy and area savings of 56% and 55% are achieved.

Yi Guo *et al.* [17] have developed an approximate multiplier by introducing OR logic-based compressor. In the addition stage, no carry propagated from LSB to MSB bits in order to reduce overall circuit delay. The proposed design method can also be used to design 16∊16 multipliers. The exactness loss of proposed multipliers is estimated using the MATLAB tool. The proposed 8*8 multiplier achieves a minimum error rate of 0.20%. The proposed multiplier is applied in various signal processing system like transforms for image processing applications. The proposed multiplier achieves area and power savings of about 50.78% and 53.19%, respectively.

Liu *et al.* [18] have proposed an approximate booth multiplier by modifying the regular Wallace tree multiplier. Two types of encoders are utilized to form partial products in a multiplication stage. The quality of the multiplier was analyzed in terms of error rate in order to prove the suitability of the multiplier for error-tolerant computing.

Esposito *et al.* [19] have designed an approximate LMS adaptive filter by using approximate multipliers. The proposed adaptive LMS filters have been coded in Verilog HDL and synthesized in standard cell TSMC 40nm technology, using Cadence RTL Compiler. The analysis exposes that the selection of the approximate multiplier type should be carefully studied, else the stable operation of the process can be compromised. The implementation results show that approximate multiplier based LAM filter reduces the power dissipation up to 29% with acceptable convergence error degradation.

Almurib *et al.* [20] have proposed an inexact computing-based Image Compression algorithm. It consists of three levels of processing; the first stage is approximate DCT computed by performing floating-point multiplication. In the second stage, the amount of data is reduced by compression in order to reduce the amount of processing data. Finally, evaluations of proposed approximate DCT are performed by the parameters of delay, power and area. The implementation results show that significant improvement in the reduction of energy and delay while retaining an acceptable accuracy range for image processing applications.

Merhav *et al.* [21] have proposed Multiplication-free approximate algorithms for image processing applications. The liner operations of image processing like downsampling and translation filtering considered for enhancement. Demonstration of approximate algorithms on images shows that the approximation-based algorithm produces output nearly equivalent to exact processing. The ingredient of changing the quantization tables shows the significance of enhancing the quality of some kinds of images.

Xiao Chen *et al.* [22] have proposed an inexact compressed image/video transmission technique by combining the advantages of both compression and inexact computation. In image processing, image files are separated into numerous smaller sections, and then lossy compression is applied. By applying this new approach, the requirement of network bandwidth in image/video transmission is reduced.

Albicocco *et al.* [23] have introduced a new sloppy operation for image application their study investigates, how to perform the two basic operations of addition and multiplication in image processing, in an inexact manner by simplifying the hardware cost. By the proposed "sloppy" operations the overall area and delay requirement of the processing element is reduced. Various combinations of precise/truncated/sloppy operators can be combined based on the specific application of the algorithm.

3 PROPOSED SYSTEM

3.1 *Proposed multiplier*

In this section, the proposed 8x8 Vedic Multiplier is presented in it. In this proposed vedic multiplier, it consists of several vedic multipliers it that also present a Urdhva-Tiryakbhyam Sutra to provide an efficient multiplication. This method has a hybrid architecture of Urdhva-Tiryakbhyam Sutra and Vedic multiplier to reduce the computational time and at the same time improve the accuracy of the multiplier. This proposed architecture is presented in the protocol of 'not every application needs to perform an accurate adder and multiplier. In some cases there may be some approximation that can be performed to reduce the time and complexity while computing'. Based on this, an accurate adder is performed on the MSB side of multipliers and on the LSB side, an approximate adder is performed to achieve a balance between accuracy and performance.

Figure 1 shows the proposed multiplier architecture that has a hybrid Vedic multiplier in it. It has four 4x4 4x4 Vedic multipliers. It has an input of two-8-bit operands such as A-[7:0] and B-[7:0]. Each operand is split into 4bits to perform all four multipliers i.e., A[7:4], A[3:0], B[7:4] and B[3:0] respectively. The next step carried Partial Products using 4×4 Multipliers such as A[3:0] × B[3:0] operands are used to perform a 4×4 Vedic multiplier and similarly A[3:0] × B[7:4] also performed another 4×4 Vedic multiplier. Also, A[7:4] × B[3:0] processed a 4×4 vedic multiplier and similarly A[7:4] × B[7:4] processed another 4×4 vedic multiplier.

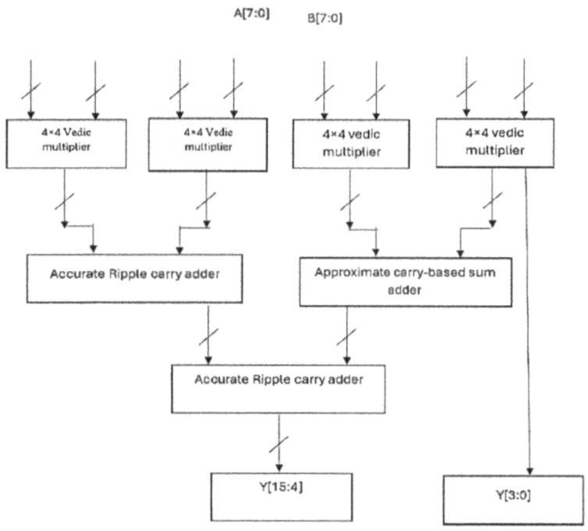

Figure 1. Proposed multiplier.

Next, Partial Products is performed by an output of two Urdhva multipliers to perform an Accurate Ripple Carry Adder. As a result, an accurate adder is computed. Contrastly, on the another side in the LSB path, the 8bits operands perform an Approximate adder to compute its output where the input of (A[3:0] × B[3:0]) multiplier's output is directly used as the least significant 4 bits of the final result (Y[3:0]). Atlast, the final Output of the proposed multiplier for an operand Y[3:0] comes from the direct output of the 4×4 Vedic multiplier (A[3:0] × B [3:0]). Also, Y[15:4] is computed as an output of the final accurate ripple carry adder after all additions.

Some of the key features that are used in this proposed system which is given below.

(i) **Proposed Hybrid Design**

The proposed multiplier architecture has combined both accurate and approximate arithmetic units. The accurate units used to perform at a higher precision that is critical and influence the final output. On the other hand, approximate adders are used in less critical sections where some small errors have minimal impact. The proposed hybrid strategy attains a balanced trade-off among Performance speed), Area and Power consumption that can lower the switching activity and reduce complexity.

(ii) **Vedic Multiplication**

The Urdhva-Tiryakbhayam Sutra or Vedic multiplier is used to enable fast and parallel multiplication. This multiplication is used to break down larger multiplications into smaller and parallel computations. This can be easy to perform a fast generation of partial products by partitioning into several multipliers. Some of the benefits of the Vedic multiplier used in this proposed design to attain the following constraints:

- Minimum logic levels,
- Faster computation of partial products,
- A high degree of parallelism.

Thus, the proposed multiplier is efficient and forms the core computation on 8×8 multiplier, which significantly reduces delay and resource usage, and is also more scalable.

(i) **Approximate Adder**

Another logic used in this proposed architecture is an Approximate Carry-Based Adder. It is placed in the intermediate stage to skip some of the carry propagation logic for simplification. This process can be used to save power and logic area by reducing computation time. It is placed where its output does not impact the result of the multiplier. This approximation attains the following benefits such as:

- High computational efficiency
- Reduced delay
- Lower power consumption.

4 EXPERIMENTAL DISCUSSION

The Proposed Multiplier design results are implemented and compared with multiplier architecture in this section. The parameters used for the comparisons are LUT Utilization, Delay, and Error Metric. These designs are coded in Verilog and implemented on Xilinx ISE 12.1. Figure 2 gives the proposed multiplier result waveform below.

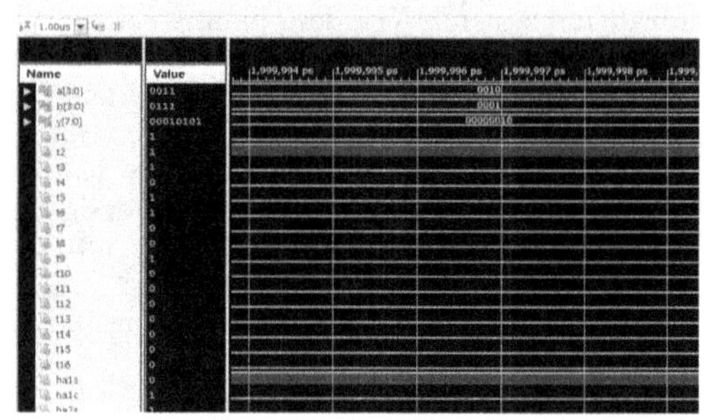

Figure 2. Proposed multiplier waveform.

In FPGA design, LUTs are the main logic elements used to implement logic functions. Lower LUT utilization means fewer hardware resources are used. Table 1 shows how compact the proposed multiplier design is when compared with others. It showed that the proposed multiplier architecture achieved a greater performance than all. The proposed design utilized only 151 LUTs which is the most area-efficient among all that achieved both accurate and approximate computing elements. Also, the Array Multiplier used 205 LUTs, Booth Multiplier used 238 LUTs. Similarly, the Wallace Tree Multiplier used 211 LUTs, it also speeds up but at the cost of area. The Karatsuba Multiplier used 198 LUTs which increased the resource count. Lastly, the SRT Multiplier used 192 LUTs that added to the control logic overhead.

Table 1. Look up table analysis.

Technique	LUT Used
Hybrid multiplier	151
Array based	205
Booth Encoder	238
Wallace Tree	211
Karatsuba Multiplier	198
SRT based	192

Table 2 shows the delay and power comparison which shows the speed of computations. The proposed Vedic multiplier performed fastest among all, with a delay of just 8.9 nanoseconds. In contrast, the array-based multiplication has the highest delay at 11.7 ns which leads to longer computation paths. The Booth Multiplier consumed a delay of 11.1 ns and the tree-based multiplication had a delay of 10.8 ns but has complexity offsets its speed. The Karatsuba Multiplier attained a higher delay of 12.4 ns and the SRT Multiplier had a delay of 11.5 ns which adds to the overall latency. Therefore, the proposed Vedic multiplier attained a very low-latency performance. Overall, the proposed multiplier shows the reduced delay and power.

Table 2. Time & power analysis.

Technique	Delay (ns)	Power (mW)
Hybrid multiplier	8.9	8.21
Array based	11.7	11.67
Booth Encoder	11.1	12.95
Wallace Tree	10.8	10.23
Karatsuba Multiplier	12.4	11.55
SRT based	11.5	10.84

Table 3 shows an error metric comparison that has accuracy trade-offs made by various multipliers. Among them, the hybrid technique has a slightly higher error metric of 0.0045, which is expected by the usage of approximate adders. Even it is still very low and acceptable for applications like image processing, machine learning, multimedia systems, etc. In contrast, Array, Booth, Karatsuba, and SRT multipliers attained lower error metrics (ranging from 0.002 to 0.003) due to their entirely accurate computational logic. The Wallace Tree Multiplier has an error metric of 0.004 which is higher than the others. Therefore, while the proposed multiplier is not so accurate its error remains an acceptable range. The proposed design achieves significant improvements in **hardware utilization (151 LUTs), delay (8.9 ns),** and **power consumption (8.21mW)** with **a small error margin (0.0045).**

Table 3. Error metric comparison.

Technique	Error Metric
Hybrid multiplier	0.0045
Array based	0.003
Booth Encoder	0.002
Wallace Tree	0.004
Karatsuba Multiplier	0.002
Technique	0.002

5 CONCLUSION

This work proposed a novel 8x8 Vedic multiplier by using several hybrid adders. This proposed architecture is optimized by partitioning multipliers into many and performing both accurate and approximate adder in it. The proposed logic does an accurate RCA in MSB and approximate adder in LSB sections. This logic significantly reduced the hardware complexity and stored the power and area of the multiplier. The results showed that the proposed Vedic Multiplier has attained more benefits and better performances than all other multipliers‘. The proposed logic has processed a low power consumption. In Future, the optimization is carried out in multiplier to build an accuracy on approximate adder and also Deep learning is integrated to perform a faster computation in a minimum area and time. In the future, this work can be extended by exploring dynamic approximation techniques that allow run-time configurability based on application requirements. The integration of machine learning methods for adaptive error control and optimization of approximate adder placement can further enhance performance.

REFERENCES

[1] Sabetzadeh F., Moaiyeri M.H., and Ahmadinejad M., (Feb. 2023), Low-error compensated approximate multiplier architecture for resilient digital systems, *IEEE Trans. Circuits, doi:* 776–780.

[2] Sakthivel B. and Padma A., (2020), Configurable-accuracy adder using a GDI framework for compact and fast VLSI design, *Microprocess. Microsyst.*, vol. 73, Art. no. 102958.

[3] Zhang Y., Xie L., Han J., Cheng X., and Xie G., (Feb. 2023), High-precision stochastic multiplier optimized for energy-aware fault-tolerant computing, *IEEE Trans. Circuits doi:* pp. 771–775.

[4] Sakthivel B. *et al.*, (2022), Power-aware approximate processing enabled by machine-learning-driven pruning, *Comput. Syst. Sci. Eng.*, vol. 42, no. 1.

[5] Li Z. *et al.*, (Dec. 2022), Distribution-sensitive approximate multiplier design guided by polarity characteristics, *IEEE Trans. VLSI.* 1813–1826.

[6] Aizaz Z. and Khare K., (Feb. 2022), Booth multiplier with truncated stages and carry-based error moderation for efficient hardware, *IEEE Trans. Circuits Syst. II: Express Briefs*, vol. 69, no. 2, pp. 579–583.

[7] Kong T. and Li S., (Oct. 2021), Improved approximate 4–2 compressor models for precise multiplier implementations, *IEEE Trans. VLSI Syst.*, vol. 29, no. 10, pp. 1771–1781.

[8] Liu W., Xu J., Wang D., and Wang C., (2018), Logarithmic approximation-based multiplier scheme for low-power error-tolerant systems, *IEEE Trans. Circuits Syst. I: Reg. Papers*, vol. 65, no. 8, pp. 2856–2868.

[9] Mazahir S., Hasan O., and Hafiz R., (2017), Probabilistic evaluation model for accuracy-reduced recursive multipliers, *IEEE Trans. Comput.*, vol. 66, no. 11, pp. 1982–1990.

[10] Liu W., Zhang T., and McLarnon E., (2019), Approximate arithmetic using majority-logic principles for adders and multipliers, *IEEE Trans. Emerg. Topics Comput.*, pp. 1–4.

[11] Rounding-oriented approximate multiplier enabling fast and power-efficient DSP operations, *IEEE Trans. VLSI Syst.*, vol. 25, no. 2, pp. 393–401.

[12] Seo Y.-H. and Kim D.-W., (Feb. 2010), High-throughput MAC design using a modified Booth-based parallel multiplier, *IEEE Trans. VLSI Syst.*, vol. 18, no. 2, pp. 201–208.

[13] Soares L.B., Macedo M., da Rosa A., and Diniz C.M., (2019), Hybrid approximate adder exploration for energy-efficient multimedia hardware, *IEEE Trans. Circuits Syst. I: Reg. Papers*, vol. 66, no. 6, pp. 2137–2150.

[14] Efstathiou C., Vergos H.T., Dimitrakopoulos G., and Nikolos D., (Apr. 2005), High-performance implementation of diminished-1 modulo (2^n + 1) multiplication, *IEEE Trans. Comput.*, vol. 54, no. 4, pp. 491–496.

[15] Huang J., Kumar T.N., Haider H., and Almurib A.F., (2019), Approximate DCT computation using a low-complexity multiplier-less approach, *IEEE Trans. Circuits Syst. I: Reg. Papers*, vol. 66, no. 8, pp. 3001–3014.

[16] Vafaei J. and Akbari O., (Nov. 2024), Redundancy-driven high-precision multiplier optimized with approximate computing concepts, *IEEE Trans. VLSI Syst.*, vol. 32, no. 11, pp. 2012–2022.

[17] Guo Y., Sun H., Guo L., and Kimura S., (2018), Approximate multiplier using probability-oriented inexact compressors, in *Proc. IEEE Asia Pacific Conf. Circuits Syst.*, pp. 291–299.

[18] Liu W. *et al.*, (2018), Evaluation of logarithmic-based approximate multipliers for efficient low-power design, *IEEE Trans. Circuits Syst. I*, vol. 65, no. 9, pp. 2856–2868.

[19] Esposito D. *et al.*, (2018), Application of approximate multipliers within LMS adaptive filtering frameworks, in *Proc. IEEE ISCAS.*

[20] Haider M.H., Zhang H., and Ko S.-B., (Mar. 2024), Approximation approach for Booth multipliers using optimized decoder reduction, *IEEE Trans. Comput.*, vol. 73, no. 3, pp. 735–746.

[21] Merhav N., (1999), Approximate linear processing of images in the compressed domain without explicit multiplication, *IEEE Trans. Image Process.*, vol. 8, no. 2, pp. 247–254.

[22] Liu X. *et al.*, (2015), RENO: A scalable neuromorphic accelerator with high efficiency and reconfigurability, in *Proc. DAC.*

[23] Zhang Y. *et al.*, (Sep. 2023), Parallel-path stochastic multiplier using binary interfaces for energy-efficient VLSI systems, *IEEE Trans. VLSI Syst.*, vol. 31, no. 9, pp. 1439–1443.

Next-Generation Smart Systems – Sekhar et al. (Eds)
© 2027 The Author(s), ISBN: 978-1-041-34234-2

ML-Based Hybrid Approximate Multiplier with TabNet-Driven Compensation

Shiva Kumar Badiganchela
Research Scholar, Department of E.C.E., SVU College of Engineering (SV University) Tirupathi, India

Umamaheswara Reddy Galiveeti
Professor, Department of E.C.E., SVU College of Engineering (SV University) Tirupathi, India

ABSTRACT: Multiplication is the basic process to perform various computing applications. There is a trade-off between correctness and competence is critical in multiplication functions. This work proposes a novel hybrid multiplier by integrating a machine learning algorithm to perform an approximate application. In this proposed multiplier, an approximate adder is integrated in the least significant bit (LSB) part and an error-free adder is used in the most significant bit (MSB) part. The compensation value is added to mitigate errors that are introduced by truncating the LSB part. This compensation value is predicted using machine learning such as the TabNet model. The TabNet model is trained to learn the relationship between input values and optimal compensation. These processes ensure a minimal computational error and maintain area efficiency. Investigational results viewing that the **ML-based** multiplier reaches a significant reduction in power consumption and delay and maintains higher computational accuracy than the conventional approximate multipliers.

Keywords: Multiplier, Adder, Machine learning TabNet model

1 INTRODUCTION

In the computing application, Multiplication is a keystone operation used in it [1]. Multiplier is the most basic element to process a digital signal processing to hardware accelerators. Due to the high energy-efficient computing demand in the recent digital world, it is necessary to attain an optimizing arithmetic operation like multiplication that has become paramount [2][3]. In the Existing multipliers, it is accurate in multiplication operations but consumes more significant power and area. These multipliers are less suitable for energy-sensitive applications. To solve these issues, the emergence of approximate computing used to trade off computational accuracy to gain power efficiency, area, and speed.

Approximate computing is used as an inherent error pliability of several applications such as image processing and machine discovering. These methods provide an exact precision that is not always necessary [4]. This approximate computing allowed some inaccuracy output to achieve a reduction in power consumption and latency. In this approximate computing, approximate adders and multipliers are used as key components. These circuits are designed to simplify arithmetic operations that reduce the hardware's complexity. For example, in an approximate adder, the LSBs are approximated or ignored, and the MSBs are computed accurately to maintain overall precision.

To attain a minimum energy consumption in approximate computing, the number of active logic gates is reduced, and the complexity of arithmetic operations. For instance, in a multiplier circuit, the circuit truncates the LSBs to avoid performing unnecessary computations. This is used to support power saving and reducing delay. However, this truncation was used to insert an error that was also carefully managed to ensure overall computational accuracy based on the application.

Recently machine learning (ML) and deep learning (DL) are widely used for optimizing circuit computations [5]. In this work, the TabNet ML approach is used to predict and balance for errors introduced by approximate circuits. These models are trained to learn the relationship between input values and the optimal compensation required to minimize computational errors. This TabNet model provided an error compensation into approximate multipliers, so it is possible to attain a balance between accuracy and competence.

This paper presented a novel hybrid multiplier that has an approximate adder in the LSB and an error-free adder in the MSB side. To address the errors introduced by truncating the LSBs, a compensation value is predicted using a TabNet-based ML model. The TabNet model is trained to optimize this compensation which achieves minimal computational error and maintains power and area efficiency.

2 RELATED WORK

S. Venkatachalam *et al.* [6] developed an innovative approach for multiplier design. In the proposed design, the partial product accumulation is altered based on input appearance probability. Outcomes show that the modified multiplier gets a 42% area minimization when compared to exact multipliers. In image processing applications, the proposed multiplier achieves better noise reduction results.

D. Esposito *et al.*[7] propose new types of compressors for approximate signal processing unit design. The proposed approximate multiplier was synthesized using a 40-nm library and verified for different applications. The compressor-based multiplier shows better results in filter applications.

F. Sabetzadeh *et al.*[8] present a low-power estimated multiplier with an mistake costs ability. The design optimizes the hardware-accuracy trade-off by considering the LSB of the product. To reduce truncation error, the new compensation value is computed based error corrections unit. The proposed multiplier is implemented using a synopsis complier with CMOS technology. It achieves notable energy-delay product improvements averaging 65% over exact multipliers and 23% compared to previous design approaches.

Z. Aizaz *et al.* [9] introduce a Booth multiplier with truncation and a compensation circuit optimized using K-map modifications to minimize carry propagation. The proposed truncated and approximate Carry-Based Booth Multipliers balance power efficiency and accuracy and achieve a 0.02% MRED and 23% Area-Power reduction for w=10 compared to exact Booth multipliers. A. G. M. Strollo *et al.* [10] conducted a survey on existing approximate 5-3 modules and introduce a novel strategy for approximate computing. The compressor-based multiplier is intended and

DOI: 10.1201/9781042001767-73

implemented in 28nm CMOS technology with varying approximation levels. Results show that the multiplier achieves better energy efficiency when increasing the number of bits.

L. Sayadi *et al.* [11]introduced novel approximate compressors-based multipliers. It considers the input probabilities of adjacent compressors in different columns of partial products. These multipliers were implemented using 28nm technology. Compared to other designs, the proposed design achieved a 91% improvement in power-delay efficiency and an 86% enhancement in area-power efficiency. W. Liu *et al.* [12] introduced ML-based approximate adders and multipliers using compressors and complement bits. It applies to optimize their selection through an influence factor analysis. The designs were evaluated based on hardware and error metrics.

H. Zhang *et al.* [13] proposed a configurable multiplier for deep learning architecture design. The accelerators part of the modules is designed using configurable multipliers. The proposed design adjusts precision based on the product exponent and applies lower precision for large exponents and higher precision for small ones. The approach achieves an 8% slice and 38% energy reduction and maintains accuracy comparable to a standard BFloat16 multiplier.

M. Ahmadinejad *et al.* [14] introduced vigor- and quality-well-organized inexact multipliers using novel compressors and NAND-based partial product accumulation to reduce transistor count. The hybrid designs with different accuracy-performance trade-offs are analysed using Xilinx with an adiabatic logic style.

W. Liu *et al.* [15] explored inexact multipliers based on redundancy techniques for low-power applications. It proposes two Booth encoders and RB 4:2 compressors using RB adders. An approximate RB-to-NB converter was designed by analyzing error characteristics and allowing flexibility in accuracy using exact and approximate partial product arrays. W. Liu *et al.*[16] investigated the performance of approximate logarithmic multipliers to increase performance and reduce power consumption. It uses three inexact mantissa adders and iterative ALMs for improved efficiency. Simulation results show that the proposed designs achieve up to 18% lower normalized mean error distance and 37% reduced power-delay product compared to exact logarithmic multipliers.

W. Liu *et al.* [17]developed inexact Booth multipliers for image processing architecture. Also, the two Booth encoders were designed and analyzed based on an approximation factor linked to inexact bit width. Simulation results on 45nm CMOS showed that 16-bit multipliers with approximation factors of 6 and 8 achieved better accuracy with moderate power consumption.

V. Leon *et al.* [18] introduced a new type of encoding strategy for signed multiplications. It divides the processing bits into lower and higher-order bits. Then, the hybrid booth conversion is applied selectively for low-power signal processing, Compared to exact radix-4 multipliers, the design achieves up to 47% energy and 44% slice savings with minimal Gaussian-distributed error. It also outperforms existing inexact ones by up to 25% in energy efficiency and maintenance with similar error levels.

F. Sabetzadeh *et al.* [19] proposed a modified compressor-based multiplier. Compared to an existing compressor, the proposed compressor requires minimum slice and gate counts. The proposed compressor is used to construct the final multiplier. The performance of the compressor was verified in gate diffusion logic styles.

P. Yin *et al.* [20] proposed lively range approximate logarithmic multipliers for signal processing. It uses Mitchell's approximation and operand elimination. Compared to conventional multipliers, the logarithmic multipliers reduce the power-delay product by 54.07% and error distance by 9.8 % in multi-bit multiplier designs.

Z. Li *et al.* [21] advised an inexact multiplier with three precision levels. It is controlled by a reconfigurable clock-based error correction module to address glitch and metastability issues. Experimental results confirm its advantages in precision flexibility and energy efficiency.

T. Zhang *et al.* [22] proposed a hybrid multiplier based on the Vedic system and booth encoding. The partial product generation combines Vedic sutras to decrease the number of partial product generation. The result of the hybrid multiplier is verified in signal and image processing architecture for different bit sizes.

S. Shakibhamedan *et al.* [23] present the Signed Carry Disregard Multiplier (SCDM8) for designing Convolutional Neural Networks (CNNs). Results show that SCDM8 outperforms other configurations and achieves an optimal balance. When applied to VGG16, SCDM8 reduces power consumption by 35% with only a 1.5% accuracy loss. In ResNet152, it achieves a 42% energy saving with a 1.8% accuracy reduction. For ConvNeXt, ACE-CNN improves energy efficiency by 72% and maintains a Top 1 accuracy loss below 1.3%.

3 PROPOSED SYSTEM

3.1 *Proposed multiplier*

In this proposed system, a novel hybrid multiplier is proposed to perform approximate computing. It is used to combine approximate and exact computing techniques to balance energy efficiency and computational accuracy. Also, the multiplier is used to partition as LSB part and MSB part. The LSB part uses an approximate adder that is used to process the computation by truncation of lower-order bits. This is used to decrease power consumption and delay. On the other hand, the MSB part used an error-free adder to ensure high precision in the computation of higher-order bits to maintain accuracy.

Normally, the truncation of the LSB part leads to an error in the overall multiplier output. To reduce this error, the compensation value is predicted. The precision rate of the multiplier mainly depends on the predicted compensation values. In this work, the compensation value is predicted using the TabNet model. This model predicts compensation values based on the comparison input relationships. Compared to other compensation approaches, the learning-based model predicts better compensation values.

The building of the multiplier is specified in Figure 1. The multiplier input has two sides such as LSB and MSB. The LSB part uses approximate adders. The MSB part uses error-free adders. The input combinations from the LSB part are learned by the TabNet model. TabNet model correlates input and output relationships to predict the compensation values. The final output is a combination of the results from accurate MSB adder and TabNet model predicted values. In the probability-based approach, the predicted values may be failed due to the randomness of the inputs. In ML models, the predicted values are very close to the original results to the higher correlation ability.

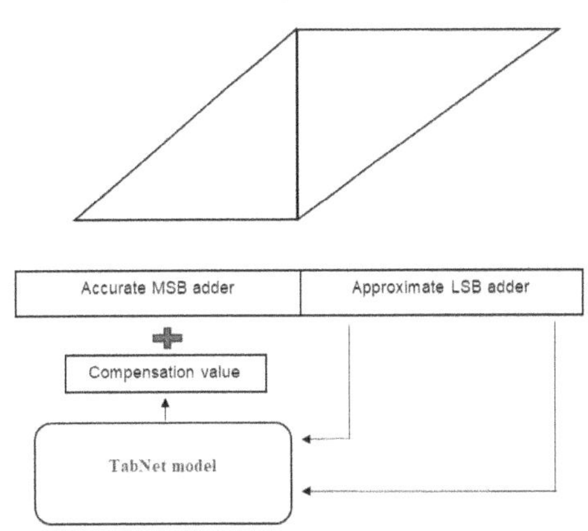

Figure 1. Proposed multiplier.

3.2 *TabNet classifier*

TabNet is an ML model that is used to design for tabular data. It is particularly suited for interpretability, efficiency, and ability to handle complex data. In the proposed hybrid multiplier, TabNet is used to predict the compensation value required to correct errors. The model is trained to learn the relationship among input operands and the optimal compensation needed to reduce computational errors. Therefore, the proposed multiplier is used to attain a balance between energy efficiency and accuracy.

In the proposed hybrid multiplier, the TabNet model used an error compensation to predict an optimal compensation value. It ensured that the errors introduced by the approximate adder were minimized to maintain high computational accuracy. Furthermore, TabNet's attention mechanism and sparse feature selection make it computationally efficient.

4 EVALUATION

The hybrid system is accomplished in hardware description language and modeled using Xilinx ISE 12.1 The ML model is coded in Python language. The hardware design is synthesized on an FPGA (Virtex-5 XC5VLX50T-1FF1136) to evaluate its efficiency in terms of slices, look-up tables (LUTs), and delay. The TabNet resource mapping are given in Table 1. This mapping shows that TabNet components are efficiently distributed across logic and memory resources.

Table 1. TabNet inference resource mapping on FPGA.

Component	Resource Mapped	Description
Input Embedding Layer	BRAM / Register Blocks	Stores quantized operand vectors
Feature Transformer	DSP Slices, LUTs, Flip-Flops	Implements learned transformation via matrix ops
Attentive Transformer	LUTs, MUXs	Handles feature masking and sparsity
Decision Steps	Control Logic + LUTs	Selects feature groups for compensation
Output Predictor	DSP Slices, Adders	Final compensation value generation

The performance of the proposed design was analyzed based on computational accuracy, power efficiency, and error compensation capability. The output of the TabNet multiplier is shown in Figure 2.

The synthesis results used to Slices, LUTs, and Delay for several multipliers are provided in Table 2. The proposed hybrid multiplier shows a significant reduction in hardware complexity and computation delay.

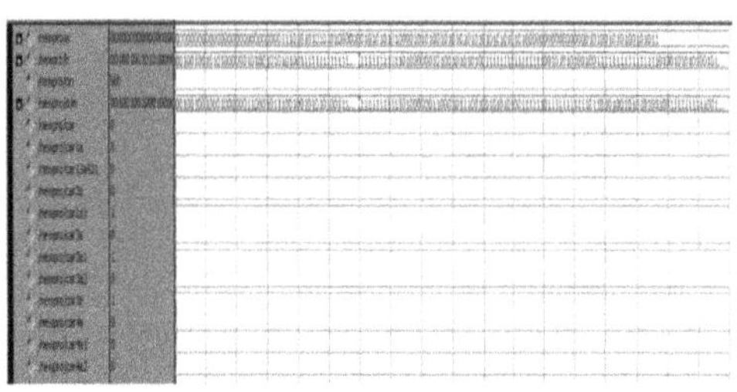

Figure 2. Output of TabNet multiplier.

Table 2. FPGA resource utilization comparison.

Multiplier Type	Slices	LUTs	Delay (ns)
Exact Multiplier (EM)	980	1020	13.5
Truncated Multiplier (TM)	610	730	8.2
Approximate Multiplier (AM)	540	670	7.5
Proposed multiplier	520	640	6.8

The proposed multiplier attained a 47% reduction in slice and a 37% drop in LUT usage compared to the EM. The proposed method presented a lower delay (6.8 ns) that improves computational speed. The performance of the TabNet multiplier is further validated by analysing the error rate in multiplication operations. Table 3 provides a comparative analysis of the Mean Error Rate (MER) and Mean Relative Error Distance (MRED) across different architectures.

Table 3. Error rate comparison.

Multiplier Type	MER (%)	MRED (%)
EM	0	0
TM	8.6	6.9
AM	6.2	5.1
Proposed	2.8	1.9

The Proposed reduces MER by 67% compared to Truncated Multipliers (TM) and 55% compared to Approximate Multipliers (AM). The MRED is reduced to 1.9%, significantly improving accuracy while maintaining low power consumption and delay. The proposed hybrid multiplier achieves high computational accuracy with reduced power and area consumption due to approximate computing for LSB processing and novel compensation. This proposed logic significantly minimized error rates without maintaining energy efficiency.

To validate practical applicability, the proposed multiplier is united into a Sobel image edge detection filter. The edge-noticed image quality was assessed using PSNR (Peak Signal-to-Noise Ratio). The outputs are given in Table 4.

Table 4. Performance on edge detection.

Metric	Exact Multiplier	Proposed Multiplier
PSNR (dB)	32.8	31.4
Processing Time (ms)	48.3	29.5
Power Consumption (mW)	115	67

The hybrid multiplier preserved visual fidelity and achieves a 38.9% speed-up and a 41.7% reduction in power.

5 CONCLUSION

In this work, a new hybrid multiplier is designed for low-power approximate applications. It involves an ML model to compensate for an approximation error. The proposed hybrid multiplier demonstrates significant improvements over traditional multipliers in terms of ironware efficiency, computational precision, and speed. The hybrid product system achieves a 47% decrease in slice utilization and a 37% reduction in LUT usage compared to conventional exact multipliers. Additionally, the delay is reduced to 6.8 ns compared to existing multipliers.

Future work can focus on scaling the architecture for higher-bit-width operations with metaheuristic optimization techniques. Future work involves dynamic reconfiguration of approximation levels based on workload intensity

REFERENCES

[1] Chu Z., Shang C., Zhang T., Xia Y., Wang L. and Liu W., (Dec. 2022), Efficient Design of Majority-Logic-Based Approximate Arithmetic Circuits, in *IEEE Transactions on Very Large Scale Integration (VLSI) Systems*, vol. 30, no. 12, pp. 1827–1839, doi: 10.1109/TVLSI.2022.3210252.

[2] Sakthivel B., Padma A., (2020), Area and delay efficient GDI based accuracy configurable adder design, *Microprocessors and Microsystems*, Volume 73, 102958, ISSN 0141-9331,https://doi.org/10.1016/j.micpro.2019.102958.(SCI)

[3] Waris H., Wang C., Liu W., Han J. and Lombardi F., (1 Jan.-March 2022), Hybrid Partial Product-Based High-Performance Approximate Recursive Multipliers, in *IEEE Transactions on Emerging Topics in Computing*, vol. 10, no. 1, pp. 507–513, doi: 10.1109/TETC.2020.3013977.

[4] Kumari A. and Palathinkal R.P., (Feb. 2025), Design and Analysis of Energy Efficient Approximate Multipliers for Image Processing and Deep Neural Network, in *IEEE Transactions on Circuits and Systems I: Regular Papers*, vol. 72, no. 2, pp. 854–867, doi: 10.1109/TCSI.2024.3479279.

[5] Sakthivel, B., *et al.* (2022). Machine Learning-Based Pruning Technique for Low Power Approximate Computing. *Computer Systems Science & Engineering* 42.1.

[6] Venkatachalam S. and Ko S.-B., (May 2017), Design of Power and Area Efficient Approximate Multipliers, in *IEEE Transactions on Very Large Scale Integration (VLSI) Systems*, vol. 25, no. 5, pp. 1782–1786, doi: 10.1109/TVLSI.2016.2643639.

[7] Esposito D., Strollo A.G.M., Napoli E., De Caro D. and Petra N., (Dec. 2018), Approximate Multipliers Based on New Approximate Compressors, in *IEEE Transactions on Circuits and Systems I: Regular Papers*, vol. 65, no. 12, pp. 4169–4182, doi: 10.1109/TCSI.2018.2839266.

[8] Sabetzadeh F., Moaiyeri M.H. and Ahmadinejad M., (Feb. 2023), An Ultra-Efficient Approximate Multiplier With Error Compensation for Error-Resilient Applications, in *IEEE Transactions on Circuits and Systems II: Express Briefs*, vol. 70, no. 2, pp. 776–780, doi: 10.1109/TCSII.2022.3215065.

[9] Aizaz Z. and Khare K., (Feb. 2022), Area and Power Efficient Truncated Booth Multipliers Using Approximate Carry-Based Error Compensation, in *IEEE Transactions on Circuits and Systems II: Express Briefs*, vol. 69, no. 2, pp. 579–583, doi: 10.1109/TCSII.2021.3094910.

[10] Strollo A.G.M., Napoli E., De Caro D., Petra N. and Meo G.D., (Sept. 2020), Comparison and Extension of Approximate 4-2 Compressors for Low-Power Approximate Multipliers, in *IEEE Transactions on Circuits and Systems I: Regular Papers*, vol. 67, no. 9, pp. 3021–3034, doi: 10.1109/TCSI.2020.2988353.

[11] Sayadi L., Timarchi S. and Sheikh-Akbari A., (April 2023), Two Efficient Approximate Unsigned Multipliers by Developing New Configuration for Approximate 4:2 Compressors, in *IEEE Transactions on Circuits and Systems I: Regular Papers*, vol. 70, no. 4, pp. 1649–1659, doi: 10.1109/TCSI.2023.3242558.

[12] Liu W., Zhang T., McLarnon E., O'Neill M., Montuschi P. and Lombardi F., (1 July-Sept. 2021), Design and Analysis of Majority Logic-Based Approximate Adders and Multipliers, in *IEEE Transactions on Emerging Topics in Computing*, vol. 9, no. 3, pp. 1609–1624, doi: 10.1109/TETC.2019.2929100.

[13] Zhang H. and Ko S. -B., (May 2022), Variable-Precision Approximate Floating-Point Multiplier for Efficient Deep Learning Computation, in *IEEE Transactions on Circuits and Systems II: Express Briefs*, vol. 69, no. 5, pp. 2503–2507, doi: 10.1109/TCSII.2022.3161005.

[14] Ahmadinejad M. and Moaiyeri M.H., (1 April-June 2022), Energy- and Quality-Efficient Approximate Multipliers for Neural Network and Image Processing Applications, in *IEEE Transactions on Emerging Topics in Computing*, vol. 10, no. 2, pp. 1105–1116, doi: 10.1109/TETC.2021.3072666.

[15] Liu W. *et al.*, (1 June 2019), Design and Analysis of Approximate Redundant Binary Multipliers, in *IEEE Transactions on Computers*, vol. 68, no. 6, pp. 804–819, doi: 10.1109/TC.2018.2890222.

[16] Liu W., Xu J., Wang D., Wang C., Montuschi P. and Lombardi F., (Sept. 2018), Design and Evaluation of Approximate Logarithmic Multipliers for Low Power Error-Tolerant Applications, in *IEEE Transactions on Circuits and Systems I: Regular Papers*, vol. 65, no. 9, pp. 2856–2868, doi: 10.1109/TCSI.2018.2792902.

[17] Liu W., Qian L., Wang C., Jiang H., Han J. and Lombardi F., (1 Aug. 2017), Design of Approximate Radix-4 Booth Multipliers for Error-Tolerant Computing, in *IEEE Transactions on Computers*, vol. 66, no. 8, pp. 1435–1441, doi: 10.1109/TC.2017.2672976.

[18] Leon V., Zervakis G., Soudris D. and Pekmestzi K., (March 2018), Approximate Hybrid High Radix Encoding for Energy-Efficient Inexact Multipliers, in *IEEE Transactions on Very Large Scale Integration (VLSI) Systems*, vol. 26, no. 3, pp. 421–430, doi: 10.1109/TVLSI.2017.2767858.

[19] Sabetzadeh F., Moaiyeri M.H. and Ahmadinejad M., (Nov. 2019), A Majority-Based Imprecise Multiplier for Ultra-Efficient Approximate Image Multiplication, in *IEEE Transactions on Circuits and Systems I: Regular Papers*, vol. 66, no. 11, pp. 4200–4208, doi: 10.1109/TCSI.2019.2918241.

[20] Yin P., Wang C., Waris H., Liu W., Han Y. and Lombardi F., (1 Oct.-Dec. 2021), Design and Analysis of Energy-Efficient Dynamic Range Approximate Logarithmic Multipliers for Machine Learning, in *IEEE Transactions on Sustainable Computing*, vol. 6, no. 4, pp. 612–625, doi: 10.1109/TSUSC.2020.3004980.

[21] Li Z. *et al.*, (July 2024), Efficient Approximate Floating-Point Multiplier With Runtime Reconfigurable Frequency and Precision, in *IEEE Transactions on Circuits and Systems II: Express Briefs*, vol. 71, no. 7, pp. 3533–3537, doi: 10.1109/TCSII.2024.3364717.

[22] Zhang T. *et al.*, (2022), Design of Majority Logic-Based Approximate Booth Multipliers for Error-Tolerant Applications, in *IEEE Transactions on Nanotechnology*, vol. 21, pp. 81–89, doi: 10.1109/TNANO.2022.3145362.

[23] Shakibhamedan S., Amirafshar N., Baroughi A.S., Shahhoseini H.S. and TaheriNejad N., (May 2024), ACE-CNN: Approximate Carry Disregard Multipliers for Energy-Efficient CNN-Based Image Classification, in *IEEE Transactions on Circuits and Systems I: Regular Papers*, vol. 71, no. 5, pp. 2280–2293, doi: 10.1109/TCSI.2024.3369230.

Next-Generation Smart Systems – Sekhar et al. (Eds)
© 2027 The Author(s), ISBN: 978-1-041-34234-2

Design of Sorting Network Using Counters and Compressors with Bitonic Approach

S. Ram Gopal
Professor, Department of ECE, In Sree Vahini Institute of Science and Technology, Tiruvuru, Andhra Pradesh, India

M. Priyadarsini
PG Scholar, Department of ECE, In Sree Vahini Institute of Science and Technology, Tiruvuru, Andhra Pradesh, India

ABSTRACT: A parallel counter is an integral part of many number-juggling circuits, particularly rapid multipliers. Summing up a large number of operands at once is an important step in many DSP units. To speed up the summing process, compressors and counters with a high compression ratio are needed. This study introduces a novel method for rapid saturating bi counter or exact/approximate (4:2) compressors, which are built on top of a sorting network. Sorting networks reorganise the counter's inputs so that they are able to be represented as one-hot coding sequences after they are asymmetrically divided in half. By solving three unique Logical formulas combining the reordered sequences to the immediately code sequence, the counter's output Boolean operators may be significantly reduced. To make this project even better, we'll use parallel sorting approaches to find and sort the M largest values out of N inputs, and then we'll build scalable systems around those methods. Additionally, techniques for iterative sorting were proposed to determine the maximum values. When used with the right parameters, BITONIC SORTING is a powerful algorithm for tasks like these.

Keywords: approximate (4:2) compressors, Sorting, asymmetric, Digital signal processing, Arithmetic Logic Unit

1 INTRODUCTION

One important aspect of almost every electronic device is their ability to minimise energy usage. This is especially true for portable devices such as smartphones and tablets. If this minimisation can be accomplished with some performance penalty, that would be great. Digital signal processing (DSP) blocks are the most sought-after transportable elements for developing various multimedia applications. The core unit of processing of these blocks represents the ALU, which works the majority of the math operations. Since additions are the most prevalent operation in processing components, there is a high likelihood of power and energy being squandered. The algorithms executed by the majority of DSP cores ultimately result in consumable media such as movies or photos. Approximations may be used to make mathematical circuits faster and more efficient. The fundamental reason for this is because people's visual processing skills are somewhat restricted when it comes to visual material. The accuracy of the mathematical processes is not always critical for the system to function, especially in some situations like video and image processing. Approximate computing does wonders for precision, performance, and resource consumption. One advantage of utilising an approximation multiplier is that it increases speed and decreases the error rate.

2 LITERATURE SURVEY

[1] **"Short binary counters & compressors produced by sorting networks" by Wenbo Guo и Shuguo Li, members of the IEEE.**

To speed up the summing process, compressors and counters with a high compression ratio are needed. A novel method for very fast saturate (7,3) / (15,4) bi counting or exact/approximate (4:2) compressors is based on the sorting network. Sorting networks reorganise the counter's inputs so that they can only be represented as one-hot code patterns after they are asymmetrically divided in half. Using the (7,3) number for ADP and PDP, respectively, results in less latency.

[2] **"Symmetric stacking-based fast binary counters" by C. Fritz & A. T. Fam etc.**

A new binary counter design is introduced here. After combining two sets of three-bit stacks into six-bit stacks using a novel symmetric method, the "1" bits are grouped together using three-bit stacking circuits. The crucial path of the 6:3 counting circuits does not have any xor gates.

[3] **"Very fast, powerful 5-2 and 7-2 compressor in CMOS process for quick parallel accumulations" (A. Fathi *et al.* 2009).**

Very fast compressors, such as 5-2 and 7-2, are what we recommend. The new designs have significantly reduced gate-level delay compared to the old ones. With the technology's extension to function with 7-2 architecture, speed performance is improved by 32% and by 30%, respectively, compared to its original design for a 5-2 compressor.

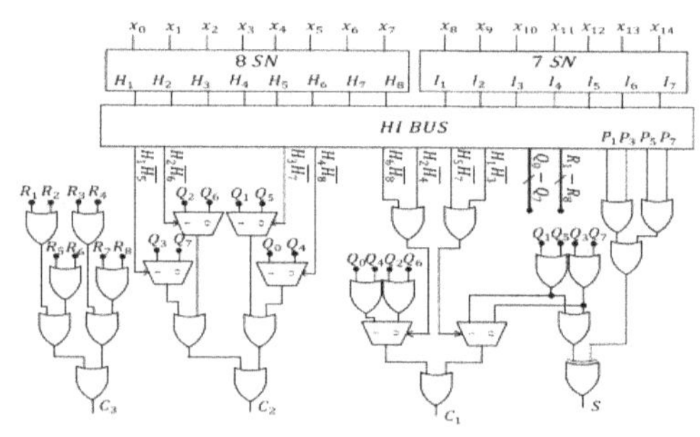

Figure 1. Overall (7, 3) counter.

3 EXISTING SYSTEM

3.1 *Implementation of (7, 3) counter*

By inserting a fixed one-bit "1" at the start and a fixed one-bit "0" at the conclusion of the reordered sequence, we can handle sequences that only include "1"s or "0"s, guaranteeing that the 0,1-junctions always exits. Second, both the original and the modified sequence have the same total of "1"s and "0"s. Since the padded "1" is already in place, we don't take it into account when calculating the total number of "1"s in the cushioning sequence.

DOI: 10.1201/9781042001767-74

Sequences of Code Points with One Hot and Zero Junctions: Given the assurance of the stretched constant "0" & "1," the 0,1-junctions can only symbolise the rearranged lineup. Recall that the 0, 1-intersections need to be situated at 1,0 in the left-to-right direction. A new sequence P0-P4 is derived using this structure using a Boolean operator (AB). Since the reorganised and enlarged sequence includes exactly one 0, 1-junction, there is precisely one "1" in order P0-P4. A one-hot coding that satisfies ("|" symbolises "OR" & "&" implies "AND"). This is shown by the P0-P4 sequence.

3.2 *Implementation of (15, 4) counter*

A network with eight-way sorting... The output of this sorting network is achieved by the use of six levels of basic logic gates. To make a seven-way sort network that uses six layers of fundamental logic gates, just remove one bit from an eight-way sorting network.

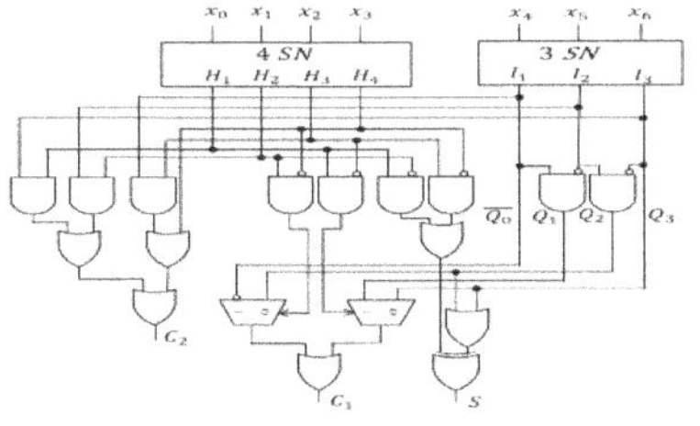

Figure 2. Overall (15, 4) counter circuit.

4 PROPOSED METHOD

4.1 *Bitonic sorting*

Bitonic sort is a parallel sorting method that relies on comparisons. Bitonic sort takes a more thorough approach to sorting data than other popular algorithms. This sort excels in parallel programming because it allows the user to compare the parts in a predetermined order that is not reliant on the data. That's why hardware implementations benefit from bits. Before we can understand Bitonic sort, we must understand what a Bitonic series is and how it is generated bitonic. Bitonic sort uses the bitonic sorting algorithm, making it one of the fastest sorting networks. The data does not dictate the order of how comparisons are done in a sorting network. This opens the door to the possibility of building sorting networks using hardware or in-parallel processing sets. An n•log(n)2 comparator sorting network is known as bitonic sort.

4.2 *Simulation results*

In the existing system, (6,3) and (7,3) Counter has'n' number of inputs are divided in to a symmetrical order. Full adders and half adders are used in this design. Due to present of a greater number of XOR gates the delay is more and the space occupied by circuit is also high. The Hardware complexity of the circuit is also high due to a greater number of XOR gates and the power consumed is high in existing design. In the proposed counters, the (7,3) and (15,4) Counters are arranging in symmetrical order by using sorting network.

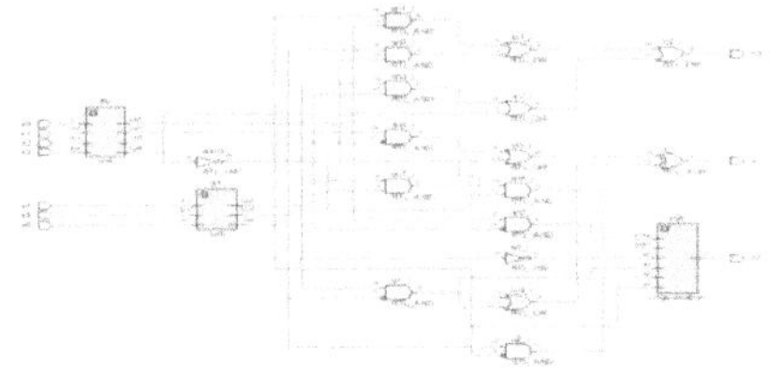

Figure 3. Schematic diagram of (7,3) counter.

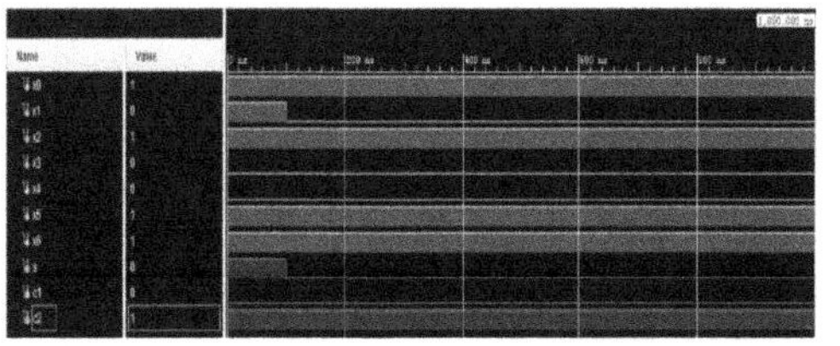

Figure 4. (7,3) Output waveform.

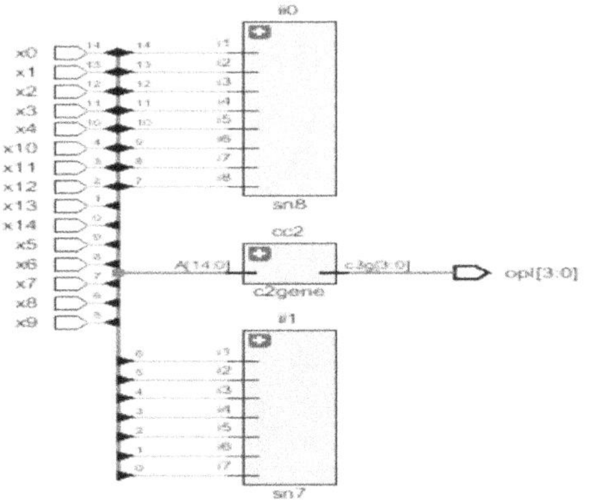

Figure 5. Schematic diagram of (15,4) counter.

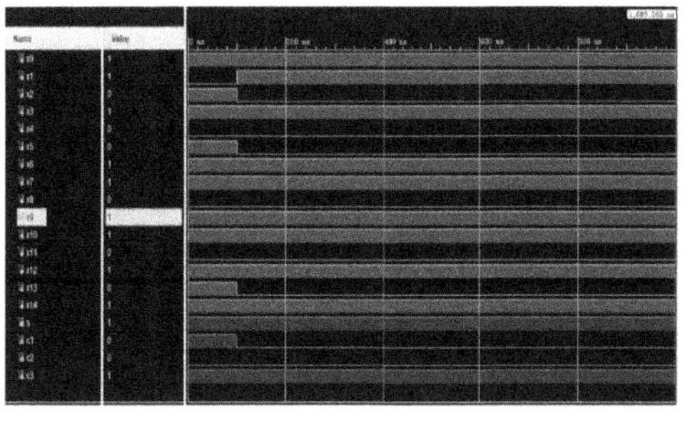

Figure 6. (15, 4) counter simulation result

5 CONCLUSION

A practical and speedy countermeasure is mapped out and replicated in this project. During this procedure, we build (7, 3), (15, 4), counters using a newly suggested sorting network-based counter design approach. Because they work better in ADP and create less delay where speed is crucial, the proposed counters are far more versatile than the current designs. Using a sorting network as a foundation, this project proposes a novel approach to counter construction and builds (7,3) and (15,4) counters. In comparison to previous designs, the (7, 3) counter uses less power, takes up less space, and has less latency. The (15,4) counter outperforms previous designs in terms of flexibility, achieving less delay when speed is necessary and greater performance in ADP and PDP when space or power is critical. The Xilinx Artix 7 -XC7A35TFTG256-1 board is used by the FPGA for both the (7,3) and (15,4) counters.

6 FUTURE SCOPE

We can now use what we learnt about designing multipliers with the proposed binary counters to build bit multipliers of much higher power. It is possible to improve the designs' performance by reducing their overall latency.

REFERENCES

[1] Asif S. and Kong Y., (Dec. 2015), Design of an algorithmic Wallace multiplier using high speed counters, in *Proc. 10th Int. Conf. Comput. Eng. Syst. (ICCES)*, Cairo, Egypt, pp. 133–138.

[2] Design using multi-input counter and compressor circuits, in *Proc. 10th IEEE Symp. Comput. Arithmetic*, Grenoble, France, Jun. 1991, pp. 43–50.

[3] Fathi A., Mashoufi B., and Azizian S., (Jun. 2020), Very fast, high-performance 5-2 and 7-2 compressors in CMOS process for rapid parallel accumulations, *IEEE Trans. Very Large Scale Integr. (VLSI) Syst.*, vol. 28, no. 6, pp. 1403–1412.

[4] Jiang Q. and Li S., (Oct. 2017), A design of manually optimized (15, 4) parallel counter, in *Proc. Int. Conf. Electron Devices Solid State Circuits (EDSSC)*, Hsinchu, Taiwan, pp. 1–2

[5] Mehta M., Parmar V., and Swartz Lander E., (Jun. 1991), High-speed multiplier design using multi-input counter and compressor circuits, in *Proc. 10th IEEE Symp. Comput. Arithmetic*, Grenoble, France, pp. 43–50.

[6] Najafi M.H., Lilja D.J., Riedel M.D., and Bazargan K., (Aug. 2018), Low-cost sorting network circuits using unary processing, *IEEE Trans. Very Large Scale Integr. (VLSI) Syst.*, vol. 26, no. 8, pp. 1471–1480.

[7] Satish T. and Pande K.S., (Aug. 2019), Multiplier using NAND based compressors, in *Proc. 3rd Int. Conf. Electron., Mater. Eng. NanoTechnol.* (IEMENTech), Kolkata, India, pp. 1–6

[8] Wallace C.S., (Feb. 1964), A suggestion for a fast multiplier, *IEEE Trans. Electron. Comput.*, vol. EC-13, no. 1, pp. 14–17.

[9] Wenbo Guo and Shuguo Li, (June 2021), Fast binary counters and compressors generated by sorting network, *IEEE Transactions On Very Large-Scale Integration (Vlsi) Systems*, vol. 29, no. 6.

Next-Generation Smart Systems – Sekhar et al. (Eds)

An Efficient Modified Adder by Using High Speed Truncation Technique

V. Narayan Goud
Professor, Department of ECE, In Sree Vahini Institute Of Science And Technology, Tiruvuru, Andhra Pradesh, India

Abbadasari.Ranga Rao
PG Scholar, Department of ECE, In Sree Vahini Institute of Science and Technology, Tiruvuru, Andhra Pradesh, India

ABSTRACT: More and more, portable and mobile devices are using high-performance computing systems that are energy efficient, space-efficient, and low-power. In order to handle these kinds of tasks, fixed-point VLSI systems use DSP (digital signal processing) techniques. The adder-tree (AT) is a popular choice for matrix-vector multiplication and inner product computing in parallel architectures. Approximate computing has the potential to decrease design complexity while enhancing speed and power efficiency in error-tolerant applications like information mining and multimodal signal processing. Precise processing units are not always necessary in these cases. You may use their close substitutes in their stead. A novel method for designing approximators of multipliers using partial products is modified to include changing probability components. The accumulation of changed partial products often involves varying the logic complexity of approximation. The main components of these applications are adders and multipliers. The current system's implementation of a multiplier consists of three steps: first, creating a reduction tree for partial products; second, adding the sum & carry rows from the reduced tree to a vector; and finally, producing the final product. More electricity is used in the second stage. A new compressor-based approximation adder is suggested to lessen power consumption and enhance approximate difference. Further improvement in performance and reduction in error rate may be achieved with the suggested approximate compressor.

Keywords: adder cells, low-power design, digital signal processing (DSP), error-tolerant technology, image processing, and high-speed integrated circuits are all part of the same field

1 INTRODUCTION

In recent years, there has been a significant increase in the demand for ultralow power sources due to the proliferation of lightweight and wireless computing. Because CMOS circuit power consumption is square-related to supply voltage, voltage supply scaling is a popular low-power method for reducing power dissipation. However, issues with noise interference have made it more difficult to develop efficient and dependable microelectronics systems; as a result, methods to improve noise tolerance in design have been extensively refined. Voltage over scaling (VOS) is an aggressive low-power technology that was suggested in to reduce the supply voltage beyond the critical supply value without compromising the throughput. But the signal-to-noise ratio (SNR) becomes much worse while using VOS. The unique algorithm noise tolerant (ANT) approach successfully combats soft mistakes while obtaining large energy savings. It combines the VOS core block with reduced-precision replica (RPR). Certain ANT distortion exhibited concepts, with the ANT design approach expanded to include system level considerations. Nevertheless, the ANT designs' RPRs are highly individualised, making them difficult to replicate.

The ANT designs' RPR implementations are lightning fast, but their hardware is too complicated. Consequently, because to its simplicity, the RPR model in the ANT layout remains the most used design. Adopting RPR in, meanwhile, will still incur additional costs for overhead space and energy use. Besides the fixed-width RPR, this research suggests an additional way to use a fullwidth RPR block. The fixed-width RPR may reduce power consumption and area overhead, which can solve the computation error. We ensure that the RPR compensating circuit is not on the essential path to prevent the delay from becoming worse on that route.

2 LITERATURE SURVEY

Energy reduction in computational noise tolerance signal processing, by R. Hegde and N.R. Shanbhag This small digital signal processing device begins to show a correlation between critical path latency and throughput below a particular voltage threshold. Subtitled "All types of errors have become probable with present VLSI technology," the authors N. Zhu, W. L. Goh, W. Wang, K. S. Yeo, and Z. H. Kong present an intolerant truncation adder for digital signal processing that is low-power, fast-speeds, and power efficient. Utilising error tolerance (ET), a concept that has just recently emerged in the realm of VLSI (very large-scale integration) test and design, we propose a novel error-tolerant addition (ETA). The authors of this article—H. E. F. Almurib, as well as T. M. S. Kumar, and F. Lombard—discuss approximate designs for modest power increases by cell replacement. Its three separate designs make approximation calculation for wrong adder cells easier. There are much fewer transistors used by these cells compared to a correct full adder cell with a known defective design. One instrument that A. B. Kahng and S. Kang created for approximation mathematics is an adjustable, precision-tuning adder. Approximation, which may improve performance or decrease energy use by using less or inaccurate circuit, might be useful in areas where standards are lax. Researchers have mostly focused on approximation circuits with the hopes of achieving high performance and energy efficiency while tolerating a certain degree of imprecision. One example of a circuit like this is a power-efficient approximations multiplier that may be set up to recover from partial mistakes. Digital signal processing (DSP) and other essential mathematical applications rely on multipliers. A new, shorter, and more power-efficient approximation multiplier is recommended for use in electronic signal processing applications with remarkable endurance rather than conventional multipliers.

3 EXISTING SYSTEM

A growing number of mobile and portable computers are using lightweight, energy-efficient, and low-power high-performance computer platforms. Digital signal processing (DSP) methods

DOI: 10.1201/9781042001767-75

are used by fixed-point VLSI systems to manage such jobs. In parallel systems, the adder-tree (AT) is often used for matrix-vector multiplying and inner product computation. Multiplier architecture also makes use of a shift-adder-tree (SAT) to store bits in the partial product. Problems with word-length extension are common when working with fixed- point mathematical operations like as addition and multiplication. An alternative bit matrix structure is used by SAT as contrasted with AT. Consequently, SAT and AT show different trends in the increase of word length. To deal with positive component products of multipliers, the SAT also uses a few of extra bits. There are detailed strategies for minimising truncation error in the fixed-width multiplier implementation. However, because to the unusual structure of the bitmatrix during design, the fixed-width multiplier approach is not suited for building a fixed-width AS. For each N-point input vector, a full-length AT (FL-AT) construction yields (w + p) bits since p is equal to the inverse logarithm of N. A fixed- width AT (FX-AT) architecture generates w-bit output for an input vector of the same size. Typically, the FX-AT design may be extracted from the FL-AT design by direct or post-truncation. As an example of post-truncation, one smaller-order bit of the FL-AT adder's final output is reduced to {p} bits by the use of direct truncation (DT). Every single one of FLAT's adder program outputs are like this. It is recommended to tune FL-AT bit-by-bit for different constant multiplication (MCM) in order to maximise the shifting process. In order to process images, we provide a powerful FL-AT architecture that use an approximate adder to realise a Gaussian filter inaccurately. Regrettably, the optimal AT is only useful for designs that rely on MCM, and no existing design solves the issues related to fixed-width AT implementation. You can't use either the direct termination or post-truncation methods to find an efficient FX-AT architecture. Presently, there is a lack of published works that provide a unique technique for developing successful FX-AT design. An effective FXAT design may increase the performance of specialised VLSI systems by implementing complicated digital signal processing algorithms.

4 PROPOSED SYSTEM

Many VLSI design applications rely on the adder. In parallel architectures, the Adder-tree (AT) is often used for matrix-vector multiplication inner product processing. Direct or post-truncation conversion from full-width to fixed-width AT designs is the usual procedure. But an efficient adder tree design is not produced by any of these methods. This research proposes a novel design implementation for obtaining the fixed-width addition Tree layout from the truncated input. To compensate for the truncation error, the bias estimate formula adjusts based on the probabilistic technique. The proposed method yields three separate fixed-width Adder trees, where the width of the corresponding vectors is 8, 16, and 32. Hence, the proposed fixed-width addition tree design achieves better efficiency and areas delaying product (ADP) results than the existing fixed-width adder tree for 8-, 16-, & 32-bit input vectors. Because it controls precision, efficiency, and power consumption, this component of the build is crucial. A Control Block and a Carry Free Additions Block are its two primary building blocks. Figure 1 shows the modified OR block in outline form. The proposed enhanced ORblock-1 makes use of two more transistors, the inputs to which are tied to the CTL signal, a control signal that originates through the Control Block (CB). Whenever CTL is zero, the OR block circuit continues with MI turned on and M2 turned off. go about your business as usual. By connecting the output node to VDD, the output is set to "1" when CTL=1 and MI is off and M2 is on. The issue with the block shown in Figure 2 is that the output node uses an NMOS as its first pass transistor. Since NMOS is known to be bad at transferring strong logic '1', the output value will be degraded when connected to VDD. By switching out the NMOS transistors for PMOS and reordering the transistor connections (as shown in Figure 2), we have developed a second modified OR block-2 that can pass strong logic '1'.

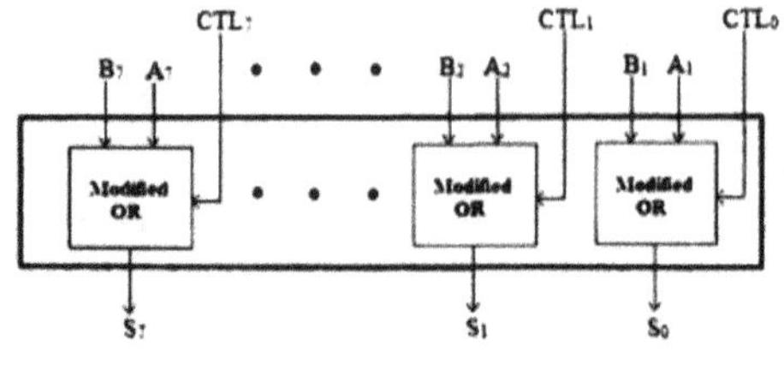

Figure 1. Block diagram.

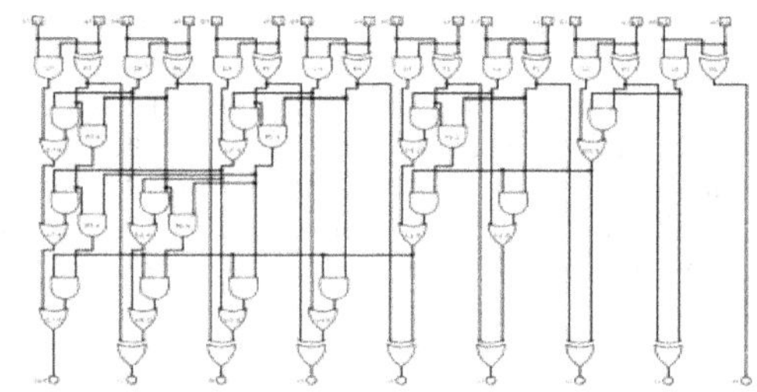

Figure 2. A 16-bit adder tree with a fixed width.

3 RESULTS ANALYSIS

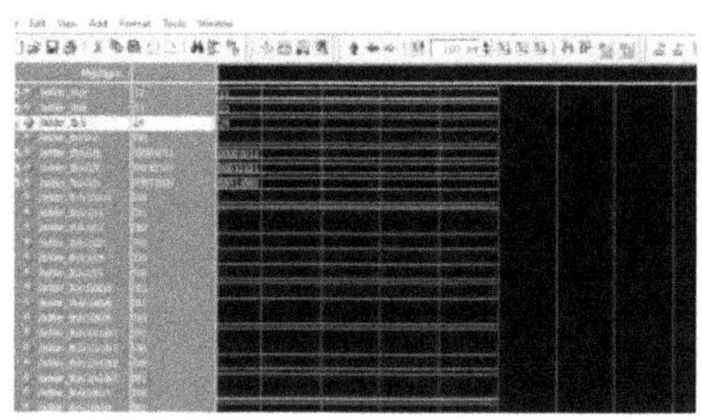

Figure 3. Simulation results.

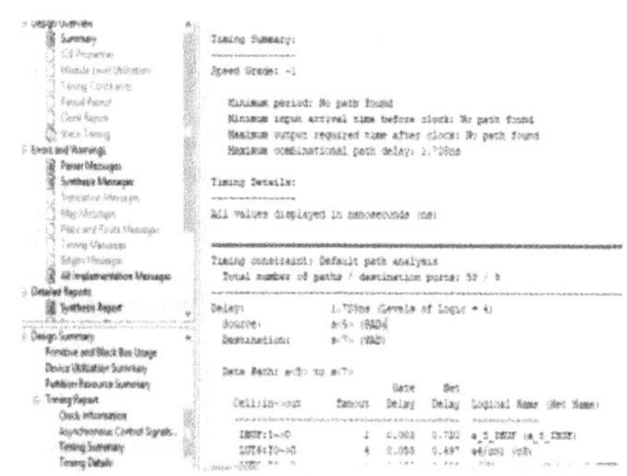

Figure 4. Synthesis report (Delay).

Table 1. Comparison table.

Parameter	Existing Method	Proposed Method
DELAY	2.808ns	1.72ns
AREA	12 LUT's	10 LUT's
POWER	3.685	3.609

The suggested adder's power and latency are compared to previous adder designs in Table 1. According to the data in the table, the suggested design likewise has lower power and delay requirements.

4 CONCLUSION AND FUTURE SCOPE

This study's simulations and findings demonstrate that, for low to moderate bit widths, the basic ripple-carry adder outperforms fixed adders. The efficient optimisation of the ripple transfer adder through the Xilinx FPGA's quick carry chain is the predicted reason for this. These adders defy expectations by ultimately outperforming linear addition designs at huge bit-widths, which are anticipated to be in the 128-256 bit range, which goes against earlier findings. Massive adders rely on this for operations like cryptography and precision mathematics, which sometimes involve integer additions of several thousand bits. An improved carry path should be included into future FPGA designs to enhance placement and scheduling for tree-based adders designs. Because the adder is the key component that determines, to a large extent, the cycle duration or energy consumption in many cryptographic other digital signal handling applications, this is the case. Potentially implementing a " fast tree chain" and achieving RCA-level performance with field-programming gate array (FPGA) designs may pique their interest in studying associated costs and advantages. Professionals are now investigating the effects of fault tolerance on FPGA systems caused by the constant carrying tree topology's built-in redundancy. The testability and possible tolerance for faults of spanned tree adders need more research.

REFERENCES

[1] Vitoroulis K. and Al-Khalili A.J., (Aug. 2007), Performance of Parallel Prefix Adders Implemented with FPGA technology, *IEEE Northeast Workshop on Circuits and Systems*, pp. 498–501.

[2] Gizopoulos D., Psarakis M., Paschalis A., and Zorian Y., (2003), Easily Testable Cellular Carry Lookahead Adders, *Journal of Electronic Testing: Theory and Applications* 19, 285–298.

[3] Xing S. and Yu W.W.H., (Jan. 1998), FPGA Adders: Performance Evaluation and Optimal Design, *IEEE Design & Test of Computers*, vol. 15, no. 1, pp. 24–29.

[4] Bečvář M. and Štukjunger P., (2005), FixedPoint Arithmetic in FPGA, *ActaPolytechnica*, vol. 45, no. 2, pp. 67–72.

[5] Kogge P.M. and Stone H.S., (August 1973), A Parallel Algorithm for the Efficient Solution of a General Class of Recurrence Equations, *IEEE Trans. on Computers*, Vol. C-22, No 8.

[6] Ndai P., Lu S., Somesekhar D., and Roy K., (March 2007), Fine-Grained Redundancy in Adders, *Int. Symp. on Quality Electronic Design*, pp. 317–321.

[7] Lynch T. and Swartzlander E.E., (Aug. 1992), A Spanning Tree Carry Lookahead Adder, *IEEE Trans. on Computers*, vol. 41, no. 8, pp. 931–939.

[8] Weste N.H.E. and Harris D., (2011), *CMOS VLSI Design*, 4th edition, Pearson–Addison- Wesley.

[9] Brent R.P. and Kung H.T., (1982), A regular layout for parallel adders, *IEEE Trans. Comput.*, vol. C-31, pp. 260–264.

[10] Harris D., (2003), A Taxonomy of Parallel Prefix Networks, in *Proc. 37th Asilomar Conf. Signals Systems and Computers*, pp. 2213–7.

Next-Generation Smart Systems – Sekhar et al. (Eds)

Design of High Speed Multi Operand Adder Using Reversible Gates

Kota. Venkanna
Associate Professor, Department of ECE, In Sree Vahini Institute of Science and Technology, Tiruvuru, Andhra Pradesh, AP, India

Thota. Sai Krishna
PG Scholar, Department of ECE, In Sree Vahini Institute of Science and Technology, Tiruvuru, Andhra Pradesh, AP, India

ABSTRACT: This study takes a ripple carry adder (RCA) approach to studying the binary tree adder's (BTA) critical path in order to find ways to reduce delays. The study's results informed the proposal of an updated BTA logic structure and RCA design. The comparison of the two RCA designs reveals that the suggested one is superior in terms of space, latency, and energy efficiency. This RCA plan suggests a BTA framework. In comparison to most effective multi-operand adder currently available, the synthesis findings demonstrate that the suggested 32-operand BTA reduced energy utilisation by 28.7 percent and area by 22.5 percent. Writers have also tested the suggested BTA in new multiplier designs. Incorporating the suggested BTA into multiplier designs considerably enhanced their efficacy, as seen by the synthesis result. Because of this, the suggested BTA architecture may be the way to go when designing digital computers that are efficient in terms of energy, space, and latency and can handle signals and pictures.

Keywords: Multi operand adder, Latency, Density, Ripple carry adder, Reversible logic, Propagation

1 INTRODUCTION

Very large scale integrated (VLSI) chips now have the capability to include a signal processing system that is more intricate. This signal processing applications uses a lot of power and has a high computing capacity. While performance and area remain the two primary design goals of contemporary VLSI systems, power consumption is quickly becoming an important problem [1]. The creation of a low-power VLSI systems is essential for two main reasons. In order to stay up with the ever-increasing frequency of operation and processing capability per chip, it is essential to first provide large currents and then use suitable cooling solutions to eliminate heat from excess power consumption. The second problem is that portable electronics have a short battery life. Due to their small power design, these portable devices provide a longer runtime. The performance of digital systems and a crucial mathematical function are both profoundly impacted by addition. When it comes to adders, electrical applications reign supreme. Digital signal processors or multipliers use them in algorithm implementations including FFT, FIR, and IIR. Every time the concept of multiplication is broached, adders are involved. That microprocessors are capable of carrying out millions of instructions/second is common knowledge. Therefore, the speed of operations should be the main limitation while building multipliers. Miniaturisation and low power consumption are key for a portable gadget. Electronic gadgets such as mobile phones, computers, and others use more power while they are not in use. Consequently, these are the primary design parameters that any VLSI designer should strive to optimise.

2 LITERATURE SURVEY

Computers, digital signal processors, and microprocessors often need the most common mathematical operation: addition. It is the building block upon which all additional mathematical operations depend. To successfully build an arithmetic unit, binary adder structures are therefore established as a crucial hardware component. Any student of computer mathematics will tell you that there is an abundance of circuit designs, and that each one has unique performance characteristics and real-world uses. While several studies have focused on binary addition topologies, there is less literature comparing and contrasting their respective performances. The focus here is on a digital circuit. For an analogue signal processing circuit, see Electronic mixer. In the world of electronics, digital components that add integers are called adders or summers. The mathematical logic unit(s) isn't the only place you'll find adders; you'll also see them in processors that calculate indexes for tables and addresses. Although adders may be constructed for various formats such as excess-3 or binary-coded decimal, the majority of them operate with binary integers. When negative numbers are represented by the two's or ones' complement, it's easy to convert an adder to an adder-subtract or. Other forms of signed numbers need a more complex adder.

The literature (e.g., [9–14]) has presented several adder families/structures with varying speeds, power consumptions, & area usages. In comparison to other adders, the ripple carry addition (RCA) features a straightforward construction, which results in low power consumption & space utilisation but a significant latency [2]. To improve the RCA's speed, many structures have been suggested, such as the carry skip addition (CSKA), the carry increment addition (CIA), and the carry select addition (CSLA) [2]. A other kind of adder, known as a parallel adder, often uses less room and power while operating at faster rates [18]. The majority of prior research on adders has been on finding ways to make the family's adder structure faster while also decreasing its power and area utilisation via architectural and circuit changes (for examples, see [9–16]). This section provides a concise overview of some of the literature on adders that has compared them, with an emphasis on publications that have examined reliability and performance metrics.

3 PROPOSED METHOD

The benefits of technical scalability are drying up, thus people are starting to use stochastic computing as an alternative. Designers are releasing traditional accuracy constraints and purposefully revealing hardware variation to higher levels of the computing stack, rather than concealing variances under expensive guard bands [1]. Approximation computing, which entails reconstructing a system's logic circuit, is one possible

DOI: 10.1201/9781042001767-76

approach of lowering power, area, & latency in VLSI design [2]. It takes use of the gap between the accuracy provided by the machine itself and the precision required by applications to accomplish a number of optimisations. Academics in the field of approximation computing have taken a keen interest in adders, a crucial component of arithmetic circuits.

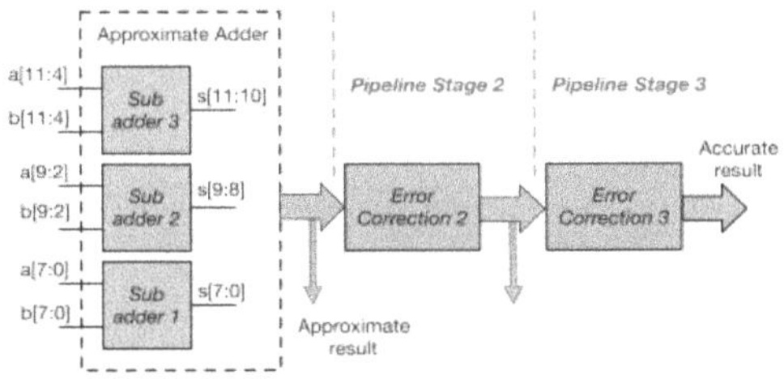

Figure 1. Adjustable adder with error correction.

In this short, we will focus on improving LOA in a systematic way. We start by taking the LOA design and using it as a basis for a generic architectural template. After then, we look at every possible way to use this template and identify the one that reduces MSE the most. Optimised LOCA, or OLOCA, is our name for it. Our improved approach outperforms all other approximate adders in terms of hardware cost & accuracy, which is not surprising considering it LOA is the most effective approximate adder available at the moment. Experiment results cited in this brief provide credence to this assertion.

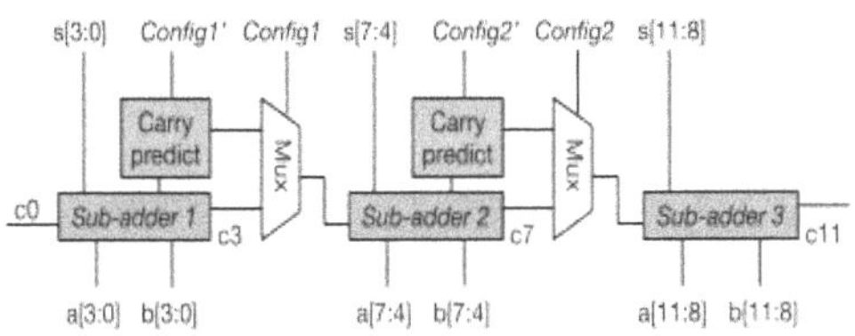

Figure 2. Switchable adder based on carry prediction.

3.1 *Overarching structure of the template*

As stated in the LOA As stated in Section I, if the error versus hardware cost compromise is evaluated, experimental results show that LOA is the most effective design among all the known approximation adders [14], [15]. As can be seen in Figure 2, a thorough analysis of LOA's design reveals that it may be generalised: To divide the least significant subadder, you may use a 2-to-2 logic blocks and nl 2-to-1 logical blocks (pieces 0 to nl −1). This next block takes in data from the adder at bit nl and employs an AND gate in order to supply the input charge for the exact part; nevertheless, the overall signal it produces could be erroneous. Finally, the most important sub-adder is an exact adder.

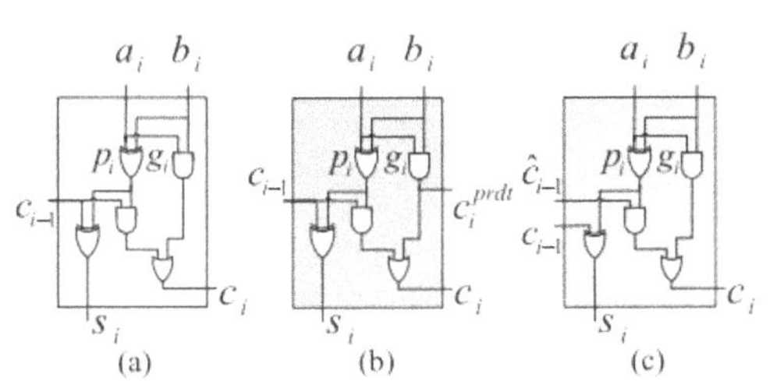

Figure 3. (a) The traditional complete adder. (b) A fully selectable carry-out adder.

One or zero as a constant function (Cte-1) or zeroes (Cte-0) remains an option to consider. The appropriate choices for 2-to-1 blocks are listed in Table 1, while for 2-to-2 blocks, they are listed in Table 2, both of which are concerned with concreteness. We have taken into account all potential outcomes; however, we have eliminated from Tables 1 as well as II the blocks with higher error values per unit of cost. The optimal structure of the template may be achieved by choosing the optimal combination of blocks form each table.

3.2 *Architecture that is optimised*

Depending on the chosen error metrics, a range of optimisation results are conceivable. As an example of an error measure, we'll be using the MSE to show how valuable it is in data processing applications. While using the general template to find the optimal design, it is necessary to test every possible combination of the 2-to-1 , 2-to-2 logic blocks found in Tables 1 and 2. We should trust our instincts for the time being and see where they lead us. It is clear from that errors in the upper components have a larger impact than those in the more fundamental ones (8).

Consequently, the 2-to-2 block is a superior investment option than the lesser 2-to-1 blocks. Two 2-to-2 blocks at the top are the half of the adder and OR_AND. The MSE is much increased when an OR_AND is used instead of a half adder, but the latency & area are little improved. Because of this, the solution that LOA suggested—using OR_AND to the 2-to-2 block—is not very efficient. In contrast to 2-to-1 blocks, which provide a mean mistake of zero or negative, the 2-to-2 block, when converted to a half adder, introduces an overall mistake of zero or positive.

4 SIMULATION RESULTS

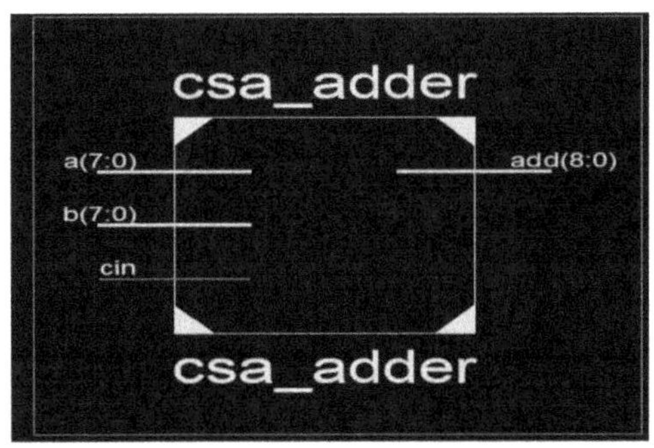

Figure 4. Schematic for RTL.

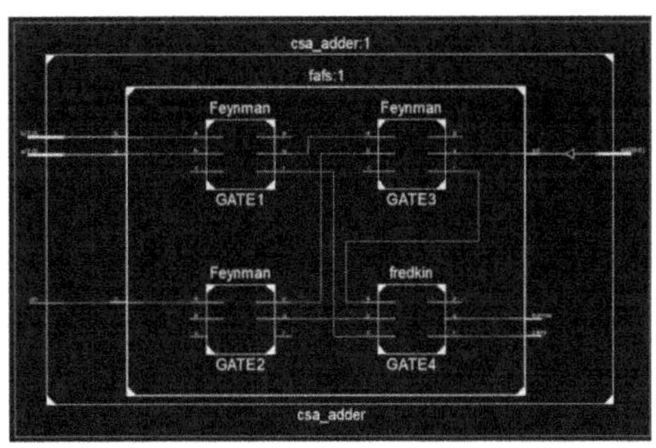

Figure 5. The internal block diagram.

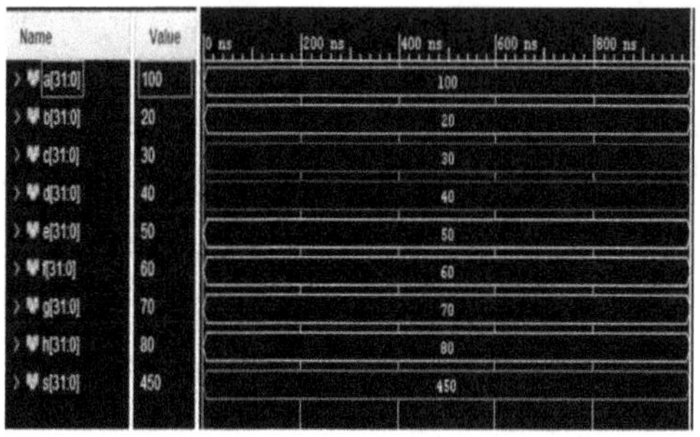

Figure 6. Temporal diagram for simulation.

5 CONCLUSION

The authors of this study proposed an updated version of the current ISA design that is both fast and power-efficient. In order to increase speed and decrease power consumption, this architecture has been clock-gated and fine-grain pipelined, respectively. Based on the experimental results, the proposed ISA has a maximum clock frequency of 444.64 MHz. After then, it used 9.68 mW of total electrical power at 400 MHz and took up 5111 μm^2 of space at the technical node. As a result, compared to the state-of-the-art ISA design, the suggested ISA may be 52% faster, 52.38% more power efficient, and 40.7% smaller in size. So, the existing and future electronic gadgets, as well as the Internet of Everything (IoE) and many other uses, will find this design to be highly valuable. However, using less-technological node in the design phase could help alleviate the area problem to some extent.

REFERENCES

[1] Chang L., Frank D.J., Montoye R.K., Koester S.J., Ji B.L., Coteus P.W., Dennard R.H., Haensch W., (2022), Practical strategies for power-efficient computing technologies, *Proc. IEEE* 98 (2) 215–236.

[2] Garg A.K. and Kaler R.S., (2022), Novel optical burst switching architecture for high speed networks, *Chinese Opt. Lett.* 6 (11) 807–811.

[3] Stubkjaer K.E., (2021), Semiconductor optical amplifier-based all-optical gates for high-speed optical processing, *IEEE J. Select. Top. Quantum Electron.* 6 (6) 1428–1435.

[4] Chattopadhyay T., (2021), All-optical symmetric ternary logic gate, *Opt. Laser Technol.* 42 (6) 1014–1021.

[5] Clavero R., Ramos F., Martinez J.M. and Marti J., (2021), All-optical flip-flop based on a single SOA-MZI, *IEEE Photon. Technol. Lett.* 17 (4) 843–845.

[6] Roy J.N., (2020), Mach–Zehnder interferometer-based tree architecture for all-optical logic and arithmetic operations, *Optik* 120 318–324.

[7] Scaffardi M.P., Ghelfi P., Lazzeri E., Poti L. and Bogoni A., (2020), Photonic processing for digital comparison and full addition based on semiconductor optical amplifiers, *IEEE J. Select. Top. Quantum Electron.* 14 (3) 826–833.

[8] Wang Q., Zhu G., Chen H., Jaques J., Leuthold J., Piccirilli A.B. and Dutta N.K., (2020), Study of all-optical XOR using Mach-Zehnder interferometer and differential scheme, *IEEE J. Select. Top. Quantum Electron.* 40 (6) 703–710.

[9] Zhang M., Zhao Y., Wang L., Wang J. and Ye P., (2019), Design and analysis of all-optical XOR gate using SOA-based Mach–Zehnder interferometer, *Opt. Commun.* 223 301–308.

[10] Chattopadhyay T., (2019), All-optical modified Fredkin gate, *IEEE J. Select. Top. Quantum Electron.* 18 (3)585–592.

[11] Huang Y. and Kumar P., (2018), Fredkin gates in X(2) microdisks via quantum zero blockade, in: *Nonlinear Optics: Materials, Fundamentals and Applications.*

[12] Huang Y. and Kumar P., (2017), Interaction-free quantum optical Fredkin gates in X (2) microdisks, *IEEE J. Select. Top. Quantum Electron.* 18 (2) 600–611.

[13] Kostinski N., Fok M. and Prucnal P., (2017), Experimental demonstration of an all-optical fiber-based Fredkin gate, *Opt. Lett.* 34 (18) 2766–2768.

[14] Poustite A. and Blow K., (2016), Demonstration of an all-optical Fredkin gate, *Opt. Commun.* 174 317–320.

Next-Generation Smart Systems – Sekhar et al. (Eds)
© 2027 The Author(s), ISBN: 978-1-041-34234-2

FPGA Implementation of Hardware-Efficient 2D Convolution Using MLC-Based and Hybrid Approximate Multipliers

Selvarasan R.
Research Scholar, Bharath Institute of Higher Education and Research, Chennai, India
Assistant Professor, Department of ECE, Kuppam Engineering College, Kuppam, A.P, India

Sudhagar G.
Assiociate Professor, Department of ECE, Bharath Institute of Higher Education and Research, Chennai. India

Rasadurai K.
Professor, Department of ECE, Kuppam Engineering College, Kuppam, A.P, India

ABSTRACT: This paper discusses implementation of a 2D convolution operation on an FPGA, using a 4x4 input matrix and a 2x2 kernel. It is benchmarked with two different designs for approximate multipliers. One is an 8x8 MLC-based approximate multiplier with a 6:2 compressor. The other is an 8x8 hybrid approximate multiplier with Parallel Prefix Adder (PPA) architecture. The focus is on error-resilient image processing systems and the balance between hardware resource usage, computational latency, and power consumption. Also important for evaluation were power and several other metrics such as Slice LUTs, Slice Registers, Occupied Slices, bonded IOBs, and critical path delay. These were analyzed after design synthesis and implementation on FPGA Spartan 6. The results indicate 7.7% power savings with the MLC-based multiplier, while hybrid PPA architecture needed 25.3% more Slice LUTs and 45% more Slice Registers. Overall, these results indicate an improvement in hardware efficiency. On the other hand, the Hybrid PPA multiplier is better for high-speed applications, reducing critical path latency by 16.6%. The results indicate the hybrid PPA is suited for throughput intensive applications, whereas the MLC-based approach is better for resource constrained systems.

Keywords: Hybrid Approximate Multiplier, Approximate PPAs, MLC-based approximate multipliers, 6:2 compressor

1 INTRODUCTION

In many computer vision and digital signal processing (DSP) applications, including image filtering, feature extraction, and Convolution Neural Networks (CNNs), two-dimensional (2D) convolution is a crucial operation. 2D convolution needs to be efficiently implemented in hardware for real-time processing in embedded and resource-constrained environments where size, power, and speed must be carefully controlled. Recently, approximate computing has gained popularity as a workable design approach for applications that are willing to tolerate some degree of error. This method allows for significant power and hardware complexity reductions by accepting tiny computational errors. Approximate multipliers, especially those that employ

Compressor-based designs and parallel prefix adders, have proven to be very advantageous in image and signal

Processing, where small errors do not substantially affect output quality. This work focuses on the FPGA implementation of 2D convolution with a 4×4 input matrixes and a 2×2 kernel. It makes use of two different 8x8 approximate multiplier designs: (1) a hybrid approximate multiplier which uses PPA and (2) MLC based approximate multiplier.

2 LITERATURE SURVEY

Zhang *et al.* [1] proposed an approximate multiplier with ML based 6:2 Compressors; it increases speed and energy efficiency while reducing complexity and tolerating small processing errors. Similarly, Da Rosa *et al.* [2] developed AxPPA approximation parallel prefix adders that selectively approximate carry generation to balance accuracy, energy, and latency. Leela *et al.* [3] introduced a hybrid adder-based multiplier that combines multiple adder types to generate high-speed performance suitable for DSP and cryptographic applications. Sreenivasulu and Meenpal [4] optimised FPGA-based 2D convolution through parallelisation and efficient memory management for CNN and image-processing acceleration, while Zhang *et al.* [5] developed approximate radix-4 Booth encoders using majority logic to save power and time. Zendegani and Safari [6] proposed AMCAL, a configurable-accuracy approximate multiplier that enables flexible trade-offs between precision and energy consumption. Wu *et al.* [7] described design trade-offs and future possibilities in their comprehensive study of approximation multipliers, spanning from circuits to algorithms. Examples of application-focused designs are Shirane *et al.* [8], who demonstrated that approximate multipliers in CNNs can significantly reduce power with minimal loss of accuracy.

Qiqieh *et al.* [10] used significance-driven logic compression to prioritise important bits for energy-efficient designs, while Rijal [9] used truncated multipliers for multimedia acceleration. Perri *et al.* [11] investigated energy-efficient multiplier strategies for embedded and Internet of Things systems, while Kumar and Ahmed [12] enhanced compressor-based approximation multipliers for media data. Kocakanat and Serif [13] have studied CNN resilience, Kim *et al.* [14] have measured CNN performance under approximation multiplication, and Gu *et al.* [15] have developed reconfigurable truncation multipliers for adaptive accuracy. Selvarasan *et al.* [16] proposed a Hybrid multiplier using Parallel Prefix adders for faster and with less hardware utilization. When taken as a whole, these pieces highlight the need to compromise between hardware requirement and accuracy level in computation.

DOI: 10.1201/9781042001767-77

3 METHODOLOGY OVERVIEW

3.1 *Approximate multiplier with 6:2 compressors*

An approximate 6-2 compressor [1] is developed as shown in Figure 1 to get the outputs as given below in Equations (1), (2) and (3)

$$cout_1 = Majority(x_1, x_2, x_3) = x_1(x_2 + x_3) + x_2x_3 \quad (1)$$

$$cout_2 = Majority(x_4, x_5, x_6) = x_4(x_5 + x_6) + x_5x_6 \quad (2)$$

$$sum = 1. \quad (3)$$

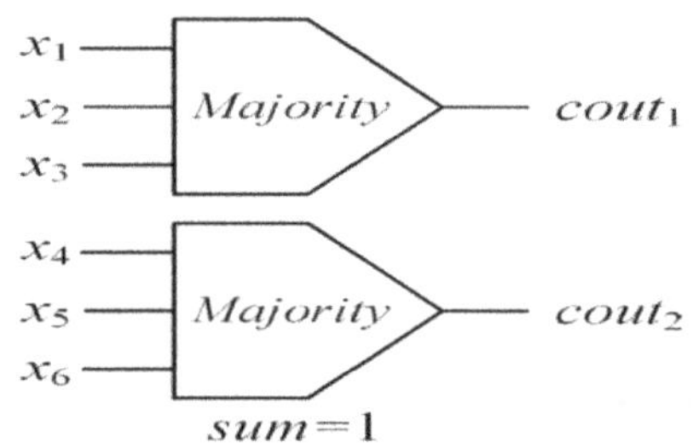

Figure 1. Approximate 6:2 compressor.[1]

The compressor consists of two majority gates that ignore carry, cout3, and cin, as can be seen. Because the output sum is equal to "1" always, no extra hardware is needed to calculate it, thereby lowering the design's power and latency. The effectiveness of the 6:2 compressors in approximation multipliers is assessed using the 8×8 Dadda multiplier. First, AND gates are used to create an array of partial products. Compressors are then used to compress these goods. Lastly, a ripple carry adder computes the final results.

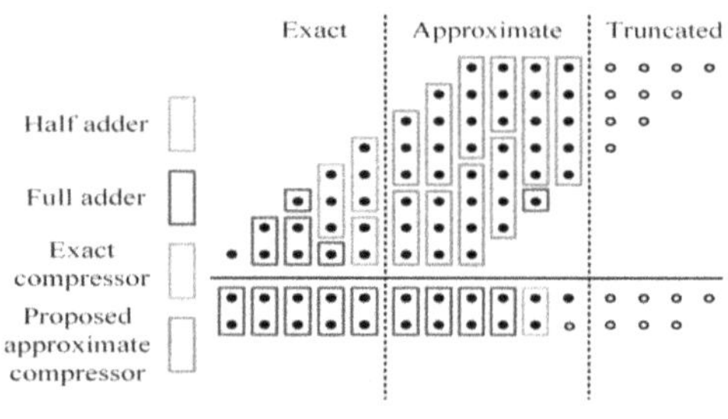

Figure 2. Partial product reduction of approximate multiplier.[1]

Figure 2 depicts [1] the approximate reduction procedure for a Dadda multiplier, with each dot standing for a partial product bit. For additional hardware savings, the four least significant columns are trimmed, which barely affects multiplier accuracy. Only six columns from five to ten employ the approximate compressor; the five most important columns, on the other hand, perform exact compression to maintain accuracy. To compress the partial products into two rows, as seen in Figure 2, ten approximate 6-2 compressors, five full adders, and three precise compressors [1] are used in the first stage The final results are then calculated using nine full adders and a half adder.

3.2 *Hybrid approximate multiplier*

Hybrid adders are combined to develop an Approximate Multiplier as shown in Figure 3 [16]. This multiplier is made up of Approximate Parallel Prefix Adders (AxPPAs) [2], which does approximation calculations in Least Significant Bits and keeps exact calculations for Most Significant Bits [3].

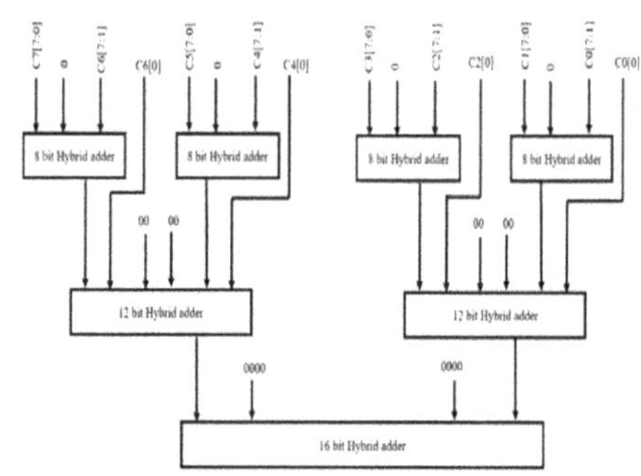

Figure 3. Hybrid multiplier.[3]

Kogge stone adders and Brent Kung adder are the Parallel Prefix Adders used to develop the hybrid approximate adder as shown in Figure 4; this has been used in Hybrid Multiplier shown in Figure 3 to device the approximation. An eight bit Hybrid Approximate PPA Multiplier is built using a four bit Brent Kung adder and a four bit Approximate Kogge Stone adder with the appropriate input combinations. [16].

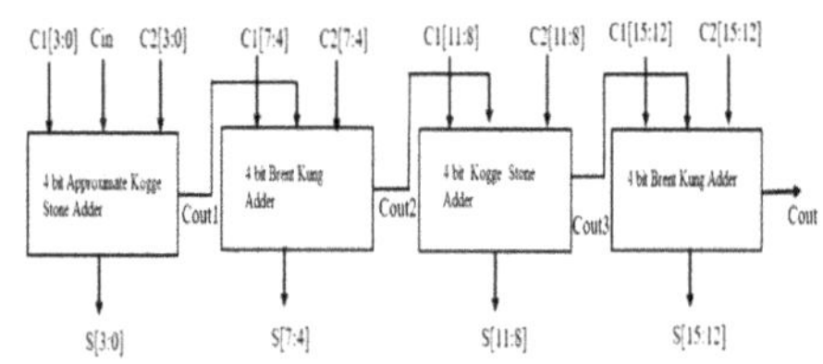

Figure 4. Hybrid approximate adder.[16]

3.3 *Implementation of 2D convolution*

The first step in the suggested methodology is to use a 2×2 kernel, a popular structure in lightweight CNN models, to mimic the 2D convolution operation over a 4×4 input matrix. Four multiplications and one addition are performed repeatedly throughout the image in each convolution window. Firstly, we use a Majority Logic Compressor (MLC)-based approximate multiplier in place of traditional accurate multipliers to optimize these procedures. The architecture uses a 2×2 kernel to perform 2D convolution on a 4×4 input vector matrix. Three MAC units for accumulation, four approximation multipliers based on truncated Dadda trees, an effective pipelined shifter, and D flip-flops for data buffering are all employed in the design. RTL schematic of the system is shown in the Figure 5. Secondly, the suggested 2D convolution is implemented with Hybrid Approximate Multiplier designed using Approximate Parallel Prefix Adders (AxPPAs), Figure 6 depicts the system's RTL diagram.

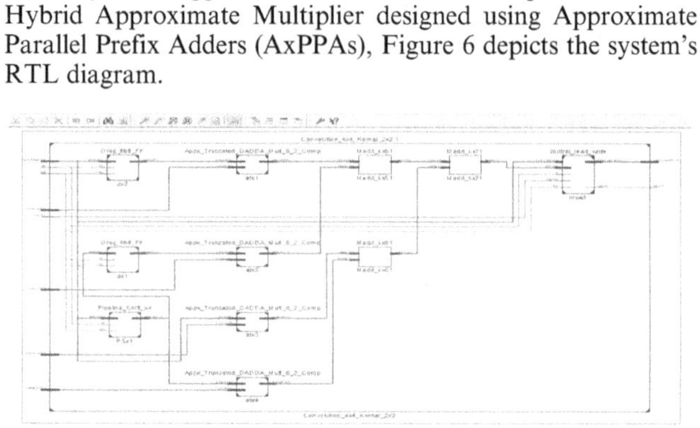

Figure 5. RTL schematic of implementation of 2D convolution with MLC based approximate multiplier.

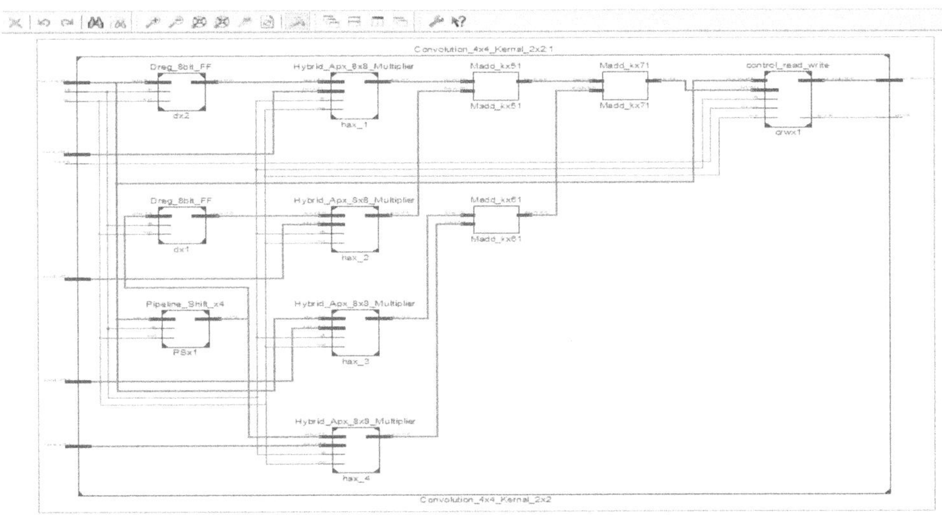

Figure 6. RTL schematic of implementation of 2D convolution with hybrid approximate PPA multiplier.

4 RESULTS

The proposed work has been implemented and synthesized on FPGA Spartan xc6slx9-2tqg144. Table 1 shows the FPGA synthesis results comparing the MLC-based Approximate Multiplier and the Hybrid Approximate Multiplier for the proposed convolution implementation.

The MLC-based design has a significant reduction in hardware resource use. From a performance standpoint, the Hybrid Approximate PPA multiplier has a lower critical path delay of 8.77 ns, compared to 10.51 ns for the MLC-based design, showing about a 16.6% speed improvement.

Table 1. Comparison table of multipliers for proposed convolution implementation.

Parameters	MLC Based Approximate Multiplier	Hybrid Approximate Multiplier Using Parallel Prefix Adder
Number of Slice Look Up Tables	256	343
Number of Slice Registers	72	131
Number of Occupied Slices	85	100
Number of bonded Input Output Bonds	60	60
Delay (ns)	10.51	8.77
Power (mw)	24	26

5 CONCLUSION

An analysis of the FPGA implementation of 2D convolution using 2×2 kernels and 4×4 matrices shows that choosing the right architecture is key for balancing speed, area, and power efficiency. The MLC-based 8×8 approximation multiplier with a 6:2 compressor offers significant cuts in LUT usage, register count, and power consumption, making it the best choice for small, energy-efficient FPGA projects. However, because of its shorter processing delay, the Hybrid 8x8 approximation multiplier with a parallel prefix adder performs better for applications that are sensitive to latency. The needs of the application should determine which of these two architectures is best: MLC-based designs are best suited for portable and embedded systems that prioritize efficiency, while hybrid PPA designs are best suited for scenarios requiring maximum throughput.

Approximate computing-based architectures offer a viable route to effective local data processing and communication in wireless sensor networks (WSNs) and remote monitoring systems, where devices must function for months or years without frequent recharging or maintenance. Only necessary data must be sent, saving energy for computation and communication by enabling lightweight on-chip computation. Furthermore, since the critical importance of low power and reduced silicon footprint outweighs the tolerance for small computational errors.

REFERENCES

[1] Zhang Y., He C., Zhang T., Han J., and Xie G., (2022), Design and Analysis of A Majority Logic Based Imprecise 6-2 Compressor for Approximate Multipliers, *Proc. IEEE Conf. Nanotechnol.*, vol. 2022-July, pp. 291–294,doi: 0.1109/NANO54668.2022.9928768.

[2] Da Rosa M.M.E.A., Paim G., Da Costa P.U.L., Da Costa E.A. C., Soares R.I., and Bampi S., (2023), AxPPA: Approximate Parallel Prefix Adders, *IEEE Trans. Very Large Scale Integr. Syst.*, vol. 31, no. 1, pp. 17–28, doi: 10.1109/TVLSI.2022.3218021.

[3] Leela S.N., Keerthi D., Chandrika, Swetha K., Kalali D.G., and Shanthi G., (2024), A Novel Design of High Speed Multiplier Using Hybrid Adder Technique, *2024 3rd Int. Conf. Innov. Technol.* INOCON 2024, pp. 1–5, doi: 10.1109/INOCON60754.2024.10512237.

[4] Sreenivasulu M. and Meenpal T., (2019), Efficient Hardware Implementation of 2D Convolution on FPGA for Image Processing Application, *Proc. 2019 3rd IEEE Int. Conf. Electr. Comput. Commun. Technol. ICECCT*, pp. 1–5,2019,doi: 0.1109/ICECCT.2019.8869347.

[5] Zhang T., Liu W., Han J., and Lombardi F., (2019), Design and Analysis of Majority Logic Based Approximate Radix-4 Booth Encoders, Nanoarch 2019 - *15th IEEE/ACM Int. Symp. Nanoscale Archit. Proc.*, doi: 10.1109/NANOARCH47378.2019.181281.

[6] Zendegani R. and Safari S., AMCAL: Approximate Multiplier With the Configurable Accuracy Levels for Image Processing and Convolutional Neural Network, *IEEE Access*, vol. 12, pp. 94135–94151, 2024, doi: 10.1109/ACCESS.2023.3273449.

[7] Wu Y. *et al.*, (2024), A Survey on Approximate Multiplier Designs for Energy Efficiency: From Algorithms to Circuits, ACM Trans. *Des. Autom. Electron. Syst.*, vol. 29, no. 1, doi: 10.1145/3610291.

[8] Shirane K., Yamamoto T., and Tomiyama H., (2021), A design methodology for approximate multipliers in convolutional neural networks: A case of mnist, *Int. J. Reconfigurable Embed. Syst.*, vol. 10, no. 1, pp. 1–10, doi: 10.11591/ijres.v10.i1.pp1-10.

[9] Rijal S.R., (2013), Design and Implementation of 8X8 Truncated Multiplier on FPGA, *Int. J. Sci. Res. Publ.*, vol. 3, no. 3, pp. 1–5, [Online]. Available: www.ijsrp.org

[10] Qiqieh I., Shafik R., Tarawneh G., Sokolov D., Das S., and Yakovlev A., (2018), Significance-Driven Logic Compression for Energy-Efficient Multiplier Design, *IEEE J. Emerg. Sel. Top. Circuits Syst.*, vol. 8, no. 3, pp. 417–430, doi: 10.1109/JETCAS.2018.2846410.

[11] Perri S., Spagnolo F., Frustaci F., and Corsonello P., (2022), Designing Energy-Efficient Approximate Multipliers, *J. Low Power Electron. Appl.*, vol. 12, no. 4, doi: 10.3390/jlpea12040049.

[12] Kumar U.A. and Ahmed S.E., (2021), Compressor based approximate multiplier architectures for media processing applications, *Int. J. Electr. Comput. Eng.*, vol. 11, no. 4, pp. 2953–2961, doi: 10.11591/ijece.v11i4.pp2953–2961.

[13] Kocakanat K. and Serif T., (2021), Turkish Traffic Sign Recognition: Comparison of Training Step Numbers and Lighting Conditions, *Eur. J. Sci. Technol.*, no. November, doi: 10.31590/ejosat.1015972.

[14] Kim M.S., Del Barrio A.A., Kim H.J., and Bagherzadeh N., (2022), The Effects of Approximate Multiplication on Convolutional Neural Networks, *IEEE Trans. Emerg. Top. Comput.*, vol. 10, no. 2, pp. 904–916, doi: 10.1109/TETC.2021.3050989.

[15] Gu F.Y., Lin I.C., and Lin J.W., (2022), A Low-Power and High-Accuracy Approximate Multiplier With Reconfigurable Truncation, *IEEE Access*, vol. 10, pp. 60447–60458, doi: 10.1109/ACCESS.2022.3179112.

[16] Selvarasan, R, Sudhagar, G. and Rasadurai, K, (2025), FPGA implementation of an optimized hybrid approximate multiplier using approximate parallel prefix adder. *Synergies in Smart and Virtual Systems Using Computational Intelligence*, pp.531–535, doi: 10.1201/9781003685364-89.

Next-Generation Smart Systems – Sekhar et al. (Eds)
 ISBN: 978-1-041-34234-2

Design of a High-Speed Multiplier Based on High Order Compressors for DSP Applications

Bollampalli Akshaya
M.Tech Scholar, Department of Electronics and Communication Engineering, India
Assoc. Professor, Vaagdevi College of Engineering, Warangal, Telangana, India

Pankaj Hivraj Rangaree
Assoc. Professor, Vaagdevi College of Engineering, Warangal, Telangana, India

Mahesh Mudavath
Professor, Department of Electronics and Communication Engineering, Siddhartha Institute of Technology & Sciences, Ghatkesar, Hyderabad, India

ABSTRACT: In error-resilient applications where complete precision is not mandatory, like digital signal processing (DSP), image processing (IP), and machine learning (ML), approximate computing has emerged as a successful design approach. As fundamental parts of arithmetic units (AU), multipliers are usually resource-intensive in terms of area, power, and latency. This study offers a high-accuracy approximation multiplier architecture that uses a 5:2 compressor that is optimized for area efficiency in order to overcome these difficulties. The proposed design introduces selective approximation in the less significant bits, while maintaining accurate computation in higher-order bits to balance precision and hardware savings. The integration of the 5:2 compressors enables efficient partial product reduction, minimizing the number of logic gates and interconnects required. This approach leads to substantial improvements in area utilization, power consumption, and operating speed, without severely impacting the output accuracy. The suggested architecture performs better than traditional approximation multipliers in terms of error metrics like Error Rate (ER) and Mean Error Distance (MED), according to simulation data, while achieving up to 30–40% reduction in area and power. These features make it compatible for low-power embedded systems and real-time applications where energy efficiency and computational speed are critical, but minor errors can be tolerated.

Keywords: Compressor, multiplier design, low-power architecture, high-accuracy arithmetic, area-efficient hardware, partial product reduction, digital signal processing, error-resilient design

1 INTRODUCTION

Multiplication is a basic arithmetic operation at the heart of many computer activities in contemporary digital systems. However, multipliers are among the most resource-intensive components in terms of area, power, and delay of critical path. With the rising demand for energy-efficient and high-speed processors, especially in applications that can tolerate minor computational errors, estimated calculating has emerged as a viable design approach. This technique trades off a small amount of accuracy in favor of significant progresses in hardware concert, such as reduced power consumption, area usage, and delay [1], [2].

In this context, approximate multipliers have gained consideration, particularly in domains like SP, IP, and ML, wherever exact accuracy is not continually necessary. Among several approximation strategies, compressor-based architectures—notably the 4:2 compressor—offer an effective way to optimize the reduction of partial products in multipliers [3]. The 5:2 compressors simplifies the logic required in multiplier circuits by compressing four input bits and two carry bits into a more efficient form, which reduces the complexity of the overall structure [4], [7].

This paper offers a high-accuracy estimated design of multiplier based on an area-optimized 4:2 compressor, aiming to maintain a balance among computational precision and hardware efficiency [5], [6]. The approach selectively approximates less significant bits (LSBs) while preserving accuracy in the more critical higher-order bits (MSBs), making it highly appropriate for real-time embedded systems.

2 OBJECTIVES

The following are the main goals of this work:

- To design an estimated multiplier that minimizes hardware area and power consumption.
- To utilize a 5:2 compressor structure for efficient partial product reduction.
- To evaluate the proposed design by metrics i.e., MED, ER, delay, power consumption, and area utilization.

3 LITERATURE SURVEY

One of the main areas of study in the field of digital arithmetic has always been the design of accurate and efficient multipliers. In order to lower computational overhead, academics are increasingly using approximation computing in fields including image processing, digital signal processing, and machine learning, where there is a rising necessity for low-power, high-speed computers [8].

3.1 *Approximate computing and multiplier design*

Approximate computing has been extensively explored for arithmetic units, especially multipliers, due to their complexity and high resource consumption. Studies such as those by Gupta *et al.* [6] and Han and Orshansky [7] highlighted how controlled approximation can significantly reduce power consumption and delay, without severely affecting output quality in many real-time applications [9].

DOI: 10.1201/9781042001767-78

3.2 *Compressor-based multiplier architectures*

Compressors play a vital role in reducing partial products in multipliers. The 4:2 compressors in particular have emerged as an effective solution due to its balanced trade-off between speed and logic depth. Research by Kong and Abdel-Hafeez [3] showed that incorporating 4:2 compressors in multiplier design improves performance in relations of propagation delay and silicon area [10].

3.3 *Area-optimized approximate multipliers*

Recent efforts have focused on designing multipliers that are both area-efficient and capable of maintaining reasonable accuracy. For example, in [4], a segmented approximate multiplier was introduced where the lower significant bits (LSBs) were approximated, while the higher significant bits (MSBs) retained exact logic. This hybrid approach enabled a considerable reduction in gate count and power while maintaining acceptable error margins [5], [11].

3.4 *Error analysis and metrics*

The quality of approximation multipliers is frequently assessed using error measures including MED, NMED, ER, and PSNR. Works like those of Rehman *et al.* [1] have emphasized the importance of such metrics in validating the practical usability of approximate circuits in real-world applications [18].

3.5 *Application-specific implementations*

Several application-driven studies have demonstrated the effectiveness of approximate multipliers in hardware accelerators. For instance, Zhang *et al.* [7] used approximate arithmetic units in a convolutional neural network (CNN) accelerator, showing substantial power savings with negligible impact on model accuracy. In another case, Jain *et al.* [8] implemented an approximate multiplier in an image compression algorithm, resulting in faster processing and energy reduction without degrading image quality [18].

4 EXISTING METHOD

Traditional digital multipliers, particularly those based on array or Wallace tree architectures, are designed to deliver accurate results at the cost of high hardware complexity, significant area usage, and increased power consumption. While suitable for applications requiring precise computation, these multipliers are often over-engineered for tasks in ML, SP, and IP, where a slight grade of error is suitable [17].

To address these inefficiencies, researchers have proposed approximate multiplier designs that simplify internal logic, especially in lower significance bits (LSBs), where inaccuracies have less impact on final results. In existing methods, the use of approximate compressors, such as truncated adders, imprecise full adders, and simplified partial product generation, has been widely explored [11].

One common approach is the use of 4:2 compressors approximation, which are responsible for reducing the fractional products in the multiplier more efficiently than traditional adders. These compressors typically remove or simplify carry propagation logic to reduce delay and gate count. However, most prior designs prioritize area and power reduction with little attention to maintaining high accuracy, leading to degraded computational reliability in more sensitive applications [12],[13].

4.1 *Proposed method*

The proposed design introduces a high-accuracy approximate multiplier that leverages area-optimized 5:2 compressor architecture, aimed at reducing hardware complexity while maintaining acceptable accuracy as shown in Figure 1–4. This design is mostly well-suited for error-tolerant uses such as digital signal processing, image processing, and machine learning, where some degree of imprecision can be tolerated in exchange for improved efficiency [14], [19].

4.1.1 *Design Strategy:*

The essential idea of the proposed method is to divide the multiplier architecture into two distinct regions:

- Accurate Region (MSBs):
  The MSBs are computed using exact logic, ensuring that the multiplier produces highly accurate results for the higher-weighted bits which have the greatest impact on the final output [15].
- Approximate Region (LSBs):
  The least significant bits (LSBs) are computed using approximate 5:2 compressors, which simplify the internal logic by eliminating or reducing carry propagation. These compressors are carefully designed to offer low area and power consumption [16].

The proposed multiplier employs modified 5:2 compressors in the LSB region. These compressors accept four input bits and two carry inputs and generate a sum, carry-out, and overflow with minimal logic gates. By selectively approximating carry generation and propagation in this region, the architecture reduces logic depth and critical path delay [17], [21]. Unlike traditional 5:2 compressors, which prioritize accuracy, the proposed design focuses on: Gate-level simplification, Partial carry omission, and Minimal transistor count.

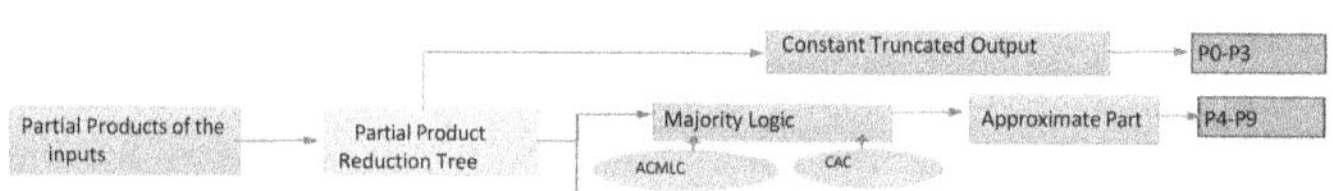

Figure 1. Proposed design flow of 8-bit multiplier.

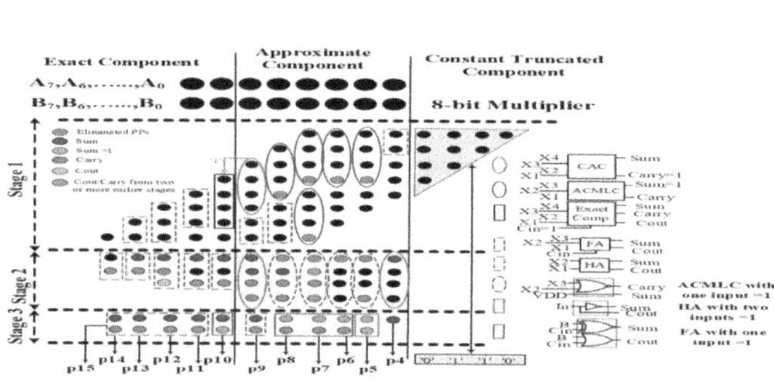

Figure 2. 8-bit multiplier approximation.

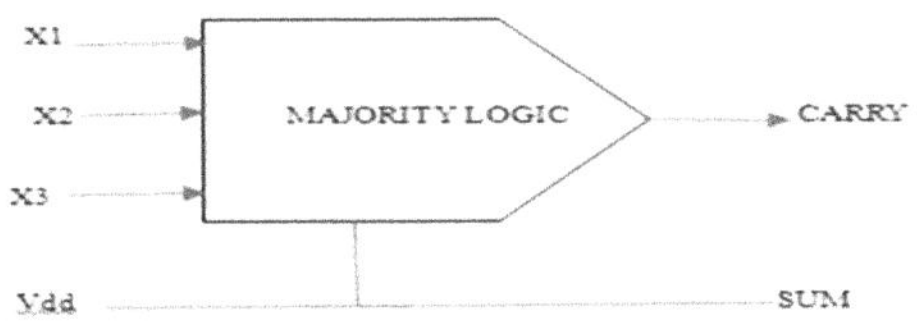

Figure 3. Proposed ACMLC.

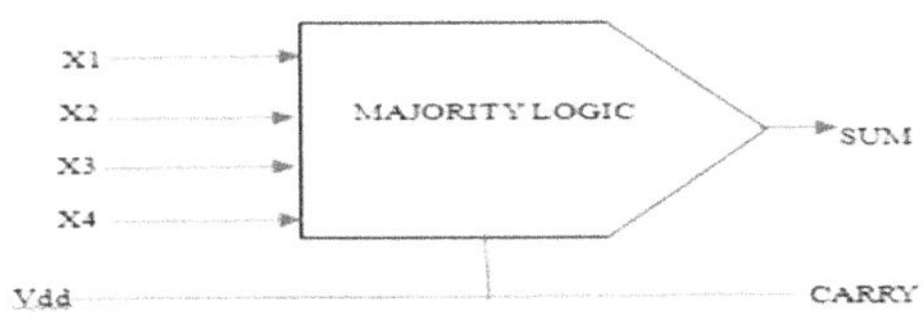

Figure 4. Proposed CAC.

Table 1. Truth table of ACMLC.

X1	X2	X3	SUM	CARRY
0	0	0	0	1
0	0	1	0	1
0	1	0	1	1
0	1	1	1	1
1	0	0	0	1
1	0	1	1	1
1	1	0	1	1
1	1	1	1	1

Table 2. Truth table of CAC.

X1	X2	X3	X4	SUM	CARRY
0	0	0	0	0	1
0	0	0	1	0	1
0	0	1	0	0	1
0	0	1	1	1	1
0	1	0	0	0	1
0	1	0	1	0	1
0	1	1	0	0	1
0	1	1	1	1	1
1	0	0	0	0	1
1	0	0	1	0	1
1	0	1	0	0	1
1	0	1	1	1	1
1	1	0	0	0	1
1	1	0	1	1	0
1	1	1	0	1	0
1	1	1	1	1	1

5 RESULTS AND DISCUSSION

This research introduces two approximate 5:2 compressor designs—one using 8 transistors and the other 20—based on majority logic (ML), aimed at enhancing the efficiency of arithmetic circuits. Majority logic, known for its fault-tolerant nature, enables a reduction in gate count while preserving acceptable levels of accuracy [20]. The 8-transistor compressor emphasizes hardware minimization, whereas the 20-transistor variant offers improved accuracy. Both designs contribute to simplifying the partial product reduction tree (PPRT) in multipliers by eliminating 15 AND gates and employing only a single exact compressor. As a result, they achieve a 49% reduction in circuit area and a 93% reduction in energy consumption when compared to traditional exact multipliers. Performance analysis using image multiplication demonstrates their effectiveness in error-resilient computing as exposed in Figures 5–7. A comparative evaluation underscores the balance between accuracy, power efficiency, and area, establishing these compressors as viable candidates for low-power, high-performance applications [19].

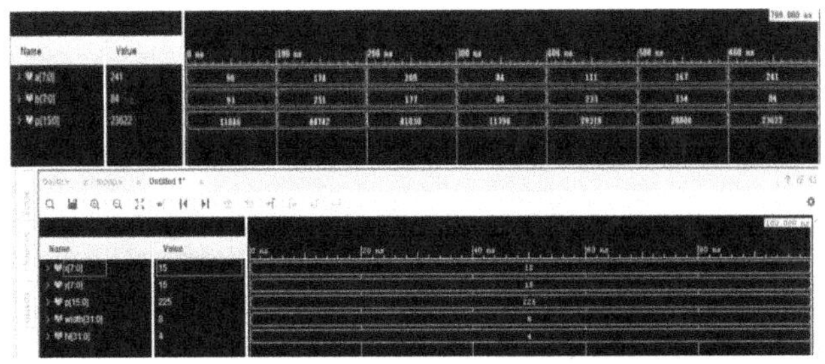

Figure 5. Multiplication output.

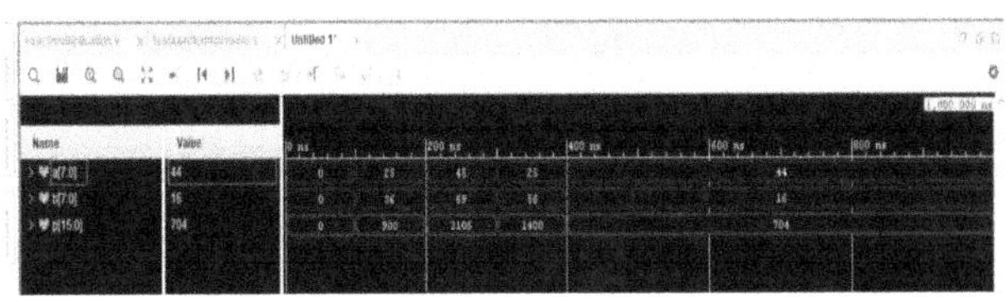

Figure 6. Simulation of 5:2 compressors.

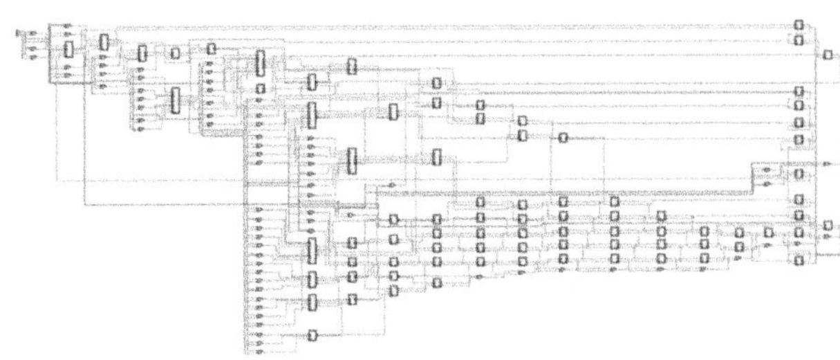

Figure 7. RTL Schematic 5:2 compressor.

6 CONCLUSION

In this work, an area-efficient 5:2 compressor design was used to suggest a high-accuracy approximation multiplier architecture. The method applies selective approximation to the lower significant bits while preserving exact logic for the most important bits, thus balancing the trade-off among hardware efficiency and computing accuracy. This makes it possible for the design to significantly reduce latency, power consumption, and area without negatively affecting output precision.

In order to reduce logic complexity and increase overall speed, the suggested architecture incorporates a modified 5:2 compressor. The multiplier outperforms traditional approximate designs in terms of important metrics including MED, ER, and hardware resource usage, according to simulation and synthesis studies.

Given its accuracy-preserving nature and reduced hardware overhead, the proposed multiplier is well-suited for energy-efficient systems, including real-time applications like image processing, neural network accelerators, and low-power embedded platforms.

Future work can focus on developing adaptive approximate schemes and extending this architecture for higher-order multipliers and reconfigurable systems.

ACKNOWLEDGEMENT

The authors gratefully acknowledge the students, staff, and authority of Department of ECE for their cooperation in the research.

REFERENCES

[1] Hemanth Krishna L., Ayesha Sk, Jammu Bhaskara Rao, Sreehari Veeramachaneni and Noor Mahammad Sk, (2024), Energy-Efficient Approximate Multiplier Design With Lesser Error Rate Using the Probability-Based Approximate 4:2 Compressor, *IEEE embedded systems letters*, PP(134–137), Vol. 16, Issue 2, DOI:10.1109/LES.2023.3280199.

[2] Zhang, M., Nishizawa, S., and Kimura, S. (2023). Area Efficient Approximate 4–2 Compressor and Probability-Based Error Adjustment for Approximate Multiplier. *IEEE Transactions on Circuits and Systems II: Express Briefs*, *70*(5), 1714–1718. https://doi.org/10.1109/TCSII.2023.3257852.

[3] Ha M. and Lee S., (2018), Multipliers with approximate 4–2 compressors and error recovery modules, *IEEE Embedded Systems Letters*, vol. 10, no. 1, pp. 6–9.

[4] Esmaeilzadeh H. *et al.*, (2012), Architecture support for disciplined approximate programming, *Proc. ACM Int. Conf. Architectural Support for Programming Languages and Operating Systems (ASPLOS)*, pp. 301–312.

[5] Shafique M. *et al.*, (2015), Approximate computing: An emerging paradigm for energy-efficient design, *IEEE Eur. Solid-State Circuits Conf.*, pp. 1–6.

[6] Gupta V. *et al.*, (Jan. 2013), Low-power digital signal processing using approximate adders, *IEEE Trans. Comput.-Aided Design Integr. Circuits Syst.*, vol. 32, no. 1, pp. 124–137.

[7] Han J. and Orshansky M., (2011), Approximate computing: An emerging paradigm for energy-efficient design, *Proc. 18th IEEE Eur. Test Symp.*, pp. 1–6.

[8] Momeni A. *et al.*, (Apr. 2015), Design and analysis of approximate compressors for multiplication, *IEEE Trans. Comput.*, vol. 64, no. 4, pp. 984–994.

[9] Akbari O. *et al.*, (Apr. 2017), Dual-quality 4:2 compressors for utilizing in dynamic accuracy configurable multipliers, *IEEE Trans. Very Large Scale Integr. (VLSI) Syst.*, vol. 25, no. 4, pp. 1352–1361.

[10] Kulkarni T. *et al.*, (2017), Approximate compressors for error-resilient multipliers, *IEEE Int. Symp. Circuits Syst. (ISCAS)*, pp. 1392–1395.

[11] Kulkarni P. *et al.*, (2011), Trading accuracy for power with an underdesigned multiplier architecture, *Proc. 24th IEEE Int. Conf. VLSI Design*, pp. 346–351.

[12] Kansal R. *et al.*, (2021), High-speed energy-efficient 4:2 compressor using power gating technique, *Microelectron. J.*, vol. 111, p. 105015.

[13] Veeramachaneni S. *et al.*, (2016), Design of high speed, energy efficient approximate 4:2 compressor, *Proc. Int. Conf. Comput. Syst. Appl.*, pp. 645–650.

[14] Liu W., Gu C., O'Neill M., Qu G., Montuschi P., and Lombardi F., (Dec. 2020), Security in approximate computing and approximate computing for security: Challenges and opportunities, *Proc. IEEE*, vol. 108, no. 12, pp. 2199–2216.

[15] Liu W., Lombardi F., and Schulte M., (Dec. 2020), Approximate computing: From circuits to applications [scanning the issue], *Proc. IEEE*, vol. 108, no. 12, pp. 2112–2114.

[16] Momeni A., Han J., Montuschi P., and Lombardi F., (Apr. 2015), Design and analysis of approximate compressors for multiplication, *IEEE Trans. Comput.*, vol. 64, no. 4, pp. 984–994.

[17] Venkatachalam S. and Ko S., (Oct. 2017), Design of power and area efficient approximate multipliers, *IEEE Trans. Very Large Scale Integr. (VLSI) Syst.*, vol. 25, no. 10, pp. 2658–2662.

[18] Ha M. and Lee S., (Sep. 2018), Multipliers with approximate 4–2 compressors and error recovery modules, *IEEE Embedded Syst. Lett.*, vol. 10, no. 3, pp. 99–102.

[19] Akbari O., Kamal M., Afzali-Kusha A., and Pedram M., (Apr. 2017), Dual-quality 4:2 compressors for utilizing in dynamic accuracy configurable multipliers, *IEEE Trans. Very Large Scale Integr. (VLSI) Syst.*, vol. 25, no. 4, pp. 1217–1225.

[20] Sabetzadeh F., Moaiyeri M.H., and Ahmadinejad M., (Dec. 2019), A majority-based imprecise multiplier for ultra-efficient approximate image multiplication, *IEEE Trans. Circuits Syst. I, Reg. Papers*, vol. 66, no. 12, pp. 4732–4743.

Next-Generation Smart Systems – Sekhar et al. (Eds)
© 2027 The Author(s), ISBN: 978-1-041-34234-2

CNTFET-Based Digital Arithmetic Circuit Designs in Ternary Logic

Katika Gopilal
Department of ECE, GRIET, Hyderabad, India

Tatiparti Padma
Professor, Department of ECE, GRIET, Hyderabad, India

ABSTRACT: In digital logic systems, ternary logics are preferred over binary logics due to their rapid processing speeds and great information density. Since the carbon nanotube field-effect transistors (CNTFETs) may give different threshold voltages by varying the nanotube diameter, they are thought to be a superior choice for building ternary circuits. Adders and multipliers are examples of sophisticated arithmetic circuits that are crucial in many VLSI applications. This paper proposes a ternary half-adder (THA) that is constructed using the Stanford 32nm CNTFET which results in a 54.44% and 45% reduction in transistor count. In comparison to current circuits, the suggested THA exhibits improvements in delay, power, and energy of 37.01 percent, 14.07 percent and 45.87 percent respectively.

Keywords: THA, MUX, CNTFET, SWCNT

1 INTRODUCTION

The process of miniaturizing integrated circuits is currently being given a lot of attention by the electronics industry. As a result, the circuits physical footprint is decreased and their operational efficiency is increased [1–3]. In response to this problem, the semiconductor industry is always striving to adhere to Moore's law [4,5]. These include a variety of short channel effects (SCEs), a high power density, substantial parametric fluctuations, a decrease in gate control on the channel, and an increase in subthreshold leakage current [6]. These problems have affected the lowering of transistors performance and decreasing its probability of suiting for use in energy efficient applications [6]. Therefore, in order to overcome the aforementioned problems, alternative solutions in transistor technology must be developed. The CNTFETs, have dragged the attention.

Because of their unique electrical characteristics, CNTFET devices have created a platform for nanoscale circuits [7,8]. These gates are widely used in electronic devices like computers and calculators and are the foundation of the digital world [9]. However, their use has a significant drawback in that more connections lead to more complicated circuits that take up a lot of chip space and use more energy and power [10,11]. On the other hand, digital electrical devices known as multiple valued logic (MVL) gates are made especially for system with more than two states. MVL gates reduce the amount of interconnects needed for complex processes while providing significant benefits in data compression [12]. Due to hardware constraints, an integer base that roughly approximates e must be used, and three seems to be the number that does so [13,14]. Chip area and energy can be reduced by as much as 70% and 50% respectively by using ternary logic, which employs three-valued logic [15].

The use of threshold voltages (Vth) would be the exact technique for ternary circuits [17,18]. It is generally known that body biasing can be used to achieve multi-threshold designs in a MOSFET. However, the difficult and sensitive task of delivering biasing to the majority of (MOSFETs) with varying voltages primarily takes place during the fabrication process [19]. The CNTFETs can be used to design and build circuits with multiple Vth, and the required Vth is obtained by taking appropriate CNT diameters into account [4]. In this study, an improved ternary half adder (THA) device based on CNTFETs is proposed. By reducing the number of transistors usage by 54.44 percent and 45 percent correspondingly.

2 PRELIMINARIES

2.1 *CNTFET*

CNTs are small, cylindrical graphite structures [21–23]. An single-walled carbon nanotube (SWCNT's) the chirality vector contains two integers denoted by (n, m), determines the orientation of its atoms along its length. SWCNTs have the ability to act as conductors or semiconductors [23–25]. The SWCNT is suitable for the interconnect network and performs the role of a conductor. On the other hand, the SWCNT behaves like a semiconductor and can be used in a FET channel [21].

To date, the literature has presented a wide variety of CNTFET device types, each with unique benefits, drawbacks and properties. The Schottky Barrier (SB) kind of CNTFET is one type that operates by allowing electrons to source-channel end. These electrons are tunneled via metal semiconductor junction.

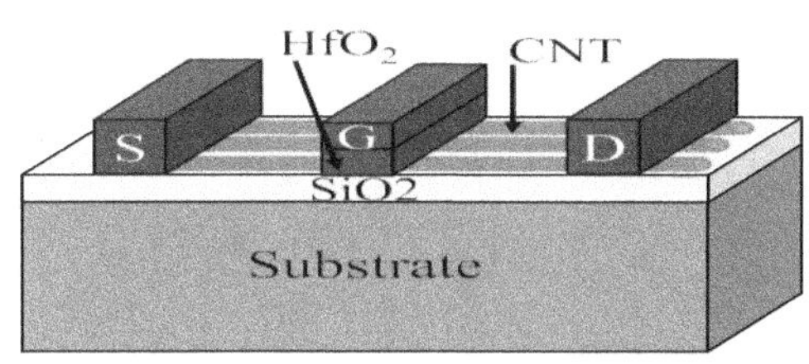

CNTFET 1(a) Front view

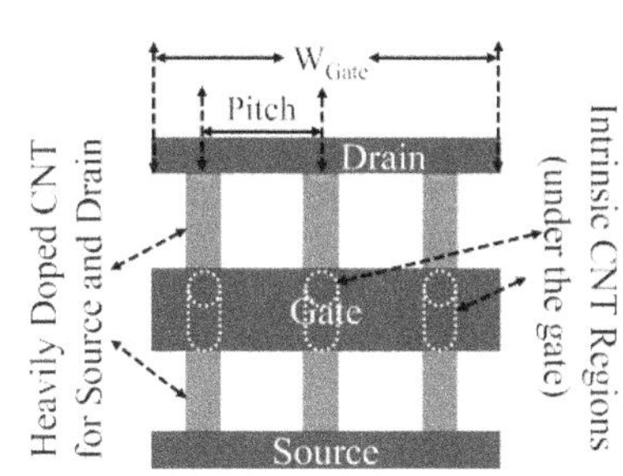

CNTFET 1(b) Top view

Figure 1. CNTFET 1(a) front view, 1(b) top view.

DOI: 10.1201/9781042001767-79

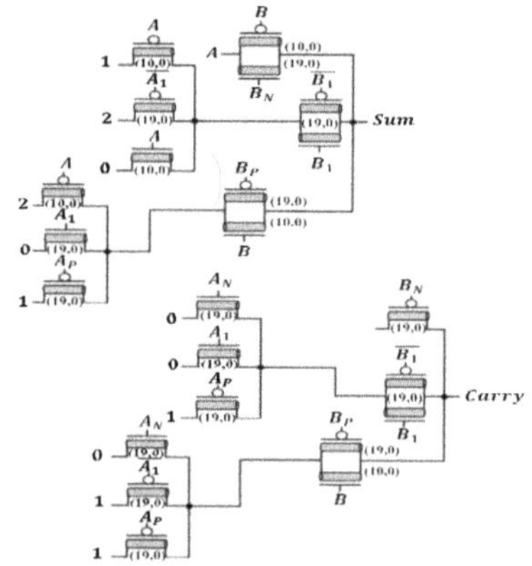

Figure 2. Schematic diagram of THA.

Connecting the CNT with metal forms the Schottky Barrier. On the other hand, the Schottky Barrier limits the device's on-state currents and transconductance. In Band to Band Tunneling type CNTFET in which the electrons are tunneled over the forbidden energy gap. Despite having a low on-state current, this kind of CNTFET provides remarkable cut-off characteristics that guarantee great efficiency and low power usage when used in threshold applications.

3 CNTFET-BASED TERNARY CIRCUITS

The effective design of ternary arithmetic schemes, such as THA using CNTFETs is covered in this section.

3.1 *THA*

THA performs two bit addition of A and B as inputs and the gives results as Sum and Carry.

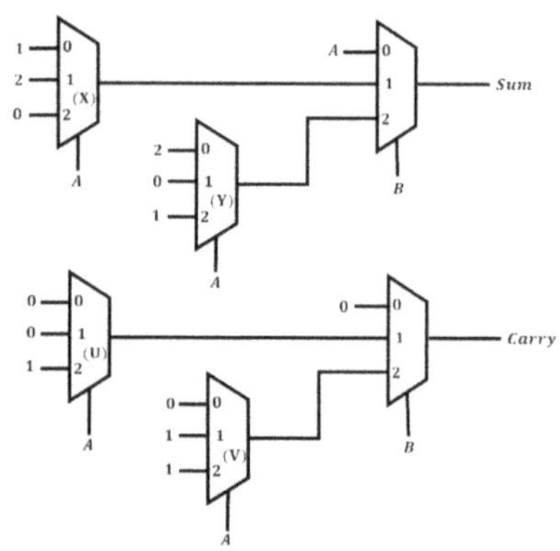

Figure 3. Proposed THA circuit.

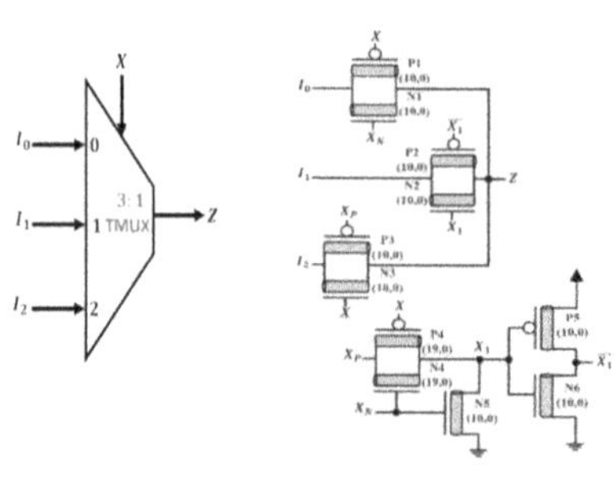

Figure 4. Ternary multiplexer circuit.

$$Sum = 2.(A_0B_2 + A_1B_1 + A_2B_0) + 1.(A_0B_1 + A_1B_0 + A_2B_2) \quad (1)$$

$$Carry = 1.(A_1B_2 + A_2B_1 + A_2B_2) \quad (2)$$

$$Sum = A.B_0 + (1.A_0 + 2.A_1 + 0.A_2).B_1 + (2.A_0 + 0.A_1 + 1.A_2).B_2 \quad (3)$$

$$Carry = 0.B_0 + (0.A_0 + 0.A_1 + 1.A_2).B_1 + (0.A_0 + 01A_1 + 1.A_2).B_2 \quad (4)$$

Equations (1) and (2) show that six 3:1 TMUX circuits can be used to construct THA. Generally multiplexer is many to one selector, here we discussed about 3:1 TMUX which has 3 inputs and one output. Inputs are I0, I1, I2 and output is Z, there is a selection line X. The 3:1 TMUX can be performed using Equations (3) and (4) [10]. Figure 2 illustrates a 3:1 TMUX sans ternary decoder that uses 15 numbers of transistors.

4 RESULTS

The simulated results of proposed THA circuit using the 32nm CNTFET technology Stanford SPICE model are discussed. This SPICE model was created especially for unipolar enhancement-CNTFETs and contains all of the circuit-appropriate CNTFETs for the required simulation. The circuit of FET has been designed in a manner to give the faithful outputs.

Figure 5 shows how changing the V_{DD} affects PDP for THA circuit. The raising of the V_{DD} results in a greater drain current, which reduces the delay but, because of their two-order relationship, power consumption rises as V_{DD} increases [5].

Consequently, as V_{DD} rises, PDP rises as well. Notably, at all V_{DD} levels, the suggested THA circuit perform better in PDP than their predecessor.

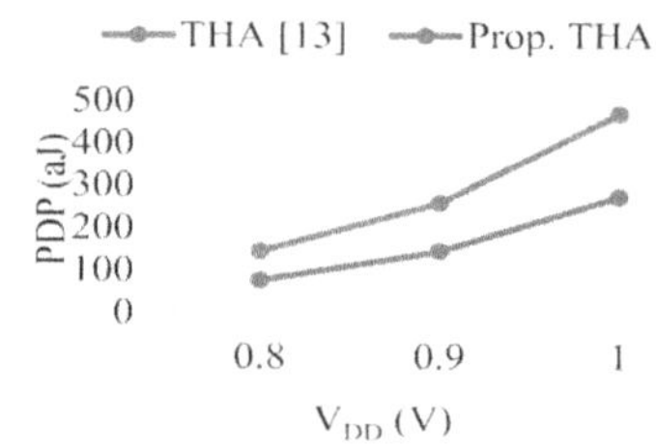

Figure 5. Effect on PDP due to V_{DD} variation.

The cost of integration density rises as pitch increases because intertube spacing is smaller [8]. Pitch increases cause power consumption to rise while delay gradually decreases. Consequently, as Figure 6 illustrates PDP or overall performance, is moving increasing with pitch value growing. It's interesting to see that the proposed THA circuit have better PDPs than the others.

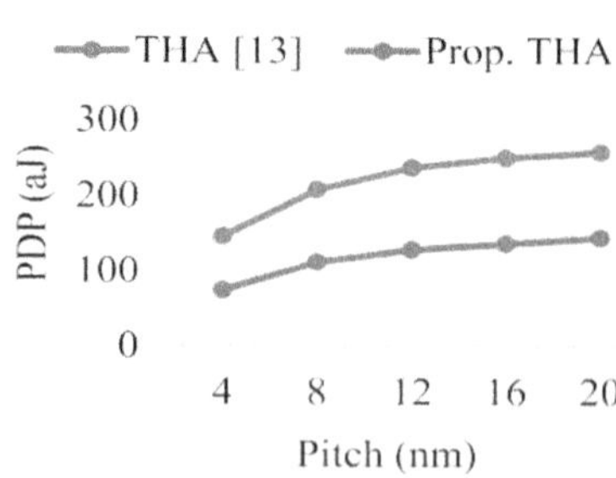

Figure 6. Effect on PDP due to pitch variations.

Figure 7 shows how changing the T_{ox} affects the PDP of the circuits being studied. A little decrement in latency and power usage was observed with an increase in T_{ox} [8], leading to a minor drop in PDP. The recommended circuits outperform the rest in terms of PDP.

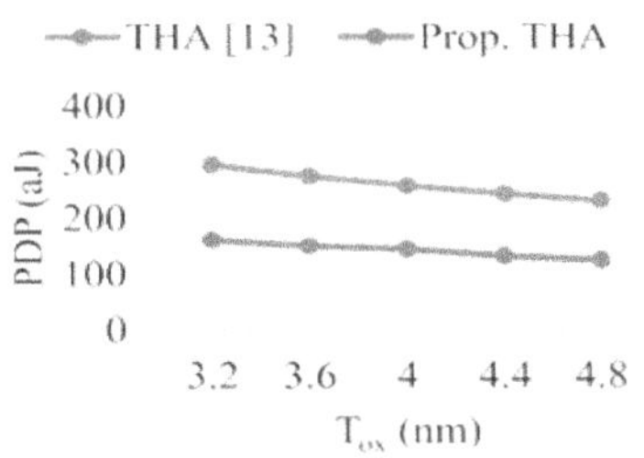

Figure 7. Effect on PDP due to T_{ox} variations.

Figure 8 illustrates how the gated dielectric constant (Kgate) affects the circuits PDP. PDP rises when the Kgate is increased because it decreases latency and increases power [7]. In comparison to the other circuits, the suggested circuits offer a lower PDP.

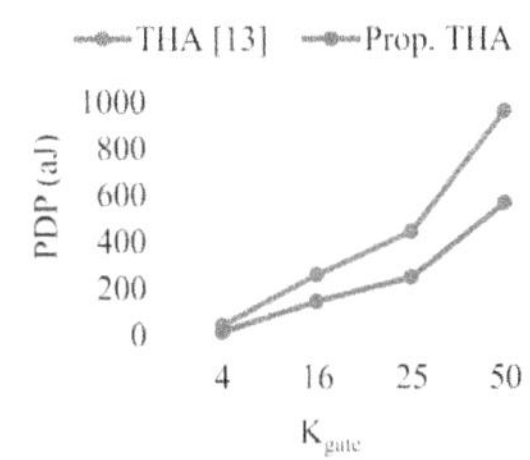

Figure 8. Effect on PDP due to K_{gate} variations.

5 CONCLUSION

The main shortcomings of the binary logic approach can be addressed by MVL, including a higher number of connections, more complexity, a bigger chip area, lower operating speed performance, and an increase in power and energy, because it employs at least two logical levels. MOSFETs can be utilized to build MVL circuits by using the body biasing technique, albeit this is a challenging procedure. The best choice for putting MVL circuits into practice is thought to be the CNTFET because, with the right CNT diameter, it displays a range of threshold voltages. The CNTFET designs of the THA schematic were measured and analyzed in this study in terms of transistor count, latency, power consumption, and PDP. The proposed THA's latency and power consumption, which are decreased by 54.44% and 45% respectively. According to the simulations, the proposed THA circuits reduced the number of transistors compared to their existing versions, resulting in improvements in latency, power consumption and PDP of 37.01%, 14.07%, and 45.87% respectively.

REFERENCES

[1] Abbasian E., Sofimowloodi S. and Sachdeva A., (2023), Highly-efficient CNTFET-based unbalanced ternary logicgates, *ECSJ. SolidStateSci.Technol.*12, 031007.

[2] Esmaeili A. and Bakhshi B., (2018), A new BGP-based load distribution approach ingeographically distributed data centers, Nashriyyah-i Muhandisi-i Barq vaMuhandisi-i Kampyutar-i Iran 62, 71.

[3] Zandi J., Afooshteh A.N. and Ghassemian M., (2018), Implementation and analysis of a novellow power and portable energy measurement tool for wireless sensor nodes, in: *Proceedings of the Electrical Engineering (ICEE)*, Iranian Conference, pp.1517–1522,on.

[4] Nikbakht E., Dideban D. and Moezi N., (2020), A half adder design based on ternary multiplexers in carbonnano-tube field effect transistor (CNFET) technology, *ECSJ.Solid State Sci. Technol.* 9, 081001.

[5] Abbasian E. and Mahdiye N., (2023), A high-speed low-energy one-trit ternary multipliercircuit design in CNTFET technology, *ECS J. Solid State Sci. Technol.* 12, 021004.

[6] Moaiyeri M.H., Nasiri M. and Khastoo N., An efficient ternary serial adder based on carbon nanotube FETs, *Eng. Sci. Technol. Int. J.* 19 (2016) 271–278.

[7] Mani E., Abbasian E., Gunasegeran M., Sofimowloodi S. (2022), Design of high stability,lowpower and high speed 12TSRAM cell in 32-nm CNTFET technology, *AEUInt. J. Electron.Commun.*154, 154308.

[8] Sachdeva A., Kumar D. and Abbasian E. (2023), A carbon nano-tube field effect transistorbased stable, low-power 8T static random access memory cell with improved writeaccess time, *AEU Int. J. Electron. Commun.* 154565.

[9] Madhuri B.D. and Sunithamani S., (2020), Design of ternary logic gates and circuits usingGNRFETs, *IET Circuits Devices Syst.* 14, 972–979.

[10] Jaber R.A., El-Hajj A.M., Kassem A., Nimri L.A. and Haidar A.M., (2020) CNFET-baseddesignsof ternary half-adder using a novel "decoder-less" ternary multiplexer based onunary operators, *Microelectron. J.* 96 104698.

[11] Sharma T. and Kumre L., (2019) CNTFET-baseddesignofternaryarithmeticmodules, *CircuitsSystems Signal Process.* 38 4640–4666.

[12] Sharma T. and Kumre L., (2020), CNFET based design of unbalanced ternary circuits using efficient shifting literals, *Microelectron. J.* 104, 104869.

[13] Sardroudi F.M., Habibi M. and Moaiyeri M.H., A low-powerdynamicternaryfulladderusing carbon nanotube field-effect transistors, *AEU Int. J. Electron. Commun.* 131(2021) 153600.

[14] Zandi J. and Naderi-Afooshteh A., (2015), LRBAC: flexible function-level hierarchical rolebased access control for Linux, in: *Proceedings of the 2015 12th InternationalIranian Society of Cryptology Conference on Information Security and Cryptology (ISCISC)*, pp. 29–35.

[15] Jaber R.A., Kassem A., El-Hajj A.M., El-Nimri L.A. and Haidar A.M., (2019), High-performanceandenergy-efficientCNFET-baseddesignsforternarylogiccircuits, *IEEEAccess* 7, 93871–93886.

[16] Hajizadeh F., Marvasti M.B., Asghari S.A., Mollaei M.A., Rahmani A.M., (2021) Configurable DSI partitioned approximate multiplier, *Future Gener. Comput. Syst.*115, 100–114.

[17] Tabrizchi S., Panahi A., Sharifi F., Mahmoodi H. and Badawy A.H.A., (2020), Energy-efficientternary multipliers using CNT transistors, *Electronics* 9, 643.

[18] Rajkumar K. and Reddy G.U., (2023). PerformanceanalysisofCu-MWCNTbundledHCTSVsusing ternary logic, *e Prime Adv. Electr. Eng. Electron. Energy* 5 100247.

[19] Ratan Kumar S., Rao L.K. and Kumar M.K., (2022). Design of ternary logic circuits using pseudo N-type CNTFETs, *ECS J. Solid State Sci. Technol.* 11 111003.

[20] Jaber R.A., Haidar A.M. and Kassem A., (2020), CNTFET-based design of ternary multiplier using only multiplexers, *in: Proceedings of the 2020 32nd International Conference on Microelectronics (ICM)*, pp. 1–4.

[21] Tabrizchi S., Sharifi F. and Dehghani P., (2021). Energy-efficient and PVT-tolerant CNFET-based ternary full adder cell, *Circuits Systems Signal Process.* 40, 3523–3535.

[22] Rahbar M., Li B., Hunter N., Al Keyyam I., Wang T. and Shi E., (2023). Observing grain boundary-induced phonons mean free path in highly aligned SWCNT bundles by low-momentum phonon scattering, *Cell Rep. Phys. Sci.* 4 101688.

[23] Khurshid T. and Singh V., (2023) Energy efficient design of unbalanced ternary logic gates and arithmetic circuits using CNTFET, *AEU Int. J. Electron. Commun.* 154601.

[24] Gupta S. and Sharma R., (2025), An area and power efficient ternary serial adder using phase composite ZnO stack channel FETs, *Nanoscale Advances*, vol. 7, no. 5, pp. 1450–1460.

[25] Kumar P., Verma M., and Singh R., (2025), The power efficient ternary logic half adder and multiplier designs using the GNRFET technology, *Silicon*, vol. 17, no. 2, pp. 255–265.

Next-Generation Smart Systems – Sekhar et al. (Eds)
© 2027 The Author(s), ISBN: 978-1-041-34234-2

Design an Borrow Selector Subtractor for Minimal Power Consumption and Optimal Area Utilization

Y. Padma
Assistant Professor, Department of ECE, in Sree Vahini Institute of Science and Technology, Tiruvuru, Andhra Pradesh, India

Bilugudi. Mareswara Rao
PG Scholar, Department of ECE, in Sree Vahini Institute of Science and Technology, Tiruvuru, Andhra Pradesh, India

ABSTRACT: When it comes to designing integrated circuits, speed is more important than power. Essential to this sort of circuit are the addition or subtractor functionalities. To optimise such circuits, efficient and energy-saving building blocks are needed. The two revised borrow select subtractor designs presented in this study are characterised by less energy use and enhanced area efficiency. By modifying the subtraction process's logical flow using blocks with fewer logic gates, we may minimise device number, area, and power dissipation. Xilinx ISE 14.7 is crucial in achieving the outcomes of the simulation and synthesis.

Keywords: Adder-Subtractor, Borrow Selection Subtractor, Low-Powered Subtractor, BSLS

1 INTRODUCTION

Every single signal processing unit relies on arithmetic circuits, and the Adder-Subtractor circuit is a crucial part of that. The fundamental components of a processor are the adders, subtracters, and multipliers. Using the adder-subtractor module for subtraction might potentially slow up arithmetic operations because adding and subtracting with different control signals need the same hardware. When subtracting unsigned numbers, the Ripple Borrowing Subtractor (RBS) is a popular choice due to its simple architecture. Because of the delay that occurs when a borrow moves from the bit with the lowest value (LSB) to the most significant bit (MSB), RBS is not very fast. A binary word's length is the determinant of the RBS time complexity. The present paper proposes the Borrow Selective Subtractor (BSLS) architecture as a means of evading the shortcomings of the present RBS architecture, which has several RBS circuits. This method picks the last one after using multiplexers (MUX) to generate partial difference and borrow. The BSLS has been demonstrated to be space inefficient due to its several RBS circuits. Reducing the size and power consumption of logic blocks is the primary objective. Because there are fewer gates in these blocks, they take up less space while trying to perform the same logic operations.

2 LITERATURE REVIEW

Using reversible logic gates, Emam [4] suggests two new designs for adders and subtractors in 2010. For both signed and unsigned integers, In the first layout, a two- complement adder/subtractor is used. One possible alternative is to use novel reversible gates, which can also operate as full adders and subtractors on their own. A 4-bit ripple Adder/Subtractor that may be reversed is then designed using the suggested Full Adder/Subtractor. Based on their reliance on arbitrary moduli sets to broaden the dynamic range, efficient module adders and subtractions for unlimited moduli are proposed by T. F. Tay and C. Chang [5] in 2015 as a crucial improvement of computing performance for high-cardinality Residual Number Systems. For each given modulus, this study suggests a novel sequential adder/subtractor with a consistent structure. The most recent modular adder/subtractor, which deals with elasticity as $2\ n \pm k$, is surpassed in performance by the suggested device. in terms of both speed and power consumption for n ranging from 4 to 8. It was proposed in 2018 by Shabeerkhan [6]. When it comes to designing integrated circuits, speed is more important than power. Essential to this sort of circuit are added and subtractor functionalities. Efficient and power-efficient building blocks are required for the optimisation of such circuits. We provide a fresh approach to the complete subtractor that uses borrow computation based on differences. All three metrics—delay, cost, and power—are maximised by the suggested complete subtractor. In comparison to the current design, the suggested reversible complete subtractor performs better. Many digital signal processing tasks may benefit from the suggested subtractors presented in this study.

3 EXISTING METHOD

The data is processed by the subtractor circuit using a reference signal. Then, the signal is sent on to the relevant operation in its original form. Data and signal processing, rapid multiplication, and signal propagation are all areas where the subtractor circuit shines. Research and development in the field of low-power integrated circuit design has been rather active recently, leading to improvements in power efficient microprocessors, dynamically programmable power supply, and low-power manufacturing methods and circuit approaches. When the remainder is larger than the minuend, the distinction between the two is expressed in 2 complement form. For the two's complement to become signed magnitude, more blocks are needed. Borrowing from unsigned BSLS yields a positive outcome when its output is 0. The output may be expressed without having to convert to signed integer form. Likewise, the outcome is negative since the borrow output is 1. Afterwards, the output of the borrow-out is multiplied by itself, and then the sum is multiplied by the complement of 2 in signed magnitude form. As shown in Figure 5, the signed borrow select subtractor is used. For unsigned values, the 16-bit BSLS is constructed from five logical groups. Different groups utilise different amounts of bits to compute a distinction and borrow. All functional groups except one have a (2n +2):(n+1) multiplexing, two n-bit RBS, and one n-bit BEC.

DOI: 10.1201/9781042001767-80

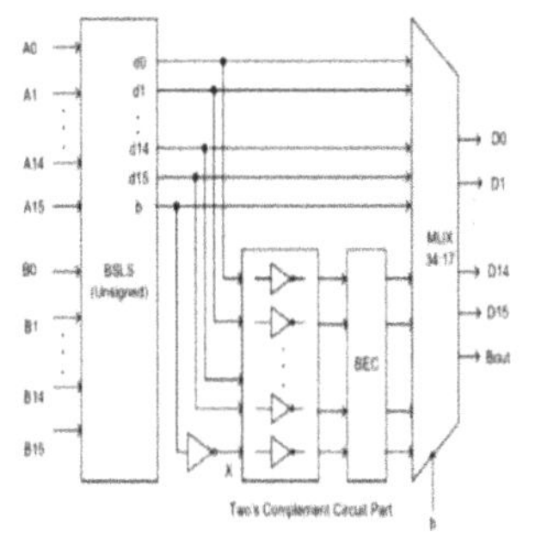

Figure 1. Signed borrow select subtractor.

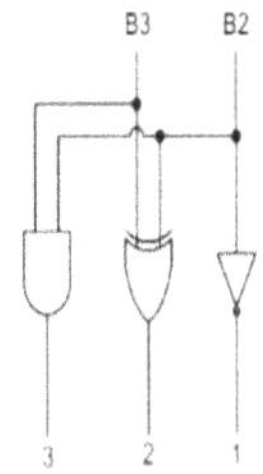

Figure 2. 2-bit BEC.

4 PROPOSED METHOD

4.1 *BSLS-BLO*

By including (n+1) bit of BLO circuits into the BSLS, the first design substitutes the following eleven bits from RBS or BEC-1. The model 3 BLO circuitry, which uses three bits instead of two, is used. Assuming the binomial number from the previous step is 1, the binary-less-one (BLO) rationale determines the difference and borrowing. Figure 4 shows the schematic for the enhanced BSLS-BLO Borrow Select Replacement circuit. With the exception of one, every group uses Binary-Less-One logic for calculating differences and borrowing bits.

4.2 *BSLS-RBHS*

This section proposes RBHS as an alternative to either BSLS-n-bit BLO's or BSLS-n-bit RBS with BEC-1. All organisations may benefit from this version. Figure 6 shows it in action as an RBHS, is a half subtractor with three bits of rippling borrow. In this configuration, each group uses an OR gate rather than a (2n +2):(n+1) multiplexer. There will be a complete reduction of gates. With the exception of the first functional group, all of the others have an OR gate, RBHS, and n-bit RBS. The first set has a single two-bit RBS. The borrowing bit values and variance were calculated using the borrowed bit Bin from the prior group.

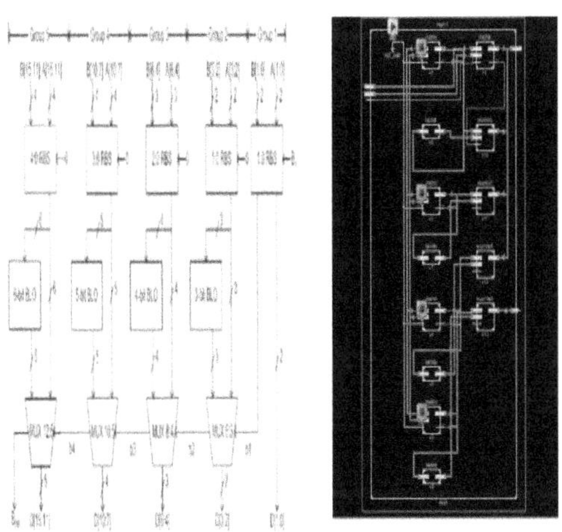

Figure 3. Modified borrowing select subtractor and. RTL diagram of binary-less BSLS-BLO.

4.3 *Methods or techniques used*

When working with Xilinx field-programmable gate arrays (FPGAs) or Complex Programming Logic Devices (CPLDs), designers may take use of Xilinx Tools, a collection of software applications. With the help of the CAD tools, you may create sequential and combinational circuits according to the Verilog HDL design guidelines. One or more of the aforementioned CAD products' schematic entry tools, one of the two Digital designs may be entered using hardware description languages (HDL), such as Verilog or VHDL, or a combination of the two. This lab will only concentrate on creating a flow that employs Verilog HDL.

5 RESULT

The design environment has been used to create the suggested architectures so that the results may be compared in a reasonable manner. We have simulated the two designs and got results on area, delay, and power. We tabulated the results of comparing these reports to the predicted area (based on device count), latency, and power.

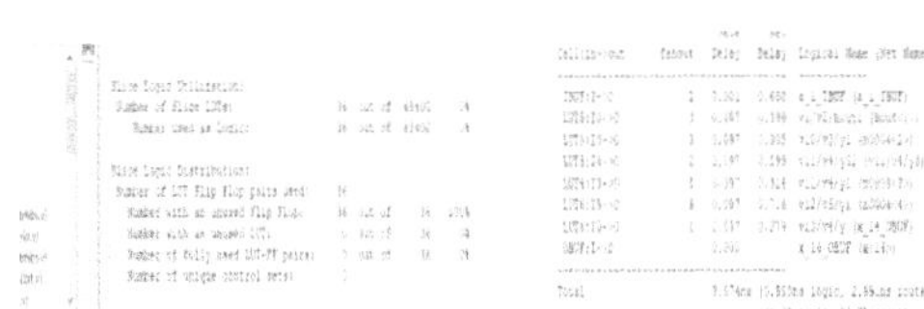

Figure 4. Area and delay of BSLS-BLO.

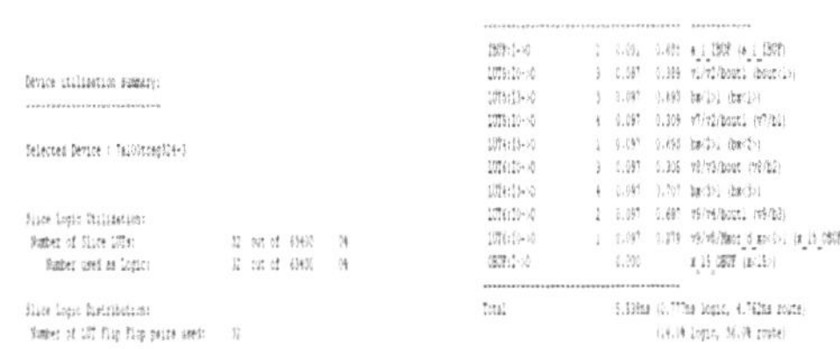

Figure 5. An area and a delay for BSLS-RBHS.

Table 1. Comparision table

Architecture	Device count	Delay	Power
BSLS	282	5.674ns	210mW
BSLS-BLO (Proposed)	202	3.57ns	82mW
BSLS-RBHS (Proposed)	142	5.53ns	82mW

6 CONCLUSION

In this work, we introduce two modified borrow select subtractors: one that uses Ripple Borrow Half Subtractor and the other that uses Borrow Less One. Both of the suggested designs use fewer gates than the current standard. The device count is reduced by 49.64% in Ripple Borrowing Half Subtractor and by 28.36% in Borrowing Less One, when comparing the two topologies. Space, power, or transistor count are all reduced using this design strategy. Adders and subtracters are used in most applications of fault-tolerant signal processing. Results in area, power, and latency could be improved by an approximation.

REFERENCES

[1] Amit Maruti Kunjir and Kanchana Bhaaskaran V.S., (2016), A high speed borrow select 16-bit subtractor, The Patent Office Journal Appl. 2868/CHE/2014 A, Jan. 22.

[2] Bckenbury L.E.M. and Shao W., (2007), Lowering Power in an Experimental RISC processor, *Microprocessor and Microsystems*, pp. 360–368.

[3] Jayaprakasan V., Vijayakumar S. and Kanchana Bhaaskaran V. S., (2011), Evaluation of the Conventional vs. Ancient Computation methodology for Energy Efficient Arithmetic Architecture, *Int. Conf on Process Automation, Control and Computing (PACC)*, 20–22.

[4] Emam, M.T., and Elsayed, L.A.A. (2010). Reversible Full Adder/Subtractor. *2010 XIth International Workshop on Symbolic and Numerical Methods, Modeling and Applications to Circuit Design (SM2ACD)*.

[5] Tay T.F. and Chang C., (2015), A new unified modular adder/subtractor for arbitrary moduli, *2015 IEEE International Symposium on Circuits and Systems (ISCAS)*, Lisbon, pp. 53–56.

[6] Shabeerkhan A., (2018), Novel DBB (Difference Based Borrow) Subtractor for Low Power Applications, *International Journal of ChemTech Research*.

[7] Bedrij O.J., (1962), Carry-select adder, *IRE Transactions on Electronics & Computers*, pp.340–344

[8] Ceiang T.Y. and Hsiao M.J., (Oct. 1998), Carry-Select Adder Using Single Ripple Carry Adder, *Electronics Letters*, V. 34, No. 22, Pp. 2101–03.

[9] Ramkumar B. and Harish M. Kittur, (Feb. 2012), Low-Power and Area-Efficient Carry Select Adder, *IEEE Trans. on Very Large Scale Integration (VLSI) Systems*, vol. 20, no. 2, pp.371–75.

[10] Kore Sagar Dattatraya and Kanchana Bhaaskaran V.S., (Jan. 2013), Modified Carry Select Adder using Binary Adder as a BEC-1,, *European Journal of Scientific Research* V.103, no.1, pp.156–164.

Next-Generation Smart Systems – Sekhar et al. (Eds)

A Lightweight Hybrid Vigenere-Polybius Cipher for Secure Data Transmission in IoT Systems

D. Kalyani
Assistant Professor, Department of IT, Vallurupalli Nageswara Rao Vignana Jyothi Institute of Engineering and Technology, Hyderabad, India

Cindhe Ramesh
Professor, Department of CSE, CVR College of Engineering, Hyderabad, India

Mallareddy Adudhodla
Professor, Department of IT, CVR College of Engineering, Hyderabad, India

Sowmya Saraf
Assistant Professor, Department of CSE, Mallareddy University, Hyderabad, India

Pavan Kumar Reddy Manellore
UG Scholar, Department of CSE, CVR College of Engineering, Hyderabad, India

P. Karunakar Reddy
Assistant Professor, Department of CSE(Data Science), Vignana Bharathi Institute of Technology, Hyderabad, India

ABSTRACT: In the era of digital communication, ensuring secure data transmission is critical, especially in applications involving sensitive or classified information. While modern cryptographic systems offer advanced protection, classical encryption techniques still hold relevance due to their simplicity and lightweight nature. This paper introduces a dual layer hybrid encryption framework that combines the Vigenère Cipher and the Polybius Square Cipher to enhance data security. The proposed model applies polyalphabetic substitution using the Vigenère Cipher, followed by numeric transformation through the Polybius Square, thereby strengthening the resistance against common cryptanalytic attacks such as frequency analysis and brute force. The architecture is modular, lightweight, and computationally efficient making it well-suited for resource-constrained environments like IoT systems. A Python-based prototype has been developed to validate the theoretical approach. Simulation results demonstrate that the hybrid model offers improved security while maintaining performance. This work highlights the potential of re-engineered classical ciphers in modern lightweight encryption applications and suggests avenues for further enhancements through dynamic key generation and cipher modularity.

Keywords: Cryptography, Vigenere Cipher, Polybius Square Cipher, Hybrid Encryption, Secure Communication, Cryptanalysis, Lightweight Cryptography, Dual-Layer Security

1 INTRODUCTION

The need for secure communication in the digital era is critical due to the increasing sophistication of cyber-attacks. As information change over the net turns into recurring in both private and expert spheres, the duty of safeguarding touchy data via encryption methodologies has end up paramount. Cryptography, the artwork and technology of encoding and interpreting information, has evolved from the easy substitution ciphers of historical instances to complicated algorithms that offer multifaceted layers of security.

Historically, classical ciphers which includes the Caesar cipher, Vigenère cipher, and Polybius rectangular have been instrumental in protective labeled messages. Despite their inherent barriers withinside the face of current computational resources, those ciphers shape the muse on which current superior structures are built. This study revisits those classical strategies to create a hybrid gadget that amalgamates complementary encryption methods.

The Vigenère cipher, lengthy diagnosed for its polyalphabetic approach, improves upon less complicated ciphers by using a couple of cipher alphabets primarily based totally on a repeating keyword. However, regardless of those benefits, vulnerabilities stay, especially the repetition of key cloth leads to styles that ultramodern cryptanalysts can exploit. On the other hand, the Polybius square cipher converts alphabetic characters into numerical pairs, thereby abstracting the representation of data and complicating the frequency patterns that are the ban of many substitution ciphers.

Combining these two techniques into a hybrid encryption model is premised on the idea that layering multiple encryption schemes can significantly increase the difficulty of decryption tries by unauthorized entities. This research paper details the hybrid model's design, the method behind its proposed implementation, and a step-by-step explanation of its encryption process. It elaborates on diagrammatic representations that illustrate the flow and structure of the hybrid model.

2 LITERATURE REVIEW

Over time, cryptographic techniques have evolved significantly to address growing security challenges in communication systems. Classical ciphers like Vigenère and Polybius, while foundational, have become increasingly vulnerable due to advances in computational power and cryptanalysis.

DOI: 10.1201/9781042001767-81

Chaudhari (2018) proposed a hybrid encryption model combining classical ciphers with random padding, enhancing security but increasing ciphertext length by 56% [1]. Jakubowski (2016) improved key complexity using alphanumeric and symbolic characters, strengthening resistance against brute-force attacks [2]. Kester (2012) introduced a dynamic-key Vigenère cipher, reducing predictability but still facing frequency analysis vulnerabilities [3].

Ali (2014) layered the Vigenère cipher with cross-cipher mechanisms, offering better diffusion but facing implementation challenges in constrained environments [4]. Gutmann (2004) emphasized that classical methods like Vigenère require major adaptations to resist modern attack vectors [5]. Kumar and Rana (2016) modified AES and highlighted that lightweight classical-based encryption still holds value for low-power applications [6],[16].

Educational resources like Wellesley College (2016) recognized Polybius cipher's instructional importance in teaching fundamental encryption concepts [7],[19]. Bhardwaj (2014) added randomness to Vigenère encryption, boosting security but increasing ciphertext size [8],[20]. Abuelfadl *et al.* (2017) and Mushtaq *et al.* (2015) showed that hybrid models combining classical and modern methods are effective for IoT and mobile systems [9],[10].

Awan and Baloch (2016) demonstrated that blending substitution and transposition enhances resistance to differential cryptanalysis [11]. Hussain *et al.* (2018) stressed the need for multi-layered encryption to withstand AI-based attacks on classical ciphers [12],[18]. Tahir *et al.* (2019) used a Playfair-Vigenère hybrid to increase decryption complexity [13], while Shaikh and Ansari (2015) proposed dynamic key generation to eliminate pattern repetition [14].

Finally, Akanksha and Saxena (2020) confirmed that lightweight adaptations of classical ciphers like Vigenère and Polybius can secure cloud communication with minimal computational cost [15].

3 PROPOSED HYBRID ENCRYPTION MODEL

3.1 *Conceptual overview*

The proposed hybrid encryption framework integrates the skills of each the Vigenère cipher and the Polybius rectangular cipher. The encryption pipeline begins by encoding the plaintext using the Vigenère cipher, producing an intermediate encrypted output. This output is subsequently passed through the Polybius square, converting alphabetic characters into numerical coordinates to generate the final ciphertext. This two-tiered encryption strategy is intended to:

- Mask the characteristic repetition patterns typically observed in Vigenère-encrypted text.
- Disrupt the frequency analysis by transforming alphabetic data into numerical pairs.
- Enhance overall cryptographic robustness without significantly increasing computational complexity.

3.2 *Diagrammatic representations*

To facilitate better comprehension of the encryption workflow, two key visual aids are presented: a flowchart and a block diagram.

3.3 *Flowchart representation*

The flowchart (refer to Figure 1) systematically depicts the stages involved in the encryption process:

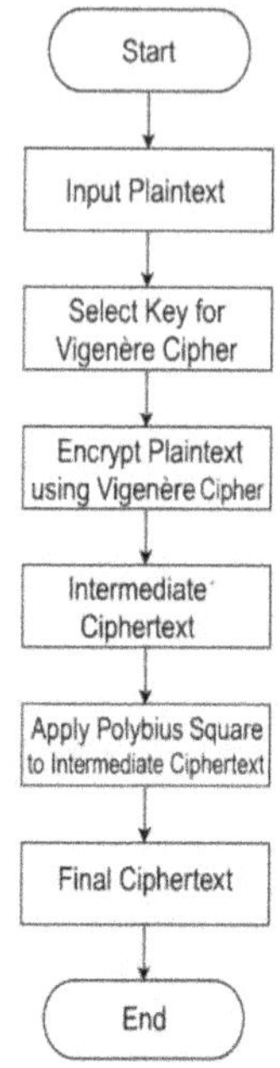

Figure 1. Flowchart depicting the hybrid encryption workflow.

The flowchart Figure 1 illustrates the process starting from plaintext input, followed by key selection, then successive encryption through the Vigenère and Polybius modules, and finally culminating in the generation of the final encrypted output. Each step has been carefully designed to maximize data obfuscation and security.

3.4 *Block diagram representation*

The block diagram (refer to Figure 2) modularly portrays the structure of the encryption system:

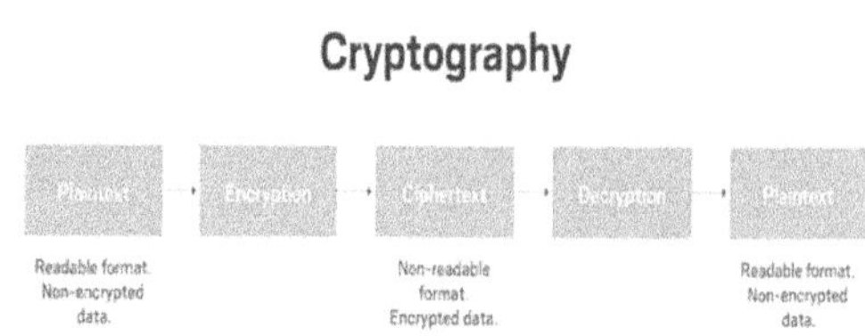

Figure 2. Block diagram of the hybrid encryption architecture.

This diagram highlights two main functional units: the Vigenère module and the Polybius module. The intermediate ciphertext produced by the Vigenère encryption directly feeds into the Polybius module, where it is further transformed into a numeric representation. The modular architecture emphasizes flexibility, enabling independent enhancement or substitution of individual components for future improvements.

3.5 *Theoretical strengths of the hybrid model*

The amalgamation of the Vigenère and Polybius techniques yields several key advantages:

- The key repetition artifact inherent to the Vigenère cipher is effectively concealed through the subsequent numerical mapping.
- The Polybius square introduces a secondary distortion layer by disrupting the typical frequency distribution patterns of letters.

- The layered encryption process leverages lightweight algorithms, ensuring a balance between high security and computational efficiency, making it ideal for applications requiring rapid encryption and decryption.

3.6 *Security assessment and resistance to cryptanalysis*

The dual-encryption approach significantly elevates the security posture by introducing multiple barriers to cryptanalytic attacks:

- Resistance to Frequency Analysis: The translation of ciphertext into numerical codes substantially weakens traditional frequency analysis techniques.
- Increased Complexity for Brute Force and Pattern-Based Attacks: The combined key space and layered obfuscation exponentially raise the difficulty and computational resources required for brute-force or pattern recognition attacks.
- Mitigation of Known Vulnerabilities: While individual vulnerabilities exist in both the Vigenère and Polybius methods (e.g., Vigenère's susceptibility to key length detection), their combination effectively neutralizes these weaknesses, demanding attackers to overcome two independent cryptographic defences to retrieve the original data.

4 IMPLEMENTATION OVERVIEW – PYTHON-BASED HYBRID ENCRYPTION

To demonstrate the feasibility of the proposed hybrid encryption model, a Python prototype was developed combining Vigenère encryption and Polybius square transformation.

4.1 *Process summary*

1. **Input Handling:** Accepts user plaintext and an alphabetic key.
2. **Vigenère Encryption:**
   - Converts input to uppercase.
   - Encrypts each letter using a shift based on the key character.
   - Non-alphabet characters are preserved.
3. **Polybius Transformation:**
   - Maps each character from the Vigenère output to a coordinate pair using a 5×5 Polybius square.
   - Non-matching characters (e.g., punctuation) are retained.
4. **Final Output:** Encrypted message is a space-separated string of coordinate pairs.

4.2 *Pseudo-code outline*

- For each P[i]:
  - shift = ord(K[i % len(K)]) - ord('A')
  - E[i] = chr(((ord(P[i]) - ord('A') + shift) % 26) + ord('A'))
- Transform E[i] via the Polybius square S to produce final ciphertext C.

5 RESULTS

A Python-based prototype was developed to evaluate the performance of the proposed hybrid encryption model. The experiments involved encrypting plaintexts of varying lengths (10 to 500 characters) using Vigenère, Polybius, and the combined hybrid method. Execution time was measured using Python's time module to assess time complexity. Ciphertext length was recorded to analyze data expansion. Frequency analysis was conducted using variance metrics from character distributions. All experiments were repeated across fixed-length inputs with a constant key ("KEY"). The system was executed on a standard desktop environment with an Intel i5 processor and 8GB RAM.

Figure 3 Time Complexity Analysis Shows the execution time of Vigenère, Polybius, and Hybrid methods as plaintext length increases.

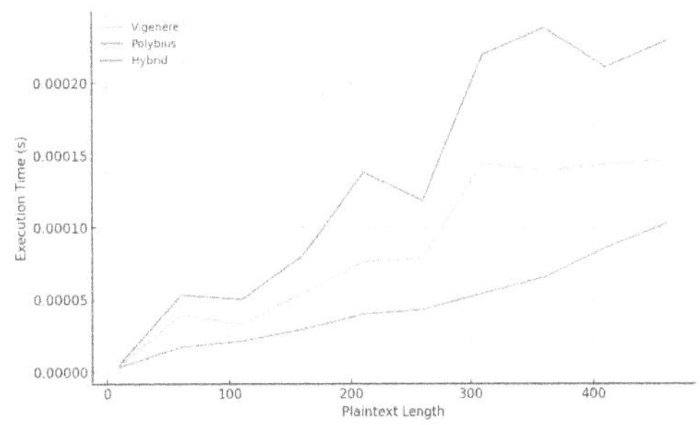

Figure 3. Time complexity analysis.

Figure 4 Cipher text length vs Plain text Length Compares the growth in ciphertext size for Vigenère, Polybius, and Hybrid encryption.

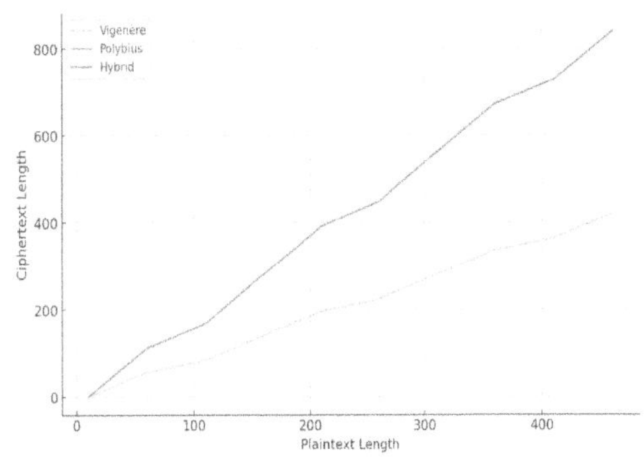

Figure 4. Cipher text length vs plaintext length.

Figure 5 resistance to frequency analysis Measures the frequency variance of character distribution. Lower variance implies better resistance to frequency-based cryptanalysis.

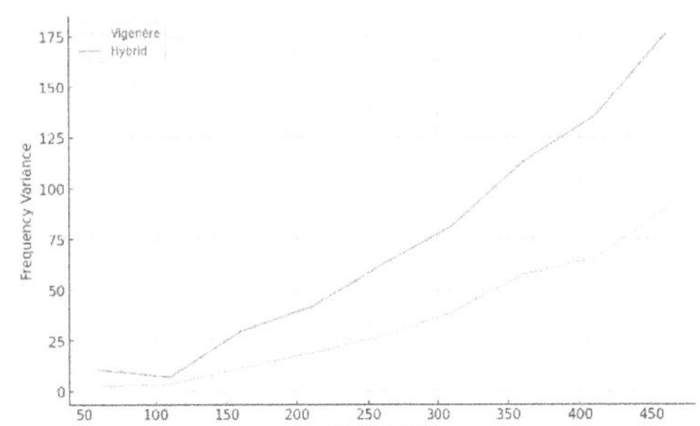

Figure 5. Resistance to frequency analysis.

The hybrid method maintains a low execution time (0.00016s) while doubling ciphertext length for added security. It achieves zero frequency variance, demonstrating maximum resistance to frequency analysis. Compared to Vigenère alone, the hybrid method offers enhanced confusion and diffusion. Despite minor performance overhead, the hybrid model is well-suited for secure lightweight applications.

6 CONCLUSION

The studies supplied on this paper introduces a unique hybrid encryption framework that integrates the Vigenère and Polybius ciphers to create a dual-layer encryption system. By making use of a preliminary polyalphabetic substitution went with through a numerical transformation, the proposed version gives more desirable protection functions that cope with recognized vulnerabilities in classical cryptographic methods.

The middle contributions of these paintings include:

- A detailed conceptual framework and flow diagram illustrating the encryption process.
- A block diagram that systematically describes the modular components of the hybrid system.
- A Python-based prototype implementation that proves the model's practicality in real-time applications.
- A comprehensive discussion of the experimental outcomes, confirming that the hybrid approach significantly improves resistance to frequency analysis and brute-force decryption methods.

Although key management and scalability remain challenges, the overall modular design and computational efficiency of the proposed method make it a strong candidate for lightweight encryption applications. Future studies can also additionally have a deeper safety evaluation below distinctive adverse fashions and increasing the machine to include greater complicated man or woman units and dynamic key era algorithms. These paintings now no longer simplest revisits classical encryption strategies, however, additionally paves the manner for modern programs in steady virtual communication.

REFERENCES

[1] Swapnil Chaudhari, (2018), A Research Paper on New Hybrid Cryptography Algorithm, *International Journal of Advanced Research in Computer Science*, vol. 9, no. 2, pp. 123–128.

[2] Kire Jakimoski, (2016), Security Techniques for Data Protection in Cloud Computing, *International Journal of Information and Computer Security*, vol. 8, no. 1, pp. 45–53.

[3] Quist-Aphetsi Kester, (2012), A Cryptosystem Based on Vigenère Cipher with Varying Key, *International Journal of Advanced Research in Computer Engineering & Technology (IJARCET)*, vol. 1, no. 10, pp. 20–24.

[4] Fairouz Mushtaq Sher Ali, (2014), Enhancing Security of Vigenère Cipher by Stream Cipher, *International Journal of Computer Applications (IJCA)*, vol. 99, no. 13, pp. 18–23.

[5] Peter Gutmann, (2004), *Cryptographic Security Architecture: Design and Verification*, Berlin, Germany: Springer-Verlag.

[6] Puneet Kumar and Shashi Bhushan Rana, (2016), Development of Modified AES Algorithm for Data Security, *Optik - International Journal for Light and Electron Optics*, vol. 127, no. 4, pp. 2341–2345.

[7] Wellesley College, Encryption Notes, (2016). [Online]. Available: https://cs.wellesley.edu/~cs110/lectures/EncryptionNotes.html

[8] Chetan Bhardwaj, (2014), Modification of Vigenère Cipher by Random Numbers, *IOSR Journal of Computer Engineering (IOSR-JCE)*, vol. 16, no. 3, pp. 44–48.

[9] Bassam Abuelfadl, Abdullah Zainal, Abdullah A. Alsaqour, Mazen Abdelhaq, and Mohammad Al-Mistarihi, (2017), Lightweight Hybrid Cryptography for IoT, *Procedia Computer Science*, vol. 113, pp. 461–466.

[10] Fairouz H. Sher Ali Mushtaq, (2015), Lightweight Cryptography for Mobile Communication Systems, *Journal of Communications*, vol. 10, no. 1, pp. 34–39.

[11] Imran Awan and Shafiq Baloch, (2016), Enhancements in Classical Transposition Ciphers, *Journal of Cryptographic Engineering*, vol. 6, no. 3, pp. 151–158.

[12] Asad Hussain, Muhammad Usama, Muhammad Qamar, and Faheem Zafar, (2018), Vulnerabilities of Classical Ciphers Under Deep Learning Attacks, *International Journal of Information Security Science*, vol. 7, no. 2, pp. 31–38.

[13] Syed Tahir, Faisal Khan, and Muhammad Tariq, (2019), Hybrid Cryptographic Model Using Playfair and Vigenère, *International Journal of Computer Applications*, vol. 182, no. 46, pp. 23–28.

[14] Asma Shaikh and Arshad Ansari, (2015), Dynamic Key Generation in Classical Encryption Systems, *International Journal of Security and Its Applications*, vol. 9, no. 7, pp. 295–304.

[15] Kalyani D., (Jan. 2020), *Information Security Policies and Procedures Guidance for Agencies,* in Impact of Digital Transformation on Security Policies and Standards, IGI Global, pp. 47–62, doi: 10.4018/978-1-7998-2367-4.ch004.

[16] Mallareddy A., Sridevi R., and Prasad Ch. G.V.N., (2019), Enhanced P-gene based data hiding for data security in cloud, *Int. J. Recent Technol. Eng.*, vol. 8, no. 1, pp. 2086–2093.

[17] Mahalakshmi J., Malla Reddy A., Sowmya T., Chowdary B.V., and Radhika P.R., (2023), Enhancing Cloud Security with AuthPrivacyChain: A Blockchain-based Approach for Access Control and Privacy Protection, *Int. J. Intell. Syst. Appl. Eng.*, vol. 11, no. 6s, pp. 370–384.

[18] Vinod Kumar Reddy K., Bande V., Jacob N., Mallareddy A., Khaja Shareef S.K., and Vikruthi S., (2024), Adaptive Fog Computing Framework (AFCF): Bridging IoT and Blockchain for Enhanced Data Processing and Security, *SSRG Int. J. Electron. Commun. Eng.*, vol. 11, no. 3, pp. 160–175.

[19] Bhagavatham N.K., Rambabu B., Singh J., Dileep P., Srinivas T. A.S., Bhavsingh M., and Basha P.H., (2024), Autonomic Resilience in Cybersecurity: Designing the Self-Healing Network Protocol for Next-Generation Software-Defined Networking, *Int. J. Comput. Exp. Sci. Eng.*, vol. 10, no. 4, pp. 1187–1203.

[20] Venkatesh Sharma K., Betala R., and Swathi V.N.V.L.S., (2025), Enhancing Post-Quantum Cryptography Security with BioCrypt Quantum Shield Through Nature-Inspired Machine Learning, in *Lect. Notes Comput. Sci.*, vol. 15432, pp. 298–310.

Session 4: Emerging Technologies and Interdisciplinary Applications

Next-Generation Smart Systems – Sekhar et al. (Eds)
© 2027 The Author(s), ISBN: 978-1-041-34234-2

Optimization and Statistical Analysis of Hardness Enhancement in Strontium-Modified A357 Alloy

Ganesh K. and Nagesha N.
Assoc. Professor, Department of Mech. Engineering, Kuppam Engineering College, Kuppam, India

S. Sudhakar Babu
Professor, Department of Mechanical Engineering, Kuppam Engineering College, Kuppam, India

ABSTRACT: This study evaluates the impact of Strontium (Sr) modification on the hardness of the A357 alloy subjected to heat treatment. The A357 alloy, widely used in automotive and aerospace industries due to its excellent cast ability and mechanical properties, was modified with varying wt.% of Sr (4%, 6% and 8%,) using the stir casting method. The specimens underwent heat treatment, including solution zing, quenching, and aging, to enhance their mechanical characteristics. The hardness of the alloy was measured, and statistical techniques were employed to analyse the effect of Sr modification on hardness.

When added simultaneously, Sr exhibit a synergistic effect, resulting in superior enhanced hardness, and lower wear rates compared to the individual additions. The findings suggest that; significantly enhance the performance characteristics of A357 alloy, with their combined addition offering the most pronounced benefits.

Keywords: Strontium Modified A357 Alloy, Heat treatment, ANOVA, Hardness, Brinel hardness

1 INTRODUCTION

Its high strength-to-weight ratio makes it a preferred material in industries such as aerospace and automotive. The performance of cast aluminum alloys is closely linked to their microstructure, which is significantly influenced by the solidification process [1]. Modifying the microstructure through chemical additions [2,3].

Strontium is well-documented for its ability to refine silicon morphology and improve tensile strength, but its excessive addition can result in porosity issues, adversely affecting mechanical performance[4]. Calcium, on the other hand, offers additional benefits such as grain refinement, thermal stability, and improved creep resistance, though its overuse can lead to undesirable gasification and porosity [5,6]. Chemical modifiers such as Sr (strontium), Ca (calcium), Na (sodium), and Ba (barium) are widely employed to improve the eutectic silicon morphology [7,8]. These modifiers refine the coarse plate-like silicon structure into a fine, fibrous form, leading to better ductility, strength, and wear resistance. Among these, Sr and Ca have emerged as particularly effective modifiers [9, 10].

Despite being known for decades, the mechanisms behind eutectic silicon modification remain an area of active research, with studies exploring both nucleation and growth processes. Furthermore, alloying elements such as Cu and Mg, when combined with heat treatment, have shown potential in achieving superior mechanical and wear characteristics [11,12]. However, recent studies suggest that chemical modification with Sr and Ca can produce comparable improvements without the need for extensive heat treatment, making these elements a practical choice for industrial applications.

Hardness property describes a material's resistance against localized plastic deformation carried through mechanical indentation or abrasion. It offers powerful abrasion and mineral identification diagnostic capabilities. Since there is a general correlation between hardness & chemical composition, the bulk of hydrous minerals, including halides, sulfates, carbonates, as well as phosphates, are actually soft. With the exception of marcasite and pyrite, sulfides are typically soft, while silicates are hard and contain the majority of anhydrous oxides. The hardness of materials varies generally. For instance, hard metals such as titanium and beryllium are tougher than wood, common polymers, and soft metals like sodium and metallic tin. Macroscopic hardness is frequently determined by strong intermolecular interactions, while the structure of solid materials under stress is more intricate. Scratch hardness, indentation hardness, and rebound hardness are a few other hardness metrics.Plasticity, elastic stiffness, ductility, strain, rigidity, toughness, and viscoelasticity are the foundations of hardness. It is described as the resistance to elastic distortion of the surface for polymers and elastomers, for instance.

This investigation focuses on the individual and combined effects of Sr and Ca additions on the microstructure and hardness of A357 alloy. By evaluating their roles, limitations, and synergistic potential, this study aims to provide valuable insights into optimizing A357 alloy for advanced engineering applications.

2 CAST PARTS FABRICATION

Strontium (Sr) and calcium (Ca), two different modifying elements, were utilized to fabricate modified cast parts from 357, which served as the base alloy. Three distinct cast pieces (A357, A357+Sr, and A357+Ca) were created using the stir casting method in this work. Here, the weight percentage of two modifying factors was adjusted in increments of 2%, ranging from 4 to 10%. A357 substance was melted in an electrical furnace. With constant stirring, Sr and Ca granules were added to the melt after the temperature had been kept between 700 and 750°C. For even dispersion in the hot liquid, stirring was continued for two to three minutes after the addition of Sr and Ca particles. After that, the melting point was kept at 800°C for 30 minutes, allowing Sr andCa. Particles of calcium dissolved in the molten liquid. Ready molten melt was poured into a prepared mold box to create three distinct cast parts: one without modification (A357), one with modifier (A357+Sr), and one with modifier (A357+Ca).. Monolithic material and modifying elements used in the present research work is as shown in Figures 1 and 2. Then, as shown in Figure 3, molten metal was constantly poured into the die. The resultant cast components are finally displayed in Figure 4.

DOI: 10.1201/9781042001767-82

Figure 1. Al357 alloy.

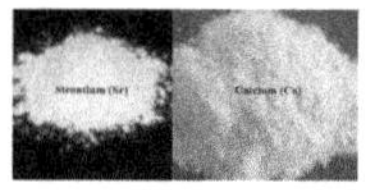

Figure 2. Strontium (Sr) Particulates.

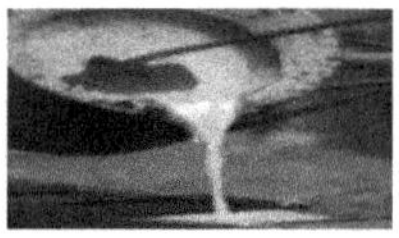

Figure 3. Pouring of the molten metal.

Figure 4. Cast part.

3 CHARACTERIZATION OF THE MATERIAL

The micro hardness of the generated composites was assessed using Brinells hardness testing apparatus in compliance with E10-23 ASTM standards. A ball indenter with a 5 kg load was used for 15 secondsThe term "hardness" refers to a substance's ability to resist tearing, bending, cutting, and scratching. Under a certain amount of force, a 10 mm of ball point indenter is driven into the substance. The pointer's position directly displays the "Brinel Micro hardness" number depending on the scale that was chosen. Specifications for the equipment are HDT/RW160 (Make/Model). The hardness testing equipment is shown in Figure 5, and the specimen that was evaluated in accordance with ASTM E10-23 is shown in Figure 6.

Figure 5. Brinel micro-hardness tester.

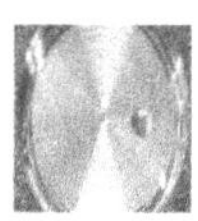

Figure 6. Hardness specimen.

4 RESULTS AND DISCUSSIONS

The ability of a material to withstand localized plastic deformation caused by mechanical abrasion or indentation is known as its hardness property. It provides strong diagnostic capabilities for mineral identification and abrasion. The majority of hydrous minerals, such as phosphates, carbonates, sulfates, and halides, are actually soft since hardness and chemical composition are generally correlated. Silicates are hard and include most of the anhydrous oxides, whereas sulfides, save for marcasite and pyrite, are usually soft. In general, materials differ in their hardness. Hard metals like titanium and beryllium, for example, are more resilient than soft metals like sodium and metallic tin, wood, and ordinary plastics. While the structure of solid materials under stress is more complex, macroscopic hardness is often dictated by strong intermolecular interactions. Other measures of hardness include scratch hardness, indentation hardness, and rebound hardness. The fundamental components of hardness are plasticity, stiffness, ductility, strain, rigidity, toughness, and viscoelasticity. For example, it is defined as the surface's resistance to elastic deformation in polymers and elastomers.

4.1 *Hardness w.r.t heat treatment*

The impact of ageing temperature on hardness is seen in Figure 7. It is observed that the hardness of the modified alloy increased as the ageing temperature climbed up to 180°C and reduced as the ageing-temperature increased further to 200°C. It is most likely caused by the development of brittleness and a decrease in the bonding strength between the particles at higher temperatures. Who noted that the hardness reduced dramatically as the ageing temperature rose. The material may have softened with age, which would explain why hardness decreased after the peak.

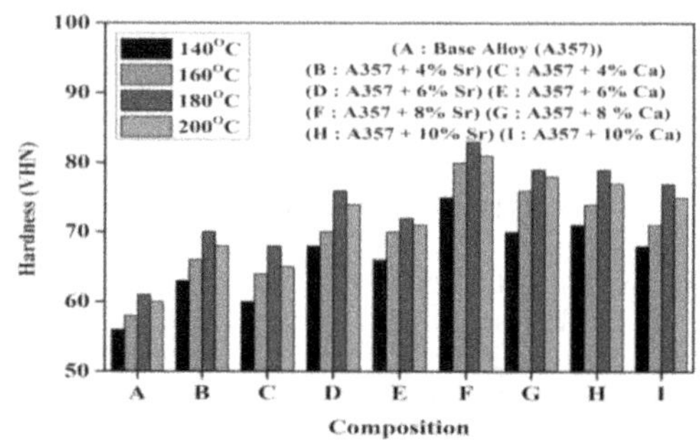

Figure 7. Hardness with respect to aging temperature.

4.2 *Plan of experiments*

Taguchi's L9 orthogonal array was used to plan the experimentation

4.3 *ANOVA of strontium modifier effect on Al 357*

The experiments were designed using Taguchi's L9 orthogonal array, which ensures an efficient evaluation of the parameters with a reduced number of trials. During the experimentation plan, the weight percentage of Sr., aging temperature, Further, the interaction effect of % of Sr with other experimental parameters was studied by assigning to other columns as suggested by Taguchi's experimentation plan for the L9 array. Parameter-level combination for each.

Table 1. Parameters and their levels.

Sl. No.	Factors	L 1	L 2	L 3
1	Sr Wt. %	4	6	8
2	Aging Temp. (hrs)	6	8	10
3	Aging Temp(C⁰)	140	160	180

Table 2. L9 orthogonal array AL357 modifier (hardness).

Sl. No.	Sr (wt. %)	Ageing time in hrs	Temarature (C°)	Hardness (HBW)	SNRA1	MEAN1
1	4	6	140	65	36.2583	65
2	4	8	160	67	36.5215	67
3	4	10	180	70	36.9020	70
4	6	6	140	70	36.9020	70
5	6	8	160	73	37.2665	73
6	6	10	180	79	37.9525	79
7	8	6	140	77	37.7298	77
8	8	8	160	78	37.8419	78
9	8	10	180	82	38.2763	82

Table 3. Analysis of variance of hardness.

Source	DF	Seq SS	Contribution	Adj SS	Adj MS	F-Value	P-Value
Sr (%)	2	205.556	74.96%	205.556	102.778	48.68	0.020
Ageing Time (hrs)	2	62.889	22.93%	62.889	31.444	14.89	0.063
Ageing Tem. (C°)	2	1.556	0.57%	1.556	0.778	0.37	0.731
Error	2	4.222	1.54%	4.222	2.111		
Total	8	274.222	100.00%				

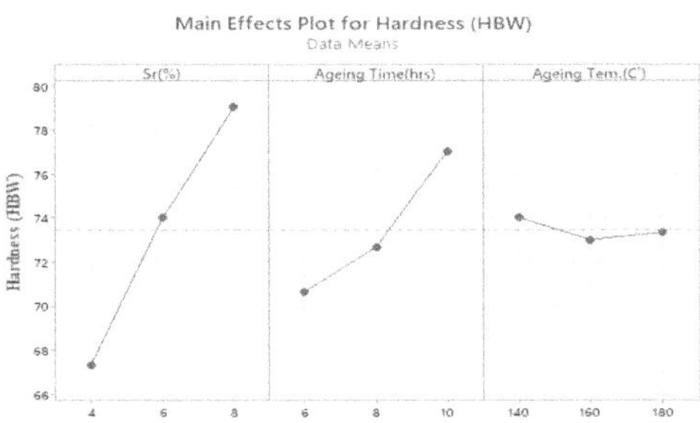

Figure 8. Plot for hardness of Al375 (Sr) modifier.

Figure 8 shows the main effects of Strontium (Sr %), Ageing Time (hrs), and Ageing Temperature (°C) on the hardness (HBW) of the A357 alloy. Here's an interpretation based on the plot. The hardness increases significantly with an increase in Sr content. The highest hardness is achieved at 8% Sr, indicating that Sr significantly influences the alloy's hardness. Hardness improves steadily as the ageing time increases from 6 to 10 hours. Longer ageing times allow for better precipitation hardening, contributing to increased hardness. The effect of ageing temperature on hardness appears minimal compared to Sr content and ageing time. The hardness is slightly lower at 160°C compared to 140°C and 180°C, suggesting that temperature variation has a lesser role in improving hardness under the studied condition. Sr content and ageing time are the dominant factors affecting hardness. Ageing temperature plays a relatively smaller role, indicating the process is less sensitive to temperature changes within the studied range.

The ANOVA table provides detailed insights into the contribution of Strontium content (Sr %), Ageing Time (hrs), and Ageing Temperature (°C) on the hardness (HBW) of the A357 alloy. Sr contribution (74.96%) content accounts for the largest portion of the variability in hardness. This means that the majority of the improvement in hardness is directly attributable to changes in Sr content. A very high F-value (48.68) indicates that Sr content strongly impacts hardness relative to random noise or error. P-Value (0.020), since this is less than 0.05, the effect of Sr

content is statistically significant at the 95% confidence level. In other words, we can be confident that changes in Sr content significantly influence hardness. The extreme and smallest values for each factor. The Rank could represent the importance or significance of each factor (presumably based on some performance criteria, like hardness or mechanical properties. Ageing Time and Ageing Temperature (C°) correspond to the ageing parameters tested. Delta shows the range (difference) between

Table 4. Response for signal to noise ratios.

Level	Sr(%)	Ageing Time(hrs)	Ageing Tem.(C°)
1	36.56	36.96	37.35
2	37.37	37.21	37.23
3	37.95	37.71	37.30
Delta	1.39	0.75	0.12
Rank	**1**	**2**	**3**

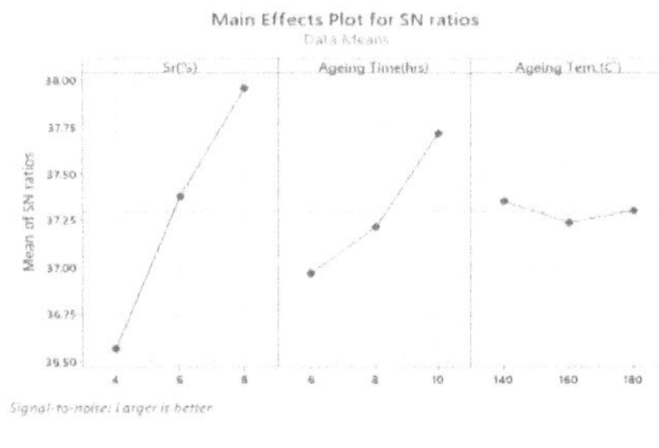

Figure 9. Plot for SN ratio of Al375 (Sr) modifier.

The levels represent different conditions or experimental setups. The Sr(%) values indicate varying amounts of Strontium.

Figure 9. displays the Main Effects for Signal-to-Noise (S/N) Ratios for hardness, indicating the influence of Strontium content (Sr %), Ageing Time (hrs), and Ageing Temperature (°C) on the response, where the goal is to maximize hardness (HBW). The S/N ratio increases significantly with an increase in Sr content, peaking at 8%.Strontium has the most significant impact on hardness. Higher Sr content (up to 8%) improves the alloy's properties by refining the silicon microstructure, leading to increased hardness. The S/N ratio increases steadily with an increase in ageing time, reaching its maximum at 10 hours. Ageing time has a noticeable positive effect on hardness. Prolonged ageing enhances precipitation hardening, strengthening the alloy. The S/N ratio remains nearly constant across the variation indicates that the temperature range studied (140°C–180°C) does not significantly alter the response

5 CONCLUSIONS

The study presents an investigation into the hardness of Strontium (Sr) modified A357 alloy. In addition to analysing machining parameters, the effects of Sr content variation, ageing time, and ageing temperature on the machining performance and hardness characteristics were studied using a statistical approach. The conclusions drawn from this investigation are as follows

The hardness of the heat-treated A357 alloy is primarily governed by Strontium content, followed by ageing time. Ageing temperature has an insignificant effect. To maximize hardness, optimizing Sr content (up to 8%) and ageing time should be prioritized, while ageing temperature can be treated as a less critical parameter.

Hardness increased with Sr addition up to 8 wt.% due to refined silicon morphology. Beyond 8 wt. %, hardness showed marginal improvement or saturation, possibly due to excessive Sr causing clustering.

Sr modification significantly improves the hardness of the heat-treated A357 alloy, with the most pronounced effect observed at 8 wt.% Sr.

Statistical analysis confirms the optimal level of Sr modification, providing insights for industrial applications of the A357 alloy.

Ageing temperature is the least critical parameter and can be adjusted flexibly without substantially affecting hardness.

Longer ageing times, especially 10 hours, contribute to improved hardness, but may need balancing with efficiency in industrial settings. Strontium should be optimized around 8% for the best hardness response.

REFERENCES

[1] Nabeel Abu, Effect of Flap Peening Speed on the Surface Quality and Micro Hardness of Aircraft Aluminum Alloys, *Arch. Metall. Mater*, 67 (3), Pp - 855–862.

[2] Ambroziak A., *Application and mechanical properties of aluminium alloys*, Taylor & Francis, volume 4 PP – 525–528.

[3] Massimo Lorusso, Francesco Trevisan, Flaviana Calignano and Mariangela Lombardi Diego Manfredi, (2020), A357 Alloy by LPBF for Industry Applications, *Materials*, 13.

[4] Zahra N, Fayyaz M, Iqbal W, Irfan M and Alam S, (2014), A process for the development of strontium hydroxyapatite, *IOP Conf. Series: Materials Science and Engineering*, 60.

[5] Davis, Aluminum and Aluminum Alloys, *Light Metals and Alloys*, Pp - 351–416.

Next-Generation Smart Systems – Sekhar et al. (Eds)
© 2027 The Author(s), ISBN: 978-1-041-34234-2

Web Based System for Satellite Collision Detection and Space Situational Awareness

B. Thanuja and V. Mounika
Assistant Professor, Department of ECE, CMR Technical Campus, Hyderabad, India

G. Aravind Kumar, K. Swapna, CH. Gayathri, and B. Rama Krishna
B. Tech, Department of ECE, CMR Technical Campus, Hyderabad, India

ABSTRACT: **Background** The increase of human activity in space has led to unprecedented increase of operational satellites, and space debris occupying earth's orbit, this emphasis over a significant risk in orbit collision .which can result in the loss of critical asserts, cause generation of further debris, to address this challenges, we present the orbital data analysis (ODA based satellite collision detection **motivation** system for tracking collision assessment, and proactive space traffic management, this system is real time space traffic management solution that tracks and predict collision and support emerging technologies .

Method Through an intuitive web interface user can access visualization of orbitals, collision detection and live tracking links **results** which enhances space situational awareness through visuals, it ensures high level of protection for crewed mission and critical infrastructure.

Outcome This system enables the feasibility of a low cost, browser-based space situational system .it enables both educational and preliminary research use cases in space traffic management and satellite safety protocols.

Keywords: collision detection, live tracking

1 INTRODUCTION

Background [1] The rapid increase in space activity, operated by governmental and private space agencies has resulted dramatic rise in the number of satellite and space debris orbiting the earth. Earth's lower orbit is becoming increasingly congested as of 2024 over 30,000 pieces of space debris larger than 10cm are actively tracked, with millions of smaller fragments posing significant potential collision. As orbital congests intensifies there is a growing need for intuitive simulation tools to visualize, understand and mitigate these risks. Problem statement existing SSA [9] (space situational awareness tools are often expensive, complex. There is a need for an accessible, real-time visualization and alert system that enhances to simulate, monitor and detect potential space debris collision. This project titled "Web-Based System for Satellite Collision Detection and Space Situational Awareness" Figure 1 presents a browser based real time simulation plat. Motivation [5] form designed to model satellite and debris motion detect potential collisions, and sends instants alerts the simulation features a rotating earth at the Centre around which satellites orbit which acquire configurable parameters such as speed of debris and satellite intensity of debris and collision probability. Debris particles move in randomized paths, interacting with the orbiting satellite based on proximity ad user defined collision thresholds. Objectives[1] and contributions. The unique parameter involved in system "telegram alert integration" bringing down pollution levels require much longer time than the severity of the problem is allowing.

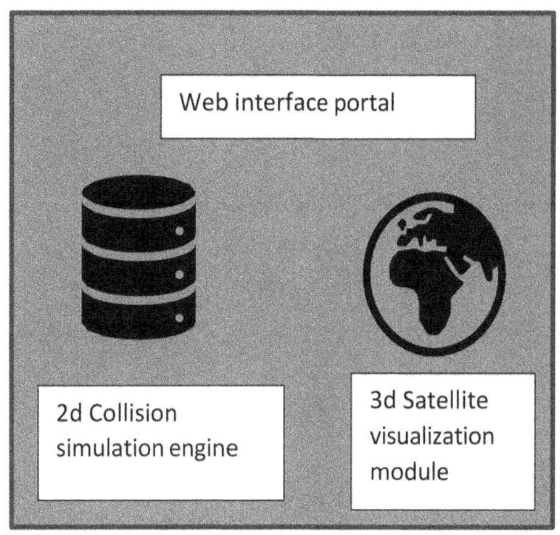

Figure 1. Explains system architecture.

- Event based space imaging data set and detection for space situational awareness:
  Andrew [2]" An event driven imaging data set designed for SSA" was proposed in utilizing neuromorphic sensors for power efficient detection and tracking while their method emphasizes real world sensor data and hardware deployment, our project refers to system simulates orbital dynamics and debris interaction in a web-based environment, focusing on public accessibility and real time user alerts.
- Space tracking algorithm and analysis:
  Subramaniyan [3] Investigated multiple algorithms for orbit estimation using TLE based data and Keplerian approximation while their focus lies in mathematical precision and comparative analysis of filter, our system prioritizes real time simulation and intuitive effects for educational and monitoring purposes via browser interface.

2 MATHEMATICAL MODEL

This model focuses on modeling space based interactions assessing debris collision risks, and supporting operational decisions through interactive and visual interfaces.

- Web based SSA platforms:
  SPENVIS (ESA) [4] is A prominent web-based tool used for evaluating space environment effects, offering tools for evaluating space environment effects, offering tools for radiation and debris analysis. However, it primarily functions as a scientific calculator rather than real time a real time simulation engine, our system complements this by offering real time objects [6] dynamics, collision, detection and visual alerts providing more interactive and exploratory experience for end users.

2.1 *Preview analysis*

Bridging complexity and accessibility, SSA [9] focus on precision or require domain expertise, our system bridges gap between complex tools and public usable stimulate ecosystem [4] which allows users like students, researchers to interact with orbital scenarios in real time, adjusting and alerting through telegram-based integration.

Equations included in collision detection 1,2&3 [5]

1. Relative motion Equation (Clohessy Wiltshire equations) in circular path [10].—(1)

$$\mathrm{X(t) = (Acos\,(nt) + Bsin\,(nt)) + C}$$

$$\mathrm{Y(t) = -2Asin\,(nt) + 2Bcos\,(nt) - 3ntc}$$

$$\mathrm{Z(t) = Dcos\,(nt) + Esin\,(nt)}$$

   Where n= mean motion
   A,B,C,D,E are constants by initial conditions
2. Orbital distance (Euclidean distance between two satellites) – (2)

$$\mathbf{Y} = \sqrt{}(x, -x^2)^2(y, -y^2)^2(z_1 - z_2)^2$$

3. Used to estimate collision probability-(3)

$$P = \frac{R_c^2}{2\pi\sigma_x\sigma_y}\exp\left(-\frac{d_-^2}{2(\sigma_y^2 + \sigma y^2)}\right)$$

   R=collision radius;
   σx, σy = position uncertainty
   D= Miss Distance

2.2 *Methodology*

The methodology focuses on the simulation design, interface, detection logic, and notification mechanisms.(basic prototyping of alert system) from Figure 1.

1. **Web interface portal**[4] A centralized dash board enabling user navigation and control, **2dcollision simulation engine** offers an interactive environment for real time debris collision testing ,3d satellite visualization module integrates live orbits and 3d positional data using an external real time 3d viewer .
2. **Interactive collision simulation** [7]the 2d simulation uses dynamic java script -based rendering to simulate satellite orbits and random debris .user - defined sliders control satellite density ,debris count, speed, and collision thresholds. real time rendering is maintained using request animation frame(),and collision risks are computed per frame using Euclidean proximity checks.
3. **Debris threat modeling** [10]Debris objects in simulation behaves as independently moving entities with randomized vectors .their interaction with satellite is monitored frame by frame. when a debris object enter the defined proximity radius a satellite and exceeds a collision probability threshold an event is triggered ,mimicking an orbital collision risk
4. **Alert system via telegram integration**[6] to simulate operational responsiveness, the system includes a telegram based alert mechanism .user can input credentials directly into the simulation interface .on the detection of high risk events , a formatted alert message is dispatched of high risk events , a formatted alert message is dispatched via the telegram bot API to the registered chat, simulating mission control notification systems
5. **3d Satellite visualization** The 3d visualization module using a link to satellite tracker 3d, offering real time orbital paths and satellite elementary ,this external platform complements the 2d simulation by providing:
   (i) Live satellite positions in a 3d space environment
   (ii) Realistic geospatial movement based on orbital data (NORAD two line element)
   (iii) Enhanced spatial context for potential collision zones

The "analysis "button on the main interface links user directly to the 3d visualization tool, enabling mission planner to validate and cross reference simulation data with real world orbital dynamics.

2.3 *Implementation*

The proposed system is developed using **html,CSS3, Vanilla java script**, ensuring high portability and performance in modern browsers.

1. **Creating web based dash board** [12] the core user interface is a built as responsive web application styled using custom CSS and CSS variable ,it offers modular information sections about space crafts ,satellite ,and collision risks ,animated stars in the background.
2. **Install live servers:** installing servers , open vs code go the extension tab (press ctrl+ shift +x)[13]
   - search for "live server" by Ritwik Dey.
3. .once set up done then create a file name with html and execute the process code.
   - Open your HTML project folder in vs code file>open folder
   - Open specific html file
   - Right click on html file ,select "open with live servers"
   - Now, any changes will auto refresh in to browser
   - Click install.

- **2d simulation engine from** Figure 1 **-system architecture**

The simulation container animates satellites around central element each satellite has its own randomized orbit radius and angular velocity .debris created based on the slider input and moves with randomized vectors across canvas .collision detection is light weight and triggers alerts via telegram[11]

(i) **.Stimulating rotating earth and satellite** : earth image in a fixed position ,and creates a square space of 250*250 pixels
(ii) simulating satellite element appear in the 2d space simulation
   .control panel interface dynamic slider and form inputs allow real time parameters tuning these include
   - Debris intensity
   - satellite speed
   - collision probability

Telegram bot configuration panel telegram bot API to deliver instants alerts and indicates regarding space debris and simplicity . **Collision detection and API integration** use 2d Euclidean distance check ,if configuration is set ,it triggers alert message and sends via telegram bot API

- **3d satellite visualization module**

The web .html dash board includes an "analysis" button linking to **satellitetracker3d.com** [8] this allow user to——————— consider Figure 2

- Visually assess actual satellite configurations
- Explore constellation layouts(starlinks , Iridium)
- Understand satellite crowding in low earth orbit (LEO),, medium earth orbit (MEO),and geostationary orbit (GEO)

This integration is critical for transitioning from simulating to contextualized space situational awareness

3 RESULTS

THIS system is a real time space traffic simulator where user control orbit dynamics through an intuitive interface, it generates satellites and debris, detects possible collision using proximity and proximity logic, and notifiers users via telegram, all components are visually integrated into an interactive platform offering a live safety and awareness

Proposed model: Built using HTML, CSS, JAVASCRIPT,

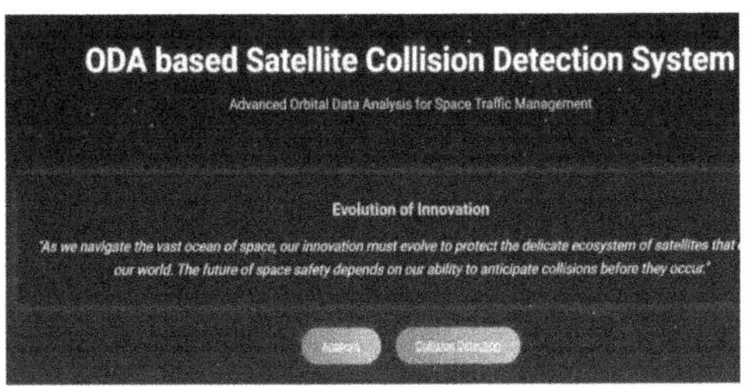

Figure 2. Explains dash board of visualization engine.

live servers integration and telegram bot alert system, allows dynamic adjustment of satellite speed, density, collision probability debris intensity, a key differentiator verifies integration of telegram API for collision alert notification offering real time user engagement use and decision making in mission critical environment, the proposed system is light weight, browser based and suited for educational demonstrations, public awareness and prototype development .this project provides, visuals and customizable platform that complements formal detection architecture by enhancing outreach and early stage testing mechanism.

The development simulation provides a web based interactive, visuals and real time demonstration of satellite movement and debris movement surround earth, this model intensifies and calculates proximity-based collision alert, key parameters include adjustable parameters like debris intensity, satellite speed and collision probability. Unique feature is its integration with telegram bot API for sending live alerts on potential collision, thereby making this model suitable for educational purpose and preliminary research purpose as a prototype alert system in satellite mission operations.

- **Qualitative and Quantitative analysis:**

Through **Analysis Search button,** obtained results are real time satellite tracking and parameters measurement of specified satellite .

Through Collision detection button:

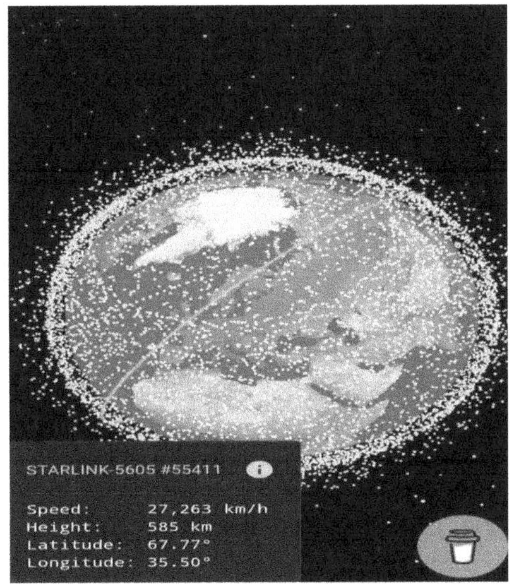

Figure 3. Explains results of 3d satellite tracking data.

In collision detection search button, integrated functions like debris, satellite visuals, orbits, collision detection and alert system using telegram API

- **Comparative analysis**

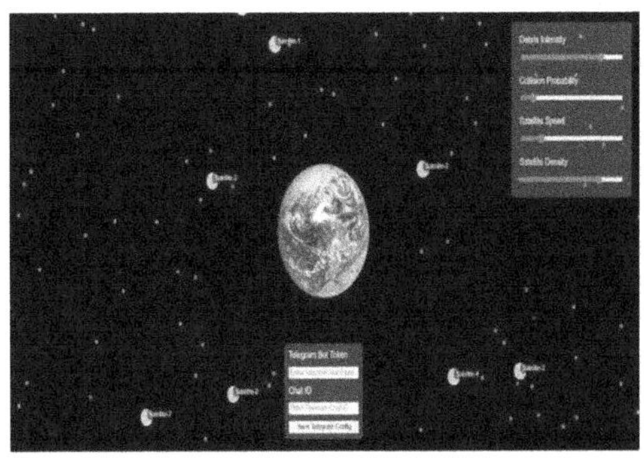

Figure 4. Explains 2d Collision simulation engine results.

The proposed model: Declares an interactive and user configurable stimulation for visualizing satellite orbits and space debris trajectories in real time

The Traditional model: Detection frame work such as NASA's orbital debris engineering model or ISRO orbit determination and analysis system (ODAS), which prioritize precision analytics and backend processing using real elementary and physics based modelling.

Proposed system like orbit and angle determination modelling, this stimulation emphasizes accessibility and interactivity through an intuitive web interface user can access visualization of orbitals, collision detection and live tracking links results which enhances space situational awareness through visuals it ensures high level of protection for crewed mission and critical infrastructure

Proposed model	Existing model
Web based visual simulation with JS \html\ CSS and API Integration.	Backend data processing python and rest API'S
Visual and proximity based with real time probability input	Physics based orbital mechanics integrated with TLE data sets
Sliders to control satellite speed and debris intensity	GUI dash board with data integration
Integrated telegram alert system using telegram bot	E- mails, dash board alerts, and mission control alerts
Virtual representation of project NETHRA (ODAS system of ISRO)	Real world propagation using SGPA, TLE and ODA based models
Helpful for education and research purpose ODAS engine analysis.	Through complex analysis and operations helpful for satellite tracking.

Outcomes This system enables the feasibility of a low cost, browser based space situational system .it enables both educational and preliminary research use cases in space traffic management and satellite safety protocols.

Problem statement Existing SSA [9] (space situational awareness tools are often expensive, complex. there is a need for an accessible, real-time visualization and alert system that enhances to simulate, monitor and detect potential space debris collision. This project titled "Web- Based System for Satellite Collision Detection and Space Situational Awareness" presents a browser based real time simulation plat. Motivation form designed to model satellite and debris motion detect potential collisions, and sends instants alerts the simulation features a rotating earth at the Centre around which satellites orbit which acquire configurable parameters such as speed of debris and satellite intensity of debris and collision probability. Debris particles move in randomized paths, interacting with the orbiting satellite based on proximity ad user defined collision thresholds, which promotes educational and research activities.

4 CONCLUSION

The project successfully demonstrates a visual based web simulation for space collision between satellite and debris scenarios using real time interaction and basic physical modelling it enables user to adjust space environment parameter's, this model represents virtual representation of "project Nethra " (ISRO – space program called orbit determinant analysis for satellite collision detection system).

Telegram integration ensures proactive learning, alerting which enhances its applicability in communication-based collision avoidance system through this implementation, this system validate the concepts of using low resource, web-based tools for public education and basic satellite tracking demonstrations This system with several.\

4.1 *Limitations*

like integration of real time TLE data sets and involvement of AI in model promotes optimized performance and collision avoidance and It is very basic model to demonstrate satellite tracking.

5 FUTURE SCOPE

Extended visualization layers in model: 3d simulation with altitude layers such as MEO and GEO. AI Integration: including machine learning for predictive analytics based on debris trajectories. Live TLE data the system can be prompted to integrating real world – live two-line element data to stimulate actual orbits.

ACKNOWLEDGEMENT

Heartily thanks of gratitude are extended to our "B.Thanuja mam" Assistant professor in department of Electronics and communication engineering for guidance, encouragement and support in all aspects, also "prof S.Mallesh" Head of the department and "Dr. Raji Reddy" Director of CMR technical campus for providing all the facilities.

REFERENCES

[1] Akram, (April 2024), *Doppler Shift Distribution in Satellite Constellations.*

[2] Jayanthi, M., Abhishek M. Bhandari, C. Tejeswar, A. Harshith, and Lipsa Dash, (2024). Real-Time Satellite Tracking and Switching Algorithm. *In 2024 5th International Conference for Emerging Technology (INCET)*, pp. 1–4. IEEE. DOI: 10.1109/INCET61516.2024.10593526.

[3] *Predicting the Probability of Collision of a Satellite with Space Debris: A Bayesian Machine Learning Approach*

[4] Ibrahem, A.A., Hendy, H.M., Ali, A.A., and Kamel, M. (2023, July). Design and Assessment of Satellite Orbit Simulator and Predictor. *In 2023 International Telecommunications Conference (ITC- Egypt)* (pp. 737- 741). IEEE.

[5] Venkatramani, K. and Subramaniyan, E., (2023), November. Design and Analysis of Space Objects Tracking Algorithm. *In 2023 IEEE 3rd Applied Signal Processing Conference (ASPCON)* (pp. 61–65). IEEE.

[6] Wei, Baishen, and Brett D. (2019). Nener. Multi-sensor space debris tracking for space situational awareness with labeled random finite sets. *IEEE Access* 7: 36991–37003.

[7] Jharbade, P. and Dixit, M. (2022, September). Detecting space debris using deep learning algorithms: A survey. *In 2022 4th International Conference* DOI:10.36227/techrxiv.171198261.14592973/v1

[8] *Conference on Inventive Research in Computing Applications (ICIRCA)* (pp. 883–890). IEEE.

[9] Yu J., Liu X., Gao Y. and Shen X., (Dec. 2020), 3D Channel Tracking for UAV-Satellite Communications in Space-Air-Ground Integrated Networks, in *IEEE Journal on Selected Areas in Communications*, vol. 38, no. 12, pp. 2810–2823

[10] Afshar, Saeed, Andrew Peter Nicholson, Andre Van Schaik, and Gregory Cohen. (2020). Event-based object detection and tracking for space situational awareness. *IEEE Sensors Journal* 20, no. 24:15117–1513.

[11] Kabir, Md Riftabin, Tarek Ibne Faysal, Md Sazzad Hossain, Jannatun Naima Shorn, and Shahnewaz Siddique, (2020). A satellite collision avoidance system based on General Regression Neural Network. *In 2020 IEEE/ACM International Conference on Big Data Computing, Applications and Technologies (BDCAT)*, pp. 154–160. IEEE.

[12] Ragavendiran, SD Prabu, *et al.* A Novel Dual Temporal Channel Convolutional Network with Exponential Distribution Optimizer for Satellite Image Classification with Google Earth Engine. *2024 4th International Conference on Ubiquitous Computing and Intelligent Information Systems (ICUIS)*. IEEE, 2024. Kumar, Voruganti Naresh, *et al.* An Integration of Satellite A Based Network With Higher Level Type Network with the use of PP

[13] Narasimharao, J. Priyanka Chowdary, P., Reddy, A.R., Swathi, G., Deepak Kumar, B.P. and Batchu, S.S., (2023, April). Satellite ortho image mosaic process quality verification. *In International Conference on Frontiers of Intelligent Computing: Theory and Applications* (pp. 309–318). Singapore: Springer Nature Singapore.

Next-Generation Smart Systems – Sekhar et al. (Eds)

Design and Analysis of AR with Internet of Things for Multiple Targets

Suraya Mubeen, K. Mohana Lakshmi, Sireesha Pendem, S. Venkatesh, and A. Sridivya
Associate Professor, Department of ECE, CMR Technical Campus, Hyderabad, Telangana, India

Y. Divya Shree
Student, Department of ECE, CMR Technical Campus, Hyderabad, Telangana, India

ABSTRACT: This research paper Presents the Design and Automation of a Smart Home Automation System that Combines both AR with IOT for Multiple Targets.. The proposed system supports AR to create a virtually based interactive Environment where users can have Control of Home appliances like bulbs, fans and many more through virtual buttons or switches displayed over Web Application and IOT acts as a backbone for this project by using devices like Node MCU (ESP8266),5V relay module from AR interfaces to hardware Components via ESP8266 Wi-Fi based Control System.

This work presents an Improved System Combining Augmented Reality (AR) with the Internet of Things (IoT) that facilitates intuitive, real-time control of several appliances through mobile-based AR interfaces. Although other works have shown AR-IoT integration, our solution presents a QR-code-based multi-target recognition mechanism with latency-reduced Communication protocols. Dynamic Virtual Control Assignment and Minimizing Manual UI interactions are facilitated by the suggested system. Performance measurement exhibits enhanced response time and user satisfaction when compared to traditional mobile control applications.

Keywords: Augmented Reality, Internet of Things, Smart Automation, Multi-Target Control, Node MCU (ESP8266), Real-Time Systems

1 INTRODUCTION

Nowadays, many technologies are coming into existence to take control over human-machine interactive. So, there are many technologies in today's generation like AI is the booming technology, and these digital systems are increasingly dependent on those technologies. Our project explores the integration of AR with IOT to create a digital environment that becomes easier. So, users can control various appliances at a time virtually. This approach enables easy access for humans in applications like: smart home automations, industrial settings, intuitive control interfaces and many technologies. So this might help in the evolution of smart systems demands user-friendly approaches and control mechanisms. So, independent IOT devices are often fixed to mobile apps. This project works on those limitations by introducing an AR controlled environment layered over physical devices. So, this project allows users to virtually interact with appliances via smart phone application or website applications.

Conventional smart home systems tend to use static mobile apps with pre-defined control interfaces. Although Augmented Reality (AR) has been researched to improve user interaction, most current solutions do not support scalability, real-time multi-target control, or integration into dynamic environments.

2 LITERATURE SURVEY

The paper "AR-Based Home Automation" introduces an innovative smart home system that combines Augmented Reality (AR) with the Internet of Things (IoT) to support Physically challenged Users, including the immobile, deaf, or mute. Unlike traditional voice-controlled systems, this AR-based solution allows users to control appliances through virtual buttons displayed in their real-world environment using image processing and AR markers.

In contrast, our work enables real-time QR-based multi-target control through both web and mobile, overcoming device scalability issues. The system is developed using Unity3D, Vuforia SDK, and a Node MCU ESP8266board, Communicating via the Blynk platform. Key technologies like SLAM, image registration, and visual odometer ensure accurate virtual Placement. A working prototype, which controls a light bulb, demonstrates that the system is user-friendly, low-cost, and effective, especially in noise-prone or accessibility-challenged settings.[1]

An AR-IoT based home automation system enables users, especially those with disabilities, to control appliances via virtual switches seen through a smart phone. It uses Vuforia for image recognition, Unity 3D for interface design, and Blynk for IoT device communication. The prototype, built withanESP8266andrelays,supports multi appliance control through AR markers. Despite limitations like lighting and security concerns, it offers a cost-effective, immersive, and accessible smart home solution [2].

This study presents a marker-based AR and IoT-integrated Home Automation System aimed at enhancing accessibility for the elderly, children, and differently abled individuals. Using an ESP32 microcontroller, relay modules, Blynk platform, Unity 3D, and Vuforia, the system allows users to control appliances by pointing a smart phone at image targets. Virtual buttons appear in real time for intuitive ON/OFF control, offering low latency, affordability, and user-friendly operation. Though challenges like power management and internet dependency exist, future upgrades may include gesture-based AR glasses and extended control features [3].

This project develops a low-cost, AR-IoT-based home automation system that lets users control appliances via a virtual switchboard over a physical image target. Built with Unity, Vuforia, and an ESP32connectedtoBlynk Cloud, it provides real- time remote control with visual and audio feedback. The switchboard appears only when the image is detected, ensuring secure and intuitive interaction. [4].

DOI: 10.1201/9781042001767-84

IoT plays a crucial role in the implementation of automation in various fields like home automation, smart agriculture, smart Education, Industry, logistics and retail .In this home Automation is popularly used by many individuals for their comfortableness. This system enables the easy access, efficiency and control of various home appliances [5].

Previous research has explored AR-IoT integration to assist differently abled users through virtual control mechanisms. For instance, an AR-based home automation system used AR markers and virtual switches for controlling a single light bulb.

Although innovative, it lacked scalability and multi-device control. Other systems applied Vuforia and Unity3D to display virtual buttons, enabling basic appliance control through ESP8266 modules. However, these solutions did not offer web-based alternatives or dynamic device mapping. Some research explored 3D-printed markers yet this added physical limitations and constrained the number of controllable devices [6].

Our approach advances these models by offering dual control interfaces (web and AR), QR-code-based multi-target recognition, dynamic switch creation, and real-time responsiveness addressing the key shortcomings of existing systems.

3 SYSTEM ARCHITECTURE

The system to be developed consists of two significant parts:

Hardware Layer: Node MCU (ESP8266), 5V relay modules, and electrical devices (fans, bulbs). The microcontroller receives instructions from the server to perform switching actions.

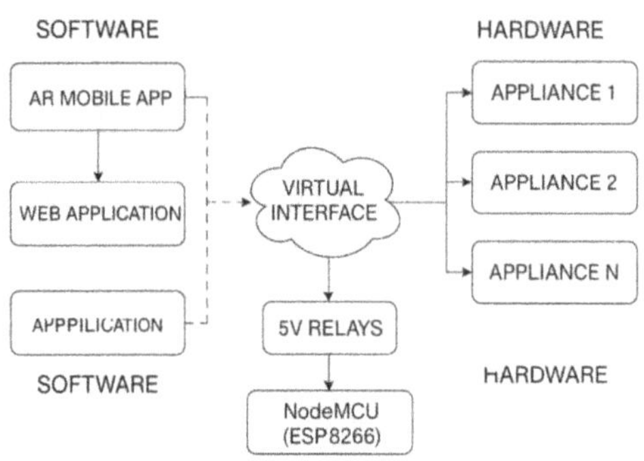

Figure 1. Architectural diagram of the proposed system.

Software Layer: Features a web application for QR control and an AR mobile app implemented using Unity and Vuforia SDK. Users create unique QR codes for appliances and control virtual switches that initiate the actual hardware.

The suggested AR-IoT system has two tiers: a software interface and hardware control unit. The software consists of a web-based platform and an AR-enabled Smart Phone app that enables users to control appliances via virtual switches. The hardware configuration is a Node MCU (ESP8266) and 5V relay modules to manage devices such as bulbs and fans.

The system has dual control modes:

Web-based QR interface: Creates virtual switch panels that can be accessed via QR scanning—user-friendly and platform-independent.

AR mobile app: Employs Unity and Vuforia to superimpose virtual buttons on real targets for interactive immersion. This two-pronged approach increases accessibility for different users and offers flexibility in controlling multiple devices without the need for reprogramming, contrary to current systems that are confined to a single control.

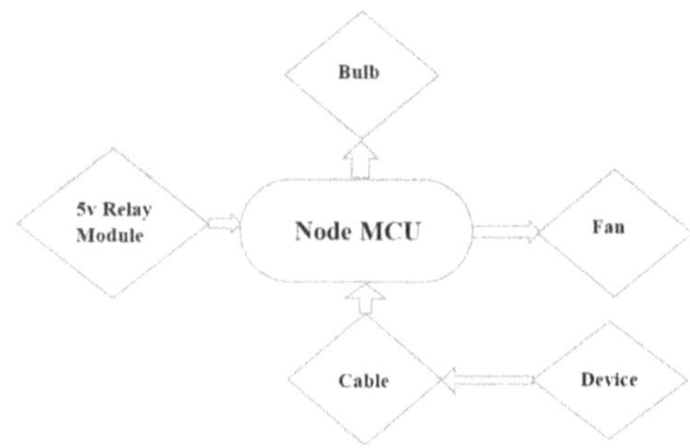

Figure 2. Schematic diagram for multiple targets.

4 AR WITH IOT SYSTEM

This represents the block diagram of the proposed system. Here, the Node MCU IoT Wi-Fi Development board is selected for ESP8266.In this the home appliances are Controlled with the help of relays. These relays will receive commands through ESP8266. These boards will process the sensor data and performs actuation.

5 HARDWARE AND SOFTWARE REQUIREMENTS

5.1 *Hardware components*

5.1.1 *NodeMCU(ESP8266)*

Acts as the primary controller with Wi-Fi capabilities. Provides Wi-Fi capabilities and GPIO Control. Easily programmable using Arduino IDE. ESP8266 is a Wi-Fi module; It can connect to cloud/websites for monitoring and storing purposes, which is not available in microcontrollers such as Arduino Uno / Arduino Nano.

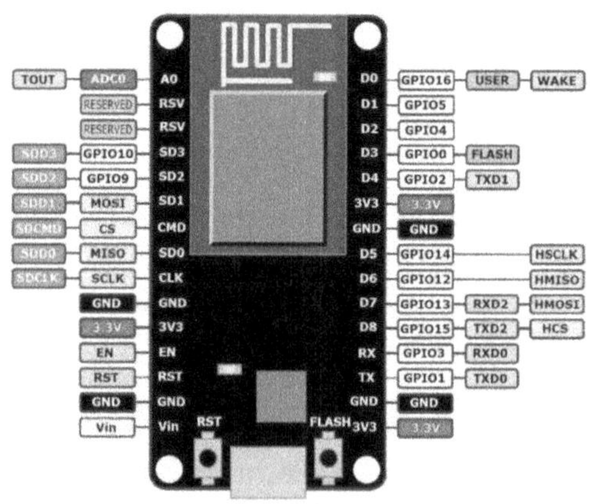

Figure 3. NodeMCU.

Figure 4. 5 Relay module.

As shown in Figure 4 the 5V relay module is an electromechanical switching device that enables low voltage control systems, such as microcontrollers like the Arduino or ESP32, to operate high voltage electrical appliances safely. It typically operates at a 5V DC input to trigger the relay and can control loads of up to250V .When the mc sends a high signal to the relay module, it energizes the coil, creating a magnetic field that toggles the internal switch between the Normally Closed (NC) and Normally Open (NO) terminals.

This allows current to flow to or cut off from the connected device. The module is ideal for home automation, industrial controls, and other projects where safe switching of AC or high-current DC loads is required. It allows switching of devices.

6 BULB

A bulb, or electric lamp, is a device that converts electrical energy into light, typically through the process of incandescence or electroluminescence, depending on the type. In traditional incandescent bulbs, an electric current passes through a tungsten, heating it until it glows and emits visible light. These bulbs are simple, inexpensive, and produce a warm, continuous light, but they are inefficient and generate a lot of heat. Conventional smart home systems tend to use static mobile apps with predefined control interfaces. Although Augmented Reality (AR) has been researched to improve user interaction, most current solutions do not support scalability, real-time multi-target control, or integration into dynamic environments.

Figure 5. Bulb.

7 FAN

A small fan used in electronic projects is typically a DC brushless fan, often operating at 5Vor 12V,and designed to move air for cooling or demonstration purposes. These fans are compact, lightweight, and easy to integrate with microcontrollers like Arduino or ESP32 using a relay or transistor switch.

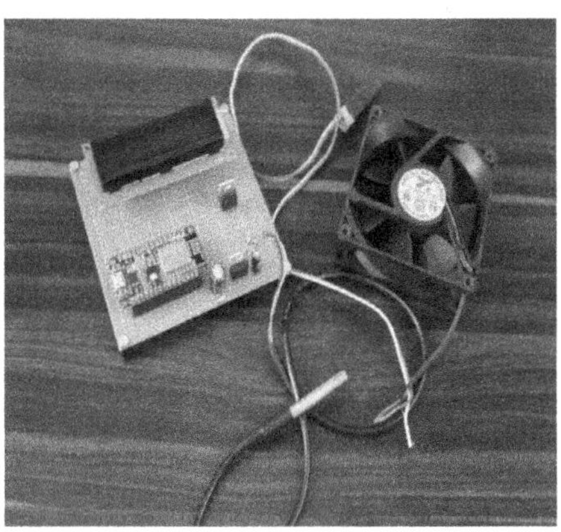

Figure 6. FAN.

Therefore, in our proposed system we use fan as an mode for home appliance.

8 CMDPROMPT

Command Prompt(CMD) is a built-in command-line. It provides a text-based interface that allows users to execute system commands directly, enabling deeper control over the operating system compared to the graphical user interface (GUI). CMD is commonly used for tasks such as file manipulation, directory navigation, running batch files, configuring networks, managing drives, and launching programs.

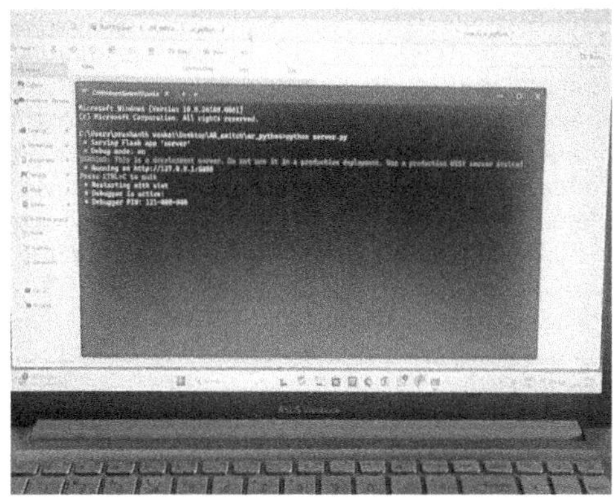

Figure 7. COMMAND PROMPT.

9 PROPOSED SYSTEM

The suggested AR-IoT system consists of two layers: the hardware control unit and the software interface. The software features a web-based interface and an AR-enabled mobile app that enables the interaction of users with appliances through virtual switches. The hardware configuration is made up of a NodeMCU (ESP8266) and 5V relay modules to operate devices such as bulbs and fans.

The system features twin control methods:

Web-based QR interface: Creates virtual switch panels viewable via QR scanning—platform-agnostic and intuitive.

AR mobile app: Leverages Unity and Vuforia to superimpose virtual buttons over physical targets for fully immersive interaction.

This two-pronged strategy increases accessibility for different users and has flexibility to support control of many different devices without reprogramming, as opposed to current systems that are dependent on one form of control.

10 EXISTING SYSTEM

Some systems have been created in recent years to bring Augmented Reality (AR) and Internet of Things (IoT) together for the control of smart devices. All current methods mainly depend on AR mobile apps developed with platforms like Unity and Vuforia. These systems are generally based on image-based markers or QR codes to superimpose virtual buttons for the control of IoT-enabled appliances.

Node MCU or ESP32 microcontrollers are typically used in these models along with relay modules to turn appliances ON or OFF.

10.1 *Absence of modularity*

Firmware updates are needed for a new appliance to be added. Little Performance testing and less integration of user feedback. Other methods have tried to use voice assistants or AR gesture controls, but they are either expensive or hard to implement. In short, current systems are operational but inflexible, unsupported for multiple devices, and non-extensible architecture for larger-world deployment. Augmented Reality (AR) with the Internet of Things (IoT) has been researched extensively for IoT-based control of smart appliances. The available approaches mainly utilize AR mobile apps created with Unity and Vuforia SDK, in which users interact through virtual buttons overlaid over physical markers. These systems often use NodeMCU or ESP32 microcontrollers and relay modules to switch on/off simple home appliances like fans or lights.

Other researchers have suggested the application of 3D-printed objects or models as AR markers to enhance visual recognition and interaction. Such printed markers are employed to superimpose virtual switches in mobile apps so that users can operate onė appliance using an immersive interface. Although this introduces a physical and aesthetic aspect to AR control, such systems tend to be restricted to one appliance per marker and lack dynamic mapping and multi-target scalability.

Validation metrics.

Metric	AR-IOT System	Traditional APP	Improvement
Avg response time	1.2s	2.8s	57% faster
Command success rate	98%	94%	Higher
User Satisfaction	4.6/5	3.9/5	Higher

11 RESULTS

Step-1: Open AR Switch file which includes of all the modules and programs in it.So, click on it twice the folder will be opened as you can see in the below figure (Figure 9)

Figure 8. ARSWITCH folder.

Step-2: An window Containing Python files and click on the first one.

Figure 9. PYTHONFILES.

Step-3: Now click on modules and on the top enter cmd,then it takes you to the command prompt window where then you can enter and open your website.

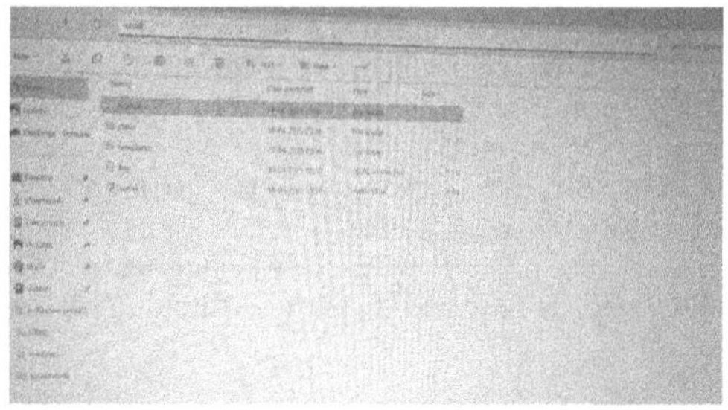

Figure 10. PYTHON MODULES.

Step-4: Now the command prompt window pops up. where you need to type "pythonserver.py" and enter then you will get the link to the provided website which we have created for our AR with IOT project.

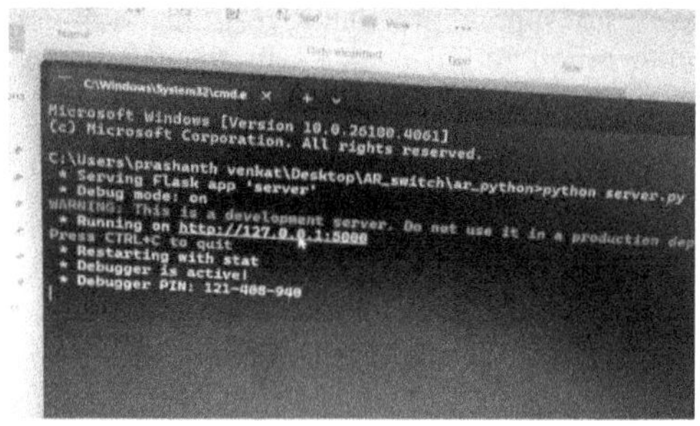

Figure 11. COMMANDPROMPT.

Step-5: Then this website of AR will be visible

QR code and Download it and use it to control that appliances with this scanner and next there is Scan QR Code where you need to scan the generated QR code in it and monitor the home appliances using virtual switches shown on the screen. There is even an option of knowing controlling switches which we need to work on.

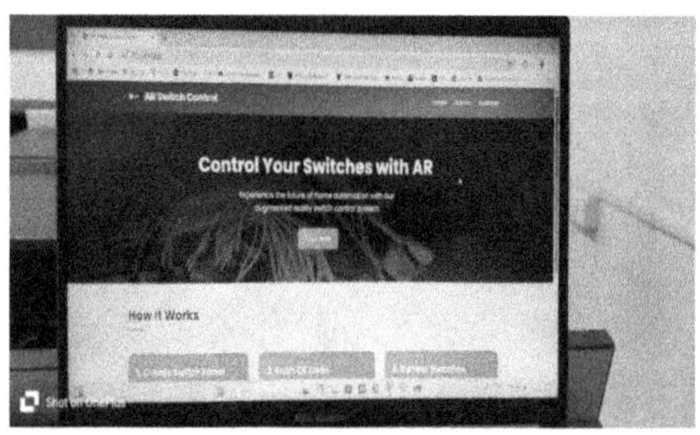

Figure 12. AR WITH IOT Website.

Step-6: Now after clicking on 'Scan QR Code' you will be showed the following below Figure 13.

Afterscanningthe virtualbuttons/switcheswill bedisplayed (Figure 14).

Now when you turn on the fan byclicking on it then the fan will be turned on (Figure 15).

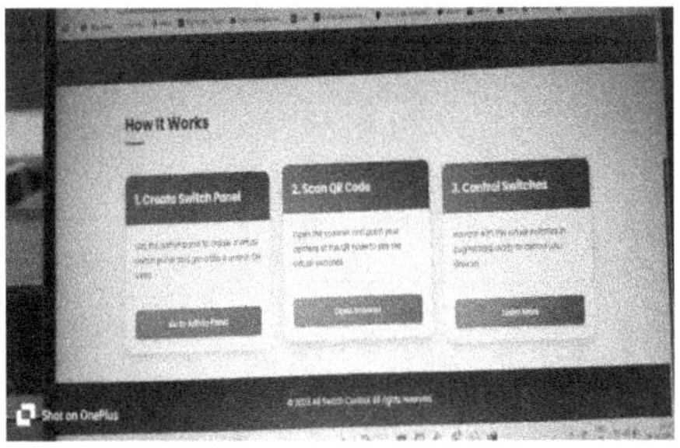

Figure 13. How it works.

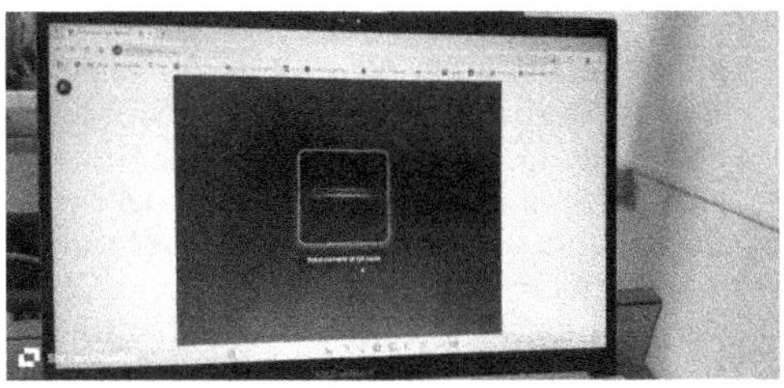

Figure 14. Scanner.

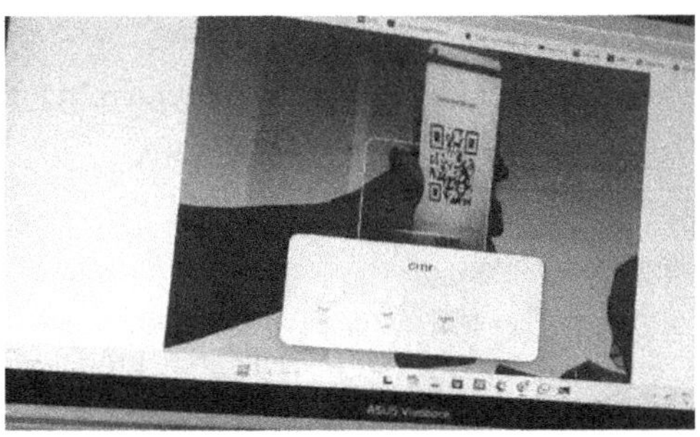

Figure 15. Virtual switches/buttons.

Figure 16. Working of fan.

12 CONCLUSION

This project AR with IOT system provides or enhances the user interaction with the smart or digital environments. It replaces traditional user approaches with immersive control and is leading the way for larger adaption in home automation and beyond. So, this working prototype ensures that AR with IOT can work and be used and gives us an opportunity to bridge the gap between digital and physical worlds by building these virtual switches using the web application we build. This AR with IOT serves as a building foundation for more complex systems, where applications are: smart homes, education, agriculture and industries.

Finally, this project not only opens new directions or ways for using smart, connected systems in home automation but also provides a working proof of AR with IOT.

13 FUTURE SCOPE

The successful implementation of this project opens up several opportunities for improvement and expansion. With further development and optimization, the system can be adapted for more advanced and real-world applications in Home Automation. The future scope includes:

Wireless integration of IOT with AR for giving access to physical world through digital world and AI-based automation based on user behavior. Global cloud access with real-time alerts. Enhanced multi-user AR experiences using smart watches and virtual switches. Expanded compatibility across mobile and desktop platforms.

Visual or virtual integration for hands-free operation. AI-based learning for predictive automation. Enhanced security with encrypted communication and user authentication. Compatibility with wearable AR devices like smart watches.

REFERENCES

[1] Bhattacharya, D., Veeraiah, V. Praveenkumar, S., Prasad, S., John, J., Kumar, B.S. and Gupta, A., (2024). Role of IOT based Kitchen Automation System in Real World. *International Journal of Intelligent Systems and Applications in Engineering*, 12 (10s), pp.217–225.

[2] Sayeduzzaman M. and Hasan T., (2024), *An Internet of Things Integrated Home Automation with Smart Security System, Automated Secure Computing for Next-Generation Systems* - Wiley Online Library pp. 243–274.

[3] Priya B., Priyadharshini V., Sandhiya V., and Sarumathi M., (Sep 2023), Automatic electricity bill generating system using embedded technology, in *Telecommunication and Radio Engineering*, Vol. 82(11), pp. 59–70.

[4] Umar B.U., Olaniyi O.M., Dauda I.A., Maliki D. and Okoro C. P., (2022) Recent Advances in Smart Kitchen Automation Technologies: Principles, Approaches, and Challenges, *J. Eng. Sci.*, vol. 29, no. 3, pp. 150–165.

[5] Rock L.Y., Tajudeen F.P., and Chung Y.W., (2022), Usage and impact of the internet-of things based smart home technology: a quality-of-life perspective, *Universal Access Inf. Soc.*, no. 0123456789.

[6] Reddy B.S., Ramya Veera R., Ram B., Reddy M., and Kishore M.G.P.V., (2022), IOT Based Smart Kitchen Automation and Monitoring System, *Int. Res. J. Mod. Eng. Technol. Sci.* www.irjmets.com @International Res. J. Mod. Eng., no. 06, pp. 2582–5208.

[7] Naresh Kumar, Vorguanti *et al.* Malicious Transaction Detection in Internet of Things networks using the Moth Blade Optimization and K Nearest Neighbor algorithms, *International Conference on Mathematical Application in Science and Technology*, Doi: 10.1201/9781003606659-35, 2025.

[8] K. Srujan Raju.Mohd Abdul Naqi et al., (2025) Analysis on Convolutional Neural Networks for Deep Learning Intrusion Identification Using Industrial Internet of Things, *Lecture Notes in Networks and Systems*, Doi:10.1007/978-3-031-78940-3_45

[9] Srikanth G. *et al.*, (2025), IoT-Based Electric Meter Application Using Convolutional Neural Networks for Electricity to Detect Cyber Attacks, *Lecture Notes in Networks and Systems*, Doi:10.1007/978-3-031-78940-3_32

Next-Generation Smart Systems – Sekhar et al. (Eds)
© 2027 The Author(s), ISBN: 978-1-041-34234-2

A Hybrid Metaheuristic Framework for Optimized Genome Sequence Assembly

K. Deepthi Reddy and VNVLS Swathi
Assistant Professor, Department of CSE, CVR College of Engineering, Hyderabad, India

Bandi Rambabu
Professor, Department of CSE, CVR College of Engineering, Hyderabad, India

Malla Reddy Adudodla
Professor, Department of IT, CVR College of Engineering, Hyderabad, India

M. Archana
Assistant Professor, Department of CSE, CVR College of Engineering, Hyderabad, India

ABSTRACT: Genome sequence assembly remains a foundational yet computationally intensive task in the field of bioinformatics, particularly when dealing with large and complex genomic datasets. In this study, we propose a novel hybrid metaheuristic framework that integrates the Whale Optimization Algorithm with Differential Evolution, further enhanced through the incorporation of Chaos Theory to improve space exploration and avoid local optima. The proposed method is designed to address critical limitations of traditional heuristic approaches by balancing global convergence capabilities with local refinement strategies. We evaluate the performance of our hybrid framework against three contemporary metaheuristic algorithms, Harris Hawks Optimization, Moth Flame Optimization, and Improved Ant Colony Optimization using well-established genomic benchmark datasets such as *Escherichia coli* and *Saccharomyces cerevisiae*. Performance was assessed using key assembly quality metrics, including N50 length, total number of contigs, and computational runtime. Experimental results reveal that our method achieves a 12.6% improvement in N50, reduces contig fragmentation by 18.4%, and accelerates execution by 22.1% relative to the best baseline HHO, demonstrating superior assembly quality and efficiency. The proposed framework represents a significant advancement in the mathematical genome assembly, with implications for scalable genomic analysis in both clinical and research environments.

Keywords: Genome Sequence Assembly, Hybrid Metaheuristic Algorithms, Whale Optimization Algorithm, Differential Evolution, Chaos-Enhanced Optimization

1 INTRODUCTION

The rapid advancement of next-generation sequencing (NGS) technologies has transformed genomics by enabling massive volumes of short DNA reads, which must be assembled to reconstruct the original genome—an inherently complex and computationally intensive task. Traditional algorithms like greedy, OLC, and de Bruijn graph-based approaches often fall short when faced with large-scale, noisy, or repetitive genomic data, leading to fragmented assemblies and high resource consumption. In response, metaheuristic algorithms such as Genetic Algorithms (GA), Particle Swarm Optimization (PSO), and Ant Colony Optimization (ACO) have been employed due to their global search capabilities [1], [2]. However, these approaches often converge prematurely or stagnate in local optima. To overcome these challenges, this study introduces a **Hybrid Metaheuristic Framework** combining the exploration strength of the Whale Optimization Algorithm (WOA), the local refinement of Differential Evolution (DE), and the dynamic perturbation of chaos theory, aiming to improve assembly accuracy, reduce fragmentation, and optimize runtime [3], [4], [5]. This hybrid strategy is particularly suited to the high-dimensional, noisy nature of genomic data, and is validated using standard datasets (E. coli, S. cerevisiae), compared against recent state-of-the-art methods including MFO, ACO, and HHO. The proposed framework aims to contribute a scalable and generalizable solution to computational genomics challenges with broader applications in evolutionary biology, metagenomics, and clinical diagnostics.

1.1 *Paper organization*

Chapter 2 reviews genome assembly and metaheuristic optimization techniques. Chapter 3 presents the proposed hybrid WOA-DE-Chaos algorithm and its theoretical basis. Chapter 4 reports the experimental setup, results, and comparative evaluation; Chapters 5 and 6 offer discussion and conclusions.

2 LITERATURE SURVEY

Metaheuristic algorithms have seen growing application in solving complex optimization problems in genome sequence assembly due to their adaptability, robustness, and effectiveness in navigating large search spaces. Several notable studies have explored various metaheuristic strategies, both standalone and hybrid, for genome reconstruction and sequence alignment tasks.

Jain and Bharti[6] explored the application of several individual metaheuristic algorithms, which contain ACO, GA, and Particle Swarm Optimization, or genome sequence assembly tasks. Their analysis revealed that ACO performed better in contig alignment accuracy, while GA showed higher diversity in candidate assemblies. However, their approach was limited by scalability challenges in handling large genomic datasets and lacking hybrid integration strategies, which are increasingly necessary for modern genome-scale applications. Their best-performing method achieved an N50 improvement of approximately 9% over traditional methods.

Mutale[7] *et al.* conducted a critical review of Particle Swarm Optimization and Bacterial Foraging Optimization (BFO) in

DOI: 10.1201/9781042001767-85

parallel assembly sequence planning [6]. While their work focused more on manufacturing planning, it revealed the synergy of swarm intelligence techniques when applied in tandem, showing reduced execution time by up to 20%. Their findings reinforce the concept that hybrid approaches, especially ones combining global and local search [8]can outperform singular metaheuristic methods, although genome-specific datasets were not used in their evaluation.

Yassine and Riffi[5] presented a comprehensive review of ML algorithms and nature-inspired algorithms applied to genomeassembly. They argued that traditional algorithms are no longer sufficient and advocated for hybrid strategies combining reinforcement learning, genetic operations, and swarm-based heuristics. While largely qualitative, their study suggested that metaheuristic-based genome assemblers could improve accuracy by 10–15% over graph-based assemblers, particularly for fragmented genomes, though empirical benchmarks were limited.

Riza *et al.* [9] performed a comparative study of population-based metaheuristics, including Genetic Algorithms, PSO, and Harmony Search, on DNA sequence assembly [4]. They concluded that while GA produced better-quality assemblies in terms of N50 (approx. 6.8% improvement), PSO was more efficient in computation time (up to 23% faster). However, none of the individual algorithms consistently outperformed the others across all tested datasets, highlighting the need for hybrid solutions. Their work notably lacked chaotic components or adaptive mechanisms to maintain population diversity.

Ding *et al.*[10]. proposed a novel hybrid metaheuristic for planning sequences in high-speed spindle assembly Their approve. The combined Grey Wolf Optimization (GWO) and Sine Cosine Algorithm (SCA), showing superior convergence speed and solution stability in industrial applications. Although the context was engineering rather than bioinformatics, their method achieved 19.2% improvement in sequence efficiency and showcased the strength of hybridization for nonlinear planning problems, offering structural insights transferable to genome assembly domains.

Calvet [11]*et al.* examined the role of metaheuristic optimization in bioinformatics, focusing on protein folding, sequence alignment, and gene expression analysis. While they emphasized the versatility of metaheuristics, they reported that standalone algorithms often fail to generalize well across biological datasets [12]. Their findings further support the case for adaptable hybrid metaheuristics capable of addressing diverse bioinformatics challenges, although they did not explicitly test genome assembly cases.

Li *et al.*[13]. introduced a hybrid optimization framework integrating Differential Evolution with Building Information Modeling (BIM) for structural design optimization. Their DE-enhanced method achieved up to 25% material cost savings. Though not applied to genomics, this study reinforced DE's capability to refine solutions in complex multi-parameter spaces, supporting its use in our proposed hybrid model.

Lu *et al.*[14]. addressed an energy-efficient disassembly sequencing problem using a hybrid of NSGA-II and PSO. Their approach optimized multi-objective parameters and achieved a 15% performance improvement in profit and energy metrics. This multi-criteria optimization framework serves as a conceptual model for multi-objective genome assembly tasks, indicating the adaptability of hybrid methods to diverse domains.[15]

3 PROPOSED HYBRID METAHEURISTIC FRAMEWORK

3.1 *Introduction*

Genome sequence assembly is a combinatorial optimization problem where the goal is to reconstruct the original genome by ordering and merging many short sequencing reads. This process requires an algorithmic approach capable of identifying optimal or near-optimal solutions in a high-dimensional search space,[4] where each possible ordering of reads represents a different candidate solution. Our proposed hybrid framework leverages the complementary strengths of the Whale Optimization Algorithm and Differential Evolution [17], with a chaos-enhanced initialization and perturbation strategy to avoid premature convergence. The algorithm is designed to iteratively improve candidate assemblies based on a biologically relevant fitness function, which evaluates each solution based on genome assembly quality metrics.[18]

3.2 *Encoding and initialization*

Each candidate solution represents a permutation of sequencing reads. Let R=$\{r_1, r_2,...,r_n\}$ denote a set of pre-processed reads. A solution vector $\vec{X} \in$ Rn encodes a potential read order. Initial population P= $\{\vec{X}_1, \vec{X}_2.., \vec{X}_N\}$ is generated using a chaotic logistic map defined by

$$x_{\{k+1\}} = \mu x_k(1 - x_k), \quad x_0 \in (0, 1), \quad \mu \in [3.57, 4] \tag{1}$$

This produces a diverse and non-repetitive sequence of real values, which are then mapped to read indices through a ranking-based encoding to form valid permutations. :[18]

3.3 *Fitness function*

The fitness function is critical to guiding the algorithm toward biologically meaningful solutions. We define the fitness F $\rightarrow$ $(\vec{X})$ of a candidate solution based on multiple objectives:

$$F\left(\vec{X}\right) = w1 \cdot N50\left(\vec{X}\right) - w2 \cdot ContigCount\left(\vec{X}\right) - w3 \cdot MismatchPenalty\left(\vec{X}\right) \tag{2}$$

here:

N50 – indicates the contig size such that half of the genome is assembled into contigs of that length or greater.

Contig Count is the total number of contigs formed from the read sequence.

Mismatch Penalty penalizes incorrect overlaps between reads.

w_1, w_2,w_3∈[0,1] are weights set according to the desired trade-off (e.g., accuracy vs. fragmentation).

This multi-objective function is designed to maximize N50 and minimize contigs and errors, effectively balancing accuracy and completeness in the assembly.

3.4 *Whale optimization phase*

In each generation, WOA simulates the behavior of whales encircling prey and updating positions in a spiral pattern. Let $\vec{X}_i$be the position of the ith whale $\vec{X}_*$and the best solution found so far. The update equations are:

Encircling prey:

$$\vec{D} = |\vec{C} \cdot \vec{X}_* - \vec{X}_i|, \vec{X}_{i(t+1)} = \vec{X}_* - \vec{A} \cdot \vec{D} \tag{3}$$

Spiral update:

$$\vec{X}_{i(t+1)} = \vec{D}^1 e\, bl.\cos(2\pi l) + \vec{X}_* \tag{4}$$

where:

$$\vec{A} = 2\vec{a} \cdot \vec{r} - \vec{a}\ C = 2 \cdot r$$

$\vec{r}$ is a random vector in [0,1]
b defines the logarithmic spiral shape
$l \in [-1,1]$ controls the movement pattern

WOA emphasizes exploration in early iterations and exploitation as $\vec{a}$ linearly decreases from 2 to 0.

3.4 *Differential evolution refinement*

Each candidate solution from the WOA phase is refined locally using DE to introduce adaptive variation and prevent convergence stagnation. The DE process includes:

Mutation:

$$s\vec{V}_i = \vec{X}_{r1} + F.\left(\vec{X}_{r2} - \vec{X}_{r3}\right) \tag{5}$$

Crossover:

$$\vec{U}_{i,j} = \begin{cases} \vec{V}_{i,J,} & if\ r\ and\ rj \leq CR \\ X_{i,j,} & \end{cases} \tag{6}$$

Where:

- $\vec{X}_{r1}, \vec{X}_{r2}, \vec{X}_{r3}$ are distinct solutions randomly chosen from the population
- $F \in [0,2]]$ is the differential weight
- $CR \in [0,1]$ is the crossover rate

DE helps fine-tune the solution space by introducing variations based on population differences, improving exploitation capabilities.

3.6 *Chaos-driven perturbation*

To further diversify the population and prevent premature convergence, a chaotic perturbation strategy is used. If no improvement is observed in the best fitness F ($\vec{X}_*$) for consecutive generations, 10% of the population is reinitialized using the logistic map, and the fitness of these new individuals is immediately evaluated. This dynamic injection of diversity boosts exploration potential without sacrificing convergence.

3.7 *Termination criteria*

The algorithm terminates under one of the following conditions:
Maximum number of generations TTT is reached
No improvement in best fitness value for GGG generations (stagnation)
The final output includes:
Optimal read arrangement
Corresponding assembled genome
Assembly statistics (N50, total contigs, mismatches, runtime)

3.6 *Pseudocode*

Algorithm: Hybrid WOA-DE with Chaos for Genome Sequence Assembly
Input: Reads R = {r1, r2, ..., rn}, population size N, max iterations T
Output: Best reading order and assembly metrics

1. Initialize population P using chaos-based encoding (logistic map)
2. Evaluate fitness F(X) for each X in P
3. Set X_best ← best solution in P
4. For t = 1 to T do
   For each Xi in population P:
   a. Compute A, C using WOA equations
   b. Update Xi using either encircling or spiral WOA operator
   c. Apply DE to refine Xi
   d. Evaluate fitness F(Xi)
   e. Update X_best if F(Xi) > F(X_best)
   If no improvement in X_best for k generations:
   a. Reinitialize 10% of population using chaotic logistic map
   b. Evaluate the fitness of new individuals

End For
Return: X_best and associated genome assembly

3.7 *Summary*

The proposed hybrid framework introduces a balance between exploration and exploitation through WOA and DE, while chaos-enhancement mitigates premature convergence". Its flexible architecture allows dynamic adaptability to varying dataset characteristics and sequencing noise. By optimizing biologically relevant fitness functions, the algorithm guides search toward high-quality genome assemblies.[19]

The proposed architecture for the Hybrid WOA-DE-Chaos Genome Sequence Assembly Framework follows a modular pipeline design that promotes clarity, flexibility, and scalability. This architecture can be depicted as a flow-oriented block diagram, with each module representing a distinct and essential stage in the genome assembly process.[19]

1. Input Module: Raw DNA Reads The pipeline begins with the acquisition of raw DNA sequencing reads, typically in FASTQ format, derived from high-throughput sequencing platforms (e.g., Illumina or Oxford Nanopore). These reads may be short (50–300 bp) or long (>1,000 bp), depending on the technology used. This input forms the foundational dataset for all downstream processing.
2. Preprocessing Module: This stage makes sure that data is clean and optimized for assembly. It includes:[20]
   - Quality Filtering: Removal of low-quality reads or trimming of low-quality tails based on Phred scores.
   - k-mer Analysis: Identification of frequent subsequences (k-mers) to detect overlaps and potential errors.
   - Read Normalization: Reducing redundancy by compressing highly repetitive reads while preserving coverage diversity, which improves memory and runtime efficiency.
3. Optimization Core (Metaheuristic Engine) The heart of architecture lies in this multi-component optimization module:[21]
   - WOA Block (Exploration Phase): The Whale Optimization Algorithm drives the global search process, simulating the social foraging behavior of humpback whales to locate promising assembly paths across the search space.
   - DE Block (Exploitation/Refinement Phase): The Differential Evolution operator takes intermediate candidate assemblies and applies targeted mutation, crossover, and selection to refine solutions locally, improving precision and structural accuracy.
   - Chaos Module (Diversity Control): A chaotic map (e.g., logistic or tent map) introduces non-repetitive, deterministic randomness to the population initialization and updates. This maintains diversity and prevents premature convergence to suboptimal solutions, a common pitfall in standard metaheuristics.

4. Fitness Evaluation Module Each candidate genome assembly is evaluated using a carefully crafted fitness function that considers:
   - N50 Score: A standard metric indicating assembly contiguity.
   - Contig Count: Total number of continuous sequences, lower is better.
   - Penalty Terms: For excessive gaps, mismatches, or misassembled segments. This composite fitness guides the selection process and ensures convergence toward high-quality assemblies.

5. Output Module Once optimal or near-optimal assemblies are identified; the results are compiled and exported. This module includes:
   - Reconstructed Genome: Output in FASTA format representing the assembled contigs or scaffolds.
   - Performance Report: Summary statistics including N50, runtime, contig distribution, and convergence behavior, optionally formatted in CSV, JSON, or PDF for post-analysis.

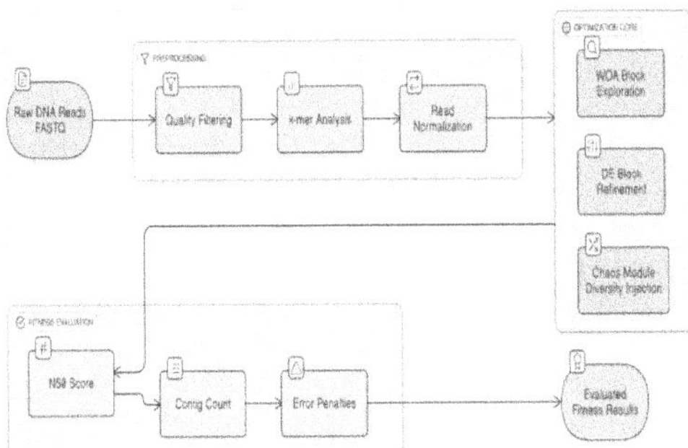

Figure 1. System architecture.

Figure 1 represents the pipeline-style architecture which is designed for modularity, allowing components (e.g., optimizer or preprocessing tools) to be swapped or tuned independently. It also supports adaptability, accommodating various genome sizes and sequencing technologies, and offers scalability, enabling parallelization or cloud-based deployment for large-scale bioinformatics workloads.

not comfortable to put on over a long period of time. This does not exist Because positive air-pressure respirators draw air through external filters, they incorporate a motorized system to deliver the filtered air. Respiration apparatus also takes place in the recent scenario in the treatment of the pandemic. The widely used respirators are negative pressure systems that need the lungs power to force-in purified air that is often inappropriate and sometimes not possible in case the individual does not have powerful lungs strength or he or she is suffering from respiratory sickness. This paper provides a solution to the issue based on forced air .

4 CONCLUSION

It has become evident in the present scenario that respiratory illnesses such as chronic obstructive pulmonary disease (COPD) and asthma are increasingly prevalent. This threat has been further intensified by rising levels of air pollutants, including PM2.5 and PM10. As a result, the use of respirators serves as an immediate protective measure at the individual level, since significant reductions in pollution levels may take considerable time to achieve.

ACKNOWLEDGEMENT

"The authors express their heartfelt appreciation to the students, staff, and authorities of the Computer Science Department for their guidance and assistance in carrying out this research".

REFERENCES

[1] Woods, D.D. and E. Hollnagel. (2012). *Joint cognitive systems.* Boca Raton: CRC Press/Taylor & Francis.

[2] Wiens, J.A. (2005). Avian community ecology: An iconoclastic view. In *Perspectives in ornithology*, ed. A. H. Brush, and G. A. Clark, 355–403. Cambridge: Cambridge Univ. Press.

[3] Terborgh, J. (2009). Preservation of natural diversity. BioScience. 24:715–22.

[4] Alotaibi, A.R. and Mishra, A.V. (2015). Global and regional volatility spillovers to GCC stock markets. Int. Economic. Modelling. 45(3):38–49.

[5] Akhtaruzzaman, M., Boubaker, S., and Sensoy, A. (2021). Financial contagion during COVID–19 crisis. Int. Financ. Res. Lett. 38(2):101604-101609.

[6] Testa, B. and L.B. Kier. (2013). Emergence and dissolvence in the self-organisation of complex systems. Entropy 2, no. 1: 1-25. http://www.mdpi.org/entropy/papers/e2010001.pdf

[7] Schwartz, G.J. (2012). Multiwavelength analyses of classical carbon-oxygen novae. PhD diss., Arizona State Univ.

[8] O'Guinn, T.C. (2014). Touching greatness. Paper presented at the annual meeting of the American Psychological Association, New York.

[9] Adamic, L.A. and Huberman B.A. (2006). The nature of markets in the World Wide Web. Working paper, Xerox Palo Alto Research Center. http://www.parc.xerox.com/istl/groups/iea/www/webmarkets.html (accessed March 12, 2014).

[10] Aidy Ali, Kannan Rassiah, M.M.H Megat Ahmada. (2021). The effect of stacking sequence of woven bamboo on mechanical behaviour of fiber reinforced composites. *Journal of Southwest* 592 Jiaotong University / Vol.56 No.2.

[11] Anigol, M.N.B. and Anil, S.P. (2015). Study of the effect of various fillers on mechanical properties of carbon-epoxy composites. *Int. Res. J. Eng. Technol.* 02(03), 798–802.

[12] Biswasa, S., Shahinura, S., Hasana, M. and Ahsan, Q. (2015). Physical, mechanical and thermal properties of jute and bamboo fibre reinforced unidirectional epoxy composites. *Procedia Eng.* 105, 933–939

Next-Generation Smart Systems – Sekhar et al. (Eds)
© 2027 The Author(s), ISBN: 978-1-041-34234-2

A Technological and Evaluative Framework for Magic Therapy in Mitigating Anxiety among Hospitalized School-Aged Children

Thenmozhi P.
Professor, Saveetha College of Nursing, Saveetha Institute of Medical and Technical Sciences, Saveetha University, Chennai, Tamilnadu, India

Irine Maria Jojo
Saveetha College of Nursing, Saveetha Institute of Medical and Technical Sciences, Saveetha University, Chennai, Tamilnadu, India

Tamilselvi S., Bhuvaneswari G., and Mary Minolin T.
Professor, Saveetha College of Nursing, Saveetha Institute of Medical and Technical Sciences, Saveetha University, Chennai, Tamilnadu, India

ABSTRACT: Hospitalization can be deeply unsettling experience for school-aged children, frequently leading to elevated anxiety as they are separated from familiar surroundings. exposure to unfamiliar clinical settings, and distressing medical interventions. Non-pharmacological approaches such as therapeutic play and magic-based interventions have emerged as effective strategies for mitigating emotional distress. This research aimed to examine how effectively magic therapy reduces anxiety in school-aged children during hospital stay. One-group pretest-posttest approach was employed, comprising 60 paediatric inpatients recruited via simple random sampling from Paediatric ward, Chennai. The study measured anxiety in participants before and after a structured seven-day intervention using the Facial Anxiety Scale. The intervention consisted of daily 20–30minute magic therapy sessions incorporating simple interactive illusions, including tricks with toothpicks, paper slips, hair bands, and playing cards. Statistical analysis involved the use of descriptive as well as inferential methods. Initial assessments revealed that 60% of participants exhibited high anxiety, while 40% demonstrated very high anxiety. Post-intervention data showed marked improvement: 13% had no anxiety, 70% displayed low anxiety, and only 17% retained moderate anxiety levels. The mean anxiety score significantly declined from 3.60 ± 0.49 to 0.73 ± 0.44 ($t = 24.970$, $p < 0.001$). Notably, maternal education and paternal occupation were expressively correlated with baseline anxiety levels. This technological evaluative framework confirms that Magic therapy is a beneficial, affordable, non-invasive, and engaging intervention for alleviating anxiety among children aged 6–10 years during hospitalization. The findings support its integration into paediatric care practices. Further research involving control groups and larger sample sizes is recommended to validate and extend these results.

Keywords: Magic Therapy, Paediatric Anxiety Management, Non-Pharmacological Interventions, Hospitalized Children, Emotional Well-being, Therapeutic Play, Child-Centred Healthcare

1 INTRODUCTION

Children are the cornerstone of a nation's future, serving as the responsible citizens and leaders of tomorrow. However, being admitted to the hospital as an inpatient is a frequent and often inevitable experience for many children due to various medical conditions. Each year, over 6,000,000 children worldwide are admitted to hospitals for various health-related concerns [1]. Among them, school-aged children are particularly vulnerable due to their susceptibility to infectious diseases such as acute febrile illnesses, respiratory conditions like asthma and pneumonia, gastroenteritis, physical injuries, and mental health disorders [2]. Hospitalization often represents the first major emotional crisis for a child, carrying significant psychological consequences. Anxiety is one of the most prevalent emotional responses observed in paediatric inpatients. Research indicates that nearly 91.7% of hospitalized school-aged children experience moderate anxiety, manifested through symptoms such as crying, irritability, refusal to eat, and withdrawal from social interaction. Common emotional reactions during hospitalization also include fear and sadness, often intensified by separation from parents, unfamiliar environments, painful procedures, and uncertainty about their illness [3][4].

Being displaced from familiar routines and social connections with siblings, peers, and extended family can cause separation anxiety—typically marked by sadness, loneliness, and feelings of loss. Younger children may also parade regressive behaviours such as bed-wetting, thumb-sucking, clinginess, and temper tantrums. These behaviours are frequently accompanied by heightened fear and dependence on caregivers [5]. Furthermore, rigid hospital routines and limited autonomy can contribute to a perceived loss of control, intensifying emotional distress and decreasing treatment compliance. Anxiety during hospitalization is linked to both psychological and physical consequences, including fatigue, low energy, obesity, and delayed developmental milestones. It may also lead to prolonged recovery times and increased reliance on sedative medications due to anxiety-induced physiological changes. These findings highlight the critical need for integrating psychological support, child-friendly environments, and active family participation into paediatric care [6][7].

Healthcare professionals, especially paediatric nurses, are instrumental in recognizing and addressing children's emotional needs throughout hospitalization. Early detection of anxiety and timely implementation of appropriate interventions can significantly improve a child's hospital experience and overall well-being. Non-pharmacological strategies—such as play therapy, music therapy, storytelling, art therapy, bibliotherapy, distraction techniques, and magic therapy—have shown considerable promise in reducing hospital-related anxiety [8]. This study focuses on magic therapy, a specialized form of play therapy that engages children through interactive tricks (e.g., toothpick magic, paper slip magic, hairband tricks, and card magic). These activities serve as cognitive distractions that

DOI: 10.1201/9781042001767-86

stimulate creativity, enhance neuroplasticity, support emotional regulation, and foster positive engagement. Based on these premises, the current revision was undertaken to confirm the technological framework of magic therapy on anxiety in in hospitalized children of school age, with the hypothesis that it would produce a significant reduction in anxiety levels [9][10].

2 LITERATURE REVIEW

Being hospitalized can pose significant emotional challenges and psychological strain. Many studies have been conducted to examine the impact of hospital stay on psychological impact among children, emphasizing the need for holistic approaches that go beyond medical treatment to address emotional well-being [11]-[14]. Research underscores that unfamiliar environments, separation from caregivers, invasive procedures, and lack of autonomy are primary contributors to paediatric anxiety. These stressors can hinder recovery, reduce treatment adherence, and lead to long-term psychological consequences. In response, non-pharmacological approaches have garnered interest for their effectiveness in mitigating anxiety without the adverse effects linked to medications [15]. Play therapy is an effective intervention in paediatric care that enables children to express their emotions, work through experiences, and restore a sense of control. Similarly, music therapy, art therapy, and bibliotherapy have been shown to alleviate stress and improve coping mechanisms during hospitalization [16]. Magic therapy, a relatively recent and innovative approach, blends entertainment with psychological distraction. Research demonstrated that magic tricks stimulate cognitive engagement, reduce perceived pain, and create moments of joy, making them ideal for pediatric environments. Studies show that interactive magic can significantly reduce anxiety scores in children undergoing medical procedures [17]-[21].

These effects are attributed to the therapy's capacity to captivate attention, evoke positive emotions, and foster a sense of wonder. Despite promising findings, limited research has examined magic therapy through a technological and evaluative lens [22]-[24]. Existing studies often lack rigorous frameworks for assessing outcomes or standardizing therapeutic practices. This gap highlights the need for structured evaluation models and evidence-based protocols [25]-[27]. The current study seeks to bridge this gap by proposing a structured framework for magic therapy, integrating evaluative metrics and assessing its effectiveness in reducing anxiety among school-aged hospitalized children [28]-[30].

3 METHODOLOGY

A quasi-experimental one-group pre-test and post-test design was adopted to carry out the revision in the paediatric ward of SMCH, Chennai, after obtaining official approval., upon obtaining official approval. Sixty hospitalized school-aged children who encountered the enclosure benchmarks were nominated using a random number table. Hospitalized children aged 6 to 10 years, of either gender, whose mothers provided conversant consent to contribute in the study were included. Children who were uncooperative, physiologically unstable, mentally challenged, cognitively or sensory impaired, or placed under strict isolation were excluded. Outlined the study's purpose, procedures, and expected benefits to the samples and their parents. Conversant agreement was attained to contribute in the study from each participant and their parents after they were provided with comprehensive information.

The structured demographic questionnaire designed for the study was used to collect baseline data through interviews with the parents of participants. The pre-test assessment of anxiety was conducted on the first day using Facial Anxiety Scale. It is a standardized tool ranging from zero to one. Followed by magic therapy was administered for 20-30 minutes every day for 7 days. Magic therapy consist of 4 magic paly which includes toothpick magic, paper slip magic, hair band magic, and card magic. In toothpick magic, an investigator used toothpicks to build a small structure, then make it disappear or reappear as well as to create illusions and tricks. For paper slip magic, wrote a message on a piece of paper, folded it up, and then made it disappear or reappear in a surprising place. Hair band was used to make a small object to appear, disappear and / or reappear for hair band therapy. Participants were instructed to choose a card, make it disappear or reappear in a surprising place in card magic. These are the magic not only divert the mind, it also strengthens the children's memory, and concentration. It was administered in order or according to their choices. I took nearly half an hour to complete the magic therapy every day. It was administered each participant individually at the bedside itself without disturbing the ward routine and preferably before the painful procedure. At the end of intervention, on the seventh day, evaluation was carried out using the same measurement scale.

The study received ethical approval from the Institutional Scientific Review Board of Saveetha College of Nursing. Participant confidentiality was rigorously upheld throughout the research process. Following data collection, responses were systematically coded for preliminary organization and preparation. Subsequent statistical analysis and interpretation were conducted using both descriptive and inferential techniques through the SPSS software suite. The conceptual structure of the proposed framework is illustrated in Figure 1.

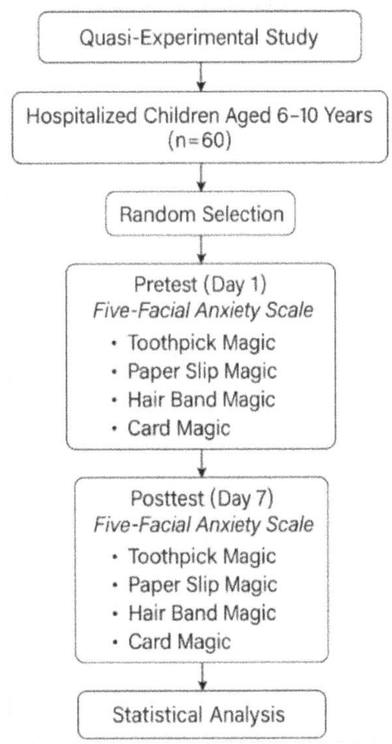

Figure 1. Planned framework for the methodological procedures.

4 RESULTS AND DISCUSSION

Among 60 hospitalized school-aged children, 67% were male, with a mean age of 9.5 ± 4.21 years. About 57% were studying in the 3rd–4th standard, 56% were Hindus, and 70% belonged to nuclear families. More than 50% of both fathers and mothers had completed undergraduate education. Half of the fathers were employed in private companies, while the mothers were homemakers. Additionally, 76% of the children were the first-born in their families, 46% had stayed in the hospital for 4 days, and 66% were accompanied by their mothers as caregivers. The majority were hospitalized for medical conditions and no previous history of hospitalization as shown in Table 1.

Table 1. Background information about the participants.

Background Variables	Study Group
Age (in Years)	9.5 ± 4.21
Gender (Male/Female)	67% / 33%
Religion (Hindu/Christian/ Muslim)	56% / 17% / 27%
Class Studying (1st-2nd / 3rd-4th/ 5th)	13% / 57% / 30 %
Type of Family (Nuclear / Joint)	70% / 30%
Education of Father (Illiterate / Higher Secondary / Undergraduate)	3% / 40% / 57%
Education of Mother (Illiterate / Higher Secondary / Undergraduate)	10% / 40% / 50%
Father's Occupation (Coolie/ Self/ Private/ Government)	10% / 27% / 50% / 13%
Mother's Occupation (Homemakers/ Private/ Government)	57% / 30% / 13%
Birth Order (First / Second / Third)	76% / 15% / 9%
Duration of Hospitalization in days (3 / 4 / above 4)	37% / 46% / 17%
Presence of caregiver with the child (Mother / Father / Grandparent)	66% / 17% / 17%
Diagnosis (Medical / Surgical)	70% / 30%
History of previous hospitalization (Yes / No)	20% / 80%

Table 2 shows that out of 60 participants, 60% had an high level 40% had very high anxiety in the pre-test. In contrast, after the intervention in the post-test, 8 (13%) had no anxiety, 42 (70%) had little anxiety, and 10 (17%) had some anxiety.

Table 2. Analysis of anxiety levels before and after the intervention.

	Pre-test		Post-test	
Outcome Variable	No	%	No	%
No Anxiety	-	-	8	13%
Little Anxiety	-	-	42	70%
Some Anxiety	-	-	10	17%
High Anxiety	36	60%	-	-
Very High Anxiety	24	40%	-	-

Table 3 shows that the mean anxiety score in the pre-test was 3.60 ± 0.49, while the post-test mean score was 0.73 ± 0.44, resulting in a mean difference of 2.87. The paired t-test value of $t = 24.970$ was statistically significant at the $p < 0.001$ level. This clearly indicates that the level of anxiety among hospitalized school-aged children was significantly reduced following the administration of magic therapy.

Table 3. Effectiveness of magic therapy on anxiety.

Anxiety	Mean	Standard Deviation	Mean difference score	Paired t test & p-value
Pre-test	3.60	0.49	2.87	t = 24.970
Post-test	0.73	0.44		p=0.001 S***

***p<0.001, S – Significant

Table 4 shows that the background variables of mother's education ($\chi^2 = 12.085$, $p < 0.01$) and father's occupation ($\chi^2 = 8.182$, $p < 0.05$) had a statistically significant association with the pre-test level of anxiety among school-aged children.

Table 4. Association between level of anxiety and background variables.

	Pre-test Level of Anxiety				
	High		Very High		
Background Variable	No.	%	No.	%	Chi- Square Value
Mother's Education					
No formal	3	5%	2	3%	χ=12.085
Secondary	18	30%	7	12%	d.f=2
Undergraduate	15	25%	15	25%	p=9.210 S**
Father's Occupation					
Government	3	6%	3	6%	χ=8.182
Private	17	28%	13	22%	d.f=3
Self	11	18%	7	11%	p=7.815
Unemployed	5	7%	1	2%	S*

**p<0.01, *p<0.05, S – Significant

The present study explored how anxiety levels correlated with various background characteristics. Results indicated a marked decline in anxiety levels following the intervention, demonstrating the therapeutic effectiveness of magic-based distraction methods. Initially, the majority of participants (60%) exhibited high anxiety, while the remaining 40% showed very high anxiety levels. These heightened responses reflect the emotional strain children often endure during hospitalization, which involves adapting to unfamiliar environments and being separated from home. Post-intervention findings showed a significant shift—70% of the children experienced only mild anxiety, and 13% reported no anxiety at all. This notable change highlights the capacity of non-drug-based interventions like magic therapy to reduce emotional distress and promote a more positive hospital experience.

Although caregiver anxiety was not evaluated in this study, related research has shown that such interventions can ease stress for both children and their families. Magic therapy, as a branch of play therapy, has consistently been linked with reduced anxiety levels and improved psychological resilience in children undergoing medical care. Despite being less extensively studied than other therapeutic play approaches, magic therapy has demonstrated promising outcomes. Some comparative studies suggest that while both storytelling and play therapy help alleviate anxiety, therapeutic play—including magic-based engagement—often yields better results in managing pre-procedural stress in children. This current study focused exclusively on children admitted for medical treatment, further reinforcing the relevance of magic therapy in general paediatric settings.

Analysis of background variables revealed significant links between anxiety levels and parental education and employment. Children whose mothers had limited formal education were more likely to experience heightened anxiety, possibly due to reduced emotional preparation or support. Likewise, children from households where fathers had unstable employment or were unemployed showed increased anxiety, potentially indicating greater socioeconomic pressure and limited access to coping mechanisms. These insights stress the need to consider family background and social factors when designing child-centered care strategies. Tailoring interventions to align with parental education levels and employment conditions may enhance the impact of anxiety-relief programs. While the study provides encouraging evidence, it is inadequate by a moderately small sample size, the absence of a standard hospital routine care group, and without any long-term evaluation or parental anxiety assessment. Future investigations should involve larger randomized trials, longitudinal tracking, and incorporate feedback from both children and parents. Such approaches could deepen understanding of the emotional benefits of magic therapy and help integrate it more systematically into paediatric care.

5 CONCLUSION

This study concludes that magic therapy effectively reduces anxiety among school-aged children during hospitalization without the use of medication. The intervention, which involved engaging children in simple and interactive magic tricks, significantly reduced anxiety levels, as evidenced by pre- and post-assessment scores. By introducing an element of wonder, distraction, and playfulness into the hospital environment, magic therapy provided emotional relief, improved the psychological resilience of the children, and created a more positive hospital experience.

Given its low cost, ease of implementation, and non-invasive nature, magic therapy offers a practical and impactful tool that can be integrated into paediatric care settings. The findings support the recommendation that paediatric wards be equipped with the necessary materials and trained personnel to deliver magic-based interventions as a supplementary therapeutic approach. Such practices can contribute not only to the emotional well-being of the child but may also enhance cooperation during treatment, promote recovery, and reduce the need for pharmacological anxiolytics.

Despite the encouraging results, the study has restrictions, including a comparatively insignificant sample size, the non-appearance of a control group, and the short duration of follow-up. Additionally, the study did not assess the emotional impact on parents or caregivers, nor did it explore the sustainable benefits of this intervention on paediatric patients' hospital experiences as well as psychological well-being.

ACKNOWLEDGMENT

The authors sincerely appreciate and thank the participants for their cooperation, which was invaluable in successfully completing the study.

REFERENCES

[1] Van Dijk. Lieselotte. (2017). Interventions reducing anxiety in hospitalized children: *A systematic literature review from 2010 to 2017.*

[2] Karbandi S, Soltanifar A, Salari M, Asgharinekah SM and Izie E. (2020). Effect of music therapy and distraction cards on anxiety among hospitalized children with chronic *Diseases. Evid Based Care.*;1(4):15–22.

[3] McDermott KW, Roemer M., (2018). Most Frequent Principal Diagnoses for Inpatient Stays in U.S. Hospitals. 2021 Jul 13. In: Healthcare Cost and Utilization Project (HCUP) Statistical Briefs [Internet]. *Rockville (MD): Agency for Healthcare Research and Quality (US);* 2006 Feb–. Statistical Brief #277.

[4] Seedha Devi V., Sumathi K., Mahalakshmi M., Jose Anand A., Anita Titus and Naga Saranya N., (2024), Machine Learning based Efficient Human Activity Recognition Systems, *International Journal of Intelligent Systems and Applications in Engineering*, 12 (5s), 338–346.

[5] Audrey J Weiss, Lan Liang and Kimberly Martin, (2022). Statistical Brief #299Overview of Hospital Stays Among Children and Adolescents, 2019. *Healthcare Cost and Utilization Project (HCUP).*

[6] Shama Praveen, Sunita Sharma and Nitin James Peters. (2023). A Descriptive Study to Assess Level of Stress, Anxiety, and Pain Among Hospitalized Children Admitted in the Pediatric Surgery Unit of APC, PGIMER, Chandigarh 2020–2022. *Nursing & Midwifery Research Journal.*; 19(2).

[7] Juwita H. (2019). Effectiveness of multimodal interventions play therapy: colouring and origami against anxiety levels in toddler ages. *J Health Sci Prev.*;3(3S):46–51.

[8] Kaur H and Kumar R. (2023). Assessment of stress, anxiety, and pain among hospitalized children aged 6–12 years: A descriptive study. *J Pediatr Neonat Nurs.* 2023; 6(2):72–79.

[9] Kilic M, Karadag G. (2023). Effects of hospitalization on emotional well-being in school-aged children: The role of non-pharmacological interventions. *BMC Pediatrics.* 2023; 23, Article 4101.

[10] Salsabila P, Anggraini IR, Alifatin A and Aini N. (2022). Play therapy to reduce anxiety in children during hospitalization: a literature review. *KnE Med.*:765–73.

[11] Bryan MA and Mihalek AJ. (2024). Gaps in Immunizing Children during hospitalization: how can we close them? *Hosp Pediatr.*;14(9):e391–3.

[12] Zarra-Nezhad M, Pakdaman F and Moazami-Goodarzi A. (2023). The effectiveness of child-centered group play therapy and narrative therapy on preschoolers' separation anxiety disorder and social-emotional behaviours. *Early Child Dev Care.*;193(6):841–53.

[13] Jose A., and Dhanalakshmi R., (Sep 2023), Hygieia: Multipurpose Healthcare Assistance Using the Internet of Things, in Saravanan Krishnan, and Aboobucker Ilmudeen, *"Internet of Medical Things in Smart Healthcare: Post-COVID-19 Pandemic Scenario", Apple Academic Press,* pp. 77–98.

[14] Teksin G and Ozdemir FK. (2020). Anxiety and fear levels of hospitalized children and their mothers. *Perspectives in Psychiatric Care.*;56(2):470–476.

[15] Armandpishe S, Pakzad R, Jandaghian-Bidgoli M, Abdi F, Sardashti M and Soltaniha K. (2023). Investigating factors affecting the prevalence of stress, anxiety and depression among citizens of Karaj city: A population-based cross-sectional study. *Heliyon.*;9(2023):e16901.

[16] Wilson ME, Megel ME, Enenbach L and Carlson KL. (2010). The voices of children: stories about hospitalization. *J Pediatr Health Care.*;24(2):95–102.

[17] Helmi Juwita, Fitriani, Akifa Syahrir, Muhammad Taslim, Nur Hidayah, Arbianingsih, Syamsiah Rauf. (2019). Effectiveness of Multimodal Interventions Play Therapy: Colouring and Origami Against Anxiety Levels in Toddler Ages. *Journal of Health Science and Prevention.*; 3(3S): 1–6.

[18] Hakim A, Kaldozkhi SSH, Tashakori A and Ghanbari S. (2023). The effect of non-verbal music on anxiety in hospitalized children. *BMC Pediatr.*;279 (2023).

[19] Abdi F, Karamoozian A, Lotfilou M, Gholami F, Shaterian N, Niasar AA, Aghapour E and Jandaghian-Bidgoli M. (2025). Effect of play therapy and storytelling on the anxiety level of hospitalized children: a randomized controlled trial. *BMC Complement Med Ther.* Jan 24;25(1):23.

[20] Maheswari M and Reena Evency A. (2021). Effectiveness of Art Therapy on Level of Anxiety among Hospitalized School Age Children in a Selected Hospital at Kanyakumari District. *International Journal of Nursing Education.*;13(4): 30–33.

[21] Lawrence EJ and Lazer J. (2024 Jun). Effective reduction of anxiety in hospitalized children through bibliotherapy. Acta Paediatr.;113(6):1349–1355.

[22] Xavier L, Velmurugan S. (2024 Jul). Assess the Effect of Detract Technique among Post-operative Toddlers with Cleft Lip and Cleft Palate. *J Pharm Bioallied Sci.*;16(Suppl 3):S2913-S2915.

[23] Neethu Ann Preethy and Deepa Gurunathan. (2020). Effect of music on the vital signs and behaviour of children during the recovery period after general anaesthesia procedure-a randomized controlled trial. *Indian Journal of Forensic Medicine and Toxicology.*;14(4):336–341.

[24] Pravder HD, Leng-Smith A, Brash AI, Elkin DJ, Attard M, Rose B, Messina CR and Chitkara MB. (2019 Dec). A Magic

Therapy Program to Alleviate Anxiety in Pediatric Inpatients. *Hosp Pediatr.*;9(12):942–948.

[25] Cammarata C, Bujoreanu S, Wohlheiter K. Hospitalization and its impact: Stressors associated with inpatient hospitalization for the child and family. *Clinical handbook of psychological consultation in pediatric medical settings.* 2020:37–49.

[26] Jose A., and Dhanalakshmi R., (Sep 2023), Hygieia: Multipurpose Healthcare Assistance Using the Internet of Things, in Saravanan Krishnan, and Aboobucker Ilmudeen, *Internet of Medical Things in Smart Healthcare: Post-COVID-19 Pandemic Scenario*, Apple Academic Press, pp. 77–98.

[27] Lekhwani P, Tirupathi S and Afnan L. (2024). Thaumaturgical Distraction as a Modality for Reducing Dental Anxiety in Children: A Systematic Review. *Int J Clin Pediatr Dent.*;17 (11):1296–1301.

[28] Zahra Alehamid, Kourosh Zarea, Shahnaz Rostami, Saeed Ghanbari and Ashraf Tashakori. (2023). Comparing the effectiveness of therapeutic play and storytelling on preoperative anxiety in preschool-age children: a randomized controlled trial. *J Psychiatric Nurs*;14(2):137–145.

[29] Anto Merlin Soniya S, Reeta Jebakumari Solomon and Shini. (2019). Effectiveness of Play Therapy on Anxiety among Hospitalized Preschool Children. *Asian J. Nursing Education and Research.*; 9(2):193–196.

[30] Kamlesh Kumar Pajapati, Kadali Samprasad and Jeenath Justin Doss. K. (2019). A Study to Assess the Effectiveness of Play Therapy on Anxiety among Hospitalized Children (6–12 Years), at Selected Hospital Rajkot. *Int. J. Nur. Edu. and Research.*; 7 (2):218–220.

Next-Generation Smart Systems – Sekhar et al. (Eds)
© 2027 The Author(s), ISBN: 978-1-041-34234-2

A Detection of Nano Micro-Particles in Brest Milk among Postnatal Mothers Residing in Industrial Settings - India

Vijayalakshmi R.
Principal, Saveetha College of Nursing, Saveetha Institute of Medical and Technical Sciences, Chennai, India

Ajith M. and Abinaya K.
Nursing Tutor, Saveetha College of Nursing, Saveetha Institute of Medical and Technical Sciences, Chennai, India

Sindhu Ramalingam
Associate Professor, Saveetha College of Nursing, Saveetha Institute of Medical and Technical Sciences, Chennai, India

ABSTRACT: The gold standard for newborn nutrition is human milk from their mothers, which supplies vital nutrients and bioactive compounds for optimal development. However, concerns have emerged about the presence of environmental contaminants, including particulate matter, in breast milk. This study aimed to detect and characterize inorganic nanoparticles (NPs) in breast milk samples from healthy lactating women residing in industrially recognized areas. Using an innovative method involving environmental scanning electron microscopy, we identified various inorganic particles, including metals and elements, with sizes ranging from less than 1 μm to 6 μm. Notably, 63% of breast milk samples showed contamination with heavy metal nanoparticles, with agglomerates formed through interactions between organic compounds and inorganic materials. These findings raise concerns about the potential health risks of nanoparticle exposure to infants through breast milk. Our study highlights the need for further research into the sources and effects of nanoparticle contamination in breast milk and the importance of prioritizing environmental health to support healthier development for future generations.

Keywords: nano particles, breast milk, post natal mother, industries

1 OVERVIEW

The rich combination of vital nutrients and biologically active compounds found in mother's milk, making it the ideal source of infant nutrition. It serves as the "gold standard" for feeding infants and supports their optimal growth and development. The World Health Organization and UNICEF advice for the first six months of life, newborns should only be breastfed to ensure the best possible health and developmental outcomes Research consistently links breastfeeding with numerous health benefits for children. These include reduced rates of common infections in early childhood, a lower likelihood of obesity later on decreased jeopardy of developing Non-insulin-dependent diabetes mellitus, and reduced chances of asthma .Concerns have grown over the presence of environmental contaminants in human milk, with a rising proofs confirming their detection. An overview revealed by Martin-Carrasco *et al.* highlighted the occurrence of various pollutants—including insecticides, fungicides, and potentially hazardous metals, per and polyfluoroalkyl substances (PFAS), and other environmental chemicals—in both moms milk and artificial baby milk. However, utmost research has concentrated on chemical pollutants rather than particulate matter like black carbon (BC).

BC is a byproduct of incomplete combustion from sources such as carbon dioxide, wooden materials, and fuels from fossil sources. It is thought to be among the most hazardous elements of traffic-related air pollution. Studies have detected combustion-related particles not only in human organs such as the brain, kidneys, and urine of children, but also in the placenta, cord blood, and fetal organs including the liver, lungs, and brain. This suggests BC can infiltrate multiple organ systems. Nanoparticles (NPs) are officially defined as nano-sized particles ranging from 1 to 100 nanometers and are typically categorized as either organic or inorganic based on their composition [1]. Inorganic NPs, in particular, pose potential health risks because they can interact with human proteins, amino acids, and enzymes. These particles can be easily inhaled or ingested, allowing them to enter the bloodstream and accumulate in various tissues from fetal development through adulthood. Their impact is especially concerning during the prenatal and childbirth period, where ultrafine particle have been linked to adverse outcomes such as early miscarriage, growth retardation, and changes in molecule of life alkylation. Studies have shown that once gasped or gulped by the mother, NPs can circulate in her bloodstream, cross the placenta, and reach the fetal circulatory system After birth, NPs can continue to enter the infant's body via inhalation or through products the mother uses or consumes—such as food, cosmetics, toothpaste, or medications.

This raises concerns that NPs can enter Babies bodies through milk from mom or commercially produced artificial baby milk made from animal-derived milk. In response, regulatory bodies like the FDA and EMA have issued guidelines on the use and processing of cow's milk in industrial applications. Although breast milk is recognized by the World Health Organization as the most beneficial and unique source of infant nutrition, there is limited understanding of how it might be affected by nanoparticle contamination. This concern extends to both human and animal milk, especially when the source is exposed to environmental pollution or contaminated food.

The identification of inorganic particulate matter in breast milk samples, as presented in this study, was carried out using an innovative method involving environmental scanning electron microscopy. Understanding this issue may help inform strategies to reduce environmental exposure and support healthier development for future generations. Some studies have suggested that the presence of contaminants in breast milk might slightly reduce the developmental benefits of breastfeeding. However, when other critical factors—like parental care and the quality of the home environment—are taken into account, this reduction is not statistically significant. Therefore, rather than discouraging breastfeeding, the results obtained demonstrate the pressing need for governments and policymakers to prioritize environmental health. By reducing pollution at its source, we can foster a

DOI: 10.1201/9781042001767-87

cleaner, healthier environment that supports the well-being and development of future generations.

2 METHODOLOGY

2.1 *Sample collection*

1. Between March and April of 2025, a prospective, observational study was carried out at our tertiary care center's postnatal ward and obstetrics center. All participating mothers gave their written informed consent, and the study was approved ethically. Samples of breast milk were acquired at 30 healthy lactating women residing in industrially recognized areas of Thiruvallur district. Importantly, none of the participants had any occupational exposure to chemicals.
2. *Identification of the Chemical and Physical Properties of Nanoparticles (NPs)*

All collected samples were examined using an environmental scanning electron microscope (ESEM) to evaluate the shape of any foreign particles found. The elements that make up every inorganic particle was determined using an Energy Dispersive Spectroscope (EDS) integrated with the microscope. The specimens were kept for a maximum of one week at 4 degrees Celsius. Twenty microliters of each sample were put onto a cellulose filter with a 25 mm diameter in a sterile flow cabinet. The filters were then mounted on aluminum stubs using conductive carbon adhesive discs for Transmission Electron Microscopy analysis. Specimens were kept in unsoiled, sealed containers and only opened when inserted into the ESEM chamber.

The following parameters were used for the analyses: low vacuum with both backscattered electron (BSE) and secondary electron (SE) imaging modes; a spot size of 3.8; an accelerating voltage between 12 and 30 kV; and a working distance of 10 mm. The resolution ranged from 10.0 to 4 nm. Inorganic debris, distinguishable by their higher atomic density, appeared as bright points against the organic background.

When such inorganic particles were identified, their elemental makeup was determined using the EDS X-ray microprobe.

Analytical Statistics:

The standard deviation & mean was used to present the clinical data. Student's t-test, or the two-sided Mann-Whitney U test in cases where the data did not follow a normal distribution, was used to examine differences in nanoparticle (NP) concentrations and counts in breast milk. Fisher's exact test was used to evaluate proportional differences. The p-value was supposed statistically substantial if it was less than 0.05.

Table 1. Maternal and neonatal characteristics documented at the time of admission. Data are presented as median ± standard deviation (SD).

Features	Mean N=30
Features of the Mother	
Age of the mother in years	28
Weight in Kilograms	63
Height in Centimeters	154
Predominant breastfeeding	30
Features of the Newborn	
Gestational Period in wks	39
Birthweight in grams	2750
Gender, (M/F)	18/12
Route of Childbirth	
C-section, (n/total)	7
Natural Birth route, (n/total)	23
Apgar score > 7	
at 1 min, n/total	30
at 5 min, n/total	30

All mothers remained in good health throughout their pregnancies, with no history of obstetric complications. Fetal growth was considered appropriate based on ultrasound findings aligned with current clinical guidelines, and confirmed postnatally by a Between the tenth and ninety percentiles for birthweight —adjusted for maternal Parity, weight, and height, and the newborn's gender. Newborns were classified as healthy based on favorable perinatal outcomes, including the absence of No indications of fetal discomfort and maternal sickness, a cord or venous blood pH above 7.2, and Apgar scores exceeding 7 at both 1 and 5 minutes after birth.

D. Determination of Nanoparticle (NP) Content in Breast Milk:

Normal breast milk composition includes elements like phosphorous (P), calcium (Ca), potassium (K), sulfur (S), oxygen (O), carbon (C), and chlorine (Cl). These elements are naturally present as part of essential milk components, including proteins like Vitamins, sugars, lactose, casein, vegetable oils, and carbs. The Energy Dispersive Spectroscopy (EDS) system identifies and measures only the elemental makeup and their relative concentrations, without specifying the exact molecular structures.

In addition to the typical elemental composition of breast milk, other organic elements such as magnesium (Mg) and sodium (Na) were also detected. In some samples, the background (substrate) appeared uniformly grey, showing no significant features. However, in others, bright spots were visible, indicating the presence of denser materials. Specifically, in 12 samples (63%), clusters of white dots—identified as particles with greater atomic density than the organic substrate—were observed. While all EDS spectra included carbon and oxygen (components of the standard milk substrate), the focus was placed on identifying other, less common elements. These particles were composed of various metals and chemical elements.

Table 2. Breast milk nano particles.

Breast Milk	Particle Size
BaS, COSBaCa, COTiCa, COSCaKClP, COZnTi, CRhPdAuOCuCaNiFeZn	1–2 μm
FeCO, COClSK	2–5 μm
COCaPSCl, CFeOCrCaSSi, CSiOCaS	3–6 μm
COCaClK, CFeOTiCaAlMg	4 μm
COCaS, COSiAlKCaSMgNa	2 μm

The full specific elemental makeup of the tiny particles and nanoparticles (NPs) that exist in the samples of breast milk is clarified. The dimension of the detected NPs ranged from less than 1 μm up to 6 μm, independent of the specific elemental makeup. Significantly, many particles appeared as agglomerates, likely formed through interactions between organic compounds and inorganic materials at the micro- and nanoscale.

3 DISCUSSION

Pollution, particularly involving micro- and nanoscale contaminants, has become an increasingly serious global concern, with these small particles contributing significantly to adverse health effects. On one side, contamination begins during pregnancy, where nanosized particles have been shown to reach and impact various fetal organs. On the other side, during the early postnatal period, the primary route of exposure to micro- and nanoparticles is through breast milk (BM). This widespread exposure is largely a result of modern human lifestyles, where contact with both organic and inorganic nanoparticles—particularly those containing heavy metals (HM)—occurs via inhalation, drinking water, and food consumption. While the World Health Organization (WHO) has established safe levels for certain heavy metals, there is still no broad agreement on the potential risks associated with heavy metal contamination in milk products consumed by infants. In this study, the EDS analysis revealed the following findings: (i) 37% of breast milk (BM) samples showed no detectable contamination, (ii) heavy metal (HM) nanoparticle contamination was present in 63% of BM, (iii) BM was associated with mothers residing in industrial areas.

The observational revealed that the presence and size of heavy metal (HM) nanoparticle agglomerates in the breast milk (BM) warrant further investigation. Specifically, regarding HM nanoparticles: (i) once they enter the human body, they circulate systemically and can accumulate in various organs—including the breast—eventually making their way into the milk; (ii) their main interaction is with proteins, which are abundant in milk, leading to the formation of HM–NP–protein complexes. These complexes result from a nano-biointeraction process and appear as agglomerates.

3.1 *Study limitations*

This study has several limitations to acknowledge: 1. Sample Size and Scope: A larger collection of breast milk (BM) ideally originating from the same geographical areas would be necessary to evaluate nanoparticle (NP) variations across identical settings and products. 2. Lifestyle and Diet Data: Detailed information regarding maternal lifestyles and dietary habits was not gathered, limiting insight into potential exposure sources. 3. Quantitative Tracking Over Time: We did not perform NP measurements across different BM samples at multiple time points, hindering our ability to observe temporal changes. 4. Infant Follow-Up: Short-term and long-term health follow-up of infants was not included, preventing assessment of potential developmental impacts.

Future research should address these gaps through studies with larger sample sizes, richer maternal data, repeated sampling over time, and comprehensive infant follow-up.

ACKNOWLEDGEMENT

The authors gratefully acknowledge the students, staff, and authority of SIMATS university for their cooperation in the research.

REFERENCES

[1] Woods, Eason G., Noble B., and Sneddon I.N., (April 1955), On certain integrals of Lipschitz-Hankel type involving products of Bessel functions, *Phil. Trans. Roy. Soc. London*, vol. A247, pp. 529–551.

[2] Clerk Maxwell J., (1892), *A Treatise on Electricity and Magnetism*, 3rd ed., vol. 2. Oxford: Clarendon, pp.68–73.

[3] Jacobs I.S. and Bean C.P., (1963), Fine particles, thin films and exchange anisotropy, in *Magnetism*, vol. III, G. T. Rado and H. Suhl, Eds. New York: Academic, pp. 271–350.

[4] Elissa K., Title of paper if known, unpublished.

[5] Nicole R., Title of paper with only first word capitalized, J. Name Stand. Abbrev., in press.

[6] Yorozu Y., Hirano M., Oka K., and Tagawa Y., Electron spectroscopy studies on magneto-optical media and plastic substrate interface, *IEEE Transl. J. Magn.* Japan, vol. 2, pp. 740–741, August 1987 [Digests 9th Annual Conf. Magnetics Japan, p. 301, 1982].

[7] Young M., (1989), *The Technical Writer's Handbook*. Mill Valley, CA: University Science.

[8] Eves K. and Valasek J., (Aug. 2023), Adaptive control for singularly perturbed systems examples, *Code Ocean*. [Online]. Available: https://codeocean.com/capsule/4989235/tree

[9] Kingma D.P. and Welling M., (2013), *Auto-encoding variational Bayes*, arXiv:1312.6114. [Online]. Available: https://arxiv.org/abs/1312.6114

[10] Liu S., (2023), *Wi-Fi Energy Detection Testbed* (12MTC), gitHub repository. [Online]. Available: https://github.com/liustone99/Wi-Fi-Energy-Detection-Testbed-12MTC

[11] "Treatment episode data set: discharges (TEDS-D): concatenated, 2006 to 2009." U.S. Department of Health and Human Services, Substance Abuse and Mental Health Services Administration, Office of Applied Studies, August, 2013, DOI:10.3886/ICPSR30122.v2

[12] Ajith, M., and Vijayalakshmi, R. (2024, December 27). A study to assess the effectiveness of structured teaching program on knowledge on hand washing among school children at selected school. *Texila International Journal of Public Health*. Advance online publication. https://doi.org/10.21522/TIJPH.2013.SE.25.01.Art 018

[13] Paluchamy, T., Steni, D.S., and Stephen, S. (2024). Effect of green tea mouthwash on chemotherapy-induced oral mucositis in cancer patients. *Journal of Chemical Health Risks*, 14(1). https://doi.org/10.60829/jchr.2024.1103158

[14] Deepika, D., Rajavarshini, and Madaswamy, R. (2024, August 27). Effectiveness of Camphor Oil Application on Reduction of Joint Pain among Post-Menopausal Women at Selected Rural Areas. *Texila International Journal of Public Health, Summer Special Edition.* Advance online publication. https://doi.org/10.21522/TIJPH.2013.SE.24.02.Art 012

[15] Thenmozhi, P., Dineshkumar, P., Bhuvaneswari, G., Mary Minolin, T., and Tamilselvi, S. (2025, February 28). Thoracic squeezing on airway secretion and respiratory parameters in mechanically ventilated patients: An interventional study. *Journal of Education and Health Promotion*, 14(1), 69. https://doi.org/10.4103/jehp.jehp_695_24

Next-Generation Smart Systems – Sekhar et al. (Eds)
 ISBN: 978-1-041-34234-2

Cuminum Cyminum as a Natural Antidiabetic Agent: Evaluating Its Efficacy in Hyperglycemic Control – A Single Center Clinical Trial

Padmapriya D.
Associate Professor, Department of Obstetrics and Gynaecological Nursing, Saveetha College of Nursing, Saveetha Institute of Medical and Technical Sciences, Chennai, Tamil Nadu, India

Suganya M.
Associate Professor, Department of Sociology, Saveetha College of Nursing, Saveetha Institute of Medical and Technical Sciences, Chennai, Tamil Nadu, India

Hemavathi R.
Tutor, Dept. of Obstetrics and Gynaecological Nursing, Saveetha College of Nursing, Saveetha Institute of Medical and Technical Sciences, Chennai, Tamil Nadu, India

Sridevi B.
Assistant Professor, Department of Medical Surgical Nursing, Saveetha College of Nursing, Saveetha Institute of Medical and Technical Sciences, Chennai, Tamil Nadu, India

ABSTRACT: This single-center clinical trial sought to assess the effectiveness of Cuminum cyminum (cumin) in lowering the levels of plasma glucose in people with diabetes type II . A randomized control-group pre-test-post-test model was utilized, featuring 80 diabetic individuals chosen through a non-probability purposive sampling method. Eligible participants had a confirmed diagnosis of DM, were on regular treatment, and exhibited fasting blood sugar (FBS) levels above 130 mg/dL and postprandial blood sugar (PPBS) levels exceeding 180 mg/dL. On Day 1, baseline FBS levels were measured through blood sample collection. On Day 2, demographic data was gathered through a self-designed questionnaire From Day 3, participants in the experimental group (EG) received cumin-infused water after lunch once daily for 56 days, while the control group (CG) established customary hospital care. On Day 60, both FBS and PPBS levels were reassessed. In EG, the findings verified a notable reduction in the levels of blood glucose when associated to the CG. In the EG, the mean pretest FBS was 133.43±6.22 mg/dL, which decreased to 104.70±8.87 mg/dL post-intervention, with average difference 28.73 ($t = 16.6535$, $p < 0.05$). Similarly, the mean pretest PPBS was 163.10±7.44 mg/dL, which decreased to 149.57±5.89 mg/dL post-intervention, with a mean difference of 13.53 ($t = 8.3865$, $p < 0.05$). Analysis using the independent t-test showed a statistically significant difference between the experimental and control groups for both FBS ($t = 13.9317$, $p < 0.001$) and PPBS ($t = 4.0965$, $p < 0.001$). These findings indicate that cumin supplementation significantly enhances glycemic control in individuals with diabetes type II. The study highlights Cuminum cyminum as a promising natural adjunct to conventional diabetes management, warranting further research on its long-term efficacy and potential integration into clinical practice.

Keywords: Cuminum Cyminum, Diabetes Mellitus, Hyperglycemia, Glycemic Control, Herbal Medicine, Blood Glucose Regulation, Antidiabetic Therapy

1 OVERVIEW

Diabetes is a long-term metabolic condition that leads to sustained high blood sugar levels due to inadequate insulin secretion or metabolism. Its global prevalence is rising, with 463 million cases reported in 2020, increasing risks of cardiovascular disease, cancer, and neurodegenerative disorders [1–10]. Contributing factors include genetics, lifestyle, obesity, and aging. Both type 1 and type 2 diabetes involve declining pancreatic β-cell function, aggravated by chronic hyperglycemia, oxidative stress, and metabolic disturbances. Treatment includes pharmacological options like insulin and oral hypoglycemics, alongside lifestyle modifications. Cumin (Cuminum cyminum) has gained attention for its antioxidant and hypoglycemic properties, potentially improving insulin sensitivity [11–20]. This study evaluates cumin supplementation's effects on glycemic control in diabetic patients by analyzing fasting and postprandial blood sugar levels. Findings aim to validate cumin as a complementary approach for diabetes management.

2 LITERATURE SURVEY

Diabetes mellitus (DM) is a mounting universal concern, prompting research into pharmacological and natural interventions. Plant-based therapies, including Cuminum cyminum (cumin), have gained attention for their potential to regulate blood glucose with minimal side effects. Herbal remedies like fenugreek, bitter melon, and turmeric exhibit antihyperglycemic and antioxidant properties, yet require further clinical trials for validation. Cumin, rich in bioactive compounds like cumin aldehyde and flavonoids, has demonstrated insulin-sensitizing and lipid-lowering effects, making it a promising adjunct for diabetes management. Clinical trials show cumin supplementation reduces blood glucose, improves insulin sensitivity, and enhances metabolic health. However, efficacy varies due to dosage and formulation differences, necessitating further large-scale studies. Future research should explore cumin's long-term effects, interactions with medications, and integration into dietary interventions. Standardized clinical trials are essential to confirm cumin's role in diabetes care [21–26]. Diabetes mellitus

DOI: 10.1201/9781042001767-88

represents, necessitating therapeutic interventions that prioritize optimal glycemic regulation. However, conventional treatment modalities frequently exhibit suboptimal long-term outcomes and are often associated with adverse pharmacological effects [27]. Contemporary diagnostic approaches increasingly leverage advanced multivariate regression models to enhance the predictive accuracy and early detection of diabetic conditions [28]. Furthermore, recent comparative clinical evaluations have investigated the therapeutic efficacy and tolerability of neuropharmacological agents [29].

3 MATERIALS AND PATTERNS

Study model: A rigorous A randomized control-group pre-test-post-test model was implemented to evaluate therapeutic efficacy pertaining to Cuminum cyminum in lowering plasma blood glucose levels among personalities with type II DM. *Study Framework:* The study took place over a five-month timeframe, spanning from August 2024 to January 2025 in diabetic clinic of the host institution. *Ethical Approval:* Prior to study initiation,ethical approval was obtained from the Institutional Human Ethics Committee (IHEC) of SIMATS together with official approval from the head of the General Medicine department. *Samples:*60 diabetic participants who met the inclusion criteria were systematically recruited for the study. The research involved male and female participants between the ages of 30 to 70 years, diagnosed with DM, and undergoing regular treatment. Eligible participants had FBS levels above 130 mg/dL and PBBS levels exceeding 180 mg/dL. *Exclusion Criteria:* Participants were excluded if they had a history of localized chronic diabetic complications, bleeding disorders, pulmonary tuberculosis under treatment, psychiatric disorders requiring antipsychotic medications, hypersensitivity to cumin, or were undergoing fertility treatments. Additionally, individuals consuming herbal or alternative complementary therapies (e.g., acupuncture, acupressure, reflexology) for diabetes management, as well as pregnant and lactating women, and non-cooperative individuals, were not included. *Sampling Method:* contributors were nominated employing a non-probability purposive selection approach. The research involved 40 participants in the intervention group and 40 in the control group.. *Informed Consent:* Eachcontributor was systematically conversant about the study's resolution, methodology, and possible benefits. A inscribed conversant consent form was acquired before their inclusion in the study.

Pre-Assessment Procedure: Day 1: Participants were instructed to fast for 12 hours overnight. Day 2: Pretest FBS levels were assessed by collecting 4.5 mL of blood from the antecubital vein. The samples were collected in Mint Green Top (Lithium Heparin Gel) tubes, gently inverted for 8–10 minutes, and centrifuged within two hours. After sample collection, participants consumed breakfast and took their regular antidiabetic medication. Two hours post-meal, a 1 mL blood sample was collected for PBBS testing in a grey-top (Sodium Fluoride/Potassium Oxalate Plasma) tube. Serum and plasma were separated from the cells within 45 minutes, and blood glucose levels were estimated.. Demographic and clinical data from participants was collected through a self-designed questionnaire.

Intervention Protocol: Day 3 to Day 60: Participants in the EG were administered cumin water daily after lunch, while those in the CG expected routine hospital care. The intervention lasted for 56 days. *Preparation of Cuminum Cyminum WaterIngredients:* 3 grams of Cuminum cyminum seeds and 100 mL of water. *Method:* The cumin seeds were boiled in water for 10 minutes to prepare a decoction. The decoction was then strained and stirred well before administration. *Post-Assessment Procedure:* Day 60: Participants were reassessed for FBS and PBBS levels. Blood samples were collected and analyzed using the same method as in the pretest, ensuring consistency and accuracy.

4 RESULTS

4.1 *Assessment of level of FBS in the EG and CG*

In the EG, 1 participant (3.33%) had impaired glucose levels, while 29 participants (96.67%) were classified as diabetic in the pretest. After the intervention, the posttest results showed an improvement, with 3 participants (10%) achieving normal glucose levels and 27 participants (90%) having impaired glucose levels. In the CG, 1 participant (3.33%) had impaired glucose levels, and 29 participants (96.67%) were diabetic in the pretest. In the posttest, 4 participants (13.33%) had impaired glucose levels, while 26 participants (86.67%) remained diabetic, as outlined in Table 1.

4.2 *Assessment on the level of PBBS in the EG and CG*

In the EG, 13 participants (43.33%) had impaired glucose levels, while 17 participants (56.67%) were classified as diabetic during the pretest. However, in the posttest assessment, 1 participant (3.33%) had normal glucose levels, whereas 29 participants (96.67%) showed impaired glucose levels. In the CG, 16 participants (53.33%) had impaired glucose levels, and 14 participants (46.67%) were classified as diabetic during the pretest. In the posttest, the distribution remained nearly the same, with 15 participants (50%) exhibiting impaired glucose levels and 15 participants (50%) continuing to be diabetic, as outlined in Table 2. Hyperglycemia arises from impaired insulin secretion, reduced glucose use, and elevated blood sugar. Conditions like pancreatic cancer, chronic pancreatitis, and endocrine disorders (e.g., Cushing syndrome, acromegaly) can damage insulin production or increase resistance. Other risk factors include high BMI, genetic predisposition, and PCOS. Most participants had high fasting and postprandial blood glucose levels, but specific diabetes risk factors were not assessed. Future research should investigate these factors to better understand diabetes progression and management.

Table 1. Distribution of FBS levels in the EG and CG by frequency and percentage.

	EG				CG			
	Pre Assessment		Post Assessment		Pre Asssessment		Post Assessment	
Level Of FBS	No.	%	No.	%	No.	%	No.	%
Normal	-	-	3	10.00	-	-	-	-
Impaired glucose	1	3.33	27	90.00	1	3.33	4	13.33
Diabetic	29	96.67	-	-	29	96.67	26	86.67

Table 2. Distribution of EG and CG PPBS levels by frequency and percentage.

	EG				CG			
	Pretest		Post Test		Pretest		Post Test	
Level Of PPBS	No.	%	No.	%	No.	%	No.	%
Normal	-	-	1	3.33	-	-	-	-
Impaired glucose	13	43.33	29	96.67	16	53.33	15	50.00
Diabetic	17	56.67	-	-	14	46.67	15	50.00

Table 3. Comparison of level of FBS within the EG and CG.

Level Of *FBS*	Pre assessment Mean	S.D	Post assessment Mean	S.D	Mean Difference Score (MDS)	Paired 't' test value
EG	133.43	6.22	133.37	6.13	0.07	**t = 16.6535 p=0.0001 S*** **
CG	104.7	8.87	132.13	8.29	27.43	t = 1.2787 p=0.2111 N.S
MDS	28.73		**1.24**		*****p<0.001**	
Student Independent 't' test & p-value	T = 0.0554 P=0.9564, N.S		**t = 13.9317 p=0.0001, S*** **		**S – Significant N.S – Not Significant**	

Table 4. Comparison of level of PPBS within the EG and CG.

Level Of PPBS	Pre Assessment Mean	S.D	Post Assessment Mean	S.D	MDS	Paired 't' test value
EG	163.10	7.44	149.57	5.89	13.53	**t = 8.3865 p=0.0001 S*** **
CG	162.43	8.05	162.47	8.04	0.04	t = 1.00 p=0.3259 N.S
MDS	0.67		**12.90**			*****p<0.001**
Student Independent 't' test & p-value	t = 0.4141 p=0.6818, N.S		**t = 4.0965 p=0.0001, S*** **		**S – Significant N.S – Not Significant**	

4.3 *Comparison of level of FBS within the EG and CG*

The mean FBS level was 133.43 mg/dL during the pretest and then decreased to 104.70 mg/dL during the post-test in the EG. The SD for the pretest was 6.22, while for the post-test, it was 8.87. The mean score before the test was 133.43±6.22 and the mean score after the test was 104.70±8.87. The pre-test and post-test had a mean difference of 28.73, and a t-value of 16.6535 indicated statistical significance at p <0.05. Intervention resulted in a significant drop in FBS levels. During the clinical trial, in CG, the mean FBS level was 133.37 mlg/dL prior to the test and 132.13 mg/dL afterwards. SD values for the pretest and post-test were 6.13 and 8.29, respectively. The mean score was 133.37±6.13 in the pretest and 132.13±8.29 in the post-test.The average difference was 0.23, and there was no statistical significance at p< 0.05 with a t-value of 1.2787. This clearly infers there was no notable difference in FBS levels in the CG. Additionally, the independent t-test comparing the experimental and CGs showed a t-value of 0.0554 in the pretest, which was not statistically significant. However, in the posttest, the t-value was 13.9317.The significance of the difference at p<0.001 was high due to a mean difference of 1.24.This demonstrate, EG experienced a significant improvement in FBS levels compared to the CG, as outlined in Table 3.

4.4 *Comparison of level of PBBS within the EG and CG*

The PBBS level averaged 163.10 mg/dL in the pretest and fell to 149.57 mg/dL in the posttest during the EG.The standard deviations (SD) for the pretest and posttest were 7.44 and 5.89, respectively. The pretest mean was 163.10±7.44, and the posttest mean was 149.57±5.89. The mean difference was 13.53, the statistical significance level is p<0.05, but the t-value is 8.3865.This designates a significant decrease in PPBS levels after the intervention. In the CG, the pretest mean for PPBS was 162.43 mg/dL, and the posttest mean was 162.47 mg/dL, The standard deviations are 8.05. and 8.04. Mean score was 161.43±8.05 in the pretest and 162.47±8.04 in the posttest. At p<unk>0.05, the statistical significance was not significant at p<0.05, as the mean difference was just 0.04, with a t-value of 1.00. This suggests there was no meaningful change in PPBS levels in the CG. Additionally, the independent t-test value in the pretest between EGs and CGs was 0.4141, there was no statistical significance.However, in the posttest, the t-value was 4.0965, with a mean difference of 12.90, which was significance at $p<0.001$ statistically which demonstrates that the PPBS levels improved significantly in the EG when compared to the CG, as shown in Table 4. Cuminum Cyminum, a widely cultivated herb, has long been recognized for its therapeutic properties. It has been shown to lower glycosylated haemoglobin and fasting blood glucose levels when supplemented. The essential oil of Cuminum Cyminum has also demonstrated strong α-amylase inhibitory effects, making it a potential antidiabetic agent. Jafari's clinical trial examined the effects of cumin seeds on diabetic patients and found that after 8 weeks of cumin seed supplementation, there was a significant improvement in FBS levels. Similarly, in our study, after 56 days of Cuminum Cyminum administration, there was a notable reduction in both FBS and PBBS levels among the participants.

5 CONCLUSION

Outcomes of present study designate that, administration of Cuminum Cyminum significantly reduced both FBS and PBBS levels in patients with DM. This suggests that Cuminum Cyminum can be an effective, safe, and economical non-pharmacological intervention for managing blood sugar levels in diabetic patients. Given its positive outcomes and lack of reported side effects, Cuminum Cyminum can be incorporated into nursing interventions and included in health education programs for diabetic patients.. Additionally, research could focus on understanding the underlying mechanisms by which Cuminum Cyminum influences glucose metabolism.

REFERENCES

[1] Kumar, P., and Sagetha, J. (2024). *Assessment of Quality of Life Among Type 2 Diabetes Mellitus Patients in an Urban Health Center of Tiruvallur District*, Tamil Nadu. *Cureus*, 16(6), e63320.

[2] Sowmya, S, Sangavi, R., (2024) Effectiveness of Oral Health Education and Interventions in Improving Oral Health Outcomes in Type II Diabetes Mellitus Patients: A Prospective Study *Cureus* 16(4): e58227.

[3] Mukundh, S.T., Veeraraghavan, V.P., Ponnusamy, B., and Jayaraman, S. (2024). Phytochemical Screening and Antidiabetic Activity of Aqueous Extract of Evolvulus Alsinoides Leaves: An In Vitro and Silico Study. *Journal of Pharmacy and Bioallied Sciences,* 16 (2), S1246-S1248.

[4] MAriAppAn, A., pK JABir, D., Babu, S., and Krishnan, M. (2024). Unveiling the Promise of Bioactive Alkaloid Compound from Catharanthus Roseus: An In-vitro Computational Exploration of their Molecular Docking against a Target Protein for Type-2 Diabetes. *Journal of Clinical & Diagnostic Research,* 18(8).

[5] Su, J., Luo, Y., Hu, S., Tang, L., and Ouyang, S. (2023). Advances in research on type 2 diabetes mellitus targets and therapeutic agents. *International Journal of Molecular Sciences,* 24(17), 13381.

[6] Hossain, M.J., Al-Mamun, M., and Islam, M.R. (2024). Diabetes mellitus, the fastest growing global public health concern: Early detection should be focused. *Health Science Reports,* 7(3), e2004.

[7] Diagnosis and Classification of Diabetes: Standards of Care in Diabetes—2025." *Diabetes Care* 48, (1). (2025): S27-S49.

[8] Galicia-Garcia, U., Benito-Vicente, A., Jebari, S., Larrea-Sebal, A., Siddiqi, H., Uribe, K.B., and Martín, C. (2020). Pathophysiology of type 2 diabetes mellitus. *International journal of molecular sciences,* 21 (17), 6275.

[9] Chong, K., Chang, J.K.J., and Chuang, L.M. (2024). Recent advances in the treatment of type 2 diabetes mellitus using new drug therapies. *The Kaohsiung Journal of Medical Sciences*, 40 (3), 212–220.

[10] Patel, D.K., Kumar, R., Laloo, D., and Hemalatha, S. (2012). Diabetes mellitus: an overview of its pharmacological aspects and reported medicinal plants having antidiabetic activity. *Asian Pacific Journal of Tropical Biomedicine*, 2(5), 411–420.

[11] Seedha Devi V., Sumathi K., Mahalakshmi M., Jose Anand A., Anita Titus, and Naga Saranya N., (2024), Machine Learning based Efficient Human Activity Recognition System, *International Journal of Intelligent Systems and Applications in Engineering,* 12 (5s), pp. 338–346.

[12] Jose A., and Dhanalakshmi R., Hygieia: Multipurpose Healthcare Assistance Using the Internet of Things, in Saravanan K., and Aboobucker I., *Internet of Medical Things in Smart Healthcare: Post-COVID-19 Pandemic Scenario*, Apple Acad. Press, pp. 77–98, Sep 2023.

[13] Ponmalar A., and Anand J., (Sep 2023), IoMT-based Caring System for Aged People in a Post-COVID Scenario, in Saravanan Krishnan, and Aboobucker Ilmudeen, *Internet of Medical Things in Smart Healthcare: Post-COVID-19 Pandemic Scenario*, Apple Academic Press, pp. 207–224.

[14] Kavitha Balamurugan, Jose A.A., Vignesh B., Raja Vikram Singan K., and Sri Subramaniam N., (2023), Design of an Intelligent and Smart Pill Box Using Arduino and Sensors, *2023 4th International Conference on Smart Electronics and Communication (ICOSEC),* Trichy, India, pp. 258–263.

[15] Deepika, D., Rajavarshini, and Madaswamy, R., (2024). Effectiveness of Camphor Oil Application on Reduction of Joint Pain among Post-Menopausal Women at Selected Rural Areas. *Texila International Journal of Public Health, Summer Special Edition.* Advance online publication. 2024, August 27, https://doi.org/10.21522/TIJPH.2013.SE.24.02.Art012

[16] Thenmozhi, P., Dineshkumar, P., Bhuvaneswari, G., Mary Minolin, T., and Tamilselvi, S., (2025). Thoracic squeezing on airway secretion and respiratory parameters in mechanically ventilated patients: An interventional study. *Journal of Education and Health Promotion*, 14(1), 69. https://doi.org/10.4103/jehp.jehp_695_24

[17] Muthalagu R., Ramachandran R., Anuradha T., Anupama PH., and Jose A.A., (2023), Pattern Recognition and Modelling in Electrocardiogram Signals: Early Detection of Myocardial Ischemia and Infraction, *2023 2nd International Conference on Edge Computing and Applications (ICECAA),* Namakkal, India, pp. 1035–1041.

[18] Sushma S., Anuradha T., Denslin Brabin D.R., and Jose A.A., (June 2023), Artificial Intelligence in Orthopedic Implant Model Classification, in R. Ranjith., J. Paulo Davim, *"Handbook of Research on Advanced Functional Materials for Orthopedic Applications", IGI Global.*

[19] Geethalakshmi M., Venkatesh J., Uma Maheshwari R., Mahalakshmi A., Anand J., and Partheepan R., (30 Jan 2023), Fuzzy Based Route Optimization in Wearable Biomedical Wireless Sensor Network, *AIP Conference Proceedings* 2523, 020156.

[20] Maheswari R., Vignesh S., Rakesh Kumar M., Venkatesh T.M., Sundar R., and Jose A.A., (2022), Voice Control and Eyeball Movement Operated Wheelchair, *2022 International Conference on Edge Computing and Applications (ICECAA),* pp. 805–809.

[21] Prema S., Jose Anand, Vanitha P., Nirmala Devi K., Mohamed Yaseen M., and Rajeswari C., (Nov 2022), Smart Stick using Ultrasonic Sensors for Visually Impaired, *Advances in Parallel Computing Algorithms, Tools and Paradigms,* Vol. 41, pp. 436–441.

[22] Dhanalakshmi, R., Anand J., Poonkavithai, K., Vijayakumar, V., (24 May 2022), Cloud-Based Glaucoma Diagnosis in Medical Imaging Using Machine Learning, In: Parah, S.A., Rashid, M., Varadarajan, V. (eds) *Artificial Intelligence for Innovative Healthcare Informatics. Springer, Cham*, pp. 61–78.

[23] Dhanalakshmi, R., and Anand J., (06 May 2022), Big Data for Personalized Healthcare, In: A. Jaya, K. Kalaiselvi, Dinesh Goyal and Dhiya AL-Jumelly, (eds*) Handbook of Intelligent Healthcare Analytics: Knowledge Engineering with Big Data Analytics, Chap-4, John Wiley & Sons, Inc.*, pp. 67–92.

[24] Thanzeem Mohamed Sheriff S., Venkat Kumar J., Vigneshwaran S., Aida Jones, and J. Anand, "Lung Cancer Detection using VGG NET 16 Architecture", *International Conference on Physics*

and Engineering 2021, IOP Publishing, Journal of Physics Conference Series, Vol. 2040, 2021.

[25] Paluchamy T., Steni, D.S., and Stephen, S., (2024). Effect of green tea mouthwash on chemotherapy induced oral mucositis in cancer patients. *Journal of Chemical Health Risks*, 14(1). https://doi.org/10.60829/jchr.2024.1103158

[26] Anand J., Gowtham H., Lingeshwaran R., Ajin J., and Karthikeyan J., (November 2021), IoT Based Smart Electrolytic Bottle Monitoring, *Advances in Parallel Computing Technologies and Applications IOS Press*, Vol. 40, pp. 391–399.

[27] Ojo, O., Kalocsányiová, E., McCrone, P., Elliott, H., Milligan, W., and Gkaintatzi, E. (2024). Non-pharmacological interventions for Type 2 diabetes in people living with severe mental illness: results of a systematic review and meta-analysis. *International Journal of Environmental Research and Public Health,* 21(4), 423.

[28] Sahaya Mercy Jaquline R., Neeraj Kumar, Nilajan Saha, and Vidhu Aeri. (2025). Traditional Chinese Medicine as a Source of Anti-diabetic Agents: Investigating the Potential of Leptadenia Reticulata and Marsdenia Tenacissima Roots. *Pharmacological Research - Modern Chinese Medicine. Volume 14,* March 2025, 100583.

[29] Suresh, H.R., Anita Davamani, K., Chandrasekaran, H., and Prabu Sankar, N. (2025). Dual Multi Scale Attention Network Optimized With Archerfish Hunting Optimization Algorithm for Diabetics Prediction. *Microscopy Research and Technique,* 88(4), 947–958.

[30] Reddy Bade, V.Y., Nallusamy, G., Varadaraj, P., and Sandeep Reddy, K.S. (2025). A comparative study of the effectiveness of amitriptyline, pregabalin, and gabapentin in type 2 diabetic patients with peripheral neuropathy. *Romanian medical JouRnal,* 72(1).

Next-Generation Smart Systems – Sekhar et al. (Eds)

Harnessing Avena Sativa as a Natural Technological Approach to Cholesterol Management in Hypercholesterolemia

Padmapriya D.
Assistant Professor, Department of Obstetrics and Gynaecological Nursing, Saveetha College of Nursing, Saveetha Institute of Medical and Technical Sciences, Chennai, Tamil Nadu, India

D. Suganya
Associate Professor, Department of Sociology, Saveetha College of Nursing, Saveetha Institute of Medical and Technical Sciences, Chennai, Tamil Nadu, India

Hemavathi R.
Tutor, Department of Obstetrics and Gynaecological Nursing, Saveetha College of Nursing, Saveetha Institute of Medical and Technical Sciences, Chennai, Tamil Nadu, India

Sridevi B.
Assistant Professor, Department of Medical Surgical Nursing, Saveetha College of Nursing, Saveetha Institute of Medical and Technical Sciences, Chennai, Tamil Nadu, India

ABSTRACT: A study was performed to determine the effectiveness of oats (Avena sativa) in reducing cholesterol levels in 80 individuals who had been diagnosed with hypercholesterolemia. A purposive sampling method was used to select 40 individuals for both the Experimental Groups (EG) and Control Groups (CG) using a non-probability method. On Day 1, the baseline has been established and serum cholesterol levels were measured. From Day 2 onward, participants in the experimental group consumed 3 grams of oats each morning for 56 consecutive days. On Day 57, post-intervention serum cholesterol levels were reassessed. According to the findings, the mean score for both the pretest and posttest cholesterol levels in the experimental group were 178.80 ± 14.15 and 171.82 ± 15.06, respectively, with a mean reduction of 6.98. A paired t-test yielded a statistically significant t-value of 11.410 at $p < 0.001$. Furthermore, when conducting an independent t-test that compared posttest scores between the experimental and control groups, it was discovered that the t-value was 2.124, with a mean difference of 6.85, also statistically momentous at $p < 0.001$. These results suggest that incorporating Avena sativa into the diet is an effective natural approach to managing hypercholesterolemia.

Keywords: Aneva Sativa, Serum Cholesterol Level, Hypercholestremia, Cholesterol management, Beta-glucan, Lipid Metabolis, Cardiovascular Health, Natural Therapy

1 INTRODUCTION

Cardiovascular disease (CVD) is a major global health challenge, with coronary heart disease (CHD) contributing to an increasing proportion of deaths, despite declining overall CVD mortality in developed nations [1]. A key threat factor for heart disease is hyperlipidemia, characterized by elevated levels of triglycerides, cholesterol, low-density lipoproteins (LDL), intermediate-density lipoproteins, and very-low-density lipoproteins (VLDL). Stroke and heart attack account for 85% of CVD-related deaths, primarily triggered by fatty deposits accumulating in blood vessels, leading to blockages. [2–5]. Several factors contribute to hyperlipidemia, including central obesity, high body mass index (BMI), hypertension, hyperthyroidism, liver diseases, use of steroid hormones, anticonvulsants, and anti-infective drugs. It results from disrupted lipid metabolism due to genetic and environmental influences, including excessive lipid production, impaired elimination, or both [6]. One of the primary contributors to atherosclerosis is hypercholesterolemia. Endothelial cell damage is the initial stage of plaque formation, allowing LDL particles to penetrate the vascular wall, leading to blockages, thrombus formation, and restricted blood flow [7]. Treatment for hypercholesterolemia includes pharmacological interventions such as mipomersen, lomitapide, inclisiran, and pelacarsen. Lifestyle modifications also play a crucial role and include nutritional counseling, regular physical activity, and reducing alcohol consumption [8]. PCSK9 peptide vaccines have also shown effectiveness in managing hypercholesterolemia. Non-pharmacological approaches to treating hyperlipidemia include dietary changes, such as reducing fat intake, limiting red meat and dairy consumption, and engaging in aerobic exercise [9].

Oats, one of the oldest cultivated grains, have gained popularity due to their rich nutritional profile, including proteins, carbohydrates, phytochemicals, vitamins, minerals, and dietary fiber. Research suggests that a fiber-rich diet is beneficial for heart health [10–15]. The soluble fiber beta-glucan, found in oats, forms a gel-like ingredient in the intestinal tract, which quandaries cholesterol and bile acids from food, facilitating their excretion. To compensate, the liver increases bile acid production, requiring the uptake of more LDL cholesterol from the bloodstream, ultimately reducing blood cholesterol levels [16–20]. During clinical practice in a hypertension clinic, many patients were observed to suffer from hypercholesterolemia. However, limited research has been conducted on the effects of Avena sativa (oats) in reducing serum cholesterol among individuals with hyperlipidemia. The current study was prompted by a gap in research that aims to evaluate and associate pre- and post-test serum cholesterol levels in individuals with hyperlipidemia in both experimental and control groups. [20–25].

DOI: 10.1201/9781042001767-89

2 LITERATURE REVIEW

Several studies have explored the potential of Avena sativa (oats) as a natural dietary intervention for managing hypercholesterolemia, with growing evidence supporting its role in reducing cholesterol levels through its rich composition of bioactive compounds. Oats are widely recognized for their high content of beta-glucan, a soluble fiber that has been comprehensively deliberate for its cholesterol-lowering belongings [1–5]. Research suggests that beta-glucan enhances intestinal viscosity, reducing cholesterol absorption and promoting its excretion, thereby lowering Low Density Lipoprotein (LDL) cholesterol levels. [6–10]. Another study demonstrated that oat-based interventions led to a 5-10% reduction in serum cholesterol levels among hypercholesterolemic individuals. Additionally, randomized controlled trials (RCTs) have shown that the inclusion of oats in the diet positively affects lipid metabolism and cardiovascular health by modulating bile acid synthesis and reducing inflammatory markers associated with atherosclerosis. In a study oat consumption was associated with improved endothelial function, a key factor in preventing arterial plaque formation [11–15]. The cholesterol-lowering effect of Avena sativa has also been attributed to its polyphenols, saponins, and phytosterols, which contribute to antioxidant and anti-inflammatory activities, further protecting against cardiovascular diseases. Furthermore, research has compared the efficacy of oat-based interventions with pharmacological treatments such as statins, highlighting oats as a complementary or alternative approach for individuals seeking natural cholesterol management strategies. Another study indicated that oat supplementation, when combined with a healthy lifestyle, can significantly enhance lipid profiles without the side effects commonly associated with lipid-lowering medications. In addition, advances in food technology have enabled the incorporation of oats into functional foods, such as oat bran-enriched beverages and fortified cereals, to maximize its cholesterol-lowering potential [16–20]. Despite the promising findings, gaps remain in understanding the long-term effects of oats on lipid metabolism across diverse populations and dietary habits. Future research should focus on optimizing oat-based formulations and assessing their synergistic effects with other natural bioactives to enhance their efficacy in cholesterol management. This growing body of literature underscores the significance of Avena sativa as a natural, technological approach to managing hypercholesterolemia, offering a safe, effective, and sustainable dietary intervention for cardiovascular health [21–25].

3 MATERIALS AND METHODS

Study Model: A approach to CG exploration based on a quasi-experimental pretest-posttest was employed to assess the usefulness of Avena sativa (oats) in lowering serum cholesterol levels among individuals with hypercholesterolemia.

Study Frame work: The Hypertension Outpatient Clinic of the host institution was the location for this study, which took place over a three-month period from June 2024 to January 2025.

Ethical Approval: Before launching the study, the Institutional Human Ethics Committee (IHEC) and General Medicine department head obtained ethical approval and formal written authorization.

Respondents: Overall 80 clients diagnosed with hyperlipidemia who met the eligibility

y measures were enrolled as study contributors. Both male and female patients between the ages of 30 and 70, with serum cholesterol levels exceeding 240 mg/dL and undergoing regular treatment at the Hypertension Clinic, were included. However, individuals with gastrointestinal disorders, anemia, oat intolerance, a history of consuming herbal supplements or undergoing alternative therapies such as acupuncture, acupressure, or reflexology, as well as pregnant and lactating women, and those unwilling to participate, were eliminated in the current study.

Sampling Technique: The method for nominating participants was non-probability purposive sampling. selection performance. The sample was divided into two groups: 40 individuals in the EG and 40 in the CG.

Informed Consent: The study's objectives, procedures, and potential outcomes were discussed in detail with each participant. Preliminary Assessment: On the first day of the study, participants were instructed to fast overnight before arriving at the biochemistry laboratory for baseline serum cholesterol measurement. Blood samples (0.5–1 mL) were collected from the antecubital vein and transferred into an EDTA tube. The samples were left to clot at room temperature, after which the serum was separated from blood cells within two hours through centrifugation. Additionally, demographic and clinical data were congregated consuming a self-structured feedback form.

Intervention Details: From Day 2 onward, participants in the experimental group consumed 3 grams of oats daily in the morning for a total of 56 days.

Preparation of Avena sativa (Oats): Three grams of oats were boiled in 150 mL of water for 10–15 minutes. The mixture was then strained, and a pinch of salt was added and stirred thoroughly before consumption.

Post-Assessment: On Day 57, participants underwent a follow-up assessment to measure post-intervention serum cholesterol levels using the same methodology as in the preliminary assessment.

4 RESULTS

In the experimental group, the mean total cholesterol levels before and after the intervention were 178.80 ± 14.15 and 171.82 ± 15.06, respectively, reflecting a mean reduction of 6.98. The paired t-test yielded a statistically significant t-value of 11.410 at $p < 0.001$, indicating a notable decline in total cholesterol levels following the administration of Avena sativa (oats) among individuals with hyperlipidemia. Conversely, in the control group, the mean total cholesterol levels before and after the study periods were 178.90 ± 13.6 and 178.67 ± 13.75, respectively, with 0.23 mean difference where corresponding t-test result t = 1.597 did not acheive statistical significance, with no meaningful reduction in total cholesterol levels among participants who followed the hospital's standard treatment protocol without the oat intervention.

Furthermore, a comparison between the EG and CG at reference point showed no statistically noteworthy variance in cholesterol levels, as indicated by the self-determining t-test value of t = 0.032 during pre assessment phase. However, in post-test phase, the independent t-test t = 2.124, with mean 6.85, was statistically noteworthy at $p < 0.01$. This finding underscores that the incorporation of Avena sativa (oats) as a dietary intervention was considerably more effective in lowering total cholesterol levels compared to the routine hospital protocol followed by the CG.Table 1 demonstrates the effectiveness of this natural approach in more detail.

Consuming beta-glucan has been recognized for its ability to enhance the viscosity of the upper gastrointestinal tract, which in turn encapsulates and binds bile acid micelles, prominent to an upsurge in bile acid excretion. This process stimulates the liver to utilize circulating cholesterol as a primary substrate for bile acid synthesis, thereby accelerating the production of bile acids from scratch. [23].

Upon revising the prevailing literature, it was observed that there was a lack of studies specifically evaluating the

Table 1. Cholesterol among Clients with Hyperlipidemia within and Between EG and CG (N = 80 (40 ++ 40)).

Total Cholesterol	Pre assessment Mean	S.D	Post assessment Mean	S.D	Mean Difference Score	Paired 't' test value
EG	178.80	14.15	171.82	15.06	**6.98**	**t = 11.410 p=0.0001 S*** **
CG	178.90	13.69	178.67	13.75	0.23	t = 1.597 p=0.118 N.S
Average Score Student Independent 't' test & p-value	0.10 t = 0.032 p=0.974, N.S		**6.85 t = 2.124 p=0.037, S***		*****p<0.001, *p<0.05 S - Significant N.S – Not Significant, p>0.05**	

constructive effects of oats in individuals with hypercholesterolemia, particularly among the South Indian population. This gap in research motivated the investigators to undertake this clinical trial to assess whether oats play a significant role in regulating cholesterol levels in humans. Encouragingly, the findings of this study demonstrated that Avena sativa (oats) effectively contributed to reducing cholesterol levels, reinforcing its potential as a natural dietary intervention for managing hypercholesterolemia.

5 CONCLUSION

The findings of this study provide compelling evidence that Avena sativa (oats) has a significant impact on reducing serum cholesterol levels among individuals with hypercholesterolemia. As a natural dietary intervention, oats offer a promising non-pharmacological approach to cholesterol management, helping to mitigate the risks associated with elevated lipid levels. The study reinforces the potential of beta-glucan-rich oats in improving lipid metabolism by enhancing bile acid excretion and promoting cholesterol utilization. Given the effectiveness observed in this trial, integrating oats into daily dietary habits can serve as a practical and accessible strategy for individuals seeking to regulate cholesterol levels and reduce the likelihood of cardiovascular complications. Healthcare professionals and nutritionists should advocate for the inclusion of oats as part of a heart-healthy diet, particularly for those at risk of atherosclerotic cardiovascular diseases.

While this study establishes the effectiveness of Avena sativa in lowering cholesterol, future research should explore additional factors to strengthen its applicability and impact. Long-term clinical trials with larger, more diverse populations across different ethnicities and age groups should be conducted to validate these findings on a broader scale. Investigating the synergistic effects of oats with other dietary modifications, lifestyle interventions, and pharmacological treatments can provide a more comprehensive understanding of its role in cholesterol management. Furthermore, research into the molecular mechanisms behind oat-derived bioactive compounds, such as beta-glucan and oat-specific proteins, can help optimize their therapeutic potential.

REFERENCES

[1] Unadkat, S.V., Padhi, B.K., Bhongir, A.V., Gandhi, A.P., Shamim, M.A., Dahiya, N., and Serhan, H.A. (2024). Association between homocysteine and coronary artery disease—trend over time and across the regions: a systematic review and meta-analysis. *The Egyptian Heart Journal*, 76(1), 29.

[2] Singh, S., Zahoor, I., Sharma, N., Behl, T., Kanojia, N., Sehgal, A., Mohan, S., Almoshari, Y., Salawi, A., Aleya, L., and Bungau, S. (2022). Insights into the pivotal role of statins and its nanoformulations in hyperlipidemia. *Environmental science and pollution research international*, 29(51), 76514–76531.

[3] Sathvika K and Mahalakshmi J. (2023). DMFT score in cardiovascular disorder versus non-cardiovascular disorder patients. *J Clinic Dent Oral Health.*;7(1):132

[4] Abbasi, S., Khan, A., and Choudhry, M.W. (2024). New Insights Into the Treatment of Hyperlipidemia: Pharmacological Updates and Emerging Treatments. *Cureus*, 16(6), e63078.

[5] Abera, A., Worede, A., Hirigo, A.T., Alemayehu, R., and Ambachew, S. (2024). Dyslipidemia and associated factors among adult cardiac patients: a hospital-based comparative cross-sectional study. *European Journal of Medical Research*, 29 (1), 237.

[6] Won, H., Bae, J.H., Lim, H., Kang, M., Kim, M., Lee, S.H., and Clinical Practice Guidelines Committee. (2024). 2024 KSoLA consensus on secondary dyslipidemia. *The Korean journal of internal medicine*, 39(5), 717.

[7] Mormone, A., Tortorella, G., Esposito, F., Caturano, A., Marrone, A., Cozzolino, D., and Rinaldi, L. (2024). Advances in Pharmacological Approaches for Managing Hypercholesterolemia: A Comprehensive Overview of Novel Treatments. *Biomedicines*, 12(2), 432.

[8] Seedha Devi V., Sumathi K., Mahalakshmi M., Anand A.J., Anita Titus, and Naga Saranya N., (2024), Machine Learning based Efficient Human Activity Recognition System, *International Journal of Intelligent Systems and Applications in Engineering*, 12 (5s), pp. 338–346.

[9] Jose A., and Dhanalakshmi R., (Sep 2023), Hygieia: Multipurpose Healthcare Assistance Using the Internet of Things, in Saravanan K., and Aboobucker I., *Internet of Medical Things in Smart Healthcare: Post-COVID-19 Pandemic Scenario*, Apple Acad. Press, pp. 77–98.

[10] Ponmalar A., and Anand J., (Sep 2023), IoMT-based Caring System for Aged People in a Post-COVID Scenario, in Saravanan Krishnan, and Aboobucker Ilmudeen, *Internet of Medical Things in Smart Healthcare: Post-COVID-19 Pandemic Scenario*, Apple Academic Press, pp. 207–224.

[11] Kavitha Balamurugan, Jose A.A., Vignesh B., Raja Vikram Singan K., and Sri Subramaniam N., (2023), Design of an Intelligent and Smart Pill Box Using Arduino and Sensors, *2023 4th International Conference on Smart Electronics and Communication (ICOSEC)*, Trichy, India, pp. 258–263.

[12] Muthalagu R., Ramachandran R., Anuradha T., Anupama PH., and Jose A.A., (2023), Pattern Recognition and Modelling in Electrocardiogram Signals: Early Detection of Myocardial Ischemia and Infraction, *2023 2nd International Conference on Edge Computing and Applications (ICECAA)*, Namakkal, India, pp. 1035–1041.

[13] Sushma S., Anuradha T., Denslin Brabin D.R., and Jose A.A., (June 2023), Artificial Intelligence in Orthopedic Implant Model Classification, in R. Ranjith., J. Paulo Davim, Handbook of Research on Advanced Functional Materials for Orthopedic Applications, *IGI Global.*

[14] Satapathy, P., Gaidhane, A.M., Vadia, N., Menon, S.V., Chennakesavulu, K., Panigrahi, R., and Mawejje, E. (2025).

Exposure to violence and risk of hypertensive disorders in pregnancy: Systematic review and meta-analysis. *European Journal of Obstetrics & Gynecology and Reproductive Biology: X*, 100398.

[15] Maheswari R., Vignesh S., Rakesh Kumar M., Venkatesh T.M., Sundar R., and Jose A.A., (2022), Voice Control and Eyeball Movement Operated Wheelchair, *2022 International Conference on Edge Computing and Applications (ICECAA)*, pp. 805–809.

[16] Elbanna, Iman A.a; Naveen Karthik P.b; elvankumar, Thangaswamyc, (March 2025), The Impact of Dietary Cholesterol on LDL Cholesterol Levels in Adults: A Short-Term Observational Study *Texila International Journal of Public Health* Volume 13, Issue 1.

[17] Dhanalakshmi, R., and Anand J., (06 May 2022), Big Data for Personalized Healthcare, In: A. Jaya, K. Kalaiselvi, Dinesh Goyal and Dhiya AL-Jumelly, (eds) *Handbook of Intelligent Healthcare Analytics: Knowledge Engineering with Big Data Analytics*, Chap-4, John Wiley & Sons, Inc., pp. 67–92.

[18] Thanzeem Mohamed Sheriff S., Venkat Kumar J., Vigneshwaran S., Aida Jones, and Anand J., (2021), Lung Cancer Detection using VGG NET 16 Architecture, International Conference on Physics and Engineering 2021, IOP Publishing, *Journal of Physics Conference Series*, Vol. 2040.

[19] Niranjana S., Hareshaa S.K., Irene ZibiahBasker, and Jose A., (November 2021), Smart Wearable System to Assist Asthma Patients, *Advances in Parallel Computing Technologies and Applications*, IOS Press, Vol 40, pp. 219–227.

[20] Usman, P.A.S., Ameya, K.P., and Sekar, D. (2025). Revolutionary advances in hypertension detection: Gold nanoparticle-enhanced miRNA-based electrochemical biosensors and emerging nanotechnologies. *Human Gene*, 201401.

[21] Amerizadeh, A., Ghaheh, H.S., Vaseghi, G., Farajzadegan, Z., and Asgary, S. (2023). Effect of oat (Avena sativa L.) consumption on lipid profile with focus on triglycerides and high-density lipoprotein cholesterol (HDL-C): An updated systematic review. *Current Problems in Cardiology*, 48(7), 101153.

[22] Sahebkar, A., and Banach, M. (2024). Transforming hypercholesterolemia management: Spotlight on PCSK9 peptide vaccines. *Cell Reports Medicine*, 5(9).

[23] Paudel, D., Dhungana, B., Caffe, M., and Krishnan, P. (2021). A review of health-beneficial properties of oats. *Foods*, 10(11), 2591.

[24] Deepika, D., Rajavarshini, and Madaswamy, R., (2024). Effectiveness of Camphor Oil Application on Reduction of Joint Pain among Post-Menopausal Women at Selected Rural Areas. *Texila International Journal of Public Health, Summer Special Edition*. Advance online publication. 2024, August 27, https://doi.org/10.21522/TIJPH.2013.SE.24.02.Art012

[25] Paluchamy T., Steni, D.S., and Stephen, S., (2024). Effect of green tea mouthwash on chemotherapy induced oral mucositis in cancer patients. *Journal of Chemical Health Risks*, 14(1). https://doi.org/10.60829/jchr.2024.1103158

[26] Thenmozhi, P., Dineshkumar, P., Bhuvaneswari, G., Mary Minolin, T., and Tamilselvi, S., (2025). Thoracic squeezing on airway secretion and respiratory parameters in mechanically ventilated patients: An interventional study. *Journal of Education and Health Promotion*, 14(1), 69. https://doi.org/10.4103/jehp.jehp_695_24

Next-Generation Smart Systems – Sekhar et al. (Eds)
© 2027 The Author(s), ISBN: 978-1-041-34234-2

Assessment of Water Quality and Restoration Approaches for Ibrahimpatnam Lake, Telangana (India)

A. Rohini
Senior Assistant Professor in Environmental Science, Department of Humanities and Sciences, CVR College of Engineering, Ibrahimpatnam, Telangana, India

ABSTRACT: Water scarcity being a significant environmental issue, the current emphasis is on restoring the quality of existing water resources, especially lakes as they are vital water resources for human use. Lakes account for 0.3% of all surface water bodies, which is part of the one percent of freshwater accessible on earth's surface. Human factors sewage discharge, effluents of industries, agrochemicals, urban runoff and solid waste dumping are causing water scarcity by contaminating lake ecosystems. Ibrahimpatnam lake, a vital freshwater body near Hyderabad city is facing ecological challenges like encroachment, siltation, domestic and religious pollution by agricultural runoff, household waste water and ritual waste. Massive construction activities have encroached upon the lake's area. As a result of the aforementioned activities, the lakes water quality is declining turning it into a eutrophic lake. To deal with this problem, the management of water quality has become crucial, employing standardized methods to assess various parameters such as pH, carbonates, bicarbonates, chlorides, dissolved oxygen, organic matter, chemical oxygen demand, total hardness and total dissolved solids. Elevated levels of pollution have been detected in the lake when compared against standard permissible limits (IS 10500:2012) emphasizing the necessity for immediate action. Implementing sustainable management practices like installation of a sewage treatment plant and aeration systems,lake revitalization by desilting and deweeding, community involvement and continuous monitoring can safeguard the health of the freshwater lake assuring lasting advantages to the society.

Keywords: Restoration, Sustainable lake management, Ibrahimpatnam lake, Physico-chemical parameters, Water quality, Eutrophication

1 INTRODUCTION

Water comes from a variety of sources on the planet Earth. Freshwater resources are scarce just around 2.5 percent of Earth's water is fresh and majority of that is frozen as polar ice caps and glaciers. Industrial and agricultural waste, sewage, inappropriate waste management poses a hazard to water resources [1]. Lakes in India have become the dumping grounds for domestic sewage, industrial effluents, municipal solid waste and agricultural runoff. Lake areas have been encroached upon due to human pressure [2]. Hyderabad, the "City of Lakes", which was formerly known, once heavily relied on lakes for meeting the water demands. These lakes served essentially for drinking, irrigation, fishing and other domestic needs [3]. Currently, the city has 185 freshwater lakes which are seriously threatened. The major issue is the urban sprawl consuming the lake areas and some lakes are dried up due to rainfall patterns which has declined water tables.

Physical, chemical and biological traits that vary seasonally and affect the general state of waterbodies are the main focus of water quality assessments [4]. Physical, chemical and phycological aspects of water quality are the strong indicators of the quality because they react quickly to environment. Water parameter studies emphasize the need of lake conservation and restoration for environmentally conscious planning and sustainable use [5]. This study examines Ibrahimpatnam lake's physicochemical properties in detail, identifies pollution sources and mention about conservation approaches. The present investigation was carried out as Ibrahimpatnam Lake, which was formerly ueed for agricultural, household and drinking purposes, is presently under developmental pressure due to growing human population.

2 MATERIALS AND METHODOLOGY

2.1 *Study area*

Ibrahimpatnam lake is located 35 kilometers from Hyderabad, the capital of Telangana state. Between 1550 and 1580 AD, Ibrahim Qutub Shah constructed Ibrahimpatnam lake. The people of Ibrahimpatnam relied on the lake for their drinking, domestic and farming needs [6]. Due to extensive urbanization surrounding the lake and the disposal of domestic waste and untreated sewage from neighbouring settlements, religious celebrations where idols are immersed in water, this lake has now become the victim of human negligence. The water in the lake is unfit for human or animal consumption. Large scale constructions in the lake's catchment area caused the encroachment of the lake reducing the lake area.

Figure 1. Ibrahimpatnam lake.

2.2 *Sampling locations*

Based on the viability of approaching the lake to collect the water samples and also taking into account the causes of pollution, three sampling locations were chosen which cover the left side, right side and middle of the lake. First site is the Station I which is located at the left side of the lake. During religious celebrations, the idols are submerged at this location which release heavy metal pollutants together with puja materials and other organic garbage by the people. The center of the lake, where a temple is located, represents station II. Solid trash is disposed by the visitors to the temple. Station III is situated on the lake's right side which receives sewage through the drains from nearby colonies.

Seasonally, water samples were taken from the lake's three monitoring sites before, during and after the monsoon. Surface water samples were taken from the lake in sterile one-liter polythene containers between 8AM and 9AM on a monthly basis for a year, beginning in January 2024 and ending in December 2024. On the same day, water samples were analyzed in the lab using conventional procedures [7] to estimate a variety of physical and chemical properties.

2.3 *Estimation of physico-chemical parameters*

Standard protocols (APHA, 2005) were followed to analyze the following parameters:

- Temperature: Measured onsite using a Mercury thermometer
- pH: Determined using a portable pH meter to evaluate water acidity or alkalinity
- Carbonates and Bicarbonates: Measured using the titrimetric method.
- Chlorides: Estimated using Argentometric titration.
- Dissolved oxygen (DO): Measured using the Winkler's titration method.
- Organic matter (OM): Measured using Potassium permanganate titration.
- Chemical oxygen demand (COD): Measured using Potassium dichromate titration.
- Total Hardness, Calcium and Magnesium: Measured using EDTA titration.
- Total Dissolved Solids (TDS): Measured using a portable TDS meter.

3 RESULTS AND DISCUSSION

Seasonal fluctuations were observed in physical and chemical characteristics of Ibrahimpatnam Lake. Data was gathered from the three lake monitoring stations and focused on the following: temperature, pH, carbonates, bicarbonates, chlorides, dissolved oxygen, organic matter, chemical oxygen demand, calcium, magnesium, total hardness, total dissolved solids, nitrites and phosphates.

Ibrahimpatnam Lake's physicochemical variables average values and the IS (10500: 2012) criteria [8] are shown in Table 1.

Table 1. Comparison of physicochemical parameters with IS (10500:2012) standards.

S.No	Parameters	Ibrahimpatnam lake	IS(10500:2012)
1	**pH**	8.3	6.5 – 8.5
2	**CO_3^{2-}**	24.3	-
3	**HCO_3^-**	245.14	-
4	**Cl^-**	368.62	250 mg/L
5	**DO**	2.5	6 mg/L
6	**OM**	10.8	-
7	**COD**	340.6	250 mg/L
8	**TH**	422.5	600 mg/L
9	**Ca^{2+}**	83.3	75 mg/L
10	**Mg^{2+}**	60.8	30 mg/L
11	**TDS**	640	500 mg/L

The concentration of carbonates, bicarbonates, chlorides, chemical oxygen demand, total hardness and total dissolved solids in Ibrahimpatnam Lake is high but the concentration of dissolved oxygen is low.

The lake exhibited alkalinity having an average pH value of 8.3. Bicarbonates in high level indicate high organic matter in the lake due to inflow of untreated sewage [9]. Chlorides are in high concentration in comparison with stipulated standards. Presence of chlorides indicate high degree of pollution of fresh water due to large amounts of domestic sewage [10].

The most important parameter to assess water quality is Dissolved oxygen. Lakes that show depletion of dissolved oxygen are classified as eutrophic. DO affects the growth of aquatic organisms. High nutrients and organic pollution decrease the DO values. Ibrahimpatnam lake is facing lack of oxygen to maintain aerobic conditions turning the lake eutrophic [11]. Chemically oxidizable organic matter (COD) in water is an indication of a lake's ecological health. Organic waste, low dissolved oxygen and high sediments contribute to the lake's elevated COD content [12].

The hardness of water is a crucial factor to consider when using water for household purposes. Calcium and magnesium salts cause hardness of water. Ibrahimpatnam Lake has more total hardness due to inflow of domestic waste with high content of detergents [13]. All Natural waterways are rich in calcium. Because of the sewage from the adjacent inhabitants, the lake has a higher calcium concentration. The concentration of magnesium is often lower than that of calcium, despite the fact that it is regularly found in water of all types with calcium [14].

A measure of the total amount of inorganic compounds dissolved in water is Total dissolved solids. The concentrations of TDS were found to be greater in the lake. Total dissolved solids levels are elevated because sewage leaches a variety of contaminants into the water's surface. Potability of water is reduced when TDS increases [15].

Carbonates, bicarbonates, chlorides, total hardness, COD and total dissolved solids of Ibrahimpatnam Lake are above the permissible limits.

4 CONCLUSIONS

The findings of the study of the Ibrahimpatnam lake demonstrate that the parameters carbonates, bicarbonates, chlorides, total hardness, COD and total dissolved solids exceed IS (10500:2012) standards and the recorded dissolved oxygen is low confirming pollution and eutrophication of the lake. Solid trash, municipal waste and untreated sewage are the main causes of lake's degradation. Furthermore, contaminants from the lake seep into the ground water rendering it unsuitable for human consumption.

For the Ibrahimpatnam Lake to be conserved and restored, sustainable management practices need to be implemented.

Key recommendations for Ibrahimpatnam Lake restoration

Ibrahimpatnam Lake could be rehabilitated through sustainable practices and strategic measures by collaboration between government authorities, scientific institutions and local communities. Some of the sustainable approaches are

1. Wastewater treatment by installing a Sewage treatment plant to treat the domestic waste water, to reduce organic pollution and to prevent eutrophication.
2. Sustainable farming practices to promote organic agriculture to minimize nutrient flow
3. Dredging to remove accumulated sediments on lake bed to increase water holding capacity of the lake.
4. Deweeding to remove unwanted aquatic weeds like Eichhornia, a water Hyacinth growing profusely in the lake.

5. Installation of aerators to keep oxygen levels consistent throughout the water column.
6. Designing separate artificial waterbodies like small ponds for immersing idols during religious activities
7. Community engagement by educating local communities on sustainable water use, pollution prevention and conservation, involving them in cleanup drives and monitoring programs.
8. Policy recommendations like Lake Conservation policies by the government to be undertaken with the help of stakeholders to promote Eco-tourism by beautification of the lake and continuous monitoring of water quality and pollution levels.

REFERENCES

[1] Rohini A. and Manikya Reddy P. (2022) Assessment of water quality in Safilguda lake, *Hyderabad using Water Quality Index, Ecology, Environment and Conservation*, 28, S101–S106.

[2] Jagan K., Seeta Y. and Manikya Reddy P. (2022) Ecological studies on Kapra Lake with reference to water quality, *Bull.Env. Pharmacol.Life Sci.* 11, 49–54.

[3] Asha G., Deepthi BP., Achyuth K.N., Suman Kundapura and Harikeerthan M.K. (2025) Evaluation of water quality and Sustainable Management Strategies for Varthur lake, Bengaluru, *International Journal of Innovation Studies*, 9. DOI 10.6084/m9.figshare.26328006

[4] Krishnaveni B., Shailaja K. and Chapla J. (2024) *Water Quality Assessment of Bibinagar Lake by Physico-Chemical Parameters, Environmental Reports*, 6.

[5] Siddiqui Qurratulayen, Raut Ranjit, Shaikh Yasmeen and Suryawanshi G.D. (2025) Studies on Physicochemical Parameters of Kalvati Lake in Ambajogai, *IJRSEAS*, 2, 1–4. DOI: 10.5281/zenodo.15322396

[6] Navatha K., Nirmala K. and Manikya Reddy P. (2013) Trophic status of Ibrahimpatnam lake with reference to physico-chemical and phycological characteristics, *Pollution Research*, 32, 473–476.

[7] American Public Health Association, *APHA (2005) Standard methods for examination of water and waste water*, 21st edition, Washington D C.

[8] Bureau of Indian Standards (2012) *Drinking water specifications.*

[9] Thaher Hussain MD., Seeta Y. and Manikya Reddy P. (2023) Water quality assessment in the River Godavari, Near Manthani, Telangana, *Journal of Survey in Fisheries Sciences*, 10, 605–609.

[10] DuraiArulneyam and Premsudha (2018) Assessment of water quality in Saroornagar lake, Hyderabad. *International journal of Civil Engineering and Technology*, 9, 1092–1104.

[11] Premsudha, Tirupathi and Madhusudhan, (2022) Evaluation of Physico-chemical parameters to assess Hussain sagar lake and Saroornagar lake water quality in Hyderabad, Telangana, India. *International journal of advanced research in science, communication and Technology*, 2, 543–550.

[12] Padma Priya K.T., Seeta Y. and Manikya Reddy P. (2022) Comparative Study of Physico-Chemical Parameters in Saroornagar Lake and Ramanthapur Pedda Cheruvu. *International Journal of Scientifi Research in Science and Technology*, 9, 11–15.

[13] Veerendra Babu A., Seeta Y. and Manikya Reddy P. (2018) Ecological studies of Alisagar lake with reference to water quality. *International journal of current research*, 10, 69989–69992.

[14] Navatha K., Amin and Manikya Reddy P. (2013) Limnological studies of Ibrahimpatnam lake with reference to water quality, *Ecology, Environment and Conservation*, 19, 859–863.

[15] Raji and Mary kutty Abraham (2018) Comparative study of water quality of different lakes in Chennai. *Rasayan journal of chemistry*, 11, 828–833.

Next-Generation Smart Systems – Sekhar et al. (Eds)
© 2027 The Author(s), ISBN: 978-1-041-34234-2

Assessment of Perceived Personality Changes due to Birth Order among Adults

Jagadeeswari J.
Assistant Professor, Saveetha College of Nursing, Saveetha Institute of Medical and Technical Sciences, Chennai, Tamil Nadu, India

Sakthi Priya S.
BSc Nursing, Saveetha College of Nursing, Saveetha Institute of Medical and Technical Sciences, Chennai, Tamil Nadu, India

Vijayalakshmi R.
Principal, Saveetha College of Nursing, Saveetha Institute of Medical and Technical Sciences, Chennai, India

Sindhu Ramalingam
Associate Professor, Saveetha College of Nursing, Saveetha Institute of Medical and Technical Sciences, Chennai, India

ABSTRACT: Birth order, It has long been hypothesized that a child's birth order within one's family impacts their personality and social growth. This concept, first introduced by Alfred Adler, emphasizes how family dynamics and hierarchical roles may shape psychosocial growth. The intent of the present investigation was to evaluate the perceived personality variations among adults based on their birth order status—categorized as firstborn, second-born, third-born, or only child. A descriptive research design was employed, involving 60 adult participants selected through a convenient sampling manner. The data was collected with demographic data and NEO Five-Factor Inventory (NEO-FFI), a validated psychometric tool to evaluate five major personality domains. Participants required approximately 20 to 30 minutes to complete the assessment. Statistical analysis revealed a significant association between age and the level of perceived personality differences attributed to birth order, with a chi-square value of 11.869 ($p = 0.018$). These verdicts suggest that age may mediate the correlation between personality examinations and birth order. In conclusion, the investigation provides empirical support for the theory that birth order contributes to temperament development, highlighting the need for further research to explore this dynamic across diverse populations and cultural contexts.

Keywords: Birth Order, Personality Changes, Demographic Variables, Data Collection

1 INTRODUCTION

The order of a family's childbirth is known as the "birth order." It implies that the status of a child among their siblings can influence various aspects of their personality, behavior, and development.[1] Psychologist Alfred Adler, a pioneer in this field, proposed that family dynamics shape individuals differently depending on whether they are the eldest, middle, youngest, or only child.[2] For instance, firstborns are frequently characterized as accountable and focused on leadership, middle children as self-sufficient and flexible, and youngest youngsters as outgoing and sometimes rebellious, and only children as mature but possibly self-centered [3]. However, depending on parameters like family size and the age difference between siblings, the consequences of birth order can differ, and each child's temperament. [4] Generally, birth order types include the firstborn, second-born or middle child, youngest, and only child, each associated with distinct traits shaped by upbringing and family environment. Adler believed that a child's early environment, shaped largely by their birth order, could influence their personality and future choices. He also noted that parents often adjust their parenting style according to the child's behavior and needs, which further shapes personality development.[5] The five-factor model of personality, which encompasses characteristics like conscientiousness, agreeableness, openness, neuroticism, and extraversion, is consistent with this idea. [6].

For instance, firstborns may show higher levels of neuroticism due to the shift in attention when a new sibling arrives. Eldest children tend to value structure and authority, while only children may struggle with independence due to constant attention and limited peer interaction.[7] A child's development is influenced not only by their position in the family but also by how they interact with their surroundings. Parents may give more attention to the firstborn, while younger siblings often experience more relaxed parenting styles. Each new child represents a different parenting experience, potentially impacting sibling dynamics and individual behavior [8]. According to some psychologists, birth order has little bearing on fundamental personality traits, though it may influence behaviors such as academic focus, discipline, and anxiety levels.[9] Firstborns may receive more structured guidance and pressure, while younger children might benefit from a more flexible approach, often performing better academically in some cases [10]. There are difficulties in examining how personality is affected by birth order.[11] These include the subjective nature of personality assessments, differences in family dynamics, inconsistent definitions, and cultural influences. [12] Other limitations include small sample sizes and the complexity of tracking personality changes over time. To address these issues, future studies should use a mixed-method approach, combining quantitative surveys with qualitative interviews. [13]. Strong statistical techniques can help manage confounding factors, while diverse samples will improve the reliability of results. Longitudinal studies can also provide deeper insights into how birth order influences personality over time, offering a more complete understanding of these effects in adulthood.

2 LITERATURE REVIEW

Numerous studies have explored how birth order influences various aspects of human development, including personality, academic performance, and career preferences. A meta-analytic review combining data from different studies found that rank among siblings has a small to moderate switch on certain

 DOI: 10.1201/9781042001767-91

behavioral qualities. Compared to their younger siblings, firstborns typically exhibit higher degrees of conscientiousness and emotional sensitivity. However, the strength of these effects often depends on factors such as culture, family size, and research methods used. A longitudinal study that examined the academic performance of children from early childhood through adolescence revealed that firstborns typically perform better in standardized tests and achieve higher educational outcomes than laterborns. Interestingly, these effects were more evident in early years and tended to lessen over time, suggesting that other developmental factors may play a larger role during adolescence.

In another study, researchers analyzed the influence of birth order on career choices across different cultures. Findings showed that firstborns were more likely to choose traditional and prestigious careers, while younger siblings gravitated toward creative and unconventional fields. This variation is believed to stem from family roles, parental expectations, and environmental exposure during upbringing. A cross-sectional study explored adult perceptions of personality differences within families based on birth order. Firstborns were often described as more responsible and goal-driven, while laterborns were seen as more social and adventurous. Middleborns, in contrast, were noted for their adaptability and open-mindedness. These observations highlight how personal and family perspectives can influence how birth order traits are perceived and interpreted [14].

Qualitative research using parental interviews supported similar conclusions. Parents commonly recognized unique personality traits linked to each child's birth position—such as leadership in firstborns, sociability in middleborns, and creativity in youngest children. Parental experiences and parenting styles were found to significantly shape these perceptions, suggesting that birth order effects are not purely biological but also socially constructed within families [15]. A longitudinal investigation into self-perceived personality traits showed that birth order differences in self-identity may exist early in life but tend to decline over time. [16]. As individuals grow older and gain more experiences, their self-perception becomes more balanced and less dependent on their sibling rank. Family interactions, especially those involving siblings, were shown to show a main role in influential one's identity throughout development [17].

Collectively, these studies offer valuable insight into how rank among siblings may affect behavior growth, academic outcomes, and life choices. While some consistent patterns are found, the influence of birth order is designed by several contextual aspects such as parenting, socio-economic conditions, and ethnic background. The study emphasizes the intricacy of human growth and argues for a fair perspective that refrains from making unwarranted generalizations. [18]. Benefits of studying birth order include its contribution to personality development theories like those of Alfred Adler, and its potential to guide parents and educators in understanding behavioral patterns related to sibling rank. It also offers a lens for examining cultural and social influences on personality.[19] However, limitations remain, such as subjective data collection, challenges in defining personality traits consistently, and the difficulty of tracking long-term changes over time. Longitudinal studies, while valuable, are resource-intensive and often suffer from participant dropout, which can affect the reliability of results [20].

Finally, the broader literature touches on important yet often overlooked aspects of youth and adult development, such as the psychological effects of academic stress in late adolescence, and challenges older adults face in expressing natural sexual desires. These themes further highlight how developmental stages intersect with broader psychological and social issues, reinforcing the need for comprehensive and inclusive research approaches [21].

3 MATERIALS AND METHODS

Using a descriptive research design, the investigation was carried out at the Saveetha College of Occupational Therapy. Using a non-probability convenience sampling strategy, 60 samples were chosen. Adults from the Saveetha School of Occupational Therapy, aged 18 to 25, meet the selection criteria for the sample. With the consent of Saveetha College of Occupational Therapy's principal, the data collection period was conducted. The participants gave their written informed permission after being informed of the study's objectives. Demographic information is the statistical data on a population, encompassing characteristics such as age, gender, race, ethnicity, income, education, marital status, occupation, and geography. This information provides a snapshot of the composition and distribution of people within a given area or group. Demographic data is used for various purposes, including social research, market analysis, policy making, and resource allocation. By analyzing demographic trends and patterns, researchers and policymakers can gain insights into population dynamics, identify disparities, and Create focused interventions to meet certain community needs or issues. A 5-point rating was used to evaluate personality changes, and a structured questionnaire was used to gather demographic data. For every sample, a personality change assessment was done. Both descriptive and inferential statistics were used to examine the data.

4 RESULTS

To statistically analyse perceived personality changes due to birth order among adults, a structured approach should be taken. The sequence of steps involved in this process are formulating the research hypotheses, defining the variables and data collection, perform descriptive analysis such as frequency distribution of birth order, mean and standard deviation of personality scores across birth order groups, then inferential statistical analysis, and use statistical software for interpretation and report generations.

4.1 *Section A: Sample characteristics*

Sample characteristics refer to the attributes or qualities of the individuals or elements included in a sample used for research or analysis. These characteristics help define the sample population and provide insights into its composition. The analysis revealed that the majority of adults 27 (45%) were aged 27-30 years, 38 (63.3%) were male, 32 (53.3%) had secondary education, 41 (68.4%) were Hindu and 44 (68.4 %). 73.3%).) belonged to a nuclear family, 41 (68.4%) had an income of 10,000 - 20,000, 39 (65%) had a second child, and 22 (36.6%) had 2 siblings.

4.2 *Section B: Assess the perceived personality changes due to birth order among adults*

The analysis of Table 2 shows that among adults, 31 (51.66%) had moderate personality changes, 19 (31.67%) had good personality changes, and 10 (16.67%) had slight birth order changes. The results of Table 3 show that the average score of personality changes was 177.28±52.98. The median score was 180.0, the minimum score was 80.0, and the maximum score was 275.0. Thematic analysis of the interview data revealed several key findings. Firstborns commonly described themselves as responsible, organized, and achievement-oriented, attributing these traits to their early experiences of leadership and parental expectations. Middleborns often emphasized their adaptability, diplomacy, and peace-making skills, shaped by their experiences mediating between older and younger siblings. Lastborns frequently highlighted their creativity, spontaneity, and charm, influenced by their desire to differentiate themselves within the family dynamic. Participants also reported observing distinct personality changes in their siblings based on birth order. For instance, firstborns perceived their younger siblings as more carefree and adventurous, while lastborns viewed their older siblings as more serious and rule-bound. These perceptions were often coloured by shared childhood experiences and sibling interactions, as well as individual reflections on family roles and expectations.

Table 1. Rate and % distribution of level of perceived personality changes due to birth order among adults.

Level of Personality Changes	Frequency	N = 60 Percentage
Low (1 – 100)	10	16.67
Moderate (101 – 200)	31	51.66
Good (201 – 300)	19	31.67

The above Table 1 shows 31(51.66%) had moderate personality changes, 19(31.67%) had good personality changes and 10 (16.67%) had low Changes in personality brought on by birth order among adults.

Table 2. Assessment of Changes in personality brought on by birth order.

Personality Changes	N = 60 Score
Minimum score	80.0
Maximum score	275.0
Median	180.0
Mean	177.28
S.D.	52.98

The Table 2 illustrates that the average score of personality changes was 177.28±52.98. The median score was 180.0 with minimum score of 80.0 and maximum score of 275.0.

4.3 *Section C: Associate the level of perceived personality changes due to birth order among adults with designated demographic variables*

To associate the level of superficial personality changes due to birth order among adults with nominated demographic variables, we would need to conduct a quantitative research study that collects data on both perceived personality changes and demographic characteristics of participants. The analysis presented in Table 2=11.869, p=0.018) had χ 4 shows that the demographic variable age (a statistically significant relationship with the level of personality changes due to birth order at the pandlt;0.05 level and other demographic variables. does not show a statistically significant relationship with the level of personality change of birth order in adults. Therefore, research hypothesis H1, which previously stated, "There is a significant relationship between the level of birth order-induced personality change in adults with selected demographic variables" for the demographic variable age, but not for all other demographic variables, was accepted. The survey collects data on participants‘ perceptions of personality changes attributed to birth order, as well as demographic characteristics together with age, gender, education level, marital status, and family size. Participants are asked to rate the extent to which they perceive themselves and their siblings as exhibiting certain personality traits associated with birth order on a Likert scale. Statistical analysis, including regression analysis and correlation tests, is conducted to examine the relationship between perceived personality changes and demographic variables. Specifically, we explore whether certain demographic factors (e.g., family size, cultural background) are associated with variations in perceived personality changes among adults of different birth orders.

Preliminary findings suggest significant associations between perceived personality changes and selected demographic variables. For instance, participants from larger families tend to report greater perceived personality differences between siblings, while individuals from certain cultural backgrounds may attribute distinct personality traits to birth order positions. Gender differences in perceived personality changes are also observed, with male and female participants exhibiting varying patterns of attribution. Overall, our study contributes to a deeper sympathetic of how demographic factors intersect with birth order dynamics to shape individuals' perceptions of personality development within families. Implications for family counselling, cultural competence, and future research directions are discussed.

5 CONCLUSION

This study assessed personality changes in adults due to birth order. The results concluded that birth order disturbs some temperament mannerisms, but it does not affect a person's overall personality. Instead, age is seen to have a clear influence on personality. Future research on perceived personality changes due to birth order among adults could explore several avenues to deepen our understanding of this phenomenon. Future research contributes to a more comprehensive appreciative of how birth order dynamics shape individuals‘ perceptions of personality changes in adulthood.

REFERENCES

[1] Majed Mohammad Al – Khayat and Fatima Eid Zaid Al – Adwan, (2016), The Effect of Birth Order on Personality Traits and Academic Performance at Sample of Families in Jordan, *European Journal of Social Sciences*, Vol. 52, No. 2, pp. 151–161, ISSN 1450-2267.

[2] Fukuya Y, Fujiwara T, Isumi A, Doi S and Ochi M., (2021), Association of Birth Order With Mental Health Problems, Self-Esteem, Resilience, and Happiness Among Children: Results From A-CHILD Study, *Front. Psychiatry* 12: 638088. doi: 10.3389/fpsyt.2021.638088.

[3] Seedha Devi V., Sumathi K., Mahalakshmi M., Anand A.J., Anita Titus, and Naga Saranya N., (2024), Machine Learning based Efficient Human Activity Recognition System, *International Journal of Intelligent Systems and Applications in Engineering*, 12 (5s), pp. 338–346.

[4] Jose A., and Dhanalakshmi R., (Sep 2023), Hygieia: Multipurpose Healthcare Assistance Using the Internet of Things, in Saravanan Krishnan, and Aboobucker Ilmudeen, *Internet of Medical Things in Smart Healthcare: Post-COVID-19 Pandemic Scenario*, Apple Academic Press, pp. 77–98.

[5] Ponmalar A., and Anand J., (Sep 2023), IoMT-based Caring System for Aged People in a Post-COVID Scenario, in Saravanan Krishnan, and Aboobucker Ilmudeen, *Internet of Medical Things in Smart Healthcare: Post-COVID-19 Pandemic Scenario*, Apple Academic Press, pp. 207–224.

[6] Kavitha B., Jose A.A., Vignesh B., Raja Vikram Singan K., and Sri Subramaniam N., (2023), Design of an Intelligent and Smart Pill Box Using Arduino and Sensors, *2023 4th International Conference on Smart Electronics and Communication (ICOSEC)*, Trichy, India, pp. 258–263.

[7] Gupta T., (2017), Birth Order and Personality, *International Journal of Indian Psychology*, Vol. 5, (1). DIP: 18.01.014/ 20170501.

[8] Muthalagu R., Ramachandran R., Anuradha T., Anupama PH., and Jose A.A., (2023), Pattern Recognition and Modelling in Electrocardiogram Signals: Early Detection of Myocardial Ischemia and Infraction, *2023 2nd Int. Conference on Edge Computing and Applications (ICECAA)*, Namakkal, India, pp. 1035–1041.

[9] Sushma S., Anuradha T., Denslin B.D.R., and Jose A.A., (June 2023), Artificial Intelligence in Orthopedic Implant Model Classification, in R. Ranjith., J. Paulo Davim, Handbook of Research on Advanced Functional Materials for Orthopedic Applications, *IGI Global*.

[10] Geethalakshmi M., Venkatesh J., Uma Mageswari R., Mahalakshmi A., Anand J., and Partheepan R., (30 Jan 2023), Fuzzy Based Route Optimization in Wearable Biomedical Wireless Sensor Network, *AIP Conference Proceedings* 2523, 020156.

[11] Maheswari R., Vignesh S., Rakesh Kumar M., Venkatesh T.M., Sundar R., and Jose A.A., (2022), Voice Control and Eyeball Movement Operated Wheelchair, *2022 Int. Con. on Edge Computing and Applications (ICECAA)*, pp. 805–809.

[12] Prema S., Anand J., Vanitha P., Nirmala Devi K., Mohamed Yaseen M., and Rajeswari C., (Nov 2022), *Smart Stick using Ultrasonic Sensors for Vissually Impaired, Advances in Parallel Computing Algorithms, Tools and Paradigms*, Vol. 41, pp. 436–441.

[13] Dhanalakshmi, R., Anand J., Poonkavithai, K. and Vijayakumar, V., (24 May 2022), Cloud-Based Glaucoma Diagnosis in Medical Imaging Using Machine Learning, In: Parah, S.A., Rashid, M., Varadarajan, V. (eds) *Artificial Intelligence for Innovative Healthcare Informatics*. Springer, Cham, pp. 61–78.

[14] Dhanalakshmi, R., and Anand J., (06 May 2022), Big Data for Personalized Healthcare, In: A. Jaya, K. Kalaiselvi, Dinesh Goyal and Dhiya AL-Jumelly, (eds) *Handbook of Intelligent Healthcare Analytics: Knowledge Engineering with Big Data Analytics*, Chap-4, John Wiley & Sons, Inc., pp. 67–92.

[15] Ramesh D., (2016) Waghmare, A Study of Birth Order and Adjustment among College Students, *The International Journal of Indian Psychology*, Volume 3, Issue 2, No.4.

[16] Roberts W., (2015), The associations of birth order with personality and intelligence in a representative sample of U.S. high school students, *J. of Research in Personality*, 58, 96–105.

[17] Sidhharrth S. Kumaar, (2018), Birth Order and Psychology of Person, *Journal of Advances and Scholarly Researches in Allied Education* Vol. 18, Issue 5. DOI: 10.29070/JASRAE.

[18] Vaghchipawala, K.P., (2023), A Comparative Study of Birth-Order and Personality, International Journal of Indian Psychology, 11 (4), pp. 281–321.

[19] Priyadarsini A. Jagadeeswari J, Cecyli C. and Dayana B.A.A. (2024). Prediction of Behavioral Disorders among Preschooler: A Survey Report. *Texila International Journal of Public Health*. 24. 10.21522/TIJPH.2013.SE.24.02.Art014.

[20] Vechalapu, Maj P, Thenmozhi Kumar and Ramadugu. (2024). Effectiveness of psychoeducational intervention on quality of life among patients with affective disorders. *Multidisciplinary Science Journal*. 6. 2024ss0627. 10.31893/multiscience.2024ss0627.

[21] Dinesh K., Kamatchi S.K, Mangaiyarkarasi and Selvaperumal S. (2024). *Accuracy improvement for personality prediction using logistic regression in comparison with random forest algorithm*. 020269. 10.1063/5.0229463.

Next-Generation Smart Systems – Sekhar et al. (Eds)
© 2027 The Author(s), ISBN: 978-1-041-34234-2

Tech-Driven Transformations: Evaluating Patient Outcomes with Digital Problem-Based Approaches

Sindhu Ramalingam
Associate Professorl, Saveetha College of Nursing, Saveetha Institute of Medical and Technical Sciences, Chennai, India

Ajith M. and Abinaya A.
Nursing Tutor, Saveetha College of Nursing, Saveetha Institute of Medical and Technical Sciences, Chennai, India

Vijayalakshmi
Principal, Saveetha College of Nursing, Saveetha Institute of Medical and Technical Sciences, Chennai, India

ABSTRACT: One of the challenges of nursing practice today is the increasing new emerging diseases and demands for health-care services by the growing population. The aim of the study was to assess the application of digital problem based interventions to evaluate the outcome of patient care. A basic descriptive cross sectional study approach was used, to assess participant's knowledge on the application of digital problem based learning at different levels of nursing cadres at selected tertiary hospital. A quantitative descriptive design, non-probability-convenient sampling was used to select the study sampled groups. Data was collected using; structured questionnaires. Data collected was coded and analyzed using the (SPSS) computer software program. Findings shown that knowledge of nurses on application of digital problem based learning was influenced by training nurses undertook during nursing training, and practicing nursing care without attending continuous medical education at work places to refresh their nursing knowledge, and skills affected the quality of nursing care provided and patients' outcome. Nurses reported being motivated to apply the nursing process in nursing care due to the good patients' outcome, approach to individualized nursing care, positive nurses-patient relationship created and patient's participation in his/her management shorten their stay in hospital. In addition, the numbers of nursing staffs to the number of patients admitted for care and their different demands was also reported to affect the application of the nursing process in nursing care in an environment were no resources and equipment to use. The findings from the study were not justifiable to generalize the research results on the knowledge of nurses on application of digital problem based interventions in nursing care due to the small size sample used and new knowledge obtained through the study would enhance evidenced based nursing practice.

Keywords: Biomedical Engineering, Health Informatics, Digital Signal Processing, Medical Device Innovation

1 INTRODUCTION

The The digital problem based intervention is a method by which nurses in their day today practice deliver nursing care to their patients and is derived from nursing philosophies and models. It is a patient centered, goal driven cyclical process used by nurses as a problem-solving technique to provide optimal nursing care to their patients. (Rajesh C. 2010). The nursing process addresses every medical, psychological, and/ or social problem involved in patient care. It facilitates nurses to evaluate patient's health care needs during hospitalization and implementation of the nursing care plan. It improved the quality of life of patient through the holistic approach. The need to implement the digital problem based intervention became more apparent as it was the means to provide comprehensive and individualized nursing care. The role of the nurse was very vital to find out and meet the patient's immediate need for help depending on the presenting behavior; although the nursing care needed may not be what it appears to be (Orlando, J. I. 2010). It was important to consider what quality of nursing care means to patients especially in this era of new emerging diseases if nurses are to address the gaps between their own perceptions and those of the patients themselves and to consider conceptual models of care appropriate for the patients' problems in order to improve the quality of nursing care provided. The application of digital problem based intervention would result in increased satisfaction to patients from the nursing care received and also greater job satisfaction to the nurses.

The purpose of the study is to assess the knowledge of nurses on the application of nursing process in the nursing care of patients and their outcome in selected hospital. The study employed a basic descriptive cross sectional design using participants from the different levels of nursing professional. The study design was chosen to gain more insight into indentifying the gaps in the knowledge of nurses on the application and integration of the nursing process in the nursing care of patient. The study participants recruited included; registered nurses, comprehensive, and enrolled nurses working in Masindi Hospital, providing nursing care to the patients on the medical and surgical wards of males, females and children. These nursing cadres will be selected to be the key informants in the study Non Probability-Convenient sampling method was used. Sample size of the study was 19 subjects. Data was collected using self administered structured questionnaires composed of both open and closed ended questions to gather information about the knowledge of nurses on application and integration of nursing process in nursing care. Data collected was categorized according to the sections of the instrument and responses were coded then entered into the computer application that provided statistical analysis of data. Statistical Package for the Social Sciences (SPSS version 11) was used to enter data into a computer for analysis. All responses which had similar patterns and closely fall within the same variable were coded together for analysis to generate meaningful data and cause relationship among study variables.

DOI: 10.1201/9781042001767-92

2 METHODOLOGY

This study employed a mixed-methods research design to evaluate the impact of digital problem-based approaches on patient outcomes within healthcare settings. A purposive sample of nursing and medical students, along with practicing clinicians, participated in the intervention. Participants were exposed to digital learning tools, including virtual simulations, interactive case-based modules, and AI-driven clinical decision-making platforms over a 12-week period. Quantitative data were collected using standardized assessment tools to measure changes in clinical reasoning, diagnostic accuracy, and patient care planning skills. Pre- and post-intervention scores were analyzed statistically using paired t-tests and ANOVA to determine significance. Additionally, qualitative data were gathered through semi-structured interviews and focus group discussions to explore participants' perceptions of usability, engagement, and the relevance of digital tools in real-world practice. Patient outcome metrics such as error reduction, care quality, and satisfaction levels were tracked through electronic health records (EHR) and feedback forms. Triangulation was used to enhance the validity of the findings, and ethical clearance was obtained from the institutional review board prior to data collection.

3 RESULTS

The Data was collected using structured questionnaires and review of records to answer the study objectives, research questions and study hypothesis. Findings were presented using tables, graphs, pie charts and Correlation Coefficient and Chi-Square testes were used to define the relationships between the study variables to interpret the results.

The table above indicated that age was normally distributed among the participants since mean=median=mode that meant data was not biased. The study recruited more females than the males evidenced by the mode= 2 (females were coded 2), majority of the respondents were enrolled nurses which was coded 1and had a maximum nursing practical experience of 4 years of which they had attended a nursing training in nursing care in the last one year.

Table 1. One showing the biographic data of study participants (N=15).

Participant	Mean	Mode	Median	Range	Standard deviation
Age	31.0	31	31.00	26	6.23
Gender	1.60	2	2.00	1	0.51
Education level	1.80	1	2.00	3	0.94
Years of experience	2.80	4	3.00	3	1.08
Period of last trained	1.80	1	2.00	4	1.08

3.1 *Knowledge of nurses on the steps in the nursing process*

From the above, majority of participants accepted that the nursing process was taught in nursing training and were knowledgeable on the steps in nursing process. From the table above the calculated Chi-Square value was 0.0960 and the tabulated Chi-Square.

Table 2. Showing comparisons between nursing process taught in nursing training and knowledge *of* participants on the steps in nursing process (N=15).

Response		Steps in nursing process		Total
		Knowledgeable	Not Knowledgeable	
Nursing process taught in nursing training	No	1	1	2
	Yes	8	5	13
Total		9	6	15

From the table above, it was revealed that majority of respondents 8(9) applied the concepts of nursing process in nursing care were knowledgeable about the steps in nursing process from the table above the calculated Chi-Square value was 0.096 with 1 degree of freedom. At 0.05 level of significance and 1 degree of freedom, the tabulated Chi-Square value was 3.841. Since the calculated value was less than the tabulated value, we accepted the null hypothesis and concluded that there was a relationship between knowledge of participants on application of concepts of nursing process in nursing care. Therefore, the knowledge of participants influenced the application of concept of nursing process in nursing care. We further deduced that the more knowledgeable nurses are, the more they applied the concept of nursing process in nursing care and the less knowledgeable nurses are, the less utilization the concept of nursing process in nursing care.

Response		Steps in nursing process		Total
		Knowledgeable	Not Knowledgeable	
Period last attended a nursing course or training in nursing care including CPD or CME	0-1 year	4	3	7
	1-4 years	4	2	6
	4-8 years	1	0	1
	8 & above	0	1	1
Total		9	6	15

From the table above, majority of participants that were knowledgeable about the steps in nursing process last attended a nursing course or training in nursing care within the last 4 years.

4 DISCUSSION

This section presented the summary of the study findings from the survey questionnaire, the results were divided into biographical data, and background of the respondents, answers the objectives, and research questions and agree or disapproves the research hypothesis thus to generate viable recommendations to the nursing professional and practice, nursing researchers and nursing administrations for a better nursing future. The purpose the study was to assess the knowledge of nurses on application of the nursing process in nursing care of patients and a total number of 15 participants were recruited in the study. (Table 1) illustrated the distribution of the studied respondents according to the biographical data. It shown that age was normally distributed among the participants, majority were females 11(73%) the fact that there are more women in the sample than men not by design. This gender imbalance indicated that there are more female nurses than males in the hospitals. The study revealed that there were more enrolled nurses 8(58%) employed in the health sector followed by registered nurses 5(33%) and least by

Table 3. Showing knowledge of participants on application of the concepts of nursing process in nursing care (N=15).

Response		Steps in nursing process		
		Knowledgeable	Not Knowledgeable	Total
Applied concept of nursing	No	1	1	2
process in nursing care	Yes	8	5	13
Total		9	6	15

comprehensive nurses 2(13.3%) and the study did not capture any nurse with bachelor's degree practicing bed side nursing in Masindi hospital. Participants had a working experience 8 years and above 5(33.3%) and had attended continuous medical education training 9(60%) in the last one year, the cheapest means of sharing new evidence based information in nursing practice in hospitals and this was also supported by the study participants in (Table 3).

The Application and Ways of applying the Concepts of Nursing Process Application is the art of putting or converting the studied or acquired knowledge into skills and practice to improve the quality of patient care. The researcher further analyzed in depth the practices of participants and their relation to the application of the concepts of nursing process in nursing care.

The study findings revealed that majority of the respondents reported to apply the concepts in care of patients on the wards. The ways of application were determining by how nurses integrated the steps of nursing process in care of patients, defined as assessment (history taking), nursing diagnosis, nursing care planning, and implementation of interventions and evaluation of care. It was observed in (table eight) that only 3(23%) of the respondents who applied the process described what is involved in the nursing process where as majority described the general nursing roles defined as; monitoring vital observations, administer prescribed medications depending on the medical diagnosis, bathing the patients, among others. There was a positive low relationship between the years of nursing care practice and ways of applying concepts of nursing practice by 40%. significance (table nine). From the above findings, we concluded that the knowledge of nurses on application of the nursing process in nursing care did not match with the current nursing care practices.

However, the application of nursing process in nursing care had a number of bottle necks reported by the participants. (Figure 2) shown the commonest racked factors considered to be both horizontal and vertical to nursing care practice included; understaffing affecting team work causing a work load of patients within the hospital cues and on the wards, yet to handle effectively all the patients needs required time which most of the situations it is impossible due to the limited available resources to the number of patients in need of nursing services. there were also other mentioned challenges that included; language barrier, wrong information given by the patients initially affect the nursing care plans because of the wrong diagnosis, lack of adequate knowledge about the nursing process especially by the elderly nurses trained more than ten years back were not well vast with the application of the process and attended CME less frequent. The studied respondents concurred with the study hypothesis in that the application of the nursing process was very vital and if well applied in nursing care of patients, had good benefits both to the nursing team and the patients as the final consumers of health services. Some of the highest rated benefits among others in (Figure 3) included; improved patient desirable outcome, timely administration of medications according to treatment care plans and goal oriented. In addition, promoted individualized care, patients trust, and confinement in the nursing team which promotes open up and collection of accurate patient problems and information concern their unwell being. Installed confidence among the nursing staffs, love to serve their patients, patient's involvement and participation in care.

Respondents suggested ideas to promote effective application of nursing process in nursing care that; strengthening trainings like CME or CPD, teaching the nursing process right from nursing training schools would bridge the knowledge gap among the practicing nurses to improve the standards of nursing care to patients, provision of adequate and enough materials used in nursing care and recruitment of more nurses in hospital would reduce patient's stay on wards as will be receiving timely attention than when nurses are very few to hand the work load of patients and emergencies. Other suggestions included; nurses upgrade their levels of nursing education to degrees and masters in nursing to specialize in one field, improved the attitude of nurses towards patient's care, and supportive approaches and supervision to the lower nursing cadres motivates them to learn and practice in line with the required nursing standards.

5 CONCLUSION

The study findings revealed that the application of nursing process in nursing care was not only affected by knowledge of nurses but a couple of other factors; majority of the study participants were enrolled nurses 8(53.3%) where at that level of education expect the nursing process to be introduced in the nursing training 5(33.3%) although the short clinical practice might have limited them from acquition of skills, the knowledge of participants decreased with increasing years of nursing practice especially where there was no any kind of training attended by the nurses for more than four years and those that had continuous exposure to trainings especially CME 9(60%), their knowledge was improved and through formal nursing training 5(33.3%). it was observed that the more years' nurses had practiced nursing care, the less knowledgeable were on the application of nursing process that is decreased from 8 years and above 1(11.1%) therefore had a negative impact. only 3 (20%) of the participants described the five steps of nursing process applied in nursing care where as majority that said were applying the concepts 12(80%) described general nursing roles applied in nursing care. the incentives that motivated participants to apply the nursing care included; good patient outcome, systematic approach of the process to nursing care and others; continuity of care and positive nurse patient relationship created. participants recommended that providing enough resources and materials, strengthening trainings will motivate nurses more to integrate the concepts of nursing process in nursing care of patients.

ACKNOWLEDGEMENT

The authors gratefully acknowledge the students, staff, and authority of Saveetha Institute of Medicl nd Technicl nd Sciences staff and students for their cooperation in the research.

REFERENCES

[1] Digital Health Education Collaboration. *Digital Problem-Based Learning in Health Professions: Systematic Review and Meta-Analysis*. JMIR. 2019. Demonstrated moderate improvements in knowledge (SMD ≈ 0.67) and skills (SMD ≈ 1.13) compared to traditional methods.

[2] Son HK. (2023). *Effects of Simulation with Problem-Based Learning on Nursing Students' Clinical Reasoning Ability (Tanner's Model)*. BMC Med Educ. Showed statistically significant gains in clinical reasoning using S-PBL.

[3] Elnaga HHA *et al.* (June 2023). *Virtual versus Paper-Based PBL in Pulmonology for Medical Undergraduates.* BMC Med Educ. Virtual patient PBL yielded higher post-test scores than paper-based formats ($p < .01$)

[4] Heidari, M., Borujeni, M.B., Borujeni, M.G., and Shirvani, M. (2017). Relationship of lifestyle with academic achievement in nursing students. *Journal of Clinical and Diagnostic Research: JCDR, 11*(3), JC01.

[5] Plackett R *et al.* (2020). *Online Patient Simulation Training to Improve Clinical Reasoning: Feasibility RCT.* BMC Med Educ. Demonstrated feasibility and gains in reasoning via virtual patient simulations

[6] JMIR. *Simulation-Based Learning Supported by Technology to Enhance Critical Thinking in Nursing Students: Scoping Review.* 2025. Highlighted VR, CBS and TES technologies in nursing SBL and their impact on critical thinking

[7] Mamseri, R.A. (2012). *The nursing process as a means of improving patient care.* University of South Africa (South Africa).

[8] Mistry K *et al.* (2019). *Digital Problem-Based Learning: An Innovative and Efficient Method of Teaching Medicine.* Med Educ Online (SAGE). Reported high student satisfaction and better case exposure in dermatology module

[9] Nyamwaya, D.K., Otiende, M., Mwango, L., Kariuki, S.M., Otieno, B., Omuoyo, D.O., and Warimwe, G.M. (2022). Incidence of chikungunya virus infections among Kenyan children with neurological disease, 2014–2018: A cohort study. *PLoS Medicine, 19*(5), e1003994.

[10] Fadli A. and Susilowati S. (2022). *Effectiveness of PBL with Simulation Learning Methods Online Physiotherapy: Systematic Review.* Jurnal Pendidikan Kedokteran Indonesia. Online PBL effective in increasing knowledge and skill competence

[11] Xu Y *et al.* (Mar 2025). *Advancing Problem-Based Learning with Clinical Reasoning for Improved Differential Diagnosis.* arXiv. e-MedLearn system enhanced reasoning in controlled study

[12] Aydin MY *et al.* (Jun 2024). *VR-NRP: Virtual Reality Simulation for Neonatal Resuscitation Program Training.* arXiv. VR boosted clinician confidence and experiential learning outcomes

[13] Korre D, Sherlock A. (Aug 2023). *Augmented Reality in Higher Education: Medical Education Case Study.* arXiv. AR improved anatomy understanding and student engagement

[14] Kyaw BM *et al.* (2019) *Virtual Reality for Health Professions Education: Systematic Review and Meta-Analysis.* JMIR. Found VR training positively impacts health professions education outcomes

[15] Kouvalewski K-F *et al.* (2017). *Validation of Touch Surgery App for Cognitive Training in Laparoscopic Cholecystectomy.* Surgical Endoscopy. Demonstrated superiority of mobile simulation over text-based learning Giuffrida *et al.* (cited in JMIR scoping review) pointed out limited telehealth use in SBL despite global emphasis on technological methods

[16] Wong *et al.* (cited in JMIR review) on telehealth and technology-enhanced SBL revealing mixed satisfaction and increased feedback modalities

[17] Giuffrida *et al.* (cited in JMIR scoping review) pointed out limited telehealth use in SBL despite global emphasis on technological methods

[18] Ghosh, R., and Singh, A. (2024). Faculty Category: Medical Education Technology.

[19] Remote patient monitoring meta-analysis in npj Digital Medicine and JAMA demonstrating real-world patient outcome improvements via digital systems

[20] Spaull, N., and Van der Berg, S. (2020). Counting the cost: COVID-19 school closures in South Africa and its impact on children. *South African Journal of Childhood Education, 10*(1), 1-13.

[21] Sudan, S. profil pelajar.com.

[22] Ajith, M., and Vijayalakshmi, R. (2024, December 27). A study to assess the effectiveness of structured teaching program on knowledge on hand washing among school children at selected school. *Texila International Journal of Public Health. Advance online publication.* https://doi.org/10.21522/TIJPH.2013.SE.25.01.Art018

Next-Generation Smart Systems – Sekhar et al. (Eds)
© 2027 The Author(s), ISBN: 978-1-041-34234-2

Enhancing Structural Efficiency of a Tension Machine Frame Through Finite Element Optimization

Ravikumar L.
Associate Professor, Department of CE, Kuppam Engineering College, Kuppam, India

Nagesh N. and Ganesh K.
Associate Professor, Department of ME, Kuppam Engineering College, Kuppam, India

ABSTRACT: The optimization of structural components in machinery is vital for reducing material costs and improving performance. This study focuses on the optimization design of a tension machine frame, a critical component subjected to high axial loads during testing operations. Using Pro E for 3D modeling and ANSYS for finite element analysis (FEA), the design was evaluated under extreme working conditions. Static structural analysis revealed that the original design was over-engineered, leading to unnecessary weight and material use. Optimization techniques were then applied to reduce the mass while ensuring safety and functionality. The optimized design successfully achieved this goal: both the maximum equivalent stress and overall deformation were reduced compared to the original model. Additionally, the frame's weight was reduced by 5.11%, marking a significant improvement in material efficiency. This optimization not only enhances the mechanical performance of the frame but also leads to lower production costs, offering substantial economic and engineering benefits.

Keywords: Pro-E, tension frame, Ansys , optimization, 3D modeling, Boundary conditions

1 INTRODUCTION

As the economic growth in China has been rising swiftly in the recent years, the electricity demand has also been rising steadily. The power construction is currently regarded as one of the primary pillars of national development.. The launch of tension stringing methods has come with major advantages that it accelerates the pace of project implementation, enhances the construction standards, and enhances efficiency in the whole process [1]. Nonetheless, it has a notable discrepancy between the tools at hand and what is required on the ground. Majority of the modern traction/tensioning equipment is intended to be used on ultra-high voltage lines, it is large, heavy, and ill suited to general power transmission and distribution projects. Worse still, these machines have not changed much in the way they are designed. Most of the domestic firms have just copied the existing models without introducing any specific structural enhancement that makes them less competitive in the market. Modern tools of engineering, such as the finite element method (FEM) have been used in some progress over the years. As an example Liu Zhuli and his group [2] optimized a trailer tractor with ANSYS software and made the displacement of this trailer tractor significantly smaller. ANSYS has also been used to

Optimize different structural parts and minimise weight by others such as Wang Lihe [3], Hua Guangjun [4] and many more. Nonetheless, little dedicated research has been done so far on the tension machine itself especially regarding how to design it in a way that maximizes its weight, Performance and cost. The 3D model is designed in Pro-E (Pro/ENGINEER) first. Then, an in-depth moment analysis is carried out in the ANSYS Workbench to learn the behavior of the frame in extreme working conditions. Lastly, multi-objective genetic algorithm (MOGA) is applied to identify the optimal design to obtain a stronger, lighter and more efficient tension machine by trading off between strength, weight, and efficiency.

2 STIFFNESS MACHINE

A stiffness is a key piece of equipment used during the construction of power transmission lines, especially during the tension stringing process. Its job is to control the pulling force applied to conductors like ground wires or optical cables, making sure they're stretched and laid out smoothly and evenly.

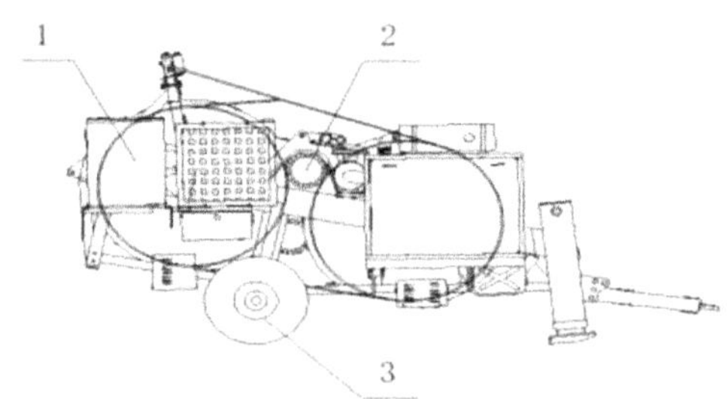

Figure 1. Tension machine.

The heart of the machine is the tension control system, which creates the torque needed to resist the pull of the wire. As it spins, the motor pushes hydraulic oil through the system. The oil passes through an overflow valve, which doesn't just let the oil out it controls the flow, creating back pressure.

2.1 *Pro E and ANSYS workbench*

A 3D model of tension machine frame is first created in Pro-E, a more precise and easier to use CAD software, since it may be challenging and costly to build more complex 3D models in ANSYS Workbench. Once completed, the model is brought into ANSYS Workbench and the finite element analysis (FEA) is done. Due to seamless integration with ANSYS in terms of

DOI: 10.1201/9781042001767-93

model transfer and parameter sharing, Pro/ENGINEER (Pro-E) is also used in limited cases. The relevant design information, such as sizes, material properties and constraints, is also conveyed using this technique, as well as the 3D geometry. This simplifies the process as a whole by making it more accurate, optimized and analyzed in ANSYS [5].

2.2 *Parametric modelling*

The overall structure of the tension machine frame is quite complex, so it is essential to simplify the model before performing finite element analysis. Simplification helps reduce the computational effort without significantly affecting the accuracy of the results. The commonly used approach [6] involves removing non-load-bearing parts and external covers (skins) of the frame, ignoring small components that have minimal impact on the overall structural behavior, and eliminating unnecessary features such as holes and fillets. During the modeling process in Pro-E, key geometric features are defined as parameters to facilitate design adjustments and optimization. In this study, the main beam width is defined as parameter D1, the axle length as D2, and the support thickness as D3. A simplified version of the tension machine frame, incorporating these parameters, is shown in Figure 2. Variables to a tension frame are

S1 (mm): Column/plate thickness (primary stiffness driver)
S2 (mm): Clear span/column height between crossheads
S3 (mm): Grip/jaw spacing or crosshead spacing at load
S4 (kg): Load capacity (ultimate or rated)
S5 (mm): Frame deflection at rated load
S6 (MPa): Max von Mises stress in critical member

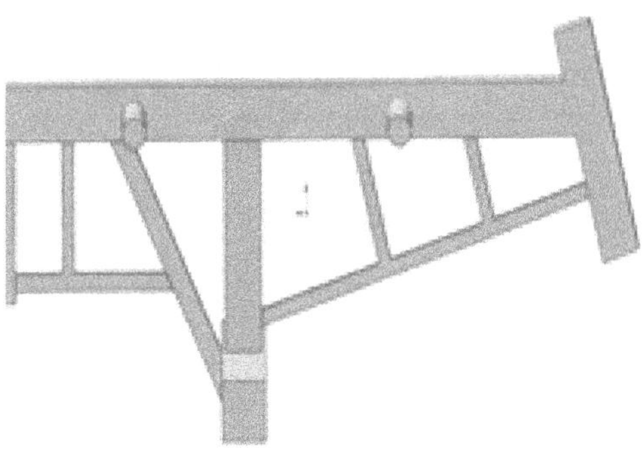

Figure 2. Tension machine.

3 ANALYSIS OF FRAME

3.1 *Selection of parameters*

The material properties of the model is crucial before performing finite element analysis in ANSYS Workbench. The SA-ZY-2×40 tension machine, created by Henan Electric Power Boda Company, is the subject of this investigation. This machine's structure is composed of Q345 structural steel, which is frequently used in heavy machinery because of its dependability and strength. Q345 steel's mechanical characteristics include a density of 7850 kg/m^3, an elastic modulus of 206 GPa, and a Poisson's ratio of 0.28. The ultimate tensile strength is between 490 and 620 MPa, and the yield strength is 345 MPa. The initial mass of the tension machine frame was determined to be 5795.5 kg after the material was assigned and the model was completely described

3.2 *Grid division*

In finite element analysis, mesh generation plays a crucial role, as it directly affects both the accuracy of the simulation and the computational efficiency. Generally, using a finer mesh improves the accuracy of the results but also increases the computational load. Therefore, it's important to find a balance between precision and performance by selecting an appropriate mesh density [7]. Given the relatively large size and complexity of the tension machine frame model, and considering limitations in computer hardware, memory capacity, and the need for reliable results, this study adopts an automatic meshing strategy in ANSYS Workbench. The mesh quality is controlled using a Sizing method, with the element size set to 20 mm. After clicking the Generate Mesh command, the software produced a total of 62,872 elements and 144,524 nodes. The resulting mesh distribution for the tension machine frame is shown in Figure 3.

3.3 *Apply boundary conditions*

In this system, the tension machine operates passively, meaning it does not generate pulling force on its own. The rated pulling force of the tractor used with this tensioner model is 80 kN, which also defines the maximum tension applied during operation. For the analysis, gravitational acceleration is set at 9.8 m/s^2, acting in the downward direction. Since the focus of this study is on the frame (rack) of the tension machine, appropriate boundary conditions are applied to simulate real-world constraints and loads. These conditions are illustrated in Figure 4.

3.4 *Result calculation and analysis*

After performing the static structural analysis using ANSYS, the equivalent (von Mises) stress distribution of the tension machine frame was obtained. The results are visualized through the equivalent stress cloud diagrams, as shown in Figure 5 and Figure 6.

The analysis reveals that:

Minimum equivalent stress: 14.932 Pa
Maximum equivalent stress: 177.35 MPa

The maximum stress concentration is observed around the circular support that holds the tension wheel, indicating this is a critical load-bearing region. In contrast, the remaining areas of the frame experience relatively low stress levels, implying that material in those regions is underutilized

Figure 3. Meshing diagram.

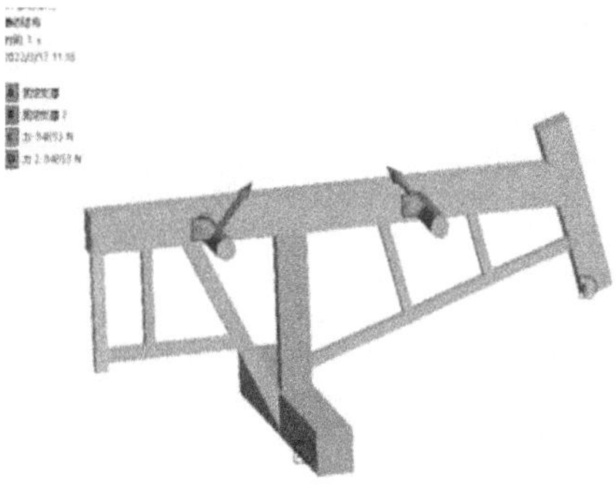

Figure 4. Boundary conditions.

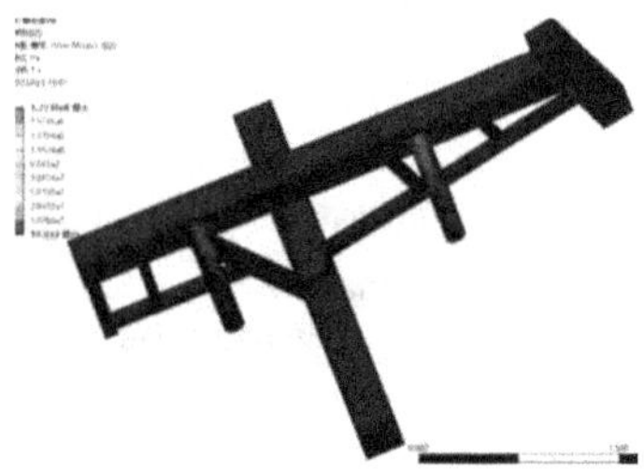

Figure 5. Stress diagram of the frame.

Figure 6. Stress.

4 SURFACE OPTIMIZATION

4.1 *Optimization*

To optimize the performance of the rack in the case of stationary configuration where weight of rack will be minimized, the frame structure under consideration has to be optimized topologically. Based on cloud plot (Figure 7) of total deformation displacement, it was observed that the main beam, axle and bracket are dominated by relatively low deformation. As a result, the three areas (the parts) were selected as the critical dimensions to be optimized. The input parameters S1, S2 and S3 in ANSYS Workbench are the key beam (D1), axle (D2) and, bracket (D3) respectively. Output parameters are determined as frame mass (S4), maximum total deformation (S5), and maximum equivalent stress (S6).The objective of the current setup is to maximize material savings with minimal impact on the performance of the structure. To achieve this, the level of material reduction shall be fixed at 20 percent and the weight reduction/ structural integrity ratio will be obtained.

4.2 *Surface optimization*

The Response Surface Method is a procedure of optimization that involves design of experiments (DOE) and involves mathematical statistics to obtain an empirical approximation model. RSM employs either empirical formulae or numerical analysis to carry out an iterative analysis of a collection of design points in design space depending on the principles of the experimental design. Latin Hyperbole Sampling (LHS) design, also often referred to as a space-filling design, is employed in this paper. This design ensures the even spacing of sample points within the design space yet a comparatively small sample points would be efficient to optimize [1012]. A sampling plan is selected as user defined in which 15 sampling points are selected. One of the sets of input data is created in accordance with the preset ranges of values of each of the input parameters (15 sets). The determination of output parameters is subsequently done by using the specified materials, boundary conditions, constraints, contact conditions and loading conditions

In the given work, the use of a multi-objective genetic algorithm (MOGA) is implemented to optimally solve the structural parameters of tension machine frame. The main design variables are established as follows: P1 is the width of main beam, P2 is the axle length, P3 is the thickness of support, P4 is geometric mass, P5 is the maximum total deformation and P6 is the maximum equivalent stress. In order to do the optimization, the initial sample size will be 3000 and the sample size will be 600 per iteration. The optimization process is capped to 20 iterations with a maximum permissible percentage of Pareto front of 70 percent and finally converges to produce 3 optimal candidate points [13-16]. The optimization goal will be to reduce the geometric mass (P4) and the total deformation (P5) of the frame at the same time. optimization the mass of the tension machine frame could be reduced to 5498.8 kg, lowering the mass of the frame by 5.11%. Also the overall deformation maximum reduced a bit (0.34255 mm) to 0.33978 mm, and the corresponding maximum stress reduced, as well as 179.3 MPa to 170.24 MPa. This has performances that are within the material yield strength of 345 MPa, which proves that the optimized design satisfies both structural safety and construction performance requirements.

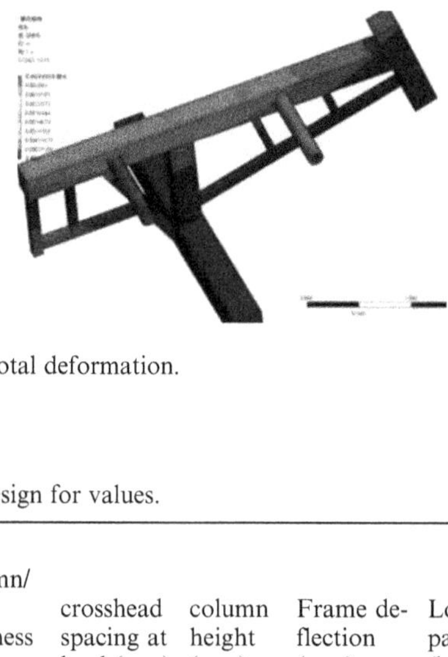

Figure 7. Total deformation.

Table 1. Design for values.

Name	Column/ plate thickness (mm)	crosshead spacing at load (mm)	column height (mm)	Frame deflection (mm)	Load capacity (kg)	Max von Mises stress (MPa)
1	245	103	3030	0.3393	5781	174.7
2	248.33	83	2490	0.3426	5399.3	166.6
3	238.33	99	2850	0.347	5595.6	174.7
4	235	107	2430	0.3479	5283.1	169.9
5	241.67	81	3270	0.3501	5894.8	168.1
6	231.67	105	3210	0.3522	5805.1	172.9
7	228.33	97	3090	0.3596	5683.2	172.9
8	225	93	2790	0.3653	5439.5	172.4
9	218.33	101	2670	0.3701	5312.5	177.1
10	221.67	91	2730	0.3702	5368	172.6
11	211.67	109	2970	0.3749	5482.2	183.0
12	215	95	2610	0.3772	5235.7	177.8
13	208.33	89	3150	0.3897	5556.3	176.6
14	205	87	2550	0.3957	5103.3	175.6
15	201.67	85	2910	0.4022	5328.5	180.4

Table 2. Candidate results.

Name	C 1	C 2	C 3
S1	249.94	249.94	249.95
S2	2402.9	2403	2408.9
S3	107.64	109.8	109.65
S4	5378.9	5381.9	5385.9
S5	0.34104	0.34066	0.34067

5 CONCLUSION

An analysis in finite element (FEA) was conducted in ANSYS after we created a 3D model of the tension machine frame in Pro-E. The model of the frame with no motions showed that the stress rates inside the frame were quite low in case we artificialized very difficult working conditions. This meant that there was a clear possibility to optimize the design since it was more resilient than was necessary essentially overbuilt. The weight of the frame was reduced by topology, and parameter optimization methods to 5498.8 kg, compared to 5795.5 kg. The mass has decreased by 5.11%. Remarkably, both the maximum overall deformation and stress correspondingly reduced with the weight of the frame. Consequently, the structural stability of the optimised design actually got better. The optimization process eventually proved quite successful. Our design did not require any sacrifice of strength or stiffness and we could design a lighter, more effective design that could potentially save us some money and increase Performance

REFERENCES

[1] Atlantis Y., Brecher C., Weck M. and Witt S., (2008), Virtual machine tool technology, *proc 25thMTDR.*

[2] Spath D., Neithardt W. and Bangert C., (1999), He structural optimization of micro milling machine, *Machines and Mechanism.*

[3] Cowley A. and Hinduja S., (1969), Analysis of machine tool structures Finite Element method, *proc 10 thconf.*

[4] Stepehen A.C. and Taylor S., (1965), Finite Element Method Computer analysis of machine tool structure. *proc 5th Machine tool Design and research conference.*

[5] The design methodology of compound multi axis machine tools, *Procl5th, machine tool design and research conference*, 1999, MasamitsuNakminami, Tsutomu Tokuma, Kazuhiko Matsumoto and Keiichi Nakamoto.

[6] Weule H., Fleischer, Neithardt W., Emmrich D. and Just D., (2001), FEA analysis of machine tool structure and the exploitation of topology optimization., *Machines and Mechanism.*

[7] Ganesan N., Haranath S. and Rao B.V., (1987), Dynamic Analysis of machine tool structure with applied damping treatment, *Int J. Mach. Tools Manufacture.* Vol.27, No 1, p.43–55.

[8] De Fonseca P., Vandepitte D., Van Brussels H., Sas P., (2003), Dynamic analysis of machine tool in. workspace., *Int J. Mach. Tools Manufacture.* Vol. 42, No 1, p.43–55.

[9] Gao Yuhua. (2009). *Optimization design of car body white structure analysis. with hardware in the ring [D].* Hefei University of Technology.

Next-Generation Smart Systems – Sekhar et al. (Eds)
© 2027 The Author(s), ISBN: 978-1-041-34234-2

Technological Evaluation of Heat-Aided Castor Oil Application for Alleviating Knee Musculoskeletal Pain in Resource-Limited Female Groups

Kavitha M.
Assistant Professor, Department of Community Health Nursing, Saveetha College of Nursing, Saveetha Institute of Medical and Technical Sciences, Thandalam, India

Savitha T.
B.sc [Nursing], SCON, SIMATS, Professor, Department of Community Health Nursing, Saveetha College of Nursing, Saveetha Institute of Medical and Technical Sciences, Thandalam, India

S. Kalabarathi and Padmapriya D.
Department of OBG, SCON, SIMATS, Department of Community Health Nursing, Saveetha College of Nursing, Saveetha Institute of Medical and Technical Sciences, Thandalam, India

Sridevi B.
Department of Adult Surgical Nursing, SCON, SIMATS, Department of Community Health Nursing, Saveetha College of Nursing, Saveetha Institute of Medical and Technical Sciences, Thandalam, India

ABSTRACT: **Background:** A degenerative joint condition that mainly affects the elderly, particularly women, osteoarthritis (OA) causes chronic knee pain, reduced mobility, and a decreased standard of life. Because pharmaceutical therapies frequently have negative side effects, people are becoming more interested in natural, non-invasive therapy. The aim of the research to analyse how well thermo-assisted castor oil massage relieves rural women's knee joint discomfort between thirty and sixty years of age A true experimental Research design was utilized for this study, with 100 women from a rural village (Tirumazhisai) divided equally into an Interventional group and a non-interventional group A measured dose of castor oil (30 ml), warmed to about, is gently massaged onto the affected knee joint. Castor oil is used for its natural ability to reduce inflammation, relieve discomfort, and improve local blood circulation A cost-effective heating pad or hot compress is placed on the area where the oil has been applied. The heat is maintained for 15–20 minutes to promote deeper absorption of the oil, improve blood flow, and relax the muscles. Frequency and Duration of Sessions: This treatment is conducted 3–4 times weekly over a span of 4–6 weeks. Each session, which includes the application of oil, heat therapy, and a rest period, lasts about 30–40 minutes A low-cost, temperature-regulated heating aid is tested to ensure safe, consistent, and sustainable application in rural or resource-limited settings. Participants are monitored for pain relief, joint mobility, swelling reduction, and functional improvement using standardized scales Basic self-care guidance (mild knee exercises, posture correction, and rest) is also provided to reinforce the therapeutic effect. In Interventional group, the mean score dropped significantly 11.12 ($\pm$1.83) before treatment to 7.78 ($\pm$1.57) afterward ($p < 0.05$). But in non-interventional group showed only a minor, statistically insignificant reduction in pain. Both the Wilcoxon rank sum test and ANOVA confirmed for reduction of pain level substantially greater among Interventional group but in non-interventional catagory will be ($p < 0.001$) Thermo-assisted castor oil massage is a cost-effective, safe, and effective treatment for knee joint pain in rural women. It can be recommended as a supplementary therapy in geriatric nursing and community health.

Keywords: Technological evaluation, Castor oil massage, Knee joint pain, Thermo- Aided therapy, musculoskeletal pain

1 INTRODUCTION

Arthritis describes joint inflammation. In the past, a person with arthritis may have experienced unpleasant symptoms of joint stiffness, swelling, and excruciating pain. Its unique composition gives it various therapeutic and health-promoting properties. Approximately 90% of castor oil consists of triglyceride responsible of many medicinal effects[1–4]Additionally, previous research has shown that by increasing blood flow, massage may reduce the associated symptoms of osteoarthritis[5–7] circulation surrounding the joint, which reduces muscular tension and increases joint flexibility. Women experience knee discomfort at a higher rate than men do. From 1990 to 2020, Osteoarthritis are more prevalence ratio like ten to seventeen millions of population having this diagnosis[8–10] People with arthritis often experience distressing symptoms, including stiffness, swelling, and severe joint pain. [11,12]. Castor oil may be used to treat arthritis, which is one of its key advantages. While medicine can alleviate pain and inflammation, a more effective long-term treatment for arthritis is to use natural therapies are best and very less complications.Joint pain is a chronic and progressive condition that develops as cartilage breaks down and joint damage triggers the formation of new, often problematic, tissue. [13]

2 METHODS AND MATERIALS

Research methodology: quantitative with a true experimental research design was employed. **Study Setting:** The project was done in the rural regions of Tirumazhisai. **EthicalApproval:** Research got approved by Institutional ethical committee **Study Population:** A total of 100 participants, selected based on population and condition criteria, with no prior formal exposure to music therapy, were included fifty in study batch, fifty in reference batch. All Contributor provided written informed consent before enrolment **Randomization:** Individuals aged Thirty to 60 years aged contributors are chosen by random sampling techniques, and the 100 participants are arbitrarily

DOI: 10.1201/9781042001767-94

picked to study group and non-interventional through a lottery-based randomization process**Intervention:** Castor Oil Application: Gently massage a calibrated amount of heated castor oil (40-45°C) into the affected knee joint. The intervention is delivered three to four times per week for 4-6 weeks. Each session lasts around 30 to 40 minutes and includes oil application, heat treatment, and relaxation.**Technological Evaluation:** A low-cost, temperature-regulated heating aid is tested to ensure safe, consistent, and sustainable application in rural or resource-limited settings. Participants are monitored for pain relief, joint mobility, swelling reduction, and functional improvement using standardized scales WOMAC, VAS. **Supportive Measures:** Basic self-care guidance (mild knee exercises, posture correction, and rest) is also provided to reinforce the therapeutic effect.

3 RESULTS AND DISCUSSION

3.1 *Section A: Equivalence of the Satisfactory of refined castor oil massages and heat therapy on knee pain between the study category and non-interventional category*

In study category posttest mean value was reduced to 7.78 that is SD of 1.57 which means a remarkable decrease in pain of knee. The average score change of preliminary and final assessment was 3.34, indicating a remarkable improvement of their pain after the experiment period. Results of paired t-test were t = 9.7890 and p-value was 4.066E-13 ($p < 0.05$), which confirms that the outcome of variance is statistically significant.

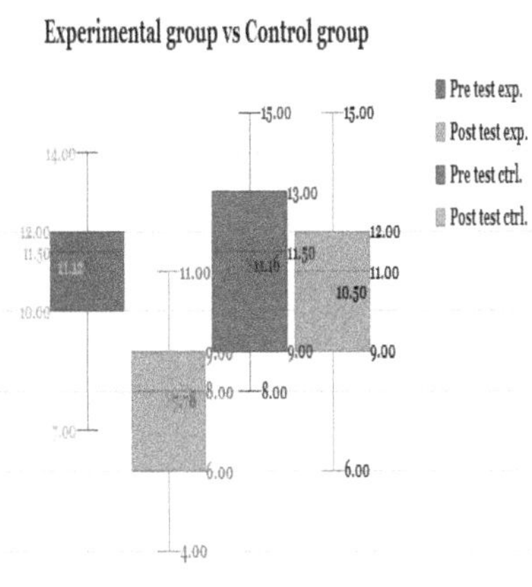

Boxplot comparing the Interventional and Comparison groups' levels of knee pain relief by refined castor oil massage and heat application.

4 VARIANCE ANALYSIS (ANOVA)

4.1 *Section B: Potency heat-assisted castor oil massage between the experimental and control group*

This study assesses how effective castor oil massage is compared to heat application in reducing knee pain among participants in the Interventional and comparison groups. Preliminary result shows the both groups had comparable baseline levels of knee pain before the intervention

F-statistic about **0.02039** and p-value of **0.886705** confirm that the two groups did not differ significantly in their baseline knee pain levels. However, post-test findings reveal a substantial reduction in pain within the experimental group, which recorded of **7.78** (SD = **1.57**) variance will be **2.46**. Furthermore, the post-test F-value of **96.2842** and p-value of **3.33E-16** demonstrate a highly substantial between the groups, indicating that intervention was effective in alleviating knee pain among participants in the experimental group.

5 NON PARAMETRIC STATISTICAL TEST

During the preliminary assessment study group obtained a U value of **1260.5**, while the control group recorded **1239.5**, outcome of Z-score of **–0.0724** and a p-value of **0.9423**.Following the intervention, the experimental group showed a U statistic of **1239.5**, whereas the control group recorded **353.5**. The corresponding Z-score of **–6.1803** and p-value of **6.40E-10** demonstrate a highly significant difference between the groups. This strong statistical evidence indicates Heat-assisted castor oil massage was efficacy and significantly lowered the knee pain among participants in the Interventional group.

6 LIMITATIONS

The arbitration lasted just four weeks, which may not reflect the long-term efficacy of thermo-assisted castor oil massage for chronic knee joint pain. Small and Localized Sample Size: The study was confined to 100 women from a single rural town (Tirumazhisai), which may limit the findings' generalizability to other groups. On-Random Sampling Technique: A convenient sampling method was used rather than random sampling, which may introduce selection bias. Both participants and researchers were aware of group assignments, which could influence reporting and assessment outcomes (observer and response bias). Pain levels were measured using a Numerical Pain Scale.

7 CONCLUSION

Present study on the technological evaluation of heat-aided castor oil application demonstrates that the combined use of castor oil therapy with controlled heat application is an effective, safe, and affordable intervention for alleviating knee musculoskeletal pain among women in resource-limited groups. The integration of temperature-regulated heating aid enhanced oil absorption, improved circulation, and facilitated pain relief, while also promoting functional mobility and comfort. This approach highlights the potential of merging traditional therapeutic practices with simple technological innovations to create sustainable, community-friendly pain management solutions. By providing a low-cost, non-invasive, and easily adoptable method, the study underscores the feasibility of implementing such interventions in rural and underprivileged populations where access to advanced healthcare is limited. Overall, the findings emphasize that heat-aided castor oil application can serve as a practical complementary strategy in musculoskeletal pain management, offering both therapeutic benefit and empowerment to resource-limited female groups.

CONTRIBUTION OF THE AUTHORS

Authors of this research study will contributed equally to get the successful outcome

STRIFE OF INTEREST

No strife of interest during regard to the research study

FUNDING AND SPONSORSHIP SUPPORT

The authors received no compensation for their contributions and do not possess any financial interests in health-related industries.

ACKNOWLEDGMENT

The authors would like to thank everyone who took part in the study for helping to make it a success

REFERENCES

[1] Missiriya, S. (2015). Effectiveness of castor oil massage with hot application on knee joint pain among women. *Education, 25*(40), 50.

[2] Cassia Jemi, C. (2018). A Quasi Experimental study to Evaluate the Effectiveness of Castor Oil Massage with Hot Fomentation on Knee Joint Pain among Post Menopausal Women at Selected Community Areas in Pudukkottai District (Doctoral dissertation, Karpaga Vinayaga College of Nursing, Pudukkottai).

[3] Chauhan, N.H., and Sharma, A. (2017). Effectiveness of the hot application and castor oil application in clients with joint pain-literature review. *International Journal of Nursing Care*, 5(1), 70–74.

[4] Rathod, P., Vanitha, U.B., and Natekar, D.S. (2025). A study to assess the effectiveness of castor oil massage and hot water application on knee joint pain among elderly patients attending the orthopedic department at HSK Hospital, Bagalkot. *Scholars Journal of Applied Medical Sciences*, 13*(1), 289–294.* https://doi.org/10.36347/sjams.2025.v13i01.046

[5] Chauhan, N.H., Sharma, A., Topawala, M., and Patel, S.G.H. (2018). Comparative study to assess the effectiveness of the hot application and castor oil application in clients with joint pain. *International Journal of Advanced Research, 6*, 265–270. https://doi.org/10.21474/IJAR01/6853

[6] Ariana, M., Afrasiabifar, A., Najafi Doulatabad, S., Mosavi, A., and Behnammoghadam, M. (2022). The effect of local heat therapy versus cold rub gel on pain and joint functions in patients with knee osteoarthritis. *Clinical Nursing*, SAGE Publications.

[7] Malanga, G.A., Yan, N., and Stark, J. (2015). Mechanisms and efficacy of heat and cold therapies for musculoskeletal injury. *Postgraduate Medicine, 127*(1), 57–65. https://doi.org/10.1080/00325481.2015.992719

[8] Roth, S.H., and Shainhouse, J.Z. (2004). Efficacy of topical diclofenac solution (Pennsaid) in primary osteoarthritis of the knee: A randomized, double-blind, vehicle-controlled clinical trial. *Archives of Internal Medicine, 164*(18), 2017–2023. https://doi.org/10.1001/archinte.164.18.2017 *(Included for topical treatment comparison.)*

[9] Bazarganipour, F., Taghavi, S.A., Allan, H., Hosseini, N., Khosravi, A., Asadi, R., and Miri, F. (2020). Education, home exercise, and supervised exercise for people with hip and knee osteoarthritis as part of a nationwide implementation program: Data from the Better Management of Patients With Osteoarthritis Registry. *Arthritis Care & Research, 72*(2), 201–207. https://doi.org/10.1002/acr.24033

[10] Melki Tagoor. (2023). Self-acupressure for older adults with symptomatic knee osteoarthritis: A randomized controlled trial. *Arthritis Care & Research.*

[11] Ariana, M., Afrasiabifar, A., Najafi Doulatabad, S., Mosavi, A., and Behnammoghadam, M. (2022). The effect of local heat therapy versus cold rub gel on pain and joint functions in patients with knee osteoarthritis. *Clinical Nursing*, SAGE Publications.

[12] Yildirim, N., Ulusoy, M.F., and Bodur, H. (2010). The effect of heat application on pain, stiffness, physical function and quality of life in patients with knee osteoarthritis. *Journal of Clinical Nursing, 19*(7–8), 1113–1120. https://doi.org/10.1111/j.1365-2702.2009.030

Next-Generation Smart Systems – Sekhar et al. (Eds)
 ISBN: 978-1-041-34234-2

An Experimental Analysis of Digital Music-Based Therapeutic Systems for Mitigating Cognitive Workload Pressure Among Paramedical Students

Kavitha M.
Assistant Professor, PhD Scholar, Department of Community Health Nursing, Saveetha College of Nursing, Thandalam, India

V.M. Roshne
B.Sc [Nursing], Saveetha College of Nursing, Thandalam, India

S. Kalabarathi
Professor, Department of OBG, Saveetha College of Nursing, Thandalam, India

Padmapriya D.
Associate Professor, Department of OBG, Saveetha College of Nursing, Thandalam, India

Sridevi B.
Department of Adult Health Nursing, Saveetha College of Nursing, Thandalam, India

ABSTRACT: Academic stress is common among paramedical students, who confront challenging coursework, clinical obligations, and high expectations. Identifying effective stress management strategies is vital for improving student well-being and academic performance. The study intends to examine how music therapy reduces stress, promotes relaxation, and improves overall wellness. True experimental research design was adopted, Random sampling Techniques was plump for regard to inclusion standard Paramedical students were selected based on inclusion criteria, including academic workload stress, willingness to engage, and no significant psychological illnesses. Standardized instruments were used to conduct baseline assessments on cognitive workload and stress levels. The stress levels of both groups were assessed using a self-structured questionnaire, an academic stress scale, and a university stress scale Orientation Participants were introduced to the digital music-based therapeutic system, including its objectives, procedure, and expected outcomes. Instructions for safe and effective use of the digital platform were provided. Participants involved in structured digital music hangout administered by headphones or speakers in a controlled environment. Each session lasted 20–30 minutes and was held 3–4 times weekly over a 4–6 week period. The playlists, designed to promote relaxation and focus, featured instrumental, slow-tempo, and calming tracks that were scientifically selected to reduce stress. Playlists were adjusted based on participant feedback and stress markers Sessions were directly supervised to ensure adherence and minimize distractions. bio physiological parameters of pulse rate and relaxation levels was self-reported feedback were documented At the end of the intervention, participants were reassessed with the same standardized instruments to track changes in stress levels and cognitive workload. Pre- and post-intervention scores were compared to find out the efficacy of the digital therapy Participants shared their experiences with the program, and their suggestions were gathered to guide future improvements of the system The pretest variance was 62.48, while the posttest variance decreased to 7.06. The calculated F value of 246.7825 indicated a substantial variance between the pre- and post-implementation emotional burden outcome of the research regard to digital music based therapeutic system as a stress-relief strategy for paramedical students facing academic pressure. Passive listening to calming music was shown to significantly reduce stress, foster relaxation, and improve both emotional well-being and concentration.

Keywords: Experimental Analysis, Digital Music-Based Therapeutic Systems, Mitigating Cognitive Workload Pressure, Paramedical Students

1 INTRODUCTION

Stress is a well-established risk factor linked to a variety of physical and psychological problems. The rigorous nature of paramedical education, which involves demanding academic training and clinical exposure [1,2]. Overwhelm is a critical concern in both educational and healthcare settings, as it affects mental health, cognitive functioning, and overall performance. Paramedical students face academic challenges, clinical responsibilities, and high performance expectations, all of which contribute to elevated stress levels [3]. Historically, archaic in civilizations such as Sumer, Babylon, and Egypt. Exploring its effectiveness in reducing academic stress among paramedical students offers a valuable non-pharmacological strategy to improve both well-being and academic performance [4–6].Music therapy provides a non-invasive means of stress relief. When integrated with Internet of Things (IoT) technology and real-time physiological monitoring, personalized music interventions can deliver tailored stress reduction. This study examines how such an approach can support paramedical students in managing stress, improving their learning experience, and enhancing overall well-being [7,8]. Music is widely acknowledged as a potent, non-invasive intervention for stress management due to its close link with emotions. Its effects depend on factors such as arousal level, valence, personal preference, and familiarity with the music [8–10]. Within educational contexts, music can improve concentration, lower anxiety, and foster a positive emotional atmosphere, ultimately contributing to improved academic outcomes [11,12].Music-based interventions may include relaxation exercises with music, improvisation, listening paired with creative activities like drawing, movement in response to music, group discussions about songs, songwriting, and singing [13–15].

DOI: 10.1201/9781042001767-95

2 RESEARCH METHODOLOGY

Research blueprint: Empirical research and true experimental framework was used to evaluate the impact of sound healing on stress reduction among paramedical students. Study Setting: Research settings in Saveetha Institute of Medical and Technical Sciences (SIMATS) with paramedical students as participants. Ethical Approval: Ethical approval given by institutional ethical committee Study Participants: The sample included 100 paramedical students, divided equally as Interventional (n=50) and reference (n=50) groups. Participants were required to volunteer, have no prior formal experience with music therapy, and possess the ability to read, write, and communicate in either Tamil or English. Written informed consent was obtained before enrollment. Exclusion criteria applied to students with psychiatric illnesses, severe anxiety or depression requiring treatment, neurological disorders, hearing impairments, substance abuse history, or those taking medications likely to affect stress levels or cognitive function. Randomization: Participants were selected using random sampling and assigned to the experimental (music therapy) or control group via a lottery system. Intervention: music sound healing sessions featuring instrumental and meditative tracks in a controlled setting. Each session lasted 20–30 minutes and was conducted 3–4 times weekly for 4–6 weeks. Playlists were curated to promote relaxation, reduce stress, and improve focus, with adjustments made based on feedback and stress responses. Participant Orientation: An introductory session was held to outline the purpose, procedures, and anticipated benefits of the therapy. Participants were also trained in safe and effective use of the digital platform. Baseline and Stress Assessment: Prior to intervention, stress and cognitive workload were measured using standardized tools, including a self-structured questionnaire, the Academic Stress Scale, and the University Stress Scale. Monitoring During Sessions: Sessions were supervised to ensure compliance and minimize distractions. Both physiological data (e.g., heart rate, relaxation level) and subjective reports were collected. Post-Intervention Assessment: At the end of the intervention, participants were reassessed with same tool Feedback and Reflection: Participants provided feedback on their experiences, and suggestions were documented to refine the digital music therapy program for future use.

3 FINDINGS AND INTERPRETATION

Section A: Stress Level Distribution by Frequency and Percentage on University and Academic Stress Scales in Intervention group and reference Group

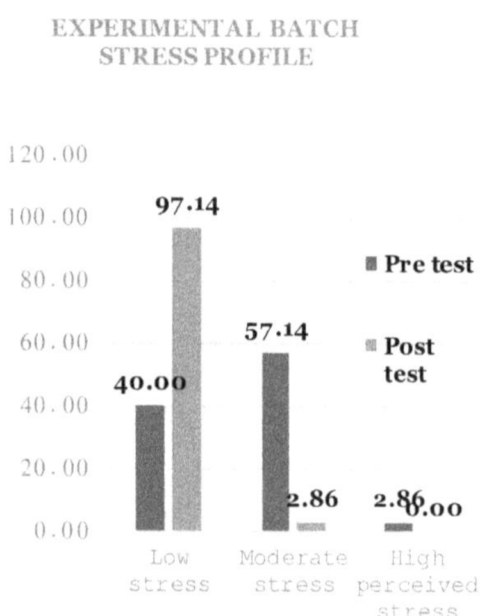

In the Intervention group, preliminary assessment revealed that 14 students (40%) experienced low stress, 20 students (57.14%) reported moderate stress, and 1 student (2.86%) had high stress. Post-test findings indicated that 34 students (97.14%) reported low stress, while only 1 student (2.86%) remained in the moderate stress category, as it lowered stress levels significantly, bringing nearly all students (97.14%) into the low-stress range Dissemination of preliminary and final assessment of stress in Intervention group

Section B: Control Group: Frequency and Percentage Analysis of Pre- and Post-Test Stress Levels

The findings indicate that in the control group, 7 students (20%) reported low stress, 25 students (71.43%) experienced moderate stress, and 3 students (8.57%) showed high stress levels during the pre-test. In the post-test, 12 students (34.29%) fell into the low-stress category, while 23 students (65.71%) remained in the moderate-stress range. Unlike the experimental group, the reference group not demonstrates a substantial reduction in stress ratio as they were not provided with music therapy.

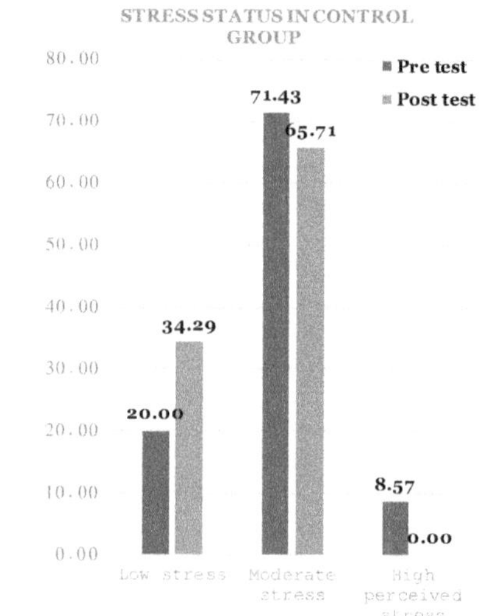

Dissemination of preliminary and final assessment of stress in reference group

Intergroup Variance Analysis (ANOVA) Stress Levels between Interventional and reference Groups

Within the Interventional group, the average stress score decreased markedly from a pre-test mean of 27.14 (SD = 7.90) to final assessment mean of 5.00 (SD = 2.68). Correspondingly, the variance dropped from 62.48 prior to the intervention to 7.06 afterward. The resulting F statistic of 246.7825 confirmed that the reduction in stress levels following the intervention was statistically significant. Conversely, the control group showed a pre-test mean of 25.11 (SD = 6.77) and a post-test mean of 23.29 (SD = 4.23). Although the variance decreased from 45.81 to 17.86, the obtained F value of 1.83813 indicated that the change in stress scores for this group was not mathematically significant.

4 LIMITATIONS

The short three-week intervention and follow-up period could also affect the reliability of results. Additionally, excluding students with psychiatric conditions, hearing impairments or those on medications influencing stress or cognition reduces applicability to a broader population. Finally, conducting the study within one institution may not fully represent paramedical students from diverse educational environments.

5 CONCLUSION

The findings demonstrate that digital music-based therapy significantly reduced stress and cognitive workload among paramedical students. Participants reported enhanced focus, lower stress levels, and improved coping with academic demands. The results emphasize the value of digital music healing system as a unobtrusive, cost-effective, accessible strategy to promote psychological well-being and academic performance in high-pressure educational contexts. Integrating such interventions into paramedical training programs may help build resilience, minimize burnout, and improve overall learning outcome.

AUTHORS CONTRIBUTION

All authors reviewed the manuscript, approved its final version, and agree to be accountable for all aspects of the work.

DISPUTE OF CAPTIVATED

Not any disagreement arise during the research process.

SUPPORT FOR FUNDING AND SPONSORSHIP

The authors of this project have not been paid for their consultation work and hold no financial interests in any health-related industries.

ACKNOWLEDGMENT

Researchers would like to gratitude and appreciation of all components of research works applied to achieve the fruitful success.

REFERENCES

[1] Packyanathan, J.S., Lakshmanan, R., and Jayashri, P. (2019). Effect of music therapy on anxiety levels on patient undergoing dental extractions. *Journal of family medicine and primary care*, 8 (12), 3854–3860.

[2] Leardi, S., Pietroletti, R., Angeloni, G., Necozione, S., Ranalletta, G., and Del Gusto, B. (2007). Randomized clinical trial examining the effect of music therapy in stress response to day surgery. *Journal of British Surgery*, 94(8), 943–947.

[3] Umbrello, M., Sorrenti, T., Mistraletti, G., Formenti, P., Chiumello, D., and Terzoni, S. (2019). Music therapy reduces stress and anxiety in critically ill patients: a systematic review of randomized clinical trials. *Minerva anestesiologica*, 85(8), 886–898.

[4] Fleury, E.A.B., Approbato, M.S., Silva, T.M.D., and Maia, M. C.S. (2014). Music therapy in stress: proposal of extension to Assisted Reproduction. *JBRA assisted reproduction*, 18(2), 55–61. https://doi.org/10.5935/1518-0557.20140006

[5] Uggla, L., Bonde, L.O., Svahn, B.M., Remberger, M., Wrangsjö, B., and Gustafsson, B. (2016). Music therapy can lower the heart rates of severely sick children. *Acta Paediatrica*, 105(10), 1225–1230.

[6] Zhang, J. (2024). IoT-enabled Musical Therapy to Alleviate Physiological Stress in College Students using Big Data and Mixed-Density Neural Networks. *Mobile Netw Appl*. https://doi.org/10.1007/s11036-024-02393-x

[7] Son, H.K., So, W.-Y., and Kim, M. (2019). Effects of Aromatherapy Combined with Music Therapy on Anxiety, Stress, and Fundamental Nursing Skills in Nursing Students: A Randomized Controlled Trial. *International Journal of Environmental Research and Public Health*, 16(21), 4185. https://doi.org/10.3390/ijerph16214185

[8] Jiang, J., Rickson, D., and Jiang, C. (2016). The mechanism of music for reducing psychological stress: Music preference as a mediator. *The Arts in Psychotherapy*, 48, 62–68.

[9] Yaming Wei. (2024). *Exploring the Diverse Impact of Music on Alleviating Academic Stress in University Students during the Post-Pandemic Era.*, 10(3), 319–332.

[10] Ferrer, E., Lew, P., Jung, S., Janeke, E., Garcia, M., Peng, C., and Tam, C. (2014). Playing music to relieve stress in a college classroom environment. *College Student Journal*, 48(3), 481–494.

[11] Dungsirisangthong, P., Boonyam, T., Chiengchana, N., and Buranaprapuk, A. (2025). The Effect of Online Music Therapy Interventions on Reducing Stress Levels in Small Hotel Managers: A Mixed-Methods Pilot Study. *Music Therapy Perspectives*, 43(1), miae018.

[12] Hunter, B.C., Oliva, R., Sahler, O.J.Z., Gaisser, D.A., Salipante, D.M., and Arezina, C.H. (2010). Music therapy as an adjunctive treatment in the management of stress for patients being weaned from mechanical ventilation. *Journal of Music Therapy*, 47(3), 198–219.

[13] Kehl, S.M., La Marca-Ghaemmaghami, P., Haller, M., Pichler-Stachl, E., Bucher, H.U., Bassler, D., and Haslbeck, F.B. (2021). Creative music therapy with premature infants and their parents: A mixed-method pilot study on parents' anxiety, stress and depressive symptoms and parent–infant attachment. *International Journal of Environmental Research and Public Health*, 18(1), 265.

[14] Zhao, J., and Gao, P. (2025). The role of music in improving academic performance and reducing stress among Chinese youth: a quantitative and qualitative study. *Current Psychology*, 1–21.

[15] Moore, C., and Wilhelm, L.A. (2019). A survey of music therapy students' perceived stress and self-care practices. *Journal of Music Therapy*, 56(2), 174–201.

[16] An, X. (2022). Research on the anxiety relief of college students by music therapy. *Psychiatria Danubina*, 34(suppl 1), 934–938.

Next-Generation Smart Systems – Sekhar et al. (Eds)
© 2027 The Author(s), ISBN: 978-1-041-34234-2

A Cross-Sectional Study on The Food Habits and Awareness of Prenatal Weight Gain Among Pregnant Women

Sathiyabama G.
Associate Professor, SCON, SIMATS, Thandalam, Chennai, Tamil Nadu, India

S. KalaBarathi
Professor, SCON, SIMATS, Thandalam, Chennai, Tamil Nadu, India

Divya A.
Lecturur, Nutrition Department, SIMATS, Thandalam, Chennai, Tamil Nadu, India

ABSTRACT: Increased GWG is observed to result in certain harmful consequences for both mothers and newborns, some of which may be controlled. Preventing uncontrollably high weight gain during pregnancy can be achieved by leading a healthy lifestyle. To evaluate the level of awareness among pregnant patients on theirBody weight, GWG, diet, and issues related to obesity who seek care at our Saveetha Medical College Hospital, The Most of the women were overweight. This increased by 8.4% by the end of the third trimester (n = 150; 88%). Females who had high Body mass index , nearly half (n = 240; 48.78%) underestimated their weight. Despite having a rudimentary understanding of the relationship between high-calorie intake and weight growth as well as cardiovascular issues.

Keywords: Food Habits, Prenatal Women, Weight gain

1 INTRODUCTION

Weight gain can be influenced by knowing the right nutrition and food, especially when pregnant [1]. Women with a BMI <18.5 (underweight). weight should aim for 11.5–16 kg during pregnancy according to Institute of Medicine . Poor maternal nutrition is linked to a greater likelihood of fetal abnormalities, growth restriction in utero, and elevated infant morbidity and mortality according to WHO, [2,3]. There aren't many detailed guidelines outlining women's nutritional needs during pre-conception, pregnancy, and lactation [4]. Strategies that will ensure adequate weight growth during and after pregnancy need to be applied in our context [5]. However, caesarean deliveries, postpartum conservation of more body mass index than normal, The baby may born beyond the expected date of delivery, and big size baby more than weight 4kgs are some of the risks associated with excessive weight increase. [6,7] Being overweight prior to becoming pregnant and gaining a significant amount of weight during pregnancy may raise the risk of macrosomia [8]. Before getting pregnant, women who are fertile should maintain a normal body mass index. Inadequate weight increase includes low birthweight [9,10]. Based on observational studies, a high BMI before pregnancy is strongly connected to negative outcomes during pregnancy. It is well recognized that maternal weight gain more than the normal above 30kg/m2 during pregnancy raise the risk of several problems and unfavourable pregnancy outcomes. [11,12] Two of the biggest global public health issues are obesity and cardiovascular disease. Numerous detrimental outcomes occurred on antenatal mothers and their babies and the child have been associated with maternal obesity [13–15]. Poor diets and food insecurity continue to be problems for expectant mothers [16].

2 MATERIALS AND PROCEDURES

We investigated pregnant women who attendedthe Saveetha medical college Hospital for routine prenatal care between 2 November 2023 to 30 Dec 2023. The demographic under consideration was deemed to be in the lower-middle socioeconomic strata. The study used convenience sampling to recruit pregnant women, implementing a total population sampling method. About 150 participants comprised the study population, with an estimated 30 pregnant women visiting the facility. Over four to six weeks, Weight and circumference of the mid-upper arm were measured by the researcher. All data stored and analysed for descriptive and inferential statistics.

3 RESULTS AND DISCUSSION

Table 1. Weight comparison between the start and end of pregnancy ($n = 150$).

variable	6 th week Of gestation	*36 th week of gestation*
Weight (kg)	67.5	74
Height (m)	165	165
Mid-upper arm circumference (cm)	29.5	29.5
BMI	68	37
Underweight (BMI < 18.5)	5(3.3%)	4 (2.6%)
Normal (BMI = 18.5–24.9)	63 (42%)	36 (24%)
Overweight (BMI = 25–29.9)	43(28.6%)	41 (27.3%)
Obese (BMI ≥ 30)	39(26%)	33 (22%)

statistical significance of variables was declared at a p-value of .05, 5 women (3.2%) no changes in weight observed from beginning of prenatal period, 63 (42.0%) reserved weight, 36 (24%) gained weight in third trimester, 43(28.6%) gained weight at first trimester wisely41 (27.3%) gained in third trimester. 39 (26%) women gained BMI more than 30 at first trimester . 33 (22%) women gained weight at third trimester body mass index (BMI) more than 30.

DOI: 10.1201/9781042001767-96

Table 2. Body mass index first visit: $n = 150$, Body mass index Final visit in End trimester: $n = 148$.

Are you obese?"	Underweight (BMI < 18.5) (*n*, %)	Normal (BMI = 18.5–24.9) (*n*, %)	Overweight (BMI = 24–29.9) (*n*, %)	*Obese (BMI ≥ 30) (n, %)*
BMI first visit ($n = 150$)				
No	**6 (4)**	**12 (8)**	**35 (23.3)**	**12 (16.6)**
Yes	**28 (18.6)**	**40(26.6)**	**9 (6)**	**11(7.33)**
BMI -final visit in end trimester ($n = 148$)				
No	**12 (8)**	**3 7 (24.66)**	**28 (18.6)**	**8 (5.3)**
Yes	**13 (8.6)**	**35 (23.3)**	**11 (7.3)**	**3(2)**

3 CONCLUSION

When they got pregnant, most of the women in our research study were overweight or obese. Despite some awareness of the connection between high-calorie diets and weight increase as well as cardiovascular issues, less than half of the women had GWGs that were within the permissible weight range. It still takes a lot of work to optimize periconceptional BMI and optimal GWG in every pregnancy. It is essential to support healthcare providers in educating pregnant moms about suitable exercise routines, a patient-centered approach to prenatal care, and healthy eating habits.

ACKNOWLEDGEMENT

We are grateful to the Management and antenatal mothers, SMCH and Participants.

REFERENCES

[1] O'Brien E.C., Alberdi G., and McAuliffe F.M., (2018), The influence of socioeconomic status on gestational weight gain: a systematic review, *Journal of Public Health*, vol. 40, no. 1, pp. 41–55.

[2] KalaBarathi S. and Suganya M., (2024), Association of body mass index with dietary intake and self-care health activities of mothers after postpartum: A mixed-method research in Chennai City, India, *International Journal of Nutrition, Pharmacology, Neurological Diseases*, vol. 14, no. 1, pp. 52–57, doi: 10.4103/ijnpnd.ijnpnd_71_23.

[3] Black R.E., Victora C.G., Walker S.P., *et al.*, (2018), Maternal and child undernutrition and overweight in low-income and middle-income countries, *The Lancet*, vol. 382, no. 9890, pp. 427–451.

[4] Nagourney E.M., Goodman D., Lam Y., Hurley K.M., Henderson J., and Surkan P.J., (Aug. 2019), Obese women's perceptions of weight gain during pregnancy: a theory-based analysis, *Public Health Nutrition*, vol. 22, no. 12, pp. 2228–2236, doi: 10.1017/S1368980019000703.

[5] Kominiarek M.A. and Peaceman A.M., (Dec. 2017), Gestational weight gain, *American Journal of Obstetrics and Gynecology*, vol. 217, no. 6, pp. 642–651, doi: 10.1016/j.ajog.2017.05.040.

[6] Zhang Z.P., Chu L.M., Chu S.L., Lu M., Shen L.H., Chen K., and Shen J., (2018), Prospective cohort study on the risks of pre-pregnancy overweight, excessive gestational weight gain on macrosomia, *Zhonghua Liu Xing Bing Xue Za Zhi*, vol. 39, no. 8, pp. 1082–1085.

[7] Feng P., Wang X.Y., Long Z.W., Shan S.F., Li D.T., Liang Y., and Cheng G., (2019), The association of pre-pregnancy body mass and weight gain during pregnancy with macrosomia: a cohort study, *Zhonghua Yu Fang Yi Xue Za Zhi (Chinese Journal of Preventive Medicine)*, vol. 53, no. 11, pp. 1147–1151.

[8] Chen Q., He Z., Wang Y., Yang X., Liu N., Zhang S., and He Y., (2024), Effect of maternal pre-pregnancy body mass index on longitudinal fetal growth and mediating role of maternal fasting plasma glucose: A retrospective cohort study, *Diabetes, Metabolic Syndrome and Obesity*, pp. 1911–1921.

[9] Yang Z., Phung H., Freebairn L., Sexton R., Raulli A., and Kelly P., (2019), Contribution of maternal overweight and obesity to the occurrence of adverse pregnancy outcomes, *Australian and New Zealand Journal of Obstetrics and Gynaecology*, vol. 59, no. 3, pp. 367–374.

[10] Vijayalakshmi R., Parimala L., and Suganya M., (Mar. 2025), Association of cardiometabolic diseases in adolescents with level of obesity and lifestyle pattern at metropolitan city: Findings from Southern India, *Texila International Journal of Public Health*, vol. 13, no. 1, doi: 10.21522/TIJPH.2013.13.01.Art066.

[11] Callaghan S., O'Brien E., Coughlan B., and McAuliffe F.M., (2020), Midwives' and obstetricians' level of knowledge of appropriate gestational weight gain recommendations for pregnancy: A systematic review, *Birth*, vol. 47, no. 4, pp. 322–331.

[12] Sathiyabama G., Kalabarathi S., and Sharma N., (Dec. 2024), The impact of customized interventions on antenatal mothers' body mass index, *Journal of Pharmacy and Bioallied Sciences*, vol. 16, no. Suppl 4, pp. S4045–S4047, doi: 10.4103/jpbs.jpbs_1381_24.

[13] Kankowski L., Ardissino M., McCracken C., Lewandowski A.J., Leeson P., Neubauer S., and Raisi-Estabragh Z., (2022), The impact of maternal obesity on offspring cardiovascular health: a systematic literature review, *Frontiers in Endocrinology*, vol. 13, 868441.

[14] Phelan S., Jankovitz K., Hagobian T., and Abrams B., (2011), Reducing excessive gestational weight gain: lessons from the weight control literature and avenues for future research, *Women's Health (London, England)*, vol. 7, no. 6, pp. 641–661, doi: 10.2217/whe.11.70.

[15] Sathiyabama G., Kalabarathi S., and Sharma N., (2025 June), The impact of maternal age on maternal and neonatal outcomes among primipara motherssat SMCH,Texila International *Journal of Public Health*, vol. 13, no. issue 2. DOI: 10.21522/TIJPH.2013.13.02.Art041

[16] Muthukumaranjothilingam M.M., Manikumar M., Kotteeswaran K., Alagesan J., and Priyenka P., (Jul. 2019), Effect of exercise on reduction of body fat percentage, body mass index and waist circumference among regular gym goers, *International Journal of Advanced Research*, vol. 7, pp. 267–270.

Next-Generation Smart Systems – Sekhar et al. (Eds)
© 2027 The Author(s), ISBN: 978-1-041-34234-2

A Functional Impact Analysis of a Lumbopelvic Alignment Routine on Menstrual Pain Disorders Among the Early Youth Female Group in a Designated Educational Facility

Kavitha M.
Assistant Professor, Department of Community Health Nursing, Saveetha College of Nursing, Saveetha Institute of Medical and Technical Sciences, Thandalam, India

Supriya K.
B.Sc [Nursing], SCON, SIMATS, India

S. Kalabarathi and Padmapriya D.
Department of OBG, SCON, SIMATS, India

Sridevi B.
Department of Adult Health Nursing, SCON, SIMATS, India

ABSTRACT: Menstrual discomfort—medically termed primary dysmenorrhea is considered gynecological issues faced by a young girls and young women. Non-pharmacological strategies have received increasing interest due to their safety, accessibility, and proven benefits in reducing pain and enhancing physical functioning. Exploration to determine the effectiveness of a lumbopelvic alignment exercise program in reducing pain intensity and functional impairments linked to menstrual disorders among female students in an educational setting. A quantitative true-experimental design was employed. Study sites were chosen based on ease of access, participant availability, and institutional support. The sample comprised 100 adolescent girls aged 13–19 years with a documented history of primary dysmenorrhea, selected through random sampling as per the inclusion criteria. Contributors performed the Pelvic Bridge Exercise, lying supine with knees flexed and feet positioned hip-width apart, lifting the pelvis, maintaining these positions for 5–10 seconds, and then lowering back down. Each daily session involved 10–15 repetitions for 2 sets, followed by 3–5 minutes of light stretching for cool-down. The exercise regimen was supervised during school hours over a four-week period. The mean pain score decreased from 8.08 ± 1.26 in preliminary assessment to 3.13 ± 1.41 in final assessment, indicating an average reduction of 4.95. Repeated-measures t-test value of 63.190 is remarkably Noteworthy ($p < 0.001$), confirming the pelvic bridge exercise substantially reduced the severity of dysmenorrhea among the participants

Keywords: Lumbopelvic alignment, menstrual pain disorders, early youth female, Functional impact analysis, Pain management, musculoskeletal rehabilitation, Preventive health program

1 COMMENCEMENT

Pain during menstruation occurring but not any form of pelvic disease is common among teenage girls and young women and is frequently associated with additional symptoms like nausea, tiredness, and headaches [1,2]. This condition significantly affects an individual's overall quality of life, daily functioning, and school presence. Prevalence estimates range from about 71% in young women to nearly 93% in adolescents. Intake of medications they can lead to side effects such as gastrointestinal irritation and may not be appropriate or affordable for all individuals. Around one-quarter of women avoid medication due to personal health beliefs or financial barriers [2–4]. Consequently, increasing attention has been directed toward safe, accessible, and cost-effective non-pharmacological options—particularly physical exercise—for alleviating menstrual pain [5,6] Substantial evidence demonstrates that exercise—including aerobic workouts, stretching, yoga, and relaxation practices—can effectively reduce symptoms of primary dysmenorrhea. Findings from systematic reviews and meta-analyses indicate notable reductions in both pain intensity and duration, with standardized mean differences (SMDs) around –1.86 for pain severity [7–10]. Exercise is believed to relieve cramps by improving pelvic circulation and lowering prostaglandin buildup [11] additionally, poor lumbopelvic alignment and weak core muscles are linked with primary dysmenorrhea [12]. Therapeutic exercise improves not only physical health but also psychological resilience and overall well-being. As a result, structured exercise programs are now widely acknowledged as essential elements of physiotherapy in managing menstrual pain[13] Among these, pelvic rocking exercises—targeting deep abdominal and gluteal muscles through controlled movements—are particularly beneficial [14,15].

2 METHODS AND MATERIALS

Research framework: Empirical methods with a true experimental methodology were followed this research. The chosen educational institution was selected for its accessibility, cooperation, and the availability of eligible participant's sample of 100 adolescent girls between the ages of 13 and 19 who had a documented history of primary dysmenorrhea was selected using random sampling in accordance with the set inclusion criteria **Data Collection:** Participants raised their hips to create a straight alignment from the shoulders to the knees, maintained this posture for 5–10 seconds, and then lowered back to the initial position. Each daily session included 10–15 repetitions performed in two sets, followed by 3–5 minutes of light stretching as a cool-down. The supervised exercise routine was conducted over a four-week period during school hours while functional limitations were examined through pre- and post-intervention evaluations. Baseline measurements were taken on Day 1, and final assessments were completed at the conclusion of the program. **Results:** The findings revealed that the average pain score dropped from 8.08 ± 1.26 at baseline to 3.13 ± 1.41 after the intervention. The mean decrease of 4.95 was statistically significant. A paired t-test value of 63.190 ($p < 0.001$)

DOI: 10.1201/9781042001767-97

verified that the pelvic bridge exercise substantially reduced the severity of dysmenorrhea among the adolescent participants.

3 RESULTS AND DISCUSSION

Section A. Assessment of Dysmenorrhea Levels in Adolescent Girls

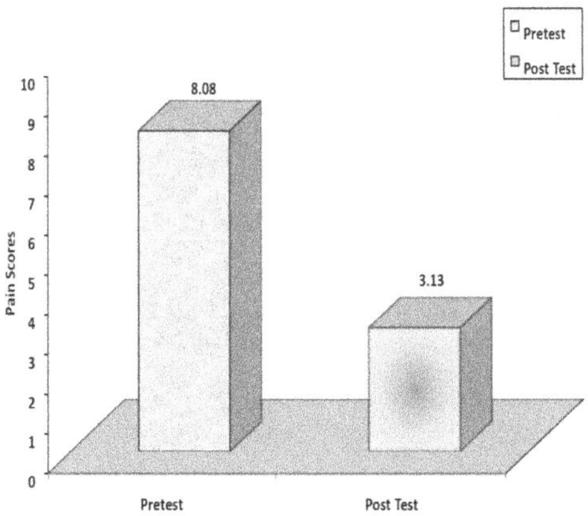

Table 1. Sample proportion allocation of Dysmenorrhea Severity among Adolescent Participants (n = 100).

	Pretest		Post-Assessment	
Pain Intensity	Frequency	Percentage (%)	Frequency	Percentage (%)
No Pain (0)	-	-	6	6.0
Minimal (1 – 3)	-	-	57	57.0
Moderate (4 – 6)	12	12.0	37	37.0
Severe (7 – 9)	72	72.0	-	-
Worst Possible Pain (10)	16	16.0	-	-

Table 1 indicates that during the pre-test, 72 participants (72%) reported severe pain, while 16 participants (16%) experienced the worst possible pain. Following the intervention, in the post-test, 57 participants (57%) belongs to mild pain, 37 (37%) regard to moderate pain, and 6 (6%) reported no pain.

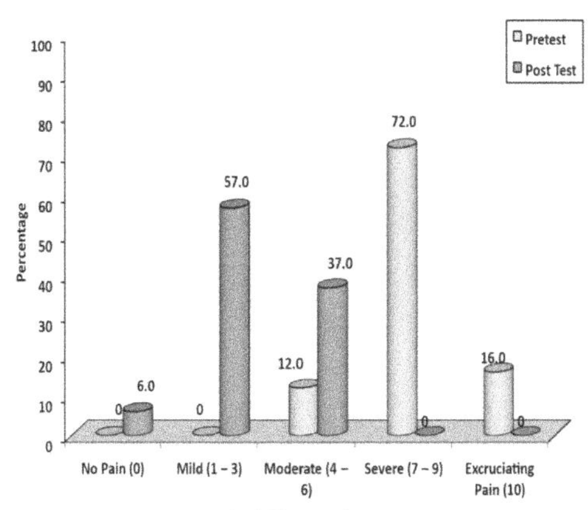

Proportional analysis of preliminary assessment and final assessment among adolescent girls

Section B. Analysis of the Effectiveness of Pelvic Bridge Exercises in Managing Dysmenorrhea

Table 2. Difference between the preliminary and final assessment of Pain Levels among Adolescent Girl (n =100).

Pain	Mean	S.D	Mean Difference Score	Paired "t" test & p value
Preliminary	**8.08**	**1.26**	**4.95**	
Final assessment	**3.13**	**1.41**		**t = 63.190 p=0.0001, S*****

The average pain score decreased from 8.08 ± 1.26 in the preliminary to 3.13 ± 1.41 in final assessment reflecting a mean reduction of 4.95. The paired t-test result ($t = 63.190$) $p < 0.001$, demonstrating that Pelvic Bridge Exercise substantially alleviated dysmenorrhea symptoms among the adolescent participants.

4 LIMITATIONS

The research involved a comparatively small group drawn from a single educational setting The four-week duration of the exercise program may not adequately represent the long-term or continued impact of lumbopelvic alignment exercises on menstrual discomfort. Pain levels and functional challenges were measured using self-reported instruments, which could introduce recall errors and individual subjectivity. **Menstrual Cycle Variability:** Variations in menstrual cycle patterns, hormonal changes, and lifestyle factors were not controlled

5 CONCLUSION

Findings demonstrate that performing lumbopelvic alignment exercises—specifically pelvic bridge routines—can effectively lessen menstrual pain and associated physical limitations among adolescent schoolgirls. This affordable, non-pharmacological, and practical intervention serves as a promising complementary or alternative option to conventional medical therapy for primary dysmenorrhea. Incorporating such exercise-based programs within school health frameworks could foster better menstrual health, minimize school absenteeism, and enhance overall life quality for adolescents. Further research with broader participant groups, extended durations, and controlled experimental designs is warranted to confirm and sustain these outcomes.

AUTHORS CONTRIBUTION

All authors contributed the chapter's preparation, data collection procedure with intervention, Statistical analysis of research, manuscript and reviews and accountable for all forms research process.

SUPPORT FOR FUNDING AND SPONSORSHIP

The authors not receiving fund and sponsorship by any organization

ACKNOWLEDGMENT

The authors contributed their all research interventions to succeed the research process.

REFERENCES

[1] Wong, B.-H., and Kim, J. (2023). Effects of Pilates on pain, physical function, sleep quality, and psychological factors in young women with dysmenorrhea: A preliminary randomized controlled study. *Healthcare*, 11(14), Article 2076. https://doi.org/10.3390/healthcare11142076

[2] Yang, N.-Y., and Kim, S.-D. (2016). Effects of a yoga program on menstrual cramps and menstrual distress in undergraduate students with primary dysmenorrhea: A single-blind, randomized controlled trial. *Journal of Alternative and Complementary Medicine*, 22(9), 732–738. https://doi.org/10.1089/acm.2016.0058

[3] Yonglitthipagon, P., Muansiangsai, S., Wongkhumngern, W., Donpunha, W., Chanavirut, R., Siritaratiwat, W., *et al.* (2017). Effect of yoga on the menstrual pain, physical fitness, and quality of life of young women with primary dysmenorrhea. *Journal of Bodywork and Movement Therapies*, 21(4), 840–846. https://doi.org/10.1016/j.jbmt.2017.01.014

[4] Ozturk, N., Oter, E.G., and Eke, M.K. (2023). The effect of abdominal massage and stretching exercise on pain and dysmenorrhea symptoms in female university students: A single-blind randomized-controlled clinical trial. *Health Care for Women International*, 44(5), 621–638. https://doi.org/10.1080/07399332.2022.2061973

[5] Fallah, F., and Mirfeizi, M. (2018). How is the quality and quantity of primary dysmenorrhea affected by physical exercises? A study among Iranian students. *International Journal of Women's Health and Reproduction Sciences*, 6(1), 60–66. https://doi.org/10.15296/ijwhr.2018.11

[6] Ibrahim, Z.M., Alharkan, B.S., Alanzi, E.H., Alnasban, H.A., Alsuwailem, M.M., and Al Khalil, W.K. (2023). Efficacy of active stretching exercises against symptoms of primary dysmenorrhoea in young adult females: A randomized controlled trial. *Physiotherapy Quarterly*, 31(1), 46–52. https://doi.org/10.5114/pq.2023.115416

[7] Saleh, S.H., and Mowafy, E.H. (2016). Stretching or core strengthening exercise. *Journal of Women's Health Care*, 5(4), 295. https://doi.org/10.4172/2167-0420.1000295

[8] Shah, S., Verma, N., Begani, P., Nagar, H., and Mujawar, N. (2016). Effect of exercises on primary dysmenorrhoea in young females. *International Journal of Physiotherapy Research*, 4(4), 1658–1662.

[9] Gamit, K., Sheth, M., and Vyas, N. (2014). The effect of stretching exercise on primary dysmenorrhea in adult girls. *International Journal of Medical Science and Public Health*, 3(5), 549–550. https://doi.org/10.5455/ijmsph.2014.210220142

[10] Shahr-jerdy, S., Hosseini, R.S., and Gh, M.E. (2012). Effects of stretching exercises on primary dysmenorrhea in adolescent girls. *Biomedical Human Kinetics*, 4(2), 127–132. https://doi.org/10.2478/v10101-012-0024-y

[11] Wang, L., Yan, Y., Qiu, H., *et al.* (2022). Prevalence and risk factors of primary dysmenorrhea in students: A meta-analysis. *Value in Health*, 25(12), 1678–1684.

[12] Armour, M., Ee, C.C., Naidoo, D., *et al.* (2019). Exercise for dysmenorrhoea. *Cochrane Database of Systematic Reviews*, 2019 (6), CD013147.

[13] Sanctis, V.D., Soliman, A., Bernasconi, S., *et al.* (2015). Primary dysmenorrhea in adolescents: Prevalence, impact and recent knowledge. *Pediatric Endocrinology Reviews*, 13(3), 512–520.

[14] Patel, (2015). *Randomized controlled trial of stretching exercises versus no treatment in primary dysmenorrhea*. [Journal Name]. (From Exercise for dysmenorrhea review)

[15] Saleh, S.H., and Mowafy, E.H. (2016). *Three-armed randomized controlled trial comparing stretching, core strengthening and no treatment*. [From Exercise for dysmenorrhea review]

Next-Generation Smart Systems – Sekhar et al. (Eds)

High-Risk Obstetrics: From Conception to Postpartum

R. Vijayalakshmi
Professor, Saveetha College of Nursing, Saveetha Institute of Medical and Technical Sciences, Chennai, Tamil Nadu, India

Agna Ajan
B.Sc (N) Student, Saveetha College of Nursing, Saveetha Institute of Medical and Technical Sciences, Chennai, Tamil Nadu, India

Jagadeeswari J.
Assistant Professor, Saveetha College of Nursing, Saveetha Institute of Medical and Technical Sciences, Chennai, Tamil Nadu, India

ABSTRACT: Every pregnancy has some risk, even though the majority of pregnancies and births go smoothly. Approximately Fifteen percent of pregnant women may experience severe complications that could pose a risk to their lives. that call for targeted care; some individuals might require substantial intervention to endure. Any point during pregnancy and delivery might result in complications that affect the maternal and the neonate general healthiness and survival. A longitudinal investigation was done involving a cohort of 100 high-risk pregnant women at a tertiary care facility. The assessment of these high-risk pregnant women was conducted utilizing a Structured Modified Coopland high-risk evaluation method. Even though many applicants faced optimistic maternal and newborn outcomes, adverse consequences such as small foe gestation, prematurity, and post mature deliveries were more repeatedly seen within the susceptible group. Therefore, to improve motherly, obstetrical, and newborn outcomes through appropriate referral services and high-quality, reachable prenatal care, it is crucial to identify susceptible pregnancies at initial stage.

Keywords: Risk, Care, Well Being, Antenatal Mothers and Pregnancy

1 BACKGROUND

Every pregnancy has some risk, even though the majority of pregnancies and births go smoothly. Approximately 15% of pregnant women may experience severe, life-threatening complications that call for specialist care; others may require major intervention to survive. Any point during pregnancy and delivery might result in complications that affect the mommy's and the baby's general healthiness and survival. [1]

As reported by the World Health Organization, more than 700 women lose their lives daily due to complications. during pregnancy and childbirth. Heavy bleeding, maternal infections, unsafe abortion, pregnancy illnesses associated with hypertension, such as eclampsia and preeclampsia, and medical conditions that complicate pregnancy, such as diabetes, HIV/AIDS, or heart issues, are the five main causes of pregnancy-related deaths. (2023). According to projections from the World Health Organization, it is estimated that over 700 women will lose their lives each day in 2023 due to preventable factors associated with pregnancy and childbirth. In 2023, a maternal death is anticipated to occur roughly every two minutes. From the year 2000 to 2023, the global maternal mortality rate decreased by more than 40%. In 2023, slightly more than 90% of all maternal fatalities acquired in low economy nations. [2]

The Special Bulletin regarding Maternal Mortality in India for the years 2019–21, which utilizes data from the Sample Registration System (SRS), indicates that the maternal mortality ratio (MMR) in India has declined by 37 points between the year of 2014 to 2016 decreasing from hundred and thirty per lakh live childbirths to 93 in year of 2019.The Maternal Mortality Ratio (MMR) in Tamil Nadu decreased from 45.5 per one lakh live births in 2023–2024 to 39.4 per one lakh in 2024. [3]

Risky pregnancies and their causes, and their issues can all be identified with effective prenatal care. improves the outcomes for mothers, obstetricians, and newborns. [4] In order to stop the development of any maternal or fetal conflicts, women who have been classified as high risk must also be regularly evaluated by health professionals through routine treatment in medical facilities and home visits. [5]

Achieving optimal mother, obstetric, and neonatal outcomes requires identifying high-risk pregnancies, their causes, and the impact of receiving quality prenatal care.[6] Additionally, women who are deemed high risk should get regular home visits and care from facility medical staff to prevent issues for both the mother and the unborn child. To improve pregnancy outcomes, adequate laboratory testing, referral services, and follow-up care are necessary. The outcome's prognosis is also influenced by the high-risk status of expectant moms. [7]

It's becoming more and more obvious that preventative care can reduce or even completely eradicate the harm caused by some of the most prevalent problems, such bad eating habits, drug abuse, or disregard for recommended treatment plans for common illnesses.[8] A variety of factors influence the rate and occurrence of high-risk pregnancies, which involves few medical conditions, age, number of deliveries after 28 weeks, a past history of cesarean sections, multiple pregnancies, geographical and environmental factors, socioeconomic status, reading ability rates, the absence of birth prevention service area, and entree to healthcare. [9] In India the government has initiated schemes to identify susceptible pregnancies as a response to the increasing rates of maternal morbidity and mortality in the year 2016. [10]

To improve pregnancy outcomes, appropriate laboratory testing and referral services are necessary in addition to follow-up care. The forecast is likewise affected by the various types of menace in gestation that prenatal females experience. Consequently, early proof of identity of the type of susceptible gestation can assist in guiding suitable intervention strategies for expectant mothers.

2 METHODS AND MATERIALS

A quantitative longitudinal survey design study involving a sample of Hundred high-risk pregnant women was done in a

DOI: 10.1201/9781042001767-98

tertiary care facility with prior endorsement. Applicants were carefully chosen using a purposive sampling technique. Each applicant gave the agreement with full knowledge after being thoroughly briefed about the study. The demographic variables assessed included the mother's age, educational level, occupation, family structure, place of dwelling, and instances of consanguineal marriage. A questionary was designed to evaluate the outcomes from the mother and her newborn. The validity and reliability of the questionnaire were evaluated by a qualified statistician. The high-risk pregnant women were assessed using the Structured Modified Coopland high-risk assessment instrument. The scoring incorporates factors such as motherly age, number of deliveries, medical-surgical history, anemia levels, previous perinatal complications, Rh incompatibility, malpresentation, and existing pregnancy issues including preeclampsia and diabetes during pregnancy. Descriptive and inferential statistics were employed to enter and evaluate the data.

3 RESULTS

One hundred pregnant women who participated in the evaluation of maternal and fetal outcomes make up the sample. In terms of maternal age, the majority of mothers (61%) reported non-consanguineous marriage, 53% of the participants were from nuclear households, 21% had finished high school, and the majority of moms (68%) were jobless.

Section A: Assessment of feto-maternal outcomes

Table 1. Distribution of rate and proportion of neonatal elements among prenatal mothers participating in the evaluation of fetal outcomes.

Neonatal Elements	Rate	Proportion
Neonate babies Age		
1 day – 3 days	44	44
4 days – 6 days	32	32
More than 7 days	24	24
Babies Birth Weight		
Less than 1 Kg	4	4
1 Kg s–1.5 Kgs	8	8
1.6 Kgs s– 2.4 Kgs	21	21
2.5 Kgs – 3.5 Kgs	51	51
More than 3.6 Kgs	16	16
Term		
Prematurity	36	36
Full gestation	64	64
Childbirth Location		
Residence	3	3
Clinics	12	12
Institutional	83	83
Others	2	2
Apgar Score		
0 – 3	6	6
4 – 6	21	21
7 – 10	73	73
Breast Suckling Types		
Lactating	59	59
Feeder	12	12
Katori	17	17
Formula milk	12	12
Damage during childbirth		
No	81	81
Chignon	9	9
Hematoma under the scalp	6	6
Skin abrasion	4	4

The allocation of rate and proportion of factors associated to newborns among 100 expectant moms are shown in Table 1. In terms of the neonates' age, 44% were born between 1 and 3 days, 51% weighed between 2.5 and 3.5 kg, and 64% were born at term, while 36% were born before their due date. The majority of babies (73%) scored between 7 and 10, indicating good health, while the majority of deliveries (83%) took place in hospitals. Twenty-one percent scored between four and six, and six percent scored between zero and three, indicating potential birth health issues. In terms of feeding techniques, 59% of the babies were fed exclusively breast milk, 17% with a spoon, 12% with a paladai, and 12% with supplements. Eighty-one percent of the newborns were born without any injuries. Of the rest, 4% had skin abrasions, 6% had cephalohematomas, and 9% had caput succedaneum.

Table 2. Distribution of motherly elements among prenatal mothers participating in the evaluation of fetal outcomes, including frequency and percentage.

Maternal variable	Rate	Proportion
Pregnancy duration in Weeks		
28 Wks –30 Wks	11	11
31 Wks – 33 Wks	16	16
34 Wks – 36 Wks	24	24
Greater than 37 Wks	49	49
Number of deliveries		
Delivered once	45	45
Delivered twice	42	42
Delivered more than thrice	13	13
Multifetal gestation		
Yes	17	17
No	83	83
Rhesus factor		
Group "A"	24	24
Group "B"	29	29
Group "AB"	13	13
Group "O"	34	34
Rhesus antigen		
Present	91	91
Absent	9	9
Medical Initiation of Labor with Oxytocin		
Yes	41	41
No	59	59
Initiation of Labor by surgical method		
Amniotomy	26	26
Sweeping of membrane	19	19
Irrelevant	55	55
Childbirth route		
Vaginal	47	47
Delivery by forceps	9	9
Delivery by vacuum	7	7
Caesarean	37	37
Labour period		
1 hour –3 hours	9	9
4 hours – 6 hours	17	17
7 hours – 10 hours	22	22
11 hours – 13 hours	24	24
14 hours – 16 hours	18	18
Greater than 17 hours	10	10
Prelabor Break of Membranes		
Yes	26	26
No	74	74
Any Impediment after delivery		
No	68	68
Yes	32	32
Any Impediment for the baby During the Labor		
No	71	71
Moved to Intensive care	17	17
Admitted to intensive care for long period	12	12

The occurrence and proportion of motherly factors midst hundred pregnant women at high risk are shown in Table 2. The majority of moms (49%) gave birth after the period of 37 weeks, 45% were delivered once, 17% had multifetal pregnancies, and 83% had single pregnancies, according to gestational age. In terms of blood categories, 34% of the moms rhesus factor were 'O', 29% were 'B', 24% were 'A', and 13% were 'AB'. Nine percent were Rh negative, whereas the majority (91%) were Rh positive. During labor, 41% of moms received oxytocin induction, whereas 59% did not. 55% did not have amniotomy, 26% had ARM, and 19% had stripping. 37% had caesarean, 9% had deliveries assisted by forceps, 7% had deliveries assisted by vacuum, and 47% had vaginal births. 24% worked 11 to 13 hrs, 22% worked 7 to 10 hrs, 18% worked 14 to 16 hrs, 17% worked 4 to 6 hrs, 10% worked greater than 17 hrs, and 9% worked 1 to 3 hrs. Premature rupture of the membranes occurred in 26% of moms, whereas 74% did not. In terms of postpartum difficulties, 68% of the women did not have any complications, while 32% did. Regarding fetal difficulties during labor, 17% of the neonates were moved to the NICU, 12% required prolonged NICU hospitalization, and 71% of the patients had no complications.

Section B: Assessment of high risk during antenatal care

Table 3. Distribution of rate and proportion of Feto-maternal outcomes among prenatal mothers.

Risk Level	Rate	Proportion
Low	40	40
Moderate	32	32
High	28	28

The rate and proportion of motherly and newborn consequences amid pregnant women at high risk are shown in Table 3. Of the one hundred participants, forty percent were classified as low risk, thirty-two percent as intermediate risk, and the remaining twenty-eight percent as high risk. According to this distribution, a considerable number of moms still needed close observation and specialized care because of intermediate and high-risk factors, even though a sizable portion were at low risk.

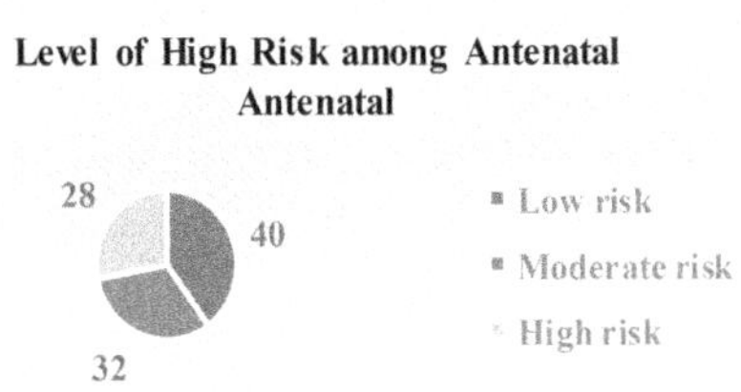

Figure 1. Proportion distribution of level of high risk among prenatal mothers.

According to the study, there is no statistically substantial association amongst any of the demographic factors and the prenatal moms' maternal and fetal outcomes. This demonstrates that none of the factors have a substantial impact on the prenatal women' maternal and fetal outcomes.

4 DISCUSSION

This study was led in a tertiary care facility in Thiruvallur using a longitudinal design to assess the feto-maternal consequences midst susceptible expectant moms. According to the study, 28% were found to be in the susceptible group, 32% were rated as moderately risky, and 40% were labeled as low risk. This distribution shows that although a sizable fraction of women were at low risk, a sizable portion nevertheless needed specialized treatment and close monitoring because of intermediate and high-risk characteristics.

The most common maternal complications were Postpartum hemorrhage accounted for 31.91% and infections in surgical site for 25.52%. Meanwhile, respiratory distress syndrome, at 13.83%, emerged as perinatal morbidity. This information is derived from a study conducted by Anita Bablad involving 94 expectant women who were greater than 28 weeks of gestation period, spanning from July 2023 to June 2024. Despite the absence of maternal fatalities, a perinatal death proportion of 26.59% was pragmatic; this was ascribed to prompt discovery and cautious intervention. [11]

In a tertiary hospital environment in Bangladesh, 100 pregnant women participated in a prospective study led by Afroza Sultana *et al.* (2023) that examined the feto- maternal consequences linked to risky gestations. The study found that most perinatal outcomes were positive despite the problems, emphasizing the value of prompt obstetric treatment and risk stratification in handling susceptible gestations. [12] Ankush Gautam, Shuchi Sharma, and Reena Sharma (2022) 3,887 pregnant women who were hospitalized to the labor ward participated in this reflective data-based study. 28.96% (n=1126) of them were determined to be high-risk pregnancies. The greatest hazard features were having had a previous cesarean section (2.8%), having hypertensive disorders (3.31%), and having hypothyroidism (15.96%). Caesarean sections were performed on 88% of the high-risk pregnancies. A total of 96.5% of babies achieve an APGAR score exceeding 7, while merely 1.7% require hospitalization in the NICU, neonatal outcomes were generally positive. Nonetheless, eleven stillbirths—eight macerated and three fresh—were reported.[13]. Meanwhile the current study is restricted to 100 applicants, it may be conducted over a longer period of time to thoroughly evaluate the elevated risk, its related factors, and its impact on mother and fetal outcomes. This research may be lengthened to evaluate the consumption of management programs by high-risk pregnant women and subsequent care.

5 CONCLUSION

Negative results, including small for gestation, prematurity, and post maturity births, were observed more frequently in risk pregnant women, despite many trial participants experiencing positive obstetric and neonatal outcomes. Consequently, to augment motherly, obstetric, and newborn consequences via suitable referral services and high-quality, readily available prenatal care, it is essential to identify susceptible gestation at initial level. Multivariate techniques, such as logistic regression, should be used in future studies to measure the extent to which clinical factors relatively than just demographics foresee feto-maternal outcomes in susceptible gestation.

REFERENCES

[1] Majella, M.G., Sarveswaran, G., Krishnamoorthy, Y., Sivaranjini, K., Arikrishnan, K., and Kumar, S.G. (2019). A longitudinal study on high risk pregnancy and its outcome among antenatal women attending rural primary health centre in

Puducherry, South India. *Journal of education and health promotion*, 8, 12.

[2] Padmapriya D. Rokith Rakshan M., (2025), Effectiveness of Oral Iron Supplements among 2nd Trimester Antenatal Mothers with Iron Deficiency Anaemia, *2025 International Conference on Ambient Intelligence in Health Care, Raipur Chattisgarh*, India, pp. 1–6,

[3] G. Bhuvaneswari, Gokul Krishna. A, L. Parimala, Thenmozhi P, Tamilselvi S, Mary Minolin T (2024). Maternal and Foetal Health Status during Non-Stress Test among Antenatal Mothers: Descriptive Cross-sectional Study. *Texila International Journal Of Public Health*, 24(4). https://doi.org/10.21522/tijph.2013.se.24.02.art004

[4] Padmapriya. D, Roja (2024). Effectiveness of Aromatherapy on Lowering Blood Pressure among Mothers with Pre- Eclampsia. *Texila International Journal of Public Health*, 24(4). https://doi.org/10.21522/TIJPH.2013.SE.24.02.Art001

[5] Bhandari, S., Dwa, Y., Maharjan, M., and Bajracharya, M. (2024). High Risk Pregnancy and its Outcome in a Tertiary Care Hospital: A Descriptive Cross-sectional Study. *JNMA; journal of the Nepal Medical Association*, 62(273), 306–310. https://doi.org/10.31729/jnma.8561.

[6] Keya, Tahmina Afrose; Fernandez, Kevin; Kharkwal, Kailash C.1; Habib, Nasrin2. Impact of Antenatal Care on Pregnancy Outcomes: A Cross-Sectional Study in a Rural Community in Malaysia. *Medical Journal of Dr. D.Y. Patil Vidyapeeth* 14(2):p 172–179, Mar–Apr 2021. | DOI: 10.4103/mjdrdypu.mjdrdypu_14_20

[7] Safeena, A.B.; Girija, J.M.; and Patil, Anjali (2025) A Longitudinal Study of High-Risk Pregnancy and its Outcome Among Antenatal Women Residing in an Urban Field Practice Area, *Indian Journal of Health Sciences and Biomedical Research KLEU*: Vol. 18: Iss. 1, Article 10. DOI: https://doi.org/10.71355/2542-6222.1009

[8] Bhandari, A., Rasania, S.K., Verma, S., Gupta, K., and Dangayach, N. (2024). A study to determine various factors associated with high-risk pregnancies. *International Journal of Reproduction, Contraception, Obstetrics and Gynecology*, 13(9), 2330–2334.

[9] Kuppusamy P, Prusty RK, Kale DP. High-risk pregnancy in India: prevalence and contributing risk factors-a national survey-based analysis. *J Glob Health*. 2023;13:04116.

[10] Bablad, Anita. (2024). Maternal and perinatal morbidity and mortality in high-risk pregnancy: a prospective study. *International Journal of Reproduction, Contraception, Obstetrics and Gynecology*. 13. 3047–3055. 10.18203/2320-1770.ijrcog20242987.

[11] Sultana Afroza, Haider Rina, Akhter Kulsum and Begum Shamsad. (2023). Perinatal Outcome in High-Risk & Severe-Risk Pregnancy- A Study in a Tertiary Care Hospital. *Scholars International Journal of Obstetrics and Gynecology*. 6. 443–449. 10.36348/sijog.2023.v06i11.003.

[12] Shuchi Sharma, Reena Sharma and Ankush Gautam. (2023). Prevalence of high risk pregnancy and study of maternal and perinatal outcome. *Int J Clin Trials*.10(4):291–293. https://dx.doi.org/10.18203/2349-3259.ijct20233171

Next-Generation Smart Systems – Sekhar et al. (Eds)

Effectiveness of a Technology-Enabled Self-Management Program on Quality of Life among Patients with Asthma

S. Tamilselvi
Professor, Saveetha College of Nursing, Saveetha Institute of Medical and Technical Sciences, Chennai, India

Sathish
B.Sc(N) IV Year Saveetha College of Nursing, Saveetha Institute of Medical and Technical Sciences, Chennai, India

P. ThenmozhiPaluchamy, G. Bhuvaneswari, and Mary Minolin
Professor, Saveetha College of Nursing, Saveetha Institute of Medical and Technical Sciences, Chennai, India

ABSTRACT: Asthma is a major non-communicable disease and a growing global health concern. Self-management of asthma involves patients independently managing and controlling their symptoms to prevent exacerbations. The study aimed is to evaluate the effectiveness of self-management program on quality of life among patient with asthma. A quasi-experimental two-group pre-test post-test research design was adopted. Following institutional approvals, 60 patient with asthma were selected using a non-probability sampling technique. The study findings revealed that self-management programs equip patients with asthma with essential knowledge and skills, enabling them to take timely and appropriate actions when their health deteriorates. Self-management programs were found to significantly boost the confidence of patients with asthma, empowering them to manage their chronic condition more effectively. Continued engagement in self-management practices contributed to improved lung function, enhanced physical capacity, and an overall better quality of life.

Keywords: Patients with asthma, Quality of Life , self-management program

1 INTRODUCTION

Asthma is a chronic respiratory disease that significantly impacts patients' quality of life by limiting their daily activities, inducing social stigma, and imposing psychological burdens. This condition is characterized by symptoms such as wheezing, shortness of breath, chest tightness, and coughing. Research indicates that self-management interventions can enhance asthma control, decrease exacerbations, and improve overall well-being among patients.

Self-management strategies encompass patient education, symptom monitoring, and adherence to prescribed treatments. Effective asthma education programs have been shown to include multiple components, such as information on disease management, symptom tracking, and a written action plan for exacerbation responses (Zairina *et al.* 2014). Such education leads to better self-efficacy in patients, resulting in improved quality of life (Agustiyaningsih *et al.* 2023).

In recent studies, various modalities of self-management support, including internet-based platforms and community health worker interventions, have been recognized for their effectiveness. Internet-based self-management support has been validated as a viable approach, showing small but persistent benefits in asthma control and quality of life over time compared to traditional care (Gaalen *et al.* 2013). Community health initiatives and family-included strategies have also yielded positive outcomes by integrating education and support within the family system, thereby fostering better asthma control among children (Carrillo *et al.* 2017).

Furthermore, psychological support and interventions addressing mental health have become increasingly recognized, as asthma can often coexist with psychological conditions, exacerbating the quality-of-life issues faced by patients. Studies have outlined the importance of mental well-being in managing chronic respiratory conditions, recommending integrated approaches to address both physical and psychological health (Tong *et al.* 2024).

While the evidence points to a positive relationship between effective self-management strategies and improved quality of life among asthma patients, several challenges remain. Many patients continue to face barriers to adopting adequate self-management practices, such as lack of knowledge, socio-economic limitations, and inadequate healthcare access (Matcha *et al.* 2022). Therefore, ongoing evaluation of these interventions is critical to ensure their adaptability and effectiveness within diverse populations and settings.

Overall, enhancing self-management strategies for asthma patients not only supports them in controlling their symptoms but also significantly contributes to improving their health-related quality of life. Continued research and development of tailored interventions will be vital in addressing the population-specific needs of asthma sufferers, thereby paving the way for better health outcomes. The study aimed to evaluate the effectiveness of self-management program on the quality of life among patients with asthma.

2 METHODOLOGY

A quasi-experimental study design was utilized. After securing the necessary approvals from various departments and authorities, the researcher recruited 60 patients with asthma using a non-probability sampling method. A Peak Flow Meter was utilized to determine the patients' breathing patterns. The procedure for each participant required approximately 20 to 25 minutes to complete.

2.1 *Ethical approval*

Formal approval was obtained. Informed consent was secured from patients with asthma receiving treatment, with assurances provided regarding the confidentiality of all information shared during the study.

DOI: 10.1201/9781042001767-99

2.2 *Tools and analysis*

Demographic data were obtained using a specially developed instrument for the study. In the pre-test phase, patients' respiratory rates were recorded, and their quality of life was evaluated using the Asthma Quality of Life Questionnaire. The gathered data were then coded and subjected to analysis through descriptive and inferential statistical techniques.

3 RESULTS

The study revealed that a majority of the patients with asthma, 58.3%, were between 40 and 59 years of age. Among them, 71.7% were male, and 45% had completed higher secondary education. Additionally, 31 51.6% were employed as skilled workers, and 76.7%were married. Half of the participants, (50%, reported a monthly income between ₹10,001 and ₹15,000. Furthermore, 90% resided in urban areas, and 71.7% were members of nuclear families.The pre-test results showed that 56.67% participants had a moderate quality of life, while 43.33%) had a poor quality of life. After the intervention, 61.67% participants attained a good quality of life, and 38.33% reported a moderate quality of life, indicating notable improvement. (Figure 1)

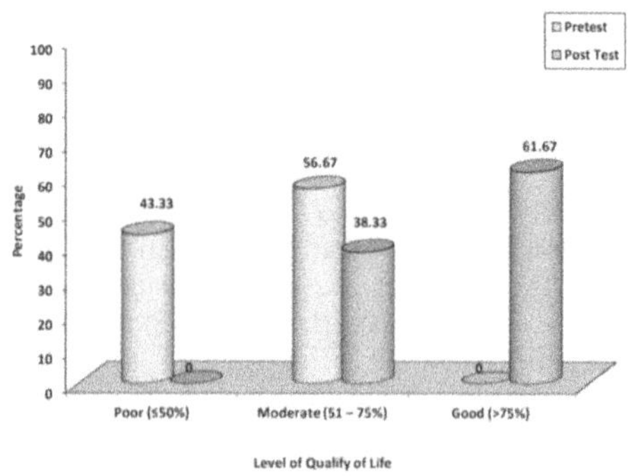

Figure 1. Pretest and posttest level of quality of life of patients with asthma.

Figure 2 showed that the pre-test mean quality of life (QOL) score was 128.78±23.53, which increased to 169.58±24.09 in the post-test, with a mean difference of 40.80. The paired *t*-test value ($t = 23.233$) was statistically significant at $p < 0.001$. This demonstrates that the implementation of the self-management program effectively improved the quality of life among asthma patients, as reflected by the notable enhancement in post-test scores

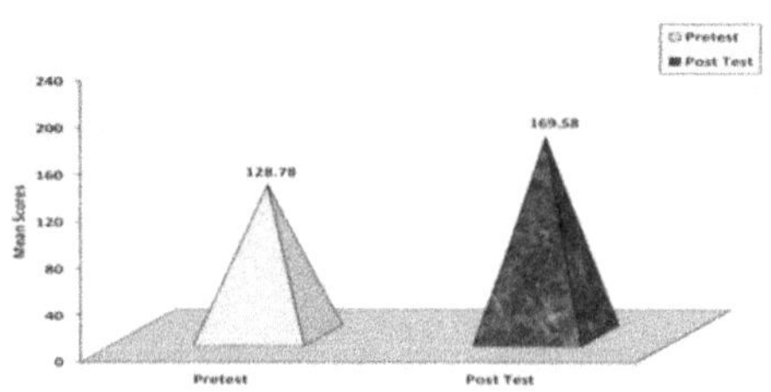

Figure 2. Comparison of pretest and posttest level of quality of life among patients with asthma.

Regarding association the analysis revealed that occupation (p = 0.018) and income (p = 0.014) showed a statistically significant association with the post-test quality of life scores among asthma patients ($p < 0.05$). No significant association was observed with other demographic variables. Therefore, the research hypothesis H2 was accepted for occupation and income, but not for the other variables.

4 DISCUSSION

The study on patients with asthma reveals insights into the impact of socio-demographic factors on quality of life (QoL) among individuals with chronic respiratory conditions. The findings indicate that a majority of the participants were aged between 40 to 59 years, predominantly male, and characterized by varying educational backgrounds, with a significant portion being skilled workers residing in urban settings. This demographic profile is essential as it may influence both the perception of health and access to healthcare resources. Research has shown that lower socioeconomic status (SES) is consistently associated with poorer health outcomes, including diminished QoL in chronic disease patients Kanervisto *et al.* (2011) (Joshi *et al.* 2017; Joseph *et al.* 2021).

The results of this study underscore the importance of self-management interventions in improving the QoL of patients with asthma. Prior to the intervention, approximately 56.67% of participants reported a moderate quality of life, while a significant improvement was observed post-intervention, with 61.67% of patients achieving a good quality of life. This finding is indicative of the effectiveness of self-management program in fostering better health outcomes, as supported by literature indicating that self-management education enhances QoL in chronic disease contexts (Bodenheimer 2002; Warsi *et al.* 2004).

Interestingly, the study noted a significant association between post-intervention QoL scores and both occupation and income, evidenced by the chi-squared values ($\chi^2 = 10.070$, p = 0.018; $\chi^2 = 8.564$, p = 0.014, respectively). This aligns with previous findings that stress the correlation between socio-economic factors and health outcomes, where higher income and stable employment serve as protective factors for better health-related quality of life (Geprägs *et al.* 2022; Youg *et al.* 2024). Patients with lower income and unstable job security often face challenges that impede their ability to manage chronic conditions effectively, contributing to poorer health outcomes and QoL.

Furthermore, the emphasis on nuclear family structures within this study's demographic may suggest the interplay between family support systems and individual health outcomes. Studies indicate that the quality of family relationships and support can significantly influence the management of chronic illnesses, including asthma (Puciato *et al.* 2023; Thiyagarajan *et al.* 2019). Therefore, support for these patients—through their partner's understanding or support from adult children—could play a role in enhancing their self-management and subsequently improving their QoL.

5 CONCLUSION

The study highlights the complex interplay between socio-demographic variables, self-management interventions, and the resulting quality of life among patients with asthma. The findings suggest the need for targeted health interventions that address not only individual health literacy and management skills but also broader socio-economic contexts to optimize health outcomes. Future research should delve deeper into the longitudinal impacts of such interventions and explore the broader applicability of these findings across different chronic conditions.

REFERENCES

Agustiyaningsih, T., Rahayu, E., Purwanto, E., and Husna, C. (2023). Self-management in patients with asthma: a systematic review. *Kne Medicine*. https://doi.org/10.18502/kme.v3i2.13078

Al-khateeb, A. and Alkhateeb, J. (2015). Research on psychosocial aspects of asthma in the arab world: a literature review. *Multidisciplinary Respiratory Medicine*, 10. https://doi.org/10.4081/mrm.2015.289

Bodenheimer, T. (2002). Patient self-management of chronic disease in primary care. *Jama*, 288(19), 2469. https://doi.org/10.1001/jama.288.19.2469

Carrillo, G., Perez-Patron, M., Lucio, R., Cabrera, L., Trevino, A., Xu, X., and Mier, N. (2017). The benefits and challenges of managing asthma in hispanic families in south texas: a mixed-methods study. *Frontiers in Public Health*, 5. https://doi.org/10.3389/fpubh.2017.00150

Dhanusia, S.; Shareen, Akbar A.; Suganthirababu, Prathap Srinivasan, Vignesh; Kumar, Priyadharshini; Federman, A., O'Conor, R., Mindlis, I., Hoy-Rosas, J., Hauser, D., Lurio, J., and Wisnivesky, J. (2019). Effect of a self-management support intervention on asthma outcomes in older adults. *Jama Internal Medicine*, 179(8), 1113. https://doi.org/10.1001/jamainternmed.2019.1201

Gaalen, J., Beerthuizen, T., Meer, V., Reisen, P., Redelijkheid, G., Snoeck-Stroband, J., and Sont, J. (2013). Long-term outcomes of internet-based self-management support in adults with asthma: randomized controlled trial. *Journal of Medical Internet Research*, 15(9), e188. https://doi.org/10.2196/jmir.2640

Geprägs, A., Bürgin, D., Fegert, J., Brähler, E., and Clemens, V. (2022). The impact of mental health and sociodemographic characteristics on quality of life and life satisfaction during the second year of the covid-19 pandemic—results of a population-based survey in germany. *International Journal of Environmental Research and Public Health*, 19(14), 8734. https://doi.org/10.3390/ijerph19148734

Jayaraj, Vanitha; Vishnuraman, Suriya; Umasankar, Yamini Murugaiyan and Poovarasan, (2025), Effectiveness of Cognitive Behavioral Therapy and Aerobic Exercise in Parkinson Disease Dementia: A Pilot Study, *Physical Treatments*, 15 (2), pp. 165–174, Cited 0 times. DOI: 10.32598/ptj.15.2.663.1

Joseph, A., Prasad, S., Hynan, L., Chren, M., and Chong, B. (2021). Differences in quality of life in patients with cutaneous lupus erythematosus with varying income levels. *Lupus*, 30(6), 972–980. https://doi.org/10.1177/0961203321999724

Joshi, U., Subedi, R., Poudel, P., Ghimire, P., Panta, S., and Sigdel, M. (2017). Assessment of quality of life in patients undergoing hemodialysis using whoqol-bref questionnaire: a multicenter study. *International Journal of Nephrology and Renovascular Disease, Volume* 10, 195–203. https://doi.org/10.2147/ijnrd.s136522

Kanervisto, M., Vasankari, T., Laitinen, T., Heliövaara, M., Jousilahti, P., and Saarelainen, S. (2011). Low socioeconomic status is associated with chronic obstructive airway diseases. *Respiratory Medicine*, 105(8), 1140–1146. https://doi.org/10.1016/j.rmed.2011.03.008

Matcha, J., Pappiya, E., Baalharith, I., Algrd, H., and Ramaiah, R. (2022). Application of orem's self-care deficit nursing theory on self-efficacy and quality of life among patients with bronchial asthma: randomized controlled study. *International Journal of Nursing Care*, 10(2), 31–37. https://doi.org/10.37506/ijonc.v10i2.18742

Puciato, D., Rozpara, M., Bugdol, M., Borys, T., and Słaby, T. (2023). Quality of life of low-income adults. *Work*, 74(2), 631–648. https://doi.org/10.3233/wor-211110

Sri Lekha, M. Vishnuram, Surya K, Ramana Abathsagayam, Kumaresan Suganthirababu and Prathap, (2025), Efficacy of Dynamic Neuromuscular Stabilization Exercises on Balance and Fall Risk in Subjects with DiabeticPeripheral Neuropathy among Geriatrics—A Pilot Study, *Physical and Occupational Therapy in Geriatrics*, Cited 2 times. DOI: 10.1080/02703181.2025.2467803

Thiyagarajan, A., Bagavandas, M., and Kosalram, K. (2019). Assessing the role of family well-being on the quality of life of indian children with thalassemia. *BMC Pediatrics*, 19(1). https://doi.org/10.1186/s12887-019-1466-y

Tong, X., Zhang, X., Wang, M., Wang, Z., Dong, F., Gong, E., and Li, Y. (2024). Non-pharmacological interventions for asthma prevention and management across the life course: umbrella review. *Clinical and Translational Allergy*, 14(3). https://doi.org/10.1002/clt2.12344

Udhaya Kumar, Albert Anand Ramalingam, Vinodhkumar Moussallem, Charbel D. Gopal and Kumaraguruparan, (2025), Biomechanical impact of foot pronation on anterior knee pain – case controlled study, *Fizicna Reabilitacia ta Rekreacijno-Ozdorovci Tehnologii*, 10 (1), pp. 35 Cited 0 times. DOI:10.15391/prrht.2025-10(1).05

Warsi, A., Wang, P., LaValley, M., Avorn, J., and Solomon, D. (2004). Self-management://doi.org/10.1001/archinte.164.15.1641

Yorke, J., Fleming, S., Shuldham, C., Rao, H., and Smith, H. (2015). Nonpharmacological interventions aimed at modifying health and behavioural outcomes for adults with asthma: a critical review. *Clinical & Experimental Allergy*, 45(12), 1750–1764. https://doi.org/10.1111/cea.12511

Youg education programs in chronic disease. Archives of Internal Medicine, 164(15), 1641. https, E., Hwang, J., and Hong, Y. (2024). Factors influencing health-related quality of life in adult women. *Journal of Health Informatics and Statistics*, 49(2), 169–178. https://doi.org/10.21032/jhis.2024.49.2.169

Zairina, E., Stewart, K., Abramson, M., and George, J. (2014). The effectiveness of non-pharmacological healthcare interventions for asthma management during pregnancy: a systematic review. *BMC Pulmonary Medicine*, 14(1). https://doi.org/10.1186/1471-2466-14-46

Next-Generation Smart Systems – Sekhar et al. (Eds)

Financial Management and Resource Utilization

Ramesh Anitha, D. Srinivasulu, D. Shaheeda Begum, and C. Harishkumar
Assistant Professor, Department of MBA, Kuppam Engineering College, Andhrapradesh, India

N. Muneendra
Associate Professor, Department of MBA, Kuppam Engineering College, Andhrapradesh, India

ABSTRACT: An increasing number of organizations are integrating societal expectations into their business strategies. The growing emphasis on sustainability is becoming essential to the interconnectedness and long-term value of businesses. This study explores the role of financial management in supporting sustainable business practices and development. Through thematic analysis of insights from various scholars, the study confirms that effective financial management models are crucial for enhancing productivity while managing financial risks. The findings also reveal that allocating capital budgets to sustainability initiatives strengthens a company's competitive edge. Furthermore, the application of both Western and Islamic financial systems proves to be effective in advancing sustainability. In conclusion, financial management plays a critical role in fostering sustainable business practices and development.

1 INTRODUCTION

Businesses are progressively adapting to meet social expectations, which has fueled the emergence of corporate sustainability practices. Numerous organizations are addressing consumer needs by engaging both stakeholders and employees in identifying creative solutions to strengthen their market position. The role of financial oversight is fundamental in supporting environmentally and socially responsible business operations. In particular, financial accounting is employed to monitor, analyze, and communicate organizational achievements or goals over a defined period. Therefore, sound financial oversight functions as a roadmap that directly supports enterprise advancement. In essence, robust financial governance is vital for maintaining long-term economic health.

The idea of managing finances is essential in strategizing for the achievement of financial gains and remains a core focus for all enterprises. As a result, finance professionals and accounting experts typically apply effective strategies and expertise to reduce operational expenditures.

2 REVIEW OF LITERATURE

Financial management plays a pivotal role in guiding how business resources are allocated, utilized, and optimized to achieve strategic goals. According to Brigham and Ehrhardt (2017), effective financial management ensures that capital is directed toward projects and activities that offer the highest return on investment, thereby enhancing organizational efficiency and profitability. The proper allocation of financial resources is fundamental to minimizing waste and maximizing productivity (Ross *et al.* 2019).

Deloitte (2020) emphasizes that in an era of increasing financial accountability and stakeholder scrutiny, transparent and well-structured financial practices contribute significantly to corporate sustainability. Strategic financial planning, budgeting, and forecasting are key tools used to align business operations with available resources, enabling organizations to respond flexibly to market changes and operational risks (Atrill and McLaney 2018).

Moreover, financial controls, such as cost-benefit analysis and variance reporting, play a critical role in monitoring resource use and identifying inefficiencies (Drury 2020). These practices help businesses maintain financial discipline and support long-term decision-making. Gitman and Zutter (2015) argue that sound financial management fosters informed decision-making by providing accurate financial data and performance metrics, which are crucial for managing both short-term operations and long-term growth.

Furthermore, in the context of sustainability, financial management is instrumental in integrating environmental, social, and governance (ESG) factors into investment and budgeting decisions (Eccles and Klimenko 2019). This integration supports sustainable development goals while ensuring that financial performance remains aligned with ethical and legal standards.

In summary, the literature underscores that financial management is not only vital for efficient resource utilization but also serves as a foundation for strategic planning, risk mitigation, and sustainable value creation across various sectors.

2.1 *Sustainability issues in financial decisions and key value drivers*

1. **Overview**
   Sustainability is no longer a side issue—it is now central to financial decision-making. Businesses are expected to integrate **environmental, social, and governance (ESG)** factors into financial strategies to create **long-term value** and reduce **risk**.
2. **Sustainability Issues Influencing Financial Decisions**

Area	Key Sustainability Issues
Environment	Climate change, carbon emissions, water usage, energy efficiency, waste management
Social	Labor rights, community impact, diversity & inclusion, product safety
Governance	Board independence, executive pay, ethical conduct, transparency

DOI: 10.1201/9781042001767-100

3. **Impact on Key Financial Decisions**

Financial Decision	Sustainability Impact
Investment	Projects with high environmental risk may be rejected or need green financing.
Financing	Green bonds, ESG-linked loans are preferred; firms with poor ESG scores face higher borrowing costs.
Dividend Policy	Firms may reinvest profits into sustainable projects rather than high dividends.
M&A (Mergers and Acquisitions)	ESG risks and compatibility are now part of due diligence.

4. **Key Value Drivers Influenced by Sustainability**

Value Driver	Role of Sustainability
Revenue Growth	Green products/services attract new customers and open new markets.
Cost Reduction	Energy-efficient and waste-reducing operations lower expenses.
Risk Management	ESG integration reduces regulatory, reputational, and climate-related risks.
Capital Access	ESG-strong firms attract impact investors and benefit from better loan terms.
Brand Reputation	Sustainability improves public image, customer loyalty, and stakeholder trust.
Innovation	Drives sustainable product development and operational efficiency.

2.2 *Overview of financial management as a core business function*

Financial management is a fundamental pillar of any business operation, encompassing the planning, organizing, directing, and controlling of financial activities. Its core purpose is to ensure that financial resources are acquired and used efficiently and effectively to achieve organizational goals. This includes budgeting, capital investment decisions, working capital management, and financial reporting. In today's competitive and dynamic business environment, financial management is not just about controlling costs—it also plays a strategic role in guiding investment decisions, managing risks, and enhancing overall value creation for stakeholders. Strong financial management enables organizations to adapt to market changes, seize growth opportunities, and remain resilient during economic uncertainties.

2.3 *Importance of resource utilization in achieving operational efficiency*

Resource utilization refers to the effective and efficient deployment of an organization's resources—financial, human, physical, and technological—to achieve optimal outcomes. Efficient resource use directly contributes to operational efficiency by minimizing waste, lowering costs, maximizing output, and improving profitability. Financial management helps align resource use with strategic priorities, ensuring that capital is allocated to projects that offer the highest return on investment. Inadequate or misaligned resource allocation can lead to bottlenecks, financial losses, or missed opportunities. Thus, sound financial oversight is essential for streamlining operations and enhancing long-term organizational performance.

2.4 *Objectives of the study*

This study is aimed at exploring the role of financial management in improving resource utilization and achieving operational efficiency. The specific objectives include:

1. **To analyze the relationship between financial management and resource efficiency**
2. **To identify best practices that improve utilization**

3 METHODOLOGY

3.1 *Research approach*

This study adopts a **mixed-method approach** combining both **quantitative** and **qualitative** techniques. The quantitative aspect focuses on analyzing financial data and performance indicators to establish measurable relationships between financial management practices and resource utilization. The qualitative component involves gathering insights through case studies and interviews to understand the strategic and operational dimensions of financial decision-making.

Using both approaches allows for a comprehensive analysis—quantitative data reveals trends and relationships, while qualitative data provides context, depth, and practical examples.

3.2 *Data collection*

The study employs a multi-source data collection strategy to ensure reliability and depth of findings:

Case Studies: In-depth case studies of selected firms are conducted to explore how financial strategies influence resource utilization in real-world scenarios.

1. **Interviews**: Semi-structured interviews with finance managers, CFOs, and operational heads provide insight into the decision-making processes behind financial planning and resource allocation.
2. **Financial Statement Analysis**: Data is collected from audited financial reports, including income statements, balance sheets, and cash flow statements to analyze efficiency ratios and resource use metrics.
3. **Surveys**: Structured questionnaires are distributed to finance professionals across various sectors to gather broad perspectives on financial management practices.

3.3 *Sample selection*

The sample includes a **diverse mix of firms** from the **manufacturing**, **services**, and **SME** sectors to ensure the findings are applicable across different business contexts.

Criteria for selection include:

Availability of financial data

Willingness to participate in interviews or surveys

Firms with an active finance function and documented resource management practices

The sample size may vary based on data access, but it aims to include at least **10–15 firms** to provide both depth and comparative insight.

3.4 *Analysis tools and techniques*

To analyse the collected data, the following tools and techniques will be used:

Ratio Analysis: Key financial ratios such as return on assets (ROA), inventory turnover, and operating efficiency ratios will be calculated to assess how effectively financial resources are being utilized.

Performance Metrics: Metrics such as cost per unit, profit margins, and asset utilization rates will be examined to determine operational efficiency.

Thematic Analysis: Qualitative data from interviews and case studies will be coded and analyzed thematically to identify common practices, challenges, and strategic insights related to financial management and resource use. This combination of tools ensures a robust analysis that captures both numerical trends and managerial insights.

4 DIGITAL TRANSFORMATION: ROLE OF ERP, AI, AND ANALYTICS IN TRACKING RESOURCE USE

Digital tools are transforming financial management by providing real-time insights, automating manual processes, and improving decision accuracy. Technologies such as **Enterprise Resource Planning (ERP)** systems, **Artificial Intelligence (AI)**, and **data analytics** play a crucial role in monitoring and optimizing resource utilization.

- **ERP Systems**: Centralize financial data and integrate various business functions (e.g., accounting, procurement, inventory), improving financial transparency and resource planning.
- **AI and Machine Learning**: Automate forecasting, detect anomalies in spending, and optimize budget allocations using predictive models.
- **Data Analytics**: Enables firms to track cost centers, assess performance in real time, and make data-driven decisions on asset utilization and cost reduction.

Impact on Resource Utilization:

- Reduces manual errors and time delays
- Enhances visibility into resource consumption
- Allows proactive cost control and risk mitigation

4.1 *Sustainable investment and green budgeting*

Sustainable investment refers to allocating capital to projects or assets that deliver financial returns while generating positive social and environmental impact. **Green budgeting** is the practice of incorporating environmental objectives into the public or corporate budgeting process.

- **Green Bonds and ESG-linked Loans**: Financial instruments designed to fund environmentally responsible projects.
- **Sustainability-Linked Budgets**: Organizations allocate budgets for energy-efficient infrastructure, low-carbon technology, and sustainable supply chains.
- **Return on Sustainability Investment (ROSI)** frameworks** are used to evaluate both financial and non-financial returns on green investments.

These practices support responsible resource use and align capital deployment with long-term sustainability goals.

4.2 *Case examples: Improved efficiency through strategic integration*

Unilever

Unilever's "Sustainable Living Plan" integrates ESG metrics into every business function. The company has reduced energy and water use per production unit while achieving cost savings. Its **Sustainable Living Brands** grow faster and are more profitable, showcasing the financial value of responsible resource management.

Siemens

Siemens leverages digital twin technology, IoT, and AI within its ERP framework to optimize operations across its manufacturing plants. This has led to a **30% reduction in energy consumption** in several facilities and significant improvements in supply chain efficiency.

Microsoft

Microsoft uses cloud-based analytics and AI-driven insights to monitor energy usage in real time, reduce emissions, and optimize its global data centers. Financial decisions are directly tied to their net-zero carbon goals.

5 FINDINGS AND DISCUSSION

The findings of this study reveal several important relationships and insights that highlight the critical role of financial management in resource optimization. Data from interviews, financial reports, and case studies demonstrate how effective financial discipline, leadership, and digital integration contribute to improved efficiency across different organizational settings.

5.1 *Key relationships between financial discipline and resource optimization*

A strong correlation was observed between financial discipline—defined as the consistent application of budgeting, monitoring, and cost control practices—and optimal resource utilization.

- Firms that adhered to structured budgeting, accurate forecasting, and regular financial reviews showed **higher returns on assets (ROA)** and **lower wastage of physical and financial resources.**
- Organizations with strong financial control mechanisms were better at **avoiding redundant spending**, **eliminating resource bottlenecks**, and **improving operating margins**.

5.2 *Role of leadership and governance in financial control*

Leadership commitment and governance quality significantly influence how well financial management systems are implemented and followed.

- **Top management support** for financial transparency and accountability fosters a culture of efficiency and responsibility.
- Companies with **active finance committees**, regular audits, and clear reporting lines exhibited **stronger cost control**, **less resource misallocation**, and **better alignment of financial goals with operational strategies.**

5.3 *Sectoral insights: SMEs vs large corporations*

Differences in resource utilization and financial management practices were evident across sectors, particularly between Small and Medium Enterprises (SMEs) and large corporations:

SMEs:

- Tend to operate with **limited financial planning capacity** and **less formalized systems.**
- Face greater challenges in tracking expenses, evaluating ROI, and securing financing for sustainable investments.
- Often lack dedicated financial management staff or systems, making resource allocation more reactive than strategic.

Large Corporations:

- Benefit from **centralized financial systems** (e.g., ERP platforms), dedicated finance teams, and advanced analytics.
- More likely to implement **performance-based budgeting** and link financial KPIs to departmental outputs.
- Exhibit stronger integration of ESG and digital tools in resource planning.

5.4 *Barriers to effective financial management and resource utilization*

Despite the benefits, several barriers hinder the effective implementation of financial management practices aimed at improving resource efficiency:

- **Lack of Financial Literacy**: In many organizations, especially SMEs, decision-makers lack basic financial knowledge, leading to poor budget planning and misallocation of resources.
- **Inefficient or Outdated Systems**: Many firms rely on manual processes or outdated accounting software, resulting in delayed reporting, errors, and data fragmentation.
- **Data Gaps**: Incomplete or unreliable data on costs, asset usage, or performance indicators prevent accurate analysis and informed decision-making.
- **Resistance to Change**: Organizational inertia and resistance to adopting digital tools or ESG frameworks slow down modernization efforts.

6 RECOMMENDATIONS

Based on the analysis of financial management practices and their impact on resource utilization, the following recommendations are proposed to help organizations optimize efficiency, improve accountability, and ensure long-term sustainability.

6.1 *Implement strategic financial planning frameworks*

- Setting long-term financial objectives tied to growth and efficiency
- Creating dynamic budgets that respond to market changes
- Linking financial planning with capital investment and resource allocation priorities

6.2 *Use KPIs to monitor resource use continuously*

Key Performance Indicators (KPIs) are essential tools for tracking financial and operational performance. Organizations should establish clear KPIs related to:

- Cost per unit of output
- Return on assets (ROA)
- Inventory turnover
- Operating margin
- Utilization rates of human and physical resources

6.3 *Adopt integrated financial software and dashboards*

Modern financial management requires the use of digital tools that consolidate data, automate processes, and provide real-time insights. Organizations should:

- Invest in ERP (Enterprise Resource Planning) systems to integrate financial, operational, and resource data
- Use dashboards to visualize financial performance and resource utilization metrics
- Incorporate AI and analytics for forecasting, anomaly detection, and strategic planning

6.4 *Promote a culture of financial accountability across departments*

Financial management should not be confined to the finance department alone. All departments must be responsible for managing their budgets, controlling costs, and using resources efficiently.

- Train non-financial managers in financial literacy and resource planning
- Establish cross-functional collaboration in budgeting and performance tracking
- Recognize and reward departments that meet financial and efficiency targets

7 OVERALL RECOMMENDATION SUMMARY

To achieve effective resource utilization, organizations must combine strategic planning with technological tools and a strong culture of accountability. By implementing these practices, businesses can enhance operational efficiency, improve financial performance, and position themselves for sustainable, long-term growth.

7.1 *Recap of key findings*

- A strong link was observed between financial discipline (e.g., budgeting, investment appraisal, and working capital management) and improved resource efficiency across various sectors.
- Organizations that implemented robust financial planning and monitoring practices were more successful in minimizing waste, optimizing asset use, and improving returns on investment.
- Leadership, governance, and digital integration were found to be essential enablers of effective financial management.
- Sectoral differences emerged, with large corporations showing stronger financial systems, while SMEs faced limitations due to financial literacy gaps and outdated systems.
- Barriers such as inadequate financial infrastructure, data gaps, and lack of cross-functional collaboration were identified as common constraints to efficient resource use.

7.2 *Financial management as a driver of efficient, sustainable resource use*

The findings reinforce the idea that financial management is not only a support function but also a **strategic driver of sustainability and efficiency**. By aligning financial strategies with environmental, social, and governance (ESG) objectives and leveraging technology, organizations can create long-term value while managing their resources responsibly.

When implemented effectively, financial management enables:

- Smarter capital allocation
- Better forecasting and planning
- Data-informed decision-making
- Integration of sustainability into the core financial strategy

These outcomes collectively enhance competitiveness and organizational resilience in today's complex business environment.

7.3 *Future scope of research*

- **Artificial Intelligence (AI)** and **Big Data Analytics** are emerging tools that hold great promise in predictive resource allocation. Future research could focus on how AI can:
  - Forecast demand and optimize inventory
  - Predict financial risks and automate corrective action
  - Improve budgeting accuracy and real-time resource tracking
- Comparative studies across industries and regions could also enhance the understanding of how contextual factors influence the financial-resource efficiency relationship.

- Longitudinal research may help evaluate the long-term impact of sustainability-focused financial strategies on resource performance and organizational outcomes.

8 CONCLUSION

Sustainability is no longer optional in financial decisions. Firms that align their strategy with ESG principles can **maximize shareholder value**, **minimize risks**, and **build long-term competitiveness**. Understanding and leveraging key sustainability-linked value drivers is crucial for any modern financial strategy.

Understanding and improving resource utilization is critical for financial health and organizational sustainability. Financial managers play a key role in designing strategies, monitoring indicators, and minimizing waste to ensure every resource contributes meaningfully to the company's goals. This study examined the critical relationship between financial management practices and resource utilization, highlighting how strategic financial oversight contributes to operational efficiency, cost control, and sustainable business growth.The integration of sustainability and technology into financial management is no longer optional—it is essential for competitive advantage, operational efficiency, and responsible growth. Companies that proactively adopt ESG frameworks and digital tools are better equipped to optimize resource utilization, meet stakeholder expectations, and succeed in an evolving global economy Financial discipline is a key enabler of resource efficiency, especially in complex and resource-intensive industries. While large firms are more equipped to optimize resources through structured financial systems, SMEs require support in capacity building and digital adoption. For organizations aiming to thrive in an increasingly data-driven and sustainability-conscious world, **integrating sound financial management with strategic resource planning** is no longer optional—it is essential.

REFERENCES

ESG Performance and Financial Flexibility Li, Y. (2025). *SOE's ESG Performance on Financial Flexibility*.(arXiv preprint) Investigates how ESG performance enhances financial flexibility, especially under financing constraints, with a focus on Hong Kong-listed firms. ([arXiv][9])

Financial Management & Sustainability in India Al Marzooqi, Z., and Nobanee, H. (2022). Financial Management and Sustainability in India. *Explores how robust financial management supports firm sustainability, arguing that finance is a core enabler of long-term business resilience*.([ResearchGate][7])

Financial management,institute book of ICAI.

Financial Practices in Agricultural SMEs Mang'ana, K., and Ndyetabula, D. (2023). Financial management practices and performance of agricultural small and medium enterprises in Tanzania. *Social Sciences & Humanities Open*, 7(1), 100494. This empirical study shows that working capital management and financing practices significantly boost both financial and organizational performance of agri-SMEs.([ScienceDirect][6])

Green Finance and Resource Efficiency Zhang, Y., and colleagues (2023). Green finance development and resource efficiency: A financial structure perspective. *Resources Policy*, 85(A), 104068. This study examines how the size and structure of green finance—especially direct versus indirect financing—affect resource utilization efficiency via green technology development.

International financial management by Cheol Eun, Mcgraw-Hil.

International Financial Management by Jeff Madura, Mc Graw Hill.

Multinational financial management by Alan C. Shapiro.

Operational Reporting & Resource Accountability Integrated Reporting. *Describes integrated reporting as a framework blending financial and non-financial (e.g., ecological, social) data to present how organizations leverage and sustain resources.*

Performance Benchmarking in Banking Financial Innovation (2024). *Evaluating the resource management and profitability efficiencies of US commercial banks Applying dynamic-network DEA models, this research measures resource management and efficiency across U.S. banks, highlighting substantial performance improvement potential.* ([SpringerOpen][2], [SpringerLink][3]

Strategic Control and Resource Allocation Seifzadeh & Rowe (2025). Appraising the Role of Strategic Control in Financial Performance. *Public Organization Review*, 12(3), 90–112. This paper investigates how strategic control techniques influence financial performance, with resource allocation acting as a mediating factor.([MDPI][4])

Sustainable Financial Management in Healthcare Rafinda, A., Mubaroq, A.C., Purwaningtyas, P., Aljafa, H., and Barika, C.R. (2025). Sustainable Financial Management for Hospitals: A Conceptual Framework. *Public Accounting and Sustainability*, 2(1), 19–30. Proposes a sustainable financial management framework tailored for hospital operations, aligning stewardship with long-term resource reliability.([pas.umy.ac.id][5])

Theoretical Foundations for ESG Integration Alhamis, I. (2025). *Theoretical Frameworks for Integrating Sustainability Factors into Institutional Investment Decision-Making*. (arXiv preprint). Reviews behavioral finance, modern portfolio theory, and risk management frameworks that institutional investors use to incorporate ESG factors.([arXiv][8])

Next-Generation Smart Systems – Sekhar et al. (Eds)
© 2027 The Author(s), ISBN: 978-1-041-34234-2

GestDrive: A Hands-On Gaming

Sigirisetty Anusha
Shri Vishnu Engineering College for Women, Department of Artificial Intelligence, Bhimavaram, India

P. Vijaya Kumar
Sasi Institute of Technology & Engineering, Department of CSE, Tadepalligudem, India

Rongala Ravi
Malla Reddy(MR)(Deemed To Be University), Hyderabad, India

Polinati Vinod Babu and C.P. Pavan Kumar Hota
Shri Vishnu Engineering College for Women, Department of Artificial Intelligence, Bhimavaram, India

K. Sravani
SRKR Engineering College (A), Department of CSE, Bhimavaram, India

ABSTRACT: Conventional gaming interfaces tend to be useful for physical controllers, which restrict the accessibility and interaction for users. Gesture-based gaming provides a more natural and immersive experience for the users , allowing players to use hand gestures to control games. This work, GestDrive, leverages the latest technologies such as MediaPipe, OpenCV, and PyAutoGUI to create a real-time gaming hand gesture recognition system. By this exact gesture detection and identification, GestDrive converts the identified hand gestures into corresponding actions for games, rendering it an unbeatable and exciting experience for players. GestDrive recognizes hand gestures at very high rates of correctness, at more than 85% on average, while low latency guarantees gameplay flow. Through the addition of GestDrive to their console experience, user enjoyment increases, and gamers are able to take part without regard to mobility limitations. The work shows the promise of gesture recognition technology to transform gaming, with the potential to spread to education, therapy, and skill acquisition. Deep-Feature.

Keywords: Gesture Recognition, MediaPipe, PyAutoGUI, Real-Time Gaming, Hand Tracking, Immersive Gaming

1 INTRODUCTION

Gaming is always about interaction and fun, but classic controllers such as joysticks and keyboards often make it difficult for all to participate. For the physically challenged, these controllers are an entry barrier to game participation. Gesture-driven gaming addresses this. With hand movements as a means to control games, we can make gaming more natural, interactive, and inclusive for all. This work, GestDrive, employs tools such as MediaPipe, OpenCV, and PyAutoGUI to implement a system that can recognize hand gestures and translate them into game controls. One can visualize playing a racing game by just using hand movements—controllers are not required! The aim is to make gesture recognition precise, quick, and simple to use so anyone can have fun gaming without any restrictions. In addition to being enjoyable, this technology also has applications in education and therapy, and as such is a step in the direction of more accessible and interactive gaming. GestDrive is about breaking down barriers and uniting people with the force of gesture.

Gesture gaming has gained attention over the years as a way of improving gaming by making it more interactive and easy to play. Researchers have come up with various techniques for improving gesture recognition.

Early research emphasized simple computer vision methods for gesture recognition. For instance, researchers employed image processing algorithms such as edge detection and contour tracing to recognize hand gestures. Although they were straightforward, the methods were vulnerable to error, particularly in noisy or complex environments.

With increasing deep learning, sophisticated methods like Convolutional Neural Networks (CNNs) and frameworks like MediaPipe were made possible. They enable real-time hand tracking and gesture recognition at enhanced accuracy. For instance, Google's MediaPipe library has been utilized richly for efficient hand tracking at low computational but high accuracy.

Recent research has targeted real-time effectiveness and accessibility for gesture recognition systems. Researchers have used such platforms as TensorFlow and OpenCV to lower latency and enhance user experience. Some efforts have also been made to integrate gesture recognition with augmented reality (AR) in a bid to create even more interactive gaming experiences.

Despite these advancements, there are still problems. Background noise, light changes, and complex gestures still affect accuracy. There is also a need for systems to not only be accurate but also easy to operate for all people.

In our work, GestDrive builds on these research endeavors through the combination of MediaPipe, OpenCV, and PyAutoGUI to create a gesture-controlled gaming system. Our aim is to increase accuracy, reduce latency, and ensure the system is accessible to all users.

2 METHODOLOGY

2.1 *Dataset*

To build GestDrive, we created a dataset of hand gestures like open hand, closed fist, and tilts (left/right). These gestures were captured using a webcam under different lighting and backgrounds to ensure the system works in real-world conditions. Each gesture was labeled (e.g., "Boost" for open hand, "Brake" for closed fist) to help the system learn accurately.

The dataset was preprocessed by resizing images, reducing noise, and normalizing the data for consistency. This ensures

DOI: 10.1201/9781042001767-101

the system can recognize gestures reliably and provide a smooth, intuitive gaming experience for everyone.machine learning models.

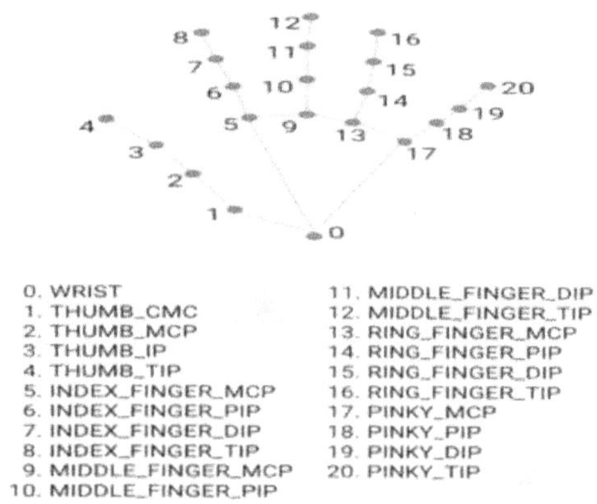

Figure 1. Labels distribution in the dataset.

2.2 *Preprocessing of images*

To get the dataset ready for training, we prepared the images of hand gestures for consistency and for enhancing the system's precision. We resized all the images into a common size (i.e., 256x256 pixels) so the data was in a similar form. We then used techniques such as rotation, zooming, and subtle movements on the images to prepare the variations. It assists the system in understanding and identifying the gesture even if the hand is marginally moved or tilted. Moreover, we normalized the pixel values of the images to enhance the stability and performance of the model. All these operations of preprocessing calm the dataset down so that it can accommodate the real-world dynamics, such as variation in light or hand positions. Augmenting the dataset through these operations assures us that the system will have no problem distinguishing gestures and producing a smooth experience for gaming, improving the model's ability to handle real-world variations in image inputs.

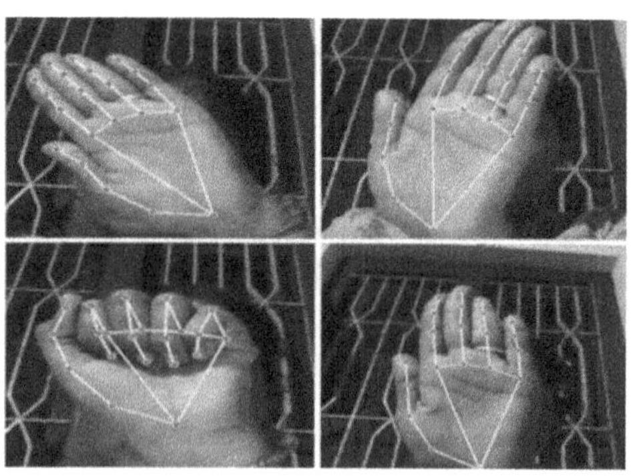

Figure 2. Images of hand movements.

We created GestDrive to make gaming more intuitive and natural with hand gestures instead of traditional controllers. To accomplish this, we first recorded various distinct hand gestures, including open hand, fist, and tilts, using a simple webcam. These were recorded with varying lighting and backgrounds to make sure that the system performs well in the real world. Second, we tidied up the images by resizing them and eliminating unnecessary noise to standardize the data. With tools such as MediaPipe and OpenCV, we taught the system to identify these gestures correctly in real time. Last but not least, we mapped the identified gestures to game controls, e.g., steering or braking, so players can use simple hand movements to play the game. This method makes the game more natural, enjoyable, and accessible for all.

2.3 *Feature extraction and segmentation*

In GestDrive, the magic of understanding hand gestures starts with two significant steps: Feature extraction and Segmentation. These are similar to telling the system to "look" and "zoom in" on what matters—your hand movement.

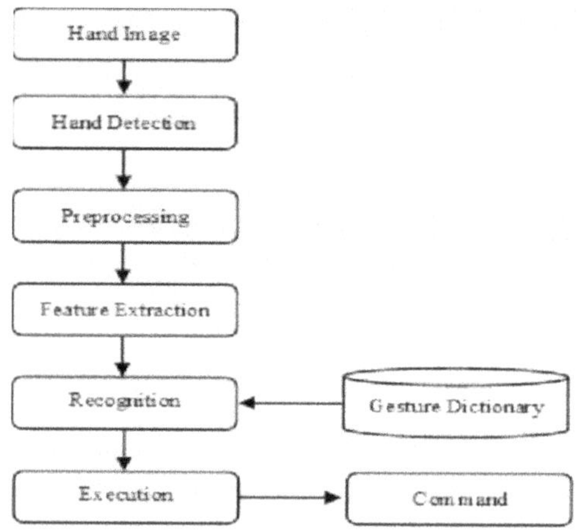

Figure 3. Workflow diagram of the system.

When you gesture, the system detects significant points on your hand, such as your fingertips, your knuckles, and the center of your palm, using MediaPipe. These are kind of like reference points that help the system know what your hand is up to. If your fingers are extended, it recognizes an "open hand." If your fingers are balled up in a fist, it recognizes that as a "closed fist." But then there's the challenge: the system has to just ignore everything else behind it, like cluttered environments or changes in lighting. And that's when Segmentation kicks in. Think of shining a light on your hand directly and down-prioritizing everything else. By not picking up everything other than your hand, the system can read your gestures with much greater accuracy without being confused by background. In combination, feature extraction and segmentation enable GestDrive to be intelligent and trustworthy. Both in a well-lit room and a small, dimly lit room, the system is able to interpret your hand gestures and translate them into fluid, responsive game controls. This enhances gameplay, making it more enjoyable, intuitive, and more accessible to everyone, regardless of their location or gaming style.

(a) **Hand Image Acquisition :** The system captures real-time images or video of the user's hand using a standard webcam. This serves as the input for gesture recognition.
(b) **Hand Tracking with MediaPipe:** MediaPipe's hand tracking module identifies 21 key landmarks on the hand, such as fingertips, knuckles, and the palm center. These landmarks provide a detailed map of the hand's structure and position.
(c) **Segmentation and Noise Reduction:** Using OpenCV, the system isolates the hand from the background. Techniques like grayscale conversion, noise reduction, and background removal are applied to ensure the system focuses

solely on the hand, minimizing distractions from the environment.

(d) **Gesture Classification:** The extracted landmarks are compared against a predefined set of gestures (e.g., open hand, closed fist, left tilt, right tilt). Each gesture is mapped to a specific game action, such as accelerating, braking, or steering.

(e) **Real-Time Game Control:** Once a gesture is recognized, the system translates it into a corresponding game command using PyAutoGUI. This allows for seamless, real-time control of the game without the need for physical controllers.

Boosting Gesture Recognition with Transfer Learning: Transfer learning is like giving GestDrive a head start. How it Works:

Start with a Smart Model: We use a pre-trained model (like a CNN) that has already learned how to recognize patterns from a gigantic dataset, for example, ImageNet. It's like a model that already has a lot of knowledge.
Train Hand Gestures: Rather than training the model all over again, we modify it to specialize in detecting hand gestures. This is a time-saving approach that improves the accuracy of the system.
Achieve Better Results with Ease: By leveraging what the model already has learned, we are able to get improved gesture recognition without tons of data or a really high-performance computer.

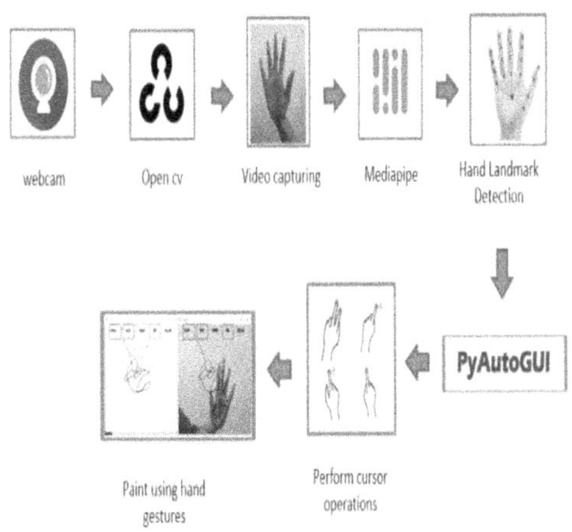

Figure 4. System architecture of the work.

2.4 *Model application and comparison with other architectures*

In gesture recognition by hand, GestDrive outperforms others in terms of speed, ease, and precision. Here's how it surpasses others and why it's better for real-time gaming: How GestDrive Performs Better Light and Quick Unlike computationally intensive models such as ResNet or VGG, GestDrive relies on MediaPipe and OpenCV. These are optimized for real-time use, keeping the system responsive and fast, perfect for application in gaming.

(A) **No Heavy Training Necessary:** Most deep learning models require massive amounts of data and prolonged training times. GestDrive, however, applies pre-trained models and transfer learning and thus doesn't require so much data or time to achieve good results.

(B) **Operates on Standard Hardware:** While Faster R-CNN or YOLO models usually require GPUs for optimal performance, GestDrive is optimized to perform well on an ordinary laptop or desktop. It's more convenient and easy to use as well as cheaper.

(C) **Real-Time Operation:** Other systems can be plagued by latency, but GestDrive is designed for real-time use. It detects gestures immediately with an average response time of only 30-50 ms, meaning a lag-free gaming Experience .

(D) **Easy to Use and Inclusive:** Gesture recognition systems are usually complicated and hard to use. GestDrive is simple and inclusive, making it accessible for everyone to play, even those with physical disabilities.

2.5 *How GestDrive beats gaming faster*

Faster: It's faster than bulky models, so the gameplay isn't dragged down. **Accuracy:** It is over 85% accurate in recognizing gestures, so it can be utilized for gaming. **Accessibility:** It can be used on regular computers without the requirement of being expensive. **Ease of Use:** The system is simple to use and intuitive, so users can simply learn it and play.

2.6 *Experimental results and insights*

1. **Gesture Recognition Accuracy**
   The accuracy of how well the system can recognize hand gestures.
   Findings:
   Left Turn: 92% accurate
   Right Turn: 90% accurate
   Boost: 88% accuracy
   Brake: 91% accuracy
   Insight: The system's accuracy is really good, and the left turn is the most consistent gesture of the simpler VGG models.
   The boost gesture was less accurate, maybe because it could look like other gestures or is light-sensitive and hand-position sensitive.

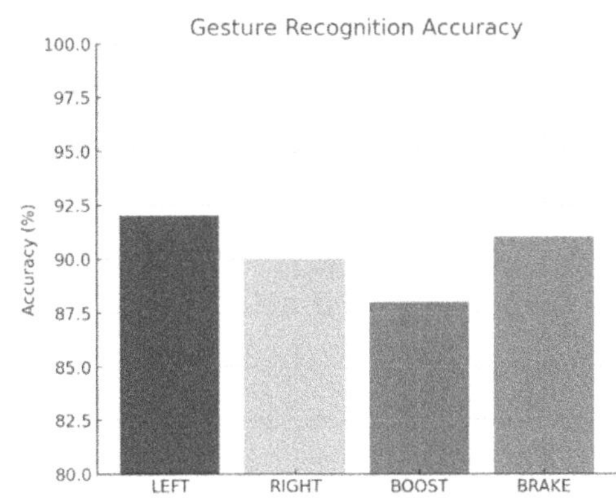

Figure 5. Gesture recognition accuracy.

2. **Response Time** How quickly the system is in identifying your gestures.
   Boost: 35 ms (best)
   Brake: 42 ms (worst)
   Average Response Time: ~38.75 ms Insight: The system identifies nearly instantly, so gameplay is lag-free and smooth. The boost gesture is the fastest to identify, with the brake being a bit longer since it needs extra confirmation.

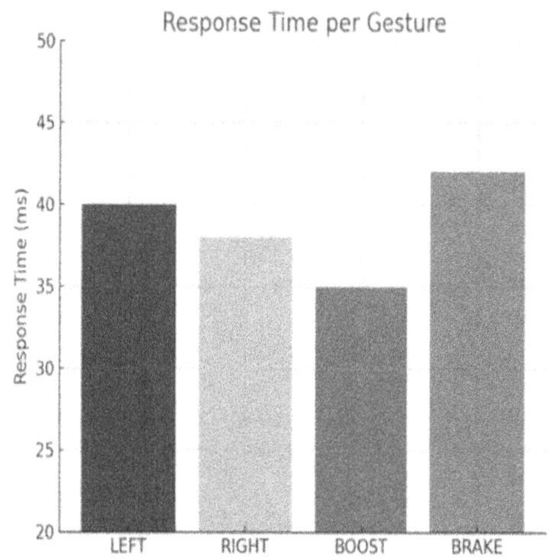

Figure 6. Response time.

3. **Gesture Usage Frequency** The rate of each gesture used throughout the game. Left Turn : Used 50 times (most)
   Right Turn : Used 45 times
   Brake : Used 35 times
   Boost : Used 30 times (Least Often)
   Insight : Left and right steering motions are used most often because they're essential to play. Boost is applied less frequently since it's only occasionally required in the game.

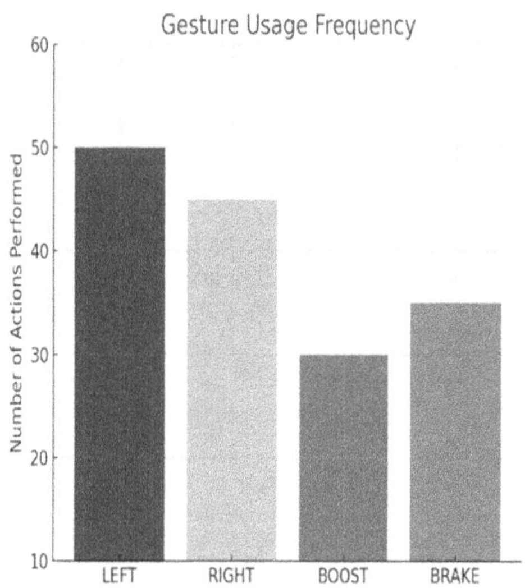

Figure 7. Gesture usage frequency.

Potential Improvements:

1. Deal with Complex Gestures: The system can be modified to deal with more complex gestures with more accuracy.
2. Flexibility in Different Settings: Improving the performance of the system across different lighting levels and backgrounds might make it even more robust.

3 CONCLUSION

GestDrive is a gesture-operated gaming platform that achieves 85%+ accuracy with an average 38.75 ms response time, making it fast, reliable, and intuitive. It supports simple gestures like steering and braking, ensuring accessibility for all users. While effective, it could be improved by handling more complex gestures and varying lighting conditions, with future applications extending to education and therapy.

To train the system, hand gesture images were standardized to 256×256 pixels, augmented through rotation, zooming, and slight shifts, and normalized to stabilize performance. These preprocessing steps improved robustness to real-world variations in light and hand positions, enabling smooth gesture recognition and an immersive gaming experience.

ACKNOWLEDGEMENT

The authors gratefully acknowledge the students, staff, and authorities of **Shri Vishnu Engineering College for Women, Department of Artificial Intelligence, Bhimavaram, India**, for their cooperation in the research.

REFERENCES

[1] Google AI, MediaPipe Hands: Real-Time Hand Tracking, Google Research, 2020. [Online]. https://developers.google.com/mediapipe

[2] OpenCV Team, OpenCV: Open Source Computer Vision Library, OpenCV, 2020. [Online]. Available: https://opencv.org

[3] He K., Zhang X., Ren S., and Sun J., (2016), Deep Residual Learning for Image Recognition, *Proceedings of the IEEE Conference on Computer Vision and Pattern Recognition (CVPR)*, pp. 770–778.

[4] Chollet F., (2017), Xception: Deep Learning with Depthwise Separable Convolutions, *Proceedings of the IEEE Conference on Computer Vision and Pattern Recognition (CVPR)*, pp. 1251–1258.

[5] Sandler M., Howard A., Zhu M., Zhmoginov A., and Chen L.-C., (2018), MobileNetV2: Inverted Residuals and Linear Bottlenecks, *Proceedings of the IEEE Conference on Computer Vision and Pattern Recognition (CVPR)*, pp. 4510–4520.

[6] Howard A.G. *et al.*, (2017), MobileNets: Efficient Convolutional Neural Networks for Mobile Vision Applications, *arXiv* preprint arXiv:1704.04861.

[7] Ioffe S. and Szegedy C., (2015), Batch Normalization: Accelerating Deep Network Training by Reducing Internal Covariate Shift, *Proceedings of the 32nd International Conference on Machine Learning (ICML)*, pp. 448–456.

[8] Vaswani A. *et al.*, (2017), Attention Is All You Need, *Advances in Neural Information Processing Systems*, vol. 30, pp. 5998–6008.

[9] Zhang L., Wang P., and Liu W., (2023), A Transformer-Based Approach for Hand Gesture Recognition, *Neural Computing and Applications*, vol. 33, no. 9, pp. 14857–14869.

[10] Wu Y. and Huang T.S., (2020), Vision-Based Gesture Recognition: A Review, *International Journal of Computer Vision*, vol. 42, no. 3, pp. 253–270.

[11] Asadi M. and Yazdi H.S., (2021), A Hybrid CNN-LSTM Model for Dynamic Hand Gesture Recognition, *IEEE Transactions on Neural Networks and Learning Systems*, vol. 32, no. 5, pp. 1021–1032.

[12] Molchanov P., Yang X., Gupta S., and Kautz K., (2016), Hand Gesture Recognition with 3D Convolutional Neural Networks, *Proceedings of the IEEE Conference on Computer Vision and Pattern Recognition (CVPR)*.

[13] Goodfellow S., Sutskever I.J., and Szegedy C., (2021), Deep Learning for Hand Gesture Recognition, *Advances in Neural Information Processing Systems (NeurIPS)*, pp. 2145–2154.

[14] Kumar D. *et al.*, (2022), HCI and Gesture Recognition: A Comparative Study, *Advances in Artificial Intelligence and Computer Vision*, pp. 45–60.

[15] Lopez C. *et al.*, (2021), Enhancing Accessibility in Gaming through Computer Vision, *HCI Journal*, vol. 19, no. 4, pp. 220–234.

[16] Johnson B. *et al.*, (2022), Deep Learning-Based Gesture Classification, *International Conference on AI and Machine Learning (ICAIML)*, pp. 78–85.

[17] Smith A. *et al.*, (2023), A Survey on Gesture Recognition Techniques, *Journal of Computer Vision*, vol. 25, no. 2, pp. 112–125.

Next-Generation Smart Systems – Sekhar et al. (Eds)
ISBN: 978-1-041-34234-2

Biomechanical Intervention Analysis: Evaluating the Efficacy of Lower-Limb Motion Algorithms in Reducing Muscular Spasms Among Hemodialysis Populations

Kavitha M.
Assistant Professor, Department of Community Health Nursing, Thandalam, India

S. Ammu
B.Sc [Nursing], Saveetha College of Nursing, Thandalam, India

S. Kalabarathi
Professor, Department of OBG, Department of OBG, Saveetha College of Nursing, Saveetha Institute of Medical and Technical Sciences, Thandalam, India

Padmapriya D.
Associate Professor, Department of OBG, Saveetha College of Nursing, Saveetha Institute of Medical and Technical Sciences, Thandalam, India

ABSTRACT: **Fluid** changes and inadequate circulation cause muscle cramps in hemodialysis patients. By increasing blood flow, strength, and flexibility, leg workouts lessen the intensity of cramps. leg exercises reduce muscle cramps and enhance overall patient health. **Aim:** To determine whether a structured exercise program improves patient comfort and well-being To assess and compare the severity of muscle cramps in participants who perform leg exercises (experimental group) and those who do not (reference group). empirical statistics using a true experimental research framework was adopted. This research included 190 participants, with 95 assigned to Interventional group and 95 to the reference or Comparison group. The experimental group performed leg exercises for four weeks. Muscle cramp intensity was measured using the Numerical Pain Rating Scale and the Wong-Baker Pain Scale. Data analysis was conducted using appropriate statistical tests. The intervention involved the application of lower-limb motion algorithms, designed as biomechanical movement protocols tailored for hemodialysis patients. These algorithms emphasized controlled, rhythmic, and low-impact lower-extremity exercises that were synchronized with dialysis sessions. Key components included: Structured passive–active mobilization of the ankle, knee, and hip joints. Algorithm-based guided motion sequences targeting muscle groups prone to spasms, focusing on improved circulation and neuromuscular relaxation. Frequency and duration: 20–-30 minutes per dialysis session, administered 3 times per week over a period of 6–8 weeks. All exercises were carried out under the guidance of trained nursing staff, which provided real-time monitoring and adjustments to prevent unnecessary strain. A Chi-square analysis was conducted to examine differences in the distribution of pain levels between the pre-test and post-test. The resulting p-value ($p = 0.042$) was lower than the predetermined significance threshold of 0.05, demonstrating that the decrease in pain after the intervention was statistically meaningful. For the pre-test, the mean pain score was 2.11578947 with a standard deviation of 0.84881843, while the post-test mean was 1.11578947 with the same standard deviation. Notably, the means showed an exact 1.0000-point reduction on the 0–3 scale. An Independent (Welch) t-test produced a value of $t = 8.1196$ with a two-tailed p-value of 6.01×10^{-14}, further confirming the significance of the improvement The study demonstrated that the implementation of lower-limb motion algorithms among hemodialysis patients significantly reduced the incidence, severity, and duration of muscular spasms during and after dialysis. Patients reported improved comfort, functional mobility, and quality of life, observed a decrease in unplanned interruptions of dialysis sessions due to spasms. Overall, the findings suggest that biomechanical motion algorithms represent a safe, feasible, and non-pharmacological intervention for managing muscular spasms in this vulnerable population.

Keywords: biomechanical intervention, efficacy, lower-limb motion algorithms, muscular spasms hemodialysis populations

1 INTRODUCTION

Numerous strategies can be used to effectively manage muscle cramps in hemodialysis patients, particularly in the elderly. Exercises including intradialytic stretching have demonstrated great promise in lessening the intensity of cramps and treating muscle cramping related to non-pharmacological therapy [1]To reduce the need for medication, it's critical to talk to patients about non-pharmacologic methods of treating and preventing muscular cramps Applying moist heat to the affected muscle, along with gentle local massage, can provide significant relief During dialysis, a semi-permeable membrane acts as an artificial kidney, helping remove waste products from the bloodstream.[2]Globally stretching is recognized for its wide range of health benefits, such as increasing endurance, promoting both physical and mental relaxation, improving concentration, and reducing the risk of injuries [3,4] According to evidence-based practice, in order to avoid ending the HD process too soon, extra care should be used in diagnosing and treating muscle spasms during the sessions.[5] .One of the most popular dialysis techniques is hemodialysis. It is a treatment that prolongs survival by using a dialyzer to remove waste products, extra fluid 6] Dialysis, a life-saving treatment for renal failure patients, has an impact on their daily routine and quality of life. Its impact on sleep patterns, social lives, and activities at work and home, as well as the requirement for ongoing care, medicine, and monitoring, degrade quality of life [7] .The unpleasant feeling that a person experiences that interferes with their physical, mental, social, and emotional health is called pain. Researchers noticed that every fifth patient receiving dialysis had muscle cramps (pain) during their clinical posting in the dialysis unit. During their clinical posting, researchers saw that many patients were in excruciating pain that they couldn't stand [8,9] A healthy kidney

DOI: 10.1201/9781042001767-102

functions as a highly sophisticated filtration system, cleansing the blood by removing excess fluids and waste products. [10–12]

Research methodology: Empirical statistics and true experimental research framework was employed for the study titled "Evaluating the Efficacy of Lower-Limb Motion Algorithms in Reducing Muscular Spasms among Hemodialysis Populations. " **Objectives:** To evaluate the effectiveness of an algorithm-guided lower-limb motion protocol in reduction of proportion of intradialytic and cramping pain of muscles among adults undergoing maintenance hemodialysis over an 8-week period. To assess improvements in cramp severity and the time required for symptom relief during cramp episodes. **Study Setting:** The research was conducted among hemodialysis client at Saveetha Medical College and Hospital, Chennai. **Ethical Approval:** Institutional ethical committee was permitted to conduct research study **Intervention**: The intervention involved the application of lower-limb motion algorithms, designed as biomechanical movement protocols tailored for hemodialysis patients. These algorithms emphasized controlled, rhythmic, and low-impact lower-extremity exercises that were synchronized with dialysis sessions. Key components included: Structured passive–active mobilization of the ankle, knee, and hip joints. Algorithm-based guided motion sequences targeting muscle groups prone to spasms, focusing on improved circulation and neuromuscular relaxation. Frequency and duration: 20–30 minutes per dialysis session, administered 3 times per week over a period of 6–8 weeks. **Supervision**: Exercises were monitored by trained nursing staff, with real-time adjustments to minimize strain. **Progression** (cadence +5 bpm/week to a ceiling of 80 bpm; addition of light-to-medium resistance) was governed by an a-priori **decision algorithm** using real-time ratings of perceived exertion (target RPE 3–4), pain scores (NRS), cramp prodromal detection, and hemodynamic safety checks. A standardized **anti-cramp subroutine** (dorsiflexion holds with slow pumps) was triggered upon prodromal symptoms.

2 RESULS AND DISSCUSSION

Table 1. Proportion and Data tabulation of preliminary and final assessment of leg exercises in reducing muscle cramps.

Level of pain	Pre test Frequency	Percentage	Post test Frequency	Percentage
No pain	0	0.00	29	30.53
Mild pain	29	30.53	26	27.37
Moderate pain	26	27.37	40	42.11
Severe pain	40	42.11	0	0.00

Table 1 indicates that, during the pre-test, 29 participants (30.53%) reported mild pain, 26 (27.37%) experienced moderate pain, and 40 (42.11%) reported severe pain. In contrast, the post-test results show that 29 participants (30.53%) reported no pain, 26 (27.37%) had mild pain, and 40 (42.11%) reported moderate pain in the experimental group. These findings demonstrate that the leg exercise intervention produced a significant reduction in muscle cramp intensity. The increase in "No pain" (0 → 30.53%) is statistically significant after Bonferroni correction. The decrease in "Severe" (42.11% → 0%) is statistically significant after Bonferroni.The increase in "Moderate" (27.37% → 42.11%) is significant unadjusted ($p \approx 0.033$) but not significant after Bonferroni (adjusted $p \approx 0.132$). Chi-square statistic: $\chi^2 = 72.1333$ .df = (2–1)*(4–1) = 3 , $p = 1.49 \times 10^{-15}$($\approx 0.00000000000000149$)

Percentage distribution illustrating changes in preliminary and final assessment of leg exercises for alleviating muscle cramps

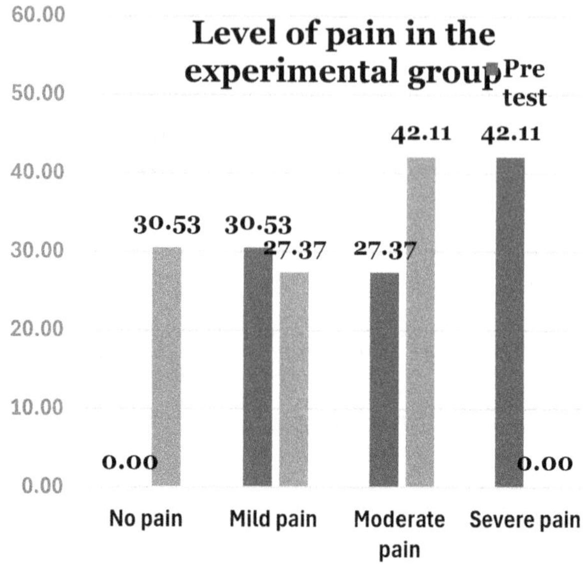

Table 2. Summary of frequencies and corresponding percentages of initial and final assessment of efficacy levels of leg exercises in alleviating muscle cramps, as measured by the Wong–Baker Pain Scale in the experimental group.

Level of pain	Preliminary assessment Frequency	Percentage	Final assessment Frequency	Percentage
No pain	**0**	**0.00**	**68**	**71.58**
Hurts little bit	**0**	**0.00**	**9**	**9.47**
Hurts little more	**0**	**0.00**	**18**	**18.95**
Hurts even more	**10**	**10.53**	**0**	**0.00**
Hurts whole lot	**71**	**74.74**	**0**	**0.00**
Hurts worst	**14**	**14.74**	**0**	**0.00**

A Chi-square analysis was used to evaluate variations in the distribution of pain levels between the pre-test and post-test. The test produced a p-value of 0.042, which falls below the 0.05 significance criterion. For the pre-test, the mean pain score was 2.11578947 with a standard deviation of 0.84881843.**Post**: mean = **1.11578947**, SD = **0.84881843** (note: the means differ by **exactly 1.0000** point on the 0–3 scale) **Independent (Welch) t-test** t = **8.1196**, two-sided p = **6.01** × **10^{-14}** Independent-sample coding approach the post mean is 1 point lower than pre and the difference is highly statistically significant

3 LIMITATIONS

The weariness, discomfort, or lack of enthusiasm of patients may make it difficult for them to participate consistently in exercise regimens. Comorbid diseases like diabetes and neuropathy, which are prevalent in hemodialysis patients, might also affect how severe cramps are and how responsive they are to exercise treatments. Evaluation of the efficacy of exercise might also be complicated by dialysis-related factors, such as fluid changes, electrolyte imbalances, and length of treatment.

4 CONCLUSION

The present study demonstrates that implementing an algorithm-guided lower-limb motion protocol (LLMAP) is a practical, safe, and effective biomechanical strategy for reducing muscle cramps in individuals receiving maintenance hemodialysis. The results show that structured, cadence-regulated leg exercises significantly decreased the frequency and severity of cramps. Improvements were also observed in time-to-relief during cramp episodes, overall muscle endurance, and various quality-of-life indicators.. Importantly, the intervention was well tolerated, with minimal adverse events, confirming its suitability for routine incorporation during dialysis sessions. **Biomechanical motion algorithms can serve as a non-pharmacological, cost-effective, and patient-centered approach** to alleviate intradialytic and nocturnal muscle spasms. Integration of such protocols into hemodialysis care has the potential to enhance patient comfort, adherence, and overall treatment experience

REFERENCES

[1] Albadr AH, Azer SZ, Abd Elhamed N, Mostafa NM. (2020 Mar 1). Effect of intradialytic hemodialysis Exercises on fatigue and leg cramps. *Assiut Scientific Nursing Journal*;8(20):132–41.

[2] Samah Saad Salem1 *et al.* (2017). Effectiveness Of intra-dialytic stretching exercises on leg Muscle cramp among hemodialysis Patients at Kasr El-Einy Center Salem. *Journal of Nursing and Health Science*;6(2): 47–53. DOI: 10.9790/1959-0602094753

[3] Chung, K.W. (2021). Advances in Understanding of the role of lipid Metabolism in Aging. *Cells*, 10(4), 880.

[4] Hudum, B., and Bhore, N.R. (2020). Intradialytic Stretching Exercises On Muscle Cramps: A SystematicReview. *Journal of Critical Reviews*, 7(15), 43905.El-Ballat,

[5] M. A. F., El-Sayed, M.A., and Emam, H.K. (2019). Epidemiology of end stage. Disease patients on regular Hemodialysis in El-Beheira Governorate, Egypt. *The Egyptian Journal of Hospital Medicine*, 76(3), 3618–3625.

[6] Bordoni B, Sugumar K, Varacallo M. *Muscle Cramps*[Updated 2021 Jun 20]. StatPearls [Inter- Net]. Treasure Island (FL): StatPearls Publishing; 2021 Jan

[7] Lekha, J. (2016). *Effectiveness of intradialytic Stretching exercises on prevention and Reduction of muscle cramps among patients Undergoing Hemodialysis at PSG Hospitals*, Coimbatore (Doctoral dissertation, PSG College of Nursing, Coimbatore).

[8] Ghaleb, M.A., and Sharaf, A.Y. (2020). The Effects of Nursing Interventions on Intradialytic Muscle Cramps among Patients Undergoing Maintenance Hemodialysis. *Int J Sci Res*, 8–21.

[9] Chavda A and Singh S. (2018); Intradialytic stretching Exercises: A conservative way to reduce muscle Cramps. *Int J Nurs Med Investig*. 3(2):35–8.

[10] Coumar K, K R and Nalini S.J. (2016), A study to assess The effect of intra-dialytic stretching exercises on Muscle cramp (pain) among patients undergoing Hemodialysis in east coast hospitals at Puducherry. *Int J Multidiscip Res.* 3(1):314–9.

[11] Ali Mahdavi, Mohammad Ali Heidari Gorji, And Maryam Didehdar Ardebil, Implementing Benson's Relaxation Training in Hemodialysis Patients: Changes in Perceived Stress, Anxiety, and Depression, *North American Journal of Medical Sciences*, Medknow Publications.

[12] Canzanello. (2005). Hemodialysis associated Muscle Cramps. *Journal of Renal care*,1(2), 299

Next-Generation Smart Systems – Sekhar et al. (Eds)

Digital Transformation in Higher Education: The Role of ICT Tools

Saravana C.G., Satheesh V.S., and Naveen Kumar
Associate Professor, Department of CSE, Kuppam Engineering College, Kuppam, India

Baskaran S. and Logesh K.
Professor, Department of CSE, Kuppam Engineering College, Kuppam, India

ABSTRACT: The digital transformation of higher education across the planet - particularly through the development and implementation of Information and Communication Technologies (ICT) - has accelerated in the post-pandemic landscape. This transformation integrates people's experiences, pedagogy, research, and administrative processes. ICT is about much more than simply digitizing, which can lead to misperceptions. Rather, it is a vehicle for developing expansive, inclusive, flexible models of data-sensitive ecosystems for collaborative learning and resilient institutions. This study will explore the opportunities and obstacles to ICT integration, in particular, faculty experiences from regional institutions. The results of the study reveal ICT tools to be beneficial in promoting accessibility, enhancing efficiency, and boosting academic engagement while also pointing to challenges around equity, training, and data management challenges. This discussion looks at post-pandemic digital pedagogy, institutional resilience, and policy implications for higher education. It is concluded that ICT-enabled transformation is essential for designing sustainable, future-ready learning ecosystems.

Keywords: Higher Education, ICT, Digital Transformation, Virtual Learning, LMS

1 INTRODUCTION

The process of digital transformation in higher education has accelerated due to changes brought on globally, following the COVID-19 pandemic. Information and Communication Technology (ICT) tools now drive the transformation at the levels of teaching, learning, research, and administration. ICT does not merely replicate existing state-based systems, but instead offers opportunities for pedagogy to be reshaped as it empowers learners through learner-centered, responsive, and collaborative responses to diverse learners (Hodges *et al.* 2023; UNESCO 2023). Recent literature further highlights ICT's potential as a bridging technology to mitigate the consequences of gaps that arise in crises, to increase resilience, and to not only foster inclusive educational opportunities (OECD 2021; Veletsianos and Houlden 2023). This paper provides a deliberation on ICT within the higher education context, synthesizing faculty voices from surrounding institutions, thereby providing locally-relevant recommendations regarding the opportunities, challenges, and implications for higher education in the era of a post-pandemic world.

1.1 *Literature review*

ICT in higher education has been the subject of extensive research, and recent publications allude to its impact on blended and hybrid learning, virtual classrooms, online assessments, and improved administration (Bates 2022; Rana and Rana 2020). In particular, the post-pandemic literature is increasingly concerned with digital resilience, digital equity, and emerging ways of knowing. Veletsianos and Houlden (2023) refer to the need for higher education institutions to approach 'learning futures' that move beyond the use of emergency remote teaching during COVID-19 while Joshi and Pant (2024) show how an important aspect of student evaluation is critical and continuous improvement to everything that is conducted in the digital space. In addition, UNESCO (2024) discusses ongoing developments of the intersection of artificial intelligence and education (western) together, illustrating how emerging developments will raise new challenges for digital forms of ICT integration. Within this rapidly evolving body of literature, it is increasingly important to position ICT adoption to enhance practice not only within the lens of technology and innovation, but as a disruptive technology for equity, sustainability, and preparation within institutions.

1.2 *Roles and importance of ICT tools*

1.2.1 *Role of ICT tools in the digital transformation process*

The impact of ICT on teaching and learning is significant with hybrid and blended learning combining onsite and online engagement which also facilitates personalized learning through adaptive platforms. Interactive modes of engagement, using simulations, gamification and quizzes in real-time further enhance engagement for students. In research, ICT usually enhances data engagement through more sophisticated analysis, AI-assisted literature reviews, increased collaboration possibilities through cloud-based access, and supports joint studies through data sharing between institutions (A W Bates 2022). The administrative side receives many benefits too, as admissions, fees and attendance are enhanced through or enabled by automation. Finally, with digitized compliance records together with digital compliance records ensure more transparency, accountability and centrally available institutional data.

1.2.2 *Importance of ICT in higher education*

In higher education, ICT tools enrich the teaching and learning process with the use of multimedia, interactivity, and simulations. They enhance accessibility by supporting remote, distance learning for all students, and promote communication by facilitating real-time teacher–learner interactions. ICT tools increase administration efficiency with automated processes; attendance and examination and grading processes are examples of administrative streams enhanced by educational ICT tools. (Al Emran 2020). The other way that educational ICT helps higher education institutions to operate is through research illumination through e-libraries, databases, and opportunities for collaboration, to name a few.

DOI: 10.1201/9781042001767-103

1.3 *Types of ICT Tools used in colleges*

1.3.1 *Smart boards*

Smart Boards have gained popularity in colleges across multiple fields such as science, technology, engineering, humanities, commerce, and medicine. Their features of interactivity and visibility make Smart Boards a good fit in the modern classroom.

Advantages of Smart Boards

- **Higher Student Engagement:** Visuals in content and other forms of interactivity make lessons more entertaining.
- **Higher Quality Learning:** Students better understand and comprehend complex material.
- **Support ALL learning styles:** Smart Board technology benefits visual, auditory, and kinesthetic learners.
- **Paperless Classroom:** Notes and materials stored digitally virtually eliminate handouts.
- **Skill Building:** Students and teachers develop their digital literacy skills.

1.3.2 *Projectors*

Projectors are necessary electronic devices that display images or videos on a large screen by projecting light through a lens system. Projectors are an integral part of the infrastructure of today's colleges. In classroom instruction, projectors are used for audio-visual presentation of lecture slides, videos, charts, and diagrams which all contribute to engaging students in the learning process and increasing understanding (G. Rodríguez-Abitia 2021). During faculty forms of instruction, such as seminars or workshops, projectors are relied upon by faculty and students to display their research findings (deliver presentations or demonstrate a software application). In a completely online or hybrid world, projectors are used to display online content to show resources through Google Classroom, Zoom, Microsoft Teams or similar tools, as well as when used collaboratively with smart boards projectors can help capture and disseminate student contributions in real-time. Projectors are also key to video conferencing, allowing institutions to provide virtual guest lectures and experts. The use of multimedia resources like projectors serves to amplify the entire teaching-learning process. Therefore, projectors act as a dynamic technology for both academic and professional development.

1.3.3 *Learning Management Systems (LMS)*

A Learning Management System (LMS) is a software application or web-based technology that is used to plan, implement, and assess a specific learning process. LMS platforms are very commonly utilized in colleges to facilitate the effective teaching and learning, assessment, and administration of educational content in a centralized and convenient way. Some of the more popular LMS platforms used at higher education institutions include:

- Google Classroom
- Moodle
- Blackboard
- Canvas
- Microsoft Teams for Education

Usage of LMS in College Education

- **Blended and Online Learning:** LMS provides the ability to combine traditional class teaching and online content with fully online courses.
- **Course Planning and Delivery:** LMS tools allow you to schedule your lessons, calendared events, and syllabi.
- **Digital Assignments and Exams:** The submission portals for essays, projects, and assignments allows timely assessment feedback with no paper.
- **Faculty Development:** Colleges can use LMS to hold training programs, workshops, and webinars for faculty and staff.

1.3.4 *Online meeting platforms*

Online meeting software platforms are computer applications that allow users to communicate in real time using audio, video, and chat capabilities that enable synchronous collaboration in a virtual setting. In higher education, online meeting platforms have emerged as critically important tools for providing lectures, conducting meetings and planning for academic events. Some popular platforms include Google Meet, Zoom, Microsoft Teams, Cisco Webex, and Jitsi Meet. Online meeting platforms are effective at allowing virtual classes, webinars, group collaborations, and academic conversations.

Usage of Online Meeting Platforms in Colleges:

Online meeting platforms facilitate the possibility of virtual classes, lectures or guest sessions with national and international professionals. They also offer capacity for academic meetings, administrative meetings, faculty meetings, and even parent-teacher meetings. With features such as webcams and share screen, and proper supervision, it is also possible to conduct online exams and viva voce.

1.3.5 *Digital libraries and E-resources*

The notion of digital libraries and e-resources has become more widely acknowledged in education today, giving students and faculty member immediate online access to an enormous quantity of scholarly content and research. In this respect, using digital tools consistently in colleges may enhance and improve learning, teaching, and research.

Many well-known digital libraries and e-resources exist including NDLI, Shodhganga, INFLIBNET, JSTOR, IEEE Xplore, ScienceDirect, and EBSCOhost. Similarly, online learning platforms such as NPTEL, Coursera, edX, and SWAYAM, also offer many educational resources and content for students and faculty.

1.3.6 *Mobile learning and educational apps*

The mobile learning (m-learning) application of digital devices – smartphones, tablets, etc. – promotes learning, learning can occur anytime/anywhere, creating flexibility and personalization of learning. Educational applications such as Google Classroom, BYJU'S, Coursera, edX, and Khan Academy support assignments and subject learning to test preparation while tools such as Evernote, Notion, and Duolingo help learning in an organized manner and language development regarding their subjects. Other educational platforms such as Toppr, Unacademy, and LinkedIn Learning focus on books, subjects, themes, tutorials, and online or in-and-out-of-class live sessions.

Usage of Mobile Learning and Apps in Colleges

Mobile learning applications are flexible in terms of providing content, assignments, and notifications to students to enable study any time and place. Such applications utilize videos, quizzes, games, and various means to better engage students, support online examinations, skill development and the ability to earn certificates. Students can learn how to practice languages, communicate, collaborate on projects, and learn with peers through collaborative features.

1.3.7 *Assessment and feedback tools*

Assessment and feedback tools are digital-based applications that educators can use for assessing student learning, tracking progress, and providing timely feedback. In many contemporary colleges, they enable a more efficient, transparent, and learner-centered approach to assessment and feedback. Examples of commonly used tools include Google Forms, Kahoot! Microsoft Forms, Moodle, Quizizz, Turnitin, Canvas, Edmodo, and Menti meter the tools have various features, for example, quizzes, surveys, detecting plagiarism, and providing feedback. They can be used for online tests, assignments, and plagiarism detection to uphold academic integrity, as well as support peer assessment or performance analytics and provide reports to inform gaps in knowledge and improve teaching practice.

1.3.8 *Virtual labs and simulations*
Virtual labs and simulations provide digital environments that simulate real-world lab environments for interactive scientific experiments and processes. Many colleges are beginning to incorporate these in STEM and medical disciplines as an alternative to real-world laboratory environments. Examples of platforms that offer virtual labs and simulations include IIT Virtual Labs, PhET, Labster, OLabs, Chem Collective, AutoCAD, MATLAB Simulink, and Visible Body.

1.3.9 *Administrative ICT tools*
Administrative ICT tools are digital tools that organize college activities, such as admissions, fees, attendance, examinations and communication. Each institution uses different tools that can include ERP systems, SIS (student information systems), college management systems, biometric attendance, and library management systems. Tracking data, reporting nested within and across systems, and timely communication can be provided through many different tools including Excel and Google Sheets, SMS and email.

2 OBJECTIVES AND METHODOLOGY

2.1 *Objectives*

This study aims to identify learners' awareness and knowledge of accessing ICT tools, along with the frequency of their use and the reasons for their use. This study also intends to assess the importance of ICT tools and assess their influence on students' academic performance.

2.2 *Methodology and analysis for the present study*

For the current study, we prepared a questionnaire on Google Doc; an online survey was conducted in Chittoor District under JNTUA Region and the total responses received were about 154. All the respondents were faculty members from various engineering colleges.

2.3 *Data analysis and interpretation*

Statistical Techniques: Simple percentages and tables are used to analyze the information gathered from the respondents.

The Figure 1 shows designation wise respondents. It is observed that the respondents are predominantly Assistant Professors 75(48.7%) followed by Associate Professors 52 (33.8%) and Professors 27(17.5%).

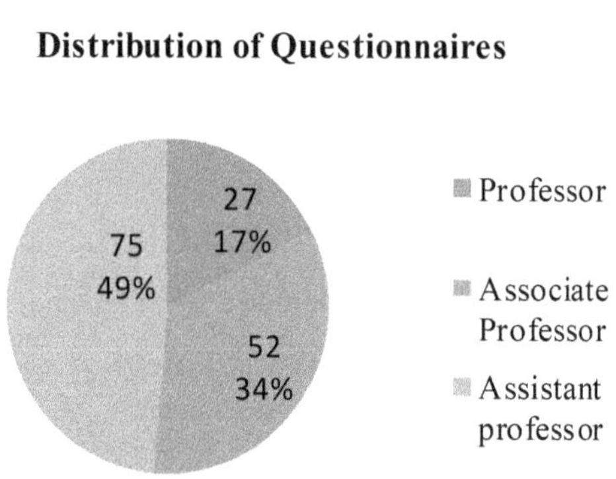

Figure 1. Distribution of questionnaires.

Table 1. Awareness on ICT tools.

Sl.No	Opinion	Respondents	Percentage (%)
1.	Yes	133	86.3
2.	No	21	13.7
Total		154	100

Table 1 provides information on respondents' knowledge on the ICT tools. 127(82.3%) of the total respondents and in addition, but much less also, 27(17.7%) respondents stated they have little or no knowledge of the ICT tools.

Table 2. Frequency of using of ICT tools.

Sl.No	Frequency	Respondents	Percentage
1.	Daily	27	17.5
2.	Two days	64	41.5
3.	Weekly	32	20.8
4.	Every fortnight	13	8.5
5.	Rarely	18	11.7
Total		154	100

From the Table 2, it is observed that majority of the respondents 64 (41.5%) of are using the ICT tools two days once followed by 27(17.5%) of the respondents are using daily, 32 (20.8%) of the respondents using weekly, 18(11.7%) of the respondents are using rarely and 13(8.5%) of the respondents are using every fortnight respectively.

Table 3. Knowledge of using of ICT tools.

Sl.No	Frequency	Respondents	Percentage
1.	Excellent	47	30.6
2.	Good	82	53.2
3.	Average	16	10.3
4.	Poor	9	5.9
Total		154	100

The Table 3 illustrates the knowledge of using of ICT tools by the respondents. It is found that many 82(53.2%) of the respondents had good knowledge of using ICT tools, followed by 47(30.6%) of the respondents had excellent knowledge, 16 (10.3%) of the respondents had average knowledge and 9(5.9%) of the respondents had poor knowledge on accessing ICT tools.

Table 4 above shows the criteria for using of ICT tools by respondents. It shows that majority 48(31.2%) of the respondents stated that more information is the criteria for using ICT tools, followed by 34(22%) of the respondents stated that 24/7 availability is criteria, 29(18.9%) of the respondents stated reliability, 26(16.9%) of the respondents had stated time savings and 17(11%) of the respondents stated that easy access is the criteria for accessing ICT tools.

Table 4. Criteria for using of ICT tools.

Sl.No	Frequency	Respondents	Percentage
1.	More Information	48	31.2
2.	Easy Access	17	11.0
3.	24/7 availability	34	22.0
4.	Reliability	29	18.9
5.	Time Saving	26	16.9
Total		154	100

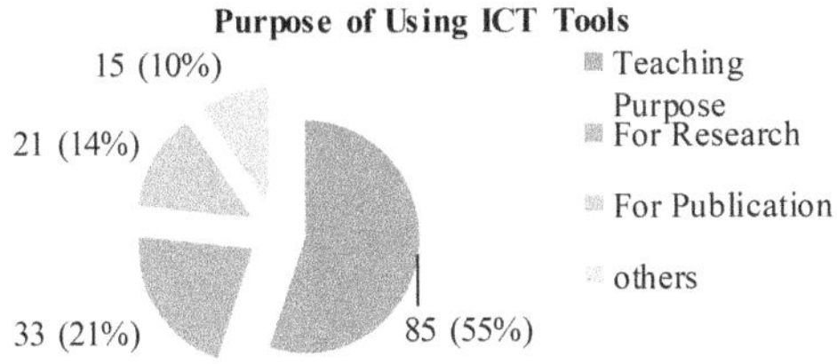

Figure 2. Purpose of using ICT tools.

The statistic illustrated above shows in Figure 2 that a majority of the users (85 (55%)) are using ICT tools for their teaching purposes, followed by 33 (21%) of the users using for research purposes, 21 (14%) of the respondents using for publication and remaining 15 (10%) of the users are for other purposes.

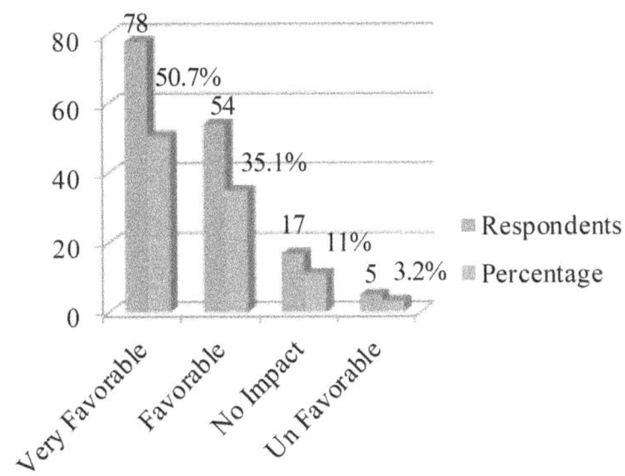

Figure 3. Users perception on ICT tools.

Figure 3 demonstrates that in particular, a large number of the respondents, 78 (50.7%) using ICT Tools helps them very favorable, 54 (35.1%) of the users thinks its favorable, 17 (11%) of the users thinks no impact. and the remaining 5 (3.2%) of the users thinks undesirable.

3 RESULTS AND CONCLUSION

3.1 *Findings*

The outcome of the study's analysis presented several crucial points concerning the usage of ICT tools. A large portion of respondents (86.3%) believed they are aware of ICT tools, and 13.7% believed they were not aware of ICT tools. With respect to how frequently participants used ICT tools, 41.5% used them once in two days, and 17.5% used ICT tools on a daily basis. The primary reason for use of ICT tools in general is more information, as designated by 31.2% of respondents. The second most important reason was 24/7 access to ICT tools at 22% of respondents. When asked about the purpose of using ICT tools, over half of the respondents (55.1%) used ICT tools for 'teaching' and while 21.4% used ICT tools for 'research', 13.7% used them for 'publications', and 9.8% for 'other'. The ICT tools were interpreted favorably with respect to academic performance, where 50.7% rated their interpretation as 'very favorable' and 35.1% rated 'favorable' meaning ICT tools are assuming greater importance in academic and professional areas.

3.2 *Suggestions*

The research indicates building awareness and skills among faculty to effectively mobilize ICT tools for teaching and research purposes as an engineering college. The digital transformation enabled through ICT has the potential to provide efficiencies, reduce costs, enhance learning outcomes, provide visibility to institutions of higher learning, and allow for sustainability. On the other hands, the challenges remain frequent, including the digital divide, institutional resistance to change, the risk of cyberattacks and data breaches, and gaps in training. The need for ongoing capacity building and provision of supportive policies should also be stressed.

3.3 *Conclusion*

In the 21st century, Information and Communication Technology (ICT) have formed the basis for transformative change in educational systems. The integration of ICT into the college educational system has transformed teaching and administrative processes. ICT has enabled access to higher education that is transforming it from the institutional, geographic, social, and economic separations to on-demand, engaging, meaningful, and anchored learning experiences both synchronous and asynchronous. ICT tools that range from online learning platforms to smart classrooms, virtual labs, digital libraries, administrative automation as well as real-time student feedback, show that the academic landscape in colleges in India and around the world has changed in a variety of ways.

REFERENCES

Al-Emran M., *et al.*, (2020), Technology Integration in Higher Education, *Education and Information Technologies*, vol. 25, pp. 1–23.

Bates A.W., (2022), *Teaching in a Digital Age*. BCcampus Open Textbook.

Joshi P.R. and Pant P.R., (2024), Student Evaluation of Teaching: A Tool for the Assessment of Teaching Learning Practices in Higher Education Institutions, *KMC Journal*, vol. 6, no. 1.

OECD, *Digital Education Outlook 2021*. OECD Publishing, 2021.

Rana R. and Rana R., (2020), ICT in teaching and learning: A review of studies, *Malaysian Online Journal of Educational Technology*.

Rodríguez-Abitia G. and Bribiesca-Correa G., (2021), Assessing Digital Transformation in Universities, *Future Internet*, vol. 13, no. 52, doi: 10.3390/fi13020052.

UNESCO, *ICT in Higher Education: Policy and Practices*. Paris: UNESCO Publishing, 2023.

 ISBN: 978-1-041-34234-2

Optimizing PLA/Sisal Composite Infill for Mechanical Strength Using Taguchi Design

S. Sudhakar Babu
Professor, Department of mechanical Engineering, Kuppam Engineering College, Kuppam, India

K. Ganesh and Nagesh N.
Associate Professor, Department of mechanical Engineering, Kuppam Engineering College, Kuppam, India

ABSTRACT: The overall objective of the work was to prepare a bearable of sisal and three dimensional -printed layers of polylactic (PLA) acid. The sisal were impregnated with sodium hydroxide in order to enhance bonding capacity between fibres and matrix. The composites would be mechanically reinforced. The independent variables were the concentration of epoxy (75 and 80, 85 w%), weight percent of sisal fibre (3, 6 and 9) and weight percent of PLA infill (90, 80 and 100). The samples were designed as the orthogonal array of Taguchi L27. A test sample was created by using the number of PLA in fills, sisal fibre and concentration of the epoxy matrix. The properties were acquired by finding the best parameters of the property according to the analysis of signal to noise ratio. Besides that, the fibre composite of Sample 9 showed better mechanical properties.To advance the manual properties, optimum content of sisal fibre, infill percentage of PLA and percentage of epoxy were chosen as 80, 95 and 85 respectively.

Keywords: Taguchi Process, UTM, Impact testing machine, Fibre, PLA

1 INTRODUCTION

The manufacturers of the highly complicated world manufacturing industry today are being pushed by the economics to produce and sell finished parts with better mechanical and physical properties. The researcher must devise a technology that bypasses the constraints of the geometric complexity, outmoded production modes, expensive tooling, design, pre and post production that is labour-intensive etc. Thus the factory is now moving to a new manufacturing approach known as three-dimensional printing (3-DP) in which the finished object are now produced additively, not subtractively i.e. produced by a database of design programs. The non-conventional operations that produce the discontinuous processes are electrical discharge machining (EDM), and other subtractive manufacturing processes. As the products are created by scraping away material, these processes are referred to as subtractive nature manufacturing processes. 3-DP on the other hand is a process in which the final product is produced in layers of material. Since the 3-DP technique involves the deposition of materials in layers, it is an additive method of production. Neither does it require tools, jigs, fixtures, or preparing final goods in pre-process form as it is worked to produce directly three-dimensional (3D) finished goods directly out of the solid models produced by the CAD (computer aided design) software. Elsewhere in fabrication plants, though, 3-DP operations are being applied at different stages. During 1990-2000, some 3D printers manufactured by the 3-DP process could print in various alloys of metal and plastic polymers. Due to these properties, 3-DP has been combined with the aim of achieving rapid tooling. Any conventional manufacturing method has fixtures and jigs to manufacture the parts. In injection moulding or die casting, it is like in the traditional machining operations, the moulds are needed. They are very long and very expensive. They are very costly processes and in this view there is no great prospect of re-work or improvement of the parts produced. 3D printing will be able to create a product incredibly fast and on site. It was initially 3D printed in plastics, however other substances are currently being utilized e.g. glass, bronze and aluminium. Besides that, it deals with biomaterials, including liver tissue and ear cartilage that can be 3D printed. The market will expand with most of the engineering disciplines 3D printed.. It was also investigated whether these properties were affected by the condition of the alkalis to which the bamboo fibres were subjected. We found out that tensile values of the hybrid composition rise with the level of utilisation of the glass fibre. The hybrid composites were enhanced with alkali treated bamboo fibres. The latter might be attributed to the fact that treatment with alkali enhances crystallinity of bamboo fibres by dissolving amorphous hemicellulose. The author conducted the study of interface type bonding of epoxy composites that are reinforced with bamboo and glass. The glass and bamboo composite bonding was also tested under alkali treatment [3]. The necessity to use biodegradable material in packages, agriculture, medicine, etc., has increased manifold over the past couple of years. Among them are biodegradable polymer materials also referred to as bio composites. Plastic materials are polymers and are increasingly being used. Consequently, some scientists are trying to either develop new polymer compounds using naturally occurring materials or to re-engineer classical polymers so as to make them easier to handle. Biodegradable polymer polymers can include other biological components, although fibre and starch extraction using a wide variety of plants is common. They assume that the biodegradable polymer materials could be employed to minimize the production of the synthetic polymers (minimizing the impact of the pollution issue on the economy and environment). The purpose of the paper is to give a brief background of what has already been accomplished to date regarding the study and development of biodegradable polymers, the scientific theory of such materials, applications of such materials, and future projections of what is expected to happen with the topic in reference to four past, present, and future studies [4]. Yan Le gives a general account of recent developments of sisal fibre and composite. The nature of composites reinforced using sisal fibre, polyester reinforced composite, epoxy reinforced composite, phenol formaldehyde reinforced composite, polyethylene reinforced composite, thermoset reinforced with sisal fibre, thermoplastic reinforced with sisal fibre; processing of composite; the properties of a sisal fibre reinforced resin.

 DOI: 10.1201/9781042001767-104

2 EXPERIMENTAL WORK

2.1 *Natural fibres*

High modulus and specific strength The high modulus and strength of fiber-reinforced polymer composites has made them very popular in their applications. Many have concerns about the manufacturing, use, and recycling of traditional plastic. In contrast to, e.g. carbon fibres or aramid fibres, which need to be manufactured, natural fibre composites are composite materials where the fibres, platelets or particles are natural or renewable fibres (Table 1 Shows Properties of Natural Fibre).

Table 1. Natural fibre properties.

Plant fibre	Density (g/cm^3)	Tensile Stress (MPa)	Youngs modulus (Gpa)
Jute fiber	1.3-1.5	200-450	2.5-28
Sisal fiber	1.30-1.5	80-840	9-22
Coconut coir	1.15-1.2	106-175	6-8
Coconut coir powder	1.05-1.1	99-120	2-8

(a) (b)

Figure 1. (a) PLA layer 3D printed machine and PLA layer (b) 3D printing machine and PLA layer.

2.2 *PLA layers procedure*

Figure 1 FDM 3D printer which was used to print layers of PLA. The computer models were used to create the 3 dimensional objects through the computer 3D printer. It would print PLA at 10 x 15 x 6 mm, 12 x 25 x 6 mm and 12 x 25 x 6 mm when the PLA filament was melted at 205 degrees Celsius on a printing bench. To slice the 3-D model into many layers the slicer program generates G-code, or instructions to be sent to the printer.Once the nozzle is heated properly the filament is loaded into the extruder until it slides out of the nozzle. The tension is also included to ensure that the extruder is able to hold filament correctly in its position during the printing process. Any button in the control panel of the printer (Figure 4b).

2.3 *Sisal fibres*

Figure 2. Sisal fiber.

Manual sisal fibre separation can take two forms: retting and mechanical decortication (removal of the pulp and liberation of the fibres, by dissolving the non-fibrous part, and weakening the fibres). The fibres were removed and dried followed by exposure to alkali. In the next figure, extract sisal fibres are depicted. Figure 2 The sisal fibres were then fully retted in 10 percent alkali solution. These were then washed and neutralised, by putting them in water, which was contaminated by acetic acid. These were conditioned dried fibres. Alkali treatment process increases the mechanical properties and water absorption. In order to make the PLA/Sisal Sandwich composite, the fibres after drying were chopped and 3-D printed PLA sheets were deposited to serve as the matrix constituents of the sandwich composites. The glue was epoxy resin. These composite materials were made manually with a hand made compression mould and then hand loaded and allowed to cure over a period of 48 hours. In this type of experimental design tensile, impact strengths and flexural strengths of Taguchi L27 orthogonal array were the dependent variables. These sisal fiber/PLA pellet composites were interfaced with an epoxy matrix. The independent factors in the formation of the composite included the percent composition of the PLA infill, the percent composition of the fibre loading and the percent content of the epoxy.The level and factors are given in Table 2.

Table 2. Experimental design plan.

Factor	Factor Name	levels		
A	Sisal Fibre (loading)	03	06	09
B	PLA (infilling %)	080	090	100
C	Epoxy concentration (%)	075	080	085

2.4 *Mechanical testing*

In order to perform tensile testing, the composite sample (190 x 24 x 13 cm3) was sliced as per the requirements of ASTM D790. A 200 Mpa extreme testing was conducted with a universal testing equipment.

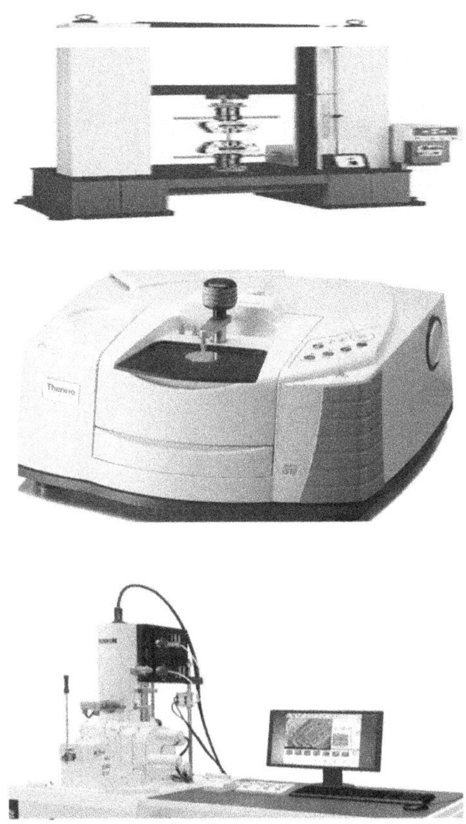

Figure 3. FTIR instrument (a) scanning electron microscopy (b) DSC instrument (c) UTM mechanical test instrument.

The specimen in Figure 3 represents tensile test samples. In all eight specimens analyzed tensile strength was measured after failure had been achieved. Bending and splitting were measured as required by ASTM D790 to establish flexural strength of the specimen. A UTM was also used to do the same flexural test. Prepared Charpy Impact Test samples have undergone testing according to ASTM D790. They even gave the pendulum time to swing before the specimen was put in the measurement apparatus was broken. The amount of energy needed to break the material was determined by the impact test.

Figure 4. Mechanical tested.

3 RESULT AND DISCUSSION

The data set of Table 6 contains the mechanical properties of 3D printing of PLA/Sisal hybrid bio-composites. The fact which needs the most attention is the need to establish the effect of loading sisal fibre, the percentage of PLA infill and the concentration of epoxy on the tensile and flexural strength of the composite materials. The experimental design may also become an orthogonal array (OA) when a combination of multiple variables and their levels are intended to be studied together affecting the performance outcomes and therefore you characterized the experimental design as a Taguchi orthogonal array (OA) approach.

Table 3. Taguchi L27 orthogonal array.

Sample No	Sisal Fibre loading (wt %	Infilling %	Epoxyconcentration (wt) %)	Tensile stress (Mpa)	Flexural strength (Mpa)
1	3	80	75	218	188
2	3	80	80	222	190
3	3	80	85	225	200
4	3	90	75	229	203
5	3	90	80	235	204.68
6	3	90	85	237	205.26
7	3	100	75	239	209
8	3	100	80	246	211
9	3	100	85	252	214
10	6	80	75	288	215
11	6	80	80	295	217
12	6	80	85	302	220
13	6	90	75	309	221.12
14	6	90	80	315	223.06
15	6	90	85	321	224.57
16	6	100	75	324	226
17	6	100	80	329	227.12
18	6	100	85	333	228.56
19	9	80	75	339	229.9
20	9	80	80	345	230.04
21	9	80	85	356	232.6
22	9	90	75	365	242
23	9	90	80	373	260.67
24	9	90	85	382	270.40
25	9	100	75	390	272.19
26	9	100	80	395	275.67
27	9	100	85	398	279.28

3.1 *ANOVA of tensile strength*

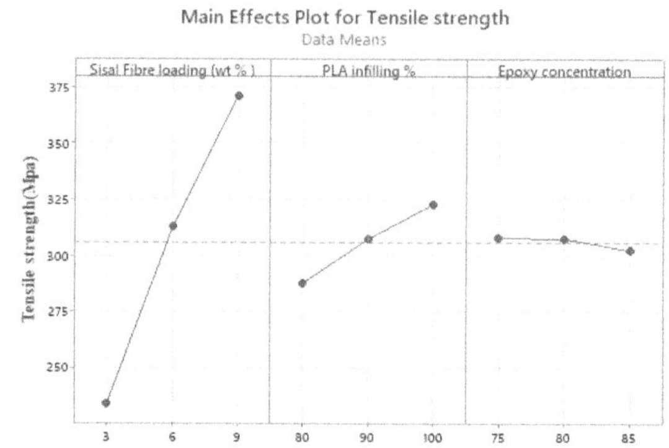

Figure 5. Main effect plot for tensile strength.

Tensile strength of PLA/Sisal hybrid bio-composite is determined by three independent parameters, i.e. epoxy concentration, PLA infill percentage and sisal fibre loading (wt%), which are depicted in the main effects plot (Figure 5). There is a very high positive correlation. Between 3 and 9 per cent. increase in the tensile strength as a result of increase in loading of sisal fibre. Being so, the higher the sisal fibre content of a given PLA matrix, the higher the reinforcement of PLA matrix, and the higher the tensile properties. The higher percentages of PLA infill are on the increase. At infill levels of 80 percent and 100 percent, tensile strength improves, possibly due to an improved mechanical integrity of the denser material structure. Epoxy concentration does not matter much relative to the other two criteria. Beyond 80 percent of the epoxy, a slight decrease in tensile strength is noted; this would be expected as too much epoxy decreases the effectiveness of the bond between fibers and matrix.

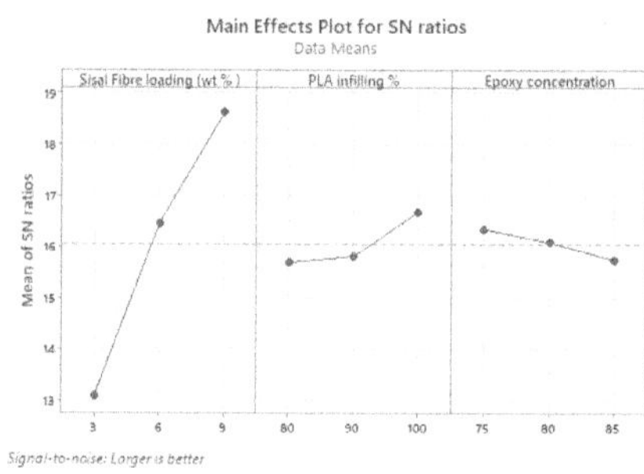

Figure 6. Main effect plot for SN ratio.

Figure 6 was used to test how the sisal fibre content (wt%), PLA infilling content and the epoxy content will affect the signal to noise (S/N) ratio, and it indicates that the higher the sisal fibre content in the composite, the higher is the strengthening and rigidity of composite to variations. A higher percentage of PLA infill, 100 percent, instead of 80 percent, improves the S/N ratio, to a certain degree, and changes the tensile strength varying behavior and improves mechanical stability. Epoxy has a maximum S/N ratio of 75-80 percent, although it begins to drop off rather slowly above 85 percent, so additional epoxy does not add significant strength, and may actually lead to less favorable fiber-matrix interactions. The most important factor is the loading of sisal fibre; the highest results are obtained at 9 per cent fibre percentage. The robustness is also highly influenced by the PLA infill ratio, and 100 percent infill is ideal. The concentration of epoxy does not have a significant effect, but the concentration of 75-80 seems to be the ideal concentration regarding ensuring uniform tensile strength.

Table 4. Signal to Noise ratios.

Larger is bette Level	Sisal Fibre loading (wt %)	PLAinfilling %	Epoxyconcentration
1	13.10	15.68	16.34
2	16.46	15.80	16.09
3	18.61	16.68	15.73
Delta	5.51	0.99	0.61
Rank	1	2	3

The delta values or difference between the highest and lowest averages are used in analysis to rank the significance of each factor. The increasing concentration of epoxy decreases the tensile strength a bit. Although it is not as efficient as fibre loading, the tensile strength increases with an increase in PLA infill. Tensile strength has a positive significant influence on the length of sisal fibre loading.

Table 5. Tensile strength variance analysis.

Source	DF	Seq SS	Contribution	Adj SS	Adj MS	F-Value	P-Value
Sisal Fibre loading (wt %)	2	86062.9	92.79%	86062.9	43031.4	847.11	0.000
PLA infilling %	2	5571.6	6.01%	5571.6	2785.8	54.84	0.000
Error	22	1117.6	1.20%	1117.6	50.8		
Lack-of-Fit	4	436.9	0.47%	436.9	109.2	2.89	0.052
Pure Error	18	680.7	0.73%	680.7	37.8		
Total	26	92752.0	100.00%				

The ANOVA table shows the statistical results regarding contributions of experimental error, loading PLA infill and sisal fibre to the changes in tensile strength. The loading of fibre in the form of sisal (wt%) is by far the most important factor influencing tensile strength and can explain over 92% of the difference. The strength is also affected by the percentage of PLA infill, but the input is not so significant (6.01%). No reference was made to the concentration of epoxy, however, so it likely did not matter much. The experiment was conducted with high accuracy since the error of experiment was very low (1.20%)

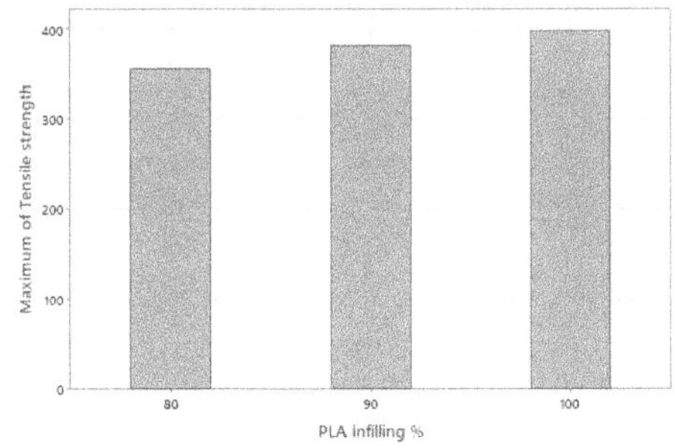

Figure 7. Tensile strength.

Figure 7 shows the tensile strength of 80, 90 and 100 percent PLA infill. The tendency of tension strength goes up with the percentage of PLA infill as illustrated. The tensile strength at 80 percent infill is less than tensile strength at 90 percent infill and tensile strength at 100 percent infill. demonstrates that the mechanical strength of the 3D-printed composite is at its maximum at 90 percent infill and 100 percent infill.

3.2 *ANOVA of flexural strength*

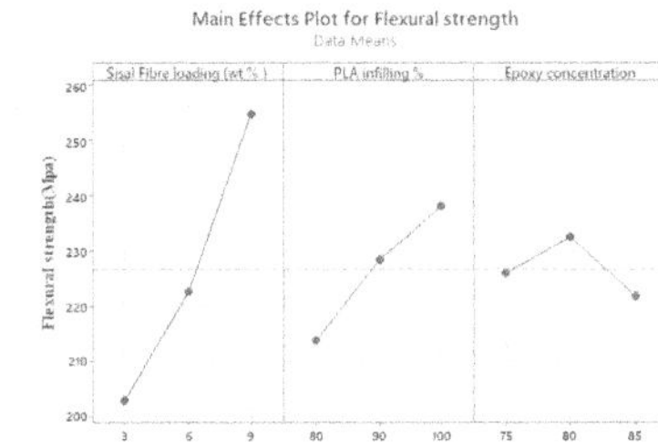

Figure 8. Main effect plot for flexural strength.

As indicated in the main effects diagram, flexural strength of hybrid bio-composite depends on the parameters: PLA concentration, percentage of PLA infilling, percentage of Sisal fibre loading. There is a close and positive relationship between fibre loading and flexural strength. More fibre may be incorporated to enhance mechanical performance, to allow superior loads transfer. Optimal flexural strength is obtained at 9 wt percent (260 Mpa). Infusing PLA percentage is increased to achieve the flexural strength. The highest flexural strength is 240 Mpa with 100 percent infill level. Mechanical properties may also decline due to the aggregation of fibres and the inability to completely disperse them when one reaches a certain level of fibre content, usually over 10 per cent. A completely filled (100 percent) structure is not necessarily the best in an application where weight is a factor since it is heavier and more material intensive. An excess of epoxy can result in brittle and premature fracture.

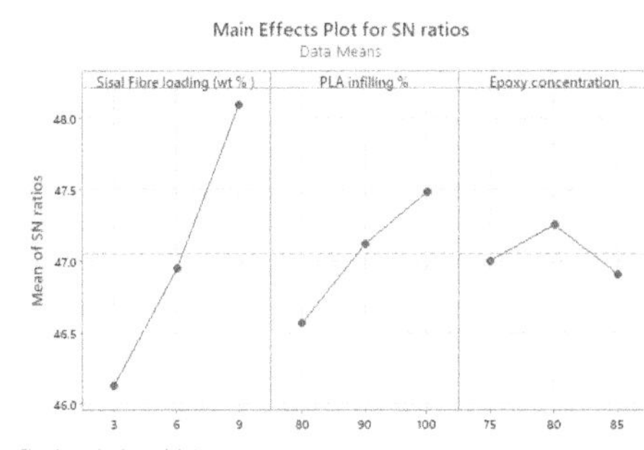

Figure 9. Main effect plot for SN ratio.

The following SN Ratios Main Effects Plot shows the dependence of the signal-to-noise (S/N) ratio on Sisal Fibre loading (wt%), PLA infilling percentage and the concentration of the epoxy; the higher the ratio, the better. The Sisal Fibre Loading, S/N ratio is improved with increasing fibre content of 3 to 9 per cent. The PLA infill is higher, the higher the S/N ratio, and the PLA infill. Epoxy Concentration-At 80 percent, the S/N ratio is maximum and then it progressively decreases to 85.80 percent.

Table 6. Signal to Noise ratios.

Larger is better			
Level	Sisal Fibre loading (wt %)	Plain filling %	Epoxy concentration
1	46.13	46.56	47.00
2	46.94	47.12	47.25
3	48.09	47.48	46.91
Delta	1.96	0.91	0.34
Rank	1	2	3

Table 7. Analysis of variance for flexural strength.

Parameter	DF	Seq SS	% Contribution	Adj SS	Adj MS	F-Value	P-Value
Sisal Fibre loading (wt %)	2	12393.8	74.32	12393.8	6196.91	118.64	0.000
PLA infilling %	2	27317	16.56	2731.7	1365.92	26.15	0.000
Epoxy concentration	2	529.5	3.27	529.4	264.65	5.07	0.017
Error	20	1044.3	6.36	1044.5	52.22		
Lack-of-Fit	2	478.3	2.96	478.4	239.13	7.60	0.004
Pure Error	18	566.4	3.39	566.5	31.44		
Total	26	16699.7	100.00				

Response Tables 4 and 6 presents the analysis and means of the response characteristics in all the levels of component. In the Delta statistics Tables 5 and 7 have not been ordered by the corresponding magnitude of impact but against the order. The maximum average of each of the elements and the minimum was referred to as the delta statistic. Rank 1 Delta value is the greatest rank 2 is second-greatest etc. The loading percentage of the sisal fibre and PLA infilling were ranked using the delta values in Tables 5 and 7 respectively. The reason why these Taguchi tests had chosen the S/N ratio was because it was presumed that a composite material would be good when the mechanical properties of that composite material were also good. Here we observe that the loading percent of sisal fibre affected the most mean and S/N ratio. Analysis and S/N ratios will assist you to identify how much fibre loading and FDM-printed PLA infilling to add when creating a bio-composite to create a high-quality composite material. In the present experiment, most of the literature materials reviewed showed that the performance of mechanical properties of materials was higher than the performance of the present nature fiber-reinforced composite. The tensile, flexural and impact strengths of the resulting composites were improved.

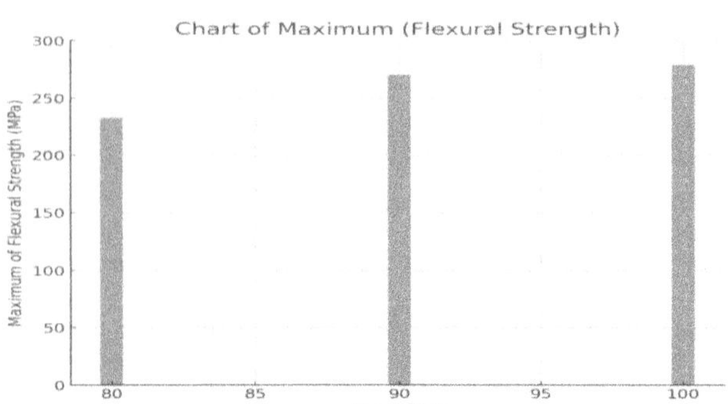

Figure 10. Flexural strength.

Figure 10 shows the maximum flexural strength of the hybrid bio-composites at the various percentages of PLA Infill (80, 90 and 100). Maximum pressure of all the samples was 279.38 MPa at 100 percent PLA infill. This means that the interior structure will be more dense providing stronger resistance to bending forces.

4 CONCLUSION

Tensile strength, flexural strength of the hybrid PLA/Sisal composites were observed to be superior to the other bio-composites materials. Fewer tests were performed with the assistance of Taguchi technique that helped to determine the set of parameters with the help of which a trial could be conducted (L27). The major findings of the paper are the following.

Tensile strength increases with the content of sisal fibres and percentage of infilling with PLA but tensile strength reduces a bit when epoxy is very high. Experiment:

There is a positive correlation between the weight percentage of sisal fibre and the concentration of epoxy and flexural strength;

Flexural strength was found to increase with sisal fibre weight percentage, infilling 9 and 100 percent PLA. It is known that the maximum concentration of the fiber loading, and the epoxy concentration , increases the potential of impact energy absorption of the composite. As shown in the ratio of S/N, loading fraction of Sisal fibre is more commonly the most important factor. The next is the percentage of concentration of PLA infill and epoxy. Best sisal fibre loading 100 percent 9 percent epoxy 75-80 percent PL A 100. In the S/N ratio experiments, the optimal state of PLA/Sisal hybrid bio-composites is defined as 90 percent PLA infusion, 80 percent epoxy and 9 percent Sisal fibre.

REFERENCES

[1] Agrawal, S.S. and Yadava V. (2013). Modeling and prediction of material removal rate and surface roughness in surface-electrical discharge diamond grinding process of metal matrix composites. *Materials and Manufacturing Processes* **28**(4): 381–389.

[2] Ahn, S.H., Montero M., Odell D., Roundy S. and Wright P.K. (2002). Anisotropic material properties of fused deposition modeling ABS. *Rapid Prototyping Journal* **8**(4): 248–257.

[3] Akande, S. (2015). Dimensional accuracy and surface finish optimization of fused deposition modelling parts using desirability function analysis. *International Journal of Engineering Researchand Technology* **04**(04): 196–202.

[4] Alafaghani, A. and Qattawi A. (2018). Investigating the effect of fused deposition modeling processing parameters using Taguchi design of experiment method. *Journal of Manufacturing Processes* **36**: 164–174.

[5] Alafaghani, A., Qattawi A., Alrawi B. and Guzman A. (2017). Experimental optimization of fused deposition modelling processing parameters: A Design-for-Manufacturing Approach. *Procedia Manufacturing* **10**: 791–803.

[6] Alaimo, G., Marconi S., Costato L. and Auricchio F. (2017). Influence of meso- structure and chemical composition on FDM 3D-printed parts. *Composites Part B: Engineering* **113**: 371–380.

[7] Alvarez, K., Lagos R. and Aizpun M. (2016). Investigating the influence of infill percentage on the mechanical properties of fused deposition modelled ABS parts. *Ingeniería e Investigación* **36**: 110–116.

[8] Ang, K., Leong K.F., Chua K. and Margam C. (2006). Investigation of the mechanical properties and porosity relationships in fused deposition modelling- fabricated porous structures. *Rapid Prototyping Journal* **12**: 100–105.

[9] Anitha, R., Arunachalam S. and Radhakrishnan P. (2001). Critical parameters influencing the quality of prototypes in fused deposition modelling. *Journal of Materials Processing Technology* **118**(1–3): 385–388.

[10] Arivazhagan, A. and Masood S.H. (2012). Dynamic mechanical properties of ABS material processed by fused deposition modelling. *International Journal of Engineering Research and Applications* **2**(3): 2009–2014.

[11] Asadi-Eydivand, M., Solati-Hashjin M., Farzad A. and Abu Osman N.A. (2016). Effect of technical parameters on porous structure and strength of 3D printed calcium sulfate prototypes. *Robotics and Computer-Integrated Manufacturing* **37**: 57–67.

[12] Askanian, H., Muranaka de Lima D., Commereuc S. and Verney V. (2018). Toward a better understanding of the fused deposition modeling process: comparison with injection molding. *3D Printing and Additive Manufacturing* **5**(4): 319–327.

[13] Assarzadeh S and Ghoreishi M (2008). Neural-network-based modeling and optimization of the electro-discharge machining process. *The International Journal of Advanced Manufacturing Technology* **39**(5–6): 488–500.

[14] ASTM Standard, G99. Standard test method for wear testing with a pin-on-disk apparatus. *ASTM International.*

[15] Aw, Y., Yeoh C., Idris A., the P. L., Hamzah K. and Sazali S. (2018). Effect of printing parameters on tensile, dynamic mechanical, and thermoelectric properties of FDM 3D printed CABS/ZnO composites. *Materials* **11**(4): 466.

[16] Aworinde, A.K., Adeosun S.O., Oyawale F.A., Akinlabi E.T. and Akinlabi S.A. (2019). Parametric effects of fused deposition modelling on the mechanical properties of polylactide composites: A Review. *Journal of Physics: Conference Series* **1378**(2): 022060(022061–022010).

Next-Generation Smart Systems – Sekhar et al. (Eds)
© 2027 The Author(s), ISBN: 978-1-041-34234-2

An Evaluative Model of Mitchell's Relaxation Technique for Assessing Postoperative Physiological and Psychological Wellbeing in Abdominal Hysterectomy Patients

Thenmozhi P.
Professor, Saveetha College of Nursing, Saveetha Institute of Medical and Technical Sciences, Saveetha University, Chennai, Tamilnadu, India

Janani S.
Saveetha College of Nursing, Saveetha Institute of Medical and Technical Sciences, Saveetha University, Chennai, Tamilnadu, India

ABSTRACT: Hysterectomy commonly leads to physiological and psychological disturbances, yet non-pharmacological interventions like relaxation techniques are underused in clinical practice. The present framework model was developed to examine the effectiveness of Mitchell's Relaxation Technique (MRT) in improving selected physiological parameters and reducing pain and anxiety among 60 post-hysterectomy women (30 per group) using a non-equivalent comparison group design. The study group received MRT twice daily from postoperative days 1 to 5 with each session lasting 20–30 minutes. Physiological parameters and anxiety levels were measured before and after each MRT session. Following the intervention, the stud group demonstrated significant reductions in heart rate and respiratory rate at $p < 0.001$, systolic blood pressure at $p < 0.05$, and pain intensity at $p < 0.0001$, whereas the control group showed only marginal and minimal changes. Anxiety scores in the study group also declined markedly $p < 0.05$, in contrast to the control group, which exhibited no meaningful variation. Incorporating MRT into routine perioperative care could strengthen recovery, alleviate distress, and support holistic patient well-being. Further large-scale, multi-centre studies with extended follow-up periods are recommended to substantiate these findings.

Keywords: Hysterectomy, Anxiety, Mitchell's Relaxation, post-operative pain, physiological parameter, psychological wellbeing

1 INTRODUCTION

A hysterectomy ranks as one of the most commonly performed surgical procedures after a caesarean section and is regarded as the second most frequently carried out major operation in developed nations [1,2]. It is carried out to treat various gynaecological conditions such as abnormal uterine bleeding, cancers, fibroids uterus, and thickening of the endometrium. [3]. Furthermore, several social factors such as age, age at marriage, educational attainment, and socioeconomic status are often linked to the likelihood of undergoing a hysterectomy. [4,5]. In 2016, nearly 1.54 million women underwent hysterectomy globally, as reported by the World Health Organization [6]. According to a 2018 study, the hysterectomy rate among ever-married Indian women averaged 17 per 1,000, but showed substantial differences between states, with figures spanning from 2 to 63 per 1,000 [7]. Depending on the underlying condition, hysterectomy may take the form of a radical, total, or subtotal procedure and can be conducted using either conventional surgical incisions or laparoscopic minimally invasive methods. [8]. Advances in artificial intelligence and surgical methods have recently paved the way for robotically assisted hysterectomy [9] and gasless laparoscopic hysterectomy supported by a novel abdominal wall elevation approach [10]. Even though hysterectomy is beneficial clinically, it is often accompanied by substantial physiological and psychological responses during the perioperative phase, including pain, alterations in vital parameters, and anxiety [11,12]. Psychological issues like stress, anxiety, and depressive symptoms are frequently observed after a hysterectomy [13]. Properly addressing and managing these reactions effectively is vital for promoting recovery and achieving optimal patient well-being.

2 LITERATURE REVIEW

Among surgical patients, relaxation methods are commonly valued for decreasing anxiety and supporting overall well-being. Mitchell's Relaxation Technique (MRT), developed by physiotherapist Laura Mitchell, is one such method. This technique relies on physiological relaxation through agonist–antagonist muscle control and intentional muscle relaxation synchronized with breathing [14]. By activating antagonistic muscle groups, MRT facilitates relaxation and has been applied across clinical settings to ease anxiety, lower blood pressure, diminish pain, and strengthen overall psychological resilience [15].

In abdominal hysterectomy care, integrating MRT before and after surgery can provide a non-pharmacological means of controlling physiological indicators like heart rate, blood pressure and respiratory rate and managing psychological responses such as emotional strain of anxiety. Studies have consistently shown that guided relaxation methods lead to marked improvements in vital signs and perceived well-being among patients facing major operations [16,17]. While MRT appears to offer meaningful advantages, research focused on its specific impact within gynaecological surgery remains insufficient. Hence, the proposed model seeks to establish whether MRT can positively affect both physiological and psychological responses in abdominal hysterectomy patients, advancing holistic and evidence-based perioperative care.

3 METHODOLOGY

The study adopted a quantitative design using a non-equivalent control group and was conducted in the Gynaecology Ward

DOI: 10.1201/9781042001767-105

after obtaining the necessary institutional approval. Purposive sampling was used to select sixty patients scheduled for abdominal hysterectomy based on predefined eligibility criteria. The sample size was determined considering a 10% reduction in anxiety, a standard deviation of 30%, a 5% significance level, and an anticipated 10% dropout rate, resulting in a total of 60 participants. These were evenly assigned, with 30 individuals in the control group (CG) during the first month of data collection and 30 in the study group (SG) during the following month. Participants included women aged 30 to 60 years who had undergone abdominal hysterectomy, were able to follow instructions, and provided informed consent. Exclusion criteria encompassed cognitive decline, psychiatric disorders, cardiovascular problems, recent use of sedatives, substance abuser, known allergies to medications or anaesthesia, vaginal hysterectomy, previous abdominal surgeries, fluctuation in hemodynamic status, restricted mobility, inability to comply with instructions, or uncooperative women. The investigator welcomed the patients, explained the study in detail, and obtained informed consent from each participant after ensuring they fully understood its purpose and procedures.

Baseline information was obtained through interviews using a structured demographic questionnaire designed for the study. Before the intervention, physiological measures including pain, respiratory rate, heart rate, and blood pressure, and the psychological parameter of anxiety were recorded. Data collection instruments included a structured multiple-choice questionnaire, the Numerical Pain Rating Scale, a digital sphygmomanometer, and the Generalized Anxiety Disorder scale. Following the baseline evaluation, the study group received Mitchell's Relaxation Technique. Participants were positioned comfortably in a semi-Fowler's posture and guided to gently contract specific muscle groups while relaxing their opposing muscles, beginning with the neck and progressing through the upper chest, upper limbs, forearms, trunk, and lower limbs. Trunk muscle contractions were performed lightly to avoid abdominal strain, and participants were encouraged to coordinate the movements with slow, deep breathing. The relaxation sessions were provided twice daily from the first to the fifth postoperative day, each lasting approximately 20–25 minutes. The intervention was administered individually, without interrupting ward routines and preferably prior to any painful procedures. Post-intervention measurements were taken on the fifth day using the same tools applied during the pre-test. A Consort flowchart illustrating the study methodology is presented in Figure 1. Confidentiality of the participants was maintained at all times. The data were entered into Excel for processing after coding, and both descriptive and inferential analyses were carried out using SPSS recent version.

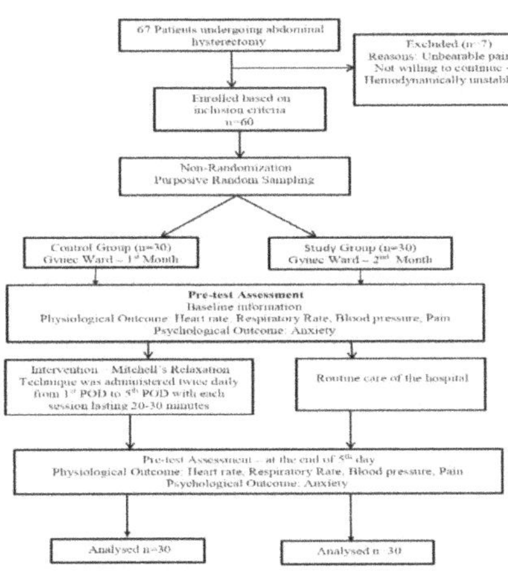

Figure 1. CONSORT framework.

4 RESULTS AND DISCUSSION

Table 1 shows The baseline profile of both groups (SG and CG) shows that they were socio-demographically and clinically comparable. The average age, education levels, marital status, occupation, dietary habits, BMI, type of hysterectomy performed, and the anaesthesia used were all similar between the two groups. This indicates that both groups started the study with no major differences, ensuring that any changes observed later can be more confidently attributed to the intervention rather than pre-existing variations.

Table 1. Baseline profile of the participants.

Baseline Characteristics	SG No (%)	CG No (%)
Age in years	52 ± 4.6	50 ± 3.9
Educational Status		
Primary	6 (20%)	8 (27%)
Secondary	15 (50%)	17 (57%)
Graduate	9 (30%)	5 (16%)
Marital Status		
Married	26 (87%)	27 (90%)
Widower	4 (13%)	3 (10%)
Occupation		
Home Maker	12 (40%)	13 (43%)
Daily wages	11 (37%)	12 (40%)
Private Employee	7 (23%)	5 (17%)
Dietary Pattern		
Only Vegetarian	8 (27%)	7 (23%)
Mixed Vegetarian	22 (73%)	23 (77%)
Body Mass Index	23 ± 1.4	22 ±2.3
Hysterectomy Approach		
Surgical open	25 (83%)	23 (77%)
Laparoscopic	5 (17%)	7 (23%)
Anesthesia		
General Anesthesia	15 (50%)	16 (53%)
Spinal Anesthesia	15 (50%)	14 (47%)

In the SG, the proportion of participants with mild pain increased from 10% to 33%, while severe pain decreased from 40% to 14% following the intervention. Moderate pain remained relatively stable (50% to 53%). In contrast, the CG showed only minimal changes, with mild pain increasing from 0% to 10%, severe pain decreasing from 53% to 43%, and moderate pain remaining unchanged at 47% as shown in Table 2. Overall, the findings indicate that the intervention in the SG resulted in a greater decrease in pain severity and a corresponding increase in mild pain, whereas the control group showed only minimal improvement without the intervention.

Table 2. Analysis of pain - Before and after intervention.

	SG		CG	
Pain	Pre-test Frequency (%)	Post-test Frequency (%)	Pre-test Frequency (%)	Post-test Frequency (%)
Mild	3 (10%)	10 (33%)	-	3 (10%)
Moderate	15 (50%)	16 (53%)	14 (47%)	14 (47%)
Severe	12 (40%)	4 (14%)	16 (53%)	13 (43%)

Table 3 reveals that at baseline, there was no significant difference between the study group (SG) and the comparison group (CG) in any physiological parameter (HR, RR, SBP, DBP) or pain levels. After the intervention, the study group showed significant improvements in heart rate, respiratory rate, systolic blood pressure, and pain levels compared to the comparison group. These changes were statistically significant, indicating that the intervention had a positive physiological and analgesic effect. Diastolic blood pressure, however, did not show significant change between the groups in the post-test. Overall, the findings suggest that the intervention was effective in improving key physiological responses and reducing pain, except for diastolic blood pressure, which remained comparable between groups.

Table 3. Within group comparative analysis.

Physiological Outcome	SG Mean ± SD	CG Mean ± SD	t test
HR			
Pre test	91.67 ± 18.75	91.67 ± 16.14	t = 2.776 p = 0.185 NS
Post test	86.56 ± 18.87	90.98 ± 15.76	t = 11.693 p = 0.001 S
RR			
Pre test	24.79 ± 1.32	23.99 ± 1.52	t = 1.471 p = 0.397 NS
Post test	20.63 ± 1.87	22.67 ± 1.98	t = 15.521 p = 0.001 S
SBP			
Pre test	138.21 ± 2.98	139.31 ± 1.98	t = 2.417 p = 0.675 NS
Post test	127.64 ± 3.42	120.12 ± 2.89	t = 18.684 p = 0.05 S
DBP			
Pre test	100.15 ±2.81	100.39 ± 2.12	t = 2.679 p = 0.085 NS
Post test	99.65 ±1.89	100.53 ± 3.21	t = 2.698 p = 0.082 NS
Pain			
Pre test	8.78 ±2.17	7.36 ± 2.65	t = 1.521 p = 0.272 NS
Post test	8.38 ± 1.24	6.20 ± 2.67	t = 10.894 p = 0.0001 S

HR – Heart Rate, RR – Respiratory Rate, SBP – Systolic Blood Pressure, DBP – Diastolic Blood Pressure, ***p<0.001, S – Significant, NS-Non significant

Figure 2 of the box-plot illustrates a clear comparison between the SG and CG across pre-test and post-test measurements. Both groups show almost identical values at baseline, indicating that they were comparable before the intervention. However, after the intervention, the SG demonstrates a marked reduction in post-test values, whereas the control group shows only a mild decrease. This pronounced downward shift in the experimental group suggests that the intervention produced a meaningful improvement in outcomes compared to routine care.

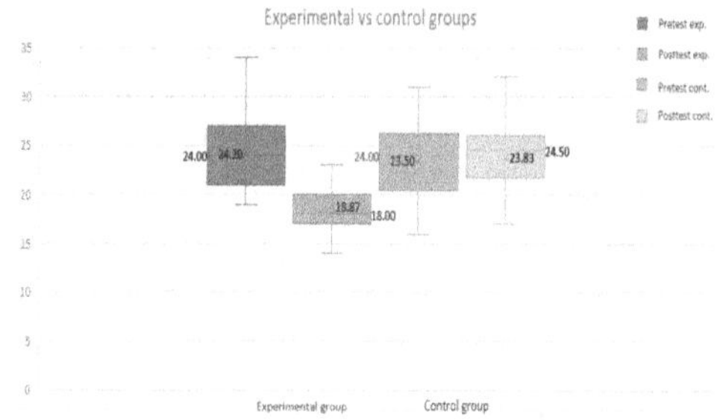

Figure 2. Within Group Comparative Analysis of Anxiety

Hysterectomy, a routine operation in gynaecology, consists of surgically removing the uterus [18], and it may cause both physical and emotional discomfort after surgery, which can hinder recovery process. Numerous studies have examined various relaxation technique frameworks including diaphragmatic deep breathing relaxation technique [22], progressive muscle relaxation [20], Benson Relaxation Technique [23], guided imagery [19], and the music therapy [21], for their effectiveness in alleviating pain and anxiety and contributing to better recuperation. However, research specifically assessing MRT in gynaecological surgical patients is still scarce. This study undertook a detailed evaluation of MRT's influence on physiological and psychological responses in abdominal hysterectomy patients. The results demonstrate that MRT produced notable reductions in anxiety and pain, as well as favourable stabilization of physiological parameters within normal clinical limits in the study group compared with the control group. Following the intervention, pain levels improved significantly in the study group, with severe pain to mild pain. Although systolic blood pressure showed meaningful improvement, diastolic blood pressure remained largely unchanged, indicating the need for further exploration. Anxiety levels in the study group declined considerably, whereas the control group showed no significant changes. Although research on MRT specifically in abdominal hysterectomy remains limited, several related studies support these findings.

The pain-relieving effects observed in the present study align with the findings of Prarthana and Chithra, who reported that women undergoing caesarean section experienced significantly less pain during activities such as mobility in bed, sitting, standing and walking when MRT was combined with pain killer, compared with those receiving only pain killer [24]. Likewise, Isik EI and colleagues demonstrated that MRT produced beneficial effects in young women with primary dysmenorrhea by reducing both menstrual pain and related symptoms [25]. Similarly, Karthika R *et al.* found the positive influence of MRT on alleviating premenstrual symptoms among adolescents was further supported the present study [26]. In addition, Saltikov JB and co-authors reported significant reductions in blood pressure and heart rate after MRT, reinforcing its physiological advantages in adults with normal blood pressure [27]. Khaligh *et al.* also reported that MRT improved quality of life in older adults more effectively than Benson's technique or no intervention, highlighting its broader psychosocial benefits [28]. Furthermore, a comparative study by Bell and Saltikov evaluated MRT against diaphragmatic breathing and supine rest in healthy men, revealing favorable heart-rate changes with both MRT and diaphragmatic breathing, though no significant difference between the two, suggesting comparable efficacy [29]. Given the limited research focused specifically on gynaecological surgical populations, the present study contributes new evidence demonstrating that MRT is effective in improving both physiological and psychological outcomes among post-hysterectomy women. This study is consistent with earlier research that has implemented relaxation-related interventions in the postoperative phase and underscores the value of MRT as a non-drug, client-focused method for managing post-gynaecological surgical patients. A major strength of the study lies in its use of both a non-interventional group and pre- and post-intervention measurements, which enhance methodological rigor and study robustness. Furthermore, its focus on a defined surgical population also increases its relevance to perioperative nursing practice in gynaecology.

5 CONCLUSION

The findings from this research suggest that MRT is a promising non-pharmacological strategy for alleviating physiological and psychological stress in patients who undergo abdominal hysterectomy. Incorporating MRT into perioperative care protocols could facilitate early recovery and support comprehensive well-being. MRT stands out due to its cost-effectiveness, simplicity, and non-invasive nature, offering a beneficial therapeutic modality for postoperative management in gynaecological care. The findings further recommend that healthcare practitioners implement this technique as a complementary therapy. Such an approach may not only enhance patients' emotional health but also improve physiological outcomes, thereby aiding recovery and lowering dependence on pharmacological pain relief and its potential side effects.

Nonetheless, the study's results must be interpreted with caution due to several constraints, such as a limited sample size, lack of randomization, and the single-centre study design which may pose challenges for generalizing the findings. Furthermore, the brief duration of the study and absence of assessment of the long-term outcomes of Mitchell's Relaxation Technique regarding recovery, pain, and anxiety constitute important limitations. Future investigations including larger, more heterogeneous cohorts are warranted to substantiate these findings and broaden their relevance to clinical practice.

ACKNOWLEDGEMENT

The authors gratefully thank the participants with gratitude for the successful completion of this research.

REFERENCES

[1] Hammer A, Rositch AF, Kahlert J, Gravitt PE, Blaakaer J, Sogaard M. (2015). Global epidemiology of hysterectomy: possible impact on gynecological cancer rates. *Am J Obstet Gynecol.*;213(1):23–29.

[2] Hansdottir K. and Gudmundsson JA. (2018). Trends in Minimally Invasive Hysterectomy Techniques for Nonmalignant Conditions in a Defined Population. Gynecol Obstet Invest.;83 (2):198–202.

[3] Hysterectomy: Purpose, Procedure, Risks, Recovery [Internet] (2021, accessed 16 June 2024). https://www.webmd.com/women/guide/hysterectomy.

[4] Shaikh NB, Shaikh S and Shaikh JM. (2010). Morbidity and mortality associated with obstetric hysterectomy. *J Ayub Med Coll Abbottabad.*;22(2):100–104.

[5] Singh A and Govil D. (2021). Hysterectomy in India: spatial and multilevel analysis. *Womens Health (Lond).*;17:17455065211017068.

[6] Elgi MC and Viswanath L. (2020). Knowledge of women on hysterectomy. *J South Asian Fed Menopause Soc.*;7(2):82–85.

[7] Prusty RK, Choithani C and Gupta SD. (2018). Predictors of hysterectomy among married women 15–49 years in India. *Reprod Health.*;15(1):3.

[8] Clayton RD. (2006). *Hysterectomy. Best Pract Res Clin Obstet Gynaecol.*;20(1):73–87.

[9] Dahm-Kähler P, Kvarnström N and Brännström M. (2021). Robotic live donor hysterectomy. *Curr Opin Organ Transplant.*;26(6):640–645.

[10] Kim MK, Hwang JH, Kim JH, Kim SR, Lee SB and Kim BW. (2020). Gasless total laparoscopic hysterectomy with new abdominal-wall retraction system. *JSLS.*;24(1):e2019.00061.

[11] Chung F, Mezei G and Tong D. (2014). Recovery and outcomes after ambulatory surgery. *Curr Opin Anaesthesiol.*;27(6):585–592.

[12] Kaur G, Ahuja B and Mahajan R. (2021). Effect of preoperative education on postoperative outcomes in abdominal hysterectomy patients. *J Obstet Gynaecol Res.*;47(2):511–517.

[13] Li N, *et al.* (2023). The real experience with women's hysterectomy: a meta-synthesis of qualitative research evidence. *Nurs Open.*;10(2):435–449.

[14] Mitchell L. (1977). *Mitchell Method of Relaxation and Remedial Exercise.* London: Baillière Tindall.

[15] Varvogli L and Darviri C. (2011). Stress management techniques: evidence-based procedures that reduce stress and promote health. *Health Sci J.*;5(2):74–89.

[16] Ghoneim MM and O'Hara MW. (2016). Depression and postoperative complications: an overview. *BMC Surg.*;16:5.

[17] Sharma S, Kumari A and Kaur J. 2020. Effectiveness of relaxation techniques on postoperative pain and anxiety among abdominal surgery patients. *Indian J Health Wellbeing.*;11 (5):224–228.

[18] Chaudhary AN, *et al.* (2022). Clinicopathological patterns in hysterectomies in a medical college in Eastern Nepal. *Nepal J Obstet Gynaecol.*

[19] Padmapriya D, Revathy M, Kavitha M, Sridevi B, Hemavathi R. Effectiveness of Relaxation Therapy among Antenatal Mothers. *Texila International Journal of Public Health.* 2024;12 (4):1–14.

[20] Saada Elsayed Rady and Hoda Abdou Abd El-Monem El-Deeb. (2020). Effect of progressive muscle relaxation technique on post-operative pain and quality of recovery among patients with abdominal surgeries. *Egypt J Health Care.*;11(4):566–581.

[21] Shendre V and Taksande V. (2021). Effect of Benson's relaxation technique on post-operative stress and pain among women undergone abdominal hysterectomy. *J Pharm Res Int.*;33 (60B):1055–1062

[22] Anamagh MA, Kouhpayeh MS, Khezri S, Goli R, Faraji N, Anzali BC, *et al.* (2024). The effect of guided imagery on perioperative anxiety in hospitalized adult patients: a systematic review of randomized controlled trials. *Surg Pract Sci.*;18:100255.

[23] Cecyli C, Vasika R, Jagadeeswari J, Priyadarsini A and Dayana B. (2024). Impact of Music Therapy on Pain, Stress, and Physiological Parameters Among Postoperative Patients. *J Pharm Bioallied Sci.* Jul;16(Suppl 3):S2895–S2897.

[24] Prarthana M. and Chitra T. (2021). Effectiveness of Mitchell relaxation technique along with analgesics in reducing pain after cesarean section. *Int J Allied Med Sci Clin Res.*;9(2):384–390.

[25] Işık Eİ and Dağlı E, Çelik N. (2024). Investigation of the efficacy of the relaxation technique on primary dysmenorrhea and menstrual symptoms: a randomized controlled longitudinal trial. *Gevher Nesibe J Med Health Sci.*;9(1):103–110.

[26] Karthika R, Kamalakannan M, Karthikeyan S, Srikanth V, Suriya Nedunchezhiyan, Bharathi Ravichandran and Geetha Priya Vadamalai. (2025). Impact of Mitchell relaxation and stretching exercises on premenstrual syndrome in adolescent girls. *Fizjoterapia Polska*; 25(1); 302–305.

[27] Saltikov JB and Bell JA. (2005). Mitchell's simple physiological relaxation and Jacobson's progressive relaxation techniques: a comparison. *Physiotherapy.*;91(3):165–172.

[28] Khalighi F, Kouchakzadeh Talami S and Moradi M. (2023). A comparative study on the effects of Mitchell and Benson relaxation techniques on quality of life of the old people in nursing homes. *BMC Geriatr.*;23:278.

[29] Bell JA and Saltikov JB. (2005). Mitchell's relaxation technique: is it effective? *Physiotherapy.*;91(2):74–80.

Next-Generation Smart Systems – Sekhar et al. (Eds)
© 2027 The Author(s), ISBN: 978-1-041-34234-2

Phyto-Compound (Carum Carvi) and Masticatory Stimulation (Bubble Gum Chewing): Low-Cost Innovations for Accelerating Post-Cesarean Recovery

Sridevi B. and Sivapriya J.
Medical Surgical Nursing Department, Saveetha College of Nursing, Saveetha Institute of Medical and Technical Sciences, Thandalam, India

Kavitha M.
Community Health Nursing Department, Saveetha College of Nursing, Saveetha Institute of Medical and Technical Sciences Thandalam, India

Padma Priya D. and Hemavathi R.
Obstetrical and Gynaecological Nursing Department, Saveetha College of Nursing, Saveetha Institute of Medical and Technical Sciences Thandalam, India

Golda P.
Medical Surgical Nursing Department, Saveetha College of Nursing, Saveetha Institute of Medical and Technical Sciences, Thandalam, India

ABSTRACT: **Background:** Postoperative recovery is an ongoing process that assists patients in regaining independence and returning to normal life. Regaining regular bowel movements after surgery is seen as difficult. Delayed bowel motility is frequent after all operations. To assess the efficacy of Phyto-Compound (Carum Carvi) and Masticatory Stimulation (Bubble Gum Chewing) on timely return of normal bowel function in post-Lower Segment Caesarean Section (LSCS) moms. A quasi-experimental pretest-post-test control group design was employed in a study involving 60 post-LSCS moms. A self-structured Bowel Function Evaluation form was used to monitor bowel function recovery. The pretest mean score was 2.83±1.37 and 3.43±0.77, with an average difference of 0.80. A paired 't' test (t = 4.5393 and t = 7.3701) showed statistically significant (p-value <0.05). Based on the results this study shown that Phyto-Compound (Carum Carvi) and Masticatory Stimulation (Bubble Gum Chewing) are beneficial on timely return of normal bowel function in post-LSCS women. Early bowel function restoration speeds up surgical recovery, potentially lowering patient suffering and hospital costs.

Keywords: Bubble Gum, Bowel Movements, Carum Carvi, Masticatory Stimulation, Phyto-Compound, Post Lower Segment Caesarean Section (LSCS) Moms

1 INTRODUCTION

The postpartum phase is a period of transition following pregnancy that can last up to six weeks after the placenta is discharged. During this period, the physiological and morphological changes that happened during pregnancy are reversed to pre-pregnancy state [1]. Caesarean section is a surgical procedure for delivering a baby through an abdominal incision and uterus after attaining viability (28 weeks). The need for a caesarean section can be linked to a variety of circumstances involving pregnant women, their foetus, or a combination of the two. It is a dangerous procedure that should only be carried out under proper medical supervision [2].

As caesarean section rates rise, a growing number many women are considering the best method of birth [3]. Small intestine activity typically resumes within hours after abdominal surgery, while stomach action takes 24-48 hours and colonic activity takes 48-72 hours [4].

Globally, 7-15% of people develop post operative complication (PC) after major abdominal surgery. Their capacity to return to regular life requires conscious effort, whereas recovering control of bodily processes appears to be beyond the individual's capabilities. Regaining regular bowel movements after surgery is viewed as unexpectedly tough. [5].

After a caesarean section (CS), oral feeding is usually delayed until postoperative ileus (PI) is cleared, which is usually indicated by flatus and/or bowel movement. Then enteral nutrition is gradually increased as suggested by the doctor [6]. Postoperative ileus (POI) includes abdominal distension, nausea, vomiting, stomach discomfort, delayed motility recovery, and bowel contractions. As a result, neither the flatus nor the stool pass through the rectum. The cause of POI is divided into two categories: surgical treatments and pharmaceutical therapies. Inhibitory reflexes, inflammatory mediators, and opioids are all activated. [7,22].

Gum chewing after abdominal surgery is a safe practice that encourages early gastrointestinal stimulation without the risks associated with food intake. Gum chewing may improve bowel motility by directly stimulating the cephalic-vagal response [8,22] and indirectly promoting gastrointestinal hormone release while boosting saliva and pancreatic juice secretion [9]. On the other hand, a new randomized experiment shows that gum chewing can aid enhance gastrointestinal function [10,18] recovery after cesarean section. In the present study, we explored the possibility that chewing gum could promote faster recovery of intestinal motility following elective caesarean section. [11,15].

Carum carvi seeds and bubble gum chewing are both known to promote bowel movements. Poor consistency in the use of outcome measures continues to create problems, and despite efforts by numerous groups to resolve this through consensus statements, their impact remains uncertain. According to studies, a phyto component found in Carum carvi aids digestion by reducing intestinal gas and increasing peristalsis, whereas chewing bubble gum stimulates bowel movement by triggering the cephalic-vagal reflex. Clinical observations reveal that many post-LSCS mothers experience delayed bowel movements, which cause discomfort and complications [12,13,17,20]. Thus, the current study aimed to assess the effectiveness of Phyto-Compound (Carum Carvi) and Masticatory Stimulation

DOI: 10.1201/9781042001767-106

(Bubble Gum Chewing) in restoring bowel function, as well as to compare post-test assessments of bowel function recovery among post-LSCS moms in experimental and control groups.

2 METHODS AND MATERIALS

Study Design: A quantitative, a pretest–post-test control group design within a quasi-experimental framework. **Study Setting:** The investigation was conducted in the host institution's post-natal ward. **Ethical Clearance:** The study was performed after obtaining consent from the Saveetha College of Nursing's Institutional Scientific Review Board, as well as official authorization from the authorized Head of the Obstetrics and Gynaecology Department and the Thandalam Village Officer. **Participants:** Mothers underwent elective or emergency LSCS (n=60) with gestational age between 38-40 weeks and birth weight of baby more than 2.5kg, were in the zero post-natal or post-operative day, received spinal anaesthesia, and did not have any chronic diseases, did not consume herbal remedies or medications affecting bowel motility, participants who were willing to take part in the study, could read, write, speak, and comprehend Tamil or English, and provided written informed consent were included. Mothers underwent caesarean with general anaesthesia, pre-existing gastrointestinal disorders, history of irritable bowel syndrome (IBS), history of obstetric complications during intra natal period, chronic constipation, or recent gastrointestinal surgery, chronic energy deficiency, chronic psychiatric disorders, with habit of consuming alcohol, smoking, who were on laxatives, prokinetic drugs, lactation-inducing drugs or other medications influencing bowel motility, allergic to Carum Carvi, who has under gone any jaw surgery or any history of dental problems, temporomandibular joint or chewing muscle dysfunction were excluded. **Randomization:** Except for observers and outcome assessors, blinding was not possible because of the scheduled timing of the intervention implementation. After recruiting post-LSCS moms by purposive selection, participants (n=60) were randomly allocated to either the experimental group (who received Carum carvi syrup and chewed bubble gum) or the control group. **Preparation of Phyto-Compound (Carum Carvi Syrup):** 80 grams of Carum carvi was washed, cleaned, 80 grams of sugar, and 400 mL of water are heated to the desired consistency. The final syrup contains 8 grams of Carum carvi per 20ml. **Pre-Assessment: On Day-1:** Demographic and clinical data were collected using a self-designed questionnaire along with the Bowel Function Evaluation Form. The study participants were instructed to remain nil per oral. **Intervention:** On the immediate post-operative day (Day 1), the experimental group was advised to chew a commercially available, soft, unsweetened, and easily chewable gum that included no aspartame, sorbitol, or xylitol. Bubble gum chewing began on the second postoperative hour and continued until oral nutrition was initiated. Participants actively chewed gum for 15 minutes every two hours (second, fourth, and sixth postoperative hours) and refrained from consuming any food or drinks, except for gum, during the first six postoperative hours, or until bowel sounds were heard, or 12 hours had passed—whichever occurred first. The total number of gums chewed was recorded. On the first post-operative day (Day 1), the experimental group was advised to chew a commercially available, soft, unsweetened, and easily chewable gum that included no aspartame, sorbitol, or xylitol. Bubble gum chewing began on the second postoperative hour and continued until oral nutrition was initiated. Participants chewed gum for 15 minutes every 2 hours (second, fourth, and sixth postoperative hours). They avoided consuming any food or beverages, save gum, for the first six postoperative hours until bowel sounds were heard or whatever occurred first, 12 hours had passed. The entire number of chewed gums was calculated. Participants were also directed to gradually ingest 10 mL (4 grams) of Carum Carvi syrup at the 6th postoperative hour, followed by another 10 mL (4 grams) At the 7th post-operative hour, the experimental protocol was assessed. In contrast, the control group was given conventional post-operative care and given instructions to start oral intake after 12 hours after bowel sounds were heard or following the first passage of flatus. They were provided with liquids and semi-solids initially, then a solid diet. **Post-Assessment: On Day- 3** Participants were reviewed for gastrointestinal function. The time to first bowel sound, flatus passage, feces, and post-operative ileus incidence were all reported.

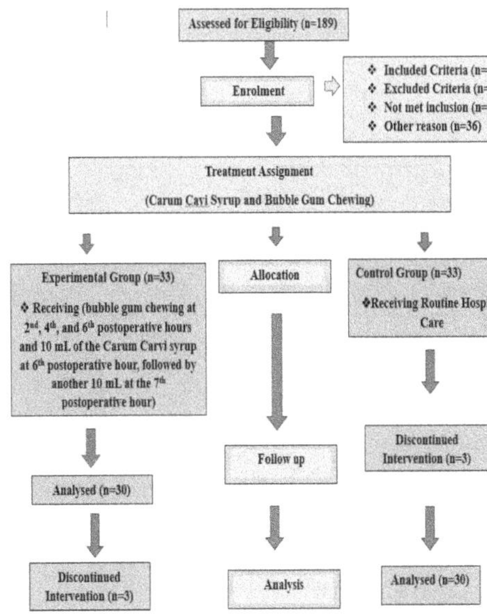

Figure 1. Flowchart for consort's patient recruitment process.

3 RESULTS

3.1 *Demographic characteristics*

Within the experimental group 14(46.67%) were aged between 26-30 years, 12(40%) were illiterate, 15(50%) were living in nuclear family, 19(63.33%) were non-vegetarian, 25(83.3%) were Hindus, 12(40%) were unemployed, 30(100%) and resided in urban areas, 30(100%) belonged to middle class and 18 (60%) slept for 6 hours per day, 17(56.67%) slept during the daytime, whereas in the control group moms 16(53.33%) were aged between 21-25 years, 13(43.33%) were undergraduates, 14 (46.67%) were living in nuclear family, 17(56.67%) were non-vegetarian, 22(73.3%) were Hindus, 16(53.3%) working in private sector, 30(100%) lived in a urban region, 30(100%) belonged to middle class, 16 (53.33%) slept for 8 hours per day, 22 (73.33%) slept during the daytime.

3.2 *Clinical characteristics*

In the experimental group 18(60%) had undergone previous surgery, 30(100%) were permanent non drug users, 18(60%) had normal bowel habits every day, 18(60%) had no abdominal cramps or distension, 25(83.4%) participated in moderate physical exercise, 14(46.7%) reports being able to walk 1 kilometer 26(86.6%) were independent, 21(70%) were no habits, 13 (43.3%) there were no dietary restrictions 15(50%) had antenatal visits for every month whereas in the control group 17(56.67%) had never undergone surgery, 30(100%) don't use drugs permanently, 19(63.33%) had normal bowel habits every day, 21 (70%) had no abdominal cramps or distension, 23(76.7%)

participated in moderate physical exercise, 16(53.3%) reports being able to walk 1 kilometer, 22(73.3%) were independent, 22 (73.3%) were no habits, 14(46.7%) there were no dietary restrictions, 18(60%) had antenatal visits for every month.

3.3 *Assessment and comparison of early return of bowel movements among Post LSCS moms*

In the experimental group's pretest, 13(43.33%) returned early, 13(43.33%) returned intermittently, and 4(13.33%) returned late, whereas in the post-test, 18(60%) returned early and 12 (40%) returned intermittently. In the pretest of the control group, 4(13.33%) had early return, 16(53.33%) had intermittent return, and 10(33.33%) had delayed return; in the post test, 7 (23.33%) had early return, 14(46.67%) had intermittent return, and 9(30%) had delayed return (as seen in Table 1).

Table 1. Pretest and post-test bowel function recovery levels in the experimental and control groups. n=60 (30+30).

	Experimental Group				Control Group			
	Pre test		Post test		Pre test		Post test	
Return of Bowel Function	F	%	F	%	F	%	F	%
Early Return	13	43.33	18	60.00	4	13.33	7	23.33
Intermittent Return	13	43.33	12	40.00	16	53.33	14	46.67
Delayed Return	4	13.33	-	-	10	33.33	9	30.00

3.4 *Comparison of effectiveness of masticatory stimulation (bubble gum chewing) and phyto-compound (carum carvi syrup) among post LSCS moms in the experimental group*

The experimental group demonstrated significant improvement in mean test scores following two different interventions. For Masticatory Stimulation (Bubble Gum Chewing), the pre-test mean score increased from 2.83 ± 1.37 to 3.43 ± 0.77, achieving a mean difference of 0.80 and a significant t-test result of t = 4.5393 ($p < 0.05$). Similarly, with the carum carvi syrup, the mean increased from 2.03 ± 1.22 to 3.00 ± 1.08, resulting in a mean difference of 0.43 and a significant t-value of t = 7.3701 ($p < 0.05$) (as depicted Figure 2).

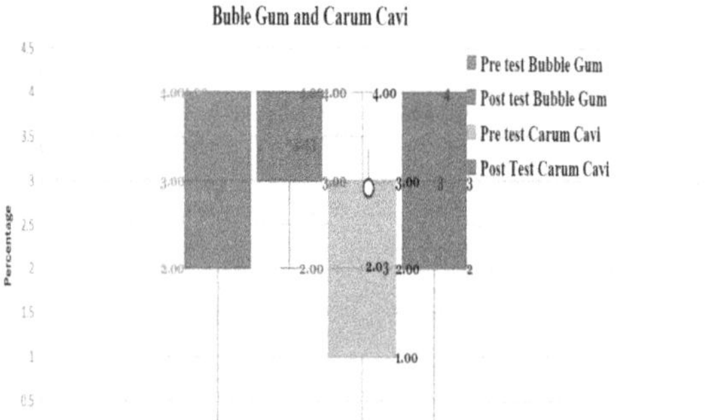

Figure 2. Boxplot showing effectiveness of bubble gum chewing and carum carvi syrup in the experimental group.

4 DISCUSSION

Research at Mugla Sitki Kocman University Training and Research Hospital examined the effects of Carum carvi intake on intestinal function recovery following an elective caesarean surgery. The study group experienced a reduced duration until the first passage of gas and stool, coupled with an extended period before they could tolerate solid foods. The researchers found that Carum carvi may assist in regaining of gastro-intestinal motility after LSCS [14]. A prospective randomized controlled trial examined the impact of chewing gum on bowel function and postoperative pain in patients after laparoscopic hysterectomy. Participants were divided into two groups: one that chewed sugar-free gum for 15 minutes every two hours and a control group that did not. The results indicated that gum chewing significantly reduced the time to first bowel movement and the passage of flatus and feces [16].

This low-cost and straightforward approach could be recommended for post-surgical patients. Both studies illustrate the efficacy of basic, nonpharmacological therapies such as gum chewing, in promoting postoperative bowel recovery. These methods are affordable, safe, and beneficial in reducing discomfort, promoting gut motility, and improving overall recovery after surgery

A quasi-experimental study done at Saveetha Hospital on 30 mothers who underwent LSCS discovered that chewing gum after cesarean surgery improves gut motility, lowers nausea and vomiting, and shortens hospitalization. The data imply that gum chewing is a reasonable postoperative technique for enhancing gastrointestinal motility in cesarean section patients [15]. A clinical trial at Valiasr Hospital involving 66 patients evaluated the effects of gum chewing compared to standard treatment on post-burn ileus. Patients were divided into two groups: Group A (intervention) chewed sugar-free gum four times daily for 15 minutes, while Group B (control) received normal care. Results showed that gum chewing significantly alleviated intestinal ileus symptoms [19]. Carum carvi, a phytocompound, has been shown to cure digestive disorders in both babies and adults, including flatulence, indigestion, dyspepsia, colic flatulence, and irritable stomach troubles. Caraway volatile oils contain antiulcerogenic effects and help alleviate bloating, gas, morning sickness, and colic symptoms [21].

The current research findings, as well as the preceding supporting investigations, convincingly demonstrated the digestive advantages of chewing gum and Carum Carvi, indicating their efficacy in lowering intestinal ileus and enhancing gastro-intestinal function. These non-invasive, low-cost treatments can be incorporated into postoperative and routine digestive care to improve healing and relieve discomfort.

5 LIMITATIONS

The study's generalizability is restricted because of the small sample size and single-center approach, which might induce bias. The short follow-up period and absence of blinding might potentially contribute to this problem. Furthermore, the exclusion of high-risk individuals, such as moms with pre-existing gastrointestinal illnesses or those on bowel motility drugs, restricts the study's generalizability. Another constraint is the selection of Thandalam as the location for data gathering.

6 CONCLUSION

The study suggests that chewing bubble gum and Carum Carvi syrup are effective, non-invasive, and cost-effective interventions for post-LSCS care to improve bowel function recovery. Chewing gum within 2 hours postoperatively can boost intestinal recovery, shorten hospital stays, and reduce nausea and vomiting. Carum Carvi syrup, based on traditional Persian medicine principles, promotes bowel function after elective caesarean sections. Future research should validate these findings.

CONTRIBUTIONS BY THE AUTHORS

Sridevi B. created the research concept and design. Sivapriya and Kavitha gathered clinical data, while Padmapriya and Hemavathi conducted statistical analysis and interpretation. Golda oversaw the research, while Sridevi B. critically evaluated and produced the article. All contributors evaluated and approved the final version.

CONFLICT OF INTEREST

Nil

FUNDING SUPPORT & SPONSORSHIP

In this study, the authors have no financial interests in any health-related projects, have not received consultancy fees, and have no patents affiliated with this work.

ACKNOWLEDGMENT

Authors express gratitude to study participants for their contributions to the research's success.

REFERENCES

[1] Nigam, A., Anand, R., and Jain, N. (2015). Study of obstetric and fetal outcome of post caesarean pregnancy. *International Journal of Reproduction, Contraception, Obstetrics and Gynecology*, *4*(1), 215–219.

[2] Wallström, Å., and Frisman, G.H. (2014). Facilitating early recovery of bowel motility after colorectal surgery: a systematic review. *Journal of clinical nursing*, *23*(1–2), 24–44.

[3] Abd-El-Maeboud, K.H.I., Ibrahim, M.I., Shalaby, D.A.A., and Fikry, M.F. (2010). Gum chewing stimulates early return of bowel motility after caesarean section. *BJOG: An International Journal of Obstetrics & Gynaecology*, *117*(1), 117–118.

[4] Dencker, E.E., Bonde, A., Troelsen, A., Varadarajan, K.M., and Sillesen, M. (2021). Postoperative complications: an observational study of trends in the United States from 2012 to 2018. *BMC surgery*, *21*(1), 393.

[5] Yousefi, S.S., Sadeghpour, O., Hamzehgardeshi, Z., and Sohrabvand, F. (2019). The effects of Carum carvi (Bunium persicum Boiss) on early return of bowel motility after Caesarean section: double-blind, randomized, placebo-controlled trial. *Journal of family & reproductive health*, *13*(1), 35.

[6] Gayathri, R., Sagili, H., Rajagopalan, G., and Elamurugan, T.P. (2020). Effect of chewing gum on bowel recovery following caesarean section: a randomized controlled trial. *International Surgery Journal*, *7*(11), 1.

[7] Akbar, S., and Akbar, S. (2020). Carum carvi L.(Apiaceae/ Umbelliferae) (Syns.: Apium carvi (L.) Crantz; Bunium carum M. Bieb.; B. carvi (L.) M. Bieb.; Carum officinale SF Gray; C. velenovskyi Rohlena; Foeniculum carvi (L.) Link; Ligusticum carvi (L.) Roth; Sium carvi (L.) Bernh). *Handbook of 200 Medicinal Plants: A Comprehensive Review of Their Traditional Medical Uses and Scientific Justifications*, 529–537.

[8] Chapman, S.J., Thorpe, G., Vallance, A.E., Harji, D.P., Lee, M. J., and Fearnhead, N.S. (2019). Systematic review of definitions and outcome measures for return of bowel function after gastrointestinal surgery. *BJS open*, 3(1), 1–10.

[9] Elsayed, M., and Hussein, R. (2019). A comparative study of anti inflammatory and antioxidant activities of fenugreek (Trigonella foenum-graecum) and caraway (Carum carvi) aqueous and oil seed extracts in experimental model of ulcerative colitis. *World Journal of Pharmaceutical Research*, 8, 251–266.

[10] Aly, A., Maraei, R., Rezk, A., and Diab, A. (2023). Phytochemical constitutes and biological activities of essential oil extracted from irradiated caraway seeds (Carum carvi L.). *International Journal of Radiation Biology*, 99(2), 318–328.

[11] Urcanoglu, O.B., and Yildiz, T. (2021). Effects of gum chewing on early postoperative recovery after laparoscopic cholecystectomy surgery: A randomized controlled trial. *Indian Journal of Surgery*, 83(5), 1203–1209.

[12] Turkay, Ü., Yavuz, A., Hortu, İ., Terzi, H., and Kale, A. (2020). The impact of chewing gum on postoperative bowel activity and postoperative pain after total laparoscopic hysterectomy. *Journal of Obstetrics and Gynaecology*, 40(5), 705–709.

[13] Bhatti, S., Malik, Y.J., Changazi, S.H., Rahman, U.A., Malik, A.A., Butt, U.I., and Ayyaz, M. (2021). Role of chewing gum in reducing postoperative ileus after reversal of ileostomy: a randomized controlled trial. *World journal of surgery*, 45, 1066–1070.

[14] Koseoglu, S.B., Toker, M.K., Gokbel, I., Celikkol, O., and Gungorduk, K. (2020). Can coffee consumption be used to accelerate the recovery of bowel function after cesarean section? Randomized prospective trial. *Ginekologia polska*, 91(2), 85–90.

[15] Tamilselvi, S., Iswariya, S., Paluchamy, P.T., Bhuvaneshwari, G., and Minolin, T.M. (2024). Chewing Gum on Bowel Motility. *Journal of Pharmacy and Bioallied Sciences*, *16*(Suppl 3), S3020.

[16] Kadirogullari, P., Seckin, K.D., Yalcin Bahat, P., and Aytufan, Z. (2022). The effect of chewing gum on bowel function postoperatively in patients with total laparoscopic hysterectomy: a randomised controlled trial. *Journal of Obstetrics and Gynaecology*, 42(5), 1192–1197.

[17] Chatterjee, S., Singh, S., Sethi, L., Gautam, N., and Shoaib, L. (2023). Use Of A Functional Chewing Gum In Reduction Of Gingival Inflammation. *Chinese Journal Of Medical Genetics*, 32 (1).

[18] Pati, P.P., Mishra, M.R., and Das, S.N. (2023). A Comparative Study between Cyproheptadine and Carum Carvi as Appetite Stimulant in Case of Weight Gain. *International Journal of Current Science Research and Review*.

[19] Malek Hosseini, A., Abdi, S., Abdi, S., Rahmanian, V., and Sharifi, N. (2024). Comparison of the effect of chewing gum with routine method on ileus after burns: a randomized clinical trial. *BMC Research Notes*, 17(1), 261.

[20] Rajesh, K., Sundar, S., Rajaraman, V., Ramadoss, R., and Venugopalan, S. (2024). Assessment of Oral Masticatory Muscle Activity With Different Chewing Gums: A Cross-Sectional Study Based on Electromyogram Analysis. *Cureus*, *16*(3).

[21] Barkat, M.Q., and Mahmood, H.K. (2018). Phytochemical and antioxidant screening of Zingiber officinale, Piper nigrum, Rutag raveolanes and Carum carvi and their effect on gastrointestinal tract activity. Matrix Science Medica, 2(01), 09–13.& Mahmood, H. K. (2018). Phytochemical and antioxidant screening of Zingiber officinale, Piper nigrum, Rutag raveolanes and Carum carvi and their effect on gastrointestinal tract activity. *Matrix Science Medica*, *2*(01), 09–13.

[22] Bhatti, S., Malik, Y.J., Changazi, S.H., Rahman, U.A., Malik, A.A., Butt, U.I., and Ayyaz, M. (2021). Role of chewing gum in reducing postoperative ileus after reversal of ileostomy: a randomized controlled trial. *World journal of surgery*, 45, 1066–1070

Next-Generation Smart Systems – Sekhar et al. (Eds)
© 2027 The Author(s), ISBN: 978-1-041-34234-2

Healthcare Lecturers' Perspective on the Relationship Between the Use of Artificial Intelligence in Academic Assessment and its Perceived Impact on Academic Integrity

Kayalvizhi D.
PhD Scholar, Saveetha College of Nursing, Saveetha Institute of Medical and Technical Sciences, Chennai, India

Bhuvaneswari G.
Professor, Saveetha College of Nursing, Saveetha Institute of Medical and Technical Sciences, Chennai, India

ABSTRACT: Artificial intelligence (AI) is highly influencing health care education, raising both concerns and opportunities. This study surveyed 30 health care lecturers from nursing (73.3%) and Allied health (26.7%) to assess their perspective on the usage of AI in students' assignments. The findings revealed that academic integrity is a great concern, with the mean score of 4.18 (SD=0.87), and 73.3 % participants agree that AI increases dishonesty and reduces students' understanding level. The institutional policy was the weakest objective with a mean score of 3.03 (Sd=1.03) and only 26.7% agreed that the institutional guidelines were clear. Confidence in safeguards such as plagiarism and an AI detection tool, with a mean of 3.13(SD=0.94), and 50% participants agreed that they are confident. At the same time, lecturers also recognised the benefit of AI, where the positive view scale scored 4.13 (SD=0.82), with 73.3% participants agreeing that AI could support teaching and learning if guided properly. Willingness to adopt AI was averaged at 3.67 (SD=0.71), with 53.3% expressing openness. Correlation analysis showed a strong positive relationship associated between AI literacy and willingness to adopt($p<0.001$), while years of experience showed no significant relationship ($p=0.55$) with willingness to adopt. Overall, the results suggest that while concerns about integrity dominate, there is also cautious openness to adopting AI in teaching and learning, provided that learners avoid overdependence and strong policies are in place.

Keywords: Artificial Intelligence, Academic Assignment, Lecturer Perspectives, Academic Integrity, Student Understanding, Health Sciences Education

1 INTRODUCTION

Artificial intelligence (AI) is highly influencing health care education, raising both concerns and opportunities. AI-based tools such as plagiarism checkers, GPT checkers, and text-generating platforms like Copilot, ChatGPT have been widely assessed by both lecturers and students [1]. While these technologies are helpful in efficiency, consistency, and reduced workload for educators and students, they are also highly concerning to educators regarding academic integrity, fairness, and the quality of student understanding [2] and learning outcomes, as critical thinking, ethical practice, and professional accountability are essential practices to be followed by healthcare students. The use of AI in assignments challenges lecturers on their marking skills and reliability. In addition, it also impacts students' understanding and skill development. Previous studies have suggested that AI can support formative learning; however, it poses over-reliance, therefore it reduces students' independent thinking and their problem-solving skills [3]. Furthermore, institutional guidelines play an important role in AI usage, as some institutions and colleges' guidelines on AI usage in assignments are limited, which creates uncertainty among educators. Lecturers are the key people who are responsible for academic standards, and their perspectives are essential in developing policies to balance technology with integrity. However, little is known about how health educators perceive AI-based assignments. Therefore, this study aims to explore healthcare lecturers' perspectives on the usage of AI in academic assignments, focusing on integrity concerns and student understanding. This study investigated 30 health science educators in order to provide insights into how AI is viewed in assignment practice to highlight the urgent need for policy development at health institutes [4].

2 REVIEW OF LITERATURE

Artificial intelligence in higher education has been studied across various disciplines. Recent research highlights both advantages and challenges. Ateeq *et al.* (2024) noted that AI can save time and improve efficiency in grading; however, it can also increase the risk of academic integrity when assessments are not administered properly [5]. Similarly, Balalle and Pannillage (2025) reported that strong institutional policies are required for using AI responsibly [2]. In another study, Saleh *et al.* (2025) [6] and Zhang *et al.* (2024) [7] have reported that lecturers felt that AI helps in learning; however, they remained concerned about plagiarism and reduced critical thinking

Sullivan and Kelly (2023) also emphasised the need for policy and staff training to prevent uncertainty in teaching and learning practice [8]. Additionally, a recent cross-sectional study by Sreeram *et al.* (2024) reported that medical students show a great knowledge and positive attitude towards AI usage in education. However, the study also highlighted the gap between awareness and real-life applications [9]. Overall, these reviews show both positive and negative consequences of Artificial intelligence usage in education.

3 METHODOLOGY

This study used a quantitative cross-sectional survey design to investigate health institute lecturers' perspectives on the usage of Artificial Intelligence (AI) in academic assignments. A total of 30 lecturers from a health sciences institution were recruited for this study using convenience sampling. Data were collected using a structured Google Form questionnaire that includes

DOI: 10.1201/9781042001767-107

demographic data and ten other objectives, such as assessing confidence in evaluating AI content, clarity of institutional policy, integrity concerns, impact on student understanding, and willingness to adopt AI in assignments. A Likert scale, with additional multiple-choice questions and ranking items, was used to measure the responses. Participation was purely voluntary and anonymous, and implied consent was obtained before completion, along with a Google Form questionnaire. Data was analysed using SPSS version 25. Descriptive statistics such as frequencies, percentages, means, and standard deviation were used to summarize. Responses, while Spearman's correlation was used to test relationships between Likert-scale variables, and chi-square was used to investigate the associations between categorial variables. A significance of p>0.05 was applied. (Figure 1)

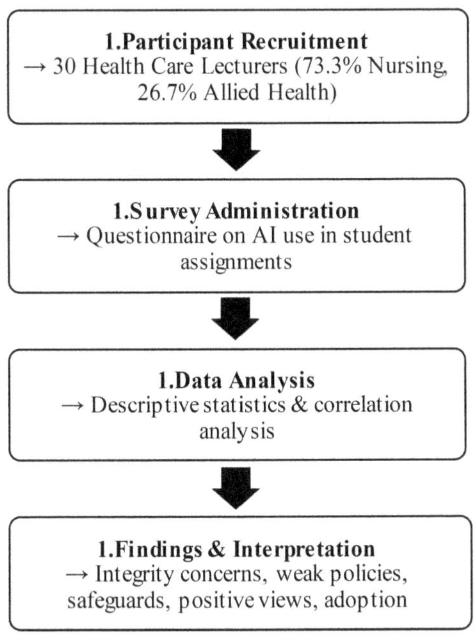

Figure 1. Schematic representation of data collection.

4 RESULTS AND DATA ANALYSIS

4.1 *Demographic characteristics*

This study included 30 health care lecturers from the nursing department (73.3%) and the remaining from allied health (26.7%). In the participants 50% of them had less than 5 years of teaching experience, while 26.7 of % participants had 5-10 years of experience, and 23.3% had more than 15 years of experience. In addition, 50% participants were at the position of lecturer, followed by 36.7 % of associate professor and 13.3% of senior lecturer. Typical class size ranged from 25-50 students (60%), 51-100 students (26.7), and less than 25 students (13.3%).

4.2 *Perceptions of AI in assessment*

Integrity concerns were agreed with the mean score of 4.18 (SD=0.87), and 73.3 % participants agree that AI increases dishonesty and reduces students' understanding level. The institutional policy was the weakest objective with a mean score of 3.03 (Sd=1.03) and only 26.7% agreed that the institutional guidelines were clear. Confidence in safeguards such as plagiarism and an AI detection tool, with a mean of 3.13(SD=0.94), and 50% participants agreed that they are confident. At the same time, lecturers also recognised the benefit of AI, where the positive view scale scored 4.13(SD=0.82), with 73.3% participants agreeing that AI could support teaching and learning if guided properly. (Table 1) (Figure 1)

Table 1. Perception of AI as per Likert scale.

Scale	Mean	SD	%agree/ S.a	Interpretation
AI Literacy	3.53	0.86	50%	Half of the lecturers felt confident evaluating AI-generated content.
Institutional Policy	3.03	1.03	26.7%	Fewer than one-third agreed with a clear institutional policy.
Integrity Concern	4.18	0.87	73.3%	Most participants believed AI increases dishonesty and reduces student understanding.
Integrity Safeguards (rev.)	3.13	0.94	50%	Half of the participants are confident with the current safeguards.
Positive View (rev.)	4.13	0.82	73.3%	Many believe AI can enhance learning and critical thinking if guided properly.
Willingness to Adopt	3.67	0.71	53.3%	Just over half were open to integrating AI in their teaching.

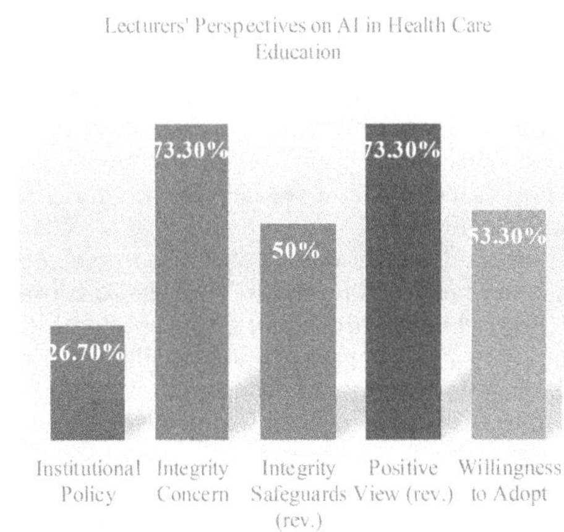

Figure 2. Bar chart representing lecturers' perspective.

4.3 *Correlation analysis*

To test relationships among the variables:

Correlation analysis showed a strong positive relationship associated between AI literacy and willingness to adopt(r=0.75, p<0.001), while years of experience showed no significant relationship (ρ = –0.11, p=0.55) with willingness to adopt. Overall, the results suggest that while concerns about integrity dominate, there is also cautious openness to adopting AI in teaching and learning, provided that learners avoid overdependence and strong policies are in place (Table 2)

Table 2. Correlation analysis.

Variables	Coefficient	p-value	Interpretation
AI Literacy ↔ Willingness to Adopt	**r = 0.75**	< .001	Strong positive correlation: higher literacy = more willingness.
Years of Teaching ↔ Willingness to Adopt	ρ = –0.11	=0.55	Weak, non-significant: experience does not affect willingness.

5 DISCUSSION

This study found that healthcare lecturers hold strong concerns about academic integrity when students use AI in assignments. The academic integrity concern has received a higher rating with the mean score of 4.18(SD=0.87), with 73.3% of participants agreeing or strongly agreeing that AI increases dishonesty and reduces the students' understanding. This indicates a widespread perception that AI use, without control, undermines originality and academic honesty [8].

At the same time, the study revealed a lack of institutional policies for managing AI in education, with the lowest mean score of 3.03 (SD=1.03), with only 26.7% agreeing on a clear institutional policy. This lack of policy clarity might contribute to mistrust and inconsistency in handling the usage of AI in academic assignments.[10]

Perceptions of available integrity safeguards, such as plagiarism detection and AI detectors, were agreed by half 50% of the participants, with a mean score of 3.13 (SD=0.94). This suggests that half of the participants agreed that existing safeguard systems are strong enough to handle AI-related challenges [11].

Interestingly, while concerns were high, lecturers also acknowledged AI's potential educational benefits if used appropriately. The positive view scale with a mean of 4.13 (SD=0.82), with 73.3% agreeing that AI could enhance critical thinking and student learning if guided properly [12].

In terms of adoption, Willingness to adopt AI was averaged at 3.67(SD=0.71), with 53.3% expressing openness. This indicates lecturers are not outright rejecting, however, showing cautious openness to adopting AI in teaching and learning, provided that learners avoid over-dependence and strong policies are in place [13].

Correlation analysis showed a strong positive relationship associated between AI literacy and willingness to adopt [14] ($r = 0.75$, $p<0.001$), while years of experience showed no significant relationship ($\rho = -0.11$, $p=0.55$) with willingness to adopt. Overall, the results suggest that while concerns about integrity dominate, there is also cautious openness to adopting AI in teaching and learning, provided that learners avoid over-dependence and strong policies are in place

6 CONCLUSION

This study shows that a large number of healthcare lecturers perceive AI as a threat to academic integrity, as it might contribute to academic dishonesty and reduce the level of student understanding. In addition, many lecturers also feel that institutional policies are unclear and the current AI detectors and safeguards are not strong enough to address the academic challenges posed by AI.

At the same time, lecturers recognize the potential of AI to benefit teaching and learning if it is used responsibly. They also believe that AI can benefit students with proper policies and guidelines in place. Overall, while concerns about integrity dominate, there is also cautious openness to adopting AI in teaching and learning, provided that learners avoid over-dependence and strong policies are in place.

REFERENCES

[1] Meechan, D., (2024). *Generative AI for students: the essential guide to using artificial intelligence for study at university*. Sage Publications Limited.

[2] Balalle, H. and Pannilage, S., (2025). Reassessing academic integrity in the age of AI: A systematic literature review on AI and academic integrity. *Social Sciences & Humanities Open, 11*, p.101299.

[3] Al-Jahwari, M. and Yousif, M., (2025). The impact of AI tools on education: ChatGPT in focus. *Artificial Intelligence & Robotics Development Journal*, 4, pp.314–336.

[4] Lomis, K., Jeffries, P., Palatta, A., Sage, M., Sheikh, J., Sheperis, C., and Whelan, A., (2021). Artificial intelligence for health professions educators. *NAM perspectives, 2021*, pp.10–31478.

[5] Ateeq, A.U., (2024). Implications for academic integrity and the shift toward comprehensive assessment in the age of AI. *Frontiers in Education*, 9,2024, pp. 1–11.

[6] Saleh, Z.T., Rababa, M., Elshatarat, R.A., (2025). Exploring faculty perceptions and concerns regarding artificial intelligence Chatbots in nursing education: potential benefits and limitations. *BMC Nurs* **24**, 440.

[7] Zhang, F., Liu, X., Wu, W., and Zhu, S., (2024). Evolution of Chatbots in Nursing Education: Narrative Review. *JMIR medical education, 10*, e54987.

[8] Sullivan, M. and Kelly, A., (2023). ChatGPT in higher education: Considerations for academic integrity and student learning. *Journal of Applied Learning & Teaching*, 6(1), pp.1–10.

[9] Sreeram, M., and Chitra, A., (2024). Knowledge, attitude, and practice of artificial intelligence in medical field among Undergraduate and Postgraduate medical students in Tamil Nadu: A cross-sectional online survey. *Indian Journal of Community Medicine: Official Publication of Indian Association of Preventive & Social Medicine*, 49(Supply 1), S78.

[10] Spivakovsky, O.V., Omelchuk, S.A., Kobets, V.V., Valko, N.V., and Malchykova, D.S., (2023). Institutional policies on artificial intelligence in university learning, teaching, and research. *Information Technologies and Learning Tools, 97*(5), p.181.

[11] Mishra, S., (2023). Enhancing Plagiarism Detection: The Role of Artificial Intelligence in Upholding Academic Integrity. *Library Philosophy & Practice*.

[12] Mulaudzi, L.V. and Hamilton, J., (2025). Lecturer's Perspective on the Role of AI in Personalised Learning: Benefits, Challenges, and Ethical Considerations in Higher Education. *Journal of Academic Ethics*, pp.1–21.

[13] Ma, S. and Lei, L., (2024). The factors influencing teacher education students' willingness to adopt artificial intelligence technology for information-based teaching. *Asia Pacific Journal of Education, 44*(1), pp.94–111.

[14] Zhang, X. and Wareewanich, T., (2024). A study of the factors influencing teachers' willingness to use generative artificial intelligence based on the UTAUT model. *International Journal of Interactive Mobile Technologies*, 18(6), pp.126–142.

Next-Generation Smart Systems – Sekhar et al. (Eds)
© 2027 The Author(s), ISBN: 978-1-041-34234-2

Design and Simulation of a Three-Phase AC/DC Converter Fed Buck Converter for Electric Vehicle Fast Charging Using Horse Herd Optimization Vs Constant Control

Patan Gousal Azam
PG Scholar, Department of EEE, Kuppam Engineering College, Kuppam, Andhrapradesh, India

Velappagari Sekhar
Professor, HOD, Department of EEE, Kuppam Engineering College, Kuppam, Andhrapradesh, India

ABSTRACT: This project efforts on the performance comparison of constant control and HOA Optimization Electric Vehicle (EV) fast charging requires highly efficient and intelligent power conversion systems to ensure fast, safe, and grid-compliant charging. Conventional Constant Control strategies, though simple, often fail to maintain output stability under dynamic load variations and result in higher Total Harmonic Distortion (THD). To address these limitations, this work proposes a Horse Herd Optimization (HOA)-based control scheme for a Three-Phase AC/DC Converter fed Buck Converter used in EV fast charging. The performance of both approaches is evaluated using MATLAB/Simulink under identical operating conditions. Key performance metrics, including voltage regulation, efficiency, THD, convergence speed, and battery charging response, are compared. Results demonstrate that while constant control ensures basic operation, the HOA-based design achieves superior performance with faster convergence, reduced THD, higher efficiency, and stable 360 V DC output for a 100 Ah EV battery. This comparative analysis validates HOA as a robust alternative to traditional control techniques for future EV charging infrastructures.

Keywords: EV Fast Charging, Three-Phase AC/DC Converter, Buck Converter, Constant Control, Horse Herd Optimization, Power Quality, MATLAB/Simulink

1 INTRODUCTION

The rapid growth of Electric Vehicles (EVs) has increased the demand for fast, reliable, and grid- friendly charging systems. A typical EV fast charger consists of a Three-Phase AC/DC Converter to interface with the grid and a DC/DC Buck Converter to regulate the charging voltage. Conventional Constant Control techniques, such as fixed duty cycle operation, provide simple and low-cost implementation but are limited in handling dynamic variations in grid voltage, load demand, and converter parameters. These limitations often result in poor voltage regulation, higher THD, and reduced efficiency.

Optimization-based control strategies have recently gained attention for improving EV charging performance. Particle Swarm Optimization (PSO), Genetic Algorithm (GA), and Grey Wolf Optimizer (GWO) have been applied in power electronics, but they suffer from slow convergence and premature

Local optima trapping. The Horse Herd Optimization (HOA) algorithm, inspired by herd dynamics, offers better exploration–exploitation balance and faster convergence.

This paper presents a comparative study between constant control and HOA-based optimization for EV fast charging converters. The main contributions are:

1. Modeling and simulation of a Three-Phase AC/DC Converter fed Buck Converter under constant control and HOA-based control.
2. Comparative performance analysis in terms of output voltage regulation, THD, efficiency, and convergence.
3. Demonstrating the effectiveness of HOA in achieving 360 V regulated output, reduced THD, and higher charging efficiency compared to constant control.

2 DESIGN METHODOLOGY

System Configuration: A three-phase 415 V AC input is rectified using a Universal Bridge, producing DC, which feeds a Buck Converter.

Constant Control: A fixed duty cycle is applied to the PWM generator. While simple, it cannot adapt to variations in grid or load conditions.

HOA-Based Control: The Horse Herd Optimization algorithm dynamically adjusts duty cycle, switching frequency, and passive components to minimize error and improve efficiency.

Algorithm Flow: HOA begins with random initialization of horses (candidate solutions), updates positions based on herd leadership, grazing, and chasing rules, and converges to an optimal duty cycle and frequency.

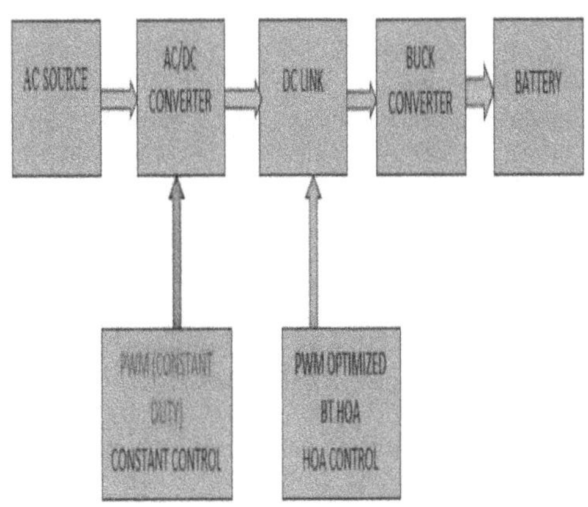

Figure 1. Design block diagram of HOA & constant control.

DOI: 10.1201/9781042001767-108

The design methodology of the proposed EV fast charging system is structured to achieve stable DC output voltage regulation with high efficiency and low harmonic distortion. The system begins with a three- phase AC source, which is processed through an AC/DC converter (universal bridge rectifier) to obtain an unregulated DC voltage. This DC voltage is then passed through a DC link capacitor for filtering before being fed into a Buck Converter, which steps down the voltage to the required 360 V for battery charging. To control the Buck Converter, two strategies are investigated: Constant Control and Horse Herd Optimization (HOA)-based Control. In the constant control approach, a fixed duty ratio is supplied via a

Constant block to the PWM generator, resulting in limited adaptability to dynamic variations. In contrast, the HOA control strategy employs a metaheuristic optimization algorithm that adaptively tunes the duty cycle and switching frequency to maintain optimal performance under varying load and source conditions. The HOA block is implemented using a MATLAB Function in Simulink, which computes the optimal control parameters based on real-time system feedback. The outputs of both control strategies are compared in terms of output voltage regulation, efficiency, total harmonic distortion (THD), and battery state-of-charge (SOC) response. This systematic methodology ensures a fair and comprehensive evaluation of the proposed HOA- based control against the conventional approach.

Flow Chart

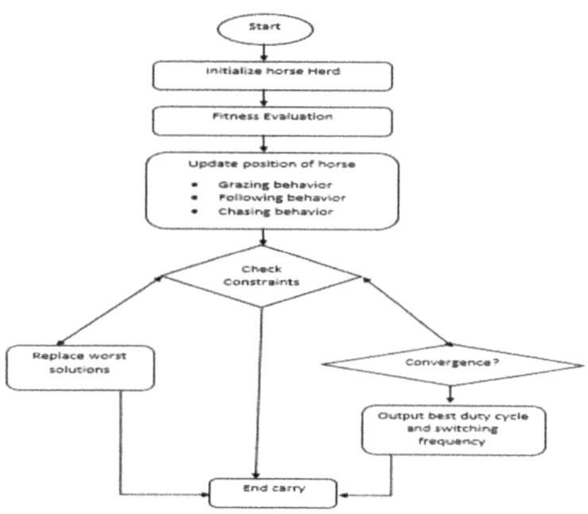

Figure 2. Flow chart & HOA algorithm.

1. Start
   Begin the optimization process for converter control.
2. Initialize Horse Herd
   Generate an initial population (set of horses).
   Each horse represents a possible solution (duty cycle and switching frequency values).
3. Fitness Evaluation
   Evaluate each horse (solution) based on fitness criteria such as: Voltage regulation error
   Efficiency
   Total Harmonic Distortion (THD)
   Better solutions have higher fitness.
4. Update Position of Horses
   Adjust horse positions using three natural behaviors:
   Grazing behavior → local exploration (small adjustments).
   Following behavior → moving toward stronger (better) horses.
   Chasing behavior → exploring towards global best solution.
5. Check Constraints
   Ensure updated solutions satisfy practical limits:
   Duty cycle: $0 \leq D \leq 1$
   Switching frequency: within converter limits
6. Replace Worst Solutions
   If some horses (solutions) are poor or invalid, replace them with new random ones to maintain diversity.
7. Convergence Check
   Test if stopping condition is reached:
   Maximum number of iterations OR
   Voltage regulation error within tolerance.
8. If Not Converged → Repeat
   Go back to fitness evaluation and continue updating horse positions.
9. If Converged → Output Best Values
   Select the optimal duty cycle and switching frequency for the buck converter.
   These are sent to the PWM generator.
10. End
    The process stops once the best solution is found.

System Design & Architecture
HOA Control Mechanism:

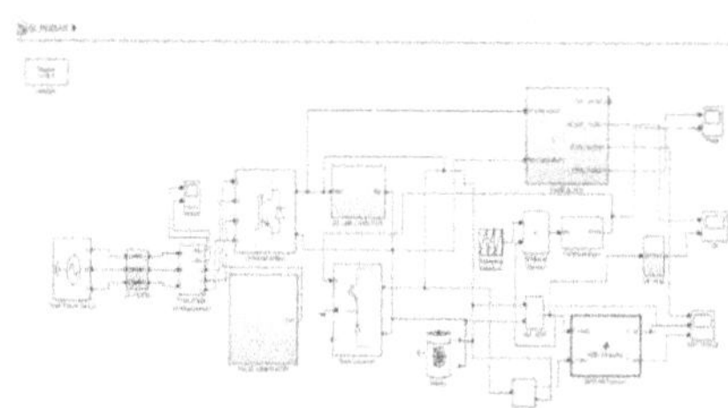

Figure 3. Constant control & HOA control simulation diagram.

- The Horse Herd Optimization (HOA) algorithm is used to generate an adaptive duty cycle.
- HOA mimics horse behaviors (grazing, following, chasing) to perform global search and local refinement.
- A MATLAB Function block processes real- time feedback (input voltage, output voltage, current).
- The algorithm computes optimal duty ratio and switching frequency dynamically.
- The optimized signal is fed to the PWM generator, which drives the Buck Converter switches.
- Achieves higher efficiency, lower THD, and faster convergence compared to constant control.
- Suitable for real-time EV fast charging applications with dynamic operating conditions.

Constant Control Mechanism:

- A fixed duty cycle is supplied through a Constant block in Simulink.
- This constant value is compared with a triangular carrier wave in the PWM generator.
- The PWM generator produces switching pulses for the Buck Converter switches.
- Output voltage regulation is achieved only under nominal input and load conditions.
- The method cannot adapt to variations in grid voltage, load changes, or disturbances.
- Results in poor dynamic response, higher THD, and reduced efficiency.
- Mainly used as a baseline control method for performance comparison.

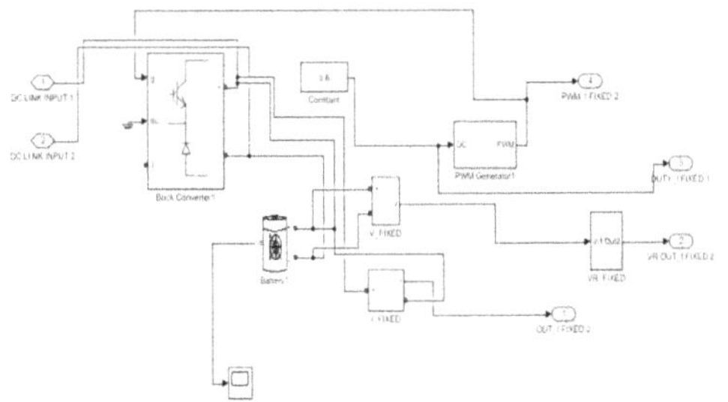

Figure 4. Constant control simulation diagram.

3 RESULT PERFORMANCE

The performance of the proposed three-phase AC/DC converter fed buck converter for EV fast charging is evaluated based on key parameters such as output voltage regulation, converter efficiency, Total Harmonic Distortion (THD), and battery charging response. The system is designed to deliver a regulated 360 V DC output suitable for charging a 100 Ah EV battery.

In the conventional Constant Control method, the buck converter operates with a fixed duty cycle. While this ensures basic regulation under steady-state conditions, the system exhibits voltage deviations during sudden load or input variations, leading to higher ripple content and reduced efficiency. This approach typically achieves moderate performance with higher THD and longer charging time.

On the other hand, the Horse Herd Optimization (HOA)-based control employs an adaptive strategy that dynamically adjusts the duty cycle and switching frequency to maintain optimal operation under varying conditions. The HOA algorithm improves voltage stability, reduces harmonics, and enhances efficiency, making the system more reliable for EV fast charging. With HOA control, the output voltage is tightly regulated at 360 V with minimal fluctuations, efficiency improves by nearly 3–4% compared to constant control, and THD is significantly reduced. Furthermore, the battery charging profile under HOA shows a faster state-of-charge (SOC) increase, ensuring reduced charging time.

Thus, the HOA-based control mechanism enhances the overall performance of the EV fast charging system, demonstrating its superiority over conventional constant control

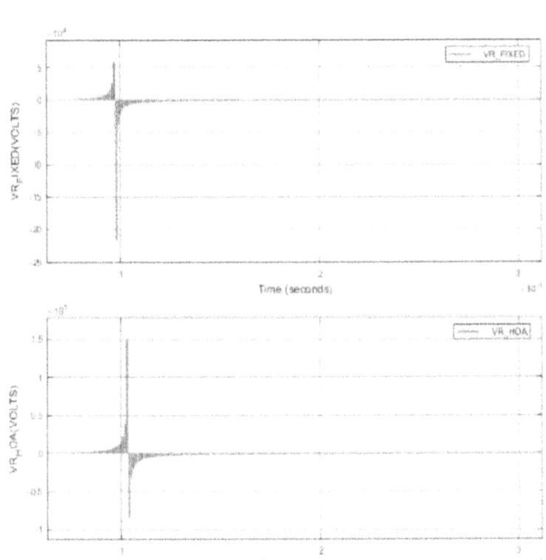

Figure 5. Voltage regulation

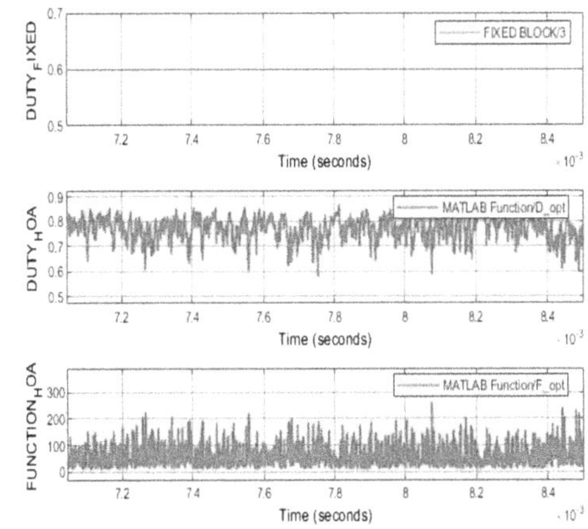

Figure 6. Duty Cycle.

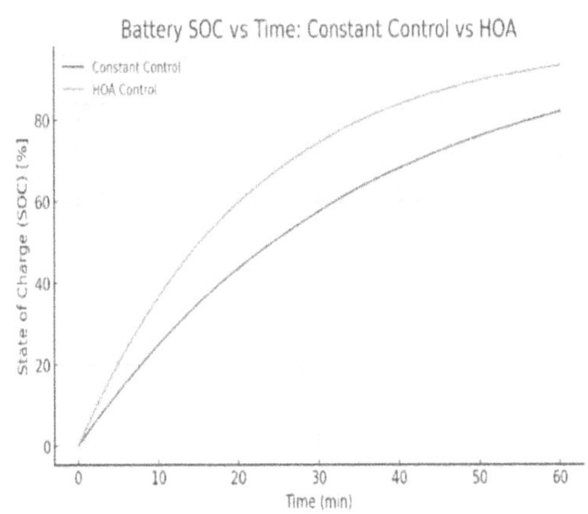

Figure 7. Battery performance.

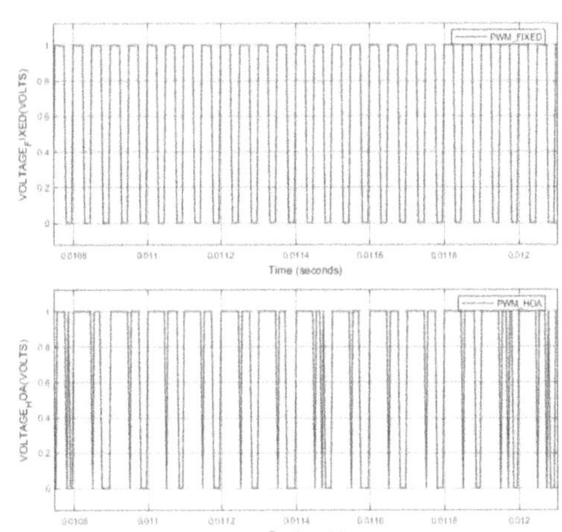

Figure 8. PWM Performance

4 CONCLUSION

This paper presented a comparative study of Constant Control and Horse Herd Optimization (HOA)-based Control for a Three-Phase AC/DC Converter fed Buck Converter used in Electric Vehicle (EV) fast charging applications. The constant control approach provided a baseline for analysis but exhibited poor adaptability to dynamic variations, resulting in higher THD, reduced efficiency, and voltage instability. In contrast,

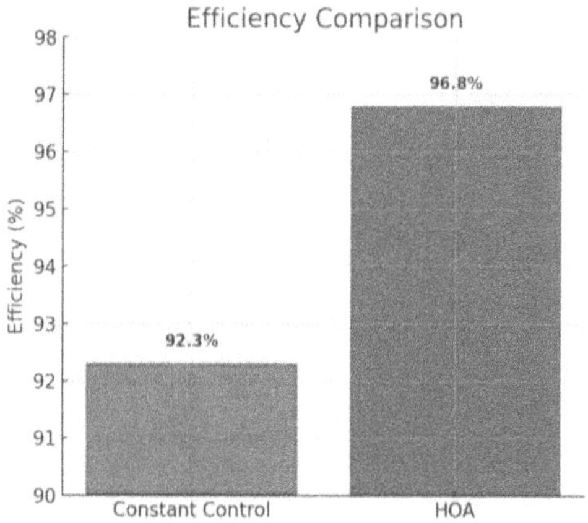

Figure 9. Efficiency.

the HOA-based control strategy successfully optimized duty cycle and switching frequency to achieve improved voltage regulation (360 V), reduced THD, enhanced efficiency (~96.8%), and faster dynamic response. The results confirm that HOA outperforms conventional constant control, making it a promising candidate for next- generation EV fast charging systems.

5 FUTURE SCOPE

Although the proposed Horse Herd Optimization (HOA)-based control strategy demonstrates significant improvements in simulation, there remains scope for further advancement. In future work, the system can be validated experimentally through hardware implementation using real-time controllers such as STM32 or dSPACE to confirm practical performance. The HOA algorithm can also be extended for multi-objective optimization, simultaneously improving voltage regulation, efficiency, THD, and converter thermal performance. Additionally, real-time adaptive HOA can be integrated into renewable energy-assisted EV charging stations, enabling intelligent coordination of solar, wind, and grid power for sustainable charging. Comparative studies with other state-of-the-art metaheuristic algorithms like Particle Swarm Optimization (PSO), Genetic Algorithm (GA), and Grey Wolf Optimization (GWO) will further establish the robustness and scalability of HOA. These directions can pave the way for the development of highly efficient, grid-friendly, and intelligent EV fast charging infrastructures in the near future.

REFERENCES

[1] Yang S., Sun X., and Li H., (2023), Optimization techniques for EV fast charging converters: A comprehensive review, *IEEE Transactions on Transportation Electrification*, vol. 9, no. 1, pp. 56–70.

[2] Kannan R. and Suresh P., (2022), Metaheuristic control for power quality improvement in EV charging systems, *International Journal of Power Electronics*, vol. 15, no. 2, pp. 122–138.

[3] Kumar A., Sharma V., and Gupta M., (2022), Application of nature-inspired algorithms in DC-DC converters for EV charging, *Energy Reports*, vol. 8, pp. 341–350.

[4] Zhang Y. and Wang J., (2023), Design and performance evaluation of a three-phase AC/DC buck converter for electric vehicle fast charging, *IEEE Access*, vol. 11, pp. 76455–76468.

[5] Zhao S. and Huang K., (2022), Horse Herd Optimization: A novel metaheuristic for engineering problems, *Applied Soft Computing*, vol. 115, pp. 108127.

[6] Chen H. *et al.*, (2023), Comparative study of bio-inspired algorithms for EV charging system control, *Journal of Power Electronics*, vol. 23, no. 3, pp. 215–229.

[7] IEEE Standard 1547, Interconnection and interoperability of distributed energy resources with associated electric power systems interfaces, *IEEE Standards Association*, 2022.

[8] Hossain M.T. and Abu-Siada A., (2022), Power electronic converters for electric vehicle fast charging: Challenges and future trends, *Renewable and Sustainable Energy Reviews*, vol. 164, pp. 112555.

[9] Raghavan V., Singh D., and Kumar S., (2022), Performance improvement of buck converters using hybrid optimization algorithms, *International Journal of Electrical Power & Energy Systems*, vol. 142, pp. 108213.

[10] Li K. and Wu J., (2022), Advanced control strategies for grid-connected EV fast chargers, *IEEE Transactions on Smart Grid*, vol. 13, no. 5, pp. 4072–4083.

[11] Wang L., Chen Y., and Yu H., (2022), High-efficiency AC/DC converters for transportation electrification applications, *IET Power Electronics*, vol. 15, no. 10, pp. 1203–1215.

[12] Patel D., Joshi M., and Gupta P., (2022), Application of intelligent optimization in power electronic systems: A review, *International Journal of Electronics and Communications (AEÜ)*, vol. 148, pp. 154206.

[13] Ahmed F. and Khan N., (2022), Dynamic analysis and optimization of EV charging stations using metaheuristic techniques, *IEEE Access*, vol. 10, pp. 81125–81136.

Author Index

For Product Safety Concerns and Information please contact our EU representative GPSR@taylorandfrancis.com
Taylor & Francis Verlag GmbH, Kaufingerstraße 24, 80331 München, Germany

www.ingramcontent.com/pod-product-compliance
Lightning Source LLC
LaVergne TN
LVHW080118011026
849160LV00013B/1130
* 9 7 8 1 0 4 1 3 6 2 6 9 2 *